S0-ARH-014

THE YOUTH BIBLE
NEW TESTAMENT

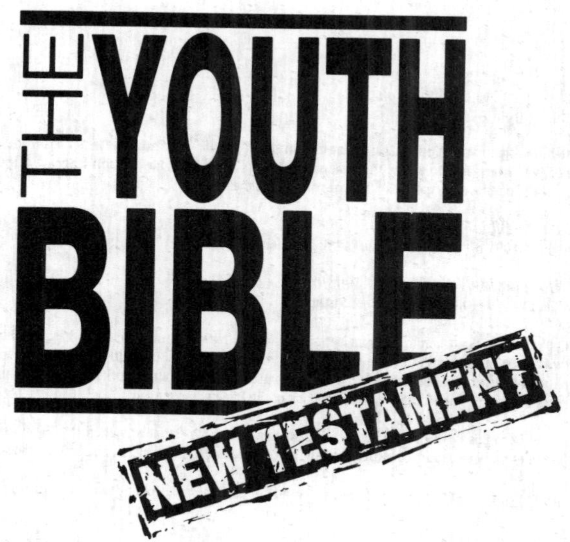

WORD
BIBLES

Group

In grateful recognition of the significant contribution the World Bible Translation Center has made to the development of the New Century Version and to the promotion of God's Word in understandable language throughout the world, a portion of the purchase price of this Bible goes to support their mission.

The Youth Bible

The Holy Bible, New Century Version

The Publisher is pleased hereby to grant permission for the New Century Version to be quoted or reprinted without prior written permission with the following qualifications: (1) up to and including one thousand verses may be quoted, except (a) the verses being quoted may not comprise as much as 50% of the work in which they are quoted and/or (b) the verses quoted may not comprise an entire book of the Bible when quoted.

Quotations from this Bible may be identified in written form with the abbreviation (NCV) in less formal documents, such as bulletins, newsletters, curriculum, media pieces, posters, transparencies, and where space is limited.

A proper copyright credit line must appear on the title or copyright page of any work quoting from The Youth Bible, as follows:

> "Scriptures quoted from The Youth Bible, New Century Version, copyright © 1991 by Word Publishing, Dallas, Texas 75039. Used by permission."

Quotations of more than one thousand verses, or quotations of the devotional and study material, or other permission requests, must be approved by Word Publishing in writing in advance of use.

The preliminary research and development on the New Century Version was done by the World Bible Translation Center, Inc., Fort Worth, Texas 76182.

Devotional and study materials were developed by Group Publishing, Inc., Loveland, CO 80539.

Library of Congress Catalog Card Number 92–34131

ISBN 0–8499–3412–5

Published by Word Publishing. Printed in the United States of America. All rights reserved.

2 3 4 9 AGF 9 8 7 6 5 4 3 2 1

CONTENTS

NEW TESTAMENT

ACKNOWLEDGMENTS

The following people contributed to *The Youth Bible:*

Group Publishing editorial team: Eugene C. Roehlkepartain (general editor), Thom Schultz, Joani Schultz, Paul Woods, Michael D. Warden, Chris Yount, Lee Sparks, Cindy Sauer, Beth Rowland, Patti Leach, Pam Clifford, Suzi Jensen and DeAnne Trujillo.

Word, Inc. team: Dan Rich, Kip Jordon, Carol Bartley, Carey Moore, Dave Moberg, Rob Birkhead, Ed Curtis, Jill Sciacca, Jim Burns, and Matt Barnhill.

Writers: Timothy R. Anderson, Nancy Brumbaugh Bayne, J. Brent Bill, Ann B. Cannon, Michael C. Carson, Dave Carver, Rick Chromey, L. Katherine Cook, Vaughn CroweTipton, Bob Darden, Karen Dockrey, Thomas J. Everson, Jim Farris, Dean Feldmeyer, Karen J. Fisher, Marty Fuller, Mike Gillespie, Mark Gilroy, Vicki Grove, Sam D. Halverson, Cindy S. Hansen, Mike Hertenstein, Margaret R. Hinchey, Tom Klaus, Rick Lawrence, Cynthia Cornwell McCachern, Elaine McCalla, Robert J. McCarty, Kevin A. Miller, Amy L.W. Nappa, Mike D.F. Nappa, Jolene L. Roehlkepartain, Ron Scates, Bob Searl, Yvonne L.D. Steindal, Gary B. Swanson, Jeffrey E. Tucker, Ramona Cramer Tucker, Annie Wamberg, Steve Wamberg, Mark Winter, Twyla Gill Wright, and Carol Davis Younger.

Designers and artists: Richard Slaton, Brian Peterson, Pat Reinheimer, David Martin, and Glyn Powell.

We would also like to thank all the young people, families and youth leaders who allowed their stories to be used in this Bible. Names and details have been changed to maintain their privacy.

No Dusting Necessary

According to a Search Institute study, 86 percent of Christian teenagers do not read the Bible when they are by themselves. Why?

"I sometimes don't understand it, so I stop."
—Mary in Nebraska

"I'm really confused."
—Andrew in Michigan

"I don't know how to read the Bible."
—Chris in Florida

If you are like most teenagers, you have had similar feelings. Sometimes the Bible seems hard to understand, hard to use, irrelevant, and even boring. So even though you know it's important, it often collects dust on a shelf.

The Youth Bible is designed specifically to help you find God's guidance in the everyday issues you face. It includes:

- The Bible text translated into clear, modern English. It's easier to read than a newspaper!
- Devotions that relate the Bible to everyday life.
- Introductions that help you understand each book of the Bible.
- "Sidelights" that give interesting—often humorous—insights into life in Bible times.

These features help you discover for yourself that the Bible is about everyday life. It's easy to use, interesting, and life-changing.

It's Easy to Use

You don't have to be a Bible scholar to use *The Youth Bible.* In fact, we have designed it so that people who have never studied the Bible can find help in God's Word. Here is all you have to do to use it.

- *Find what's on your mind*—When you are dealing with a topic or problem, just look it up in the "Topical Devotion Guide." This guide lists more than two hundred fifty devotions on topics that interest teenagers.
- *Read the devotion*—The devotions tell true stories or give interesting information to help you think about the topic. Then read the related Bible passage and think about the questions, which will help you understand and apply the passage.
- *Find related passages*—Each devotion suggests other Bible passages that can speak to your need. Just look them up. And you don't have to already know where to find 2 Timothy or 1 Corinthians in the Bible. Just use the page numbers listed on the Contents page.
- *Learn about the Bible*—This Bible doesn't assume you know who people are or what events take place. It explains in simple language the ideas and events that are important for understanding Bible passages. And if you don't know where to find something you want to study, use the Dictionary/Topical Concordance in the back of the book or the Topical Devotion Guide index in the front to help you.

It's Interesting

On the surface, many parts of the Bible may seem boring. But when you start digging, you discover that even these kinds of books are fascinating. These features help bring the Bible to life:

• *Introductions*—Each book of the Bible has a short, easy-to-read introduction to help you understand the book and its purpose. Most introductions also include time lines and maps or diagrams to help you see when and where things happened.

• *Sidelights*—Throughout the New Testament you'll find over one hundred forty boxes with interesting and fun information about life in Bible times and about the Bible itself. This information will not only add interest to your Bible reading, but it will help you understand many passages. Besides, you will amaze your friends with your knowledge!

It's Life-Changing

One warning: Don't use this Bible unless you want your life to be changed. The devotions are written to challenge you to grow in your faith. They encourage you to examine your own life and to relate the scriptural principles to what you say, do, and think.

Of course, the Bible can do all these things even without the devotions, introductions, and sidelights that are added. It's God's Word, and it doesn't need our help. But sometimes *we* need help; we need guidance and direction to get us started. *The Youth Bible* gives that help. Once you start using it, it won't have much time to collect dust on the bookshelf.

The Editors, Group Publishing

FIVE BIBLE STUDY TIPS

1. Pray. Ask God to guide you as you read. Your prayer doesn't have to be fancy. You might just pray, "Help me, God, to discover you and your will as I read my Bible."

2. Read. Read a devotion and the Bible passage related to it. If the passage is not clear the first time you read it, read it again. Also check out the introduction at the beginning of the book that helps you understand the book's purpose.

3. Think. Think about the questions listed in the devotion. It may help to ask yourself: What's going on in the passage? How is the world similar or different than it was then? How does the passage fit into my faith?

4. Do. What is God saying to you through this passage? What changes or new directions does the passage call for? Decide what you can do to respond to the truth in the passage, and do it. Use the ideas in the devotional section labeled "Consider . . ." to get you started. It could change your life!

5. Ask. If a passage confuses or bothers you, talk to someone about it. Ask a parent, youth leader, pastor, Sunday school teacher, or trusted friend to help you understand.

USING THE YOUTH BIBLE IN GROUPS

Though designed especially for individual use, *The Youth Bible* has many features that also make it excellent for group use. Use it with your youth group or in a Bible study group with friends. Try these suggestions:

Decide—Find out what topics interest or concern group members. Then see the Topical Devotion Guide to find the devotions on those themes.

Compare—Have different people (or small groups) look at different devotions on the same topic. Compare the stories and the passages. Where do they overlap? What new insights do you gain from the differences?

Be open—Let people express their thoughts and feelings. Listen for different perspectives. When someone says something controversial, you might ask, "Would anyone like to respond to that?"

Commit—Decide specific ways group members can apply what they have learned from the Bible. Encourage each other to keep the commitments you make to yourselves and to God.

Topical Devotion Guide

This devotion guide helps you find devotions on topics that interest or concern you. Refer to it when you are dealing with a particular problem or issue, or use it as a topical reading plan. Simply decide what topic you want to study and then read one devotion each day on that topic until you have read all the devotions and passages.

PREFACE

The Bible is God's message to humanity. He has spoken to all peoples and all generations. Of course, God first accomplished this by directly addressing his people, the Israelites in the Old Testament and the young church in the New Testament, in a language they could understand.

The original text of the Bible was written in Hebrew, Aramaic, and Greek—languages of the people. Since God intends to address all people of all ages through his Word, each generation and language group must translate the Bible into its own language.

These facts, that the Bible is God's message and that it is ultimately addressed to all people in every age, require that a translation be both accurate and clear. These are the two overarching principles that stand behind the *New Century Version.*

An Accurate Translation

The first concern of the *New Century Version* is that the translation be faithful to the manuscripts in the original languages. A team composed of the World Bible Translation Center and fifty additional, highly qualified and experienced Bible scholars and translators was assembled. This team included people with experience on the *New International Version*, the *New American Standard Bible*, and the *New King James Version.* The scholars came from a variety of theological colleges, universities, and seminaries in the United States, Canada, Australia, and Great Britain.

These translators recognize that the most accurate translations are those which pay close attention to the meanings of words in their broader context, rather than those which simply treat words as isolated entities. They understand that a contemporary English translation must sometimes depart from the word order of the original languages to reflect accurately the meaning of God's Word to a modern English-speaking audience.

Further, it is true that translation involves interpretive decisions. With this in mind, it is important to note that the breadth of scholarship which stands behind the *New Century Version* ensures an unbiased translation.

Last, it should be mentioned that the best available Hebrew and Greek texts were used, principally the third edition of the United Bible Societies' Greek text and the latest edition of the Biblia Hebraica, along with the Septuagint.

A Clear Translation

The second concern was to make the language clear enough for all people to read the Bible and understand it for themselves. In maintaining clear language, several guidelines were followed. Vocabulary choice has been based upon *The Living Word Vocabulary* by Dr. Edgar Dale and Dr. Joseph O'Rourke (Worldbook-Childcraft International, 1981), which is the standard used by the editors of *The World Book Encyclopedia* to determine appropriate vocabulary. For difficult words that have no simpler synonyms, footnotes and dictionary references are provided. Footnotes appear at the bottom of the page and are indicated in the text by a raised letter ([n]) for "note." The dictionary/topical concordance is located at the back of the Bible with references indicated in the text by a raised letter ([d]).

The *New Century Version* aids understanding by using contemporary references for measurements and geographical locations when it is feasible. For instance, terms such as "shekels," "cubits," "omer," and "hin" have been converted to modern equivalents. Where geographical references are identical, the modern name has been used, such as the "Mediterranean Sea" instead of "Great Sea" or "Western Sea." Also, to minimize confusion, the most familiar name for a place is used consistently, instead of using variant names for the same place. "Lake Galilee" is used throughout rather than its variant forms, "Sea of Kinnereth," "Lake Gennesaret," and "Sea of Tiberias."

Ancient customs are often unfamiliar to modern readers. Customs such as shaving a man's beard to shame him or ritually walking between the halves of a dead animal to seal an agreement are meaningless to many modern-day readers. So these are clarified either in the text or in a footnote.

Since *meanings* of words change with time, care has been taken to avoid potential misunderstandings. To do so, the *New Century Version* uses contemporary language in place of the archaic language often found in translations. Frequently in the Old Testament God tells his people to "devote" something to him, as when he tells the Israelites to devote Jericho and everything in it to him. While we might understand this to mean he is telling them to keep it safe and holy, the exact opposite is true. He is telling them to destroy it totally as an offering to him. The *New Century Version* communicates the idea clearly by translating "devoted," in these situations, as "destroyed as an offering to the Lord."

Where there was potential for confusion, *rhetorical questions* have been stated according to their implied answer. The psalmist's question, "Who, O God, is like you?" has been stated more directly as, "God, there is no one like you."

Figures of speech have been translated according to their meanings. For instance, the expression, "the Virgin Daughter of Zion," which is frequently used in the Old Testament, is simply and accurately translated "the people of Jerusalem" so that the meaning is not obscured by the figure of speech.

Idiomatic expressions of the biblical languages are translated to communicate the same meaning to today's reader that would have been understood by the original audience. For example, the Hebrew idiom "he rested with his fathers" is translated by its meaning—"he died."

Obscure terms have been clarified. Terms are often obscure in the Bible because they are part of the ancient culture which God directly addressed in his revelation. In the Old Testament, for instance, God frequently condemns the people for their "high places" and "Asherah poles." The *New Century Version* translates these according to their meanings, which would have been understood by the Hebrews. "High places" is translated "places where gods were worshiped" and "Asherah poles" is translated "Asherah idols."

Gender language has also been translated with a concern for clarity. To avoid the misconception that "man," "mankind," and "he" are exclusively masculine when they are being used in a generic sense, this translation has chosen to use less ambiguous language, such as "people," "humans," and "human beings," and has carefully worked throughout to choose gender language that would accurately convey the intent of the original writers. Specifically and exclusively masculine and feminine references in the text have been retained.

Following in the tradition of other English versions, the *New Century Version* indicates the divine name YHWH, the Tetragrammaton, by putting LORD, and sometimes GOD, in capital letters. This is to distinguish it from Adonai, another Hebrew word that is translated "Lord."

Every attempt has been made to maintain proper English style, while clarifying concepts and communication. The beauty of Hebrew parallelism in poetry has been retained, and the images of the ancient languages have been captured in equivalent English images wherever possible, but in all cases, clarity of communication with the modern reader has taken precedence over preservation of the ancient form.

Study Aids

Other features to enhance understanding of the text include a topical devotion guide, subject headings throughout to identify speakers and topics, book introductions to give a synopsis of each book's theme, a dictionary/topical concordance of biblical words and concepts, and footnotes identifying Old Testament quotations in the New Testament.

Our Prayer

It is with great humility and prayerfulness that this Bible is presented. We acknowledge the infallibility of God's Word and yet our own human frailty. We pray that God has worked through us as his vessels so that we all might better learn his truth for ourselves and that it might richly grow in our lives. It is to his glory that this Bible is given.

THE PUBLISHER

NEW TESTAMENT

MATTHEW

Why Read This Book:

- Learn how Jesus filled the role of the Messiah—the Savior whose coming was anticipated in the Old Testament (Matthew 1—3).
- Find guidelines for living (Matthew 5—7).
- Understand Jesus' power as shown through many miracles and stories (Matthew 8—20).
- See what happened to Jesus that led to his death and resurrection (Matthew 21—28).

Behind the Scenes:

When candidates announce they are running for political office, the press begins a flurry of investigation. Reporters check the candidate's background and experience. Where is he from? What's her family like? Is he trustworthy? Has she done what she says she's done?

The book of Matthew is something like stories about new candidates. This Gospel digs into Jesus' background. It tells his relationship to the Jewish faith—how he fulfills Old Testament prophecies about a Messiah or Savior. That's why the book quotes Old Testament passages more than any other book in the New

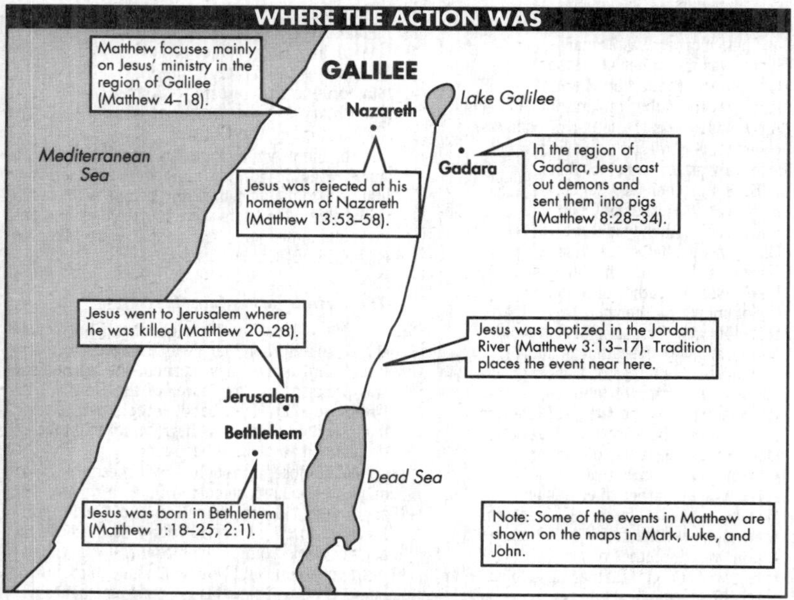
WHERE THE ACTION WAS
Matthew focuses mainly on Jesus' ministry in the region of Galilee (Matthew 4–18).
GALILEE
Lake Galilee
Nazareth
Mediterranean Sea
Gadara
In the region of Gadara, Jesus cast out demons and sent them into pigs (Matthew 8:28–34).
Jesus was rejected at his hometown of Nazareth (Matthew 13:53–58).
Jesus went to Jerusalem where he was killed (Matthew 20–28).
Jesus was baptized in the Jordan River (Matthew 3:13–17). Tradition places the event near here.
Jerusalem
Bethlehem
Dead Sea
Jesus was born in Bethlehem (Matthew 1:18–25, 2:1).
Note: Some of the events in Matthew are shown on the maps in Mark, Luke, and John.

WHEN THE ACTION WAS

Jesus was born
Jesus was crucified, rose from the dead, and went to heaven
Paul began his missionary work
Fire destroyed Rome
BC/AD
25AD
50AD
75AD
100AD
Jesus began his ministry
Romans destroyed the Temple in Jerusalem

Behind the Scenes (cont.):

Testament. And because the Jews expected a political messiah to establish a kingdom on earth, this book emphasizes Jesus' teachings about what his kingdom would be like.

The book of Matthew uses a straightforward, biographical approach to tell stories of Jesus' life and teachings. It begins by telling about his birth (chapters 1—2), then focuses on his ministry, primarily around Lake Galilee, where he grew up (chapters 3—18). Then the book moves to tell about events in Jerusalem that ultimately led to Jesus' death (chapters 19—27). The book concludes with Jesus' resurrection and last instructions to his disciples (chapter 28).

Matthew is a good source for examining what Jesus did and said while he was on earth. By reading it, we learn what Jesus expects of us if we intend to follow him.

The Family History of Jesus

1 This is the family history of Jesus Christ. He came from the family of David, and David came from the family of Abraham.

2 Abraham was the father[n] of Isaac.
Isaac was the father of Jacob.
Jacob was the father of Judah and his brothers.
3 Judah was the father of Perez and Zerah.
(Their mother was Tamar.)
Perez was the father of Hezron.
Hezron was the father of Ram.
4 Ram was the father of Amminadab.
Amminadab was the father of Nahshon.
Nahshon was the father of Salmon.
5 Salmon was the father of Boaz.
(Boaz's mother was Rahab.)
Boaz was the father of Obed.
(Obed's mother was Ruth.)
Obed was the father of Jesse.
6 Jesse was the father of King David.
David was the father of Solomon.
(Solomon's mother had been Uriah's wife.)
7 Solomon was the father of Rehoboam.
Rehoboam was the father of Abijah.
Abijah was the father of Asa.
8 Asa was the father of Jehoshaphat.
Jehoshaphat was the father of Jehoram.
Jehoram was the ancestor of Uzziah.
9 Uzziah was the father of Jotham.
Jotham was the father of Ahaz.
Ahaz was the father of Hezekiah.
10 Hezekiah was the father of Manasseh.
Manasseh was the father of Amon.
Amon was the father of Josiah.
11 Josiah was the grandfather of Jehoiachin and his brothers.
(This was at the time that the people were taken to Babylon.)
12 After they were taken to Babylon:
Jehoiachin was the father of Shealtiel.
Shealtiel was the grandfather of Zerubbabel.
13 Zerubbabel was the father of Abiud.
Abiud was the father of Eliakim.
Eliakim was the father of Azor.
14 Azor was the father of Zadok.
Zadok was the father of Akim.
Akim was the father of Eliud.
15 Eliud was the father of Eleazar.
Eleazar was the father of Matthan.
Matthan was the father of Jacob.
16 Jacob was the father of Joseph.
Joseph was the husband of Mary,
and Mary was the mother of Jesus.
Jesus is called the Christ.[d]

17 So there were fourteen generations from
Abraham to David. And there were fourteen generations from David until the people were taken
to Babylon. And there were fourteen generations
from the time when the people were taken to
Babylon until Christ was born.

The Birth of Jesus Christ

18 This is how the birth of Jesus Christ came
about. His mother Mary was engaged[n] to marry
Joseph, but before they married, she learned she
was pregnant by the power of the Holy Spirit.[d]
19 Because Mary's husband, Joseph, was a good
man, he did not want to disgrace her in public, so
he planned to divorce her secretly.

20 While Joseph thought about these things, an
angel of the Lord came to him in a dream. The
angel said, "Joseph, descendant[d] of David, don't
be afraid to take Mary as your wife, because the
baby in her is from the Holy Spirit. 21 She will give
birth to a son, and you will name him Jesus,[n]
because he will save his people from their sins."

22 All this happened to bring about what the
Lord had said through the prophet:[d] 23 "The virgin[d] will be pregnant. She will have a son, and

father "Father" in Jewish lists of ancestors can sometimes mean grandfather or more distant relative.
engaged For the Jewish people an engagement was a lasting agreement, which could only be broken by a divorce. If a bride was unfaithful, it was considered adultery, and she could be put to death.
Jesus The name Jesus means "salvation."

they will name him Immanuel,"[n] which means "God is with us."

24When Joseph woke up, he did what the Lord's angel had told him to do. Joseph took Mary as his wife, 25but he did not have sexual relations with her until she gave birth to the son. And Joseph named him Jesus.

Wise Men Come to Visit Jesus

2 Jesus was born in the town of Bethlehem in Judea during the time when Herod was king. When Jesus was born, some wise men from the east came to Jerusalem. 2They asked, "Where is the baby who was born to be the king of the Jews? We saw his star in the east and have come to worship him."

3When King Herod heard this, he was troubled, as well as all the people in Jerusalem. 4Herod called a meeting of all the leading priests and teachers of the law and asked them where the Christ[d] would be born. 5They answered, "In the town of Bethlehem in Judea. The prophet[d] wrote about this in the Scriptures:[d]

6'But you, Bethlehem, in the land of Judah,
are important among the tribes[d] of Judah.
A ruler will come from you

"The virgin . . . Immanuel" Quotation from Isaiah 7:14.

FOLLOWING GOD

Taking a Stand

As a young man in Germany, Martin Luther feared he wasn't good enough for God. He even became a monk, hoping to avoid God's anger. Luther tested the patience of other monks as he beat himself with whips and slept without a blanket in the frigid German winter. He confessed every tiny thought or deed, just in case it might be evil.

Regardless of his quirks, Luther grew as a highly skilled Bible professor. But he still felt spiritually distressed by his fear of an angry, judging God. While preparing lectures on the Psalms and later on Paul's letter to the Romans, he discovered something that would change his life: He couldn't earn God's approval. God loved him as he was! He knew now that God really loved him, no matter how unlovable he was. He was happy for the first time in his life. He began teaching and preaching his newfound faith, and criticizing many church policies of the day.

Predictably, the religious authorities disapproved. A long-standing rewards system required people to earn their salvation. The authorities gave Luther a clear choice: Take back everything he had written and said, or be kicked out of the church, lose his job and perhaps lose his life.

Luther had to choose between following God and going along with the system. At a dramatic trial before several authorities, he looked at his accusers and said, "Here I stand. I can do no other."

He was thrown out of the church, and he had to hide in a remote castle from would-be assassins. Yet, his view of a loving God instead of a punishing one ignited the flame that grew into a bonfire of church reform in the sixteenth century.

*In **Matthew 1:18–25**, Joseph, like Luther, had to choose between following God and taking the easy way out.*

- *What factors might have made both Luther's and Joseph's decisions difficult?*
- *Do you ever find yourself facing a situation in which following God looks like the most difficult way? What direction or comfort does this Bible story give you?*

CONSIDER . . .

- writing out a tough decision you're now facing. Based on what you have read in the passage, list your options for following God, and choose.
- encouraging friends who are facing hard choices to follow God's direction, although it may seem difficult.

FOR MORE, SEE . . .

- Exodus 3:1–15
- Luke 2:1–7
- 1 Timothy 4:6–10

who will be like a shepherd for my people
Israel.' " *Micah 5:2*
7Then Herod had a secret meeting with the
wise men and learned from them the exact time
they first saw the star. 8He sent the wise men to
Bethlehem, saying, "Look carefully for the child.
When you find him, come tell me so I can worship him too."
9After the wise men heard the king, they left.
The star that they had seen in the east went before them until it stopped above the place where
the child was. 10When the wise men saw the star,
they were filled with joy. 11They came to the
house where the child was and saw him with his
mother, Mary, and they bowed down and worshiped him. They opened their gifts and gave him
treasures of gold, frankincense,[d] and myrrh.[d]
12But God warned the wise men in a dream not
to go back to Herod, so they returned to their own
country by a different way.

Jesus' Parents Take Him to Egypt

13After they left, an angel of the Lord came to
Joseph in a dream and said, "Get up! Take the
child and his mother and escape to Egypt, because
Herod is starting to look for the child so he can
kill him. Stay in Egypt until I tell you to return."
14So Joseph got up and left for Egypt during the
night with the child and his mother. 15And Joseph
stayed in Egypt until Herod died. This happened

WORSHIP

Enjoying God's Gifts

Sean Sutcliffe hated Sunday mornings. "Sunday meant church, and that meant boring," he said. He felt boredom start with the first note of the organ, and steadily suffered as worship went on. The best part to him was driving out of the church parking lot on the way to lunch.

"Much of what happened there just didn't seem important," he said. "We sang a few old songs, read a few scriptures, listened to somebody talk for thirty minutes—how did any of that really worship God?"

The only thing that kept Sean's interest in church was the youth group. One Sunday evening, the group gathered at a nearby lake. They started a campfire, and somebody played soft guitar while everyone watched a spectacular sunset. Sean sat in silence, enjoying the sunset's reflection on the still lake, until the last pink streak faded in the sky. "That's the most beautiful thing I've ever seen," he said.

Caroline McGee overheard him. She had been sitting so quietly he hadn't noticed her. She asked him, "Do you think God hears us when we say things like that? Do you think God likes it when we enjoy a sunset?"

"Yeah," Sean replied. Then suddenly something "clicked" for Sean about worship. "Maybe part of worship is enjoying something God made," he said. "To watch a sunset, or a butterfly, or the rain, and to be thankful that God had such good taste. Am I right?"

The next time he worshiped at church, he looked around at the people. Many of their faces wore the same expression of awe Sean had felt at the lake. Maybe this feeling of "wow!" is worship, he thought. It isn't the motions you go through. It's when you see or hear or remember things so good that you have to catch your breath, and then thank and praise God for them.

In **Matthew 2:1–12**, read about the "wow!" the wise men must have felt when they saw and worshiped the infant Jesus.

- In what ways might the wise men have felt as Sean did while he watched the sunset?
- When have you experienced a sense of "wow!" in worship, either in or out of church?

C O N S I D E R . . .

- noticing the ways your church worships God and finding out the meaning of each part of the service.
- visiting a few other churches with your family or friends, and seeing what each church does differently.

F O R M O R E , S E E . . .

- Psalm 19:1–6
- Luke 9:28–36
- Revelation 4:1–11

to bring about what the Lord had said through the
prophet:[d] "I called my son out of Egypt."[n]

Herod Kills the Baby Boys

16 When Herod saw that the wise men had
tricked him, he was furious. So he gave an order
to kill all the baby boys in Bethlehem and in the
surrounding area who were two years old or
younger. This was in keeping with the time he
learned from the wise men. 17 So what God had
said through the prophet[d] Jeremiah came true:

18 "A voice was heard in Ramah
of painful crying and deep sadness:
Rachel crying for her children.
She refused to be comforted,
because her children are dead." *Jeremiah 31:15*

Joseph and Mary Return

19 After Herod died, an angel of the Lord spoke
to Joseph in a dream while he was in Egypt. 20 The
angel said, "Get up! Take the child and his
mother and go to the land of Israel, because the

"I called . . . Egypt." Quotation from Hosea 11:1.

FREEDOM

Going to a Safe Place

White journalist Donald Woods openly opposed the South African government's cruel policies toward its black people. In the early 1970s, Woods began to publish a newspaper that chronicled the government's repressive actions.

Woods befriended several leaders in the black liberation movement, including Steve Biko; and he grew even more committed to freedom for blacks. In spite of government and police warnings, Woods refused to turn his back on his friends.

The political situation soon worsened in South Africa. The police stepped up arrests of black leaders, who were later found tortured and often dead. In 1977, Steve Biko was arrested. Woods worked furiously for his friend's release, but faced unbending opposition from officials.

When Woods personally discovered the dead body of his tortured friend, he blasted the official explanation that Biko's death was accidental. While questioning the doctor who had determined the cause of Biko's death, Woods heard the doctor tearfully admit to falsifying the autopsy report. Woods, in his raging grief, openly accused the government of murdering Biko. South Africa's response was to arrest Woods.

After Woods was held under house arrest for three months, his friends in the liberation movement devised a plan for him to escape from the country. After escaping the guards, he crossed the country disguised as a priest. Along the way, sympathizers risked their lives to see him safely along. But he finally made it to the bordering country of Lesotho.

Woods's family also escaped and joined him in Lesotho. They moved to England, where Woods wrote the story of South Africa's cruelty. If he had not been able to escape, his story and Steve Biko's would not have been told. Because of changes in South Africa, Woods has been able to return. His story—and others like it—directly influenced these changes.

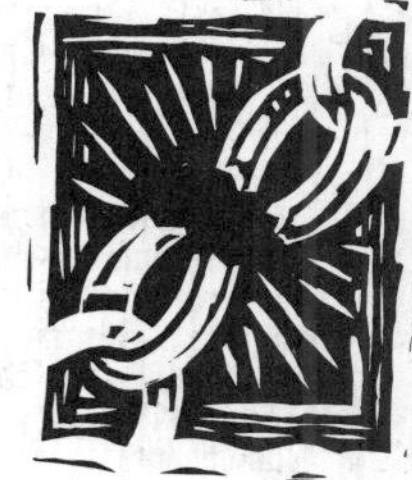

Joseph, Mary, and Jesus also had to flee from their country so Jesus could grow up and fulfill God's purpose for him. Read their story in **Matthew 2:13–23**.

- Why did Joseph and Mary and Donald Woods temporarily leave their homes instead of facing their persecutors?
- Have you ever had to leave a "comfort zone" in your life to follow God? What happened?

C O N S I D E R . . .

- watching the movie Cry Freedom (about Donald Woods) and talking about whether God's freedom is similar or different, and why.
- looking up the word freedom in the dictionary, and then defining "Christian freedom" in your own words.

F O R M O R E , S E E . . .

- Exodus 12:31–50
- John 8:31–36
- Galatians 5:13–15

people who were trying to kill the child are now
dead."

> **SIDELIGHT:** The "three kings" traditionally associated with Matthew 2:1–12 were probably neither "three" nor "kings." Some sources suggest as many as a hundred of these philosophers, doctors, and astrologers visited Jesus. Now that would make a Christmas play! The traditional idea of "three" comes from the three gifts they brought—gold, frankincense, and myrrh.

21So Joseph took the child and his mother and
went to Israel. 22But he heard that Archelaus was
now king in Judea since his father Herod had
died. So Joseph was afraid to go there. After being
warned in a dream, he went to the area of Galilee,
23to a town called Nazareth, and lived there. And
so what God had said through the prophets[d] came
true: "He will be called a Nazarene."[n]

The Work of John the Baptist

3 About that time John the Baptist[d] began
preaching in the desert area of Judea. 2John
said, "Change your hearts and lives because the
kingdom of heaven is near." 3John the Baptist is
the one Isaiah the prophet[d] was talking about
when he said:

"This is a voice of one
  who calls out in the desert:
'Prepare the way for the Lord.
  Make the road straight for him.' " *Isaiah 40:3*

4John's clothes were made from camel's hair,
and he wore a leather belt around his waist. For
food, he ate locusts[d] and wild honey. 5Many people came from Jerusalem and Judea and all the
area around the Jordan River to hear John. 6They
confessed their sins, and he baptized them in the
Jordan River.

7Many of the Pharisees[d] and Sadducees[d] came
to the place where John was baptizing people.
When John saw them, he said, "You are all
snakes! Who warned you to run away from God's
coming punishment? 8Do the things that show
you really have changed your hearts and lives.
9And don't think you can say to yourselves, 'Abraham is our father.' I tell you that God could make
children for Abraham from these rocks. 10The ax
is now ready to cut down the trees, and every tree
that does not produce good fruit will be cut down
and thrown into the fire.[n]

11"I baptize you with water to show that your
hearts and lives have changed. But there is one
coming after me who is greater than I am, whose
sandals I am not good enough to carry. He will
baptize you with the Holy Spirit[d] and fire. 12He
will come ready to clean the grain, separating the
good grain from the chaff.[d] He will put the good
part of the grain into his barn, but he will burn the
chaff with a fire that cannot be put out."[n]

Jesus Is Baptized by John

13At that time Jesus came from Galilee to the
Jordan River and wanted John to baptize him.
14But John tried to stop him, saying, "Why do you
come to me to be baptized? I need to be baptized
by you!"

15Jesus answered, "Let it be this way for now.
We should do all things that are God's will." So
John agreed to baptize Jesus.

16As soon as Jesus was baptized, he came up
out of the water. Then heaven opened, and he
saw God's Spirit[d] coming down on him like a
dove. 17And a voice from heaven said, "This is my
Son, whom I love, and I am very pleased with
him."

> **SIDELIGHT:** John the Baptist's diet wouldn't go over well at an all-church potluck dinner. He dined on locusts and wild honey (Matthew 3:4). Some people speculate that he might have been part of the desert Qumran community, people who lived in caves in cliffs above the Dead Sea. In the Qumran caves, some of the earliest manuscripts of the Bible and other writings—known as the Dead Sea Scrolls—were discovered in 1947.

The Temptation of Jesus

4 Then the Spirit[d] led Jesus into the desert to
be tempted by the devil. 2Jesus ate nothing
for forty days and nights. After this, he was very
hungry. 3The devil came to Jesus to tempt him,
saying, "If you are the Son of God, tell these rocks
to become bread."

4Jesus answered, "It is written in the Scriptures,[d] 'A person does not live by eating only
bread, but by everything God says.' "[n]

Nazarene A person from the city of Nazareth, a name probably meaning "branch" (see Isaiah 11:1).
The ax . . . fire. This means that God is ready to punish his people who do not obey him.
He will . . . out. This means that Jesus will come to separate good people from bad people, saving the good and punishing the bad.
'A person . . . says.' Quotation from Deuteronomy 8:3.

5 Then the devil led Jesus to the holy city of
Jerusalem and put him on a high place of the Temple.[d] 6 The devil said, "If you are the Son of God,
jump down, because it is written in the Scriptures:

'He has put his angels in charge of you.
They will catch you in their hands
so that you will not hit your foot on a
rock.' "

Psalm 91:11-12

7 Jesus answered him, "It also says in the Scriptures, 'Do not test the Lord your God.' "[n]

8 Then the devil led Jesus to the top of a very
high mountain and showed him all the kingdoms
of the world and all their splendor. 9 The devil
said, "If you will bow down and worship me, I
will give you all these things."
10 Jesus said to the devil, "Go away from me,
Satan! It is written in the Scriptures, 'You must
worship the Lord your God and serve only
him.' "[n]
11 So the devil left Jesus, and angels came and
took care of him.

'Do . . . God.' Quotation from Deuteronomy 6:16.
'You . . . him.' Quotation from Deuteronomy 6:13.

GOD'S WILL

God's Surprises

It was February, and time to begin rehearsals for Wheeler High School's senior play. Trina Cook eagerly auditioned for a part, convinced she would make the cast. But when the list was posted, Trina couldn't find her name on it.

She tried to hide her disappointment as she walked toward her last class of the day. Mr. Hendon, the director, caught up with her. "Trina," he said, "I meant to talk to you before the names were posted. We know you would have worked hard and done a good job for us. But you've had a lot of honors already, so we decided to let some of the others have a chance. I hope you're not too disappointed."

"Thanks, Mr. Hendon," she answered. "Thanks for explaining it to me." She still felt sad, but she didn't want him to know. In a way, she understood what he was saying.

A week later, Trina cringed as sharp pains shot through her stomach. Soon she was in the hospital, recovering from an emergency appendectomy. Mr. Hendon came to visit her. "It's a good thing you didn't put me in the senior play," she said. "You'd be looking for a replacement now."

A few weeks later, the missions committee at Trina's church decided to produce a drama about a woman who had spent her life in missions efforts. By this time Trina had regained her strength. She was chosen to play the leading role.

At every rehearsal, the cast prayed that God would use their efforts through the play to touch someone's heart.

Trina had no idea that she would be the one whose heart would be touched: On the evening of the performance, she committed her life to God's service and went on to be a missionary.

Disappointments, closed doors, and unexpected events often lead to surprises of God's will for our lives. Just as Trina was surprised by her road to a missionary career, John the Baptist was surprised to learn that God's will was for him to baptize the Messiah, instead of vice versa. You'll find the story of Jesus' baptism in **Matthew 3:13–17**.

- Why were both John the Baptist and Trina surprised by God's will?
- How has God used ironic or unusual circumstances in your life to do his will? How did you respond in those situations?

CONSIDER . . .

- Writing a list of prayer concerns. As you pray, follow each with, "We know that in everything God works for the good of those who love him" (Romans 8:28).
- thinking of unexpected events that have happened to you in the last month, and how God might be leading you. Then act on one of those leads.

FOR MORE, SEE . . .

- Isaiah 55:8–11
- Luke 3:1–20
- 1 Corinthians 1:18–25

Jesus Begins Work in Galilee

12When Jesus heard that John had been put in
prison, he went back to Galilee. 13He left Nazareth and went to live in Capernaum, a town near
Lake Galilee, in the area near Zebulun and Naphtali. 14Jesus did this to bring about what the
prophet[d] Isaiah had said:

15"Land of Zebulun and land of Naphtali
along the sea,
beyond the Jordan River.
This is Galilee where the non-Jewish people
live.
16These people who live in darkness
will see a great light.
They live in a place covered with the
shadows of death,
but a light will shine on them." *Isaiah 9:1-2*

Jesus Chooses Some Followers

17From that time Jesus began to preach, saying,
"Change your hearts and lives, because the kingdom of heaven is near."
18As Jesus was walking by Lake Galilee, he saw
two brothers, Simon (called Peter) and his brother
Andrew. They were throwing a net into the lake
because they were fishermen. 19Jesus said, "Come
follow me, and I will make you fish for people."
20So Simon and Andrew immediately left their
nets and followed him.
21As Jesus continued walking by Lake Galilee,
he saw two other brothers, James and John, the
sons of Zebedee. They were in a boat with their
father Zebedee, mending their nets. Jesus told
them to come with him. 22Immediately they left
the boat and their father, and they followed Jesus.

Jesus Teaches and Heals People

23Jesus went everywhere in Galilee, teaching in
the synagogues,[d] preaching the Good News[d]
about the kingdom of heaven, and healing all the
people's diseases and sicknesses. 24The news
about Jesus spread all over Syria, and people
brought all the sick to him. They were suffering
from different kinds of diseases. Some were in
great pain, some had demons,[d] some were epileptics,[n] and some were paralyzed. Jesus healed all
of them. 25Many people from Galilee, the Ten
Towns,[n] Jerusalem, Judea, and the land across
the Jordan River followed him.

Jesus Teaches the People

5 When Jesus saw the crowds, he went up on
a hill and sat down. His followers came to
him, 2and he began to teach them, saying:

3"Those people who know they have great
spiritual needs are happy,
because the kingdom of heaven belongs to
them.
4Those who are sad now are happy,
because God will comfort them.
5Those who are humble are happy,
because the earth will belong to them.
6Those who want to do right more than
anything else are happy,
because God will fully satisfy them.
7Those who show mercy to others are happy,
because God will show mercy to them.
8Those who are pure in their thinking are
happy,
because they will be with God.
9Those who work to bring peace are happy,
because God will call them his children.
10Those who are treated badly for doing good
are happy,
because the kingdom of heaven belongs to
them.

11"People will insult you and hurt you. They
will lie and say all kinds of evil things about you
because you follow me. But when they do, you
will be happy. 12Rejoice and be glad, because you
have a great reward waiting for you in heaven.
People did the same evil things to the prophets[d]
who lived before you.

You Are like Salt and Light

13"You are the salt of the earth. But if the salt
loses its salty taste, it cannot be made salty again.
It is good for nothing, except to be thrown out
and walked on.
14"You are the light that gives light to the
world. A city that is built on a hill cannot be hidden. 15And people don't hide a light under a bowl.
They put it on a lampstand so the light shines for
all the people in the house. 16In the same way,
you should be a light for other people. Live so that
they will see the good things you do and will
praise your Father in heaven.

The Importance of the Law

17"Don't think that I have come to destroy the
law of Moses or the teaching of the prophets.[d] I
have not come to destroy them but to bring about
what they said. 18I tell you the truth, nothing will
disappear from the law until heaven and earth are
gone. Not even the smallest letter or the smallest
part of a letter will be lost until everything has
happened. 19Whoever refuses to obey any command and teaches other people not to obey that

epileptics People with a disease that causes them sometimes to lose control of their bodies and maybe faint, shake strongly, or not be able to move.

Ten Towns In Greek, called "Decapolis." It was an area east of Lake Galilee that once had ten main towns.

command will be the least important in the kingdom of heaven. But whoever obeys the commands and teaches other people to obey them will
be great in the kingdom of heaven. 20I tell you
that if you are no more obedient than the teachers
of the law and the Pharisees,[d] you will never enter the kingdom of heaven.

Jesus Teaches About Anger

21"You have heard that it was said to our people long ago, 'You must not murder anyone.[n]
Anyone who murders another will be judged.'
22But I tell you, if you are angry with a brother or
sister,[n] you will be judged. If you say bad things
to a brother or sister, you will be judged by the
council. And if you call someone a fool, you will
be in danger of the fire of hell.
23"So when you offer your gift to God at the
altar, and you remember that your brother or sister has something against you, 24leave your gift
there at the altar. Go and make peace with that
person, and then come and offer your gift.

You . . . anyone. Quotation from Exodus 20:13; Deuteronomy 5:17.
brother . . . sister Although the Greek text reads "brother" here and throughout this book, Jesus' words were meant for the entire church, including men and women.

HAPPINESS

The Secret of Real Happiness

Young Francesco had it all: money, friends, power. His father was one of the wealthiest businessmen in the city-state of Assisi, in twelfth-century Italy. Francesco partied away his teenage years, often carousing in the streets until dawn.

But something was missing. When the parties ended, he felt depressed.

To try to find happiness and purpose, Francesco trained to be a knight. At twenty-one, he gallantly rode off to war against the neighboring city-state of Perugia. After a disastrous battlefield decision, he and his soldiers were taken prisoners. In a dungeon Francesco caught a fever that almost killed him. The enemy released him, and he somehow stumbled back to Assisi. He had left as a proud knight; he returned as a sad, sick failure.

These experiences made Francesco reexamine his life. He spent days in prayer, poring over Jesus' Sermon on the Mount in Matthew 5—7. He saw a chance for genuine happiness by following Jesus' teachings about storing treasures in heaven instead of on earth, not worrying about tomorrow, and trusting God. He began to run through meadows, singing like the birds and flinging his arms open to embrace the wind and sun. He gave away all his possessions and lived in caves because he didn't want to be burdened with "things." He traded his expensive clothing for a shepherd's robe.

His relationships with other people changed too. For the first time, he was happy. He spent his days helping the poor, homeless, and disabled. He went to the local leper colony and embraced people who had once nauseated him. He attracted several friends who shared his poverty and worked beside him, ministering to the poor of their community.

Francesco was named St. Francis shortly after his death, and remains one of the most beloved of all Christians. Eight hundred years later, people still seek the secret to the happiness St. Francis of Assisi found.

One of the passages that changed Francesco's life was **Matthew 5:1–12**. Read how Jesus' secret to happiness transformed St. Francis's life.

- What do you find in Jesus' words that could so powerfully change Francesco's depression to happiness?
- How does Jesus' secret for happiness compare to what you've been taught about happiness?

CONSIDER . . .

- looking at the "things" in your bedroom that make you happy and asking yourself which of them would make Jesus happy.
- writing each verse of this passage on a separate card, and then putting a different one on your mirror for eight days.

FOR MORE, SEE . . .

- Psalm 4
- Luke 6:17–49
- John 15:5–11

25“If your enemy is taking you to court, become
friends quickly, before you go to court. Otherwise, your enemy might turn you over to the
judge, and the judge might give you to a guard to
put you in jail. 26I tell you the truth, you will not
leave there until you have paid everything you
owe.

Jesus Teaches About Sexual Sin

27“You have heard that it was said, ‘You must
not be guilty of adultery.’[n] 28But I tell you that if
anyone looks at a woman and wants to sin sexually with her, in his mind he has already done that
sin with the woman. 29If your right eye causes you
to sin, take it out and throw it away. It is better
to lose one part of your body than to have your
whole body thrown into hell. 30If your right hand
causes you to sin, cut it off and throw it away. It
is better to lose one part of your body than for
your whole body to go into hell.

Jesus Teaches About Divorce

31“It was also said, ‘Anyone who divorces his
wife must give her a written divorce paper.’[n]
32But I tell you that anyone who divorces his wife
forces her to be guilty of adultery.[d] The only reason for a man to divorce his wife is if she has
sexual relations with another man. And anyone

‘You . . . adultery.’ Quotation from Exodus 20:14; Deuteronomy 5:18.
‘Anyone . . . divorce paper.’ Quotation from Deuteronomy 24:1.

SHARING FAITH

Salt and Light

Brett Clanton’s image of a homeless person had always been of a bag lady rummaging through dumpsters. He was afraid of poor people. And he was a little scared as he and his youth group traveled to San Antonio, Texas, to help in a homeless shelter for a week.

Brett and the other young people spent their days with homeless families—serving food, helping them find clothing, reading the Bible with them, playing with their children. By the end of the week the image of the faceless bag lady was gone from Brett’s mind. These people were now his friends.

The group went to the city’s famous river walk on their last evening of the trip, and they saw street people along the way. “I saw a man asleep on a bench, and I started to make a wide path to avoid him, and I suddenly realized that I knew him!” Brett later told the church. “I knew his name, where he was from—and I wasn’t afraid. Then I realized that all homeless people have names and home towns, and that becoming homeless could happen to any of us.”

One Wednesday evening the young people shared their experiences with the whole church. The next day, several of the adults from Brett’s church attended a meeting of more than thirty-five area ministers. These adults had been so moved by the young people’s stories that they shared them with leaders from the other churches.

The truth that Brett and the others had learned in San Antonio had spread from a few teenagers to an entire church, and then to a gathering of area ministers. The group now sponsors a task force on local poverty and hunger. The young people energized the task force members to respond to poverty in their community.

Brett discovered the contagious power of being the salt of the earth and light of the world as Jesus describes in **Matthew 5:13–16**. Jesus promises that when faith is shared, things change.

- How did Brett’s youth group act as salt and light in San Antonio and in their home town?
- How can you be “salt and light” in your world, as Jesus describes in the passage?

CONSIDER . . .

- telling someone you know about your faith this week.
- choosing two people you know who seem most like “salt and light” and asking them what they’ve learned as they have shared their faith.

FOR MORE, SEE . . .

- Isaiah 9:2–7
- 2 Corinthians 4:1–6
- 1 John 1:5–6

who marries that divorced woman is guilty of
adultery.

Make Promises Carefully

33"You have heard that it was said to our people long ago, 'Don't break your promises, but
keep the promises you make to the Lord.'[n] 34But
I tell you, never swear an oath. Don't swear an
oath using the name of heaven, because heaven
is God's throne. 35Don't swear an oath using the
name of the earth, because the earth belongs to
God. Don't swear an oath using the name of Jerusalem, because that is the city of the great King.
36Don't even swear by your own head, because
you cannot make one hair on your head become
white or black. 37Say only yes if you mean yes,
and no if you mean no. If you say more than yes
or no, it is from the Evil One.

Don't Fight Back

38"You have heard that it was said, 'An eye for
an eye, and a tooth for a tooth.'[n] 39But I tell you,
don't stand up against an evil person. If someone
slaps you on the right cheek, turn to him the other

'Don't . . . Lord.' This refers to Leviticus 19:12; Numbers 30:2; Deuteronomy 23:21.
'An eye . . . tooth.' Quotation from Exodus 21:24; Leviticus 24:20; Deuteronomy 19:21.

ANGER

Beating the Bully

Life wasn't going well for twelve-year-old Keith Jenkins. His parents had recently divorced, and he and his mom had moved from their farm to a nearby city. Keith felt alone in his new school, which seemed huge. But now there was another problem. Another student, Brian, had threatened to beat up Keith after school. And he meant it.

After the last bell on Thursday, Keith tried to slip out of school without being seen. He wanted to get home quickly. As he turned a corner, Brian was waiting for him.

Keith's heart pounded with fear. Brian attacked and landed blow after blow. Keith tried to fight back, but Brian was several years older and much stronger. After a few minutes of a one-sided fight, Brian left his victim lying on the sidewalk. Keith got up slowly and walked the rest of the way home. At the front door, his mother saw his torn clothes, his bloody face and hands. Keith told what happened and asked, "Mom, why are people like that? Why does Brian like to hurt other people?"

"I don't know, honey," she answered. "It doesn't make sense. There must be something wrong with him." Keith knew that she was upset, though she was trying to hide her anger toward Brian.

Later that evening, Keith looked at his reflection in the hall mirror. His face was already puffy and purple. He looked at his mom and said, "I look pretty weird, don't I?"

She laughed, and then he began to laugh. "You've certainly looked better," she said, with a sad smile. "How do you feel?"

"Sore," he said. "And a little scared. But you know what? I'm not really mad at Brian. What you said about there being something wrong—I think there is. I thought I'd hate him. But I don't. I feel kind of sorry for him. I don't think anybody likes him. Maybe that's why he does those things."

Jesus offers several ways to respond when we're angered and hurt by others. In **Matthew 5:17–26**, read how Jesus might have reacted in Keith's situation.

- Did Keith react in the way Jesus commands? Why or why not?
- If Brian had beaten you up, how would you have handled your anger and hurt? What are some ways to handle the situation according to the passage?

CONSIDER . . .

- watching how some TV characters handle their anger. What would happen in the real world if people handled their anger in those ways?
- making peace with someone with whom you have a conflict before the next time you attend worship.

FOR MORE, SEE . . .

- Proverbs 15:1
- Matthew 5:38–48
- Ephesians 4:17–32

cheek also. 40If someone wants to sue you in court
and take your shirt, let him have your coat also.

> **SIDELIGHT:** The coat (or robe) in Matthew 5:40 was a prized possession in Jesus' day. It was often the only protection poor people had from cold nights. That's why the Old Testament protected it (Exodus 22:26-27). And rich people showed their wealth by the number and quality of coats or robes they had (see James 5:1-2).

41If someone forces you to go with him one mil
go with him two miles. 42If a person asks you fo
something, give it to him. Don't refuse to give t
someone who wants to borrow from you.

Love All People

43"You have heard that it was said, 'Love you
neighbor[n] and hate your enemies.' 44But I say t
you, love your enemies. Pray for those who hu
you. 45If you do this, you will be true children o
your Father in heaven. He causes the sun to ris
on good people and on evil people, and he send
rain to those who do right and to those who d
wrong. 46If you love only the people who lov

Love your neighbor Quotation from Leviticus 19:18.

SEXUALITY

A Special Gift

Anna Bradley, thirteen, felt her life turning upside down. Her body was changing so fast she couldn't figure out what was happening. Along with the physical changes, she had new feelings she didn't understand.

A couple of years earlier, she didn't even like being around boys. Now she was fascinated by them. Especially Larry. He was so cute! She hung around outside the science lab just to see him when he came out. When he said "hi" to her in the hall, she felt like she was melting inside. "What's going on here?" she asked herself. "What's happening to me?"

She finally got the courage to ask her youth leader, Deanna.

"You're beginning to change from a young girl into a young woman," Deanna said.

"You mean my feelings—these desires—aren't bad?"

"How could they be bad if God put them there? But God also expects you to use this gift wisely."

"But what will the kids at school say if I tell them I want to stay a virgin until I marry? What will boys say if I go on a date with them?"

"You can tell them this is your decision, and that's all there is to it. If they're your friends, they'll respect your decision."

"What about the waiting part? Will it be hard to control myself all that time?"

"You can do it. People can control themselves—although some may not think they can, and many simply don't want to. But it's possible, and it'll be worth it. You'll discover how God's gift of sexuality is so wonderful in a committed marriage relationship."

Jesus considered sexuality a special gift from God. As such he spoke of the serious consequence of sex being used outside of marriage. **Matthew 5:27–37** has some rather harsh things to say about specific sexual behaviors. Read the passage and think about what Anna might think as she reads it.

- How does Deanna's advice relate to Jesus' teaching in the passage?
- Why do you think Jesus took sexual relations so seriously?

CONSIDER . . .

- talking about sexuality with a parent or an adult whom you trust. Write your questions first if that's helpful. Be honest about your feelings.
- organizing a discussion group at your church—perhaps a panel with adults and youth—on issues involving sexuality and teenagers.

FOR MORE, SEE . . .

- Genesis 1:26–28
- Song of Solomon 2:1–17
- 1 Corinthians 7:1–15

you, you will get no reward. Even the tax collectors do that. 47And if you are nice only to your friends, you are no better than other people. Even those who don't know God are nice to their friends. 48So you must be perfect, just as your Father in heaven is perfect.

Jesus Teaches About Giving

6 "Be careful! When you do good things, don't do them in front of people to be seen by them. If you do that, you will have no reward from your Father in heaven.

2"When you give to the poor, don't be like the
hypocrites.[d] They blow trumpets in the synagogues[d] and on the streets so that people will see
them and honor them. I tell you the truth, those
hypocrites already have their full reward. 3So
when you give to the poor, don't let anyone know
what you are doing. 4Your giving should be done
in secret. Your Father can see what is done in
secret, and he will reward you.

Jesus Teaches About Prayer

5"When you pray, don't be like the hypocrites.[d]

PEACE

The Second Mile

Tracy Collins pulled her car into the driveway and groaned when she saw that the front door was ajar. "Not again!" she fumed. She knew her apartment had been robbed for the third time.

When the police arrived, they helped her take inventory of what was missing. "Not that there was much left to take," she said. "He really cleaned me out the first time."

The police were virtually positive who the thief was. After the previous burglary, one of the officers had let the name slip: Tim O'Conner. They recognized his "style." A warrant for his arrest had been issued months earlier.

Tracy worked in an inner-city mission distributing food and clothing to needy people. Among the volunteers were adults placed on probation for nonviolent crimes. Instead of going to jail, they were required to provide community service.

Several weeks after the third burglary, Tracy interviewed a new probationer, filling out a form that would record the hours worked. "What's your name?" she asked, her pen ready on the correct line.

"Tim O'Conner," he said.

Tracy choked, and looked into the young man's eyes. He sat calmly, waiting for the next question. He was well-dressed, well-groomed, and had good manners. She shook her head as if to clear it, and turned the document back to the first page, searching for the line that would tell her why he had been convicted. "Burglary of a habitation," it read.

"Is something wrong?" he asked in a polite voice.

"He has no idea I'm one of his victims," she thought angrily. Then her anger turned into compassion as she wondered what made him break into other people's homes. "No," she answered. "Let's finish this form."

After they finished the interview, Tim was given an assignment. "Thanks," he said. "I'm glad the judge sent me here."

"So am I," Tracy said.

Tracy was surprised when she didn't feel like striking back at Tim. Then she realized Jesus' words in **Matthew 5:38–48** must have helped her handle her anger in a peaceful manner.

- In light of the passage, do you think Tracy did the right thing?
- Does "turning the other cheek" mean that Jesus wants people to walk all over your rights? Why or why not?

CONSIDER . . .

- listing the "normal" ways for handling conflicts, and then listing the "cheek-turning," peaceful ways next to them. Promise yourself to "turn the other cheek" the next time a conflict arises.
- walking away from a fight or keeping your cool in an argument in the future.

FOR MORE, SEE . . .

- Psalm 37
- Luke 6:27–36
- Colossians 3:12–13

They love to stand in the synagogues[d] and on the
street corners and pray so people will see them.
I tell you the truth, they already have their full
reward. 6When you pray, you should go into your
room and close the door and pray to your Father
who cannot be seen. Your Father can see what is
done in secret, and he will reward you.

> **SIDELIGHT:** Jews in Jesus' day had plenty of opportunities to give to people in need, which could lead to the problems Jesus talked about in Matthew 6:1–4. Jerusalem had a "chamber of secrets" where people quietly left gifts. Then the needy could slip in unnoticed and claim goods without embarrassment.

7"And when you pray, don't be like those people who don't know God. They continue saying
things that mean nothing, thinking that God will
hear them because of their many words. 8Don't
be like them, because your Father knows the
things you need before you ask him. 9So when
you pray, you should pray like this:
'Our Father in heaven,
may your name always be kept holy.
10May your kingdom come
and what you want be done,
here on earth as it is in heaven.
11Give us the food we need for each day.
12Forgive us for our sins,
just as we have forgiven those who sinned
against us.
13And do not cause us to be tempted,
but save us from the Evil One.'
14Yes, if you forgive others for their sins, your Father in heaven will also forgive you for your sins.
15But if you don't forgive others, your Father in
heaven will not forgive your sins.

Jesus Teaches About Worship

16"When you give up eating,[n] don't put on a
sad face like the hypocrites.[d] They make their
faces look sad to show people they are giving up
eating. I tell you the truth, those hypocrites already have their full reward. 17So when you give
up eating, comb your hair and wash your face.
18Then people will not know that you are giving
up eating, but your Father, whom you cannot see,
will see you. Your Father sees what is done in
secret, and he will reward you.

God Is More Important than Money

19"Don't store treasures for yourselves here on
earth where moths and rust will destroy them and
thieves can break in and steal them. 20But store
your treasures in heaven where they cannot be
destroyed by moths or rust and where thieves
cannot break in and steal them. 21Your heart will
be where your treasure is.
22"The eye is a light for the body. If your eyes
are good, your whole body will be full of light.
23But if your eyes are evil, your whole body will
be full of darkness. And if the only light you have
is really darkness, then you have the worst darkness.
24"No one can serve two masters. The person will hate one master and love the other,
or will follow one master and refuse to follow
the other. You cannot serve both God and
worldly riches.

Don't Worry

25"So I tell you, don't worry about the food or
drink you need to live, or about the clothes you
need for your body. Life is more than food, and
the body is more than clothes. 26Look at the birds
in the air. They don't plant or harvest or store
food in barns, but your heavenly Father feeds
them. And you know that you are worth much
more than the birds. 27You cannot add any time
to your life by worrying about it.
28"And why do you worry about clothes? Look
at how the lilies in the field grow. They don't
work or make clothes for themselves. 29But I tell
you that even Solomon with his riches was not
dressed as beautifully as one of these flowers.
30God clothes the grass in the field, which is alive
today but tomorrow is thrown into the fire. So
you can be even more sure that God will clothe
you. Don't have so little faith! 31Don't worry and
say, 'What will we eat?' or 'What will we drink?'
or 'What will we wear?' 32The people who don't
know God keep trying to get these things, and
your Father in heaven knows you need them.
33The thing you should want most is God's kingdom and doing what God wants. Then all these
other things you need will be given to you. 34So
don't worry about tomorrow, because tomorrow
will have its own worries. Each day has enough
trouble of its own.

Be Careful About Judging Others

7 "Don't judge other people, or you will be
judged. 2You will be judged in the same way
that you judge others, and the amount you give
to others will be given to you.
3"Why do you notice the little piece of dust in
your friend's eye, but you don't notice the big
piece of wood in your own eye? 4How can you say

give up eating This is called "fasting." The people would give up eating for a special time of prayer and worship to God. It was also done to show sadness and disappointment.

to your friend, 'Let me take that little piece of dust out of your eye'? Look at yourself! You still have that big piece of wood in your own eye. 5You hypocrite![d] First, take the wood out of your own eye. Then you will see clearly to take the dust out of your friend's eye.

6"Don't give holy things to dogs, and don't throw your pearls before pigs. Pigs will only trample on them, and dogs will turn to attack you.

Ask God for What You Need

7"Ask, and God will give to you. Search, and you will find. Knock, and the door will open for you. 8Yes, everyone who asks will receive. Everyone who searches will find. And everyone who knocks will have the door opened.

9"If your children ask for bread, which of you would give them a stone? 10Or if your children ask for a fish, would you give them a snake? 11Even though you are bad, you know how to give good gifts to your children. How much more your heavenly Father will give good things to those who ask him!

The Most Important Rule

12"Do to others what you want them to do to you. This is the meaning of the law of Moses and the teaching of the prophets.[d]

The Way to Heaven Is Hard

13"Enter through the narrow gate. The gate is wide and the road is wide that leads to hell, and many people enter through that gate. 14But the gate is small and the road is narrow that leads to true life. Only a few people find that road.

WORRYING

Sweating It Out

Jason Taylor stood at the coach's door, staring a long time at the recently posted roster. There it was: His name was on the list. He had made the junior varsity basketball team. Jason let out a deep sigh of relief and offered a silent thanks to God.

Anxiety was Jason's trademark. He worried about everything. In the two-day waiting period between tryouts and team roster, Jason couldn't sleep, concentrate on school, or eat much of anything. These worries were added to his stress of being a new kid in school. His family had moved from Georgia to Seattle over the summer.

His new friend Marc, seeing Jason staring at the roster, came over and shared Jason's happy time. "I knew you'd make it," Marc said, slapping him on the back. "Congratulations!"

Jason shook his head. "Since seventh grade," he said, "I had been looking forward to going to Stone Mountain High. Coach Wilson said I had a good chance of making junior varsity there this year. But then Dad told us we'd have to move here to Seattle because of his transfer to the new branch office. I didn't think I'd have a chance to make the team here. I've been sweating it out all summer. It even made me get off to a bad start on my grades."

"I told you there wasn't anything to worry about," Marc said.

"Easy for you to say," Jason thought. Suddenly a new worry hit Jason: "What if I'm not good enough to start?"

People today worry about many things, as did the people in Jesus' earthly ministry. He reminded them often not to worry. Read Jesus' practical teachings about worrying in **Matthew 6:25–34**.

- How could the analogy of the birds and flowers apply to Jason's life? How are the two kinds of worry different?
- If God doesn't want you to use time for worrying, how does he want you to use it?

C O N S I D E R . . .

- taking ten to fifteen minutes to watch a bird. Why do you think Jesus saw birds as examples of how you could live?
- listing some things you're worried about. Analyze each item on the list and decide if it's something you can change or something you should leave in God's hands.

F O R   M O R E ,   S E E . . .

- Psalm 46
- Luke 10:41–42
- Philippians 4:5–7

People Know You by Your Actions

15“Be careful of false prophets.[d] They come to
you looking gentle like sheep, but they are really
dangerous like wolves. 16You will know these
people by what they do. Grapes don’t come from
thornbushes, and figs don’t come from thorny
weeds. 17In the same way, every good tree produces good fruit, but a bad tree produces bad
fruit. 18A good tree cannot produce bad fruit, and
a bad tree cannot produce good fruit. 19Every tree
that does not produce good fruit is cut down and
thrown into the fire. 20In the same way, you will
know these false prophets by what they do.

21“Not all those who say that I am their Lord
will enter the kingdom of heaven. The only people who will enter the kingdom of heaven are
those who do what my Father in heaven wants.
22On the last day many people will say to me,
‘Lord, Lord, we spoke for you, and through you
we forced out demons[d] and did many miracles.’[d]
23Then I will tell them clearly, ‘Get away from
me, you who do evil. I never knew you.’

Two Kinds of People

24“Everyone who hears my words and obeys
them is like a wise man who built his house on
rock. 25It rained hard, the floods came, and the
winds blew and hit that house. But it did not fall,
because it was built on rock. 26Everyone who
hears my words and does not obey them is like
a foolish man who built his house on sand.
27It rained hard, the floods came, and the winds
blew and hit that house, and it fell with a big
crash.”

28When Jesus finished saying these things, the
people were amazed at his teaching, 29because he
did not teach like their teachers of the law. He
taught like a person who had authority.

Jesus Heals a Sick Man

8 When Jesus came down from the hill, great
crowds followed him. 2Then a man with a
skin disease came to Jesus. The man bowed down
before him and said, “Lord, you can heal me if
you will.”

3Jesus reached out his hand and touched the
man and said, “I will. Be healed!” And immediately the man was healed from his disease. 4Then
Jesus said to him, “Don’t tell anyone about this.
But go and show yourself to the priest[n] and offer

show . . . priest The law of Moses said a priest must say when a Jewish person with a skin disease was well.

CULTS

Deadly Deception

Malaya is home for a species of praying mantis that’s made a career of looking like a flower. But this “flower” kills unsuspecting bugs.

Pink, petal-like structures flank its spindly legs. Part of its green thorax simulates the stem of an orchid. A few brown markings here and there make it look slightly wilted. When a soft breeze blows, the mantis even simulates the flower’s gentle, swaying motion.

But this unusual insect is as deadly as it is beautiful. If a butterfly mistakes the mantis for an orchid, the mantis strikes with frightful speed and captures the butterfly in pink, vice-like forelegs.

Like butterflies, Christians need to be aware that not everything is as it appears. Many cults may look appealing, just as the praying mantis looks like an orchid to an unsuspecting butterfly. Learn how you can watch out for this kind of deception in **Matthew 7:15–29**.

- How is a butterfly captured by a praying mantis like those who build their houses on the sand?
- Who are some modern-day “false prophets” or groups you have heard of or been contacted by? How might Jesus react to them?

CONSIDER . . .

- praying for ways to resist the temptations of cults, and then investing time to grow in your faith in Christ.
- praying for those caught in cults, and sharing your faith with non-Christians.

FOR MORE, SEE . . .

- 1 Kings 18:1–40
- Mark 13:14–23
- 2 Peter 2:1–22

the gift Moses commanded[n] for people who are made well. This will show the people what I have done."

Jesus Heals a Soldier's Servant

5When Jesus entered the city of Capernaum, an army officer came to him, begging for help. 6The officer said, "Lord, my servant is at home in bed. He can't move his body and is in much pain."

7Jesus said to the officer, "I will go and heal him."

8The officer answered, "Lord, I am not worthy for you to come into my house. You only need to command it, and my servant will be healed. 9I, too, am a man under the authority of others, and I have soldiers under my command. I tell one soldier, 'Go,' and he goes. I tell another soldier, 'Come,' and he comes. I say to my servant, 'Do this,' and my servant does it.

10When Jesus heard this, he was amazed. He said to those who were following him, "I tell you the truth, this is the greatest faith I have found, even in Israel. 11Many people will come from the east and from the west and will sit and eat with Abraham, Isaac, and Jacob in the kingdom of heaven. 12But those people who should be in the kingdom will be thrown outside into the darkness, where people will cry and grind their teeth with pain."

13Then Jesus said to the officer, "Go home. Your servant will be healed just as you believed he would." And his servant was healed that same hour.

Jesus Heals Many People

14When Jesus went to Peter's house, he saw that Peter's mother-in-law was sick in bed with a fever. 15Jesus touched her hand, and the fever left her. Then she stood up and began to serve Jesus.

16That evening people brought to Jesus many who had demons.[d] Jesus spoke and the demons left them, and he healed all the sick. 17He did these things to bring about what Isaiah the prophet[d] had said:

"He took our suffering on him
and carried our diseases." *Isaiah 53:4*

People Want to Follow Jesus

18When Jesus saw the crowd around him, he told his followers to go to the other side of the lake. 19Then a teacher of the law came to Jesus and said, "Teacher, I will follow you any place you go."

20Jesus said to him, "The foxes have holes to live in, and the birds have nests, but the Son of Man[d] has no place to rest his head."

21Another man, one of Jesus' followers, said to him, "Lord, first let me go and bury my father."

22But Jesus told him, "Follow me, and let the people who are dead bury their own dead."

Jesus Calms a Storm

23Jesus got into a boat, and his followers went with him. 24A great storm arose on the lake so that waves covered the boat, but Jesus was sleeping. 25His followers went to him and woke him, saying, "Lord, save us! We will drown!"

26Jesus answered, "Why are you afraid? You don't have enough faith." Then Jesus got up and gave a command to the wind and the waves, and it became completely calm.

27The men were amazed and said, "What kind of man is this? Even the wind and the waves obey him!"

Jesus Heals Two Men with Demons

28When Jesus arrived at the other side of the lake in the area of the Gadarene[n] people, two men who had demons[d] in them met him. These men lived in the burial caves and were so dangerous that people could not use the road by those caves. 29They shouted, "What do you want with us, Son of God? Did you come here to torture us before the right time?"

30Near that place there was a large herd of pigs feeding. 31The demons begged Jesus, "If you make us leave these men, please send us into that herd of pigs."

32Jesus said to them, "Go!" So the demons left the men and went into the pigs. Then the whole herd rushed down the hill into the lake and were drowned. 33The herdsmen ran away and went into town, where they told about all of this and what had happened to the men who had demons. 34Then the whole town went out to see Jesus. When they saw him, they begged him to leave their area.

Jesus Heals a Paralyzed Man

9 Jesus got into a boat and went back across the lake to his own town. 2Some people brought to Jesus a man who was paralyzed and lying on a mat. When Jesus saw the faith of these people, he said to the paralyzed man, "Be encouraged, young man. Your sins are forgiven."

3Some of the teachers of the law said to themselves, "This man speaks as if he were God. That is blasphemy!"[n]

4Knowing their thoughts, Jesus said, "Why are

Moses commanded Read about this in Leviticus 14:1-32.
Gadarene From Gadara, an area southeast of Lake Galilee.
blasphemy Saying things against God or not showing respect for God.

you thinking evil thoughts? 5Which is easier: to
say, 'Your sins are forgiven,' or to tell him, 'Stand
up and walk'? 6But I will prove to you that the
Son of Man[d] has authority on earth to forgive
sins." Then Jesus said to the paralyzed man,
"Stand up, take your mat, and go home." 7And
the man stood up and went home. 8When the
people saw this, they were amazed and praised
God for giving power like this to human beings.

Jesus Chooses Matthew

9When Jesus was leaving, he saw a man named
Matthew sitting in the tax collector's booth. Jesus
said to him, "Follow me," and he stood up and
followed Jesus.
10As Jesus was having dinner at Matthew's
house, many tax collectors and "sinners" came
and ate with Jesus and his followers. 11When the
Pharisees[d] saw this, they asked Jesus' followers,
"Why does your teacher eat with tax collectors
and sinners?"
12When Jesus heard them, he said, "It is not the
healthy people who need a doctor, but the sick.

> **SIDELIGHT:** As a tax collector, Matthew was hardly Mr. Popularity (Matthew 9:9–13). He could tax you for crossing a bridge—and also tax your cart, its axle, and the engine (or donkey). And you thought toll roads were bad!

13Go and learn what this means: 'I want kindness
more than I want animal sacrifices.'[n] I did
not come to invite good people but to invite sinners."

'I want . . . sacrifices.' Quotation from Hosea 6:6.

NON-CHRISTIANS

How to Win Friends

Carlos Trujillo thought he had found a simple solution to negative peer influence: just avoid non-Christians. But then he got a job at a fast-food restaurant.

Because he was a team worker, Carlos often helped others finish their work. One day he helped Todd, another worker, wipe off the last table before their shift ended.

"Thanks for your help, Carlos," Todd said. "I've really got to hustle tonight because I have to study for a huge chemistry exam tomorrow. Mrs. Stafford's tests are really tough."

"You take chemistry from Mrs. Stafford, too?" Carlos asked. "Why don't we study together?"

Todd and Carlos spent two hours at the library reviewing for the test. Although he later learned that Todd had never been inside a church, Carlos discovered they had a lot in common. "Maybe," Carlos thought, "God has a good reason for Todd and me to be friends."

Over time, Carlos began to reach out in friendship to other non-Christians. His initial fear of how non-Christians would be a bad influence on him quickly disappeared. In fact, he discovered that many of his non-Christian friends were hungry for the truth of Christ.

In **Matthew 9:9–13**, Jesus chose to eat with Matthew, a tax collector, and other "sinners." This action raised pious eyebrows among the religious leaders. Read Jesus' response to their criticism.

- Why might the Pharisees have agreed with Carlos's initial plan to avoid non-Christians?
- What do these verses say to you about reaching non-Christians in your world?

CONSIDER . . .

- inviting someone at school or at work to attend church with you, or bringing that person to your next youth group outing.
- taking time this week to establish a relationship with a non-Christian or unchurched friend.

FOR MORE, SEE . . .

- Isaiah 56:1–8
- Luke 12:8–9
- James 2:14–26

Jesus' Followers Are Criticized

14Then the followers of John[n] came to Jesus and said, "Why do we and the Pharisees[d] often give up eating for a certain time,[n] but your followers don't?"

15Jesus answered, "The friends of the bridegroom are not sad while he is with them. But the time will come when the bridegroom will be taken from them, and then they will give up eating.

16"No one sews a patch of unshrunk cloth over a hole in an old coat. If he does, the patch will shrink and pull away from the coat, making the hole worse. 17Also, people never pour new wine into old leather bags. Otherwise, the bags will break, the wine will spill, and the wine bags will be ruined. But people always pour new wine into new wine bags. Then both will continue to be good."

Jesus Gives Life to a Dead Girl and Heals a Sick Woman

18While Jesus was saying these things, a leader of the synagogue[d] came to him. He bowed down before Jesus and said, "My daughter has just died. But if you come and lay your hand on her, she will live again." 19So Jesus and his followers stood up and went with the leader.

20Then a woman who had been bleeding for twelve years came behind Jesus and touched the edge of his coat. 21She was thinking, "If I can just touch his clothes, I will be healed."

22Jesus turned and saw the woman and said, "Be encouraged, dear woman. You are made well because you believed." And the woman was healed from that moment on.

23Jesus continued along with the leader and went into his house. There he saw the funeral musicians and many people crying. 24Jesus said, "Go away. The girl is not dead, only asleep." But the people laughed at him. 25After the crowd had been thrown out of the house, Jesus went into the girl's room and took hold of her hand, and she stood up. 26The news about this spread all around the area.

Jesus Heals More People

27When Jesus was leaving there, two blind men followed him. They cried out, "Have mercy on us, Son of David!"[d]

28After Jesus went inside, the blind men went with him. He asked the men, "Do you believe that I can make you see again?"

They answered, "Yes, Lord."

29Then Jesus touched their eyes and said, "Because you believe I can make you see again, it will happen." 30Then the men were able to see. But Jesus warned them strongly, saying, "Don't tell anyone about this." 31But the blind men left and spread the news about Jesus all around that area.

32When the two men were leaving, some people brought another man to Jesus. This man could not talk because he had a demon[d] in him. 33After Jesus forced the demon to leave the man, he was able to speak. The crowd was amazed and said, "We have never seen anything like this in Israel."

34But the Pharisees[d] said, "The prince of demons is the one that gives him power to force demons out."

35Jesus traveled through all the towns and villages, teaching in their synagogues,[d] preaching the Good News[d] about the kingdom, and healing all kinds of diseases and sicknesses. 36When he saw the crowds, he felt sorry for them because they were hurting and helpless, like sheep without a shepherd. 37Jesus said to his followers, "There are many people to harvest but only a few workers to help harvest them. 38Pray to the Lord, who owns the harvest, that he will send more workers to gather his harvest."[n]

Jesus Sends Out His Apostles

10 Jesus called his twelve followers together and gave them authority to drive out evil spirits and to heal every kind of disease and sickness. 2These are the names of the twelve apostles:[d] Simon (also called Peter) and his brother Andrew; James son of Zebedee, and his brother John; 3Philip and Bartholomew; Thomas and Matthew, the tax collector; James son of Alphaeus, and Thaddaeus; 4Simon the Zealot[d] and Judas Iscariot, who turned against Jesus.

5Jesus sent out these twelve men with the following order: "Don't go to the non-Jewish people or to any town where the Samaritans[d] live. 6But go to the people of Israel, who are like lost sheep. 7When you go, preach this: 'The kingdom of heaven is near.' 8Heal the sick, raise the dead to life again, heal those who have skin diseases, and force demons[d] out of people. I give you these powers freely, so help other people freely. 9Don't carry any money with you — gold or silver or copper. 10Don't carry a bag or extra clothes or sandals or a walking stick. Workers should be given what they need.

11"When you enter a city or town, find some

John John the Baptist, who preached to people about Christ's coming (Matthew 3, Luke 3).
give up . . . time This is called "fasting." The people would give up eating for a special time of prayer and worship to God. It was also done to show sadness and disappointment.
"There are . . . harvest." As a farmer sends workers to harvest the grain, Jesus sends his followers to bring people to God.

worthy person there and stay in that home until
you leave. 12When you enter that home, say,
'Peace be with you.' 13If the people there welcome you, let your peace stay there. But if they
don't welcome you, take back the peace you
wished for them. 14And if a home or town refuses
to welcome you or listen to you, leave that place
and shake its dust off your feet.[n] 15I tell you the
truth, on the Judgment Day it will be better for
the towns of Sodom and Gomorrah[n] than for the
people of that town.

Jesus Warns His Apostles

16"Listen, I am sending you out like sheep
among wolves. So be as smart as snakes and as
innocent as doves. 17Be careful of people, because
they will arrest you and take you to court and
whip you in their synagogues.[d] 18Because of me
you will be taken to stand before governors and
kings, and you will tell them and the non-Jewish
people about me. 19When you are arrested, don't
worry about what to say or how to say it. At that
time you will be given the things to say. 20It will
not really be you speaking but the Spirit of your
Father speaking through you.
21"Brothers will give their own brothers to be
killed, and fathers will give their own children to
be killed. Children will fight against their own

shake . . . feet. A warning. It showed that they had rejected these people.
Sodom and Gomorrah Two cities that God destroyed because the people were so evil.

SICKNESS

Giving the World Friends

Rebecca Smathers, a high school junior, dances, walks, and runs. No big deal for most of us—but for Rebecca those abilities prove God's power. For not long ago, she was almost completely paralyzed.

In her freshman year, Rebecca felt her muscles slowly becoming numb. She started avoiding golf and softball practices. Play rehearsals caused excruciating pain. Her mother finally took her to a doctor, and Rebecca was admitted to the hospital that same day.

A spinal tap confirmed she had Guillain Barr Syndrome, a rare condition in which a virus attacks the nervous system, causing paralysis in all of the motor functions. Although she began various drug and physical treatments, Rebecca's condition worsened. "The syndrome spread, and I could no longer sit upright in bed by myself," she recalls.

Doctors gave her little chance for recovery. However, Rebecca believes the care and prayers of others made the difference. "My spirits have been strengthened because of the love from family and friends," Rebecca says. "Daily I received phone calls, cards, and flowers. My room was crowded with friends every day. It was a time for fellowship and support, not only for me, but also for my family and friends."

The doctors continued treatment, and Rebecca slowly recovered.

"Some people say the Lord doesn't give us answers we can see or touch, yet we all see and touch our family and friends," Rebecca says. "The Lord answered my prayers with a family who stroked my hair and sat next to me day and night while I lay motionless.

"The Lord brought me friends who told me, 'You will get better, because I'm praying for you.' I thank God for the answers he's given me."

Rebecca's doctors were amazed at the healing power of faith. Yet **Matthew 9:35—10:8** tells how Jesus commissioned the disciples to heal the sick.

- How well did the people who prayed and stayed with Rebecca follow Jesus' commission to the apostles?
- Why does God care not only about your physical health, but also your spiritual health?

CONSIDER . . .

- doing one activity this week to better your health and well-being.
- visiting someone in a hospital or nursing home and praying with him or her.

FOR MORE, SEE . . .

- 2 Kings 20:1–11
- Psalm 30:2–3
- Luke 18:35–43

parents and have them put to death. 22All people
will hate you because you follow me, but those
people who keep their faith until the end will be
saved. 23When you are treated badly in one city,
run to another city. I tell you the truth, you will
not finish going through all the cities of Israel before the Son of Man[d] comes.
24"A student is not better than his teacher, and
a servant is not better than his master. 25A student
should be satisfied to become like his teacher; a
servant should be satisfied to become like his master. If the head of the family is called Beelzebul,[d]
then the other members of the family will be
called worse names!

Fear God, Not People

26"So don't be afraid of those people, because
everything that is hidden will be shown. Everything that is secret will be made known. 27I tell
you these things in the dark, but I want you to tell
them in the light. What you hear whispered in
your ear you should shout from the housetops.
28Don't be afraid of people, who can kill the body
but cannot kill the soul. The only one you should
fear is the one who can destroy the soul and the
body in hell. 29Two sparrows cost only a penny,
but not even one of them can die without your
Father's knowing it. 30God even knows how
many hairs are on your head. 31So don't be
afraid. You are worth much more than many sparrows.

Tell People About Your Faith

32"All those who stand before others and say
they believe in me, I will say before my Father in
heaven that they belong to me. 33But all who
stand before others and say they do not believe in
me, I will say before my Father in heaven that
they do not belong to me.
34"Don't think that I came to bring peace to the
earth. I did not come to bring peace, but a sword.

SELF-ESTEEM

Playing Your Part

The second-period algebra test had been a disaster for Charlene Markham. Then she had slipped and fallen in the hallway in front of two dozen other students. As she sat in sixth-period band practice, her mind was everywhere except on the sheets of music.

"Sometimes I wonder if my being here at Springbrook High makes any difference at all," she thought as the band music filled the room. "It's like the flutists' part in this medley. All you can hear are the trumpets and trombones, anyway."

As an experiment, Charlene raised the flute to her lips but only pretended to play. "See," she thought after the piece, "no one even noticed."

Just before the bell rang, Mr. Westmore, the band director, instructed the students to put away their instruments. Then he asked Charlene to stay after the bell.

"Why didn't you play in the Sousa medley?" he asked.

Charlene was stunned that he knew what she had done. She didn't answer him.

"Charlene," he said kindly, yet firmly, "we need every part in a piece of music to make it complete. The director looks for everyone to be playing his or her part."

Somehow Charlene felt better knowing she had been missed. "Maybe I have a part to play after all," she thought. Learn what Jesus says about your importance in **Matthew 10:24–33**.

- How does the Bible passage speak to Charlene's feelings of worthlessness?
- How does knowing that God loves you affect your feelings about yourself?

CONSIDER . . .

- investing thirty minutes today in an activity for your own growth, health and well-being.
- listing all of the "sections" in God's "band" (the church) you can think of, such as pastors, leaders, choirs and so forth. Pick the one section that you're most interested in, and volunteer to "play" in it.

FOR MORE, SEE . . .

- Psalm 8:3–9
- Romans 5:1–11
- 1 Corinthians 12:12–31

35I have come so that
'a son will be against his father,
a daughter will be against her mother,
a daughter-in-law will be against her
mother-in-law.
36 A person's enemies will be members of his
own family.' *Micah 7:6*

37"Those who love their father or mother more than they love me are not worthy to be my followers. Those who love their son or daughter more than they love me are not worthy to be my followers. 38Whoever is not willing to carry the cross and follow me is not worthy of me. 39Those who try to hold on to their lives will give up true life. Those who give up their lives for me will hold on to true life. 40Whoever accepts you also accepts me, and whoever accepts me also accepts the One who sent me. 41Whoever meets a prophet[d] and accepts him will receive the reward of a prophet. And whoever accepts a good person because that person is good will receive the reward of a good person. 42Those who give one of these little ones a cup of cold water because they are my followers will truly get their reward."

Jesus and John the Baptist

11 After Jesus finished telling these things to his twelve followers, he left there and went to the towns in Galilee to teach and preach.

2John the Baptist[d] was in prison, but he heard about what Christ was doing. So John sent some of his followers to Jesus. 3They asked him, "Are you the One who is to come, or should we wait for someone else?"

4Jesus answered them, "Go tell John what you hear and see: 5The blind can see, the crippled can walk, and people with skin diseases are healed. The deaf can hear, the dead are raised to life, and the Good News[d] is preached to the poor. 6Those who do not stumble in their faith because of me are blessed."

7As John's followers were leaving, Jesus began talking to the people about John. Jesus said, "What did you go out into the desert to see? A reed[n] blown by the wind? 8What did you go out to see? A man dressed in fine clothes? No, those who wear fine clothes live in kings' palaces. 9So

reed It means that John was not ordinary or weak like grass blown by the wind.

PRIORITIES

Doing the Right Thing

Dad appeared in Marcia Sloan's bedroom doorway. "What's all this I hear about you going to a Christian college next year?" he asked.

This was the moment she had been dreading. "It's true, Dad. That's what I've decided."

"Ever since you started going to that church, you've been getting weird ideas," he said. "If you want to go to medical school, you'll need the quality of education that you can get at a state school."

Then he dropped the ultimatum: "If you go to that Christian college, don't look to us for financial support."

Marcia's father kept his promise. But Marcia firmly believed that the Christian college was God's will for her.

Marcia's freshman year in college was difficult. Because she had to pay her own tuition, she worked several hours part-time in the evenings. But she kept going, knowing she had made a smart choice.

Jesus cautioned that following him would not always be easy. Read in **Matthew 10:34–42** about the difficult choices Christians may face.

- How was Marcia's predicament like that described in the passage?
- What does this passage say about your priorities in your family and in other areas of life?

C O N S I D E R . . .

- giving encouragement to a Christian friend whose parents are not believers.
- taking your mom or dad out for dessert after dinner one night this week, and talking with them about your goals and priorities.

F O R M O R E , S E E . . .

- Genesis 22:1–18
- Exodus 20:12
- 1 John 3:1–3

why did you go out? To see a prophet?[d] Yes, and
I tell you, John is more than a prophet. 10This was
written about him:

'I will send my messenger ahead of you,
who will prepare the way for you.' *Malachi 3:1*

11I tell you the truth, John the Baptist is greater
than any other person ever born, but even the
least important person in the kingdom of heaven
is greater than John. 12Since the time John the
Baptist came until now, the kingdom of heaven
has been going forward in strength, and people
have been trying to take it by force. 13All the
prophets and the law of Moses told about what
would happen until the time John came. 14And if
you will believe what they said, you will believe
that John is Elijah, whom they said would come.
15You people who can hear me, listen!

16"What can I say about the people of this time?
What are they like? They are like children sitting
in the marketplace, who call out to each other,

17'We played music for you, but you did not
dance;
we sang a sad song, but you did not cry.'

18John came and did not eat or drink like other
people. So people say, 'He has a demon.'[d] 19The
Son of Man[d] came, eating and drinking, and people say, 'Look at him! He eats too much and
drinks too much wine, and he is a friend of tax
collectors and sinners.' But wisdom is proved to
be right by what it does."

Jesus Warns Unbelievers

20Then Jesus criticized the cities where he did
most of his miracles,[d] because the people did not
change their lives and stop sinning. 21He said,
"How terrible for you, Korazin! How terrible for
you, Bethsaida! If the same miracles I did in you
had happened in Tyre and Sidon,[n] those people
would have changed their lives a long time ago.
They would have worn rough cloth and put ashes

Tyre and Sidon Towns where wicked people lived.

FAITH

The Faith Difference

Next time friends ask you, "Does your faith make a difference?" remember these statistics about teenagers in the United States*:

1. Teenagers who have never used illegal drugs—61 percent of regular churchgoers, versus 39 percent of nonchurchgoers.
2. Teenagers who have never had sexual intercourse—61 percent of regular churchgoers, versus 35 percent of nonchurchgoers.
3. Teenagers who believe in a personal God—87 percent of regular churchgoers, versus 64 percent of nonchurchgoers.
4. Teenagers who read the Bible weekly—58 percent of regular churchgoers, versus 17 percent of nonchurchgoers.
5. Teenagers who plan to go to college—57 percent of regular churchgoers, versus 33 percent of nonchurchgoers.

Faith isn't a "heady" thing. It's something that affects everything we do. As the statistics above illustrate, a committed faith makes a visible, real difference in the way we live. In **Matthew 11:2–11** the followers of John the Baptist asked Jesus whether he was the Christ. Read how he responded.

- Why is faith a powerful force in the miracles of Jesus as well as the behavior of regular churchgoers?
- What difference does faith make in your own life? Have you seen the signs of God's work that are listed in the passage?

CONSIDER . . .

- surveying your own behavior in comparison to the statistics. How well did you fit the categories?
- drawing up your own survey and interviewing both churchgoers and nonchurchgoers. Share your results with others at church and school.

FOR MORE, SEE . . .

- Judges 6:11–24
- Luke 13:1–9
- James 5:13–18

*Eugene C. Roehlkepartain ed., The Youth Ministry Resource Book; (Loveland, CO: Group Books, 1988).

on themselves to show they had changed. 22But
I tell you, on the Judgment Day it will be better
for Tyre and Sidon than for you. 23And you, Capernaum,[n] will you be lifted up to heaven? No,
you will be thrown down to the depths. If the
miracles I did in you had happened in Sodom,[n]
its people would have stopped sinning, and it
would still be a city today. 24But I tell you, on the
Judgment Day it will be better for Sodom than for
you."

Jesus Offers Rest to People

25At that time Jesus said, "I praise you, Father,
Lord of heaven and earth, because you have hidden these things from the people who are wise
and smart. But you have shown them to those
who are like little children. 26Yes, Father, this is
what you really wanted.
27"My Father has given me all things. No one
knows the Son, except the Father. And no one
knows the Father, except the Son and those
whom the Son chooses to tell.
28"Come to me, all of you who are tired and
have heavy loads, and I will give you rest. 29Ac-
cept my teachings and learn from me, because I
am gentle and humble in spirit, and you will find
rest for your lives. 30The teaching that I ask you
to accept is easy; the load I give you to carry is
light."

Jesus Is Lord of the Sabbath

12 At that time Jesus was walking through
some fields of grain on a Sabbath[d] day.
His followers were hungry, so they began to pick
the grain and eat it. 2When the Pharisees[d] saw
this, they said to Jesus, "Look! Your followers
are doing what is unlawful to do on the Sabbath
day."
3Jesus answered, "Have you not read what David did when he and the people with him were
hungry? 4He went into God's house, and he and
those with him ate the holy bread, which was
lawful only for priests to eat. 5And have you not
read in the law of Moses that on every Sabbath
day the priests in the Temple[d] break this law
about the Sabbath day? But the priests are not
wrong for doing that. 6I tell you that there is
something here that is greater than the Temple.

Korazin . . . Bethsaida . . . Capernaum Towns by Lake Galilee where Jesus preached to the people.
Sodom A city that God destroyed because the people were so evil.

WORRYING

Making It Through Your Day

Why did everyone else seem to have such a carefree life? Stacy Campbell wondered.

For more than a year her mother had been threatening to leave her father. Her school counselor told her she would have to raise her grades in physics and math if she ever wanted to take engineering in college. While other students received allowances, Stacy worked long hours at a "lousy" part-time job. And Grandma Campbell had just gone into a nursing home because she couldn't care for herself anymore.

Stacy usually fell into bed after midnight. But she often had trouble going to sleep. Even in her sleep she couldn't find rest; the day's problems crept into her dreams.

But then one evening she stumbled across a way to unwind at day's end. She began to spend a little time reading her Bible and praying just before going to bed. In time, this habit helped to settle her down, set her mind at peace and place her day's troubles in God's care.

Jesus offered ways to cope with the stresses of life. Read about his promise in **Matthew 11:25–30**.

- What truth in this passage did Stacy stumble upon?
- What kinds of stresses do you have that you can take to Jesus?

CONSIDER . . .

- writing a thank-you note to Jesus for helping you cope with problems.
- setting aside ten minutes a day for one week for Bible reading and prayer. Perhaps begin by reading a psalm and a chapter of Proverbs each day. Many of the psalms are prayers you can use.

FOR MORE, SEE . . .

- Psalm 4
- Luke 11:5–13
- Jude 24–25

7The Scripture[d] says, 'I want kindness more than I want animal sacrifices.'[n] You don't really know what those words mean. If you understood them, you would not judge those who have done nothing wrong.

8"So the Son of Man[d] is Lord of the Sabbath day."

> **SIDELIGHT:** It was hard not to break Sabbath laws in Jesus' day (Matthew 12:1–8). The Pharisees believed thirty-nine different actions violated Sabbath laws. You couldn't take a trip, light a fire, get a drink, or pick up anything that weighed more than two figs. How much does a TV remote control weigh?

Jesus Heals a Man's Hand

9Jesus left there and went into their synagogue,[d] 10where there was a man with a crippled hand. They were looking for a reason to accuse Jesus, so they asked him, "Is it right to heal on the Sabbath[d] day?"[n]

11Jesus answered, "If any of you has a sheep, and it falls into a ditch on the Sabbath day, you will help it out of the ditch. 12Surely a human being is more important than a sheep. So it is lawful to do good things on the Sabbath day."

13Then Jesus said to the man with the crippled hand, "Hold out your hand." The man held out his hand, and it became well again, like the other hand. 14But the Pharisees[d] left and made plans to kill Jesus.

Jesus Is God's Chosen Servant

15Jesus knew what the Pharisees[d] were doing, so he left that place. Many people followed him, and he healed all who were sick. 16But Jesus warned the people not to tell who he was. 17He did these things to bring about what Isaiah the prophet[d] had said:

18"Here is my servant whom I have chosen.
I love him, and I am pleased with him.
I will put my Spirit[d] upon him,
and he will tell of my justice to all people.
19He will not argue or cry out;
no one will hear his voice in the streets.
20He will not break a crushed blade of grass
or put out even a weak flame
until he makes justice win the victory.
21 In him will the non-Jewish people find
hope." *Isaiah 42:1-4*

Jesus' Power Is from God

22Then some people brought to Jesus a man who was blind and could not talk, because he had a demon.[d] Jesus healed the man so that he could talk and see. 23All the people were amazed and said, "Perhaps this man is the Son of David!"[d]

24When the Pharisees[d] heard this, they said, "Jesus uses the power of Beelzebul,[d] the ruler of demons, to force demons out of people."

25Jesus knew what the Pharisees were thinking, so he said to them, "Every kingdom that is divided against itself will be destroyed. And any city or family that is divided against itself will not continue. 26And if Satan forces out himself, then Satan is divided against himself, and his kingdom will not continue. 27You say that I use the power of Beelzebul to force out demons. If that is true, then what power do your people use to force out demons? So they will be your judges. 28But if I use the power of God's Spirit[d] to force out demons, then the kingdom of God has come to you.

29"If anyone wants to enter a strong person's house and steal his things, he must first tie up the strong person. Then he can steal the things from the house.

30"Whoever is not with me is against me. Whoever does not work with me is working against me. 31So I tell you, people can be forgiven for every sin and everything they say against God. But whoever speaks against the Holy Spirit will not be forgiven. 32Anyone who speaks against the Son of Man[d] can be forgiven, but anyone who speaks against the Holy Spirit will not be forgiven, now or in the future.

People Know You by Your Words

33"If you want good fruit, you must make the tree good. If your tree is not good, it will have bad fruit. A tree is known by the kind of fruit it produces. 34You snakes! You are evil people, so how can you say anything good? The mouth speaks the things that are in the heart. 35Good people have good things in their hearts, and so they say good things. But evil people have evil in their hearts, so they say evil things. 36And I tell you that on the Judgment Day people will be responsible for every careless thing they have said. 37The words you have said will be used to judge you. Some of your words will prove you right, but some of your words will prove you guilty."

The People Ask for a Miracle

38Then some of the Pharisees[d] and teachers of the law answered Jesus, saying, "Teacher, we want to see you work a miracle[d] as a sign."

39Jesus answered, "Evil and sinful people are

'I . . . sacrifices.' Quotation from Hosea 6:6.
"Is it right . . . day?" It was against Jewish law to work on the Sabbath day.

the ones who want to see a miracle for a sign. But
no sign will be given to them, except the sign of
the prophet[d] Jonah. 40Jonah was in the stomach
of the big fish for three days and three nights. In
the same way, the Son of Man[d] will be in the
grave three days and three nights. 41On the Judgment Day the people from Nineveh[n] will stand
up with you people who live now, and they will
show that you are guilty. When Jonah preached
to them, they were sorry and changed their lives.
And I tell you that someone greater than Jonah is
here. 42On the Judgment Day, the Queen of the
South[n] will stand up with you people who live
today. She will show that you are guilty, because
she came from far away to listen to Solomon's
wise teaching. And I tell you that someone greater
than Solomon is here.

People Today Are Full of Evil

43"When an evil spirit comes out of a person,
it travels through dry places, looking for a place to
rest, but it doesn't find it. 44So the spirit says, 'I
will go back to the house I left.' When the spirit
comes back, it finds the house still empty, swept
clean, and made neat. 45Then the evil spirit goes
out and brings seven other spirits even more evil
than it is, and they go in and live there. So the
person has even more trouble than before. It is
the same way with the evil people who live today."

Jesus' True Family

46While Jesus was talking to the people, his
mother and brothers stood outside, trying to find
a way to talk to him. 47Someone told Jesus, "Your
mother and brothers are standing outside, and
they want to talk to you."
48He answered, "Who is my mother? Who are
my brothers?" 49Then he pointed to his followers
and said, "Here are my mother and my brothers.
50My true brother and sister and mother are those
who do what my Father in heaven wants."

A Story About Planting Seed

13 That same day Jesus went out of the
house and sat by the lake. 2Large crowds
gathered around him, so he got into a boat and sat
down, while the people stood on the shore. 3Then
Jesus used stories to teach them many things. He
said: "A farmer went out to plant his seed. 4While
he was planting, some seed fell by the road, and
the birds came and ate it all up. 5Some seed fell
on rocky ground, where there wasn't much dirt.
That seed grew very fast, because the ground was
not deep. 6But when the sun rose, the plants dried
up, because they did not have deep roots. 7Some
other seed fell among thorny weeds, which grew
and choked the good plants. 8Some other seed fell
on good ground where it grew and produced a
crop. Some plants made a hundred times more,
some made sixty times more, and some made
thirty times more. 9You people who can hear me,
listen."

Why Jesus Used Stories to Teach

10The followers came to Jesus and asked, "Why
do you use stories to teach the people?"
11Jesus answered, "You have been chosen to
know the secrets about the kingdom of heaven,
but others cannot know these secrets. 12Those
who have understanding will be given more, and
they will have all they need. But those who do not
have understanding, even what they have will be
taken away from them. 13This is why I use stories
to teach the people: They see, but they don't
really see. They hear, but they don't really hear or
understand. 14So they show that the things Isaiah
said about them are true:

'You will listen and listen, but you will not
understand.
You will look and look, but you will not
learn.
15For the minds of these people have become
stubborn.
They do not hear with their ears,
and they have closed their eyes.
Otherwise they might really understand
what they see with their eyes
and hear with their ears.
They might really understand in their minds
and come back to me and be healed.'

Isaiah 6:9-10

16But you are blessed, because you see with your
eyes and hear with your ears. 17I tell you the
truth, many prophets[d] and good people wanted to
see the things that you now see, but they did not
see them. And they wanted to hear the things that
you now hear, but they did not hear them.

Jesus Explains the Seed Story

18"So listen to the meaning of that story about
the farmer. 19What is the seed that fell by the
road? That seed is like the person who hears the
message about the kingdom but does not understand it. The Evil One comes and takes away what
was planted in that person's heart. 20And what is
the seed that fell on rocky ground? That seed is
like the person who hears the teaching and
quickly accepts it with joy. 21But he does not let
the teaching go deep into his life, so he keeps it

Nineveh The city where Jonah preached to warn the people. Read Jonah 3.
Queen of the South The Queen of Sheba. She traveled a thousand miles to learn God's wisdom from Solomon. Read 1 Kings 10:1-13.

only a short time. When trouble or persecution comes because of the teaching he accepted, he quickly gives up. [22]And what is the seed that fell among the thorny weeds? That seed is like the person who hears the teaching but lets worries about this life and the temptation of wealth stop that teaching from growing. So the teaching does not produce fruit[n] in that person's life. [23]But what is the seed that fell on the good ground? That seed is like the person who hears the teaching and understands it. That person grows and produces fruit, sometimes a hundred times more, sometimes sixty times more, and sometimes thirty times more."

A Story About Wheat and Weeds

[24]Then Jesus told them another story: "The kingdom of heaven is like a man who planted good seed in his field. [25]That night, when everyone was asleep, his enemy came and planted weeds among the wheat and then left. [26]Later, the wheat sprouted and the heads of grain grew, but the weeds also grew. [27]Then the man's servants came to him and said, 'You planted good seed in your field. Where did the weeds come from?' [28]The man answered, 'An enemy planted weeds.' The servants asked, 'Do you want us to pull up the weeds?' [29]The man answered, 'No, because when you pull up the weeds, you might also pull up the wheat. [30]Let the weeds and the wheat grow together until the harvest time. At harvest time I will tell the workers, "First gather the weeds and tie them together to be burned. Then gather the wheat and bring it to my barn." ' "

Stories of Mustard Seed and Yeast

[31]Then Jesus told another story: "The kingdom of heaven is like a mustard seed that a man planted in his field. [32]That seed is the smallest of all seeds, but when it grows, it is one of the largest garden plants. It becomes big enough for the wild birds to come and build nests in its branches."

[33]Then Jesus told another story: "The kingdom of heaven is like yeast that a woman took and hid in a large tub of flour until it made all the dough rise."

[34]Jesus used stories to tell all these things to the

produce fruit To produce fruit means to have in your life the good things God wants.

FOLLOWING GOD

Tuned In

One beautiful spring morning, an experienced hiker was walking with a friend down Fifth Avenue in Manhattan. The streets rumbled with the sounds of weekday rush-hour traffic. Suddenly the hiker stopped. "Listen," he said. "I hear a cricket."

"That's nonsense!" his friend scoffed. "Why do you think you hear a lowly cricket in all this downtown uproar?"

"I'm sure I do," the hiker said. "Watch this." He pulled a dime from his pocket and dropped it on the pavement. Almost all of the people nearby stopped at the sound of the coin hitting the concrete.

"All of us are tuned to certain things," the hiker said to his friend. "Our ears hear what they are tuned to. Mine happen to be tuned to crickets."

In a similar way we need to be open to God's word. Jesus said we need "eyes to see" and "ears to hear" before we can tune in to the gospel. Read how to gain a new view of your faith in **Matthew 13:1–23**.

- How was the hiker's hearing the cricket like the ability to hear Jesus' message?
- Why do you think Jesus compares following God to being the "good ground" for the seed of faith?

CONSIDER . . .

- looking around your room or yard as if you've never seen it before. What do you see, hear or feel that's gone unnoticed? Then do the same process at your church. How can you follow God in ways you may not have noticed?
- listing three specific things you can do in the next week to better see and hear ways to follow God.

FOR MORE, SEE . . .

- 1 Samuel 3:1–21
- Isaiah 42:18–20
- 1 Corinthians 13:8–13

people; he always used stories to teach them.
35This is as the prophet[d] said:

"I will speak using stories;
I will tell things that have been secret since
the world was made." *Psalm 78:2*

Jesus Explains About the Weeds

36Then Jesus left the crowd and went into the
house. His followers came to him and said, "Explain to us the meaning of the story about the
weeds in the field."

37Jesus answered, "The man who planted the
good seed in the field is the Son of Man.[d] 38The
field is the world, and the good seed are all of
God's children who belong to the kingdom. The
weeds are those people who belong to the Evil
One. 39And the enemy who planted the bad seed
is the devil. The harvest time is the end of the
world, and the workers who gather are God's angels.

40"Just as the weeds are pulled up and burned
in the fire, so it will be at the end of the world.
41The Son of Man will send out his angels, and
they will gather out of his kingdom all who cause
sin and all who do evil. 42The angels will throw
them into the blazing furnace, where the people
will cry and grind their teeth with pain. 43Then
the good people will shine like the sun in the kingdom of their Father. You people who can hear
me, listen.

Stories of a Treasure and a Pearl

44"The kingdom of heaven is like a treasure hidden in a field. One day a man found the treasure,
and then he hid it in the field again. He was so
happy that he went and sold everything he owned
to buy that field.

45"Also, the kingdom of heaven is like a man
looking for fine pearls. 46When he found a very
valuable pearl, he went and sold everything he
had and bought it.

A Story of a Fishing Net

47"Also, the kingdom of heaven is like a net
that was put into the lake and caught many different kinds of fish. 48When it was full, the fishermen
pulled the net to the shore. They sat down and
put all the good fish in baskets and threw away
the bad fish. 49It will be this way at the end of the
world. The angels will come and separate the evil
people from the good people. 50The angels will
throw the evil people into the blazing furnace,
where people will cry and grind their teeth with
pain."

SIN

A Crafty Enemy

Life in the Arctic would be pretty safe for a ringed seal if it weren't for its enemy the polar bear.

This crafty predator probably uses more strategies than any other animal in capturing and killing its prey. It may spend thirty minutes in the water approaching a resting seal on an ice floe, surfacing silently to see where the prey is and then submerging again. It may drift like a small harmless iceberg to within striking distance, and then explode from the water so suddenly and ferociously that the seal has no time to react.

When it's stalking on the ice, the polar bear slithers along on its chest and forelegs. It will build mounds of snow to hide behind while it waits at the edge of a breathing hole. It can surface in the seal's den and catch it sleeping there. Or it can dive so quickly into the den from above that the seal cannot escape.

We, too, must be wary of a crafty enemy. You can read about the enemy in Jesus' parable of the wheat and weeds in **Matthew 13:24–30**.

- How are the polar bear's tactics similar to the enemy's in the passage?
- How can you be prepared for the traps of the enemy in your life?

CONSIDER . . .

- separating the forms of entertainment that you enjoy into categories of "wheat" and "weeds." Consider giving up one (or more) of the "weeds."
- looking up references to "Satan" and "devil" in the "Dictionary with Topical Concordance" at the back of this Bible. Share what you learn with friends.

FOR MORE, SEE . . .

- Genesis 3:1–9
- Hebrews 3:12–14
- 1 Peter 5:8–9

51Jesus asked his followers, "Do you understand all these things?"
They answered, "Yes, we understand."
52Then Jesus said to them, "So every teacher of
the law who has been taught about the kingdom
of heaven is like the owner of a house. He brings
out both new things and old things he has saved."

Jesus Goes to His Hometown

53When Jesus finished teaching with these stories, he left there. 54He went to his hometown
and taught the people in the synagogue,[d] and they
were amazed. They said, "Where did this man get
this wisdom and this power to do miracles?[d] 55He
is just the son of a carpenter. His mother is Mary,
and his brothers are James, Joseph, Simon, and
Judas. 56And all his sisters are here with us.
Where then does this man get all these things?"
57So the people were upset with Jesus.
But Jesus said to them, "A prophet[d] is honored
everywhere except in his hometown and in his
own home."
58So he did not do many miracles there because
they had no faith.

How John the Baptist Was Killed

14 At that time Herod, the ruler of Galilee,
heard the reports about Jesus. 2So he
said to his servants, "Jesus is John the Baptist,[d]
who has risen from the dead. That is why he can
work these miracles."[d]
3Sometime before this, Herod had arrested
John, tied him up, and put him into prison. Herod
did this because of Herodias, who had been the
wife of Philip, Herod's brother. 4John had been
telling Herod, "It is not lawful for you to be married to Herodias." 5Herod wanted to kill John, but
he was afraid of the people, because they believed
John was a prophet.[d]
6On Herod's birthday, the daughter of Herodias
danced for Herod and his guests, and she pleased
him. 7So he promised with an oath to give her
anything she wanted. 8Herodias told her daughter
what to ask for, so she said to Herod, "Give me
the head of John the Baptist here on a platter."
9Although King Herod was very sad, he had made
a promise, and his dinner guests had heard him.
So Herod ordered that what she asked for be

HAPPINESS

Real Treasure

When seventeen-year-old Derek Green bought his first car—a "previously owned" model—he expected to hit the road and leave his problems in the dust.

The car, Derek expected, would give him more time to do as he pleased. It would get him out of the house and away from his parents' fighting all the time. It would surely improve his standing with girls.

But only a week later, with three friends in the car, a fan belt broke on the way to a football game.

One month later, he had to buy two new tires.

Now he discovered, twenty miles from home, that the radiator was leaking. As the traffic swished past on the freeway, Derek and his friend Phil sat in the front seat of the car, watching the steam rise from under the hood.

"I always looked forward to owning my own car," Derek said. "But sometimes I feel as if the car owns me."

Derek learned an ageless truth that the more things we acquire, the more they use our time and energy. Possessions rarely bring the happiness expected, and often bring just the opposite. The Bible talks often about the spiritual kingdom and the only true happiness. Read three of Jesus' parables on the kingdom in **Matthew 13:44–52**.

- What are the differences between Derek's car and the "treasure hidden in a field" mentioned in the passage?
- What is the true value of the things you treasure?

CONSIDER . . .

- praying that God will help you value the things in life that truly last.
- interviewing an elderly Christian about the things that have meant the most in his or her lifetime.

FOR MORE, SEE . . .

- Ecclesiastes 3:1–8
- Philippians 4:4–9
- Revelation 3:14–22

done. 10He sent soldiers to the prison to cut off John's head. 11And they brought it on a platter and gave it to the girl, and she took it to her mother. 12John's followers came and got his body and buried it. Then they went and told Jesus.

More than Five Thousand Fed

13When Jesus heard what had happened to John, he left in a boat and went to a lonely place by himself. But the crowds heard about it and followed him on foot from the towns. 14When he arrived, he saw a great crowd waiting. He felt sorry for them and healed those who were sick.

15When it was evening, his followers came to him and said, "No one lives in this place, and it is already late. Send the people away so they can go to the towns and buy food for themselves."

16But Jesus answered, "They don't need to go away. You give them something to eat."

17They said to him, "But we have only five loaves of bread and two fish."

18Jesus said, "Bring the bread and the fish to me." 19Then he told the people to sit down on the grass. He took the five loaves and the two fish and, looking to heaven, he thanked God for the food. Jesus divided the bread and gave it to his followers, who gave it to the people. 20All the people ate and were satisfied. Then the followers filled twelve baskets with the leftover pieces of food. 21There were about five thousand men there who ate, not counting women and children.

> **SIDELIGHT:** The fish mentioned in Matthew 14:17–21 may have referred to the small, sardine-like fish that were plentiful in Lake Galilee. The poor usually ate this fish with barley bread.

Jesus Walks on the Water

22Immediately Jesus told his followers to get into the boat and go ahead of him across the lake. He stayed there to send the people home. 23After he had sent them away, he went by himself up into the hills to pray. It was late, and Jesus was there alone. 24By this time, the boat was already far away from land. It was being hit by waves, because the wind was blowing against it.

25Between three and six o'clock in the morning, Jesus came to them, walking on the water. 26When his followers saw him walking on the water, they were afraid. They said, "It's a ghost!" and cried out in fear.

27But Jesus quickly spoke to them, "Have courage! It is I. Do not be afraid."

28Peter said, "Lord, if it is really you, then command me to come to you on the water."

29Jesus said, "Come."

And Peter left the boat and walked on the water to Jesus. 30But when Peter saw the wind and the waves, he became afraid and began to sink. He shouted, "Lord, save me!"

31Immediately Jesus reached out his hand and caught Peter. Jesus said, "Your faith is small. Why did you doubt?"

32After they got into the boat, the wind became calm. 33Then those who were in the boat worshiped Jesus and said, "Truly you are the Son of God!"

34When they had crossed the lake, they came to shore at Gennesaret. 35When the people there recognized Jesus, they told people all around there that Jesus had come, and they brought all their sick to him. 36They begged Jesus to let them touch just the edge of his coat, and all who touched it were healed.

Obey God's Law

15 Then some Pharisees[d] and teachers of the law came to Jesus from Jerusalem. They asked him, 2"Why don't your followers obey the unwritten laws which have been handed down to us? They don't wash their hands before they eat."

3Jesus answered, "And why do you refuse to obey God's command so that you can follow your own teachings? 4God said, 'Honor your father and your mother,'[n] and 'Anyone who says cruel things to his father or mother must be put to death.'[n] 5But you say a person can tell his father or mother, 'I have something I could use to help you, but I have given it to God already.' 6You teach that person not to honor his father or his mother. You rejected what God said for the sake of your own rules. 7You are hypocrites![d] Isaiah was right when he said about you:

8'These people show honor to me with words,
but their hearts are far from me.
9Their worship of me is worthless.
The things they teach are nothing but
human rules.' " *Isaiah 29:13*

10After Jesus called the crowd to him, he said, "Listen and understand what I am saying. 11It is not what people put into their mouths that makes them unclean.[d] It is what comes out of their mouths that makes them unclean."

12Then his followers came to him and asked, "Do you know that the Pharisees are angry because of what you said?"

'Honor . . . mother.' Quotation from Exodus 20:12; Deuteronomy 5:16.
'Anyone . . . death.' Quotation from Exodus 21:17.

13 Jesus answered, "Every plant that my Father in heaven has not planted himself will be pulled up by the roots. 14 Stay away from the Pharisees; they are blind leaders. And if a blind person leads a blind person, both will fall into a ditch."

15 Peter said, "Explain the example to us."

16 Jesus said, "Do you still not understand?
17 Surely you know that all the food that enters the mouth goes into the stomach and then goes out of the body.
18 But what people say with their mouths comes from the way they think; these are the things that make people unclean.
19 Out of the mind come evil thoughts, murder, adultery,[d] sexual sins, stealing, lying, and speaking evil of others.
20 These things make people unclean; eating with unwashed hands does not make them unclean."

Jesus Helps a Non-Jewish Woman

21 Jesus left that place and went to the area of Tyre and Sidon.
22 A Canaanite woman from that area came to Jesus and cried out, "Lord, Son of David,[d] have mercy on me! My daughter has a demon,[d] and she is suffering very much."

23 But Jesus did not answer the woman. So his followers came to Jesus and begged him, "Tell the woman to go away. She is following us and shouting."

24 Jesus answered, "God sent me only to the lost sheep, the people of Israel."

25 Then the woman came to Jesus again and bowed before him and said, "Lord, help me!"

26 Jesus answered, "It is not right to take the children's bread and give it to the dogs."

FEAR

The Handicap

Curt Ryan was "cool." Nothing seemed to unnerve him. That's why the youth group was surprised when he strongly objected to the idea of a weekend service retreat at a home for mentally and physically disabled people.

"Why don't you like the idea?" someone asked.

"It's stupid, that's all!" Curt said.

"Are you scared, or what?" someone else asked.

"Yeah, right," Curt responded sarcastically.

The group decided to go ahead, and planned the retreat. Curt grudgingly went along, and kept up his "cool" veneer. But inside, Curt was afraid of the people at the home. He coped with his fear by avoiding any contact with residents.

But he couldn't avoid the dance. Curt walked in late and leaned against a wall in a dark corner. Sally, one of the residents, saw him and rushed up in her wheelchair. She tugged at his arm. "Dance with me," she pleaded.

He pretended he had not heard her.

"Please dance with me," she persisted. "Please?"

Reluctantly, Curt agreed. Although he felt awkward at first, Curt's fears soon faded. He discovered Sally was fun. She had a sharp wit. Sally actually made Curt feel comfortable.

"I was scared," he admitted later. "I didn't know what to expect. Then I saw the love and care these people give. They are just like me. I am the one who was handicapped."

Like Curt's fear of the residents, Peter, one of Jesus' disciples, often suffered from fear. Read how he was afraid to walk on water in **Matthew 14:22–33**.

- How are Curt's and Peter's reactions to fear similar?
- Would you have stayed in the boat or gotten out to walk on the water? Why?

CONSIDER . . .

- dividing a piece of paper equally. On the left side list fears. On the right side list ways to overcome fears. Share it with a friend. Pray for one another.
- taking a step this week in overcoming one of your fears. For example, if you're shy, go up to someone at school or church and introduce yourself.

FOR MORE, SEE . . .

- Psalm 27
- Mark 4:35–41
- 1 Corinthians 2:1–5

27The woman said, "Yes, Lord, but even the
dogs eat the crumbs that fall from their masters'
table."
28Then Jesus answered, "Woman, you have
great faith! I will do what you asked." And at that
moment the woman's daughter was healed.

Jesus Heals Many People

29After leaving there, Jesus went along the
shore of Lake Galilee. He went up on a hill and
sat there.
30Great crowds came to Jesus, bringing with
them the lame, the blind, the crippled, those who
could not speak, and many others. They put them
at Jesus' feet, and he healed them. 31The crowd
was amazed when they saw that people who
could not speak before were now able to speak.
The crippled were made strong. The lame could
walk, and the blind could see. And they praised
the God of Israel for this.

More than Four Thousand Fed

32Jesus called his followers to him and said, "I
feel sorry for these people, because they have already been with me three days, and they have
nothing to eat. I don't want to send them away
hungry. They might faint while going home."
33His followers asked him, "How can we get
enough bread to feed all these people? We are far
away from any town."
34Jesus asked, "How many loaves of bread do
you have?"
They answered, "Seven, and a few small fish."
35Jesus told the people to sit on the ground.
36He took the seven loaves of bread and the fish
and gave thanks to God. Then he divided the food
and gave it to his followers, and they gave it to the
people. 37All the people ate and were satisfied.
Then his followers filled seven baskets with the
leftover pieces of food. 38There were about four
thousand men there who ate, besides women and
children. 39After sending the people home, Jesus
got into the boat and went to the area of Maga-
dan.

The Leaders Ask for a Miracle

16 The Pharisees[d] and Sadducees[d] came to
Jesus, wanting to trick him. So they
asked him to show them a miracle[d] from God.
2Jesus answered, "At sunset you say we will

PERSISTENCE

Go for the Gold

In 1972 Mark Spitz was an Olympic hero. He competed in seven swimming events, won seven gold medals, and set seven world records. Spitz remains a legend.

Almost twenty years later, Spitz is attempting a comeback. He wants to compete again in the Olympics, hoping to beat his time in the 100-meter butterfly. That time would have placed him eighth in the 1988 Olympics.

It takes persistence to prepare for competition. Spitz admits the closest he's been to water since his 1972 accomplishments is in the shower or his son's wading pool.

Why do it? "I just want to see if I can," Spitz says. "God gifted me with a certain talent and ability. You've got to get hungry if you want to prove something. I'm hungry to prove myself."

His coach believes in Spitz. "If anyone can do it, Mark can," he says. "He's a winner, a master competitor."

In a way similar to Spitz's dedication to his swimming dream, a woman pursued Jesus to heal her daughter. Read **Matthew 15:21–28** to see how she showed great persistence and faith.

- How is Spitz's persistence similar to the mother's in the passage?
- When have you been persistent like the mother? What happened?

C O N S I D E R . . .

- looking for examples of persistent people in newspapers or on television. What qualities do they possess? Write five of those qualities on a card. Tape it to your mirror as a reminder.
- setting a realistic goal for a project or task you've been putting off. Share it with a friend and ask him or her to help you reach your goal.

F O R M O R E , S E E . . .

- Ruth 1:1–18
- Mark 5:25–34
- Ephesians 6:10–20

have good weather, because the sky is red. 3And
in the morning you say that it will be a rainy day,
because the sky is dark and red. You see these
signs in the sky and know what they mean. In the
same way, you see the things that I am doing
now, but you don't know their meaning. 4Evil
and sinful people ask for a miracle as a sign, but
they will not be given any sign, except the sign of
Jonah."[n] Then Jesus left them and went away.

Guard Against Wrong Teachings

5Jesus' followers went across the lake, but they
had forgotten to bring bread. 6Jesus said to them,
"Be careful! Beware of the yeast of the Pharisees[d]
and the Sadducees."[d]
7His followers discussed the meaning of this,
saying, "He said this because we forgot to bring
bread."
8Knowing what they were talking about, Jesus
asked them, "Why are you talking about not having bread? Your faith is small. 9Do you still not
understand? Remember the five loaves of bread
that fed the five thousand? And remember that
you filled many baskets with the leftovers? 10Or
the seven loaves of bread that fed the four thousand and the many baskets you filled then also?
11I was not talking to you about bread. Why don't
you understand that? I am telling you to beware
of the yeast of the Pharisees and the Sadducees."
12Then the followers understood that Jesus was
not telling them to beware of the yeast used in
bread but to beware of the teaching of the Pharisees and the Sadducees.

SIDELIGHT: The city of Caesarea Philippi (Matthew 16:13) where Peter declared Jesus was God's Son, was north of Lake Galilee in an area that wasn't Jewish. In fact, it had a pagan shrine to Pan, a Greek and Roman nature god.

Peter Says Jesus Is the Christ

13When Jesus came to the area of Caesarea Philippi, he asked his followers, "Who do people say
the Son of Man[d] is?"
14They answered, "Some say you are John the
Baptist.[d] Others say you are Elijah, and still others
say you are Jeremiah or one of the prophets."[d]
15Then Jesus asked them, "And who do you say
I am?"
16Simon Peter answered, "You are the Christ,[d]
the Son of the living God."
17Jesus answered, "You are blessed, Simon son
of Jonah, because no person taught you that. My
Father in heaven showed you who I am. 18So I tell
you, you are Peter.[n] On this rock I will build my
church, and the power of death will not be able
to defeat it. 19I will give you the keys of the kingdom of heaven; the things you don't allow on
earth will be the things that God does not allow,
and the things you allow on earth will be the
things that God allows." 20Then Jesus warned his
followers not to tell anyone he was the Christ.

Jesus Says that He Must Die

21From that time on Jesus began telling his followers that he must go to Jerusalem, where the
older Jewish leaders, the leading priests, and the
teachers of the law would make him suffer many
things. He told them he must be killed and then
be raised from the dead on the third day.
22Peter took Jesus aside and told him not to talk
like that. He said, "God save you from those
things, Lord! Those things will never happen to
you!"
23Then Jesus said to Peter, "Go away from me,
Satan![n] You are not helping me! You don't care
about the things of God, but only about the things
people think are important."
24Then Jesus said to his followers, "If people
want to follow me, they must give up the things
they want. They must be willing even to give up
their lives to follow me. 25Those who want to save
their lives will give up true life, and those who
give up their lives for me will have true life. 26It
is worth nothing for them to have the whole
world if they lose their souls. They could never
pay enough to buy back their souls. 27The Son of
Man[d] will come again with his Father's glory and
with his angels. At that time, he will reward them
for what they have done. 28I tell you the truth,
some people standing here will see the Son of
Man coming with his kingdom before they die."

Jesus Talks with Moses and Elijah

17 Six days later, Jesus took Peter, James,
and John, the brother of James, up on a
high mountain by themselves. 2While they
watched, Jesus' appearance was changed; his face
became bright like the sun, and his clothes became white as light. 3Then Moses and Elijah[n] appeared to them, talking with Jesus.
4Peter said to Jesus, "Lord, it is good that we

sign of Jonah Jonah's three days in the fish are like Jesus' three days in the tomb. The story about Jonah is in the book of Jonah.
Peter The Greek name "Peter," like the Aramaic name "Cephas," means "rock."
Satan Name for the devil, meaning "the enemy." Jesus means that Peter was talking like Satan.
Moses and Elijah Two of the most important Jewish leaders in the past. Moses had given them the law, and Elijah was an important prophet.

are here. If you want, I will put up three tents
here—one for you, one for Moses, and one for
Elijah."

> **SIDELIGHT:** *When Peter suggested camping out in Matthew 17:4, he may have been thinking about the annual Feast of Shelters. During this harvest festival, Jews from everywhere came to Jerusalem and built shelters or booths in the streets and town square—anywhere with a little space. It made for bad traffic jams, but was cheaper than staying in a hotel.*

5While Peter was talking, a bright cloud covered them. A voice came from the cloud and said,
"This is my Son, whom I love, and I am very
pleased with him. Listen to him!"
6When his followers heard the voice, they were
so frightened they fell to the ground. 7But Jesus
went to them and touched them and said, "Stand
up. Don't be afraid." 8When they looked up, they
saw Jesus was now alone.
9As they were coming down the mountain,
Jesus commanded them not to tell anyone about
what they had seen until the Son of Man[d] had
risen from the dead.
10Then his followers asked him, "Why do the
teachers of the law say that Elijah must come
first?"
11Jesus answered, "They are right to say that
Elijah is coming and that he will make everything
the way it should be. 12But I tell you that Elijah
has already come, and they did not recognize
him. They did to him whatever they wanted to
do. It will be the same with the Son of Man; those
same people will make the Son of Man suffer."
13Then the followers understood that Jesus was
talking about John the Baptist.[d]

Jesus Heals a Sick Boy

14When Jesus and his followers came back to
the crowd, a man came to Jesus and bowed before

FAITH

T-e-a-c-h-e-r

A fever left Helen Keller blind and deaf at birth. She was imprisoned in a dark, silent world.

In 1887, when Helen was seven, Anne Sullivan, herself partially blind, became Helen's teacher. Anne had great vision and hope. She believed Helen held untapped and unseen abilities.

Months passed with very little progress, but Anne still believed.

Then, finally, Anne witnessed the results of faith. Helen was playing at the water pump. Anne finger-spelled "w-a-t-e-r" into her free hand. Anne wrote in her journal, "The word coming so close upon the sensation of cold water rushing over her hand seemed to startle her. A new light came into her face. She understood! Then turning around she asked my name. I spelled "T-e-a-c-h-e-r."

Thanks to Anne's faith, Helen's dark, lonely life opened wide to the light of communication and learning. Helen graduated with honors from Radcliffe College, and went on to a distinguished career as an educator, speaker and author. Helen and "Teacher" were lifelong companions.

"Teacher's" faith brought Helen out of darkness and into light. In **Matthew 16:13–20**, read how Jesus had faith in Peter, even when Peter wasn't sure of his own faith.

- How was Anne's and Helen's friendship similar to Jesus' and Peter's?
- Anne's faith enabled her to teach Helen. Peter's faith helped him become a church leader. What does your faith help you do?

CONSIDER. . .

- helping young children grow in their faith by volunteering to help one Sunday in the church nursery, Sunday school or vacation church school.
- writing a Haiku poem that expresses faith. A Haiku poem has three lines. The first and third lines each have seven syllables. The middle line has five.

FOR MORE, SEE. . .

- Nehemiah 9:6–8
- Mark 8:27–38
- Hebrews 11

him. 15The man said, "Lord, have mercy on my
son. He has epilepsy[n] and is suffering very much,
because he often falls into the fire or into the water. 16I brought him to your followers, but they
could not cure him."
17Jesus answered, "You people have no faith,
and your lives are all wrong. How long must I put
up with you? How long must I continue to be
patient with you? Bring the boy here." 18Jesus
commanded the demon[d] inside the boy. Then the
demon came out, and the boy was healed from
that time on.
19The followers came to Jesus when he was
alone and asked, "Why couldn't we force the demon out?"
20Jesus answered, "Because your faith is too
small. I tell you the truth, if your faith is as big as
a mustard seed, you can say to this mountain,
'Move from here to there,' and it will move. All
things will be possible for you." 21 [n]

Jesus Talks About His Death

22While Jesus' followers were gathering in Galilee, he said to them, "The Son of Man[d] will be
handed over to people, 23and they will kill him.
But on the third day he will be raised from the
dead." And the followers were filled with sadness.

Jesus Talks About Paying Taxes

24When Jesus and his followers came to Capernaum, the men who collected the Temple[d] tax
came to Peter. They asked, "Does your teacher
pay the Temple tax?"
25Peter answered, "Yes, Jesus pays the tax."
Peter went into the house, but before he could
speak, Jesus said to him, "What do you think? The
kings of the earth collect different kinds of taxes.
But who pays the taxes—the king's children or
others?"
26Peter answered, "Other people pay the
taxes."
Jesus said to Peter, "Then the children of the
king don't have to pay taxes. 27But we don't want
to upset these tax collectors. So go to the lake and
fish. After you catch the first fish, open its mouth
and you will find a coin. Take that coin and give
it to the tax collectors for you and me."

Who Is the Greatest?

18 At that time the followers came to Jesus
and asked, "Who is greatest in the kingdom of heaven?"
2Jesus called a little child to him and stood the
child before his followers. 3Then he said, "I tell
you the truth, you must change and become
like little children. Otherwise, you will never
enter the kingdom of heaven. 4The greatest
person in the kingdom of heaven is the one
who makes himself humble like this child.
5"Whoever accepts a child in my name accepts
me. 6If one of these little children believes in me,
and someone causes that child to sin, it would be
better for that person to have a large stone tied
around the neck and be drowned in the sea.
7How terrible for the people of the world because
of the things that cause them to sin. Such things
will happen, but how terrible for the one who
causes them to happen! 8If your hand or your foot
causes you to sin, cut it off and throw it away. It
is better for you to lose part of your body and live
forever than to have two hands and two feet and
be thrown into the fire that burns forever. 9If your
eye causes you to sin, take it out and throw it
away. It is better for you to have only one eye and
live forever than to have two eyes and be thrown
into the fire of hell.

A Lost Sheep

10"Be careful. Don't think these little children
are worth nothing. I tell you that they have angels
in heaven who are always with my Father in
heaven. 11 [n]
12"If a man has a hundred sheep but one of the
sheep gets lost, he will leave the other ninety-nine
on the hill and go to look for the lost sheep. 13I
tell you the truth, he is happier about that one
sheep than about the ninety-nine that were never
lost. 14In the same way, your Father in heaven
does not want any of these little children to be
lost.

When a Person Sins Against You

15"If your fellow believer sins against you, go
and tell him in private what he did wrong. If he
listens to you, you have helped that person to be
your brother or sister again. 16But if he refuses to
listen, go to him again and take one or two other
people with you. 'Every case may be proved by
two or three witnesses.'[n] 17If he refuses to listen
to them, tell the church. If he refuses to listen to
the church, then treat him like a person who does
not believe in God or like a tax collector.
18"I tell you the truth, the things you don't allow on earth will be the things God does not allow. And the things you allow on earth will be the
things that God allows.
19"Also, I tell you that if two of you on earth

pilepsy A disease that causes a person sometimes to lose control of his body and maybe faint, shake strongly, or not be able to move.
'erse 21 Some Greek copies add verse 21: "That kind of spirit comes out only if you use prayer and give up eating."
'erse 11 Some Greek copies add verse 11: "The Son of Man came to save lost people."
Every . . . witnesses.' Quotation from Deuteronomy 19:15.

agree about something and pray for it, it will be
done for you by my Father in heaven. 20This is
true because if two or three people come together
in my name, I am there with them."

An Unforgiving Servant

21Then Peter came to Jesus and asked, "Lord,
when my fellow believer sins against me, how
many times must I forgive him? Should I forgive
him as many as seven times?"
22Jesus answered, "I tell you, you must forgive
him more than seven times. You must forgive him
even if he does wrong to you seventy-seven times.
23"The kingdom of heaven is like a king who
decided to collect the money his servants owed
him. 24When the king began to collect his money,
a servant who owed him several million dollars
was brought to him. 25But the servant did not
have enough money to pay his master, the king.
So the master ordered that everything the servant
owned should be sold, even the servant's wife
and children. Then the money would be used to
pay the king what the servant owed.
26"But the servant fell on his knees and begged,
'Be patient with me, and I will pay you everything
I owe.' 27The master felt sorry for his servant and
told him he did not have to pay it back. Then he
let the servant go free.
28"Later, that same servant found another servant who owed him a few dollars. The servant
grabbed him around the neck and said, 'Pay me
the money you owe me!'
29"The other servant fell on his knees and
begged him, 'Be patient with me, and I will pay
you everything I owe.'
30"But the first servant refused to be patient. He

FRIENDS

I Hate You!

"What's going on?" Dad asked Suzanne, his fourteen-year-old daughter. "I was outside the house and heard your screaming."

"I hate her!" Suzanne yelled. "How could Vicki do this to me?" Suzanne Hinton and Vicki Linder had grown up together. As kids they had played with Barbie dolls and built tree forts. They had walked to school together and shared lunches. In middle school they were still friends.

Then Jean Lawlor moved to town. Jean caused trouble. To Suzanne it seemed Jean enjoyed setting Suzanne and Vicki against each other.

Dad listened as Suzanne alternated between crying and telling him what was going on. Jean had told Vicki that Suzanne was interested in Todd, Vicki's boyfriend. Jean later told Vicki that Suzanne had asked Todd out on a date, which wasn't true. Suzanne and Vicki had just argued on the phone, screaming at each other before Vicki slammed down the receiver.

"Can you believe it?" Suzanne wailed. "Vicki believed Jean—not me! I hate Jean! And Vicki! They betrayed me!"

"Sounds like you have a major conflict," Dad said.

"It's their fault!" Suzanne cried.

"The issue is: What are you going to do?" Dad said.

Sooner or later, conflict will erupt in most friendships. Jesus taught his followers several guidelines for dealing with conflict. Read **Matthew 18:15–20** and see how Suzanne, Vicki, and Jean might find ways to settle their differences.

- If Suzanne follows Jesus' teachings, what can she do to resolve her conflict with Vicki and Jean?
- How might Jesus' prescription for dealing with conflict help you in your friendships?

C O N S I D E R . . .

- making a list of friends with whom you have conflicts. Pray daily for strength to help you deal with these conflicts.
- writing about a friendship that's bothering you. Using Jesus' plan as a model, write your own plan for improving the friendship. What will you do and say?

F O R M O R E , S E E . . .

- Genesis 4:1–15
- Luke 6:27–36
- Galatians 2:11–14

threw the other servant into prison until he could
pay everything he owed. 31When the other servants saw what had happened, they were very
sorry. So they went and told their master all that
had happened.
32"Then the master called his servant in and
said, 'You evil servant! Because you begged me to
forget what you owed, I told you that you did not
have to pay anything. 33You should have showed
mercy to that other servant, just as I showed
mercy to you.' 34The master was very angry and
put the servant in prison to be punished until he
could pay everything he owed.
35"This king did what my heavenly Father will
do to you if you do not forgive your brother or
sister from your heart."

Jesus Teaches About Divorce

19 After Jesus said all these things, he left
Galilee and went into the area of Judea
on the other side of the Jordan River. 2Large
crowds followed him, and he healed them there.
3Some Pharisees[d] came to Jesus and tried to
trick him. They asked, "Is it right for a man to
divorce his wife for any reason he chooses?"
4Jesus answered, "Surely you have read in the
Scriptures:[d] When God made the world, 'he
made them male and female.'[n] 5And God said,
'So a man will leave his father and mother and be
united with his wife, and the two will become
one body.'[n] 6So there are not two, but one. God
has joined the two together, so no one should separate them."
7The Pharisees asked, "Why then did Moses
give a command for a man to divorce his wife by
giving her divorce papers?"
8Jesus answered, "Moses allowed you to divorce your wives because you refused to accept
God's teaching, but divorce was not allowed in
the beginning. 9I tell you that anyone who di-

'he made . . . female.' Quotation from Genesis 1:27 or 5:2.
'So . . . body.' Quotation from Genesis 2:24.

FORGIVENESS

So Sorry

Kerrie Trent was in trouble, and she knew it. She hadn't even cracked the textbook, and the history exam would determine her grade in the class.

She sat behind Matt Kimmerly, who was a smart student. He would help, she thought. "Psst, Matt," she whispered, poking him with her pencil. "Question five. Gimme a clue."

Matt shrugged.

Kerrie poked him again with the pencil. Matt turned. "Cut it out," he hissed.

"Matt, come up here, and bring your exam," interrupted Ms. Miller, the history teacher. As Matt walked to Ms. Miller's desk, Kerrie pretended to work on her exam.

"I won't tolerate cheating," Ms. Miller said quietly to Matt. She tossed the exam into the wastebasket. Matt tried to explain what had happened, but she didn't believe him. "Take your seat, and be quiet for the rest of the period," she snapped.

Kerrie saw Matt's face as he walked back toward his seat. His eyes showed his deep anger and hurt. "Why?" he whispered. Kerrie looked away.

As school let out, Kerrie saw Matt in the hall and tried to tell him how sorry she was. But Matt ignored her. At midnight, she still couldn't get Matt's hurt out of her mind. She knew what to do. "Tomorrow," she thought, "I'll tell Ms. Miller what really happened, but will Matt ever forgive me?"

Both Kerrie and Matt could learn from the story Jesus told in **Matthew 18:21–35**.

- How is Kerrie's and Matt's struggle similar to the one in Jesus' story?
- Which character in Jesus' parable do you identify with most often? Why?

C O N S I D E R . . .

- listing things you find difficult to forgive. Put them in order, from least to most difficult to forgive. What factors make forgiveness difficult?
- thinking of two people: one who has hurt you most, and one you have hurt the most. Pray for strength, and then do one thing to help bring forgiveness to both people.

F O R M O R E , S E E . . .

- Jonah 3
- Micah 7:18–20
- Luke 17:1–4

vorces his wife and marries another woman is
guilty of adultery.[d] The only reason for a man to
divorce his wife is if his wife has sexual relations
with another man."
10The followers said to him, "If that is the only
reason a man can divorce his wife, it is better not
to marry."
11Jesus answered, "Not everyone can accept
this teaching, but God has made some able to accept it. 12There are different reasons why some
men cannot marry. Some men were born without
the ability to become fathers. Others were made
that way later in life by other people. And some
men have given up marriage because of the kingdom of heaven. But the person who can marry
should accept this teaching about marriage."[n]

> **SIDELIGHT:** Divorce has always been a controversial subject—even in Jesus' day. While some religious leaders said someone could only get a divorce because of unfaithfulness, others argued that a husband could divorce a wife for burning supper, wearing the wrong thing in public, or even talking to another man. Jesus entered the debate in Matthew 19:1–12.

Jesus Welcomes Children

13Then the people brought their little children
to Jesus so he could put his hands on them[n] and
pray for them. His followers told them to stop,
14but Jesus said, "Let the little children come to
me. Don't stop them, because the kingdom of
heaven belongs to people who are like these children." 15After Jesus put his hands on the children,
he left there.

A Rich Young Man's Question

16A man came to Jesus and asked, "Teacher,
what good thing must I do to have life forever?"
17Jesus answered, "Why do you ask me about
what is good? Only God is good. But if you want
to have life forever, obey the commands."
18The man asked, "Which commands?"
Jesus answered, " 'You must not murder anyone; you must not be guilty of adultery;[d] you
must not steal; you must not tell lies about your
neighbor; 19honor your father and mother;[n] and
love your neighbor as you love yourself.' "[n]
20The young man said, "I have obeyed all these
things. What else do I need to do?"
21Jesus answered, "If you want to be perfect
then go and sell your possessions and give th
money to the poor. If you do this, you will hav
treasure in heaven. Then come and follow me."
22But when the young man heard this, he le
sorrowfully, because he was rich.
23Then Jesus said to his followers, "I tell yo
the truth, it will be hard for a rich person to ente
the kingdom of heaven. 24Yes, I tell you that it i
easier for a camel to go through the eye of a nee
dle than for a rich person to enter the kingdom o
God."
25When Jesus' followers heard this, they wer
very surprised and asked, "Then who can b
saved?"
26Jesus looked at them and said, "This is some
thing people cannot do, but God can do a
things."
27Peter said to Jesus, "Look, we have left every
thing and followed you. So what will we have?
28Jesus said to them, "I tell you the truth, whe
the age to come has arrived, the Son of Man[d] wi
sit on his great throne. All of you who followe
me will also sit on twelve thrones, judging th
twelve tribes[d] of Israel. 29And all those who hav
left houses, brothers, sisters, father, mother, chi
dren, or farms to follow me will get much mo
than they left, and they will have life foreve
30Many who have the highest place now will hav
the lowest place in the future. And many wh
have the lowest place now will have the highe
place in the future.

A Story About Workers

20 "The kingdom of heaven is like a perso
who owned some land. One mornin
he went out very early to hire some people t
work in his vineyard. 2The man agreed to pay th
workers one coin[n] for working that day. Then h
sent them into the vineyard to work. 3About nin
o'clock the man went to the marketplace and sa
some other people standing there, doing nothin
4So he said to them, 'If you go and work in m
vineyard, I will pay you what your work is worth
5So they went to work in the vineyard. The ma
went out again about twelve o'clock and thre
o'clock and did the same thing. 6About fiv
o'clock the man went to the marketplace aga
and saw others standing there. He asked the
'Why did you stand here all day doing nothing
7They answered, 'No one gave us a job.' The ma
said to them, 'Then you can go and work in m
vineyard.'
8"At the end of the day, the owner of the vin

But . . . marriage. This may also mean, "The person who can accept this teaching about not marrying should accept it."
put his hands on them Showing that Jesus gave special blessings to these children.
'You . . . mother.' Quotation from Exodus 20:12-16; Deuteronomy 5:16-20.
'love . . . yourself.' Quotation from Leviticus 19:18.
coin A Roman denarius. One coin was the average pay for one day's work.

yard said to the boss of all the workers, 'Call the
workers and pay them. Start with the last people
I hired and end with those I hired first.'
9"When the workers who were hired at five
o'clock came to get their pay, each received one
coin. 10When the workers who were hired first
came to get their pay, they thought they would be
paid more than the others. But each one of them
also received one coin. 11When they got their
coin, they complained to the man who owned the
land. 12They said, 'Those people were hired last
and worked only one hour. But you paid them the
same as you paid us who worked hard all day in
the hot sun.' 13But the man who owned the vineyard said to one of those workers, 'Friend, I am
being fair to you. You agreed to work for one coin.
14So take your pay and go. I want to give the man
who was hired last the same pay that I gave you.
15I can do what I want with my own money. Are
you jealous because I am good to those people?'
16"So those who have the last place now will
have the first place in the future, and those who
have the first place now will have the last place
in the future."

Jesus Talks About His Own Death

17While Jesus was going to Jerusalem, he took
his twelve followers aside privately and said to

JUSTICE

It's Not Fair!

For months, Laura Steiner, seventeen, prepared her chemistry project for the area science fair competition. In previous years Laura had won several ribbons, but she had never won a chance to go to state. As a senior, this was her last chance.

Laura's fourteen-year-old brother, Kenneth, a freshman, also entered the science fair. Scientific concepts came to him easier than they did to Laura. Kenneth put together his project on the solar system in just a few days.

On the opening day of the fair, Laura, Kenneth, and their parents arrived in the family car. Laura rushed to see her project that simulated a nuclear reaction, while her brother and parents went to see Kenneth's entry. Laura couldn't wait to see the prize she expected from the judges.

But there was no ribbon. "Have the judges been here?" she cried. Yes, they have, she was told. "Then there's been some mistake!"

Kenneth ran up to Laura. "I won first prize!" yelled Kenneth. "I'm going to state!"

"That's unfair!" wailed Laura, who started sobbing. "Your project isn't even unique."

When she had settled down a bit, her parents tried to comfort her, but weren't very successful. "It just isn't fair," Laura muttered time and again. "I worked so hard, but Kenneth just threw his together at the last minute."

Then Mom reminded her of a time when Laura and Kenneth were younger. "Remember when you beat Kenneth in the skiing competition, after he had taught you to ski?" Mom asked. "He didn't think that was fair, but you didn't mind winning."

Laura was still disappointed, but started feeling happy for her brother. "Congratulations, and good luck at state," she finally told him.

No doubt you have been told, "Life isn't fair." Laura obviously found this out. God's view of justice and fairness puzzled many of the people in Jesus' time. Many assumed God would be better to them than to others. Read Jesus' response to their assumption in **Matthew 20:1–16**.

- How are Laura's complaints similar to those of the vineyard workers in Jesus' parable?
- If you were one of the first workers hired, how would you have felt? What would your reaction have been if you were among the last hired?

CONSIDER . . .

- looking for examples of "fairness" and "justice" in the news. Talk with your friends about whether these examples fit their views.
- asking a lawyer or judge to define justice. Ask your pastor to define justice. Then come up with your own definition.

FOR MORE, SEE . . .

- Job 8:3–6
- Luke 14:12–24
- 2 Thessalonians 1:3–12

them, 18“Look, we are going to Jerusalem. The
Son of Man[d] will be turned over to the leading
priests and the teachers of the law, and they will
say that he must die. 19They will give the Son of
Man to the non-Jewish people to laugh at him and
beat him with whips and crucify him. But on the
third day, he will be raised to life again.”

A Mother Asks Jesus a Favor

20Then the wife of Zebedee came to Jesus with
her sons. She bowed before him and asked him to
do something for her.

21Jesus asked, “What do you want?”

She said, “Promise that one of my sons will sit
at your right side and the other will sit at your left
side in your kingdom.”

22But Jesus said, “You don’t understand what
you are asking. Can you drink the cup that I am
about to drink?”[n]

The sons answered, “Yes, we can.”

23Jesus said to them, “You will drink from my
cup. But I cannot choose who will sit at my right
or my left; those places belong to those for whom
my Father has prepared them.”

24When the other ten followers heard this, they
were angry with the two brothers.

> **SIDELIGHT:** James and John, the sons of Zebedee, were nicknamed “the sons of thunder” (Matthew 20:20–24; see Mark 3:17). The nicknames may have come from their booming voices or their short tempers. Either way, the name would look great on a wrestling team roster.

25Jesus called all the followers together and
said, “You know that the rulers of the non-Jewish
people love to show their power over the people.
And their important leaders love to use all their
authority. 26But it should not be that way among
you. Whoever wants to become great among you
must serve the rest of you like a servant. 27Who-
ever wants to become first among you must serve
the rest of you like a slave. 28In the same way, the
Son of Man[d] did not come to be served. He came
to serve others and to give his life as a ransom for
many people.”

Jesus Heals Two Blind Men

29When Jesus and his followers were leaving
Jericho, a great many people followed him. 30Two
blind men sitting by the road heard that Jesus was
going by, so they shouted, “Lord, Son of David,[d]
have mercy on us!”

31The people warned the blind men to be quiet,
but they shouted even more, “Lord, Son of David,
have mercy on us!”

32Jesus stopped and said to the blind men,
“What do you want me to do for you?”

33They answered, “Lord, we want to see.”

34Jesus felt sorry for the blind men and touched
their eyes, and at once they could see. Then they
followed Jesus.

Jesus Enters Jerusalem as a King

21 As Jesus and his followers were coming
closer to Jerusalem, they stopped at
Bethphage at the hill called the Mount of Olives.[d]
From there Jesus sent two of his followers 2and
said to them, “Go to the town you can see there.
When you enter it, you will quickly find a donkey
tied there with its colt. Untie them and bring
them to me. 3If anyone asks you why you are taking the donkeys, say that the Master needs them,
and he will send them at once.”

4This was to bring about what the prophet[d] had
said:

5“Tell the people of Jerusalem,
 ‘Your king is coming to you.
He is gentle and riding on a donkey,
 on the colt of a donkey.’ ”

Isaiah 62:11; Zechariah 9:9

6The followers went and did what Jesus told
them to do. 7They brought the donkey and the
colt to Jesus and laid their coats on them, and
Jesus sat on them. 8Many people spread their
coats on the road. Others cut branches from the
trees and spread them on the road. 9The people
were walking ahead of Jesus and behind him,
shouting,

“Praise[n] to the Son of David![d]
God bless the One who comes in the name
 of the Lord! *Psalm 118:26*
Praise to God in heaven!”

10When Jesus entered Jerusalem, all the city
was filled with excitement. The people asked,
“Who is this man?”

11The crowd said, “This man is Jesus, the
prophet from the town of Nazareth in Galilee.”

Jesus Goes to the Temple

12Jesus went into the Temple[d] and threw out
all the people who were buying and selling there.
He turned over the tables of those who were exchanging different kinds of money, and he upset
the benches of those who were selling doves.

drink . . . drink Jesus used the idea of drinking from a cup to ask if they could accept the same terrible things that would happen to him.

Praise Literally, “Hosanna,” a Hebrew word used at first in praying to God for help. At this time it was probably a shout of joy used in praising God or his Messiah.

13Jesus said to all the people there, "It is written
in the Scriptures,[d] 'My Temple will be called a
house for prayer.'[n] But you are changing it into
a 'hideout for robbers.' "[n]
14The blind and crippled people came to Jesus
in the Temple, and he healed them. 15The leading
priests and the teachers of the law saw that Jesus
was doing wonderful things and that the children
were praising him in the Temple, saying,
"Praise[n] to the Son of David."[d] All these things
made the priests and the teachers of the law very
angry.
16They asked Jesus, "Do you hear the things
these children are saying?"
Jesus answered, "Yes. Haven't you read in the
Scriptures, 'You have taught children and babies
to sing praises'?"[n]
17Then Jesus left and went out of the city to
Bethany, where he spent the night.

The Power of Faith

18Early the next morning, as Jesus was going
back to the city, he became hungry. 19Seeing a fig
tree beside the road, Jesus went to it, but there
were no figs on the tree, only leaves. So Jesus said
to the tree, "You will never again have fruit." The
tree immediately dried up.
20When his followers saw this, they were
amazed. They asked, "How did the fig tree dry up
so quickly?"
21Jesus answered, "I tell you the truth, if you
have faith and do not doubt, you will be able to
do what I did to this tree and even more. You will
be able to say to this mountain, 'Go, fall into the
sea.' And if you have faith, it will happen. 22If you
believe, you will get anything you ask for in
prayer."

Leaders Doubt Jesus' Authority

23Jesus went to the Temple,[d] and while he was
teaching there, the leading priests and the older
leaders of the people came to him. They said,
"What authority do you have to do these things?
Who gave you this authority?"
24Jesus answered, "I also will ask you a question. If you answer me, then I will tell you what
authority I have to do these things. 25Tell me:
When John baptized people, did that come from
God or just from other people?"
They argued about Jesus' question, saying, "If
we answer, 'John's baptism was from God,' Jesus
will say, 'Then why didn't you believe him?' 26But
if we say, 'It was from people,' we are afraid of
what the crowd will do because they all believe
that John was a prophet."[d]
27So they answered Jesus, "We don't know."
Jesus said to them, "Then I won't tell you what
authority I have to do these things.

A Story About Two Sons

28"Tell me what you think about this: A man
had two sons. He went to the first son and said,
'Son, go and work today in my vineyard.' 29The
son answered, 'I will not go.' But later the son
changed his mind and went. 30Then the father
went to the other son and said, 'Son, go and work
today in my vineyard.' The son answered, 'Yes,
sir, I will go and work,' but he did not go.
31Which of the two sons obeyed his father?"
The priests and leaders answered, "The first
son."
Jesus said to them, "I tell you the truth, the tax
collectors and the prostitutes[d] will enter the kingdom of God before you do. 32John came to show
you the right way to live. You did not believe him,
but the tax collectors and prostitutes believed
him. Even after seeing this, you still refused to
change your ways and believe him.

A Story About God's Son

33"Listen to this story: There was a man who
owned a vineyard. He put a wall around it and
dug a hole for a winepress[d] and built a tower.
Then he leased the land to some farmers and left
for a trip. 34When it was time for the grapes to be
picked, he sent his servants to the farmers to get
his share of the grapes. 35But the farmers grabbed
the servants, beat one, killed another, and then
killed a third servant with stones. 36So the man
sent some other servants to the farmers, even
more than he sent the first time. But the farmers
did the same thing to the servants that they had
done before. 37So the man decided to send his son
to the farmers. He said, 'They will respect my
son.' 38But when the farmers saw the son, they
said to each other, 'This son will inherit the vineyard. If we kill him, it will be ours!' 39Then the
farmers grabbed the son, threw him out of the
vineyard, and killed him. 40So what will the
owner of the vineyard do to these farmers when
he comes?"
41The priests and leaders said, "He will surely
kill those evil men. Then he will lease the vineyard to some other farmers who will give him his
share of the crop at harvest time."

'My Temple . . . prayer.' Quotation from Isaiah 56:7.
'hideout for robbers.' Quotation from Jeremiah 7:11.
Praise Literally, "Hosanna," a Hebrew word used at first in praying to God for help. At this time it was probably a shout of joy used in praising God or his Messiah.
'You . . . praises' Quotation from the Septuagint (Greek) version of Psalm 8:2.

[42]Jesus said to them, "Surely you have read this
in the Scriptures:[d]

'The stone that the builders rejected
became the cornerstone.[d]
The Lord did this,
and it is wonderful to us.' *Psalm 118:22-23*

[43]"So I tell you that the kingdom of God will be
taken away from you and given to people who do
the things God wants in his kingdom. [44]The person who falls on this stone will be broken, and on
whomever that stone falls, that person will be
crushed."[n]

[45]When the leading priests and the Pharisees[d]
heard these stories, they knew Jesus was talking
about them. [46]They wanted to arrest him, but
they were afraid of the people, because the people
believed that Jesus was a prophet.[d]

Verse 44 Some copies do not have verse 44.

A Story About a Wedding Feast

22 Jesus again used stories to teach the people. He said, [2]"The kingdom of heaven is
like a king who prepared a wedding feast for his
son. [3]The king invited some people to the feast.
When the feast was ready, the king sent his servants to tell the people, but they refused to come.
[4]"Then the king sent other servants, saying,
'Tell those who have been invited that my feast
is ready. I have killed my best bulls and calves for
the dinner, and everything is ready. Come to the
wedding feast.'
[5]"But the people refused to listen to the servants and left to do other things. One went to
work in his field, and another went to his business. [6]Some of the other people grabbed the servants, beat them, and killed them. [7]The king was

HYPOCRISY

Sunday Christians

It was Saturday night and Jay Nelson was ready to party. On Saturday nights all streets led to the warehouse. After a tough week at school, it was party time!

The warehouse was in a secluded spot at the edge of town. The party was in full swing when Jay arrived. Beer flowed freely. People danced wildly to the full-volume music.

"Hey, Jay," a familiar voice cried.

Jay turned to see Chris Freedman, a new kid at school.

"I didn't know you'd be here," Chris said.

"Oh, yeah," Jay said easily as he hoisted a can of beer. "This is the place for all the cool people."

The next morning Jay's head was pounding. He dragged himself off to Sunday school. The teacher met him at the door. "Jay," she said. "There's someone new I'd like you to meet, Chris Freedman."

Chris's eyes widened. "This is great!" he said. "My folks made me come. But you're here, so this must be the cool place to be, huh?"

"Class," the teacher said. "Today's lesson will focus on telling others about God's love. Jay, would you please lead us in prayer?"

As he prayed, Jay had to come face-to-face with his own hypocrisy. Jesus told stories about living with integrity. Read one in **Matthew 21:28–32**.

- Which son in Jesus' story is most like Jay? Why?
- How are you like the son who said he wouldn't work but went anyway?
- How are you like the son who said he would work but didn't?

C O N S I D E R . . .

- looking up "hypocrite" in a dictionary. Jot down the definitions. Read what Jesus says about hypocrisy in Matthew 7:1-5 and Matthew 23:1-12. Write Jesus' advice under the definitions. Keep the paper as a reminder to guard against hypocrisy in your life.
- noticing the sets on TV shows you watch this week—how the sets make the show seem "real" when it isn't at all. Then think of one "set" in your life and do one thing today to be more authentic.

F O R M O R E , S E E . . .

- Psalm 51
- Matthew 7:1–5
- Luke 11:37–44

furious and sent his army to kill the murderers
and burn their city.
8“After that, the king said to his servants, ‘The
wedding feast is ready. I invited those people, but
they were not worthy to come. 9So go to the
street corners and invite everyone you find to
come to my feast.’ 10So the servants went into the
streets and gathered all the people they could
find, both good and bad. And the wedding hall
was filled with guests.
11“When the king came in to see the guests, he
saw a man who was not dressed for a wedding.
12The king said, ‘Friend, how were you allowed
to come in here? You are not dressed for a wedding.’ But the man said nothing. 13So the king told
some servants, ‘Tie this man’s hands and feet.
Throw him out into the darkness, where people
will cry and grind their teeth with pain.’
14“Yes, many people are invited, but only a few
are chosen.”

Is It Right to Pay Taxes or Not?

15Then the Pharisees[d] left that place and made
plans to trap Jesus in saying something wrong.

PRIORITIES

What Are You Worth?

“I’m worth $353.21 today,” Craig Madison remarked as he modeled the clothes he had purchased during his shopping binge. “These,” he said as he removed new sunglasses, “$40.”

“This leather jacket—$100. Check out these running shoes—$80.” Craig continued to tick off his value in new goods, including sales tax.

A few months later, Craig joined his church’s drama group, which traveled all summer across the country. When the group arrived in a town, members would set up a huge circus tent and perform several times. It was hard work, but lots of fun.

The least favorite part for Craig was the afternoon matinee, a play especially for young children. Craig didn’t like little kids. They “bugged” him, he said. Until the group performed at an orphanage.

Almost immediately, six-year-old Billy liked Craig. Wherever Craig sat, Billy climbed in his lap. During the performance, Billy watched the play with awe. At one point, Billy yelled, “Hi, Craig!”

After the performance, Billy was back in Craig’s lap. “Do you believe in this Jesus guy?” Billy asked.

“Yeah, I think so,” Craig said.

“You think he’d love me?” Billy pressed.

“He loves everyone,” Craig said.

“No one ever loved me before,” Billy said.

Craig didn’t know what to say. Suddenly all his possessions didn’t seem so important. He handed his sunglasses to Billy. “Are these worth a lot?” Billy asked.

“Just $40,” said Craig. “But Billy, you’re worth much, much more. That’s what Jesus is about.”

Sometimes it’s easy to forget what’s really important. To help keep us on track, Jesus told a parable in **Matthew 22:1–14** about life’s priorities. He wanted the people to know that his top priority is to live for God and do his will.

- How is Craig’s initial love of stuff like the attitude of the wedding guests? Why did his priorities change?
- How are your priorities sometimes like those of the wedding guests?

CONSIDER . . .

- reviewing your activities of the past week. Which of them reflect your desires for the best use of time? Which ones don’t?
- inviting your parent to list his or her priorities for you while you list your own. Compare the lists and discuss differences and similarities.

FOR MORE, SEE . . .

- Ecclesiastes 2:1–11
- Luke 12:13–21
- 1 Timothy 6:17–19

16They sent some of their own followers and some people from the group called Herodians.[n] They said, "Teacher, we know that you are an honest man and that you teach the truth about God's way. You are not afraid of what other people think about you, because you pay no attention to who they are. 17So tell us what you think. Is it right to pay taxes to Caesar[d] or not?"

18But knowing that these leaders were trying to trick him, Jesus said, "You hypocrites![d] Why are you trying to trap me? 19Show me a coin used for paying the tax." So the men showed him a coin.[n] 20Then Jesus asked, "Whose image and name are on the coin?"

21The men answered, "Caesar's."

Then Jesus said to them, "Give to Caesar the things that are Caesar's, and give to God the things that are God's."

22When the men heard what Jesus said, they were amazed and left him and went away.

Some Sadducees Try to Trick Jesus

23That same day some Sadducees[d] came to Jesus and asked him a question. (Sadducees believed that people would not rise from the dead.) 24They said, "Teacher, Moses said if a married man dies without having children, his brother must marry the widow and have children for him. 25Once there were seven brothers among us. The first one married and died. Since he had no children, his brother married the widow. 26Then the second brother also died. The same thing happened to the third brother and all the other brothers. 27Finally, the woman died. 28Since all seven men had married her, when people rise from the dead, whose wife will she be?"

29Jesus answered, "You don't understand, because you don't know what the Scriptures[d] say, and you don't know about the power of God. 30When people rise from the dead, they will not marry, nor will they be given to someone to marry. They will be like the angels in heaven. 31Surely you have read what God said to you about rising from the dead. 32God said, 'I am the God of Abraham, the God of Isaac, and the God of Jacob.'[n] God is the God of the living, not the dead."

33When the people heard this, they were amazed at Jesus' teaching.

The Most Important Command

34When the Pharisees[d] learned that the Sadducees[d] could not argue with Jesus' answers to them, the Pharisees met together. 35One Pharisee, who was an expert on the law of Moses, asked Jesus this question to test him: 36"Teacher, which command in the law is the most important?"

37Jesus answered, " 'Love the Lord your God with all your heart, all your soul, and all your mind.'[n] 38This is the first and most important command. 39And the second command is like the first: 'Love your neighbor as you love yourself.'[n] 40All the law and the writings of the prophets depend on these two commands."

Jesus Questions the Pharisees

41While the Pharisees[d] were together, Jesus asked them, 42"What do you think about the Christ?[d] Whose son is he?"

They answered, "The Christ is the Son of David."[d]

43Then Jesus said to them, "Then why did David call him 'Lord'? David, speaking by the power of the Holy Spirit,[d] said,

44'The Lord said to my Lord:
Sit by me at my right side,
until I put your enemies under your
control.' *Psalm 110:*

45David calls the Christ 'Lord,' so how can the Christ be his son?"

46None of the Pharisees could answer Jesus' question, and after that day no one was brave enough to ask him any more questions.

Jesus Accuses Some Leaders

23 Then Jesus said to the crowds and to his followers, 2"The teachers of the law and the Pharisees[d] have the authority to tell you what the law of Moses says. 3So you should obey and follow whatever they tell you, but their lives are not good examples for you to follow. They tell you to do things, but they themselves don't do them. 4They make strict rules and try to force people to obey them, but they are unwilling to help those who struggle under the weight of their rules.

5"They do good things so that other people will see them. They make the boxes[n] of Scriptures that they wear bigger, and they make their special prayer clothes very long. 6Those Pharisees and teachers of the law love to have the most important seats at feasts and in the synagogues.[d] 7They love people to greet them with respect in the marketplaces, and they love to have people call them 'Teacher.'

Herodians A political group that followed Herod and his family.
coin A Roman denarius. One coin was the average pay for one day's work.
'I am . . . Jacob.' Quotation from Exodus 3:6.
'Love . . . mind.' Quotation from Deuteronomy 6:5.
'Love . . . yourself.' Quotation from Leviticus 19:18.
boxes Small leather boxes containing four important Scriptures. Some Jews tied these to the forehead and left arm, probably show they were very religious.

8“But you must not be called ‘Teacher,’ because you have only one Teacher, and you are all
brothers and sisters together. 9And don’t call any
person on earth ‘Father,’ because you have one
Father, who is in heaven. 10And you should not
be called ‘Master,’ because you have only one
Master, the Christ.[d] 11Whoever is your servant is
the greatest among you. 12Whoever makes himself great will be made humble. Whoever makes
himself humble will be made great.
13“How terrible for you, teachers of the law and
Pharisees! You are hypocrites![d] You close the door
for people to enter the kingdom of heaven. You
yourselves don’t enter, and you stop others who
are trying to enter. 14 [n]
15“How terrible for you, teachers of the law and
Pharisees! You are hypocrites! You travel across
land and sea to find one person who will change
to your ways. When you find that person, you
make him more fit for hell than you are.
16“How terrible for you! You guide the people,
but you are blind. You say, ‘If people swear by the
Temple[d] when they make a promise, that means
nothing. But if they swear by the gold that is in
the Temple, they must keep that promise.’ 17You
are blind fools! Which is greater: the gold or the
Temple that makes that gold holy? 18And you say,
‘If people swear by the altar when they make a
promise, that means nothing. But if they swear by
the gift on the altar, they must keep that promise.’
19You are blind! Which is greater: the gift or
the altar that makes the gift holy? 20The person
who swears by the altar is really using the altar
and also everything on the altar. 21And the person who swears by the Temple is really using
the Temple and also everything in the Temple.
22The person who swears by heaven is also using God’s throne and the One who sits on that
throne.
23“How terrible for you, teachers of the law and
Pharisees! You are hypocrites! You give to God
one-tenth of everything you earn—even your

Verse 14 Some Greek copies add verse 14: “How terrible for you, teachers of the law and Pharisees. You are hypocrites. You take away widows’ houses, and you say long prayers so that people will notice you. So you will have a worse punishment.”

HYPOCRISY

Being an Example

Stuart Jacobs attended the same high school as David Springer. Stuart was a “brain.” He got A’s in all his courses except gym. He wore thick glasses, stuttered, and looked like an unmade bed. He had few friends. Stuart didn’t fit in.

David heard about a game some guys had started to play at lunch at one of the school’s doorways. A long, sloping ramp led to the door. David arrived and found Stuart chasing quarters down the ramp. The guys took turns rolling quarters. Stuart, who longed for acceptance from the guys, always chased the quarters. If he caught them before a certain crack in the ramp, he got to keep them. He didn’t realize he was being laughed at.

“C’mon, David!” his friends called, “It’s your turn to roll a quarter for Stuart.” David didn’t know what to do. He didn’t want to disappoint the guys, but he didn’t want to hurt Stuart’s feelings, either.

His pastor’s words during a recent sermon came back to him, “You may be the only one through whom others see Christ.”

“What am I going to do?” David wondered.

Jesus told his followers that their words needed to reflect their actions. Read how Jesus taught about the differences between real faith and fake faith in **Matthew 23:1–12**.

- If David followed his pastor’s advice and Jesus’ teachings, what did he do?
- Have you ever sensed your faith was just an act? How can you change?

C O N S I D E R . . .

- writing a variety of conclusions to David’s story based on Jesus’ teachings in the passage.
- identifying one way you can “make yourself humble” this week, and do it.

F O R M O R E , S E E . . .

- Leviticus 19:15–18
- Mark 12:28–44
- Luke 6:37–42

mint, dill, and cumin.[n] But you don't obey the
really important teachings of the law—justice,
mercy, and being loyal. These are the things you
should do, as well as those other things. 24You
guide the people, but you are blind! You are like
a person who picks a fly out of a drink and then
swallows a camel![n]

> **SIDELIGHT:** When Jesus criticized the Pharisees for picking flies out of their drinks (Matthew 23:24), he mentioned one of the five smallest items in the Bible. Others are fleas (1 Samuel 24:14), ants (Proverbs 6:6), tiny pen marks (Matthew 5:18), and mustard seeds (Mark 4:31).

25"How terrible for you, teachers of the law and
Pharisees! You are hypocrites! You wash the outside of your cups and dishes, but inside they are
full of things you got by cheating others and by
pleasing only yourselves. 26Pharisees, you are
blind! First make the inside of the cup clean,
and then the outside of the cup can be truly
clean.
27"How terrible for you, teachers of the law and
Pharisees! You are hypocrites! You are like tombs
that are painted white. Outside, those tombs look
fine, but inside, they are full of the bones of dead
people and all kinds of unclean things. 28It is the
same with you. People look at you and think you
are good, but on the inside you are full of hypocrisy and evil.
29"How terrible for you, teachers of the law and
Pharisees! You are hypocrites! You build tombs
for the prophets,[d] and you show honor to the
graves of those who lived good lives. 30You say, 'If
we had lived during the time of our ancestors, we
would not have helped them kill the prophets.'
31But you give proof that you are children of those
who murdered the prophets. 32And you will complete the sin that your ancestors started.
33"You are snakes! A family of poisonous
snakes! How are you going to escape God's judgment? 34So I tell you this: I am sending to you
prophets and wise men and teachers. Some of
them you will kill and crucify. Some of them you
will beat in your synagogues and chase from town
to town. 35So you will be guilty for the death of
all the good people who have been killed on
earth—from the murder of that good man Abel to
the murder of Zechariah[n] son of Berakiah, whom
you murdered between the Temple and the altar.
36I tell you the truth, all of these things will happen to you people who are living now.

Jesus Feels Sorry for Jerusalem

37"Jerusalem, Jerusalem! You kill the prophets[d]
and stone to death those who are sent to you.
Many times I wanted to gather your people as a
hen gathers her chicks under her wings, but you
did not let me. 38Now your house will be left completely empty. 39I tell you, you will not see me
again until that time when you will say, 'God
bless the One who comes in the name of the
Lord.' "[n]

The Temple Will Be Destroyed

24 As Jesus left the Temple[d] and was walking away, his followers came up to show
him the Temple's buildings. 2Jesus asked, "Do
you see all these buildings? I tell you the truth,
not one stone will be left on another. Every stone
will be thrown down to the ground."
3Later, as Jesus was sitting on the Mount of Olives,[d] his followers came to be alone with him.
They said, "Tell us, when will these things happen? And what will be the sign that it is time for
you to come again and for this age to end?"
4Jesus answered, "Be careful that no one fools
you. 5Many will come in my name, saying, 'I am
the Christ,'[d] and they will fool many people. 6You
will hear about wars and stories of wars that are
coming, but don't be afraid. These things must
happen before the end comes. 7Nations will fight
against other nations; kingdoms will fight against
other kingdoms. There will be times when there
is no food for people to eat, and there will be
earthquakes in different places. 8These things are
like the first pains when something new is about
to be born.
9"Then people will arrest you, hand you over to
be hurt, and kill you. They will hate you because
you believe in me. 10At that time, many will lose
their faith, and they will turn against each other
and hate each other. 11Many false prophets[d] will
come and cause many people to believe lies.
12There will be more and more evil in the world,
so most people will stop showing their love for
each other. 13But those people who keep their
faith until the end will be saved. 14The Good
News[d] about God's kingdom will be preached in
all the world, to every nation. Then the end will
come.

mint, dill, and cumin Small plants grown in gardens and used for spices. Only very religious people would be careful enough to give a tenth of these plants.
You . . . camel! Meaning, "You worry about the smallest mistakes but commit the biggest sin."
Abel . . . Zechariah In the order of the books of the Hebrew Old Testament, the first and last men to be murdered.
'God . . . Lord.' Quotation from Psalm 118:26.

[15]"Daniel the prophet spoke about 'the destroying terror.'[n] You will see this standing in the holy
place." (You who read this should understand
what it means.) [16]"At that time, the people in Judea should run away to the mountains. [17]If people
are on the roofs[n] of their houses, they must not
go down to get anything out of their houses. [18]If
people are in the fields, they must not go back to
get their coats. [19]At that time, how terrible it will
be for women who are pregnant or have nursing
babies! [20]Pray that it will not be winter or a Sabbath[d] day when these things happen and you
have to run away, [21]because at that time there
will be much trouble. There will be more trouble
than there has ever been since the beginning of
the world until now, and nothing as bad will ever
happen again. [22]God has decided to make that terrible time short. Otherwise, no one would go on
living. But God will make that time short to help
the people he has chosen. [23]At that time, someone might say to you, 'Look, there is the Christ!'
Or another person might say, 'There he is!'
But don't believe them. [24]False Christs and false
prophets will come and perform great wonders
and miracles.[d] They will try to fool even the
people God has chosen, if that is possible.
[25]Now I have warned you about this before
it happens.

[26]"If people tell you, 'The Christ is in the
desert,' don't go there. If they say, 'The Christ is
in the inner room,' don't believe it. [27]When the

'the destroying terror' Mentioned in Daniel 9:27; 12:11 (see also Daniel 11:31).
roof In Bible times houses were built with flat roofs. The roof was used for drying things such as flax and fruit. And it was used as an extra room, as a place for worship, and as a place to sleep in the summer.

LEADERSHIP

Leading a Just Cause

On November 1, 1872, Susan B. Anthony walked into a polling place, demanding to be registered to vote. She voted in the national election. Two weeks later a U.S. marshal arrested her for "voting without lawful right." The judge wouldn't allow a jury trial. Her sentence was to pay a $100 fine and the cost of the trial. "Your Honor," declared Anthony. "I shall never pay one dollar of your unjust penalty."

She never did.

Anthony was long-familiar with the controversy and conflict of reform movements. Years earlier, she had worked for the American Anti-Slavery Society. She regarded slavery as evil and un-Christian. She published the first women's newspaper and organized the first women's union. Now Anthony was at the front of the National Women's Suffrage Movement, working tirelessly for women's voting rights.

The work was often discouraging. The press mocked her. She was denied entry into meetings. She was attacked by angry mobs. But these persecutions didn't stop her. She lectured, lobbied Congress and organized petitions.

In 1920, Anthony's efforts helped to pass the Nineteenth Amendment to the U.S. Constitution, assuring everyone the right to vote regardless of gender. But Anthony never got the chance to vote under the new amendment. She had died fourteen years earlier.

Those who lead movements for justice usually suffer ridicule, persecution, and sometimes death. Read in **Matthew 23:34–39**, what Jesus thinks about those who persecute the prophets of God.

- Why do you think people fear and persecute leaders such as Susan B. Anthony and the ones Jesus describes?
- When has your unpopular stance caused you persecution?

CONSIDER . . .

- reading through one of the prophets of the Old Testament such as Amos, trying to understand why his messages were ridiculed and rejected.
- listening to leaders who have differing opinions, keeping your mind open for truth— even if it's uncomfortable.

FOR MORE, SEE . . .

- Jeremiah 3:11–13
- Ezekiel 20:13–20
- 2 Timothy 3:1–9

Son of Man[d] comes, he will be seen by everyone,
like lightning flashing from the east to the west.
28Wherever the dead body is, there the vultures
will gather.
29"Soon after the trouble of those days,

'the sun will grow dark,
and the moon will not give its light.
The stars will fall from the sky.
And the powers of the heavens will be
shaken.' *Isaiah 13:10; 34:4*

30"At that time, the sign of the Son of Man will
appear in the sky. Then all the peoples of the
world will cry. They will see the Son of Man coming on clouds in the sky with great power and
glory. 31He will use a loud trumpet to send
his angels all around the earth, and they will
gather his chosen people from every part of the
world.
32"Learn a lesson from the fig tree: When its
branches become green and soft and new leaves
appear, you know summer is near. 33In the same
way, when you see all these things happening,
you will know that the time is near, ready to
come. 34I tell you the truth, all these things will
happen while the people of this time are still living. 35Earth and sky will be destroyed, but the
words I have said will never be destroyed.

When Will Jesus Come Again?

36"No one knows when that day or time will
be, not the angels in heaven, not even the Son.
Only the Father knows. 37When the Son of Man[d]
comes, it will be like what happened during
Noah's time. 38In those days before the flood, people were eating and drinking, marrying and giving
their children to be married, until the day Noah
entered the boat. 39They knew nothing about
what was happening until the flood came and destroyed them. It will be the same when the Son
of Man comes. 40Two men will be in the field.
One will be taken, and the other will be left.
41Two women will be grinding grain with a

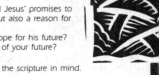

FUTURE

The Rock

In San Francisco Bay an abandoned penitentiary sits on Alcatraz Island. For years it served as a prison for hardened criminals. Its prisoners called it "The Rock."

Whitey Thompson was a "solid con." He grew up in an abusive home. He ran away. Whitey seemed to have no future.

After a failed bank robbery, Whitey was sent to jail, where he fought with guards and other prisoners. Being sent to "The Rock" seemed logical. It was end of the line for those considered hopeless criminals.

Ironically, Whitey's life turned around at Alcatraz. Whitey began to think about his future, which led him to find hope in Jesus.

Instead of killing time, he learned new skills, including painting. He painted beautiful landscapes. Guards, prisoners, and visitors admired his art.

Whitey was released directly from Alcatraz to the streets. It wasn't easy to keep looking toward the future and to build a new life. But Whitey finds strength in Jesus.

Now Whitey returns to Alcatraz as a guest of the National Park Service, which runs the former prison as a tourist attraction. His eyes twinkle when tourists ask how he survived. "Here I was on The Rock," he says. "Now I've found the true Rock."

The future lies in Jesus. In **Matthew 24:36–44**, read Jesus' promises to return. This promise not only gives hope for the future, but also a reason for living today, as Whitey discovered.

- What did Whitey discover in Jesus to help him find hope for his future?
- How does knowing Christ will return affect your view of your future?

C O N S I D E R . . .

- making a list of the things you want to achieve. Keep the scripture in mind. If Jesus came tomorrow would you be ready?
- telling a cynical friend about the hope for the future you have in Jesus.

F O R M O R E , S E E . . .

- Psalm 33:13–22
- Luke 12:35–40
- 1 Thessalonians 5:1–11

mill.[n] One will be taken, and the other will be
left.
42"So always be ready, because you don't know
the day your Lord will come. 43Remember this: If
the owner of the house knew what time of night
a thief was coming, the owner would watch and
not let the thief break in. 44So you also must be
ready, because the Son of Man will come at a time
you don't expect him.
45"Who is the wise and loyal servant that the
master trusts to give the other servants their food
at the right time? 46When the master comes and
finds the servant doing his work, the servant will
be blessed. 47I tell you the truth, the master will
choose that servant to take care of everything he
owns. 48But suppose that evil servant thinks to
himself, 'My master will not come back soon,'
49and he begins to beat the other servants and eat
and get drunk with others like him? 50The master
will come when that servant is not ready and is
not expecting him. 51Then the master will cut
him in pieces and send him away to be with the
hypocrites,[d] where people will cry and grind their
teeth with pain.

A Story About Ten Bridesmaids

25 "At that time the kingdom of heaven will
be like ten bridesmaids who took their
lamps and went to wait for the bridegroom. 2Five
of them were foolish and five were wise. 3The five
foolish bridesmaids took their lamps, but they did
not take more oil for the lamps to burn. 4The wise

mill Two large, round, flat rocks used for grinding grain to make flour.

DECISION MAKING

Always Be Ready

Kent Andrews was discouraged as he drove to work. He could hear Mom's words from a few months ago echo in his mind. "Kent, you must get your act together," she'd said. "It's your senior year and time is running out. You need to decide about college. Don't you want to go?"

What a worry wart, he had thought at the time. Of course he wanted to go to college. His grades were okay. He just needed to decide where to go. Weren't they all the same? Kent was sick of school anyway, and wanted to have fun with his friends in his senior year.

Kent hadn't counted on the state standardized test. The state allowed students to graduate only if they passed the basic skills test. Fairly easy stuff—if you were ready. But it had seemed a better idea to Kent to party than to study.

Kent had failed the test. He had missed the admissions deadlines for most colleges anyway, and most of the financial aid had already been doled out.

So, instead of receiving his diploma with his friends, Kent had watched graduation from the bleachers in the school gym. Instead of packing for college in the fall like his friends, he was sacking groceries at a local supermarket.

As Kent tied his apron for work, he thought about his friends in college. He realized it was his own fault he wasn't there with them. Next year, Kent vowed, I'll be ready.

Jesus told a story about poor preparation and poor decisions. Read it in **Matthew 25:1–13**.

- How are the stories of Kent and the ten girls similar? How did poor decision making play a role in both stories?
- When have you had to live with the consequences of a poor decision similar to that of the ten girls in Jesus' story? How would better decisions have helped you?

C O N S I D E R . . .

- dividing a piece of paper in half. On the left side list things about which you have made poor decisions in the past. On the right side write one thing you could do in each instance to make a better choice next time.
- asking a parent to tell about a tough decision he or she has made and what happened as a result of the choice.

F O R M O R E . S E E . . .

- Proverbs 8:10
- Luke 12:35–48
- John 7:16–18

bridesmaids took their lamps and more oil in jars. 5Because the bridegroom was late, they became sleepy and went to sleep.

6"At midnight someone cried out, 'The bridegroom is coming! Come and meet him!' 7Then all the bridesmaids woke up and got their lamps ready. 8But the foolish ones said to the wise, 'Give us some of your oil, because our lamps are going out.' 9The wise bridesmaids answered, 'No, the oil we have might not be enough for all of us. Go to the people who sell oil and buy some for yourselves.'

10"So while the five foolish bridesmaids went to buy oil, the bridegroom came. The bridesmaids who were ready went in with the bridegroom to the wedding feast. Then the door was closed and locked.

11"Later the others came back and said, 'Sir, sir, open the door to let us in.' 12But the bridegroom answered, 'I tell you the truth, I don't want to know you.'

13"So always be ready, because you don't know the day or the hour the Son of Man[d] will come.

A Story About Three Servants

14"The kingdom of heaven is like a man who was going to another place for a visit. Before he left, he called for his servants and told them to take care of his things while he was gone. 15He gave one servant five bags of gold, another servant two bags of gold, and a third servant one bag of gold, to each one as much as he could handle. Then he left. 16The servant who got five bags went quickly to invest the money and earned five more bags. 17In the same way, the servant who had two bags invested them and earned two more. 18But the servant who got one bag went out and dug a hole in the ground and hid the master's money.

19"After a long time the master came home and asked the servants what they did with his money. 20The servant who was given five bags of gold brought five more bags to the master and said, 'Master, you trusted me to care for five bags of gold, so I used your five bags to earn five more.' 21The master answered, 'You did well. You are a good and loyal servant. Because you were loyal with small things, I will let you care for much greater things. Come and share my joy with me.'

22"Then the servant who had been given two bags of gold came to the master and said, 'Master, you gave me two bags of gold to care for, so I used your two bags to earn two more.' 23The master answered, 'You did well. You are a good and loyal servant. Because you were loyal with small things, I will let you care for much greater things. Come and share my joy with me.'

24"Then the servant who had been given one bag of gold came to the master and said, 'Master, I knew that you were a hard man. You harvest things you did not plant. You gather crops where you did not sow any seed. 25So I was afraid and went and hid your money in the ground. Here is your bag of gold.' 26The master answered, 'You are a wicked and lazy servant! You say you knew that I harvest things I did not plant and that I gather crops where I did not sow any seed. 27So you should have put my gold in the bank. Then, when I came home, I would have received my gold back with interest.'

28"So the master told his other servants, 'Take the bag of gold from that servant and give it to the servant who has ten bags of gold. 29Those who have much will get more, and they will have much more than they need. But those who do not have much will have everything taken away from them.' 30Then the master said, 'Throw that useless servant outside, into the darkness where people will cry and grind their teeth with pain.'

The King Will Judge All People

31"The Son of Man[d] will come again in his great glory, with all his angels. He will be King and sit on his great throne. 32All the nations of the world will be gathered before him, and he will separate them into two groups as a shepherd separates the sheep from the goats. 33The Son of Man will put the sheep on his right and the goats on his left.

34"Then the King will say to the people on his right, 'Come, my Father has given you his blessing. Receive the kingdom God has prepared for you since the world was made. 35I was hungry, and you gave me food. I was thirsty, and you gave me something to drink. I was alone and away from home, and you invited me into your house. 36I was without clothes, and you gave me something to wear. I was sick, and you cared for me. I was in prison, and you visited me.'

37"Then the good people will answer, 'Lord, when did we see you hungry and give you food, or thirsty and give you something to drink? 38When did we see you alone and away from home and invite you into our house? When did we see you without clothes and give you something to wear? 39When did we see you sick or in prison and care for you?'

40"Then the King will answer, 'I tell you the truth, anything you did for even the least of my people here, you also did for me.'

41"Then the King will say to those on his left, 'Go away from me. You will be punished. Go into the fire that burns forever that was prepared for the devil and his angels. 42I was hungry, and you gave me nothing to eat. I was thirsty and you gave me nothing to drink. 43I was alone and away from home, and you did not invite me into your house. I was without clothes, and

you gave me nothing to wear. I was sick and in prison, and you did not care for me.'
44"Then those people will answer, 'Lord, when
did we see you hungry or thirsty or alone and
away from home or without clothes or sick or in
prison? When did we see these things and not
help you?'
45"Then the King will answer, 'I tell you the
truth, anything you refused to do for even the
least of my people here, you refused to do for me.'
46"These people will go off to be punished forever, but the good people will go to live forever."

The Plan to Kill Jesus

26 After Jesus finished saying all these
things, he told his followers, 2"You
know that the day after tomorrow is the day of the
Passover[d] Feast. On that day the Son of Man[d] will
be given to his enemies to be crucified."
3Then the leading priests and the older Jewish
leaders had a meeting at the palace of the high
priest, named Caiaphas. 4At the meeting, they
planned to set a trap to arrest Jesus and kill him.
5But they said, "We must not do it during the
feast, because the people might cause a riot."

Perfume for Jesus' Burial

6Jesus was in Bethany at the house of Simon,
who had a skin disease. 7While Jesus was there,
a woman approached him with an alabaster[d] jar
filled with expensive perfume. She poured this
perfume on Jesus' head while he was eating.

SERVICE

Are You Jesus?

Eric Schwartz dressed in army surplus fatigues and roared through the city on his motorcycle. He wore his hair long and his beard full, which made him look older than his eighteen years. Eric was proud of his tough image—it was his "style."

Because of his tough image, it was no surprise when he was arrested for shoplifting. Since Eric was a first-time offender, the judge sentenced him to several hours of community service instead of jail.

Eric chose to "do his time" at The Shepherd's Table, a soup kitchen for the homeless. He peeled potatoes, served food, and mopped floors. The sights, sounds, and smells depressed him. It was a place for the poor, broken, lonely, and afraid—people who reminded him a lot of himself.

Eric began to talk with the people. He had expected to find just a bunch of drunken bums, but, instead, he met a surprising variety of people caught in the poverty trap.

There was a Vietnam War veteran who worked, but never had money at month's end. An older woman had lost her home after her husband had died. A young mother with three small children lived in one room. A family who had lost a farm struggled to find work in the city. The stories broke his heart.

He didn't feel so "tough" after a while. In fact, he began to enjoy how he felt when he served others. One evening after supper, he was wiping tables when he felt a tug at his camouflage pants. A young girl looked up to him.

"Mister," whispered the child. "Are you Jesus?"

The question startled him. "Huh?" he asked, confused.

"You must be Jesus," she insisted. "Momma told me Jesus loves poor people like us."

When Eric shared the story with the soup kitchen manager, she showed him **Matthew 25:31–46**. "That's why we're here," she said.

- What did serving teach Eric about being Jesus' follower?
- When have you seen someone as Jesus describes: hungry, thirsty, sick, without warm clothes, alone, or imprisoned? What was your reaction?

CONSIDER . . .

- listing all the people with whom you come in contact in a typical day. Decide something you can do to serve those people.
- thinking of Jesus each time you see someone in need. How do your thoughts affect your attitude toward that person?

FOR MORE, SEE . . .

- Lamentations 3:26–27
- Luke 10:25–37
- John 13:1–17

8His followers were upset when they saw
the woman do this. They asked, "Why waste
that perfume? 9It could have been sold for a
great deal of money and the money given to
the poor."
10Knowing what had happened, Jesus said,
"Why are you troubling this woman? She did an
excellent thing for me. 11You will always have
the poor with you, but you will not always
have me. 12This woman poured perfume on
my body to prepare me for burial. 13I tell you
the truth, wherever the Good News[d] is
preached in all the world, what this woman has
done will be told, and people will remember
her."

Judas Becomes an Enemy of Jesus

14Then one of the twelve apostles, Judas Iscar-
iot, went to talk to the leading priests. 15He said,
"What will you pay me for giving Jesus to you?"
And they gave him thirty silver coins. 16After that,
Judas watched for the best time to turn Jesus in.

Jesus Eats the Passover Meal

17On the first day of the Feast[d] of Unleavened
Bread, the followers came to Jesus. They said,
"Where do you want us to prepare for you to eat
the Passover[d] meal?"
18Jesus answered, "Go into the city to a certain
man and tell him, 'The Teacher says: The chosen

FRIENDS

Diary of a Backstabber

November 1: I knew something was wrong when I came out from work and saw Drew. He should have been at basketball practice. "I need to talk to you," he said, and my stomach tightened. "Lisa, I hate to do this, but there's no good way to break up. . ."

He droned on, but I didn't hear anything past the "break up" part. "And I want to still be friends," he said. FRIENDS! He dumps me and still wants to be friends!

November 30: I can't stand seeing Drew at school. And now he's hanging around the mall with his skateboarding friends.

December 6: Tonight I saw some workers dismantling a Winter Wonderland display at the mall lobby. When I got to the store, I asked my manager what happened.

"It was skateboarders," she said. "A bunch of 'em sneaked in after hours and trashed the whole thing. They rode their skateboards all over, using the fake snowdrifts as ramps."

December 11: During prayer requests at youth group, I spoke up. "I think we should pray for Drew, since the incident at the mall with the skateboarders and all."

December 13: The rumors about Drew spread to school. Then in fifth hour, he was called out of class. After school let out, I ran into him. He didn't look good.

"Are you okay?" I asked, surprised that I felt so concerned.

"Yeah, I guess so," Drew answered. "Have you heard what everyone's saying about me, Lisa?"

"Uh, yeah," I stammered, not looking him in the eye.

"It wasn't us!" he says. "Sure, we hang around the mall some, but we'd never do something like that. I can't imagine who'd think we had. You don't know who turned in our names, do you?"

"No, Drew I don't," I said. Because she felt hurt, Lisa betrayed Drew and got him into a lot of trouble. We don't know Judas's motives for betraying Jesus, but we do know what happened. Read about it in **Matthew 26:14–25**.

- What feelings might Lisa and Judas have experienced as each betrayed a friend?
- If you had been in the room with Jesus and the disciples, what would you have said or done?

C O N S I D E R . . .

- making a commitment not to betray your friends by spreading rumors or gossip about them.
- forgiving a friend who has betrayed you. Try to settle your differences.

F O R M O R E , S E E . . .

- Isaiah 53:4–6
- Mark 14:10–21
- Acts 1:12–26

time is near. I will have the Passover with my
followers at your house.' " 19The followers did
what Jesus told them to do, and they prepared the
Passover meal.

20In the evening Jesus was sitting at the table
with his twelve followers. 21As they were eating,
Jesus said, "I tell you the truth, one of you will
turn against me."

22This made the followers very sad. Each one
began to say to Jesus, "Surely, Lord, I am not the
one who will turn against you, am I?"

23Jesus answered, "The man who has dipped
his hand with me into the bowl is the one who
will turn against me. 24The Son of Man[d] will die,
just as the Scriptures[d] say. But how terrible it will
be for the person who hands the Son of Man over
to be killed. It would be better for him if he had
never been born."

25Then Judas, who would give Jesus to his enemies, said to Jesus, "Teacher, surely I am not the
one, am I?"

Jesus answered, "Yes, it is you."

The Lord's Supper

26While they were eating, Jesus took some
bread and thanked God for it and broke it. Then
he gave it to his followers and said, "Take this
bread and eat it; this is my body."

27Then Jesus took a cup and thanked God for
it and gave it to the followers. He said, "Every one
of you drink this. 28This is my blood which is the
new agreement that God makes with his people.
This blood is poured out for many to forgive their
sins. 29I tell you this: I will not drink of this fruit
of the vine[n] again until that day when I drink it
new with you in my Father's kingdom."

30After singing a hymn, they went out to the
Mount of Olives.[d]

Jesus' Followers Will Leave Him

31Jesus told his followers, "Tonight you will all
stumble in your faith on account of me, because
it is written in the Scriptures:[d]

'I will kill the shepherd,
and the sheep will scatter.' *Zechariah 13:7*

32But after I rise from the dead, I will go ahead of
you into Galilee."

33Peter said, "Everyone else may stumble in
their faith because of you, but I will not."

34Jesus said, "I tell you the truth, tonight before
the rooster crows you will say three times that
you don't know me."

35But Peter said, "I will never say that I don't
know you! I will even die with you!" And all the
other followers said the same thing.

Jesus Prays Alone

36Then Jesus went with his followers to a place
called Gethsemane. He said to them, "Sit here
while I go over there and pray." 37He took Peter
and the two sons of Zebedee with him, and he
began to be very sad and troubled. 38He said to
them, "My heart is full of sorrow, to the point of
death. Stay here and watch with me."

39After walking a little farther away from them,
Jesus fell to the ground and prayed, "My Father,
if it is possible, do not give me this cup[n] of suffering. But do what you want, not what I want."
40Then Jesus went back to his followers and found
them asleep. He said to Peter, "You men could
not stay awake with me for one hour? 41Stay
awake and pray for strength against temptation.
The spirit wants to do what is right, but the body
is weak."

42Then Jesus went away a second time and
prayed, "My Father, if it is not possible for this
painful thing to be taken from me, and if I must
do it, I pray that what you want will be done."

43Then he went back to his followers, and again
he found them asleep, because their eyes were
heavy. 44So Jesus left them and went away and
prayed a third time, saying the same thing.

45Then Jesus went back to his followers and
said, "Are you still sleeping and resting? The time
has come for the Son of Man[d] to be handed over
to sinful people. 46Get up, we must go. Look, here
comes the man who has turned against me."

Jesus Is Arrested

47While Jesus was still speaking, Judas, one of
the twelve apostles,[d] came up. With him were
many people carrying swords and clubs who had
been sent from the leading priests and the older
Jewish leaders of the people. 48Judas had planned
to give them a signal, saying, "The man I kiss
is Jesus. Arrest him." 49At once Judas went to
Jesus and said, "Greetings, Teacher!" and kissed
him.

50Jesus answered, "Friend, do what you came
to do."

Then the people came and grabbed Jesus and
arrested him. 51When that happened, one of
Jesus' followers reached for his sword and pulled
it out. He struck the servant of the high priest and
cut off his ear.

52Jesus said to the man, "Put your sword back
in its place. All who use swords will be killed with
swords. 53Surely you know I could ask my Father,
and he would give me more than twelve armies
of angels. 54But it must happen this way to bring
about what the Scriptures[d] say."

fruit of the vine Product of the grapevine; this may also be translated "wine."
cup Jesus is talking about the terrible things that will happen to him. Accepting these things will be very hard, like drinking a cup of something bitter.

55Then Jesus said to the crowd, "You came to
get me with swords and clubs as if I were a criminal. Every day I sat in the Temple[d] teaching, and
you did not arrest me there. 56But all these things
have happened so that it will come about as the
prophets[d] wrote." Then all of Jesus' followers left
him and ran away.

Jesus Before the Leaders

57Those people who arrested Jesus led him to
the house of Caiaphas, the high priest, where the
teachers of the law and the older Jewish leaders
were gathered. 58Peter followed far behind to the
courtyard of the high priest's house, and he sat
down with the guards to see what would happen
to Jesus.
59The leading priests and the whole Jewish
council tried to find something false against Jesus
so they could kill him. 60Many people came and
told lies about him, but the council could find no
real reason to kill him. Then two people came and
said, 61"This man said, 'I can destroy the Temple[d]
of God and build it again in three days.' "
62Then the high priest stood up and said to
Jesus, "Aren't you going to answer? Don't you
have something to say about their charges against
you?" 63But Jesus said nothing.

> **SIDELIGHT:** Practically every legal rule was broken to convict Jesus (Matthew 26:57–67). Jewish law prohibited trials at night, during Passover, and without legitimate witnesses—all of which happened in Jesus' trial. Any good judge would declare a mistrial today.

Again the high priest said to Jesus, "I command
you by the power of the living God: Tell us if you
are the Christ,[d] the Son of God."
64Jesus answered, "Those are your words. But
I tell you, in the future you will see the Son of
Man[d] sitting at the right hand of God, the Powerful One, and coming on clouds in the sky."
65When the high priest heard this, he tore his
clothes and said, "This man has said things that
are against God! We don't need any more witnesses; you all heard him say these things against
God. 66What do you think?"
The people answered, "He should die."
67Then the people there spat in Jesus' face and
beat him with their fists. Others slapped him.
68They said, "Prove to us that you are a prophet,[d]
you Christ! Tell us who hit you!"

Peter Says He Doesn't Know Jesus

69At that time, as Peter was sitting in the courtyard, a servant girl came to him and said, "You
also were with Jesus of Galilee."
70But Peter said to all the people there that he
was never with Jesus. He said, "I don't know
what you are talking about."
71When he left the courtyard and was at the
gate, another girl saw him. She said to the people
there, "This man was with Jesus of Nazareth."
72Again, Peter said he was never with him, saying, "I swear I don't know this man Jesus!"
73A short time later, some people standing
there went to Peter and said, "Surely you are one
of those who followed Jesus. The way you talk
shows it."
74Then Peter began to place a curse on himself
and swear, "I don't know the man." At once, a
rooster crowed. 75And Peter remembered what
Jesus had told him: "Before the rooster crows,
you will say three times that you don't know me."
Then Peter went outside and cried painfully.

Jesus Is Taken to Pilate

27 Early the next morning, all the leading
priests and older leaders of the people
decided that Jesus should die. 2They tied him, led
him away, and turned him over to Pilate, the governor.

Judas Kills Himself

3Judas, the one who had given Jesus to his enemies, saw that they had decided to kill Jesus.
Then he was very sorry for what he had done. So
he took the thirty silver coins back to the priests
and the leaders, 4saying, "I sinned; I handed over
to you an innocent man."
The leaders answered, "What is that to us?
That's your problem, not ours."
5So Judas threw the money into the Temple.[d]
Then he went off and hanged himself.
6The leading priests picked up the silver coins
in the Temple and said, "Our law does not allow
us to keep this money with the Temple money,
because it has paid for a man's death." 7So they
decided to use the coins to buy Potter's Field as
a place to bury strangers who died in Jerusalem.
8That is why that field is still called the Field of
Blood. 9So what Jeremiah the prophet[d] had said
came true: "They took thirty silver coins. That is
how little the Israelites thought he was worth.
10They used those thirty silver coins to buy the
potter's field, as the Lord commanded me."[n]

Pilate Questions Jesus

11Jesus stood before Pilate the governor, and

"They . . . commanded me." See Zechariah 11:12-13 and Jeremiah 32:6-9.

Pilate asked him, "Are you the king of the Jews?"
Jesus answered, "Those are your words."
12When the leading priests and the older leaders accused Jesus, he said nothing.
13So Pilate said to Jesus, "Don't you hear them
accusing you of all these things?"
14But Jesus said nothing in answer to Pilate,
and Pilate was very surprised at this.

Pilate Tries to Free Jesus

15Every year at the time of Passover[d] the governor would free one prisoner whom the people
chose. 16At that time there was a man in prison,
named Barabbas, who was known to be very bad.
17When the people gathered at Pilate's house, Pilate said, "Whom do you want me to set free:
Barabbas or Jesus who is called the Christ?"[d] 18Pi-
late knew that the people turned Jesus in to him
because they were jealous.
19While Pilate was sitting there on the judge's
seat, his wife sent this message to him: "Don't do
anything to that man, because he is innocent. Today I had a dream about him, and it troubled me
very much."
20But the leading priests and older leaders convinced the crowd to ask for Barabbas to be freed
and for Jesus to be killed.
21Pilate said, "I have Barabbas and Jesus.
Which do you want me to set free for you?"
The people answered, "Barabbas."
22Pilate asked, "So what should I do with Jesus,
the one called the Christ?"
They all answered, "Crucify him!"
23Pilate asked, "Why? What wrong has he
done?"
But they shouted louder, "Crucify him!"
24When Pilate saw that he could do nothing
about this and that a riot was starting, he took
some water and washed his hands[n] in front of
the crowd. Then he said, "I am not guilty of this
man's death. You are the ones who are causing
it!"
25All the people answered, "We and our children will be responsible for his death."
26Then he set Barabbas free. But Jesus was
beaten with whips and handed over to the soldiers to be crucified.
27The governor's soldiers took Jesus into the
governor's palace, and they all gathered around
him. 28They took off his clothes and put a red robe
on him. 29Using thorny branches, they made a
crown, put it on his head, and put a stick in his
right hand. Then the soldiers bowed before Jesus
and made fun of him, saying, "Hail, King of the
Jews!" 30They spat on Jesus. Then they took his
stick and began to beat him on the head. 31After
they finished, the soldiers took off the robe and
put his own clothes on him again. Then they led
him away to be crucified.

Jesus Is Crucified

32As the soldiers were going out of the city with
Jesus, they forced a man from Cyrene, named Simon, to carry the cross for Jesus. 33They all came
to the place called Golgotha, which means the
Place of the Skull. 34The soldiers gave Jesus wine
mixed with gall[n] to drink. He tasted the wine but
refused to drink it. 35When the soldiers had crucified him, they threw lots[d] to decide who would
get his clothes. 36The soldiers sat there and continued watching him. 37They put a sign above
Jesus' head with a charge against him. It said:
THIS IS JESUS, THE KING OF THE JEWS. 38Two robbers
were crucified beside Jesus, one on the right and
the other on the left. 39People walked by and insulted Jesus and shook their heads, 40saying, "You
said you could destroy the Temple[d] and build it
again in three days. So save yourself! Come down
from that cross if you are really the Son of God!"
41The leading priests, the teachers of the law,
and the older Jewish leaders were also making fun
of Jesus. 42They said, "He saved others, but he
can't save himself! He says he is the king of Israel!
If he is the king, let him come down now from the
cross. Then we will believe in him. 43He trusts in
God, so let God save him now, if God really wants
him. He himself said, 'I am the Son of God.' "
44And in the same way, the robbers who were
being crucified beside Jesus also insulted him.

Jesus Dies

45At noon the whole country became dark, and
the darkness lasted for three hours. 46About three
o'clock Jesus cried out in a loud voice, "Eli, Eli,
lama sabachthani?" This means, "My God, my
God, why have you rejected me?"
47Some of the people standing there who heard
this said, "He is calling Elijah."
48Quickly one of them ran and got a sponge and
filled it with vinegar and tied it to a stick and gave
it to Jesus to drink. 49But the others said, "Don't
bother him. We want to see if Elijah will come to
save him."
50But Jesus cried out again in a loud voice and
died.
51Then the curtain in the Temple[n] was torn
into two pieces, from the top to the bottom. Also,
the earth shook and rocks broke apart. 52The

washed his hands He did this as a sign to show that he wanted no part in what the people did.
gall Probably a drink of wine mixed with drugs to help a person feel less pain.
curtain in the Temple A curtain divided the Most Holy Place from the other part of the Temple. That was the special building in Jerusalem where God commanded the Jewish people to worship him.

graves opened, and many of God's people who
had died were raised from the dead. 53They came
out of the graves after Jesus was raised from the
dead and went into the holy city, where they appeared to many people.
54When the army officer and the soldiers guarding Jesus saw this earthquake and everything else
that happened, they were very frightened and
said, "He really was the Son of God!"
55Many women who had followed Jesus from
Galilee to help him were standing at a distance
from the cross, watching. 56Mary Magdalene, and
Mary the mother of James and Joseph, and the
mother of James and John were there.

Jesus Is Buried

57That evening a rich man named Joseph, a follower of Jesus from the town of Arimathea, came
to Jerusalem. 58Joseph went to Pilate and asked to
have Jesus' body. So Pilate gave orders for the soldiers to give it to Joseph. 59Then Joseph took the
body and wrapped it in a clean linen cloth. 60He
put Jesus' body in a new tomb that he had cut out
of a wall of rock, and he rolled a very large stone
to block the entrance of the tomb. Then Joseph
went away. 61Mary Magdalene and the other
woman named Mary were sitting near the tomb.

The Tomb of Jesus Is Guarded

62The next day, the day after Preparation[d] Day,
the leading priests and the Pharisees[d] went to Pilate. 63They said, "Sir, we remember that while
that liar was still alive he said, 'After three days
I will rise from the dead.' 64So give the order for
the tomb to be guarded closely till the third day.
Otherwise, his followers might come and steal the
body and tell people that he has risen from the
dead. That lie would be even worse than the first
one."
65Pilate said, "Take some soldiers and go guard
the tomb the best way you know." 66So they all
went to the tomb and made it safe from thieves

SADNESS

Does Anybody Care?

"Louise!" Mom yelled. "Joyce is on the phone!" Joyce Berg was Louise Stone's best friend. They were inseparable.

Joyce's voice was soft when Louise picked up the phone. It didn't sound like her. "Louise, my dad died," Joyce said.

Silence.

Louise's mind raced. She knew he had been sick. But Joyce and Louise were only sixteen. Parents don't die now!

"What can I do?" Louise asked.

"Can you come over?" Joyce replied.

Louise went. The sadness was overwhelming. Joyce was quiet. Her mom cried a lot. Her brother stayed in his room. Louise babysat, answered phones, collected casseroles from visitors. She went to the funeral and hugged Joyce a lot.

Back home Mom and Louise talked. "I couldn't do anything," Louise said as she wept. "It was awful. I couldn't take away her sadness. I didn't know how to tell her I cared."

For several weeks both Joyce and Louise remained sad. Although they knew this was temporary, they didn't realize that the death of Joyce's dad would leave them vulnerable to sad feelings for months, even years. There was no way to avoid their grief; it was just something to go through.

Sadness and grief are normal feelings when someone close to you dies. After Jesus was crucified, his friends were terribly sad. Read what they did in **Matthew 27:57–61**.

- What feelings seem common to Jesus' friends and Louise?
- What ways might this the passage suggest for helping hurting friends?

C O N S I D E R . . .

- making a list of your hurting friends. Carry it with you. It will remind you to reach out to those friends, especially after the immediate crisis has passed.
- memorizing Romans 8:38-39. Use it to strengthen you in sad times.

F O R M O R E , S E E . . .

- Ecclesiastes 7:2–4
- Luke 23:44–56
- John 11:28–44

by sealing the stone in the entrance and putting soldiers there to guard it.

Jesus Rises from the Dead

28 The day after the Sabbath[d] day was the first day of the week. At dawn on the first day, Mary Magdalene and another woman named Mary went to look at the tomb.
2At that time there was a strong earthquake. An angel of the Lord came down from heaven, went to the tomb, and rolled the stone away from the entrance. Then he sat on the stone. 3He was shining as bright as lightning, and his clothes were white as snow. 4The soldiers guarding the tomb
shook with fear because of the angel, and they became like dead men.
5The angel said to the women, "Don't be afraid. I know that you are looking for Jesus, who has been crucified. 6He is not here. He has risen from the dead as he said he would. Come and see the place where his body was. 7And go quickly
and tell his followers, 'Jesus has risen from the dead. He is going into Galilee ahead of you, and you will see him there.' " Then the angel said, "Now I have told you."

SIDELIGHT: The stones in front of tombs in Jesus' day were large, disk-shaped boulders (Matthew 28:2). They were placed in grooves so that they would roll down and block the entrance to the cave-like tombs, making them difficult to move.

8The women left the tomb quickly. They were afraid, but they were also very happy. They ran to tell Jesus' followers what had happened. 9Sud-
denly, Jesus met them and said, "Greetings." The

FOLLOWING GOD

Not Me, Lord!

"How do I know what God wants me to do?" Beth Berger asked her pastor. Beth was a college junior struggling with her future. She was home on Christmas break, looking for a summer job.

"Obviously, you want to follow God," Pastor Jones said. "Try listening. You'll be surprised at what you hear."

"I don't want to be a pastor!" Beth shot back. "I'm not sure I feel called to do that."

"You don't have to be in full-time ministry to follow God," he said quietly. "Following God takes different paths. Why not explore other possibilities?"

Beth stayed open to God's calling. She was offered a position for the summer at a church camp. She accepted. She worked with children, led Bible studies, planned and led worship and music, cared for animals and camped outdoors. She listened for God and learned what it meant to be a follower.

She returned to college energized for her senior year. "I discovered I'm good at things like teaching. I even like Bible studies," she wrote to Pastor Jones. "I still don't know what I'll do. But I'll keep finding ways to follow God."

Beth learned that following God may at first seem scary. But after the initial "Yes, send me," serving God brings adventure, growth and true joy. Read **Matthew 28:16–20** to find Jesus' commission and promise for those who agree to follow him.

- What did Beth learn about following God? How is this similar to Jesus' command?
- How do you follow God? How do you seek to make others followers of God?

CONSIDER . . .

- writing a scenario in which you befriend people who have never heard about Jesus. How will you teach them about faith?
- listing the ways the careers you're interested in could minister and spread God's kingdom.

FOR MORE, SEE . . .

- Exodus 3
- John 21
- Acts 1:7–11

women came up to him, took hold of his feet, and worshiped him. [10]Then Jesus said to them, "Don't be afraid. Go and tell my followers to go on to Galilee, and they will see me there."

The Soldiers Report to the Leaders

[11]While the women went to tell Jesus' followers, some of the soldiers who had been guarding the tomb went into the city to tell the leading priests everything that had happened. [12]Then the priests met with the older Jewish leaders and made a plan. They paid the soldiers a large amount of money [13]and said to them, "Tell the people that Jesus' followers came during the night and stole the body while you were asleep. [14]If the governor hears about this, we will satisfy him and save you from trouble." [15]So the soldiers kept the money and did as they were told. And that story is still spread among the Jewish people even today.

Jesus Talks to His Followers

[16]The eleven followers went to Galilee to the mountain where Jesus had told them to go. [17]On the mountain they saw Jesus and worshiped him, but some of them did not believe it was really Jesus. [18]Then Jesus came to them and said, "All power in heaven and on earth is given to me. [19]So go and make followers of all people in the world. Baptize them in the name of the Father and the Son and the Holy Spirit.[a] [20]Teach them to obey everything that I have taught you, and I will be with you always, even until the end of this age."

MARK

Why Read This Book:

- Learn about the healings and miracles Jesus performed (Mark 2—8).
- Listen to Jesus' teachings about following him (Mark 9—12).
- See how Jesus was victorious even though people killed him (Mark 14—16).

Behind the Scenes:

The Gospel of Mark is a lot like an evening newscast. It's filled with short, quick "news bites" about Jesus' life. It moves quickly from scene to scene, and is filled with action and drama.

Unlike a newsmagazine, it doesn't linger on any scene. Instead, it cuts quickly from one scene to the next. So Mark is packed with simple, vivid stories. The Greek word translated "immediately" or "then" appears more than forty times in just sixteen chapters!

The book begins with a short segment on John the Baptist, who announced Jesus' coming. Then it tells about Jesus' miracles and activities in the region of Lake Galilee. Finally, the action moves to Jerusalem, where Jesus was arrested and killed. Then he rose from the grave.

Unlike the other three Gospels, this book appears to be addressed to people

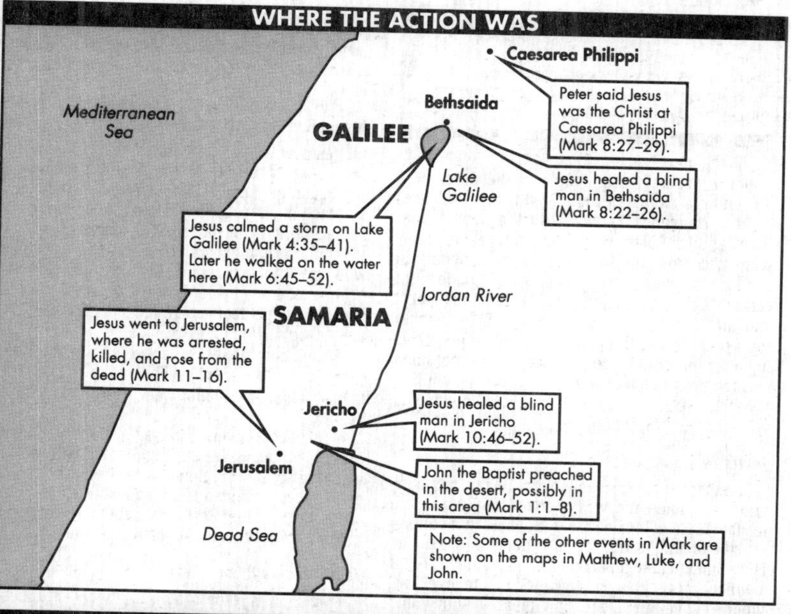

WHERE THE ACTION WAS
Caesarea Philippi
Peter said Jesus was the Christ at Caesarea Philippi (Mark 8:27–29).
Bethsaida
Mediterranean Sea
GALILEE
Lake Galilee
Jesus healed a blind man in Bethsaida (Mark 8:22–26).
Jesus calmed a storm on Lake Galilee (Mark 4:35–41). Later he walked on the water here (Mark 6:45–52).
Jordan River
SAMARIA
Jesus went to Jerusalem, where he was arrested, killed, and rose from the dead (Mark 11–16).
Jericho
Jesus healed a blind man in Jericho (Mark 10:46–52).
Jerusalem
John the Baptist preached in the desert, possibly in this area (Mark 1:1–8).
Dead Sea
Note: Some of the other events in Mark are shown on the maps in Matthew, Luke, and John.

WHEN THE ACTION WAS

Jesus was born	Jesus was crucified, rose from the dead, and went to heaven	Paul began his missionary work	Fire destroyed Rome	
BC/AD	25AD	50AD	75AD	100AD
	Jesus began his ministry		Romans destroyed the Temple in Jerusalem	

Behind the Scenes (cont.): who weren't from the area where Jesus lived. Since this audience wasn't as familiar with stories about Jesus, this book is a simple introduction to who Jesus was, what he did and why he came into the world.

So it's a great place to begin learning the basics!

John Prepares for Jesus

1 This is the beginning of the Good News[d] about Jesus Christ, the Son of God,[n] 2as the prophet[d] Isaiah wrote:

"I will send my messenger ahead of you,
who will prepare your way." *Malachi 3:1*

3"This is a voice of one
who calls out in the desert:
'Prepare the way for the Lord.
Make the road straight for him.' " *Isaiah 40:3*

> **SIDELIGHT:** John the Baptist quoted from Isaiah about preparing the way for the Lord (Mark 1:2–3), a passage of scripture describing an ancient practice for traveling oriental kings. Whenever a ruler went places without roads, a crew of workers went ahead to smooth out rough places for the king's chariot.

4John was baptizing people in the desert and preaching a baptism of changed hearts and lives for the forgiveness of sins. 5All the people from Judea and Jerusalem were going out to him. They confessed their sins and were baptized by him in the Jordan River. 6John wore clothes made from camel's hair, had a leather belt around his waist, and ate locusts[d] and wild honey. 7This is what John preached to the people: "There is one coming after me who is greater than I; I am not good enough even to kneel down and untie his sandals. 8I baptize you with water, but he will baptize you with the Holy Spirit."[d]

Jesus Is Baptized

9At that time Jesus came from the town of Nazareth in Galilee and was baptized by John in the Jordan River. 10Immediately, as Jesus was coming up out of the water, he saw heaven open. The Holy Spirit[d] came down on him like a dove, 11and a voice came from heaven: "You are my Son, whom I love, and I am very pleased with you."

12Then the Spirit sent Jesus into the desert. 13He was in the desert forty days and was tempted by Satan. He was with the wild animals, and the angels came and took care of him.

Jesus Chooses Some Followers

14After John was put in prison, Jesus went int Galilee, preaching the Good News[d] from God 15He said, "The right time has come. The king dom of God is near. Change your hearts and live and believe the Good News!"

16When Jesus was walking by Lake Galilee, h saw Simon[n] and his brother Andrew throwing net into the lake because they were fishermen 17Jesus said to them, "Come follow me, and I wi make you fish for people." 18So Simon and An drew immediately left their nets and followe him.

19Going a little farther, Jesus saw two mor brothers, James and John, the sons of Zebedee They were in a boat, mending their nets. 20Jesu immediately called them, and they left their fathe in the boat with the hired workers and followe Jesus.

Jesus Forces Out an Evil Spirit

21Jesus and his followers went to Capernaum On the Sabbath[d] day He went to the synagogue and began to teach. 22The people were amazed a his teaching, because he taught like a person wh had authority, not like their teachers of the law 23Just then, a man was there in the synagogu who had an evil spirit in him. He shoutec 24"Jesus of Nazareth! What do you want with us Did you come to destroy us? I know who yo are — God's Holy One!"

25Jesus commanded the evil spirit, "Be quie Come out of the man!" 26The evil spirit shook th man violently, gave a loud cry, and then came ou of him.

27The people were so amazed they asked eac other, "What is happening here? This man teaching something new, and with authority. H even gives commands to evil spirits, and the obey him." 28And the news about Jesus sprea quickly everywhere in the area of Galilee.

Jesus Heals Many People

29As soon as Jesus and his followers left the sy agogue,[d] they went with James and John to th home of Simon[n] and Andrew. 30Simon's mothe in-law was sick in bed with a fever, and the pe ple told Jesus about her. 31So Jesus went to h

the Son of God Some Greek copies omit these words.
Simon Simon's other name was Peter.

bed, took her hand, and helped her up. The fever
left her, and she began serving them.
32That evening, after the sun went down, the
people brought to Jesus all who were sick and had
demons[d] in them. 33The whole town gathered at
the door. 34Jesus healed many who had different
kinds of sicknesses, and he forced many demons
to leave people. But he would not allow the demons to speak, because they knew who he was.
35Early the next morning, while it was still
dark, Jesus woke and left the house. He went to
a lonely place, where he prayed. 36Simon and his
friends went to look for Jesus. 37When they found
him, they said, "Everyone is looking for you!"
38Jesus answered, "We should go to other
towns around here so I can preach there too. That
is the reason I came." 39So he went everywhere
in Galilee, preaching in the synagogues and forcing out demons.

Jesus Heals a Sick Man

40A man with a skin disease came to Jesus. He
fell to his knees and begged Jesus, "You can heal
me if you will."
41Jesus felt sorry for the man, so he reached out
his hand and touched him and said, "I will. Be
healed!" 42Immediately the disease left the man,
and he was healed.
43Jesus told the man to go away at once, but he
warned him strongly, 44"Don't tell anyone about
this. But go and show yourself to the priest. And
offer the gift Moses commanded for people who
are made well.[n] This will show the people what
I have done." 45The man left there, but he began
to tell everyone that Jesus had healed him, and so
he spread the news about Jesus. As a result, Jesus
could not enter a town if people saw him. He
stayed in places where nobody lived, but people
came to him from everywhere.

Moses . . . well Read about this in Leviticus 14:1-32.

FOLLOWING GOD

Leaving Everything

Li Tang grew up in the Chinese capital of Beijing. All her life, Li's family and friends had taught her that God was not real. Li believed what others told her, but she hoped that someday she would find that there really is a God.

When Li was seventeen years old, she found a Bible in an old library. She opened it and began reading about God loving people and sending his Son to the world.

Li was amazed. Why had she never heard about this before? She wanted to know more about this God and follow him. How could she? She decided she would leave everything—her family, her friends and even her country—to follow Jesus.

Her parents weren't thrilled with Li's decision to study Christianity, but they wanted her to be happy. Many of her friends couldn't understand why she wanted to leave. Wasn't ancestor worship good enough for her?

Li moved to England to study and learn more about Jesus so she could someday return to tell others about him. While there, she met Christians who helped her learn and grow.

"You really experience the change in your life," Li reflected after she decided to follow Jesus. "It's really a difference."

Jesus asked people to follow him. Often, following meant leaving many things behind. Yet following also meant gaining a friend like Jesus. Read about Jesus' first followers in **Mark 1:14–20.**

- How did what Li had to give up compare with what the disciples had to give up to follow Jesus?
- What have you had to give up to follow Jesus? What do you need to give up now to follow Jesus more fully?

C O N S I D E R . . .

- making a small, wooden cross to carry in your pocket or purse as a reminder of what it means to follow Jesus.
- interviewing two Christian friends about what it means to them to follow Jesus.

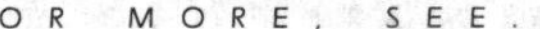

F O R   M O R E ,   S E E . . .

- Ruth 1:11–18
- Matthew 4:12–22
- John 1:35–42

Jesus Heals a Paralyzed Man

2 A few days later, when Jesus came back to
Capernaum, the news spread that he was at
home. 2Many people gathered together so that
there was no room in the house, not even outside
the door. And Jesus was teaching them God's
message. 3Four people came, carrying a paralyzed
man. 4Since they could not get to Jesus because
of the crowd, they dug a hole in the roof right
above where he was speaking. When they got
through, they lowered the mat with the paralyzed
man on it. 5When Jesus saw the faith of these
people, he said to the paralyzed man, "Young
man, your sins are forgiven."
6Some of the teachers of the law were sitting
there, thinking to themselves, 7"Why does this
man say things like that? He is speaking as if he
were God. Only God can forgive sins."
8Jesus knew immediately what these teachers
of the law were thinking. So he said to them,
"Why are you thinking these things? 9Which is
easier: to tell this paralyzed man, 'Your sins are
forgiven,' or to tell him, 'Stand up. Take your mat
and walk'? 10But I will prove to you that the Son
of Man[d] has authority on earth to forgive sins." So
Jesus said to the paralyzed man, 11"I tell you,
stand up, take your mat, and go home." 12Imme-
diately the paralyzed man stood up, took his mat,
and walked out while everyone was watching
him.
The people were amazed and praised God.
They said, "We have never seen anything like
this!"
13Jesus went to the lake again. The whole
crowd followed him there, and he taught them.
14While he was walking along, he saw a man
named Levi son of Alphaeus, sitting in the tax collector's booth. Jesus said to him, "Follow me,"
and he stood up and followed Jesus.
15Later, as Jesus was having dinner at Levi's

FORGIVENESS

The Christmas Gift

"I can't stand him! He's the one who left us. Why should I have to ruin my Christmas by spending it with him?" Juanita shouted at her mother through sobs.

"Honey, that was three years ago," Ellen Gonzales said. She put her hand on her daughter's shoulder. "A lot has happened since then. We're different people now—and happier too."

"That doesn't make it right. He still left us," Juanita countered.

Ellen sat down beside Juanita. "Your father needed work, and there was nothing here for him. He had to go someplace where he could feel useful and needed. I never believed he really wanted to leave us."

"But he did leave us," Juanita said. "And he never came back."

"You're right. But that doesn't mean he doesn't love you. Now he wants you to understand, to forgive him, and to get to know him again. Could you please forgive your father and go to his house for a few days for Christmas?" Ellen asked sympathetically.

"I guess I never really understood why he left, Mom." Juanita thought for a moment, then said, "I don't really want to, but I guess I could spend part of my Christmas vacation with Dad."

As Juanita reached for the phone, Ellen smiled and said quietly, "Maybe forgiveness can be your Christmas gift to your dad."

Forgiveness can bring healing to people and relationships. Read **Mark 2:1–12** to see how Jesus' miracle resulted in forgiveness and healing.

- How did Jesus' and Juanita's forgiveness bring about healing?
- Who needs a healing word of forgiveness from you?

C O N S I D E R . . .

- calling someone you've not talked with for a long time because of a misunderstanding.
- listing people you need to forgive, forgiving each person and then performing an act of service for each one to bring about healing.

F O R   M O R E ,   S E E . . .

- Psalm 130
- Luke 5:17–26
- Hebrews 12:14–15

house, many tax collectors and "sinners" were
eating there with Jesus and his followers. Many
people like this followed Jesus. 16When the teachers of the law who were Pharisees[d] saw Jesus eating with the tax collectors and "sinners," they
asked his followers, "Why does he eat with tax
collectors and sinners?"
17Jesus heard this and said to them, "It is not
the healthy people who need a doctor, but the
sick. I did not come to invite good people but to
invite sinners."

SIDELIGHT: Most of Jesus' ministry took place around Lake Galilee (for example, see Mark 2:13-14). This lake is the world's lowest fresh-water lake, with a surface 680 feet below sea level. Despite the lake's prominence in Jesus' ministry, it's only mentioned three times in the Old Testament (Numbers 34:11, Joshua 12:3, and Joshua 13:27).

Jesus' Followers Are Criticized

18Now the followers of John[n] and the Phari-
sees[d] often gave up eating for a certain time.[n]
Some people came to Jesus and said, "Why do
John's followers and the followers of the Phari-

John John the Baptist, who preached to the Jewish people about Christ's coming (Mark 1:4-8).
gave . . . time This is called "fasting." The people would give up eating for a special time of prayer and worship to God. It was also done to show sadness and disappointment.

CELEBRATING

Party Blues

Allison Vollaro's graduation party really drew a crowd. She had invited all her friends, which came to around thirty. Beyond that, her parents had invited several relatives and friends.

People filled every nook and corner in the house. A group of guys talked and joked on the sun deck. Several of the girls gathered in the kitchen and laughed at each other's stories. And a large assortment of other people crammed into the living room, talking about the graduation ceremony and chuckling at the antics of some of the kids.

Everyone was having a great time. Everyone, that is, except Allison. She stood quietly in a corner of the kitchen, only half-listening to the girls' conversation.

"What's wrong, Al?" asked Kriss Mitchell, walking quietly over to Allison. "You seem lost in your thoughts."

"Yeah, I guess I am," Allison said with a weak smile. "It's just that now that I'm out of school, I don't know what's going to happen to my friendships. I love you all so much; it makes me sad to think of you not being in my life anymore."

Kriss touched Allison on the arm. "Hey, listen, none of us knows what's going to happen from one day to the next. We may all get to stay together forever, or we may not. We just can't know for sure. But," Kriss added with a smile, "we're here today. So let's go join the others and have some fun, okay? After all, it is your party."

"Okay, okay," Allison said jokingly. Then she reached out and grabbed Kriss's hand. "Thanks, Kriss. I needed to hear that."

Kriss helped Allison realize the importance of celebrating good things that come along, even though they may not last. Jesus helped his disciples understand the same truth. Read the story Jesus used in **Mark 2:18–22**.

- How was Allison like the Pharisees' disciples in this passage?
- How can you celebrate Jesus' presence in your life, as this passage directs?

CONSIDER . . .

- writing all the ways Jesus reveals his presence in your life, then thanking God for being so real to you.
- throwing a party to celebrate friendship and God's love.

FOR MORE, SEE . . .

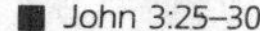

- Isaiah 62:1–9
- Matthew 9:14–17
- John 3:25–30

sees often give up eating, but your followers
don't?"
19Jesus answered, "The friends of the bridegroom do not give up eating while the bridegroom is still with them. As long as the
bridegroom is with them, they cannot give up
eating. 20But the time will come when the bridegroom will be taken from them, and then they
will give up eating.
21"No one sews a patch of unshrunk cloth
over a hole in an old coat. Otherwise, the patch
will shrink and pull away—the new patch
will pull away from the old coat. Then the
hole will be worse. 22Also, no one ever pours
new wine into old leather bags. Otherwise,
the new wine will break the bags, and the
wine will be ruined along with the bags. But
new wine should be put into new leather bags."

Jesus Is Lord of the Sabbath

23One Sabbath[d] day, as Jesus was walking
through some fields of grain, his followers began
to pick some grain to eat. 24The Pharisees[d] said to
Jesus, "Why are your followers doing what is not
lawful on the Sabbath day?"
25Jesus answered, "Have you never read what
David did when he and those with him were hungry and needed food? 26During the time of Abia-
thar the high priest, David went into God's house
and ate the holy bread, which is lawful only for
priests to eat. And David also gave some of the
bread to those who were with him."
27Then Jesus said to the Pharisees, "The Sabbath day was made to help people; they were not
made to be ruled by the Sabbath day. 28So then,
the Son of Man[d] is Lord even of the Sabbath day."

FREEDOM

Free to Choose

Angela Ferrara stared out the window of her second-story bedroom. Her father had just told the family he was taking a job in California. They would move at the end of February.

Angela cried as she thought about the friends she would have to leave and the basketball team she would have to quit. It wasn't fair. She wanted to be angry at her dad for moving during her last year in junior high school. If only they could wait until June.

She had pleaded with her parents not to move, but they wouldn't change their minds. Angela had no choice. The family would have to stay together, and she knew her parents expected her to cooperate.

"Can I come in?"

Surprised, Angela turned and saw her dad standing in the doorway of her room. Angela hesitated. "Yeah, I guess," she said finally.

"Your mother and I have been thinking. And we think you're old enough to make good decisions about your life, Angela," her dad began. "You may stay with your Aunt Sarah until school is out if you'd like to."

Angela's expression changed from disgust to a smile. "You mean I have a choice?" Angela asked incredulously. "I can decide for myself?"

"We don't want the family to be separated," her dad said. "But, on the other hand, we don't want to force you to make a move in the middle of the school year. It's up to you."

Angela's parents trusted her to make a responsible decision. In a similar way, God gives us guidelines for our lives, but trusts us to use those guidelines responsibly. Read **Mark 2:23—3:6** to see how Jesus encouraged people to follow those guidelines.

- What similarities are there between Jesus' use of guidelines and Angela's parents' decision to let Angela decide for herself?
- What kind of judging attitudes have you had toward people that are similar to the Pharisees' attitudes?

- talking to your parents about the purpose of family rules you don't understand.
- asking kids from other Christian churches about their beliefs. Celebrate the freedom you each have to be different!

- Amos 5:21–24
- Matthew 12:1–14
- Luke 6:1–11

Jesus Heals a Man's Hand

3 Another time when Jesus went into a synagogue,[d] a man with a crippled hand was there. 2Some people watched Jesus closely to see if he would heal the man on the Sabbath[d] day so they could accuse him.

3Jesus said to the man with the crippled hand, "Stand up here in the middle of everyone."

4Then Jesus asked the people, "Which is lawful on the Sabbath day: to do good or to do evil, to save a life or to kill?" But they said nothing to answer him.

5Jesus was angry as he looked at the people, and he felt very sad because they were stubborn. Then he said to the man, "Hold out your hand." The man held out his hand and it was healed. 6Then the Pharisees[d] left and began making plans with the Herodians[n] about a way to kill Jesus.

Many People Follow Jesus

7Jesus left with his followers for the lake, and a large crowd from Galilee followed him. 8Also many people came from Judea, from Jerusalem, from Idumea, from the lands across the Jordan River, and from the area of Tyre and Sidon. When they heard what Jesus was doing, many people came to him. 9When Jesus saw the crowds, he told his followers to get a boat ready for him to keep people from crowding against him. 10He had healed many people, so all the sick were pushing toward him to touch him. 11When evil spirits saw Jesus, they fell down before him and shouted, "You are the Son of God!" 12But Jesus strongly warned them not to tell who he was.

Jesus Chooses His Twelve Apostles

13Then Jesus went up on a mountain and called to him the men he wanted, and they came to him. 14Jesus chose twelve men and called them apostles.[d] He wanted them to be with him, and he wanted to send them out to preach 15and to have the authority to force demons[d] out of people. 16These are the twelve men he chose: Simon (Jesus named him Peter), 17James and John, the sons of Zebedee (Jesus named them Boanerges, which means "Sons of Thunder"), 18Andrew, Philip, Bartholomew, Matthew, Thomas, James the son of Alphaeus, Thaddaeus, Simon the Zealot,[d] 19and Judas Iscariot, who later turned against Jesus.

Some People Say Jesus Has a Devil

20Then Jesus went home, but again a crowd gathered. There were so many people that Jesus and his followers could not eat. 21When his family heard this, they went to get him because they thought he was out of his mind. 22But the teachers of the law from Jerusalem were saying, "Beelzebul[d] is living inside him! He uses power from the ruler of demons[d] to force demons out of people."

23So Jesus called the people together and taught them with stories. He said, "Satan will not force himself out of people. 24A kingdom that is divided cannot continue, 25and a family that is divided cannot continue. 26And if Satan is against himself and fights against his own people, he cannot continue; that is the end of Satan. 27No one can enter a strong person's house and steal his things unless he first ties up the strong person. Then he can steal things from the house. 28I tell you the truth, all sins that people do and all the things people say against God can be forgiven. 29But anyone who speaks against the Holy Spirit[d] will never be forgiven; he is guilty of a sin that continues forever."

30Jesus said this because the teachers of the law said that he had an evil spirit inside him.

Jesus' True Family

31Then Jesus' mother and brothers arrived. Standing outside, they sent someone in to tell him to come out. 32Many people were sitting around Jesus, and they said to him, "Your mother and brothers are waiting for you outside."

33Jesus asked, "Who are my mother and my brothers?" 34Then he looked at those sitting around him and said, "Here are my mother and my brothers! 35My true brother and sister and mother are those who do what God wants."

A Story About Planting Seed

4 Again Jesus began teaching by the lake. A great crowd gathered around him, so he sat down in a boat near the shore. All the people stayed on the shore close to the water. 2Jesus taught them many things, using stories. He said, 3"Listen! A farmer went out to plant his seed. 4While he was planting, some seed fell by the road, and the birds came and ate it up. 5Some seed fell on rocky ground where there wasn't much dirt. That seed grew very fast, because the ground was not deep. 6But when the sun rose, the plants dried up because they did not have deep roots. 7Some other seed fell among thorny weeds, which grew and choked the good plants. So those plants did not produce a crop. 8Some other seed fell on good ground and began to grow. It got taller and produced a crop. Some plants made thirty times more, some made sixty times more, and some made a hundred times more."

9Then Jesus said, "You people who can hear me, listen!"

Herodians A political group that followed Herod and his family.

Jesus Tells Why He Used Stories

10Later, when Jesus was alone, the twelve apostles[d] and others around him asked him about the stories.

> **SIDELIGHT:** Jesus' story about planting seeds (Mark 4:1–9) not only has spiritual truth, but tells a lot about farming in those days. After plowing a field, farmers would walk through the field scattering seeds around the field. Then they would go back over the field dragging branches across to cover the seeds and protect them from birds and strong winds.

11Jesus said, "You can know the secret about the kingdom of God. But to other people I tell everything by using stories 12so that:

'They will look and look, but they will not
learn.
They will listen and listen, but they will not
understand.
If they did learn and understand,
they would come back to me and be
forgiven.' "

Isaiah 6:9-10

Jesus Explains the Seed Story

13Then Jesus said to his followers, "Don't you understand this story? If you don't, how will you understand any story? 14The farmer is like a person who plants God's message in people.
15Sometimes the teaching falls on the road. This is like the people who hear the teaching of God, but Satan quickly comes and takes away the teaching that was planted in them. 16Others are like the seed planted on rocky ground. They hear the teaching and quickly accept it with joy. 17But since they don't allow the teaching to go deep into their lives, they keep it only a short time. When trouble or persecution comes because of the teaching they accepted, they quickly give up. 18Others are like the seed planted among the thorny weeds. They hear

EVIL

Fearful Escape

Susan Platt was small, tired, and afraid. Her troubled eyes continually darted around the crowded bus stop. Everyone looked suspicious to Susan and made her want to run somewhere—anywhere—to get away from those who might find her and take her back.

Susan had a good reason to be afraid. Although she looked like any other teenager in Los Angeles, Susan was different from most. For the past six years, Susan had been involved in a coven that pledged itself to worship Satan. It had seemed fun when she started. Now, at eighteen, she wanted out.

Susan pulled at the sleeves of her sweater. Her arms must not be seen. They would expose her. Carved into her flesh were Satanic symbols to identify her as a devout Satanist. These marks were only an outward sign of the evil she had witnessed.

Susan had met some Christians a few years earlier. They had tried to tell her the truth about God's love and had offered to help her escape to a new way of life. She had refused then, but now she was going to find them.

Susan scanned the bus stop one last time. Seeing that no one was following her, she breathed a sigh of relief. As she climbed up the bus steps, Susan thought about how each step she took brought her closer to the freedom Jesus offered.

Since the beginning of time, Satan has lied to people, telling them his way is right and God's way is evil. **Mark 3:20–35** shows one instance when Satan convinced people that Jesus himself had an evil spirit.

- Why did Susan and the people in Jesus' day fear Satan?
- What promise do you see in this passage that helps you in the face of evil?

CONSIDER . . .

- praying for your church and family to be united so they can stand against evil.
- identifying an evil influence in your life and working to get rid of it.

FOR MORE, SEE . . .

- Genesis 3
- Matthew 9:32–34
- John 10:19–21

the teaching, 19 but the worries of this life, the temptation of wealth, and many other evil desires keep the teaching from growing and producing fruit[n] in their lives. 20 Others are like the seed planted in the good ground. They hear the teaching and accept it. Then they grow and produce fruit—sometimes thirty times more, sometimes sixty times more, and sometimes a hundred times more."

Use What You Have

21 Then Jesus said to them, "Do you hide a lamp under a bowl or under a bed? No! You put the lamp on a lampstand. 22 Everything that is hidden will be made clear and every secret thing will be made known. 23 You people who can hear me, listen!

24 "Think carefully about what you hear. The way you give to others is the way God will give to you, but God will give you even more. 25 Those who have understanding will be given more. But those who do not have understanding, even what they have will be taken away from them."

Jesus Uses a Story About Seed

26 Then Jesus said, "The kingdom of God is like someone who plants seed in the ground. 27 Night and day, whether the person is asleep or awake, the seed still grows, but the person does not know how it grows. 28 By itself the earth produces grain. First the plant grows, then the head, and then all the grain in the head. 29 When the grain is ready, the farmer cuts it, because this is the harvest time."

A Story About Mustard Seed

30 Then Jesus said, "How can I show you what the kingdom of God is like? What story can I use to explain it? 31 The kingdom of God is like a mustard seed, the smallest seed you plant in the ground. 32 But when planted, this seed grows and becomes the largest of all garden plants. It produces large branches, and the wild birds can make nests in its shade."

33 Jesus used many stories like these to teach the crowd God's message—as much as they could understand. 34 He always used stories to

producing fruit To produce fruit means to have in your life the good things God wants.

FAITH

It's Alive!

Witness, if you will, one of the most efficient, self-contained structures in nature. It possesses—on its own—almost everything it needs to survive and grow. It has its own coat, its own embryo and its own food supply.

It can even impregnate itself. That's right; each one has the male and female components it needs to create a fertilized egg.

The reproductive system is incredible, but it does need extra help to grow. After fertilization, it remains dormant until warm, moist conditions promote germination.

Then its coat softens and the metabolism rate in the cells increases. It drinks water and even starts "breathing," while a simple digestion begins. The digested food travels to new areas of growth that emerge when cell division begins.

And congratulations, Mr. and Mrs. Seed, it's a plant!

The incredible seed is a lot like the kingdom of God. Read **Mark 4:26–34** to see how.

- How is a seed's reproductive system like faith's growth process in you?
- According to this passage, what benefits can come from faith's growth in you? What benefits can come from many people growing in faith?

CONSIDER . . .

- working in a garden and drawing other parallels between the plant world and faith. Write your own parable to illustrate those parallels.
- choosing one quality from 2 Peter 1:5-9 to add to your faith. Create one project to help develop that quality.

FOR MORE, SEE . . .

- Ecclesiastes 11:1–6
- Matthew 13:24–32
- Luke 13:18–20

teach them. But when he and his followers were alone, Jesus explained everything to them.

Jesus Calms a Storm

35That evening, Jesus said to his followers, "Let's go across the lake." 36Leaving the crowd behind, they took him in the boat just as he was. There were also other boats with them. 37A very strong wind came up on the lake. The waves came over the sides and into the boat so that it was already full of water. 38Jesus was at the back of the boat, sleeping with his head on a cushion. His followers woke him and said, "Teacher, don't you care that we are drowning!"

39Jesus stood up and commanded the wind and said to the waves, "Quiet! Be still!" Then the wind stopped, and it became completely calm.

40Jesus said to his followers, "Why are you afraid? Do you still have no faith?"

41The followers were very afraid and asked each other, "Who is this? Even the wind and the waves obey him!"

A Man with Demons Inside Him

5 Jesus and his followers went to the other side of the lake to the area of the Gerasene people. 2When Jesus got out of the boat, instantly a man with an evil spirit came to him from the burial caves. 3This man lived in the caves, and no one could tie him up, not even with a chain. 4Many times people had used chains to tie the man's hands and feet, but he always broke them off. No one was strong enough to control him. 5Day and night he would wander around the burial caves and on the hills, screaming and cutting himself with stones. 6While Jesus was still far away, the man saw him, ran to him, and fell down before him.

7The man shouted in a loud voice, "What do you want with me, Jesus, Son of the Most High God? I command you in God's name not to torture me!" 8He said this because Jesus was saying to him, "You evil spirit, come out of the man."

9Then Jesus asked him, "What is your name?"

He answered, "My name is Legion,[n] because we are many spirits." 10He begged Jesus again and again not to send them out of that area.

11A large herd of pigs was feeding on a hill near there. 12The demons[d] begged Jesus, "Send us into the pigs; let us go into them." 13So Jesus allowed them to do this. The evil spirits left the man and went into the pigs. Then the herd of pigs — about two thousand of them — rushed down the hill into the lake and were drowned.

14The herdsmen ran away and went to the town and to the countryside, telling everyone about this. So people went out to see what had happened. 15They came to Jesus and saw the man who used to have the many evil spirits, sitting, clothed, and in his right mind. And they were frightened. 16The people who saw this told the others what had happened to the man who had the demons living in him, and they told about the pigs. 17Then the people began to beg Jesus to leave their area.

18As Jesus was getting back into the boat, the man who was freed from the demons begged to go with him.

19But Jesus would not let him. He said, "Go home to your family and tell them how much the Lord has done for you and how he has had mercy on you." 20So the man left and began to tell the people in the Ten Towns[n] about what Jesus had done for him. And everyone was amazed.

Jesus Gives Life to a Dead Girl and Heals a Sick Woman

21When Jesus went in the boat back to the other side of the lake, a large crowd gathered around him there. 22A leader of the synagogue,[d] named Jairus, came there, saw Jesus, and fell at his feet. 23He begged Jesus, saying again and again, "My daughter is dying. Please come and put your hands on her so she will be healed and will live." 24So Jesus went with him.

A large crowd followed Jesus and pushed very close around him. 25Among them was a woman who had been bleeding for twelve years. 26She had suffered very much from many doctors and had spent all the money she had, but instead of improving, she was getting worse. 27When the woman heard about Jesus, she came up behind him in the crowd and touched his coat. 28She thought, "If I can just touch his clothes, I will be healed." 29Instantly her bleeding stopped, and she felt in her body that she was healed from her disease.

30At once Jesus felt power go out from him. So he turned around in the crowd and asked, "Who touched my clothes?"

31His followers said, "Look at how many people are pushing against you! And you ask, 'Who touched me?' "

32But Jesus continued looking around to see who had touched him. 33The woman, knowing that she was healed, came and fell at Jesus' feet. Shaking with fear, she told him the whole truth. 34Jesus said to her, "Dear woman, you are made well because you believed. Go in peace; be healed of your disease."

Legion Means very many. A legion was about five thousand men in the Roman army.
Ten Towns In Greek, called "Decapolis." It was an area east of Lake Galilee that once had ten main towns.

35While Jesus was still speaking, some people
came from the house of the synagogue leader.
They said, "Your daughter is dead. There is no
need to bother the teacher anymore."
36But Jesus paid no attention to what they said.
He told the synagogue leader, "Don't be afraid;
just believe."
37Jesus let only Peter, James, and John the
brother of James go with him. 38When they came
to the house of the synagogue leader, Jesus found
many people there making lots of noise and crying
loudly. 39Jesus entered the house and said to
them, "Why are you crying and making so much
noise? The child is not dead, only asleep." 40But
they laughed at him. So, after throwing them out
of the house, Jesus took the child's father and
mother and his three followers into the room
where the child was. 41Taking hold of the girl's
hand, he said to her, "Talitha, koum!" (This
means, "Young girl, I tell you to stand up!") 42At
once the girl stood right up and began walking.
(She was twelve years old.) Everyone was completely amazed. 43Jesus gave them strict orders
not to tell people about this. Then he told them
to give the girl something to eat.

Jesus Goes to His Hometown

6 Jesus left there and went to his hometown,
and his followers went with him. 2On the
Sabbath[d] day he taught in the synagogue.[d] Many
people heard him and were amazed, saying,
"Where did this man get these teachings? What
is this wisdom that has been given to him? And
where did he get the power to do miracles?[d] 3He
is just the carpenter, the son of Mary and the
brother of James, Joseph, Judas, and Simon. And
his sisters are here with us." So the people were
upset with Jesus.
4Jesus said to them, "A prophet[d] is honored everywhere except in his hometown and with his
own people and in his own home." 5So Jesus was
not able to work any miracles there except to heal
a few sick people by putting his hands on them.
6He was amazed at how many people had no
faith.

Then Jesus went to other villages in that area
and taught. 7He called his twelve followers together and got ready to send them out two by two
and gave them authority over evil spirits. 8This is
what Jesus commanded them: "Take nothing for
your trip except a walking stick. Take no bread,

SICKNESS

Miracles Happen

Doris Flynn's face was streaked with tears. "They say there's no hope," she sobbed, reaching for another tissue. "My granddaughter has a tumor the size of a baseball. It has completely surrounded her kidneys."

She continued haltingly: "The doctors aren't sure if other organs are involved. They don't think she'll live long."

Betty Hall placed her hand on Doris's shoulder. "Miracles do happen, Doris. We need to pray for a miracle."

"I've given up on God. Even he can't heal Wendy now. And besides, I don't think he's listening anymore."

Doris was wrong. Even the doctors were wrong. A new medicine was added to Wendy's treatment, and she was healed.

God heals. He can use doctors, nurses, and medicine to accomplish his purposes. Sometimes he even heals without their help. Read **Mark 5:21–43** to see how Jesus healed two people.

- How were the three healings—Wendy, the woman (verses 25–34) and the little girl—different from each other?
- Does God still heal the way Jesus did in this passage?

CONSIDER . . .

- writing a letter as though you were going to send it to someone who asked for healing and didn't receive it. Encourage that imaginary person to accept God's will.
- walking down the hallway of a local hospital and silently praying for God's healing for each patient.

FOR MORE, SEE . . .

- Psalm 103:1–5
- Matthew 9:1–26
- James 5:13–18

no bag, and no money in your pockets. 9Wear sandals, but take only the clothes you are wearing. 10When you enter a house, stay there until you leave that town. 11If the people in a certain place refuse to welcome you or listen to you, leave that place. Shake its dust off your feet[n] as a warning to them."

12So the followers went out and preached that people should change their hearts and lives. 13They forced many demons[d] out and put olive oil on many sick people and healed them.

How John the Baptist Was Killed

14King Herod heard about Jesus, because he was now well known. Some people said, "He is John the Baptist,[d] who has risen from the dead. That is why he can work these miracles."[d]

15Others said, "He is Elijah."[n]

Other people said, "Jesus is a prophet,[d] like the prophets who lived long ago."

16When Herod heard this, he said, "I killed John by cutting off his head. Now he has risen from the dead!"

17Herod himself had ordered his soldiers to arrest John and put him in prison in order to please his wife, Herodias. She had been the wife of Philip, Herod's brother, but then Herod had married her. 18John had been telling Herod, "It is not lawful for you to be married to your brother's wife." 19So Herodias hated John and wanted to kill him. But she couldn't, 20because Herod was afraid of John and protected him. He knew John was a good and holy man. Also, though John's preaching always bothered him, he enjoyed listening to John.

21Then the perfect time came for Herodias to cause John's death. On Herod's birthday, he gave a dinner party for the most important government leaders, the commanders of his army, and the most important people in Galilee. 22When the daughter of Herodias came in and danced, she pleased Herod and the people eating with him.

So King Herod said to the girl, "Ask me for anything you want, and I will give it to you." 23He promised her, "Anything you ask for I will give to you—up to half of my kingdom."

24The girl went to her mother and asked, "What should I ask for?"

Her mother answered, "Ask for the head of John the Baptist."[d]

25At once the girl went back to the king and said to him, "I want the head of John the Baptist right now on a platter."

26Although the king was very sad, he had made a promise, and his dinner guests had heard it. So he did not want to refuse what she asked. 27Immediately the king sent a soldier to bring John's head. The soldier went and cut off John's head in the prison 28and brought it back on a platter. He gave it to the girl, and the girl gave it to her mother. 29When John's followers heard this, they came and got John's body and put it in a tomb.

SIDELIGHT: Herod the Great wasn't the great guy his name might imply. Besides beheading John the Baptist (Mark 6:14–29), he murdered his own kids, prompting the saying, "It's safer to be Herod's pig than Herod's son."

More than Five Thousand Fed

30The apostles[d] gathered around Jesus and told him about all the things they had done and taught. 31Crowds of people were coming and going so that Jesus and his followers did not even have time to eat. He said to them, "Come away by yourselves, and we will go to a lonely place to get some rest."

32So they went in a boat by themselves to a lonely place. 33But many people saw them leave and recognized them. So from all the towns they ran to the place where Jesus was going, and they got there before him. 34When he arrived, he saw a great crowd waiting. He felt sorry for them, because they were like sheep without a shepherd. So he began to teach them many things.

35When it was late in the day, his followers came to him and said, "No one lives in this place, and it is already very late. 36Send the people away so they can go to the countryside and towns around here to buy themselves something to eat."

37But Jesus answered, "You give them something to eat."

They said to him, "We would all have to work a month to earn enough money to buy that much bread!"

38Jesus asked them, "How many loaves of bread do you have? Go and see."

When they found out, they said, "Five loaves and two fish."

39Then Jesus told his followers to have the people sit in groups on the green grass. 40So they sat in groups of fifty or a hundred. 41Jesus took the five loaves and two fish and, looking up to heaven, he thanked God for the food. He divided the bread and gave it to his followers for them to give to the people. Then he divided the two fish among them all. 42All the people ate and were satisfied. 43The followers filled twelve baskets

Shake . . . feet A warning. It showed that they were rejecting these people.
Elijah A man who spoke for God and who lived hundreds of years before Christ. See 1 Kings 17.

with the leftover pieces of bread and fish. [44]There
were five thousand men who ate.

Jesus Walks on the Water

[45]Immediately Jesus told his followers to get
into the boat and go ahead of him to Bethsaida
across the lake. He stayed there to send the people home. [46]After sending them away, he went
into the hills to pray.
[47]That night, the boat was in the middle of the
lake, and Jesus was alone on the land. [48]He saw
his followers struggling hard to row the boat, because the wind was blowing against them. Between three and six o'clock in the morning, Jesus
came to them, walking on the water, and he
wanted to walk past the boat. [49]But when they
saw him walking on the water, they thought he
was a ghost and cried out. [50]They all saw him and
were afraid. But quickly Jesus spoke to them and
said, "Have courage! It is I. Do not be afraid."
[51]Then he got into the boat with them, and the
wind became calm. The followers were greatly
amazed. [52]They did not understand about the miracle of the five loaves, because their minds were
closed.
[53]When they had crossed the lake, they came
to shore at Gennesaret and tied the boat there.
[54]When they got out of the boat, people immedi-

HUNGER AND POVERTY

The Multiplication Principle

"We have only three thousand cans. I wanted to collect ten thousand," Kristen Green complained to Mr. Rossetti, the principal of St. Francis De Sales High School in Columbus, Ohio. Mr. Rossetti was the one who had asked Kristen to chair her school's canned food drive for the soup kitchen.

Mr. Rossetti listened but didn't say much. Later that day during the school pep rally, he surprised Kristen by asking her to speak to the students about the food drive.

Kristen spoke about a man she had met at the local soup kitchen who each night asked for an extra plate of food for his dying wife. Kristen also told about a hungry woman who shared her orange with the person sitting beside her. She continued, "We think of starving people being in Ethiopia, but these people live three blocks from this school." Kristen challenged the students to meet the goal of ten thousand cans of food in the next week.

After the pep rally, students asked Kristen how they could help. Suddenly everyone was mobilized: The football team went door to door in the Columbus neighborhoods, asking for donations of canned goods. The Fellowship of Christian Athletes collected $1,500 worth of food in one night. Kristen and a friend asked area grocers for food donations.

By Wednesday, the goal of ten thousand cans was met—a goal people had thought was unrealistic. (Only four thousand cans had been collected the year before.) Kristen decided not to tell anyone the goal was reached before the deadline. On Friday, people cheered when she announced the total: 17,299 cans!

Kristen and others filled three school buses with the food. As they delivered the food to the soup kitchen, people standing in line thanked them and patted them on the back.

"We knew we were making a difference," Kristen says. "People were going to be able to eat."

Jesus and his disciples were also confronted with the challenge of feeding hungry people. Read **Mark 6:30–44** to see how Jesus fed a hungry mob.

- How is the multiplication of canned food at De Sales High similar to Jesus multiplying food for the multitude? How is it different?
- How have you seen Jesus increase your gifts or resources to help others?

C O N S I D E R . . .

- giving up eating a meal and spending time in prayer for those who have less to eat than you do. Donate the money you would have spent on the meal to World Vision, Special Programs, Pasadena, CA 91131, or to another relief agency.
- organizing a canned food drive at your church or school.

F O R   M O R E ,   S E E . . .

- 2 Kings 4:42–44
- Matthew 14:13–21
- John 6:1–15

ately recognized Jesus. 55They ran everywhere in
that area and began to bring sick people on mats
wherever they heard he was. 56And everywhere
he went — into towns, cities, or countryside — the
people brought the sick to the marketplaces. They
begged him to let them touch just the edge of his
coat, and all who touched it were healed.

Obey God's Law

7 When some Pharisees[d] and some teachers of
the law came from Jerusalem, they gathered
around Jesus. 2They saw that some of Jesus' followers ate food with hands that were not clean,[d]
that is, they hadn't washed them. 3(The Pharisees
and all the Jews never eat before washing their
hands in a special way according to their unwritten laws. 4And when they buy something in the
market, they never eat it until they wash themselves in a special way. They also follow many
other unwritten laws, such as the washing of
cups, pitchers, and pots.)
5The Pharisees and the teachers of the law said
to Jesus, "Why don't your followers obey the unwritten laws which have been handed down to
us? Why do your followers eat their food with
hands that are not clean?"
6Jesus answered, "Isaiah was right when he
spoke about you hypocrites.[d] He wrote,

'These people show honor to me with words,
but their hearts are far from me.
7Their worship of me is worthless.
The things they teach are nothing but
human rules.' *Isaiah 29:13*

8You have stopped following the commands of
God, and you follow only human teachings."
9Then Jesus said to them, "You cleverly ignore
the commands of God so you can follow your
own teachings. 10Moses said, 'Honor your father
and your mother,'[n] and 'Anyone who says cruel
things to his father or mother must be put to
death.'[n] 11But you say a person can tell his father
or mother, 'I have something I could use to help
you, but it is Corban — a gift to God.' 12You no
longer let that person use that money for his fa-

'Honor . . . mother' Quotation from Exodus 20:12; Deuteronomy 5:16.
'Anyone . . . death.' Quotation from Exodus 21:17.

HYPOCRISY

An Open Letter to God

Craig Mackey was tired of seeing what he called "the Dr. Jekyll and Mr. Hyde" sides of his father. In his frustration, he wrote this letter to God.

Dear God,

There are a few things I just don't understand about people and the way they act. Let me tell you what I mean.

Take my dad, for example. Don't get me wrong. He's a nice guy; he goes to church with us and everything. But when it comes to his business, he really changes. Dad's always talking about how he really "got the best of that guy" in a business deal or how he "beat her out of a contract." It just doesn't seem very Christian.

Oh, and another place is on the highway. My dad gets really angry at other drivers and sometimes even yells at them.

And, oh well, I guess I just don't understand. It just doesn't seem very Christian.

Can you help me understand, God?

Craig

Hypocrisy is common. Even in Jesus' day, Jesus' followers were troubled by hypocrites. Read **Mark 7:1–23** to learn more about the situation.

- What was hypocritical about Craig's dad's actions and the Pharisees' actions?
- According to this passage, what's the cure for hypocrisy?

C O N S I D E R . . .

- evaluating your own life for any hypocrisies and applying the "cure" to get rid of them.
- writing a letter to Craig that responds to his frustrations.

F O R M O R E , S E E . . .

- Isaiah 29:13–14
- Matthew 15:1–20
- Romans 14:13–18

ther or his mother. 13By your own rules, which you teach people, you are rejecting what God said. And you do many things like that."

14After Jesus called the crowd to him again, he said, "Every person should listen to me and understand what I am saying. 15There is nothing people put into their bodies that makes them unclean. People are made unclean by the things that come out of them." 16 [n]

17When Jesus left the people and went into the house, his followers asked him about this story. 18Jesus said, "Do you still not understand? Surely you know that nothing that enters someone from the outside can make that person unclean. 19It does not go into the mind, but into the stomach. Then it goes out of the body." (When Jesus said this, he meant that no longer was any food unclean for people to eat.)

20And Jesus said, "The things that come out of people are the things that make them unclean. 21All these evil things begin inside people, in the mind: evil thoughts, sexual sins, stealing, murder, adultery,[d] 22greed, evil actions, lying, doing sinful things, jealousy, speaking evil of others, pride, and foolish living. 23All these evil things come from inside and make people unclean."

Jesus Helps a Non-Jewish Woman

24Jesus left that place and went to the area around Tyre. When he went into a house, he did not want anyone to know he was there, but he could not stay hidden. 25A woman whose daughter had an evil spirit in her heard that he was there. So she quickly came to Jesus and fell at his feet. 26She was Greek, born in Phoenicia, in Syria. She begged Jesus to force the demon[d] out of her daughter.

27Jesus told the woman, "It is not right to take the children's bread and give it to the dogs. First let the children eat all they want."

28But she answered, "Yes, Lord, but even the dogs under the table can eat the children's crumbs."

29Then Jesus said, "Because of your answer, you may go. The demon has left your daughter."

30The woman went home and found her daughter lying in bed; the demon was gone.

Jesus Heals a Deaf Man

31Then Jesus left the area around Tyre and went through Sidon to Lake Galilee, to the area of the Ten Towns.[n] 32While he was there, some people brought a man to him who was deaf and could not talk plainly. The people begged Jesus to put his hand on the man to heal him.

33Jesus led the man away from the crowd, by himself. He put his fingers in the man's ears and then spit and touched the man's tongue. 34Looking up to heaven, he sighed and said to the man, "Ephphatha!" (This means, "Be opened.") 35Instantly the man was able to hear and to use his tongue so that he spoke clearly.

36Jesus commanded the people not to tell anyone about what happened. But the more he commanded them, the more they told about it. 37They were completely amazed and said, "Jesus does everything well. He makes the deaf hear! And those who can't talk he makes able to speak."

More than Four Thousand People Fed

8 Another time there was a great crowd with Jesus that had nothing to eat. So Jesus called his followers and said, 2"I feel sorry for these people, because they have already been with me for three days, and they have nothing to eat. 3If I send them home hungry, they will faint on the way. Some of them live a long way from here."

4Jesus' followers answered, "How can we get enough bread to feed all these people? We are far away from any town."

5Jesus asked, "How many loaves of bread do you have?"

They answered, "Seven."

6Jesus told the people to sit on the ground. Then he took the seven loaves, gave thanks to God, and divided the bread. He gave the pieces to his followers to give to the people, and they did so. 7The followers also had a few small fish. After Jesus gave thanks for the fish, he told his followers to give them to the people also. 8All the people ate and were satisfied. Then his followers filled seven baskets with the leftover pieces of food. 9There were about four thousand people who ate. After they had eaten, Jesus sent them home. 10Then right away he got into a boat with his followers and went to the area of Dalmanutha.

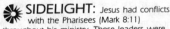

> **SIDELIGHT:** Jesus had conflicts with the Pharisees (Mark 8:11) throughout his ministry. These leaders were respected for their accurate interpretations of Jewish law. The historian Josephus estimates that six thousand Pharisees lived in Palestine during Jesus' years.

The Leaders Ask for a Miracle

11The Pharisees[d] came to Jesus and began to ask him questions. Hoping to trap him, they asked Jesus for a miracle[d] from God. 12Jesus sighed

Verse 16 Some Greek copies add verse 16: "You people who can hear me, listen!"
Ten Towns In Greek, called "Decapolis." It was an area east of Lake Galilee that once had ten main towns.

deeply and said, "Why do you people ask for a
miracle as a sign? I tell you the truth, no sign will
be given to you." 13Then Jesus left the Pharisees
and went in the boat to the other side of the lake.

Guard Against Wrong Teachings

14His followers had only one loaf of bread with
them in the boat; they had forgotten to bring
more. 15Jesus warned them, "Be careful! Beware
of the yeast of the Pharisees[d] and the yeast of
Herod."
16His followers discussed the meaning of this,
saying, "He said this because we have no bread."
17Knowing what they were talking about, Jesus
asked them, "Why are you talking about not having bread? Do you still not see or understand? Are
your minds closed? 18You have eyes, but you
don't really see. You have ears, but you don't
really listen. Remember when 19I divided five
loaves of bread for the five thousand? How many
baskets did you fill with leftover pieces of food?"
They answered, "Twelve."
20"And when I divided seven loaves of bread
for the four thousand, how many baskets did you
fill with leftover pieces of food?"
They answered, "Seven."
21Then Jesus said to them, "Don't you understand yet?"

Jesus Heals a Blind Man

22Jesus and his followers came to Bethsaida.
There some people brought a blind man to Jesus
and begged him to touch the man. 23So Jesus took
the blind man's hand and led him out of the village. Then he spit on the man's eyes and put his
hands on the man and asked, "Can you see
now?"
24The man looked up and said, "Yes, I see people, but they look like trees walking around."
25Again Jesus put his hands on the man's eyes.

SICKNESS

She Made a Difference

In the 1940s, more than 500,000 people in the city of Calcutta (5 percent of the city's population) literally lived and died in the streets. With summer temperatures normally above 115 degrees and winter temperatures hovering in the high 90s, the city could seem like hell on earth. It was there that the "poorest of the poor" lived, plagued by leprosy, tuberculosis, pneumonia and, most of all, poverty.

What hope was there in such a place? Surely no one could make a difference there. But Agnes thought differently. She believed that God was calling her to bring hope to these poor and downtrodden people.

In her journal, Agnes, now known as Mother Teresa, described her first day in the slums as a day of meeting Christ. She met Christ face to face there—the hungry Christ, the naked Christ, the sick Christ, the homeless Christ. She said the touch of him in this distressing disguise gave her great joy, peace, and strength.

So, clad in a white sari edged with blue, Mother Teresa began her work. She and a group of nuns taught the children of the poor. They provided care for lepers who could get help nowhere else. They built shelters and hospitals so the poor would have a place out of the streets. They fed the hungry and loved the unlovable. They literally changed the face of Calcutta.

Jesus' love flowed through Mother Teresa to touch people. Jesus' love always makes a difference. When Jesus touches sick people, their lives are never the same. Read **Mark 7:31–37** and imagine how the sick people who met Jesus must have felt.

- How is Mother Teresa's hands-on approach to ministry like Jesus' approach?
- Which of Jesus' actions in this passage are most important to people who are sick?

CONSIDER . . .

- doing a task that you don't like to do (such as cleaning a bathroom) for a homebound member of your church.
- talking to your pastor about how your church can minister to people with AIDS.

FOR MORE, SEE . . .

- Leviticus 13
- Matthew 8:1–4
- Luke 17:11–19

Then the man opened his eyes wide and they were healed, and he was able to see everything clearly. 26Jesus told him to go home, saying, "Don't go into the town."

Peter Says Jesus Is the Christ

27Jesus and his followers went to the towns around Caesarea Philippi. While they were traveling, Jesus asked them, "Who do people say I am?"

28They answered, "Some say you are John the Baptist.[d] Others say you are Elijah,[n] and others say you are one of the prophets."[d]

29Then Jesus asked, "But who do you say I am?"

Peter answered, "You are the Christ."[d]

30Jesus warned his followers not to tell anyone who he was.

31Then Jesus began to teach them that the Son of Man[d] must suffer many things and that he would be rejected by the older Jewish leaders, the leading priests, and the teachers of the law. He told them that the Son of Man must be killed and then rise from the dead after three days. 32Jesus told them plainly what would happen. Then Peter took Jesus aside and began to tell him not to talk like that. 33But Jesus turned and looked at his followers. Then he told Peter not to talk that way. He said, "Go away from me, Satan![n] You don't care about the things of God, but only about things people think are important."

34Then Jesus called the crowd to him, along with his followers. He said, "If people want to follow me, they must give up the things they want. They must be willing even to give up their lives to follow me. 35Those who want to save their lives will give up true life. But those who give up their lives for me and for the Good News[d] will have true life. 36It is worth nothing for them to have the whole world if they lose their souls. 37They could never pay enough to buy back their souls. 38The people who live now are living in a sinful and evil time. If people are ashamed of me and my teaching, the Son of Man[d] will be ashamed of them when he comes with his Father's glory and with the holy angels."

9 Then Jesus said to the people, "I tell you the truth, some people standing here will see the kingdom of God come with power before they die."

Jesus Talks with Moses and Elijah

2Six days later, Jesus took Peter, James, and John up on a high mountain by themselves. While they watched, Jesus' appearance was changed. 3His clothes became shining white, whiter than any person could make them. 4Then Elijah and Moses[n] appeared to them, talking with Jesus.

5Peter said to Jesus, "Teacher, it is good that we are here. Let us make three tents—one for you, one for Moses, and one for Elijah." 6Peter did not know what to say, because he and the others were so frightened.

7Then a cloud came and covered them, and a voice came from the cloud, saying, "This is my Son, whom I love. Listen to him!"

8Suddenly Peter, James, and John looked around, but they saw only Jesus there alone with them.

9As they were coming down the mountain, Jesus commanded them not to tell anyone about what they had seen until the Son of Man[d] had risen from the dead.

10So the followers obeyed Jesus, but they discussed what he meant about rising from the dead.

11Then they asked Jesus, "Why do the teachers of the law say that Elijah must come first?"

12Jesus answered, "They are right to say that Elijah must come first and make everything the way it should be. But why does the Scripture[d] say that the Son of Man will suffer much and that people will treat him as if he were nothing? 13I tell you that Elijah has already come. And people did to him whatever they wanted to do, just as the Scriptures said it would happen."

Jesus Heals a Sick Boy

14When Jesus, Peter, James, and John came back to the other followers, they saw a great crowd around them and the teachers of the law arguing with them. 15But as soon as the crowd saw Jesus, the people were surprised and ran to welcome him.

16Jesus asked, "What are you arguing about?"

17A man answered, "Teacher, I brought my son to you. He has an evil spirit in him that stops him from talking. 18When the spirit attacks him, it throws him on the ground. Then my son foams at the mouth, grinds his teeth, and becomes very stiff. I asked your followers to force the evil spirit out, but they couldn't."

19Jesus answered, "You people have no faith. How long must I stay with you? How long must I put up with you? Bring the boy to me."

20So the followers brought him to Jesus. As soon as the evil spirit saw Jesus, it made the boy lose control of himself, and he fell down and rolled on the ground, foaming at the mouth.

Elijah A man who spoke for God and who lived hundreds of years before Christ. See 1 Kings 17.
Satan Name for the devil meaning "the enemy." Jesus means that Peter was talking like Satan.
Elijah and Moses Two of the most important Jewish leaders in the past. Moses had given them the law, and Elijah was an important prophet.

21 Jesus asked the boy's father, "How long has
this been happening?"
The father answered, "Since he was very
young. 22 The spirit often throws him into a fire
or into water to kill him. If you can do anything for him, please have pity on us and help
us."
23 Jesus said to the father, "You said, 'If you
can!' All things are possible for the one who believes."
24 Immediately the father cried out, "I do believe! Help me to believe more!"
25 When Jesus saw that a crowd was quickly
gathering, he ordered the evil spirit, saying, "You
spirit that makes people unable to hear or speak,
I command you to come out of this boy and never
enter him again!"
26 The evil spirit screamed and caused the boy
to fall on the ground again. Then the spirit came
out. The boy looked as if he were dead, and many
people said, "He is dead!" 27 But Jesus took
hold of the boy's hand and helped him to stand
up.
28 When Jesus went into the house, his followers began asking him privately, "Why couldn't we
force that evil spirit out?"
29 Jesus answered, "That kind of spirit can only
be forced out by prayer."

Jesus Talks About His Death

30 Then Jesus and his followers left that place
and went through Galilee. He didn't want anyone
to know where he was, 31 because he was teaching his followers. He said to them, "The Son of
Man[d] will be handed over to people, and they will
kill him. After three days, he will rise from the
dead." 32 But the followers did not understand
what Jesus meant, and they were afraid to ask
him.

Who Is the Greatest?

33 Jesus and his followers went to Capernaum.
When they went into a house there, he asked
them, "What were you arguing about on the
road?" 34 But the followers did not answer, because their argument on the road was about
which one of them was the greatest.
35 Jesus sat down and called the twelve apostles[d] to him. He said, "Whoever wants to be the
most important must be last of all and servant of
all."

FAITH

Over a Cliff

Ethan Magness peered anxiously over his shoulder down the steep cliff. The bottom of the deep ravine appeared to be miles away. Standing on the edge of the rocks, he heard the rappelling instructor yell, "Just lean straight back into the air; the ropes will hold you."

"I can't lean back," Ethan thought. "How do I know the ropes will hold me?"

"Come on, Ethan, are you afraid?" Ellie asked.

Sweat poured down his face as he thought about the cliff. He was afraid, but he didn't want anyone to know it—especially not Ellie.

"Come on, Ethan," the instructor encouraged. "It's all right; just have faith in the ropes. They'll hold you."

Ethan held his breath and leaned back. He was swinging in the air, but the ropes did hold! Cautiously, he let out the tension on the rope and slid down. Finally he reached the bottom. Whew!

Just as it took faith for Ethan to rappel, it also took faith for the disciples to believe in Jesus. Read **Mark 9:1–9** to see an experience the disciples had with Jesus.

- How is Ethan's faith in his ropes similar to the faith the disciples needed to believe in Jesus?
- How can you overcome hard-to-believe things that stand in the way of your faith in Jesus?

CONSIDER . . .

- listing obstacles to your faith on separate sheets of paper and tearing up each sheet.
- doing one risky thing to demonstrate your faith. For example, tell a non-Christian friend about Jesus or take a stand for or against a social issue.

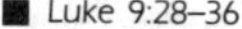

FOR MORE, SEE . . .

- Psalm 130
- Matthew 17:1–9
- Luke 9:28–36

36Then Jesus took a small child and had him
stand among them. Taking the child in his arms,
he said, 37"Whoever accepts a child like this in my
name accepts me. And whoever accepts me accepts the One who sent me."

Anyone Not Against Us Is for Us

38Then John said, "Teacher, we saw someone
using your name to force demons[d] out of a person. We told him to stop, because he does not
belong to our group."
39But Jesus said, "Don't stop him, because anyone who uses my name to do powerful things will
not easily say evil things about me. 40Whoever is
not against us is with us. 41I tell you the truth,
whoever gives you a drink of water because you
belong to the Christ[d] will truly get his reward.
42"If one of these little children believes in me,
and someone causes that child to sin, it would be
better for that person to have a large stone tied
around his neck and be drowned in the sea. 43If
your hand causes you to sin, cut it off. It is better
for you to lose part of your body and live forever
than to have two hands and go to hell, where the
fire never goes out. 44 [n] 45If your foot causes you
to sin, cut it off. It is better for you to lose part of
your body and to live forever than to have two
feet and be thrown into hell. 46 [n] 47If your eye
causes you to sin, take it out. It is better for you
to enter the kingdom of God with only one eye
than to have two eyes and be thrown into hell.
48In hell the worm does not die; the fire is never
put out. 49Every person will be salted with fire.
50"Salt is good, but if the salt loses its salty taste,
you cannot make it salty again. So, be full of salt,
and have peace with each other."

Verse 44 Some Greek copies of Mark add verse 44, which is the same as verse 48.
Verse 46 Some Greek copies of Mark add verse 46, which is the same as verse 48.

POPULARITY

Everyone Is Going

Sam Collins slammed his locker shut. It was Friday afternoon; the final bell had rung. He needed to catch Roy and Justin before they got on their bus to be sure all of them were meeting at the football game that night.

As Sam turned from his locker, his foot caught on a wheel. It was Alex O'Brien's wheelchair. Alex had broken his neck the previous spring in a diving accident and was paralyzed from the shoulders down.

"Hey, Sam, what are you guys doin' tonight?" Alex asked.

"Well, uh. . . ." Sam hesitated as his eyes searched the hall for the other guys, but Alex didn't wait for an answer.

"Would you like to come over to my place? My mom said she'd pick up some videos. Could you open my locker and put away the books in my backpack, please?"

Sam impatiently unloaded the backpack, opened the locker, and deposited the books. As Sam closed the locker, Alex asked again, "Well? What about tonight?"

Sam glanced down the empty hallway. The buses were pulling away. It was too late to make plans with Justin and Roy. Alex needed a friend. But everyone would be going to the game.

Sam thought for a moment and then smiled at Alex. "What time do you want me to come over?"

The disciples also had to make a decision about what it meant to be popular. They were arguing about who was the greatest or most popular. **Read Mark 9:30–37** to see how Jesus turned the tables on them.

- How would Sam's actions make him important in the kingdom of God?
- When have you had to decide between doing what's popular and what's right? How was that experience like the incident in this passage?

CONSIDER . . .

- having lunch with an unpopular classmate.
- doing a household chore that everyone in your family dislikes doing.

FOR MORE, SEE . . .

- Proverbs 11:24–26
- Matthew 18:1–5
- Philippians 2:5–7

Jesus Teaches About Divorce

10 Then Jesus left that place and went into the area of Judea and across the Jordan River. Again, crowds came to him, and he taught them as he usually did.

> **SIDELIGHT:** In the original Greek language of the New Testament, the word for "hell" (Mark 9:45-49) is Gehenna, which is based on the Hebrew name of the Hinnom Valley southwest of Jerusalem. The description is appropriate. In ancient times, this valley was used for infant sacrifices (see Jeremiah 32:35). It later became Jerusalem's smelly garbage dump—not a place you would want to spend eternity!

2Some Pharisees[d] came to Jesus and tried to trick him. They asked, "Is it right for a man to divorce his wife?"

3Jesus answered, "What did Moses command you to do?"

4They said, "Moses allowed a man to write out divorce papers and send her away."[n]

5Jesus said, "Moses wrote that command for you because you were stubborn. 6But when God made the world, 'he made them male and female.'[n] 7'So a man will leave his father and mother and be united with his wife, 8and the two will become one body.'[n] So there are not two, but one. 9God has joined the two together, so no one should separate them."

10Later, in the house, his followers asked Jesus again about the question of divorce. 11He answered, "Anyone who divorces his wife and marries another woman is guilty of adultery[d] against her. 12And the woman who divorces her husband and marries another man is also guilty of adultery."

Jesus Accepts Children

13Some people brought their little children to Jesus so he could touch them, but his followers told them to stop. 14When Jesus saw this, he was upset and said to them, "Let the little children come to me. Don't stop them, because the kingdom of God belongs to people who are like these children. 15I tell you the truth, you must accept the kingdom of God as if you were a little child, or you will never enter it." 16Then Jesus took the children in his arms, put his hands on them, and blessed them.

A Rich Young Man's Question

17As Jesus started to leave, a man ran to him and fell on his knees before Jesus. The man asked, "Good teacher, what must I do to have life forever?"

18Jesus answered, "Why do you call me good? Only God is good. 19You know the commands: 'You must not murder anyone. You must not be guilty of adultery.[d] You must not steal. You must not tell lies about your neighbor. You must not cheat. Honor your father and mother.' "[n]

20The man said, "Teacher, I have obeyed all these things since I was a boy."

21Jesus, looking at the man, loved him and said, "There is one more thing you need to do. Go and sell everything you have, and give the money to the poor, and you will have treasure in heaven. Then come and follow me."

22He was very sad to hear Jesus say this, and he left sorrowfully, because he was rich.

23Then Jesus looked at his followers and said, "How hard it will be for the rich to enter the kingdom of God!"

24The followers were amazed at what Jesus said. But he said again, "My children, it is very hard to enter the kingdom of God! 25It is easier for a camel to go through the eye of a needle than for a rich person to enter the kingdom of God."

26The followers were even more surprised and said to each other, "Then who can be saved?"

27Jesus looked at them and said, "This is something people cannot do, but God can. God can do all things."

28Peter said to Jesus, "Look, we have left everything and followed you."

29Jesus said, "I tell you the truth, all those who have left houses, brothers, sisters, mother, father, children, or farms for me and for the Good News[d] 30will get more than they left. Here in this world they will have a hundred times more homes, brothers, sisters, mothers, children, and fields. And with those things, they will also suffer for their belief. But in the age that is coming they will have life forever. 31Many who have the highest place now will have the lowest place in the future. And many who have the lowest place now will have the highest place in the future."

Jesus Talks About His Death

32As Jesus and the people with him were on the

"Moses . . . away." Quotation from Deuteronomy 24:1.
'he made . . . female.' Quotation from Genesis 1:27.
'So . . . body.' Quotation from Genesis 2:24.
'You . . . mother.' Quotation from Exodus 20:12-16; Deuteronomy 5:16-20.

road to Jerusalem, he was leading the way. His
followers were amazed, but others in the crowd
who followed were afraid. Again Jesus took the
twelve apostles[d] aside and began to tell them
what was about to happen in Jerusalem. 33He
said, "Look, we are going to Jerusalem. The Son
of Man[d] will be turned over to the leading priests
and the teachers of the law. They will say that he
must die, and they will turn him over to the non-
Jewish people, 34who will laugh at him and spit
on him. They will beat him with whips and crucify him. But on the third day, he will rise to life
again."

Two Followers Ask Jesus a Favor

35Then James and John, sons of Zebedee, came
to Jesus and said, "Teacher, we want to ask you
to do something for us."

36Jesus asked, "What do you want me to do for
you?"

37They answered, "Let one of us sit at your
right side and one of us sit at your left side in your
glory in your kingdom."

38Jesus said, "You don't understand what you
are asking. Can you drink the cup that I must
drink? And can you be baptized with the
same kind of baptism that I must go through?"[n]

39They answered, "Yes, we can."

Jesus said to them, "You will drink the same
cup that I will drink, and you will be baptized with the same baptism that I must go
through. 40But I cannot choose who will sit at
my right or my left; those places belong to
those for whom they have been prepared."

41When the other ten followers heard this, they
began to be angry with James and John.

42Jesus called them together and said, "The
non-Jewish people have rulers. You know that
those rulers love to show their power over the
people, and their important leaders love to use all
their authority. 43But it should not be that way
among you. Whoever wants to become great
among you must serve the rest of you like a servant. 44Whoever wants to become the first among
you must serve all of you like a slave. 45In the
same way, the Son of Man[d] did not come to be
served. He came to serve others and to give his
life as a ransom for many people."

Can you . . . through? Jesus was asking if they could suffer the same terrible things that would happen to him.

FAITH

Christmas In June, July . . .

Corky Adams is unique. He's a real trendsetter. For example, he always wears one red sock and one green sock to remind himself that every day is Christmas. His socks are a perfect reflection of the way he lives his Christian faith with others.

Corky often plays with children and talks with elderly folks in his neighborhood. Once he drove a thousand miles to comfort someone whose friend had died suddenly. He is also a gifted photographer who captures the best of each person he photographs.

Corky is a joy to be around. His beaming smile lights up his cheeks as though he were Santa Claus himself. When friends see him, their natural reaction is to smile and give him a hug. His faith is alive with wonder and joy—much like the excitement of a child who has just discovered that dirt and water make mud.

What's most amazing about Corky, though, is that he's thirty-five years old!

Jesus, himself, challenges us, no matter how old or young we are, to live the childlike faith and joy that Corky lives each day. Read **Mark 10:13–16** to see how Jesus requires childlike faith.

- How does Corky reflect the kingdom of God in a childlike way?
- In what ways do you feel challenged to be more childlike in your own faith?

CONSIDER . . .

- listing the questions you had about God as a child, then writing the answers you have discovered as you've grown.
- playing with a little child. Build with blocks; paint with your fingers. Read stories. Notice the childlike qualities, such as curiosity, innocence, and trust. Then work at applying those qualities to your faith.

FOR MORE, SEE . . .

- Isaiah 11:1–6
- Mark 9:33–37
- Romans 8:14–17

Jesus Heals a Blind Man

46Then they came to the town of Jericho. As
Jesus was leaving there with his followers and a
great many people, a blind beggar named Bartimaeus son of Timaeus was sitting by the road.
47When he heard that Jesus from Nazareth was
walking by, he began to shout, "Jesus, Son of David,[d] have mercy on me!"
48Many people warned the blind man to be
quiet, but he shouted even more, "Son of David,
have mercy on me!"
49Jesus stopped and said, "Tell the man to come
here."
So they called the blind man, saying, "Cheer
up! Get to your feet. Jesus is calling you." 50The
blind man jumped up, left his coat there, and
went to Jesus.
51Jesus asked him, "What do you want me to
do for you?"
The blind man answered, "Teacher, I want to
see."
52Jesus said, "Go, you are healed because you
believed." At once the man could see, and he followed Jesus on the road.

Jesus Enters Jerusalem as a King

11 As Jesus and his followers were coming
closer to Jerusalem, they came to the
towns of Bethphage and Bethany near the Mount
of Olives.[d] From there Jesus sent two of his followers 2and said to them, "Go to the town you
can see there. When you enter it, you will quickly
find a colt tied, which no one has ever ridden.
Untie it and bring it here to me. 3If anyone asks
you why you are doing this, tell him its Master
needs the colt, and he will send it at once."
4The followers went into the town, found a colt
tied in the street near the door of a house, and
untied it. 5Some people were standing there and
asked, "What are you doing? Why are you untying that colt?" 6The followers answered the way
Jesus told them to answer, and the people let
them take the colt.
7They brought the colt to Jesus and put their
coats on it, and Jesus sat on it. 8Many people
spread their coats on the road. Others cut
branches in the fields and spread them on the
road. 9The people were walking ahead of Jesus
and behind him, shouting,

MONEY

What's Important?

"I have made many millions, but they have brought me no happiness. I would barter them all for the days I sat on an office stool in Cleveland and counted myself rich on $3 a week." —John Rockefeller, a multi-millionaire

"The care of $200 million is too great a load for any brain or back to bear. It is enough to kill anyone. There is no pleasure in it." —W.H. Vanderbilt, who inherited a fortune

"I am the most miserable man on earth." —John Jacob Astor, who died leaving $5 million

"Millionaires seldom smile." —Andrew Carnegie, a millionaire

Each of these people, who had lots of money, knew other things were more important than money. Jesus tried to teach the same lesson to the young man in **Mark 10:17–30**. Read how he responded.

- How is what Jesus said similar to the quotes from these millionaires?
- How does your "wealth" help or hinder your faith?

CONSIDER . . .

- drawing a treasure chest and "filling" it with all the things that are most valuable to you. Evaluate what Jesus would think of your treasure.
- giving someone $10 with no strings attached and for no particular reason—just for the fun of it. How does it make you feel?

FOR MORE, SEE . . .

- Deuteronomy 14:22–29
- Luke 21:1–4
- Acts 3:1–10

"Praise[n] God!
God bless the One who comes in the name
of the Lord! *Psalm 118:26*
10God bless the kingdom of our father David!
That kingdom is coming!
Praise to God in heaven!"
11Jesus entered Jerusalem and went into the
Temple.[d] After he had looked at everything, since
it was already late, he went out to Bethany with
the twelve apostles.[d]
12The next day as Jesus was leaving Bethany,
he became hungry. 13Seeing a fig tree in leaf
from far away, he went to see if it had any figs
on it. But he found no figs, only leaves, because
it was not the right season for figs. 14So Jesus
said to the tree, "May no one ever eat fruit from
you again." And Jesus' followers heard him say
this.

Jesus Goes to the Temple

15When Jesus returned to Jerusalem, he went
into the Temple[d] and began to throw out those
who were buying and selling there. He turned
over the tables of those who were exchanging different kinds of money, and he upset the benches
of those who were selling doves. 16Jesus refused
to allow anyone to carry goods through the Temple courts. 17Then he taught the people, saying,
"It is written in the Scriptures,[d] 'My Temple will
be called a house for prayer for people from all
nations.'[n] But you are changing God's house into
a 'hideout for robbers.'"[n]
18The leading priests and the teachers of the
law heard all this and began trying to find a way
to kill Jesus. They were afraid of him, because all
the people were amazed at his teaching. 19That
evening, Jesus and his followers left the city.

Praise Literally, "Hosanna," a Hebrew word used at first in praying to God for help, but at this time it was probably a shout of joy used in praising God or his Messiah.
'My Temple . . . nations.' Quotation from Isaiah 56:7.
'hideout for robbers.' Quotation from Jeremiah 7:11.

SERVICE

Volunteer of the Year

Wanted: Class clown. Poor study habits a must.

If you asked her teachers, this job advertisement fit Denise Delgado perfectly. She never did her homework, and she was constantly cutting up in class. Denise had a definite gift of getting people to notice her.

Yet, Denise also had a gift her teachers failed to recognize. During her senior year, Denise volunteered at a special school for autistic children. Autistic children are difficult to work with because they seldom respond to those around them. However, Denise loved working with the kids. She soaked in any affirmation they would give her—a nod of the head, the glance of an eye, or a rare smile. Teachers and parents alike marveled at Denise's success in helping their children.

When she graduated, the special school awarded Denise a scholarship to study special education. The "class clown" even became a celebrity when the local United Way recognized her as the Youth Volunteer of the Year.

Like Denise early in high school, Jesus' followers sometimes searched for recognition among their peers. They didn't understand that Jesus required them to be servants first of all. John and James were two such people. Read about their encounter with Jesus in **Mark 10:35–45**.

- How was Denise's response similar to the challenge Jesus gave his followers?
- Which servant characteristics that Jesus talks about in this passage do you have?

CONSIDER. . .

- encouraging someone you usually compete with, and being excited when he or she does something better than you.
- going to a sports event and writing down the encouraging things people say to their favorite team. Use those things to encourage the people around you.

FOR MORE, SEE. . .

- 1 Samuel 3:1–10
- Luke 22:24–27
- John 13:1–17

The Power of Faith

20The next morning as Jesus was passing by with his followers, they saw the fig tree dry and dead, even to the roots. 21Peter remembered the tree and said to Jesus, "Teacher, look! The fig tree you cursed is dry and dead!"

> **SIDELIGHT:** The people whom Jesus threw out of the Temple were merchants who took advantage of those in Jerusalem on religious pilgrimages (Mark 11:15–17). They exchanged foreign currency for money to use in the Temple—with an extra charge, of course. Others sold doves to be used in Temple sacrifices.

22Jesus answered, "Have faith in God. 23I tell you the truth, you can say to this mountain, 'Go, fall into the sea.' And if you have no doubts in your mind and believe that what you say will happen, God will do it for you. 24So I tell you to believe that you have received the things you ask for in prayer, and God will give them to you. 25When you are praying, if you are angry with someone, forgive him so that your Father in heaven will also forgive your sins." 26 [n]

Leaders Doubt Jesus' Authority

27Jesus and his followers went again to Jerusalem. As Jesus was walking in the Temple,[d] the leading priests, the teachers of the law, and the older leaders came to him. 28They said to him, "What authority do you have to do these things? Who gave you this authority?"

29Jesus answered, "I will ask you one question. If you answer me, I will tell you what authority I have to do these things. 30Tell me: When John baptized people, was that authority from God or just from other people?"

31They argued about Jesus' question, saying, "If we answer, 'John's baptism was from God,' Jesus will say, 'Then why didn't you believe him?' 32But

Verse 26 Some early Greek copies add verse 26: "But if you don't forgive other people, then your Father in heaven will not forgive your sins."

PERSISTENCE

The Long Run

"We don't know if your baby will live through the night," the doctors told two-pound Patti Maslowski's new parents. She was born in 1966, when few babies born three months premature survived.

But Patti was a fighter from the start.

By the time she reached high school, she was an excellent student and an all-district volleyball star. She was also the regional track champion in the 3,200-meter run. When she finished eighth in her first state track meet, everyone was confident she had a great running future.

But then a back injury before her junior year changed her plans. No longer could she run like she used to. So she found a new way to give of herself—by becoming the track team manager.

Patti explains why she perseveres: "My persistence comes from making the most of each opportunity I'm given. I wasn't expected to live in the first place, so now I just want to use the gifts I've been blessed with to the best of my ability."

At one point in Jesus' ministry, he met a blind man who also exhibited Patti's perseverance. Read about the blind man in **Mark 10:46–52**.

- Why did Patti and the blind man persevere?
- How does your faith in Jesus help you persevere in pursuing your goals?

C O N S I D E R . . .

- making a plan of action to improve performance in one area of your life. Then spend the time needed to make progress. Evaluate your progress every month.
- setting short- and long-term goals. Write them in a pocket calendar, and keep the calendar in your purse or wallet.

F O R   M O R E ,   S E E . . .

- Isaiah 35:1–10
- Luke 5:17–25
- Hebrews 10:32–39

if we say, 'It was from other people,' the crowd
will be against us." (These leaders were afraid of
the people, because all the people believed that
John was a prophet.[d])
33So they answered Jesus, "We don't know."
Jesus said to them, "Then I won't tell you what
authority I have to do these things."

A Story About God's Son

12 Jesus began to use stories to teach the
people. He said, "A man planted a vineyard. He put a wall around it and dug a hole for
a winepress[d] and built a tower. Then he leased
the land to some farmers and left for a trip. 2When
it was time for the grapes to be picked, he sent a
servant to the farmers to get his share of the
grapes. 3But the farmers grabbed the servant and
beat him and sent him away empty-handed.
4Then the man sent another servant. They hit him
on the head and showed no respect for him. 5So
the man sent another servant, whom they killed.
The man sent many other servants; the farmers
beat some of them and killed others.
6"The man had one person left to send, his son
whom he loved. He sent him last of all, saying,
'They will respect my son.'
7"But the farmers said to each other, 'This son
will inherit the vineyard. If we kill him, it will be
ours.' 8So they took the son, killed him, and
threw him out of the vineyard.
9"So what will the owner of the vineyard do?
He will come and kill those farmers and will give
the vineyard to other farmers. 10Surely you have
read this Scripture:[d]

'The stone that the builders rejected
became the cornerstone.[d]
11The Lord did this,
and it is wonderful to us.' " *Psalm 118:22-23*

12The Jewish leaders knew that the story was
about them. So they wanted to find a way to arrest Jesus, but they were afraid of the people. So
the leaders left him and went away.

Is It Right to Pay Taxes or Not?

13Later, the Jewish leaders sent some Phari-

WORSHIP

1964

On August 18, 1964, the Beatles boarded a plane in London and flew to San Francisco to begin their first coast-to-coast concert tour of North America. The "Fab Four" expected to perform before more people in their thirty-one-day tour than any other act in music history. What they didn't expect was "Beatlemania."

When the musicians arrived, they were greeted at the airport by five thousand screaming fans. At the hotel where they stayed, they were greeted by four thousand more. And that was just the beginning.

In the months that followed, the Beatles found themselves confronted by mobs raging with excitement. The foursome often had to travel in secret to avoid crowds. At their concerts, the music was often drowned out by excited, screaming fans.

Some might think the Beatles loved the attention. But they didn't.

"It wasn't as much fun for us as it was for all of you," commented George Harrison, the band's guitarist, when asked about Beatlemania. People worshiped the Beatles—even though they were just human beings and didn't really deserve that kind of adoration.

Everyone longs to worship something, to have a hero to look up to. That was true even in Jesus' time. **Mark 11:1–11** describes a worship scene that resembled Beatlemania—except the one worshiped was worthy of people's praise. Check it out.

- How is the story in the passage like Beatlemania?
- If you had been in Jerusalem at the time of the passage, how would you have worshiped Jesus? How do you worship him today?

CONSIDER . . .

- going to a Christian concert to discover a new way to worship.
- writing a song or poem of worship to Jesus, thanking him for what he's done for you.

FOR MORE, SEE . . .

- Psalm 66
- Matthew 21:1–11
- Luke 19:28–40

sees[d] and Herodians[n] to Jesus to trap him in saying something wrong. 14They came to him and
said, "Teacher, we know that you are an honest
man. You are not afraid of what other people
think about you, because you pay no attention to
who they are. And you teach the truth about
God's way. Tell us: Is it right to pay taxes to Caesar[d] or not? 15Should we pay them, or not?"

But knowing what these men were really trying to do, Jesus said to them, "Why are you trying
to trap me? Bring me a coin to look at." 16They
gave Jesus a coin, and he asked, "Whose image
and name are on the coin?"

They answered, "Caesar's."

17Then Jesus said to them, "Give to Caesar the
things that are Caesar's, and give to God the
things that are God's." The men were amazed at
what Jesus said.

Some Sadducees Try to Trick Jesus

18Then some Sadducees[d] came to Jesus and
asked him a question. (Sadducees believed that
people would not rise from the dead.) 19They said,
"Teacher, Moses wrote that if a man's brother
dies, leaving a wife but no children, then that man
must marry the widow and have children for his
brother. 20Once there were seven brothers. The
first brother married and died, leaving no children. 21So the second brother married the widow,
but he also died and had no children. The same
thing happened with the third brother. 22All seven
brothers married her and died, and none of the
brothers had any children. Finally the woman
died too. 23Since all seven brothers had married
her, when people rise from the dead, whose wife
will she be?"

24Jesus answered, "Why don't you understand?
Don't you know what the Scriptures[d] say, and
don't you know about the power of God? 25When
people rise from the dead, they will not marry,
nor will they be given to someone to marry. They
will be like the angels in heaven. 26Surely you
have read what God said about people rising from
the dead. In the book in which Moses wrote
about the burning bush,[n] it says that God told
Moses, 'I am the God of Abraham, the God of
Isaac, and the God of Jacob.'[n] 27God is the God
of the living, not the dead. You Sadducees are
wrong!"

The Most Important Command

28One of the teachers of the law came and
heard Jesus arguing with the Sadducees.[d] Seeing
that Jesus gave good answers to their questions,
he asked Jesus, "Which of the commands is most
important?"

29Jesus answered, "The most important command is this: 'Listen, people of Israel! The Lord
our God is the only Lord. 30Love the Lord your
God with all your heart, all your soul, all your
mind, and all your strength.'[n] 31The second
command is this: 'Love your neighbor as
you love yourself.'[n] There are no commands
more important than these."

32The man answered, "That was a good answer, Teacher. You were right when you said
God is the only Lord and there is no other God
besides him. 33One must love God with all his
heart, all his mind, and all his strength. And one
must love his neighbor as he loves himself. These
commands are more important than all the animals and sacrifices we offer to God."

34When Jesus saw that the man answered him
wisely, Jesus said to him, "You are close to the
kingdom of God." And after that, no one was
brave enough to ask Jesus any more questions.

35As Jesus was teaching in the Temple,[d] he
asked, "Why do the teachers of the law say that
the Christ[d] is the son of David? 36David himself,
speaking by the Holy Spirit,[d] said:

'The Lord said to my Lord:
Sit by me at my right side,
until I put your enemies under your
control.' *Psalm 110:1*

37David himself calls the Christ 'Lord,' so how can
the Christ be his son?" The large crowd listened
to Jesus with pleasure.

38Jesus continued teaching and said, "Beware
of the teachers of the law. They like to walk
around wearing fancy clothes, and they love for
people to greet them with respect in the marketplaces. 39They love to have the most important
seats in the synagogues[d] and at feasts. 40But they
cheat widows and steal their houses and then try
to make themselves look good by saying long
prayers. They will receive a greater punishment."

True Giving

41Jesus sat near the Temple[d] money box and
watched the people put in their money. Many
rich people gave large sums of money. 42Then a
poor widow came and put in two small copper
coins, which were only worth a few cents.

43Calling his followers to him, Jesus said, "I tell
you the truth, this poor widow gave more than all
those rich people. 44They gave only what they did
not need. This woman is very poor, but she gave
all she had; she gave all she had to live on."

Herodians A political group that followed Herod and his family.
burning bush Read Exodus 3:1-12 in the Old Testament.
'I am . . . Jacob.' Quotation from Exodus 3:6.
'Listen . . . strength.' Quotation from Deuteronomy 6:4-5.
'Love . . . yourself.' Quotation from Leviticus 19:18.

The Temple Will Be Destroyed

13 As Jesus was leaving the Temple,[d] one of
his followers said to him, "Look,
Teacher! How beautiful the buildings are! How
big the stones are!"
2Jesus said, "Do you see all these great buildings? Not one stone will be left on another. Every
stone will be thrown down to the ground."

> **SIDELIGHT:** Jesus' prediction that the Temple would be destroyed (Mark 13:1–2) came true within about forty years. In A.D. 70, the Romans surrounded and sacked Jerusalem, burning the Temple to the ground. Today, the Muslim shrine called the "Dome of the Rock" stands on the Temple site.

3Later, as Jesus was sitting on the Mount of Olives,[d] opposite the Temple, he was alone with Peter, James, John, and Andrew. They asked Jesus,
4"Tell us, when will these things happen? And
what will be the sign that they are going to happen?"
5Jesus began to answer them, "Be careful that
no one fools you. 6Many people will come in my
name, saying, 'I am the One,' and they will fool
many people. 7When you hear about wars and
stories of wars that are coming, don't be afraid.
These things must happen before the end comes.
8Nations will fight against other nations, and kingdoms against other kingdoms. There will be earthquakes in different places, and there will be times
when there is no food for people to eat. These
things are like the first pains when something
new is about to be born.
9"You must be careful. People will arrest you
and take you to court and beat you in their synagogues.[d] You will be forced to stand before kings
and governors, to tell them about me. This will
happen to you because you follow me. 10But before these things happen, the Good News[d] must
be told to all people. 11When you are arrested and
judged, don't worry ahead of time about what
you should say. Say whatever is given you to say

GIVING

Under Construction

Stephen Chang was shy and short. He was one of those teenagers who seemed to slip into the background at big events. He was so quiet that most of the time no one noticed he was even there.

One thing, however, that did stand out about Stephen was how hard he worked. When the youth group picked up leaves for a fund-raiser, Stephen had the most bags of leaves. And when litter filled the youth group room during a meeting, Stephen stayed after to clean up.

It was Stephen's hard work that Joe Heaton recalled when he asked him to design a planter box for a youth group prayer service. Stephen responded enthusiastically, immediately drawing up blueprints for the planter. He created a large cross-shaped planter box. It was beautiful.

The youth group members then planted mustard seeds in the box. As the seeds grew, tended by Stephen's loving care, they reminded the class members of their own growth as Christians.

Aside from Joe, few people knew it was Stephen who had created the planter. No one even knew Stephen had cared for the plants.

In some ways, Stephen is like the widow Jesus talked about in **Mark 12:38–44**. Read this passage to discover Jesus' message.

- How were Stephen's gifts like the kind of giving Jesus described?
- According to this passage, what are things we should not do to be "religious"?

CONSIDER. . .

- doing something anonymously to help someone. For example, you could send money to someone, or you could rake someone's leaves without his knowing about it.
- committing to contribute a percentage of your income to your church.

FOR MORE, SEE. . .

- Malachi 3:8–12
- Matthew 6:19–24
- 1 Timothy 6:6–10

at that time, because it will not really be you
speaking; it will be the Holy Spirit.[d]
12"Brothers will give their own brothers to be
killed, and fathers will give their own children to
be killed. Children will fight against their own
parents and cause them to be put to death. 13All
people will hate you because you follow me, but
those people who keep their faith until the end
will be saved.
14"You will see 'the destroying terror'[n] standing where it should not be." (You who read this
should understand what it means.) "At that time,
the people in Judea should run away to the mountains. 15If people are on the roofs[n] of their
houses, they must not go down or go inside to get
anything out of their houses. 16If people are in the
fields, they must not go back to get their coats.
17At that time, how terrible it will be for women
who are pregnant or have nursing babies! 18Pray
that these things will not happen in winter, 19be-
cause those days will be full of trouble. There will
be more trouble than there has ever been since
the beginning, when God made the world, until
now, and nothing as bad will ever happen again.
20God has decided to make that terrible time
short. Otherwise, no one would go on living.
But God will make that time short to help the
people he has chosen. 21At that time, someone
might say to you, 'Look, there is the Christ!'[d]
Or another person might say, 'There he is!'
But don't believe them. 22False Christs and false
prophets[d] will come and perform great wonders and miracles.[d] They will try to fool even
the people God has chosen, if that is possible.
23So be careful. I have warned you about all
this before it happens.
24"During the days after this trouble comes,
'the sun will grow dark,
and the moon will not give its light.
25The stars will fall from the sky.

'the destroying terror' Mentioned in Daniel 9:27; 12:11 (cf. Daniel 11:31).
roofs In Bible times houses were built with flat roofs. The roof was used for drying things such as flax and fruit. And it was used as an extra room, as a place for worship, and as a place to sleep in the summer.

FUTURE

Be Prepared

NEW MADRID, MO.—In November 1990, grocery store shelves were cleared and ice chests packed with emergency items such as food, water, first-aid kits, flashlights and radios. People were frightened. Some people wouldn't even sleep in their own homes; they slept in their cars and pick-up trucks instead. Many residents even left the area.

"I'm terrified of this," resident Anna Harper said. "I feel like it's some terminal illness. I don't want to believe it, but there is so much talk about it."

Residents of this small town were preparing for the earthquake that Iben Browning, a business consultant from New Mexico, had predicted. He said tidal forces were unusually high and could trigger an earthquake of 6.5 to 7.5 on the Richter scale forty-eight hours before or after December 3, along the New Madrid Fault.

While many residents of the small town scurried about to prepare for the catastrophe, others were calm about it. After all, these residents said, it's not as though they didn't already know they were living on a fault line.

December 3 came and went, and there was no earthquake.

In **Mark 13:24–33**, Jesus warns his followers of a certain day they need to be prepared for in the future.

- According to this passage, no one knows when Jesus will return. To prepare for that day, which people should we be like—the people who prepared at the last minute or those who were ready at all times?
- If Jesus were to return today, would you be ready?

C O N S I D E R . . .

- deciding what things you would put in an "emergency kit" to prepare for the end of the world; for example, faith or courage. Think about what you need to do to have those things ready.
- asking your pastor or youth leader to teach a course on the "end times."

F O R M O R E , S E E . . .

- Genesis 9:1–17
- Luke 21:25–36
- 1 Thessalonians 4:13—5:11

And the powers of the heavens will be
shaken.' *Isaiah 13:10; 34:4*

26"Then people will see the Son of Man[d] coming in clouds with great power and glory. 27Then he will send his angels all around the earth to gather his chosen people from every part of the earth and from every part of heaven.

28"Learn a lesson from the fig tree: When its branches become green and soft and new leaves appear, you know summer is near. 29In the same way, when you see these things happening, you will know that the time is near, ready to come. 30I tell you the truth, all these things will happen while the people of this time are still living. 31Earth and sky will be destroyed, but the words I have said will never be destroyed.

32"No one knows when that day or time will be, not the angels in heaven, not even the Son. Only the Father knows. 33Be careful! Always be ready, because you don't know when that time will be. 34It is like a man who goes on a trip. He leaves his house and lets his servants take care of it, giving each one a special job to do. The man tells the servant guarding the door always to be watchful. 35So always be ready, because you don't know when the owner of the house will come back. It might be in the evening, or at midnight, or in the morning while it is still dark, or when the sun rises. 36Always be ready. Otherwise he might come back suddenly and find you sleeping. 37I tell you this, and I say this to everyone: 'Be ready!' "

The Plan to Kill Jesus

14 It was now only two days before the Passover[d] and the Feast[d] of Unleavened Bread. The leading priests and teachers of the law were trying to find a trick to arrest Jesus and kill him. 2But they said, "We must not do it during the feast, because the people might cause a riot."

A Woman with Perfume for Jesus

3Jesus was in Bethany at the house of Simon, who had a skin disease. While Jesus was eating there, a woman approached him with an alabaster[d] jar filled with very expensive perfume, made of pure nard.[d] She opened the jar and poured the perfume on Jesus' head.

4Some who were there became upset and said to each other, "Why waste that perfume? 5It was worth a full year's work. It could have been sold and the money given to the poor." And they got very angry with the woman.

6Jesus said, "Leave her alone. Why are you troubling her? She did an excellent thing for me. 7You will always have the poor with you, and you can help them anytime you want. But you will not always have me. 8This woman did the only thing she could do for me; she poured perfume on my body to prepare me for burial. 9I tell you the truth, wherever the Good News[d] is preached in all the world, what this woman has done will be told, and people will remember her."

> **SIDELIGHT:** The perfume the woman poured on Jesus' feet at Bethany (Mark 14:3–9) might have made many modern perfumes seem cheap. Called spikenard, it was taken from pink-blossomed plants in the Himalayan Mountains of northern India.

Judas Becomes an Enemy of Jesus

10One of the twelve apostles, Judas Iscariot, went to talk to the leading priests to offer to hand Jesus over to them. 11These priests were pleased about this and promised to pay Judas money. So he watched for the best time to turn Jesus in.

Jesus Eats the Passover Meal

12It was now the first day of the Feast[d] of Unleavened Bread when the Passover[d] lamb was sacrificed. Jesus' followers said to him, "Where do you want us to go and prepare for you to eat the Passover meal?"

13Jesus sent two of his followers and said to them, "Go into the city and a man carrying a jar of water will meet you. Follow him. 14When he goes into a house, tell the owner of the house, 'The Teacher says: Where is my guest room in which I can eat the Passover meal with my followers?' 15The owner will show you a large room upstairs that is furnished and ready. Prepare the food for us there."

16So the followers left and went into the city. Everything happened as Jesus had said, so they prepared the Passover meal.

17In the evening, Jesus went to that house with the twelve. 18While they were all eating, Jesus said, "I tell you the truth, one of you will turn against me—one of you eating with me now."

19The followers were very sad to hear this. Each one began to say to Jesus, "I am not the one, am I?"

20Jesus answered, "It is one of the twelve—the one who dips his bread into the bowl with me. 21The Son of Man[d] will die, just as the Scriptures[d] say. But how terrible it will be for the person who hands the Son of Man over to be killed. It would be better for him if he had never been born."

The Lord's Supper

22While they were eating, Jesus took some bread and thanked God for it and broke it. Then he gave it to his followers and said, "Take it; this is my body."

23Then Jesus took a cup and thanked God for
it and gave it to the followers, and they all drank
from the cup.
24Then Jesus said, "This is my blood which is
the new agreement that God makes with his people. This blood is poured out for many. 25I tell you
the truth, I will not drink of this fruit of the vine[n]
again until that day when I drink it new in the
kingdom of God."
26After singing a hymn, they went out to the
Mount of Olives.[d]

Jesus' Followers Will Leave Him

27Then Jesus told the followers, "You will all
stumble in your faith, because it is written in the
Scriptures:[d]
'I will kill the shepherd,
and the sheep will scatter.' *Zechariah 13:7*
28But after I rise from the dead, I will go ahead of
you into Galilee."
29Peter said, "Everyone else may stumble in
their faith, but I will not."
30Jesus answered, "I tell you the truth, tonight
before the rooster crows twice you will say three
times you don't know me."
31But Peter insisted, "I will never say that I
don't know you! I will even die with you!" And
all the other followers said the same thing.

Jesus Prays Alone

32Jesus and his followers went to a place called
Gethsemane. He said to them, "Sit here while I
pray." 33Jesus took Peter, James, and John with
him, and he began to be very sad and troubled.
34He said to them, "My heart is full of sorrow, to
the point of death. Stay here and watch."
35After walking a little farther away from them,
Jesus fell to the ground and prayed that, if possible, he would not have this time of suffering. 36He
prayed, "Abba,[n] Father! You can do all things.
Take away this cup[n] of suffering. But do what
you want, not what I want."
37Then Jesus went back to his followers and
found them asleep. He said to Peter, "Simon, are

fruit of the vine Product of the grapevine; this may also be translated "wine."
Abba Name that a child called his father.
cup Jesus is talking about the terrible things that will happen to him. Accepting these things will be very hard, like drinking a cup of something bitter.

DEATH

Loving Memories

"Peace I leave with you." That's the message Rudy Beranek lived and died.

Peace and hope. Those were Rudy's constant themes in life. And as he prepared for his death, he continued to share those gifts.

He invited two funeral homes to work together on his funeral services, because the funeral director of each was his close friend. He then asked two flower shops to design floral arrangements, again, because he valued each shop owner's friendship.

For Rudy, the most important thing in life was people working together for the good of all, sharing their gifts and appreciating others' gifts. It was as if by inviting businesses to collaborate in preparing with him for his death that he was inviting them to recognize what was most important in life.

Rudy also asked people at each church he had served to donate college scholarships for children to have a Christian education. And he invited each church's choir to share its gift of song at his funeral.

He wanted no one to be left out. In short, Rudy said "I love you" to the people whom his life had touched.

Jesus, like Rudy, shared his life as he gathered his friends together for his last meal. Read about this special gathering in **Mark 14:12–26**.

- How did Jesus, like Rudy, prepare people for his death?
- How can you remember Jesus' death for you every day?

CONSIDER . . .

- visiting the grave or a favorite spot of a friend or relative who has died. Recall the ways that person taught you through his or her life.
- creating a symbol of Jesus' death and carrying it in your pocket or purse every day.

FOR MORE, SEE . . .

- Exodus 12:1–17
- Luke 22:7–20
- John 13:21–30

you sleeping? Couldn't you stay awake with me for one hour? 38 Stay awake and pray for strength against temptation. The spirit wants to do what is right, but the body is weak."

39 Again Jesus went away and prayed the same thing. 40 Then he went back to his followers, and again he found them asleep, because their eyes were very heavy. And they did not know what to say to him.

41 After Jesus prayed a third time, he went back to his followers and said to them, "Are you still sleeping and resting? That's enough. The time has come for the Son of Man[d] to be handed over to sinful people. 42 Get up, we must go. Look, here comes the man who has turned against me."

Jesus Is Arrested

43 At once, while Jesus was still speaking, Judas, one of the twelve apostles,[d] came up. With him were many people carrying swords and clubs who had been sent from the leading priests, the teachers of the law, and the older Jewish leaders.

44 Judas had planned a signal for them, saying, "The man I kiss is Jesus. Arrest him and guard him while you lead him away." 45 So Judas went straight to Jesus and said, "Teacher!" and kissed him. 46 Then the people grabbed Jesus and arrested him. 47 One of his followers standing nearby pulled out his sword and struck the servant of the high priest and cut off his ear.

48 Then Jesus said, "You came to get me with swords and clubs as if I were a criminal. 49 Every day I was with you teaching in the Temple,[d] and you did not arrest me there. But all these things have happened to make the Scriptures[d] come true." 50 Then all of Jesus' followers left him and ran away.

51 A young man, wearing only a linen cloth, was following Jesus, and the people also grabbed him. 52 But the cloth he was wearing came off, and he ran away naked.

Jesus Before the Leaders

53 The people who arrested Jesus led him to the house of the high priest, where all the leading priests, the older Jewish leaders, and the teachers of the law were gathered. 54 Peter followed far behind and entered the courtyard of the high priest's house. There he sat with the guards, warming himself by the fire.

55 The leading priests and the whole Jewish council tried to find something that Jesus had done wrong so they could kill him. But the council could find no proof of anything. 56 Many people came and told false things about him, but all said different things—none of them agreed.

57 Then some people stood up and lied about Jesus, saying, 58 "We heard this man say, 'I will destroy this Temple[d] that people made. And three days later, I will build another Temple not made by people.'" 59 But even the things these people said did not agree.

60 Then the high priest stood before them and asked Jesus, "Aren't you going to answer? Don't you have something to say about their charges against you?" 61 But Jesus said nothing; he did not answer.

The high priest asked Jesus another question: "Are you the Christ,[d] the Son of the blessed God?"

62 Jesus answered, "I am. And in the future you will see the Son of Man[d] sitting at the right hand of God, the Powerful One, and coming on clouds in the sky."

63 When the high priest heard this, he tore his clothes and said, "We don't need any more witnesses! 64 You all heard him say these things against God. What do you think?"

They all said that Jesus was guilty and should die. 65 Some of the people there began to spit at Jesus. They blindfolded him and beat him with their fists and said, "Prove you are a prophet!"[d] Then the guards led Jesus away and beat him.

Peter Says He Doesn't Know Jesus

66 While Peter was in the courtyard, a servant girl of the high priest came there. 67 She saw Peter warming himself at the fire and looked closely at him.

Then she said, "You also were with Jesus, that man from Nazareth."

68 But Peter said that he was never with Jesus. He said, "I don't know or understand what you are talking about." Then Peter left and went toward the entrance of the courtyard. And the rooster crowed.[n]

69 The servant girl saw Peter there, and again she said to the people who were standing nearby, "This man is one of those who followed Jesus." 70 Again Peter said that it was not true.

A short time later, some people were standing near Peter saying, "Surely you are one of those who followed Jesus, because you are from Galilee, too."

71 Then Peter began to place a curse on himself and swear, "I don't know this man you're talking about!"

72 At once, the rooster crowed the second time. Then Peter remembered what Jesus had told him: "Before the rooster crows twice, you will say three times that you don't know me." Then Peter lost control of himself and began to cry.

And . . . crowed. A few, early Greek copies leave out this phrase.

Pilate Questions Jesus

15 Very early in the morning, the leading
priests, the older leaders, the teachers of
the law, and all the Jewish council decided what
to do with Jesus. They tied him, led him away,
and turned him over to Pilate, the governor.
2Pilate asked Jesus, "Are you the king of the
Jews?"
Jesus answered, "Those are your words."
3The leading priests accused Jesus of many
things. 4So Pilate asked Jesus another question,
"You can see that they are accusing you of many
things. Aren't you going to answer?"
5But Jesus still said nothing, so Pilate was very
surprised.

Pilate Tries to Free Jesus

6Every year at the time of the Passover[d] the
governor would free one prisoner whom the people chose. 7At that time, there was a man named
Barabbas in prison who was a rebel and had committed murder during a riot. 8The crowd came to

PEER PRESSURE

Curfew Capers

"It's our last night at camp. Can't we please stay up late to talk?" Missy Goette and Michael Davenport begged.

The two spokespeople had been designated by their peers to negotiate an extended curfew with Wayne Broderick, the camp director. Wayne listened patiently. Then he reminded them that "we all agreed on Sunday evening that the camp curfew would be midnight. We still have one day's activities to rest up for, so we will not change the curfew."

Missy and Michael reluctantly agreed and relayed the news to their friends. Most accepted the verdict.

Nonetheless, Mary McCain and Justin Weimer convinced Missy to secretly rendezvous at 4 A.M. to celebrate their last night together.

Just after leaving their dorms, the three friends came face-to-face with Wayne.

"What are you doing out here?" he growled.

Missy tried to explain: "We were just talking. We wanted to have more time together before we have to leave."

"What about curfew?" asked Wayne.

"We agreed to a midnight curfew," Justin admitted.

Wayne continued by asking, "What are the consequences for breaking a guideline?"

Mary spoke quietly as tears filled her eyes. "We have to call our parents to pick us up from camp early."

After daybreak, Wayne had the three call their parents. Soon they were heading homeward with their families.

Peer pressure, like that Mary, Justin, and Missy experienced, can be destructive. Read **Mark 15:1–20** to see how a type of peer pressure led to Jesus' death.

- Why did Pilate, the crowd who shouted for Barabbas to be released, and the kids who came together at 4 A.M. give in to pressure?
- If you had been in the shouting crowd, how would you have withstood the pressure to kill Jesus? How can you use those same actions to withstand peer pressure today?

C O N S I D E R . . .

- listing situations in which you experience strong peer pressure to do wrong. Beside each situation, write what you can do or say to withstand the pressure.
- forming a "Pressure Valve Team" with friends. Whenever a teammate is pressured to do something wrong, relieve that negative pressure by providing positive pressure to do what's right.

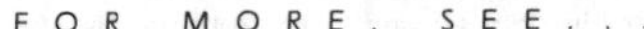

F O R M O R E , S E E . . .

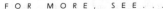

- Proverbs 1:10–19
- Luke 23:1–25
- John 18:28—19:16

Pilate and began to ask him to free a prisoner as
he always did.
9So Pilate asked them, "Do you want me to free
the king of the Jews?" 10Pilate knew that the leading priests had turned Jesus in to him because
they were jealous. 11But the leading priests had
persuaded the people to ask Pilate to free Barabbas, not Jesus.
12Then Pilate asked the crowd again, "So what
should I do with this man you call the king of the
Jews?"
13They shouted, "Crucify him!"
14Pilate asked, "Why? What wrong has he
done?"
But they shouted even louder, "Crucify him!"
15Pilate wanted to please the crowd, so he freed
Barabbas for them. After having Jesus beaten with
whips, he handed Jesus over to the soldiers to be
crucified.

> **SIDELIGHT:** The kind of beating Jesus experienced (Mark 15:15) was a gruesome practice among the Romans. The whip was made of leather, lead, and bone, and could tear out eyes, sever veins, and rip open stomachs. It was a customary part of the death sentence.

16The soldiers took Jesus into the governor's
palace (called the Praetorium) and called all the
other soldiers together. 17They put a purple robe
on Jesus and used thorny branches to make a
crown for his head. 18They began to call out to
him, "Hail, King of the Jews!" 19The soldiers beat
Jesus on the head many times with a stick. They
spit on him and made fun of him by bowing on
their knees and worshiping him. 20After they finished, the soldiers took off the purple robe and put
his own clothes on him again. Then they led him
out of the palace to be crucified.

Jesus Is Crucified

21A man named Simon from Cyrene, the father
of Alexander and Rufus, was coming from the
fields to the city. The soldiers forced Simon to
carry the cross for Jesus. 22They led Jesus to the
place called Golgotha, which means the Place of
the Skull. 23The soldiers tried to give Jesus wine
mixed with myrrh[d] to drink, but he refused. 24The
soldiers crucified Jesus and divided his clothes
among themselves, throwing lots[d] to decide what
each soldier would get.
25It was nine o'clock in the morning when they
crucified Jesus. 26There was a sign with this
charge against Jesus written on it: THE KING OF THE
JEWS. 27They also put two robbers on crosses beside Jesus, one on the right, and the other on the
left. 28 [n] 29People walked by and insulted Jesus
and shook their heads, saying, "You said you
could destroy the Temple[d] and build it again in
three days. 30So save yourself! Come down from
that cross!"
31The leading priests and the teachers of the
law were also making fun of Jesus. They said to
each other, "He saved other people, but he can't
save himself. 32If he is really the Christ,[d] the king
of Israel, let him come down now from the cross.
When we see this, we will believe in him." The
robbers who were being crucified beside Jesus
also insulted him.

Jesus Dies

33At noon the whole country became dark, and
the darkness lasted for three hours. 34At three
o'clock Jesus cried in a loud voice, "Eloi, Eloi,
lama sabachthani." This means, "My God, my
God, why have you rejected me?"
35When some of the people standing there
heard this, they said, "Listen! He is calling Elijah."
36Someone there ran and got a sponge, filled it
with vinegar, tied it to a stick, and gave it to Jesus
to drink. He said, "We want to see if Elijah will
come to take him down from the cross."
37Then Jesus cried in a loud voice and died.
38The curtain in the Temple[n] was torn into
two pieces, from the top to the bottom. 39When
the army officer who was standing in front of the
cross saw what happened when Jesus died, he
said, "This man really was the Son of God!"
40Some women were standing at a distance
from the cross, watching; among them were
Mary Magdalene, Salome, and Mary the mother
of James and Joseph. (James was her youngest
son.) 41These women had followed Jesus in Galilee and helped him. Many other women were
also there who had come with Jesus to Jerusalem.

Jesus Is Buried

42This was Preparation[d] Day. (That means the
day before the Sabbath[d] day.) That evening, 43Jo-
seph from Arimathea was brave enough to go to
Pilate and ask for Jesus' body. Joseph, an important member of the Jewish council, was one of the
people who was waiting for the kingdom of God
to come. 44Pilate was amazed that Jesus would
have already died, so he called the army officer
who had guarded Jesus and asked him if Jesus had
already died. 45The officer told Pilate that he was

erse 28 Some Greek copies add verse 28: "And the Scripture came true that says, 'They put him with criminals.' "
rtain in the Temple A curtain divided the Most Holy Place from the other part of the Temple. That was the special building in Jerusalem where God commanded the Jewish people to worship him.

dead, so Pilate told Joseph he could have the
body. 46Joseph bought some linen cloth, took the
body down from the cross, and wrapped it in the
linen. He put the body in a tomb that was cut out
of a wall of rock. Then he rolled a very large stone
to block the entrance of the tomb. 47And Mary
Magdalene and Mary the mother of Joseph saw
the place where Jesus was laid.

> **SIDELIGHT:** Most people who were crucified in Jesus' day were left on the cross or were simply discarded in a mass grave. By requesting Jesus' body for burial, Joseph saved Jesus from that final indignity (Mark 15:42–47).

Jesus Rises from the Dead

16 The day after the Sabbath[d] day, Mary
Magdalene, Mary the mother of James,
and Salome bought some sweet-smelling spices to
put on Jesus' body. 2Very early on that day, the
first day of the week, soon after sunrise, the
women were on their way to the tomb. 3They
said to each other, "Who will roll away for us the
stone that covers the entrance of the tomb?"
4Then the women looked and saw that the
stone had already been rolled away, even thoug
it was very large. 5The women entered the tom
and saw a young man wearing a white robe an
sitting on the right side, and they were afraid.
6But the man said, "Don't be afraid. You ar
looking for Jesus from Nazareth, who has bee
crucified. He has risen from the dead; he is nc
here. Look, here is the place they laid him. 7Nov
go and tell his followers and Peter, 'Jesus is goin
into Galilee ahead of you, and you will see hir
there as he told you before.' "
8The women were confused and shaking wit
fear, so they left the tomb and ran away. They di
not tell anyone about what happened, becaus
they were afraid.

Verses 9-20 are not included in two of the best and oldest Greek manuscripts of Mark.

Some Followers See Jesus

[9After Jesus rose from the dead early on th
first day of the week, he showed himself first t
Mary Magdalene. One time in the past, he ha
forced seven demons[d] out of her. 10After Ma
saw Jesus, she went and told his followers, wh
were very sad and were crying. 11But Mary to

JESUS CHRIST

Unexpected Savior

Jesus painted no pictures. Yet some of the greatest artists were inspired by him to paint their greatest works.

Jesus wrote no poetry. Yet hundreds of the world's greatest poems pay tribute to him.

Jesus composed no music. Yet Haydn, Handel, Beethoven, Bach, and other great musicians wrote some of their greatest music to praise him.

Jesus preached and taught for only three years. The philosopher Socrates taught for forty years, Plato for fifty years, and Aristotle for forty years. Yet more people follow what Jesus taught than follow the three philosophers combined.

Jesus died on a cross as a criminal. Yet even a guard who helped put him to death recognized that he was God's Son. Read **Mark 15:33–39** to see how Jesus showed he was God's Son even in his death.

- What unexpected things do you see in Jesus' life as described by the passage and by the comparisons above?
- How does this passage strengthen your faith in Jesus as God's Son?

CONSIDER . . .

- listing everything you would expect a king to do. Then compare it to what you read in the Bible about Jesus. Identify similarities and differences.
- rereading the passage, putting yourself in the place of the officer. How would you have responded to this situation? What would you have said?

FOR MORE, SEE . . .

- Isaiah 53
- Matthew 16:21–28
- John 19:28–37

them that Jesus was alive. She said that she had
seen him, but the followers did not believe her.
12Later, Jesus showed himself to two of his followers while they were walking in the country,
but he did not look the same as before. 13These
followers went back to the others and told them
what had happened, but again, the followers did
not believe them.

Jesus Talks to the Apostles

14Later Jesus showed himself to the eleven
apostles while they were eating, and he criticized
them because they had no faith. They were stubborn and refused to believe those who had seen
him after he had risen from the dead.
15Jesus said to his followers, "Go everywhere in
the world, and tell the Good News[d] to everyone.
16Anyone who believes and is baptized will be
saved, but anyone who does not believe will be
punished. 17And those who believe will be able to
do these things as proof: They will use my name
to force out demons.[d] They will speak in new languages.[n] 18They will pick up snakes and drink
poison without being hurt. They will touch the
sick, and the sick will be healed."
19After the Lord Jesus said these things to his
followers, he was carried up into heaven, and he
sat at the right side of God. 20The followers went
everywhere in the world and told the Good News
to people, and the Lord helped them. The Lord
proved that the Good News they told was true by
giving them power to work miracles.[d]]

languages This can also be translated "tongues."

LIFE

A Light in the Darkness

Devon Sparks was heavily into drugs by the time he was fourteen. After being arrested for helping his friends steal a radio, he was placed in an alternative school. But he kept slipping further and further downhill.

He became more distant from his family and friends. And he started using drugs daily to try to escape the pain he felt inside.

One day Devon couldn't stand the pain any longer. He hated himself, and he didn't want to go on living. He felt trapped. The darkness was overwhelming, and he just couldn't see a way out.

Finally, he cried out to God. "Please," he pleaded, "please help me."

Almost immediately he sensed a peace and calm inside, as if the darkness was replaced with a new hope. In the next weeks, he began attending Narcotics Anonymous support meetings and joined a Christian fellowship. Devon had a new beginning.

"Turning my life over to God's direction is the toughest decision I've ever made," Devon later explained. "But my faith is beginning to pay off. I'm making new friends. I found a job. I'm taking art classes. I feel alive. It's a day-to-day struggle to stay free of drugs, but I'm headed in the right direction for once in my life."

Devon was beginning to experience the life and power of Jesus' resurrection. Read about the resurrection in **Mark 16:1–8**.

- How was Devon's new life similar to Jesus' resurrection? How was it different?
- How is your response to Jesus' resurrection like or unlike the women's reactions in this passage?

CONSIDER . . .

- asking God to "roll away" an obstacle in your life with his resurrection power.
- listing the ways you can "stop the pain" you may be experiencing like Devon stopped his pain. Ask others for help if you need to.

FOR MORE, SEE . . .

- Exodus 14
- Matthew 28:1–10
- John 20:1–18

SHARING FAITH

Pass It On!

Geri Rainbolt was frightened when she stepped up to the microphone. She wasn't sure God could use her story to help other people. But she began speaking anyway.

"Two years ago I went out drinking with several friends. I drank so much I passed out. My friends panicked. Was I dying? Would I be okay? They didn't know what to do.

"So they drove me to Kristi Coll's house. Her parents would know what to do. They were always around when we needed them.

"Kristi's parents called my dad. He came and picked me up, drove me home and carried me to my room. I don't remember anything—just waking up the next morning.

"My dad came in to talk with me. Tears filled his eyes. He was so afraid of losing me.

"Right then, I realized I never knew how much I could hurt my father. I really love him, but I had hurt him.

"And that's the message I want to share with you today. The things that keep me—that keep us—from loving our parents or friends are the same things that can keep us from growing in our relationship with God."

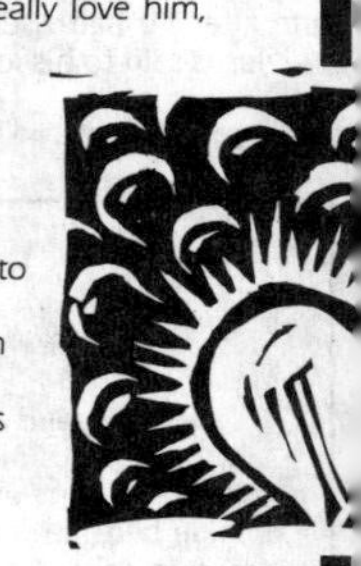

The room was silent as the teenagers soaked in the truth of Geri's message. Geri could sense God's power as she stepped away from the microphone. She had indeed passed on a truth about faith they all needed to hear.

In **Mark 16:19–20**, Jesus' first followers experienced the same power in telling others about Jesus.

- How is Geri's talk similar to the disciples telling the Good News? How is it different?
- How can you tell others the Good News?

CONSIDER . . .

- telling a non-Christian friend about Jesus.
- asking your pastor or youth leader to lead a training course on telling others about Christ.

FOR MORE, SEE . . .

- 1 Kings 18
- Luke 24:44–53
- Acts 1:1–14

LUKE

Why Read This Book:

- Discover the Bible's only stories about Jesus' childhood (Luke 2).
- See how Jesus ministered to all people, especially the poor and the outcast (Luke 4—8).
- Enjoy some of Jesus' most famous stories (Luke 10, 15—16).
- Learn how Jesus gave his life for our sins (Luke 22—24).

Behind the Scenes:

Imagine never hearing that Jesus was laid in a manger when he was born (Luke 2:7–11). Imagine not knowing the parable of the Good Samaritan (Luke 10:25–37). Or the parable of the son who left home, which is also known as the Prodigal Son (Luke 15:11–32). Imagine not knowing about Jesus' encounter with Zacchaeus (Luke 19:1–10).

We wouldn't have any of these stories without the Gospel of Luke.

Though the books of Matthew, Mark, and John tell many stories about Jesus, they don't include about one-third of the material in Luke. Luke is the most complete account of Jesus' life. Written by a doctor, it's a detailed, organized picture of Jesus' life and ministry.

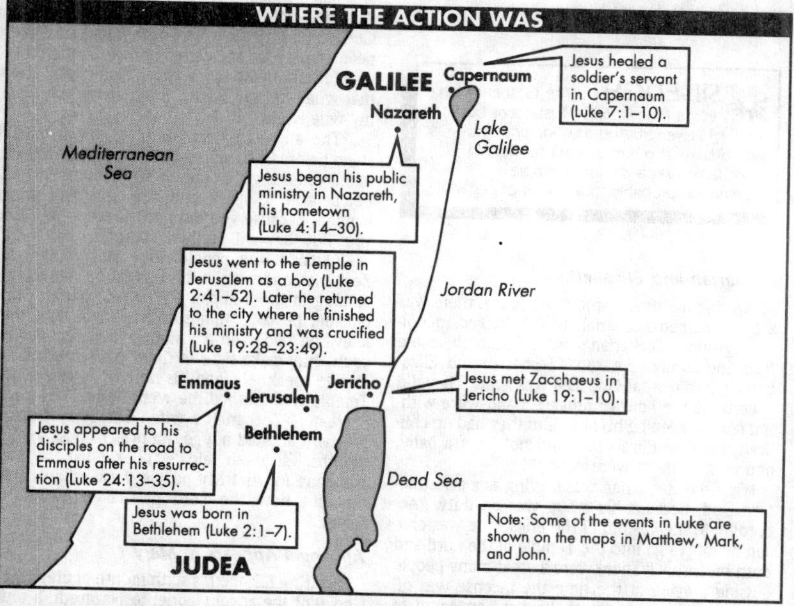
WHERE THE ACTION WAS
GALILEE
Capernaum
Jesus healed a soldier's servant in Capernaum (Luke 7:1–10).
Nazareth
Lake Galilee
Mediterranean Sea
Jesus began his public ministry in Nazareth, his hometown (Luke 4:14–30).
Jesus went to the Temple in Jerusalem as a boy (Luke 2:41–52). Later he returned to the city where he finished his ministry and was crucified (Luke 19:28–23:49).
Jordan River
Emmaus
Jerusalem
Jericho
Jesus met Zacchaeus in Jericho (Luke 19:1–10).
Jesus appeared to his disciples on the road to Emmaus after his resurrection (Luke 24:13–35).
Bethlehem
Dead Sea
Jesus was born in Bethlehem (Luke 2:1–7).
Note: Some of the events in Luke are shown on the maps in Matthew, Mark, and John.
JUDEA

WHEN THE ACTION WAS

Jesus was born — **BC/AD**

Jesus began his ministry — **25AD**

Jesus was crucified, rose from the dead, and went to heaven

Paul began his missionary work — **50AD**

Fire destroyed Rome

Romans destroyed the Temple in Jerusalem — **75AD**

100AD

Behind the Scenes (cont.): As you read the Gospel of Luke, you'll discover some important emphases. First, this book emphasizes that Jesus came for all people, not just the Jews. You'll also see Jesus' particular concern for women, the poor and the outcasts of the world. Then the book shows Jesus as God's Spirit-led Son who came to offer eternal life to all people who follow him.

Luke 19:10 says that "the Son of Man came to find lost people and save them." This book tells, in detail, the story of his coming. If you like the Gospel of Luke, check out the sequel: the book of Acts. It's written by the same author, and continues the story where Luke leaves off.

Luke Writes About Jesus' Life

1 Many have tried to report on the things that happened among us. 2They have written the same things that we learned from others—the people who saw those things from the beginning and served God by telling people his message. 3Since I myself have studied everything carefully from the beginning, most excellent[n] Theophilus, it seemed good for me to write it out for you. I arranged it in order 4to help you know that what you have been taught is true.

> **SIDELIGHT:** The Gospel of Luke is the longest New Testament book, with 1,151 verses. And the book of Acts—which Luke also wrote—isn't far behind. Since Luke was a doctor, a simple prescription probably took reams of paper!

Zechariah and Elizabeth

5During the time Herod ruled Judea, there was a priest named Zechariah who belonged to Abijah's group.[n] Zechariah's wife, Elizabeth, came from the family of Aaron. 6Zechariah and Elizabeth truly did what God said was good. They did everything the Lord commanded and were without fault in keeping his law. 7But they had no children, because Elizabeth could not have a baby, and both of them were very old.

8One day Zechariah was serving as a priest before God, because his group was on duty. 9According to the custom of the priests, he was chosen by lot[d] to go into the Temple of the Lord and burn incense.[d] 10There were a great many people outside praying at the time the incense was offered. 11Then an angel of the Lord appeared to Zechariah, standing on the right side of the incense table. 12When he saw the angel, Zechariah was startled and frightened. 13But the angel said to him, "Zechariah, don't be afraid. God has heard your prayer. Your wife, Elizabeth, will give birth to a son, and you will name him John. 14He will bring you joy and gladness, and many people will be happy because of his birth. 15John will be a great man for the Lord. He will never drink wine or beer, and even from birth, he will be filled with the Holy Spirit.[d] 16He will help many people of Israel return to the Lord their God. 17He will go before the Lord in spirit and power like Elijah. He will make peace between parents and their children and will bring those who are not obeying God back to the right way of thinking, to make a people ready for the coming of the Lord."

18Zechariah said to the angel, "How can I know that what you say is true? I am an old man, and my wife is old, too."

19The angel answered him, "I am Gabriel. I stand before God, who sent me to talk to you and to tell you this good news. 20Now, listen! You will not be able to speak until the day these things happen, because you did not believe what I told you. But they will really happen."

21Outside, the people were still waiting for Zechariah and were surprised that he was staying so long in the Temple. 22When Zechariah came outside, he could not speak to them, and they knew he had seen a vision in the Temple. He could only make signs to them and remained unable to speak. 23When his time of service at the Temple was finished, he went home.

24Later, Zechariah's wife, Elizabeth, became pregnant and did not go out of her house for five months. Elizabeth said, 25"Look what the Lord has done for me! My people were ashamed[n] of me, but now the Lord has taken away that shame."

An Angel Appears to Mary

26During Elizabeth's sixth month of pregnancy God sent the angel Gabriel to Nazareth, a town in Galilee, 27to a virgin.[d] She was engaged to marry a man named Joseph from the family of David. Her name was Mary. 28The angel came to

excellent This word was used to show respect to an important person like a king or ruler.
Abijah's group The Jewish priests were divided into twenty-four groups. See 1 Chronicles 24.
ashamed The Jewish people thought it was a disgrace for women not to have children.

her and said, "Greetings! The Lord has blessed
you and is with you."
29But Mary was very startled by what the angel
said and wondered what this greeting might
mean.
30The angel said to her, "Don't be afraid, Mary;
God has shown you his grace. 31Listen! You will
become pregnant and give birth to a son, and you
will name him Jesus. 32He will be great and
will be called the Son of the Most High. The
Lord God will give him the throne of King David,
his ancestor. 33He will rule over the people
of Jacob forever, and his kingdom will never
end."
34Mary said to the angel, "How will this happen since I am a virgin?"
35The angel said to Mary, "The Holy Spirit[d] will
come upon you, and the power of the Most High
will cover you. For this reason the baby will be
holy and will be called the Son of God. 36Now
Elizabeth, your relative, is also pregnant with a
son though she is very old. Everyone thought she
could not have a baby, but she has been pregnant
for six months. 37God can do anything!"
38Mary said, "I am the servant of the Lord. Let
this happen to me as you say!" Then the angel
went away.

Mary Visits Elizabeth

39Mary got up and went quickly to a town in
the hills of Judea. 40She came to Zechariah's
house and greeted Elizabeth. 41When Elizabeth
heard Mary's greeting, the unborn baby inside her
jumped, and Elizabeth was filled with the Holy
Spirit.[d] 42She cried out in a loud voice, "God has
blessed you more than any other woman, and he
has blessed the baby to which you will give birth.
43Why has this good thing happened to me, that
the mother of my Lord comes to me? 44When I
heard your voice, the baby inside me jumped with
joy. 45You are blessed because you believed that
what the Lord said to you would really happen."

Mary Praises God

46Then Mary said,
"My soul praises the Lord;
47 my heart rejoices in God my Savior,
48because he has shown his concern for his
humble servant girl.

GOD'S POWER

Power in Letting Go

Joni Eareckson loved to swim when she was young. She was an excellent diver too, and had even thought about trying out for the Olympics.

When she was seventeen, Joni and her friends went swimming in Chesapeake Bay. Joni dove into the unfamiliar waters, expecting to feel that cool, free-floating feeling she had come to love. Instead, she felt nothing. As her head struck the bottom, her spinal cord snapped—leaving her paralyzed from the neck down for the rest of her life.

Joni felt depressed and angry at the prospect of spending the rest of her life in a wheelchair. Most of her anger was aimed at God. "Oh God, how can you do this to me?" she prayed. "What have you done to me?"

Though God has never healed her physically, he did heal Joni's soul. And over the years she has grown into a beautiful free spirit. She sums it up this way: "When I had no choice but acceptance, trust, and surrender . . . it was as if I had finally gained emotional independence—through complete dependence on God."

Read **Luke 1:26–38** to see how God brought forth life in another teenage girl because she was ready to accept, trust, and surrender.

- How was Mary's response to God's actions different from or similar to Joni's?
- In what specific ways would you like to see God's power change your life?

CONSIDER . . .

- underlining the verses in this passage that speak most to you, and memorizing them.
- asking God to help you understand his unlimited power and the ways he chooses to use (or not to use) it.

FOR MORE, SEE . . .

- Psalm 31:14–24
- 2 Corinthians 12:7–10
- James 1:1–5

From now on, all people will say that I am
blessed,
49 because the Powerful One has done great
things for me.
His name is holy.
50God will show his mercy forever and ever
to those who worship and serve him.
51He has done mighty deeds by his power.
He has scattered the people who are
proud
and think great things about themselves.
52He has brought down rulers from their
thrones
and raised up the humble.
53He has filled the hungry with good things
and sent the rich away with nothing.
54He has helped his servant, the people of
Israel,
remembering to show them mercy
55as he promised to our ancestors,
to Abraham and to his children forever."
56Mary stayed with Elizabeth for about three
months and then returned home.

The Birth of John

57When it was time for Elizabeth to give birth,
she had a boy. 58Her neighbors and relatives heard
how good the Lord was to her, and they rejoiced
with her.
59When the baby was eight days old, they came
to circumcise[d] him. They wanted to name him
Zechariah because this was his father's name,
60but his mother said, "No! He will be named
John."
61The people said to Elizabeth, "But no one in
your family has this name." 62Then they made
signs to his father to find out what he would like
to name him.
63Zechariah asked for a writing tablet and
wrote, "His name is John," and everyone was surprised. 64Immediately Zechariah could talk again,
and he began praising God. 65All their neighbors
became alarmed, and in all the mountains of Judea people continued talking about all these
things. 66The people who heard about them wondered, saying, "What will this child be?" because
the Lord was with him.

Zechariah Praises God

67Then Zechariah, John's father, was filled with
the Holy Spirit and prophesied:[d]
68"Let us praise the Lord, the God of Israel,
because he has come to help his people and
has given them freedom.

BRAGGING

A Tale of Two Teenagers

Ted and Ed were graduating seniors. One was voted most popular; the other most respected. Both graduated with many awards.

Ed never talked about himself. He never seemed to mind not being in the spotlight.

But Ted had to be the center of attention. If he thought others missed the significance of his accomplishments, he quickly filled them in.

They were two of the state's best cross-country runners. Ted almost always finished first, and Ed almost always came in right behind him. They were both comfortable with that, and always managed to congratulate and praise each other after a race. In their final state meet, however, Ed finished first. Ted couldn't congratulate or praise him, or even accept congratulations for himself. He was only comfortable with being Number One.

Ted bragged a lot to get attention, but Ed didn't. Read **Luke 1:39–56** to see how God blessed a young girl, who didn't brag or take credit for herself.

- If Mary were in high school today, what do you think she would be like?
- Are you more like Ed or Ted? How does Mary's prayer in this passage apply to you?

C O N S I D E R . . .

- drawing a line with two endpoints labeled ED and TED. Place a pencil point where you think you fit on the line, and another where you would like to be on the line. Ask God to help you reach your goal.
- thinking of someone you know who is like Ed, and spending more time with that person.

F O R M O R E , S E E . . .

- Jeremiah 9:23–24
- Romans 12:3–5
- Philippians 2:5–11

69 He has given us a powerful Savior
from the family of God's servant David.
70 He said that he would do this
through his holy prophets[d] who lived long ago:
71 He promised he would save us from our enemies
and from the power of all those who hate us.
72 He said he would give mercy to our fathers
and that he would remember his holy promise.
73 God promised Abraham, our father,
74 that he would save us from the power of our enemies
so we could serve him without fear,
75 being holy and good before God as long as we live.

76 "Now you, child, will be called a prophet of the Most High God.
You will go before the Lord to prepare his way.
77 You will make his people know that they will be saved
by having their sins forgiven.
78 With the loving mercy of our God,
a new day from heaven will dawn upon us.
79 It will shine on those who live in darkness,
in the shadow of death.
It will guide us into the path of peace."

80 And so the child grew up and became strong
in spirit. John lived in the desert until the time
when he came out to preach to Israel.

The Birth of Jesus

2 At that time, Augustus Caesar[d] sent an order
that all people in the countries under Roman
rule must list their names in a register. 2 This was
the first registration;[n] it was taken while Quirinius was governor of Syria. 3 And all went to their
own towns to be registered.

4 So Joseph left Nazareth, a town in Galilee, and
went to the town of Bethlehem in Judea, known
as the town of David. Joseph went there because
he was from the family of David. 5 Joseph registered with Mary, to whom he was engaged[n] and
who was now pregnant. 6 While they were in
Bethlehem, the time came for Mary to have the
baby, 7 and she gave birth to her first son. Because
there were no rooms left in the inn, she wrapped
the baby with pieces of cloth and laid him in a box
where animals are fed.

Shepherds Hear About Jesus

8 That night, some shepherds were in the fields
nearby watching their sheep. 9 Then an angel of

> **SIDELIGHT:** When Mary wrapped Jesus with cloths (Luke 2:7), he probably couldn't move his arms because he was wrapped so tightly. In biblical times, people believed a good six-month "wrapping" prevented arms and legs from becoming crooked.

the Lord stood before them. The glory of the Lord
was shining around them, and they became very
frightened. 10 The angel said to them, "Do not be
afraid. I am bringing you good news that will be
a great joy to all the people. 11 Today your Savior
was born in the town of David. He is Christ,[d] the
Lord. 12 This is how you will know him: You will
find a baby wrapped in pieces of cloth and lying
in a feeding box."

13 Then a very large group of angels from
heaven joined the first angel, praising God and
saying:

14 "Give glory to God in heaven,
and on earth let there be peace among the people who please God."

15 When the angels left them and went back to
heaven, the shepherds said to each other, "Let's
go to Bethlehem. Let's see this thing that has happened which the Lord has told us about."

16 So the shepherds went quickly and found
Mary and Joseph and the baby, who was lying in
a feeding box. 17 When they had seen him, they
told what the angels had said about this child.
18 Everyone was amazed at what the shepherds
said to them. 19 But Mary treasured these things
and continued to think about them. 20 Then the
shepherds went back to their sheep, praising God
and thanking him for everything they had seen
and heard. It had been just as the angel had told
them.

21 When the baby was eight days old, he was
circumcised[d] and was named Jesus, the name
given by the angel before the baby began to grow
inside Mary.

Jesus Is Presented in the Temple

22 When the time came for Mary and Joseph to
do what the law of Moses taught about being
made pure,[n] they took Jesus to Jerusalem to
present him to the Lord. 23 (It is written in the law

registration Census. A counting of all the people and the things they own.
engaged For the Jewish people, an engagement was a lasting agreement. It could only be broken by divorce.
pure The law of Moses said that forty days after a Jewish woman gave birth to a son, she must be cleansed by a ceremony at the Temple. Read Leviticus 12:2-8.

of the Lord: "Every firstborn[d] male shall be given
to the Lord.")[n] 24 Mary and Joseph also went to
offer a sacrifice, as the law of the Lord says: "You
must sacrifice two doves or two young pigeons."[n]

Simeon Sees Jesus

25 In Jerusalem lived a man named Simeon who
was a good man and godly. He was waiting for the
time when God would take away Israel's sorrow,
and the Holy Spirit[d] was in him. 26 Simeon had
been told by the Holy Spirit that he would not die
before he saw the Christ[d] promised by the Lord.
27 The Spirit led Simeon to the Temple.[d] When
Mary and Joseph brought the baby Jesus to the
Temple to do what the law said they must do,
28 Simeon took the baby in his arms and thanked
God:

29 "Now, Lord, you can let me, your servant,
die in peace as you said.
30 With my own eyes I have seen your
salvation,
31 which you prepared before all people.
32 It is a light for the non-Jewish people to see
and an honor for your people, the
Israelites."

33 Jesus' father and mother were amazed at
what Simeon had said about him. 34 Then Simeon
blessed them and said to Mary, "God has chosen
this child to cause the fall and rise of many in
Israel. He will be a sign from God that many people will not accept 35 so that the thoughts of many
will be made known. And the things that will happen will make your heart sad, too."

Anna Sees Jesus

36 There was a prophetess,[d] Anna, from the family of Phanuel in the tribe[d] of Asher. Anna was
very old. She had once been married for seven
years. 37 Then her husband died, and she was a
widow for eighty-four years. Anna never left the
Temple but worshiped God, going without food
and praying day and night. 38 Standing there at
that time, she thanked God and spoke about Jesus
to all who were waiting for God to free Jerusalem.

Joseph and Mary Return Home

39 When Joseph and Mary had done everything
the law of the Lord commanded, they went home
to Nazareth, their own town in Galilee. 40 The little child grew and became strong. He was filled
with wisdom, and God's goodness was upon him.

"Every . . . Lord." Quotation from Exodus 13:2.
"You . . . pigeons." Quotation from Leviticus 12:8.

WORSHIP

Awesome Stuff

When you look up at the sky on a clear night, did you know:

- the nearest star to earth is four light-years away?
- the light your eyeball sees from a star may have begun its journey toward you—at 186,000 miles per second—before the birth of Christ?
- some of the stars you see in a night sky may not be stars but whole galaxies? They may be millions of stars that are so incredibly far away they appear to be just one pinpoint of light.
- our little corner of the universe is one of only a few places with light and activity? Most of space is vast emptiness with no stars or planets.
- the earth's place in the universe may be comparable to the place occupied by a grain of sand in our world? Awe-inspiring, isn't it? In **Luke 2:8–21** the shepherds also learned how worship can grow out of seeing beyond ourselves into God's awesome realm.
- How do the facts of Jesus' birth and the vastness of our universe compare or contrast?
- What does it tell you to know that the same God who made and watches over us became a human just so we could know him?

CONSIDER . . .

- listing five ways you can worship God more, then doing them.
- sitting under a starry sky and pondering God's vast power.

FOR MORE, SEE . . .

- Psalm 8:3–9
- Habbakuk 3:17–19
- Acts 4:24–31

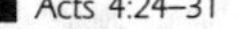

Jesus As a Boy

41Every year Jesus' parents went to Jerusalem
for the Passover[d] Feast. 42When he was twelve
years old, they went to the feast as they always
did. 43After the feast days were over, they started
home. The boy Jesus stayed behind in Jerusalem,
but his parents did not know it. 44Thinking that
Jesus was with them in the group, they traveled
for a whole day. Then they began to look for him
among their family and friends. 45When they did
not find him, they went back to Jerusalem to look
for him there. 46After three days they found Jesus
sitting in the Temple[d] with the teachers, listening
to them and asking them questions. 47All who
heard him were amazed at his understanding and
answers. 48When Jesus' parents saw him, they
were astonished. His mother said to him, "Son,
why did you do this to us? Your father and I were
very worried about you and have been looking for
you."
49Jesus said to them, "Why were you looking
for me? Didn't you know that I must be in my
Father's house?" 50But they did not understand
the meaning of what he said.
51Jesus went with them to Nazareth and was
obedient to them. But his mother kept in her
mind all that had happened. 52Jesus became wiser
and grew physically. People liked him, and he
pleased God.

The Preaching of John

3 It was the fifteenth year of the rule of Tiberius Caesar.[d] These men were under Caesar:
Pontius Pilate, the ruler of Judea; Herod, the ruler
of Galilee; Philip, Herod's brother, the ruler of
Iturea and Trachonitis; and Lysanias, the ruler of
Abilene. 2Annas and Caiaphas were the high
priests. At this time, the word of God came to
John son of Zechariah in the desert. 3He went all
over the area around the Jordan River preaching
a baptism of changed hearts and lives for the forgiveness of sins. 4As it is written in the book of
Isaiah the prophet:[d]

"This is a voice of one
who calls out in the desert:

FAMILY

Laboratory of Faith

"Jen, I don't want to leave." Jen Peters knew Kay Stone was serious. "Christianity is so much easier here. Everyone follows God, gets along, and it feels so good to get away from the pressure."

Kay's youth group had spent a weekend together in a mountain cabin. They had had a lot of fun and spent time learning about God. But now it was time to go home.

"Maybe I should take time off from school and stay here—or maybe even go to school in another town," Kay wondered aloud.

A few caring questions from Jen helped Kay talk about the real issue in her life. She was under stress at home, and the weekend away had provided a sense of escape. She didn't want to go back to the way it was.

"Kay, God has taught you much this weekend. And for every lesson he teaches, he provides a laboratory to test your new understanding and put it to work. Your family just might be your laboratory."

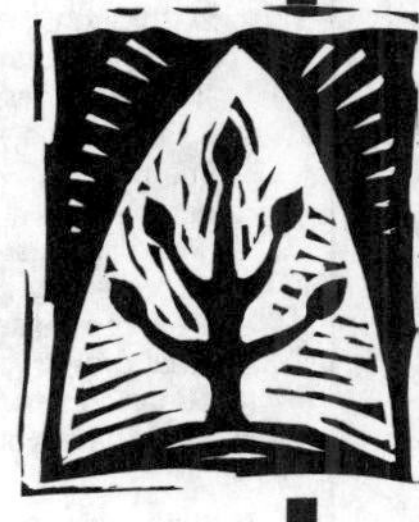

Kay thought for a moment, then nodded in agreement.

"Yeah," Kay sighed. "I guess there's no better place for God to help me grow."

Good or bad, families can challenge you to grow as a person and a Christian. **Luke 2:22–40** speaks of how God used Jesus' family to help him.

- Why does Kay need her family, even though things are hard? Why did Jesus need his family?
- Who are the "Simeons" and "Annas" in your life who help you see God's work in your life and your family? Why are these people important to you?

CONSIDER . . .

- telling your parent one good lesson you have learned because of your family.
- talking to a trusted adult if your family struggles feel overwhelming.

FOR MORE, SEE . . .

- Proverbs 22:6
- Matthew 12:46–50
- Ephesians 6:1–3

'Prepare the way for the Lord.
Make the road straight for him.
5Every valley should be filled in,
and every mountain and hill should be made flat.
Roads with turns should be made straight,
and rough roads should be made smooth.
6And all people will know about the salvation of God!' " *Isaiah 40:3-5*

7To the crowds of people who came to be baptized by John, he said, "You are all snakes! Who
warned you to run away from God's coming punishment? 8Do the things that show you really
have changed your hearts and lives. Don't begin
to say to yourselves, 'Abraham is our father.' I tell
you that God could make children for Abraham
from these rocks. 9The ax is now ready to cut
down the trees, and every tree that does not produce good fruit will be cut down and thrown into
the fire."[n]

10The people asked John, "Then what should
we do?"

11John answered, "If you have two shirts, share
with the person who does not have one. If you
have food, share that also."

12Even tax collectors came to John to be baptized. They said to him, "Teacher, what should
we do?"

13John said to them, "Don't take more taxes
from people than you have been ordered to take."

14The soldiers asked John, "What about us?
What should we do?"

John said to them, "Don't force people to give you money, and don't lie about them. Be satisfied with the pay you get."

15Since the people were hoping for the Christ[d]
to come, they wondered if John might be the
one.

16John answered everyone, "I baptize you with
water, but there is one coming who is greater

The ax . . . fire. This means that God is ready to punish his people who do not obey him.

SPIRITUAL GROWTH

Who Am I?

When Brian Ziegler was a boy, he used to love to make mud pies by the outdoor faucet on the side of his house. His mom would give him old pie pans, and he'd fill them with just the right mix of dirt and water.

"You had to be careful to mix it right," Brian recalls. "Too much dirt, and your pie would crumble. Too much water, and it would ooze."

As Brian got older, he didn't make mud pies as often. But he still enjoyed working with his hands to create. In junior high, Brian got into an art class and learned the basics of sculpture design.

"I was hooked from then on," Brian says with a smile. "I loved the idea of taking an image in my hands, and making it a reality in the clay. It's been fun ever since!"

Brian now works as a sculptor part-time after school. He has won several awards for his work through the school system, and plans to attend an art school in New York after he graduates.

"I want to design sculptures like you see around big corporate skyscrapers," says Brian, "and still have my own business."

Brian grins. "Wow, I never realized you could turn making mud pies into a career."

Brian's interest and skill in sculpting grew as he got older. In the same way, our ability to understand and appreciate God grows as we get older and expose ourselves to more of God's ways. Jesus also experienced this spiritual growth process. Read about it in **Luke 2:41–52**, especially verse 52.

- What do Jesus and Brian have in common based on the passage?
- How have you "continued to learn more and more" in the past year?

CONSIDER . . .

- thinking about all the ways you have changed in the past year, and thanking God for helping you grow spiritually.
- keeping a prayer journal to help log spiritual growth in your life.

FOR MORE, SEE . . .

- 1 Samuel 2:26
- Ephesians 4:4–16
- 1 Corinthians 13:11–13

than I am. I am not good enough to untie his sandals. He will baptize you with the Holy Spirit[d] and fire. 17He will come ready to clean the grain, separating the good grain from the chaff.[d] He will put the good part of the grain into his barn, but he will burn the chaff with a fire that cannot be put out."[n] 18And John continued to preach the Good News,[d] saying many other things to encourage the people.

19But John spoke against Herod, the governor, because of his sin with Herodias, the wife of Herod's brother, and because of the many other evil things Herod did. 20So Herod did something even worse: He put John in prison.

Jesus Is Baptized by John

21When all the people were being baptized by
John, Jesus also was baptized. While Jesus was
praying, heaven opened 22and the Holy Spirit[d]
came down on him in the form of a dove. Then a voice came from heaven, saying, "You are my Son, whom I love, and I am very pleased with you."

The Family History of Jesus

23When Jesus began his ministry, he was about thirty years old. People thought that Jesus was Joseph's son.

Joseph was the son[n] of Heli.
24Heli was the son of Matthat.
Matthat was the son of Levi.
Levi was the son of Melki.
Melki was the son of Jannai.
Jannai was the son of Joseph.
25Joseph was the son of Mattathias.
Mattathias was the son of Amos.
Amos was the son of Nahum.
Nahum was the son of Esli.
Esli was the son of Naggai.
26Naggai was the son of Maath.
Maath was the son of Mattathias.
Mattathias was the son of Semein.
Semein was the son of Josech.
Josech was the son of Joda.
27Joda was the son of Joanan.
Joanan was the son of Rhesa.
Rhesa was the son of Zerubbabel.

He will . . . out. This means that Jesus will come to separate good people from bad people, saving the good and punishing the bad.
son "Son" in Jewish lists of ancestors can sometimes mean grandson or more distant relative.

JUSTICE

Quiet Disasters

If forty thousand people were to die from an earthquake or hurricane, would it make the news? Of course.

But forty thousand people die every day—from hunger. And when was the last time you saw that on the news?

If you saw a rich person feasting while a poor child starved at the doorstep, would you be angry? Of course.

But did you know that the United States has less than 6 percent of the world's population, yet consumes more than 33 percent of the world's resources?

It may be hard to see yourself as superwealthy, especially when you compare your income with those of kids around you. But when compared to the average world citizen, you have great wealth. And you have a lot to offer a hurting world.

Luke 3:1–18 records John's advice to the people of his day who practiced "religion," but weren't supporting "justice." Read the passage to hear the warning he gives them—and us.

- What group of people might John relay his message to today?
- According to this passage, how should we define justice?

CONSIDER . . .

- writing a short speech that John the Baptist might deliver to your church.
- doing something to promote justice in the world. For example, spearhead a canned food drive, or volunteer at a local relief agency.

FOR MORE, SEE . . .

- Jeremiah 2:34–35
- Matthew 3:1–12
- John 1:19–34

Zerubbabel was the grandson of Shealtiel.
Shealtiel was the son of Neri.
28Neri was the son of Melchi.
Melchi was the son of Addi.
Addi was the son of Cosam.
Cosam was the son of Elmadam.
Elmadam was the son of Er.
29Er was the son of Joshua.
Joshua was the son of Eliezer.
Eliezer was the son of Jorim.
Jorim was the son of Matthat.
Matthat was the son of Levi.
30Levi was the son of Simeon.
Simeon was the son of Judah.
Judah was the son of Joseph.
Joseph was the son of Jonam.
Jonam was the son of Eliakim.
31Eliakim was the son of Melea.
Melea was the son of Menna.
Menna was the son of Mattatha.
Mattatha was the son of Nathan.
Nathan was the son of David.
32David was the son of Jesse.
Jesse was the son of Obed.
Obed was the son of Boaz.
Boaz was the son of Salmon.
Salmon was the son of Nahshon.
33Nahshon was the son of Amminadab.
Amminadab was the son of Admin.
Admin was the son of Arni.
Arni was the son of Hezron.
Hezron was the son of Perez.
Perez was the son of Judah.
34Judah was the son of Jacob.
Jacob was the son of Isaac.
Isaac was the son of Abraham.
Abraham was the son of Terah.
Terah was the son of Nahor.
35Nahor was the son of Serug.
Serug was the son of Reu.
Reu was the son of Peleg.
Peleg was the son of Eber.
Eber was the son of Shelah.
36Shelah was the son of Cainan.
Cainan was the son of Arphaxad.
Arphaxad was the son of Shem.
Shem was the son of Noah.
Noah was the son of Lamech.
37Lamech was the son of Methuselah.
Methuselah was the son of Enoch.
Enoch was the son of Jared.
Jared was the son of Mahalalel.
Mahalalel was the son of Kenan.
38Kenan was the son of Enosh.
Enosh was the son of Seth.
Seth was the son of Adam.
Adam was the son of God.

Jesus Is Tempted by the Devil

4 Jesus, filled with the Holy Spirit,[d] returned
from the Jordan River. The Spirit led Jesus
into the desert 2where the devil tempted Jesus for
forty days. Jesus ate nothing during that time, and
when those days were ended, he was very hungry.
3The devil said to Jesus, "If you are the Son of
God, tell this rock to become bread."
4Jesus answered, "It is written in the Scriptures:[d] 'A person does not live by eating only
bread.' "[n]
5Then the devil took Jesus and showed him all
the kingdoms of the world in an instant. 6The
devil said to Jesus, "I will give you all these kingdoms and all their power and glory. It has all been
given to me, and I can give it to anyone I wish.
7If you worship me, then it will all be yours."
8Jesus answered, "It is written in the Scriptures: 'You must worship the Lord your God and
serve only him.' "[n]
9Then the devil led Jesus to Jerusalem and put
him on a high place of the Temple.[d] He said to
Jesus, "If you are the Son of God, jump down. 10It
is written in the Scriptures:

'He has put his angels in charge of you
to watch over you.' *Psalm 91:11*

11It is also written:

'They will catch you in their hands
so that you will not hit your foot on a
rock.' " *Psalm 91:12*

12Jesus answered, "But it also says in the Scriptures: 'Do not test the Lord your God.' "[n]
13After the devil had tempted Jesus in every
way, he left him to wait until a better time.

Jesus Teaches the People

14Jesus returned to Galilee in the power of the
Holy Spirit,[d] and stories about him spread all
through the area. 15He began to teach in their synagogues,[d] and everyone praised him.

SIDELIGHT: *If you don't like being noticed when you visit different churches, you wouldn't have visited many synagogues in Jesus' day. It was customary for the synagogue leader to invite visitors to address the congregation. Jesus took advantage of the opportunity to preach in Luke 4:14–19.*

'A person . . . bread.' Quotation from Deuteronomy 8:3.
'You . . . him.' Quotation from Deuteronomy 6:13.
'Do . . . God.' Quotation from Deuteronomy 6:16.

16Jesus traveled to Nazareth, where he had
grown up. On the Sabbath[d] day he went to the
synagogue, as he always did, and stood up to read.
17The book of Isaiah the prophet[d] was given to
him. He opened the book and found the place
where this is written:
18"The Lord has put his Spirit in me,
because he appointed me to tell the Good
News[d] to the poor.
He has sent me to tell the captives they are
free
and to tell the blind that they can see
again. *Isaiah 61:1*
God sent me to free those who have been
treated unfairly *Isaiah 58:6*
19 and to announce the time when the Lord
will show his kindness." *Isaiah 61:2*
20Jesus closed the book, gave it back to the assistant, and sat down. Everyone in the synagogue
was watching Jesus closely. 21He began to say to
them, "While you heard these words just now,
they were coming true!"
22All the people spoke well of Jesus and were
amazed at the words of grace he spoke. They
asked, "Isn't this Joseph's son?"
23Jesus said to them, "I know that you will tell
me the old saying: 'Doctor, heal yourself.' You
want to say, 'We heard about the things you did
in Capernaum. Do those things here in your own

SIN

Proving Self

In his small high school in upstate New York, Josh Hartley was a star. He played everything from baseball to football, and enjoyed knowing he had helped win most of the trophies in the school display case. Some people thought he was stuck-up, but that didn't bother him much. The important thing was that everyone knew who Josh Hartley was.

Then things changed. Josh's mother got a new job in another part of the state. So Josh had to move from his small-town school to a supersize suburban school near New York City.

No problem, thought Josh. I may not be able to play every sport here, but I can still make my mark somewhere.

But time after time, Josh met with disappointment. He would try out, but when teams were posted, his name never appeared. And even if he had made the teams, the trophy case filled an entire hallway of the school. No chance of recognition there.

For the first time in his life Josh began to get in trouble. It was little things at first—skipping school and picking fights between classes. But then the problems began to get worse. Josh seemed out of control. He didn't care about school anymore, or much of anything else.

One year later, Josh was put in the county correctional center for arson. He had torched the high school field house.

Josh was released from prison on the condition that he receive counseling. After much therapy and prayer, Josh's attitude and outlook on life improved.

After Josh got out of prison, he told his parents, "I just didn't know who I was anymore. I wasn't an athlete. I didn't belong anywhere. So I found other ways to prove myself and get noticed."

Josh tried to prove himself in unhealthy ways. In **Luke 4:1–13** Satan also tempted Jesus to prove his identity by sinning against God. Read the passage to see how Jesus defeated the temptation to sin.

- What temptations did both Josh and Jesus face?
- Based on Jesus' example, what can you do to keep from sinning the next time you're tempted?

CONSIDER . . .

- identifying ways you want to "prove yourself and get noticed." Talk about one of the ways with a parent or trusted friend.
- telling a trusted friend about a sin you struggle with and asking him or her to pray for you.

FOR MORE, SEE . . .

- Genesis 3:1–6
- Matthew 4:1–11
- Mark 12:28–34

town!' " 24Then Jesus said, "I tell you the truth,
a prophet is not accepted in his hometown. 25But
I tell you the truth, there were many widows in
Israel during the time of Elijah. It did not rain in
Israel for three and one-half years, and there was
no food anywhere in the whole country. 26But Elijah was sent to none of those widows, only to a
widow in Zarephath, a town in Sidon. 27And there
were many with skin diseases living in Israel during the time of the prophet Elisha. But none of
them were healed, only Naaman, who was from
the country of Syria."

28When all the people in the synagogue heard
these things, they became very angry. 29They got
up, forced Jesus out of town, and took him to the
edge of the cliff on which the town was built.
They planned to throw him off the edge, 30but
Jesus walked through the crowd and went on his
way.

Jesus Forces Out an Evil Spirit

31Jesus went to Capernaum, a city in Galilee,
and on the Sabbath[d] day, he taught the people.
32They were amazed at his teaching, because he
spoke with authority. 33In the synagogue[d] a man
who had within him an evil spirit shouted in a
loud voice, 34"Jesus of Nazareth! What do you
want with us? Did you come to destroy us? I
know who you are—God's Holy One!"

35Jesus commanded the evil spirit, "Be quiet!
Come out of the man!" The evil spirit threw the
man down to the ground before all the people and
then left the man without hurting him.

36The people were amazed and said to each
other, "What does this mean? With authority and
power he commands evil spirits, and they come
out." 37And so the news about Jesus spread to every place in the whole area.

Jesus Heals Many People

38Jesus left the synagogue[d] and went to the
home of Simon.[n] Simon's mother-in-law was sick
with a high fever, and they asked Jesus to help
her. 39He came to her side and commanded the

Simon Simon's other name was Peter.

GOD'S WILL

Against the Grain

In the spring of 1981, a worker at a nuclear weapons plant near Amarillo, Texas, made an appointment to see Bishop Leroy Matthiesen of the diocese of Amarillo.

"I'm pushing sixty," said Bill Hobbles. "I've worked for Pantex for seventeen years, and I'm worried that, as a Christian, what I'm doing with my life may be morally wrong."

Bishop Matthiesen listened to Bill's dilemma, and decided to take action. Knowing that the plant was a cornerstone of the local economy, the bishop issued a public statement calling for workers in the nuclear-weapons industry to search their consciences and consider quitting and finding other jobs.

He was accused of treason in the papers and was publicly invited to accept a one-way ticket to the totalitarian country of his choice. Moreover, a local agency cut off all funds for one of his social-service programs.

An important part of living out our faith means following God's will as we understand it—even when our view is unpopular. And as Jesus found in **Luke 4:16–30**, sometimes it's hardest to follow God's will when we are with those who know us best.

- How is the bishop's experience like Jesus' experience in the passage? How are their experiences different?
- Drawing from the passage, how should you respond when you feel you must take a stand that others—even Christians—disagree with?

CONSIDER . . .

- choosing one way you will stand up for your beliefs at school, even though it may be unpopular with some people. For example, stick up for someone who is being picked on or take a stand on a controversial issue.
- writing out all the questions you have about God's will for your life and then talking to your youth pastor about them.

FOR MORE, SEE . . .

- Jeremiah 1:4–10
- Mark 6:1–6
- Romans 12:1–2

fever to leave. It left her, and immediately she got
up and began serving them.
40When the sun went down, the people
brought those who were sick to Jesus. Putting his
hands on each sick person, he healed every one
of them. 41Demons[d] came out of many people,
shouting, "You are the Son of God." But Jesus
commanded the demons and would not allow
them to speak, because they knew Jesus was the
Christ.[d]
42At daybreak, Jesus went to a lonely place, but
the people looked for him. When they found him,
they tried to keep him from leaving. 43But Jesus
said to them, "I must preach about God's kingdom to other towns, too. This is why I was sent."
44Then he kept on preaching in the synagogues[d] of Judea.

Jesus' First Followers

5 One day while Jesus was standing beside
Lake Galilee, many people were pressing all
around him to hear the word of God. 2Jesus saw
two boats at the shore of the lake. The fishermen
had left them and were washing their nets. 3Jesus
got into one of the boats, the one that belonged
to Simon,[n] and asked him to push off a little from
the land. Then Jesus sat down and continued to
teach the people from the boat.
4When Jesus had finished speaking, he said to
Simon, "Take the boat into deep water, and put
your nets in the water to catch some fish."
5Simon answered, "Master, we worked hard all
night trying to catch fish, and we caught nothing.
But you say to put the nets in the water, so I will."
6When the fishermen did as Jesus told them, they
caught so many fish that the nets began to break.
7They called to their partners in the other boat to
come and help them. They came and filled both
boats so full that they were almost sinking.
8When Simon Peter saw what had happened,
he bowed down before Jesus and said, "Go away
from me, Lord. I am a sinful man!" 9He and the
other fishermen were amazed at the many fish
they caught, as were 10James and John, the sons
of Zebedee, Simon's partners.

Jesus said to Simon, "Don't be afraid. From
now on you will fish for people." 11When the men
brought their boats to the shore, they left everything and followed Jesus.

Jesus Heals a Sick Man

12When Jesus was in one of the towns, there
was a man covered with a skin disease. When he
saw Jesus, he bowed before him and begged him,
"Lord, you can heal me if you will."
13Jesus reached out his hand and touched the
man and said, "I will. Be healed!" Immediately
the disease disappeared. 14Then Jesus said, "Don't
tell anyone about this, but go and show yourself
to the priest[n] and offer a gift for your healing, as
Moses commanded.[n] This will show the people
what I have done."
15But the news about Jesus spread even more.
Many people came to hear Jesus and to be healed
of their sicknesses, 16but Jesus often slipped away
to be alone so he could pray.

Jesus Heals a Paralyzed Man

17One day as Jesus was teaching the people, the
Pharisees[d] and teachers of the law from every
town in Galilee and Judea and from Jerusalem
were there. The Lord was giving Jesus the power
to heal people. 18Just then, some men were carrying on a mat a man who was paralyzed. They
tried to bring him in and put him down before
Jesus. 19But because there were so many people
there, they could not find a way in. So they went
up on the roof and lowered the man on his mat
through the ceiling into the middle of the crowd
right before Jesus. 20Seeing their faith, Jesus said,
"Friend, your sins are forgiven."

SIDELIGHT: If you think access to buildings is a new problem for disabled people, read Luke 5:18–20. The friends probably had to dig through layers of clay, reeds, grass, and branches to make a hole in the roof, since that's how most roofs were made in Jesus' time. The roofs were supported by wooden beams, which stretched from wall to wall.

21The Jewish teachers of the law and the Pharisees thought to themselves, "Who is this man
who is speaking as if he were God? Only God can
forgive sins."
22But Jesus knew what they were thinking and
said, "Why are you thinking these things?
23Which is easier: to say, 'Your sins are forgiven,'
or to say, 'Stand up and walk'? 24But I will prove
to you that the Son of Man[d] has authority on earth
to forgive sins." So Jesus said to the paralyzed
man, "I tell you, stand up, take your mat, and go
home."
25At once the man stood up before them,
picked up his mat, and went home, praising God.
26All the people were fully amazed and began
to praise God. They were filled with much re-

Simon Simon's other name was Peter.
show . . . priest The law of Moses said a priest must say when a Jewish person with a skin disease was well.
Moses commanded Read about this in Leviticus 14:1-32.

spect and said, "Today we have seen amazing things!"

Levi Follows Jesus

27After this, Jesus went out and saw a tax collector named Levi sitting in the tax collector's booth. Jesus said to him, "Follow me!" 28So Levi got up, left everything, and followed him.

29Then Levi gave a big dinner for Jesus at his house. Many tax collectors and other people were eating there, too. 30But the Pharisees[d] and the men who taught the law for the Pharisees began to complain to Jesus' followers, "Why do you eat and drink with tax collectors and sinners?"

31Jesus answered them, "It is not the healthy people who need a doctor, but the sick. 32I have not come to invite good people but sinners to change their hearts and lives."

Jesus Answers a Question

33They said to Jesus, "John's followers often give up eating[n] for a certain time and pray, just as the Pharisees[d] do. But your followers eat and drink all the time."

34Jesus said to them, "You cannot make the friends of the bridegroom give up eating while he is still with them. 35But the time will come when the bridegroom will be taken away from them, and then they will give up eating."

36Jesus told them this story: "No one takes cloth off a new coat to cover a hole in an old coat. Otherwise, he ruins the new coat, and the cloth from the new coat will not be the same as the old cloth. 37Also, no one ever pours new wine into old leather bags. Otherwise, the new wine will break the bags, the wine will spill out, and the leather bags will be ruined. 38New wine must be put into new leather bags. 39No one after drinking old wine wants new wine, because he says, 'The old wine is better.' "

Jesus Is Lord over the Sabbath

6 One Sabbath[d] day Jesus was walking through some fields of grain. His followers picked the heads of grain, rubbed them in their hands, and ate them. 2Some Pharisees[d] said, "Why do you do what is not lawful on the Sabbath day?"

3Jesus answered, "Have you not read what David did when he and those with him were hungry? 4He went into God's house and took and ate the holy bread, which is lawful only for priests to eat. And he gave some to the people who were with him." 5Then Jesus said to the Pharisees, "The Son of Man[d] is Lord of the Sabbath day."

Jesus Heals a Man's Hand

6On another Sabbath[d] day Jesus went into the synagogue[d] and was teaching, and a man with a crippled right hand was there. 7The teachers of the law and the Pharisees[d] were watching closely to see if Jesus would heal on the Sabbath day so they could accuse him. 8But he knew what they were thinking, and he said to the man with the crippled hand, "Stand up here in the middle of everyone." The man got up and stood there. 9Then Jesus said to them, "I ask you, which is lawful on the Sabbath day: to do good or to do evil, to save a life or to destroy it?" 10Jesus looked around at all of them and said to the man, "Hold out your hand." The man held out his hand, and it was healed.

11But the Pharisees and the teachers of the law were very angry and discussed with each other what they could do to Jesus.

Jesus Chooses His Apostles

12At that time Jesus went off to a mountain to pray, and he spent the night praying to God. 13The next morning, Jesus called his followers to him and chose twelve of them, whom he named apostles:[d] 14Simon (Jesus named him Peter), his brother Andrew, James, John, Philip, Bartholomew, 15Matthew, Thomas, James son of Alphaeus, Simon (called the Zealot[d]), 16Judas son of James, and Judas Iscariot, who later turned Jesus over to his enemies.

Jesus Teaches and Heals

17Jesus and the apostles[d] came down from the mountain, and he stood on level ground. A large group of his followers was there, as well as many people from all around Judea, Jerusalem, and the seacoast cities of Tyre and Sidon. 18They all came to hear Jesus teach and to be healed of their sicknesses, and he healed those who were troubled by evil spirits. 19All the people were trying to touch Jesus, because power was coming from him and healing them all.

20Jesus looked at his followers and said,

"You people who are poor are happy,
because the kingdom of God belongs to
you.
21You people who are now hungry are happy,
because you will be satisfied.
You people who are now crying are happy,
because you will laugh with joy.

22"People will hate you, shut you out, insult you, and say you are evil because you follow the Son of Man.[d] But when they do, you will be happy. 23Be full of joy at that time, because you have a great reward waiting for you in heaven.

give up eating This is called "fasting." The people would give up eating for a special time of prayer and worship to God. It was also done to show sadness and disappointment.

Their ancestors did the same things to the prophets.[d]
24“But how terrible it will be for you who are
rich,
because you have had your easy life.
25How terrible it will be for you who are full
now,
because you will be hungry.
How terrible it will be for you who are
laughing now,
because you will be sad and cry.
26“How terrible when everyone says only good
things about you, because their ancestors said the
same things about the false prophets.

Love Your Enemies

27“But I say to you who are listening, love your
enemies. Do good to those who hate you, 28bless
those who curse you, pray for those who are cruel
to you. 29If anyone slaps you on one cheek, offer
him the other cheek, too. If someone takes your
coat, do not stop him from taking your shirt.
30Give to everyone who asks you, and when
someone takes something that is yours, don’t ask
for it back. 31Do to others what you would want
them to do to you. 32If you love only the people
who love you, what praise should you get? Even
sinners love the people who love them. 33If you
do good only to those who do good to you, what
praise should you get? Even sinners do that! 34If
you lend things to people, always hoping to get
something back, what praise should you get?
Even sinners lend to other sinners so that they can
get back the same amount! 35But love your enemies, do good to them, and lend to them without
hoping to get anything back. Then you will have
a great reward, and you will be children of the
Most High God, because he is kind even to people
who are ungrateful and full of sin. 36Show mercy,
just as your Father shows mercy.

Look at Yourselves

37“Don’t judge other people, and you will not
be judged. Don’t accuse others of being guilty,
and you will not be accused of being guilty. Forgive, and you will be forgiven. 38Give, and you
will receive. You will be given much. Pressed
down, shaken together, and running over, it will
spill into your lap. The way you give to others is
the way God will give to you.”
39Jesus told them this story: “Can a blind person lead another blind person? No! Both of them
will fall into a ditch. 40A student is not better than
the teacher, but the student who has been fully
trained will be like the teacher.
41“Why do you notice the little piece of dust in
your friend’s eye, but you don’t notice the big
piece of wood in your own eye? 42How can you
say to your friend, ‘Friend, let me take that little
piece of dust out of your eye’ when you cannot
see that big piece of wood in your own eye! You
hypocrite![d] First, take the wood out of your own
eye. Then you will see clearly to take the dust out
of your friend’s eye.

Two Kinds of Fruit

43“A good tree does not produce bad fruit, nor
does a bad tree produce good fruit. 44Each tree is
known by its own fruit. People don’t gather figs
from thornbushes, and they don’t get grapes from
bushes. 45Good people bring good things out of
the good they stored in their hearts. But evil people bring evil things out of the evil they stored in
their hearts. People speak the things that are in
their hearts.

Two Kinds of People

46“Why do you call me, ‘Lord, Lord,’ but do not
do what I say? 47I will show you what everyone
is like who comes to me and hears my words and
obeys. 48That person is like a man building a
house who dug deep and laid the foundation on
rock. When the floods came, the water tried to
wash the house away, but it could not shake it,
because the house was built well. 49But the one
who hears my words and does not obey is like a
man who built his house on the ground without
a foundation. When the floods came, the house
quickly fell and was completely destroyed.”

Jesus Heals a Soldier’s Servant

7 When Jesus finished saying all these things
to the people, he went to Capernaum.
2There was an army officer who had a servant
who was very important to him. The servant was
so sick he was nearly dead. 3When the officer
heard about Jesus, he sent some older Jewish
leaders to him to ask Jesus to come and heal his
servant. 4The men went to Jesus and begged him,
saying, “This officer is worthy of your help. 5He
loves our people, and he built us a synagogue.”[d]
6So Jesus went with the men. He was getting
near the officer’s house when the officer sent
friends to say, “Lord, don’t trouble yourself, because I am not worthy to have you come into my
house. 7That is why I did not come to you myself.
But you only need to command it, and my servant
will be healed. 8I, too, am a man under the authority of others, and I have soldiers under my
command. I tell one soldier, ‘Go,’ and he goes.
I tell another soldier, ‘Come,’ and he comes.
I say to my servant, ‘Do this,’ and my servant
does it.”
9When Jesus heard this, he was amazed. Turning to the crowd that was following him, he said,
“I tell you, this is the greatest faith I have found
anywhere, even in Israel.”

[10]Those who had been sent to Jesus went back to the house where they found the servant in good health.

Jesus Brings a Man Back to Life

[11]Soon afterwards Jesus went to a town called Nain, and his followers and a large crowd traveled with him. [12]When he came near the town gate, he saw a funeral. A mother, who was a widow, had lost her only son. A large crowd from the town was with the mother while her son was being carried out. [13]When the Lord saw her, he felt very sorry for her and said, "Don't cry." [14]He went up and touched the coffin, and the people who were carrying it stopped. Jesus said, "Young man, I tell you, get up!" [15]And the son sat up and began to talk. Then Jesus gave him back to his mother.

[16]All the people were amazed and began praising God, saying, "A great prophet[d] has come to us! God has come to help his people."

[17]This news about Jesus spread through all Judea and into all the places around there.

John Asks a Question

[18]John's followers told him about all these things. He called for two of his followers [19]and sent them to the Lord to ask, "Are you the One who is to come, or should we wait for someone else?"

SIDELIGHT: The coffin where the boy lay when Jesus brought him back to life (Luke 7:11–15) wasn't like coffins today. In fact, it was probably just a board on which they laid the body. Just like today, wealthier people sometimes had more elaborate "funeral biers," as they were called.

[20]When the men came to Jesus, they said, "John the Baptist[d] sent us to you with this question: 'Are you the One who is to come, or should we wait for someone else?' "

[21]At that time, Jesus healed many people of

LEADERSHIP

Fish Out of Water

"Whales Commit Mass Suicide"

The 1986 newspaper headline alerted the community in Cape Cod about the baffling incident that had happened the night before. A herd, or "pod," of ninety-four whales beached themselves on the shores of Cape Cod. They just swam up onto the sand . . . and died.

That wasn't the first or last time whales have committed this strange act around the world. Newspapers periodically report stories of whales beaching themselves.

Several theories try to explain why whales do this. One of them is that the whales are following a basic herd instinct. Every pod has a leader. And if the leader becomes ill or disoriented, it might react by beaching itself. But since it's the leader, the other whales simply follow, even though it means death.

Sound crazy? Maybe, but it's not so unlike the way many people act. It's easy to follow leaders who say they have got the right answers, or know the truth.

People who pretend to have life's answers but live destructively are called hypocrites. In **Luke 6:39–49**, Jesus was saddened and angered to find hypocrisy in the religious leaders around him.

- How is the lead whale like the blind leaders Jesus talks about in this passage?
- What leaders do kids follow, even though the leaders' lifestyles seem destructive?

CONSIDER . . .

- listing "good fruits" and "bad fruits" you see in your own life, then asking God to take away the bad fruit.
- telling people whom you look to as leaders about the "good fruits" you see in their lives.

FOR MORE, SEE . . .

- Isaiah 29:13
- Amos 8:4–8
- James 1:19–27

their sicknesses, diseases, and evil spirits, and he
gave sight to many blind people. 22Then Jesus answered John's followers, "Go tell John what you
saw and heard here. The blind can see, the crippled can walk, and people with skin diseases are
healed. The deaf can hear, the dead are raised to
life, and the Good News[d] is preached to the poor.
23Those who do not stumble in their faith because
of me are blessed!"

24When John's followers left, Jesus began talking to the people about John: "What did you go
out into the desert to see? A reed[n] blown by the
wind? 25What did you go out to see? A man
dressed in fine clothes? No, people who have fine
clothes and much wealth live in kings' palaces.
26But what did you go out to see? A prophet?[d]
Yes, and I tell you, John is more than a prophet.
27This was written about him:

'I will send my messenger ahead of you,
who will prepare the way for you.' *Malachi 3:1*

28I tell you, John is greater than any other person
ever born, but even the least important person in
the kingdom of God is greater than John."

29(When the people, including the tax collectors, heard this, they all agreed that God's teaching was good, because they had been baptized by
John. 30But the Pharisees[d] and experts on the law
refused to accept God's plan for themselves; they
did not let John baptize them.)

31Then Jesus said, "What shall I say about the
people of this time? What are they like? 32They
are like children sitting in the marketplace, calling
to one another and saying,

'We played music for you, but you did not
dance;
we sang a sad song, but you did not cry.'

33John the Baptist came and did not eat bread or
drink wine, and you say, 'He has a demon[d] in
him.' 34The Son of Man[d] came eating and drinking, and you say, 'Look at him! He eats too much
and drinks too much wine, and he is a friend of
tax collectors and sinners!' 35But wisdom is
proved to be right by what it does."

A Woman Washes Jesus' Feet

36One of the Pharisees[d] asked Jesus to eat with

reed It means that John was not ordinary or weak like grass blown by the wind.

FAITH

Surrender

In Officer's Training School, Roger Curtis learned to speak to an officer in a specific way. First you say, "Sir." Then you say your name, "Candidate Curtis." Then you answer the question or respond to the officer. Then finish with, "Sir." Officers try their hardest to confuse you. For example:

Officer: "Candidate Curtis!"

Candidate: "Sir, Candidate Curtis, yes, Sir!"

Officer: "You've got a thread on your uniform, Curtis!"

Candidate: "Sir, Candidate Curtis, yes, Sir!"

Officer: "Tell you what I'm gonna do; I'm gonna pull it, and I want you to make a noise like a cannon."

Candidate: "Sir, Candidate Curtis, yes, Sir!"

Officer: "I pulled it!"

Candidate: "Sir, Candidate Curtis, boom, Sir!"

Maybe this approach sounds foolish to you. But in battle, the most important thing soldiers can do is to place themselves completely under the authority of their superior—even if they don't understand the reasoning behind the orders. That's real faith. **Luke 7:1–10** describes another soldier who understood that kind of faith, and reaped the benefits of it.

- How is the soldier in this passage like Candidate Curtis?
- Is your faith as strong as the officer's in this passage? Why or why not?

CONSIDER...

- trusting God with a part of your life you have never had the faith to let go of before.
- memorizing Hebrews 11:1 to learn God's definition of faith.

FOR MORE, SEE...

- Genesis 22:1–18
- Matthew 14:22–35
- Hebrews 11

him, so Jesus went into the Pharisee's house and
sat at the table. 37A sinful woman in the town
learned that Jesus was eating at the Pharisee's
house. So she brought an alabaster[d] jar of perfume
38and stood behind Jesus at his feet, crying. She
began to wash his feet with her tears, and she
dried them with her hair, kissing them many
times and rubbing them with the perfume.
39When the Pharisee who asked Jesus to come to
his house saw this, he thought to himself, "If Jesus
were a prophet,[d] he would know that the woman
touching him is a sinner!"
40Jesus said to the Pharisee, "Simon, I have
something to say to you."

Simon said, "Teacher, tell me."
41Jesus said, "Two people owed money to the
same banker. One owed five hundred coins[n] and
the other owed fifty. 42They had no money to pay
what they owed, but the banker told both of them
they did not have to pay him. Which person will
love the banker more?"
43Simon, the Pharisee, answered, "I think it
would be the one who owed him the most
money."

Jesus said to Simon, "You are right." 44Then
Jesus turned toward the woman and said to Simon, "Do you see this woman? When I came into
your house, you gave me no water for my feet,
but she washed my feet with her tears and dried
them with her hair. 45You gave me no kiss of
greeting, but she has been kissing my feet since I
came in. 46You did not put oil on my head, but she

coins Roman denarii. One coin was the average pay for one day's work.

NON-CHRISTIANS

Beyond the Great Divide

Janice Jenson was a riot. There was just no denying that. Tasha Smith hated her world history course, but Janice, who sat next to her, had a way of summing up every lecture that made it all seem like a funny movie. Her silly faces and off-the-wall comments sent Tasha rolling every time.

Tasha had to admit she liked Janice. But that made Tasha uneasy. She wasn't sure she was supposed to like Janice.

Janice had a reputation for wildness around school. She was a heavy drinker and usually had a whole string of boyfriends begging for her attention—which she freely gave. She was bad news, and everybody knew it.

"Tasha, why are hanging around with that girl?" her church friends would sometimes ask. "She could hurt your Christian witness."

Before long, Tasha began to get angry about her friends' attitude—and the internal struggle over Janice she still fought.

"How will people who don't know you ever get the chance if I'm unwilling to get to know them first?" Tasha asked God one day.

"They won't," a voice seemed to respond. Tasha smiled. She knew what she had to do now. She gladly spends time with her non-Christian friends—and shares Christ's love with them.

Tasha struggled with accepting non-Christians when others thought it was wrong. Jesus had to deal with the same problem within the religious community of his time. Read about his encounter with a "sinful woman" in **Luke 7:36–50**.

- What feelings do Tasha's church friends and the Pharisee in the passage share?
- If Jesus were a student in your school, whom might he spend the most time with?

CONSIDER . . .

- scanning your yearbook and asking God to lead you to people he wants you to spend time with.
- talking with your youth pastor about doing a youth group study on friendship evangelism.

FOR MORE, SEE . . .

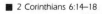

- Isaiah 61:1–2
- John 4:1–41
- 2 Corinthians 6:14–18

poured perfume on my feet. 47I tell you that her many sins are forgiven, so she showed great love. But the person who is forgiven only a little will love only a little."

48Then Jesus said to her, "Your sins are forgiven."

49The people sitting at the table began to say among themselves, "Who is this who even forgives sins?"

50Jesus said to the woman, "Because you believed, you are saved from your sins. Go in peace."

The Group with Jesus

8 After this, while Jesus was traveling through some cities and small towns, he preached and told the Good News[d] about God's kingdom. The twelve apostles[d] were with him, 2and also some women who had been healed of sicknesses and evil spirits: Mary, called Magdalene, from whom seven demons[d] had gone out; 3Joanna, the wife of Chuza (the manager of Herod's house); Susanna; and many others. These women used their own money to help Jesus and his apostles.

A Story About Planting Seed

4When a great crowd was gathered, and people were coming to Jesus from every town, he told them this story:

5"A farmer went out to plant his seed. While he was planting, some seed fell by the road. People walked on the seed, and the birds ate it up. 6Some seed fell on rock, and when it began to grow, it died because it had no water. 7Some seed fell among thorny weeds, but the weeds grew up with it and choked the good plants. 8And some seed fell on good ground and grew and made a hundred times more."

As Jesus finished the story, he called out, "You people who can hear me, listen!"

9Jesus' followers asked him what this story meant.

10Jesus said, "You have been chosen to know the secrets about the kingdom of God. But I use stories to speak to other people so that:

'They will look, but they may not see.
They will listen, but they may not
understand.' *Isaiah 6:9*

11"This is what the story means: The seed is God's message. 12The seed that fell beside the road is like the people who hear God's teaching, but the devil comes and takes it away from them so they cannot believe it and be saved. 13The seed that fell on rock is like those who hear God's teaching and accept it gladly, but they don't allow the teaching to go deep into their lives. They believe for a while, but when trouble comes, they give up. 14The seed that fell among the thorny weeds is like those who hear God's teaching, but they let the worries, riches, and pleasures of this life keep them from growing and producing good fruit. 15And the seed that fell on the good ground is like those who hear God's teaching with good, honest hearts and obey it and patiently produce good fruit.

Use What You Have

16"No one after lighting a lamp covers it with a bowl or hides it under a bed. Instead, the person puts it on a lampstand so those who come in will see the light. 17Everything that is hidden will become clear, and every secret thing will be made known. 18So be careful how you listen. Those who have understanding will be given more. But those who do not have understanding, even what they think they have will be taken away from them."

Jesus' True Family

19Jesus' mother and brothers came to see him, but there was such a crowd they could not get to him. 20Someone said to Jesus, "Your mother and your brothers are standing outside, wanting to see you."

21Jesus answered them, "My mother and my brothers are those who listen to God's teaching and obey it!"

Jesus Calms a Storm

22One day Jesus and his followers got into a boat, and he said to them, "Let's go across the lake." And so they started across. 23While they were sailing, Jesus fell asleep. A very strong wind blew up on the lake, causing the boat to fill with water, and they were in danger.

24The followers went to Jesus and woke him, saying, "Master! Master! We will drown!"

Jesus got up and gave a command to the wind and the waves. They stopped, and it became calm. 25Jesus said to his followers, "Where is your faith?"

The followers were afraid and amazed and said to each other, "Who is this that commands even the wind and the water, and they obey him?"

A Man with Demons Inside Him

26Jesus and his followers sailed across the lake from Galilee to the area of the Gerasene people. 27When Jesus got out on the land, a man from the town who had demons[d] inside him came to Jesus. For a long time he had worn no clothes and had lived in the burial caves, not in a house. 28When he saw Jesus, he cried out and fell down before him. He said with a loud voice, "What do you want with me, Jesus, Son of the Most High God? I beg you, don't torture me!" 29He said this because Jesus was commanding the evil spirit to come out of the man. Many times it had taken

hold of him. Though he had been kept under
guard and chained hand and foot, he had broken
his chains and had been forced by the demon out
into a lonely place.
30Jesus asked him, "What is your name?"
He answered, "Legion,"[n] because many demons were in him. 31The demons begged Jesus
not to send them into eternal darkness.[n] 32A
large herd of pigs was feeding on a hill, and the
demons begged Jesus to allow them to go into the
pigs. So Jesus allowed them to do this. 33When
the demons came out of the man, they went into
the pigs, and the herd ran down the hill into the
lake and was drowned.
34When the herdsmen saw what had happened, they ran away and told about this in the
town and the countryside. 35And people went to
see what had happened. When they came to
Jesus, they found the man sitting at Jesus' feet,
clothed and in his right mind, because the demons were gone. But the people were frightened.
36The people who saw this happen told the others
how Jesus had made the man well. 37All the people of the Gerasene country asked Jesus to leave,
because they were all very afraid. So Jesus got into
the boat and went back to Galilee.
38The man whom Jesus had healed begged to
go with him, but Jesus sent him away, saying,
39"Go back home and tell people how much God
has done for you." So the man went all over town
telling how much Jesus had done for him.

Jesus Gives Life to a Dead Girl and Heals a Sick Woman

40When Jesus got back to Galilee, a crowd welcomed him, because everyone was waiting for
him. 41A man named Jairus, a leader of the synagogue,[d] came to Jesus and fell at his feet, begging
him to come to his house. 42Jairus' only daughter,
about twelve years old, was dying.
While Jesus was on his way to Jairus' house,
the people were crowding all around him. 43A
woman was in the crowd who had been bleeding
for twelve years, but no one was able to heal her.
44She came up behind Jesus and touched the edge
of his coat, and instantly her bleeding stopped.
45Then Jesus said, "Who touched me?"
When all the people said they had not touched
him, Peter said, "Master, the people are all
around you and are pushing against you."
46But Jesus said, "Someone did touch me, because I felt power go out from me." 47When the
woman saw she could not hide, she came forward, shaking, and fell down before Jesus. While
all the people listened, she told why she had
touched him and how she had been instantly
healed. 48Jesus said to her, "Dear woman, you are
made well because you believed. Go in peace."
49While Jesus was still speaking, someone came
from the house of the synagogue leader and said
to him, "Your daughter is dead. Don't bother the
teacher anymore."
50When Jesus heard this, he said to Jairus,
"Don't be afraid. Just believe, and your daughter
will be well."
51When Jesus went to the house, he let only
Peter, John, James, and the girl's father and
mother go inside with him. 52All the people were
crying and feeling sad because the girl was dead,
but Jesus said, "Stop crying. She is not dead,
only asleep."
53The people laughed at Jesus because they
knew the girl was dead. 54But Jesus took hold of
her hand and called to her, "My child, stand up!"
55Her spirit came back into her, and she stood up
at once. Then Jesus ordered that she be given
something to eat. 56The girl's parents were
amazed, but Jesus told them not to tell anyone
what had happened.

Jesus Sends Out the Apostles

9 Jesus called the twelve apostles[d] together
and gave them power and authority over all
demons[d] and the ability to heal sicknesses. 2He
sent the apostles out to tell about God's kingdom
and to heal the sick. 3He said to them, "Take
nothing for your trip, neither a walking stick, bag,
bread, money, or extra clothes. 4When you enter
a house, stay there until it is time to leave. 5If
people do not welcome you, shake the dust off of
your feet[n] as you leave the town, as a warning
to them."
6So the apostles went out and traveled through
all the towns, preaching the Good News[d] and
healing people everywhere.

Herod Is Confused About Jesus

7Herod, the governor, heard about all the
things that were happening and was confused,
because some people said, "John the Baptist[d]
has risen from the dead." 8Others said, "Elijah has
come to us." And still others said, "One of the
prophets[d] who lived long ago has risen from the
dead." 9Herod said, "I cut off John's head, so who
is this man I hear such things about?" And Herod
kept trying to see Jesus.

More than Five Thousand Fed

10When the apostles[d] returned, they told Jesus

"Legion" Means very many. A legion was about five thousand men in the Roman army.
eternal darkness Literally, "the abyss," something like a pit or a hole that has no end.
shake . . . feet A warning. It showed that they had rejected these people.

everything they had done. Then Jesus took them with him to a town called Bethsaida where they could be alone together. 11But the people learned where Jesus went and followed him. He welcomed them and talked with them about God's kingdom and healed those who needed to be healed.

12Late in the afternoon, the twelve apostles came to Jesus and said, "Send the people away. They need to go to the towns and countryside around here and find places to sleep and something to eat, because no one lives in this place."

13But Jesus said to them, "You give them something to eat."

They said, "We have only five loaves of bread and two fish, unless we go buy food for all these people." 14(There were about five thousand men there.)

Jesus said to his followers, "Tell the people to sit in groups of about fifty people."

15So the followers did this, and all the people sat down. 16Then Jesus took the five loaves of bread and two fish, and looking up to heaven, he thanked God for the food. Then he divided the food and gave it to the followers to give to the people. 17They all ate and were satisfied, and what was left over was gathered up, filling twelve baskets.

Jesus Is the Christ

18One time when Jesus was praying alone, his followers were with him, and he asked them, "Who do the people say I am?"

19They answered, "Some say you are John the Baptist.[d] Others say you are Elijah.[n] And others say you are one of the prophets[d] from long ago who has come back to life."

20Then Jesus asked, "But who do you say I am?"

Peter answered, "You are the Christ[d] from God."

21Jesus warned them not to tell anyone, saying, 22"The Son of Man[d] must suffer many things. He will be rejected by the older Jewish leaders, the leading priests, and the teachers of the law. He will be killed and after three days will be raised from the dead."

23Jesus said to all of them, "If people want to follow me, they must give up the things they want. They must be willing to give up their lives daily to follow me. 24Those who want to save their lives will give up true life. But those who give up their lives for me will have true life. 25It is worth nothing for them to have the whole world if they themselves are destroyed or lost. 26If people are ashamed of me and my teaching, then the Son of Man[d] will be ashamed of them when he comes in his glory and with the glory of the Father and the holy angels. 27I tell you the truth, some people standing here will see the kingdom of God before they die."

Jesus Talks with Moses and Elijah

28About eight days after Jesus said these things, he took Peter, John, and James and went up on a mountain to pray. 29While Jesus was praying, the appearance of his face changed, and his clothes became shining white. 30Then two men, Moses and Elijah,[n] were talking with Jesus. 31They appeared in heavenly glory, talking about his departure which he would soon bring about in Jerusalem. 32Peter and the others were very sleepy, but when they awoke fully, they saw the glory of Jesus and the two men standing with him. 33When Moses and Elijah were about to leave, Peter said to Jesus, "Master, it is good that we are here. Let us make three tents—one for you, one for Moses, and one for Elijah." (Peter did not know what he was talking about.)

34While he was saying these things, a cloud came and covered them, and they became afraid as the cloud covered them. 35A voice came from the cloud, saying, "This is my Son, whom I have chosen. Listen to him!"

36When the voice finished speaking, only Jesus was there. Peter, John, and James said nothing and told no one at that time what they had seen.

Jesus Heals a Sick Boy

37The next day, when they came down from the mountain, a large crowd met Jesus. 38A man in the crowd shouted to him, "Teacher, please come and look at my son, because he is my only child. 39An evil spirit seizes my son, and suddenly he screams. It causes him to lose control of himself and foam at the mouth. The evil spirit keeps on hurting him and almost never leaves him. 40I begged your followers to force the evil spirit out, but they could not do it."

41Jesus answered, "You people have no faith, and your lives are all wrong. How long must I stay with you and put up with you? Bring your son here."

42While the boy was coming, the demon[d] threw him on the ground and made him lose control of himself. But Jesus gave a strong command to the evil spirit and healed the boy and gave him

Elijah A man who spoke for God and who lived hundreds of years before Christ. See 1 Kings 17.
Moses and Elijah Two of the most important Jewish leaders in the past. Moses had given them the law, and Elijah was an important prophet.

back to his father. 43All the people were amazed
at the great power of God.

Jesus Talks About His Death

While everyone was wondering about all that
Jesus did, he said to his followers, 44"Don't forget
what I tell you now: The Son of Man[d] will be
handed over to people." 45But the followers did
not understand what this meant; the meaning
was hidden from them so they could not understand. But they were afraid to ask Jesus about it.

Who Is the Greatest?

46Jesus' followers began to have an argument
about which one of them was the greatest. 47Jesus
knew what they were thinking, so he took a little
child and stood the child beside him. 48Then Jesus
said, "Whoever accepts this little child in my
name accepts me. And whoever accepts me accepts the One who sent me, because whoever is
least among you all is really the greatest."

Anyone Not Against Us Is for Us

49John answered, "Master, we saw someone
using your name to force demons[d] out of people.
We told him to stop, because he does not belong
to our group."
50But Jesus said to him, "Don't stop him, because whoever is not against you is for you."

A Town Rejects Jesus

51When the time was coming near for Jesus to
depart, he was determined to go to Jerusalem.
52He sent some men ahead of him, who went into
a town in Samaria to make everything ready for
him. 53But the people there would not welcome
him, because he was set on going to Jerusalem.
54When James and John, followers of Jesus, saw
this, they said, "Lord, do you want us to call
fire down from heaven and destroy those people?"[n]

Verse 54 Here, some Greek copies add: ". . . as Elijah did."

DECISION MAKING

A Soldier Decides

On June 5, 1944, Dwight Eisenhower sat at a table surrounded by all his advisers. The decision, however, was his alone.

It appeared there just might be a brief break in the horrible weather they were having. The question was whether to send the largest amphibious invasion force ever assembled across the stormy English Channel to attack Hitler's "Fortress Europe." Their efforts had been fruitless before, but the success of this mission was essential if the war was to be won.

Conditions of tide and moon wouldn't be right again for weeks, and by then the element of surprise could be lost. On the other hand, the predicted gale force winds in the channel could swamp the landing crafts and drown the entire army before it reached shore. All the eyes looked to General Eisenhower. He knew if he made the wrong choice, the results could be disastrous. After long minutes of silence, he spoke.

"We go!" he said.

The D-Day invasion was on, and the outcome of the war was decided—in favor of Britain and the Allies.

Making big decisions is hard, especially since we usually don't know all the consequences of our choices. In **Luke 9:51–62**, Jesus pointed out that important decisions can involve letting go of the past and taking a stand.

- How was General Eisenhower unlike the would-be followers in this passage?
- Are you willing to say to Jesus, "I'll follow you any place you go"? If not, what's holding you back?

CONSIDER . . .

- writing out all the important decisions you need to make soon and asking advice from several people you trust.
- asking your parent or youth leader to give his or her insight on how you can make better decisions.

FOR MORE, SEE . . .

- Joshua 24:14–15
- Proverbs 8
- Acts 5:1–11

55But Jesus turned and scolded them. 56Then[n] they went to another town.

> **SIDELIGHT:** The disciples' reaction to Jesus' not being welcomed in a Samaritan town (Luke 9:51–56) would have been common in Jesus' day, given the hatred between Jews and Samaritans at that time. A hundred years earlier, Jews had destroyed a Samaritan temple. Then, during the night, Samaritans had strewn human bones on the steps of the Jewish Temple in Jerusalem. To see Jesus' attitude toward the Samaritans, read John 4:5–10.

Following Jesus

57As they were going along the road, someone said to Jesus, "I will follow you any place you go."

58Jesus said to them, "The foxes have holes to live in, and the birds have nests, but the Son of Man[d] has no place to rest his head."

59Jesus said to another man, "Follow me!"

But he said, "Lord, first let me go and bury my father."

60But Jesus said to him, "Let the people who are dead bury their own dead. You must go and tell about the kingdom of God."

61Another man said, "I will follow you, Lord, but first let me go and say good-bye to my family."

62Jesus said, "Anyone who begins to plow a field but keeps looking back is of no use in the kingdom of God."

Jesus Sends Out the Seventy-Two

10 After this, the Lord chose seventy-two[n] others and sent them out in pairs ahead of him into every town and place where he planned to go. 2He said to them, "There are a great many people to harvest, but there are only a few workers. So pray to God, who owns the harvest, that he will send more workers to help gather his harvest. 3Go now, but listen! I am sending you out like sheep among wolves. 4Don't carry a purse, a bag, or sandals, and don't waste time talking with people on the road. 5Before you go into a house, say, 'Peace be with this house.' 6If peaceful people live there, your blessing of peace will stay with them, but if not, then your blessing will come back to you. 7Stay in the peaceful house, eating and drinking what the people there give you. A worker should be given his pay. Don't move from house to house. 8If you go into a town and the people welcome you, eat what they give you. 9Heal the sick who live there, and tell them, 'The kingdom of God is near you.' 10But if you go into a town, and the people don't welcome you, then go into the streets and say, 11'Even the dirt from your town that sticks to our feet we wipe off against you.[n] But remember that the kingdom of God is near.' 12I tell you, on the Judgment Day it will be better for the people of Sodom[n] than for the people of that town.

Jesus Warns Unbelievers

13"How terrible for you, Korazin! How terrible for you, Bethsaida! If the miracles[d] I did in you had happened in Tyre and Sidon,[n] those people would have changed their lives long ago. They would have worn rough cloth and put ashes on themselves to show they had changed. 14But on the Judgment Day it will be better for Tyre and Sidon than for you. 15And you, Capernaum,[n] will you be lifted up to heaven? No! You will be thrown down to the depths!

16"Whoever listens to you listens to me, and whoever refuses to accept you refuses to accept me. And whoever refuses to accept me refuses to accept the One who sent me."

Satan Falls

17When the seventy-two[n] came back, they were very happy and said, "Lord, even the demons[d] obeyed us when we used your name!"

18Jesus said, "I saw Satan fall like lightning from heaven. 19Listen, I have given you power to walk on snakes and scorpions, power that is greater than the enemy has. So nothing will hurt you. 20But you should not be happy because the spirits obey you but because your names are written in heaven."

Jesus Prays to the Father

21Then Jesus rejoiced in the Holy Spirit[d] and said, "I praise you, Father, Lord of heaven and earth, because you have hidden these things from the people who are wise and smart. But you have shown them to those who are like little children. Yes, Father, this is what you really wanted.

22"My Father has given me all things. No one knows who the Son is, except the Father. And no

Verse 55-56 Some copies read: "But Jesus turned and scolded them. And Jesus said, 'You don't know what kind of spirit you belong to. 56The Son of Man did not come to destroy the souls of people but to save them.' Then"
seventy-two Many Greek copies read seventy.
dirt . . . you A warning. It showed that they had rejected these people.
Sodom City that God destroyed because the people were so evil.
Tyre and Sidon Towns where wicked people lived.
Korazin, Bethsaida, Capernaum Towns by Lake Galilee where Jesus preached to the people.

one knows who the Father is, except the Son and those whom the Son chooses to tell."

23Then Jesus turned to his followers and said privately, "You are blessed to see what you now see. 24I tell you, many prophets[d] and kings wanted to see what you now see, but they did not, and they wanted to hear what you now hear, but they did not."

The Good Samaritan

25Then an expert on the law stood up to test Jesus, saying, "Teacher, what must I do to get life forever?"

26Jesus said, "What is written in the law? What do you read there?"

27The man answered, "Love the Lord your God with all your heart, all your soul, all your strength, and all your mind."[n] Also, "Love your neighbor as you love yourself."[n]

28Jesus said to him, "Your answer is right. Do this and you will live."

29But the man, wanting to show the importance of his question, said to Jesus, "And who is my neighbor?"

30Jesus answered, "As a man was going down from Jerusalem to Jericho, some robbers attacked him. They tore off his clothes, beat him, and left him lying there, almost dead. 31It happened that a Jewish priest was going down that road. When he saw the man, he walked by on the other side. 32Next, a Levite[n] came there, and after he went over and looked at the man, he walked by on the

"Love . . . mind." Quotation from Deuteronomy 6:5.
"Love . . . yourself." Quotation from Leviticus 19:18.
Levite Levites were members of the tribe of Levi who helped the Jewish priests with their work in the Temple. Read 1 Chronicles 23:24-32.

SHARING FAITH

Unknown Soldiers

Spitballs and paper airplanes were flying everywhere. One student was demonstrating his amazing mastery of crude sounds. Poor Edward Kimball. He was only nineteen, but he was responsible for this Sunday school class of half-crazed junior high boys. He did his best, but they were more concerned about spitballs, practical jokes, and nasty sounds than about God.

Ed was warm, gentle, and shy. But to the boys, he came across as dull. Many adults had serious doubts about Ed's future as a Sunday school teacher.

But Ed was persistent. He really cared about those boys. Realizing his weaknesses as a teacher, he decided he might be more successful meeting the boys one-to-one. One sunny day in April he paced up and down a Boston street, trying to get up nerve to walk into a shoe store where Dwight, one of his students, worked. Finally he did. In frightened, faltering words he told Dwight how God had made a difference in his life. When he looked up the boy was crying.

Not many people today remember what Ed did. Thousands of lives, however, were touched by Dwight L. Moody, the famous evangelist, who on that day in 1855 was led to faith in Christ by Edward Kimball.

It wasn't easy for Ed to share his faith. In **Luke 10:1–12**, Jesus explains that the way won't be easy, but his heart will guide and strengthen us as we obey him.

- Do you think some of the seventy-two people in this passage felt as "ungifted" as Ed did? Why did Jesus choose them? (See especially verse 2.)
- According to this passage, which quality was most important to Jesus: talent or obedience? Why is that?

C O N S I D E R . . .

- asking God to show you how you can be more obedient to him in sharing your faith.
- reading a book about Dwight L. Moody's life and ministry.

F O R   M O R E ,   S E E . . .

- Isaiah 6:1–8
- Matthew 28:16–20
- Mark 6:7–13

other side of the road.
33Then a Samaritan[n] trav-
eling down the road came to where the hurt man
was. When he saw the man, he felt very sorry for
him.
34The Samaritan went to him, poured olive
oil and wine[n] on his wounds, and bandaged
them. Then he put the hurt man on his own donkey and took him to an inn where he cared for
him.
35The next day, the Samaritan brought out
two coins,[n] gave them to the innkeeper, and
said, 'Take care of this man. If you spend more
money on him, I will pay it back to you when I
come again.'"

36Then Jesus said, "Which one of these three
men do you think was a neighbor to the man who
was attacked by the robbers?"

37The expert on the law answered, "The one
who showed him mercy."

SIDELIGHT: The Jerusalem-to-Jericho road where the man was robbed in Jesus' story (Luke 10:30) was notoriously dangerous. With a 3,600 foot drop in only seventeen miles, this narrow, steep, twisting path—nicknamed "The Bloody Way"—was the notorious hangout of robbers.

Samaritan Samaritans were people from Samaria. These people were part Jewish, but the Jews did not accept them as true Jews. Samaritans and Jews disliked each other.
olive oil and wine Oil and wine were used like medicine to soften and clean wounds.
coins Roman denarii. One coin was the average pay for one day's work.

SERVICE

Sweating on a Shingle

Minnie Burgeon wasn't looking forward to the rainy season.

"Oh, it's worse now than it was before they worked on it," says Minnie, who last year paid $2,000 to replace the roof on her home.

The roofing company Minnie used had done several jobs in her area— mostly for the elderly—and then had disappeared.

Minnie had no money to get the roof replaced again, so she contacted the Samaritan Connection, a service organization that matches people in need with volunteer labor.

The timing was bad. It was June, and hot. Everyone wanted to be swimming and boating, not baking on a rooftop. One youth group volunteered its time and energy for Minnie, but once the group members had spent a few hours tearing shingles off the sweltering roof, their resolve to help others waned.

"Hey, I'm sorry, but I don't think I can stay very long. I've got stuff around the house I'm supposed to do."

"Yeah, I've got a date tonight, and I've gotta do my hair."

"I told a friend I'd meet her at the mall in a little while, so I can't stay long."

The leader knew he had to do something or lose the whole work crew. He brought them downstairs to meet Minnie. She pointed to the water stains above her bed and talked about how she would lie in bed and worry as water dripped on her. Then she said, "Jesus has been good to me to send me you Samaritans."

Nobody left. Nobody complained again. They all finished the job and felt great. Minnie was no longer just a "service project." She was a neighbor.

Read **Luke 10:25–37** to find out who God says your neighbor is.

- How is your youth group like the one in the story? How is it like the men who encountered the hurt man in the passage?
- What can you do to become more like the Samaritan in the passage?

CONSIDER . . .

- helping a friend or neighbor with a job around the house.
- listing four ways you could serve others better and then doing one each week for the next four weeks.

FOR MORE, SEE . . .

- Matthew 22:34–46
- Mark 12:28–34
- Philippians 2:1–4

Jesus said to him, "Then go and do what he
did."

Mary and Martha

38While Jesus and his followers were traveling,
Jesus went into a town. A woman named Martha
let Jesus stay at her house. 39Martha had a sister
named Mary, who was sitting at Jesus' feet and
listening to him teach. 40But Martha was busy
with all the work to be done. She went in and
said, "Lord, don't you care that my sister has left
me alone to do all the work? Tell her to help me."
41But the Lord answered her, "Martha, Martha, you are worried and upset about many
things. 42Only one thing is important. Mary has
chosen the better thing, and it will never be taken
away from her."

Jesus Teaches About Prayer

11 One time Jesus was praying in a certain
place. When he finished, one of his followers said to him, "Lord, teach us to pray as Joh
taught his followers."
2Jesus said to them, "When you pray, say:
'Father, may your name always be kept holy.
May your kingdom come.
3Give us the food we need for each day.
4Forgive us for our sins,
because we forgive everyone who has don
wrong to us.
And do not cause us to be tempted.' "

Continue to Ask

5Then Jesus said to them, "Suppose one of yo
went to your friend's house at midnight and sa
to him, 'Friend, loan me three loaves of bread. 6
friend of mine has come into town to visit me, b
I have nothing for him to eat.' 7Your friend insic
the house answers, 'Don't bother me! The do
is already locked, and my children and I are i
bed. I cannot get up and give you anything.' 8I te
you, if friendship is not enough to make him g
up to give you the bread, your boldness will mak

WORRYING

First Letter Home

Dear Mom and Dad,

I hate college! I wish I were back home in Toledo in high school. I worry about tests. I worry about dates. I worry if anyone likes me. My studying never feels like it does me any good. I don't feel comfortable with friends like I did in high school. I even wake up and worry about the weather.

I never used to worry! What's happening to me?

Love, Moira

Dear Moira,

Sorry to hear you're so worried. We could tell you "don't worry," but even we know better.

One suggestion: Don't rely on others, or your accomplishments, or your busyness for your self-concept. If you do, there'll be lots of worry in your future. Take some time and sit still with God. He has less worrisome ways of helping us know who we are—apart from those other things. Rely on him to show you what he thinks of you.

Love, Mom & Dad

P.S. Don't worry!

Moira Jackson needed to see that she was loved and accepted just as she was, without doing anything. Read how Jesus helped another busy, fretful, worrying woman see that truth in **Luke 10:38–42**.

- Can you think of a time you acted like Martha in this passage?
- How would your "worry level" change if you had a better sense of God's love for you?

CONSIDER . . .

- sitting for five minutes in God's presence and just listening.
- writing out all your concerns and then talking to God about each one.

FOR MORE, SEE . . .

- Psalm 131
- Matthew 6:25–34
- 1 Peter 5:6–7

him get up and give you whatever you need. 9So
I tell you, ask, and God will give to you. Search,
and you will find. Knock, and the door will open
for you. 10Yes, everyone who asks will receive.
The one who searches will find. And everyone
who knocks will have the door opened. 11If your
children ask for a fish, which of you would give
them a snake instead? 12Or, if your children ask
for an egg, would you give them a scorpion?
13Even though you are bad, you know how to give
good things to your children. How much more
your heavenly Father will give the Holy Spirit[d] to
those who ask him!"

Jesus' Power Is from God

14One time Jesus was sending out a demon[d]
that could not talk. When the demon came out,
the man who had been unable to speak, then
spoke. The people were amazed. 15But some of
them said, "Jesus uses the power of Beelzebul,[d]
the ruler of demons, to force demons out of people."
16Other people, wanting to test Jesus, asked
him to give them a sign from heaven. 17But knowing their thoughts, he said to them, "Every kingdom that is divided against itself will be destroyed. And a family that is divided against itself
will not continue. 18So if Satan is divided against
himself, his kingdom will not continue. You say
that I use the power of Beelzebul to force out demons. 19But if I use the power of Beelzebul to
force out demons, what power do your people use
to force demons out? So they will be your judges.
20But if I use the power of God to force out
demons, then the kingdom of God has come to
you.
21"When a strong person with many weapons
guards his own house, his possessions are safe.
22But when someone stronger comes and defeats
him, the stronger one will take away the weapons
the first man trusted and will give away the possessions.
23"Anyone who is not with me is against me,
and anyone who does not work with me is working against me.

The Empty Person

24"When an evil spirit comes out of a person,
it travels through dry places, looking for a place to
rest. But when it finds no place, it says, 'I will go
back to the house I left.' 25And when it comes

PRAYER

Countdown to Victory

"Oh, I'll never get it right. There's just no cure. It's hopeless."

Maybe that's what a lot of scientists were thinking in the first part of the twentieth century, when a disease called polio crippled and killed millions. Hundreds of researchers looked frantically for a cure. But it seemed like an impossible task. Then in 1954, Dr. Jonas Salk announced that after two hundred attempts he had developed a vaccine. This terrible disease disappeared virtually overnight.

Later, a reporter asked Dr. Salk how it felt to have had two hundred failures and only one success. Salk replied that he had never experienced two hundred failures. He had learned two hundred lessons. And those lessons had enabled him to create a usable vaccine. Rather than viewing each unsuccessful attempt as a tragedy, Dr. Salk chose to see it as an opportunity to learn.

Dr. Salk saw a need and didn't stop until the need was met. Similarly, persistent prayer is what Jesus recommends as one of the best ways to find answers in life. Read the story Jesus told in **Luke 11:1–13**.

- How is Dr. Salk like the man who needed bread in Jesus' story?
- Based on the passage, how should you pray about problems you really care about?

CONSIDER . . .

- writing about seven concerns that are important to you, and praying about a different concern each day this week.
- making a pact with a friend to become your "prayer partner" for the next month. Meet at least once a week to share requests and pray for each other.

FOR MORE, SEE . . .

- Psalm 130
- Matthew 6:1–15
- Luke 18:1–8

back, it finds that house swept clean and made neat. 26Then the evil spirit goes out and brings seven other spirits more evil than it is, and they go in and live there. So the person has even more trouble than before."

People Who Are Truly Happy

27As Jesus was saying these things, a woman in the crowd called out to Jesus, "Happy is the mother who gave birth to you and nursed you."

28But Jesus said, "No, happy are those who hear the teaching of God and obey it."

The People Want a Miracle

29As the crowd grew larger, Jesus said, "The people who live today are evil. They want to see a miracle[d] for a sign, but no sign will be given them, except the sign of Jonah.[n] 30As Jonah was a sign for those people who lived in Nineveh, the Son of Man[d] will be a sign for the people of this time. 31On the Judgment Day the Queen of the South[n] will stand up with the people who live now. She will show they are guilty, because she came from far away to listen to Solomon's wise teaching. And I tell you that someone greater than Solomon is here. 32On the Judgment Day the people of Nineveh will stand up with the people who live now, and they will show that you are guilty. When Jonah preached to them, they were sorry and changed their lives. And I tell you that someone greater than Jonah is here.

Be a Light for the World

33"No one lights a lamp and puts it in a secret place or under a bowl, but on a lampstand so the people who come in can see. 34Your eye is a light for the body. When your eyes are good, your whole body will be full of light. But when your eyes are evil, your whole body will be full of darkness. 35So be careful not to let the light in you become darkness. 36If your whole body is full of light, and none of it is dark, then you will shine bright, as when a lamp shines on you."

Jesus Accuses the Pharisees

37After Jesus had finished speaking, a Pharisee[d] asked Jesus to eat with him. So Jesus went in and sat at the table. 38But the Pharisee was surprised when he saw that Jesus did not wash his hands[n] before the meal. 39The Lord said to him, "You Pharisees clean the outside of the cup and the dish, but inside you are full of greed and evil. 40You foolish people! The same one who made what is outside also made what is inside. 41So give what is in your dishes to the poor, and then you will be fully clean. 42How terrible for you Pharisees! You give God one-tenth of even your mint, your rue, and every other plant in your garden. But you fail to be fair to others and to love God. These are the things you should do while continuing to do those other things. 43How terrible for you Pharisees, because you love to have the most important seats in the synagogues,[d] and you love to be greeted with respect in the marketplaces. 44How terrible for you, because you are like hidden graves, which people walk on without knowing."

Jesus Talks to Experts on the Law

45One of the experts on the law said to Jesus, "Teacher, when you say these things, you are insulting us, too."

46Jesus answered, "How terrible for you, you experts on the law! You make strict rules that are very hard for people to obey, but you yourselves don't even try to follow those rules. 47How terrible for you, because you build tombs for the prophets[d] whom your ancestors killed! 48And now you show that you approve of what your ancestors did. They killed the prophets, and you build tombs for them! 49This is why in his wisdom God said, 'I will send prophets and apostles[d] to them. They will kill some, and they will treat others cruelly.' 50So you who live now will be punished for the deaths of all the prophets who were killed since the beginning of the world— 51from the killing of Abel to the killing of Zechariah,[n] who died between the altar and the Temple.[d] Yes, I tell you that you who are alive now will be punished for them all.

52"How terrible for you, you experts on the law. You have taken away the key to learning about God. You yourselves would not learn, and you stopped others from learning, too."

53When Jesus left, the teachers of the law and the Pharisees[d] began to give him trouble, asking him questions about many things, 54trying to catch him saying something wrong.

Don't Be Like the Pharisees

12 So many thousands of people had gathered that they were stepping on each other. Jesus spoke first to his followers, saying "Beware of the yeast of the Pharisees,[d] because they are hypocrites.[d] 2Everything that is hidden will be shown, and everything that is secret will be made known. 3What you have said in the dark will be heard in the light, and what you have

sign of Jonah Jonah's three days in the fish are like Jesus' three days in the tomb. See Matthew 12:40.
Queen of the South The Queen of Sheba. She traveled a thousand miles to learn God's wisdom from Solomon. Read 1 Kings 10:1-3.
wash his hands This was a Jewish religious custom that the Pharisees thought was very important.
Abel . . . Zechariah In the Hebrew Old Testament, the first and last men to be murdered.

whispered in an inner room will be shouted from the housetops.

4"I tell you, my friends, don't be afraid of people who can kill the body but after that can do nothing more to hurt you. 5I will show you the one to fear. Fear the one who has the power to kill you and also to throw you into hell. Yes, this is the one you should fear.

6"Five sparrows are sold for only two pennies, and God does not forget any of them. 7But God even knows how many hairs you have on your head. Don't be afraid. You are worth much more than many sparrows.

Don't Be Ashamed of Jesus

8"I tell you, all those who stand before others and say they believe in me, I, the Son of Man,[d] will say before the angels of God that they belong to me. 9But all who stand before others and say they do not believe in me, I will say before the angels of God that they do not belong to me.

10"Anyone who speaks against the Son of Man[d] can be forgiven, but anyone who speaks against the Holy Spirit[d] will not be forgiven.

11"When you are brought into the synagogues[d] before the leaders and other powerful people, don't worry about how to defend yourself or what to say. 12At that time the Holy Spirit will teach you what you must say."

Jesus Warns Against Selfishness

13Someone in the crowd said to Jesus, "Teacher, tell my brother to divide with me the property our father left us."

14But Jesus said to him, "Who said I should

BRAGGING

Cliffhangers

Pugslie Selman was by far the biggest kid around, and he didn't mind letting everyone know it. In a neighborhood full of tough guys, this loner was the undisputed champion. His real name was John, but nobody used it. The few guys he hung around with called him "Pugs," and most everyone else simply tried to stay out of his way.

Today was different, though. Instead of pushing people around, Pugs was on a ledge forty feet high, crying like a baby. He had come rock climbing with his buddies, and now he was stuck. He was afraid to try to go back down the way he had come up, but he couldn't trust the rope around his waist (or the boy who was holding it) enough to lean out and grab the rock above his head. So he clung to the cliff and cried.

Predictably, everyone on the ground laughed at Pugslie. They were yelling and joking about the "giant wimp." But then things changed. Paul Woods, a little guy that Pugslie liked to push around, climbed up the cliff face. "Everything will be all right, Pugs, " said Paul. "You'll be fine. Just follow me."

Then Paul climbed ahead of Pugslie, showing him each place to put his feet and hands. Before long, the guys on the ground were cheering Pugslie as he climbed over the top of the cliff and raised his fist into the air.

Pugslie is still big, and he's still tough. But because of Paul, Pugslie doesn't brag about his size so much. Paul showed Pugs that everyone has special gifts.

Jesus told a story about another man who thought he was big and tough. Like Pugslie, he had an "I'm the best" attitude. Read about his "fall" in **Luke 12:13–21**.

- What similarities can you see between Pugslie and the rich man in the passage?
- In what ways do you "store things up" for yourself? What does this passage say to you about that?

CONSIDER . . .

- listing the positive qualities of three of your friends and thanking God for giving them those gifts.
- looking up the word humility in the dictionary, and asking God to help you be humble.

FOR MORE, SEE . . .

- Daniel 4:19–37
- 1 Corinthians 1:26–31
- Ephesians 2:8–9

judge or decide between you?" 15Then Jesus said to them, "Be careful and guard against all kinds of greed. Life is not measured by how much one owns."

16Then Jesus told this story: "There was a rich man who had some land, which grew a good crop. 17He thought to himself, 'What will I do? I have no place to keep all my crops.' 18Then he said, 'This is what I will do: I will tear down my barns and build bigger ones, and there I will store all my grain and other goods. 19Then I can say to myself, "I have enough good things stored to last for many years. Rest, eat, drink, and enjoy life!"'

20"But God said to him, 'Foolish man! Tonight your life will be taken from you. So who will get those things you have prepared for yourself?'

21"This is how it will be for those who store up things for themselves and are not rich toward God."

SIDELIGHT: The rich man in Jesus' story (Luke 12:16–21) would probably have been a millionaire today. Most farmers stored their food supply in clay jars of various sizes. To have a barn or grain silo would indicate extreme wealth. Archaeologists have discovered some underground grain silos that are twenty-five feet wide and more than twenty feet deep.

Don't Worry

22Jesus said to his followers, "So I tell you, don't worry about the food you need to live, or about the clothes you need for your body. 23Life is more than food, and the body is more than clothes. 24Look at the birds. They don't plant or harvest, they don't have storerooms or barns, but God feeds them. And you are worth much more than birds. 25You cannot add any time to your life by worrying about it. 26If you cannot do even the little things, then why worry about the big things? 27Consider how the lilies grow; they don't work or make clothes for themselves. But I tell you that even Solomon with his riches was not dressed as beautifully as one of these flowers. 28God clothes the grass in the field, which is alive today but tomorrow is thrown into the fire. So how much more will God clothe you? Don't have so little faith! 29Don't always think about what you will eat or what you will drink, and don't keep worrying. 30All the people in the world are trying to get these things, and your Father knows you need them. 31But seek God's kingdom, and all the other things you need will be given to you.

Don't Trust in Money

32"Don't fear, little flock, because your Fathe[r] wants to give you the kingdom. 33Sell your posses-sions and give to the poor. Get for yourselve[s] purses that will not wear out, the treasure i[n] heaven that never runs out, where thieves can'[t] steal and moths can't destroy. 34Your heart will b[e] where your treasure is.

Always Be Ready

35"Be dressed, ready for service, and have you[r] lamps shining. 36Be like servants who are waitin[g] for their master to come home from a weddin[g] party. When he comes and knocks, the servant[s] immediately open the door for him. 37They will b[e] blessed when their master comes home, becaus[e] he sees that they were watching for him. I tell yo[u] the truth, the master will dress himself to serv[e] and tell the servants to sit at the table, and he wi[ll] serve them. 38Those servants will be happy whe[n] he comes in and finds them still waiting, even [if] it is midnight or later.

39"Remember this: If the owner of the hous[e] knew what time a thief was coming, he woul[d] not allow the thief to enter his house. 40So yo[u] also must be ready, because the Son of Man[d] wi[ll] come at a time when you don't expect him!"

Who Is the Trusted Servant?

41Peter said, "Lord, did you tell this story to [us] or to all people?"

42The Lord said, "Who is the wise and truste[d] servant that the master trusts to give the oth[er] servants their food at the right time? 43When th[e] master comes and finds the servant doing h[is] work, the servant will be blessed. 44I tell you th[e] truth, the master will choose that servant to tak[e] care of everything he owns. 45But suppose the se[r]vant thinks to himself, 'My master will not com[e] back soon,' and he begins to beat the other se[r]vants, men and women, and to eat and drink an[d] get drunk. 46The master will come when that se[r]vant is not ready and is not expecting him. Th[en] the master will cut him in pieces and send hi[m] away to be with the others who don't obey.

47"The servant who knows what his mast[er] wants but is not ready, or who does not do wh[at] the master wants, will be beaten with ma[ny] blows! 48But the servant who does not kno[w] what his master wants and does things th[at] should be punished will be beaten with fe[w] blows. From everyone who has been given muc[h] much will be demanded. And from the o[ne] trusted with much, much more will be expecte[d].

Jesus Causes Division

49"I came to set fire to the world, and [I] wish it were already burning! 50I have a b[a]

tism[n] to suffer through, and I feel very
troubled until it is over. 51Do you think I came
to give peace to the earth? No, I tell you, I came
to divide it. 52From now on, a family with five
people will be divided, three against two, and
two against three. 53They will be divided: father
against son and son against father, mother against
daughter and daughter against mother, mother-
in-law against daughter-in-law and daughter-
in-law against mother-in-law."

Understanding the Times

54Then Jesus said to the people, "When you see
clouds coming up in the west, you say, 'It's going
to rain,' and it happens. 55When you feel the wind
begin to blow from the south, you say, 'It will be
a hot day,' and it happens. 56Hypocrites![d] You
know how to understand the appearance of the
earth and sky. Why don't you understand what is
happening now?

I . . . baptism Jesus was talking about the suffering he would soon go through.

MONEY

It's Only Money!

By the time he was thirty, Millard Fuller had achieved the American Dream. He was worth more than $1 million and lived a lifestyle that showed it. He drove a fancy car, lived in a huge house, owned lots of land, and generally enjoyed the things his money could buy. He and his wife, Linda, had just about anything that a young couple could want, except. . . .

Except what? Well, they weren't sure. All Millard and Linda did know was that they weren't happy.

"We just thought there must be something more to life," Millard explains.

On the advice of a friend, Millard and Linda turned to God. They spent time reading the Bible and praying with other Christians at Koinonia Farms. What could they do? What should they do?

"By seeing other Christians' lifestyles," explains Linda, "we quickly saw there was much more to life than the success money can bring. We realized God had a purpose for us. And we were determined to find out what it was."

Finally, they received the answer to their prayers. They believed God wanted them to start something new. Something big. They believed God wanted them to start over.

So they did. They sold off their businesses and their big house, and gave the money away. They sold their land, their boats, their horses, their cattle. In fact, they got rid of just about everything.

After this, they didn't go on tour to brag about how kind they were, or how many points they had earned with God. Instead, they continued to pray about what God was calling them toward. For more than five years, they worked at various mission stations, continuing to pray. Finally, at God's prompting, they formed Habitat for Humanity, a world-wide group that seeks to eliminate all substandard housing. Because the Fullers were able to give everything away and listen to God, thousands of families go to bed each night in safe, secure homes.

One of the passages that helped the Fullers make their decision was **Luke 12:32–40**. Read it and see if you can understand their actions.

- How did these verses influence the Fullers?
- What can you do to apply Jesus' words in this passage?

CONSIDER . . .

- deciding to give a specific portion of your money to your church or other charity.
- keeping a list of all the money you spend in a week. Sit down with your list and see who really determines how you spend it. Then pray for the freedom to give everything to God.

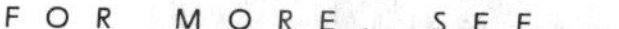

FOR MORE, SEE . . .

- Isaiah 58:6–11
- Matthew 6:19–21
- 2 Corinthians 9:6–9

Settle Your Problems

57"Why can't you decide for yourselves what is
right? 58If your enemy is taking you to court, try
hard to settle it on the way. If you don't, your
enemy might take you to the judge, and the judge
might turn you over to the officer, and the officer
might throw you into jail. 59I tell you, you will not
get out of there until you have paid everything
you owe."

Change Your Hearts

13 At that time some people were there
who told Jesus that Pilate[n] had killed
some people from Galilee while they were worshiping. He mixed their blood with the blood of
the animals they were sacrificing to God. 2Jesus
answered, "Do you think this happened to them
because they were more sinful than all others
from Galilee? 3No, I tell you. But unless you
change your hearts and lives, you will be destroyed as they were! 4What about those eighteen
people who died when the tower of Siloam fell on
them? Do you think they were more sinful than
all the others who live in Jerusalem? 5No, I tell
you. But unless you change your hearts and lives,
you will all be destroyed too!"

The Useless Tree

6Jesus told this story: "A man had a fig tree
planted in his vineyard. He came looking for some
fruit on the tree, but he found none. 7So the man
said to his gardener, 'I have been looking for fruit
on this tree for three years, but I never find any.
Cut it down. Why should it waste the ground?'
8But the servant answered, 'Master, let the tree
have one more year to produce fruit. Let me dig

Pilate Pontius Pilate was the Roman governor of Judea from A.D. 26 to A.D. 36.

SPIRITUAL GROWTH

Every Day Counts

Tim Richard was a friend of mine, in an unusual way. We met by accident and had very little in common. We liked different foods, different sports, different girls, and we each had our own definition of a "good time." We did share two things, though: we had the same birthday and we loved the same God. Sometimes this was all we could agree on, but we usually enjoyed our time together.

When we were eighteen, Tim died suddenly of a heart attack. He said he wasn't feeling well, and he passed out by the time the paramedics got to him. He was dead hours later. Through my tears, I realized that I didn't have anyone to share my birthday with. And I wasn't so sure about the God that I loved. Why did this happen? Everybody knows that teenagers aren't supposed to die, right?

A few days later, Tim's family and friends got together to mourn his death. As we sat around talking, somebody told a story about Tim that brought a smile to our faces. Before long, all of Tim's old jokes were flying, along with stories of how his short life had touched each of us. In that conversation, we saw that Tim had tried to live each day as though it were an important chance to serve God and others.

I think of my friend Tim often, because his life and death challenged me. I realized I don't know what will happen. So I must work to make each day count.

When people asked Jesus about their friends who had died, he gave them a challenge to use their days well. Read about it in **Luke 13:1–9**.

- How is Tim's story like the stories in the passage?
- What can you do to prepare yourself to "bear fruit" and so avoid being like the useless tree in the passage?

CONSIDER . . .

- imagining that you have only two weeks to live. Decide what your priorities would be, then do them.
- buying two small potted plants and taking one to a person who is sick, elderly or shut-in. Keep the other in your room as a reminder to pray for your special friend—and as a reminder to always try to bear fruit for God's kingdom.

FOR MORE, SEE . . .

- Psalm 90
- Matthew 7:15–23
- Galatians 6:7–10

up the dirt around it and put on some fertilizer. 9If the tree produces fruit next year, good. But if not, you can cut it down.' "

Jesus Heals on the Sabbath

10Jesus was teaching in one of the synagogues[d] on the Sabbath[d] day. 11A woman was there who, for eighteen years, had an evil spirit in her that made her crippled. Her back was always bent; she could not stand up straight. 12When Jesus saw her, he called her over and said, "Woman, you are free from your sickness." 13Jesus put his hands on her, and immediately she was able to stand up straight and began praising God.

14The synagogue leader was angry because Jesus healed on the Sabbath day. He said to the people, "There are six days when one has to work. So come to be healed on one of those days, and not on the Sabbath day."

15The Lord answered, "You hypocrites![d] Doesn't each of you untie your work animals and lead them to drink water every day—even on the Sabbath day? 16This woman that I healed, a daughter of Abraham, has been held by Satan for eighteen years. Surely it is not wrong for her to be freed from her sickness on a Sabbath day!" 17When Jesus said this, all of those who were criticizing him were ashamed, but the entire crowd rejoiced at all the wonderful things Jesus was doing.

Stories of Mustard Seed and Yeast

18Then Jesus said, "What is God's kingdom like? What can I compare it with? 19It is like a mustard seed that a man plants in his garden. The seed grows and becomes a tree, and the wild birds build nests in its branches."

20Jesus said again, "What can I compare God's kingdom with? 21It is like yeast that a woman took and hid in a large tub of flour until it made all the dough rise."

The Narrow Door

22Jesus was teaching in every town and village as he traveled toward Jerusalem. 23Someone said to Jesus, "Lord, will only a few people be saved?"

Jesus said, 24"Try hard to enter through the narrow door, because many people will try to enter there, but they will not be able. 25When the owner of the house gets up and closes the door, you can stand outside and knock on the door and say, 'Sir, open the door for us.' But he will answer, 'I don't know you or where you come from.' 26Then you will say, 'We ate and drank with you, and you taught in the streets of our town.' 27But he will say to you, 'I don't know you or where you come from. Go away from me, all you who do evil!' 28You will cry and grind your teeth with pain when you see Abraham, Isaac, Jacob, and all the prophets[d] in God's kingdom, but you yourselves thrown outside. 29People will come from the east, west, north, and south and will sit down at the table in the kingdom of God. 30There are those who have the lowest place in life now who will have the highest place in the future. And there are those who have the highest place now who will have the lowest place in the future."

Jesus Will Die in Jerusalem

31At that time some Pharisees[d] came to Jesus and said, "Go away from here! Herod wants to kill you!"

32Jesus said to them, "Go tell that fox Herod, 'Today and tomorrow I am forcing demons[d] out and healing people. Then, on the third day, I will reach my goal.' 33Yet I must be on my way today and tomorrow and the next day. Surely it cannot be right for a prophet[d] to be killed anywhere except in Jerusalem.

34"Jerusalem, Jerusalem! You kill the prophets and stone to death those who are sent to you. Many times I wanted to gather your people as a hen gathers her chicks under her wings, but you would not let me. 35Now your house is left completely empty. I tell you, you will not see me until that time when you will say, 'God bless the One who comes in the name of the Lord.' "[n]

Healing on the Sabbath

14 On a Sabbath[d] day, when Jesus went to eat at the home of a leading Pharisee,[d] the people were watching Jesus very closely. 2And in front of him was a man with dropsy.[n] 3Jesus said to the Pharisees and experts on the law, "Is it right or wrong to heal on the Sabbath day?" 4But they would not answer his question. So Jesus took the man, healed him, and sent him away. 5Jesus said to the Pharisees and teachers of the law, "If your child or ox falls into a well on the Sabbath day, will you not pull him out quickly?" 6And they could not answer him.

Don't Make Yourself Important

7When Jesus noticed that some of the guests were choosing the best places to sit, he told this story: 8"When someone invites you to a wedding feast, don't take the most important seat, because someone more important than you may have been invited. 9The host, who invited both of you, will come to you and say, 'Give this person your seat.' Then you will be embarrassed and will have

'God . . . Lord.' Quotation from Psalm 118:26.
dropsy A sickness that causes the body to swell larger and larger.

to move to the last place. 10So when you are invited, go sit in a seat that is not important. When
the host comes to you, he may say, 'Friend, move
up here to a more important place.' Then all the
other guests will respect you. 11All who make
themselves great will be made humble, but those
who make themselves humble will be made
great."

You Will Be Rewarded

12Then Jesus said to the man who had invited
him, "When you give a lunch or a dinner, don't
invite only your friends, your family, your other
relatives, and your rich neighbors. At another
time they will invite you to eat with them, and
you will be repaid. 13Instead, when you give a
feast, invite the poor, the crippled, the lame, and
the blind. 14Then you will be blessed, because
they have nothing and cannot pay you back. But
you will be repaid when the good people rise from
the dead."

A Story About a Big Banquet

15One of those at the table with Jesus heard
these things and said to him, "Happy are the people who will share in the meal in God's kingdom."
16Jesus said to him, "A man gave a big banquet

ETERNAL LIFE

Good Enough

Terry Wilson's favorite saying seemed to be "good enough."

"Hey, Terry!" his friend, Josh Simms, yelled. "How'd baseball tryouts go?"

"Good enough," he said.

"Did you clean your room?" Terry's mom would ask.

"Good enough," was the inevitable response.

"What about that song you were working on for Sunday, Terry?" his youth minister asked. "Will it be ready for Sunday service?"

The amazing thing about Terry is that whatever he did, it almost always was good enough. He usually did make the team or pass the test or win the award. If he wanted to, Terry could make anything he tried come out "good enough." It was even more surprising that he usually accomplished these feats without trying too hard. If a particular task was too demanding or required too much commitment, Terry simply shifted his energy into something else that promised an easier victory.

One summer Terry asked his friend Josh to be his prayer partner. They arranged to meet each week, and it started out well.

But then Terry started coming late, or not at all. Josh was always there, but Terry eventually quit. The commitment was too much, it seemed. That fall, after leaving home for the first time, Terry called Josh, in tears. He was so lonely and felt so "dead" inside. Josh sympathized with his friend and prayed for him, but there was little else he could do. If Terry's faith wasn't "good enough," it was his own fault.

Terry discovered that living the Christian life wasn't as easy as other things he had tried. And he had trouble paying the price to follow God. When Jesus talked about living with God forever, he said that it starts with giving your all to live for God here on earth. Listen to his words in **Luke 13:22–30**.

- What did Jesus say to the people who, like Terry, thought their lives were "good enough" to be worthy of eternal life?
- What are obstacles that keep you from the "narrow road" that leads to living with God forever?

CONSIDER . . .

- writing a short story or poem that describes what you think life in heaven will be like.
- selecting five goals that will help you walk the "narrow road" of eternal life with God. Put a copy of them in an envelope and give it to a trusted friend. Ask him or her to mail it to you in six months. Do your best to achieve the goals!

FOR MORE, SEE . . .

- Hosea 6:1–6
- Matthew 7:13–23
- Hebrews 6:7–12

and invited many people. 17When it was time to
eat, the man sent his servant to tell the guests,
'Come. Everything is ready.'
18"But all the guests made excuses. The first
one said, 'I have just bought a field, and I must go
look at it. Please excuse me.' 19Another said, 'I
have just bought five pairs of oxen; I must go and
try them. Please excuse me.' 20A third person
said, 'I just got married; I can't come.' 21So the
servant returned and told his master what had
happened. Then the master became angry and
said, 'Go at once into the streets and alleys of
the town, and bring in the poor, the crippled,
the blind, and the lame.' 22Later the servant
said to him, 'Master, I did what you commanded,
but we still have room.' 23The master said to the
servant, 'Go out to the roads and country lanes,
and urge the people there to come so my house
will be full. 24I tell you, none of those whom I invited first will eat with me.' "

SIDELIGHT: A party invitation in Jesus' day (Luke 14:15–24) included the day but never the hour. When the party was ready, slaves would go get the guests. To reject an invitation you had earlier accepted was the ultimate insult—as this story illustrates!

FRIENDS

A New Kind of Friend

Seventeen-year-old Amanda Hughes doesn't worry much about friends. Her attractive smile, engaging personality and sincere personal warmth make people simply want to be with her.

When she went on the service project, Amanda wasn't concerned about being in a new group. Questions like "will they like me?" never entered her mind. She was just excited about this new experience.

Amanda was surprised the first day she worked. She had expected to work on new home construction, interacting only with her crew. But her crew was renovating an existing home—a home full of people, one of whom, Charles, was close to her own age. For perhaps the first time in her life, she was nervous about making a friend. Her skin was a different color, and her life experience was vastly different. She and Charles seemed to have little in common.

Amanda cried as she told her prayer group of her desire to befriend Charles and his family. How could she do it? They were just so different.

One day, instead of taking her break with the work crew, she challenged Charles to a game of basketball. It was no contest, but they had a great time. The next day, he offered to help her paint, and again they had a lot of fun.

On their last work day, Amanda asked Charles if she could have his address and write to him.

"That'd be great," he exclaimed.

After exchanging addresses and phone numbers, they exchanged hugs. Amanda laughed inside as she thought about her confusion, and thanked God for helping bring two of his children just a little bit closer.

Sometimes we're friends only with those who are just like us. See how Jesus felt about that subject by reading **Luke 14:7–14**.

- How did Amanda demonstrate her understanding of Jesus' words in this passage?
- What do these verses say about you and your circle of friends?

CONSIDER . . .

- sending an anonymous letter to one of your friends. Fill it with encouragement from scripture, as well as other affirmations.
- arranging for your youth group to visit another church, preferably one of a different tradition and location (for instance, if you're in the suburbs, visit a city church). See what you can learn from each other.

FOR MORE, SEE . . .

- Ruth 1
- Philemon 4–7
- 1 John 4:13–21

The Cost of Being Jesus' Follower

25Large crowds were traveling with Jesus, and
he turned and said to them, 26"If anyone comes
to me but loves his father, mother, wife, children,
brothers, or sisters — or even life — more than me,
he cannot be my follower. 27Whoever is not willing to carry the cross and follow me cannot be my
follower. 28If you want to build a tower, you first
sit down and decide how much it will cost, to see
if you have enough money to finish the job. 29If
you don't, you might lay the foundation, but you
would not be able to finish. Then all who would
see it would make fun of you, 30saying, 'This person began to build but was not able to finish.'
31"If a king is going to fight another king, first
he will sit down and plan. He will decide if he and
his ten thousand soldiers can defeat the other king
who has twenty thousand soldiers. 32If he can't,
then while the other king is still far away, he will
send some people to speak to him and ask for
peace. 33In the same way, you must give up everything you have to be my follower.

Don't Lose Your Influence

34"Salt is good, but if it loses its salty taste, you
cannot make it salty again. 35It is no good for the
soil or for manure; it is thrown away.
"You people who can hear me, listen."

A Lost Sheep, a Lost Coin

15 The tax collectors and sinners all came
to listen to Jesus. 2But the Pharisees[d] and
the teachers of the law began to complain: "Look,
this man welcomes sinners and even eats with
them."
3Then Jesus told them this story: 4"Suppose
one of you has a hundred sheep but loses one of
them. Then he will leave the other ninety-nine
sheep in the open field and go out and look for the

FOLLOWING GOD

The Choice to Follow

André Bolte is a likable guy. He's athletic, funny, good-looking, and charming. In fact, when André joined the youth group at First Church, attendance went up. He was eager to learn more about following God and making friends.

André was also eager to please others. So it wasn't long before he agreed to participate in Bible study, Sunday school and other activities. After a few years, you couldn't go to any youth group event without seeing André or hearing how wonderful he was. And he was a great follower of God.

As time passed, André stayed active in the group. But new things came up, too. He started playing sports at school. He joined a couple of academic clubs. He got a new girlfriend. He got a job and a car.

André didn't want his friends to think he had forgotten them, so he kept volunteering for jobs in the group. He got so busy, though, that he began to do them poorly, or just forgot about them.

He still comes around the youth group occasionally. Not long ago, he came to encourage the younger kids to keep active—"Just like I am," he said. They didn't say much, though. Afterward, Michelle Jones commented: "André is a lot of talk and no action. He never does what he says he will. It seems pretty useless to me."

André wanted to follow God, but his overloaded lifestyle got in the way. When people asked Jesus what it takes to truly follow God, he had them make some hard choices. Read Jesus' requirements in **Luke 14:25–33**.

- How is André's situation like that of the king mentioned in the passage?
- What does this passage say about your priorities and following God?

CONSIDER . . .

- listing your top five priorities in life and taping the list to your mirror. Each day, pray for the chance to follow God in those areas of your life.
- keeping a daily log for the coming week, writing down everything you do and how long it takes. At the end of the week, compare your daily log to your priorities. What does it say about your schedule?

FOR MORE, SEE . . .

- Psalm 119:105–115
- Luke 9:23–26
- Philippians 3:8–11

lost sheep until he finds it. 5 And when he finds it,
he happily puts it on his shoulders 6 and goes
home. He calls to his friends and neighbors and
says, 'Be happy with me because I found my lost
sheep.' 7 In the same way, I tell you there is more
joy in heaven over one sinner who changes his
heart and life, than over ninety-nine good people
who don't need to change.
8 "Suppose a woman has ten silver coins,[n] but
loses one. She will light a lamp, sweep the house,
and look carefully for the coin until she finds it.
9 And when she finds it, she will call her friends
and neighbors and say, 'Be happy with me because I have found the coin that I lost.' 10 In the
same way, there is joy in the presence of the angels of God when one sinner changes his heart
and life."

The Son Who Left Home

11 Then Jesus said, "A man had two sons. 12 The
younger son said to his father, 'Give me my share
of the property.' So the father divided the property between his two sons. 13 Then the younger
son gathered up all that was his and traveled far
away to another country. There he wasted his
money in foolish living. 14 After he had spent everything, a time came when there was no food
anywhere in the country, and the son was poor

silver coins Roman denarii. One coin was the average pay for one day's work.

GOD'S LOVE

Stubborn Love

Stan Geary sat dumbfounded at the dining room table in Arlo Lane's house. For years Arlo had told stories about how he hated his mom because she didn't really care about him. Arlo had accused her of trying to control him, choose his friends for him, even determine the music he listened to.

He didn't really believe his mother loved him.

Arlo's mom had wanted him to stop smoking marijuana. She told him how hurtful the drug is, how addictive it can be. But Arlo claimed it was all a front—his mom just wanted to control him. She got her pleasure out of ruling his life, he thought.

But now, Stan didn't know what to believe. He knew at least some of Arlo's stories must have been true, but a quick glance around the table told him that they weren't true anymore. As Arlo and his mom laughed and joked, it was obvious that something—no, everything—had changed.

Stan didn't understand it, but he liked it. Later, when the guys were outside working on Arlo's ten-speed bike, Stan asked what had changed.

"It was awesome," Arlo said. "After one of our battles, Mom and I were both really upset. She started crying, you know? I yelled something like, 'What do you have to cry about?' She said she was crying because she loved me, and the drugs were hurting me."

"At that moment I looked at her and realized she was telling the truth. I don't know how—something just clicked inside. I realized she really does love me. So we decided to start all over again. It hasn't been easy, but I've quit smoking marijuana. Things have gotten a lot better!"

Arlo discovered how God's love can change things for the better. Jesus told stories that show how God's love can change people's lives. Check them out in **Luke 15:1–10**.

- How do you think the love Jesus talked about in this passage helped Arlo's relationship with his mom to change?
- What can you do to help you feel God's love for you?

C O N S I D E R . . .

- writing what you think God's love is like, then comparing your ideas with 1 Corinthians 13:4–7.
- reading the words to "Amazing Grace" from a hymnal. Rewrite them to fit your own life. Then sing your own song of thanks to God for his love!

F O R M O R E , S E E . . .

- Zephaniah 3:14–17
- John 3:16
- 1 John 3:1–3

and hungry. 15So he got a job with one of the
citizens there who sent the son into the fields to
feed pigs. 16The son was so hungry that he
wanted to eat the pods the pigs were eating, but
no one gave him anything. 17When he realized
what he was doing, he thought, 'All of my father's
servants have plenty of food. But I am here, almost dying with hunger. 18I will leave and return
to my father and say to him, "Father, I have
sinned against God and have done wrong to you.
19I am no longer worthy to be called your son, but
let me be like one of your servants." ' 20So the son
left and went to his father.

"While the son was still a long way off, his father saw him and felt sorry for his son. So the
father ran to him and hugged and kissed him.
21The son said, 'Father, I have sinned against God
and have done wrong to you. I am no longer worthy to be called your son.' 22But the father said to
his servants, 'Hurry! Bring the best clothes and
put them on him. Also, put a ring on his finger
and sandals on his feet. 23And get our fat calf and
kill it so we can have a feast and celebrate. 24My
son was dead, but now he is alive again! He was
lost, but now he is found!' So they began to celebrate.

25"The older son was in the field, and as he
came closer to the house, he heard the sound of
music and dancing. 26So he called to one of the
servants and asked what all this meant. 27The servant said, 'Your brother has come back, and your
father killed the fat calf, because your brother
came home safely.' 28The older son was angry and
would not go in to the feast. So his father went
out and begged him to come in. 29But the older
son said to his father, 'I have served you like a
slave for many years and have always obeyed your
commands. But you never gave me even a young
goat to have at a feast with my friends. 30But your
other son, who wasted all your money on prostitutes,[d] comes home, and you kill the fat calf for
him!' 31The father said to him, 'Son, you are al-

REBELLION

I'm Outta Here

"Have you seen Liz?" the nervous voice asked. "It's past midnight and she's not home yet. We had another argument. . . . Her mother and I are . . . worried."

How could this be happening? Liz Cole was great—very popular and liked by everyone in her group. Her parents were model church members. They seemed like the "perfect" family. But this night revealed that they weren't so "perfect" after all.

Three hours later, Liz came up the front steps. She looked angry. "I'm outta here. I just came home for some clothes."

"Your dad and I were worried, " her mother said.

She sneered. "I've got nothing to say to you."

But then she sat down, crying. She cried for a long time. In fact, all three of them did. And it turned out that they had plenty to say to each other. Before long, they were talking about how this "perfect" family had been spending a lot of energy concentrating on the rules and regulations involved with being so perfect, and not enough time telling how much they loved each other. The word love was used a lot more that night than it had been in a long time.

The Coles now know they don't have the perfect family. But they do love each other and have created a family where rebellion has been replaced by gentleness, respect, and forgiveness.

Liz's family was almost torn apart by rebellion. Jesus told a story about another family that dealt with rebellion. Read about it in **Luke 15:11–32**.

- What similarities and differences do you see between Liz's story and the one Jesus told?
- What things make you feel like rebelling? What might this passage say to you?

CONSIDER . . .

- walking around your block three times. Each time, pray about a different problem in your family life that makes you feel like rebelling.
- rewriting the story in Luke 15:11–32 to fit your family situation.

FOR MORE, SEE . . .

- Daniel 9:3–19
- John 3:16–21
- Hebrews 3:12—4:13

ways with me, and all that I have is yours. 32We
had to celebrate and be happy because your
brother was dead, but now he is alive. He was
lost, but now he is found.' "

True Wealth

16 Jesus also said to his followers, "Once
there was a rich man who had a manager to take care of his business. This manager
was accused of cheating him. 2So he called the
manager in and said to him, 'What is this I hear
about you? Give me a report of what you have
done with my money, because you can't be my
manager any longer.' 3The manager thought
to himself, 'What will I do since my master
is taking my job away from me? I am not
strong enough to dig ditches, and I am
ashamed to beg. 4I know what I'll do so that
when I lose my job people will welcome me
into their homes.'

5"So the manager called in everyone who owed
the master any money. He asked the first one,
'How much do you owe?' 6He answered, 'Eight
hundred gallons of olive oil.' The manager said to
him, 'Take your bill, sit down quickly, and write
four hundred gallons.' 7Then the manager asked
another one, 'How much do you owe?' He answered, 'One thousand bushels of wheat.' Then
the manager said to him, 'Take your bill and write
eight hundred bushels.' 8So, the master praised
the dishonest manager for being smart. Yes,
worldly people are smarter with their own kind
than spiritual people are.

9"I tell you, make friends for yourselves using
worldly riches so that when those riches are gone,
you will be welcomed in those homes that continue forever. 10Whoever can be trusted with a
little can also be trusted with a lot, and whoever
is dishonest with a little is dishonest with a lot. 11If
you cannot be trusted with worldly riches, then
who will trust you with true riches? 12And if you
cannot be trusted with things that belong to
someone else, who will give you things of your
own?

13"No servant can serve two masters. The servant will hate one master and love the other, or

MONEY

Tool or Master?

Money was tight for John Wesley. When he began his ministry in the 1700s, he had to budget to survive. After making careful calculations, he determined that he would need about sixty-five dollars a year to live on. Remember, this was a long time ago! Because there was little inflation during that time, John stayed on that yearly budget for the rest of his life. When he first made that decision, his annual income was about seventy dollars. John was able to give away five dollars that first year.

Later in his life, after he had written several books and become a famous minister, his income often exceeded three thousand dollars per year. But John still held to his budget and lived on sixty-five dollars. He gave the rest of the money to people who needed it or to charities that would help tell others about God's love for them.

How could John do this? Was it hard? We don't know the answers to those questions. All we do know is that at an early age John Wesley decided to make sure that money would be his servant, not his master.

John Wesley, who started the Christian movement we know as Methodism, understood the truth Jesus talks about in **Luke 16:1–13**. Read the passage to learn Jesus' view on money.

- How did John Wesley apply Jesus' teaching in this passage to his own life?
- How would heeding these verses change your spending habits?

CONSIDER . . .

- looking through the advertisements of two or three current magazines to see what they reveal about our society's view of money and material goods. How does society's view of money compare with Jesus'?
- making a commitment to give money to a worthwhile organization, such as your denomination's hunger-relief program, or an interdenominational hunger-relief organization.

FOR MORE, SEE . . .

- Proverbs 30:7–9
- Luke 16:19–31
- James 1:9–11

will follow one master and refuse to follow the other. You cannot serve both God and worldly riches."

God's Law Cannot Be Changed

[14]The Pharisees,[d] who loved money, were listening to all these things and made fun of Jesus.
[15]He said to them, "You make yourselves look
good in front of people, but God knows what is really in your hearts. What is important to people is hateful in God's sight.
[16]"The law of Moses and the writings of the
prophets[d] were preached until John[n] came. Since then the Good News[d] about the kingdom of God is being told, and everyone tries to enter it by
force. [17]It would be easier for heaven and earth to
pass away than for the smallest part of a letter in the law to be changed.

Divorce and Remarriage

[18]"If a man divorces his wife and marries another woman, he is guilty of adultery,[d] and the man who marries a divorced woman is also guilty of adultery."

The Rich Man and Lazarus

[19]Jesus said, "There was a rich man who always
dressed in the finest clothes and lived in luxury
every day. [20]And a very poor man named Lazarus,
whose body was covered with sores, was laid at
the rich man's gate. [21]He wanted to eat only the
small pieces of food that fell from the rich man's table. And the dogs would come and lick his
sores. [22]Later, Lazarus died, and the angels car-
ried him to the arms of Abraham.[d] The rich man
died, too, and was buried. [23]In the place of the
dead, he was in much pain. The rich man saw

John John the Baptist, who preached to people about Christ's coming (Matthew 3, Luke 3).

DECISION MAKING

But I Didn't Think . . .

Sixteen-year-old Alan McPherson was in a daze as he walked out of Mr. Lloyd's English class. His friends and classmates swirled by him in a rush to get to sixth period for their final exam of the day.

"How was I supposed to know all that stuff?" he asked out loud.

"Oh, come on, Alan," said his friend, Casey Adams. "You've known for weeks that our whole exam would come from Moby Dick. Don't act surprised now."

"Yeah, but it all seemed so complicated. There were so many details!"

"Tell the truth, Alan. Did you even read the book?" he asked.

He moaned. "Of course not! You know I watched the movie. It's a stupid book anyway. What do I care about Ahab and the Pequod or whatever? I didn't have time. I thought all I'd need was the basic plot, not every little detail."

"You know whose fault that is," Casey sighed as he left Alan by the lockers. "See ya later."

Alan did know whose fault it was. If only he could turn back the clock, he thought. If only he had made the right decision. Then he could have passed the test.

Alan made the wrong decision, and suffered for it. Fortunately, Alan's test was not a life-or-death matter. **Luke 16:19–31** records a story about another man's exam. But this man's test had eternal consequences.

- What similarities do you think exist between Alan and the rich man in the passage?
- How was the decision the rich man faced like decisions you face in life?

C O N S I D E R . . .

- using a concordance to find times Jesus talked about the importance of making wise choices. Look up "wisdom," "choice," "decide," or "decision."
- listing all the decisions you face right now, and asking your youth leader for advice on what choices would be best.

F O R M O R E , S E E . . .

- Proverbs 8:10–11
- Isaiah 58:3–9
- Romans 7:15–25

Abraham far away with Lazarus at his side. 24He
called, 'Father Abraham, have mercy on me! Send
Lazarus to dip his finger in water and cool my
tongue, because I am suffering in this fire!' 25But
Abraham said, 'Child, remember when you were
alive you had the good things in life, but bad
things happened to Lazarus. Now he is comforted
here, and you are suffering. 26Besides, there is a
big pit between you and us, so no one can cross
over to you, and no one can leave there and come
here.' 27The rich man said, 'Father, then please
send Lazarus to my father's house. 28I have five
brothers, and Lazarus could warn them so that
they will not come to this place of pain.' 29But
Abraham said, 'They have the law of Moses and
the writings of the prophets;[d] let them learn from
them.' 30The rich man said, 'No, father Abraham! If someone goes to them from the dead,
they would believe and change their hearts and
lives.' 31But Abraham said to him, 'If they will
not listen to Moses and the prophets, they
will not listen to someone who comes back
from the dead.' "

SIDELIGHT: To say that the rich man in Luke 16:19–31 wore "the finest clothes" would indicate the man spent a lot of money on his wardrobe. The outer clothes were purple, a sign of true wealth and royalty. Some of his clothes might have been made out of an Egyptian yellowed flax that was so luxurious it was called "woven air."

Sin and Forgiveness

17 Jesus said to his followers, "Things that
cause people to sin will happen, but how
terrible for the person who causes them to happen! 2It would be better for you to be thrown into
the sea with a large stone around your neck than
to cause one of these little ones to sin. 3So be
careful!

"If another follower sins, warn him, and if he
is sorry and stops sinning, forgive him. 4If he sins
against you seven times in one day and says that
he is sorry each time, forgive him."

FRIENDS

Helping Each Other

Everyone wants friends, and those friends have a great influence on our lives. That influence can be harmful, as it is when people push us to vandalize property, get sexually involved, or use drugs. But—as students in an Atlanta, Georgia, high school discovered—friends can also be positive influences.

Older teenagers decided they could use their influence on younger teenagers to make a positive difference. So they started a program to convince junior high kids that they could avoid sex before marriage and still be popular.

Did it make a difference?

- By the end of the eighth grade, students who didn't participate in the program were five times more likely to be sexually active than those who participated.
- A year later, the rate of sexual activity among those who had gone through this "peer-to-peer" program was 33 percent less than the rate of those not in the program.

Jesus talked about how friends can affect each other's behavior. He told people to use "positive peer pressure," rather than give in to others' sin. Read all about it in **Luke 17:1–10**.

- How does the Atlanta high school story relate to this passage?
- How does this passage help you evaluate your friendships? How does it challenge you to help your friends?

CONSIDER . . .

- listing activities you could do with your friends that would be both fun and positive.
- spending more time with the strong Christians in your youth group.

FOR MORE, SEE . . .

- Exodus 32:1–29
- Romans 1:11–12
- James 5:19–20

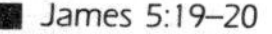

How Big Is Your Faith?

5The apostles[d] said to the Lord, "Give us more
faith!"
6The Lord said, "If your faith were the size of
a mustard seed, you could say to this mulberry
tree, 'Dig yourself up and plant yourself in the
sea,' and it would obey you.

Be Good Servants

7"Suppose one of you has a servant who has
been plowing the ground or caring for the sheep.
When the servant comes in from working in the
field, would you say, 'Come in and sit down to
eat'? 8No, you would say to him, 'Prepare something for me to eat. Then get yourself ready and
serve me. After I finish eating and drinking, you
can eat.' 9The servant does not get any special
thanks for doing what his master commanded.
10It is the same with you. When you have done
everything you are told to do, you should say, 'We
are unworthy servants; we have only done the
work we should do.' "

Be Thankful

11While Jesus was on his way to Jerusalem, he
was going through the area between Samaria and
Galilee. 12As he came into a small town, ten men
who had a skin disease met him there. They did
not come close to Jesus 13but called to him,
"Jesus! Master! Have mercy on us!"
14When Jesus saw the men, he said, "Go and
show yourselves to the priests."[n]
As the ten men were going, they were healed.
15When one of them saw that he was healed, he
went back to Jesus, praising God in a loud voice.
16Then he bowed down at Jesus' feet and thanked

show . . . priests The law of Moses said a priest must say when a Jewish person with a skin disease became well.

THANKFULNESS

Attitude of Gratitude

Bruce Hallman's father shook his head doubtfully. "I don't see how we can do it, son," he said.

Bruce knew his father was right, but it still hurt to think about missing the big trip. All of the guys in the jazz band were looking forward to that summer trip, but Bruce's dad had been unemployed for a while. So money was tight—too tight to allow an eleventh grader to go to Europe for a month.

As Bruce left the room, he asked God to somehow show him a way. He continued to pray about it, and not long afterward a family in his church asked him to do some yardwork. Not much, but it was something. Soon more jobs came in, mostly from families who knew that Bruce was saving his money for the trip.

All spring, Bruce was busier than he had ever been. And that summer, he went to Europe with the band. The families he had worked for had provided the means to get there.

That was a long time ago, but Bruce hasn't forgotten those families. He's a youth minister now, committed to helping kids find their way out of rough spots. "I know I can't go back and thank all those families who helped me," Bruce says. "I don't even remember some of their names. But I figure I can express my thanks to God for all the good things in my life by helping others."

Sometimes we only think of thankfulness when something really special happens to us. People like Bruce, though, understand what Jesus said about always being thankful. Read Jesus' words in **Luke 17:11–19**.

- How is Bruce like the leper who returned to Jesus?
- What things in your life make you feel like running after Jesus just to say "thanks!"?

CONSIDER . . .

- writing a letter to God, thanking him for all the good things in your life.
- keeping stamps and blank postcards handy all the time. When people do something nice for you, send them a note of thanks.

FOR MORE, SEE . . .

- Psalm 100
- Acts 3:1–10
- 1 Thessalonians 5:15–18

him. (And this man was a Samaritan.[d]) 17Jesus
said, "Weren't ten men healed? Where are the
other nine? 18Is this Samaritan the only one who
came back to thank God?" 19Then Jesus said to
him, "Stand up and go on your way. You were
healed because you believed."

SIDELIGHT: The "skin disease" described in Luke 17:11-19 is often called leprosy. It was a dreaded disease, and people who had it were isolated from other people because they were unclean (see Leviticus 13:42-46). Most scholars agree leprosy in the Bible isn't the same disease we call leprosy today, but it's not clear exactly what the disease was.

God's Kingdom Is Within You

20Some of the Pharisees[d] asked Jesus, "When
will the kingdom of God come?"
Jesus answered, "God's kingdom is coming,
but not in a way that you will be able to see with
your eyes. 21People will not say, 'Look, here it is!'
or, 'There it is!' because God's kingdom is
within[n] you."
22Then Jesus said to his followers, "The time
will come when you will want very much to see
one of the days of the Son of Man.[d] But you will
not see it. 23People will say to you, 'Look, there
he is!' or, 'Look, here he is!' Stay where you are;
don't go away and search.

When Jesus Comes Again

24"When the Son of Man[d] comes again, he will
shine like lightning, which flashes across the sky
and lights it up from one side to the other. 25But
first he must suffer many things and be rejected
by the people of this time. 26When the Son of Man
comes again, it will be as it was when Noah lived.
27People were eating, drinking, marrying, and giving their children to be married until the day
Noah entered the boat. Then the flood came and
killed them all. 28It will be the same as during the
time of Lot. People were eating, drinking, buying,
selling, planting, and building. 29But the day Lot
left Sodom,[n] fire and sulfur rained down from
the sky and killed them all. 30This is how it will
be when the Son of Man comes again.
31"On that day, a person who is on the roof and
whose belongings are in the house should not go
inside to get them. A person who is in the field
should not go back home. 32Remember Lot's
wife.[n] 33Those who try to keep their lives will
lose them. But those who give up their lives will
save them. 34I tell you, on that night two people
will be sleeping in one bed; one will be taken and
the other will be left. 35There will be two women
grinding grain together; one will be taken, and
the other will be left." 36 [n]
37The followers asked Jesus, "Where will this
be, Lord?"
Jesus answered, "Where there is a dead body,
there the vultures will gather."

God Will Answer His People

18 Then Jesus used this story to teach his
followers that they should always pray
and never lose hope. 2"In a certain town there
was a judge who did not respect God or care
about people. 3In that same town there was a
widow who kept coming to this judge, saying,
'Give me my rights against my enemy.' 4For a
while the judge refused to help her. But afterwards, he thought to himself, 'Even though I
don't respect God or care about people, 5I will see
that she gets her rights. Otherwise she will continue to bother me until I am worn out.' "
6The Lord said, "Listen to what the unfair judge
said. 7God will always give what is right to his
people who cry to him night and day, and he will
not be slow to answer them. 8I tell you, God will
help his people quickly. But when the Son of
Man[d] comes again, will he find those on earth
who believe in him?"

Being Right with God

9Jesus told this story to some people who
thought they were very good and looked down on
everyone else: 10"A Pharisee[d] and a tax collector
both went to the Temple[d] to pray. 11The Pharisee
stood alone and prayed, 'God, I thank you that I
am not like other people who steal, cheat, or take
part in adultery,[d] or even like this tax collector. 12I
give up eating[n] twice a week, and I give one-
tenth of everything I get!'
13"The tax collector, standing at a distance,
would not even look up to heaven. But he beat on
his chest because he was so sad. He said, 'God,
have mercy on me, a sinner.' 14I tell you, when
this man went home, he was right with God, but
the Pharisee was not. All who make themselves
great will be made humble, but all who make
themselves humble will be made great."

within Or "among."
Sodom City that God destroyed because the people were so evil.
Lot's wife A story about what happened to Lot's wife is found in Genesis 19:15-17, 26.
Verse 36 A few Greek copies add verse 36: "Two people will be in the field. One will be taken, and the other will be left."
give up eating This is called "fasting." The people would give up eating for a special time of prayer and worship to God. It was also done to show sadness and disappointment.

Who Will Enter God's Kingdom?

[15]Some people brought even their babies to
Jesus so he could touch them. When the followers
saw this, they told them to stop. [16]But Jesus called
for the children, saying, "Let the little children
come to me. Don't stop them, because the kingdom of God belongs to people who are like these
children. [17]I tell you the truth, you must accept
the kingdom of God as if you were a child, or you
will never enter it."

A Rich Man's Question

[18]A certain leader asked Jesus, "Good Teacher,
what must I do to have life forever?"
[19]Jesus said to him, "Why do you call me good?
Only God is good. [20]You know the commands:
'You must not be guilty of adultery.[d] You must not
murder anyone. You must not steal. You must
not tell lies about your neighbor. Honor your
father and mother.' "[n]
[21]But the leader said, "I have obeyed all these
commands since I was a boy."
[22]When Jesus heard this, he said to him, "There
is still one more thing you need to do. Sell
everything you have and give it to the poor,
and you will have treasure in heaven. Then
come and follow me." [23]But when the man
heard this, he became very sad, because he
was very rich.
[24]Jesus looked at him and said, "It is very hard
for rich people to enter the kingdom of God. [25]It
is easier for a camel to go through the eye of a
needle than for a rich person to enter the kingdom
of God."

Who Can Be Saved?

[26]When the people heard this, they asked,
"Then who can be saved?"
[27]Jesus answered, "God can do things that are
not possible for people to do."

'You . . . mother.' Quotation from Exodus 20:12-16; Deuteronomy 5:16-20.

BRAGGING

Maximum Ruler

In October 1989, pictures of General Manuel Noriega shaking his fist at the world made headlines everywhere. As dictator of the country of Panama, he'd just thwarted an attempt to remove him from power. Some reports indicated he tortured and murdered as many as seventy-five rebel soldiers after the attempted coup.

Noriega controlled the Panamanian government pridefully, as if he owned it. He held mock elections where his people frightened away voters. He reportedly financed his lifestyle through illegal drug trade and commonly mocked and belittled his enemies, including the United States.

In December, his arrogance reached its peak. He boasted that he was Panama's "maximum leader," daring anyone to disagree.

Someone did.

That month the United States invaded Panama and removed Noriega from power. Within days, he was on his way to face drug charges in a Florida courtroom.

On New Year's Day, the world again saw Manuel Noriega's picture in the headlines. This time, though, the pictures showed a handcuffed man dressed in prison clothes being taken away to jail.

Jesus talked about how God views bragging and prideful people. Read what he said in **Luke 18:9–14**.

- What attitude did both General Noriega and the Pharisee in this passage display?
- How can pride interfere in your relationship with Christ?

CONSIDER . . .

- looking up the word pride in a dictionary and thinking about what part pride plays in bragging.
- writing the second half of Luke 18:14 on a 4" X 6" card and placing it on your mirror as an encouragement to avoid arrogance.

FOR MORE, SEE . . .

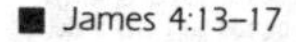

- Jeremiah 9:23–24
- 1 Corinthians 4:6–7
- James 4:13–17

28Peter said, "Look, we have left everything
and followed you."
29Jesus said, "I tell you the truth, all those who
have left houses, wives, brothers, parents, or children for the kingdom of God 30will get much
more in this life. And in the age that is coming,
they will have life forever."

Jesus Will Rise from the Dead

31Then Jesus took the twelve apostles[d] aside
and said to them, "We are going to Jerusalem.
Everything the prophets[d] wrote about the Son of
Man[d] will happen. 32He will be turned over to
those who are not Jews. They will laugh at him,
insult him, spit on him, 33beat him with whips,
and kill him. But on the third day, he will rise to
life again." 34The apostles did not understand this;
the meaning was hidden from them, and they did
not realize what was said.

Jesus Heals a Blind Man

35As Jesus came near the city of Jericho, a blind
man was sitting beside the road, begging. 36When
he heard the people coming down the road, he
asked, "What is happening?"
37They told him, "Jesus, from Nazareth, is going by."
38The blind man cried out, "Jesus, Son of David,[d] have mercy on me!"
39The people leading the group warned the
blind man to be quiet. But the blind man shouted
even more, "Son of David, have mercy on me!"
40Jesus stopped and ordered the blind man to
be brought to him. When he came near, Jesus
asked him, 41"What do you want me to do for
you?"
He said, "Lord, I want to see."
42Jesus said to him, "Then see. You are healed
because you believed."
43At once the man was able to see, and he followed Jesus, thanking God. All the people who
saw this praised God.

Zacchaeus Meets Jesus

19 Jesus was going through the city of
Jericho. 2A man was there named

SELF-ESTEEM

Geek in Glasses

The workers in the Los Angeles Lakers' front office first noticed Kurt Rambis during training camp. "Who invited the geek in the glasses to camp?" they asked.

On the court Kurt adjusted his black horn-rimmed glasses and continued his workout. With 20/400 vision, thick, scraggly hair and an awkward style, no one expected him to make one of the best teams in basketball.

Despite the way others looked at him, Kurt still believed he had much to contribute to the Lakers. It didn't matter if he didn't look or play like the other guys, as long as what he did made this a better—and winning—team.

And Kurt Rambis was right.

He not only made the team but became a starter. He earned a reputation as a tough defensive player and rebounder. Through the 1980s his talents helped the Lakers win four NBA championships. During his time there, the Lakers became known as the "team of the '80s."

Not bad for a "geek in glasses."

Kurt believed his deficiency shouldn't stop him from striving to reach his potential. The Bible tells about someone else who got recognition even though others looked down on him. Read Zacchaeus's story in **Luke 19:1–10**.

- How are Kurt Rambis and Zacchaeus similar? different?
- How does seeing the way Jesus treated Zacchaeus help you believe in your own potential?

CONSIDER . . .

- listing things you like about yourself and thanking God for making you special.
- giving one sincere compliment to your friends, family, or others each day for the next week.

FOR MORE, SEE . . .

- Judges 6:11–16; 7:19–22
- 1 Samuel 16:1–13
- 1 Timothy 4:12

Zacchaeus, who was a very important tax collector, and he was wealthy. 3He wanted to see
who Jesus was, but he was not able because he
was too short to see above the crowd. 4He ran
ahead to a place where Jesus would come,
and he climbed a sycamore tree so he could
see him. 5When Jesus came to that place, he
looked up and said to him, "Zacchaeus, hurry
and come down! I must stay at your house
today."

6Zacchaeus came down quickly and welcomed
him gladly. 7All the people saw this and began to complain, "Jesus is staying with a sinner!"

8But Zacchaeus stood and said to the Lord, "I
will give half of my possessions to the poor. And
if I have cheated anyone, I will pay back four
times more."

9Jesus said to him, "Salvation has come to this
house today, because this man also belongs to the
family of Abraham. 10The Son of Man[d] came to
find lost people and save them."

SIDELIGHT: Asking to stay at Zacchaeus's house, as Jesus did in Luke 19:1–10, would have been seen as scandalous. As a tax collector, Zacchaeus was thought of as a thief or a swindler. Many tax collectors would charge more than the fair amount and keep the "profits" for themselves—a practice approved by the Roman government.

A Story About Three Servants

11As the people were listening to this, Jesus told
them a story because he was near Jerusalem and
they thought God's kingdom would appear immediately. 12He said: "A very important man went to
a country far away to be made a king and then to
return home. 13So he called ten of his servants
and gave a coin[n] to each servant. He said, 'Do
business with this money until I get back.' 14But
the people in the kingdom hated the man. So they

coin A Greek "mina." One mina was enough money to pay a person for working three months.

MONEY

Earning Potential

Norm Wakefield has a lot to be proud of.

His son Joel earns a good salary during the school year as a physical education teacher. During summers Joel works as a trainer for baseball's Oakland Athletics. Through his work in Oakland, he has earned a World Series championship ring, valued at seven thousand dollars.

Norm's daughter Annette may never make as much money as Joel. Hampered by a learning disability, she'll take a little longer than usual to finish high school. During the summer she earns the minimum wage working with kids at the community center. She also gets income from babysitting. When she took part in the Special Olympics, she did well enough to win a second-place ribbon.

When Norm was asked to speak at a junior high graduation, he took with him to show both Joel's championship ring and Annette's track ribbon. Their abilities brought them different rewards monetarily. But in their father's eyes, they are both champions.

Annette and Joel both did their best. Jesus talks about God's view of making the most of what you have. Read his words in **Luke 19:11–27**.

- Which character in the passage is most like Joel? like Annette? like you?
- According to this passage, what does God expect you to do with the gifts he has given you?

CONSIDER . . .

- evaluating how thoughtfully you spend your money.
- looking for ways you can invest what God has given you—whether it's money or talents—to make the most of what God has given to you.

FOR MORE, SEE . . .

- Ecclesiastes 5:10–17
- Matthew 6:31–33
- Matthew 25:14–30

sent a group to follow him and say, 'We don't want this man to be our king.'

15"But the man became king. When he returned home, he said, 'Call those servants who have my money so I can know how much they earned with it.'

16"The first servant came and said, 'Sir, I earned ten coins with the one you gave me.' 17The king said to the servant, 'Excellent! You are a good servant. Since I can trust you with small things, I will let you rule over ten of my cities.'

18"The second servant said, 'Sir, I earned five coins with your one.' 19The king said to this servant, 'You can rule over five cities.'

20"Then another servant came in and said to the king, 'Sir, here is your coin which I wrapped in a piece of cloth and hid. 21I was afraid of you, because you are a hard man. You even take money that you didn't earn and gather food that you didn't plant.' 22Then the king said to the servant, 'I will condemn you by your own words, you evil servant. You knew that I am a hard man, taking money that I didn't earn and gathering food that I didn't plant. 23Why then didn't you put my money in the bank? Then when I came back, my money would have earned some interest.'

24"The king said to the men who were standing by, 'Take the coin away from this servant and give it to the servant who earned ten coins.' 25They said, 'But sir, that servant already has ten coins.' 26The king said, 'Those who have will be given more, but those who do not have anything will have everything taken away from them. 27Now where are my enemies who didn't want me to be king? Bring them here and kill them before me.' "

Jesus Enters Jerusalem as a King

28After Jesus said this, he went on toward Jerusalem. 29As Jesus came near Bethphage and Bethany, towns near the hill called the Mount of Olives,[d] he sent out two of his followers. 30He said, "Go to the town you can see there. When you enter it, you will find a colt tied there, which no one has ever ridden. Untie it and bring it here to me. 31If anyone asks you why you are untying it, say that the Master needs it."

32The two followers went into town and found the colt just as Jesus had told them. 33As they were untying it, its owners came out and asked the followers, "Why are you untying our colt?"

34The followers answered, "The Master needs it." 35So they brought it to Jesus, threw their coats on the colt's back, and put Jesus on it. 36As Jesus rode toward Jerusalem, others spread their coats on the road before him.

37As he was coming close to Jerusalem, on the way down the Mount of Olives, the whole crowd of followers began joyfully shouting praise to God for all the miracles[d] they had seen. 38They said,

"God bless the king who comes in the name
of the Lord! *Psalm 118:26*
There is peace in heaven and glory to God!"

39Some of the Pharisees[d] in the crowd said to Jesus, "Teacher, tell your followers not to say these things."

40But Jesus answered, "I tell you, if my followers didn't say these things, then the stones would cry out."

Jesus Cries for Jerusalem

41As Jesus came near Jerusalem, he saw the city and cried for it, 42saying, "I wish you knew today what would bring you peace. But now it is hidden from you. 43The time is coming when your enemies will build a wall around you and will hold you in on all sides. 44They will destroy you and all your people, and not one stone will be left on another. All this will happen because you did not recognize the time when God came to save you."

Jesus Goes to the Temple

45Jesus went into the Temple[d] and began to throw out the people who were selling things there. 46He said, "It is written in the Scriptures,[d] 'My Temple will be a house for prayer.'[n] But you have changed it into a 'hideout for robbers'!"[n]

47Jesus taught in the Temple every day. The leading priests, the experts on the law, and some of the leaders of the people wanted to kill Jesus. 48But they did not know how they could do it, because all the people were listening closely to him.

Jewish Leaders Question Jesus

20 One day Jesus was in the Temple,[d] teaching the people and telling them the Good News.[d] The leading priests, teachers of the law, and older Jewish leaders came up to talk with him, 2saying, "Tell us what authority you have to do these things? Who gave you this authority?"

3Jesus answered, "I will also ask you a question. Tell me: 4When John baptized people, was that authority from God or just from other people?"

5They argued about this, saying, "If we answer, 'John's baptism was from God,' Jesus will say, 'Then why did you not believe him?' 6But if we say, 'It was from other people,' all the people will stone us to death, because they believe John was a prophet."[d] 7So they answered that they didn't know where it came from.

'My Temple . . . prayer.' Quotation from Isaiah 56:7.
'hideout for robbers' Quotation from Jeremiah 7:11.

8Jesus said to them, "Then I won't tell you
what authority I have to do these things."

A Story About God's Son

9Then Jesus told the people this story: "A man
planted a vineyard and leased it to some farmers.
Then he went away for a long time. 10When it
was time for the grapes to be picked, he sent a
servant to the farmers to get some of the grapes.
But they beat the servant and sent him away
empty-handed. 11Then he sent another servant.
They beat this servant also, and showed no respect for him, and sent him away empty-handed.
12So the man sent a third servant. The farmers
wounded him and threw him out. 13The owner of
the vineyard said, 'What will I do now? I will send
my son whom I love. Maybe they will respect
him.' 14But when the farmers saw the son, they
said to each other, 'This son will inherit the vineyard. If we kill him, it will be ours.' 15So the farmers threw the son out of the vineyard and killed
him.

"What will the owner of this vineyard do to
them? 16He will come and kill those farmers and
will give the vineyard to other farmers."

When the people heard this story, they said,
"Let this never happen!"

17But Jesus looked at them and said, "Then
what does this verse mean:

'The stone that the builders rejected
became the cornerstone'?[d] *Psalm 118:22*

18Everyone who falls on that stone will be broken,
and the person on whom it falls, that person will
be crushed!"

19The teachers of the law and the leading
priests wanted to arrest Jesus at once, because
they knew the story was about them. But they
were afraid of what the people would do.

Is It Right to Pay Taxes or Not?

20So they watched Jesus and sent some spies
who acted as if they were sincere. They wanted
to trap Jesus in saying something wrong so they
could hand him over to the authority and power
of the governor. 21So the spies asked Jesus,
"Teacher, we know that what you say and teach

EVIL

Grim Snapshots

In April, fifteen-year-old Jason Thomas was thrilled to receive a new pair of expensive sneakers. In May he was dead. Someone had strangled him, stolen his shoes, and left his body.

Due to an accident as an infant, Carol Miller suffers from severe physical handicaps. Many in the youth group have reached out to her in spite of the differences. Yet, one day a young girl insensitively told Carol she thought Carol was disgusting and hated being around her. The girl walked away leaving Carol to cry alone.

When the Detroit Pistons won their second straight NBA championship, the city wanted to "celebrate." Looting and rioting caused untold damage. Hundreds were injured. Seven people were killed.

Bad news, huh? We would like to say those things never happened, or just sweep them under a rug somewhere. But they did happen. And other bad things continue to happen all around us, all the time.

While we are sometimes tempted to close our eyes to evil in the world, Jesus never avoided the reality of evil. However, he was also quick to point out that God can and will triumph over it. Read a parable he told about evil in **Luke 20:9–19**.

- What motivates people to mistreat each other the way they did in the parable and the snapshots above?
- How do you see God's power conquering evil in the world as this passage describes?

CONSIDER . . .

- praying for God to use you to overcome evil with good.
- writing letters of encouragement through a pen pal program to a prison inmate.

FOR MORE, SEE . . .

- Proverbs 24:19–20
- Matthew 21:33–43
- Romans 12:17–21

is true. You pay no attention to who people are, and you always teach the truth about God's way. 22Tell us, is it right for us to pay taxes to Caesar[d] or not?"

23But Jesus, knowing they were trying to trick him, said, 24"Show me a coin. Whose image and name are on it?"

They said, "Caesar's."

25Jesus said to them, "Then give to Caesar the things that are Caesar's, and give to God the things that are God's."

26So they were not able to trap Jesus in anything he said in the presence of the people. And being amazed at his answer, they became silent.

> **SIDELIGHT:** The Sadducees—who didn't believe in the resurrection of the dead (Luke 20:27)—were major rivals of the Pharisees in Jesus' time. In later years, the Sadducees were often considered heretics by other Jews.

Some Sadducees Try to Trick Jesus

27Some Sadducees,[d] who believed people would not rise from the dead, came to Jesus. 28They asked, "Teacher, Moses wrote that if a man's brother dies and leaves a wife but no children, then that man must marry the widow and have children for his brother. 29Once there were seven brothers. The first brother married and died, but had no children. 30Then the second brother married the widow, and he died. 31And the third brother married the widow, and he died. The same thing happened with all seven brothers; they died and had no children. 32Finally, the woman died also. 33Since all seven brothers had married her, whose wife will she be when people rise from the dead?"

34Jesus said to them, "On earth, people marry and are given to someone to marry. 35But those who will be worthy to be raised from the dead and live again will not marry, nor will they be given to someone to marry. 36In that life they are like angels and cannot die. They are children of God, because they have been raised from the dead. 37Even Moses clearly showed that the dead are raised to life. When he wrote about the burning bush,[n] he said that the Lord is 'the God of Abraham, the God of Isaac, and the God of Jacob.'[n] 38God is the God of the living, not the dead, because all people are alive to him."

39Some of the teachers of the law said, "Teacher, your answer was good." 40No one was brave enough to ask him another question.

Is the Christ the Son of David?

41Then Jesus said, "Why do people say that the Christ[d] is the Son of David?[d] 42In the book of Psalms, David himself says:

'The Lord said to my Lord:
Sit by me at my right side,
43 until I put your enemies under your control.'[n] *Psalm 110:1*

44David calls the Christ 'Lord,' so how can the Christ be his son?"

Jesus Accuses Some Leaders

45While all the people were listening, Jesus said to his followers, 46"Beware of the teachers of the law. They like to walk around wearing fancy clothes, and they love for people to greet them with respect in the marketplaces. They love to have the most important seats in the synagogues[d] and at feasts. 47But they cheat widows and steal their houses and then try to make themselves look good by saying long prayers. They will receive a greater punishment."

True Giving

21 As Jesus looked up, he saw some rich people putting their gifts into the Temple[d] money box.[n] 2Then he saw a poor widow putting two small copper coins into the box. 3He said, "I tell you the truth, this poor widow gave more than all those rich people. 4They gave only what they did not need. This woman is very poor, but she gave all she had to live on."

The Temple Will Be Destroyed

5Some people were talking about the Temple[d] and how it was decorated with beautiful stones and gifts offered to God.

But Jesus said, 6"As for these things you are looking at, the time will come when not one stone will be left on another. Every stone will be thrown down."

7They asked Jesus, "Teacher, when will these things happen? What will be the sign that they are about to take place?"

8Jesus said, "Be careful so you are not fooled. Many people will come in my name, saying, 'I am the One' and, 'The time has come!' But don't follow them. 9When you hear about wars and riots, don't be afraid, because these things must happen first, but the end will come later."

10Then he said to them, "Nations will fight

burning bush Read Exodus 3:1-12 in the Old Testament.
'the God of . . . Jacob' These words are taken from Exodus 3:6.
until . . . control Literally, "until I make your enemies a footstool for your feet."
money box A special box in the Jewish place of worship where people put their gifts to God.

against other nations, and kingdoms against other kingdoms. 11 In various places there will be great earthquakes, sicknesses, and a lack of food. Fearful events and great signs will come from heaven.

12 "But before all these things happen, people will arrest you and treat you cruelly. They will judge you in their synagogues[d] and put you in jail and force you to stand before kings and governors, because you follow me. 13 But this will give you an opportunity to tell about me. 14 Make up your minds not to worry ahead of time about what you will say. 15 I will give you the wisdom to say things that none of your enemies will be able to stand against or prove wrong. 16 Even your parents, brothers, relatives, and friends will turn against you, and they will kill some of you. 17 All people will hate you because you follow me. 18 But none of these things can really harm you. 19 By continuing to have faith you will save your lives.

Jerusalem Will Be Destroyed

20 "When you see armies all around Jerusalem, you will know it will soon be destroyed. 21 At that time, the people in Judea should run away to the mountains. The people in Jerusalem must get out, and those who are near the city should not go in. 22 These are the days of punishment to bring about all that is written in the Scriptures.[d] 23 How terrible it will be for women who are pregnant or have nursing babies! Great trouble will come upon this land, and God will be angry with these people. 24 They will be killed by the sword and taken as prisoners to all nations. Jerusalem will be crushed by non-Jewish people until their time is over.

Don't Fear

25 "There will be signs in the sun, moon, and stars. On earth, nations will be afraid and confused because of the roar and fury of the sea. 26 People will be so afraid they will faint, wondering what is happening to the world, because the powers of the heavens will be shaken. 27 Then people will see the Son of Man[d] coming in a cloud with power and great glory. 28 When these things begin to happen, look up and hold your heads

PEER PRESSURE

Friends in Deed

Lance O'Pry was a student at Lamar High School in Rosenberg, Texas, when he learned he had cancer. He was told he would have to undergo painful chemotherapy if he hoped to live.

For Lance the pain was even harder to take knowing the treatment would make his hair fall out. Would he fit in at school? What would his friends say? Would they avoid him because they were embarrassed by his baldness? Would he be laughed at and mocked? He knew his classmates' reactions could make having the awful disease even more unbearable.

What he didn't know—but soon discovered—was that his friends really cared. To make sure Lance would fit in, Jason, Korl, Mac, Tim, Johnny, Donnie, Jeff, and Doug all shaved their heads.

A stranger to Rosenberg might wonder why nine students at Lamar High study, laugh, joke and go on dates wearing shiny, bald heads. But one of those bald heads knows the power of positive peer pressure. That makes all the difference.

Peer pressure can be good or bad. The Bible talks about a negative kind of peer pressure that many Christians will face. Read **Luke 21:5–19**, especially verse 16, to find out more about it.

- Lance faced rejection at school. How will Christians face rejection by the world, according to this passage?
- What encouragement does this passage give you to stand up to pressure from people who try to get you to compromise what you believe?

CONSIDER...

- making a list of pressures that challenge your relationships with God and your friends, then asking your youth leader for advice on how to overcome those pressures.
- making a pact with your friends to always encourage each other to follow God.

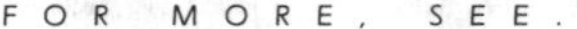

FOR MORE, SEE...

- 1 Samuel 20:28–42
- Matthew 10:16–23
- 1 Corinthians 15:33

high, because the time when God will free you is near!"

Jesus' Words Will Live Forever

29Then Jesus told this story: "Look at the fig tree and all the other trees. 30When their leaves appear, you know that summer is near. 31In the same way, when you see these things happening, you will know that God's kingdom is near.

32"I tell you the truth, all these things will happen while the people of this time are still living. 33Earth and sky will be destroyed, but the words I have spoken will never be destroyed.

Be Ready All the Time

34"Be careful not to spend your time feasting, drinking, or worrying about worldly things. If you do, that day might come on you suddenly, 35like a trap on all people on earth. 36So be ready all the time. Pray that you will be strong enough to escape all these things that will happen and that you will be able to stand before the Son of Man."[d]

37During the day, Jesus taught the people in the Temple,[d] and at night he went out of the city and stayed on the Mount of Olives.[d] 38Every morning all the people got up early to go to the Temple to listen to him.

Judas Becomes an Enemy of Jesus

22 It was almost time for the Feast[d] of Unleavened Bread, called the Passover[d] Feast. 2The leading priests and teachers of the law were trying to find a way to kill Jesus, because they were afraid of the people.

3Satan entered Judas Iscariot, one of Jesus' twelve apostles.[d] 4Judas went to the leading priests and some of the soldiers who guarded the Temple[d] and talked to them about a way to hand Jesus over to them. 5They were pleased and agreed to give Judas money. 6He agreed and watched for the best time to hand Jesus over to them when he was away from the crowd.

Jesus Eats the Passover Meal

7The Day of Unleavened[d] Bread came when the Passover[d] lambs had to be sacrificed. 8Jesus said to Peter and John, "Go and prepare the Passover meal for us to eat."

9They asked, "Where do you want us to prepare it?" 10Jesus said to them, "After you go into the city, a man carrying a jar of water will meet you. Follow him into the house that he enters, 11and tell the owner of the house, 'The Teacher says: Where is the guest room in which I may eat the Passover meal with my followers?' 12Then he will show you a large, furnished room upstairs. Prepare the Passover meal there."

13So Peter and John left and found everything as Jesus had said. And they prepared the Passover meal.

The Lord's Supper

14When the time came, Jesus and the apostles[d] were sitting at the table. 15He said to them, "I wanted very much to eat this Passover[d] meal with you before I suffer. 16I will not eat another Passover meal until it is given its true meaning in the kingdom of God."

17Then Jesus took a cup, gave thanks, and said, "Take this cup and share it among yourselves. 18I will not drink again from the fruit of the vine[n] until God's kingdom comes."

19Then Jesus took some bread, gave thanks, broke it, and gave it to the apostles, saying, "This is my body, which I am giving for you. Do this to remember me." 20In the same way, after supper, Jesus took the cup and said, "This cup is the new agreement that God makes with his people. This new agreement begins with my blood which is poured out for you.

Who Will Turn Against Jesus?

21"But one of you will turn against me, and his hand is with mine on the table. 22What God has planned for the Son of Man[d] will happen, but how terrible it will be for that one who turns against the Son of Man."

23Then the apostles[d] asked each other which one of them would do that.

Be Like a Servant

24The apostles[d] also began to argue about which one of them was the most important. 25But Jesus said to them, "The kings of the non-Jewish people rule over them, and those who have authority over others like to be called 'friends of the people.' 26But you must not be like that. Instead, the greatest among you should be like the youngest, and the leader should be like the servant. 27Who is more important: the one sitting at the table or the one serving? You think the one at the table is more important, but I am like a servant among you.

28"You have stayed with me through my struggles. 29Just as my Father has given me a kingdom, I also give you a kingdom 30so you may eat and drink at my table in my kingdom. And you will sit on thrones, judging the twelve tribes[d] of Israel.

Don't Lose Your Faith!

31"Simon, Simon, Satan has asked to test all of you as a farmer sifts his wheat. 32I have prayed that you will not lose your faith! Help your brothers be stronger when you come back to me."

fruit of the vine Product of the grapevine; this may also be translated "wine."

33But Peter said to Jesus, "Lord, I am ready to
go with you to prison and even to die with you!"
34But Jesus said, "Peter, before the rooster
crows this day, you will say three times that you
don't know me."

Be Ready for Trouble

35Then Jesus said to the apostles,[d] "When I sent
you out without a purse, a bag, or sandals, did you
need anything?"
They said, "No."
36He said to them, "But now if you have a purse
or a bag, carry that with you. If you don't have a
sword, sell your coat and buy one. 37The Scripture[d] says, 'He was treated like a criminal,'[n] and
I tell you this scripture must have its full meaning.
It was written about me, and it is happening
now."
38His followers said, "Look, Lord, here are two
swords."
He said to them, "That is enough."

Jesus Prays Alone

39Jesus left the city and went to the Mount of
Olives,[d] as he often did, and his followers went
with him. 40When he reached the place, he said
to them, "Pray for strength against temptation."
41Then Jesus went about a stone's throw away
from them. He kneeled down and prayed, 42"Father, if you are willing, take away this cup[n] of
suffering. But do what you want, not what I
want." 43Then an angel from heaven appeared to
him to strengthen him. 44Being full of pain, Jesus
prayed even harder. His sweat was like drops of
blood falling to the ground. 45When he finished
praying, he went to his followers and found them
asleep because of their sadness. 46Jesus said to
them, "Why are you sleeping? Get up and pray for
strength against temptation."

Jesus Is Arrested

47While Jesus was speaking, a crowd came up,
and Judas, one of the twelve apostles,[d] was leading them. He came close to Jesus so he could kiss
him.
48But Jesus said to him, "Judas, are you using
the kiss to give the Son of Man[d] to his enemies?"
49When those who were standing around him

'He . . . criminal' Quotation from Isaiah 53:12.
cup Jesus is talking about the painful things that will happen to him. Accepting these things will be hard, like drinking a cup of something bitter.

JEALOUSY

When Others Succeed

"Few men have the strength to honor a friend's success without envy." —Aeschylus

"Lots of people know a good thing the minute the other fellow sees it first." —Job E. Hedges

"The man who keeps busy helping the man below him won't have time to envy the man above him—and there may not be anybody above him anyway." —Henrietta C. Mears

"The greatest among you should be like the youngest, and the leader should be like the servant." —Jesus Christ

For more about what Jesus said to his jealous disciples—who were arguing about prestige—read **Luke 22:24–30**.

- What similarities and differences are there between what Jesus said and what these famous people said about jealousy?
- How are you like and unlike the disciples in the passage? What would Jesus say to you?

C O N S I D E R . . .

- stopping yourself next time you feel jealous toward someone. Instead, do an act of service for that person.
- setting three goals for the coming week that will help you overcome jealous feelings you have toward someone you know.

F O R M O R E , S E E . . .

- Genesis 37:2–28
- 1 Samuel 18:6–11
- 1 Peter 2:1

saw what was happening, they said, "Lord,
should we strike them with our swords?" 50And
one of them struck the servant of the high priest
and cut off his right ear.
51Jesus said, "Stop! No more of this." Then he
touched the servant's ear and healed him.
52Those who came to arrest Jesus were the
leading priests, the soldiers who guarded the
Temple,[d] and the older Jewish leaders. Jesus said
to them, "You came out here with swords and
clubs as though I were a criminal. 53I was with
you every day in the Temple, and you didn't arrest me there. But this is your time—the time
when darkness rules."

Peter Says He Doesn't Know Jesus

54They arrested Jesus, and led him away, and
brought him into the house of the high priest. Peter followed far behind them. 55After the soldiers
started a fire in the middle of the courtyard and
sat together, Peter sat with them. 56A servant girl
saw Peter sitting there in the firelight, and looking
closely at him, she said, "This man was also with
him."
57But Peter said this was not true; he said,
"Woman, I don't know him."
58A short time later, another person saw Peter
and said, "You are also one of them."
But Peter said, "Man, I am not!"
59About an hour later, another man insisted,
"Certainly this man was with him, because he is
from Galilee, too."
60But Peter said, "Man, I don't know what you
are talking about!"
At once, while Peter was still speaking, a
rooster crowed. 61Then the Lord turned and
looked straight at Peter. And Peter remembered
what the Lord had said: "Before the rooster crows
this day, you will say three times that you don't
know me." 62Then Peter went outside and cried
painfully.

The People Make Fun of Jesus

63The men who were guarding Jesus began
making fun of him and beating him.
64They blindfolded him and said, "Prove that
you are a prophet,[d] and tell us who hit you."
65They said many cruel things to Jesus.

GOD'S WILL

Daring to Follow

Bruce Olson believed strongly that God wanted him to live with the savage Motilone Indians in the jungles of South America. So, this skinny, shy, Minnesota boy set out to find them.

The Motilones were an isolated and fierce group. They hated white people and had killed or wounded all who tried to contact them. Bruce's first encounter with them came when they shot an arrow through his thigh. Then they captured him and forced him to walk hours to their village.

The months that followed were filled with pain, hunger and loneliness. But Bruce wouldn't give up. God had sent him. Eventually Bruce learned the Motilones' language and began communicating with his captors. They called him "Bruchko."

The Motilones have now come to love and respect Bruchko. Through him many people have met Jesus and have benefited from Bruchko's medical and agricultural expertise.

All because he dared to follow God.

Bruce knew what God wanted him to do, and he wouldn't stop until he had accomplished it. Jesus also refused to give up on God's will. Read about his experience in **Luke 22:39–46**, when he prayed the night before he was to suffer beatings and a cruel death.

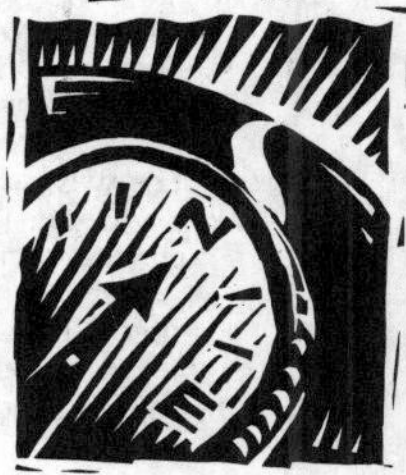

- Knowing it would be hard, why do you think both Jesus and Bruchko insisted on following God's leadership?
- Jesus followed God's will all his life. What makes following God's will possible even when it's tough for you?

CONSIDER . . .

- placing an object in your room that will remind you to seek God's desires.
- reading Bruce Olson's autobiography, titled Bruchko, published by Creation House.

FOR MORE, SEE . . .

- Psalm 143:8–11
- Matthew 26:36–46
- Mark 14:32–42

Jesus Before the Leaders

66When day came, the council of the older
leaders of the people, both the leading priests and
the teachers of the law, came together and led
Jesus to their highest court. 67They said, "If you
are the Christ,[d] tell us."

Jesus said to them, "If I tell you, you will not
believe me. 68And if I ask you, you will not answer. 69But from now on, the Son of Man[d] will sit
at the right hand of the powerful God."

70They all said, "Then are you the Son of God?"

Jesus said to them, "You say that I am."

71They said, "Why do we need witnesses now?
We ourselves heard him say this."

Pilate Questions Jesus

23 Then the whole group stood up and led
Jesus to Pilate.[n] 2They began to accuse
Jesus, saying, "We caught this man telling things
that mislead our people. He says that we should
not pay taxes to Caesar,[d] and he calls himself the
Christ,[d] a king."

3Pilate asked Jesus, "Are you the king of the
Jews?"

Jesus answered, "Those are your words."

4Pilate said to the leading priests and the people, "I find nothing against this man."

5They were insisting, saying, "But Jesus makes
trouble with the people, teaching all around Judea. He began in Galilee, and now he is here."

Pilate Sends Jesus to Herod

6Pilate heard this and asked if Jesus was from
Galilee. 7Since Jesus was under Herod's authority,
Pilate sent Jesus to Herod, who was in Jerusalem
at that time. 8When Herod saw Jesus, he was very
glad, because he had heard about Jesus and had
wanted to meet him for a long time. He was hoping to see Jesus work a miracle.[d] 9Herod asked
Jesus many questions, but Jesus said nothing.

Pilate Pontius Pilate was the Roman governor of Judea from A.D. 26 to A.D. 36.

SUFFERING

The Price of Goals

In West Perrine, Florida, Lee Lawrence had a dream.

"Can you imagine," he said, "all the churches in the neighborhood . . . marching up Homestead Avenue to let the drug pushers know we won't take it anymore?"

The drug dealers didn't like Lee or his vision. Twice he was shot at while getting out of his car. The grocery store he owned was vandalized; then someone tried to burn it down. Refusing to give up, Lee got several pushers arrested. His store became a drug-free haven for the neighborhood kids.

The dealers vowed to strike back.

In March 1989, Lee walked outside his store and was met by a man shooting a semiautomatic rifle. The first shot knocked Lee to the ground. A second man shot Lee again as he lay on the pavement. Minutes later he was dead. But his vision was not.

On Lee Lawrence's funeral day, more than three thousand people from area churches linked arms and marched up Homestead Avenue singing, "We shall overcome: drugs and crime must go!"

It was a dream come true. And the start of a turnaround in West Perrine.

Lee was willing to face hardship—even death—to see his goal become a reality. Jesus also endured hardship because of his mission to reclaim humanity from sin. Read about it in **Luke 22:63–71**.

- What price were both Lee and Jesus willing to pay to see their goals become reality?
- How was Jesus' response in this passage like the way you respond when others attack your faith? How is your response different from Jesus'?

CONSIDER . . .

- writing down three goals you would be willing to suffer for.
- looking through a newspaper to find three people who are suffering for doing right, and praying for them each day this week.

FOR MORE, SEE . . .

- Exodus 3:6–10
- Mark 14:62–65
- 1 Peter 2:18–25

10The leading priests and teachers of the law were standing there, strongly accusing Jesus. 11After Herod and his soldiers had made fun of Jesus, they dressed him in a kingly robe and sent him back to Pilate. 12In the past, Pilate and Herod had always been enemies, but on that day they became friends.

Jesus Must Die

13Pilate called the people together with the leading priests and the Jewish leaders. 14He said to them, "You brought this man to me, saying he makes trouble among the people. But I have questioned him before you all, and I have not found him guilty of what you say. 15Also, Herod found nothing wrong with him; he sent him back to us. Look, he has done nothing for which he should die. 16So, after I punish him, I will let him go free." 17 [n]

18But the people shouted together, "Take this man away! Let Barabbas go free!" 19(Barabbas was a man who was in prison for his part in a riot in the city and for murder.)

20Pilate wanted to let Jesus go free and told this to the crowd. 21But they shouted again, "Crucify him! Crucify him!"

22A third time Pilate said to them, "Why? What wrong has he done? I can find no reason to kill him. So I will have him punished and set him free."

23But they continued to shout, demanding that Jesus be crucified. Their yelling became so loud that 24Pilate decided to give them what they wanted. 25He set free the man who was in jail for rioting and murder, and he handed Jesus over to them to do with him as they wished.

Jesus Is Crucified

26As they led Jesus away, Simon, a man from Cyrene, was coming in from the fields. They forced him to carry Jesus' cross and to walk behind him.

27A large crowd of people was following Jesus, including some women who were sad and crying for him. 28But Jesus turned and said to them, "Women of Jerusalem, don't cry for me. Cry for yourselves and for your children. 29The time is coming when people will say, 'Happy are the women who cannot have children and who have no babies to nurse.' 30Then people will say to the mountains, 'Fall on us!' And they will say to the hills, 'Cover us!' 31If they act like this now when life is good, what will happen when bad times come?" [n]

32There were also two criminals led out with Jesus to be put to death. 33When they came to a place called the Skull, the soldiers crucified Jesus and the criminals — one on his right and the other on his left. 34Jesus said, "Father, forgive them, because they don't know what they are doing." [n]

> **SIDELIGHT:** If Jesus had been crucified like most Roman prisoners were executed, he was probably nailed to a capital T-shaped (Roman) cross rather than the Italian cross that most churches now display (Luke 23:32–33).

The soldiers threw lots[d] to decide who would get his clothes. 35The people stood there watching. And the leaders made fun of Jesus, saying, "He saved others. Let him save himself if he is God's Chosen One, the Christ."[d]

36The soldiers also made fun of him, coming to Jesus and offering him some vinegar. 37They said, "If you are the king of the Jews, save yourself!" 38At the top of the cross these words were written: THIS IS THE KING OF THE JEWS.

39One of the criminals on a cross began to shout insults at Jesus: "Aren't you the Christ? Then save yourself and us."

40But the other criminal stopped him and said, "You should fear God! You are getting the same punishment he is. 41We are punished justly, getting what we deserve for what we did. But this man has done nothing wrong." 42Then he said, "Jesus, remember me when you come into your kingdom."

43Jesus said to him, "I tell you the truth, today you will be with me in paradise." [n]

Jesus Dies

44It was about noon, and the whole land became dark until three o'clock in the afternoon, 45because the sun did not shine. The curtain in the Temple [n] was torn in two. 46Jesus cried out in a loud voice, "Father, I give you my life." After Jesus said this, he died.

47When the army officer there saw what happened, he praised God, saying, "Surely this was a good man!"

48When all the people who had gathered there

Verse 17 A few Greek copies add verse 17: "Every year at the Passover Feast, Pilate had to release one prisoner to the people."
If . . . come? Literally, "If they do these things in the green tree, what will happen in the dry?"
Verse 34 Some early Greek copies do not have this part of the verse.
paradise A place where people who are obedient to God go when they die.
curtain in the Temple A curtain divided the Most Holy Place from the other part of the Temple, the special building in Jerusalem where God commanded the Jewish people to worship him.

to watch saw what happened, they returned
home, beating their chests because they were so
sad. 49But those who were close friends of Jesus,
including the women who had followed him from
Galilee, stood at a distance and watched.

Joseph Takes Jesus' Body

50There was a good and religious man named
Joseph who was a member of the Jewish council.
51But he had not agreed to the other leaders' plans
and actions against Jesus. He was from the Jewish
town of Arimathea and was waiting for the kingdom of God to come. 52Joseph went to Pilate to
ask for the body of Jesus. 53He took the body
down from the cross, wrapped it in cloth, and put
it in a tomb that was cut out of a wall of rock. This
tomb had never been used before. 54This was late
on Preparation[d] Day, and when the sun went
down, the Sabbath[d] day would begin.
55The women who had come from Galilee with
Jesus followed Joseph and saw the tomb and how
Jesus' body was laid. 56Then the women left to
prepare spices and perfumes.

On the Sabbath day they rested, as the law of
Moses commanded.

Jesus Rises from the Dead

24 Very early on the first day of the week,
at dawn, the women came to the tomb,
bringing the spices they had prepared. 2They
found the stone rolled away from the entrance of
the tomb, 3but when they went in, they did not
find the body of the Lord Jesus. 4While they were
wondering about this, two men in shining clothes
suddenly stood beside them. 5The women were
very afraid and bowed their heads to the ground.
The men said to them, "Why are you looking for
a living person in this place for the dead? 6He is
not here; he has risen from the dead. Do you remember what he told you in Galilee? 7He said the
Son of Man[d] must be handed over to sinful people, be crucified, and rise from the dead on the

FORGIVENESS

Lasting Impact

Dr. Boris Kornfeld was a prisoner in Siberia. Because of his medical skills, he regularly performed surgery for both prisoners and staff.

One day while repairing a guard's artery, which had been cut by a knife wound, he seriously considered stitching the wound in a way that would cause the guard to bleed to death. Shocked by his own hatred and bitterness, he quietly said the words from the Lord's Prayer:

"Forgive us for our sins, just as we have forgiven those who sinned against us."

Weeks later, Dr. Kornfeld was examining a patient who had just had surgery for cancer. Sensing a spiritual depth in the man, Kornfeld retold the story of the earlier incident. He shared his secret faith with the patient.

That night, someone who was angry at the doctor sneaked into his sleeping quarters and smashed his head. Kornfeld died a few hours later.

But his confession did not die. The patient who heard it became a Christian. When he left the prison camp, he went on to tell the world of his experiences there.

The patient was the Christian writer Aleksandr Solzhenitsyn.

Dr. Kornfeld's forgiveness of guards in the terrible prison camps had a great impact on Solzhenitsyn's life—and, as a result, on the world. The Bible tells of an even greater sacrifice and act of forgiveness—Jesus dying on the cross for all people's sins. Read about the forgiveness in **Luke 23:26–43**.

- How was Dr. Kornfeld's forgiveness of the guard like and unlike Jesus' forgiveness of the thief in the passage?
- If you were watching Jesus on the cross, and knew he was God's son, what would you ask forgiveness for?

CONSIDER . . .

- writing a short song to thank God for forgiving you.
- creating a symbol of forgiveness and putting it in your locker or on your notebooks at school to remind you that God's forgiveness is always available.

FOR MORE, SEE . . .

- Isaiah 53:1–12
- Mark 15:21–21
- John 19:17–27

third day." 8Then the women remembered what Jesus had said.

9The women left the tomb and told all these things to the eleven apostles[d] and the other followers. 10It was Mary Magdalene, Joanna, Mary the mother of James, and some other women who told the apostles everything that had happened at the tomb. 11But they did not believe the women, because it sounded like nonsense. 12But Peter got up and ran to the tomb. Bending down and looking in, he saw only the cloth that Jesus' body had been wrapped in. Peter went away to his home, wondering about what had happened.

Jesus on the Road to Emmaus

13That same day two of Jesus' followers were going to a town named Emmaus, about seven miles from Jerusalem. 14They were talking about everything that had happened. 15While they were talking and discussing, Jesus himself came near and began walking with them, 16but they were kept from recognizing him. 17Then he said, "What are these things you are talking about while you walk?"

The two followers stopped, looking very sad. 18The one named Cleopas answered, "Are you the only visitor in Jerusalem who does not know what just happened there?"

19Jesus said to them, "What are you talking about?"

They said, "About Jesus of Nazareth. He was a prophet[d] who said and did many powerful things before God and all the people. 20Our leaders and the leading priests handed him over to be sentenced to death, and they crucified him. 21But we were hoping that he would free Israel. Besides this, it is now the third day since this happened. 22And today some women among us amazed us. Early this morning they went to the tomb, 23but they did not find his body there. They came and told us that they had seen a vision of angels who said that Jesus was alive! 24So some of our group went to the tomb, too. They found it just as the women said, but they did not see Jesus."

25Then Jesus said to them, "You are foolish and slow to believe everything the prophets said. 26They said that the Christ[d] must suffer these things before he enters his glory." 27Then starting with what Moses and all the prophets had said about him, Jesus began to explain everything that had been written about himself in the Scriptures.[d]

28They came near the town of Emmaus, and Jesus acted as if he were going farther. 29But they begged him, "Stay with us, because it is late; it is almost night." So he went in to stay with them.

30When Jesus was at the table with them, he took some bread, gave thanks, divided it, and

LIFE

Good News

Bob Delker's family members mourned the day he died, but they also knew others would live now because of him. Bob had decided to give his body to medicine. That meant that people who desperately needed organ donations would receive them. For these people, Bob's death brought new life.

A few received badly needed bone transplants. Some critically injured burn victims received skin grafts. Corneas from Bob's eyes allowed two blind people to see.

In all, Bob's final gift helped thirty-four people. Countless others have been inspired to become organ donors because of Bob's example.

Bob's death brought new life to many people. Similarly, the sad news of Jesus' death meant the possibility of new life for all people everywhere, for Jesus rose from the dead. But unlike Bob Delker, Jesus didn't stay dead. Read **Luke 24:1–11** to discover what happened.

- How is an organ transplant a little like Jesus' coming back from the dead?
- How does Jesus' rising from the dead make a difference in your life?

CONSIDER . . .

- listing the ways that Christ's death has given you life.
- growing a plant in your room as a reminder of the spiritual life Jesus gives you.

FOR MORE, SEE . . .

- Psalm 36:7–9
- Mark 16:1–8
- John 20:1–18

gave it to them. 31And then, they were allowed to recognize Jesus. But when they saw who he was, he disappeared. 32They said to each other, "It felt like a fire burning in us when Jesus talked to us on the road and explained the Scriptures to us."

33So the two followers got up at once and went back to Jerusalem. There they found the eleven apostles[d] and others gathered. 34They were saying, "The Lord really has risen from the dead! He showed himself to Simon."

35Then the two followers told what had happened on the road and how they recognized Jesus when he divided the bread.

Jesus Appears to His Followers

36While the two followers were telling this, Jesus himself stood right in the middle of them and said, "Peace be with you."

37They were fearful and terrified and thought they were seeing a ghost. 38But Jesus said, "Why are you troubled? Why do you doubt what you see? 39Look at my hands and my feet. It is I myself! Touch me and see, because a ghost does not have a living body as you see I have."

40After Jesus said this, he showed them his hands and feet. 41While they still could not believe it because they were amazed and happy, Jesus said to them, "Do you have any food here?" 42They gave him a piece of broiled fish. 43While the followers watched, Jesus took the fish and ate it.

44He said to them, "Remember when I was with you before? I said that everything written about me must happen—everything in the law of Moses, the books of the prophets,[d] and the Psalms."

45Then Jesus opened their minds so they could understand the Scriptures.[d] 46He said to them, "It is written that the Christ[d] would suffer and rise from the dead on the third day 47and that a change of hearts and lives and forgiveness of sins would be preached in his name to all nations, starting at Jerusalem. 48You are witnesses of these things. 49I will send you what my Father has promised, but you must stay in Jerusalem until you have received that power from heaven."

Jesus Goes Back to Heaven

50Jesus led his followers as far as Bethany, and he raised his hands and blessed them. 51While he was blessing them, he was separated from them and carried into heaven. 52They worshiped him and returned to Jerusalem very happy. 53They stayed in the Temple[d] all the time, praising God.

JOHN

Why Read This Book:

- Be reminded that Jesus Christ is fully human and fully divine (John 1).
- Find stories that reveal Jesus' glory as giver of eternal life (John 2—11).
- Learn the importance of Jesus' death and resurrection (John 13—21).

Behind the Scenes:

Imagine meeting someone for the first time. The conversation begins with "Hi, I'm Barb. I go to Central High. I live in Rogers Park." If the conversation continues, you might talk about hobbies, interests, background, and other information.

But you still wouldn't really know that person. If you saw each other regularly, you would begin to understand each other's personality, values, and uniquenesses.

In some ways, the first three Gospels (Matthew, Mark, and Luke) are like the first part of a relationship with Jesus Christ. Through these books, we get to know stories about Jesus and what he did. But the Gospel of John digs deeper into who Jesus was, why he lived, and the meaning of his life.

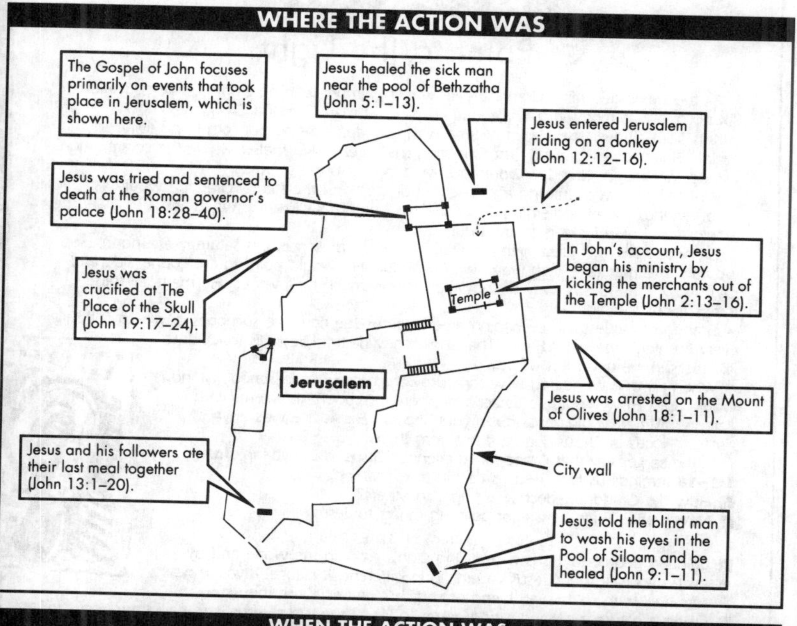
WHERE THE ACTION WAS
The Gospel of John focuses primarily on events that took place in Jerusalem, which is shown here.
Jesus healed the sick man near the pool of Bethzatha (John 5:1–13).
Jesus entered Jerusalem riding on a donkey (John 12:12–16).
Jesus was tried and sentenced to death at the Roman governor's palace (John 18:28–40).
Jesus was crucified at The Place of the Skull (John 19:17–24).
In John's account, Jesus began his ministry by kicking the merchants out of the Temple (John 2:13–16).
Temple
Jerusalem
Jesus was arrested on the Mount of Olives (John 18:1–11).
Jesus and his followers ate their last meal together (John 13:1–20).
City wall
Jesus told the blind man to wash his eyes in the Pool of Siloam and be healed (John 9:1–11).

WHEN THE ACTION WAS

BC/AD — Jesus was born
25AD — Jesus began his ministry
Jesus was crucified, rose from the dead, and went to heaven
50AD
Fire destroyed Rome
Romans destroyed the Temple in Jerusalem
75AD
100AD

Behind the Scenes (cont.):

This fourth Gospel is quite different from the other three. Like the others, it tells about what Jesus said and did. But it goes a step further by interpreting Jesus' significance as God's Son.

Many new believers turn first to this Gospel to discover what it means to be a Christian. That's not surprising, given the book's purpose as stated in John 20:31: "These [things] are written so that you may believe that Jesus is the Christ, the Son of God. Then, by believing, you may have life through his name."

Christ Comes to the World

1 In the beginning there was the Word.[n] The
Word was with God, and the Word was
God. 2He was with God in the beginning. 3All
things were made by him, and nothing was made
without him. 4In him there was life, and that life
was the light of all people. 5The Light shines in the
darkness, and the darkness has not overpowered
it.

6There was a man named John[n] who was sent
by God. 7He came to tell people the truth about
the Light so that through him all people could

Word The Greek word is "logos," meaning any kind of communication; it could be translated "message." Here, it means Christ, because Christ was the way God told people about himself.

John John the Baptist, who preached to people about Christ's coming (Matthew 3, Luke 3).

JESUS CHRIST

Point to the Light

All the kids called him "Grandpa." He was a plumber with an eighth-grade education. But no one was more articulate about Jesus Christ than Grandpa Craig.

Kids from all over spent a lot of time with Grandpa—eating popcorn in his living room, having Bible studies, praying, just "shooting the breeze." No matter where the conversation wandered, though, Grandpa would always bring it around to Jesus.

Whenever we were talking about school or dating or the future, Grandpa would say, "That reminds me of something Jesus said . . ." or, "That's just like when Jesus . . ." and he would reveal new insights to us about Jesus.

Grandpa's life was filled with the reality of Jesus' presence. On Saturday afternoons, we would sometimes take long walks with Grandpa. He would point to the countryside and say, "Now, that's Jesus' way of showing us how much he loves us. He made all these things for us to enjoy."

Grandpa saw Jesus in everything around him. "See how the sun goes down so faithfully every evening?" he would ask. "That shows how faithful Jesus is to us. Just like the sun, he never lets us down."

When anyone wondered how to act toward a new kid in school, Grandpa would ask, "How would Jesus act if he were in school?" Problems with parents? "What would Jesus do in your shoes?" His advice was always simple: "Focus on Jesus. Figure it out from there."

In the same way that Grandpa experienced Jesus in everything, **John 1:1–18** reminds us that Jesus is central to everything.

- How did Grandpa reflect Jesus' light to others?
- How can your life be a light pointing others to Jesus?

CONSIDER . . .

- pointing people to Jesus by noticing God's work in the world and by asking yourself what Jesus would do in different situations. If you're not sure, talk with a Christian friend or church member about the issue.
- taking a nature walk and sitting down to list all the ways Jesus is revealed through creation and then sharing your list with a friend.

FOR MORE, SEE . . .

- Isaiah 53:1–12
- Philippians 2:5–11
- Colossians 1:15–20

ıear about the Light and believe. 8John was not
he Light, but he came to tell people the truth
bout the Light. 9The true Light that gives light to
ll was coming into the world!
10The Word was in the world, and the world
vas made by him, but the world did not know
.im. 11He came to the world that was his own,
ut his own people did not accept him. 12But to
ll who did accept him and believe in him he gave
ıe right to become children of God. 13They did
ot become his children in any human way—by
ny human parents or human desire. They were
orn of God.
14The Word became a human and lived among
s. We saw his glory—the glory that belongs to
ıe only Son of the Father—and he was full of

> **SIDELIGHT:** Did you know Jesus was a great camper? When John 1:14 says "The Word became a human and lived among us," the literal Greek words say he "pitched his tent" among us. No fancy houses here!

race and truth. 15John tells the truth about him
ıd cries out, saying, "This is the One I told you
bout: 'The One who comes after me is greater
ıan I am, because he was living before me.' "
16Because he was full of grace and truth, from
m we all received one gift after another. 17The
w was given through Moses, but grace and truth
ıme through Jesus Christ. 18No one has ever
en God. But God the only Son is very close to
e Father,[n] and he has shown us what God is
ke.

›hn Tells People About Jesus

19Here is the truth John[n] told when the Jews
Jerusalem sent priests and Levites to ask him,
Vho are you?"
20John spoke freely and did not refuse to an-
ver. He said, "I am not the Christ."[d]
21So they asked him, "Then who are you? Are
u Elijah?"[n]
He answered, "No, I am not."
"Are you the Prophet?"[n] they asked.
He answered, "No."
22Then they said, "Who are you? Give us an
swer to tell those who sent us. What do you say
out yourself?"
23John told them in the words of the prophet
Isaiah:

"I am the voice of one
calling out in the desert:
'Make the road straight for the Lord.' "
Isaiah 40:3

24Some Pharisees[d] who had been sent asked
John: 25"If you are not the Christ or Elijah or the
Prophet, why do you baptize people?"
26John answered, "I baptize with water, but
there is one here with you that you don't know
about. 27He is the One who comes after me. I am
not good enough to untie the strings of his sandals."
28This all happened at Bethany on the other
side of the Jordan River, where John was baptizing people.
29The next day John saw Jesus coming toward
him. John said, "Look, the Lamb of God,[n] who
takes away the sin of the world! 30This is the One
I was talking about when I said, 'A man will come
after me, but he is greater than I am, because he
was living before me.' 31Even I did not know who
he was, although I came baptizing with water so
that the people of Israel would know who he is."
32-33Then John said, "I saw the Spirit come
down from heaven in the form of a dove and rest
on him. Until then I did not know who the Christ
was. But the God who sent me to baptize with
water told me, 'You will see the Spirit[d] come
down and rest on a man; he is the One who will
baptize with the Holy Spirit.' 34I have seen this
happen, and I tell you the truth: This man is the
Son of God."

The First Followers of Jesus

35The next day John[n] was there again with
two of his followers. 36When he saw Jesus walking by, he said, "Look, the Lamb of God!"[n]
37The two followers heard John say this, so
they followed Jesus. 38When Jesus turned and saw
them following him, he asked, "What are you
looking for?"
They said, "Rabbi, where are you staying?"
("Rabbi" means "Teacher.")
39He answered, "Come and see." So the two
men went with Jesus and saw where he was staying and stayed there with him that day. It was
about four o'clock in the afternoon.
40One of the two men who followed Jesus after
they heard John speak about him was Andrew,
Simon Peter's brother. 41The first thing Andrew

: . . . Father This could be translated, "But the only God is very close to the Father." Also, some Greek copies say, "But the only Son is very close to the Father."
n John the Baptist, who preached to people about Christ's coming (Matthew 3, Luke 3).
jah A man who spoke for God. He lived hundreds of years before Christ and was expected to return before Christ (Malachi 4:5-6).
›phet They probably meant the prophet that God told Moses he would send (Deuteronomy 18:15-19).
nb of God Name for Jesus. Jesus is like the lambs that were offered for a sacrifice to God.

did was to find his brother Simon and say to him,
"We have found the Messiah." ("Messiah" means
"Christ."[d])
42Then Andrew took Simon to Jesus. Jesus
looked at him and said, "You are Simon son of
John. You will be called Cephas." ("Cephas"
means "Peter."[n])
43The next day Jesus decided to go to Galilee.
He found Philip and said to him, "Follow me."
44Philip was from the town of Bethsaida, where
Andrew and Peter lived. 45Philip found Nathanael
and told him, "We have found the man that Moses wrote about in the law, and the prophets[d] also
wrote about him. He is Jesus, the son of Joseph,
from Nazareth."
46But Nathanael said to Philip, "Can anything
good come from Nazareth?"
Philip answered, "Come and see."
47As Jesus saw Nathanael coming toward him,
he said, "Here is truly an Israelite. There is nothing false in him."
48Nathanael asked, "How do you know me?"
Jesus answered, "I saw you when you were under the fig tree, before Philip told you about me."
49Then Nathanael said to Jesus, "Teacher, you
are the Son of God; you are the King of Israel."
50Jesus said to Nathanael, "Do you believe simply because I told you I saw you under the fig
tree? You will see greater things than that." 51And
Jesus said to them, "I tell you the truth, you will
all see heaven open and 'angels of God going up
and coming down'[n] on the Son of Man."[d]

The Wedding at Cana

2 Two days later there was a wedding in the
town of Cana in Galilee. Jesus' mother was
there, 2and Jesus and his followers were also invited to the wedding. 3When all the wine was
gone, Jesus' mother said to him, "They have no
more wine."
4Jesus answered, "Dear woman, why come to
me? My time has not yet come."
5His mother said to the servants, "Do whatever
he tells you to do."
6In that place there were six stone water jars
that the Jews used in their washing ceremony.[n]
Each jar held about twenty or thirty gallons.
7Jesus said to the servants, "Fill the jars with
water." So they filled the jars to the top.
8Then he said to them, "Now take some out
and give it to the master of the feast."
So they took the water to the master. 9When
he tasted it, the water had become wine. He did
not know where the wine came from, but the
servants who had brought the water knew. Th
master of the wedding called the bridegroo
10and said to him, "People always serve the be
wine first. Later, after the guests have been drin
ing awhile, they serve the cheaper wine. But yo
have saved the best wine till now."
11So in Cana of Galilee Jesus did his first mir
cle.[d] There he showed his glory, and his followe
believed in him.

> **SIDELIGHT:** The wedding at Cana (John 2:1–11) wouldn't have involved a short ceremony followed by a cake-and-punch reception. In Jesus' day, weddings usually lasted about a week. On the first day, the couple exchanged vows under a canopy. Then, for the next six days or more, the couple and all the guests celebrated with dancing, games, music, food, and wine.

Jesus in the Temple

12After this, Jesus went to the town of Cape
naum with his mother, brothers, and follower
They stayed there for just a few days. 13When
was almost time for the Jewish Passover[d] Fea
Jesus went to Jerusalem. 14In the Temple[d]
found people selling cattle, sheep, and doves.
saw others sitting at tables, exchanging differe
kinds of money. 15Jesus made a whip out of cor
and forced all of them, both the sheep and catt
to leave the Temple. He turned over the tabl
and scattered the money of those who were e
changing it. 16Then he said to those who we
selling pigeons, "Take these things out of he
Don't make my Father's house a place for buyi
and selling!"
17When this happened, the followers reme
bered what was written in the Scriptures:[d] "M
strong love for your Temple completely contr
me."[n]
18The Jews said to Jesus, "Show us a mirac
to prove you have the right to do these thing
19Jesus answered them, "Destroy this temp
and I will build it again in three days."
20The Jews answered, "It took forty-six years
build this Temple! Do you really believe you c
build it again in three days?"
21(But the temple Jesus meant was his ov
body. 22After Jesus was raised from the dead,
followers remembered that Jesus had said th

Peter The Greek name "Peter," like the Aramaic name "Cephas," means "rock."
'angels . . . down' These words are from Genesis 28:12.
washing ceremony The Jewish people washed themselves in special ways before eating, before worshiping in the Temple and at other special times.
"My . . . me." Quotation from Psalm 69:9.

Then they believed the Scripture[d] and the words
Jesus had said.)
23When Jesus was in Jerusalem for the Passover
Feast, many people believed in him because they
saw the miracles he did. 24But Jesus did not trust
himself to them because he knew them all. 25He
did not need anyone to tell him about people, because he knew what was in people's minds.

Nicodemus Comes to Jesus

3 There was a man named Nicodemus who
was one of the Pharisees[d] and an important
Jewish leader. 2One night Nicodemus came to
Jesus and said, "Teacher, we know you are a
teacher sent from God, because no one can do the
miracles[d] you do unless God is with him."
3Jesus answered, "I tell you the truth, unless
one is born again, he cannot be in God's kingdom."
4Nicodemus said, "But if a person is already
old, how can he be born again? He cannot enter
his mother's body again. So how can a person be
born a second time?"
5But Jesus answered, "I tell you the truth, unless one is born from water and the Spirit,[d] he
cannot enter God's kingdom. 6Human life comes
from human parents, but spiritual life comes from
the Spirit. 7Don't be surprised when I tell you,
'You must all be born again.' 8The wind blows
where it wants to and you hear the sound of it,
but you don't know where the wind comes from
or where it is going. It is the same with every
person who is born from the Spirit."
9Nicodemus asked, "How can this happen?"
10Jesus said, "You are an important teacher in
Israel, and you don't understand these things? 11I
tell you the truth, we talk about what we know,
and we tell about what we have seen, but you
don't accept what we tell you. 12I have told you
about things here on earth, and you do not be-

ANGER

Constructive Anger

They wander the streets late at night in the toughest parts of town. Jackets with their emblem let anyone who can see know exactly who they are.

They are not the Crips or Bloods. They are not even a gang. They are "Mad Dads"—men who have dedicated themselves to fight the influences of gangs and substance abuse in Omaha, Nebraska.

Neighborhoods feel the difference when the Mad Dads come around. These men educate adults about the needs of young people. They clean up gang graffiti, work with local businesses to find jobs for kids who need them, and encourage kids to stay in school and out of trouble.

Often, volunteer patrols of Mad Dads watch for gang or drug-related activities, and then report them to the police.

Mad Dads formed out of the founders' shared anger against gang violence and drug pushing in their neighborhoods. They finally got angry enough to take positive action.

Eddie Staton, one of the founders, said, "For too long, we, as black men, were silent. And people took our silence to mean we didn't care about drugs, alcohol, or gangs. So we took action. As parents, as black fathers in particular . . . we are actively involved in preventative measures against the influences of gangs, drugs, and alcohol."

Jesus became angry at bad influences too. Read **John 2:12–22** to see what Jesus did with his anger.

- How are the Mad Dads' actions like Jesus' actions in this passage? How are they different?
- When have you been so angry at wrongdoing that you took action against it like Jesus or the Mad Dads did?

CONSIDER. . .

- stopping the next time you get angry, and praying that your anger will produce something positive.
- memorizing Ephesians 4:26. What does the verse mean to you? Meditate on it so it can help you the next time you are angry.

FOR MORE, SEE. . .

- Psalm 103:7–13
- Ephesians 4:26–27
- James 1:19–20

lieve me. So you will not believe me if I tell you
about things of heaven. 13The only one who has
ever gone up to heaven is the One who came
down from heaven—the Son of Man.[d]
14"Just as Moses lifted up the snake in the
desert,[n] the Son of Man must also be lifted up.
15So that everyone who believes can have eternal
life in him.
16"God loved the world so much that he gave
his one and only Son so that whoever believes in
him may not be lost, but have eternal life. 17God
did not send his Son into the world to judge the
world guilty, but to save the world through him.
18People who believe in God's Son are not judged
guilty. Those who do not believe have already
been judged guilty, because they have not believed in God's one and only Son. 19They are
judged by this fact: The Light has come into the
world, but they did not want light. They wanted
darkness, because they were doing evil things.
20All who do evil hate the light and will not come
to the light, because it will show all the evil things
they do. 21But those who follow the true way
come to the light, and it shows that the things
they do were done through God."

Jesus and John the Baptist

22After this, Jesus and his followers went into
the area of Judea, where he stayed with his followers and baptized people. 23John was also baptizing in Aenon, near Salim, because there was
plenty of water there. People were going there to
be baptized. 24(This was before John was put into
prison.)
25Some of John's followers had an argument
with a Jew about religious washing.[n] 26So they
came to John and said, "Teacher, remember the
man who was with you on the other side of the
Jordan River, the one you spoke about so much?
He is baptizing, and everyone is going to him."
27John answered, "A man can get only what
God gives him. 28You yourselves heard me say, 'I

Moses . . . desert When the Israelites were dying from snake bites, God told Moses to put a brass snake on a pole. The people who looked at the snake were healed (Numbers 21:4-9).

religious washing The Jewish people washed themselves in special ways before eating, before worshiping in the Temple, and at other special times.

ETERNAL LIFE

The Ultimate Price

Brian Watkins had been in New York City before. Brian loved the annual trip his family made from Provo, Utah, to watch the U.S. Open together in New York.

One Sunday during the 1990 tournament, Brian was waiting with his parents in a Manhattan subway station when a gang approached them. Surrounding the Watkinses, they robbed Brian's father, then began beating Brian's mother.

Brian fought back to defend his mother. The attackers turned from Brian's mother to Brian. In the struggle, one of the robbers pulled a knife and stabbed Brian to death.

Brian Watkins paid the ultimate price because he couldn't stand watching the ones he loved be hurt. Jesus, God's Son, willingly paid the ultimate price for us because he doesn't want us to be hurt forever.

In **John 3:1–21**, Jesus talks about the gift of eternal life that his death would provide.

- How were Brian's feelings for his parents like God's desires for us? How were they different?
- According to this passage (especially verses 16–18), what must we do to receive all God desires for us?

CONSIDER . . .

- writing John 3:16 on paper, placing it in a box, and gift wrapping the box. Give the box to a friend to keep in his or her room as a reminder of God's gift of eternal life.
- asking your pastor or youth leader what eternal life is, then comparing the answer to what Jesus said in this passage.

FOR MORE, SEE . . .

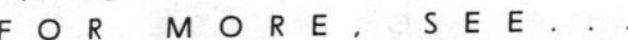

- Isaiah 12
- 1 Timothy 1:12–17
- 1 John 5:1–12

am not the Christ,[d] but I am the one sent to prepare the way for him.' 29The bride belongs only to
the bridegroom. But the friend who helps the
bridegroom stands by and listens to him. He is
thrilled that he gets to hear the bridegroom's
voice. In the same way, I am really happy. 30He
must become greater, and I must become less important.

The One Who Comes from Heaven

31"The One who comes from above is greater
than all. The one who is from the earth belongs
to the earth and talks about things on the earth.
But the One who comes from heaven is greater
than all. 32He tells what he has seen and heard,
but no one accepts what he says. 33Whoever accepts what he says has proven that God is true.
34The One whom God sent speaks the words of
God, because God gives him the Spirit[d] fully.
35The Father loves the Son and has given him
power over everything. 36Those who believe in
the Son have eternal life, but those who do not
obey the Son will never have life. God's anger
stays on them."

Jesus and a Samaritan Woman

4 The Pharisees[d] heard that Jesus was making
and baptizing more followers than John, 2al-
though Jesus himself did not baptize people, but
his followers did. 3Jesus knew that the Pharisees
had heard about him, so he left Judea and went
back to Galilee. 4But on the way he had to go
through the country of Samaria.

5In Samaria Jesus came to the town called Sychar, which is near the field Jacob gave to his son
Joseph. 6Jacob's well was there. Jesus was tired
from his long trip, so he sat down beside the well.
It was about twelve o'clock noon. 7When a Samaritan[d] woman came to the well to get some
water, Jesus said to her, "Please give me a drink."
8(This happened while Jesus' followers were in
town buying some food.)

9The woman said, "I am surprised that you ask
me for a drink, since you are a Jewish man and
I am a Samaritan woman." (Jewish people are not
friends with Samaritans.[n])

10Jesus said, "If you only knew the free gift of
God and who it is that is asking you for water, you
would have asked him, and he would have given
you living water."

11The woman said, "Sir, where will you get this
living water? The well is very deep, and you have
nothing to get water with. 12Are you greater than
Jacob, our father, who gave us this well and drank
from it himself along with his sons and flocks?"

13Jesus answered, "Everyone who drinks this
water will be thirsty again, 14but whoever drinks
the water I give will never be thirsty. The water
I give will become a spring of water gushing up
inside that person, giving eternal life."

15The woman said to him, "Sir, give me this
water so I will never be thirsty again and will not
have to come back here to get more water."

16Jesus told her, "Go get your husband and
come back here."

17The woman answered, "I have no husband."
Jesus said to her, "You are right to say you have
no husband. 18Really you have had five husbands,
and the man you live with now is not your husband. You told the truth."

19The woman said, "Sir, I can see that you are
a prophet.[d] 20Our ancestors worshiped on this
mountain, but you Jews say that Jerusalem is the
place where people must worship."

21Jesus said, "Believe me, woman. The time is
coming when neither in Jerusalem nor on this
mountain will you actually worship the Father.
22You Samaritans worship something you don't
understand. We understand what we worship,
because salvation comes from the Jews. 23The
time is coming when the true worshipers will
worship the Father in spirit and truth, and that
time is here already. You see, the Father too is
actively seeking such people to worship him.
24God is spirit, and those who worship him must
worship in spirit and truth."

25The woman said, "I know that the Messiah is
coming." (Messiah is the One called Christ.[d])
"When the Messiah comes, he will explain everything to us."

26Then Jesus said, "I am he — I, the one talking
to you."

27Just then his followers came back from town
and were surprised to see him talking with a
woman. But none of them asked, "What do you
want?" or "Why are you talking with her?"

28Then the woman left her water jar and went
back to town. She said to the people, 29"Come
and see a man who told me everything I ever did.
Do you think he might be the Christ?" 30So the
people left the town and went to see Jesus.

SIDELIGHT: Jesus risked getting into lots of trouble when he talked with the Samaritan woman (see John 4:1–30). Jewish law forbade teachers to speak to women, Jews to talk to Samaritans, and the "righteous" to mingle with "sinners." Kinda made it hard to have any friends, don't you think?

Jewish people . . . Samaritans. This can also be translated "Jewish people don't use things that Samaritans have used."

31 Meanwhile, his followers were begging him,
"Teacher, eat something."
32 But Jesus answered, "I have food to eat that
you know nothing about."
33 So the followers asked themselves, "Did
somebody already bring him food?"
34 Jesus said, "My food is to do what the One
who sent me wants me to do and to finish his
work. 35 You have a saying, 'Four more months till
harvest.' But I tell you, open your eyes and look
at the fields ready for harvest now. 36 Already, the
one who harvests is being paid and is gathering
crops for eternal life. So the one who plants and
the one who harvests celebrate at the same time.
37 Here the saying is true, 'One person plants, and
another harvests.' 38 I sent you to harvest a crop
that you did not work on. Others did the work,
and you get to finish up their work."[n]
39 Many of the Samaritans in that town believed
in Jesus because of what the woman said: "He
told me everything I ever did." 40 When the Samaritans came to Jesus, they begged him to stay
with them, so he stayed there two more days.
41 And many more believed because of the things
he said.
42 They said to the woman, "First we believed
in Jesus because of your speech, but now we believe because we heard him ourselves. We know

But I . . . their work. As a farmer sends workers to harvest grain, Jesus sends his followers out to bring people to God.

JUDGING OTHERS

Prejudice

The bell rang. Creative writing was over for another day. Burt Moore stared at his short story.

His classmates walked by, some commenting as they passed. "What an imagination you have in there!" Burt wasn't sure if it was a compliment or not. "I'd love to hear you try reading it yourself, freak." He was sure that wasn't a compliment.

Burt waited for the classroom traffic to clear, then made his way to his next class: trigonometry.

Mr. Springer, his teacher, greeted him at the doorway. "Hi, Burt!" he yelled. "How are you today?"

Burt just nodded and wondered, once again, why people treated him like he was deaf.

When Burt began attending public school in junior high, one of the toughest adjustments was learning how to interact with others. Some people were great. They shared Burt's interest in chess and science fiction, and made special efforts to make him their friend. Others, though, openly insulted him for being different.

Burt learned a lot about prejudice in junior high and high school. Because of his severe cerebral palsy, some people expected Burt to be stupid. He always took special pleasure in blowing away stereotypes by writing a creative short story or taking the toughest math class offered.

Burt was different from others in some ways. His speech was often difficult to understand. He communicated by typing with touchsticks strapped to his hands. And he traveled by moving a joystick attached to his wheelchair.

But Burt had a lot more in common with those around him than many people thought. A lot of them refused to see beyond his wheelchair or his inability to speak as they did. And their prejudice was tough on Burt.

Jesus also had to overcome people's prejudice. Read **John 4:5–42** about how Jesus dealt with prejudice toward himself and others.

- How did Burt break down prejudice in the same way Jesus did?
- What prejudices do you have? How would Jesus respond to those prejudices?

CONSIDER. . .

- writing a letter to the editor of your school or local newspaper concerning a prejudice you see. Describe ways to combat that prejudice.
- regularly eating lunch at school with someone who has been hurt by prejudice.

FOR MORE, SEE. . .

- Psalm 9:7–10
- Acts 10:1–33
- Galatians 3:26–29

that this man really is the Savior of the world."

Jesus Heals an Officer's Son

43Two days later, Jesus left and went to Galilee. 44(Jesus had said before that a prophet[d] is not respected in his own country.) 45When Jesus arrived in Galilee, the people there welcomed him. They had seen all the things he did at the Passover[d] Feast in Jerusalem, because they had been there, too.

46Jesus went again to visit Cana in Galilee where he had changed the water into wine. One of the king's important officers lived in the city of Capernaum, and his son was sick. 47When he heard that Jesus had come from Judea to Galilee, he went to Jesus and begged him to come to Capernaum and heal his son, because his son was almost dead. 48Jesus said to him, "You people must see signs and miracles[d] before you will believe in me."

49The officer said, "Sir, come before my child dies."

50Jesus answered, "Go. Your son will live."

The man believed what Jesus told him and went home. 51On the way the man's servants came and met him and told him, "Your son is alive."

52The man asked, "What time did my son begin to get well?"

They answered, "Yesterday at one o'clock the fever left him."

53The father knew that one o'clock was the exact time that Jesus had said, "Your son will live." So the man and all the people who lived in his house believed in Jesus.

54That was the second miracle Jesus did after coming from Judea to Galilee.

Jesus Heals a Man at a Pool

5 Later Jesus went to Jerusalem for a special Jewish feast. 2In Jerusalem there is a pool with five covered porches, which is called Bethzatha[n] in the Jewish language.[n] This pool is near the Sheep Gate. 3Many sick people were lying on the porches beside the pool. Some were blind, some were crippled, and some were paralyzed.[n] 5A man was lying there who had been sick for thirty-eight years. 6When Jesus saw the man and knew that he had been sick for such a long time, Jesus asked him, "Do you want to be well?"

7The sick man answered, "Sir, there is no one to help me get into the pool when the water starts moving. While I am coming to the water, someone else always gets in before me."

8Then Jesus said, "Stand up. Pick up your mat and walk." 9And immediately the man was well; he picked up his mat and began to walk.

The day this happened was a Sabbath[d] day. 10So the Jews said to the man who had been healed, "Today is the Sabbath. It is against our law for you to carry your mat on the Sabbath day."

11But he answered, "The man who made me well told me, 'Pick up your mat and walk.' "

12Then they asked him, "Who is the man who told you to pick up your mat and walk?"

13But the man who had been healed did not know who it was, because there were many people in that place, and Jesus had left.

14Later, Jesus found the man at the Temple[d] and said to him, "See, you are well now. Stop sinning so that something worse does not happen to you."

15Then the man left and told the Jews that Jesus was the one who had made him well.

16Because Jesus was doing this on the Sabbath day, the Jews began to persecute him. 17But Jesus said to them, "My Father never stops working, and so I keep working, too."

18This made the Jews try still harder to kill him. They said, "First Jesus was breaking the law about the Sabbath day. Now he says that God is his own Father, making himself equal with God!"

Jesus Has God's Authority

19But Jesus said, "I tell you the truth, the Son can do nothing alone. The Son does only what he sees the Father doing, because the Son does whatever the Father does. 20The Father loves the Son and shows the Son all the things he himself does. But the Father will show the Son even greater things than this so that you can all be amazed. 21Just as the Father raises the dead and gives them life, so also the Son gives life to those he wants to. 22In fact, the Father judges no one, but he has given the Son power to do all the judging 23so that all people will honor the Son as much as they honor the Father. Anyone who does not honor the Son does not honor the Father who sent him.

24"I tell you the truth, whoever hears what I say and believes in the One who sent me has eternal life. That person will not be judged guilty but has already left death and entered life. 25I tell you the truth, the time is coming and is already here when the dead will hear the voice of the Son of God, and those who hear will have life. 26Life comes from the Father himself, and he has allowed the Son to have life in himself as well.

Bethzatha Also called Bethsaida or Bethesda, a pool of water north of the Temple in Jerusalem.
Jewish language Hebrew or Aramaic, the languages of the Jewish people in the first century.
Verse 3 Some Greek copies add "and they waited for the water to move." A few later copies add verse 4: "Sometimes an angel of the Lord came down to the pool and stirred up the water. After the angel did this, the first person to go into the pool was healed from any sickness he had."

27And the Father has given the Son the power to
judge, because he is the Son of Man.[d] 28Don't be
surprised at this: A time is coming when all who
are dead and in their graves will hear his voice.
29Then they will come out of their graves. Those
who did good will rise and have life forever, but
those who did evil will rise to be judged guilty.

Jesus Is God's Son

30"I can do nothing alone. I judge only the way
I am told, so my judgment is fair. I don't try to
please myself, but I try to please the One who sent
me.

31"If only I tell people about myself, what I say
is not true. 32But there is another who tells about
me, and I know that the things he says about me
are true.

33"You have sent people to John, and he has
told you the truth. 34It is not that I accept such
human telling; I tell you this so you can be saved.
35John was like a burning and shining lamp, and
you were happy to enjoy his light for a while.

36"But I have a proof about myself that is
greater than that of John. The things I do, which
are the things my Father gave me to do, prove
that the Father sent me. 37And the Father himself
who sent me has given proof about me. You have
never heard his voice or seen what he looks like.
38His teaching does not live in you, because you
don't believe in the One the Father sent. 39You
carefully study the Scriptures[d] because you think
they give you eternal life. They do in fact tell
about me, 40but you refuse to come to me to have
that life.

41"I don't need praise from people. 42But I
know you—I know that you don't have God's
love in you. 43I have come from my Father and
speak for him, but you don't accept me. But when
another person comes, speaking only for himself,
you will accept him. 44You try to get praise from
each other, but you do not try to get the praise
that comes from the only God. So how can you
believe? 45Don't think that I will stand before the
Father and say you are wrong. The one who says
you are wrong is Moses, the one you hoped
would save you. 46If you really believed Moses,
you would believe me, because Moses wrote
about me. 47But if you don't believe what Moses
wrote, how can you believe what I say?"

More than Five Thousand Fed

6 After this, Jesus went across Lake Galilee (or,
Lake Tiberias). 2Many people followed him
because they saw the miracles[d] he did to heal the
sick. 3Jesus went up on a hill and sat down there
with his followers. 4It was almost the time for the
Jewish Passover[d] Feast.

5When Jesus looked up and saw a large crowd
coming toward him, he said to Philip, "Where can
we buy enough bread for all these people to eat?"
6(Jesus asked Philip this question to test him, because Jesus already knew what he planned to do.)

7Philip answered, "We would all have to work
a month to buy enough bread for each person to
have only a little piece."

8Another one of his followers, Andrew, Simon
Peter's brother, said, 9"Here is a boy with five
loaves of barley bread and two little fish, but that
is not enough for so many people."

> **SIDELIGHT:** There were three types of bread in Jesus' day: small loaves (that would look like our biscuits), round loaves (about the size of basketballs), and flat loaves (large, bread-like pancakes). The boy who gave loaves to Jesus gave the first type (John 6:9). His were made from barley, indicating he was probably poor.

10Jesus said, "Tell the people to sit down." This
was a very grassy place, and about five thousand
men sat down there. 11Then Jesus took the loaves
of bread, thanked God for them, and gave them
to the people who were sitting there. He did the
same with the fish, giving as much as the people
wanted.

12When they had all had enough to eat, Jesus
said to his followers, "Gather the leftover pieces
of fish and bread so that nothing is wasted." 13So
they gathered up the pieces and filled twelve baskets with the pieces left from the five barley
loaves.

14When the people saw this miracle[d] that Jesus
did, they said, "He must truly be the Prophet[n]
who is coming into the world."

15Jesus knew that the people planned to come
and take him by force and make him their king,
so he left and went into the hills alone.

Jesus Walks on the Water

16That evening Jesus' followers went down to
Lake Galilee. 17It was dark now, and Jesus had not
yet come to them. The followers got into a boat
and started across the lake to Capernaum. 18By
now a strong wind was blowing, and the waves
on the lake were getting bigger. 19When they had
rowed the boat about three or four miles, they
saw Jesus walking on the water, coming toward
the boat. The followers were afraid, 20but Jesus
said to them, "It is I. Do not be afraid." 21Then
they were glad to take him into the boat. At once

Prophet They probably meant the prophet that God told Moses he would send (Deuteronomy 18:15-19).

the boat came to land at the place where they
wanted to go.

The People Seek Jesus

22The next day the people who had stayed on
the other side of the lake knew that Jesus had not
gone in the boat with his followers but that they
had left without him. And they knew that only
one boat had been there. 23But then some boats
came from Tiberias and landed near the place
where the people had eaten the bread after the
Lord had given thanks. 24When the people saw
that Jesus and his followers were not there now,
they got into boats and went to Capernaum to
find Jesus.

Jesus, the Bread of Life

25When the people found Jesus on the other
side of the lake, they asked him, "Teacher, when
did you come here?"

26Jesus answered, "I tell you the truth, you
aren't looking for me because you saw me do
miracles.[d] You are looking for me because you
ate the bread and were satisfied. 27Don't work
for the food that spoils. Work for the food
that stays good always and gives eternal life.
The Son of Man[d] will give you this food, because on him God the Father has put his power."

28The people asked Jesus, "What are the things
God wants us to do?"

29Jesus answered, "The work God wants you to
do is this: Believe the One he sent."

30So the people asked, "What miracle will you
do? If we see a miracle, we will believe you. What
will you do? 31Our fathers ate the manna[d] in the

PRIORITIES

Proms and Personalities

"So who are you going to the prom with this year?" Heather Keith asked.

"I'm waiting for Brett to ask me. He's got the greatest car, and his parents have loads of money. So I know we'd have a blast," Laurie Hull answered.

"I didn't know you liked Brett Howard. How long has this been going on?"

Laurie tossed her hair back. "Oh, I don't like him."

Heather didn't have to say anything. Her shocked look said it all.

"I don't have to like him to go to the prom with him," Laurie explained. "I just think we'd look good together. And he can afford the kind of evening I want."

Over the next few weeks, Laurie asked her friends to drop hints to Brett. She even teased him at lunch one day, asking if he had anyone with whom to share his Trans Am for the prom.

A week before the prom, though, Brett hadn't asked Laurie to the prom. Three other guys had asked the bubbly cheerleader, but Laurie thought they were too weird. They didn't have very much money, and she wasn't about to be seen with any of them.

Prom night came, and Laurie stayed home watching television. While her friends had a great time, Laurie ate popcorn and wondered why Brett had never asked her.

Laurie had focused on what she could get from people, rather than on the people themselves. But when she did, she came up empty-handed.

Jesus frequently challenged people to make people rather than things a priority. Read **John 6:24–51** to see how people tended to give Jesus' miracles higher priority than they gave Jesus himself.

- What was most important to Laurie and the people in this passage?
- How can you make people a priority in your life?

C O N S I D E R . . .

- looking at your class members' photographs in a recent yearbook. Ask God to help you focus on your classmates as people and not on what you can get from them.
- telling five friends or family members the things you appreciate about them. Focus only on inner qualities and not on what you can get from them.

F O R M O R E , S E E . . .

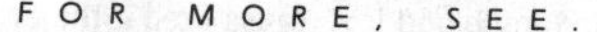

- 1 Samuel 16:6–13
- Matthew 6:25–34
- James 2:1–9

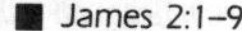

desert. This is written in the Scriptures:[d] 'He gave
them bread from heaven to eat.' "[n]
32Jesus said, "I tell you the truth, it was not
Moses who gave you bread from heaven; it is my
Father who is giving you the true bread from
heaven. 33God's bread is the One who comes
down from heaven and gives life to the world."
34The people said, "Sir, give us this bread always."
35Then Jesus said, "I am the bread that gives
life. Whoever comes to me will never be hungry,
and whoever believes in me will never be thirsty.
36But as I told you before, you have seen me and
still don't believe. 37The Father gives me my people. Every one of them will come to me, and I will
always accept them. 38I came down from heaven
to do what God wants me to do, not what I want
to do. 39Here is what the One who sent me wants
me to do: I must not lose even one whom God
gave me, but I must raise them all on the last day.
40Those who see the Son and believe in him have
eternal life, and I will raise them on the last day.
This is what my Father wants."
41The Jews began to complain about Jesus because he said, "I am the bread that comes down
from heaven." 42They said, "This is Jesus, the son
of Joseph. We know his father and mother. How
can he say, 'I came down from heaven'?"
43But Jesus answered, "Stop complaining to
each other. 44The Father is the One who sent me.
No one can come to me unless the Father draws
him to me, and I will raise that person up on the
last day. 45It is written in the prophets,[d] 'They will
all be taught by God.'[n] Everyone who listens to
the Father and learns from him comes to me. 46No
one has seen the Father except the One who is
from God; only he has seen the Father. 47I tell you
the truth, whoever believes has eternal life. 48I am
the bread that gives life. 49Your ancestors ate the
manna in the desert, but still they died. 50Here is
the bread that comes down from heaven. Anyone
who eats this bread will never die. 51I am the living bread that came down from heaven. Anyone
who eats this bread will live forever. This bread
is my flesh, which I will give up so that the world
may have life."
52Then the Jews began to argue among themselves, saying, "How can this man give us his flesh
to eat?"
53Jesus said, "I tell you the truth, you must eat
the flesh of the Son of Man and drink his blood.
Otherwise, you won't have real life in you.
54Those who eat my flesh and drink my blood
have eternal life, and I will raise them up on the
last day. 55My flesh is true food, and my blood is
true drink. 56Those who eat my flesh and drink
my blood live in me, and I live in them. 57The
living Father sent me, and I live because of the
Father. So whoever eats me will live because of
me. 58I am not like the bread your ancestors ate.
They ate that bread and still died. I am the bread
that came down from heaven, and whoever eats
this bread will live forever." 59Jesus said all these
things while he was teaching in the synagogue[d] in
Capernaum.

The Words of Eternal Life

60When the followers of Jesus heard this, many
of them said, "This teaching is hard. Who can accept it?"
61Knowing that his followers were complaining
about this, Jesus said, "Does this teaching bother
you? 62Then will it also bother you to see the Son
of Man[d] going back to the place where he came
from? 63It is the Spirit that gives life. The flesh
doesn't give life. The words I told you are spirit,
and they give life. 64But some of you don't believe." (Jesus knew from the beginning who did
not believe and who would turn against him.)
65Jesus said, "That is the reason I said, 'If the Father does not bring a person to me, that one cannot come.' "
66After Jesus said this, many of his followers left
him and stopped following him.
67Jesus asked the twelve followers, "Do you
want to leave, too?"
68Simon Peter answered him, "Lord, where
would we go? You have the words that give eternal life. 69We believe and know that you are the
Holy One from God."
70Then Jesus answered, "I chose all twelve of
you, but one of you is a devil."
71Jesus was talking about Judas, the son of Simon Iscariot. Judas was one of the twelve, but
later he was going to turn against Jesus.

Jesus' Brothers Don't Believe

7 After this, Jesus traveled around Galilee. He
did not want to travel in Judea, because the
Jews there wanted to kill him. 2It was time for the
Jewish Feast[d] of Shelters. 3So Jesus' brothers said
to him, "You should leave here and go to Judea
so your followers there can see the miracles[d] you
do. 4Anyone who wants to be well known does
not hide what he does. If you are doing these
things, show yourself to the world." 5(Even Jesus'
brothers did not believe in him.)
6Jesus said to his brothers, "The right time for
me has not yet come, but any time is right for you.
7The world cannot hate you, but it hates me, because I tell it the evil things it does. 8So you go to
the feast. I will not go yet to this feast, because the

'He gave . . . eat.' Quotation from Psalm 78:24.
'They . . . God.' Quotation from Isaiah 54:13.

right time for me has not yet come." 9After saying
this, Jesus stayed in Galilee.
10But after Jesus' brothers had gone to the feast,
Jesus went also. But he did not let people see him.
11At the feast the Jews were looking for him and
saying, "Where is that man?"
12Within the large crowd there, many people
were whispering to each other about Jesus. Some
said, "He is a good man."
Others said, "No, he fools the people." 13But no
one was brave enough to talk about Jesus openly,
because they were afraid of the Jews.

Jesus Teaches at the Feast

14When the feast was about half over, Jesus
went to the Temple[d] and began to teach. 15The
Jews were amazed and said, "This man has never
studied in school. How did he learn so much?"
16Jesus answered, "The things I teach are not
my own, but they come from him who sent me.
17If people choose to do what God wants, they
will know that my teaching comes from God and
not from me. 18Those who teach their own ideas
are trying to get honor for themselves. But those
who try to bring honor to the one who sent him
speak the truth, and there is nothing false in
them. 19Moses gave you the law,[n] but none of
you obeys that law. Why are you trying to kill
me?"
20The people answered, "A demon[d] has come
into you. We are not trying to kill you."
21Jesus said to them, "I did one miracle,[d] and
you are all amazed. 22Moses gave you the law
about circumcision.[d] (But really Moses did not
give you circumcision; it came from our ancestors.) And yet you circumcise a baby on a Sabbath[d] day. 23If a baby can be circumcised on a
Sabbath day to obey the law of Moses, why are
you angry at me for healing a person's whole body
on the Sabbath day? 24Stop judging by the way
things look, but judge by what is really right."

Is Jesus the Christ?

25Then some of the people who lived in Jerusa-

law Moses gave God's people the law that God gave him on Mount Sinai (Exodus 34:29-32).

LIFE

Along for the Ride

Angie Baldwin had kept quiet about her heart problem so long that even the memories of surgeries and long hospital stays didn't seem real to her. She lived the life of an amazingly active, fun-loving eighth grader.

So when her school band took a trip to an amusement park, Angie reluctantly delivered her mother's note to the band director. The note said Angie shouldn't ride the "thrill rides."

Angie refused at first to join her boyfriend on one of the park's featured thrill rides. She kept quiet about her heart while he teased her about being chicken.

Angie finally gave in. The initial ride kind of took her breath, but she wasn't feeling too bad at the end of it.

Just as her second venture was beginning, Angie passed out. The ride operator stopped the ride, got Angie out, and called an ambulance.

Three hours later, Angie was having another heart surgery. In the middle of the operation, her heart stopped for twenty seconds. Angie might have died had she not been plugged into life-support equipment.

Angie has fully recovered, but her brush with death has made her more aware of how fragile life can be. And she's more open about her heart condition and her restrictions.

Life is a wonderful gift. Read **John 6:59–69** to see how Jesus said he was the only one who could give life.

- What words of assurance would Angie find in the passage?
- What do you appreciate most about the life Jesus has given you?

CONSIDER . . .

- buying or picking a flower to display in your room as a reminder of the gift of life.
- spending an afternoon taking pictures of the things you most enjoy about life, then creating a photo arrangement once they are developed.

FOR MORE, SEE . . .

- Leviticus 17:10–14
- Psalm 104:33–35
- Hebrews 9:11–15

lem said, "This is the man they are trying to kill. 26But he is teaching where everyone can see and hear him, and no one is trying to stop him. Maybe the leaders have decided he really is the Christ.[d] 27But we know where this man is from. And when the real Christ comes, no one will know where he comes from."

28Jesus, teaching in the Temple,[d] cried out, "Yes, you know me, and you know where I am from. But I have not come by my own authority. I was sent by the One who is true, whom you don't know. 29But I know him, because I am from him, and he sent me."

30When Jesus said this, the people tried to take him. But no one was able to touch him, because it was not yet the right time. 31But many of the people believed in Jesus. They said, "When the Christ comes, will he do more miracles[d] than this man has done?"

The Leaders Try to Arrest Jesus

32The Pharisees[d] heard the crowd whispering these things about Jesus. So the leading priests and the Pharisees sent some Temple[d] guards to arrest him. 33Jesus said, "I will be with you a little while longer. Then I will go back to the One who sent me. 34You will look for me, but you will not find me. And you cannot come where I am."

35The Jews said to each other, "Where will this man go so we cannot find him? Will he go to the Greek cities where our people live and teach the Greek people there? 36What did he mean when he said, 'You will look for me, but you will not find me,' and 'You cannot come where I am'?"

Jesus Talks About the Spirit

37On the last and most important day of the feast Jesus stood up and said in a loud voice, "Let anyone who is thirsty come to me and drink. 38If anyone believes in me, rivers of living water will flow out from that person's heart, as the Scripture[d] says." 39Jesus was talking about the Holy Spirit.[d] The Spirit had not yet been given, because Jesus had not yet been raised to glory. But later, those who believed in Jesus would receive the Spirit.

The People Argue About Jesus

40When the people heard Jesus' words, some of them said, "This man really is the Prophet."[n]

41Others said, "He is the Christ."[d]

Still others said, "The Christ will not come from Galilee. 42The Scripture[d] says that the Christ will come from David's family and from Bethlehem, the town where David lived." 43So the people did not agree with each other about Jesus. 44Some of them wanted to arrest him, but no one was able to touch him.

Some Leaders Won't Believe

45The Temple[d] guards went back to the leading priests and the Pharisees,[d] who asked, "Why didn't you bring Jesus?"

46The guards answered, "The words he says are greater than the words of any other person who has ever spoken!"

47The Pharisees answered, "So Jesus has fooled you also! 48Have any of the leaders or the Pharisees believed in him? No! 49But these people, who know nothing about the law, are under God's curse."

50Nicodemus, who had gone to see Jesus before, was in that group.[n] He said, 51"Our law does not judge a man without hearing him and knowing what he has done."

52They answered, "Are you from Galilee, too? Study the Scriptures,[d] and you will learn that no prophet[d] comes from Galilee."

Some early Greek manuscripts do not contain 7:53—8:11.

[53And everyone left and went home.

The Woman Caught in Adultery

8 Jesus went to the Mount of Olives.[d] 2But early in the morning he went back to the Temple,[d] and all the people came to him, and he sat and taught them. 3The teachers of the law and the Pharisees[d] brought a woman who had been caught in adultery.[d] They forced her to stand before the people. 4They said to Jesus, "Teacher, this woman was caught having sexual relations with a man who is not her husband. 5The law of Moses commands that we stone to death every woman who does this. What do you say we should do?" 6They were asking this to trick Jesus so that they could have some charge against him.

But Jesus bent over and started writing on the ground with his finger. 7When they continued to ask Jesus their question, he raised up and said, "Anyone here who has never sinned can throw the first stone at her." 8Then Jesus bent over again and wrote on the ground.

9Those who heard Jesus began to leave one by one, first the older men and then the others. Jesus was left there alone with the woman standing before him. 10Jesus raised up again and asked her,

Prophet They probably meant the prophet God told Moses he would send (Deuteronomy 18:15-19).
Nicodemus . . . group. The story about Nicodemus going and talking to Jesus is in John 3:1-21.

"Woman, where are they? Has no one judged you
guilty?"
11She answered, "No one, sir."
Then Jesus said, "I also don't judge you guilty.
You may go now, but don't sin anymore."]

Jesus Is the Light of the World

12Later, Jesus talked to the people again, saying,
"I am the light of the world. The person who follows me will never live in darkness but will have
the light that gives life."
13The Pharisees[d] said to Jesus, "When you talk
about yourself, you are the only one to say these
things are true. We cannot accept what you say."
14Jesus answered, "Yes, I am saying these
things about myself, but they are true. I know
where I came from and where I am going. But
you don't know where I came from or where I am
going. 15You judge by human standards. I am not
judging anyone. 16But when I do judge, my judging is true, because I am not alone. The Father
who sent me is with me. 17Your own law says that
when two witnesses say the same thing, you must
accept what they say. 18I am one of the witnesses
who speaks about myself, and the Father who
sent me is the other witness."

> **SIDELIGHT:** When the teachers of the law and the Pharisees brought the woman caught in adultery to Jesus, they were more interested in tricking Jesus than in doing what was right (John 8:1–11). Though the woman was "caught in adultery," they didn't accuse the man involved—even though the law demanded that both be executed if guilty (Leviticus 20:10).

SEXUALITY

Once Forgiven, What Then?

Stephanie Broussard silently wept as Ross Walker sat next to her in the front seat of his dad's Buick, buttoning his shirt. The silence seemed to swallow them.

"Ross, we said we'd never do this again," she finally said through her tears.

"Well, we didn't mean to. . . . It just happened," Ross responded.

"That's what you always say." The two sat silently for a long time, and then Stephanie finally spoke, "I don't think we should see each other anymore."

Ross didn't say anything. He just stared out the window. But Stephanie knew by his sniffling that he was crying.

Stephanie reached across and touched his arm. "I'm sorry, Ross, but I just can't keep doing this to us—or to God. We just keep doing it over and over, and then asking God to forgive us."

Ross jerked his head around and looked at Stephanie. "But God does forgive us, Steph," Ross argued. "We won't do it again."

Stephanie started crying even harder. "No, Ross, we say that every time. I'm serious this time. We can't keep sinning and expect God to forgive us. I love you, but this hurts too much. Please take me home."

In **John 8:1–11**, Jesus faced a woman caught in sexual sin. Read what he said to her.

- How are Ross and Stephanie similar to the woman caught in adultery? How are they different?
- What does this passage tell us about Jesus' perspective on sexual sin and the person who commits it? What is there in your life that needs to hear his "don't sin anymore"?

CONSIDER. . .

- evaluating the movies you watch or music you listen to and deciding what view of sexuality they promote.
- acting on one area of your life where Jesus is telling you to "go and not sin anymore." Tell a friend or parent about the area, and ask that person to support you in your decision.

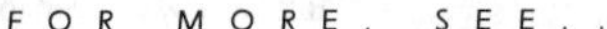

FOR MORE, SEE. . .

- Psalm 51:1–19
- I Corinthians 6:12–20
- Ephesians 6:10–18

19They asked, "Where is your father?"
Jesus answered, "You don't know me or my
Father. If you knew me, you would know my Father, too." 20Jesus said these things while he was
teaching in the Temple,[d] near where the money
is kept. But no one arrested him, because the right
time for him had not yet come.

The People Misunderstand Jesus

21Again, Jesus said to the people, "I will leave
you, and you will look for me, but you will die in
your sins. You cannot come where I am going."
22So the Jews asked, "Will Jesus kill himself? Is
that why he said, 'You cannot come where I am
going'?"
23Jesus said, "You people are from here below,
but I am from above. You belong to this world,
but I don't belong to this world. 24So I told you
that you would die in your sins. Yes, you will die
in your sins if you don't believe that I am he."
25They asked, "Then who are you?"
Jesus answered, "I am what I have told you
from the beginning. 26I have many things to say
and decide about you. But I tell people only the
things I have heard from the One who sent me,
and he speaks the truth."
27The people did not understand that he was
talking to them about the Father. 28So Jesus said
to them, "When you lift up the Son of Man,[d] you
will know that I am he. You will know that these
things I do are not by my own authority but that
I say only what the Father has taught me. 29The
One who sent me is with me. I always do what
is pleasing to him, so he has not left me alone."
30While Jesus was saying these things, many people believed in him.

Freedom from Sin

31So Jesus said to the Jews who believed in
him, "If you continue to obey my teaching, you
are truly my followers. 32Then you will know the
truth, and the truth will make you free."
33They answered, "We are Abraham's children,
and we have never been anyone's slaves. So why
do you say we will be free?"
34Jesus answered, "I tell you the truth, everyone who lives in sin is a slave to sin. 35A slave does
not stay with a family forever, but a son belongs
to the family forever. 36So if the Son makes you
free, you will be truly free. 37I know you are Abraham's children, but you want to kill me because
you don't accept my teaching. 38I am telling you
what my Father has shown me, but you do what
your father has told you."
39They answered, "Our father is Abraham."
Jesus said, "If you were really Abraham's children, you would do the things Abraham did. 40I
am a man who has told you the truth which I
heard from God, but you are trying to kill me.
Abraham did nothing like that. 41So you are doing
the things your own father did."
But they said, "We are not like children who
never knew who their father was. God is our Father; he is the only Father we have."
42Jesus said to them, "If God were really your
Father, you would love me, because I came from
God and now I am here. I did not come by my
own authority; God sent me. 43You don't understand what I say, because you cannot accept my
teaching. 44You belong to your father the devil,
and you want to do what he wants. He was a
murderer from the beginning and was against the
truth, because there is no truth in him. When he
tells a lie, he shows what he is really like, because
he is a liar and the father of lies. 45But because I
speak the truth, you don't believe me. 46Can any
of you prove that I am guilty of sin? If I am telling
the truth, why don't you believe me? 47The person who belongs to God accepts what God says.
But you don't accept what God says, because you
don't belong to God."

Jesus Is Greater than Abraham

48The Jews answered, "We say you are a Samaritan[d] and have a demon[d] in you. Are we not
right?"
49Jesus answered, "I have no demon in me. I
give honor to my Father, but you dishonor me. 50I
am not trying to get honor for myself. There is
One who wants this honor for me, and he is the
judge. 51I tell you the truth, whoever obeys my
teaching will never die."
52The Jews said to Jesus, "Now we know that
you have a demon in you! Even Abraham and the
prophets[d] died. But you say, 'Whoever obeys my
teaching will never die.' 53Do you think you are
greater than our father Abraham, who died? And
the prophets died, too. Who do you think you
are?"
54Jesus answered, "If I give honor to myself,
that honor is worth nothing. The One who gives
me honor is my Father, and you say he is your
God. 55You don't really know him, but I know
him. If I said I did not know him, I would be a
liar like you. But I do know him, and I obey what
he says. 56Your father Abraham was very happy
that he would see my day. He saw that day and
was glad."
57The Jews said to him, "You have never seen
Abraham! You are not even fifty years old."
58Jesus answered, "I tell you the truth, before
Abraham was even born, I am!" 59When Jesus
said this, the people picked up stones to throw at
him. But Jesus hid himself, and then he left the
Temple.[d]

Jesus Heals a Man Born Blind

9 As Jesus was walking along, he saw a man
who had been born blind. [2]His followers
asked him, "Teacher, whose sin caused this man
to be born blind—his own sin or his parents'
sin?"
[3]Jesus answered, "It is not this man's sin or his
parents' sin that made him be blind. This man
was born blind so that God's power could be
shown in him. [4]While it is daytime, we must continue doing the work of the One who sent me.
Night is coming, when no one can work. [5]While
I am in the world, I am the light of the world."
[6]After Jesus said this, he spit on the ground and
made some mud with it and put the mud on the
man's eyes. [7]Then he told the man, "Go and wash
in the Pool of Siloam." (Siloam means Sent.) So
the man went, washed, and came back seeing.
[8]The neighbors and some people who had earlier seen this man begging said, "Isn't this the
same man who used to sit and beg?"
[9]Some said, "He is the one," but others said,
"No, he only looks like him."
The man himself said, "I am the man."
[10]They asked, "How did you get your sight?"
[11]He answered, "The man named Jesus made
some mud and put it on my eyes. Then he told me
to go to Siloam and wash. So I went and washed,
and then I could see."
[12]They asked him, "Where is this man?"
"I don't know," he answered.

SIDELIGHT: Sending the blind man to wash in the Pool of Siloam would clearly have been symbolic for the people in Jesus' day (John 9:7). This pool was the source for water used for religious ceremonies. It was also Jerusalem's primary water source.

Pharisees Question the Healing

[13]Then the people took to the Pharisees[d] the

SIN

Blind Side

"I actually thought no one could tell I was drinking." Josh Perez studied his hands for a moment before he looked up at the group. "I got caught the first time I got drunk. I thought about quitting then. But my friends were into it, so I kept drinking with them."

Josh paused and took a deep breath. Then he continued, "Before long, I didn't need them as an excuse to drink. I enjoyed it so much I drank every chance I could." A few other teenagers in the group nodded knowingly. Josh relaxed a bit.

"I figured I was maintaining pretty well. I kept my position on the baseball team and my grades hadn't slipped too far. I tried to be careful with curfews and covering the alcohol on my breath.

"One day, my dad made some comment to me about how I was gonna end up just like him. That shocked me! Dad's an alcoholic. And it scared me.

"So I talked to my youth leader, and he suggested I get into this support group," Josh said as his eyes swept over the teenagers seated in a circle. "I really thought I had everyone fooled. I guess the only one blind to my drinking problem was me."

Jesus encountered blind people of all kinds. Read **John 9:1–41** to see the key to true sight.

- What are the similarities and differences between Josh's blindness and the Pharisees' blindness? Between Josh's blindness and that of the man blind from birth?
- What does this Bible passage tell us about being blind to sin?

CONSIDER . . .

- asking God to open your eyes to areas where you are blind to sin.
- asking a good friend to tell you about a blind spot in your life, then working to change it.

FOR MORE, SEE . . .

- Isaiah 6:9–10
- Matthew 15:1–20
- Ephesians 5:6–15

man who had been blind. 14The day Jesus had made mud and healed his eyes was a Sabbath[d] day. 15So now the Pharisees asked the man, "How did you get your sight?"

He answered, "He put mud on my eyes, I washed, and now I see."

16So some of the Pharisees were saying, "This man does not keep the Sabbath day, so he is not from God."

But others said, "A man who is a sinner can't do miracles[d] like these." So they could not agree with each other.

17They asked the man again, "What do you say about him since it was your eyes he opened?"

The man answered, "He is a prophet."[d]

18The Jews did not believe that he had been blind and could now see again. So they sent for the man's parents 19and asked them, "Is this your son who you say was born blind? Then how does he now see?"

20His parents answered, "We know that this is our son and that he was born blind. 21But we don't know how he can now see. We don't know who opened his eyes. Ask him. He is old enough to speak for himself." 22His parents said this because they were afraid of the Jews, who had already decided that anyone who said Jesus was the Christ[d] would be put out of the synagogue.[d] 23That is why his parents said, "He is old enough. Ask him."

24So for the second time, they called the man who had been blind. They said, "You should give God the glory by telling the truth. We know that this man is a sinner."

25He answered, "I don't know if he is a sinner. One thing I do know: I was blind, and now I see."

26They asked, "What did he do to you? How did he make you see again?"

27He answered, "I already told you, and you didn't listen. Why do you want to hear it again? Do you want to become his followers, too?"

28Then they insulted him and said, "You are his follower, but we are followers of Moses. 29We know that God spoke to Moses, but we don't even know where this man comes from."

30The man answered, "This is a very strange thing. You don't know where he comes from, and yet he opened my eyes. 31We all know that God does not listen to sinners, but he listens to anyone who worships and obeys him. 32Nobody has ever heard of anyone giving sight to a man born blind. 33If this man were not from God, he could do nothing."

34They answered, "You were born full of sin! Are you trying to teach us?" And they threw him out.

Spiritual Blindness

35When Jesus heard that they had thrown him out, Jesus found him and said, "Do you believe in the Son of Man?"[d]

36He asked, "Who is the Son of Man, sir, so that I can believe in him?"

37Jesus said to him, "You have seen him. The Son of Man is the one talking with you."

38He said, "Lord, I believe!" Then the man worshiped Jesus.

39Jesus said, "I came into this world so that the world could be judged. I came so that the blind[n] would see and so that those who see will become blind."

40Some of the Pharisees[d] who were nearby heard Jesus say this and asked, "Are you saying we are blind, too?"

41Jesus said, "If you were blind, you would not be guilty of sin. But since you keep saying you see, your guilt remains."

The Shepherd and His Sheep

10 Jesus said, "I tell you the truth, the person who does not enter the sheepfold by the door, but climbs in some other way, is a thief and a robber. 2The one who enters by the door is the shepherd of the sheep. 3The one who guards the door opens it for him. And the sheep listen to the voice of the shepherd. He calls his own sheep by name and leads them out. 4When he brings all his sheep out, he goes ahead of them, and they follow him because they know his voice. 5But they will never follow a stranger. They will run away from him because they don't know his voice." 6Jesus told the people this story, but they did not understand what it meant.

SIDELIGHT: When Jesus described a sheepfold in John 10:1–6, his listeners would have understood immediately, since sheep were the most common animal of that region. Sheepfolds consisted of low buildings to protect the flock during bad weather, and an outdoor pen that had a wall around it. The wall was covered with sharp thorny brush to keep out thieves and predators.

Jesus Is the Good Shepherd

7So Jesus said again, "I tell you the truth, I am the door for the sheep. 8All the people who came before me were thieves and robbers. The sheep did not listen to them. 9I am the door, and the person who enters through me will be saved and

blind Jesus is talking about people who are spiritually blind, not physically blind.

will be able to come in and go out and find pas-
ture. 10A thief comes to steal and kill and destroy,
but I came to give life—life in all its fullness.
11"I am the good shepherd. The good shepherd
gives his life for the sheep. 12The worker who is
paid to keep the sheep is different from the shepherd who owns them. When the worker sees a
wolf coming, he runs away and leaves the sheep
alone. Then the wolf attacks the sheep and scat-
ters them. 13The man runs away because he is
only a paid worker and does not really care about
the sheep.
14-15"I am the good shepherd. I know my sheep,
as the Father knows me. And my sheep know me,
as I know the Father. I give my life for the sheep.
16I have other sheep that are not in this flock, and
I must bring them also. They will listen to my
voice, and there will be one flock and one shepherd. 17The Father loves me because I give my life
so that I can take it back again. 18No one takes it
away from me; I give my own life freely. I have
the right to give my life, and I have the right to
take it back. This is what my Father commanded
me to do."
19Again the Jews did not agree with each other
because of these words of Jesus. 20Many of them
said, "A demon[d] has come into him and made
him crazy. Why listen to him?"
21But others said, "A man who is crazy with a
demon does not say things like this. Can a demon
open the eyes of the blind?"

Jesus Is Rejected

22The time came for the Feast[d] of Dedication at
Jerusalem. It was winter, 23and Jesus was walking
in the Temple[d] in Solomon's Porch.[d] 24The Jews
gathered around him and said, "How long will
you make us wonder about you? If you are the
Christ,[d] tell us plainly."
25Jesus answered, "I told you already, but you
did not believe. The miracles[d] I do in my Father's
name show who I am. 26But you don't believe,
because you are not my sheep. 27My sheep listen
to my voice; I know them, and they follow me.
28I give them eternal life, and they will never die,
and no one can steal them out of my hand. 29My
Father gave my sheep to me. He is greater than
all, and no person can steal my sheep out of my
Father's hand. 30The Father and I are one."

GOD'S LOVE

Shepherds and Sheep

Sheep can be incredibly smart. For instance, most sheep can distinguish their shepherd's voice from any other voice. A few exceptional sheep can even be taught how to come when called and how to sit like a dog (well, almost) on command.

On the other hand, sheep can seem completely brainless. It's not unusual to see sheep trying to walk through a barbed wire fence or casually strolling straight off the edge of a cliff. To make matters worse, where one goes, others tend to follow.

The hardest thing about being a shepherd is keeping the sheep where they should be. Certain sheep seem determined to go where they could be harmed. Modern shepherds use a device called a "hobbler" on sheep's hind legs to keep them from moving freely. Before hobblers were invented, shepherds often broke a sheep's leg to keep it from the great danger of wandering away from the flock. It was all part of caring for the sheep.

Jesus seemed to understand sheep well. Read **John 10:1–30** to discover how Jesus saw his followers as sheep and himself as their shepherd.

- How is Jesus' care of his people similar to the care of a shepherd for sheep?
- How are people today—including yourself—like sheep?

CONSIDER . . .

- underlining the things in this passage that the shepherd does and circling the things sheep do. Then turn to Psalm 23 and do the same thing.
- reading A Shepherd Looks at Psalm 23 by W. Phillip Keller (Zondervan) to learn more about sheep and their shepherd.

FOR MORE, SEE . . .

- Psalm 23
- Ezekiel 34:11–31
- Luke 15:1–7

31 Again the Jews picked up stones to kill Jesus.
32 But he said to them, "I have done many good
works from the Father. Which of these good
works are you killing me for?"
33 The Jews answered, "We are not killing you
because of any good work you did, but because
you speak against God. You are only a human, but
you say you are the same as God!"
34 Jesus answered, "It is written in your law that
God said, 'I said, you are gods.'[n] 35 This Scripture[d] called those people gods who received
God's message, and Scripture is always true. 36 So
why do you say that I speak against God because
I said, 'I am God's Son'? I am the one God chose
and sent into the world. 37 If I don't do what my
Father does, then don't believe me. 38 But if I do
what my Father does, even though you don't believe in me, believe what I do. Then you will
know and understand that the Father is in me and
I am in the Father."
39 They tried to take Jesus again, but he escaped
from them.
40 Then he went back across the Jordan River to
the place where John had first baptized. Jesus
stayed there, 41 and many people came to him and
said, "John never did a miracle, but everything
John said about this man is true." 42 And in that
place many believed in Jesus.

The Death of Lazarus

11 A man named Lazarus was sick. He lived
in the town of Bethany, where Mary and
her sister Martha lived. 2 Mary was the woman
who later put perfume on the Lord and wiped his
feet with her hair. Mary's brother was Lazarus,
the man who was now sick. 3 So Mary and Martha
sent someone to tell Jesus, "Lord, the one you
love is sick."
4 When Jesus heard this, he said, "This sickness
will not end in death. It is for the glory of God,
to bring glory to the Son of God." 5 Jesus loved
Martha and her sister and Lazarus. 6 But when he
heard that Lazarus was sick, he stayed where he
was for two more days. 7 Then Jesus said to his
followers, "Let's go back to Judea."
8 The followers said, "But Teacher, the Jews

'I . . . gods.' Quotation from Psalm 82:6.

DEATH

Sharing Sadness

They went through the church doors, signed the guest registry and made their way to a back pew. Neither of them knew Polly's father, but they had decided to go to his funeral because Polly Brinkman was their classmate.

It wasn't a comfortable situation for Steve Parks or Don Shackelford, but they couldn't begin to imagine how tough it must have been for Polly. As they filed past the open coffin after the service, Polly looked up at them and kind of smiled and cried at the same time.

The next Thursday Polly came back to school and made it a point to talk with Don and Steve before class. "I really want to thank you guys for being at my dad's funeral Saturday. It means a lot to me," Polly said.

"We didn't know what else we could do to help," Don offered.

"That was enough," Polly said. "Just knowing I had friends there made a difference. I didn't feel so alone. Your being around made the service easier to take. It was like you shared some of the hurt."

Jesus understood what it was like to grieve with friends. Read **John 11:1–45** to see how Jesus shared his friends' grief and how Jesus' presence at a funeral made a difference.

- How did Steve's and Don's actions compare with Jesus' actions?
- What does Jesus' reactions to Lazarus's death teach us about dealing with sadness?

CONSIDER . . .

- telling a trusted friend about the death of someone who was important to you. Openly express your emotions.
- asking your pastor or youth leader to help you and a group of friends devise things you can do when a friend's family member dies.

FOR MORE, SEE . . .

- Isaiah 61:1–3
- Romans 12:9–15
- Revelation 21:1–4

there tried to stone you to death only a short time
ago. Now you want to go back there?"
9Jesus answered, "Are there not twelve hours
in the day? If anyone walks in the daylight, he will
not stumble, because he can see by this world's
light. 10But if anyone walks at night, he stumbles
because there is no light to help him see."
11After Jesus said this, he added, "Our friend
Lazarus has fallen asleep, but I am going there to
wake him."
12The followers said, "But Lord, if he is only
asleep, he will be all right."
13Jesus meant that Lazarus was dead, but his
followers thought he meant Lazarus was really
sleeping. 14So then Jesus said plainly, "Lazarus is
dead. 15And I am glad for your sakes I was not
there so that you may believe. But let's go to him
now."
16Then Thomas (the one called Didymus) said
to the other followers, "Let us also go so that we
can die with him."

Jesus in Bethany

17When Jesus arrived, he learned that Lazarus
had already been dead and in the tomb for four
days. 18Bethany was about two miles from Jerusalem. 19Many of the Jews had come there to comfort Martha and Mary about their brother.
20When Martha heard that Jesus was coming,
she went out to meet him, but Mary stayed home.
21Martha said to Jesus, "Lord, if you had been
here, my brother would not have died. 22But I
know that even now God will give you anything
you ask."
23Jesus said, "Your brother will rise and live
again."
24Martha answered, "I know that he will rise
and live again in the resurrection[n] on the last
day."
25Jesus said to her, "I am the resurrection and
the life. Those who believe in me will have life
even if they die. 26And everyone who lives and
believes in me will never die. Martha, do you believe this?"
27Martha answered, "Yes, Lord. I believe that
you are the Christ,[d] the Son of God, the One coming to the world."

Jesus Cries

28After Martha said this, she went back and
talked to her sister Mary alone. Martha said, "The
Teacher is here and he is asking for you." 29When
Mary heard this, she got up quickly and went to
Jesus. 30Jesus had not yet come into the town but
was still at the place where Martha had met him.
31The Jews were with Mary in the house, com-
forting her. When they saw her stand and leave
quickly, they followed her, thinking she was going to the tomb to cry there.
32But Mary went to the place where Jesus was.
When she saw him, she fell at his feet and said,
"Lord, if you had been here, my brother would
not have died."
33When Jesus saw Mary crying and the Jews
who came with her also crying, he was upset and
was deeply troubled. 34He asked, "Where did you
bury him?"
"Come and see, Lord," they said.
35Jesus cried.
36So the Jews said, "See how much he loved
him."
37But some of them said, "If Jesus opened the
eyes of the blind man, why couldn't he keep Lazarus from dying?"

Jesus Raises Lazarus

38Again feeling very upset, Jesus came to the
tomb. It was a cave with a large stone covering
the entrance. 39Jesus said, "Move the stone
away."
Martha, the sister of the dead man, said, "But,
Lord, it has been four days since he died. There
will be a bad smell."

SIDELIGHT: Lazarus had been dead four days before Jesus arrived (John 11:39). That would have made bringing him back to life particularly miraculous to people in Jesus' day. They believed that a soul stayed with a body for three days and then left.

40Then Jesus said to her, "Didn't I tell you that
if you believed you would see the glory of God?"
41So they moved the stone away from the entrance. Then Jesus looked up and said, "Father, I
thank you that you heard me. 42I know that you
always hear me, but I said these things because of
the people here around me. I want them to believe that you sent me." 43After Jesus said this, he
cried out in a loud voice, "Lazarus, come out!"
44The dead man came out, his hands and feet
wrapped with pieces of cloth, and a cloth around
his face.
Jesus said to them, "Take the cloth off of him
and let him go."

The Plan to Kill Jesus

45Many of the Jews, who had come to visit
Mary and saw what Jesus did, believed in him.
46But some of them went to the Pharisees[d] and
told them what Jesus had done. 47Then the lead-

resurrection Being raised from the dead to live again.

ing priests and Pharisees called a meeting of the
Jewish council. They asked, "What should we do?
This man is doing many miracles.[d] 48 If we let him
continue doing these things, everyone will believe
in him. Then the Romans will come and take
away our Temple[d] and our nation."
49 One of the men there was Caiaphas, the high
priest that year. He said, "You people know nothing! 50 You don't realize that it is better for one
man to die for the people than for the whole nation to be destroyed."
51 Caiaphas did not think of this himself. As high
priest that year, he was really prophesying[d] that
Jesus would die for the Jewish nation 52 and for
God's scattered children to bring them all together and make them one.
53 That day they started planning to kill Jesus.
54 So Jesus no longer traveled openly among the
Jews. He left there and went to a place near the
desert, to a town called Ephraim and stayed there
with his followers.
55 It was almost time for the Jewish Passover[d]
Feast. Many from the country went up to Jerusalem before the Passover to do the special things
to make themselves pure. 56 The people looked for
Jesus and stood in the Temple asking each other,
"Is he coming to the Feast? What do you think?"
57 But the leading priests and the Pharisees had
given orders that if anyone knew where Jesus
was, he must tell them. Then they could arrest
him.

Jesus with Friends in Bethany

12 Six days before the Passover[d] Feast,
Jesus went to Bethany, where Lazarus
lived. (Lazarus is the man Jesus raised from the
dead.) 2 There they had a dinner for Jesus. Martha
served the food, and Lazarus was one of the people eating with Jesus. 3 Mary brought in a pint of
very expensive perfume made from pure nard.[d]
She poured the perfume on Jesus' feet, and then
she wiped his feet with her hair. And the sweet
smell from the perfume filled the whole house.
4 Judas Iscariot, one of Jesus' followers who
would later turn against him, was there. Judas
said, 5 "This perfume was worth three hundred
coins.[n] Why wasn't it sold and the money given
to the poor?" 6 But Judas did not really care about
the poor; he said this because he was a thief. He
was the one who kept the money box, and he
often stole from it.
7 Jesus answered, "Leave her alone. It was right

coins One coin, a denarius, was the average pay for one day's work.

SERVICE

Life on the Altar

Chuckie Johnston could be making a lot of money selling drugs. Or he could have a steady job as a bodyguard in his old neighborhood. Instead, he lives and works with former addicts at Boston Outreach, a Christian rehabilitation program.

Chuckie could have been part of a network that destroyed thousands of lives. Instead, he is helping hundreds of people break the bondage of drug abuse.

Gertrude Falk could have been a school administrator in a good school in the United States. She could have lived in a beautiful home and retired with a great pension. Rather, she has spent all of her adult life living in a modest home on a little island in Haiti. Thousands of kids over the years have received an education, medical care, adequate nutrition, and a chance to hear about Jesus Christ because of Gertrude's gifts.

Chuckie and Gertrude have given their lives to serve others. They have no regrets, because they know the secret of service—gratitude. In **John 12:1–11**, we read that Mary also knew the secret of service.

- In what ways is Mary's service similar to or different from Chuckie's and Gertrude's service to the Lord?
- If Jesus were in your house today, how might you serve him?

CONSIDER . . .

- listing all the things God has done for you and thanking him for those things.
- becoming involved in an ongoing act of service to others by joining a volunteer service organization.

FOR MORE, SEE . . .

- Isaiah 1:11–17
- Romans 12:1–2
- James 1:26–27

for her to save this perfume for today, the day for me to be prepared for burial. 8You will always have the poor with you, but you will not always have me."

The Plot Against Lazarus

9A large crowd of Jews heard that Jesus was in Bethany. So they went there to see not only Jesus but Lazarus, whom Jesus raised from the dead. 10So the leading priests made plans to kill Lazarus, too. 11Because of Lazarus many of the Jews were leaving them and believing in Jesus.

Jesus Enters Jerusalem

12The next day a great crowd who had come to Jerusalem for the Passover[d] Feast heard that Jesus was coming there. 13So they took branches of palm trees and went out to meet Jesus, shouting,

"Praise[n] God!
God bless the One who comes in the name
of the Lord!
God bless the King of Israel!" *Psalm 118:25-26*

14Jesus found a colt and sat on it. This was as the Scripture[d] says,

15"Don't be afraid, people of Jerusalem!
Your king is coming,
sitting on the colt of a donkey." *Zechariah 9:9*

16The followers of Jesus did not understand this at first. But after Jesus was raised to glory, they remembered that this had been written about him and that they had done these things to him.

People Tell About Jesus

17There had been many people with Jesus when he raised Lazarus from the dead and told him to come out of the tomb. Now they were telling others about what Jesus did. 18Many people went out to meet Jesus, because they had heard about this miracle.[d] 19So the Pharisees[d] said to each other, "You can see that nothing is going right for us. Look! The whole world is following him."

Jesus Talks About His Death

20There were some Greek people, too, who came to Jerusalem to worship at the Passover[d] Feast. 21They went to Philip, who was from Bethsaida in Galilee, and said, "Sir, we would like to see Jesus." 22Philip told Andrew, and then Andrew and Philip told Jesus.

23Jesus said to them, "The time has come for the Son of Man[d] to receive his glory. 24I tell you the truth, a grain of wheat must fall to the ground and die to make many seeds. But if it never dies, it remains only a single seed. 25Those who love their lives will lose them, but those who hate their lives in this world will keep true life forever. 26Whoever serves me must follow me. Then my servant will be with me everywhere I am. My Father will honor anyone who serves me.

27"Now I am very troubled. Should I say, 'Father, save me from this time'? No, I came to this time so I could suffer. 28Father, bring glory to your name!"

Then a voice came from heaven, "I have brought glory to it, and I will do it again."

29The crowd standing there, who heard the voice, said it was thunder.

But others said, "An angel has spoken to him."

30Jesus said, "That voice was for your sake, not mine. 31Now is the time for the world to be judged; now the ruler of this world will be thrown down. 32If I am lifted up from the earth, I will draw all people toward me." 33Jesus said this to show how he would die.

34The crowd said, "We have heard from the law that the Christ[d] will live forever. So why do you say, 'The Son of Man must be lifted up'? Who is this 'Son of Man'?"

35Then Jesus said, "The light will be with you for a little longer, so walk while you have the light. Then the darkness will not catch you. If you walk in the darkness, you will not know where you are going. 36Believe in the light while you still have it so that you will become children of light." When Jesus had said this, he left and hid himself from them.

Some People Won't Believe in Jesus

37Though Jesus had done many miracles[d] in front of the people, they still did not believe in him. 38This was to bring about what Isaiah the prophet[d] had said:

"Lord, who believed what we told them?
Who saw the Lord's power in this?"
Isaiah 53:1

39This is why the people could not believe: Isaiah also had said,

40"He has blinded their eyes,
and he has closed their minds.
Otherwise they would see with their eyes
and understand in their minds
and come back to me and be healed."
Isaiah 6:10

41Isaiah said this because he saw Jesus' glory and spoke about him.

42But many believed in Jesus, even many of the leaders. But because of the Pharisees,[d] they did not say they believed in him for fear they would be put out of the synagogue.[d] 43They loved praise from people more than praise from God.

44Then Jesus cried out, "Whoever believes in

Praise Literally, "Hosanna," a Hebrew word used at first in praying to God for help, but at this time it was probably a shout of joy used in praising God or his Messiah.

me is really believing in the One who sent me.
45Whoever sees me sees the One who sent me. 46I
have come as light into the world so that whoever
believes in me would not stay in darkness.
47"Anyone who hears my words and does not
obey them, I do not judge, because I did not come
to judge the world, but to save the world. 48There
is a judge for those who refuse to believe in me
and do not accept my words. The word I have
taught will be their judge on the last day. 49The
things I taught were not from myself. The Father
who sent me told me what to say and what to
teach. 50And I know that eternal life comes from
what the Father commands. So whatever I say is
what the Father told me to say."

Jesus Washes His Followers' Feet

13 It was almost time for the Jewish Passover[d] Feast. Jesus knew that it was time
for him to leave this world and go back to the
Father. He had always loved those who were his
own in the world, and he loved them all the way
to the end.
2Jesus and his followers were at the evening
meal. The devil had already persuaded Judas Iscariot, the son of Simon, to turn against Jesus.
3Jesus knew that the Father had given him power
over everything and that he had come from God
and was going back to God. 4So during the meal
Jesus stood up and took off his outer clothing.
Taking a towel, he wrapped it around his waist.
5Then he poured water into a bowl and began to
wash the followers' feet, drying them with the
towel that was wrapped around him.
6Jesus came to Simon Peter, who said to him,
"Lord, are you going to wash my feet?"
7Jesus answered, "You don't understand now
what I am doing, but you will understand later."
8Peter said, "No, you will never wash my feet."
Jesus answered, "If I don't wash your feet, you
are not one of my people."
9Simon Peter answered, "Lord, then wash not
only my feet, but wash my hands and my head,
too!"
10Jesus said, "After a person has had a bath, his
whole body is clean. He needs only to wash his
feet. And you men are clean,[d] but not all of you."
11Jesus knew who would turn against him, and
that is why he said, "Not all of you are clean."
12When he had finished washing their feet, he

DEATH

Life From the Ashes

Forest fires swept through nearly half of Yellowstone National Park's 2.2 million acres in the summer of 1988. At first, it seemed life in the park could never be the same. The fire seemed like a total disaster.

But it wasn't. Foresters pointed out that lodgepole pine trees had cones on them that would only open under intense heat—almost as though they were designed to respond to a forest fire. Yellowstone's dry climate kept dead wood from decaying quickly, so the ashes from the fire provided nutrients to the ground that could actually mean better growth for years to come. Bluebirds and woodpeckers would benefit from open areas the fire had created. Other animals would flourish with the nearly tenfold increase in plant species that the newly fortified and uncovered earth could offer.

No one at Yellowstone looks forward to forest fires. But it is known that fires, however devastating they seem, don't mean the end of things.

The devastation of death can be sudden and tragic—like the devastation of a forest fire. But new life can result. Read **John 12:20–36** to discover what Jesus said about death and new growth.

- How might an ecologist's attitude toward forest fires be like Jesus' attitude toward death?
- What does the Bible passage say to you about death?

CONSIDER . . .

- writing on a sheet of paper about an area of your life in which you need to give something up and then burying the paper in your backyard. A week later, dig it up and evaluate your progress in letting go.
- walking through a park or forest to notice examples in nature of how death gives way to new growth.

FOR MORE, SEE . . .

- Ecclesiastes 3:1–8
- 2 Corinthians 4:16—5:10
- 1 John 1:5–7

put on his clothes and sat down again. He asked,
"Do you understand what I have just done for
you? 13You call me 'Teacher' and 'Lord,' and you
are right, because that is what I am. 14If I, your
Lord and Teacher, have washed your feet, you
also should wash each other's feet. 15I did this as
an example so that you should do as I have done
for you. 16I tell you the truth, a servant is not
greater than his master. A messenger is not
greater than the one who sent him. 17If you know
these things, you will be happy if you do them.
18"I am not talking about all of you. I know
those I have chosen. But this is to bring about
what the Scripture[d] said: 'The man who ate at my
table has turned against me.'[n] 19I am telling you
this now before it happens so that when it happens, you will believe that I am he. 20I tell you the
truth, whoever accepts anyone I send also accepts
me. And whoever accepts me also accepts the
One who sent me."

Jesus Talks About His Death

21After Jesus said this, he was very troubled. He
said openly, "I tell you the truth, one of you will
turn against me."
22The followers all looked at each other, because they did not know whom Jesus was talking
about. 23One of the followers sitting[n] next to

'The man . . . me.' Quotation from Psalm 41:9.
sitting Literally, "lying." The people of that time ate lying down and leaning on one arm.

SERVICE

The Lowly Star

Jerry Richardson was an all-state running back and linebacker for a high school football team that was considered one of the best in the nation. He was fast. He was remarkably strong. And opposing players hated to see him walk onto the field.

Jerry's teammate, Scott Cunningham, on the other hand, was nothing special on the football field. He played Jerry's same position on offense—running back. He made the team only because the head coach found a place for every player who lasted through the rigorous two-a-day practices. Scott boasted few athletic skills, but he did have the courage to pick himself up after each ferocious hit and do it all again.

Since he rarely played in games, Scott never knew the thrill of the crowd chanting his name after a big play. What he heard, most often, was "Jer-ry! Jer-ry! Jer-ry!"

That's why what happened at the yearbook-signing party after Scott and Jerry's senior year was so remarkable. Scott saw Jerry walking toward him with a smile on his face.

Softly Jerry said, "I'd like to sign your yearbook, Scott. Would you sign mine?"

Scott nervously handed over his yearbook. A couple of minutes later, Jerry handed it back, smiled and squeezed Scott's shoulder. Scott never saw Jerry again. But he will always remember what Jerry wrote in his yearbook: "You have to be the greatest influence on me because of the size of your heart. You are the best player I know, from the standpoint of desire and heart. Glad to have you on my side. Luck always, Jerry."

Just as Jerry humbled himself in front of his classmates, Jesus humbled himself and washed his disciples' feet—a task normally reserved for servants, not kings. Read about it in **John 13:1–17**.

- How was Jerry's note to Scott similar to Jesus' washing the disciple's feet?
- At first, some of Jesus' disciples were uncomfortable with Jesus washing their feet. How would you feel if someone like Jerry washed your feet or did something equal to that?

C O N S I D E R . . .

- thinking about someone in your life who could use some encouragement. Write a note to that person, listing the qualities you appreciate about him or her. Sign the note and then secretly slip it into his or her locker or notebook.
- planning a get-together for your friends and inviting someone who is normally not invited to parties or events.

F O R M O R E , S E E . . .

- Nehemiah 5:1–13
- Matthew 20:20–28
- Galatians 5:13–15

Jesus was the follower Jesus loved. 24Simon Peter
motioned to him to ask Jesus whom he was talking about.
25That follower leaned closer to Jesus and
asked, "Lord, who is it?"

SIDELIGHT: Parents may tell kids to wash their hands before dinner, but they probably don't insist on clean feet. In Jesus' day, washing feet was important, since people wore sandals and their feet got sore from walking everywhere. But, more importantly, washing a guest's feet was a sign of hospitality (John 13:1–20). Try it next time you have a party!

26Jesus answered, "I will dip this bread into the
dish. The man I give it to is the man who will turn
against me." So Jesus took a piece of bread,
dipped it, and gave it to Judas Iscariot, the son of
Simon. 27As soon as Judas took the bread, Satan
entered him. Jesus said to him, "The thing that
you will do — do it quickly." 28No one at the table
understood why Jesus said this to Judas. 29Since
he was the one who kept the money box, some
of the followers thought Jesus was telling him to
buy what was needed for the feast or to give
something to the poor.
30Judas took the bread Jesus gave him and immediately went out. It was night.
31When Judas was gone, Jesus said, "Now the
Son of Man[d] receives his glory, and God receives
glory through him. 32If God receives glory
through him, then God will give glory to the Son

FRIENDS

The Tough Choice

Melissa Spencer had a secret problem. Two months earlier, she and her boyfriend Matt had had sexual intercourse. It was her first time. Now she was pregnant. And Matt, immature and desperate, was pressuring her to "get rid" of the baby. When Melissa refused, he beat her. Life seemed dark and hopeless to her. She was afraid to tell anyone about her problems, especially her single mom.

But Melissa's best friend, Jessica Bullard, knew, and that secret tormented Jessica. Melissa had made Jessica promise to keep quiet about her secret.

"If you tell anyone," warned Melissa, "I'll hate you forever." But Jessica could barely contain her rage when she saw how Matt was abusing Melissa.

Though she knew she was risking a strong friendship, Jessica decided to get help for Melissa before it was too late. She asked to meet with Melissa's aunt and uncle and, sobbing, told them Melissa's story.

They thanked Jessica for her honesty and courage, then they found Melissa and gently confronted her with the truth. After Melissa's initial shock, she broke down crying, asking them for help.

Melissa was angry with Jessica for violating her trust. But in less than a week, she forgave Jessica and told her how relieved she was that Jessica had told.

Melissa got the help she needed. And she gave birth to a healthy little girl who was adopted by a couple who could never have children.

Just as Jessica risked something important to her for the good of her friend, Jesus encourages those who follow him to love each other with a self-sacrificing love. Read about this kind of love in **John 13:31–35**.

- How is Jessica's decision to tell Melissa's secret similar to Jesus' decision to go to the cross?
- What's one way you can love your best friend the way Jesus loved his disciples?

CONSIDER . . .

- talking to a friend who has been doing something that concerns you.
- making a pact with a friend, promising each other to be open to criticism and direction regarding the choices you each make in life.

FOR MORE, SEE . . .

- 1 Samuel 20
- Proverbs 17:17
- 1 John 4:7–8

through himself. And God will give him glory
quickly."
33Jesus said, "My children, I will be with you
only a little longer. You will look for me, and what
I told the Jews, I tell you now: Where I am going
you cannot come.
34"I give you a new command: Love each
other. You must love each other as I have loved
you. 35All people will know that you are my followers if you love each other."

Peter Will Say He Doesn't Know Jesus

36Simon Peter asked Jesus, "Lord, where are
you going?"
Jesus answered, "Where I am going you cannot
follow now, but you will follow later."
37Peter asked, "Lord, why can't I follow you
now? I am ready to die for you!"
38Jesus answered, "Are you ready to die for
me? I tell you the truth, before the rooster crows,
you will say three times that you don't know me."

Jesus Comforts His Followers

14 Jesus said, "Don't let your hearts be troubled. Trust in God, and trust in me.
2There are many rooms in my Father's house; I
would not tell you this if it were not true. I am
going there to prepare a place for you. 3After I go
and prepare a place for you, I will come back and
take you to be with me so that you may be where
I am. 4You know the way to the place where I am
going."
5Thomas said to Jesus, "Lord, we don't know
where you are going. So how can we know the
way?"
6Jesus answered, "I am the way, and the truth,
and the life. The only way to the Father is through
me. 7If you really knew me, you would know my
Father, too. But now you do know him, and you
have seen him."
8Philip said to him, "Lord, show us the Father.
That is all we need."

DOUBT

Riding Out the Storm

Robin Graham is the youngest person in history to sail around the world alone. But success didn't come easily for him. He left on his three-year odyssey as a sixteen-year-old boy thrill-seeker. Adventure was like a drug to him.

His trip changed something deep inside him. A violent storm almost capsized his little sloop, the Dove. In the midst of the torrent, the Dove's mast snapped in two, and Robin barely survived a waterspout—a water-filled tornado.

But that wasn't the worst of it. When his boat entered the doldrums, a windless, currentless part of the ocean near the equator, Robin almost went crazy with despair and doubt. At one point, he completely gave up hope that he would ever make it out of the doldrums, so he splashed kerosene all over his boat and set it on fire. Fortunately, Robin snapped to his senses and doused the fire before it did serious damage.

Three years after his departure, Robin sailed into the Los Angeles harbor to cheering crowds, honking cars, and blasting steam whistles. He had made it. And, more importantly, he had wrestled two great enemies—doubt and despair—and found himself stronger as a result.

Robin Graham is a courageous hero. But he had crippling doubts about himself, just like the "heroes of the faith" who first followed Jesus. Read about them in **John 14:1–14**.

- How were Robin's doubts like the doubts the disciples experienced after Jesus told them he was leaving them?
- What doubts have you had about your life that seem impossible for God to solve?

CONSIDER . . .

- writing on paper, "The one thing I doubt the most is. . ." and finishing the sentence. Then ask a friend to pray with you about your doubt.
- writing out one nagging doubt you have about God. Then tape your "doubt" to a specific date on a calendar at least a week from today. Ask God to give you insight into your doubt by that date.

FOR MORE, SEE . . .

- Jonah
- Matthew 14:22–33
- James 1:2–8

⁹Jesus answered, "I have been with you a long
time now. Do you still not know me, Philip?
Whoever has seen me has seen the Father. So
why do you say, 'Show us the Father'? 10Don't
you believe that I am in the Father and the Father
is in me? The words I say to you don't come from
me, but the Father lives in me and does his own
work. 11Believe me when I say that I am in the
Father and the Father is in me. Or believe because
of the miracles[d] I have done. 12I tell you the truth,
whoever believes in me will do the same things
that I do. Those who believe will do even greater
things than these, because I am going to the Father. 13And if you ask for anything in my name,
I will do it for you so that the Father's glory will
be shown through the Son. 14If you ask me for
anything in my name, I will do it.

The Promise of the Holy Spirit

15"If you love me, you will obey my commands. 16I will ask the Father, and he will give
you another Helper[n] to be with you forever—
17the Spirit[d] of truth. The world cannot accept
him, because it does not see him or know him.
But you know him, because he lives with you and
he will be in you.

18"I will not leave you all alone like orphans; I
will come back to you. 19In a little while the world
will not see me anymore, but you will see me.
Because I live, you will live, too. 20On that day

Helper "Counselor" or "Comforter." Jesus is talking about the Holy Spirit.

PEACE

The True Champion

Four decades after his death, an obscure Scottish sprinter named Eric Liddell became a household name after the Oscar-winning movie Chariots of Fire profiled his heroics in the 1924 Olympic Games. The movie told of Liddell's strong Christian convictions, his competitive spirit that was harnessed by his love for God, and his decision to drop out of the Olympic 100-meter dash because the race was scheduled for Sunday, a day he believed was to be a day of rest for Christians.

Later, Liddell shocked the sports world by competing in and winning the Olympic 400-meter race—an event he had not intended to enter. The actor who played Liddell in the film, Ian Charleson, said, "What I admired about him was his serenity. My whole personality changed during the time I was doing the part. I became very slow and laconic."

After his Olympic victory, Liddell returned to China where he continued his work as a Christian missionary. When war broke out, he and other Westerners were rounded up by Japanese troops and held as "civil internees." During Liddell's two years in the camp, he was cut off from his wife and children. Liddell worked long hours—with little complaint—to organize a sports and recreation program for teenagers. He also helped people in any way he could and tutored students at night.

Toward the end of the war, Liddell died fighting the onslaught of a brain tumor. He died the same way he always ran—fighting for every inch on the outside, but at peace inside.

Annie Buchan, a close friend, was with him when he died. Before slipping into a coma from which he would never recover, Eric told his friend, "Annie, it's complete surrender."

Eric Liddell knew by experience the kind of peace Jesus promises those who follow him. Read about that peace in **John 14:15–29**.

- Have you experienced the kind of peace Eric Liddell knew and Jesus talked about?
- What does the passage tell you about how to know God's peace? What's one thing in your life you feel you need peace about?

CONSIDER . . .

- watching for times you don't feel at peace, then stopping to pray for fifteen seconds.
- planning to take a few hours or even a day or two for a "personal retreat" with God. Spend the time reading the Bible, praying and worshiping.

FOR MORE, SEE . . .

- Psalm 119:162–165
- Philippians 4:6–9
- James 3:13–18

you will know that I am in my Father, and that you are in me and I am in you. 21Those who know my commands and obey them are the ones who love me, and my Father will love those who love me. I will love them and will show myself to them."

22Then Judas (not Judas Iscariot) said, "But, Lord, why do you plan to show yourself to us and not to the rest of the world?"

23Jesus answered, "If people love me, they will obey my teaching. My Father will love them, and we will come to them and make our home with them. 24Those who do not love me do not obey my teaching. This teaching that you hear is not really mine; it is from my Father, who sent me.

25"I have told you all these things while I am with you. 26But the Helper will teach you everything and will cause you to remember all that I told you. This Helper is the Holy Spirit whom the Father will send in my name.

27"I leave you peace; my peace I give you. I do not give it to you as the world does. So don't let your hearts be troubled or afraid. 28You heard me say to you, 'I am going, but I am coming back to you.' If you loved me, you should be happy that I am going back to the Father, because he is greater than I am. 29I have told you this now, before it happens, so that when it happens, you will believe. 30I will not talk with you much longer, because the ruler of this world is coming. He has no power over me, 31but the world must know that I love the Father, so I do exactly what the Father told me to do.

"Come now, let us go.

Jesus Is Like a Vine

15 "I am the true vine; my Father is the gardener. 2He cuts off every branch of mine that does not produce fruit. And he trims and cleans every branch that produces fruit so that it will produce even more fruit. 3You are already clean[d] because of the words I have spoken to you. 4Remain in me, and I will remain in you. A branch cannot produce fruit alone but must remain in the vine. In the same way, you cannot produce fruit alone but must remain in me.

5"I am the vine, and you are the branches. If any remain in me and I remain in them, they produce much fruit. But without me they can do nothing. 6If any do not remain in me, they are like a branch that is thrown away and then dies. People pick up dead branches, throw them into the fire, and burn them. 7If you remain in me and follow my teachings, you can ask anything you want, and it will be given to you. 8You should produce much fruit and show that you are my followers, which brings glory to my Father. 9I loved you as the Father loved me. Now remain in my love. 10I have obeyed my Father's commands, and I remain in his love. In the same way, if you obey my commands, you will remain in my love. 11I have told you these things so that you can have the same joy I have and so that your joy will be the fullest possible joy.

SIDELIGHT: Jesus' listeners would have quickly understood Jesus' comparison of himself to the vine in John 15:1–11, since vineyards were common in Israel. Growing a good harvest of grapes required intensive, long-term work. Each year, the vines had to be pruned heavily, hoed, thinned, and sometimes irrigated. Without such care, the harvest would be poor and the grapes bitter.

12"This is my command: Love each other as I have loved you. 13The greatest love a person can show is to die for his friends. 14You are my friends if you do what I command you. 15I no longer call you servants, because a servant does not know what his master is doing. But I call you friends, because I have made known to you everything I heard from my Father. 16You did not choose me; I chose you. And I gave you this work: to go and produce fruit, fruit that will last. Then the Father will give you anything you ask for in my name. 17This is my command: Love each other.

Jesus Warns His Followers

18"If the world hates you, remember that it hated me first. 19If you belonged to the world, it would love you as it loves its own. But I have chosen you out of the world, so you don't belong to it. That is why the world hates you. 20Remember what I told you: A servant is not greater than his master. If people did wrong to me, they will do wrong to you, too. And if they obeyed my teaching, they will obey yours, too. 21They will do all this to you on account of me, because they do not know the One who sent me. 22If I had not come and spoken to them, they would not be guilty of sin, but now they have no excuse for their sin. 23Whoever hates me also hates my Father. 24I did works among them that no one else has ever done. If I had not done these works, they would not be guilty of sin. But now they have seen what I have done, and yet they have hated both me and my Father. 25But this happened so that what is written in their law would be true: 'They hated me for no reason.'[n]

'They . . . reason.' These words could be from Psalm 35:19 or Psalm 69:4.

[26]"I will send you the Helper[n] from the Father; he is the Spirit of truth who comes from the
Father. When he comes, he will tell about me,
[27]and you also must tell people about me, because
you have been with me from the beginning.
16 "I have told you these things to keep you
from giving up. [2]People will put you out
of their synagogues.[d] Yes, the time is coming
when those who kill you will think they are offering service to God. [3]They will do this because
they have not known the Father and they have
not known me. [4]I have told you these things now
so that when the time comes you will remember
that I warned you.

The Work of the Holy Spirit

"I did not tell you these things at the beginning,
because I was with you then. [5]Now I am going
back to the One who sent me. But none of you
asks me, 'Where are you going?' [6]Your hearts are
filled with sadness because I have told you these
things. [7]But I tell you the truth, it is better for you
that I go away. When I go away, I will send the
Helper[n] to you. If I do not go away, the Helper

Helper "Counselor" or "Comforter." Jesus is talking about the Holy Spirit.

SPIRITUAL GROWTH

Cheri's Gift

Michele remembers exactly why she tried to meet Cheri Bruce the first time. They sang together in the Girls Performance Choir their senior year, and Cheri's talent dazzled Michele. Cheri wrote her own songs and could play piano with the kind of intensity and skill Michele envied.

But there was something about Cheri that defied description. She had an honesty about her—a fearless security that made Michele feel safe and challenged at the same time.

One day Michele decided to stay after choir and talk to Cheri. That became the first of many long, intense conversations. The inner strength Michele had always sensed in Cheri was rooted, she found, in a deep faith in Christ.

She seemed to know more about God than anyone Michele had ever met. Michele herself had grown up going to church, and had opinions about God. But Cheri told Michele about a God she had come to know personally.

One day as they rode together in her car, Cheri said, "The Bible says God hates sin, and that's why it's so important for us to recognize our sin and ask God's forgiveness."

"So what?" Michele said. "I don't drink, swear, smoke, or do drugs. I don't have anything to confess."

But Cheri didn't miss a beat. "Michele, all of us sin. I know you've lied to your parents about going out with that older actor guy you met. Don't you realize that lying to your parents is sin in God's eyes?"

Cheri was getting a little too bold, and suddenly Michele felt very uncomfortable. "If I'm a Christian and you're a Christian, why are we so different?" Michele asked.

"The big question is, 'How much do you need God in your life?' " Cheri responded. "Everyone needs God, but not everyone knows they need him."

That conversation in the car has been locked in Michele's memory since that day, because that day she really put her faith in Christ and began spending time in prayer, Bible reading, and church so as to grow closer to Jesus—as Jesus told all Christians to do in **John 15:1–17**.

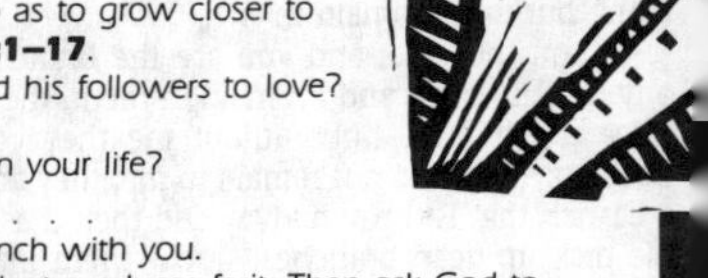

- Did Cheri love Michele the way Jesus commanded his followers to love? Why or why not?
- What kind of "spiritual fruit" do you see ripening in your life?

CONSIDER . . .

- inviting someone you respect spiritually to have lunch with you.
- asking someone who gardens to explain how a plant produces fruit. Then ask God to make you produce more "spiritual fruit" in your life.

FOR MORE, SEE . . .

- Psalm 1
- Matthew 7:24–27
- Matthew 13:3–23

will not come. 8When the Helper comes, he will
prove to the people of the world the truth about
sin, about being right with God, and about judgment. 9He will prove to them that sin is not believing in me. 10He will prove to them that being
right with God comes from my going to the Father and not being seen anymore. 11And the
Helper will prove to them that judgment happened when the ruler of this world was judged.
12"I have many more things to say to you, but
they are too much for you now. 13But when the
Spirit[d] of truth comes, he will lead you into all
truth. He will not speak his own words, but he
will speak only what he hears, and he will tell you
what is to come. 14The Spirit of truth will bring
glory to me, because he will take what I have to
say and tell it to you. 15All that the Father has is
mine. That is why I said that the Spirit will take
what I have to say and tell it to you.

Sadness Will Become Happiness

16"After a little while you will not see me, and
then after a little while you will see me again."
17Some of the followers said to each other,
"What does Jesus mean when he says, 'After a
little while you will not see me, and then
after a little while you will see me again'? And
what does he mean when he says, 'Because I am
going to the Father'?" 18They also asked, "What
does he mean by 'a little while'? We don't understand what he is saying."
19Jesus saw that the followers wanted to ask

HOLY SPIRIT

The Improbable Disciple

Nicky Cruz was a murderous, uncontrollable gang leader who had killed before and would likely kill again. Without overstating the truth, Cruz was the most unlikely prospect for Christian conversion. He was also one of the first gang members whom David Wilkerson, a rural minister, met on the rough streets of New York City.

Wilkerson left his comfortable surroundings and started a missionary outreach to gang members in New York during the late 1960s. He was idealistic, and sometimes his efforts to gain a foothold for Christ among the vicious gang culture failed miserably.

Time after time, Nicky rejected David's pleas to seek God's forgiveness—once threatening the thin, quaking minister with a knife to his throat. But David replied, "You can cut me to pieces, Nicky, but every piece will still cry out, 'I love you.' "

David invited Nicky to attend a city-wide revival meeting he was organizing for gang members. Impressed by the man's courage, Nicky told David he and his gang would be there.

Nicky did show up at the revival, and David invited him to collect the offering. Nicky and his gang did and then headed for the backstage exit, snickering at the gullible preacher.

But on the way out, Nicky felt a heavy, almost overpowering weight on his shoulders. He stopped. He couldn't escape the fearful truth: The Jesus about whom David had spoken required something of him. Nicky and his gang returned to meet David on stage. At the end of the meeting, Nicky told David, "I've given my heart to God."

Today Nicky works with tough, inner-city teenagers, helping them turn from drugs and violence and follow Christ. Jesus said one of the Holy Spirit's main responsibilities is to prove the truth to people who are like Nicky Cruz used to be. Read about the Holy Spirit in **John 16:4–15**.

- According to verse 8, how did the Holy Spirit influence Nicky Cruz's change of heart?
- When have you felt the Holy Spirit working with you? Explain.

C O N S I D E R . . .

- listing ten words that could replace the word "Holy" and ten words that could replace the word "Spirit." Mix and match the words to come up with combinations such as "Perfect Presence" or "Pure Companion."
- spending five minutes at the end of each day, thinking of ways the Holy Spirit was with you throughout the day.

F O R M O R E , S E E . . .

- Psalm 51:10–13
- Luke 11:5–13
- Acts 2:1–36

him about this, so he said to them, "Are you asking each other what I meant when I said, 'After
a little while you will not see me, and then
after a little while you will see me again'? 20I tell
you the truth, you will cry and be sad, but the
world will be happy. You will be sad, but your
sadness will become joy. 21When a woman gives
birth to a baby, she has pain, because her time
has come. But when her baby is born, she for-
gets the pain, because she is so happy that a child
has been born into the world. 22It is the same
with you. Now you are sad, but I will see you
again and you will be happy, and no one will take
away your joy. 23In that day you will not ask me
for anything. I tell you the truth, my Father will
give you anything you ask for in my name. 24Un-
til now you have not asked for anything in my
name. Ask and you will receive, so that your joy
will be the fullest possible joy.

Victory over the World

25"I have told you these things, using stories
that hide the meaning. But the time will come
when I will not use stories like that to tell you
things; I will speak to you in plain words about
the Father. 26In that day you will ask the Father
for things in my name. I mean, I will not need to
ask the Father for you. 27The Father himself loves
you. He loves you because you loved me and believed that I came from God. 28I came from the
Father into the world. Now I am leaving the
world and going back to the Father."

29Then the followers of Jesus said, "You are
speaking clearly to us now and are not using stories that are hard to understand. 30We can see
now that you know all things. You can answer a
person's question even before it is asked. This
makes us believe you came from God."

31Jesus answered, "So now you believe? 32Lis-
ten to me; a time is coming when you will be
scattered, each to his own home. That time is
now here. You will leave me alone, but I am
never really alone, because the Father is with me.

33"I told you these things so that you can have
peace in me. In this world you will have trouble,
but be brave! I have defeated the world."

SIDELIGHT: Jesus' prayer in John 17 is the longest prayer in the New Testament. But Nehemiah holds the record for the longest Bible prayer with his prayer of praise, confession, and covenant in Nehemiah 9:5–37.

Jesus Prays for His Followers

17 After Jesus said these things, he looked
toward heaven and prayed, "Father, the
time has come. Give glory to your Son so that the

PRAYER

Do You Have a Prayer?

Does prayer have a place in your life? Read about other teenagers' prayer attitudes and practices as discovered in a Search Institute survey:

- Eighty-three percent say they often pray for God's help when they have problems.
- Eighty-three percent say they often pray that God will help other people.
- Sixty-five percent say they pray at least once a week outside church and other than before meals.
- Yet only 15 percent say personal prayer is an important influence in their life.
- No wonder 90 percent of teenagers are interested in learning how to pray.

Read **John 17:1–26** to see how Jesus prayed.

- What might the teenagers in the survey ask Jesus if they talked to him about his prayer?
- What does Jesus' prayer in this passage reveal about what is most important to him? How are your own priorities reflected in your prayers?

CONSIDER . . .

- making a prayer list of the people and things you consider most important to pray for. Use it daily, and keep track of answers.
- forming a prayer group to study prayer and pray together each week.

FOR MORE, SEE . . .

- 2 Samuel 7:18–29
- Ephesians 6:18–19
- Hebrews 4:14–16

Son can give glory to you. 2You gave the Son
power over all people so that the Son could give
eternal life to all those you gave him. 3And this is
eternal life: that people know you, the only true
God, and that they know Jesus Christ, the One
you sent. 4Having finished the work you gave
me to do, I brought you glory on earth. 5And
now, Father, give me glory with you; give me
the glory I had with you before the world was
made.

6"I showed what you are like to those you gave
me from the world. They belonged to you, and
you gave them to me, and they have obeyed your
teaching. 7Now they know that everything you
gave me comes from you. 8I gave them the teachings you gave me, and they accepted them. They
knew that I truly came from you, and they believed that you sent me. 9I am praying for them.
I am not praying for people in the world but for
those you gave me, because they are yours. 10All
I have is yours, and all you have is mine. And my
glory is shown through them. 11I am coming to
you; I will not stay in the world any longer. But
they are still in the world. Holy Father, keep them
safe by the power of your name, the name you
gave me, so that they will be one, just as you and
I are one. 12While I was with them, I kept them
safe by the power of your name, the name you
gave me. I protected them, and only one of them,
the one worthy of destruction, was lost so that the
Scripture[d] would come true.

13"I am coming to you now. But I pray these
things while I am still in the world so that these
followers can have all of my joy in them. 14I have
given them your teaching. And the world has
hated them, because they don't belong to the
world, just as I don't belong to the world. 15I am
not asking you to take them out of the world but
to keep them safe from the Evil One. 16They don't
belong to the world, just as I don't belong to the
world. 17Make them ready for your service
through your truth; your teaching is truth. 18I
have sent them into the world, just as you sent me
into the world. 19For their sake, I am making myself ready to serve so that they can be ready for
their service of the truth.

20"I pray for these followers, but I am also praying for all those who will believe in me because
of their teaching. 21Father, I pray that they can be
one. As you are in me and I am in you, I pray that
they can also be one in us. Then the world will
believe that you sent me. 22I have given these people the glory that you gave me so that they can be
one, just as you and I are one. 23I will be in them
and you will be in me so that they will be completely one. Then the world will know that you
sent me and that you loved them just as much as
you loved me.

24"Father, I want these people that you gave
me to be with me where I am. I want them to see
my glory, which you gave me because you loved
me before the world was made. 25Father, you are
the One who is good. The world does not know
you, but I know you, and these people know you
sent me. 26I showed them what you are like, and
I will show them again. Then they will have the
same love that you have for me, and I will live in
them."

Jesus Is Arrested

18 When Jesus finished praying, he went
with his followers across the Kidron Valley. On the other side there was a garden, and
Jesus and his followers went into it.

2Judas knew where this place was, because
Jesus met there often with his followers. Judas
was the one who turned against Jesus. 3So Judas
came there with a group of soldiers and some
guards from the leading priests and the Pharisees.[d] They were carrying torches, lanterns, and
weapons.

4Knowing everything that would happen to
him, Jesus went out and asked, "Who is it you are
looking for?"

5They answered, "Jesus from Nazareth."

"I am he," Jesus said. (Judas, the one who
turned against Jesus, was standing there with
them.) 6When Jesus said, "I am he," they moved
back and fell to the ground.

7Jesus asked them again, "Who is it you are
looking for?"

They said, "Jesus of Nazareth."

8"I told you that I am he," Jesus said. "So if you
are looking for me, let the others go." 9This happened so that the words Jesus said before would
come true: "I have not lost any of the ones you
gave me."

10Simon Peter, who had a sword, pulled it out
and struck the servant of the high priest, cutting
off his right ear. (The servant's name was Mal-
chus.) 11Jesus said to Peter, "Put your sword back.
Shouldn't I drink the cup[n] the Father gave me?"

Jesus Is Brought Before Annas

12Then the soldiers with their commander and
the Jewish guards arrested Jesus. They tied him
13and led him first to Annas, the father-in-law of
Caiaphas, the high priest that year. 14Caiaphas
was the one who told the Jews that it would be
better if one man died for all the people.

up Jesus is talking about the painful things that will happen to him. Accepting these things will be very hard, like drinking a cup of something bitter.

Peter Says He Doesn't Know Jesus

15Simon Peter and another one of Jesus' followers went along after Jesus. This follower knew the
high priest, so he went with Jesus into the high
priest's courtyard. 16But Peter waited outside near
the door. The follower who knew the high
priest came back outside, spoke to the girl at
the door, and brought Peter inside. 17The girl
at the door said to Peter, "Aren't you also one
of that man's followers?"

Peter answered, "No, I am not!"
18It was cold, so the servants and guards h
built a fire and were standing around it, warmi
themselves. Peter also was standing with the
warming himself.

The High Priest Questions Jesus

19The high priest asked Jesus questions abo
his followers and his teaching. 20Jesus answere
"I have spoken openly to everyone. I have alwa

FEAR

Letting Go

Brad Parks, Dean Brown, and Eric Unrau grew up together. In the summer they played football, rode trail bikes, and shot BB guns. In the fall they signed up for the same classes and held all-night Monopoly tournaments. In the winter they skied; in the spring they went camping. The years they had spent together made them feel like brothers.

But during their senior year in high school, something changed. Dean and Eric started drinking. They insisted on seeing the raunchiest movies in town. They each talked about how far they had gotten with their girlfriends.

All the while, Brad went along with them. But he felt worse and worse about himself. The changes he saw in Dean and Eric disgusted him. But Brad didn't have many friends in school. He couldn't risk alienating the ones he did have. He was afraid they would reject him. For months, this fear overpowered the sick feeling he had whenever he was with his friends.

One night, Dean called Brad and told him to be ready to leave for the movies in a half-hour.

"What are we going to see?" asked Brad.

"Eric found out how to sneak into a steamy show downtown. It starts in an hour."

Something broke in Brad. He was angry about his wasted weekends, about the terrible things he had said and done with his friends, and about letting God down.

"I'm sorry. I just can't go with you guys tonight," Brad said. "I can't stand the kind of movies we've seen lately. I'm not going to do that kind of stuff with you anymore."

Shocked, Dean tried to convince Brad to come anyway. But Brad wouldn't budge. Furious, Dean hung up the phone.

Dean and Eric abruptly broke off all contact with Brad. They spread terrible rumors about him at school and threatened to beat him up. A five-minute conversation had cost Brad his two closest friends. But it won him something far more valuable: the ability to face his fears and overcome them.

Just as Brad struggled to stand up to his friends, the apostle Peter was too afraid to admit he followed Jesus when he thought his life might be threatened. Read about Peter's struggle in **John 18:1–27**.

- How were Brad's fears similar to the apostle Peter's fears? How were they different?
- If you had been in Peter's shoes, what would you have said to the people who asked if you knew Jesus?

C O N S I D E R . . .

- writing one thing you have been afraid to tell a friend this last month, then thinking of a creative way to face your fear.
- listing the activities and topics of conversation you have participated in with your friends this last week. Circle things Jesus would never do or say, and mark a star beside things he would do or say.

F O R M O R E , S E E . . .

- Psalm 118:5–9
- Matthew 10:26–32
- Acts 2:14–42

taught in synagogues[d] and in the Temple,[d] where all the Jews come together. I never said anything in secret. 21So why do you question me? Ask the people who heard my teaching. They know what I said."

22When Jesus said this, one of the guards standing there hit him. The guard said, "Is that the way you answer the high priest?"

> **SIDELIGHT:** The sword Simon Peter used in John 18:10–11 was probably similar to a modern machete. Roman soldiers of this time used lightweight, well-balanced swords that were about two feet long for close-range combat. The sword is the most common weapon mentioned in the Bible, appearing more than four hundred times from Genesis to Revelation.

23Jesus answered him, "If I said something wrong, then show what it was. But if what I said is true, why do you hit me?"

24Then Annas sent Jesus, who was still tied, to Caiaphas the high priest.

Peter Says Again He Doesn't Know Jesus

25As Simon Peter was standing and warming himself, they said to him, "Aren't you one of that man's followers?"

Peter said it was not true; he said, "No, I am not."

26One of the servants of the high priest was there. This servant was a relative of the man whose ear Peter had cut off. The servant said, "Didn't I see you with him in the garden?"

27Again Peter said it wasn't true. At once a rooster crowed.

Jesus Is Brought Before Pilate

28Early in the morning they led Jesus from Caiaphas's house to the Roman governor's palace. They would not go inside the palace, because they did not want to make themselves unclean;[n] they wanted to eat the Passover[d] meal. 29So Pilate went outside to them and asked, "What charges do you bring against this man?"

30They answered, "If he were not a criminal, we wouldn't have brought him to you."

31Pilate said to them, "Take him yourselves and judge him by your own law."

"But we are not allowed to put anyone to death," the Jews answered. 32(This happened so that what Jesus said about how he would die would come true.)

33Then Pilate went back inside the palace and called Jesus to him and asked, "Are you the king of the Jews?"

34Jesus said, "Is that your own question, or did others tell you about me?"

35Pilate answered, "I am not Jewish. It was your own people and their leading priests who handed you over to me. What have you done wrong?"

36Jesus answered, "My kingdom does not belong to this world. If it belonged to this world, my servants would fight so that I would not be given over to the Jews. But my kingdom is from another place."

37Pilate said, "So you are a king!"

Jesus answered, "You are the one saying I am a king. This is why I was born and came into the world: to tell people the truth. And everyone who belongs to the truth listens to me."

38Pilate said, "What is truth?" After he said this, he went out to the Jews again and said to them, "I find nothing against this man. 39But it is your custom that I free one prisoner to you at Passover time. Do you want me to free the 'king of the Jews'?"

40They shouted back, "No, not him! Let Barabbas go free!" (Barabbas was a robber.)

19 Then Pilate ordered that Jesus be taken away and whipped. 2The soldiers made a crown from some thorny branches and put it on Jesus' head and put a purple robe around him. 3Then they came to him many times and said, "Hail, King of the Jews!" and hit him in the face.

4Again Pilate came out and said to them, "Look, I am bringing Jesus out to you. I want you to know that I find nothing against him." 5So Jesus came out, wearing the crown of thorns and the purple robe. Pilate said to them, "Here is the man!"

6When the leading priests and the guards saw Jesus, they shouted, "Crucify him! Crucify him!"

But Pilate answered, "Crucify him yourselves, because I find nothing against him."

7The Jews answered, "We have a law that says he should die, because he said he is the Son of God."

8When Pilate heard this, he was even more afraid. 9He went back inside the palace and asked Jesus, "Where do you come from?" But Jesus did not answer him. 10Pilate said, "You refuse to speak to me? Don't you know I have power to set you free and power to have you crucified?"

11Jesus answered, "The only power you have over me is the power given to you by God. The

unclean Going into a non-Jewish place would make them unfit to eat the Passover Feast, according to Jewish law.

man who turned me in to you is guilty of a greater
sin."
12After this, Pilate tried to let Jesus go. But the
Jews cried out, "Anyone who makes himself king
is against Caesar. If you let this man go, you are
no friend of Caesar."
13When Pilate heard what they were saying, he
brought Jesus out and sat down on the judge's
seat at the place called The Stone Pavement. (In
the Jewish language[n] the name is Gabbatha.)
14It was about noon on Preparation[d] Day of Passover[d] week. Pilate said to the Jews, "Here is your
king!"
15They shouted, "Take him away! Take him
away! Crucify him!"

Pilate asked them, "Do you want me to crucify
your king?"

The leading priests answered, "The only king
we have is Caesar."
16So Pilate handed Jesus over to them to be crucified.

Jesus Is Crucified

The soldiers took charge of Jesus. 17Carrying
his own cross, Jesus went out to a place called
The Place of the Skull, which in the Jewish language[n] is called Golgotha. 18There they crucified
Jesus. They also crucified two other men, one on
each side, with Jesus in the middle. 19Pilate wrote
a sign and put it on the cross. It read: JESUS OF
NAZARETH, THE KING OF THE JEWS. 20The sign was
written in the Jewish language, in Latin, and in
Greek. Many of the Jews read the sign, because
the place where Jesus was crucified was near
the city. 21The leading Jewish priests said to Pilate, "Don't write, 'The King of the Jews.' But
write, 'This man said, "I am the King of the
Jews." ' "
22Pilate answered, "What I have written, I have
written."
23After the soldiers crucified Jesus, they took
his clothes and divided them into four parts, with
each soldier getting one part. They also took his
long shirt, which was all one piece of cloth, woven from top to bottom. 24So the soldiers said to
each other, "We should not tear this into parts.
Let's throw lots[d] to see who will get it." This
happened so that this Scripture would come
true:[d]

"They divided my clothes among them,
and they threw lots[d] for my clothing."

Psalm 22:18

So the soldiers did this.

> **SIDELIGHT:** The "long shirt" the soldiers gambled for (John 19:23–24) was, in reality, like Jesus' undergarment. Crucifixions were often done with the criminals naked to make the execution even more humiliating.

25Standing near his cross were Jesus' mother,
his mother's sister, Mary the wife of Clopas, and
Mary Magdalene. 26When Jesus saw his mother
and the follower he loved standing nearby, he said
to his mother, "Dear woman, here is your son."
27Then he said to the follower, "Here is your
mother." From that time on, the follower took her
to live in his home.

Jesus Dies

28After this, Jesus knew that everything had
been done. So that the Scripture[d] would come
true, he said, "I am thirsty."[n] 29There was a ja
full of vinegar there, so the soldiers soaked
sponge in it, put the sponge on a branch of a hys
sop plant, and lifted it to Jesus' mouth. 30When
Jesus tasted the vinegar, he said, "It is finished."
Then he bowed his head and died.
31This day was Preparation[d] Day, and the nex
day was a special Sabbath[d] day. Since the Jews di
not want the bodies to stay on the cross on th
Sabbath day, they asked Pilate to order that th
legs of the men be broken[n] and the bodies b
taken away. 32So the soldiers came and broke th
legs of the first man on the cross beside Jesus
Then they broke the legs of the man on the othe
cross beside Jesus. 33But when the soldiers cam
to Jesus and saw that he was already dead, the
did not break his legs. 34But one of the soldier
stuck his spear into Jesus' side, and at once bloo
and water came out. 35(The one who saw thi
happen is the one who told us this, and whateve
he says is true. And he knows that he tells th
truth, and he tells it so that you might believe
36These things happened to make the Scriptur
come true: "Not one of his bones will be bro
ken."[n] 37And another Scripture says, "They wi
look at the one they stabbed."[n]

Jesus Is Buried

38Later, Joseph from Arimathea asked Pilate
he could take the body of Jesus. (Joseph was
secret follower of Jesus, because he was afraid
the Jews.) Pilate gave his permission, so Josep

Jewish language Hebrew or Aramaic, the languages of the Jewish people in the first century.
"I am thirsty." Read Psalms 22:15; 69:21.
broken The breaking of their bones would make them die sooner.
"Not one . . . broken." Quotation from Psalm 34:20. The idea is from Exodus 12:46; Numbers 9:12.
"They . . . stabbed." Quotation from Zechariah 12:10.

came and took Jesus' body away. 39Nicodemus,
who earlier had come to Jesus at night, went with
Joseph. He brought about seventy-five pounds of
myrrh[d] and aloes.[d] 40These two men took Jesus'
body and wrapped it with the spices in pieces of
linen cloth, which is how the Jewish people bury
the dead. 41In the place where Jesus was crucified, there was a garden. In the garden was a new
tomb that had never been used before. 42The men
laid Jesus in that tomb because it was nearby, and
the Jews were preparing to start their Sabbath[d]
day.

Jesus' Tomb Is Empty

20 Early on the first day of the week, Mary
Magdalene went to the tomb while it
was still dark. When she saw that the large stone
had been moved away from the tomb, 2she ran to
Simon Peter and the follower whom Jesus loved.
Mary said, "They have taken the Lord out of the
tomb, and we don't know where they have put
him."

3So Peter and the other follower started for the
tomb. 4They were both running, but the other follower ran faster than Peter and reached the tomb
first. 5He bent down and looked in and saw the
strips of linen cloth lying there, but he did not go
in. 6Then following him, Simon Peter arrived and
went into the tomb and saw the strips of linen
lying there. 7He also saw the cloth that had been
around Jesus' head, which was folded up and laid
in a different place from the strips of linen. 8Then
the other follower, who had reached the tomb
first, also went in. He saw and believed. 9(They
did not yet understand from the Scriptures[d] that
Jesus must rise from the dead.)

DEATH

Good-bye to a Pigtail-Puller

Danny Finnegan was Irish through and through. His red hair clashed with his light blue eyes—eyes that always seemed to laugh with mischief. Danny and his wife were Christine's parents' best friends. And he was the only adult she can remember who made a special effort to make her feel important.

In church on Sundays he would always sit behind Christine, where he could tug on her pigtails without ever taking his eyes off the minister. He would ride with Christine's family in the station wagon after church because he had never learned how to drive. And always, he would lean back and shout over the dull roar created by her brothers and sisters, "Christine, please sing 'Danny Boy' for me. You have such a beautiful voice. Please, Christine, sing for me."

Beaming with pride, she would always oblige. And when she had sung the last note, she always heard Danny's hearty laugh amid her brothers' and sisters' groans.

Danny loved Christine. He was one of those people you're sure will live forever just because a world without Danny wouldn't seem a whole world at all.

But one day Danny's doctor told him he was dying of cancer. Though years had passed since Danny had pulled on Christine's pigtails in church, she was stunned. She wrote Danny a long, loving letter when she heard he wouldn't last much longer.

A month later, Danny died. But before he slipped away, he made one last phone call to Christine's parents to tell them about "the most beautiful letter."

It was hard to see someone die who had been so full of life. Joseph and Nicodemus knew what it was like to lose somebody who made life worth living. Read about what they did for Jesus in **John 19:38–42**.

- How was the letter to Danny Finnegan like Joseph's and Nicodemus's burying Jesus?
- If you had been there, what would have been your first reaction to Jesus' death? What would you have done for Jesus?

C O N S I D E R . . .

- writing a letter to a friend or relative, telling him or her how your life has been enriched by his or her presence in it.
- asking someone who has lost a loved one to talk about that loved one.

F O R M O R E , S E E . . .

- Psalm 116
- Luke 24:1–8
- Hebrews 9:23–28

Jesus Appears to Mary Magdalene

10Then the followers went back home. 11But Mary stood outside the tomb, crying. As she was crying, she bent down and looked inside the tomb. 12She saw two angels dressed in white, sitting where Jesus' body had been, one at the head and one at the feet.

13They asked her, "Woman, why are you crying?"

She answered, "They have taken away my Lord, and I don't know where they have put him." 14When Mary said this, she turned around and saw Jesus standing there, but she did not know it was Jesus.

15Jesus asked her, "Woman, why are you crying? Whom are you looking for?"

Thinking he was the gardener, she said to him, "Did you take him away, sir? Tell me where you put him, and I will get him."

16Jesus said to her, "Mary."

Mary turned toward Jesus and said in the Jewish language,[n] "Rabboni." (This means Teacher.)

17Jesus said to her, "Don't hold on to me, because I have not yet gone up to the Father. But go to my brothers and tell them, 'I am going back to my Father and your Father, to my God and your God.' "

18Mary Magdalene went and said to the followers, "I saw the Lord!" And she told them what Jesus had said to her.

Jesus Appears to His Followers

19When it was evening on the first day of the week, the followers were together. The doors were locked, because they were afraid of the Jews. Then Jesus came and stood right in the middle of them and said, "Peace be with you." 20After he said this, he showed them his hands and his side. The followers were thrilled when they saw the Lord.

21Then Jesus said again, "Peace be with you. As the Father sent me, I now send you." 22After he said this, he breathed on them and said, "Receive the Holy Spirit.[d] 23If you forgive anyone his sins, they are forgiven. If you don't forgive them, they are not forgiven."

Jesus Appears to Thomas

24Thomas (called Didymus), who was one of the twelve, was not with them when Jesus came. 25The other followers kept telling Thomas, "We saw the Lord."

But Thomas said, "I will not believe it until I see the nail marks in his hands and put my finger where the nails were and put my hand into his side."

26A week later the followers were in the house again, and Thomas was with them. The doors were locked, but Jesus came in and stood right in the middle of them. He said, "Peace be with you." 27Then he said to Thomas, "Put your finger here, and look at my hands. Put your hand here in my side. Stop being an unbeliever and believe."

28Thomas said to him, "My Lord and my God!"

29Then Jesus told him, "You believe because you see me. Those who believe without seeing me will be truly happy."

Why John Wrote This Book

30Jesus did many other miracles[d] in the presence of his followers that are not written in this book. 31But these are written so that you may believe that Jesus is the Christ,[d] the Son of God. Then, by believing, you may have life through his name.

Jesus Appears to Seven Followers

21 Later, Jesus showed himself to his followers again—this time at Lake Galilee.[n] This is how he showed himself: 2Some of the followers were together: Simon Peter, Thomas (called Didymus), Nathanael from Cana in Galilee, the two sons of Zebedee, and two other followers. 3Simon Peter said, "I am going out to fish."

The others said, "We will go with you." So they went out and got into the boat. They fished that night but caught nothing.

4Early the next morning Jesus stood on the shore, but the followers did not know it was Jesus. 5Then he said to them, "Friends, did you catch any fish?"

They answered, "No."

6He said, "Throw your net on the right side of the boat, and you will find some." So they did, and they caught so many fish they could not pull the net back into the boat.

7The follower whom Jesus loved said to Peter, "It is the Lord!" When Peter heard him say this, he wrapped his coat around himself. (Peter had taken his clothes off.) Then he jumped into the water. 8The other followers went to shore in the boat, dragging the net full of fish. They were not very far from shore, only about a hundred yards. 9When the followers stepped out of the boat and onto the shore, they saw a fire of hot coals. There were fish on the fire, and there was bread.

10Then Jesus said, "Bring some of the fish you just caught."

11Simon Peter went into the boat and pulled the net to the shore. It was full of big fish, one

Jewish language Hebrew or Aramaic, the languages of the Jewish people in the first century.
Lake Galilee Literally, "Sea of Tiberias."

hundred fifty-three in all, but even though there
were so many, the net did not tear. [12]Jesus said
to them, "Come and eat." None of the followers
dared ask him, "Who are you?" because they
knew it was the Lord. [13]Jesus came and took the
bread and gave it to them, along with the fish.
[14]This was now the third time Jesus showed
himself to his followers after he was raised from
the dead.

SIDELIGHT: Barbecued fish for breakfast, anyone? That's what Jesus served when he appeared to his disciples (see John 21:4–13). Cooking fish on an open, charcoal fire was common in Jesus' day. He may have served them musht fish (now known as St. Peter's fish), which is one of the most common fish in Lake Galilee.

Jesus Talks to Peter

[15]When they finished eating, Jesus said to Simon Peter, "Simon son of John do you love me
more than these?"

He answered, "Yes, Lord, you know that I love you."

Jesus said, "Feed my lambs."

[16]Again Jesus said, "Simon son of John do you
love me?"

He answered, "Yes, Lord, you know that I love you."

Jesus said, "Take care of my sheep."

[17]A third time he said, "Simon son of John do
you love me?"

DOUBT

The Death of Doubt

Tim Simpson and his brothers had fought with their dad through the years. He was a salesman, a community leader, a church leader and a strong disciplinarian. He expected a lot from his four sons; his standards were high and generally inflexible. Going to church wasn't an option; it was expected.

Tim loved his dad, but it had always been a fearful, distant love. He had never really known, deep inside, whether his dad loved him. He saw God the same way—as a fearful, distant ruler he was forced to obey. So he wasn't sure if God loved him either. Until one cold November day.

Tim's dad had asked Tim to go out to breakfast with him—just the two of them. Tim didn't know what to think. What have I done? he wondered.

So Tim and his dad climbed into the family's beat-up station wagon and went to breakfast together. They didn't say much in the car, and Tim could see that his dad had something important to tell him.

After a tense, awkward breakfast, his dad laid down his fork, looked at Tim and said: "I know we haven't always seen eye to eye. And I know I've made life tough on you. But I don't ever want you to forget what I'm about to say to you. I love you as much as a father can love his son. And nothing will ever change that."

The words came with a power and a peace that enveloped Tim. Something changed between him and his dad in that moment. And something changed between Tim and God in that moment.

Tim felt, for the first time, the assurance of God's love for him.

Like Tim, the disciples sometimes had a hard time believing God. They doubted many of the promises Jesus had told them. And the chief doubter among them was Thomas. Read about Thomas's doubt in **John 20:19–31**.

- How did Tim's doubts about his father's love for him compare to Thomas's doubts about Jesus rising from the dead?
- When have you doubted the love of someone close to you?

C O N S I D E R . . .

- taking a twenty-minute walk and asking God to demonstrate his love for you in something you see.
- reaffirming your love to a friend or family member who may be doubting your love.

F O R M O R E , S E E . . .

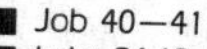

- Job 40—41
- Luke 24:13–53
- Romans 14:14–23

Peter was hurt because Jesus asked him the
third time, "Do you love me?" Peter said, "Lord,
you know everything; you know that I love
you!"
He said to him, "Feed my sheep. 18I tell you the
truth, when you were younger, you tied your
own belt and went where you wanted. But when
you are old, you will put out your hands and
someone else will tie you and take you where you
don't want to go." 19(Jesus said this to show how
Peter would die to give glory to God.) Then Jesus
said to Peter, "Follow me!"
20Peter turned and saw that the follower Jesus
loved was walking behind them. (This was the
follower who had leaned against Jesus at the supper and had said, "Lord, who will turn against
you?") 21When Peter saw him behind them, he
asked Jesus, "Lord, what about him?"
22Jesus answered, "If I want him to live until I
come back, that is not your business. You follow
me."
23So a story spread among the followers that
this one would not die. But Jesus did not say he
would not die. He only said, "If I want him to live
until I come back, that is not your business."
24That follower is the one who is telling these
things and who has now written them down. We
know that what he says is true.
25There are many other things Jesus did. If every one of them were written down, I suppose the
whole world would not be big enough for all the
books that would be written.

CELEBRATING

A Dark Victory

All year long, Tracy Howell's volleyball coach assured the team they were the best in the state. For most of the year, the state rankings agreed with her. Hilltop High's varsity volleyball team ranked Number One going into the district playoffs. Winning the district championship was the first step on the way to the state championship.

But Hilltop lost its first three playoff matches. One more, and they were out. With each loss, the girls became more depressed. Before their fourth match, the coach couldn't even get them "up" for it. The fans stayed away when they began losing.

Privately, Tracy told her best friend, "I know we're good, but I don't think we can win."

Hilltop's ranking slipped to sixth in state, and the experts labeled them the "dark horse" in the state playoffs. Seeded next to last in the tournament, Hilltop was paired against the best teams in state. They won their first match and surprised even themselves. In the second match, they lost their first game, but won the last two. They went into the state finals with renewed fan support.

In the third match, the games were tight. Hilltop won the first game, 18–16, but lost the second, 17–15. When the last point was scored in the final game, Hilltop had won 19–17.

The fans rushed onto the court and mobbed the Hilltop players. In the middle of the screaming crowd, Tracy felt out of place. She expected to feel all the ecstatic emotions she had dreamed of. But she felt more relief than anything.

That same joyful relief is what Jesus' disciples must have felt when Jesus rose from the dead and showed himself to them. Read about the disciples' experience in **John 21:1–14**.

- How do Tracy's up-and-down emotions compare with the disciples' emotions after Jesus was crucified and then appeared to them?
- When have you felt the kind of joy the disciples experienced on the shores of Lake Galilee? Explain.

CONSIDER . . .

- sending a "Celebrate Life" box to a faraway friend. Include confetti, party hats, party favors, snacks, and notes of encouragement to celebrate life.
- celebrating Christmas—the birth of Jesus—one day during the next two weeks. Plan a party, invite your friends, decorate in Christmas colors and ornaments, watch Christmas movies on video, and close by thanking God for his goodness in sending Christ.

FOR MORE, SEE . . .

- Psalm 126
- Luke 15:1–7
- James 1:2–4

ACTS

Why Read This Book:

- Discover how the Christian church was born (Acts 1—9).
- Recognize that God wants all people to have faith in him (Acts 10—12).
- Be encouraged to tell others about your faith, as the early Christians did (Acts 13—28).

Behind the Scenes:

It looked like everything was over. Jesus was dead—executed by the Romans. After three years with Jesus, the disciples weren't sure what to do next. Maybe go back to fishing and tax-collecting and the other things they did before Jesus came along.

But three days later, Jesus rose from the dead, and the world has never been the same. The book of Acts tells how that event began changing the world.

Written by Luke, Acts picks up where the Gospel of Luke leaves off. It tells how Jesus went up into heaven, then sent his Holy Spirit fifty days later (Acts 2). The rest of the book tells how the Good News of Jesus Christ spread rapidly throughout the world. Most of the book focuses on two people: Peter and Paul. Peter had been Jesus' disciple, and he quickly became a prominent leader in the early church. Through the book of Acts, we see him struggling to learn—and teach others—what it means to follow Jesus. Peter became a courageous leader who risked his life many times to share his faith.

Unlike Peter, Paul began as an enemy of Christians. But through a miraculous conversion (Acts 9), he became a devout Christian and great church leader. Acts tells about his travels to spread the Good News. And Acts provides the context for many of the topics Paul writes about in his letters (such as 1 Corinthians and Philippians).

Acts tells about a time Christians were endangered by religious and political authorities. Many churches had to meet in hiding, and Christian leaders were

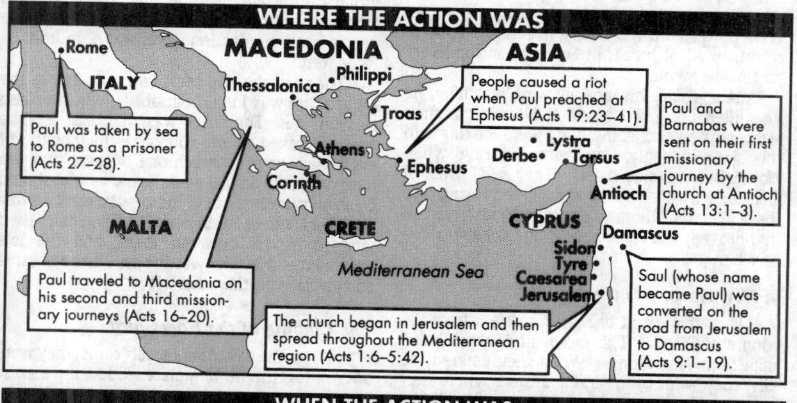

WHEN THE ACTION WAS

Jesus was born	The church began soon after Jesus went to heaven	Paul began his missionary work	Fire destroyed Rome	
BC/AD	25AD	50AD	75AD	100AD
	Jesus began his ministry	Paul became a Christian	Romans destroyed the Temple in Jerusalem	

Behind the Scenes (cont.): *regularly thrown in jail—or killed—for what they believed and taught. Yet the early Christians didn't back down. Their determination can encourage us to live our faith and tell others about it—even when we are tempted to hide it.*

Luke Writes Another Book

1 To Theophilus.

The first book I wrote was about everything Jesus began to do and teach 2until the day he was taken up into heaven. Before this, with the help of the Holy Spirit,[d] Jesus told the apostles he had chosen what they should do. 3After his death, he showed himself to them and proved in many ways that he was alive. The apostles saw Jesus during the forty days after he was raised from the dead, and he spoke to them about the kingdom of God. 4Once when he was eating with them, he told them not to leave Jerusalem. He said, "Wait here to receive the promise from the Father which I told you about. 5John baptized people with water, but in a few days you will be baptized with the Holy Spirit."

Jesus Is Taken Up Into Heaven

6When the apostles[d] were all together, they asked Jesus, "Lord, are you now going to give the kingdom back to Israel?"

7Jesus said to them, "The Father is the only One who has the authority to decide dates and times. These things are not for you to know. 8But when the Holy Spirit[d] comes to you, you will receive power. You will be my witnesses—in Jerusalem, in all of Judea, in Samaria, and in every part of the world."

9After he said this, as they were watching, he was lifted up, and a cloud hid him from their sight. 10As he was going, they were looking into the sky. Suddenly, two men wearing white clothes stood beside them. 11They said, "Men of Galilee, why are you standing here looking into the sky? Jesus, whom you saw taken up from you into heaven, will come back in the same way you saw him go."

A New Apostle Is Chosen

12Then they went back to Jerusalem from the Mount of Olives.[d] (This mountain is about half a mile from Jerusalem.) 13When they entered the city, they went to the upstairs room where they were staying. Peter, John, James, Andrew, Philip, Thomas, Bartholomew, Matthew, James son of Alphaeus, Simon (known as the Zealot[d]), and Judas son of James were there. 14They all continued praying together with some women, including Mary the mother of Jesus, and Jesus' brothers.

15During this time there was a meeting of the believers (about one hundred twenty of them). Peter stood up and said, 16-17"Brothers and sisters,[n] in the Scriptures[d] the Holy Spirit[d] said through David something that must happen involving Judas. He was one of our own group and served together with us. He led those who arrested Jesus." 18(Judas bought a field with the money he got for his evil act. But he fell to his death, his body burst open, and all his intestines poured out. 19Everyone in Jerusalem learned about this so they named this place Akeldama. In their language Akeldama means "Field of Blood.") 20"In the Book of Psalms," Peter said, "this is written:

'May his place be empty;
leave no one to live in it.' *Psalm 69:25*

And it is also written:

'Let another man replace him as leader.' *Psalm 109:8*

21-22"So now a man must become a witness with us of Jesus' being raised from the dead. He must be one of the men who were part of our group during all the time the Lord Jesus was among us—from the time John was baptizing people until the day Jesus was taken up from us to heaven."

23They put the names of two men before the group. One was Joseph Barsabbas, who was also called Justus. The other was Matthias. 24-25The apostles prayed, "Lord, you know the thoughts of everyone. Show us which one of these two you have chosen to do this work. Show us who should be an apostle[d] in place of Judas, who turned away and went where he belongs." 26Then they used lots[d] to choose between them, and the lots showed that Matthias was the one. So he became an apostle with the other eleven.

The Coming of the Holy Spirit

2 When the day of Pentecost[d] came, they were all together in one place. 2Suddenly a noise like a strong, blowing wind came from heaven and filled the whole house where they were sitting. 3They saw something like flames of fire that were separated and stood over each person there.

Brothers and sisters Although the Greek text says "Brothers" here and throughout this book, the words of the speakers were meant for the entire church, including men and women.

4They were all filled with the Holy Spirit,[d] and
they began to speak different languages[n] by the
power the Holy Spirit was giving them.

SIDELIGHT: Before the birth of the church, Pentecost (Acts 2:1–4) was a major time of celebration among Jews. This festival celebrated the wheat harvest with religious ceremonies, eating, drinking, and music. The festivities surrounding the event may be why skeptics thought the disciples were drunk (Acts 2:13).

5There were some religious Jews staying in Jerusalem who were from every country in the
world. 6When they heard this noise, a crowd
came together. They were all surprised, because
each one heard them speaking in his own language. 7They were completely amazed at this.
They said, "Look! Aren't all these people that we
hear speaking from Galilee? 8Then how is it possible that we each hear them in our own languages? We are from different places: 9Parthia,
Media, Elam, Mesopotamia, Judea, Cappadocia,
Pontus, Asia, 10Phrygia, Pamphylia, Egypt, the areas of Libya near Cyrene, Rome 11(both Jews and
those who had become Jews), Crete, and Arabia.
But we hear them telling in our own languages
about the great things God has done!" 12They
were all amazed and confused, asking each other,
"What does this mean?"
13But others were making fun of them, saying,
"They have had too much wine."

Peter Speaks to the People

14But Peter stood up with the eleven apostles,[d]
and in a loud voice he spoke to the crowd: "My
fellow Jews, and all of you who are in Jerusalem,
listen to me. Pay attention to what I have to say.
15These people are not drunk, as you think; it is
only nine o'clock in the morning! 16But Joel the
prophet[d] wrote about what is happening here today:
17'God says: In the last days
I will pour out my Spirit[d] on all kinds of
people.
Your sons and daughters will prophesy.[d]
Your young men will see visions,
and your old men will dream dreams.

languages This can also be translated "tongues."

HOLY SPIRIT

The Third Rail

The largest subway in the world is in New York City. It is an electric-powered, underground railway system. Every day, the system's 6,200 cars carry 3.5 million people to their destinations. Each year, more than a billion people use the subway.

The subway trains get their power through a "third rail," which runs alongside the 723 miles of subway tracks and supplies 600 volts of electricity to each train.

Without the third rail's power, the whole system would fail, and millions of people would be stranded. At all times, the successful operation of the subway system depends on the power of the third rail. Like the third rail is the subway's source of power, the Holy Spirit is the source of power for Christians. As we connect with the Spirit, we have the power we need to live the Christian life. Read **Acts 2:1–21** to discover how the Holy Spirit first empowered Christians.

- As the third rail empowers the subway, how does the Holy Spirit empower Christians?
- According to this passage, what are some evidences of the Holy Spirit's power?

C O N S I D E R . . .

- telling people from another culture about Jesus. Depend on the Holy Spirit to help you communicate clearly.
- finding out about the beginning of your congregation. What similarities do you see between that beginning and the beginning of the church in Acts 2?

F O R M O R E , S E E . . .

- Joel 2:28–29
- John 14:15–26
- 1 Corinthians 12:1–11

18At that time I will pour out my Spirit
also on my male slaves and female slaves,
and they will prophesy.
19I will show miracles[d]
in the sky and on the earth:
blood, fire, and thick smoke.
20The sun will become dark,
the moon red as blood,
before the overwhelming and glorious day
of the Lord will come.
21Then anyone who calls on the Lord
will be saved.' *Joel 2:28-32*

22"People of Israel, listen to these words: Jesus
from Nazareth was a very special man. God
clearly showed this to you by the miracles,[d] wonders, and signs he did through Jesus. You all know
this, because it happened right here among you.
23Jesus was given to you, and with the help of
those who don't know the law, you put him to
death by nailing him to a cross. But this was God's
plan which he had made long ago; he knew all
this would happen. 24God raised Jesus from the
dead and set him free from the pain of death, because death could not hold him. 25For David said
this about him:
'I keep the Lord before me always.
Because he is close by my side,
I will not be hurt.
26So I am glad, and I rejoice.
Even my body has hope,
27because you will not leave me in the grave.
You will not let your Holy One rot.
28You will teach me how to live a holy life.
Being with you will fill me with joy.'
Psalm 16:8-11

29"Brothers and sisters, I can tell you truly that
David, our ancestor, died and was buried. His
grave is still here with us today. 30He was a
prophet[d] and knew God had promised him that
he would make a person from David's family a
king just as he was.[n] 31Knowing this before it
happened, David talked about the Christ[d] rising
from the dead. He said:
'He was not left in the grave.
His body did not rot.'
32So Jesus is the One whom God raised from the
dead. And we are all witnesses to this. 33Jesus was
lifted up to heaven and is now at God's right side.
The Father has given the Holy Spirit[d] to Jesus as
he promised. So Jesus has poured out that Spirit,
and this is what you now see and hear. 34David
was not the one who was lifted up to heaven, but
he said:
'The Lord said to my Lord,
"Sit by me at my right side,
35 until I put your enemies under your
control." '[n] *Psalm 110:1*

36"So, all the people of Israel should know this
truly: God has made Jesus—the man you nailed
to the cross—both Lord and Christ."

37When the people heard this, they felt guilty
and asked Peter and the other apostles, "What
shall we do?"

38Peter said to them, "Change your hearts and
lives and be baptized, each one of you, in the
name of Jesus Christ for the forgiveness of your
sins. And you will receive the gift of the Holy
Spirit. 39This promise is for you, for your children,
and for all who are far away. It is for everyone the
Lord our God calls to himself."

40Peter warned them with many other words.
He begged them, "Save yourselves from the evil
of today's people!" 41Then those people who accepted what Peter said were baptized. About
three thousand people were added to the number
of believers that day. 42They spent their time
learning the apostles' teaching, sharing, breaking
bread,[n] and praying together.

The Believers Share

43The apostles[d] were doing many miracles[d] and
signs, and everyone felt great respect for God.
44All the believers were together and shared everything. 45They would sell their land and the
things they owned and then divide the money
and give it to anyone who needed it. 46The believers met together in the Temple[d] every day. They
ate together in their homes, happy to share their
food with joyful hearts. 47They praised God and
were liked by all the people. Every day the Lord
added those who were being saved to the group
of believers.

Peter Heals a Crippled Man

3 One day Peter and John went to the Temple[d]
at three o'clock, the time set each day for the
afternoon prayer service. 2There, at the Temple
gate called Beautiful Gate, was a man who had
been crippled all his life. Every day he was carried
to this gate to beg for money from the people going into the Temple. 3The man saw Peter and
John going into the Temple and asked them for
money. 4Peter and John looked straight at him
and said, "Look at us!" 5The man looked at them,
thinking they were going to give him some

God . . . was See 2 Samuel 7:13; Psalm 132:11.
until . . . control Literally, "until I make your enemies a footstool for your feet."
breaking bread This may mean a meal as in verse 46, or the Lord's Supper, the special meal Jesus told his followers to eat to remember him (Luke 22:14-20).

money. [6]But Peter said, "I don't have any silver or gold, but I do have something else I can give you. By the power of Jesus Christ from Nazareth, stand up and walk!" [7]Then Peter took the man's right hand and lifted him up. Immediately the man's feet and ankles became strong. [8]He jumped up, stood on his feet, and began to walk. He went into the Temple with them, walking and jumping and praising God. [9-10]All the people recognized him as the crippled man who always sat by the Beautiful Gate begging for money. Now they saw this same man walking and praising God, and they were amazed. They wondered how this could happen.

Peter Speaks to the People

[11]While the man was holding on to Peter and John, all the people were amazed and ran to them at Solomon's Porch.[d] [12]When Peter saw this, he said to them, "People of Israel, why are you surprised? You are looking at us as if it were our own power or goodness that made this man walk. [13]The God of Abraham, Isaac, and Jacob, the God of our ancestors, gave glory to Jesus, his servant. But you handed him over to be killed. Pilate decided to let him go free, but you told Pilate you did not want Jesus. [14]You did not want the One who is holy and good but asked Pilate to give you

CHURCH

The Place to Belong

Rebecca Fisher yearned to fit in. She wanted people to like her and be her friend. That's why she joined every organization she could at school. She still didn't feel like she fit in, but at least she was busy.

During French club meeting one day, Lee Brungardt invited Rebecca to church. She grimaced at the thought, remembering the church she had attended with her mother years before. Each service had been one long, boring sermon with her mom telling her to be quiet. That was not Rebecca's idea of fun. She "had a commitment already," she lied to Lee.

But Lee persisted. Finally Rebecca agreed to endure one service—just to get him to leave her alone.

She didn't say much to him. When Lee and Rebecca arrived for Sunday school the next Sunday morning, the kids were standing around talking and laughing. Several of them recognized Rebecca and welcomed her. During the Bible study, the teacher called Rebecca by name and asked her opinion. Several kids invited Rebecca and Lee to sit with them during the worship service. And during the sermon, the pastor told interesting stories. Rebecca never felt bored.

After the worship service, all the kids went to Jason Hawley's house for lunch and to complete plans for their mission project. Rebecca helped make posters.

All the way home, Rebecca couldn't stop talking about how much she had liked Lee's church. "It just seems like I fit there, you know?" she commented.

"Yeah, I know." Lee smiled. "So, I guess you'll need a ride next week?"

Rebecca laughed and asked, "What do you think?"

People are attracted to places where people really care and teach God's Word. Read **Acts 2:36–47** to see how the first church attracted people by the way its people lived and worshiped together.

- How does the church in Acts compare with Lee's church?
- Which qualities does the Acts church have in common with your church? Which qualities of this church are different from your church's?

C O N S I D E R . . .

- befriending visitors who come to your church. Ask them to sit with you or invite them to other church activities.
- doing a specific job in your church, such as greeting visitors or writing for the newsletter. Become one of the people who makes church more of what God wants it to be.

F O R M O R E , S E E . . .

- Isaiah 2:2–5
- Acts 4:32–35
- Romans 12

a murderer[n] instead. 15And so you killed the One
who gives life, but God raised him from the dead.
We are witnesses to this. 16It was faith in Jesus
that made this crippled man well. You can see this
man, and you know him. He was made completely well because of trust in Jesus, and you all
saw it happen!

17"Brothers and sisters, I know you did those
things to Jesus because neither you nor your leaders understood what you were doing. 18God said
through the prophets[d] that his Christ[d] would suffer and die. And now God has made these things
come true in this way. 19So you must change your
hearts and lives! Come back to God, and he will
forgive your sins. Then the Lord will send the
time of rest. 20And he will send Jesus, the One he
chose to be the Christ. 21But Jesus must stay in
heaven until the time comes when all things will
be made right again. God told about this time long
ago when he spoke through his holy prophets.
22Moses said, 'The Lord your God will give you a
prophet like me, who is one of your own people.
You must listen to everything he tells you. 23Any-
one who does not listen to that prophet will die,
cut off from God's people.'[n] 24Samuel, and all the
other prophets who spoke for God after Samuel,
told about this time now. 25You are descendants[d]
of the prophets. You have received the agreement
God made with your ancestors. He said to your
father Abraham, 'Through your descendants[d] all
the nations on the earth will be blessed.'[n] 26God
has raised up his servant Jesus and sent him to

murderer Barabbas, the man the crowd asked Pilate to set free instead of Jesus (Luke 23:18).
'The Lord . . . people.' Quotation from Deuteronomy 18:15, 19.
'Through . . . blessed.' Quotation from Genesis 22:18; 26:4.

GOD'S LOVE

Power to Heal

"Hey, freak! Why don't you join the circus?"

"Aaagh! It's Frankenstein's brother."

Rocky Dennis had heard cruel jeers like this all his life. Rocky had been born with a disease known as lionitis. This disease multiplied calcium deposits at an abnormal rate throughout Rocky's skull and progressively disfigured Rocky's face.

But Rocky displayed remarkable friendship, joy, and confidence—even with the people who were most cruel. He wouldn't accept rejection. When people made fun of his face, he responded with better jokes. Rocky loved people in a way that made them forget what he looked like. His comfort with himself put other people at ease.

Mask, the movie about Rocky's life, portrays how Rocky loved a blind and beautiful teenage girl. Because the girl couldn't see his physical deformity, his inner beauty captured her heart. Rocky opened up the world to her. He showed her color by placing things in her hands: Blue was an ice cube; red was a hot rock; the hot rock cooled to pink; white was a mass of cotton balls.

But not everyone could see Rocky's beauty. After meeting Rocky, the blind girl's parents blocked further contact with him. The only girl who had ever really seen Rocky was taken away from him.

Rocky had reason to be frustrated, angry and sad. But he overcame bad with good. He continued to care for people and was patient with those who were blinded by his deformity.

Jesus also knew the pain of rejection, but he kept loving people anyway, as we see in **Acts 3:11–19**.

- How were Rocky's attitude and actions similar to Jesus' attitude and actions?
- According to this passage, what is the Christlike way to respond to rejection?

CONSIDER . . .

- listing things you could say to people who reject you.
- developing a friendship with someone other people reject.

FOR MORE, SEE . . .

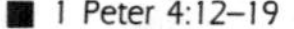

- Isaiah 53:1–6
- Matthew 5:43–48
- 1 Peter 4:12–19

you first to bless you by turning each of you away
from doing evil."

Peter and John at the Council

4 While Peter and John were speaking to the
people, Jewish priests, the captain of the soldiers that guarded the Temple,[d] and Sadducees[d]
came up to them. 2They were upset because the
two apostles[d] were teaching the people and were
preaching that people will rise from the dead
through the power of Jesus. 3The Jewish leaders
grabbed Peter and John and put them in jail. Since
it was already night, they kept them in jail until
the next day. 4But many of those who had heard
Peter and John preach believed the things they
said. There were now about five thousand in the
group of believers.
5The next day the Jewish rulers, the older Jewish leaders, and the teachers of the law met in
Jerusalem. 6Annas the high priest, Caiaphas, John,
and Alexander were there, as well as everyone
from the high priest's family. 7They made Peter
and John stand before them and then asked them,
"By what power or authority did you do this?"
8Then Peter, filled with the Holy Spirit,[d] said to
them, "Rulers of the people and you older leaders,
9are you questioning us about a good thing that
was done to a crippled man? Are you asking us
who made him well? 10We want all of you and all
the Jewish people to know that this man was
made well by the power of Jesus Christ from Nazareth. You crucified him, but God raised him from
the dead. This man was crippled, but he is now
well and able to stand here before you because of
the power of Jesus. 11Jesus is
'the stone[n] that you builders rejected,
which has become the cornerstone.'[d]

Psalm 118:22

12Jesus is the only One who can save people. His
name is the only power in the world that has been
given to save people. We must be saved through
him."
13The Jewish leaders saw that Peter and John
were not afraid to speak, and they understood
that these men had no special training or education. So they were amazed. Then they realized

stone A symbol meaning Jesus.

SHARING FAITH

Responding to Opportunities

"C'mon, Manuel. Don't let me down! Mrs. Reece trusts you," Rick Jantzen pleaded. "She would let you into the classroom to use the lab at night, and you could copy the test key while you're there. She'd never know."

"I just can't. I can't use Mrs. Reece's trust that way," Manuel Salazar said. "And besides, it's wrong to cheat."

"Why can't you do it just this once? No one will know!" Rick persisted.

"I will know and so will Jesus," Manuel answered.

"But Jesus wants you to make good grades, doesn't he?" Rick challenged.

"Yeah, he does. This just isn't the way to make those good grades."

Rick finally quit pressuring Manuel to compromise his faith. In fact, over time Rick even started asking Manuel questions about "this Jesus who runs your life."

Caught in a tough situation, Manuel shared his faith by showing how it influenced his actions. Read how Peter and John took advantage of an opportunity to talk about Jesus in **Acts 4:1–13**.

- What obstacles did Manuel and Peter have to overcome to talk about their faith?
- What basic facts about Jesus did Peter consider essential in discussing his faith?

CONSIDER . . .

- writing down ways you could share your faith with a non-Christian. Use one of these ways with someone this week.
- enlisting a friend to role-play faith-sharing situations. Role-play talking to people who are skeptical, open, rebellious or interested.

FOR MORE, SEE . . .

- Daniel 1:3–16
- Matthew 10:16–20
- Colossians 4:5–6

that Peter and John had been with Jesus. 14Because they saw the healed man standing there beside the two apostles, they could say nothing against them. 15After the Jewish leaders ordered them to leave the meeting, they began to talk to each other. 16They said, "What shall we do with these men? Everyone in Jerusalem knows they have done a great miracle,[d] and we cannot say it is not true. 17But to keep it from spreading among the people, we must warn them not to talk to people anymore using that name."

18So they called Peter and John in again and told them not to speak or to teach at all in the name of Jesus. 19But Peter and John answered them, "You decide what God would want. Should we obey you or God? 20We cannot keep quiet. We must speak about what we have seen and heard." 21The Jewish leaders warned the apostles again and let them go free. They could not find a way to punish them, because all the people were praising God for what had been done. 22The man who received the miracle of healing was more than forty years old.

SIDELIGHT: The council before which Peter appeared in Acts 4:1–22 was the Sanhedrin, the Jewish equivalent of the Supreme Court. It was likely composed of Jerusalem's religious and political leaders. Its main job was to protect Jewish life, custom, and law.

The Believers Pray

23After Peter and John left the meeting of Jewish leaders, they went to their own group and told them everything the leading priests and the older Jewish leaders had said to them. 24When the believers heard this, they prayed to God together, "Lord, you are the One who made the sky, the earth, the sea, and everything in them. 25By the Holy Spirit,[d] through our father David your servant, you said:

'Why are the nations so angry?
Why are the people making useless plans?
26The kings of the earth prepare to fight,
and their leaders make plans together
against the Lord
and his Christ.'[d] *Psalm 2:1-2*

27These things really happened when Herod, Pontius Pilate, those who are not Jews, and the Jewish people all came together against Jesus here in Jerusalem. Jesus is your holy servant, the One you made to be the Christ. 28These people made your plan happen because of your power and your will. 29And now, Lord, listen to their threats. Lord, help us, your servants, to speak your word without fear. 30Help us to be brave by showing us your power to heal. Give proofs and make miracles[d] happen by the power of Jesus, your holy servant."

31After they had prayed, the place where they were meeting was shaken. They were all filled with the Holy Spirit,[d] and they spoke God's word without fear.

The Believers Share

32The group of believers were united in their hearts and spirit. All those in the group acted as though their private property belonged to everyone in the group. In fact, they shared everything. 33With great power the apostles[d] were telling people that the Lord Jesus was truly raised from the dead. And God blessed all the believers very much. 34No one in the group needed anything. From time to time those who owned fields or houses sold them, brought the money, 35and gave it to the apostles. Then the money was given to anyone who needed it.

36One of the believers was named Joseph, a Levite born in Cyprus. The apostles called him Barnabas (which means "one who encourages"). 37Joseph owned a field, sold it, brought the money, and gave it to the apostles.

Ananias and Sapphira Die

5 But a man named Ananias and his wife Sapphira sold some land. 2He kept back part of the money for himself; his wife knew about this and agreed to it. But he brought the rest of the money and gave it to the apostles.[d] 3Peter said, "Ananias, why did you let Satan rule your thoughts to lie to the Holy Spirit[d] and to keep for yourself part of the money you received for the land? 4Before you sold the land, it belonged to you. And even after you sold it, you could have used the money any way you wanted. Why did you think of doing this? You lied to God, not to us!" 5-6When Ananias heard this, he fell down and died. Some young men came in, wrapped up his body, carried it out, and buried it. And everyone who heard about this was filled with fear.

7About three hours later his wife came in, but she did not know what had happened. 8Peter said to her, "Tell me, was the money you got for your field this much?"

Sapphira answered, "Yes, that was the price."

9Peter said to her, "Why did you and your husband agree to test the Spirit of the Lord? Look! The men who buried your husband are at the door, and they will carry you out." 10At that moment Sapphira fell down by his feet and died. When the young men came in and saw that she was dead, they carried her out and buried her beside her husband. 11The whole church and all the others who heard about these things were filled with fear.

The Apostles Heal Many

12The apostles[d] did many signs and miracles[d]
among the people. And they would all meet together on Solomon's Porch.[d] 13None of the others
dared to join them, but all the people respected
them. 14More and more men and women believed in the Lord and were added to the group
of believers. 15The people placed their sick on
beds and mats in the streets, hoping that when
Peter passed by at least his shadow might fall on
them. 16Crowds came from all the towns around
Jerusalem, bringing their sick and those who were
bothered by evil spirits, and all of them were
healed.

Leaders Try to Stop the Apostles

17The high priest and all his friends (a group
called the Sadducees[d]) became very jealous.
18They took the apostles[d] and put them in jail.
19But during the night, an angel of the Lord
opened the doors of the jail and led the apostles
outside. The angel said, 20"Go stand in the Tem-

PRIORITIES

Who's the Boss?

Richard Wurmbrand fidgeted in his chair as he listened to Gheorghe Gheorghiu-Dej, the Communist Party boss, deliver his speech. Gheorghe promised the post-World War II clergy of Romania that his government would pay the clergy from tax revenues if communism and Christianity would work together.

Most of the audience cheered, and a leader promised that the clergy would cooperate with the state.

But Richard didn't cheer. He had already been imprisoned and beaten several times for his faith. He knew speaking out could again cost him his freedom.

Richard's wife, Sabrina, sat beside him. "Go and wash this shame from the face of Christ!" she demanded.

Richard pleaded that he would probably be taken away if he spoke out against the communists.

"I don't need a coward," Sabrina replied.

Gathering his courage, Richard asked permission to speak and was welcomed forward by the organizers, who apparently anticipated a unity speech. Instead, Richard began by saying it was the duty of pastors to glorify God, not earthly powers. He encouraged the clergy to support the eternal kingdom of God, not the fleeting powers of Romania.

As he continued, someone suddenly began to clap. And another person also clapped. Soon, the clapping erupted into waves of applause.

"Stop! Your right to speak has been withdrawn," ordered the Minister of Cults ("cults" included religious bodies of all kinds in Romania).

"My right to speak comes from God," Richard declared. He kept speaking until his microphone was disconnected.

Soon after, Richard was imprisoned. The Romanian communists instituted their state religion and the Ministry of Cults ran the church.

Like Richard, the apostles recognized the priority of obeying God and speaking out for him. Read **Acts 5:17–32** to see how they spoke out for Jesus even when threatened by imprisonment.

- Based on the story and the Bible passage, what were the top priorities for Richard Wurmbrand and the apostles?
- When have you faced opposition for your faith? How was that experience like and unlike the scripture passage?

CONSIDER . . .

- making a poster of Acts 5:29 and writing around the border five priorities you believe God wants you to follow. Then make a weekly schedule that reflects those priorities.
- talking with a friend about times you have had to do something unpopular to make your faith your top priority.

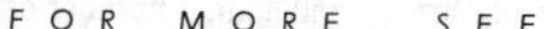

FOR MORE, SEE . . .

- Psalm 119:17–24
- Matthew 10:32–36
- 2 Corinthians 11:23–29

ple[d] and tell the people everything about this new
life." 21When the apostles heard this, they obeyed
and went into the Temple early in the morning
and continued teaching.
When the high priest and his friends arrived,
they called a meeting of the Jewish leaders and all
the important older Jewish men. They sent some
men to the jail to bring the apostles to them.
22But, upon arriving, the officers could not find
the apostles. So they went back and reported to
the Jewish leaders. 23They said, "The jail was
closed and locked, and the guards were standing
at the doors. But when we opened the doors, the
jail was empty!" 24Hearing this, the captain of the
Temple guards and the leading priests were confused and wondered what was happening.
25Then someone came and told them, "Listen!
The men you put in jail are standing in the Temple teaching the people." 26Then the captain and
his men went out and brought the apostles back.
But the soldiers did not use force, because they
were afraid the people would stone them to
death.
27The soldiers brought the apostles to the meeting and made them stand before the Jewish leaders. The high priest questioned them, 28saying,
"We gave you strict orders not to continue teaching in that name. But look, you have filled Jerusalem with your teaching and are trying to make us
responsible for this man's death."
29Peter and the other apostles answered, "We
must obey God, not human authority! 30You
killed Jesus by hanging him on a cross. But God,
the God of our ancestors, raised Jesus up from the
dead! 31Jesus is the One whom God raised to be
on his right side, as Leader and Savior. Through
him, all Jewish people could change their hearts
and lives and have their sins forgiven. 32We saw
all these things happen. The Holy Spirit,[d] whom
God has given to all who obey him, also proves
these things are true."
33When the Jewish leaders heard this, they became angry and wanted to kill them. 34But a Pharisee[d] named Gamaliel stood up in the meeting. He
was a teacher of the law, and all the people respected him. He ordered the apostles to leave the
meeting for a little while. 35Then he said, "People
of Israel, be careful what you are planning to do
to these men. 36Remember when Theudas appeared? He said he was a great man, and about
four hundred men joined him. But he was killed,
and all his followers were scattered; they were
able to do nothing. 37Later, a man named Judas
came from Galilee at the time of the registration.[n] He also led a group of followers and was
killed, and all his followers were scattered. 38And
so now I tell you: Stay away from these men, and
leave them alone. If their plan comes from human
authority, it will fail. 39But if it is from God, you
will not be able to stop them. You might even be
fighting against God himself!"
The Jewish leaders agreed with what Gamaliel
said. 40They called the apostles in, beat them, and
told them not to speak in the name of Jesus again.
Then they let them go free. 41The apostles left the
meeting full of joy because they were given the
honor of suffering disgrace for Jesus. 42Every day
in the Temple and in people's homes they continued teaching the people and telling the Good
News—that Jesus is the Christ.[d]

SIDELIGHT: Relationships between Jews and non-Jewish people were strained in Bible times. This prejudice shows up in Acts 6:1 where Greek (non-Jewish) Christians complained that their widows weren't receiving a fair share of the church's distributions. The book of Acts is filled with other stories that highlight the tensions between Jewish and non-Jewish Christians.

Seven Leaders Are Chosen

6 The number of followers was growing. But
during this same time, the Greek-speaking
followers had an argument with the other Jewish
followers. The Greek-speaking widows were not
getting their share of the food that was given out
every day. 2The twelve apostles[d] called the whole
group of followers together and said, "It is not
right for us to stop our work of teaching God's
word in order to serve tables. 3So, brothers and
sisters, choose seven of your own men who are
good, full of the Spirit[d] and full of wisdom. We
will put them in charge of this work. 4Then we
can continue to pray and to teach the word of
God."
5The whole group liked the idea, so they chose
these seven men: Stephen (a man with great faith
and full of the Holy Spirit), Philip,[n] Procorus, Ni-
canor, Timon, Parmenas, and Nicolas (a man
from Antioch who had become a Jew). 6Then
they put these men before the apostles, who
prayed and laid their hands[n] on them.
7The word of God was continuing to spread.
The group of followers in Jerusalem increased,
and a great number of the Jewish priests believed
and obeyed.

registration Census. A counting of all the people and the things they own.
Philip Not the apostle named Philip.
laid their hands The laying on of hands had many purposes, including the giving of a blessing, power, or authority.

Stephen Is Accused

[8]Stephen was richly blessed by God who gave
him the power to do great miracles[d] and signs
among the people. [9]But some Jewish people were
against him. They belonged to the synagogue[d] of
Free Men[n] (as it was called), which included
Jewish people from Cyrene, Alexandria, Cilicia,
and Asia. They all came and argued with Stephen.
[10]But the Spirit[d] was helping him to speak with
wisdom, and his words were so strong that they
could not argue with him. [11]So they secretly
urged some men to say, "We heard Stephen speak
against Moses and against God."
[12]This upset the people, the older Jewish leaders, and the teachers of the law. They came and
grabbed Stephen and brought him to a meeting of
the Jewish leaders. [13]They brought in some people to tell lies about Stephen, saying, "This man
is always speaking against this holy place and the
law of Moses. [14]We heard him say that Jesus from
Nazareth will destroy this place and that Jesus
will change the customs Moses gave us." [15]All the
people in the meeting were watching Stephen
closely and saw that his face looked like the face
of an angel.

Stephen's Speech

7 The high priest said to Stephen, "Are these
things true?"
[2]Stephen answered, "Brothers and fathers, lis-

Free Men Jewish people who had been slaves or whose fathers had been slaves, but were now free.

HONESTY

Rumors

"Shhhhh! There she is."

The girls in the back of the room stopped giggling and whispering when Zoe Ketner arrived at her first-period world history class on Monday morning.

"What's going on?" Zoe asked uncomfortably as she sat next to her best friend, Marlene Riddle.

Marlene shot a dirty look at the girls in the back of the room: "Someone is saying you're 'easy,' " she said. "There's a note in the guys' bathroom that says 'Zoe's fine, so get in line.' "

Zoe couldn't believe it. She felt like someone had just kicked her in the chest.

Just then, Mark Warren leaned across the aisle and asked, "Hey, Zoe, can I be next in line?"

Zoe burst into tears and ran from the room. Her mind raced as she stumbled through the empty hallway. Where could such a false rumor have come from? Who could say such ugly things?

Then she remembered what Ben Pullman, her ex-boyfriend, had said. After begging her not to break up, he warned that she would be sorry if she did.

"This must be what he meant," Zoe thought as she leaned against a locker and slid down to sit on the floor.

Zoe knew it would take a long time to clear her reputation. But she was determined that, no matter what, it would be cleared.

"Lord," she prayed, "help me be strong." Zoe maintained her high standards in dating, and in time the rumors died down.

Stephen was also a victim of lies and rumors, but he remained faithful to God, as we read in **Acts 6:8–15**.

- How could Zoe and Stephen be strong in the face of lies and rumors?
- When has someone told lies about you the way these people did about Stephen? How did you respond?

C O N S I D E R . . .

- thinking of a tactful way to respond to people who spread rumors. Always talk to the person who is being talked about rather than spread rumors.
- deciding what you will do to clear your reputation if someone spreads dishonest rumors about you.

F O R M O R E , S E E . . .

- Leviticus 19:16–17
- Matthew 26:57–68
- James 3:1–12

ten to me. Our glorious God appeared to Abraham, our ancestor, in Mesopotamia before he
lived in Haran. 3God said to Abraham, 'Leave
your country and your relatives, and go to the
land I will show you.'[n] 4So Abraham left the
country of Chaldea and went to live in Haran.
After Abraham's father died, God sent him to this
place where you now live. 5God did not give
Abraham any of this land, not even a foot of it. But
God promised that he would give this land to him
and his descendants,[d] even before Abraham had
a child. 6This is what God said to him: 'Your
descendants will be strangers in a land they don't
own. The people there will make them slaves and
will mistreat them for four hundred years. 7But I
will punish the nation where they are slaves.
Then your descendants will leave that land and
will worship me in this place.'[n] 8God made an
agreement with Abraham, the sign of which was
circumcision.[d] And so when Abraham had his son
Isaac, Abraham circumcised him when he was
eight days old. Isaac also circumcised his son Jacob, and Jacob did the same for his sons, the
twelve ancestors[n] of our people.

9"Jacob's sons became jealous of Joseph and
sold him to be a slave in Egypt. But God was with
him 10and saved him from all his troubles. The
king of Egypt liked Joseph and respected him because of the wisdom God gave him. The king
made him governor of Egypt and put him in
charge of all the people in his palace.

11"Then all the land of Egypt and Canaan became so dry that nothing would grow, and the
people suffered very much. Jacob's sons, our ancestors, could not find anything to eat. 12But
when Jacob heard there was grain in Egypt, he
sent his sons there. This was their first trip to
Egypt. 13When they went there a second time,
Joseph told his brothers who he was, and the king
learned about Joseph's family. 14Then Joseph sent
messengers to invite Jacob, his father, to come to
Egypt along with all his relatives (seventy-five persons altogether). 15So Jacob went down to Egypt,
where he and his sons died. 16Later their bodies
were moved to Shechem and put in a grave there.
(It was the same grave Abraham had bought for
a sum of money from the sons of Hamor in Shechem.)

17"The promise God made to Abraham was
soon to come true, and the number of people in
Egypt grew large. 18Then a new king, who did not
know who Joseph was, began to rule Egypt.
19This king tricked our people and was cruel to
our ancestors, forcing them to leave their babies
outside to die. 20At this time Moses was born, and
he was very beautiful. For three months Moses
was cared for in his father's house. 21When they
put Moses outside, the king's daughter adopted
him and raised him as if he were her own son.
22The Egyptians taught Moses everything they
knew, and he was a powerful man in what he said
and did.

23"When Moses was about forty years old, he
thought it would be good to visit his own people,
the people of Israel. 24Moses saw an Egyptian mis-
treating an Israelite, so he defended the Israelite
and punished the Egyptian by killing him. 25Mo-
ses thought his own people would understand
that God was using him to save them, but they
did not. 26The next day when Moses saw two
men of Israel fighting, he tried to make peace between them. He said, 'Men, you are brothers.
Why are you hurting each other?' 27The man who
was hurting the other pushed Moses away and
said, 'Who made you our ruler and judge? 28Are
you going to kill me as you killed the Egyptian
yesterday?'[n] 29When Moses heard him say this,
he left Egypt and went to live in the land of Midian where he was a stranger. While Moses lived
in Midian, he had two sons.

30"Forty years later an angel appeared to Moses
in the flames of a burning bush as he was in the
desert near Mount Sinai. 31When Moses saw this,
he was amazed and went near to look closer. Moses heard the Lord's voice say, 32'I am the God of
your ancestors, the God of Abraham, Isaac, and
Jacob.'[n] Moses began to shake with fear and was
afraid to look. 33The Lord said to him, 'Take off
your sandals, because you are standing on holy
ground. 34I have seen the troubles my people have
suffered in Egypt. I have heard their cries and
have come down to save them. And now, Moses,
I am sending you back to Egypt.'[n]

35"This Moses was the same man the two men
of Israel rejected, saying, 'Who made you a ruler
and judge?'[n] Moses is the same man God sent
to be a ruler and savior, with the help of the angel
that Moses saw in the burning bush. 36So Moses
led the people out of Egypt. He worked miracles[d]
and signs in Egypt, at the Red Sea,[d] and then in
the desert for forty years. 37This is the same Moses
that said to the people of Israel, 'God will give
you a prophet[d] like me, who is one of your own

'Leave . . . you.' Quotation from Genesis 12:1.
'Your descendants . . . place.' Quotation from Genesis 15:13-14 and Exodus 3:12.
twelve ancestors Important ancestors of the Jewish people; the leaders of the twelve Jewish tribes.
'Who . . . yesterday?' Quotation from Exodus 2:14.
'I am . . . Jacob.' Quotation from Exodus 3:6.
'Take . . . Egypt.' Quotation from Exodus 3:5-10.
'Who . . . judge?' Quotation from Exodus 2:14.

people.'[n] 38This is the Moses who was with the gathering of the Israelites in the desert. He was with the angel that spoke to him at Mount Sinai, and he was with our ancestors. He received commands from God that give life, and he gave those commands to us.

39"But our ancestors did not want to obey Moses. They rejected him and wanted to go back to Egypt. 40They said to Aaron, 'Make us gods who will lead us. Moses led us out of Egypt, but we don't know what has happened to him.'[n] 41So the people made an idol that looked like a calf. Then they brought sacrifices to it and were proud of what they had made with their own hands. 42But God turned against them and did not try to stop them from worshiping the sun, moon, and stars. This is what is written in the book of the prophets: God says,

'People of Israel, you did not bring me
sacrifices and offerings
while you traveled in the desert for forty
years.
43You have carried with you
the tent to worship Molech[d]
and the idols of the star god Rephan that
you made to worship.
So I will send you away beyond Babylon.'

Amos 5:25-27

44"The Holy Tent[d] where God spoke to our ancestors was with them in the desert. God told Moses how to make this Tent, and he made it like the plan God showed him. 45Later, Joshua led our ancestors to capture the lands of the other nations. Our people went in, and God forced the other people out. When our people went into this new land, they took with them this same Tent they had received from their ancestors. They kept it until the time of David, 46who pleased God and asked God to let him build a house for him, the God of Jacob. 47But Solomon was the one who built the Temple.[d]

48"But the Most High does not live in houses that people build with their hands. As the prophet says:

49'Heaven is my throne,
and the earth is my footstool.
So do you think you can build a house for
me? says the Lord.
Do I need a place to rest?
50Remember, my hand made all these things!' "

Isaiah 66:1-2

51Stephen continued speaking: "You stubborn people! You have not given your hearts to God, nor will you listen to him! You are always against what the Holy Spirit[d] is trying to tell you, just as your ancestors were. 52Your ancestors tried to hurt every prophet who ever lived. Those prophets said long ago that the One who is good would come, but your ancestors killed them. And now you have turned against and killed the One who is good. 53You received the law of Moses, which God gave you through his angels, but you haven't obeyed it."

Stephen Is Killed

54When the leaders heard this, they became furious. They were so mad they were grinding their teeth at Stephen. 55But Stephen was full of the Holy Spirit.[d] He looked up to heaven and saw the glory of God and Jesus standing at God's right side. 56He said, "Look! I see heaven open and the Son of Man[d] standing at God's right side."

57Then they shouted loudly and covered their ears and all ran at Stephen. 58They took him out of the city and began to throw stones at him to kill him. And those who told lies against Stephen left their coats with a young man named Saul. 59While they were throwing stones, Stephen prayed, "Lord Jesus, receive my spirit." 60He fell on his knees and cried in a loud voice, "Lord, do not hold this sin against them." After Stephen said this, he died.

8 Saul agreed that the killing of Stephen was good.

Troubles for the Believers

On that day the church of Jerusalem began to be persecuted,[d] and all the believers, except the apostles,[d] were scattered throughout Judea and Samaria.

2And some religious people buried Stephen and cried loudly for him. 3Saul was also trying to destroy the church, going from house to house, dragging out men and women and putting them in jail. 4And wherever they were scattered, they told people the Good News.[d]

Philip Preaches in Samaria

5Philip[n] went to the city of Samaria and preached about the Christ.[d] 6When the people there heard Philip and saw the miracles[d] he was doing, they all listened carefully to what he said. 7Many of these people had evil spirits in them, but Philip made the evil spirits leave. The spirits made a loud noise when they came out. Philip also healed many weak and crippled people there. 8So the people in that city were very happy.

9But there was a man named Simon in that city. Before Philip came there, Simon had practiced magic and amazed all the people of Samaria.

'God . . . people.' Quotation from Deuteronomy 18:15.
'Make . . . him.' Quotation from Exodus 32:1.
Philip Not the apostle named Philip.

He bragged and called himself a great man. 10All
the people — the least important and the most important — paid attention to Simon, saying, "This
man has the power of God, called 'the Great
Power'!" 11Simon had amazed them with his
magic so long that the people became his followers. 12But when Philip told them the Good News[d]
about the kingdom of God and the power of Jesus
Christ, men and women believed Philip and were
baptized. 13Simon himself believed, and after he
was baptized, he stayed very close to Philip.
When he saw the miracles and the powerful
things Philip did, Simon was amazed.

14When the apostles[d] who were still in Jerusalem heard that the people of Samaria had accepted the word of God, they sent Peter and John
to them. 15When Peter and John arrived, they
prayed that the Samaritan believers might receive
the Holy Spirit.[d] 16These people had been baptized in the name of the Lord Jesus, but the
Holy Spirit had not yet come upon any of them.
17Then, when the two apostles began laying
their hands on the people, they received the
Holy Spirit.

18Simon saw that the Spirit was given to
people when the apostles laid their hands on
them. So he offered the apostles money, 19saying,
"Give me also this power so that anyone on
whom I lay my hands will receive the Holy
Spirit."

20Peter said to him, "You and your money
should both be destroyed, because you thought
you could buy God's gift with money. 21You cannot share with us in this work since your heart is
not right before God. 22Change your heart! Turn
away from this evil thing you have done, and pray
to the Lord. Maybe he will forgive you for thinking this. 23I see that you are full of bitter jealousy
and ruled by sin."

24Simon answered, "Both of you pray for me to
the Lord so the things you have said will not happen to me."

25After Peter and John told the people what
they had seen Jesus do and after they had spoken
the message of the Lord, they went back to Jerusalem. On the way, they went through many Samaritan towns and preached the Good News to
the people.

ANGER

Rage

Ann, thirteen, appeared to be a model student and a devoted daughter. But one night, Ann brought two guys into her bedroom and called her father to come upstairs. Using a knife and a length of pipe, the three teenagers slashed and bludgeoned him to death. Ann had been psychologically abused by her father.

Alan, fourteen, was the school scapegoat. Gangly and clumsy, with few friends, he was the target of daily harassment and beatings. One morning in late January, Alan headed to school carrying one of his father's high-power rifles and ammunition. When he got there, he opened fire in the hallway, killing the school's principal and wounding two teachers and one student. He thought his actions might win his harsh father's approval.

A group of Jewish leaders, religious and proper, faithfully practiced the regulations of their faith. When Stephen, a Christian disciple, started preaching about Jesus, the Jewish leaders went berserk. They carried Stephen out of the city and hurled stones at him until he was dead.

Read **Acts 7:51–60** to get the full story of how these Jewish leaders let their anger lead to destruction.

- What caused Ann's, Alan's, and the Jewish leaders' rage?
- Why was Stephen able to respond to his killers the way he did?

C O N S I D E R . . .

- counting to ten before expressing your anger so you won't do something you'll later regret.
- seeking professional help if your anger turns to rage. Protect yourself and others by learning how to handle anger.

F O R M O R E , S E E . . .

- Deuteronomy 13:6–11
- Ephesians 4:26–32
- James 1:19–20

Philip Teaches an Ethiopian

26An angel of the Lord said to Philip,[n] "Get
ready and go south to the road that leads down
to Gaza from Jerusalem—the desert road." 27So
Philip got ready and went. On the road he saw a
man from Ethiopia, a eunuch.[d] He was an important officer in the service of Candace, the queen of the Ethiopians; he was responsible for taking care of all her money. He had gone to Jerusalem to worship. 28Now, as he was on his way
home, he was sitting in his chariot reading from
the Book of Isaiah, the prophet.[d] 29The Spirit[d]
said to Philip, "Go to that chariot and stay near it."

30So when Philip ran toward the chariot, he heard the man reading from Isaiah the prophet. Philip asked, "Do you understand what you are reading?"

31He answered, "How can I understand unless someone explains it to me?" Then he invited
Philip to climb in and sit with him. 32The portion
of Scripture[d] he was reading was this:

"He was like a sheep being led to be killed.
He was quiet, as a lamb is quiet while its wool is being cut;
he never opened his mouth.
33 He was shamed and was treated unfairly.
He died without children to continue his family.
His life on earth has ended." *Isaiah 53:7-8*

34The officer said to Philip, "Please tell me,
who is the prophet talking about—himself or
someone else?" 35Philip began to speak, and starting with this same Scripture, he told the man the Good News[d] about Jesus.

36While they were traveling down the road,
they came to some water. The officer said, "Look, here is water. What is stopping me from being

Philip Not the apostle named Philip.

BIBLE STUDY

Creative Questions

"Lately I've been wondering if there really is a God," Kevin Morgan said and looked down at his shoes. "I mean, how do I know Christianity isn't just wishful thinking?"

Kevin looked around the room for someone to answer his questions. Everyone was silent.

Finally, Jeremy Coffey spoke up. "I like to hit it from the opposite point of view. I try to prove there isn't a God."

Then everyone started talking at once.

"That leads to even harder questions," said someone in the corner. "How can you explain everything in this world if there isn't a Creator?"

"And why do people get mad at things like murder and child abuse if there isn't a God who shows the difference between right and wrong?"

"Yeah! And what about people's need for religion? Why would they want to worship God if there is no God?"

The questions went on and on. Finally, the kids were silent. Jeremy looked around and smiled. "Believing there is no God takes more faith than realizing there is one," he said. "Thanks for stretching my faith."

There's nothing wrong with sincere questions because they lead to real answers. An Ethiopian asked questions that led to faith in Jesus in **Acts 8:26–40**.

- How do you think his questions led Kevin to deeper faith? How did the Ethiopian's questions lead him to God's salvation?
- What questions would you ask about the passage the Ethiopian had read?

CONSIDER . . .

- listing the questions you have about God and searching for answers to those questions.
- writing down questions as you read the Bible. Ask these questions during Sunday school or youth group.

FOR MORE, SEE . . .

- Isaiah 53:7–8
- John 20:24–29
- Hebrews 6:1–3

baptized?" [37][n] [38]Then the officer commanded
the chariot to stop. Both Philip and the officer
went down into the water, and Philip baptized
him. [39]When they came up out of the water, the
Spirit of the Lord took Philip away; the officer
never saw him again. And the officer continued
on his way home, full of joy. [40]But Philip appeared
in a city called Azotus and preached the Good
News in all the towns on the way from Azotus to
Caesarea.

SIDELIGHT: Acts 8:26–40 tells of what is likely the conversion of the first African. He came from an area south of Egypt called Nubia. Philip had traveled about fifty miles from Jerusalem to witness to this man.

Saul Is Converted

9 In Jerusalem Saul was still threatening the
followers of the Lord by saying he would kill
them. So he went to the high priest [2]and asked
him to write letters to the synagogues[d] in the city
of Damascus. Then if Saul found any followers of
Christ's Way, men or women, he would arrest
them and bring them back to Jerusalem.
[3]So Saul headed toward Damascus. As he came
near the city, a bright light from heaven suddenly
flashed around him. [4]Saul fell to the ground and
heard a voice saying to him, "Saul, Saul! Why are
you persecuting me?"
[5]Saul said, "Who are you, Lord?"
The voice answered, "I am Jesus, whom you
are persecuting. [6]Get up now and go into the city.
Someone there will tell you what you must do."
[7]The people traveling with Saul stood there but
said nothing. They heard the voice, but they saw

Verse 37 Some late copies of Acts add verse 37: "Philip answered, 'If you believe with all your heart, you can.' The officer said, 'I believe that Jesus Christ is the Son of God.' "

FOLLOWING GOD

Show and Tell

Charles Blondin stretched an eleven-hundred-foot tightrope across Niagara Falls on June 30, 1859. About twenty-five thousand spectators gathered to watch the incredible stunt. Charles stood in front of the crowd and asked, "How many believe I can walk across Niagara Falls?"

"We believe!" the crowd roared. And so Charles walked safely across Niagara Falls, one hundred sixty feet in the air.

Five days later, he asked, "How many believe I can walk across Niagara Falls blindfolded and pushing a wheelbarrow?"

The crowd cheered. And Charles did it again.

Two weeks later, the crowd gathered again. "How many believe I can walk across with a person on my back?" he asked.

The crowd screamed: "Of course! We believe!"

Charles looked straight at a person in the front. "You, sir. Climb on!" The man refused.

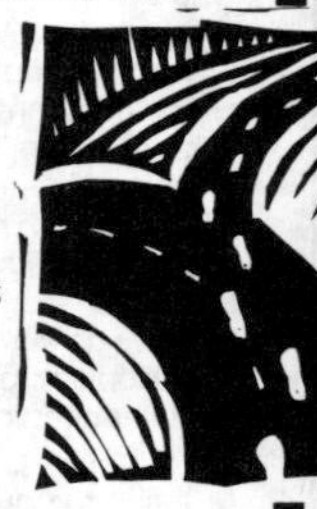

There's a big difference between talking about faith and acting on that faith. In **Acts 9:1–20**, Saul and Ananias both learned what it meant to act on their faith.

- Which was most difficult to act on: Charles's challenge or Jesus' instructions to Saul and Ananias? Why?
- What did Ananias's actions communicate to Saul?

C O N S I D E R . . .

- becoming an "Ananias" to a friend who is struggling with his or her faith. Provide encouragement and support as that person searches for what it means to follow God.
- writing the story of a time when you have experienced God's love. Then tell a friend your story.

F O R M O R E , S E E . . .

- Exodus 4:1–17
- Acts 22:1–16
- James 2:14–18

no one. 8Saul got up from the ground and opened
his eyes, but he could not see. So those with Saul
took his hand and led him into Damascus. 9For
three days Saul could not see and did not eat or
drink.
10There was a follower of Jesus in Damascus
named Ananias. The Lord spoke to Ananias in a
vision, "Ananias!"
Ananias answered, "Here I am, Lord."
11The Lord said to him, "Get up and go to
Straight Street. Find the house of Judas,[n] and ask
for a man named Saul from the city of Tarsus. He
is there now, praying. 12Saul has seen a vision in
which a man named Ananias comes to him and
lays his hands on him. Then he is able to see
again."
13But Ananias answered, "Lord, many people
have told me about this man and the terrible
things he did to your holy people in Jerusalem.
14Now he has come here to Damascus, and the
leading priests have given him the power to arrest
everyone who worships you."
15But the Lord said to Ananias, "Go! I have chosen Saul for an important work. He must tell
about me to those who are not Jews, to kings, and
to the people of Israel. 16I will show him how
much he must suffer for my name."
17So Ananias went to the house of Judas. He
laid his hands on Saul and said, "Brother Saul, the
Lord Jesus sent me. He is the one you saw on the
road on your way here. He sent me so that you
can see again and be filled with the Holy Spirit."[d]
18Immediately, something that looked like fish
scales fell from Saul's eyes, and he was able to see
again! Then Saul got up and was baptized. 19After
he ate some food, his strength returned.

Saul Preaches in Damascus

Saul stayed with the followers of Jesus in Damascus for a few days. 20Soon he began to preach
about Jesus in the synagogues,[d] saying, "Jesus is
the Son of God."
21All the people who heard him were amazed.
They said, "This is the man who was in Jerusalem
trying to destroy those who trust in this name! He
came here to arrest the followers of Jesus and take
them back to the leading priests."
22But Saul grew more powerful. His proofs that
Jesus is the Christ[d] were so strong that the Jewish
people in Damascus could not argue with him.
23After many days, some Jewish people made
plans to kill Saul. 24They were watching the city
gates day and night, but Saul learned about their
plan. 25One night some followers of Saul helped
him leave the city by lowering him in a basket
through an opening in the city wall.

Saul Preaches in Jerusalem

26When Saul went to Jerusalem, he tried to join
the group of followers, but they were all afraid of
him. They did not believe he was really a follower. 27But Barnabas accepted Saul and took him
to the apostles.[d] Barnabas explained to them that
Saul had seen the Lord on the road and the Lord
had spoken to Saul. Then he told them how
boldly Saul had preached in the name of Jesus in
Damascus.
28And so Saul stayed with the followers, going
everywhere in Jerusalem, preaching boldly in the
name of the Lord. 29He would often talk and argue with the Jewish people who spoke Greek, but
they were trying to kill him. 30When the followers
learned about this, they took Saul to Caesarea and
from there sent him to Tarsus.
31The church everywhere in Judea, Galilee,
and Samaria had a time of peace and became
stronger. Respecting the Lord by the way they
lived, and being encouraged by the Holy Spirit,[d]
the group of believers continued to grow.

Peter Heals Aeneas

32As Peter was traveling through all the area,
he visited God's people who lived in Lydda.
33There he met a man named Aeneas, who was
paralyzed and had not been able to leave his bed
for the past eight years. 34Peter said to him, "Aeneas, Jesus Christ heals you. Stand up and make
your bed." Aeneas stood up immediately. 35All
the people living in Lydda and on the Plain of
Sharon saw him and turned to the Lord.

Peter Heals Tabitha

36In the city of Joppa there was a follower
named Tabitha (whose Greek name was Dorcas).
She was always doing good deeds and kind acts.
37While Peter was in Lydda, Tabitha became sick
and died. Her body was washed and put in a room
upstairs. 38Since Lydda is near Joppa and the followers in Joppa heard that Peter was in Lydda,
they sent two messengers to Peter. They begged
him, "Hurry, please come to us!" 39So Peter got
ready and went with them. When he arrived,
they took him to the upstairs room where all the
widows stood around Peter, crying. They showed
him the shirts and coats Tabitha had made when
she was still alive. 40Peter sent everyone out of the
room and kneeled and prayed. Then he turned to
the body and said, "Tabitha, stand up." She
opened her eyes, and when she saw Peter, she sat
up. 41He gave her his hand and helped her up.
Then he called the saints[d] and the widows into
the room and showed them that Tabitha was
alive. 42People everywhere in Joppa learned about

Judas This is not either of the apostles named Judas.

this, and many believed in the Lord. 43Peter
stayed in Joppa for many days with a man named
Simon who was a tanner.

Peter Teaches Cornelius

10 At Caesarea there was a man named
Cornelius, an officer in the Italian group
of the Roman army. 2Cornelius was a religious
man. He and all the other people who lived in his
house worshiped the true God. He gave much of
his money to the poor and prayed to God often.
3One afternoon about three o'clock, Cornelius
clearly saw a vision. An angel of God came to him
and said, "Cornelius!"

4Cornelius stared at the angel. He became
afraid and said, "What do you want, Lord?"

The angel said, "God has heard your prayers.
He has seen that you give to the poor, and he
remembers you. 5Send some men now to Joppa to
bring back a man named Simon who is also called
Peter. 6He is staying with a man, also named Simon, who is a tanner and has a house beside the
sea." 7When the angel who spoke to Cornelius
left, Cornelius called two of his servants and a
soldier, a religious man who worked for him.
8Cornelius explained everything to them and sent
them to Joppa.

9About noon the next day as they came near
Joppa, Peter was going up to the roof[n] to pray.
10He was hungry and wanted to eat, but while the
food was being prepared, he had a vision. 11He
saw heaven opened and something coming down
that looked like a big sheet being lowered to earth
by its four corners. 12In it were all kinds of animals, reptiles, and birds. 13Then a voice said to
Peter, "Get up, Peter; kill and eat."

14But Peter said, "No, Lord! I have never eaten
food that is unholy or unclean."[d]

15But the voice said to him again, "God has
made these things clean so don't call them 'unholy'!" 16This happened three times, and at once
the sheet was taken back to heaven.

17While Peter was wondering what this vision
meant, the men Cornelius sent had found Simon's house and were standing at the gate.
18They asked, "Is Simon Peter staying here?"

19While Peter was still thinking about the vision, the Spirit[d] said to him, "Listen, three men
are looking for you. 20Get up and go downstairs.
Go with them without doubting, because I have
sent them to you."

21So Peter went down to the men and said, "I
am the one you are looking for. Why did you
come here?"

22They said, "A holy angel spoke to Cornelius,
an army officer and a good man; he worships
God. All the Jewish people respect him. The angel
told Cornelius to ask you to come to his house so
that he can hear what you have to say." 23So Peter
asked the men to come in and spend the night.

The next day Peter got ready and went with
them, and some of the followers from Joppa
joined him. 24On the following day they came to
Caesarea. Cornelius was waiting for them and
had called together his relatives and close friends.
25When Peter entered, Cornelius met him, fell at
his feet, and worshiped him. 26But Peter helped
him up, saying, "Stand up. I too am only a human." 27As he talked with Cornelius, Peter went
inside where he saw many people gathered. 28He
said, "You people understand that it is against our
Jewish law for Jewish people to associate with or
visit anyone who is not Jewish. But God has
shown me that I should not call any person 'unholy' or 'unclean.' 29That is why I did not argue
when I was asked to come here. Now, please tell
me why you sent for me."

30Cornelius said, "Four days ago, I was praying
in my house at this same time—three o'clock in
the afternoon. Suddenly, there was a man standing before me wearing shining clothes. 31He said,
'Cornelius, God has heard your prayer and has
seen that you give to the poor and remembers
you. 32So send some men to Joppa and ask Simon
Peter to come. Peter is staying in the house of a
man, also named Simon, who is a tanner and has
a house beside the sea.' 33So I sent for you immediately, and it was very good of you to come. Now
we are all here before God to hear everything the
Lord has commanded you to tell us."

34Peter began to speak: "I really understand
now that to God every person is the same. 35In
every country God accepts anyone who worships
him and does what is right. 36You know the message that God has sent to the people of Israel is the
Good News[d] that peace has come through Jesus
Christ. Jesus is the Lord of all people! 37You know
what has happened all over Judea, beginning in
Galilee after John[n] preached to the people about
baptism. 38You know about Jesus from Nazareth,
that God gave him the Holy Spirit[d] and power.
You know how Jesus went everywhere doing
good and healing those who were ruled by the
devil, because God was with him. 39We saw what
Jesus did in Judea and in Jerusalem, but the Jews
in Jerusalem killed him by hanging him on a cross.
40Yet, on the third day, God raised Jesus to life
and caused him to be seen, 41not by all the people,
but only by the witnesses God had already cho-

roof In Bible times houses were built with flat roofs. The roof was used for drying things such as flax and fruit. And it was used as an extra room, as a place for worship, and as a place to sleep in the summer.

John John the Baptist, who preached to people about Christ's coming (Luke 3).

sen. And we are those witnesses who ate and
drank with him after he was raised from the dead.
42He told us to preach to the people and to tell
them that he is the one whom God chose to be
the judge of the living and the dead. 43All the
prophets say it is true that all who believe in Jesus
will be forgiven of their sins through Jesus'
name."
44While Peter was still saying this, the Holy
Spirit[d] came down on all those who were listening. 45The Jewish believers who came with Peter
were amazed that the gift of the Holy Spirit had
been given even to those who were not Jews.
46These Jewish believers heard them speaking in
different languages[n] and praising God. Then Peter said, 47"Can anyone keep these people from
being baptized with water? They have received
the Holy Spirit just as we did!" 48So Peter ordered
that they be baptized in the name of Jesus Christ.
Then they asked Peter to stay with them for a few
days.

Peter Returns to Jerusalem

11 The apostles[d] and the believers in Judea
heard that some who were not Jewish
had accepted God's teaching too. 2But when Peter came to Jerusalem, some Jewish believers argued with him. 3They said, "You went into the
homes of people who are not circumcised[d] and
ate with them!"
4So Peter explained the whole story to them.
5He said, "I was in the city of Joppa, and while I
was praying, I had a vision. I saw something that
looked like a big sheet being lowered from heaven
by its four corners. It came very close to me. 6I
looked inside it and saw animals, wild beasts, reptiles, and birds. 7I heard a voice say to me, 'Get
up, Peter. Kill and eat.' 8But I said, 'No, Lord! I
have never eaten anything that is unholy or unclean.'[d] 9But the voice from heaven spoke again,
'God has made these things clean, so don't call
them unholy.' 10This happened three times. Then
the whole thing was taken back to heaven.

languages This can also be translated "tongues."

JUDGING OTHERS

The Color of Hatred

"It's not that blacks are bad," John Metzger says. "There are quite a few, well, not quite a few, but a sizable number of nonwhites who are intelligent."

John is a racist. He believes whites are the "chosen people"—that all nonwhite races should live in their own territories, away from whites. He is also the leader of the Aryan Youth Movement, otherwise known as "skinheads."

John doesn't look like a skinhead. His blond hair is cut conservatively. He has a respectable job and dresses like most guys his age.

But John's racist beliefs are deeply ingrained. His father leads a group of adult racists called the White Aryan Resistance. When other kids were growing up with stories about Goldilocks and the three bears, John listened to stories of hatred and prejudice at his father's knee.

Skinheads in John's Aryan Youth Movement have been linked to such brutalities as beating people to death, terrorizing people of nonwhite origin, and even nailing a former skinhead to a cross. And they have done these things all in the name of preserving their race.

Prejudice has blinded John and other racists to the fact that God loves all people the same. In **Acts 10:34–48**, Peter challenges the people of his day to see others from God's perspective and lay aside their prejudices.

- How was prejudice in Peter's day different from John Metzger's prejudice? How are they similar?
- According to this passage, what is the cure for prejudice?

CONSIDER...

- observing people in a mall. Evaluate which people you do or don't have prejudices toward. Then ask God to remove any prejudices you may have.
- getting to know someone you have prejudged. Think about the ways the person is different from what you had expected.

FOR MORE, SEE...

- Genesis 3:20
- John 4:1–27
- Acts 11:1–18

11Right then three men who were sent to me from Caesarea came to the house where I was staying. 12The Spirit[d] told me to go with them without doubting. These six believers here also went with me, and we entered the house of Cornelius. 13He told us about the angel he saw standing in his house. The angel said to him, 'Send some men to Joppa and invite Simon Peter to come. 14By the words he will say to you, you and all your family will be saved.' 15When I began my speech, the Holy Spirit came on them just as he came on us at the beginning. 16Then I remembered the words of the Lord. He said, 'John baptized with water, but you will be baptized with the Holy Spirit.' 17Since God gave them the same gift he gave us who believed in the Lord Jesus Christ, how could I stop the work of God?"

18When the Jewish believers heard this, they stopped arguing. They praised God and said, "So God is allowing even those who are not Jewish to turn to him and live."

The Good News Comes to Antioch

19Many of the believers were scattered when they were persecuted after Stephen was killed. Some of them went as far as Phoenicia, Cyprus, and Antioch telling the message to others, but only to Jews. 20Some of these believers were people from Cyprus and Cyrene. When they came to Antioch, they spoke also to Greeks, telling them the Good News[d] about the Lord Jesus. 21The Lord was helping the believers, and a large group of people believed and turned to the Lord.

22The church in Jerusalem heard about all of this, so they sent Barnabas to Antioch. 23-24Barnabas was a good man, full of the Holy Spirit[d] and full of faith. When he reached Antioch and saw how God had blessed the people, he was glad. He encouraged all the believers in Antioch always to obey the Lord with all their hearts, and many people became followers of the Lord.

25Then Barnabas went to the city of Tarsus to look for Saul, 26and when he found Saul, he brought him to Antioch. For a whole year Saul and Barnabas met with the church and taught many people there. In Antioch the followers were called Christians for the first time.

27About that time some prophets[d] came from Jerusalem to Antioch. 28One of them, named Agabus, stood up and spoke with the help of the Holy Spirit. He said, "A very hard time is coming to the whole world. There will be no food to eat." (This happened when Claudius ruled.) 29The believers all decided to help the followers who lived in Judea, as much as each one could. 30They gathered the money and gave it to Barnabas and Saul, who brought it to the elders[d] in Judea.

SIDELIGHT: The name "Christian" (Acts 11:26) may have originally been an insult. It meant "devotees of the Anointed One" or "followers of Christ." The term was widely used by the end of the first century.

Herod Agrippa Hurts the Church

12 During that same time King Herod began to mistreat some who belonged to the church. 2He ordered James, the brother of John, to be killed by the sword. 3Herod saw that the Jewish people liked this, so he decided to arrest Peter, too. (This happened during the time of the Feast[d] of Unleavened Bread.)

4After Herod arrested Peter, he put him in jail and handed him over to be guarded by sixteen soldiers. Herod planned to bring Peter before the people for trial after the Passover[d] Feast. 5So Peter was kept in jail, but the church prayed earnestly to God for him.

Peter Leaves the Jail

6The night before Herod was to bring him to trial, Peter was sleeping between two soldiers, bound with two chains. Other soldiers were guarding the door of the jail. 7Suddenly, an angel of the Lord stood there, and a light shined in the cell. The angel struck Peter on the side and woke him up. "Hurry! Get up!" the angel said. And the chains fell off Peter's hands. 8Then the angel told him, "Get dressed and put on your sandals." And Peter did. Then the angel said, "Put on your coat and follow me." 9So Peter followed him out, but he did not know if what the angel was doing was real; he thought he might be seeing a vision. 10They went past the first and second guards and came to the iron gate that separated them from the city. The gate opened by itself for them, and they went through it. When they had walked down one street, the angel suddenly left him.

11Then Peter realized what had happened. He thought, "Now I know that the Lord really sent his angel to me. He rescued me from Herod and from all the things the Jewish people thought would happen."

12When he considered this, he went to the home of Mary, the mother of John Mark. Many people were gathered there, praying. 13Peter knocked on the outside door, and a servant girl named Rhoda came to answer it. 14When she recognized Peter's voice, she was so happy she forgot to open the door. Instead, she ran inside and told the group, "Peter is at the door!"

15They said to her, "You are crazy!" But she

kept on saying it was true, so they said, "It must be Peter's angel."

[16]Peter continued to knock, and when they opened the door, they saw him and were amazed. [17]Peter made a sign with his hand to tell them to be quiet. He explained how the Lord led him out of the jail, and he said, "Tell James and the other believers what happened." Then he left to go to another place.

[18]The next day the soldiers were very upset and wondered what had happened to Peter. [19]Herod looked everywhere for him but could not find him. So he questioned the guards and ordered that they be killed.

The Death of Herod Agrippa

Later Herod moved from Judea and went to the city of Caesarea, where he stayed. [20]Herod was very angry with the people of Tyre and Sidon, but the people of those cities all came in a group to him. After convincing Blastus, the king's personal servant, to be on their side, they asked Herod for peace, because their country got its food from his country.

[21]On a chosen day Herod put on his royal robes, sat on his throne, and made a speech to the people. [22]They shouted, "This is the voice of a god, not a human!" [23]Because Herod did not give the glory to God, an angel of the Lord immediately caused him to become sick, and he was eaten by worms and died.

[24]God's message continued to spread and reach people.

[25]After Barnabas and Saul finished their task in Jerusalem, they returned to Antioch, taking John Mark with them.

Barnabas and Saul Are Chosen

13 In the church at Antioch there were these prophets[d] and teachers: Barnabas, Simeon (also called Niger), Lucius (from the city of Cyrene), Manaen (who had grown up with Herod, the ruler), and Saul. [2]They were all worshiping the Lord and giving up eating for a certain time.[n] During this time the Holy Spirit[d] said to them, "Set apart for me Barnabas and Saul to do a special work for which I have chosen them."

[3]So after they gave up eating and prayed, they laid their hands on[n] Barnabas and Saul and sent them out.

Barnabas and Saul in Cyprus

[4]Barnabas and Saul, sent out by the Holy Spirit,[d] went to the city of Seleucia. From there they sailed to the island of Cyprus. [5]When they came to Salamis, they preached the Good News[d] of God in the Jewish synagogues.[d] John Mark was with them to help.

[6]They went across the whole island to Paphos where they met a Jewish magician named Bar-Jesus. He was a false prophet[d] [7]who always stayed close to Sergius Paulus, the governor and a smart man. He asked Barnabas and Saul to come to him, because he wanted to hear the message of God. [8]But Elymas, the magician, was against them. (Elymas is the name for Bar-Jesus in the Greek language.) He tried to stop the governor from believing in Jesus. [9]But Saul, who was also called Paul, was filled with the Holy Spirit. He looked straight at Elymas [10]and said, "You son of the devil! You are an enemy of everything that is right! You are full of evil tricks and lies, always trying to change the Lord's truths into lies. [11]Now the Lord will touch you, and you will be blind. For a time you will not be able to see anything—not even the light from the sun."

Then everything became dark for Elymas, and he walked around, trying to find someone to lead him by the hand. [12]When the governor saw this, he believed because he was amazed at the teaching about the Lord.

Paul and Barnabas Leave Cyprus

[13]Paul and those with him sailed from Paphos and came to Perga, in Pamphylia. There John Mark left them to return to Jerusalem. [14]They continued their trip from Perga and went to Antioch, a city in Pisidia. On the Sabbath[d] day they went into the synagogue[d] and sat down. [15]After the law of Moses and the writings of the prophets[d] were read, the leaders of the synagogue sent a message to Paul and Barnabas: "Brothers, if you have any message that will encourage the people, please speak."

[16]Paul stood up, raised his hand, and said, "You Israelites and you who worship God, please listen! [17]The God of the Israelites chose our ancestors. He made the people great during the time they lived in Egypt, and he brought them out of that country with great power. [18]And he was patient with them for forty years in the desert. [19]God destroyed seven nations in the land of Canaan and gave the land to his people. [20]All this happened in about four hundred fifty years.

"After this, God gave them judges until the time of Samuel the prophet. [21]Then the people asked for a king, so God gave them Saul son of Kish. Saul was from the tribe[d] of Benjamin and was king for forty years. [22]After God took him away, God made David their king. God said about

giving up . . . time This is called "fasting." The people would give up eating for a special time of prayer and worship to God. It was also done to show sadness and disappointment.

laid their hands on The laying on of hands had many purposes, including the giving of a blessing, power, or authority.

him: 'I have found in David son of Jesse the kind
of man I want. He will do all I want him to do.'
23So God has brought Jesus, one of David's
descendants,[d] to Israel to be its Savior,[d] as he
promised. 24Before Jesus came, John[n] preached
to all the people of Israel about a baptism of
changed hearts and lives. 25When he was finishing his work, he said, 'Who do you think I am?
I am not the Christ.[d] He is coming later, and I am
not worthy to untie his sandals.'
26"Brothers, sons of the family of Abraham, and
those of you who are not Jews who worship God,
listen! The news about this salvation has been
sent to us. 27Those who live in Jerusalem and
their leaders did not realize that Jesus was the
Savior. They did not understand the words that
the prophets wrote, which are read every Sabbath[d] day. But they made them come true when
they said Jesus was guilty. 28They could not find
any real reason for Jesus to be put to death, but
they asked Pilate to have him killed. 29When they
had done to him all that the Scriptures[d] had said,
they took him down from the cross and laid him
in a tomb. 30But God raised him up from the dead!
31After this, for many days, those who had gone
with Jesus from Galilee to Jerusalem saw him.
They are now his witnesses to the people. 32We
tell you the Good News[d] about the promise God
made to our ancestors. 33God has made this promise come true for us, his children, by raising
Jesus from the dead. We read about this also in
Psalm 2:

'You are my Son.
Today I have become your Father.' *Psalm 2:7*

34God raised Jesus from the dead, and he will
never go back to the grave and become dust. So
God said:

'I will give you the holy and sure blessings
that I promised to David.' *Isaiah 55:3*

35But in another place God says:

'You will not let your Holy One rot.' *Psalm 16:10*

36David did God's will during his lifetime. Then
he died and was buried beside his ancestors, and
his body did rot in the grave. 37But the One God
raised from the dead did not rot in the grave.
38-39Brothers, understand what we are telling you:
You can have forgiveness of your sins through
Jesus. The law of Moses could not free you from
your sins. But through Jesus everyone who believes is free from all sins. 40Be careful! Don't let
what the prophets said happen to you:

John John the Baptist, who preached to people about Christ's coming (Luke 3).

BIBLE STUDY

Putting the Pieces Together

Jigsaw puzzles can drive you crazy. When first you dump hundreds of jigsaw puzzle pieces from the box, you fear you will never get the puzzle together. But because you know the pieces have to fit together eventually, you separate border pieces from inside pieces. The border goes together reasonably well, so you move on to notice pieces that are related and may form a figure in the puzzle.

Each time you fit a piece, you feel more hopeful. Completing certain sections may bring cries of victory and, "Come see what we finished!" Sometimes along the way, it gets discouraging, but you keep at it. Bit by bit, the picture begins to take shape. The pieces are no longer meaningless but related and relevant. When only a few pieces remain, you can see exactly where they belong. The triumph of the final assembly makes the hours of work worth it.

Sometimes Bible study can be like a jigsaw puzzle. Understanding the Bible and the God described in it also happens piece by piece. In **Acts 13:22–33**, Paul put together some pieces about Jesus for his listeners.

- How is this passage like the picture on the front of a puzzle box?
- What are the three most important pieces to you in this passage?

C O N S I D E R . . .

- listing at least ten things you already understand about Jesus.
- keeping a journal of discoveries you make during group and individual Bible studies. Reread this journal to remind yourself of the pieces of truth you've learned.

F O R   M O R E ,   S E E . . .

- Deuteronomy 6:4–9
- Romans 15:4
- 2 Timothy 3:14–17

41'Listen, you people who doubt!
You can wonder, and then die.
I will do something in your lifetime
that you won't believe even when you are
told about it!' " *Habakkuk 1:5*
42While Paul and Barnabas were leaving the
synagogue, the people asked them to tell them
more about these things on the next Sabbath.
43When the meeting was over, many Jews and
those who had changed to the Jewish religion and
who worshiped God followed Paul and Barnabas
from that place. Paul and Barnabas were persuading them to continue trusting in God's grace.
44On the next Sabbath day, almost everyone in
the city came to hear the word of the Lord. 45See-
ing the crowd, the Jewish people became very
jealous and said insulting things and argued
against what Paul said. 46But Paul and Barnabas
spoke very boldly, saying, "We must speak the
message of God to you first. But you refuse to
listen. You are judging yourselves not worthy of
having eternal life! So we will now go to the people of other nations. 47This is what the Lord told
us to do, saying:
'I have made you a light for the nations;
you will show people all over the world the
way to be saved.' " *Isaiah 49:6*
48When those who were not Jewish heard Paul
say this, they were happy and gave honor to the
message of the Lord. And the people who were
chosen to have life forever believed the message.
49So the message of the Lord was spreading
through the whole country. 50But the Jewish people stirred up some of the important religious
women and the leaders of the city. They started
trouble against Paul and Barnabas and forced
them out of their area. 51So Paul and Barnabas
shook the dust off their feet[n] and went to Ico-

shook . . . feet A warning. It showed that they had rejected these people.

JEALOUSY

A Door to Greater Evil

Report card day. Dale Castle dreaded walking into his house. He figured his parents had already seen Denise's report card, and he knew his would never compare to hers.

"They'll probably give her a new car or something for every A," Dale thought to himself.

As Dale opened the front door, he heard his parents talking in the living room.

"Denise, this is an outstanding report card—as usual," his dad gushed.

"We're so proud of you, honey. You've worked so hard," his mother added.

Dale tried to sneak by his parents, but just as he rounded the corner his mother called out: "Dale, come here. Let's see how you did this semester."

"Oh great," Dale thought, "here comes World War III." Dale walked into the living room and handed his mother his crumpled report card from his back pocket.

She unfolded it and said, "Well, these are fine grades, son." Then she handed it to his dad.

"Hmmm," his dad mused. "Looks like you brought up that grade in biology. Good work."

"Yeah, right," Dale fumed. "I know it's not as good as Denise's. Nothing I do is ever as good as her."

He stormed out of the room, leaving his family in shock.

Dale let his jealousy of Denise affect his response to his parents. In **Acts 13:44–52**, some Jewish leaders allowed their jealousy to affect the way they treated Paul and Barnabas.

- Why were Dale and the Jewish leaders jealous? What were the consequences of Dale's and the Jewish leaders' jealousy?
- When have you been jealous of someone? What were the consequences of your jealousy?

CONSIDER . . .

- making a list of your talents and things you are good at, then reading the list when you are tempted to be jealous of someone else.
- thanking God for someone you are jealous of. Be excited when that person does well.

FOR MORE, SEE . . .

- Genesis 37
- Psalm 37:1–8
- Acts 17:5–9

nium. 52But the followers were filled with joy and
the Holy Spirit.[d]

Paul and Barnabas in Iconium

14 In Iconium, Paul and Barnabas went as
usual to the Jewish synagogue.[d] They
spoke so well that a great many Jews and Greeks
believed. 2But some of the Jews who did not believe excited the non-Jewish people and turned
them against the believers. 3Paul and Barnabas
stayed in Iconium a long time and spoke bravely
for the Lord. He showed that their message about
his grace was true by giving them the power to
work miracles[d] and signs. 4But the city was divided. Some of the people agreed with the Jews,
and others believed the apostles.[d]
5Some who were not Jews, some Jews, and
some of their rulers wanted to mistreat Paul and
Barnabas and to stone them to death. 6When Pau
and Barnabas learned about this, they ran away t
Lystra and Derbe, cities in Lycaonia, and to th
areas around those cities. 7They announced th
Good News[d] there, too.

Paul in Lystra and Derbe

8In Lystra there sat a man who had been bor
crippled; he had never walked. 9As this man wa
listening to Paul speak, Paul looked straight
him and saw that he believed God could he
him. 10So he cried out, "Stand up on your feet!
The man jumped up and began walking aroun
11When the crowds saw what Paul did, the
shouted in the Lycaonian language, "The go
have become like humans and have come dow
to us!" 12Then the people began to call Barnab
"Zeus"[n] and Paul "Hermes,"[n] because he w

"Zeus" The Greeks believed in many gods, of whom Zeus was most important.
"Hermes" The Greeks believed he was a messenger for the other gods.

HEROES

Admire, Don't Worship

Mandy Rios admired everything about her pastor. When he first came to her church, she was immediately drawn to his dynamic personality, warm smile and genuine concern for people.

The pastor always had time to listen. He always talked about how great the young people of the church were, praising their character and service. Mandy believed that God must be just like her pastor.

Whenever the youth group had a controversial discussion, Mandy would go to her pastor later and ask what he thought. Mandy would explain what he said in the next youth group meeting. To Mandy, he knew everything.

Eleven months after coming to Mandy's church, her pastor left suddenly to go to another church. He answered none of Mandy's letters, nor did he return her phone calls. He never even said good-bye.

Mandy was crushed and heartbroken. How could he treat her church like this? How could he treat her like this when she had respected him so much? Mandy felt betrayed. Could she ever trust a pastor again?

Worshiping a person always leads to disappointment. Her pastor turned out to be human—with human faults and inconsistencies. In **Acts 14:8–18**, God used Paul and Barnabas to work miracles, but even they weren't worthy of worship.

- What led Mandy to worship her pastor, and the people to worship Paul and Barnabas?
- Based on Paul's and Barnabas's words, what are appropriate ways to treat spiritual leaders?

CONSIDER . . .

- thanking God for the good qualities of people you admire. Ask God to help you keep your admiration in proper perspective.
- getting to know someone you admire and learning about his or her human and less-admirable qualities as well.

FOR MORE, SEE . . .

- Exodus 20:2–6
- Daniel 3
- 1 Corinthians 4:1–7

the main speaker. 13The priest in the temple of Zeus, which was near the city, brought some bulls and flowers to the city gates. He and the people wanted to offer a sacrifice to Paul and Barnabas. 14But when the apostles,[d] Barnabas and Paul, heard about it, they tore their clothes. They ran in among the people, shouting, 15"Friends, why are you doing these things? We are only human beings like you. We are bringing you the Good News[d] and are telling you to turn away from these worthless things and turn to the living God. He is the One who made the sky, the earth, the sea, and everything in them. 16In the past, God let all the nations do what they wanted. 17Yet he proved he is real by showing kindness, by giving you rain from heaven and crops at the right times, by giving you food and filling your hearts with joy." 18Even with these words, they were barely able to keep the crowd from offering sacrifices to them.

SIDELIGHT: Paul and Barnabas faced a real case of mistaken identity when they visited Lystra, a town in the center of modern-day Turkey (Acts 14:8–18). The people in the region believed a myth that the Greek gods Zeus and Hermes had previously visited the area. When Paul and Barnabas healed a cripple, the people thought the gods had returned, putting the Christian missionaries in an awkward situation.

19Then some Jewish people came from Antioch and Iconium and persuaded the people to turn against Paul. So they threw stones at him and dragged him out of town, thinking they had killed him. 20But the followers gathered around him, and he got up and went back into the town. The next day he and Barnabas left and went to the city of Derbe.

The Return to Antioch in Syria

21Paul and Barnabas told the Good News[d] in Derbe, and many became followers. Paul and Barnabas returned to Lystra, Iconium, and Antioch, 22making the followers of Jesus stronger and helping them stay in the faith. They said, "We must suffer many things to enter God's kingdom." 23They chose elders[d] for each church, by praying and giving up eating for a certain time.[n] These elders had trusted the Lord, so Paul and Barnabas put them in the Lord's care.

24Then they went through Pisidia and came to Pamphylia. 25When they had preached the message in Perga, they went down to Attalia. 26And from there they sailed away to Antioch where the believers had put them into God's care and had sent them out to do this work. Now they had finished.

27When they arrived in Antioch, Paul and Barnabas gathered the church together. They told the church all about what God had done with them and how God had made it possible for those who were not Jewish to believe. 28And they stayed there a long time with the followers.

The Meeting at Jerusalem

15 Then some people came to Antioch from Judea and began teaching the non-Jewish believers: "You cannot be saved if you are not circumcised[d] as Moses taught us." 2Paul and Barnabas were against this teaching and argued with them about it. So the church decided to send Paul, Barnabas, and some others to Jerusalem where they could talk more about this with the apostles[d] and elders.[d]

3The church helped them leave on the trip, and they went through the countries of Phoenicia and Samaria, telling all about how those who were not Jewish had turned to God. This made all the believers very happy. 4When they arrived in Jerusalem, they were welcomed by the apostles, the elders, and the church. Paul, Barnabas, and the others told about everything God had done with them. 5But some of the believers who belonged to the Pharisee[d] group came forward and said, "The non-Jewish believers must be circumcised. They must be told to obey the law of Moses."

6The apostles and the elders gathered to consider this problem. 7After a long debate, Peter stood up and said to them, "Brothers, you know that in the early days God chose me from among you to preach the Good News[d] to those who are not Jewish. They heard the Good News from me, and they believed. 8God, who knows the thoughts of everyone, accepted them. He showed this to us by giving them the Holy Spirit,[d] just as he did to us. 9To God, those people are not different from us. When they believed, he made their hearts pure. 10So now why are you testing God by putting a heavy load around the necks of the non-Jewish believers? It is a load that neither we nor our ancestors were able to carry. 11But we believe that we and they too will be saved by the grace of the Lord Jesus."

12Then the whole group became quiet. They listened to Paul and Barnabas tell about all the miracles[d] and signs that God did through them among the non-Jewish people. 13After they finished speaking, James said, "Brothers, listen to

giving . . . time This is called "fasting." The people would give up eating for a special time of prayer and worship to God. It was also done to show sadness and disappointment.

me. 14Simon has told us how God showed his love
for the non-Jewish people. For the first time he is
accepting from among them a people to be his
own. 15The words of the prophets[d] agree with this
too:

16'After these things I will return.
The kingdom of David is like a fallen tent.
But I will rebuild its ruins,
and I will set it up.
17Then those people who are left alive may ask
the Lord for help,
and the other nations that belong to me,
says the Lord,
who will make it happen.
18 And these things have been known for a
long time.' *Amos 9:11-12*

19"So I think we should not bother the non-
Jewish people who are turning to God. 20Instead,
we should write a letter to them telling them
these things: Stay away from food that has been
offered to idols (which makes it unclean[d]), any
kind of sexual sin, eating animals that have been
strangled, and blood. 21They should do these
things, because for a long time in every city the
law of Moses has been taught. And it is still read
in the synagogue[d] every Sabbath[d] day."

Letter to Non-Jewish Believers

22The apostles,[d] the elders,[d] and the whole
church decided to send some of their men with
Paul and Barnabas to Antioch. They chose Judas
Barsabbas and Silas, who were respected by the
believers. 23They sent the following letter with
them:

From the apostles and elders, your brothers.

To all the non-Jewish believers in Antioch, Syria, and Cilicia:

Greetings!

24We have heard that some of our group
have come to you and said things that trouble and upset you. But we did not tell them
to do this. 25We have all agreed to choose
some messengers and send them to you with
our dear friends Barnabas and Paul— 26peo-
ple who have given their lives to serve our
Lord Jesus Christ. 27So we are sending Judas
and Silas, who will tell you the same things.
28It has pleased the Holy Spirit[d] that you
should not have a heavy load to carry, and
we agree. You need to do only these things:
29Stay away from any food that has been offered to idols, eating any animals that have
been strangled, and blood, and any kind of
sexual sin. If you stay away from these
things, you will do well.

Good-bye.

30So they left Jerusalem and went to Antioc
where they gathered the church and gave ther
the letter. 31When they read it, they were ver
happy because of the encouraging message. 32Ju
das and Silas, who were also prophets,[d] said man
things to encourage the believers and make ther
stronger. 33After some time Judas and Silas we
sent off in peace by the believers, and they wer
back to those who had sent them. 34 [n]

35But Paul and Barnabas stayed in Antioch an
along with many others, preached the Goo
News[d] and taught the people the message of th
Lord.

Paul and Barnabas Separate

36After some time, Paul said to Barnabas, "W
should go back to all those towns where w
preached the message of the Lord. Let's visit th
believers and see how they are doing."

37Barnabas wanted to take John Mark wit
them, 38but he had left them at Pamphylia; he di
not continue with them in the work. So Paul di
not think it was a good idea to take him. 39Pa
and Barnabas had such a serious argument abo
this that they separated and went different way
Barnabas took Mark and sailed to Cyprus, 40b
Paul chose Silas and left. The believers in Antioc
put Paul into the Lord's care, 41and he we
through Syria and Cilicia, giving strength to th
churches.

Timothy Goes with Paul

16 Paul came to Derbe and Lystra, where
follower named Timothy lived. Tim
thy's mother was Jewish and a believer, but h
father was a Greek.

2The believers in Lystra and Iconium respect
Timothy and said good things about him. 3Pa
wanted Timothy to travel with him, but all th
Jews living in that area knew that Timothy's
ther was Greek. So Paul circumcised[d] Timothy
please the Jews. 4Paul and those with him tra
eled from town to town and gave the decisio
made by the apostles[d] and elders[d] in Jerusale
for the people to obey. 5So the churches b
came stronger in the faith and grew larger eve
day.

Paul Is Called Out of Asia

6Paul and those with him went through the
eas of Phrygia and Galatia since the Holy Spir
did not let them preach the Good News[d] in th
country of Asia. 7When they came near the cou
try of Mysia, they tried to go into Bithynia, but t
Spirit of Jesus did not let them. 8So they passed
Mysia and went to Troas. 9That night Paul saw

Verse 34 Some Greek copies add verse 34: ". . . but Silas decided to remain there."

a vision a man from Macedonia. The man stood
and begged, "Come over to Macedonia and help
us." 10After Paul had seen the vision, we immediately prepared to leave for Macedonia, understanding that God had called us to tell the Good
News to those people.

Lydia Becomes a Christian

11We left Troas and sailed straight to the island
of Samothrace. The next day we sailed to Neapolis.[n] 12Then we went by land to Philippi, a Roman colony[n] and the leading city in that part of
Macedonia. We stayed there for several days.

13On the Sabbath[d] day we went outside the city
gate to the river where we thought we would find
a special place for prayer. Some women had gathered there, so we sat down and talked with them.
14One of the listeners was a woman named Lydia
from the city of Thyatira whose job was selling
purple cloth. She worshiped God, and he opened
her mind to pay attention to what Paul was saying. 15She and all the people in her house were
baptized. Then she invited us to her home, saying, "If you think I am truly a believer in the Lord,
then come stay in my house." And she persuaded
us to stay with her.

Neapolis City in Macedonia. It was the first city Paul visited on the continent of Europe.
Roman colony A town begun by Romans with Roman laws, customs, and privileges.

GOD'S WILL

Close to Your Heart

Sandra Graham was one semester away from high school graduation, and she had no idea what she would do with her life. She had been praying for God to show her his will, but still there were no answers.

One Sunday after church, Ted Holt, a Sunday school teacher, asked Sandra to come home with his family of eight for dinner.

All through the meal, they talked about Sandra's plans after graduation. "What do you think God wants you to do, Sandra?" Ted asked as they finished dessert.

"I don't know. I've been praying about it, but God just doesn't seem to answer," Sandra lamented.

Ted's voice softened. "What do you want to do?" he asked.

"God's will," she answered.

Again, Ted asked, "But what do you want to do?"

Sandra was confused. "That's it. I want to do God's will."

Ted smiled. "Sandra, I have six kids, and I want nothing more than for each of my kids to be happy. I'll do almost anything to make that happen."

Sandra nodded, not sure what this had to do with her decision.

Ted laughed heartily when he saw her confusion. "Sandra, God is your father, and he wants you to be happy. He's probably been showing you all the time what his will is."

"He has?" Sandra asked incredulously.

"Yes, he has. Look into your heart. I'll bet your desires will point you toward God's will."

Sandra did find God's will. After she graduated from college, she used her love for drama to teach others how to communicate their faith. In **Acts 16:6–10**, Paul also found God's will.

- What was Ted trying to help Sandra learn about finding God's will? In the passage, how did God show his will to Paul and the others?
- Do you think God still reveals his will to people as he did in the passage? In what other ways do people learn God's will?

CONSIDER . . .

- keeping track of what happens to you in the coming week. See if any patterns emerge that show God leading you in a particular direction.
- interviewing an older person in your church about what he or she has learned about discovering and doing God's will.

FOR MORE, SEE . . .

- Psalm 32:6–11
- Matthew 6:9–13
- Luke 22:41–43

Paul and Silas in Jail

16Once, while we were going to the place for prayer, a servant girl met us. She had a special spirit[n] in her, and she earned a lot of money for her owners by telling fortunes. 17This girl followed Paul and us, shouting, "These men are servants of the Most High God. They are telling you how you can be saved."

18She kept this up for many days. This bothered Paul, so he turned and said to the spirit, "By the power of Jesus Christ, I command you to come out of her!" Immediately, the spirit came out.

19When the owners of the servant girl saw this, they knew that now they could not use her to make money. So they grabbed Paul and Silas and dragged them before the city rulers in the marketplace. 20They brought Paul and Silas to the Roman rulers and said, "These men are Jews and are making trouble in our city. 21They are teaching things that are not right for us as Romans to do."

22The crowd joined the attack against them. The Roman officers tore the clothes of Paul and Silas and had them beaten with rods. 23Then Paul and Silas were thrown into jail, and the jailer was ordered to guard them carefully. 24When he heard this order, he put them far inside the jail and pinned their feet down between large blocks of wood.

25About midnight Paul and Silas were praying and singing songs to God as the other prisoners listened. 26Suddenly, there was a strong earthquake that shook the foundation of the jail. Then all the doors of the jail broke open, and all the prisoners were freed from their chains. 27The jailer woke up and saw that the jail doors were open. Thinking that the prisoners had already escaped, he got his sword and was about to kill himself.[n] 28But Paul shouted, "Don't hurt yourself! We are all here."

29The jailer told someone to bring a light. Then he ran inside and, shaking with fear, fell down before Paul and Silas. 30He brought them outside and said, "Men, what must I do to be saved?"

31They said to him, "Believe in the Lord Jesus and you will be saved — you and all the people in your house." 32So Paul and Silas told the message of the Lord to the jailer and all the people in his house. 33At that hour of the night the jailer took Paul and Silas and washed their wounds. Then he and all his people were baptized immediately. 34After this the jailer took Paul and Silas home and gave them food. He and his family were very happy because they now believed in God.

35The next morning, the Roman officers sen the police to tell the jailer, "Let these men g free."

36The jailer said to Paul, "The officers have sen an order to let you go free. You can leave now Go in peace."

37But Paul said to the police, "They beat us i public without a trial, even though we are Roma citizens.[n] And they threw us in jail. Now the want to make us go away quietly. No! Let then come themselves and bring us out."

38The police told the Roman officers what Pa said. When the officers heard that Paul and Sila were Roman citizens, they were afraid. 39So the came and told Paul and Silas they were sorry an took them out of jail and asked them to leave th city. 40So when they came out of the jail, the went to Lydia's house where they saw some c the believers and encouraged them. Then the left.

Paul and Silas in Thessalonica

17 Paul and Silas traveled through Amphi olis and Apollonia and came to Thessal nica where there was a Jewish synagogue.[d] 2Pa went into the synagogue as he always did, and o each Sabbath[d] day for three weeks, he talked wi the Jews about the Scriptures.[d] 3He explained an proved that the Christ[d] must die and then ri from the dead. He said, "This Jesus I am tellir you about is the Christ." 4Some of the Jews we convinced and joined Paul and Silas, along wi many of the Greeks who worshiped God ar many of the important women.

5But the Jews became jealous. So they got som evil men from the marketplace, formed a mo and started a riot. They ran to Jason's house, loc ing for Paul and Silas, wanting to bring them o to the people. 6But when they did not find the they dragged Jason and some other believers the leaders of the city. The people were yellin "These people have made trouble everywhere the world, and now they have come here to 7Jason is keeping them in his house. All of the do things against the laws of Caesar,[d] saying the is another king, called Jesus."

8When the people and the leaders of the ci heard these things, they became very ups 9They made Jason and the others put up a sum money. Then they let the believers go free.

Paul and Silas Go to Berea

10That same night the believers sent Paul a Silas to Berea where they went to the Jewish sy

spirit This was a spirit from the devil, which caused her to say she had special knowledge.
kill himself He thought the leaders would kill him for letting the prisoners escape.
Roman citizens Roman law said that Roman citizens must not be beaten before they had a trial.

gogue.[d] 11These Jews were more willing to listen
than the Jews in Thessalonica. The Bereans were
eager to hear what Paul and Silas said and studied
the Scriptures[d] every day to find out if these
things were true. 12So, many of them believed, as
well as many important Greek women and men.
13But the Jews in Thessalonica learned that Paul
was preaching the word of God in Berea, too. So
they came there, upsetting the people and making
trouble. 14The believers quickly sent Paul away to
the coast, but Silas and Timothy stayed in Berea.
15The people leading Paul went with him to Athens.
Then they carried a message from Paul back
to Silas and Timothy for them to come to him as
soon as they could.

Paul Preaches in Athens

16While Paul was waiting for Silas and Timothy
in Athens, he was troubled because he saw that
the city was full of idols. 17In the synagogue,[d] he
talked with the Jews and the Greeks who worshiped
God. He also talked every day with people
in the marketplace.

18Some of the Epicurean and Stoic philosophers[n]
argued with him, saying, "This man

Epicurean and Stoic philosophers Philosophers were those who searched for truth. Epicureans believed that pleasures, especially pleasures of the mind, were the goal of life. Stoics believed that life should be without feelings of joy or grief.

FRIENDS

A Way Out

Keivan McClure was delighted to land a job at the steak house. He needed every penny he could earn for college. Few of his co-workers were Christians, but Keivan didn't let that bother him. He tried to make friends with them, and he talked about faith and church when he had a chance.

One night after closing, the entire crew decided to go to a drive-in movie and out for pizza. The chosen movie was one with lots of violence and nudity, so Keivan decided not to go.

"I'll meet you after the movie for pizza," Keivan said.

"What's the matter? Our movie choice not good enough for Mr. Holier-Than-Thou?" one of the crew chided.

Keivan knew he didn't deserve that, so he just repeated his request: "That's not what I said or meant. I'll see you for pizza."

"Yeah, right, church-boy," another crew member taunted. "You can't handle the scary stuff, so you're running away."

Most of the other crew members laughed. Keivan didn't know what to say.

Finally, Conrad Langley, the crew leader, spoke up. "Hey, get off his back," he said. "Keivan's a Christian and doesn't watch that junk. I'm a Christian too, and I'm not going either."

The crew was silent. Keivan was surprised. He knew Conrad was a nice guy, but Conrad had never said anything about being a Christian before.

After that night, things got better at work. Keivan and Conrad became close friends, and the crew members showed more respect for their beliefs.

Committed Christian friends. They're a great help when the going gets rough. In **Acts 17:1–15**, Paul and Silas were rescued from discouraging circumstances by friends who cared.

- How was the way Conrad helped Keivan similar to the way the believers helped Paul?
- When has someone helped you in the same way the believers helped Paul? When have you supported another Christian?

CONSIDER . . .

- keeping a journal where you write about times you are discouraged. Later, re-read entries and reflect on how God pulled you through.
- encouraging a Christian friend who is in a difficult situation to be strong and hang in there.

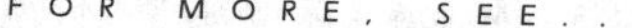

FOR MORE, SEE . . .

- Ecclesiastes 4:9–12
- Matthew 10:21–23
- 1 Timothy 1:1–3

doesn't know what he is talking about. What is
he trying to say?" Others said, "He seems to be
telling us about some other gods," because Paul
was telling them about Jesus and his rising from
the dead. 19They got Paul and took him to a
meeting of the Areopagus,[n] where they said,
"Please explain to us this new idea you have
been teaching. 20The things you are saying are
new to us, and we want to know what this teaching means." 21(All the people of Athens and
those from other countries who lived there always used their time to talk about the newest
ideas.)

22Then Paul stood before the meeting of the
Areopagus and said, "People of Athens, I can see
you are very religious in all things. 23As I was going through your city, I saw the objects you worship. I found an altar that had these words written
on it: TO A GOD WHO IS NOT KNOWN. You worship
a god that you don't know, and this is the God I
am telling you about! 24The God who made the
whole world and everything in it is the Lord of the
land and the sky. He does not live in temples built
by human hands. 25This God is the One who gives
life, breath, and everything else to people. He
does not need any help from them; he has everything he needs. 26God began by making one person, and from him came all the different people
who live everywhere in the world. God decided
exactly when and where they must live. 27God
wanted them to look for him and perhaps search
all around for him and find him, though he is not
far from any of us: 28'We live in him. We walk in
him. We are in him.' Some of your own poets
have said: 'For we are his children.' 29Since we
are God's children, you must not think that God
is like something that people imagine or make
from gold, silver, or rock. 30In the past, people did
not understand God, and he ignored this. But
now, God tells all people in the world to change
their hearts and lives. 31God has set a day that
he will judge all the world with fairness, by the
man he chose long ago. And God has proved
this to everyone by raising that man from the
dead!"

32When the people heard about Jesus being
raised from the dead, some of them laughed. But
others said, "We will hear more about this from
you later." 33So Paul went away from them. 34But
some of the people believed Paul and joined him.
Among those who believed was Dionysius, a
member of the Areopagus, a woman named Dam-
aris, and some others.

Areopagus A council or group of important leaders in Athens. They were like judges.

NON-CHRISTIANS

A Starting Place

Jay Dugan is a talented musician. His friend explained God as a director who "conducts" every element of life to move in harmony.

Amanda Roady has moved nine times in eleven years. Her friend explained God as the friend who goes with us no matter where we move or what new situation we face.

Jason Gaddy is a soccer star. His friend explained God as a coach who insists on practice, works to tone our life muscles, teaches strategy for difficult experiences, and cheers every play from the sidelines.

Some Greek leaders thought there must be a god they did not know. In **Acts 17:22–31**, Paul focused on their understanding of that god to guide them to a full knowledge of the true God.

- Why is it effective to explain God by using things people already understand?
- What images did Paul use to describe God in this passage?

C O N S I D E R . . .

- underlining phrases about God in Acts 17:22–31 that someone who has never been in church could understand. Use these phrases to explain God to your non-Christian friends.
- thinking of a way to explain Jesus to a non-Christian friend. Begin with an image your friend will relate to.

F O R M O R E , S E E . . .

- Exodus 3:12–15
- John 4:5–25
- 1 Corinthians 9:19–23

Paul in Corinth

18 Later Paul left Athens and went to Corinth. [2]Here he met a Jew named Aquila who had been born in the country of Pontus. But Aquila and his wife, Priscilla, had recently moved to Corinth from Italy, because Claudius[n] commanded that all Jews must leave Rome. Paul went to visit Aquila and Priscilla. [3]Because they were tentmakers, just as he was, he stayed with them and worked with them. [4]Every Sabbath[d] day he talked with the Jews and Greeks in the synagogue,[d] trying to persuade them to believe in Jesus.

> **SIDELIGHT:** Claudius (Acts 18:2) ruled Rome thirteen years and was partially paralyzed. He kicked Christians out of Rome for allegedly starting riots that threatened the Roman peace—a common charge against early Christians.

[5]Silas and Timothy came from Macedonia and joined Paul in Corinth. After this, Paul spent all his time telling people the Good News,[d] showing the Jews that Jesus is the Christ.[d] [6]But they would not accept Paul's teaching and said some evil things. So he shook off the dust from his clothes[n] and said to them, "If you are not saved, it will be your own fault! I have done all I can do! After this, I will go only to those who are not Jewish." [7]Paul left the synagogue and moved into the home of Titius Justus, next to the synagogue. This man worshiped God. [8]Crispus was the leader of that synagogue, and he and all the people living in his house believed in the Lord. Many others in Corinth also listened to Paul and believed and were baptized.

[9]During the night, the Lord told Paul in a vision: "Don't be afraid. Continue talking to people and don't be quiet. [10]I am with you, and no one will hurt you because many of my people are in this city." [11]Paul stayed there for a year and a half, teaching God's word to the people.

Paul Is Brought Before Gallio

[12]When Gallio was the governor of the country of Southern Greece, some of the Jews came together against Paul and took him to the court. [13]They said, "This man is teaching people to worship God in a way that is against our law."

[14]Paul was about to say something, but Gallio spoke to the Jews, saying, "I would listen to you Jews if you were complaining about a crime or some wrong. [15]But the things you are saying are only questions about words and names—arguments about your own law. So you must solve this problem yourselves. I don't want to be a judge of these things." [16]And Gallio made them leave the court.

[17]Then they all grabbed Sosthenes, the leader of the synagogue,[d] and beat him there before the court. But this did not bother Gallio.

Paul Returns to Antioch

[18]Paul stayed with the believers for many more days. Then he left and sailed for Syria, with Priscilla and Aquila. At Cenchrea Paul cut off his hair,[n] because he had made a promise to God. [19]Then they went to Ephesus, where Paul left Priscilla and Aquila. While Paul was there, he went into the synagogue[d] and talked with the Jews. [20]When they asked him to stay with them longer, he refused. [21]But as he left, he said, "I will come back to you again if God wants me to." And so he sailed away from Ephesus.

[22]When Paul landed at Caesarea, he went and gave greetings to the church in Jerusalem. After that, Paul went to Antioch. [23]He stayed there for a while and then left and went through the regions of Galatia and Phrygia. He traveled from town to town in these regions, giving strength to all the followers.

Apollos in Ephesus and Corinth

[24]A Jew named Apollos came to Ephesus. He was born in the city of Alexandria and was a good speaker who knew the Scriptures[d] well. [25]He had been taught about the way of the Lord and was always very excited when he spoke and taught the truth about Jesus. But the only baptism Apollos knew about was the baptism that John[n] taught. [26]Apollos began to speak very boldly in the synagogue,[d] and when Priscilla and Aquila heard him, they took him to their home and helped him better understand the way of God. [27]Now Apollos wanted to go to the country of Southern Greece. So the believers helped him and wrote a letter to the followers there, asking them to accept him. These followers had believed in Jesus because of God's grace, and when Apollos arrived, he helped them very much. [28]He argued very strongly with the Jews before all the people, clearly proving with the Scriptures that Jesus is the Christ.[d]

Claudius The emperor (ruler) of Rome, A.D. 41-54.
shook . . . clothes This was a warning to show that Paul was finished talking to the Jews in that city.
cut . . . hair Jews did this to show that the time of a special promise to God was finished.
John John the Baptist, who preached to people about Christ's coming (Luke 3).

Paul in Ephesus

19 While Apollos was in Corinth, Paul was
visiting some places on the way to Ephesus. There he found some followers 2and asked
them, "Did you receive the Holy Spirit[d] when you
believed?"
They said, "We have never even heard of a
Holy Spirit."
3So he asked, "What kind of baptism did you
have?"
They said, "It was the baptism that John[n]
taught."
4Paul said, "John's baptism was a baptism of
changed hearts and lives. He told people to believe in the one who would come after him, and
that one is Jesus."
5When they heard this, they were baptized in
the name of the Lord Jesus. 6Then Paul laid his
hands on them,[n] and the Holy Spirit came upon
them. They began speaking different languages[n]
and prophesying.[d] 7There were about twelve people in this group.
8Paul went into the synagogue[d] and spoke out
boldly for three months. He talked with the Jews
and persuaded them to accept the things he said
about the kingdom of God. 9But some of the Jews
became stubborn. They refused to believe and
said evil things about the Way of Jesus before all
the people. So Paul left them, and taking the followers with him, he went to the school of a man
named Tyrannus. There Paul talked with people
every day 10for two years. Because of his work,
every Jew and Greek in the country of Asia heard
the word of the Lord.

John John the Baptist, who preached to people about Christ's coming (Luke 3).
laid his hands on them The laying on of hands had many purposes, including the giving of a blessing, power, or authority.
languages This can also be translated "tongues."

FAITH

Growing Up

Checkmark the items that are true of your relationship with God. I understand God better now than when I first started learning about him. I genuinely enjoy being involved in activities related to my faith. God helps me love and care for people. My relationships are better as a result of my faith in God. I understand scripture better than I used to. I ask God to help me solve problems. My friends and family know I'm a Christian. I take time each day to pray. I know God loves me. I ask God to forgive me when I do something wrong. I am honest with God about my feelings. I tell people about Jesus. My relationship with God deeply influences my actions.

Now rate yourself:

- 6 to 13 checkmarks—Your faith is definitely growing. You are experiencing the type of growth described in Acts 19:1–7.
- 3 to 5 checkmarks—Be careful that your faith is not stagnating. Read the items you didn't checkmark, and begin building those things into your life. Be encouraged by Acts 19:1–7.
- 0 to 2 checkmarks—Your faith is wilting. Water it with the Word of God and get involved with other Christians soon—before your faith withers. Be challenged by Acts 19:1–7.

In **Acts 19:1–7**, Paul explained truth that the followers did not know. When they heard all that God had done for them, they were changed—and their faith could grow.

- How did Paul help people's faith grow? What items in the checklist would be true for the people in the passage?
- How did the people in this passage express their faith?

CONSIDER . . .

- pretending it's yearbook signing time. Write an entry to Jesus telling ways your relationship has grown, what you appreciate about him and how you hope your relationship will grow in the next year.
- choosing one item from the checklist to begin building into your life.

FOR MORE, SEE . . .

- Psalm 15
- 1 Corinthians 3:1–9
- Colossians 1:9–14

The Sons of Sceva

11God used Paul to do some very special miracles.[d] 12Some people took handkerchiefs and clothes that Paul had used and put them on the sick. When they did this, the sick were healed and evil spirits left them.

13But some Jews also were traveling around and making evil spirits go out of people. They tried to use the name of the Lord Jesus to force the evil spirits out. They would say, "By the same Jesus that Paul talks about, I order you to come out!" 14Seven sons of Sceva, a leading Jewish priest, were doing this.

15But one time an evil spirit said to them, "I know Jesus, and I know about Paul, but who are you?"

16Then the man who had the evil spirit jumped on them. Because he was so much stronger than all of them, they ran away from the house naked and hurt. 17All the people in Ephesus—Jews and Greeks—learned about this and were filled with fear and gave great honor to the Lord Jesus. 18Many of the believers began to confess openly and tell all the evil things they had done. 19Some of them who had used magic brought their magic books and burned them before everyone. Those books were worth about fifty thousand silver coins.[n]

20So in a powerful way the word of the Lord kept spreading and growing.

21After these things, Paul decided to go to Jerusalem, planning to go through the countries of Macedonia and Southern Greece and then on to Jerusalem. He said, "After I have been to Jerusalem, I must also visit Rome." 22Paul sent Timothy and Erastus, two of his helpers, ahead to Macedonia, but he himself stayed in Asia for a while.

Trouble in Ephesus

23And during that time, there was some serious trouble in Ephesus about the Way of Jesus. 24A man named Demetrius, who worked with silver, made little silver models that looked like the temple of the goddess Artemis.[n] Those who did this work made much money. 25Demetrius had a meeting with them and some others who did the same kind of work. He told them, "Men, you know that we make a lot of money from our business. 26But look at what this man Paul is doing. He has convinced and turned away many people in Ephesus and in almost all of Asia! He says the gods made by human hands are not real. 27There is a danger that our business will lose its good name, but there is also another danger: People will begin to think that the temple of the great goddess Artemis is not important. Her greatness will be destroyed, and Artemis is the goddess that everyone in Asia and the whole world worships."

28When the others heard this, they became very angry and shouted, "Artemis, the goddess of Ephesus, is great!" 29The whole city became confused. The people grabbed Gaius and Aristarchus, who were from Macedonia and were traveling with Paul, and ran to the theater. 30Paul wanted to go in and talk to the crowd, but the followers did not let him. 31Also, some leaders of Asia who were friends of Paul sent him a message, begging him not to go into the theater. 32Some people were shouting one thing, and some were shouting another. The meeting was completely confused; most of them did not know why they had come together. 33The Jews put a man named Alexander in front of the people, and some of them told him what to do. Alexander waved his hand so he could explain things to the people. 34But when they saw that Alexander was a Jew, they all shouted the same thing for two hours: "Great is Artemis of Ephesus!"

35Then the city clerk made the crowd be quiet. He said, "People of Ephesus, everyone knows that Ephesus is the city that keeps the temple of the great goddess Artemis and her holy stone[n] that fell from heaven. 36Since no one can say this is not true, you should be quiet. Stop and think before you do anything. 37You brought these men here, but they have not said anything evil against our goddess or stolen anything from her temple. 38If Demetrius and those who work with him have a charge against anyone they should go to the courts and judges where they can argue with each other. 39If there is something else you want to talk about, it can be decided at the regular town meeting of the people. 40I say this because some people might see this trouble today and say that we are rioting. We could not explain this, because there is no real reason for this meeting." 41After the city clerk said these things, he told the people to go home.

Paul In Macedonia and Greece

20 When the trouble stopped, Paul sent for the followers to come to him. After he encouraged them and then told them good-bye, he left and went to the country of Macedonia. 2He said many things to strengthen the followers in the different places on his way through Macedonia. Then he went to Greece, 3where he stayed for three months. He was ready to sail for Syria, but some Jews were planning something against him. So Paul decided to go back through Macedo-

fifty thousand silver coins Probably drachmas. One coin was enough to pay a worker for one day's labor.
Artemis A Greek goddess that the people of Asia Minor worshiped.
holy stone Probably a meteorite or stone that the people thought looked like Artemis.

nia to Syria. 4The men who went with him were Sopater son of Pyrrhus, from the city of Berea; Aristarchus and Secundus, from the city of Thessalonica; Gaius, from Derbe; Timothy; and Tychicus and Trophimus, two men from the country of Asia. 5These men went on ahead and waited for us at Troas. 6We sailed from Philippi after the Feast[d] of Unleavened Bread. Five days later we met them in Troas, where we stayed for seven days.

Paul's Last Visit to Troas

7On the first day of the week,[n] we all met together to break bread,[n] and Paul spoke to the group. Because he was planning to leave the next day, he kept on talking until midnight. 8We were all together in a room upstairs, and there were many lamps in the room. 9A young man named Eutychus was sitting in the window. As Paul continued talking, Eutychus was falling into a deep sleep. Finally, he went sound asleep and fell to the ground from the third floor. When they picked him up, he was dead. 10Paul went down to Eutychus, knelt down, and put his arms around him. He said, "Don't worry. He is alive now." 11Then Paul went upstairs again, broke bread, and ate. He spoke to them a long time, until it was early morning, and then he left. 12They took the young man home alive and were greatly comforted.

The Trip from Troas to Miletus

13We went on ahead of Paul and sailed for the city of Assos, where he wanted to join us on the ship. Paul planned it this way because he wanted to go to Assos by land. 14When he met us there, we took him aboard and went to Mitylene. 15We sailed from Mitylene and the next day came to a place near Chios. The following day we sailed to Samos, and the next day we reached Miletus. 16Paul had already decided not to stop at Ephesus, because he did not want to stay too long in the country of Asia. He was hurrying to be in Jerusalem on the day of Pentecost,[d] if that were possible.

The Elders from Ephesus

17Now from Miletus Paul sent to Ephesus and called for the elders[d] of the church. 18When they came to him, he said, "You know about my life from the first day I came to Asia. You know the way I lived all the time I was with you. 19The Jews made plans against me, which troubled me very much. But you know I always served the Lord unselfishly, and I often cried. 20You know I preached to you and did not hold back anything that would help you. You know that I taught you in public and in your homes. 21I warned both Jews and Greeks to change their lives and turn to God and believe in our Lord Jesus. 22But now I must obey the Holy Spirit[d] and go to Jerusalem. I don't know what will happen to me there. 23I know only that in every city the Holy Spirit tells me that troubles and even jail wait for me. 24I don't care about my own life. The most important thing is that I complete my mission, the work that the Lord Jesus gave me—to tell people the Good News[d] about God's grace.

25"And now, I know that none of you among whom I was preaching the kingdom of God will ever see me again. 26So today I tell you that if any of you should be lost, I am not responsible, 27because I have told you everything God wants you to know. 28Be careful for yourselves and for all the people the Holy Spirit has given to you to care for. You must be like shepherds to the church of God,[n] which he bought with the death of his own son. 29I know that after I leave, some people will come like wild wolves and try to destroy the flock. 30Also, some from your own group will rise up and twist the truth and will lead away followers after them. 31So be careful! Always remember that for three years, day and night, I never stopped warning each of you, and I often cried over you.

32"Now I am putting you in the care of God and the message about his grace. It is able to give you strength, and it will give you the blessings God has for all his holy people. 33When I was with you, I never wanted anyone's money or fine clothes. 34You know I always worked to take care of my own needs and the needs of those who were with me. 35I showed you in all things that you should work as I did and help the weak. I taught you to remember the words Jesus said: 'It is more blessed to give than to receive.' "

36When Paul had said this, he knelt down with all of them and prayed. 37-38And they all cried because Paul had said they would never see him again. They put their arms around him and kissed him. Then they went with him to the ship.

Paul Goes to Jerusalem

21 After we all said good-bye to them, we sailed straight to the island of Cos. The next day we reached Rhodes, and from there we went to Patara. 2There we found a ship going to Phoenicia, so we went aboard and sailed away. 3We sailed near the island of Cyprus, seeing it to

first day of the week Sunday, which for the Jews began at sunset on our Saturday. But if in this part of Asia a different system of time was used, then the meeting was on our Sunday night.
break bread Probably the Lord's Supper, the special meal that Jesus told his followers to eat to remember him (Luke 22:14-20).
of God Some Greek copies say, "of the Lord."

the north, but we sailed on to Syria. We stopped at Tyre because the ship needed to unload its cargo there. 4We found some followers in Tyre and stayed with them for seven days. Through the Holy Spirit[d] they warned Paul not to go to Jerusalem. 5When we finished our visit, we left and continued our trip. All the followers, even the women and children, came outside the city with us. After we all knelt on the beach and prayed, 6we said good-bye and got on the ship, and the followers went back home.

7We continued our trip from Tyre and arrived at Ptolemais, where we greeted the believers and stayed with them for a day. 8The next day we left Ptolemais and went to the city of Caesarea. There we went into the home of Philip the preacher,[d] one of the seven helpers,[n] and stayed with him. 9He had four unmarried daughters who had the gift of prophesying.[d] 10After we had been there for some time, a prophet named Agabus arrived from Judea. 11He came to us and borrowed Paul's belt and used it to tie his own hands and feet. He said, "The Holy Spirit says, 'This is how the Jews in Jerusalem will tie up the man who wears this belt. Then they will give him to those who are not Jews.' "

12When we all heard this, we and the people there begged Paul not to go to Jerusalem. 13But he said, "Why are you crying and making me so sad? I am not only ready to be tied up in Jerusalem, I am ready to die for the Lord Jesus!"

14We could not persuade him to stay away from Jerusalem. So we stopped begging him and said, "We pray that what the Lord wants will be done."

15After this, we got ready and started on our way to Jerusalem. 16Some of the followers from Caesarea went with us and took us to the home of Mnason, where we would stay. He was from Cyprus and was one of the first followers.

Paul Visits James

17In Jerusalem the believers were glad to see us. 18The next day Paul went with us to visit James, and all the elders[d] were there. 19Paul greeted them and told them everything God had done among the non-Jewish people through him. 20When they heard this, they praised God. Then they said to Paul, "Brother, you can see that many thousands of Jews have become believers. And they think it is very important to obey the law of Moses. 21They have heard about your teaching, that you tell the Jews who live among those who are not Jews to leave the law of Moses. They have heard that you tell them not to circumcise[d] their children and not to obey Jewish customs. 22What should we do? They will learn that you have come. 23So we will tell you what to do: Four of our men have made a promise to God. 24Take these men with you and share in their cleansing ceremony.[n] Pay their expenses so they can shave their heads.[n] Then it will prove to everyone that what they have heard about you is not true and that you follow the law of Moses in your own life. 25We have already sent a letter to the non-Jewish believers. The letter said: 'Do not eat food that has been offered to idols, or blood, or animals that have been strangled. Do not take part in sexual sin.' "

26The next day Paul took the four men and shared in the cleansing ceremony with them. Then he went to the Temple[d] and announced the time when the days of the cleansing ceremony would be finished. On the last day an offering would be given for each of the men.

27When the seven days were almost over, some Jews from Asia saw Paul at the Temple. They caused all the people to be upset and grabbed Paul. 28They shouted, "People of Israel, help us! This is the man who goes everywhere teaching against the law of Moses, against our people, and against this Temple. Now he has brought some Greeks into the Temple and has made this holy place unclean!"[d] 29(The Jews said this because they had seen Trophimus, a man from Ephesus, with Paul in Jerusalem. The Jews thought that Paul had brought him into the Temple.)

SIDELIGHT: When Paul was accused of making the Temple unclean, he was being accused of a crime punishable by death (Acts 21:28). Archaeologists have found a temple inscription that says: "No foreigner is to enter. . . . Whoever is caught will render himself liable to the consequent penalty of death."

30All the people in Jerusalem became upset. Together they ran, took Paul, and dragged him out of the Temple. The Temple doors were closed immediately. 31While they were trying to kill Paul, the commander of the Roman army in Jerusalem learned that there was trouble in the whole city. 32Immediately he took some officers and soldiers and ran to the place where the crowd was gathered. When the people saw them, they stopped beating Paul. 33The commander went to Paul and arrested him. He told his soldiers to tie Paul with

helpers The seven men chosen for a special work described in Acts 6:1-6.
cleansing ceremony The special things Jews did to end the Nazirite promise.
shave their heads The Jews did this to show that their promise was finished.

two chains. Then he asked who he was and what he had done wrong. 34Some in the crowd were yelling one thing, and some were yelling another. Because of all this confusion and shouting, the commander could not learn what had happened. So he ordered the soldiers to take Paul to the army building. 35When Paul came to the steps, the soldiers had to carry him because the people were ready to hurt him. 36The whole mob was following them, shouting, "Kill him!"

37As the soldiers were about to take Paul into the army building, he spoke to the commander, "May I say something to you?"

The commander said, "Do you speak Greek? 38I thought you were the Egyptian who started some trouble against the government not long ago and led four thousand killers out to the desert."

39Paul said, "No, I am a Jew from Tarsus in the country of Cilicia. I am a citizen of that important city. Please, let me speak to the people."

40The commander gave permission, so Paul stood on the steps and waved his hand to quiet the people. When there was silence, he spoke to them in the Jewish language.[n]

Paul Speaks to the People

22 Paul said, "Friends, fellow Jews, listen to my defense to you." 2When the Jews heard him speaking the Jewish language,[n] they became very quiet. Paul said, 3"I am a Jew, born in Tarsus in the country of Cilicia, but I grew up in this city. I was a student of Gamaliel,[n] who carefully taught me everything about the law of our ancestors. I was very serious about serving God, just as are all of you here today. 4I persecuted the people who followed the Way of Jesus, and some of them were even killed. I arrested men and women and put them in jail. 5The high priest and the whole council of older Jewish leaders can tell you this is true. They gave me letters to the Jewish brothers in Damascus. So I was going there to arrest these people and bring them back to Jerusalem to be punished.

6"About noon when I came near Damascus, a bright light from heaven suddenly flashed all around me. 7I fell to the ground and heard a voice saying, 'Saul, Saul, why are you persecuting me?' 8I asked, 'Who are you, Lord?' The voice said, 'I am Jesus from Nazareth whom you are persecuting.' 9Those who were with me did not hear the voice, but they saw the light. 10I said, 'What shall I do, Lord?' The Lord answered, 'Get up and go to Damascus. There you will be told about all the things I have planned for you to do.' 11I could not see, because the bright light had made me blind. So my companions led me into Damascus.

12"There a man named Ananias came to me. He was a religious man; he obeyed the law of Moses, and all the Jews who lived there respected him. 13He stood by me and said, 'Brother Saul, see again!' Immediately I was able to see him. 14He said, 'The God of our ancestors chose you long ago to know his plan, to see the Righteous One, and to hear words from him. 15You will be his witness to all people, telling them about what you have seen and heard. 16Now, why wait any longer? Get up, be baptized, and wash your sins away, trusting in him to save you.'

17"Later, when I returned to Jerusalem, I was praying in the Temple,[d] and I saw a vision. 18I saw the Lord saying to me, 'Hurry! Leave Jerusalem now! The people here will not accept the truth about me.' 19But I said, 'Lord, they know that in every synagogue[d] I put the believers in jail and beat them. 20They also know I was there when Stephen, your witness, was killed. I stood there agreeing and holding the coats of those who were killing him!' 21But the Lord said to me, 'Leave now. I will send you far away to the non-Jewish people.' "

22The crowd listened to Paul until he said this. Then they began shouting, "Kill him! Get him out of the world! He should not be allowed to live!" 23They shouted, threw off their coats,[n] and threw dust into the air.[n]

24Then the commander ordered the soldiers to take Paul into the army building and beat him. He wanted to make Paul tell why the people were shouting against him like this. 25But as the soldiers were tying him up, preparing to beat him, Paul said to an officer nearby, "Do you have the right to beat a Roman citizen[n] who has not been proven guilty?"

26When the officer heard this, he went to the commander and reported it. The officer said, "Do you know what you are doing? This man is a Roman citizen."

27The commander came to Paul and said, "Tell me, are you really a Roman citizen?"

He answered, "Yes."

28The commander said, "I paid a lot of money to become a Roman citizen."

But Paul said, "I was born a citizen."

29The men who were preparing to question Paul moved away from him immediately. The commander was frightened because he had already tied Paul, and Paul was a Roman citizen.

Jewish language Hebrew or Aramaic, the languages of the Jews in the first century.
Gamaliel A very important teacher of the Pharisees, a Jewish religious group (Acts 5:34).
threw off their coats This showed that the Jews were very angry with Paul.
threw dust into the air This showed even greater anger.
Roman citizen Roman law said that Roman citizens must not be beaten before they had a trial.

Paul Speaks to Jewish Leaders

30The next day the commander decided to
learn why the Jews were accusing Paul. So he
ordered the leading priests and the Jewish council
to meet. The commander took Paul's chains off.
Then he brought Paul out and stood him before
their meeting.

23 Paul looked at the Jewish council and
said, "Brothers, I have lived my life without guilt feelings before God up to this day." 2Ana-
nias,[n] the high priest, heard this and told the
men who were standing near Paul to hit him on
the mouth. 3Paul said to Ananias, "God will hit
you, too! You are like a wall that has been painted
white. You sit there and judge me, using the law
of Moses, but you are telling them to hit me, and
that is against the law."

4The men standing near Paul said to him, "You
cannot insult God's high priest like that!"

5Paul said, "Brothers, I did not know this man
was the high priest. It is written in the Scriptures,[d]
'You must not curse a leader of your people.' "[n]

6Some of the men in the meeting were Sadducees,[d] and others were Pharisees.[d] Knowing this,
Paul shouted to them, "My brothers, I am a Pharisee, and my father was a Pharisee. I am on trial
here because I believe that people will rise from
the dead."

7When Paul said this, there was an argument
between the Pharisees and the Sadducees, and
the group was divided. 8(The Sadducees do not
believe in angels or spirits or that people will rise
from the dead. But the Pharisees believe in them
all.) 9So there was a great uproar. Some of the
teachers of the law, who were Pharisees, stood up
and argued, "We find nothing wrong with this
man. Maybe an angel or a spirit did speak to him."

10The argument was beginning to turn into
such a fight that the commander was afraid the
Jews would tear Paul to pieces. So he told the
soldiers to go down and take Paul away and put
him in the army building.

11The next night the Lord came and stood by
Paul. He said, "Be brave! You have told people in
Jerusalem about me. You must do the same in
Rome."

12In the morning some of the Jews made a plan
to kill Paul, and they took an oath not to eat or
drink anything until they had killed him. 13There
were more than forty Jews who made this plan.
14They went to the leading priests and the older
Jewish leaders and said, "We have taken an oath
not to eat or drink until we have killed Paul. 15So
this is what we want you to do: Send a message
to the commander to bring Paul out to you as
though you want to ask him more questions. We
will be waiting to kill him while he is on the way
here."

16But Paul's nephew heard about this plan and
went to the army building and told Paul. 17Then
Paul called one of the officers and said, "Take this
young man to the commander. He has a message
for him."

18So the officer brought Paul's nephew to the
commander and said, "The prisoner, Paul, asked
me to bring this young man to you. He wants to
tell you something."

19The commander took the young man's hand
and led him to a place where they could be alone.
He asked, "What do you want to tell me?"

20The young man said, "The Jews have decided
to ask you to bring Paul down to their council
meeting tomorrow. They want you to think they
are going to ask him more questions. 21But don't
believe them! More than forty men are hiding and
waiting to kill Paul. They have all taken an oath
not to eat or drink until they have killed him.
Now they are waiting for you to agree."

22The commander sent the young man away,
ordering him, "Don't tell anyone that you have
told me about their plan."

Paul Is Sent to Caesarea

23Then the commander called two officers and
said, "I need some men to go to Caesarea. Get
two hundred soldiers, seventy horsemen, and two
hundred men with spears ready to leave at nine
o'clock tonight. 24Get some horses for Paul to ride
so he can be taken to Governor Felix safely."
25And he wrote a letter that said:

> 26From Claudius Lysias.
> To the Most Excellent Governor Felix:
> Greetings.
>
> 27The Jews had taken this man and
> planned to kill him. But I learned that he is
> a Roman citizen, so I went with my soldiers
> and saved him. 28I wanted to know why
> they were accusing him, so I brought him
> before their council meeting. 29I learned that
> the Jews said Paul did some things that were
> wrong by their own laws, but no charge was
> worthy of jail or death. 30When I was told
> that some of the Jews were planning to kill
> Paul, I sent him to you at once. I also told
> those Jews to tell you what they have against
> him.

31So the soldiers did what they were told and
took Paul and brought him to the city of Antipatris
that night. 32The next day the horsemen went
with Paul to Caesarea, but the other soldiers went
back to the army building in Jerusalem. 33When

Ananias This is not the same man named Ananias in Acts 22:12.
'You . . . people.' Quotation from Exodus 22:28.

the horsemen came to Caesarea and gave the letter to the governor, they turned Paul over to him.
34The governor read the letter and asked Paul,
"What area are you from?" When he learned that
Paul was from Cilicia, 35he said, "I will hear your
case when those who are against you come here,
too." Then the governor gave orders for Paul to
be kept under guard in Herod's palace.

Paul Is Accused

24 Five days later Ananias, the high priest,
went to the city of Caesarea with some
of the older Jewish leaders and a lawyer named
Tertullus. They had come to make charges against
Paul before the governor. 2Paul was called into
the meeting, and Tertullus began to accuse him,
saying, "Most Excellent Felix! Our people enjoy
much peace because of you, and many wrong
things in our country are being made right
through your wise help. 3We accept these things
always and in every place, and we are thankful for
them. 4But not wanting to take any more of your
time, I beg you to be kind and listen to our few
words. 5We have found this man to be a trouble-
maker, stirring up the Jews everywhere in the
world. He is a leader of the Nazarene[d] group.
6Also, he was trying to make the Temple[d] unclean,[d] but we stopped him.[n] 8By asking him
questions yourself, you can decide if all these
things are true." 9The other Jews agreed and said
that all of this was true.

10When the governor made a sign for Paul to
speak, Paul said, "Governor Felix, I know you
have been a judge over this nation for a long time.
So I am happy to defend myself before you. 11You
can learn for yourself that I went to worship in
Jerusalem only twelve days ago. 12Those who are
accusing me did not find me arguing with anyone
in the Temple or stirring up the people in the synagogues[d] or in the city. 13They cannot prove the
things they are saying against me now. 14But I will
tell you this: I worship the God of our ancestors
as a follower of the Way of Jesus. The Jews say
that the Way of Jesus is not the right way. But I
believe everything that is taught in the law of Moses and that is written in the books of the Prophets.[d] 15I have the same hope in God that they
have—the hope that all people, good and bad,
will surely be raised from the dead. 16This is why
I always try to do what I believe is right before
God and people.

17"After being away from Jerusalem for several
years, I went back to bring money to my people
and to offer sacrifices. 18I was doing this when
they found me in the Temple. I had finished the
cleansing ceremony and had not made any trouble; no people were gathering around me. 19But
there were some Jews from the country of Asia
who should be here, standing before you. If I have
really done anything wrong, they are the ones
who should accuse me. 20Or ask these Jews here
if they found any wrong in me when I stood before the Jewish council in Jerusalem. 21But I did
shout one thing when I stood before them: 'You
are judging me today because I believe that people will rise from the dead!' "

22Felix already understood much about the
Way of Jesus. He stopped the trial and said,
"When commander Lysias comes here, I will de-
cide your case." 23Felix told the officer to keep
Paul guarded but to give him some freedom and
to let his friends bring what he needed.

Paul Speaks to Felix and His Wife

24After some days Felix came with his wife,
Drusilla, who was Jewish, and asked for Paul to
be brought to him. He listened to Paul talk about
believing in Christ Jesus. 25But Felix became
afraid when Paul spoke about living right, self-
control, and the time when God will judge the
world. He said, "Go away now. When I have
more time, I will call for you." 26At the same time
Felix hoped that Paul would give him some
money, so he often sent for Paul and talked with
him.

SIDELIGHT: The Judean governor Felix was greedy, brutal, and incompetent. He once killed four hundred men suspected of terrorist activities—without a trial. When Paul wouldn't pay him a bribe, Felix left the apostle in jail for two years, until Felix was succeeded in office (Acts 24:1–27).

27But after two years, Felix was replaced by
Porcius Festus as governor. But Felix had left Paul
in prison to please the Jews.

Paul Asks to See Caesar

25 Three days after Festus became governor, he went from Caesarea to Jerusa-
lem. 2There the leading priests and the important
Jewish leaders made charges against Paul before
Festus. 3They asked Festus to do them a favor.
They wanted him to send Paul back to Jerusalem,
because they had a plan to kill him on the way.
4But Festus answered that Paul would be kept in
Caesarea and that he himself was returning there
soon. 5He said, "Some of your leaders should go

Verse 6 Some Greek copies add 6b-8a: "And we wanted to judge him by our own law. 7But the officer Lysias came and used much force to take him from us. 8And Lysias commanded those who wanted to accuse Paul to come to you."

with me. They can accuse the man there in Caesarea, if he has really done something wrong."
6 Festus stayed in Jerusalem another eight or ten
days and then went back to Caesarea. The next
day he told the soldiers to bring Paul before him.
Festus was seated on the judge's seat 7 when Paul
came into the room. The Jewish people who had
come from Jerusalem stood around him, making
serious charges against him, which they could not
prove. 8 This is what Paul said to defend himself:
"I have done nothing wrong against the Jewish
law, against the Temple,[d] or against Caesar."[d]
9 But Festus wanted to please the Jews. So he
asked Paul, "Do you want to go to Jerusalem for
me to judge you there on these charges?"
10 Paul said, "I am standing at Caesar's judgment seat now, where I should be judged. I have
done nothing wrong to the Jews; you know this
is true. 11 If I have done something wrong and the
law says I must die, I do not ask to be saved from
death. But if these charges are not true, then no
one can give me to them. I want Caesar to hear
my case!"
12 Festus talked about this with his advisors.
Then he said, "You have asked to see Caesar, so
you will go to Caesar!"

Paul Before King Agrippa

13 A few days later King Agrippa and Bernice
came to Caesarea to visit Festus. 14 They stayed
there for some time, and Festus told the king
about Paul's case. Festus said, "There is a man
that Felix left in prison. 15 When I went to Jerusalem, the leading priests and the older Jewish leaders there made charges against him, asking me to
sentence him to death. 16 But I answered, 'When
a man is accused of a crime, Romans do not hand
him over until he has been allowed to face his
accusers and defend himself against their
charges.' 17 So when these Jews came here to
Caesarea for the trial, I did not waste time. The
next day I sat on the judge's seat and commanded
that the man be brought in. 18 The Jews stood up
and accused him, but not of any serious crime as
I thought they would. 19 The things they said were
about their own religion and about a man named
Jesus who died. But Paul said that he is still alive.
20 Not knowing how to find out about these questions, I asked Paul, 'Do you want to go to Jerusalem and be judged there?' 21 But he asked to be
kept in Caesarea. He wants a decision from the
emperor.[n] So I ordered that he be held until I
could send him to Caesar.[d]"
22 Agrippa said to Festus, "I would also like to
hear this man myself."
Festus said, "Tomorrow you will hear him."
23 The next day Agrippa and Bernice appeared
with great show, acting like very important people. They went into the judgment room with the
army leaders and the important men of Caesarea.
Then Festus ordered the soldiers to bring Paul in.
24 Festus said, "King Agrippa and all who are gathered here with us, you see this man. All the Jewish people, here and in Jerusalem, have complained to me about him, shouting that he should
not live any longer. 25 When I judged him, I found
no reason to order his death. But since he asked
to be judged by Caesar, I decided to send him.
26 But I have nothing definite to write the emperor
about him. So I have brought him before all of
you—especially you, King Agrippa. I hope you
can question him and give me something to write.
27 I think it is foolish to send a prisoner to Caesar
without telling what charges are against him."

Paul Defends Himself

26 Agrippa said to Paul, "You may now
speak to defend yourself."
Then Paul raised his hand and began to speak.
2 He said, "King Agrippa, I am very happy to stand
before you and will answer all the charges the
Jewish people make against me. 3 You know so
much about all the Jewish customs and the things
the Jews argue about, so please listen to me patiently.
4 "All the Jewish people know about my whole
life, how I lived from the beginning in my own
country and later in Jerusalem. 5 They have
known me for a long time. If they want to, they
can tell you that I was a good Pharisee.[d] And the
Pharisees obey the laws of the Jewish religion
more carefully than any other group. 6 Now I am
on trial because I hope for the promise that God
made to our ancestors. 7 This is the promise that
the twelve tribes[d] of our people hope to receive
as they serve God day and night. My king, the
Jews have accused me because I hope for this
same promise! 8 Why do any of you people think
it is impossible for God to raise people from the
dead?
9 "I, too, thought I ought to do many things
against Jesus from Nazareth. 10 And that is what I
did in Jerusalem. The leading priests gave me the
power to put many of God's people in jail, and
when they were being killed, I agreed it was a
good thing. 11 In every synagogue,[d] I often punished them and tried to make them speak against
Jesus. I was so angry against them I even went to
other cities to find them and punish them.
12 "One time the leading priests gave me permission and the power to go to Damascus. 13 On
the way there, at noon, I saw a light from heaven.
It was brighter than the sun and flashed all around
me and those who were traveling with me. 14 We

emperor The ruler of the Roman Empire, which was almost all the known world.

all fell to the ground. Then I heard a voice speaking to me in the Jewish language,[n] saying, 'Saul,
Saul, why are you persecuting me? You are only
hurting yourself by fighting me.' 15I said, 'Who are
you, Lord?' The Lord said, 'I am Jesus, the one
you are persecuting. 16Stand up! I have chosen
you to be my servant and my witness—you will
tell people the things that you have seen and the
things that I will show you. This is why I have
come to you today. 17I will keep you safe from
your own people and also from those who are not
Jewish. I am sending you to them 18to open their
eyes so that they may turn away from darkness to
the light, away from the power of Satan and to
God. Then their sins can be forgiven, and they
can have a place with those people who have
been made holy by believing in me.'
19"King Agrippa, after I had this vision from
heaven, I obeyed it. 20I began telling people that
they should change their hearts and lives and turn
to God and do things to show they really had
changed. I told this first to those in Damascus,
then in Jerusalem, and in every part of Judea, and
also to those who are not Jewish. 21This is why
the Jews took me and were trying to kill me in the
Temple.[d] 22But God has helped me, and so I stand
here today, telling all people, small and great,
what I have seen. But I am saying only what Moses and the prophets[d] said would happen — 23that
the Christ[d] would die, and as the first to rise from
the dead, he would bring light to the Jewish and
non-Jewish people."

Paul Tries to Persuade Agrippa

24While Paul was saying these things to defend
himself, Festus said loudly, "Paul, you are out of
your mind! Too much study has driven you
crazy!"
25Paul said, "Most excellent Festus, I am not
crazy. My words are true and sensible. 26King
Agrippa knows about these things, and I can
speak freely to him. I know he has heard about all
of these things, because they did not happen off
in a corner. 27King Agrippa, do you believe what
the prophets[d] wrote? I know you believe."
28King Agrippa said to Paul, "Do you think you
can persuade me to become a Christian in such a
short time?"
29Paul said, "Whether it is a short or a long
time, I pray to God that not only you but every
person listening to me today would be saved and
be like me—except for these chains I have."
30Then King Agrippa, Governor Festus, Bernice, and all the people sitting with them stood up
31and left the room. Talking to each other, they
said, "There is no reason why this man should die
or be put in jail." 32And Agrippa said to Festus,
"We could let this man go free, but he has asked
Caesar[d] to hear his case."

Paul Sails for Rome

27 It was decided that we would sail for Italy. An officer named Julius, who served
in the emperor's[n] army, guarded Paul and some
other prisoners. 2We got on a ship that was from
the city of Adramyttium and was about to sail to
different ports in the country of Asia. Aristarchus,
a man from the city of Thessalonica in Macedonia, went with us. 3The next day we came to Sidon. Julius was very good to Paul and gave him
freedom to go visit his friends, who took care of
his needs. 4We left Sidon and sailed close to the
island of Cyprus, because the wind was blowing
against us. 5We went across the sea by Cilicia and
Pamphylia and landed at the city of Myra, in
Lycia. 6There the officer found a ship from Alexandria that was going to Italy, so he put us on it.
7We sailed slowly for many days. We had a
hard time reaching Cnidus because the wind was
blowing against us, and we could not go any farther. So we sailed by the south side of the island
of Crete near Salmone. 8Sailing past it was hard.
Then we came to a place called Fair Havens, near
the city of Lasea.
9We had lost much time, and it was now dangerous to sail, because it was already after the Day
of Cleansing.[n] So Paul warned them, 10"Men, I
can see there will be a lot of trouble on this trip.
The ship, the cargo, and even our lives may be
lost." 11But the captain and the owner of the ship
did not agree with Paul, and the officer believed
what the captain and owner of the ship said.
12Since that harbor was not a good place for the
ship to stay for the winter, most of the men decided that the ship should leave. They hoped we
could go to Phoenix and stay there for the winter.
Phoenix, a city on the island of Crete, had a harbor which faced southwest and northwest.

The Storm

13When a good wind began to blow from the
south, the men on the ship thought, "This is the
wind we wanted, and now we have it." So they
pulled up the anchor, and we sailed very close to
the island of Crete. 14But then a very strong wind
named the "northeaster" came from the island.
15The ship was caught in it and could not sail
against it. So we stopped trying and let the wind

Jewish language Hebrew or Aramaic, the languages of the Jews in the first century.
emperor The ruler of the Roman Empire, which was almost all the known world.
Day of Cleansing An important Jewish holy day in the fall of the year. This was the time of year that bad storms arose on the sea.

carry us. 16When we went below a small island
named Cauda, we were barely able to bring in the
lifeboat. 17After the men took the lifeboat in, they
tied ropes around the ship to hold it together. The
men were afraid that the ship would hit the sand-
banks of Syrtis,[n] so they lowered the sail and let
the wind carry the ship. 18The next day the storm
was blowing us so hard that the men threw out
some of the cargo. 19A day later with their own
hands they threw out the ship's equipment.
20When we could not see the sun or the stars for
many days, and the storm was very bad, we lost
all hope of being saved.

21After the men had gone without food for a
long time, Paul stood up before them and said,
"Men, you should have listened to me. You
should not have sailed from Crete. Then you
would not have all this trouble and loss. 22But
now I tell you to cheer up because none of you
will die. Only the ship will be lost. 23Last night an
angel came to me from the God I belong to and
worship. 24The angel said, 'Paul, do not be afraid.
You must stand before Caesar.[d] And God has
promised you that he will save the lives of everyone sailing with you.' 25So men, have courage. I
trust in God that everything will happen as his
angel told me. 26But we will crash on an island."

27On the fourteenth night we were still being
carried around in the Adriatic Sea.[n] About midnight the sailors thought we were close to land,
28so they lowered a rope with a weight on the end
of it into the water. They found that the water
was one hundred twenty feet deep. They went a
little farther and lowered the rope again. It was
ninety feet deep. 29The sailors were afraid that we
would hit the rocks, so they threw four anchors
into the water and prayed for daylight to come.
30Some of the sailors wanted to leave the ship,
and they lowered the lifeboat, pretending they
were throwing more anchors from the front of the
ship. 31But Paul told the officer and the other soldiers, "If these men do not stay in the ship, your
lives cannot be saved." 32So the soldiers cut the
ropes and let the lifeboat fall into the water.

33Just before dawn Paul began persuading all
the people to eat something. He said, "For the
past fourteen days you have been waiting and
watching and not eating. 34Now I beg you to eat
something. You need it to stay alive. None of you
will lose even one hair off your heads." 35After he
said this, Paul took some bread and thanked God
for it before all of them. He broke off a piece and
began eating. 36They all felt better and started eating, too. 37There were two hundred seventy-six
people on the ship. 38When they had eaten all
they wanted, they began making the ship lighter
by throwing the grain into the sea.

The Ship Is Destroyed

39When daylight came, the sailors saw land.
They did not know what land it was, but they saw
a bay with a beach and wanted to sail the ship to
the beach if they could. 40So they cut the ropes to
the anchors and left the anchors in the sea. At the
same time, they untied the ropes that were holding the rudders. Then they raised the front sail
into the wind and sailed toward the beach. 41But
the ship hit a sandbank. The front of the ship
stuck there and could not move, but the back of
the ship began to break up from the big waves.

42The soldiers decided to kill the prisoners so
none of them could swim away and escape. 43But
Julius, the officer, wanted to let Paul live and did
not allow the soldiers to kill the prisoners. Instead
he ordered everyone who could swim to jump
into the water first and swim to land. 44The rest
were to follow using wooden boards or pieces of
the ship. And this is how all the people made it
safely to land.

SIDELIGHT: Paul often experienced rough waters while sailing (Acts 27:13–44). Storms, a common occurrence in the Mediterranean Sea, made travel hazardous for wooden trading ships. Today, one Greek island, only nine miles long, has four hundred churches that were built by sailors who were fulfilling vows they made to God in the midst of perilous storms.

Paul on the Island of Malta

28 When we were safe on land, we learned
that the island was called Malta. 2The
people who lived there were very good to us. Because it was raining and very cold, they made a
fire and welcomed all of us. 3Paul gathered a pile
of sticks and was putting them on the fire when
a poisonous snake came out because of the heat
and bit him on the hand. 4The people living on
the island saw the snake hanging from Paul's
hand and said to each other, "This man must be
a murderer! He did not die in the sea, but Justice[n] does not want him to live." 5But Paul shook
the snake off into the fire and was not hurt. 6The
people thought that Paul would swell up or fall
down dead. They waited and watched him for a
long time, but nothing bad happened to him. So
they changed their minds and said, "He is a god!"

Syrtis Shallow area in the sea near the Libyan coast.
Adriatic Sea The sea between Greece and Italy, including the central Mediterranean.
Justice The people thought there was a god named Justice who would punish bad people.

7There were some fields around there owned
by Publius, an important man on the island. He
welcomed us into his home and was very good to
us for three days. 8Publius' father was sick with a
fever and dysentery.[n] Paul went to him, prayed,
and put his hands on the man and healed him.
9After this, all the other sick people on the island
came to Paul, and he healed them, too. 10-11The
people on the island gave us many honors. When
we were ready to leave, three months later, they
gave us the things we needed.

Paul Goes to Rome

We got on a ship from Alexandria that had
stayed on the island during the winter. On the
front of the ship was the sign of the twin gods.[n]
12We stopped at Syracuse for three days. 13From
there we sailed to Rhegium. The next day a wind
began to blow from the south, and a day later we
came to Puteoli. 14We found some believers there
who asked us to stay with them for a week. Finally, we came to Rome. 15The believers in Rome
heard that we were there and came out as far as
the Market of Appius[n] and the Three Inns[n] to
meet us. When Paul saw them, he was encouraged and thanked God.

Paul in Rome

16When we arrived at Rome, Paul was allowed
to live alone, with the soldier who guarded him.
17Three days later Paul sent for the Jewish leaders there. When they came together, he said,
"Brothers, I have done nothing against our people
or the customs of our ancestors. But I was arrested in Jerusalem and given to the Romans. 18Af-
ter they asked me many questions, they could find
no reason why I should be killed. They wanted to
let me go free, 19but the Jewish people there argued against that. So I had to ask to come to Rome
to have my trial before Caesar.[d] But I have no
charge to bring against my own people. 20That is
why I wanted to see you and talk with you. I am
bound with this chain because I believe in the
hope of Israel."

21They answered Paul, "We have received no
letters from Judea about you. None of our Jewish
brothers who have come from there brought
news or told us anything bad about you. 22But we
want to hear your ideas, because we know that
people everywhere are speaking against this religious group."

23Paul and the Jewish people chose a day for a
meeting and on that day many more of the Jews
met with Paul at the place he was staying. He
spoke to them all day long. Using the law of Moses and the prophets'[d] writings, he explained the
kingdom of God, and he tried to persuade them
to believe these things about Jesus. 24Some believed what Paul said, but others did not. 25So
they argued and began leaving after Paul said one
more thing to them: "The Holy Spirit[d] spoke the
truth to your ancestors through Isaiah the
prophet, saying,

26'Go to this people and say:
You will listen and listen, but you will not
understand.
You will look and look, but you will not
learn,
27because these people have become stubborn.
They don't hear with their ears,
and they have closed their eyes.
Otherwise, they might really understand
what they see with their eyes
and hear with their ears.
They might really understand in their minds
and come back to me and be healed.'

Isaiah 6:9-10

28"I want you to know that God has also sent
his salvation to those who are not Jewish, and
they will listen!" 29 [n]

30Paul stayed two full years in his own rented
house and welcomed all people who came to visit
him. 31He boldly preached about the kingdom of
God and taught about the Lord Jesus Christ, and
no one tried to stop him.

dysentery A sickness like diarrhea.
twin gods Statues of Castor and Pollux, gods in old Greek tales.
Market of Appius A town about twenty-seven miles from Rome.
Three Inns A town about thirty miles from Rome.
Verse 29 Some late Greek copies add verse 29: "After Paul said this, the Jews left. They were arguing very much with each other."

ROMANS

Why Read This Book:

- Understand that all people have sinned (Romans 1—3).
- Learn how Jesus Christ pays for our sins (Romans 4—8).
- Be challenged to live the Christian life (Romans 12—15).

Behind the Scenes:

Suppose a school friend sat down with you in the cafeteria and asked, out of the blue, "What do you believe?" What would you say?

The Book of Romans is the apostle Paul's answer to that question: What do you believe? For more than twenty years, he had been a missionary, spreading the good news about Jesus Christ. He wanted to visit the Roman church, but before he went, he wanted the Roman Christians to understand what he believed.

So he wrote them this letter, which many people believe is the best, most powerful summary of Christian beliefs in the Bible. The letter explains how all people have sinned and how God sent Jesus to pay for those sins and make people right with God (Romans 3:22–28). Then it explains what it means to live as Christians.

The Book of Romans is packed with powerful statements about God and faith. From this book we can learn how God's love for us overcomes the power of sin in our lives and how we can live lives that please God.

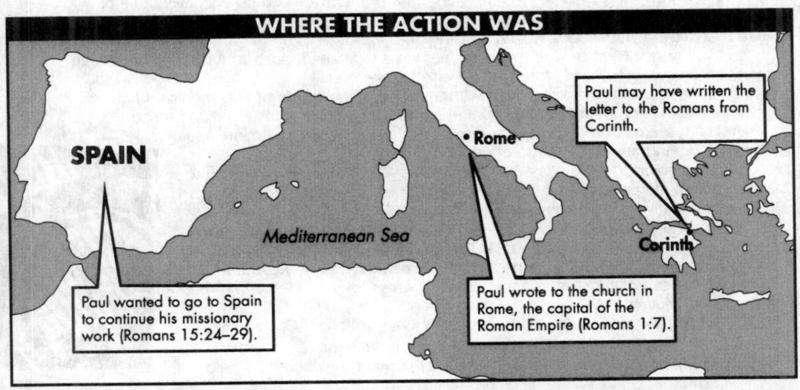
WHERE THE ACTION WAS
SPAIN
Rome
Mediterranean Sea
Corinth
Paul may have written the letter to the Romans from Corinth.
Paul wanted to go to Spain to continue his missionary work (Romans 15:24–29).
Paul wrote to the church in Rome, the capital of the Roman Empire (Romans 1:7).

WHEN THE ACTION WAS

BC/AD — 25AD — 50AD — 75AD — 100AD

- Jesus was born
- Jesus began his ministry
- The church began soon after Jesus went to heaven
- Paul became a Christian
- Paul began his missionary work
- Paul wrote Romans
- Fire destroyed Rome
- Romans destroyed the Temple in Jerusalem

1 From Paul, a servant of Christ Jesus. God
called me to be an apostle[d] and chose me to
tell the Good News.[d]
2God promised this Good News long ago
through his prophets,[d] as it is written in the Holy
Scriptures.[d] 3-4The Good News is about God's
Son, Jesus Christ our Lord. As a man, he was born
from the family of David. But through the Spirit[d]
of holiness he was appointed to be God's Son with
great power by rising from the dead. 5Through
Christ, God gave me the special work of an apostle, which was to lead people of all nations to believe and obey. I do this work for him. 6And you
who are in Rome are also called to belong to Jesus
Christ.
7To all of you in Rome whom God loves and
has called to be his holy people:
Grace and peace to you from God our Father
and the Lord Jesus Christ.

A Prayer of Thanks

8First I want to say that I thank my God
through Jesus Christ for all of you, because people
everywhere in the world are talking about your
faith. 9God, whom I serve with my whole heart
by telling the Good News[d] about his Son, knows

GOD'S WILL

Mother Hale

"My husband and I had dreams of what we were going to do with our children," recalls Clara McBride Hale of her life in the early part of the 1900s. "We dreamed that they'd grow up and be what they want to be and have a good life."

But Clara's husband died when their children, Lorraine and Nathan, were five and six. And during that time, untrained women could only work domestic jobs, such as housecleaning. Clara had to support her children, but she didn't want to leave them alone all day while she went to work.

"So I decided to take in other people's children," Clara continues. "They were coming for five days and going home Saturday and Sunday. But they got so they didn't want to go home. They wanted to stay with me altogether. So the parents would give me an extra dollar, and that meant I kept them all the time."

What started as a "survival" business bloomed into a lifetime ministry for Clara, who came to be known by the children and their parents as "Mother Hale."

"I raised forty," Mother Hale recalls. "Every one of them went to college, every one of them graduated, and they have lovely jobs. I have singers, dancers, preachers, and things like that. No big names or anything, but they're happy."

In 1969, when Mother Hale was sixty-four years old, she decided to retire. She had raised forty children and felt ready for someone else to take over.

"Then my daughter sent me a girl with an addict baby. Inside of two months, I had twenty-two babies living in a five-room apartment. My decision to stop didn't mean anything. It seems as though God wanted them. He kept sending them, and he kept making a way for me to make it.

"I'm not going to retire again," Mother Hale says. "Until I die, I'm going to keep doing. My people need me. They need somebody that's not taking from them and is giving them something."

Mother Hale recognized that she had a God-given purpose for living, and she gave herself fully to that purpose. The apostle Paul also gave himself fully to God's purpose for his life, as he asserts in **Romans 1:1–7**. Read the passage to see what Paul says about God's purpose for your life.

- How is Mother Hale like Paul in this passage?
- According to this passage, why should we want to follow God's will?

CONSIDER . . .

- making a commitment to read the Book of Romans this month, to help you discover God's will for your life.
- writing out God's purpose for your life according to the passage. Then pray for God to make his purpose become reality in your life.

FOR MORE, SEE . . .

- Jeremiah 1:4–8
- Matthew 12:46–50
- 1 Thessalonians 4:3–8

that I always mention you 10every time I pray. I
pray that I will be allowed to come to you, and

> **SIDELIGHT:** The recipients of the letter to the Romans lived in the capital of the giant, powerful Roman Empire (Romans 1:7). The Romans built a 250,000-mile long highway system that would have circled the equator ten times if it had been one long road.

this will happen if God wants it. 11I want very
much to see you, to give you some spiritual gift
to make you strong. 12I mean that I want us to
help each other with the faith we have. Your faith
will help me, and my faith will help you. 13Broth-
ers and sisters,[n] I want you to know that I
planned many times to come to you, but this has
not been possible. I wanted to come so that I
could help you grow spiritually as I have helped
the other non-Jewish people.

14I have a duty to all people — Greeks and those
who are not Greeks, the wise and the foolish.
15That is why I want so much to preach the Good
News to you in Rome.

16I am proud of the Good News, because it is
the power God uses to save everyone who believes — to save the Jews first, and also to save
those who are not Jews. 17The Good News shows
how God makes people right with himself — that
it begins and ends with faith. As the Scripture[d]
says, "But those who are right with God will live
by trusting in him."[n]

All People Have Done Wrong

18God's anger is shown from heaven against all
the evil and wrong things people do. By their own
evil lives they hide the truth. 19God shows his anger because some knowledge of him has been
made clear to them. Yes, God has shown himself
to them. 20There are things about him that people
cannot see — his eternal power and all the things
that make him God. But since the beginning of
the world those things have been easy to understand by what God has made. So people have no
excuse for the bad things they do. 21They knew
God, but they did not give glory to God or thank
him. Their thinking became useless. Their foolish
minds were filled with darkness. 22They said they
were wise, but they became fools. 23They traded
the glory of God who lives forever for the worship
of idols made to look like earthly people, birds,
animals, and snakes.

24Because they did these things, God left them
and let them go their sinful way, wanting only to
do evil. As a result, they became full of sexual sin,
using their bodies wrongly with each other.
25They traded the truth of God for a lie. They worshiped and served what had been created instead
of the God who created those things, who should
be praised forever. Amen.

26Because people did those things, God left
them and let them do the shameful things they
wanted to do. Women stopped having natural sex
and started having sex with other women. 27In
the same way, men stopped having natural sex
and began wanting each other. Men did shameful
things with other men, and in their bodies they
received the punishment for those wrongs.

28People did not think it was important to have
a true knowledge of God. So God left them and
allowed them to have their own worthless thinking and to do things they should not do. 29They
are filled with every kind of sin, evil, selfishness,
and hatred. They are full of jealousy, murder,
fighting, lying, and thinking the worst about each
other. They gossip 30and say evil things about
each other. They hate God. They are rude and
conceited and brag about themselves. They in-
vent ways of doing evil. They do not obey their
parents. 31They are foolish, they do not keep their
promises, and they show no kindness or mercy to
others. 32They know God's law says that those
who live like this should die. But they themselves
not only continue to do these evil things, they
applaud others who do them.

You People Also Are Sinful

2 If you think you can judge others, you are
wrong. When you judge them, you are really
judging yourself guilty, because you do the same
things they do. 2God judges those who do wrong
things, and we know that his judging is right.
3You judge those who do wrong, but you do
wrong yourselves. Do you think you will be able
to escape the judgment of God? 4He has been very
kind and patient, waiting for you to change, but
you think nothing of his kindness. Perhaps you do
not understand that God is kind to you so you will
change your hearts and lives. 5But you are stubborn and refuse to change, so you are making
your own punishment even greater on the day he
shows his anger. On that day everyone will see
God's right judgments. 6God will reward or punish every person for what that person has done.
7Some people, by always continuing to do good,
live for God's glory, for honor, and for life that has
no end. God will give them life forever. 8But other

Brothers and sisters Although the Greek text says "Brothers" here and throughout this book, Paul's words were meant for the entire church, including men and women.
"But those . . . him." Quotation from Habakkuk 2:4.

people are selfish. They refuse to follow truth and,
instead, follow evil. God will give them his punishment and anger. 9He will give trouble and suffering to everyone who does evil—to the Jews
first and also to those who are not Jews. 10But he
will give glory, honor, and peace to everyone who
does good—to the Jews first and also to those
who are not Jews. 11For God judges all people in
the same way.

12People who do not have the law and who are
sinners will be lost, although they do not have the
law. And, in the same way, those who have the
law and are sinners will be judged by the law.
13Hearing the law does not make people right
with God. It is those who obey the law who will
be right with him. 14(Those who are not Jews do
not have the law, but when they freely do what
the law commands, they are the law for themselves. This is true even though they do not have
the law. 15They show that in their hearts they
know what is right and wrong, just as the law
commands. And they show this by their consciences. Sometimes their thoughts tell them they
did wrong, and sometimes their thoughts tell
them they did right.) 16All these things will happen on the day when God, through Christ Jesus,
will judge people's secret thoughts. The Good
News[d] that I preach says this.

The Jews and the Law

17What about you? You call yourself a Jew. You
trust in the law of Moses and brag that you are
close to God. 18You know what he wants you to
do and what is important, because you have
learned the law. 19You think you are a guide for
the blind and a light for those who are in darkness. 20You think you can show foolish people
what is right and teach those who know nothing.
You have the law; so you think you know everything and have all truth. 21You teach others, so
why don't you teach yourself? You tell others not
to steal, but you steal. 22You say that others must
not take part in adultery,[d] but you are guilty of
that sin. You hate idols, but you steal from temples. 23You brag about having God's law, but you
bring shame to God by breaking his law, 24just as
the Scriptures[d] say: "Those who are not Jews
speak against God's name because of you."[n]

25If you follow the law, your circumcision[d] has
meaning. But if you break the law, it is as if you
were never circumcised. 26People who are not
Jews are not circumcised, but if they do what the
law says, it is as if they were circumcised. 27You
Jews have the written law and circumcision, but
you break the law. So those who are not circumcised in their bodies, but still obey the law, will
show that you are guilty. 28They can do this because a person is not a true Jew if he is only a Jew
in his physical body; true circumcision is not only
on the outside of the body. 29A person is a Jew
only if he is a Jew inside; true circumcision is
done in the heart by the Spirit,[d] not by the written
law. Such a person gets praise from God rather
than from people.

3 So, do Jews have anything that other people
do not have? Is there anything special about
being circumcised? 2Yes, of course, there is in every way. The most important thing is this: God
trusted the Jews with his teachings. 3If some Jews
were not faithful to him, will that stop God from
doing what he promised? 4No! God will continue
to be true even when every person is false. As the
Scriptures[d] say:

"So you will be shown to be right when you
speak,
and you will win your case." *Psalm 51:4*

5When we do wrong, that shows more clearly
that God is right. So can we say that God is wrong
to punish us? (I am talking as people might talk.)
6No! If God could not punish us, he could not
judge the world.

7A person might say, "When I lie, it really gives
him glory, because my lie shows God's truth. So
why am I judged a sinner?" 8It would be the same
to say, "We should do evil so that good will
come." Some people find fault with us and say we
teach this, but they are wrong and deserve the
punishment they will receive.

All People Are Guilty

9So are we Jews better than others? No! We
have already said that Jews and those who are not
Jews are all guilty of sin. 10As the Scriptures[d] say:

"There is no one who always does what is
right,
not even one.
11 There is no one who understands.
There is no one who looks to God for help.
12All have turned away.
Together, everyone has become useless.
There is no one who does anything good;
there is not even one." *Psalm 14:1-3*
13"Their throats are like open graves;
they use their tongues for telling lies." *Psalm 5:9*
"Their words are like snake poison." *Psalm 140:3*
14 "Their mouths are full of cursing and hate." *Psalm 10:7*
15"They are always ready to kill people.
16 Everywhere they go they cause ruin and
misery.
17They don't know how to live in peace." *Isaiah 59:7-8*
18 "They have no fear of God." *Psalm 36:1*

[n] **"Those . . . you."** Quotation from Isaiah 52:5; Ezekiel 36:20.

[19]We know that the law's commands are for
those who have the law. This stops all excuses
and brings the whole world under God's judgment, [20]because no one can be made right with
God by following the law. The law only shows us
our sin.

How God Makes People Right

[21]But God has a way to make people right with
him without the law, and he has now shown us
that way which the law and the prophets[d] told us
about. [22]God makes people right with himself
through their faith in Jesus Christ. This is true for
all who believe in Christ, because all people are
the same: [23]All have sinned and are not good
enough for God's glory, [24]and all need to be made
right with God by his grace, which is a free gift.
They need to be made free from sin through Jesus
Christ. [25]God gave him as a way to forgive sin
through faith in the blood of Jesus' death. This
showed that God always does what is right and
fair, as in the past when he was patient and did
not punish people for their sins. [26]And God gave
Jesus to show today that he does what is right.
God did this so he could judge rightly and so he
could make right any person who has faith in
Jesus.

[27]So do we have a reason to brag about ourselves? No! And why not? It is the way of faith
that stops all bragging, not the way of trying to
obey the law. [28]A person is made right with God
through faith, not through obeying the law. [29]Is
God only the God of the Jews? Is he not also the
God of those who are not Jews? [30]Of course he is,
because there is only one God. He will make Jews
right with him by their faith, and he will also
make those who are not Jews right with him
through their faith. [31]So do we destroy the law by
following the way of faith? No! Faith causes us to
be what the law truly wants.

The Example of Abraham

4 So what can we say that Abraham,[n] the father of our people, learned about faith? [2]If

Abraham Most respected ancestor of the Jews. Every Jew hoped to see Abraham.

FORGIVENESS

Only a Car

Uncle Carl let Derek borrow his new, red convertible for the prom. It was less than two weeks old.

The magical night ended much too early for Derek, about 3 A.M., when he dropped off his date at her house and started the long drive across town to home. The next thing he knew, he was waking up, skidding madly across the deserted suburban road, scraping the side of the car against a guardrail before he could come to a stop.

He drove home, parked the car against the curb, and sat on the front porch, waiting for morning to come. His stomach was in a knot. He didn't even try to sleep.

At 8 A.M., Derek stood next to his uncle as he silently examined the foot-wide scar that now marred the fender and door of his new car. Uncle Carl's breathing was slow and measured. The silence seemed to go on forever.

How could Derek ever make this up to him? How could he pay for the damage or heal the hurt he saw in his face?

Finally, the older man placed his hand on Derek's shoulder and gave it a reassuring squeeze. He shrugged, smiled a lopsided smile, and said, "It's only a car."

At that moment, Derek knew something of the kind of forgiveness Paul was talking about when he wrote **Romans 3:21–28**.

- How is Uncle Carl's act of forgiveness like the forgiveness Paul talks about in this passage?
- According to the passage, how do we receive God's forgiveness?

CONSIDER . . .

- writing about a way someone has hurt you recently and then tearing up the paper and forgiving the hurt.
- talking to a friend you've hurt and asking for forgiveness.

FOR MORE, SEE . . .

- Psalm 103:10–13
- Luke 6:27–36
- Hebrews 8:10–13

Abraham was made right by the things he did, he
had a reason to brag. But this is not God's view,
3because the Scripture[d] says, "Abraham believed
God, and God accepted Abraham's faith, and that
faith made him right with God."[n]
4When people work, their pay is not given as
a gift, but as something earned. 5But people cannot do any work that will make them right with
God. So they must trust in him, who makes even
evil people right in his sight. Then God accepts
their faith, and that makes them right with him.
6David said the same thing. He said that people
are truly blessed when God, without paying attention to good deeds, makes people right with himself.

7"Happy are they
whose sins are forgiven,
whose wrongs are pardoned.
8Happy is the person
whom the Lord does not consider guilty."
Psalm 32:1-2

9Is this blessing only for those who are circum-

"Abraham . . . God." Quotation from Genesis 15:6.

FAITH

Free Approval

Ed Marx really liked Julie Hempstead. In fact, he was totally crazy about her.

Julie was funny, smart, beautiful—everything Ed wanted in a girl. For weeks, Ed watched Julie as she went from class to class. He watched her while she ate lunch. He watched her as she walked home from school.

Finally, after weeks of planning, he got up the nerve to ask her out.

"Hi, Ed. What's up?" Julie asked with that smile Ed loved so much.

"Um, I was wondering . . ." he said, clearing his throat. "I was wondering if you'd like to go do something Friday night." Ed couldn't believe his heart could pound so hard.

"Sure, I'd love to," Julie responded without missing a beat.

That was the first of many evenings together for the new couple. Julie really liked Ed. He was funny and sensitive. And, of course, Ed liked Julie, but he couldn't believe she could be interested in him.

As they continued to date, Ed kept doing things for Julie to keep her interested. He bought her gifts. He offered to run errands for her. One day, he even offered her his car so she wouldn't have to walk to school.

"Ed, I don't want your car," Julie said.

"It's okay, really," Ed assured her. "I want you to have it."

"No, Ed, you don't understand." Julie took a deep breath. "You don't need to try so hard. I already like you. You really don't need to do anything to win my love. So just relax, okay? You're starting to drive me crazy."

Ed felt embarrassed. "It's hard to believe, that's all," he said.

"Well, believe it," Julie said, grinning, and she kissed him.

Ed had a hard time believing Julie could love him unless he did things to earn her affection. **Romans 4:1–12** tells a similar story about Abraham, who discovered that God's favor is also based on believing. Read the passage to see why we can't earn God's approval through our actions.

- How does Ed's response to Julie differ from Abraham's response to God in the passage?
- According to the passage, what does God require for you to have a relationship with him?

CONSIDER . . .

- thinking of ways you might try to earn God's love and then asking God to help you accept his love by faith.
- writing out how you think God sees you, and having your youth leader do the same.
- Compare the two descriptions, and ask God to increase your faith to believe the truth about how he sees you.

FOR MORE, SEE . . .

- Genesis 15:1–6
- Galatians 3:6–27
- Ephesians 2:8–9

cised[d] or also for those who are not circumcised? We have already said that God accepted Abraham's faith and that faith made him right with God. 10So how did this happen? Did God accept Abraham before or after he was circumcised? It was before his circumcision. 11Abraham was circumcised to show that he was right with God through faith before he was circumcised. So Abraham is the father of all those who believe but are not circumcised; he is the father of all believers who are accepted as being right with God. 12And Abraham is also the father of those who have been circumcised and who live following the faith that our father Abraham had before he was circumcised.

God Keeps His Promise

13Abraham[n] and his descendants[d] received the promise that they would get the whole world. He did not receive that promise through the law, but through being right with God by his faith. 14If people could receive what God promised by following the law, then faith is worthless. And God's promise to Abraham is worthless, 15because the law can only bring God's anger. But if there is no law, there is nothing to disobey.

16So people receive God's promise by having faith. This happens so the promise can be a free gift. Then all of Abraham's children can have that promise. It is not only for those who live under the law of Moses but for anyone who lives with faith like that of Abraham, who is the father of us all. 17As it is written in the Scriptures:[d] "I am making you a father of many nations."[n] This is true before God, the God Abraham believed, the God who gives life to the dead and who creates something out of nothing.

18There was no hope that Abraham would have children. But Abraham believed God and continued hoping, and so he became the father of many nations. As God told him, "Your descendants also will be too many to count."[n] 19Abraham was almost a hundred years old, much past the age for having children, and Sarah could not have children. Abraham thought about all this, but his faith in God did not become weak. 20He never doubted that God would keep his promise, and he never stopped believing. He grew stronger in his faith and gave praise to God. 21Abraham felt sure that God was able to do what he had promised. 22So, "God accepted Abraham's faith, and that faith made him right with God."[n] 23Those words ("God accepted Abraham's faith") were written not only for Abraham 24but also for us. God will accept us also because we believe in the One who raised Jesus our Lord from the dead. 25Jesus was given to die for our sins, and he was raised from the dead to make us right with God.

Right with God

5 Since we have been made right with God by our faith, we have peace with God. This happened through our Lord Jesus Christ, 2who has brought us into that blessing of God's grace that we now enjoy. And we are happy because of the hope we have of sharing God's glory. 3We also have joy with our troubles, because we know that these troubles produce patience. 4And patience produces character, and character produces hope. 5And this hope will never disappoint us, because God has poured out his love to fill our hearts. He gave us his love through the Holy Spirit,[d] whom God has given to us.

6When we were unable to help ourselves, at the moment of our need, Christ died for us, although we were living against God. 7Very few people will die to save the life of someone else. Although perhaps for a good person someone might possibly die. 8But God shows his great love for us in this way: Christ died for us while we were still sinners.

9So through Christ we will surely be saved from God's anger, because we have been made right with God by the blood of Christ's death. 10While we were God's enemies, he made friends with us through the death of his Son. Surely, now that we are his friends, he will save us through his Son's life. 11And not only that, but now we are also very happy in God through our Lord Jesus Christ. Through him we are now God's friends again.

Adam and Christ Compared

12Sin came into the world because of what one man did, and with sin came death. This is why everyone must die—because everyone sinned. 13Sin was in the world before the law of Moses, but sin is not counted against us as breaking a command when there is no law. 14But from the time of Adam to the time of Moses, everyone had to die, even those who had not sinned by breaking a command, as Adam had.

Adam was like the One who was coming in the future. 15But God's free gift is not like Adam's sin. Many people died because of the sin of that one man. But the grace from God was much greater;

Abraham Most respected ancestor of the Jews. Every Jew hoped to see Abraham.
"I . . . nations." Quotation from Genesis 17:5.
"Your . . . count." Quotation from Genesis 15:5.
"God . . . God." Quotation from Genesis 15:6.

many people received God's gift of life by the
grace of the one man, Jesus Christ. 16After Adam
sinned once, he was judged guilty. But the gift of
God is different. God's free gift came after many
sins, and it makes people right with God. 17One
man sinned, and so death ruled all people because
of that one man. But now those people who accept God's full grace and the great gift of being
made right with him will surely have true life and
rule through the one man, Jesus Christ.

18So as one sin of Adam brought the punishment of death to all people, one good act that
Christ did makes all people right with God. And
that brings true life for all. 19One man disobeyed
God, and many became sinners. In the same way,
one man obeyed God, and many will be made
right. 20The law came to make sin worse. But
when sin grew worse, God's grace increased.
21Sin once used death to rule us, but God gave
people more of his grace so that grace could rule
by making people right with him. And this brings
life forever through Jesus Christ our Lord.

Dead to Sin but Alive in Christ

6 So do you think we should continue sinning
so that God will give us even more grace?

> **SIDELIGHT:** Adam—the man in the Garden of Eden (Genesis 1–4)—seems to get blamed for more than his share of sin in Romans 5:12–21. But don't feel too sorry for him. Paul uses Adam to represent all people. That's not surprising when you know that "adam" means "human."

2No! We died to our old sinful lives, so how can
we continue living with sin? 3Did you forget that
all of us became part of Christ when we were
baptized? We shared his death in our baptism.
4When we were baptized, we were buried with
Christ and shared his death. So, just as Christ was

FRIENDS

What Are Friends For?

Sometimes Lisa Kretch got frustrated with her friends. It seemed like she was constantly bailing them out of something.

Take Coreen Mills for instance. She was flunking algebra. And Nancy Olton had just broken up with her boyfriend and was depressed all the time. Luann Winger was gaining weight like crazy, and all she did was complain about it and eat.

And as if that weren't enough, last week all three of these friends had gone to a party and had drunk several beers. Lisa had to drive them home so they wouldn't have a wreck.

Sometimes it seemed like Lisa's friends were trying to cause her problems. It was all getting to be too much. Too much concern, too much pain.

Maybe she should just find new friends, she thought. It would sure make her life easier. But . . .

"Hi, Lisa!" Coreen said, setting her tray down beside Lisa's at the cafeteria table. "Boy, this algebra is a bear. Can you help me with a couple of things?"

This was it. The true test. Was Lisa strong enough? She gathered her courage, took a deep breath, paused, and said, "Sure, Coreen. What are friends for?" And she meant it.

Lisa learned that friendship means commitment, even when friends disappoint you. **Romans 5:1–19** calls God our friend. Read the passage to discover how committed he is to us.

- How is Lisa's friendship with her friends like God's friendship with us in Jesus Christ?
- How can you model your friendship with God in human friendships?

CONSIDER . . .

- writing down the names of three friends and praying for them each day this week.
- writing a card, buying a flower, or doing a favor for a friend, just to say I'm committed to you.

FOR MORE, SEE . . .

- Job 2:11–13
- Proverbs 17:17
- John 15:13–16

raised from the dead by the wonderful power of
the Father, we also can live a new life.
[5]Christ died, and we have been joined with him
by dying too. So we will also be joined with
him by rising from the dead as he did. [6]We know
that our old life died with Christ on the cross
so that our sinful selves would have no power
over us and we would not be slaves to sin. [7]Any-
one who has died is made free from sin's control.
[8]If we died with Christ, we know we will also
live with him. [9]Christ was raised from the dead,
and we know that he cannot die again. Death has
no power over him now. [10]Yes, when Christ died,
he died to defeat the power of sin one time—
enough for all time. He now has a new life, and
his new life is with God. [11]In the same way, you
should see yourselves as being dead to the power
of sin and alive with God through Christ Jesus.
[12]So, do not let sin control your life here on
earth so that you do what your sinful self wants
to do. [13]Do not offer the parts of your body to
serve sin, as things to be used in doing evil. Instead, offer yourselves to God as people who have
died and now live. Offer the parts of your body to
God to be used in doing good. [14]Sin will not be
your master, because you are not under law but
under God's grace.

Be Slaves of Righteousness

[15]So what should we do? Should we sin because we are under grace and not under law? No!
[16]Surely you know that when you give yourselves

FREEDOM

A Slave to Freedom

Tom Stipe wouldn't have been late for Biology 101 if he hadn't fallen. And he wouldn't have fallen if he hadn't been running. And he wouldn't have been running if he had gotten out of bed on time.

But he didn't get out of bed on time. He had forgotten to set his alarm. And his roommate—a guy he could hardly stand—hadn't bothered to wake him up, even though they were in the same class.

College wasn't everything Tom had hoped it would be.

It wasn't the classes. They were hard, sure, but Tom was no stranger to the books. And it wasn't the basketball practice. Practice was always rough, but you expected that and planned for it. It wasn't even Jack, the bothersome roommate. Tom had roomed with his brother at home, and they had rarely gotten along for more than a few minutes at a time.

It was the freedom, Tom realized with a start. Or, more to the point, it was the responsibility that came with the freedom. That was the part Tom disliked.

In high school, Tom had resented the way everyone controlled his time. His mother woke him in the morning. His teachers prodded him to work during the day and sent work home with him at night. Tom longed to be free.

But now that he was in college, Tom discovered that the freedom he had longed for came with one looming catch: responsibility. He was free to do what he wanted, but he also had to live with the consequences of his actions.

Tom learned that freedom and responsibility always come together. **Romans 6:1–12** talks about freedom too, and the responsibility that comes with it.

- How is Tom's struggle with freedom similar to the struggle for freedom Paul writes about in the passage?
- What does the passage say we need to do to gain freedom?

CONSIDER . . .

- drawing a line down the center of a page. On the left side, list all the freedoms you want to gain. On the right, list all the responsibilities that will come with those freedoms. With a parent, design a plan for helping you gain those freedoms responsibly.
- evaluating how you use your free time to see if you use it responsibly. If not, start using some of your time to do something on a regular basis to serve others.

FOR MORE, SEE . . .

- Psalm 119:41–48
- John 8:31–32, 34–36
- 1 Peter 2:16

like slaves to obey someone, then you are really
slaves of that person. The person you obey is your
master. You can follow sin, which brings spiritual
death, or you can obey God, which makes you
right with him. 17In the past you were slaves to
sin — sin controlled you. But thank God, you fully
obeyed the things that you were taught. 18You
were made free from sin, and now you are slaves
to goodness. 19I use this example because this is
hard for you to understand. In the past you offered the parts of your body to be slaves to sin and
evil; you lived only for evil. In the same way now
you must give yourselves to be slaves of goodness.
Then you will live only for God.

20In the past you were slaves to sin, and goodness did not control you. 21You did evil things,
and now you are ashamed of them. Those things
only bring death. 22But now you are free from sin
and have become slaves of God. This brings you
a life that is only for God, and this gives you life
forever. 23When people sin, they earn what sin
pays — death. But God gives us a free gift — life
forever in Christ Jesus our Lord.

An Example from Marriage

7 Brothers and sisters, all of you understand
the law of Moses. So surely you know that
the law rules over people only while they are
alive. 2For example, a woman must stay married
to her husband as long as he is alive. But if her
husband dies, she is free from the law of marriage.
3But if she marries another man while her husband is still alive, the law says she is guilty of adultery.[d] But if her husband dies, she is free from the
law of marriage. Then if she marries another man,
she is not guilty of adultery.

4In the same way, my brothers and sisters, your
old selves died, and you became free from the law
through the body of Christ. This happened so that
you might belong to someone else — the One who
was raised from the dead — and so that we might
be used in service to God. 5In the past, we were
ruled by our sinful selves. The law made us want
to do sinful things that controlled our bodies, so
the things we did were bringing us death. 6In the
past, the law held us like prisoners, but our old
selves died, and we were made free from the law.
So now we serve God in a new way with the
Spirit,[d] and not in the old way with written rules.

Our Fight Against Sin

7You might think I am saying that sin and the
law are the same thing. That is not true. But the
law was the only way I could learn what sin
meant. I would never have known what it means
to want to take something belonging to someone
else if the law had not said, "You must not want
to take your neighbor's things."[n] 8And sin found
a way to use that command and cause me to want
all kinds of things I should not want. But without
the law, sin has no power. 9I was alive before I
knew the law. But when the law's command
came to me, then sin began to live, 10and I died.
The command was meant to bring life, but for me
it brought death. 11Sin found a way to fool me by
using the command to make me die.

12So the law is holy, and the command is holy
and right and good. 13Does this mean that something that is good brought death to me? No! Sin
used something that is good to bring death to me.
This happened so that I could see what sin is
really like; the command was used to show that
sin is very evil.

The War Within Us

14We know that the law is spiritual, but I am
not spiritual since sin rules me as if I were its
slave. 15I do not understand the things I do. I do
not do what I want to do, and I do the things I
hate. 16And if I do not want to do the hated things
I do, that means I agree that the law is good. 17But
I am not really the one who is doing these hated
things; it is sin living in me that does them. 18Yes,
I know that nothing good lives in me — I mean
nothing good lives in the part of me that is earthly
and sinful. I want to do the things that are good,
but I do not do them. 19I do not do the good
things I want to do, but I do the bad things I do
not want to do. 20So if I do things I do not want
to do, then I am not the one doing them. It is sin
living in me that does those things.

21So I have learned this rule: When I want to
do good, evil is there with me. 22In my mind, I am
happy with God's law. 23But I see another law
working in my body, which makes war against
the law that my mind accepts. That other law
working in my body is the law of sin, and it makes
me its prisoner. 24What a miserable man I am!
Who will save me from this body that brings me
death? 25I thank God for saving me through Jesus
Christ our Lord!

So in my mind I am a slave to God's law, but
in my sinful self I am a slave to the law of sin.

Be Ruled by the Spirit

8 So now, those who are in Christ Jesus are
not judged guilty. 2Through Christ Jesus the
law of the Spirit[d] that brings life made me free
from the law that brings sin and death. 3The law
was without power, because the law was made
weak by our sinful selves. But God did what the
law could not do. He sent his own Son to earth
with the same human life that others use for sin.
By sending his Son to be an offering to pay for sin,

"You . . . things." Quotation from Exodus 20:17.

God used a human life to destroy sin. 4He did this
so that we could be the kind of people the law
correctly wants us to be. Now we do not live following our sinful selves, but we live following the
Spirit.
5Those who live following their sinful selves
think only about things that their sinful selves want.
But those who live following the Spirit are
thinking about the things the Spirit wants them to
do. 6If people's thinking is controlled by the sinful
self, there is death. But if their thinking is controlled by the Spirit, there is life and peace. 7When
people's thinking is controlled by the sinful self,
they are against God, because they refuse to obey
God's law and really are not even able to
obey God's law. 8Those people who are ruled by
their sinful selves cannot please God.
9But you are not ruled by your sinful selves.
You are ruled by the Spirit, if that Spirit of God
really lives in you. But the person who does not
have the Spirit of Christ does not belong to Christ.
10Your body will always be dead because of sin.

DRUGS AND ALCOHOL

Not Alone . . .

Seven years, five months, three days. That's how long Shelly Everett had been sober. Counting today. And she didn't mind talking about it to her fellow Alcoholics Anonymous (AA) members. It helped her stick with recovery.

"I started drinking in high school," she explained. "But I didn't start abusing it until I was in college. By the time I was out of school and in a career position, I was an alcoholic."

Shelly went on to tell how a marriage and the addition of two children didn't change her drinking habits much. "I managed to keep up with my responsibilities, both at home and at work," she said. "As long as I did that, I convinced myself that I had it under control."

But then things changed. A messy divorce. Trouble at work. And a daughter who almost died from rheumatic fever.

"I began to drink more often—for comfort, and sometimes, to forget. Eventually, events in my life began to blur together. I was never sober.

"And the worse I felt about myself the more I drank. Finally, I just wanted to die. So I tried to drink myself to death. Five days later I woke up in a hospital room attached to a bunch of machines. The doctors say I didn't even know who I was. I lay there and cried. I couldn't eat. I couldn't sleep. I was a failure. I couldn't even kill myself right." Shelly pulled a tissue from the box beside her. The AA leader motioned her to continue.

"Then," she went on, "the hospital chaplain walked in, and there's this little dumpy woman with him. They both just sit down by my bed. And this little dumpy woman asked, 'You wanna quit drinking?' "

Now Shelly's tears came in full flood. "I just bawled like a baby. I wanted to quit, but I didn't know how! Then she says, 'You don't have to do it alone. You've got me and Reverend Benjamin here and a whole flock of folks willing to help. And you've got God, too, honey. Don't forget about God.' "

Shelly blew her nose on the tissue and looked around at the faces of her friends. "For the first time I realized I wasn't alone. And I haven't had a drink since that day—all because you, and God, are keeping me sober."

Shelly learned she wasn't alone in her struggle. And God made a difference in her life. The apostle Paul made a similar discovery. Read about it in **Romans 7:14–25**.

- How is Shelly's addiction like the "battle" Paul describes in this passage?
- What are ways God shows that he is with you when you're pressured to use alcohol or drugs?

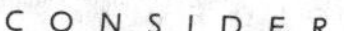

CONSIDER . . .

- encouraging a friend who is dealing with issues like Shelly's to seek professional help.
- finding an appropriate support group in your community if you struggle with a drinking or drug problem. Your pastor or a counselor can help you.

FOR MORE, SEE . . .

- Proverbs 23:29–32
- Isaiah 5:11–12
- Luke 21:34–36

But if Christ is in you, then the Spirit gives you
life, because Christ made you right with God.
[11]God raised Jesus from the dead, and if God's
Spirit is living in you, he will also give life to your
bodies that die. God is the One who raised Christ
from the dead, and he will give life through his
Spirit that lives in you.
[12]So, my brothers and sisters, we must not be
ruled by our sinful selves or live the way our sinful
selves want. [13]If you use your lives to do the
wrong things your sinful selves want, you will die
spiritually. But if you use the Spirit's help to stop
doing the wrong things you do with your body,
you will have true life.
[14]The true children of God are those who let
God's Spirit lead them. [15]The Spirit we received
does not make us slaves again to fear; it makes us
children of God. With that Spirit we cry out, "Father."[n] [16]And the Spirit himself joins with our
spirits to say we are God's children. [17]If we are
God's children, we will receive blessings from
God together with Christ. But we must suffer as
Christ suffered so that we will have glory as Christ
has glory.

"Father" Literally, "Abba, Father." Jewish children called their fathers "Abba."

SPIRITUAL GROWTH

Living for God

To buy or not to buy. That was the question.

Carrie Munson was the only one in her class who didn't have a school jacket. Well, nearly the only one. Most of the kids had them—navy blue and white, with a hood that rolled up into the zippered collar when you didn't want it over your head.

And Cline's Sporting Goods had a special offer this weekend. They would put the school name on the back of the coat and your initials on the front—no charge. But only if you bought it this weekend.

"Let's see," Carrie thought aloud. "That's a savings of . . . $8 for the school name and $3 for my initials . . . that's $11 savings!"

True, it wasn't a fortune, but with Carrie's meager allowance, every penny counted.

There was just one problem. Carrie had pledged to give $13 each month to the church to help fund the new homeless shelter. And if she bought the jacket, she would have only $11 left.

That's $2 short, Carrie thought. And the pledge is due this Sunday.

"Ugh!" Carrie grunted in frustration. Why had she made such a big pledge? Thirteen dollars! That was almost a fourth of her income! And besides, the jacket was on sale now. If Carrie didn't buy it this weekend, it would cost her $11 dollars more next week, and she wouldn't have enough money then—especially if she paid her pledge.

"What should I do?" Carrie asked, looking at the ceiling of the sporting goods store. Slowly, her eyebrows unfurled, her tense shoulders relaxed, and she walked out of the store—away from the jacket she wanted.

When Carrie got home, she went to her bedroom, pulled $13 out of her purse, and put it in the Bible next to her bed.

"If you want me to have the jacket, you'll provide a way," she prayed. "But I don't want to break my promise to you just to get what I want."

Carrie discovered it's not always easy to do what's right, especially when our own desires get in the way. **Romans 8:6–17** talks about why spiritual growth is sometimes hard.

- How is the conflict described in this passage like what happened to Carrie?
- According to this passage, what should you do the next time your own desires conflict with God's?

CONSIDER . . .

- asking God's forgiveness for times you have chosen your desires over his.
- listing all the ways your desires might conflict with God's and asking God to help you grow through following his desires for your life.

FOR MORE, SEE . . .

- Psalm 1:1–3
- Colossians 3:1–10
- Hebrews 12:1–13

Our Future Glory

18The sufferings we have now are nothing compared to the great glory that will be shown to us.
19Everything God made is waiting with excitement for God to show his children's glory completely. 20Everything God made was changed to
become useless, not by its own wish but because
God wanted it and because all along there was
this hope: 21that everything God made would be
set free from ruin to have the freedom and glory
that belong to God's children.
22We know that everything God made has
been waiting until now in pain, like a woman
ready to give birth. 23Not only the world, but we
also have been waiting with pain inside us. We
have the Spirit[d] as the first part of God's promise.
So we are waiting for God to finish making us his
own children, which means our bodies will be
made free. 24We were saved, and we have this
hope. If we see what we are waiting for, that is
not really hope. People do not hope for something
they already have. 25But we are hoping for something we do not have yet, and we are waiting for
it patiently.
26Also, the Spirit helps us with our weakness.
We do not know how to pray as we should. But
the Spirit himself speaks to God for us, even begs
God for us with deep feelings that words cannot
explain. 27God can see what is in people's hearts.
And he knows what is in the mind of the Spirit,
because the Spirit speaks to God for his people in
the way God wants.
28We know that in everything God works for
the good of those who love him. They are the

PATIENCE

Looking Back

Pierce Richman had been a Christian about six months before the problems started.

What problems? "Well, I lost my job," Pierce recalls. "Then the transmission on my car went out, and I had no money to repair it. But that wasn't the real problem. My girlfriend broke up with me. I really wanted to marry this girl, but she said I wasn't what she wanted in a husband. That really hurt."

About that time Pierce's old desires began to well up. Before he had become a Christian at age eighteen, he had lived a loose lifestyle, filled with drinking and taking drugs and sleeping with girlfriends.

"I came to Christ to get away from all that," he recalls. "But when all these problems started, I began to feel really insecure. It was all I could do not to go out and get drunk or call up one of my old girlfriends. I felt gross inside. I began to wonder whether I was really a Christian."

But Pierce didn't go back to his old lifestyle. Even though he didn't understand why all these things were happening to him, he knew God was in control. So he waited.

"Things didn't get better right away," Pierce says, "but I knew I had made the right decision. And that helped me believe even more that, if I was patient, God would come through for me. And he did!"

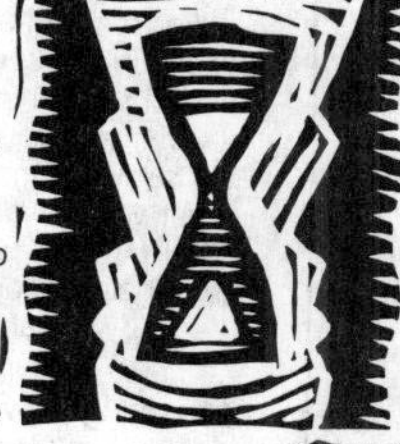

Pierce and his girlfriend got back together, and he got a new job—better than the other one. Now Pierce knows the value of obeying God even when you don't know what God is doing.

Pierce learned that becoming like Christ takes patience. Paul talked about how all creation is waiting patiently for us to become like Christ. Read why in **Romans 8:22–30.**

- How does Pierce demonstrate the patience the passage describes?
- According to the passage, what is God's ultimate purpose for you? Why do we need patience to wait for his purpose to be fulfilled?

CONSIDER . . .

- dreaming about the kind of person you want to be ten years from now. Then ask God to give you patience to let him make you into the person he wants you to be.
- working on a project that takes a long time to finish, such as a quilt or a model ship. Use the experience to learn more about patience.

FOR MORE, SEE . . .

- Lamentations 3:25–26
- Hebrews 11:8–16
- James 5:7–11

people he called, because that was his plan. 29God
knew them before he made the world, and he
decided that they would be like his Son so that
Jesus would be the firstborn[n] of many brothers.
30God planned for them to be like his Son; and
those he planned to be like his Son, he also called;
and those he called, he also made right with
him; and those he made right, he also glorified.

God's Love in Christ Jesus

31So what should we say about this? If God is
with us, no one can defeat us. 32He did not spare
his own Son but gave him for us all. So with Jesus,
God will surely give us all things. 33Who can accuse the people God has chosen? No one, because
God is the One who makes them right. 34Who can
say God's people are guilty? No one, because
Christ Jesus died, but he was also raised from the
dead, and now he is on God's right side, begging God for us. 35Can anything separate us from
the love Christ has for us? Can troubles or problems or sufferings or hunger or nakedness or
danger or violent death? 36As it is written in the
Scriptures:[d]

"For you we are in danger of death all the
time.

firstborn Here this probably means that Christ was the first in God's family to share God's glory.

WORRYING

Let It Rain!

When Ray Jordon was a teenager, his friend Scott Wright and he would help bale hay each summer for seventy-year-old Bailey Tag, a rancher who lived near their town. Mr. Tag baled the hay onto the ground. Then he would drive the tractor, and Ray would walk behind it, picking up bales and throwing them up to Scott on the wagon, where he would stack them.

It was hot, miserable, sticky, dirty work. But the pay was good.

One day as the three ate their lunches under a big oak tree, the sky began to darken in the west and the sound of thunder rolled toward them.

Mr. Tag sat, eating his apple and looking at the clouds. "Beautiful, aren't they?" he remarked. "Rain'll cool things off a might, I 'spect."

"What about the hay?" Scott asked.

Mr. Tag looked at his apple. "Let me finish this, and we'll get the hay to the barn. We've got time."

Scott looked at Ray, and they both looked out over the field where the other bales waited to be picked up.

"Mr. Tag," said Ray, "those clouds look like they're moving this way."

He looked at them, paused, then nodded. "Maybe."

Ray swept the field with his arm. "But, what about the other bales? I mean, what if the rain is moving this way? What'll we do?"

Mr. Tag looked at Ray, smiled around a bite of his apple and winked. "Why, we'll let it rain," he said. "What else can we do?"

So that's what they did. They let it rain. The bales got wet, and they had to dry in the sun for a few days before they could be picked up. But they got picked up. What else could have been done?

After all, worrying wouldn't stop the rain. **Romans 8:31–39** says there are some things we never have to worry about. Read the passage to find out what we can be sure of.

- How does worrying about the hay differ from worrying about God's love?
- What assurance do these verses offer you when you worry about losing your special relationship with God?

C O N S I D E R . . .

- writing down all the things you worry about, then crossing out the ones you can't do anything about. Create a plan for doing something about the others.
- reading a fun novel, going camping, or doing something similar—to help you let go of your worries and trust God.

F O R M O R E , S E E . . .

- Psalm 91
- Psalm 131
- Matthew 6:25–34

People think we are worth no more than
sheep to be killed." *Psalm 44:22*

37But in all these things we have full victory
through God who showed his love for us. 38Yes,
I am sure that neither death, nor life, nor angels,
nor ruling spirits, nothing now, nothing in the future, no powers, 39nothing above us, nothing below us, nor anything else in the whole world will
ever be able to separate us from the love of God
that is in Christ Jesus our Lord.

God and the Jewish People

9 I am in Christ, and I am telling you the truth;
I do not lie. My conscience is ruled by the
Holy Spirit,[d] and it tells me I am not lying. 2I have
great sorrow and always feel much sadness. 3I
wish I could help my Jewish brothers and sisters,
my people. I would even wish that I were cursed
and cut off from Christ if that would help them.
4They are the people of Israel, God's chosen children. They have seen the glory of God, and they
have the agreements that God made between
himself and his people. God gave them the law of
Moses and the right way of worship and his promises. 5They are the descendants[d] of our great ancestors, and they are the earthly family into which
Christ was born, who is God over all. Praise him
forever![n] Amen.

6It is not that God failed to keep his promise to
them. But only some of the people of Israel are
truly God's people,[n] 7and only some of Abraham's[n] descendants are true children of Abraham. But God said to Abraham: "The descendants I promised you will be from Isaac."[n] 8This
means that not all of Abraham's descendants are
God's true children. Abraham's true children are
those who become God's children because of the
promise God made to Abraham. 9God's promise
to Abraham was this: "At the right time I will
return, and Sarah will have a son."[n] 10And that
is not all. Rebekah's sons had the same father, our
father Isaac. 11-12But before the two boys were
born, God told Rebekah, "The older will serve the
younger."[n] This was before the boys had done
anything good or bad. God said this so that the
one chosen would be chosen because of God's
own plan. He was chosen because he was the one
God wanted to call, not because of anything he
did. 13As the Scripture[d] says, "I loved Jacob, but
I hated Esau."[n]

14So what should we say about this? Is God
unfair? In no way. 15God said to Moses, "I will
show kindness to anyone to whom I want to
show kindness, and I will show mercy to anyone
to whom I want to show mercy."[n] 16So God will
choose the one to whom he decides to show
mercy; his choice does not depend on what people want or try to do. 17The Scripture says to the
king of Egypt: "I made you king for this reason:
to show my power in you so that my name will
be talked about in all the earth."[n] 18So God
shows mercy where he wants to show mercy, and
he makes stubborn the people he wants to make
stubborn.

19So one of you will ask me: "Then why does
God blame us for our sins? Who can fight his
will?" 20You are only human, and human beings
have no right to question God. An object should
not ask the person who made it, "Why did you
make me like this?" 21The potter can make anything he wants to make. He can use the same clay
to make one thing for special use and another
thing for daily use.

22It is the same way with God. He wanted to
show his anger and to let people see his power.
But he patiently stayed with those people he was
angry with — people who were made ready to be
destroyed. 23He waited with patience so that he
could make known his rich glory to the people
who receive his mercy. He has prepared these
people to have his glory, 24and we are those people whom God called. He called us not from the
Jews only but also from those who are not Jews.
25As the Scripture says in Hosea:

"I will say, 'You are my people'
to those I had called 'not my people.'
And I will show my love
to those people I did not love." *Hosea 2:1, 23*

26"They were called,
'You are not my people,'
but later they will be called
'children of the living God.'" *Hosea 1:10*

27And Isaiah cries out about Israel:

"The people of Israel are many,
like the grains of sand by the sea.
But only a few of them will be saved,
28 because the Lord will quickly and
completely punish the people on the
earth." *Isaiah 10:22-23*

29It is as Isaiah said:

born . . . forever! This can also mean, "born. May God, who rules over all things, be praised forever!"
God's people Literally, "Israel," the people God chose to bring his blessings to the world.
Abraham Most respected ancestor of the Jews. Every Jew hoped to see Abraham.
'The descendants . . . Isaac." Quotation from Genesis 21:12.
'At . . . son." Quotation from Genesis 18:10, 14.
'The older . . . younger." Quotation from Genesis 25:23.
'I . . . Esau." Quotation from Malachi 1:2-3.
'I . . . mercy." Quotation from Exodus 33:19.
'I . . . earth." Quotation from Exodus 9:16.

"The Lord All-Powerful
allowed a few of our descendants to live.
Otherwise we would have been completely
destroyed
like the cities of Sodom and Gomorrah."[n]

Isaiah 1:9

30So what does all this mean? Those who are
not Jews were not trying to make themselves
right with God, but they were made right with
God because of their faith. 31The people of Israel
tried to follow a law to make themselves right
with God. But they did not succeed, 32because
they tried to make themselves right by the things
they did instead of trusting in God to make them
right. They stumbled over the stone that causes
people to stumble. 33As it is written in the Scripture:

"I will put in Jerusalem a stone that causes
people to stumble,
a rock that makes them fall.
Anyone who trusts in him will never be
disappointed."

Isaiah 8:14; 28:16

> **SIDELIGHT:** Early Christians often argued about what was required to be a Christian (Romans 9:1–33). Some Jewish Christians wanted the non-Jewish ones to obey all the Jewish laws. If their beliefs had won the day, we would all have to eat kosher pickles!

10

Brothers and sisters, the thing I want
most is for all the Jews to be saved. That
is my prayer to God. 2I can say this about them:
They really try to follow God, but they do not
know the right way. 3Because they did not know
the way that God makes people right with him,
they tried to make themselves right in their own
way. So they did not accept God's way of making
people right. 4Christ ended the law so that everyone who believes in him may be right with God.

5Moses writes about being made right by following the law. He says, "A person who obeys
these things will live because of them."[n] 6But
this is what the Scripture says about being made
right through faith: "Don't say to yourself, 'Who
will go up into heaven?' " (That means, "Who
will go up to heaven and bring Christ down to
earth?") 7"And do not say, 'Who will go down
into the world below?' " (That means, "Who will
go down and bring Christ up from the dead?")
8This is what the Scripture says: "The word is
near you; it is in your mouth and in your heart."[n]
That is the teaching of faith that we are telling. 9If
you use your mouth to say, "Jesus is Lord," and
if you believe in your heart that God raised Jesus
from the dead, you will be saved. 10We believe
with our hearts, and so we are made right with
God. And we use our mouths to say that we believe, and so we are saved. 11As the Scripture says,
"Anyone who trusts in him will never be disappointed."[n] 12That Scripture says "anyone" because there is no difference between those who
are Jews and those who are not. The same Lord
is the Lord of all and gives many blessings to all
who trust in him, 13as the Scripture says, "Anyone
who calls on the Lord will be saved."[n]

14But before people can ask the Lord for help,
they must believe in him; and before they can
believe in him, they must hear about him; and for
them to hear about the Lord, someone must tell
them; 15and before someone can go and tell them,
that person must be sent. It is written, "How
beautiful is the person who comes to bring good
news."[n]

16But not all the Jews accepted the good news.
Isaiah said, "Lord, who believed what we told
them?"[n] 17So faith comes from hearing the Good
News,[d] and people hear the Good News when
someone tells them about Christ.

18But I ask: Didn't people hear the Good
News? Yes, they heard—as the Scripture says:

"Their message went out through all the
world;
their words go everywhere on earth."

Psalm 19:

19Again I ask: Didn't the people of Israel under
stand? Yes, they did understand. First, Moses
says:

"I will use those who are not a nation to
make you jealous.
I will use a nation that does not understand
to make you angry."

Deuteronomy 32:2

20Then Isaiah is bold enough to say:

"I was found by those who were not asking
me for help.
I made myself known to people who were
not looking for me."

Isaiah 65:

21But about Israel God says,

"All day long I stood ready to accept
people who disobey and are stubborn."

Isaiah 65:

Sodom and Gomorrah Two cities that God destroyed because the people were so evil.
"A person . . . them." Quotation from Leviticus 18:5.
Verses 6-8 Quotations from Deuteronomy 9:4; 30:12-14; Psalm 107:26.
"Anyone . . . disappointed." Quotation from Isaiah 28:16.
"Anyone . . . saved." Quotation from Joel 2:32.
"How . . . news." Quotation from Isaiah 52:7.
"Lord, . . . them?" Quotation from Isaiah 53:1.

God Shows Mercy to All People

11 So I ask: Did God throw out his people?
No! I myself am an Israelite from the
family of Abraham, from the tribe[d] of Benjamin.
2God chose the Israelites to be his people before
they were born, and he has not thrown his people
out. Surely you know what the Scripture[d] says
about Elijah, how he prayed to God against the
people of Israel. 3"Lord," he said, "they have
killed your prophets,[d] and they have destroyed
your altars. I am the only prophet left, and now
they are trying to kill me, too."[n] 4But what answer did God give Elijah? He said, "But I have left
seven thousand people in Israel who have never
bowed down before Baal."[n] 5It is the same now.
There are a few people that God has chosen by his
grace. 6And if he chose them by grace, it is not for
the things they have done. If they could be made
God's people by what they did, God's gift of grace
would not really be a gift.

"They . . . too." Quotation from 1 Kings 19:10, 14.
"But . . . Baal." Quotation from 1 Kings 19:18.

SHARING FAITH

Why Didn't You Say Something?

Mark Shipp went to church on Sundays. He didn't make a big thing of it, but he sang in the choir and went to Bible study. He was even on the youth council. Mark was trying to do what was right without being . . . pushy.

Just about every Friday, his school buddy, Jack, would invite him to play touch football: "So, what'cha got planned this weekend, Mark?"

Mark would shrug, "Oh, you know . . ."

"Tell me about it! Clean this, straighten that, mow the grass, wash the car! I work harder on Saturdays than I do on school days."

Mark would smile knowingly and shrug, "That's the truth."

"That's why I take Sunday off. Me, Tim, Larry, and some other guys get together in the morning to play football. Do ya wanna come?"

Mark would evade the question, "Oh, I'd like to, Jack. I really would, but I can't. I've already made plans."

"Sure. Well, if you ever change your mind, the invitation stands," Jack would say and then off he would go with a smile.

Then one Friday late in the year, the ritual took a different turn.

Mark had just evaded the question, explaining that he really wanted to play touch football but couldn't, and Jack just nodded as usual. But this time, Jack didn't walk away. He just stood there, looking at Mark.

Finally, he spoke. "Mark, for the past year I've invited you to play touch football, but you can't because you go to church."

Mark was caught off guard. "Oh, well, yeah, I go to church, but that . . ."

"For a year I've been inviting you to play football, and never once have you invited me to church," Jack continued, scratching his head. "Why?"

Mark needed to read Paul's admonition in **Romans 10:8–18** to learn how important it is to tell others about your faith in Christ and not just assume they don't want to know.

- What does this passage say about Mark's attitude toward telling others about his faith in Christ?
- According to the passage, why is it important that you tell others about your faith in Christ?

CONSIDER . . .

- putting your faith story into words. How, in a hundred words, has your faith affected your life?
- inviting a non-Christian friend to go to church with you this Sunday.

FOR MORE, SEE . . .

- Jeremiah 1:4–8
- Matthew 10:32–33
- Acts 2

7So this is what has happened: Although the
Israelites tried to be right with God, they did not
succeed, but the ones God chose did become
right with him. The others were made stubborn
and refused to listen to God. 8As it is written in
the Scriptures:[d]

"God gave the people a dull mind so they
could not understand." *Isaiah 29:10*

"He closed their eyes so they could not see
and their ears so they could not hear.
This continues until today." *Deuteronomy 29:4*

9And David says:

"Let their own feasts trap them and cause
their ruin;
let their feasts cause them to stumble and
be paid back.
10Let their eyes be closed so they cannot see
and their backs be forever weak from
troubles." *Psalm 69:22-23*

11So I ask: When the Jews fell, did that fall destroy them? No! But their mistake brought salvation to those who are not Jews, in order to make
the Jews jealous. 12The Jews' mistake brought
rich blessings for the world, and the Jews' loss
brought rich blessings for the non-Jewish people.
So surely the world will receive much richer
blessings when enough Jews become the kind of
people God wants.

13Now I am speaking to you who are not Jews.
I am an apostle[d] to those who are not Jews, and
since I have that work, I will make the most of it.
14I hope I can make my own people jealous and,
in that way, help some of them to be saved.
15When God turned away from the Jews, he became friends with other people in the world. So
when God accepts the Jews, surely that will bring
them life after death.

16If the first piece of bread is offered to God,
then the whole loaf is made holy. If the roots of
a tree are holy, then the tree's branches are holy
too.

17It is as if some of the branches from an olive
tree have been broken off. You non-Jewish people
are like the branch of a wild olive tree that has
been joined to that first tree. You now share the
strength and life of the first tree, the Jews. 18So do
not brag about those branches that were broken
off. If you brag, remember that you do not support
the root, but the root supports you. 19You will say,
"Branches were broken off so that I could be
joined to their tree." 20That is true. But those
branches were broken off because they did not
believe, and you continue to be part of the tree
only because you believe. Do not be proud, but be
afraid. 21If God did not let the natural branches of
that tree stay, then he will not let you stay if you
don't believe.

22So you see that God is kind and also very
strict. He punishes those who stop following him.
But God is kind to you, if you continue following
in his kindness. If you do not, you will be cut of
from the tree. 23And if the Jews will believe ir
God again, he will accept them back. God is able
to put them back where they were. 24It is not nat
ural for a wild branch to be part of a good tree
And you who are not Jews are like a branch cu
from a wild olive tree and joined to a good olive
tree. But since those Jews are like a branch tha
grew from the good tree, surely they can be joine
to their own tree again.

25I want you to understand this secret, brother
and sisters, so you will understand that you do no
know everything: Part of Israel has been mad
stubborn, but that will change when many who
are not Jews have come to God. 26And that is how
all Israel will be saved. It is written in the Scrip
tures:

"The Savior will come from Jerusalem;
he will take away all evil from the family o
Jacob.[n]
27And I will make this agreement with those
people
when I take away their sins."
Isaiah 59:20-21; 27

28The Jews refuse to accept the Good News,
so they are God's enemies. This has happened t
help you who are not Jews. But the Jews are sti
God's chosen people, and he loves them ver
much because of the promises he made to the
ancestors. 29God never changes his mind abou
the people he calls and the things he gives them
30At one time you refused to obey God. But nov
you have received mercy, because those peopl
refused to obey. 31And now the Jews refuse t
obey, because God showed mercy to you. Bu
this happened so that they also can receiv
mercy from him. 32God has given all people ove
to their stubborn ways so that he can show
mercy to all.

Praise to God

33Yes, God's riches are very great, and his wi
dom and knowledge have no end! No one ca
explain the things God decides or understand h
ways. 34As the Scripture[d] says,

"Who has known the mind of the Lord,
or who has been able to give him advice?"
Isaiah 40:

35"No one has ever given God anything
that he must pay back." *Job 41:*

36Yes, God made all things, and everything co
tinues through him and for him. To him be tl
glory forever! Amen.

Jacob Father of the twelve family groups of Israel, the people God chose to be his people.

Give Your Lives to God

12 So brothers and sisters, since God has
shown us great mercy, I beg you to offer
your lives as a living sacrifice to him. Your offering
must be only for God and pleasing to him, which
is the spiritual way for you to worship. 2Do not
change yourselves to be like the people of this
world, but be changed within by a new way of
thinking. Then you will be able to decide what
God wants for you; you will know what is good
and pleasing to him and what is perfect. 3Because
God has given me a special gift, I have something
to say to everyone among you. Do not think you
are better than you are. You must decide what
you really are by the amount of faith God has
given you. 4Each one of us has a body with many
parts, and these parts all have different uses. 5In
the same way, we are many, but in Christ we are
all one body. Each one is a part of that body, and
each part belongs to all the other parts. 6We all
have different gifts, each of which came because
of the grace God gave us. The person who has the
gift of prophecy[d] should use that gift in agreement
with the faith. 7Anyone who has the gift of serving
should serve. Anyone who has the gift of teaching should teach. 8Whoever has the gift of
encouraging others should encourage. Whoever
has the gift of giving to others should give freely.
Anyone who has the gift of being a leader should
try hard when he leads. Whoever has the gift of
showing mercy to others should do so with joy.
9Your love must be real. Hate what is evil, and
hold on to what is good. 10Love each other like
brothers and sisters. Give each other more honor
than you want for yourselves. 11Do not be lazy but
work hard, serving the Lord with all your heart.
12Be joyful because you have hope. Be patient
when trouble comes, and pray at all times.

GOD'S LOVE

Free Gifts

Aaron Spell volunteered in an inner-city free store, where he sorted used clothing and helped people pick out things they needed.

One Friday, while Aaron was walking to the bus stop near the store, he passed a house that was having a yard sale. He recognized one of the kids as the child of a woman who often came to the free store. After a few moments of talking to the child, he began to recognize more than just the little boy.

There, piled on the old card tables, were stacks of blue jeans, sweatshirts, socks, shoes, and mittens that Aaron had seen earlier that week at the free store. He was outraged! These people didn't take the clothing from the store because they needed it. They took it so they could sell it! What a rip-off!

"It just doesn't seem right," Aaron complained to Jim Knudson, the store manager, later that week. "We gave them those clothes so they'd have something to wear, not so they could sell them."

"Well, it seems they needed the clothes either way," responded Jim. "They needed the clothes to sell for cash so they could buy other things. Besides, we help these people because we care about them, not because they always respond the way we want them to."

"It sounds risky," Aaron said.

"Love always is," answered Jim.

Jim helped Aaron see that their love wasn't something people should have to earn. God's love is like that too. Read **Romans 11:29–36** to find a description of God's merciful gift of love for us.

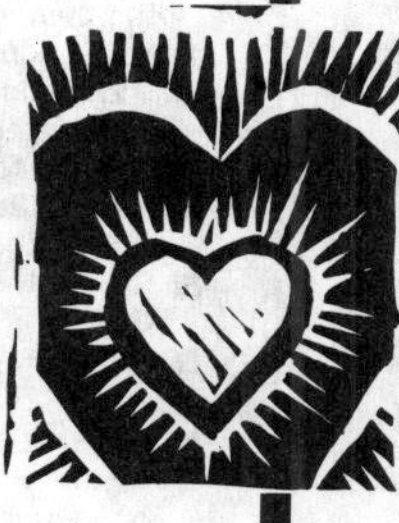

- How is the free store like God's love for us?
- What would happen to your relationship with God if his love depended on your doing what he wanted?

CONSIDER . . .

- writing out five reasons God's love can never be taken away from you. Read Romans 8:31–39 for a few hints.
- giving a dollar to someone you meet who is in need—without knowing how that person will use the money.

FOR MORE, SEE . . .

- Psalm 103:6–14
- Ephesians 2:4–7
- 1 John 4:7–12

13 Share with God's people who need help. Bring
strangers in need into your homes.
14 Wish good for those who harm you; wish
them well and do not curse them. 15 Be happy
with those who are happy, and be sad with those
who are sad. 16 Live in peace with each other. Do
not be proud, but make friends with those who
seem unimportant. Do not think how smart you
are.
17 If someone does wrong to you, do not pay
him back by doing wrong to him. Try to do what
everyone thinks is right. 18 Do your best to live in
peace with everyone. 19 My friends, do not try to
punish others when they wrong you, but wait
for God to punish them with his anger. It is written: "I will punish those who do wrong; I will
repay them,"[n] says the Lord. 20 But you should
do this:

"If your enemy is hungry, feed him;
if he is thirsty, give him a drink.
Doing this will be like pouring burning coals
on his head." *Proverbs 25:21-22*

"I . . . them" Quotation from Deuteronomy 32:35.

FOLLOWING GOD

Bouncing Betties

The Bouncing Betty was the worst kind of land mine in the Vietnam War. It was loaded with a spring so when you stepped on it, it flew into the air, about waist high, then exploded. It was designed to blow people apart and to strike terror in the hearts of young soldiers.

The plan worked on Craig Morrison.

He was on patrol one day with five other guys and this little Vietnamese guy who was supposed to be their guide. They had been out about three hours, walking quietly through the bush, just looking and listening and trying not to get shot.

Then they came to a clearing, maybe a hundred feet across. The situation had "Bouncing Betty" written all over it. And Craig just knew snipers were hiding in the jungle on the other side, waiting for him and his buddies to step into that clearing. But the bush was too thick to go around the clearing, so they had no choice but to go through.

The Vietnamese guide signaled for quiet and pointed to his feet then spread his fingers on both hands. "Stay quiet," he whispered. "Follow me. Place your feet where I place mine. Stay ten yards behind the guy in front of you."

Craig had never been so scared in his life. The guide went ten yards out into the clearing and then motioned for Craig to follow.

Slowly now. Despite his fears, he managed to keep putting his feet in the impressions left by the guide. He kept his head down, waiting for a sniper's bullet to send him to the ground.

And then it was over. He took a deep breath and realized he had made it across. Shaking violently, he looked up and saw the little Vietnamese guy smiling at him. It was nice to have someone in whose steps you could walk.

Craig learned that to get through rough times he had to deny his own desires and follow someone he could trust, someone who knew the way. **Romans 12:1–16** talks about God as the one who knows the way for our lives. Read the passage to see how we can walk in his steps.

- How is the way Craig followed the guide similar to the way you follow God?
- According to the passage, why should you follow God? (See verses 1–2.)

CONSIDER . . .

- asking your youth leader to read Romans 12:6–8. Have the leader tell you which gifts he thinks you have. Then ask God to give you more opportunities to use your gift.
- writing how your life would change if you walked each day in Christ's steps by following his instructions in this passage.

FOR MORE, SEE . . .

- Psalm 119:9–16
- Luke 9:23–26
- Luke 14:25–33

21 Do not let evil defeat you, but defeat evil by
doing good.

Christians Should Obey the Law

13 All of you must yield to the government
rulers. No one rules unless God has
given him the power to rule, and no one rules
now without that power from God. 2 So those
who are against the government are really against
what God has commanded. And they will bring
punishment on themselves. 3 Those who do right
do not have to fear the rulers; only those who do
wrong fear them. Do you want to be unafraid of
the rulers? Then do what is right, and they will
praise you. 4 The ruler is God's servant to help
you. But if you do wrong, then be afraid. He has
the power to punish; he is God's servant to punish those who do wrong. 5 So you must yield to the
government, not only because you might be punished, but because you know it is right.
6 This is also why you pay taxes. Rulers are
working for God and give their time to their

GOVERNMENT

An Inch Is as Good as a Mile

Darren Smithers wrote a column for his high school newspaper. It wasn't a big column, but it was fun. He wrote humorously about cafeteria food, class workload, or the latest bungle of the notoriously bad basketball team. He had gotten the job because his best friend, Mitch Salinas, was the editor. And much to their surprise, the column had become one of the paper's most popular features, even among kids who attended other schools.

One Monday on the way to class, Darren saw a student in a wheelchair and an older woman trying—unsuccessfully—to push the wheelchair over the curb.

When Darren stopped to help, he noticed a wheelchair ramp cut into the curb just a few yards away. But the yellow paint that marked it off had faded, and someone had parked in front of it.

"Unbelievable," Darren said, shaking his head.

"Believe it," said the student in the wheelchair, whose name was Bruce McCoy. "It happens all the time. That's why my mom has to come with me. More than half the ramps haven't been painted in five years. People just ignore them."

Darren smelled a story. He agreed to meet Bruce and his mom the next day. They would bring their extra wheelchair, and Darren would spend the day trying to get around school in it.

That's how Darren discovered that the main elevator stopped two inches below the floor level (as good as two miles when you're in a wheelchair). He had trouble negotiating the super-narrow doors in the band room. And he discovered high water fountains everywhere and over a hundred obstacles all over the campus. And that was in just six hours!

The next day, Darren wrote about his experiences, but somehow that just didn't seem like enough. He also attended student council meetings and talked to the principal about the problem.

A few months later, Darren talked to Bruce again. But this time his mom wasn't with him. "She doesn't need to come with me anymore," he said. "For some reason, the principal just seemed to wake up."

"Maybe somebody tapped him on the shoulder," Darren said.

Romans 13:1–10 encourages us to do what's right in serving our government. In Paul's day, that meant carefully following the laws laid out by Rome. But in today's democracy, it can mean helping to shape policy—just as Darren did. Read the passage to see what else Paul said about your relationship with the government.

- Would Paul have approved of Darren's actions? Why or why not?
- What's one thing you can do to apply this passage to your situation?

CONSIDER . . .

- running for a place in your school's student council.
- writing a letter to your congressional representative, relating your concerns about the disabled, education, or some other issue you care about.

FOR MORE, SEE . . .

- 1 Samuel 8:1–22
- Matthew 22:17–21
- 1 Peter 2:13–17

work. [7]Pay everyone, then, what you owe. If you owe any kind of tax, pay it. Show respect and honor to them all.

SIDELIGHT: Relations with the government were important to Roman Christians, since they lived in the capital city. When Paul wrote Romans 13:1–7, about obeying the government, Christians were tolerated—sometimes even protected—by the state. Within a few years, though, Christians would face the constant threat of torture and execution.

Loving Others

[8]Do not owe people anything, except always owe love to each other, because the person who loves others has obeyed all the law. [9]The law says, "You must not be guilty of adultery.[d] You must not murder anyone. You must not steal. You must not want to take your neighbor's things."[n] All these commands and all others are really only one rule: "Love your neighbor as you love yourself."[n] [10]Love never hurts a neighbor, so loving is obeying all the law.

[11]Do this because we live in an important time. It is now time for you to wake up from your sleep, because our salvation is nearer now than when we first believed. [12]The "night"[n] is almost finished, and the "day"[n] is almost here. So we should stop doing things that belong to darkness and take up the weapons used for fighting in the light. [13]Let us live in a right way, like people who belong to the day. We should not have wild parties or get drunk. There should be no sexual sins of any kind, no fighting or jealousy. [14]But clothe yourselves with the Lord Jesus Christ and forget about satisfying your sinful self.

Do Not Criticize Other People

14 Accept into your group someone who is weak in faith, and do not argue about opinions. [2]One person believes it is right to eat all kinds of food.[n] But another, who is weak, believes it is right to eat only vegetables. [3]The one who knows that it is right to eat any kind of food must not reject the one who eats only vegetables. And the person who eats only vegetables must not think that the one who eats all foods is wrong, because God has accepted that person. [4]You cannot judge another person's servant. The master decides if the servant is doing well or not. And the Lord's servant will do well because the Lord helps him do well.

[5]Some think that one day is more important than another, and others think that every day is the same. Let all be sure in their own mind. [6]Those who think one day is more important than other days are doing that for the Lord. And those who eat all kinds of food are doing that for the Lord, and they give thanks to God. Others who refuse to eat some foods do that for the Lord, and they give thanks to God. [7]We do not live or die for ourselves. [8]If we live, we are living for the Lord, and if we die, we are dying for the Lord. So living or dying, we belong to the Lord.

[9]The reason Christ died and rose from the dead to live again was so he would be Lord over both the dead and the living. [10]So why do you judge your brothers or sisters in Christ? And why do you think you are better than they are? We will all stand before God to be judged, [11]because it is written in the Scriptures:[d]

" 'As surely as I live,' says the Lord,
'Everyone will bow before me;
everyone will say that I am God.' "

Isaiah 45:23

[12]So each of us will have to answer to God.

Do Not Cause Others to Sin

[13]For that reason we should stop judging each other. We must make up our minds not to do anything that will make another Christian sin. [14]I am in the Lord Jesus, and I know that there is no food that is wrong to eat. But if a person believes something is wrong, that thing is wrong for him. [15]If you hurt your brother's or sister's faith because of something you eat, you are not really following the way of love. Do not destroy someone's faith by eating food he thinks is wrong, because Christ died for him. [16]Do not allow what you think is good to become what others say is evil. [17]In the kingdom of God, eating and drinking are not important. The important things are living right with God, peace, and joy in the Holy Spirit.[d] [18]Anyone who serves Christ by living this way is pleasing God and will be accepted by other people.

[19]So let us try to do what makes peace and helps one another. [20]Do not let the eating of food destroy the work of God. All foods are all right to

"You . . . things." Quotation from Exodus 20:13-15, 17.
"Love . . . yourself." Quotation from Leviticus 19:18.
"night" This is used as a symbol of the sinful world we live in. This world will soon end.
"day" This is used as a symbol of the good time that is coming, when we will be with God.
all . . . food The Jewish law said there were some foods Jews should not eat. When Jews became Christians, some of them did not understand they could now eat all foods.

eat, but it is wrong to eat food that causes someone else to sin. 21It is better not to eat meat or
drink wine or do anything that will cause your
brother or sister to sin.
22Your beliefs about these things should be kept
secret between you and God. People are happy if
they can do what they think is right without feeling guilty. 23But those who eat something without
being sure it is right are wrong because they did
not believe it was right. Anything that is done
without believing it is right is a sin.
15 We who are strong in faith should help
the weak with their weaknesses, and not
please only ourselves. 2Let each of us please our
neighbors for their good, to help them be stronger
in faith. 3Even Christ did not live to please himself. It was as the Scriptures[d] said: "When people
insult you, it hurts me."[n] 4Everything that was
written in the past was written to teach us. The
Scriptures give us patience and encouragement so
that we can have hope. 5Patience and encouragement come from God. And I pray that God will
help you all agree with each other the way Christ
Jesus wants. 6Then you will all be joined together,
and you will give glory to God the Father of our
Lord Jesus Christ. 7Christ accepted you, so you
should accept each other, which will bring glory
to God. 8I tell you that Christ became a servant
of the Jews to show that God's promises to the
Jewish ancestors are true. 9And he also did this so

"When . . . me." Quotation from Psalm 69:9.

DRUGS AND ALCOHOL

The Lost Weekend

"It was just beer. It wasn't like they were alcoholics or drug addicts or anything, right?"

The teenagers in the small Sunday school class nodded their heads, but they didn't speak. What was there to say? So JoAnn Pearson kept talking.

"Well, so we'd do it every weekend. We'd usually go to a ball game or a dance or a party or something on Friday night. Then we'd go get some beer and chips and stuff and go back to Lonnie Brock's house. Her parents were never home.

"Then we'd just drink beer all weekend. Just, you know, get a buzz on Friday and keep it until Sunday night. Then, after a while it was more than a buzz. We started getting really drunk. And we'd just stay drunk all weekend.

"To tell you the truth, it was getting kinda scary, but I didn't know what to do. Then, one day I woke up with a terrible hangover. I was so wasted. And it was Sunday and I didn't know where I was. I mean, I couldn't remember anything that had happened since Friday night. That really scared me.

"I remember kneeling next to the commode in the bathroom and thinking, whoa, this has gone too far. I lost a whole weekend.

"And that's why I'm here," JoAnn concluded. "I decided to go to church more and see if God could help me straighten out my life. He can, can't he?"

"Yes, he can," said Chip Shoenig. "And we'll be there to help too. Right, guys?"

And everyone nodded.

JoAnn learned the hard way that to be free she had to turn away from alcohol. **Romans 13:11–14** also talks about the need to turn away from drunkenness to follow God. Read the passage to see what it says about drinking and drugs.

- According to this passage, how did JoAnn's decision move her from darkness to light?
- What reasons does the passage give for avoiding drunkenness?

CONSIDER . . .

- examining your own drug or alcohol use in light of this passage. What would God want you to do (or stop doing)?
- helping a drug-abusing friend find help through a local substance abuse program or your church.

FOR MORE, SEE . . .

- Proverbs 23:19–21
- Luke 21:34–36
- Galatians 5:16–25

that those who are not Jews could give glory to
God for the mercy he gives to them. It is written
in the Scriptures:
"So I will praise you among the non-Jewish
people.
I will sing praises to your name." *Psalm 18:49*
10The Scripture also says,
"Be happy, you who are not Jews, together
with his people." *Deuteronomy 32:43*
11Again the Scripture says,
"All you who are not Jews, praise the Lord.
All you people, sing praises to him."
Psalm 117:1
12And Isaiah says,
"A new king will come from the family of
Jesse.[n]
He will come to rule over the non-Jewish
people,
and they will have hope because of him."
Isaiah 11:10
13I pray that the God who gives hope will fill
you with much joy and peace while you trust in
him. Then your hope will overflow by the power
of the Holy Spirit.[d]

Paul Talks About His Work

14My brothers and sisters, I am sure that
you are full of goodness. I know that you have
all the knowledge you need and that you are
able to teach each other. 15But I have written
to you very openly about some things I wanted

Jesse Jesse was the father of David, king of Israel. Jesus was from their family.

DECISION MAKING

Different Strokes for Different Folks

"I'd be mortified!" Rachael Whalen said.

"Everyone would laugh at us!" Dora Parolini shouted.

"We can't let her do it. We'll just have to talk to her, that's all," Janeen Holt reasoned.

Laura Booker shook her head and tried to calm them. "It won't do any good. Her church says you can't wear skirts or dresses above the knee."

"But that's stupid," said Dora. "How can you be a cheerleader and not wear a short skirt? Everyone does it!"

"Yeah," Janeen added. "And besides, Linda knew when she tried out that we wore short skirts."

"Why can't we just let her wear her skirt longer than ours?" Laura asked. "Is it really such a big deal? I mean, I don't think there's anything wrong with our outfits. But if she does, why can't we let her do it her way?"

Rachael sighed loudly. "They're called uniforms! We're supposed to look the same."

"I still don't think it's that big a deal," Laura said. "We're talking about two inches of fabric. No one's asking us to lengthen our skirts. She just wants to be allowed to wear hers longer."

There was a long pause as Laura looked at the other girls. Finally Rachael said, "Okay! Okay, I guess it's all right. Different strokes for different folks, huh?"

Laura smiled. It was nice to know that sometimes everyone could "win."

Linda had made a decision based on her beliefs, even though she knew others would disagree. **Romans 14:5–12** challenges us all to make decisions based on our faith.

- How is Linda like the people mentioned in the passage?
- How might this passage affect the way you make decisions about your faith?

CONSIDER . . .

- talking to your youth leader about your church's beliefs. Ask how your church decided to believe the things it does.
- making decisions about your lifestyle based on what the Bible teaches. Work toward changing activities that go against your beliefs.

FOR MORE, SEE . . .

- 1 Kings 12:1–20
- Matthew 7:13–14
- Acts 5:12–32

you to remember. I did this because God gave
me this special gift: 16to be a minister of Christ
Jesus to those who are not Jews. I served God
by teaching his Good News,[d] so that the non-
Jewish people could be an offering that God
would accept—an offering made holy by the
Holy Spirit.[d]
17So I am proud of what I have done for God
in Christ Jesus. 18I will not talk about anything
except what Christ has done through me in leading those who are not Jews to obey God. They
have obeyed God because of what I have said and
done, 19because of the power of miracles[d] and the
great things they saw, and because of the power
of the Holy Spirit. I preached the Good News
from Jerusalem all the way around to Illyricum,
and so I have finished that part of my work. 20I
always want to preach the Good News in places
where people have never heard of Christ, because
I do not want to build on the work someone else
has already started. 21But it is written in the Scriptures:[d]

"Those who were not told about him will
see,

FRIENDS

Accepted

Karen Flock carried her tray into the cafeteria, looking for her friends. As usual, they were sitting by the windows, in the traditional "senior corner." Karen carried her tray to the table and sat down, but she had trouble staying with their conversation. Her mind was on something else.

A girl named Amy.

Amy Powell was a freshman whom Karen had seen at church. Amy was new to the school and, Karen could see, desperately lonely. Amy ate her lunch alone every day. Not because she wanted to—you could see that in her eyes. She ate alone because sophomores, juniors, and seniors didn't eat with underclassmen, and other freshmen were afraid to eat with her.

They weren't afraid of Amy. It was Kara Holland they were afraid of. Kara was queen of the freshman class. She and her "court" of five pretty girls ruled freshman society. They decided who was "in" and who was "out," and, for undisclosed reasons, Amy was definitely "out."

The more Karen thought about Amy's situation, the more angry she became. It's time to stop this dumb game, she thought. So Karen picked up her tray and walked across the cafeteria to where Amy was sitting. Amy wouldn't look up at her, so she said, "Hi, Amy."

"Hi."

"Is this seat saved?" she asked, pulling out a chair and sitting down.

"No." She looked up briefly, then back to her plate.

"So, how do you like the school?"

Amy shrugged.

"Hi, Amy!" two voices said as they walked by. Girls. Freshmen. Then they giggled.

Now Amy looked up at Karen. She smiled, shyly.

It would be okay, now, she knew. No freshman ever questioned the acceptance of a senior.

Karen accepted Amy even though others had rejected her. Paul talks about the foolishness of rejecting others, since we have all been accepted equally by Christ. Read what else Paul said about accepting others in **Romans 15:4–13**.

- Based on this passage, what might Paul have said to Karen and her friends?
- How does knowing that Christ has accepted other people help you accept them too?

CONSIDER . . .

- sitting by people you don't know this week and getting to know them.
- thinking of people at school or church whom you don't like and asking God to help you accept them as he does.

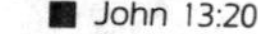

FOR MORE, SEE . . .

- Job 2:11–13
- 1 Samuel 18:1–4
- John 13:20

and those who have not heard about him
will understand." *Isaiah 52:15*

Paul's Plan to Visit Rome

22This is the reason I was stopped many times from coming to you. 23Now I have finished my work here. Since for many years I have wanted to come to you, 24I hope to visit you on my way to Spain. After I enjoy being with you for a while, I hope you can help me on my trip. 25Now I am going to Jerusalem to help God's people. 26The believers in Macedonia and Southern Greece were happy to give their money to help the poor among God's people at Jerusalem. 27They were happy to do this, and really they owe it to them. These who are not Jews have shared in the Jews' spiritual blessings, so they should use their material possessions to help the Jews. 28After I am sure the poor in Jerusalem get the money that has been given for them, I will leave for Spain and stop and visit you. 29I know that when I come to you I will bring Christ's full blessing.

30Brothers and sisters, I beg you to help me in my work by praying to God for me. Do this because of our Lord Jesus and the love that the Holy Spirit[d] gives us. 31Pray that I will be saved from the non-believers in Judea and that this help I bring to Jerusalem will please God's people there. 32Then, if God wants me to, I will come to you with joy, and together you and I will have a time of rest. 33The God who gives peace be with you all. Amen.

Greetings to the Christians

16 I recommend to you our sister Phoebe, who is a helper[n] in the church in Cenchrea. 2I ask you to accept her in the Lord in the way God's people should. Help her with anything she needs, because she has helped me and many other people also.

3Give my greetings to Priscilla and Aquila, who work together with me in Christ Jesus 4and who risked their own lives to save my life. I am thankful to them, and all the non-Jewish churches are thankful as well. 5Also, greet for me the church that meets at their house.

Greetings to my dear friend Epenetus, who was the first person in the country of Asia to follow Christ. 6Greetings to Mary, who worked very hard for you. 7Greetings to Andronicus and Junia, my relatives, who were in prison with me. They are very important apostles. They were believers in Christ before I was. 8Greetings to Ampliatus, my dear friend in the Lord. 9Greetings to Urbanus, a worker together with me for Christ. And greetings to my dear friend Stachys. 10Greetings to Apelles, who was tested and proved that he truly loves Christ. Greetings to all those who are in the family of Aristobulus. 11Greetings to Herodion, my fellow citizen. Greetings to all those in the family of Narcissus who belong to the Lord. 12Greetings to Tryphena and Tryphosa, women who work very hard for the Lord. Greetings to my dear friend Persis, who also has worked very hard for the Lord. 13Greetings to Rufus, who is a special person in the Lord, and to his mother, who has been like a mother to me also. 14Greetings to Asyncritus, Phlegon, Hermes, Patrobas, Hermas, and all the brothers who are with them. 15Greetings to Philologus and Julia, Nereus and his sister, and Olympas, and to all God's people with them. 16Greet each other with a holy kiss. All of Christ's churches send greetings to you.

17Brothers and sisters, I ask you to look out for those who cause people to be against each other and who upset other people's faith. They are against the true teaching you learned, so stay away from them. 18Such people are not serving our Lord Christ but are only doing what pleases themselves. They use fancy talk and fine words to fool the minds of those who do not know about evil. 19All the believers have heard that you obey, so I am very happy because of you. But I want you to be wise in what is good and innocent in what is evil.

20The God who brings peace will soon defeat Satan and give you power over him.

The grace of our Lord Jesus be with you.

21Timothy, a worker together with me, sends greetings, as well as Lucius, Jason, and Sosipater, my relatives.

22I am Tertius, and I am writing this letter from Paul. I send greetings to you in the Lord.

23Gaius is letting me and the whole church here use his home. He also sends greetings to you, as do Erastus, the city treasurer, and our brother Quartus. 24 [n]

25Glory to God who can make you strong in

SIDELIGHT: Since the early Christians didn't have churches to go to, they usually met in homes (Romans 16:3–5). Priscilla and Aquila might have been wealthy and had a large house where Christians could gather for worship. You would probably have to clean your room more often if this were still standard practice.

helper Literally, "deaconess." This might mean the same as one of the special women helpers in 1 Timothy 3:11.
Verse 24 Some Greek copies add verse 24: "The grace of our Lord Jesus Christ be with all of you. Amen."

faith by the Good News[d] that I tell people and by the message about Jesus Christ. The message about Christ is the secret that was hidden for long ages past but is now made known.
26It has been made clear through the writings of the prophets.[d] And by the command of the eternal God it is made known to all nations that they might believe and obey.
27To the only wise God be glory forever through Jesus Christ! Amen.

BIBLE STUDY

Recipe

Ray Marx had baked bread before. Hundreds of times.

Well, two times anyway.

"It's a simple loaf of white bread. How hard could that be?" Ray wondered aloud. "A little yeast, a little oil, a little flour—nothing to it."

Ray put all the ingredients into the big bowl his mother always used, added more flour until the mixture was a big ball, and dumped it onto the counter.

As Ray kneaded the dough he imagined how surprised and happy his parents would be when he presented his homemade bread for breakfast the next morning. It was their twenty-fifth anniversary.

Ray covered the big ball of dough with a light coating of butter, flipped it into the bowl, covered it with plastic wrap, and set it aside in a warm corner of the room to rise.

"See, nothing to it," he said smugly. "Didn't even have to look at the recipe."

Now all he had to do was wait for it to rise. Thirty minutes. Nothing. An hour. Nothing.

"It just sat there in the bowl like a . . . like a big lump of dough. Why wasn't it rising?" Ray asked himself.

He checked the expiration date on the yeast package. No problem; it wouldn't expire for another three months. So what could it be?

Reluctantly, he went to the cookbook.

"Let's see," he mused. "Flour, oil, yeast, sugar . . .

"Sugar! Of course!"

Without sugar, the yeast couldn't do its job. No wonder the bread wasn't rising! He had left out a small but vital ingredient.

Ray's bread couldn't rise without sugar. In the same way, Paul says that a Christian can't reach a mature faith without having the right ingredients in his or her life. Read **Romans 16:22–27** to see what those ingredients are.

- What, according to Paul, is the effect of God's message on people's lives?
- According to this passage, what ingredients might you be lacking to bring you to Christian maturity?

CONSIDER . . .

- asking your parent or Sunday school teacher to give you a recipe for Bible study. Ask what steps you should follow in studying the Bible.
- regularly attending your youth group's weekly Bible study. If you don't have one, ask your youth leader to start one.

FOR MORE, SEE . . .

- Joshua 1:8
- Psalm 19:7–11
- Revelation 1:1–3

1 CORINTHIANS

Why Read This Book:

- Hear down-to-earth advice about dealing with church problems (1 Corinthians 1—10).
- Learn the importance of working together as Christians (1 Corinthians 11—13).
- Discover the promise of Christ's victory over death (1 Corinthians 14—16).

Behind the Scenes:

If you have ever gone on a road trip with a band, youth group, or sports team, you know what it's like. At first, everything goes well. Everyone has fun being together. But as the miles and days pass, things get tense. Roommates have fights. Bossy people get on other people's nerves. Clowns become irritating. By the time you're home, you're glad you only see those people a few hours a day!

The Christians at Corinth may have had similar feelings. Located in one of the largest and most important cities in Greece, church members came from all over the world. Their backgrounds were different. Their incomes were different. Their beliefs were different. And those differences were dividing the church. To complicate things, many were immature Christians.

In this letter to the Corinthians, the apostle Paul addresses the issues that were dividing the church. These included competition, pride, differences in theology, sexual immorality, lawsuits, marriage and singleness, food offered to idols, and worship. He expresses his beliefs on the issues, challenging the church to follow Christ in all things.

At the heart of the letter, Paul focuses on what it means to be Christians together (1 Corinthians 12—13), respecting each other's uniqueness and gifts, and, above all, loving each other with God's love.

This letter is a problem-solving letter. As you read, you can almost picture Paul referring to a list of questions he has heard from the people, then answering each one. His advice is specific and practical.

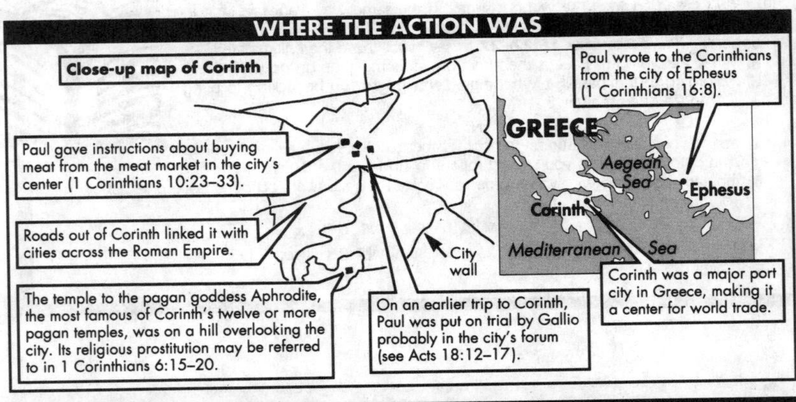

WHEN THE ACTION WAS

BC/AD	Jesus was born
	Jesus began his ministry
25AD	The church began soon after Jesus went to heaven
	Paul began his missionary work
50AD	Paul founded the church in Corinth
	Paul wrote 1 Corinthians
	Fire destroyed Rome
75AD	Romans destroyed the Temple in Jerusalem
100AD	

Behind the Scenes (cont.): In many ways, the Corinthian Christians lived in a culture a lot like ours. They faced many of the same temptations and problems we face today. This book gives a unique glimpse into their world. And it gives us practical insights into how to live in our complex world today.

---

1 From Paul. God called me to be an apostle[d]
of Christ Jesus because that is what God
wanted. Also from Sosthenes, our brother in
Christ.
2To the church of God in Corinth, to you
who have been made holy in Christ Jesus.
You were called to be God's holy people with
all people everywhere who pray in the name
of the Lord Jesus Christ—their Lord and ours:
3Grace and peace to you from God our Father
and the Lord Jesus Christ.

Paul Gives Thanks to God

4I always thank my God for you because of the
grace God has given you in Christ Jesus. 5I thank
God because in Christ you have been made rich

HEROES

How Hard They Fall

Phil Edwards's youth group was selected to sing at a Christian music conference. The young people were so excited; they would be singing on the same stage as many contemporary Christian artists.

Phil hoped to meet some of the musicians—especially those in one particular band. Phil had their albums, and he had gone to a few of their concerts. He had T-shirts with their group logo on them, and his room was plastered with their posters. Phil was even a trivia expert on the group. He could tell you the band members' birthdays, birthplaces, favorite foods and even their pet peeves. Phil practically worshiped this band!

On the day of the performance, when Phil and his youth group went backstage to prepare for the performance, Phil was distracted. He searched the area to get a glimpse of the band.

He didn't have to look far. He heard arguing from a back corner and looked to see the lead guitarist yelling at a stagehand. Two other band members were smoking under a No Smoking sign by the door, and the lead singer was walking right toward Phil.

As the singer walked past, Phil touched the singer's shoulder to get his attention.

"Hey, punk! What do you think this is? Public property?" the singer growled and jerked away.

Phil couldn't even speak. He just melted back into his group in shock.

When Phil went home that night, he tore down all his posters and shoved them into his trash can. He couldn't believe he had been so stupid. Phil had thought these guys were perfect just because they could sing. Phil vowed he would never again forget that even famous people are just human, and can disappoint others.

Knowing whom to trust and admire isn't a new problem. People back in Bible times also had a hard time figuring out just who should be their hero. Read about one such struggle in **1 Corinthians 1:1–17**.

- In what ways is Phil's "hero worship" similar to that of the Corinthians in this passage? In what ways is it different?
- According to this passage (especially verses 10–13), what happens if we worship human heroes?

CONSIDER . . .

- evaluating whether people whom you admire deserve your respect. Then look for heroes that point you toward Christ.
- going out with your best friend for "hero" sandwiches at your local sub shop. With every bite, give one reason that only Jesus can be a real hero.

FOR MORE, SEE . . .

- Proverbs 4:20–27
- Romans 15:1–6
- 1 Timothy 4:12–16

in every way, in all your speaking and in all your knowledge. 6Just as our witness about Christ has been guaranteed to you, 7so you have every gift from God while you wait for our Lord Jesus Christ to come again. 8Jesus will keep you strong until the end so that there will be no wrong in you on the day our Lord Jesus Christ comes again. 9God, who has called you to share everything with his Son, Jesus Christ our Lord, is faithful.

SIDELIGHT: You have heard of the Suez Canal in Egypt and the Panama Canal in Panama. But have you heard of the Corinth Track? Because Corinth was located on a small strip of land (see map p.262), the city built a five-mile rock track across the land to roll cargo and small ships. By using this track, sailors not only had a shorter trip, but they avoided a dangerous sea journey.

Problems in the Church

10I beg you, brothers and sisters,[n] by the name of our Lord Jesus Christ that all of you agree with each other and not be split into groups. I beg that you be completely joined together by having the same kind of thinking and the same purpose. 11My brothers and sisters, some people from Chloe's family have told me quite plainly that there are quarrels among you. 12This is what I mean: One of you says, "I follow Paul"; another says, "I follow Apollos"; another says, "I follow Peter"; and another says, "I follow Christ." 13Christ has been divided up into different groups! Did Paul die on the cross for you? No! Were you baptized in the name of Paul? No! 14I thank God I did not baptize any of you except Crispus and Gaius 15so that now no one can say you were baptized in my name. 16(I also baptized the family of Stephanas, but I do not remember that I baptized anyone else.) 17Christ did not send me to baptize people but to preach the Good News.[d] And he sent me to preach the Good News without using words of human wisdom so that the cross[n] of Christ would not lose its power.

Christ Is God's Power and Wisdom

18The teaching about the cross is foolishness to those who are being lost, but to us who are being saved it is the power of God. 19It is written in the Scriptures:[d]

"I will cause the wise men to lose their
wisdom;
I will make the wise men unable to
understand." *Isaiah 29:14*

20Where is the wise person? Where is the educated person? Where is the skilled talker of this world? God has made the wisdom of the world foolish. 21In the wisdom of God the world did not know God through its own wisdom. So God chose to use the message that sounds foolish to save those who believe. 22The Jews ask for miracles,[d] and the Greeks want wisdom. 23But we preach a crucified Christ. This is a big problem to the Jews, and it is foolishness to those who are not Jews. 24But Christ is the power of God and the wisdom of God to those people God has called—Jews and Greeks. 25Even the foolishness of God is wiser than human wisdom, and the weakness of God is stronger than human strength.

26Brothers and sisters, look at what you were when God called you. Not many of you were wise in the way the world judges wisdom. Not many of you had great influence. Not many of you came from important families. 27But God chose the foolish things of the world to shame the wise, and he chose the weak things of the world to shame the strong. 28He chose what the world thinks is unimportant and what the world looks down on and thinks is nothing in order to destroy what the world thinks is important. 29God did this so that no one can brag in his presence. 30Because of God you are in Christ Jesus, who has become for us wisdom from God. In Christ we are put right with God, and have been made holy, and have been set free from sin. 31So, as the Scripture[d] says, "If someone wants to brag, he should brag only about the Lord."[n]

The Message of Christ's Death

2 Dear brothers and sisters, when I came to you, I did not come preaching God's secret with fancy words or a show of human wisdom. 2I decided that while I was with you I would forget about everything except Jesus Christ and his death on the cross. 3So when I came to you, I was weak and fearful and trembling. 4My teaching and preaching were not with words of human wisdom that persuade people but with proof of the power that the Spirit[d] gives. 5This was so that your faith would be in God's power and not in human wisdom.

brothers and sisters Although the Greek text says "brothers" here and throughout this book, Paul's words were meant for the entire church, including men and women.
cross Paul uses the cross as a picture of the gospel, the story of Christ's death and rising from the dead to pay for people's sins. The cross, or Christ's death, was God's way to save people.
"If . . . Lord." Quotation from Jeremiah 9:24.

God's Wisdom

6However, I speak a wisdom to those who are
mature. But this wisdom is not from this world or
from the rulers of this world, who are losing their
power. 7I speak God's secret wisdom, which he
has kept hidden. Before the world began, God
planned this wisdom for our glory. 8None of the
rulers of this world understood it. If they had,
they would not have crucified the Lord of glory.
9But as it is written in the Scriptures:[d]

"No one has ever seen this,
  and no one has ever heard about it.
No one has ever imagined
  what God has prepared for those
  who love him." *Isaiah 64:4*

10But God has shown us these things through
the Spirit.[d]

The Spirit searches out all things, even the deep
secrets of God. 11Who knows the thoughts that
another person has? Only a person's spirit that
lives within him knows his thoughts. It is the
same with God. No one knows the thoughts of
God except the Spirit of God. 12Now we did not
receive the spirit of the world, but we received
the Spirit that is from God so that we can know
all that God has given us. 13And we speak about
these things, not with words taught us by human
wisdom but with words taught us by the Spirit.
And so we explain spiritual truths to spiritual people. 14A person who does not have the Spirit does
not accept the truths that come from the Spirit of
God. That person thinks they are foolish and cannot understand them, because they can only be
judged to be true by the Spirit. 15The spiritual
person is able to judge all things, but no one
can judge him. The Scripture says:

16"Who has known the mind of the Lord?
  Who has been able to teach him?" *Isaiah 40:13*

But we have the mind of Christ.

Following People Is Wrong

3 Brothers and sisters, in the past I could not
talk to you as I talk to spiritual people. I had
to talk to you as I would to people without the
Spirit—babies in Christ. 2The teaching I gave you
was like milk, not solid food, because you were

PRIORITIES

Is This All There Is?

When Howard Hughes was forty-five, he was one of the most glamorous men in America. He owned an airline and hotels around the world. He dated actresses, flew exotic test aircraft, and worked on top-secret CIA contracts.

Twenty years later, Howard Hughes was the world's richest man—with $2.3 billion. But he was also one of the world's most pathetic. He lived in small, dark rooms in his hotels. He preferred to keep his life without sun and without joy. He had a scraggly beard down to his waist, long hair, and two-inch-long fingernails. His body had wasted away to a mere one hundred pounds.

He spent most of his time watching movies over and over—sometimes watching the same movie 150 times. He lay naked in bed, deathly afraid of germs. Life had lost its meaning for him.

Finally, emaciated and hooked on drugs, Howard Hughes died at age sixty-seven, because he didn't have a medical device his company had helped to develop.

Howard Hughes had it all—worldly wisdom, wealth, power, fame. He had all the things the world considers important. But they weren't enough. Read **1 Corinthians 1:18–31** to see what Paul says is really important in life.

- How was Howard Hughes's life an illustration of this passage?
- According to this passage, what does God say is most important for Christians?

C O N S I D E R . . .

- doing something "foolish"—such as helping someone who doesn't deserve it—as a sign of your faith.
- tearing out words and pictures from a magazine that show what the world says is important and what God says is important. Make a separate pile for each category.

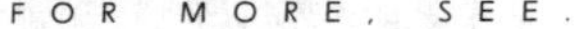

F O R M O R E , S E E . . .

- Psalm 139:1–18
- 2 Corinthians 11:16–31
- 1 John 3:1–3

not able to take solid food. And even now you are
not ready. [3]You are still not spiritual, because
there is jealousy and quarreling among you, and
this shows that you are not spiritual. You are acting like people of the world. [4]One of you says, "I
belong to Paul," and another says, "I belong to
Apollos." When you say things like this, you are
acting like people of the world.

[5]Is Apollos important? No! Is Paul important?
No! We are only servants of God who helped you
believe. Each one of us did the work God gave us
to do. [6]I planted the seed, and Apollos watered it.
But God is the One who made it grow. [7]So the
one who plants is not important, and the one who
waters is not important. Only God, who makes
things grow, is important. [8]The one who plants
and the one who waters have the same purpose,
and each will be rewarded for his own work. [9]We
are God's workers, working together; you are like
God's farm, God's house.

> **SIDELIGHT:** Even though Apollos isn't mentioned much in the Bible, he appears to have been an influential church leader. For a while he was a leader in Corinth, and may have been a better preacher than Paul (1 Corinthians 3:1–9).

[10]Using the gift God gave me, I laid the foundation of that house like an expert builder. Others
are building on that foundation, but all people
should be careful how they build on it. [11]The
foundation that has already been laid is Jesus
Christ, and no one can lay down any other foun-

SCHOOL

The Powerful Way

It was disgusting! While Scott Douglas was at the evening play practice, someone had smeared animal guts all over his car. Scott just stood in the parking lot, looking shocked.

Things had not been the same since he had seriously committed his life to Christ. Many of his friends didn't understand. They thought Scott was snubbing them when he wouldn't party with them. The verbal abuse came first. Then a few flattened tires. Then vicious rumors.

But this? This was sick!

Scott's best friend, Jeff Stevens, walked up behind him. When he noticed the car, Jeff blew up. "Man! . . . I can't believe . . . the nerve of those. . . ." Jeff was so angry he couldn't even finish his sentences. "We know who's behind this," he fumed. "Enough is enough! Let's go bash some heads!"

Scott shook his head and began to smile. "No way. Two bucks and some elbow grease, and we'll never know it happened. Besides, aren't we supposed to act more like Jesus? Do you think Jesus would bash heads now?"

Jeff looked at his friend and began to smile. "You're something, buddy. You're also right. Okay. To the car wash we go!"

Scott Douglas had plenty of reasons to take revenge. But, instead, Scott prayed for those people and treated them as he would anyone else. People noticed. During his final months at high school, people who knew what Scott had been through asked what his secret was.

It was tough for Scott to live the Christian life at school. But because he didn't fight back, Scott's actions demonstrated God's power. To find out more about demonstrating God's power at school, read **1 Corinthians 2:1–11**.

- How do Scott's actions show the difference between God's wisdom and the world's wisdom?
- According to this passage, what should be our attitude as we talk about and demonstrate our faith?

CONSIDER. . .

- imagining you were with Paul when he was experiencing some of the feelings he talks about in this passage. Write what you would say to encourage him.
- demonstrating God's power at school by not getting angry if people ridicule your faith.

FOR MORE, SEE. . .

- Joshua 6
- Ephesians 3:14–21
- 2 Timothy 1:6–8

dation. 12But if people build on that foundation,
using gold, silver, jewels, wood, grass, or straw,
13their work will be clearly seen, because the Day
of Judgment[n] will make it visible. That Day will
appear with fire, and the fire will test everyone's
work to show what sort of work it was. 14If the
building that has been put on the foundation still
stands, the builder will get a reward. 15But if the
building is burned up, the builder will suffer loss.
The builder will be saved, but it will be as one
who escaped from a fire.
16Don't you know that you are God's temple
and that God's Spirit[d] lives in you? 17If anyone
destroys God's temple, God will destroy that person, because God's temple is holy and you are
that temple.
18Do not fool yourselves. If you think you are
wise in this world, you should become a fool so
that you can become truly wise, 19because the
wisdom of this world is foolishness with God. It
is written in the Scriptures,[d] "He catches those
who are wise in their own clever traps."[n] 20It is
also written in the Scriptures, "The Lord knows
what wise people think. He knows their thoughts
are just a puff of wind."[n] 21So you should not
brag about human leaders. All things belong to
you: 22Paul, Apollos, and Peter; the world, life,
death, the present, and the future—all these be-

Day of Judgment The day Christ will come to judge all people and take his people home to live with him.
"He . . . traps." Quotation from Job 5:13.
"The Lord . . . wind." Quotation from Psalm 94:11.

POPULARITY

It's Not Who You Know . . .

Even in grade school, Steven Curtis Chapman faced a dilemma: to be popular by the "in" crowd's terms or to be popular on his own terms. Steven's faith was important to him, and he didn't want to compromise it.

At the same time, he just wanted to be everyone's friend. "I wanted to get along with everybody," Steven, the 1990 Gospel Music Association's Artist of the Year, explains now. So he decided to live what he believed and hope people would like him anyway.

It wasn't easy. He used to get together to play guitars with one guy. "Then [this guy] went the direction of the jock crowd," Steven recalls. "I went into music. He was the cool sports guy that everybody wanted to be friends with, and I saw this split happening and it really bothered me."

It didn't seem right that they couldn't be friends, just because they had different interests.

So Steven challenged the system. He continued to be himself and pursue interests even if they were "unpopular." He tried to be the best Christian he could be, and he treated people the same—no matter what clique they were in.

By the end of his high school years, people recognized what Steven had done. Steven's classmates voted to give him the highest honors possible at Heath High School, naming him "Mr. Heath" and "Mr. Senior."

Steven thinks he got the awards, "not so much for myself, but as a representative of a group of people who said, 'We are going to stand for what's good and right.' "

Steven had proven that it's not whom you know but who you are that matters most of all. Read **1 Corinthians 3:1–23** to see how Paul helped the Corinthian church understand this principle.

- Why do people such as Steven's classmates and the Corinthians value having the right connections? How does this attitude divide people?
- What does this passage tell us we should focus on, instead of focusing on popularity?

C O N S I D E R . . .

- evaluating whether your efforts to be popular please God.
- working with friends to create a "Popularity/Clique Survey" to distribute at school. Determine how cliques affect relationships.

F O R M O R E , S E E . . .

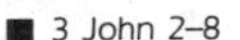

- Daniel 1:1–21
- Mark 10:42–45
- 3 John 2–8

long to you. 23And you belong to Christ, and
Christ belongs to God.

Apostles Are Servants of Christ

4 People should think of us as servants of
Christ, the ones God has trusted with his secrets. 2Now in this way those who are trusted
with something valuable must show they are worthy of that trust. 3As for myself, I do not care if I
am judged by you or by any human court. I do not
even judge myself. 4I know of no wrong I have
done, but this does not make me right before the
Lord. The Lord is the One who judges me. 5So do
not judge before the right time; wait until the
Lord comes. He will bring to light things that are
now hidden in darkness, and will make known
the secret purposes of people's hearts. Then God
will praise each one of them.
6Brothers and sisters, I have used Apollos and
myself as examples so you could learn through us
the meaning of the saying, "Follow only what is
written in the Scriptures."[d] Then you will not be
more proud of one person than another. 7Who
says you are better than others? What do you
have that was not given to you? And if it was
given to you, why do you brag as if you did not
receive it as a gift?
8You think you already have everything you
need. You think you are rich. You think you have
become kings without us. I wish you really were
kings so we could be kings together with you.
9But it seems to me that God has put us apostles[d]
in last place, like those sentenced to die. We are

SERVICE

Worthy of the Trust

"Son, please don't go."

Bill Dukes's eyes met his father's. "Dad, I believe God wants me in Brazil this year. We've been waiting on the missionary board for a long time. Now the appointment is here. I've got to go."

Bill nearly broke down as he watched his dad's eyes fill with tears. The doctors didn't think Bill's dad had long to live. If Bill left for Brazil, his father might die before Bill could come home.

"Look, Dad, I know you want me to stay. I want to be around you too. But I have to ask what God wants. And as far as I can tell now, he wants me in Brazil."

As Bill drove away from his parents' house, his mind replayed doubts others had expressed about his decision:

"A wife, one boy, and a baby on the way. You're crazy!"

"Do you really think God would call you away from your father now?"

"We need pastors in this country. Why don't you stay?"

Bill weighed his options. Jesus had given him so much that Bill felt he had a responsibility to fulfill.

For eight years, Bill and his family worked in South America. And, against all predictions by doctors and the expectations of Bill's family, Bill's father was alive to welcome him home.

"I'm convinced that God is faithful," Bill says, "especially in those times when someone has to make a hard choice to be faithful in serving God."

The Corinthian Christians needed to be reminded of the same thing, and so do we. Read how Paul makes the point clear in **1 Corinthians 4:1–5**.

- How would Bill's feelings about his life compare with Paul's feelings in this passage?
- How do you feel about God's knowing and judging the secrets of your heart?

C O N S I D E R . . .

- thanking God for a servant whose faithfulness has helped you in some way. Ask God to help you do the same for someone else.
- evaluating any commitments to serve you have made and haven't kept. Begin fulfilling those commitments this week.

F O R M O R E , S E E . . .

- Joshua 24:14–15
- Luke 16:10–12
- Ephesians 4:11–16

like a show for the whole world to see—angels
and people. 10We are fools for Christ's sake, but
you are very wise in Christ. We are weak, but you
are strong. You receive honor, but we are
shamed. 11Even to this very hour we do not have
enough to eat or drink or to wear. We are often
beaten, and we have no homes in which to live.
12We work hard with our own hands for our food.
When people curse us, we bless them. When they
hurt us, we put up with it. 13When they tell evil
lies about us, we speak nice words about them.
Even today, we are treated as though we were the
garbage of the world—the filth of the earth.

14I am not trying to make you feel ashamed. I
am writing this to give you a warning as my own
dear children. 15For though you may have ten
thousand teachers in Christ, you do not have
many fathers. Through the Good News[d] I became
your father in Christ Jesus, 16so I beg you, please
follow my example. 17That is why I am sending to
you Timothy, my son in the Lord. I love Timothy,
and he is faithful. He will help you remember my
way of life in Christ Jesus, just as I teach it in all
the churches everywhere.

18Some of you have become proud, thinking
that I will not come to you again. 19But I will
come to you very soon if the Lord wishes. Then
I will know what the proud ones do, not what
they say, 20because the kingdom of God is present
not in talk but in power. 21Which do you want:
that I come to you with punishment or with love
and gentleness?

Wickedness in the Church

5 It is actually being said that there is sexual
sin among you. And it is a kind that does not
happen even among people who do not know
God. A man there has his father's wife. 2And you
are proud! You should have been filled with sadness so that the man who did this should be put
out of your group. 3I am not there with you in
person, but I am with you in spirit. And I have
already judged the man who did that sin as if I
were really there. 4When you meet together in
the name of our Lord Jesus, and I meet with you
in spirit with the power of our Lord Jesus, 5then
hand this man over to Satan. So his sinful self[n]
will be destroyed, and his spirit will be saved on
the day of the Lord.

6Your bragging is not good. You know the saying, "Just a little yeast makes the whole batch of
dough rise." 7Take out all the old yeast so that you
will be a new batch of dough without yeast,
which you really are. For Christ, our Passover[d]
lamb, has been sacrificed. 8So let us celebrate this
feast, but not with the bread that has the old
yeast—the yeast of sin and wickedness. Let us
celebrate this feast with the bread that has no
yeast—the bread of goodness and truth.

9I wrote you in my earlier letter not to associate
with those who sin sexually. 10But I did not mean
you should not associate with those of this world
who sin sexually, or with the greedy, or robbers,
or those who worship idols. To get away from
them you would have to leave this world. 11I am
writing to tell you that you must not associate
with those who call themselves believers in Christ
but who sin sexually, or are greedy, or worship
idols, or abuse others with words, or get drunk,
or cheat people. Do not even eat with people like
that.

12-13It is not my business to judge those who are
not part of the church. God will judge them. But
you must judge the people who are part of the
church. The Scripture[d] says, "You must get rid of
the evil person among you."[n]

> **SIDELIGHT:** Corinth was known for lawsuits (1 Corinthians 6:1). Trials were social events, and sitting on the jury was a privilege. One record tells of a jury with six thousand people on it.

Judging Problems Among Christians

6 When you have something against another
Christian, how can you bring yourself to go
before judges who are not right with God? Why
do you not let God's people decide who is right?
2Surely you know that God's people will judge the
world. So if you are to judge the world, are you
not able to judge small cases as well? 3You know
that in the future we will judge angels, so surely
we can judge the ordinary things of this life. 4If
you have ordinary cases that must be judged, are
you going to appoint people as judges who mean
nothing to the church? 5I say this to shame you.
Surely there is someone among you wise enough
to judge a complaint between believers. 6But now
one believer goes to court against another believer—and you do this in front of unbelievers!

7The fact that you have lawsuits against each
other shows that you are already defeated. Why
not let yourselves be wronged? Why not let yourselves be cheated? 8But you yourselves do wrong
and cheat, and you do this to other believers!

9-10Surely you know that the people who do
wrong will not inherit God's kingdom. Do not be
fooled. Those who sin sexually, worship idols,
take part in adultery,[d] those who are male prosti-

sinful self Literally, "flesh." This could also mean his body.
"You . . . you." Quotation from Deuteronomy 17:7; 19:19; 22:21, 24; 24:7.

tutes,[d] or men who have sexual relations with
other men, those who steal, are greedy, get
drunk, lie about others, or rob — these people will
not inherit God's kingdom. 11In the past, some of
you were like that, but you were washed clean.
You were made holy, and you were made right
with God in the name of the Lord Jesus Christ and
in the Spirit of our God.

Use Your Bodies for God's Glory

12"I am allowed to do all things," but all things
are not good for me to do. "I am allowed to do
all things," but I will not let anything make me its
slave. 13"Food is for the stomach, and the stomach
for food," but God will destroy them both. The
body is not for sexual sin but for the Lord, and the
Lord is for the body. 14By his power God has
raised the Lord from the dead and will also raise
us from the dead. 15Surely you know that your
bodies are parts of Christ himself. So I must never
take the parts of Christ and join them to a prostitute![d] 16It is written in the Scriptures,[d] "The two
will become one body."[n] So you should know
that anyone who joins with a prostitute becomes
one body with the prostitute. 17But the one who
joins with the Lord is one spirit with the Lord.
18So run away from sexual sin. Every other sin
people do is outside their bodies, but those who
sin sexually sin against their own bodies. 19You
should know that your body is a temple for the
Holy Spirit[d] who is in you. You have received
the Holy Spirit from God. So you do not belong
to yourselves, 20because you were bought by God
for a price. So honor God with your bodies.

About Marriage

7 Now I will discuss the things you wrote me
about. It is good for a man not to have sexual
relations with a woman. 2But because sexual sin
is a danger, each man should have his own wife,
and each woman should have her own husband.
3The husband should give his wife all that he
owes her as his wife. And the wife should give her
husband all that she owes him as her husband.

"The two . . . body." Quotation from Genesis 2:24.

BRAGGING

Honest to God!

Nothing ordinary ever seemed to happen to Ray Fulton. His stories of extravagant family vacations, chance meetings of famous people, and doing unbelievable feats were too amazing to be true. When Henry McCormick questioned the facts of his stories, Ray would get defensive. He would insist he was being truthful by pledging, "Honest to God!"

Finally, Henry caught Ray in a blatant lie. One Saturday morning he called to tell Henry he had gotten a ticket to a rock concert that had been sold out for more than two months. He wouldn't show Henry the ticket for fear of losing it, he said, nor would he explain how he got it. Yet he tried to make Henry believe he had an "inside" source. He promised to tell all about the concert the next day.

But that night, during the very hour of the concert, Henry spotted Ray with his family at a mall more than fifty miles from the concert site! Henry confronted Ray the next day, and he still insisted he had been at the concert. When Henry told him he had seen him at the mall, he finally admitted he had exaggerated a little—but he had bought the group's latest album, he said.

Henry's friendship with Ray crumbled after that. He was tired of sorting truth from fiction whenever Ray bragged. Bragging ruined Henry's friendship with Ray. Read **1 Corinthians 5:6–8** to see what Paul thought about bragging.

- How was Ray's bragging like the yeast Paul writes about in this passage?
- What effects has bragging had in your relationships?

C O N S I D E R . . .

- listing specific ways people can keep from bragging.
- asking God to show you if you have been guilty of bragging. If so, tell the modest truth to the people you bragged to.

F O R M O R E , S E E . . .

- Isaiah 10:8–15
- Jeremiah 9:23–24
- James 4:13–17

4The wife does not have full rights over her own
body; her husband shares them. And the husband
does not have full rights over his own body; his
wife shares them. 5Do not refuse to give your bodies to each other, unless you both agree to stay
away from sexual relations for a time so you can
give your time to prayer. Then come together
again so Satan cannot tempt you because of a lack
of self-control. 6I say this to give you permission
to stay away from sexual relations for a time. It is
not a command to do so. 7I wish that everyone
were like me, but each person has his own gift
from God. One has one gift, another has another
gift.

8Now for those who are not married and for the
widows I say this: It is good for them to stay unmarried as I am. 9But if they cannot control themselves, they should marry. It is better to marry
than to burn with sexual desire.

10Now I give this command for the married
people. (The command is not from me; it is from
the Lord.) A wife should not leave her husband.
11But if she does leave, she must not marry again,
or she should make up with her husband. Also the
husband should not divorce his wife.

12For all the others I say this (I am saying this,
not the Lord): If a Christian man has a wife who
is not a believer, and she is happy to live with
him, he must not divorce her. 13And if a Christian
woman has a husband who is not a believer, and
he is happy to live with her, she must not divorce
him. 14The husband who is not a believer is made
holy through his believing wife. And the wife who
is not a believer is made holy through her believing husband. If this were not true, your children
would not be clean,[d] but now your children are
holy.

15But if those who are not believers decide to
leave, let them leave. When this happens, the
Christian man or woman is free. But God called
us to live in peace. 16Wife, you don't know;
maybe you will save your husband. And husband,
you don't know; maybe you will save your wife.

Live as God Called You

17But in any case each one of you should continue to live the way God has given you to live—
the way you were when God called you. This is
a rule I make in all the churches. 18If a man was
already circumcised[d] when he was called, he
should not undo his circumcision. If a man was
without circumcision when he was called, he
should not be circumcised. 19It is not important if
a man is circumcised or not. The important thing
is obeying God's commands. 20Each one of you
should stay the way you were when God called

DRUGS AND ALCOHOL

Serving Something

"I never believed I'd lose control." For the first time in two years, Mikal Hun's eyes, mind and heart were clear. And it was the first time she had ever discussed her alcohol addiction with Carl Nelson, her youth leader.

"I didn't become alcoholic overnight. It was a gradual thing for me. First, it was an occasional sneak drink at a friend's house when her parents were gone. Then it was a few beers at parties. It wasn't long before I needed drinks. Before and after school as well as during lunch break, and even between classes—any time was the right time because I needed them just to feel human."

Choking back tears, Mikal continued: "I couldn't see it then because of my addiction. But I now know I sold myself into slavery—one drink at a time. My body, my heart, my mind became a slave to beer and wine coolers."

As Mikal covered her face and sobbed, a warm tear slowly rolled from Carl's eye and down his cheek. He felt with her the tragedy of her experience and recalled the warning in **1 Corinthians 6:12–20**.

- How did the slavery Paul warned of become a reality in Mikal's life?
- How can food or sex, like alcohol, enslave people?

CONSIDER . . .

- looking at magazine ads for alcoholic beverages. Determine what the advertisers are communicating about using alcohol.
- talking with an adult if you have a problem with drugs and alcohol.

FOR MORE, SEE . . .

- Proverbs 20:1
- Matthew 4:8–11
- Romans 1:18–25

you. 21If you were a slave when God called you, do not let that bother you. But if you can be free, then make good use of your freedom. 22Those who were slaves when the Lord called them are free persons who belong to the Lord. In the same way, those who were free when they were called are now Christ's slaves. 23You all were bought at a great price, so do not become slaves of people. 24Brothers and sisters, each of you should stay as you were when you were called, and stay there with God.

Questions About Getting Married

25Now I write about people who are not married. I have no command from the Lord about this; I give my opinion. But I can be trusted, because the Lord has shown me mercy. 26The present time is a time of trouble, so I think it is good for you to stay the way you are. 27If you have a wife, do not try to become free from her. If you are not married, do not try to find a wife. 28But if you decide to marry, you have not sinned. And if a girl who has never married decides to marry, she has not sinned. But those who marry will have trouble in this life, and I want you to be free from trouble.

29Brothers and sisters, this is what I mean: We do not have much time left. So starting now, those who have wives should live as if they had no wives. 30Those who are crying should live as if they were not crying. Those who are happy should live as if they were not happy. Those who buy things should live as if they own nothing. 31Those who use the things of the world should live as if they were not using them, because this world in its present form will soon be gone.

32I want you to be free from worry. A man who is not married is busy with the Lord's work, trying to please the Lord. 33But a man who is married is busy with things of the world, trying to please his wife. 34He must think about two things — pleasing his wife and pleasing the Lord. A woman who is not married or a girl who has never married is busy with the Lord's work. She wants to be holy in body and spirit. But a married woman is busy with things of the world, as to how she can please her husband. 35I am saying this to help you, not to limit you. But I want you to live in the right way, to give yourselves fully to the Lord without concern for other things.

36If a man thinks he is not doing the right thing with the girl he is engaged to, if she is almost past the best age to marry and he feels he should marry her, he should do what he wants. They should get married. It is no sin. 37But if a man is sure in his mind that there is no need for marriage, and has

LOVE

Keeping in Focus

- The best way to draw a straight line is to focus on its ending point.
- The best way to take a test is to shut out all distractions and focus only on the questions.
- The best way to drive a car safely is to focus on the road and the traffic around you.
- The best way to become an accomplished musician or athlete is to focus your time and talent on training and practice.
- The best way to build lifelong friendships is to focus on being friendly and communicating honestly.
- The best way to accomplish things is to focus on goals.
- The best way to love God is to focus on knowing Christ and doing his will.

For more about the importance of keeping love's focus, read **1 Corinthians 7:29–35**.

- How does focusing on loving God affect the way you use your time?
- What things listed in this passage distract you from focusing your love on God?

CONSIDER . . .

- asking God to reveal any distractions in your life that keep you from focusing your love on him.
- transforming the relationships in your life to help you focus on loving God. For example, you and a friend could have a Bible study together, or you and your mom or dad could pray together once a week.

FOR MORE, SEE . . .

- Genesis 5:21–24
- Matthew 10:34–38
- Philippians 3:12–14

his own desires under control, and has decided
not to marry the one to whom he is engaged, he
is doing the right thing. 38So the man who marries
his girl does right, but the man who does not
marry will do better.
39A woman must stay with her husband as long
as he lives. But if her husband dies, she is free to
marry any man she wants, but she must marry in
the Lord. 40The woman is happier if she does not
marry again. This is my opinion, but I believe I
also have God's Spirit.

About Food Offered to Idols

8 Now I will write about meat that is sacrificed
to idols. We know that "we all have knowledge." Knowledge puffs you up with pride, but
love builds up. 2If you think you know something,
you do not yet know anything as you should. 3But
if any person loves God, that person is known by
God.
4So this is what I say about eating meat sacrificed to idols: We know that an idol is really nothing in the world, and we know there is only one
God. 5Even though there are things called gods,
in heaven or on earth (and there are many "gods"
and "lords"), 6for us there is only one God—our
Father. All things came from him, and we live for
him. And there is only one Lord—Jesus Christ.
All things were made through him, and we also
were made through him.
7But not all people know this. Some people are
still so used to idols that when they eat meat, they
still think of it as being sacrificed to an idol. Because their conscience is weak, when they eat it,
they feel guilty. 8But food will not bring us closer
to God. Refusing to eat does not make us less
pleasing to God, and eating does not make us better in God's sight.
9But be careful that your freedom does not
cause those who are weak in faith to fall into sin.
10You have "knowledge," so you eat in an idol's
temple.[n] But someone who is weak in faith
might see you eating there and be encouraged to
eat meat sacrificed to idols while thinking it is

idol's temple Building where a god is worshiped.

FREEDOM

Free to Do Good

Holly Boyd was overweight. All the kids made fun of her when she tried to play games with them. And when refreshments were served, they would say things such as "Hurry! Hide the food. Here comes Holly."

One night after youth group, youth leader Max Barrett found Holly crying in an empty room.

She told Max about how much it hurt when kids made fun of her and how she wanted to lose weight but couldn't. Max couldn't relate to Holly's weight problem; he was a runner and never seemed to gain weight. But he could empathize with the pain she felt.

"I'll tell you what, Holly," he offered, "you give up sweets and so will I. And why don't you start running with me?"

Holly agreed. The two ran together three times a week. And at youth group meetings while the kids were eating junk food, Max and Holly munched on veggies.

In four months, Holly had lost thirty pounds. She felt better about herself. Holly told Max she couldn't have done it without him.

Max could have eaten whatever he wanted, but he gave up his freedom to help Holly. Read **1 Corinthians 8:1–13** to see how Paul encourages Christians to use their freedom to help others.

- How do Max's actions demonstrate the principles of this passage?
- How would your friends describe your use of the freedom you have in Jesus Christ?

CONSIDER . . .

- changing an area of your life if your freedom is hurting others.
- talking to a new Christian and asking what he or she thinks about how Christians use their freedom.

FOR MORE, SEE . . .

- Deuteronomy 30:11–20
- 1 Corinthians 10:23–24
- 1 Timothy 4:10–12

wrong to do so. 11This weak believer for whom Christ died is ruined because of your "knowledge." 12When you sin against your brothers and sisters in Christ like this and cause them to do what they feel is wrong, you are also sinning against Christ. 13So if the food I eat causes them to fall into sin, I will never eat meat again so that I will not cause any of them to sin.

Paul Is like the Other Apostles

9 I am a free man. I am an apostle.[d] I have seen Jesus our Lord. You people are all an example of my work in the Lord. 2If others do not accept me as an apostle, surely you do, because you are proof that I am an apostle in the Lord.

3This is the answer I give people who want to judge me: 4Do we not have the right to eat and drink? 5Do we not have the right to bring a believing wife with us when we travel as do the other apostles and the Lord's brothers and Peter? 6Are Barnabas and I the only ones who must work to earn our living? 7No soldier ever serves in the army and pays his own salary. No one ever plants a vineyard without eating some of the grapes. No person takes care of a flock without drinking some of the milk.

8I do not say this by human authority; God's law also says the same thing. 9It is written in the law of Moses: "When an ox is working in the grain, do not cover its mouth to keep it from eating."[n] When God said this, was he thinking only about oxen? No. 10He was really talking about us. Yes, that Scripture[d] was written for us, because it goes on to say: "The one who plows and the one who works in the grain should hope to get some of the grain for their work." 11Since we planted spiritual seed among you, is it too much if we should harvest from you some things for this life? 12If others have the right to get something from you, surely we have this right, too. But we do not use it. No, we put up with everything ourselves so that we will not keep anyone from believing the Good News[d] of Christ. 13Surely you know that those who work at the Temple[d] get their food from the Temple, and those who serve at the altar get part of what is offered at the altar. 14In the same way, the Lord has commanded that those who tell the Good News should get their living from this work.

15But I have not used any of these rights. And I am not writing this now to get anything from you. I would rather die than to have my reason for bragging taken away. 16Telling the Good News does not give me any reason for bragging. Telling the Good News is my duty—something I must do. And how terrible it will be for me if I do not tell the Good News. 17If I preach because it is my own choice, I have a reward. But if I preach and it is not my choice to do so, I am only doing the duty that was given to me. 18So what reward do I get? This is my reward: that when I tell the Good News I can offer it freely. I do not use my full rights in my work of preaching the Good News.

19I am free and belong to no one. But I make myself a slave to all people to win as many as I can. 20To the Jews I became like a Jew to win the Jews. I myself am not ruled by the law. But to those who are ruled by the law I became like a person who is ruled by the law. I did this to win those who are ruled by the law. 21To those who are without the law I became like a person who is without the law. I did this to win those people who are without the law. (But really, I am not without God's law—I am ruled by Christ's law.) 22To those who are weak, I became weak so I could win the weak. I have become all things to all people so I could save some of them in any way possible. 23I do all this because of the Good News and so I can share in its blessings.

24You know that in a race all the runners run, but only one gets the prize. So run to win! 25All those who compete in the games use self-control so they can win a crown. That crown is an earthly thing that lasts only a short time, but our crown will never be destroyed. 26So I do not run without a goal. I fight like a boxer who is hitting something—not just the air. 27I treat my body hard and make it my slave so that I myself will not be disqualified after I have preached to others.

SIDELIGHT: Paul's reference to "running the race" in 1 Corinthians 9:24–27 would have reminded the Corinthians of the Isthmian Games, held every two years in Corinth's coliseum. These games were the most famous athletic competition of their time except for the ancient Olympics. The games might have included wrestling, boxing, chariot races, and foot races.

Warnings from Israel's Past

10 Brothers and sisters, I want you to know what happened to our ancestors who followed Moses. They were all under the cloud and all went through the sea. 2They were all baptized as followers of Moses in the cloud and in the sea. 3They all ate the same spiritual food, 4and all drank the same spiritual drink. They drank from that spiritual rock that followed them, and that

"When an ox . . . eating." Quotation from Deuteronomy 25:4.

rock was Christ. 5But God was not pleased with
most of them, so they died in the desert.
6And these things happened as examples for us,
to stop us from wanting evil things as those people
did. 7Do not worship idols, as some of them did.
Just as it is written in the Scriptures:[d] "They sat
down to eat and drink, and then they got up and
sinned sexually."[n] 8We must not take part in sexual sins, as some of them did. In one day twenty-
three thousand of them died because of their sins.
9We must not test Christ as some of them did;
they were killed by snakes. 10Do not complain as
some of them did; they were killed by the angel
that destroys.
11The things that happened to those people are
examples. They were written down to teach us,
because we live in a time when all these things of
the past have reached their goal. 12If you think
you are strong, you should be careful not to fall.
13The only temptation that has come to you is that
which everyone has. But you can trust God, who
will not permit you to be tempted more than you
can stand. But when you are tempted, he will also
give you a way to escape so that you will be able
to stand it.
14So, my dear friends, run away from the worship of idols. 15I am speaking to you as to intelligent people; judge for yourselves what I say. 16We
give thanks for the cup of blessing,[n] which is a
sharing in the blood of Christ. And the bread that
we break is a sharing in the body of Christ. 17Be-
cause there is one loaf of bread, we who are many
are one body, because we all share that one loaf.
18Think about the Israelites: Do not those who
eat the sacrifices share in the altar? 19I do not
mean that the food sacrificed to an idol is important. I do not mean that an idol is anything at all.
20But I say that what is sacrificed to idols is offered
to demons,[d] not to God. And I do not want you
to share anything with demons. 21You cannot
drink the cup of the Lord and the cup of demons
also. You cannot share in the Lord's table and the

"They . . . sexually." Quotation from Exodus 32:6.
cup of blessing The cup of the fruit of the vine that Christians thank God for and drink at the Lord's Supper.

SHARING FAITH

Giving It All

In 1873, Lottie Moon went to China as a missionary. She reached out to the Chinese people in the face of tremendous persecution, and she challenged Christians back in the United States to give more money to help people hear the gospel.

In 1911, war and famine hit China. Lottie was evacuated to Japan, but she regularly gave a large part of her small salary to her starving Chinese friends.

She wrote to her mission board asking for help time and again. But the board was heavily in debt and could hardly pay its missionary salaries. Nothing was budgeted for famine relief.

The famine worsened. Lottie drew out the last of her savings from a bank to send to relief workers. "I pray that no missionary will ever be as lonely as I have been," she wrote in her bank book.

Lottie vowed not to eat as long as her Chinese friends were starving. On Christmas Eve night, 1912, she lapsed into unconsciousness. The nurse who was with her watched her clasping and unclasping her hands in the Chinese fashion of greeting. The nurse bent over her and heard her saying the name of a Chinese friend. Even in her last minutes, Lottie's heart and mind were focused on the people she loved.

Lottie Moon died, having given everything she had to the Chinese people. Paul writes about this kind of love in **1 Corinthians 9:16–27**.

- How did Lottie Moon demonstrate this passage with her life?
- How can the methods in this passage help you effectively reach a non-Christian friend?

C O N S I D E R . . .

- getting to know a non-Christian friend so you can share your faith.
- giving to a missionary organization to help spread the gospel.

F O R M O R E , S E E . . .

- Isaiah 61
- Matthew 10:1–15
- Matthew 28:16–20

table of demons. [22]Are we trying to make the Lord
jealous? We are not stronger than he is, are we?

How to Use Christian Freedom

[23]"We are allowed to do all things," but all
things are not good for us to do. "We are allowed
to do all things," but not all things help others
grow stronger. [24]Do not look out only for yourselves. Look out for the good of others also.
[25]Eat any meat that is sold in the meat market.
Do not ask questions to see if it is meat you think
is wrong to eat. [26]You may eat it, "because the
earth belongs to the Lord, and everything in it."[n]
[27]Those who are not believers may invite you
to eat with them. If you want to go, eat anything
that is put before you. Do not ask questions to see
if you think it might be wrong to eat. [28]But if anyone says to you, "That food was offered to idols,"
do not eat it. Do not eat it because of that person
who told you and because eating it might be
thought to be wrong. [29]I don't mean you think it
is wrong, but the other person might. But why,
you ask, should my freedom be judged by someone else's conscience? [30]If I eat the meal with
thankfulness, why am I criticized because of
something for which I thank God?
[31]The answer is, if you eat or drink, or if you
do anything, do it all for the glory of God. [32]Never
do anything that might hurt others—Jews,
Greeks, or God's church— [33]just as I, also, try to
please everybody in every way. I am not trying to
do what is good for me but what is good for most
people so they can be saved.

11 Follow my example, as I follow the example of Christ.

Being Under Authority

[2]I praise you because you remember me in everything, and you follow closely the teachings just
as I gave them to you. [3]But I want you to understand this: The head of every man is Christ, the
head of a woman is the man,[n] and the head of

"because . . . it" Quotation from Psalms 24:1; 50:12; 89:11.
the man This could also mean "her husband."

SEXUALITY

It Could Happen to Me

As Christians, Todd Pierce and Larry Gatchell shared the same sexual values. Both believed it was important to wait until marriage to have sexual intercourse. But Todd and Larry differed in their attitude toward the temptation.

"No problem!" Todd would often say. "That's not going to happen to me. I can wait."

But Larry would say: "Hey, it's a problem for me. I know it could happen to me."

Because of their different perspectives, Todd and Larry lived different lifestyles. Convinced of his ability to remain chaste, Todd flirted with girls, and with the danger of becoming sexually involved. Barely a teenager, Todd began to solo date with his "steady" girlfriends.

Realizing his own vulnerability to become sexually active, Larry didn't take the same risks as Todd. Larry would usually group date and never got too serious with any girl.

Todd and Larry met together once a week before school to pray and read the Bible. One day, as Todd read the scripture aloud, Larry heard Todd's voice crack, then go silent. Looking up, he saw Todd wiping tears from his eyes.

After a while, Todd spoke: "I've really blown it, Larry. I said I'd never do it before marriage, but I did. I guess I only fooled myself by thinking I was too strong to be so weak."

Read **1 Corinthians 10:1–13**, to see Paul's warnings about temptation.

- Which of these verses do you believe would have spoken the strongest to Todd?
- What ways has God provided to help us deal with sexual temptation?

CONSIDER . . .

- designing an "escape plan" for whenever you are tempted with sexual sin.
- listing situations when you might be tempted sexually. Then decide how you will avoid those situations.

FOR MORE, SEE . . .

- Genesis 39:6–12
- 2 Samuel 11
- Ephesians 5:1–5

Christ is God. 4Every man who prays or prophesies[d] with his head covered brings shame to his
head. 5But every woman who prays or prophesies
with her head uncovered brings shame to her
head. She is the same as a woman who has
her head shaved. 6If a woman does not cover her
head, she should have her hair cut off. But since
it is shameful for a woman to cut off her hair or
to shave her head, she should cover her head.
7But a man should not cover his head, because he
is the likeness and glory of God. But woman is
man's glory. 8Man did not come from woman, but
woman came from man. 9And man was not made
for woman, but woman was made for man. 10So
that is why a woman should have a symbol of
authority on her head, because of the angels.

11But in the Lord women are not independent
of men, and men are not independent of women.
12This is true because woman came from man,
but also man is born from woman. But everything
comes from God. 13Decide this for yourselves: Is
it right for a woman to pray to God with her head
uncovered? 14Even nature itself teaches you that
wearing long hair is shameful for a man. 15But
long hair is a woman's glory. Long hair is given to
her as a covering. 16Some people may still want to
argue about this, but I would add that neither we
nor the churches of God have any other practice.

The Lord's Supper

17In the things I tell you now I do not praise
you, because when you come together you do
more harm than good. 18First, I hear that when
you meet together as a church you are divided,
and I believe some of this. 19(It is necessary to
have differences among you so that it may be
clear which of you really have God's approval.)
20When you come together, you are not really eating the Lord's Supper.[n] 21This is because when
you eat, each person eats without waiting for the
others. Some people do not get enough to eat,
while others have too much to drink. 22You can
eat and drink in your own homes! You seem to
think God's church is not important, and you em-
barrass those who are poor. What should I tell
you? Should I praise you? I do not praise you for
doing this.

23The teaching I gave you is the same teaching
I received from the Lord: On the night when the
Lord Jesus was handed over to be killed, he took
bread 24and gave thanks for it. Then he broke the
bread and said, "This is my body; it is for you. Do
this to remember me." 25In the same way, after
they ate, Jesus took the cup. He said, "This cup
is the new agreement that is sealed with the blood
of my death. When you drink this, do it to remember me." 26Every time you eat this bread and
drink this cup you are telling others about the
Lord's death until he comes.

27So a person who eats the bread or drinks the
cup of the Lord in a way that is not worthy of it
will be guilty of sinning against the body and the
blood of the Lord. 28Look into your own hearts
before you eat the bread and drink the cup, 29be-
cause all who eat the bread and drink the cup
without recognizing the body eat and drink judgment against themselves. 30That is why many in
your group are sick and weak, and many have
died. 31But if we judged ourselves in the right
way, God would not judge us. 32But when the
Lord judges us, he punishes us so that we will not
be destroyed along with the world.

33So my brothers and sisters, when you come
together to eat, wait for each other. 34Anyone
who is too hungry should eat at home so that in
meeting together you will not bring God's judgment on yourselves. I will tell you what to do
about the other things when I come.

Gifts from the Holy Spirit

12 Now, brothers and sisters, I want you to
understand about spiritual gifts. 2You
know the way you lived before you were believers. You let yourselves be influenced and led away
to worship idols—things that could not speak.
3So I want you to understand that no one who is
speaking with the help of God's Spirit says, "Jesus
be cursed." And no one can say, "Jesus is Lord,"
without the help of the Holy Spirit.[d]

4There are different kinds of gifts, but they are
all from the same Spirit. 5There are different ways
to serve but the same Lord to serve. 6And there
are different ways that God works through people
but the same God. God works in all of us in everything we do. 7Something from the Spirit can be
seen in each person, for the common good. 8The
Spirit gives one person the ability to speak with
wisdom, and the same Spirit gives another the
ability to speak with knowledge. 9The same Spirit
gives faith to one person. And, to another, that
one Spirit gives gifts of healing. 10The Spirit gives
to another person the power to do miracles,[d] to
another the ability to prophesy.[d] And he gives to
another the ability to know the difference between good and evil spirits. The Spirit gives one
person the ability to speak in different kinds of
languages[n] and to another the ability to interpret
those languages. 11One Spirit, the same Spirit,
does all these things, and the Spirit decides what
to give each person.

Lord's Supper The meal Jesus told his followers to eat to remember him (Luke 22:14-20).
languages This can also be translated "tongues."

The Body of Christ Works Together

12A person's body is only one thing, but it has many parts. Though there are many parts to a body, all those parts make only one body. Christ is like that also. 13Some of us are Jews, and some are Greeks. Some of us are slaves, and some are free. But we were all baptized into one body through one Spirit.[d] And we were all made to share in the one Spirit.

14The human body has many parts. 15The foot might say, "Because I am not a hand, I am not part of the body." But saying this would not stop the foot from being a part of the body. 16The ear might say, "Because I am not an eye, I am not part of the body." But saying this would not stop the ear from being a part of the body. 17If the whole body were an eye, it would not be able to hear. If the whole body were an ear, it would not be able to smell. 18-19If each part of the body were the same part, there would be no body. But truly God put all the parts, each one of them, in the body as he wanted them. 20So then there are many parts, but only one body.

21The eye cannot say to the hand, "I don't need you!" And the head cannot say to the foot, "I don't need you!" 22No! Those parts of the body that seem to be the weaker are really necessary. 23And the parts of the body we think are less deserving are the parts to which we give the most honor. We give special respect to the parts we want to hide. 24The more respectable parts of our body need no special care. But God put the body together and gave more honor to the parts that need it 25so our body would not be divided. God wanted the different parts to care the same for each other. 26If one part of the body suffers, all the other parts suffer with it. Or if one part of our body is honored, all the other parts share its honor.

27Together you are the body of Christ, and each one of you is a part of that body. 28In the church God has given a place first to apostles,[d] second to prophets,[d] and third to teachers. Then God has

WORSHIP

Remember Me?

The second Sunday in March is a special day for Sharon Ebell's family. Each year on this date, her family gathers for a meal. When the table is cleared, the family photo albums are brought out and passed around.

Everyone smiles and giggles to see how each family member has changed from picture to picture over the years. The giggles sometimes erupt into laughter when the pictures prompt funny stories about family members. Sharon's favorite is the one about her dad being chased by a skunk when he was a teenager.

And there are always tears when the family sees the photos of its absent members. No eye is dry when photos of Jonathan, Sharon's younger brother, are passed around. He died of cystic fibrosis when he was five.

Some of Sharon's friends think her family's habit is a little weird. A few have even wondered if it isn't like worshiping the dead.

But Sharon shrugs off their comments. "It's just how we remember the people who've been important to our family. I never met my grandparents, but I feel like I know them. I've seen their pictures and heard stories about them at least once a year for as long as I can remember," she explains. "I don't think we worship our dead relatives; we just celebrate their lives."

As Christians, we don't worship the dead. But we do worship one who died and rose from the dead. Read **1 Corinthians 11:23–26** to see how Paul explains one way in which Christians can celebrate Jesus' life and work.

- How is the celebration Paul describes similar to the celebration in Sharon's family? How is it different?
- What do you do in your church and life to remember Jesus?

CONSIDER . . .

- creating other celebrations to remember Jesus. For example, a candlelight dinner could remind you that Jesus is the light of the world.
- talking with your pastor about the ways your church follows this scripture.

FOR MORE, SEE . . .

- Exodus 12:14–20
- Exodus 16:31–36
- Luke 22:14–20

given a place to those who do miracles,[d] those
who have gifts of healing, those who can help others, those who are able to govern, and those who
can speak in different languages.[n] 29Not all are
apostles. Not all are prophets. Not all are teachers.
Not all do miracles. 30Not all have gifts of healing.
Not all speak in different languages. Not all interpret those languages. 31But you should truly want
to have the greater gifts.

Love Is the Greatest Gift

And now I will show you the best way of all.
13 I may speak in different languages[n] of
people or even angels. But if I do not
have love, I am only a noisy bell or a crashing
cymbal. 2I may have the gift of prophecy.[d] I may
understand all the secret things of God and have

SIDELIGHT: The Bible's famous "love chapter" (1 Corinthians 13) stands in sharp contrast to the kind of "love" for which Corinth was infamous. Above Corinth on the hill of Acropolis was the temple of Aphrodite, who was the Greek goddess of love. Prostitute-priestesses worked in that temple, supposedly "cleansing" men of sin through perverse sexual acts.

languages This can also be translated "tongues."

SELF-ESTEEM

Be Yourself

Susan Klopp wanted to be like Melody Malen. Melody was smart. She was in the National Honor Society. And teachers said Melody was the best student in their classes.

Susan wanted that recognition too. So she started doing what Melody did. When Melody got a wedge haircut, Susan did the same. When Melody joined the yearbook staff, so did Susan.

But as Susan got involved with the yearbook staff, she began to doubt herself. She felt out of place. Susan hated matching all the mug shots with the names of the students. She liked talking, not working by herself writing about the rifle team's accomplishments.

Susan's best friend, Gina Andrews, confronted Susan one day.

"What are you trying to do? You looked better in long hair," Gina said.

"What's wrong with my hair?" Susan asked.

"It's just not you," Gina replied. "Just like you should be on the debate team, not the yearbook staff. You're a better debater than a writer. In fact, if you didn't have that nose, I'd swear you were just another Melody."

"That's not true!" Susan sputtered.

"Oh, no?" Gina asked. "Just look in the mirror sometime. And ask yourself who you are."

At first Susan dismissed Gina's comments. But the more she worked on the yearbook, the emptier she felt. Susan missed her friend Gina. She missed being on the debate team. She missed her old self.

So Susan quit the yearbook staff, realizing that she had to choose her own life—not copy Melody's. Susan started hanging around with Gina and joined the debate team again. It felt good to be back.

Susan finally recognized the importance of being herself and using her own talents. Read **1 Corinthians 12:1–11** to see what Paul says about gifts.

- What does this passage say about whether it was wise for Susan to copy Melody?
- How does this passage make you feel about your own gifts, or about the gifts of others?

CONSIDER . . .

- meeting with your Christian friends to identify each other's gifts.
- rereading this passage with your family, substituting your name and other family members' names who best fit the gifts described.

FOR MORE, SEE . . .

- Genesis 49:2–28
- Romans 12:4–8
- Ephesians 4:11–12

all knowledge, and I may have faith so great I can
move mountains. But even with all these things,
if I do not have love, then I am nothing. 3I may
give away everything I have, and I may even give
my body as an offering to be burned.[n] But I gain
nothing if I do not have love.

4Love is patient and kind. Love is not jealous,
it does not brag, and it is not proud. 5Love is not
rude, is not selfish, and does not get upset with
others. Love does not count up wrongs that have
been done. 6Love is not happy with evil but is
happy with the truth. 7Love patiently accepts all
things. It always trusts, always hopes, and always
remains strong.

8Love never ends. There are gifts of prophecy,[d]
but they will be ended. There are gifts of speaking
in different languages, but those gifts will stop.
There is the gift of knowledge, but it will come to
an end. 9The reason is that our knowledge and
our ability to prophesy are not perfect. 10But
when perfection comes, the things that are not
perfect will end. 11When I was a child, I talked
like a child, I thought like a child, I reasoned like
a child. When I became a man, I stopped those
childish ways. 12It is the same with us. Now we
see a dim reflection, as if we were looking into a
mirror, but then we shall see clearly. Now I know
only a part, but then I will know fully, as God has
known me. 13So these three things continue forever: faith, hope, and love. And the greatest of
these is love.

Desire Spiritual Gifts

14 You should seek after love, and you
should truly want to have the spiritual
gifts, especially the gift of prophecy.[d] 2I will explain why. Those who have the gift of speaking in
different languages[n] are not speaking to people;
they are speaking to God. No one understands

Verse 3 Other Greek copies read: "hand over my body in order that I may brag."
languages This can also be translated "tongues."

CHURCH

Watching Every Detail

Michelangelo spent four years painting the 132-foot-long by 44-foot-wide ceiling of the Sistine Chapel. Every day for hours, Michelangelo would lie on his back on the scaffolding, perfecting the details of the continuous, unbroken compositions that contained hundreds of figures from the book of Genesis.

The color. The curves of the lines. The facial expressions. The shadows. The hair. The noses. The fingers. Every detail was important.

But the ceiling was sixty feet from the floor. Those admiring Michelangelo's work could see the mastery of his work, but they couldn't see the details from so far away.

One day one of Michelangelo's friends asked Michelangelo why he spent so many hours painstakingly perfecting each detail—details no one would ever be able to see. "After all, who will know whether it is perfect or not?" Michelangelo's friend asked.

"I will," Michelangelo replied.

Michelangelo saw the many possibilities of details for the ceiling of the Sistine Chapel. And he knew when all those details came together, they would make a masterpiece.

That's what **1 Corinthians 12:12–27** is all about. Read what Paul says about the importance of many parts making one body—the church.

- According to the passage, why are details so important?
- How can this passage help you see the important gifts each person brings to your church?

CONSIDER . . .

- asking a teenager, a middle-aged adult, and a senior citizen ways they contribute to church and why those contributions are important. Then evaluate your own contributions.
- getting involved in the church and using your talents. If you sing, join the choir. If you're good at art, make posters to publicize events.

FOR MORE, SEE . . .

- 1 Kings 5:5–18
- Colossians 3:11–17
- 1 Peter 4:7–11

them; they are speaking secret things through the
Spirit.[d] 3But those who prophesy are speaking to
people to give them strength, encouragement,
and comfort. 4The ones who speak in different
languages are helping only themselves, but those
who prophesy are helping the whole church. 5I
wish all of you had the gift of speaking in different
kinds of languages, but more, I wish you would
prophesy. Those who prophesy are greater than
those who can only speak in different languages—unless someone is there who can explain what is said so that the whole church can
be helped.
6Brothers and sisters, will it help you if I come
to you speaking in different languages? No! It will
help you only if I bring you a new truth or some
new knowledge, or prophecy, or teaching. 7It is
the same as with lifeless things that make
sounds—like a flute or a harp. If they do not
make clear musical notes, you will not know
what is being played. 8And in a war, if the trumpet does not give a clear sound, who will prepare
for battle? 9It is the same with you. Unless you
speak clearly with your tongue, no one can understand what you are saying. You will be talking
into the air! 10It may be true that there are all
kinds of sounds in the world, and none is without
meaning. 11But unless I understand the meaning
of what someone says to me, I will be a foreigner
to him, and he will be a foreigner to me. 12It is the

LOVE

Love Never Ends

Everyone knew Lisa Wilson and Gregg Hillburn as Lisa and Gregg—almost as though their names were one word. They had been dating for four years. They cheered for the football team together. They ate lunch together. They did everything together. Nothing could separate them.

Until Gregg started to party.

At first he and Lisa went to parties to be with their friends. Sure there was alcohol, but Lisa and Gregg didn't drink.

After a while, though, Gregg began accepting a glass of beer. Then he started getting drunk. Lisa hated it.

Sometimes Lisa tried talking to Gregg about the problem. But he always got mad. One time he even broke up with her on the spot and called her nasty names. Lisa wanted to scream back at him, but instead she went to his parents.

Tears streaked Lisa's face as she told Gregg's mom and dad what was happening. After she finished, Gregg's dad told Lisa about his own former drinking problem. He knew Gregg needed professional help.

Over the next few months, Lisa wanted to give up on Gregg. Although he was seeing a professional counselor, he was furious at Lisa for "turning him in." He accused her of ruining his life. And he said he never wanted to see her again.

But Lisa patiently waited for Gregg to recover. Although Gregg's words hurt her, Lisa hung on to her memories of the Gregg she first knew. When Gregg eventually admitted his problem, he thanked Lisa for loving him during the times when he was so unlovable.

Lisa loved Gregg with the kind of love described in **1 Corinthians 13:1–13**. Through the tough times, Lisa stuck with Gregg, and a few years later they were married. Gregg has remained sober to this day.

- How do Lisa's actions reflect the message of this scripture?
- How can this passage help you know what true love is all about?

CONSIDER . . .

- copying this scripture passage onto the inside cover of a notebook. The next time someone stretches your patience, read this scripture for advice on how to respond.
- hanging in there with a friend or relative you are about to give up on. Keep loving this person through a difficult time.

FOR MORE, SEE . . .

- Song of Solomon 8:6–7
- Matthew 5:43–48
- Romans 13:9–10

same with you. Since you want spiritual gifts very
much, seek most of all to have the gifts that help
the church grow stronger.
13The one who has the gift of speaking in a different language should pray for the gift to interpret what is spoken. 14If I pray in a different language, my spirit is praying, but my mind does
nothing. 15So what should I do? I will pray with
my spirit, but I will also pray with my mind. I will
sing with my spirit, but I will also sing with my
mind. 16If you praise God with your spirit, those
persons there without understanding cannot say
amen[n] to your prayer of thanks, because they do
not know what you are saying. 17You may be
thanking God in a good way, but the other person
is not helped.
18I thank God that I speak in different kinds of
languages more than all of you. 19But in the
church meetings I would rather speak five words
I understand in order to teach others than thousands of words in a different language.
20Brothers and sisters, do not think like children. In evil things be like babies, but in your
thinking you should be like adults. 21It is written
in the Scriptures:[d]

"With people who use strange words and
foreign languages
I will speak to these people.
But even then they will not listen to me,"
Isaiah 28:11-12

says the Lord.
22So the gift of speaking in different kinds of
languages is a proof for those who do not believe,
not for those who do believe. And prophecy is for
people who believe, not for those who do not believe. 23Suppose the whole church meets together
and everyone speaks in different languages. If
some people come in who do not understand or

amen To say amen means to agree with the things that were said.

FRIENDS

Inside Lingo

What do the following acronyms mean?

- MS-DOS
- SIMM
- SCSI
- MB
- ROM
- RAM
- DPI
- RGB
- PC
- CD-ROM
- CPU

If you know computers, you probably know what most of these acronyms stand for. And when you talk with other computer people, you might rattle off these abbreviations and have a great conversation.

But if you don't work with computers, few of these abbreviations make any sense. And you may feel left out when others use them around you.

Cliques work in a similar way. People on the "inside" may talk the same way, act the same way, and like the same kinds of things. They easily exclude others and make them feel unwanted.

In **1 Corinthians 14:13–20**, Paul talks about including other people in worship, and his advice has a lot to say about cliques.

- According to this passage, why is it better to speak five understandable words than thousands of words that no one understands? What does this say about cliques?
- How did you feel not knowing what the words at the beginning of this devotion were all about? What does the Scripture say to you about "insiders" and "outsiders"?

CONSIDER . . .

- getting together with your friends and discussing ways you exclude others. Choose one way to improve.
- thumbing through your yearbook, looking for someone who used to be—but is no longer—in your group of friends. Call that person and ask how he or she is doing.

FOR MORE, SEE . . .

- Ruth 2
- Jonah 4
- Philemon

do not believe, they will say you are crazy. 24But suppose everyone is prophesying and some people come in who do not believe or do not understand. If everyone is prophesying, their sin will be shown to them, and they will be judged by all that they hear. 25The secret things in their hearts will be made known. So they will bow down and worship God saying, "Truly, God is with you."

Meetings Should Help the Church

26So, brothers and sisters, what should you do? When you meet together, one person has a song, and another has a teaching. Another has a new truth from God. Another speaks in a different language,[n] and another person interprets that language. The purpose of all these things should be to help the church grow strong. 27When you meet together, if anyone speaks in a different language, it should be only two, or not more than three, who speak. They should speak one after the other, and someone else should interpret. 28But if there is no interpreter, then those who speak in a different language should be quiet in the church meeting. They should speak only to themselves and to God.

29Only two or three prophets[d] should speak, and the others should judge what they say. 30If a message from God comes to another person who is sitting, the first speaker should stop. 31You can all prophesy one after the other. In this way all the people can be taught and encouraged. 32The spirits of prophets are under the control of the prophets themselves. 33God is not a God of confusion but a God of peace.

As is true in all the churches of God's people, 34women should keep quiet in the church meetings. They are not allowed to speak, but they must yield to this rule as the law says. 35If they want to learn something, they should ask their own husbands at home. It is shameful for a woman to speak in the church meeting. 36Did God's teaching come from you? Or are you the only ones to whom it has come?

37Those who think they are prophets or spiritual persons should understand that what I am writing to you is the Lord's command. 38Those who ignore this will be ignored by God.

39So my brothers and sisters, you should truly want to prophesy. But do not stop people from using the gift of speaking in different kinds of languages. 40But let everything be done in a right and orderly way.

The Good News About Christ

15 Now, brothers and sisters, I want you to remember the Good News[d] I brought to you. You received this Good News and continue strong in it. 2And you are being saved by it if you continue believing what I told you. If you do not, then you believed for nothing.

3I passed on to you what I received, of which this was most important: that Christ died for our sins, as the Scriptures[d] say; 4that he was buried and was raised to life on the third day as the Scriptures say; 5and that he was seen by Peter and then by the twelve apostles.[d] 6After that, Jesus was seen by more than five hundred of the believers at the same time. Most of them are still living today, but some have died. 7Then he was seen by James and later by all the apostles. 8Last of all he was seen by me—as by a person not born at the normal time. 9All the other apostles are greater than I am. I am not even good enough to be called an apostle, because I persecuted the church of God. 10But God's grace has made me what I am, and his grace to me was not wasted. I worked harder than all the other apostles. (But it was not I really; it was God's grace that was with me.) 11So if I preached to you or the other apostles preached to you, we all preach the same thing, and this is what you believed.

We Will Be Raised from the Dead

12Now since we preached that Christ was raised from the dead, why do some of you say that people will not be raised from the dead? 13If no one is ever raised from the dead, then Christ has not been raised. 14And if Christ has not been raised, then our preaching is worth nothing, and your faith is worth nothing. 15And also, we are guilty of lying about God, because we testified of him that he raised Christ from the dead. But if people are not raised from the dead, then God never raised Christ. 16If the dead are not raised, Christ has not been raised either. 17And if Christ has not been raised, then your faith has nothing to it; you are still guilty of your sins. 18And those in Christ who have already died are lost. 19If our hope in Christ is for this life only, we should be pitied more than anyone else in the world.

20But Christ has truly been raised from the dead—the first one and proof that those who sleep in death will also be raised. 21Death has come because of what one man did, but the rising from death also comes because of one man. 22In Adam all of us die. In the same way, in Christ all of us will be made alive again. 23But everyone will be raised to life in the right order. Christ was first to be raised. When Christ comes again, those who belong to him will be raised to life, 24and then the end will come. At that time Christ will destroy all rulers, authorities, and powers, and he will hand over the kingdom to God the Father. 25Christ must rule until he puts all enemies under his con-

language This can also be translated "tongue."

trol. 26The last enemy to be destroyed will be
death. 27The Scripture[d] says that God put all
things under his control.[n] When it says "all
things" are under him, it is clear this does not
include God himself. God is the One who put everything under his control. 28After everything has
been put under the Son, then he will put himself
under God, who had put all things under him.
Then God will be the complete ruler over everything.
29If the dead are never raised, what will people
do who are being baptized for the dead? If the
dead are not raised at all, why are people being
baptized for them?
30And what about us? Why do we put ourselves in danger every hour? 31I die every day.
That is true, brothers and sisters, just as it is true
that I brag about you in Christ Jesus our Lord. 32If
I fought wild animals in Ephesus only with human hopes, I have gained nothing. If the dead are
not raised, "Let us eat and drink, because tomorrow we will die."[n]
33Do not be fooled: "Bad friends will ruin good
habits." 34Come back to your right way of thinking and stop sinning. Some of you do not know
God—I say this to shame you.

SIDELIGHT: Though Paul probably didn't fight wild animals himself (1 Corinthians 15:32), it's likely he is referring to the Roman "sport" of putting prisoners in an arena, then releasing wild animals to maul the prisoners while huge crowds watched. Animals used in this activity included lions, bears, leopards, rhinoceroses, crocodiles, tigers, and elephants. A decade after Paul wrote this letter, Christians faced this kind of persecution.

What Kind of Body Will We Have?

35But someone may ask, "How are the dead
raised? What kind of body will they have?" 36Fool-
ish person! When you sow a seed, it must die in

God put . . . control. From Psalm 8:6.
"Let us . . . die." Quotation from Isaiah 22:13; 56:12.

FAITH

Stick With It

It's not easy to become an emperor butterfly. To emerge into the world, the butterfly must force its way through the neck of a flask-shaped cocoon. Getting through this opening takes hours of intense struggle. The insect must squirm and wiggle to push its way through the confining threads.

If you watched an emperor butterfly's struggle, you might feel sorry for the struggling insect and snip the confining threads to make an easier exit. But if you did, the butterfly would never develop its wings. Instead, it would spend most of its life crawling, never able to spread its wings and fly.

Entomologists who study this butterfly believe the pressure on the insect's body forces the essential juices into the wings, thus preparing the wings for flight. Without the pressure, the wings would never become strong.

Sometimes having faith is difficult. Like the emperor butterfly, we struggle. We feel overwhelmed—tested. And we wish someone could step in and take away the struggle.

But our faith grows through those struggles, as Paul reminds us in **1 Corinthians 15:1–11**.

- According to this passage, what are we to continue to believe in?
- How can the example of the people's faith in this passage encourage you when you struggle with your faith?

CONSIDER . . .

- calling one of your grandparents or an older person in your congregation. Ask that person about his or her faith journey—including the ups and downs.
- talking to a friend about the ways you have grown after a difficult time.

FOR MORE, SEE . . .

- Genesis 22
- Daniel 3
- Hebrews 11

the ground before it can live and grow. 37And
when you sow it, it does not have the same
"body" it will have later. What you sow is only a
bare seed, maybe wheat or something else. 38But
God gives it a body that he has planned for it,
and God gives each kind of seed its own body.
39All things made of flesh are not the same: People
have one kind of flesh, animals have another,
birds have another, and fish have another. 40Also
there are heavenly bodies and earthly bodies. But
the beauty of the heavenly bodies is one kind,
and the beauty of the earthly bodies is another.
41The sun has one kind of beauty, the moon has
another beauty, and the stars have another. And
each star is different in its beauty.

42It is the same with the dead who are raised
to life. The body that is "planted" will ruin and
decay, but it is raised to a life that cannot be destroyed. 43When the body is "planted," it is without honor, but it is raised in glory. When the body
is "planted," it is weak, but when it is raised, it
is powerful. 44The body that is "planted" is a
physical body. When it is raised, it is a spiritual
body.

There is a physical body, and there is also a
spiritual body. 45It is written in the Scriptures:[d]
"The first man, Adam, became a living person."[n]
But the last Adam became a spirit that gives life.
46The spiritual did not come first, but the physical
and then the spiritual. 47The first man came from
the dust of the earth. The second man came
from heaven. 48People who belong to the earth
are like the first man of earth. But those people
who belong to heaven are like the man of heav-
en. 49Just as we were made like the man of earth,
so we will also be made like the man of heaven.

50I tell you this, brothers and sisters: Flesh and
blood cannot have a part in the kingdom of God.
Something that will ruin cannot have a part in
something that never ruins. 51But look! I tell you
this secret: We will not all sleep in death, but we
will all be changed. 52It will take only a second—
as quickly as an eye blinks—when the last trumpet sounds. The trumpet will sound, and those
who have died will be raised to live forever, and
we will all be changed. 53This body that can be
destroyed must clothe itself with something that
can never be destroyed. And this body that dies
must clothe itself with something that can never
die. 54So this body that can be destroyed will
clothe itself with that which can never be destroyed, and this body that dies will clothe itself
with that which can never die. When this happens, this Scripture will be made true:

"Death is destroyed forever in victory."
Isaiah 25:8

55"Death, where is your victory?
Death, where is your pain?" *Hosea 13:14*

"The first . . . person." Quotation from Genesis 2:7.

DEATH

Life After Death?

What do teenagers think about death? According to a Gallup Youth Poll, two-thirds of teenagers believe in life after death. But while most teenagers believe in life after death, most teenagers also fear death. According to a Youth Monitor Poll:

- Three out of four teenagers worry that one of their parents will die.
- Half worry about themselves dying.
- Two other major worries—being in a car accident or a plane crash—also hint at this fear of death.

Fearing death is natural for most people. But Paul says death isn't final for Christians. Read about the other side of death in **1 Corinthians 15:12–28**.

- Why does Paul talk about Christ when explaining being raised from the dead?
- How does this passage help you deal with your fears about death?

CONSIDER . . .

- going to a church cemetery and reading the epitaphs on gravestones. Decide how you can develop the faith and hope indicated by the sayings.
- drinking a soft drink with your youth leader and talking about your fears concerning death.

FOR MORE, SEE . . .

- Isaiah 57:1–2
- John 5:24–29
- Hebrews 2:14–15

56Death's power to hurt is sin, and the power of sin is the law. 57But we thank God! He gives us the victory through our Lord Jesus Christ.

58So my dear brothers and sisters, stand strong. Do not let anything change you. Always give yourselves fully to the work of the Lord, because you know that your work in the Lord is never wasted.

The Gift for Other Believers

16 Now I will write about the collection of money for God's people. Do the same thing I told the Galatian churches to do: 2On the first day of every week, each one of you should put aside money as you have been blessed. Save it up so you will not have to collect money after I come. 3When I arrive, I will send whomever you approve to take your gift to Jerusalem. I will send them with letters of introduction, 4and if it seems good for me to go also, they will go along with me.

Paul's Plans

5I plan to go through Macedonia, so I will come to you after I go through there. 6Perhaps I will stay with you for a time or even all winter. Then you can help me on my trip, wherever I go. 7I do not want to see you now just in passing. I hope to stay a longer time with you if the Lord allows it. 8But I will stay at Ephesus until Pentecost,[d] 9because a good opportunity for a great and growing work has been given to me now. And there are many people working against me.

10If Timothy comes to you, see to it that he has nothing to fear with you, because he is working for the Lord just as I am. 11So none of you should treat Timothy as unimportant, but help him on his trip in peace so that he can come back to me. I am expecting him to come with the brothers.

12Now about our brother Apollos: I strongly encouraged him to visit you with the other brothers. He did not at all want to come now; he will come when he has the opportunity.

Paul Ends His Letter

13Be alert. Continue strong in the faith. Have courage, and be strong. 14Do everything in love.

15You know that the family of Stephanas were the first believers in Southern Greece and that they have given themselves to the service of God's people. I ask you, brothers and sisters, 16to follow the leading of people like these and anyone else who works and serves with them.

ETERNAL LIFE

We Will All Be Changed

Coal, buried deep within the earth, sometimes encounters intense pressure and heat. When it does, over time, a diamond results.

Under the right conditions, the mineral beryl transforms into an emerald, another precious stone. But if beryl contains impurities and undergoes the same conditions, the result is aquamarine—which is only a semiprecious stone.

When rocks with specks of gold are melted, the weighty gold deposits sink to the bottom, and the impurities are scraped from the top. After the process is repeated several times, only pure gold remains.

As minerals change under the right conditions, our bodies will change at death. In **1 Corinthians 15:35–58**, Paul talks about the transformation and refining that will occur in our bodies.

- How will the change in our bodies be similar to what happens to coal, beryl, and gold-specked rocks? How will it be different?
- How does the value of eternal life compare to the value of precious stones?

CONSIDER . . .

- drawing a picture of what you think heaven will be like.
- hanging a "We Will All Be Changed" sign in your closet to remind you how our earthly bodies will change.

FOR MORE, SEE . . .

- Psalm 73:23–28
- Job 19:25–27
- Revelation 22:1–5

[17]I am happy that Stephanas, Fortunatus, and
Achaicus have come. You are not here, but they
have filled your place. [18]They have refreshed my
spirit and yours. You should recognize the value
of people like these.

[19]The churches in the country of Asia send
greetings to you. Aquila and Priscilla greet you in
the Lord, as does the church that meets in their
house. [20]All the brothers and sisters here send
greetings. Give each other a holy kiss when you
meet.

[21]I, Paul, am writing this greeting with my own
hand.

[22]If anyone does not love the Lord, let him be
separated from God—lost forever!

Come, O Lord!

[23]The grace of the Lord Jesus be with you.

[24]My love be with all of you in Christ Jesus.

2 CORINTHIANS

Why Read This Book:

- Explore what it means to be a minister for Christ (2 Corinthians 1—7).
- Be challenged to give generously to God's work (2 Corinthians 8—9).
- See what Christians have to brag about (2 Corinthians 10—13).

Behind the Scenes:

"One of the striking differences between a cat and a lie is that the cat has only nine lives." —Mark Twain, American humorist

The apostle Paul wouldn't have laughed at that quote while he was writing 2 Corinthians. Any mention of lying would not have been a laughing matter.

Just three or four years earlier, Paul had started the church in Corinth, a major city in modern-day Greece. He had carefully guided and helped the people grow in their faith, as can be seen in 1 Corinthians. The church was special to him.

But then someone started spreading lies and rumors about Paul, trying to discredit him. He was inconsistent, they said. He was deceptive, arrogant, and boastful. He didn't have the right credentials. He was emotionally unstable. And the list continued. Even worse, the people believed the lies, and were turning to other, false leaders for guidance.

The slanderous lies angered and upset Paul personally. But he worried most that the church was being led away from Jesus Christ. Though he didn't like doing it, Paul's enemies had forced him to defend his ministry. He sent a harsh, stinging letter, which we don't have (see 2 Corinthians 2:3–4). He demanded that the church turn away from the false teachers and discipline the person who insulted him. Much to the apostle's relief, the church followed his advice and reaffirmed its loyalty to him (see 2 Corinthians 7:6–16). The crisis was over.

In 2 Corinthians, a thankful Paul rebuilds the relationship that had been strained by the sharp words. He also clears up any remaining misunderstanding that might

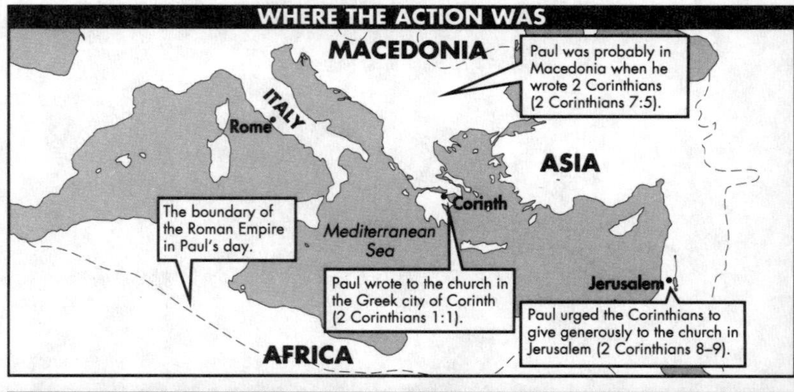

WHERE THE ACTION WAS
MACEDONIA
Paul was probably in Macedonia when he wrote 2 Corinthians (2 Corinthians 7:5).
ITALY
Rome
ASIA
Corinth
The boundary of the Roman Empire in Paul's day.
Mediterranean Sea
Paul wrote to the church in the Greek city of Corinth (2 Corinthians 1:1).
Jerusalem
Paul urged the Corinthians to give generously to the church in Jerusalem (2 Corinthians 8–9).
AFRICA
WHEN THE ACTION WAS
Jesus was born
The church began soon after Jesus went to heaven
Paul began his missionary work
Fire destroyed Rome
BC/AD
25AD
50AD
75AD
100AD
Jesus began his ministry
Paul founded the church in Corinth
Paul wrote 2 Corinthians
Romans destroyed the Temple in Jerusalem

Behind the Scenes (cont.): be present in the church. Finally, he urges the Corinthians to give generously to the offering he was collecting for the struggling church in Jerusalem.

Because of the conflict that prompted the letter, 2 Corinthians gives us an intimate picture of the struggles and dangers Paul faced because of his ministry. In the process, the book gives us a detailed picture of what it means to follow Christ and to be a minister of the Good News.

Though the book focuses on being a minister, its insights and guidance apply to all Christians. It gives courage to overcome discouragement. It encourages us to share freely with others. And it reminds us to find our strength in Christ. That's good advice for all people!

---

1 From Paul, an apostle[d] of Christ Jesus. I am an apostle because that is what God wanted. Also from Timothy our brother in Christ.

To the church of God in Corinth, and to all of God's people everywhere in Southern Greece:

[2]Grace and peace to you from God our Father and the Lord Jesus Christ.

> **SIDELIGHT:** The Corinthian church was made up of a diverse group of people who came to this major city from around the world. Paul hints at this when he addresses them in 2 Corinthians 1:2 with "grace," a Greek greeting, and "peace," a Hebrew greeting.

Paul Gives Thanks to God

[3]Praise be to the God and Father of our Lord Jesus Christ. God is the Father who is full of mercy and all comfort. [4]He comforts us every time we have trouble, so when others have trouble, we can comfort them with the same comfort God gives us. [5]We share in the many sufferings of Christ. In the same way, much comfort comes to us through Christ. [6]If we have troubles, it is for your comfort and salvation, and if we have comfort, you also have comfort. This helps you to accept patiently the same sufferings we have. [7]Our hope for you is strong, knowing that you share in our sufferings and also in the comfort we receive.

[8]Brothers and sisters,[n] we want you to know about the trouble we suffered in Asia. We had great burdens there that were beyond our own strength. We even gave up hope of living. [9]Truly, in our own hearts we believed we would die. But this happened so we would not trust in ourselves but in God, who raises people from the dead. [10]God saved us from these great dangers of death, and he will continue to save us. We have put our hope in him, and he will save us again. [11]And you can help us with your prayers. Then many people will give thanks for us—that God blessed us because of their many prayers.

The Change in Paul's Plans

[12]This is what we are proud of, and I can say it with a clear conscience: In everything we have done in the world, and especially with you, we have had an honest and sincere heart from God. We did this by God's grace, not by the kind of wisdom the world has. [13-14]We write to you only what you can read and understand. And I hope that as you have understood some things about us, you may come to know everything about us. Then you can be proud of us, as we will be proud of you on the day our Lord Jesus Christ comes again.

[15]I was so sure of all this that I made plans to visit you first so you could be blessed twice. [16]I planned to visit you on my way to Macedonia and again on my way back. I wanted to get help from you for my trip to Judea. [17]Do you think that I made these plans without really meaning it? Or maybe you think I make plans as the world does, so that I say yes, yes and at the same time no, no.

[18]But if you can believe God, you can believe that what we tell you is never both yes and no. [19]The Son of God, Jesus Christ, that Silas and Timothy and I preached to you, was not yes and no. In Christ it has always been yes. [20]The yes to all of God's promises is in Christ, and through Christ we say yes to the glory of God. [21]Remember, God is the One who makes you and us strong in Christ. God made us his chosen people. [22]He put his mark on us to show that we are his, and he put his Spirit[d] in our hearts to be a guarantee for all he has promised.

[23]I tell you this, and I ask God to be my witness that this is true: The reason I did not come back to Corinth was to keep you from being punished or hurt. [24]We are not trying to control your faith. You are strong in faith. But we are workers with you for your own joy.

2 So I decided that my next visit to you would not be another one to make you sad. [2]If I

Brothers and sisters Although the Greek text says "Brothers" here and throughout this book, Paul's words were meant for the entire church, including men and women.

make you sad, who will make me glad? Only you can make me glad—particularly the person whom I made sad. 3I wrote you a letter for this reason: that when I came to you I would not be made sad by the people who should make me happy. I felt sure of all of you, that you would share my joy. 4When I wrote to you before, I was very troubled and unhappy in my heart, and I wrote with many tears. I did not write to make you sad, but to let you know how much I love you.

Forgive the Sinner

5Someone there among you has caused sadness, not to me, but to all of you. I mean he caused sadness to all in some way. (I do not want to make it sound worse than it really is.) 6The punishment that most of you gave him is enough for him. 7But now you should forgive him and comfort him to keep him from having too much sadness and giving up completely. 8So I beg you to show that you love him. 9I wrote you to test you and to see if you obey in everything. 10If you forgive someone, I also forgive him. And what I have forgiven—if I had anything to forgive—I forgave it for you, as if Christ were with me. 11I did this so that Satan would not win anything from us, because we know very well what Satan's plans are.

Paul's Concern in Troas

12When I came to Troas to preach the Good News[d] of Christ, the Lord gave me a good opportunity there. 13But I had no peace, because I did not find my brother Titus. So I said good-bye to them at Troas and went to Macedonia.

Victory Through Christ

14But thanks be to God, who always leads us in victory through Christ. God uses us to spread his knowledge everywhere like a sweet-smelling perfume. 15Our offering to God is this: We are the sweet smell of Christ among those who are being saved and among those who are being lost. 16To those who are lost, we are the smell of death that brings death, but to those who are being saved, we are the smell of life that brings life. So who is able to do this work? 17We do not sell the word of God for a profit as many other people do. But in Christ we speak the truth before God, as messengers of God.

Servants of the New Agreement

3 Are we starting to brag about ourselves again? Do we need letters of introduction to you or from you, like some other people? 2You yourselves are our letter, written on our hearts, known and read by everyone. 3You show that you are a letter from Christ sent through us. This letter is not written with ink but with the Spirit[d] of the living God. It is not written on stone tablets[n] but on human hearts.

4We can say this, because through Christ we feel certain before God. 5We are not saying that we can do this work ourselves. It is God who makes us able to do all that we do. 6He made us able to be servants of a new agreement from himself to his people. This new agreement is not a written law, but it is of the Spirit. The written law brings death, but the Spirit gives life.

7The law that brought death was written in words on stone. It came with God's glory, which made Moses' face so bright that the Israelites could not continue to look at it. But that glory later disappeared. 8So surely the new way that brings the Spirit has even more glory. 9If the law that judged people guilty of sin had glory, surely the new way that makes people right with God has much greater glory. 10That old law had glory but it really loses its glory when it is compared to the much greater glory of this new way. 11If that law which disappeared came with glory, then this new way which continues forever has much greater glory.

12We have this hope, so we are very bold. 13We are not like Moses, who put a covering over his face so the Israelites would not see it. The glory was disappearing, and Moses did not want them to see it end. 14But their minds were closed, and even today that same covering hides the meaning when they read the old agreement. That covering is taken away only through Christ. 15Even today, when they read the law of Moses, there is a covering over their minds. 16But when a person changes and follows the Lord, that covering is taken away. 17The Lord is the Spirit, and where the Spirit of the Lord is, there is freedom. 18Our faces, then, are not covered. We all show the Lord's glory, and we are being changed to be like him. This change in us brings ever greater glory, which comes from the Lord, who is the Spirit.

Preaching the Good News

4 God, with his mercy, gave us this work to do, so we don't give up. 2But we have turned away from secret and shameful ways. We use no trickery, and we do not change the teaching of God. We teach the truth plainly, showing everyone who we are. Then they can know in their hearts what kind of people we are in God's sight. 3If the Good News[d] that we preach is hidden, it is hidden only to those who are lost. 4The devil who rules this world has blinded the minds of those who do not believe. They cannot see the

stone tablets Meaning the law of Moses that was written on stone tablets (Exodus 24:12; 25:16).

light of the Good News — the Good News about
the glory of Christ, who is exactly like God. 5We
do not preach about ourselves, but we preach that
Jesus Christ is Lord and that we are your servants
for Jesus. 6God once said, "Let the light shine out
of the darkness!" This is the same God who made
his light shine in our hearts by letting us know the
glory of God that is in the face of Christ.

Spiritual Treasure in Clay Jars

7We have this treasure from God, but we are
like clay jars that hold the treasure. This shows
that the great power is from God, not from us.
8We have troubles all around us, but we are not
defeated. We do not know what to do, but we do
not give up the hope of living. 9We are persecuted, but God does not leave us. We are hurt

SIDELIGHT: Hiding treasures in clay jars was a common practice in biblical times, since people wouldn't suspect anything valuable was in the cheap jar (2 Corinthians 4:7). It's sort of like hiding your money in a sock.

NON-CHRISTIANS

Trying Too Hard

Dave Hildebrant tried to live a perfect Christian life. He went to church and was active in his youth group. He faithfully read the Bible and shared his faith with others.

Dave's problem was that he got carried away.

At school Dave constantly talked about his beliefs. In history class he challenged everything his teacher said. In science class he blasted theories and ideas as un-Christian. During lunch he commented on others' food, telling them that God wanted them to treat their bodies like a temple. Between classes he witnessed in the halls.

At first, teachers and students listened to him. But soon, people around him grew irritated. Teachers began to cut him off, and students just laughed. The more they laughed or ignored him the harder he tried. Finally, even other Christians began to sneer. They started calling him "the preacher" and "super Christian."

Holly Myers was also a Christian. Although she, too, was tired of Dave's style, she felt sorry when others put him down. One day Dave complained to Holly that no one ever listened.

"Maybe you're trying too hard," Holly suggested. "After all, we don't have to be preaching all the time. We just need to let God's love shine through."

Over the next few weeks, whenever Holly saw Dave she just smiled. For a long time Dave didn't seem to have heard her. He just kept on preaching and witnessing, and students kept on making fun of him.

Slowly, Dave began following Holly's advice. He still lived out his faith, but instead of being obnoxious, he expressed it with a smile, a kind word or an offer of help. And, for the first time, people began responding positively to Dave's efforts.

Sometimes we get so tied up in trying to convert others that we don't let God's love show through us to non-Christians. Read **2 Corinthians 4:3–12** to discover more about the treasure of God's love and how to share your faith with the world.

- How does Dave's discovery relate to Paul's belief that we are clay jars holding the treasure of God's love?
- How have you shared God's treasure with a non-Christian?

CONSIDER . . .

- asking God to teach you how to respect others while you share your beliefs with them.
- inviting a friend who doesn't go to church to come with you to worship. Introduce him or her to your Christian friends.

FOR MORE, SEE . . .

- Genesis 18:16–33
- Matthew 28:16–20
- Colossians 3:12–17

sometimes, but we are not destroyed. 10We carry
the death of Jesus in our own bodies so that the
life of Jesus can also be seen in our bodies. 11We
are alive, but for Jesus we are always in danger of
death so that the life of Jesus can be seen in our
bodies that die. 12So death is working in us, but
life is working in you.

13It is written in the Scriptures,[d] "I believed, so
I spoke."[n] Our faith is like this, too. We believe,
and so we speak. 14God raised the Lord Jesus from
the dead, and we know that God will also raise
us with Jesus. God will bring us together with
you, and we will stand before him. 15All these
things are for you. And so the grace of God that
is being given to more and more people will bring
increasing thanks to God for his glory.

Living by Faith

16So we do not give up. Our physical body i
becoming older and weaker, but our spirit insid
us is made new every day. 17We have small trou
bles for a while now, but they are helping us gai
an eternal glory that is much greater than th
troubles. 18We set our eyes not on what we se
but on what we cannot see. What we see will las
only a short time, but what we cannot see wil
last forever.

5 We know that our body—the tent we live i
here on earth—will be destroyed. But whe
that happens, God will have a house for us. It wil
not be a house made by human hands; instead, i
will be a home in heaven that will last forever
2But now we groan in this tent. We want God t

"I . . . spoke." Quotation from Psalm 116:10.

FAITH

Unseen Water

Frank Zeigler's ranch in Wyoming had been in his family for years, but had never been used. It was full of cactus and rocks. Surely the land could be used for something, Frank thought. He thought of raising sheep, but sheep couldn't live there without water. He thought of mining the minerals that had been discovered long ago, but there was no water to process the ore.

Frank felt he was missing something—something he couldn't see. He just needed water, but there was none for miles around.

"I know there is more," he told his wife. "I just know there is. God is always giving us gifts, but half the time we don't see them."

One day as he rode across the barren range, he suddenly stopped. He piled up five or six rocks and called a drilling company. Frank told them to drill a deep water well where he had piled the rocks.

At first the owners laughed. "There's no water on that land. You know that," they teased.

But he insisted. "I just have a feeling it's there," he said. Finally they agreed to drill. Months later, they hit water almost one mile underground.

Astonished, the drilling crew asked how he knew water was down there. Frank shrugged. "I just knew," he said. "I guess I had the faith that there was more there than my eyes could see."

As Frank did, it's important for us to have faith not just in things seen but in things unseen as well. To learn more, read **2 Corinthians 4:13–18**.

- How does Frank's search for water parallel the faith described in the passage? How does it differ?
- Which part of this passage gives you the greatest sense of hope in your faith?

CONSIDER . . .

- thinking about things you know exist even though you can't see them, such as air and electricity. List ways you know God exists even though you can't see him.
- stepping out in faith in an area where you may not have all the "facts" but still believe what you're doing is God's will.

FOR MORE, SEE . . .

- Psalm 116
- Romans 8:18–28
- Colossians 3:1–4

give us our heavenly home, 3because it will clothe
us so we will not be naked. 4While we live in this
body, we have burdens, and we groan. We do not
want to be naked, but we want to be clothed with
our heavenly home. Then this body that dies will
be fully covered with life. 5This is what God made
us for, and he has given us the Spirit[d] to be a
guarantee for this new life.

6So we always have courage. We know that
while we live in this body, we are away from the
Lord. 7We live by what we believe, not by what
we can see. 8So I say that we have courage. We
really want to be away from this body and be at
home with the Lord. 9Our only goal is to please
God whether we live here or there, 10because we
must all stand before Christ to be judged. Each of
us will receive what we should get—good or
bad—for the things we did in the earthly body.

Becoming Friends with God

11Since we know what it means to fear the
Lord, we try to help people accept the truth about
us. God knows what we really are, and I hope
that in your hearts you know, too. 12We are not
trying to prove ourselves to you again, but we are
telling you about ourselves so you will be proud
of us. Then you will have an answer for those
who are proud about things that can be seen
rather than what is in the heart. 13If we are out
of our minds, it is for God. If we have our right
minds, it is for you. 14The love of Christ controls
us, because we know that One died for all, so all
have died. 15Christ died for all so that those who
live would not continue to live for themselves. He
died for them and was raised from the dead so
that they would live for him.

16From this time on we do not think of anyone
as the world does. In the past we thought of
Christ as the world thinks, but we no longer think
of him in that way. 17If anyone belongs to Christ,
there is a new creation. The old things have gone;
everything is made new! 18All this is from God.
Through Christ, God made peace between us and
himself, and God gave us the work of telling ev-

FOLLOWING GOD

Daring to Believe

Christopher Wren, a young English architect in the early 1700s, had the chance of a lifetime. He had won the job of building a new cathedral in London. He prayed and worked to design a cathedral with a magnificently arched ceiling stretching toward heaven.

But when the church was almost finished, other architects in London claimed the building was flawed. They said six additional pillars were needed or else the roof would fall.

Wren genuinely believed God was guiding him in building the cathedral. Still, the other architects were older and more experienced. So, instead of reacting angrily, he listened and prayed. After much discussion he agreed to add the pillars.

At least that's what everyone thought.

After the cathedral was finished, Wren left London. Fifty years later, after his death, workers were repainting the ceiling when they discovered something strange. Each of the six additional pillars was a few inches short of the vaulted ceiling.

Wren had been right. And he had proven it.

Like Christopher Wren we are called to follow God as best we know how, which often requires courage and creativity. To learn more about following God read **2 Corinthians 5:6–17**.

- How does Christopher Wren's decision to follow God's call in his heart relate to Paul's advice to live by believing in Christ?
- How have you made choices that reflect the challenge of verse 9? What happened?

CONSIDER . . .

- choosing a creative way to follow God this week, such as writing, drawing, painting, or singing.
- interviewing your pastor, a teacher, or a friend about times he or she struggled with decisions to follow God, and what happened.

FOR MORE, SEE . . .

- Isaiah 65:17–25
- John 14:1–7
- Philippians 1:19–20

eryone about the peace we can have with him.
19God was in Christ, making peace between the
world and himself. In Christ, God did not hold the
world guilty of its sins. And he gave us this message of peace. 20So we have been sent to speak for
Christ. It is as if God is calling to you through us.
We speak for Christ when we beg you to be at
peace with God. 21Christ had no sin, but God
made him become sin so that in Christ we could
become right with God.

6 We are workers together with God, so we
beg you: Do not let the grace that you received from God be for nothing. 2God says,

"At the right time I heard your prayers.
On the day of salvation I helped you."
Isaiah 49:8

I tell you that the "right time" is now, and the
"day of salvation" is now.
3We do not want anyone to find fault with our
work, so nothing we do will be a problem for anyone. 4But in every way we show we are servants
of God: in accepting many hard things, in troubles, in difficulties, and in great problems. 5We are
beaten and thrown into prison. We meet those
who become upset with us and start riots. We
work hard, and sometimes we get no sleep or
food. 6We show we are servants of God by our
pure lives, our understanding, patience, and kind-

SERVICE

Doing What We Can

Joanni Glade wasn't like the other kids in the youth group. Born with the neuromuscular disease Charcot-marie-toothe, she couldn't walk without crutches.

This was her first year in the youth group, and though she had been very active, the other kids assumed she wouldn't go on the two-week summer service project. But Joanni shocked them when she made it clear she was going.

A few youth group members went to Joanni. "We know you want to go, but don't you think it would be better for everyone if you stayed at home?" they asked. "Aren't you afraid you'll get hurt?" Joanni firmly replied she was going.

When the group arrived at the service project, their assignment was to repair a home in the middle of a dry, treeless yard. Everyone had an assignment. Some kids repaired the roof, some replaced siding, and some painted.

Joanni began painting, but quickly discovered she didn't have the strength to lift the brush over and over. By the end of the first day she felt like a failure. "I guess everyone was right. I really am useless here," she thought.

The same people who had talked to her earlier approached her again. "Maybe it would be better if you went home," they urged. "It's not that we don't care; it's just that we're here to help these other people." After a while Joanni disappeared, and no one could find her. Later she reappeared with a tired but happy smile on her face.

The next day Joanni didn't go with the group to the work site. An hour later, a supply truck arrived at the work site with lumber, nails, shingles and water. Joanni sat in the cab with a list of supplies. For two weeks Joanni kept track of supplies and saw to it that work groups had what they needed. By the end of the project, the project directors talked about hiring her the next year as their supply coordinator.

Joanni took the message of **2 Corinthians 5:20—6:10** seriously. In spite of the doubts of others she served God in her own unique way.

- How were Joanni's actions similar to the kind of service the passage talks about?
- When have you served God and others in ways that are reflected in this passage? What was the result?

CONSIDER . . .

- taking an inventory of your skills, gifts and abilities, and deciding how you can use them in God's service.
- including people with disabilities as full and equal servants in your youth group and church.

FOR MORE, SEE . . .

- Jeremiah 1:4–10
- Matthew 4:16–19
- James 2:14–26

ness, by the Holy Spirit,[d] by true love, 7by speaking the truth, and by God's power. We use our
right living to defend ourselves against everything. 8Some people honor us, but others blame
us. Some people say evil things about us, but others say good things. Some people say we are liars,
but we speak the truth. 9We are not known, but
we are well known. We seem to be dying, but we
continue to live. We are punished, but we are not
killed. 10We have much sadness, but we are always rejoicing. We are poor, but we are making
many people rich in faith. We have nothing, but
really we have everything.

11We have spoken freely to you in Corinth and
have opened our hearts to you. 12Our feelings of
love for you have not stopped, but you have
stopped your feelings of love for us. 13I speak to
you as if you were my children. Do to us as we
have done—open your hearts to us.

> **SIDELIGHT:** Paul was no stranger to the local bars—prison bars, that is (2 Corinthians 6:5). According to Clement of Rome, Paul was imprisoned at least seven times. Among the places he was locked up were Philippi, Jerusalem, and Rome. Paul's life ended in prison when he was executed by the Roman government.

Warning About Non-Christians

14You are not the same as those who do not
believe. So do not join yourselves to them. Good
and bad do not belong together. Light and darkness cannot share together. 15How can Christ and
Belial, the devil, have any agreement? What can
a believer have together with a nonbeliever?
16The temple of God cannot have any agreement
with idols, and we are the temple of the living
God. As God said: "I will live with them and walk
with them. And I will be their God, and they will
be my people."[n]

17"Leave those people,
and be separate, says the Lord.
Touch nothing that is unclean,[d]
and I will accept you."

Isaiah 52:11; Ezekiel 20:34, 41

18"I will be your father,
and you will be my sons and daughters,
says the Lord Almighty." *2 Samuel 7:14; 7:8*

7 Dear friends, we have these promises from
God, so we should make ourselves pure—
free from anything that makes body or soul unclean. We should try to become holy in the way
we live, because we respect God.

Paul's Joy

2Open your hearts to us. We have not done
wrong to anyone, we have not ruined the faith of
anyone, and we have not cheated anyone. 3I do
not say this to blame you. I told you before that
we love you so much we would live or die with
you. 4I feel very sure of you and am very proud
of you. You give me much comfort, and in all of
our troubles I have great joy.

5When we came into Macedonia, we had no
rest. We found trouble all around us. We had
fighting on the outside and fear on the inside. 6But
God, who comforts those who are troubled, comforted us when Titus came. 7We were comforted,
not only by his coming but also by the comfort
you gave him. Titus told us about your wish to see
me and that you are very sorry for what you did.
He also told me about your great care for me, and
when I heard this, I was much happier.

8Even if my letter made you sad, I am not sorry
I wrote it. At first I was sorry, because it made you
sad, but you were sad only for a short time. 9Now
I am happy, not because you were made sad, but
because your sorrow made you change your lives.
You became sad in the way God wanted you to,
so you were not hurt by us in any way. 10The kind
of sorrow God wants makes people change their
hearts and lives. This leads to salvation, and you
cannot be sorry for that. But the kind of sorrow
the world has brings death. 11See what this sorrow—the sorrow God wanted you to have—has
done to you: It has made you very serious. It
made you want to prove you were not wrong. It
made you angry and afraid. It made you want to
see me. It made you care. It made you want the
right thing to be done. You proved you were innocent in the problem. 12I wrote that letter, not because of the one who did the wrong or because
of the person who was hurt. I wrote the letter
so you could see, before God, the great care
you have for us. 13That is why we were comforted.

Not only were we very comforted, we were
even happier to see that Titus was so happy. All
of you made him feel much better. 14I bragged to
Titus about you, and you showed that I was right.
Everything we said to you was true, and you have
proved that what we bragged about to Titus is
true. 15And his love for you is stronger when he
remembers that you were all ready to obey. You
welcomed him with respect and fear. 16I am very
happy that I can trust you fully.

"I . . . people." Quotation from Leviticus 26:11-12; Jeremiah 32:38; Ezekiel 37:27.

Christian Giving

8 And now, brothers and sisters, we want you
to know about the grace God gave the
churches in Macedonia. 2They have been tested
by great troubles, and they are very poor. But they
gave much because of their great joy. 3I can tell
you that they gave as much as they were able and
even more than they could afford. No one told
them to do it. 4But they begged and pleaded with
us to let them share in this service for God's people. 5And they gave in a way we did not expect:
They first gave themselves to the Lord and to us.
This is what God wants. 6So we asked Titus to
help you finish this special work of grace since he
is the one who started it. 7You are rich in everything—in faith, in speaking, in knowledge, in
truly wanting to help, and in the love you learned
from us. In the same way, be strong also in the
grace of giving.

8I am not commanding you to give. But I want
to see if your love is true by comparing you with
others that really want to help. 9You know the
grace of our Lord Jesus Christ. You know that
Christ was rich, but for you he became poor so
that by his becoming poor you might become
rich.

10This is what I think you should do: Last year
you were the first to want to give, and you were
the first who gave. 11So now finish the work you
started. Then your "doing" will be equal to your
"wanting to do." Give from what you have. 12If
you want to give, your gift will be accepted. It will
be judged by what you have, not by what you do
not have. 13We do not want you to have troubles
while other people are at ease, but we want ev-

GIVING

The Little Things

Linda Dale was Judy Grantham's friend, and she had come on the ski trip to be with Judy. The Bible studies and prayertimes were okay, but she had really come to ski. After a day of skiing, Linda was on the bus, feeling exhausted and cold. Her socks were soaked and the bus was freezing. Shivering and surrounded by people she barely knew, she hoped Judy would come soon.

Jennifer Davis was cold, too. She was a regular group member, and noticed Linda sitting alone, cold and miserable. Going over to Linda, she asked, "Are you okay? You look like a Popsicle."

"I'm just so cold," Linda said. "My feet are freezing. Maybe Judy will have an extra pair of dry socks she can loan me."

"I have an extra pair of socks I'd be glad to give you," Jennifer said.

Linda hesitated, but then she said, "Would you? That would be wonderful."

Jennifer found the socks and gave them to Linda, along with some dry gloves and a scarf. By the time Judy boarded the bus, Linda and Jennifer were laughing about their day of skiing.

Later that night Linda asked Judy, "Why did Jennifer give me all those clothes when she was just as cold as I was?"

"Because giving is a part of being a Christian," Judy said. Then they talked for hours about why Judy was a Christian, and what it meant to give.

After the ski trip, Linda began coming to youth group regularly. While she still enjoyed the fun stuff, she also began asking more questions during Bible studies and offered prayers during worship. It took a while, but slowly she developed a solid faith.

In a world that assumes life's purpose is to take and keep, Jennifer's giving showed Linda that Christianity is different. Jennifer took **2 Corinthians 8:5–15** to heart.

- Looking at the passage, why did Jennifer share dry socks with Linda?
- In what ways does the passage challenge you to give to others?

CONSIDER . . .

- doing one unexpected chore around the house as a way to give of yourself.
- organizing a benefit fund-raiser to help a Christian mission or service project.

FOR MORE, SEE . . .

- Exodus 22:25–27
- Acts 20:32–35
- Philippians 2:5–7

erything to be equal. 14At this time you have
plenty. What you have can help others who are
in need. Then later, when they have plenty, they
can help you when you are in need, and all will
be equal. 15As it is written in the Scriptures,[d] "The
person who gathered more did not have too
much, nor did the person who gathered less have
too little."[n]

Titus and His Companions Help

16I thank God because he gave Titus the same
love for you that I have. 17Titus accepted what we
asked him to do. He wanted very much to go to
you, and this was his own idea. 18We are sending
with him the brother who is praised by all the
churches because of his service in preaching the
Good News.[d] 19Also, this brother was chosen by
the churches to go with us when we deliver this
gift of money. We are doing this service to bring
glory to the Lord and to show that we really want
to help.

20We are being careful so that no one will criticize us for the way we are handling this large gift.
21We are trying hard to do what the Lord accepts
as right and also what people think is right.

22Also, we are sending with them our brother,
who is always ready to help. He has proved this
to us in many ways, and he wants to help even
more now, because he has much faith in you.

23Now about Titus—he is my partner who is
working with me to help you. And about the
other brothers—they are sent from the churches,
and they bring glory to Christ. 24So show these
men the proof of your love and the reason we are
proud of you. Then all the churches can see it.

Help for Fellow Christians

9 I really do not need to write you about this
help for God's people. 2I know you want to
help. I have been bragging about this to the people in Macedonia, telling them that you in Southern Greece have been ready to give since last
year. And your desire to give has made most of
them ready to give also. 3But I am sending the
brothers to you so that our bragging about you in
this will not be empty words. I want you to be
ready, as I said you would be. 4If any of the people
from Macedonia come with me and find that you
are not ready, we will be ashamed that we were
so sure of you. (And you will be ashamed, too!)
5So I thought I should ask these brothers to go to
you before we do. They will finish getting in order
the generous gift you promised so it will be ready
when we come. And it will be a generous gift—
not one that you did not want to give.

6Remember this: The person who plants a little
will have a small harvest, but the person who
plants a lot will have a big harvest. 7Each one
should give as you have decided in your heart to
give. You should not be sad when you give, and
you should not give because you feel forced to
give. God loves the person who gives happily.
8And God can give you more blessings than you
need. Then you will always have plenty of everything—enough to give to every good work. 9It is
written in the Scriptures:[d]

"He gives freely to the poor.
The things he does are right and will
continue forever." *Psalm 112:9*

10God is the One who gives seed to the farmer
and bread for food. He will give you all the seed
you need and make it grow so there will be a great
harvest from your goodness. 11He will make you
rich in every way so that you can always give
freely. And your giving through us will cause
many to give thanks to God. 12This service you do
not only helps the needs of God's people, it also
brings many more thanks to God. 13It is a proof
of your faith. Many people will praise God because you obey the Good News[d] of Christ—the
gospel you say you believe—and because you
freely share with them and with all others. 14And
when they pray, they will wish they could be with
you because of the great grace that God has given
you. 15Thanks be to God for his gift that is too
wonderful for words.

Paul Defends His Ministry

10 I, Paul, am begging you with the gentleness and the kindness of Christ. Some
people say that I am easy on you when I am with
you and bold when I am away. 2They think we
live in a worldly way, and I plan to be very bold
with them when I come. I beg you that when I
come I will not need to use that same boldness
with you. 3We do live in the world, but we do not
fight in the same way the world fights. 4We fight
with weapons that are different from those the
world uses. Our weapons have power from God
that can destroy the enemy's strong places. We
destroy people's arguments 5and every proud
thing that raises itself against the knowledge of
God. We capture every thought and make it give
up and obey Christ. 6We are ready to punish anyone there who does not obey, but first we want
you to obey fully.

7You must look at the facts before you. If you
feel sure that you belong to Christ, you must remember that we belong to Christ just as you do.
8It is true that we brag freely about the authority
the Lord gave us. But this authority is to build you
up, not to tear you down. So I will not be
ashamed. 9I do not want you to think I am trying
to scare you with my letters. 10Some people say,

"The person . . . little." Quotation from Exodus 16:18.

"Paul's letters are powerful and sound important, but when he is with us, he is weak. And his speaking is nothing." 11They should know this: We are not there with you now, so we say these things in letters. But when we are there with you, we will show the same authority that we show in our letters.

SIDELIGHT: Paul may have been a great missionary, but he would have never made it on the front of a fashion magazine. A nonbiblical book called Acts of Paul and Thecla described him as "a man small of stature, with bald head and crooked legs . . . with eyebrows meeting and nose somewhat hooked." His critics said: "He is weak. And his speaking is nothing" (2 Corinthians 10:10).

12We do not dare to compare ourselves with those who think they are very important. They use themselves to measure themselves, and they judge themselves by what they themselves are. This shows that they know nothing. 13But we will not brag about things outside the work that was given us to do. We will limit our bragging to the work that God gave us, and this includes our work with you. 14We are not bragging too much, as we would be if we had not already come to you. But we have come to you with the Good News[d] of Christ. 15We limit our bragging to the work that is ours, not what others have done. We hope that as your faith continues to grow, you will help our work to grow much larger. 16We want to tell the Good News in the areas beyond your city. We do not want to brag about work that has already been done in another person's area. 17But, "If someone wants to brag, he should brag only about the Lord."[n] 18It is not those who say they are good who are accepted but those who the Lord thinks are good.

Paul and the False Apostles

11 I wish you would be patient with me even when I am a little foolish, but you are already doing that. 2I am jealous over you with a jealousy that comes from God. I promised to give you to Christ, as your only husband. I want to give you as his pure bride. 3But I am afraid that your minds will be led away from your true and pure following of Christ just as Eve was tricked by the snake with his evil ways. 4You are very patient with anyone who comes to you and preaches a different Jesus from the one we preached. You are very willing to accept a spirit or gospel that is different from the Spirit[d] and Good News[d] you received from us.

5I do not think that those "great apostles" are any better than I am. 6I may not be a trained speaker, but I do have knowledge. We have shown this to you clearly in every way.

7I preached God's Good News to you without pay. I made myself unimportant to make you important. Do you think that was wrong? 8I accepted pay from other churches, taking their money so I could serve you. 9If I needed something when I was with you, I did not trouble any of you. The brothers who came from Macedonia gave me all that I needed. I did not allow myself to depend on you in any way, and I will never depend on you. 10No one in Southern Greece will stop me from bragging about that. I say this with the truth of Christ in me. 11And why do I not depend on you? Do you think it is because I do not love you? God knows that I love you.

12And I will continue doing what I am doing now, because I want to stop those people from having a reason to brag. They would like to say that the work they brag about is the same as ours. 13Such men are not true apostles[d] but are workers who lie. They change themselves to look like apostles of Christ. 14This does not surprise us. Even Satan changes himself to look like an angel of light.[n] 15So it does not surprise us if Satan's servants also make themselves look like servants who work for what is right. But in the end they will be punished for what they do.

Paul Tells About His Sufferings

16I tell you again: No one should think I am a fool. But if you think so, accept me as you would accept a fool. Then I can brag a little, too. 17When I brag because I feel sure of myself, I am not talking as the Lord would talk but as a fool. 18Many people are bragging about their lives in the world. So I will brag too. 19You are wise, so you will gladly be patient with fools! 20You are even patient with those who order you around, or use you, or trick you, or think they are better than you, or hit you in the face. 21It is shameful to me to say this, but we were too "weak" to do those things to you!

But if anyone else is brave enough to brag, then I also will be brave and brag. (I am talking as a fool.) 22Are they Hebrews?[n] So am I. Are they Israelites? So am I. Are they from Abraham's family? So am I. 23Are they serving Christ? I am serving him more. (I am crazy to talk like this.) I have

"If . . . Lord." Quotation from Jeremiah 9:24.
angel of light Messenger from God. The devil fools people so that they think he is from God.
Hebrews A name for the Jews that some Jews were very proud of.

worked much harder than they. I have been in prison more often. I have been hurt more in beatings. I have been near death many times. 24Five times the Jews have given me their punishment of thirty-nine lashes with a whip. 25Three different times I was beaten with rods. One time I was almost stoned to death. Three times I was in ships that wrecked, and one of those times I spent a night and a day in the sea. 26I have gone on many travels and have been in danger from rivers, thieves, my own people, the Jews, and those who are not Jews. I have been in danger in cities, in places where no one lives, and on the sea. And I have been in danger with false Christians. 27I have done hard and tiring work, and many times I did not sleep. I have been hungry and thirsty, and many times I have been without food. I have been cold and without clothes. 28Besides all this, there is on me every day the load of my concern for all the churches. 29I feel weak every time someone is weak, and I feel upset every time someone is led into sin.

30If I must brag, I will brag about the things that show I am weak. 31God knows I am not lying. He is the God and Father of the Lord Jesus Christ, and he is to be praised forever. 32When I was in Damascus, the governor under King Aretas wanted to arrest me, so he put guards around the city. 33But my friends lowered me in a basket through a hole in the city wall. So I escaped from the governor.

A Special Blessing in Paul's Life

12 I must continue to brag. It will do no good, but I will talk now about visions and revelations[n] from the Lord. 2I know a man in Christ who was taken up to the third heaven fourteen years ago. I do not know whether the man was in his body or out of his body, but God knows. 3-4And I know that this man was taken up to paradise.[n] I don't know if he was in his body or away from his body, but God knows. He heard things he is not able to explain, things that no human is allowed to tell. 5I will brag about a man like that, but I will not brag about myself, except about my weaknesses. 6But if I wanted to brag about myself, I would not be a fool, because I would be telling the truth. But I will not brag about myself. I do not want people to think more of me than what they see me do or hear me say.

7So that I would not become too proud of the wonderful things that were shown to me, a painful physical problem[n] was given to me. This problem was a messenger from Satan, sent to beat me and keep me from being too proud. 8I begged the Lord three times to take this problem away from me. 9But he said to me, "My grace is enough for you. When you are weak, my power is made perfect in you." So I am very happy to brag about my weaknesses. Then Christ's power can live in me. 10For this reason I am happy when I have weaknesses, insults, hard times, sufferings, and all kinds of troubles for Christ. Because when I am weak, then I am truly strong.

Paul's Love for the Christians

11I have been talking like a fool, but you made me do it. You are the ones who should say good things about me. I am worth nothing, but those "great apostles" are not worth any more than I am! 12When I was with you, I patiently did the things that prove I am an apostle[d]—signs, wonders, and miracles.[d] 13So you received everything that the other churches have received. Only one thing was different: I was not a burden to you. Forgive me for this!

14I am now ready to visit you the third time, and I will not be a burden to you. I want nothing from you, except you. Children should not have to save up to give to their parents. Parents should save to give to their children. 15So I am happy to give everything I have for you, even myself. If I love you more, will you love me less?

16It is clear I was not a burden to you, but you think I was tricky and lied to catch you. 17Did I cheat you by using any of the messengers I sent to you? No, you know I did not. 18I asked Titus to go to you, and I sent our brother with him. Titus did not cheat you, did he? No, you know that Titus and I did the same thing and with the same spirit.

19Do you think we have been defending ourselves to you all this time? We have been speaking in Christ and before God. You are our dear friends, and everything we do is to make you stronger. 20I am afraid that when I come, you will not be what I want you to be, and I will not be what you want me to be. I am afraid that among you there may be arguing, jealousy, anger, selfish fighting, evil talk, gossip, pride, and confusion. 21I am afraid that when I come to you again, my God will make me ashamed before you. I may be saddened by many of those who have sinned because they have not changed their hearts or turned from their sexual sins and the shameful things they have done.

Final Warnings and Greetings

13 I will come to you for the third time. "Every case must be proved by two or

revelations Revelation is making known a truth that was hidden.
paradise A place where good people go when they die.
painful physical problem Literally, "thorn in the flesh."

three witnesses."[n] 2When I was with you the
second time, I gave a warning to those who had
sinned. Now I am away from you, and I give a
warning to all the others. When I come to you
again, I will not be easy with them. 3You want
proof that Christ is speaking through me. My
proof is that he is not weak among you, but he is
powerful. 4It is true that he was weak when he
was killed on the cross, but he lives now by God's
power. It is true that we are weak in Christ, but
for you we will be alive in Christ by God's power.
5Look closely at yourselves. Test yourselves to
see if you are living in the faith. You know that
Jesus Christ is in you—unless you fail the test.
6But I hope you will see that we ourselves have
not failed the test. 7We pray to God that you will
not do anything wrong. It is not important to see
that we have passed the test, but it is important
that you do what is right, even if it seems we have
failed. 8We cannot do anything against the truth,
but only for the truth. 9We are happy to be weak,
if you are strong, and we pray that you will become complete. 10I am writing this while I am
away from you so that when I come I will not
have to be harsh in my use of authority. The Lord
gave me this authority to build you up, not to tear
you down.
11Now, brothers and sisters, I say good-bye.
Try to be complete. Do what I have asked you
to do. Agree with each other, and live in peace.
Then the God of love and peace will be with
you.

SIDELIGHT: *Want to start rumors in your youth group? Then put 2 Corinthians 13:12 into practice. This custom of kissing other Christians arose spontaneously in the early church, and later became a regular part of worship. It's still a custom in some Near Eastern cultures.*

12Greet each other with a holy kiss. 13All of
God's holy people send greetings to you.
14The grace of the Lord Jesus Christ, the love
of God, and the fellowship of the Holy Spirit[d] be
with you all.

GALATIANS

Why Read This Book:

- See the dangers of listening to false teachers (Galatians 1–2).
- Discover the freedom we have through faith in Christ (Galatians 3).
- Find out how Christians should use their freedom (Galatians 5–6).

Behind the Scenes:

What do you have to do to be a Christian? Do you have to practice certain rituals? Do you have to follow certain rules?

Those were controversial questions in the early church, as we discover in Paul's letter to the Galations. Not long before, Paul had started the churches in Galatia. But soon after he left, people began questioning his beliefs and authority. They said non-Jewish people who became Christians also had to follow Jewish laws and rituals to be true Christians—a perspective that was splitting the early church (see Acts 15).

When Paul heard what was happening, he wrote this letter to confront the problem. "You have already accepted the Good News. If anyone is preaching something different to you, he should be judged guilty!" he blasts in Galatians 1:9. Then Paul gets to the heart of the Christian faith. He explains that people can't do anything to earn God's promises. Those promises are free gifts for all people, to be received by faith in Christ. Instead of being the law's prisoners, Christians live in freedom.

Someone always seems to be telling us that serving God means following a long list of dos and don'ts. Paul's letter to the Galatians reminds us that being a Christian isn't a matter of what we do or don't do; it's a matter of accepting what Jesus Christ did for us. Now that's Good News!

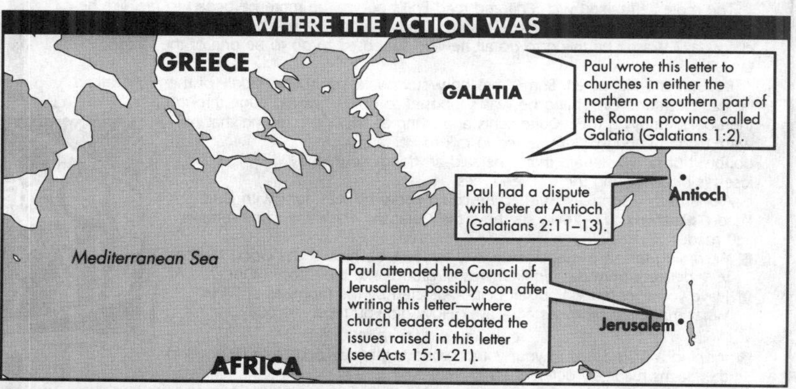
WHERE THE ACTION WAS
GREECE
GALATIA
Paul wrote this letter to churches in either the northern or southern part of the Roman province called Galatia (Galatians 1:2).
Antioch
Paul had a dispute with Peter at Antioch (Galatians 2:11–13).
Mediterranean Sea
Paul attended the Council of Jerusalem—possibly soon after writing this letter—where church leaders debated the issues raised in this letter (see Acts 15:1–21).
Jerusalem
AFRICA

WHEN THE ACTION WAS

BC/AD	20AD	30AD	40AD	50AD	60AD	70AD
Jesus was born	The church began soon after Jesus went to heaven			Paul started churches in Galatia	Fire destroyed Rome	
	Jesus began his ministry	Paul became a Christian		Paul wrote Galatians	Romans destroyed the Temple in Jerusalem	

1 From Paul, an apostle.[d] I was not chosen to
be an apostle by human beings, nor was I
sent from human beings. I was made an apostle
through Jesus Christ and God the Father who
raised Jesus from the dead. 2This letter is also from
all those of God's family[n] who are with me.
To the churches in Galatia:[n]
3Grace and peace to you from God our Father
and the Lord Jesus Christ. 4Jesus gave himself for
our sins to free us from this evil world we live in,
as God the Father planned. 5The glory belongs to
God forever and ever. Amen.

The Only Good News

6God, by his grace through Christ, called you to
become his people. So I am amazed that you are
turning away so quickly and believing something
different than the Good News.[d] 7Really, there is
no other Good News. But some people are confusing you; they want to change the Good News

those . . . family The Greek text says "brothers."
Galatia Probably the same country where Paul preached and began churches on his first missionary trip. Read the book of Acts, chapters 13 and 14.

CULTS

Good News, Bad News

Jeff Davis had gone to church off and on since he was little, but he had never felt he really needed God. That is, until last summer. Nearly everything Jeff did seemed to go wrong. He got fired from his summer job, then he totaled his car. Now his dad had moved out and wanted a divorce. Jeff began to wonder if maybe he could use help with his life.

He immediately thought of Phil Rogers. Nothing seemed to faze him. He seemed to have an inside track on the supernatural. He constantly read spiritual books and encouraged other kids to read them.

So Jeff started talking with Phil during lunch. Phil had an answer for every question Jeff asked. He made everything seem so simple and clear-cut. Phil talked about what it took to be one of the "Chosen Ones"—a new religious group Phil was involved with. "Wow," Jeff thought. "This guy really knows his stuff!"

Of course, Phil explained the Bible differently than Jeff had ever heard, but Phil seemed to know what he was talking about. It all seemed so simple. All you had to do is follow a list of rules and requirements, and you would be fine.

The more Jeff talked with Phil and read Phil's books, the more he began to feel like he, too, might finally be on the inside track to God. After all, wasn't he learning new things every day? Wasn't he trying to do all he was supposed to do to be one of the Chosen Ones?

But Jeff still wondered. Sometimes he would wake up in the middle of the night, afraid he had not done everything he was supposed to do. He would page through the books, studying the requirements and trying to shake the feeling that he wasn't good enough. Jeff wanted to talk to Phil about his doubts, but he was afraid that if he said anything, he might lose his place among the Chosen Ones.

Alone in the night, Jeff wished he could know he was right with God. Read **Galatians 1:1–10** to see how the Galatians made the same mistake Jeff made.

- According to this passage (especially verses 4–6), how is the Good News very different from the requirements of groups like the Chosen Ones?
- Have you ever found yourself being attracted by the promises of a cult? What made the promises attractive? How did you resist the pull?

CONSIDER . . .

- forming a Bible study in your youth group to prepare people to respond to the claims made by different cults.
- sharing the Good News with someone in a cult. Take an older Christian with you who knows about the specific cult.

FOR MORE, SEE . . .

- Deuteronomy 13:1–4
- Matthew 7:13–20
- 1 John 4:1–6

of Christ. 8We preached to you the Good News.
So if we ourselves, or even an angel from heaven,
should preach to you something different, we
should be judged guilty! 9I said this before, and
now I say it again: You have already accepted the
Good News. If anyone is preaching something different to you, he should be judged guilty!

> **SIDELIGHT:** If Paul wrote Galatians early in his missionary career—as some scholars believe—it may have been the first New Testament book written, dated less than twenty years after Jesus lived. Other scholars think either 1 Thessalonians or James was the first book written.

10Do you think I am trying to make people accept me? No, God is the One I am trying to
please. Am I trying to please people? If I still
wanted to please people, I would not be a servant
of Christ.

Paul's Authority Is from God

11Brothers and sisters,[n] I want you to know
that the Good News[d] I preached to you was not
made up by human beings. 12I did not get it from
humans, nor did anyone teach it to me, but Jesus
Christ showed it to me.

13You have heard about my past life in the Jewish religion. I attacked the church of God and
tried to destroy it. 14I was becoming a leader in
the Jewish religion, doing better than most other
Jews of my age. I tried harder than anyone else to
follow the teachings handed down by our ancestors.

15But God had special plans for me and set me
apart for his work even before I was born. He
called me through his grace 16and showed his son
to me so that I might tell the Good News about
him to those who are not Jewish. When God
called me, I did not get advice or help from any
person. 17I did not go to Jerusalem to see those
who were apostles[d] before I was. But, without
waiting, I went away to Arabia and later went
back to Damascus.

18After three years I went to Jerusalem to meet
Peter and stayed with him for fifteen days. 19I met
no other apostles, except James, the brother of the
Lord. 20God knows that these things I write are
not lies. 21Later, I went to the areas of Syria and
Cilicia.

22In Judea the churches in Christ had never
met me. 23They had only heard it said, "This man
who was attacking us is now preaching the same
faith that he once tried to destroy." 24And these
believers praised God because of me.

Other Apostles Accepted Paul

2 After fourteen years I went to Jerusalem
again, this time with Barnabas. I also took
Titus with me. 2I went because God showed me
I should go. I met with the believers there, and in
private I told their leaders the Good News[d] that
I preach to the non-Jewish people. I did not want
my past work and the work I am now doing to be
wasted. 3Titus was with me, but he was not
forced to be circumcised,[d] even though he was a
Greek. 4We talked about this problem because
some false believers had come into our group secretly. They came in like spies to overturn the
freedom we have in Christ Jesus. They wanted to
make us slaves. 5But we did not give in to those
false believers for a minute. We wanted the truth
of the Good News to continue for you.

6Those leaders who seemed to be important
did not change the Good News that I preach. (It
doesn't matter to me if they were "important" or
not. To God everyone is the same.) 7But these
leaders saw that I had been given the work of
telling the Good News to those who are not Jewish, just as Peter had the work of telling the Jews.
8God gave Peter the power to work as an apostle[d]
for the Jewish people. But he also gave me the
power to work as an apostle for those who are not
Jews. 9James, Peter, and John, who seemed to be
the leaders, understood that God had given me
this special grace, so they accepted Barnabas and
me. They agreed that they would go to the Jewish
people and that we should go to those who are
not Jewish. 10The only thing they asked us was to
remember to help the poor—something I really
wanted to do.

Paul Shows that Peter Was Wrong

11When Peter came to Antioch, I challenged
him to his face, because he was wrong. 12Peter ate
with the non-Jewish people until some Jewish
people sent from James came to Antioch. When
they arrived, Peter stopped eating with those who
weren't Jewish, and he separated himself from
them. He was afraid of the Jews. 13So Peter was
a hypocrite,[d] as were the other Jewish believers
who joined with him. Even Barnabas was influenced by what these Jewish believers did. 14When
I saw they were not following the truth of the
Good News,[d] I spoke to Peter in front of them all.

Brothers and sisters Although the Greek text says "Brothers" here and throughout this book, Paul's words were meant for the entire church, including men and women.

I said, "Peter, you are a Jew, but you are not living like a Jew. You are living like those who are not Jewish. So why do you now try to force those who are not Jewish to live like Jews?"

[15]We were not born as non-Jewish "sinners," but as Jews. [16]Yet we know that a person is made right with God not by following the law, but by trusting in Jesus Christ. So we, too, have put our faith in Christ Jesus, that we might be made right with God because we trusted in Christ. It is not because we followed the law, because no one can be made right with God by following the law.

[17]We Jews came to Christ, trying to be made right with God, and it became clear that we are sinners, too. Does this mean that Christ encourages sin? No! [18]But I would really be wrong to begin teaching again those things that I gave up. [19]It was the law that put me to death, and I died to the law so that I can now live for God. [20]I was put to death on the cross with Christ, and I do not live anymore—it is Christ who lives in me. I still live in my body, but I live by faith in the Son of God who loved me and gave himself to save me. [21]By saying these things I am not going against God's grace. Just the opposite, if the law could make us right with God, then Christ's death would be useless.

FAITH

You'd Better Believe It!

Pastor Crosby offered to take everyone out for pizza after Bible study. The kids cheered. Then the pastor disappeared upstairs to make a phone call.

"Did you hear that?" David asked James. "He's gonna buy us pizza!"

"There's no such thing as a free lunch, Dave. Look over there." James pointed toward a pile of brand new brooms, mops, buckets and sponges stacked against the wall. "When Crosby gets back, he's gonna tell us we've gotta clean the basement to pay for our lunch."

David had to admit James's theory made sense.

"Well, I'm starving," James continued. "If we gotta clean up, we might as well get going." He walked over and picked up one of the brooms.

"What are you guys doing?" Laura Moore asked.

"Well, what are you doing?" David asked sarcastically.

Laura was confused. "I'm waiting to go to lunch."

The boys laughed. "The sooner we get this basement cleaned, the sooner we can eat," David said, raising a storm of dust with his broom.

Laura started coughing. "You guys are making a big mess."

A few minutes later, Pastor Crosby walked into the dust storm. "What's going on down here? I thought I told you guys we were going out to lunch."

David stepped forward with a sheepish grin. "We figured you'd have us clean the basement before lunch, so we decided to get a head start."

"I just ordered pizzas at that new restaurant across town," Pastor Crosby said. "Let's go!"

James and David didn't believe their pastor's promise. Read **Galatians 2:11–21** to see how the apostle Peter didn't have faith in God's promises to him.

- How is the boys' lack of faith in their pastor's promise similar to Peter's lack of faith in God's promises?
- How have you acted like Peter in this passage and not believed God loves you and accepts you?

CONSIDER . . .

- making a list of good deeds you have done to make God love and accept you. Then tear up the list to symbolize that faith—not good deeds—earns eternal life.
- looking for "free" offers of things that really aren't free. Compare these things to God's free gift of eternal life through faith. Think about why it's hard for people to believe God's gift is really free.

FOR MORE, SEE . . .

- Genesis 15:1–6
- Romans 3:21–31
- Ephesians 2:4–10

Blessing Comes Through Faith

3 You people in Galatia were told very clearly about the death of Jesus Christ on the cross. But you were foolish; you let someone trick you. 2Tell me this one thing: How did you receive the Holy Spirit?[d] Did you receive the Spirit by following the law? No, you received the Spirit because you heard the Good News[d] and believed it. 3You began your life in Christ by the Spirit. Now are you trying to make it complete by your own power? That is foolish. 4Were all your experiences wasted? I hope not! 5Does God give you the Spirit and work miracles[d] among you because you follow the law? No, he does these things because you heard the Good News and believed it.

6The Scriptures[d] say the same thing about Abraham: "Abraham believed God, and God accepted Abraham's faith, and that faith made him right with God."[n] 7So you should know that the true children of Abraham are those who have faith. 8The Scriptures, telling what would happen in the future, said that God would make the non-Jewish people right through their faith. This Good News was told to Abraham beforehand, as the Scripture says: "All nations will be blessed through you."[n] 9So all who believe as Abraham believed are blessed just as Abraham was. 10But those who depend on following the law to make them right are under a curse, because the Scriptures say, "Anyone will be cursed who does not always obey what is written in the Book of the Law."[n] 11Now it is clear that no one can be made right with God by the law, because the Scriptures say, "Those who are right with God will live by trusting in him."[n] 12The law is not based on faith. It says, "A person who obeys these things will live because of them."[n] 13Christ took away the curse the law put on us. He changed places with us and put himself under that curse. It is written in the Scriptures, "Anyone whose body is displayed on a tree[n] is cursed." 14Christ did this so that God's blessing promised to Abraham might come through Jesus Christ to those who are not Jews. Jesus died so that by our believing we could receive the Spirit that God promised.

The Law and the Promise

15Brothers and sisters, let us think in human terms: Even an agreement made between two persons is firm. After that agreement is accepted by both people, no one can stop it or add anything to it. 16God made promises both to Abraham and to his descendant.[d] God did not say, "and to your descendants." That would mean many people. But God said, "and to your descendant." That means only one person; that person is Christ. 17This is what I mean: God had an agreement with Abraham and promised to keep it. The law, which came four hundred thirty years later, cannot change that agreement and so destroy God's promise to Abraham. 18If the law could give us Abraham's blessing, then the promise would not be necessary. But that is not possible, because God freely gave his blessings to Abraham through the promise he had made.

19So what was the law for? It was given to show that the wrong things people do are against God's will. And it continued until the special descendant, who had been promised, came. The law was given through angels who used Moses for a mediator[n] to give the law to people. 20But a mediator is not needed when there is only one side, and God is only one.

The Purpose of the Law of Moses

21Does this mean that the law is against God's promises? Never! That would be true only if the law could make us right. But God did not give a law that can bring life. 22Instead, the Scriptures[d] showed that the whole world is bound by sin. This was so the promise would be given through faith to people who believe in Jesus Christ.

SIDELIGHT: The Greek word translated "guardian" in Galatians 3:24 could almost be translated "babysitter." It refers to the person—usually a slave—who was responsible for taking care of young children (see also Galatians 4:1-7). Possibly half of the population of the Roman Empire were slaves during New Testament times.

23Before this faith came, we were all held prisoners by the law. We had no freedom until God showed us the way of faith that was coming. 24In other words, the law was our guardian leading us to Christ so that we could be made right with God through faith. 25Now the way of faith has come, and we no longer live under a guardian.

"Abraham . . . God." Quotation from Genesis 15:6.
"All . . . you." Quotation from Genesis 12:3 and 18:18.
"Anyone . . . Law." Quotation from Deuteronomy 27:26.
"Those . . . him." Quotation from Habakkuk 2:4.
"A person . . . them." Quotation from Leviticus 18:5.
displayed on a tree Deuteronomy 21:22-23 says that when a person was killed for doing wrong, the body was hung on a tree to show shame. Paul means that the cross of Jesus was like that.
mediator A person who helps one person talk to or give something to another person.

26-27You were all baptized into Christ, and so
you were all clothed with Christ. This means that
you are all children of God through faith in Christ
Jesus. 28In Christ, there is no difference between
Jew and Greek, slave and free person, male and
female. You are all the same in Christ Jesus. 29You
belong to Christ, so you are Abraham's descendants.[d] You will inherit all of God's blessings because of the promise God made to Abraham.

4 I want to tell you this: While those who will
inherit their fathers' property are still children, they are no different from slaves. It does not
matter that the children own everything. 2While
they are children, they must obey those who are
chosen to care for them. But when the children
reach the age set by their fathers, they are free. 3It
is the same for us. We were once like children,
slaves to the useless rules of this world. 4But
when the right time came, God sent his Son who
was born of a woman and lived under the law.
5God did this so he could buy freedom for those
who were under the law and so we could become
his children.

6Since you are God's children, God sent the
Spirit of his Son into your hearts, and the Spirit[d]
cries out, "Father."[n] 7So now you are not a slave;
you are God's child, and God will give you the
blessing he promised, because you are his child.

"Father" Literally, "Abba, Father." Jewish children called their fathers "Abba."

JUDGING OTHERS

Inside Out

In this corner: Harold Milburn, Sunday school superintendent, board member, businessman. Gray suit and tie, starched shirt, thick glasses.

In that corner: Josh Kincaid, would-be radical, always off on some wild project to save the world, usually involving loud music. Orange-dyed mohawk, ripped jeans, T-shirt, earring.

Mohawk sizes up Starched Shirt. "He'll turn me down before I even ask. Old people are like that. Narrow-minded, afraid of anything new."

Starched Shirt sizes up Mohawk: "Oh, boy. Here we go. Another crazy idea. And if I say no, he'll call me old-fashioned."

"Hi, Josh. What's up?"

"We want to fix up the old fellowship hall for a place to have a weekly Bible study."

Starched Shirt frowns.

So does Mohawk. "I knew it," he thinks. "You think anybody who doesn't look like you can't be trusted."

"Hmmm," Starched Shirt muses. "These kids sure dress funny, but their hearts are in the right place."

"Sounds like a great idea to me," Starched Shirt finally says. "What's your first topic?"

Mohawk is down for the count. "Uh, the importance of prayer," he manages to get out.

"Now there's a subject I could always use some help with," Starched Shirt says.

"Well, Mr. Milburn," Mohawk grins, "why don't you join us sometime?"

Though people may be different on the outside, they are the same in Jesus Christ. Read this truth in **Galatians 3:23–29**.

- How are Starched Shirt and Mohawk—or as it says in this passage, a Jew and a Greek—no different in Christ?
- What criteria besides what is in this passage have you used to judge another Christian?

C O N S I D E R . . .

- tearing out pictures of five people from a magazine. On each picture, write five preconceptions you have about people like that person. Check your perceptions by getting to know people in each category.
- visiting a church with a different culture. For example, if you are from a Spanish-speaking church, visit a Vietnamese church.

F O R M O R E , S E E . . .

- 1 Samuel 16:1–13
- Romans 2:28–29
- 2 Corinthians 5:11–12

Paul's Love for the Christians

[8]In the past you did not know God. You were
slaves to gods that were not real. [9]But now you
know the true God. Really, it is God who knows
you. So why do you turn back to those weak and
useless rules you followed before? Do you want to
be slaves to those things again? [10]You still follow
teachings about special days, months, seasons,
and years. [11]I am afraid for you, that my work for
you has been wasted.

[12]Brothers and sisters, I became like you, so I
beg you to become like me. You were very good
to me before. [13]You remember that it was because
of an illness that I came to you the first time,
preaching the Good News.[d] [14]Though my sickness was a trouble for you, you did not hate me
or make me leave. But you welcomed me as an
angel from God, as if I were Jesus Christ himself!
[15]You were very happy then, but where is that joy
now? I am ready to testify that you would have
taken out your eyes and given them to me if that
were possible. [16]Now am I your enemy because
I tell you the truth?

[17]Those people[n] are working hard to persuade

Those people They are the false teachers who were bothering the believers in Galatia (Galatians 1:7).

GOD'S LOVE

Too Good to Be True?

"Yours Free! Just Call and Claim Your Prize! No Obligation!" It was a once-in-a-lifetime offer that Jackie Sondheim couldn't refuse when it arrived in the mail.

Sure, Jackie had heard that some of these offers were scams. But this looked like a sure bet. It guaranteed she would get "a luxurious fur coat" or a "limited edition Mercedes sports car with all the extras."

"Everyone's a winner" the card boasted. "Call now to learn what you won!"

"What could it hurt," Jackie thought to herself, picking up the phone.

Sure enough, she had won! The fur coat was being packed for her. And, the contest's agent asked if she would also consider another special offer. For only $395 (charge it, if you like), she could receive beauty tips from "the nation's foremost beauty experts" in an exclusive newsletter for teenage girls called "Lookin' Good."

Plus, she would have access to a toll-free "Looks Line." She could call the number any time, day or night, and receive personal consultations on anything from shoes to eye shadow—for the rest of her life. It was just a one-time fee, Jackie told herself. And it was good for a lifetime. So she placed her order with her mom's credit card.

Jackie's excitement turned to displeasure when she received the genuine dyed rabbit fur coat. She knew she had been taken when the one-page "Lookin' Good" newsletter arrived, complete with revolutionary beauty tips such as "thoroughly wash your face each night before going to bed."

Something that had seemed like a dream just a few days earlier now seemed like a nightmare. It had sounded too good to be true. And it was.

All around us are too-good-to-be-true offers. Most are hoaxes. **Galatians 4:4–7** tells about an offer of God's love that seems too good to be true, but really is true!

- What differences do you see between the once-in-a-lifetime offer Jackie fell for and the once-for-all-times offer of God's love that's described in the passage?
- What parts of God's offer of love are most appealing to you? How have you responded to that offer?

CONSIDER . . .

- using the form and style of a junk-mail offer to write a postcard about God's offer of love. Send it to a friend who needs some encouragement.
- talking to a friend who was adopted about what it feels like to be specially chosen by parents. Discuss similarities and differences between that experience and the experience of being a child of God.

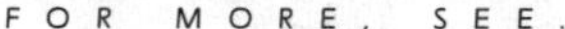

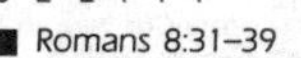

FOR MORE, SEE . . .

- Isaiah 64:8–9
- Matthew 7:7–11
- Romans 8:31–39

you, but this is not good for you. They want
to persuade you to turn against us and follow
only them. 18It is good for people to show
interest in you, but only if their purpose is
good. This is always true, not just when I am
with you. 19My little children, again I feel the
pain of childbirth for you until you truly become like Christ. 20I wish I could be with you
now and could change the way I am talking
to you, because I do not know what to think
about you.

The Example of Hagar and Sarah

21Some of you still want to be under the law.
Tell me, do you know what the law says? 22The
Scriptures[d] say that Abraham had two sons. The
mother of one son was a slave woman, and the
mother of the other son was a free woman.
23Abraham's son from the slave woman was born
in the normal human way. But the son from the
free woman was born because of the promise God
made to Abraham.

24This story teaches something else: The two
women are like the two agreements between God
and his people. One agreement is the law that
God made on Mount Sinai,[n] and the people
who are under this agreement are like slaves. The
mother named Hagar is like that agreement. 25She
is like Mount Sinai in Arabia and is a picture of the
earthly Jewish city of Jerusalem. This city and its
people, the Jews, are slaves to the law. 26But the
heavenly Jerusalem, which is above, is like the
free woman. She is our mother. 27It is written in
the Scriptures:

"Be happy, Jerusalem.
  You are like a woman who never gave
    birth to children.
Start singing and shout for joy.
  You never felt the pain of giving birth,
but you will have more children
  than the woman who has a husband."

Isaiah 54:1

28My brothers and sisters, you are God's children because of his promise, as Isaac was then.
29The son who was born in the normal way
treated the other son badly. It is the same today.
30But what does the Scripture say? "Throw out
the slave woman and her son. The son of the slave
woman should not inherit anything. The son of
the free woman should receive it all."[n] 31So, my
brothers and sisters, we are not children of the
slave woman, but of the free woman.

Keep Your Freedom

5 We have freedom now, because Christ made
us free. So stand strong. Do not change and
go back into the slavery of the law. 2Listen, I Paul
tell you that if you go back to the law by being
circumcised,[d] Christ does you no good. 3Again, I
warn every man: If you allow yourselves to be
circumcised, you must follow all the law. 4If you
try to be made right with God through the law,
your life with Christ is over—you have left God's
grace. 5But we have the true hope that comes
from being made right with God, and by the Spirit
we wait eagerly for this hope. 6When we are in
Christ Jesus, it is not important if we are circumcised or not. The important thing is faith—the
kind of faith that works through love.

> **SIDELIGHT:** Circumcision (Galatians 5:2–6) was an important ritual for Jews, symbolizing bringing a baby boy into God's family. A festive occasion marked each circumcision, which was usually performed by the boy's father.

7You were running a good race. Who stopped
you from following the true way? 8This change
did not come from the One who chose you. 9Be
careful! "Just a little yeast makes the whole batch
of dough rise." 10But I trust in the Lord that you
will not believe those different ideas. Whoever is
confusing you with such ideas will be punished.
11My brothers and sisters, I do not teach that a
man must be circumcised. If I teach circumcision,
why am I still being attacked? If I still taught circumcision, my preaching about the cross would
not be a problem. 12I wish the people who are
bothering you would castrate[n] themselves!
13My brothers and sisters, God called you to be
free, but do not use your freedom as an excuse to
do what pleases your sinful self. Serve each other
with love. 14The whole law is made complete in
this one command: "Love your neighbor as you
love yourself."[n] 15If you go on hurting each other
and tearing each other apart, be careful, or you
will completely destroy each other.

The Spirit and Human Nature

16So I tell you: Live by following the Spirit.[d]
Then you will not do what your sinful selves
want. 17Our sinful selves want what is against the

Mount Sinai Mountain in Arabia where God gave his laws to Moses (Exodus 19 and 20).
"Throw . . . all." Quotation from Genesis 21:10.
castrate To cut off part of the male sex organ. Paul uses this word because it is similar to "circumcision." Paul wanted to show that he is very upset with the false teachers.
"Love . . . yourself." Quotation from Leviticus 19:18.

Spirit, and the Spirit wants what is against our
sinful selves. The two are against each other, so
you cannot do just what you please. [18]But if
the Spirit is leading you, you are not under the
law.

[19]The wrong things the sinful self does are
clear: being sexually unfaithful, not being pure,
taking part in sexual sins, [20]worshiping gods, doing witchcraft,[d] hating, making trouble, being
jealous, being angry, being selfish, making people
angry with each other, causing divisions among
people, [21]feeling envy, being drunk, having wild
and wasteful parties, and doing other things like
these. I warn you now as I warned you before:
Those who do these things will not inherit God's
kingdom. [22]But the Spirit produces the fruit of
love, joy, peace, patience, kindness, goodness,
faithfulness, [23]gentleness, self-control. There is no
law that says these things are wrong. [24]Those who
belong to Christ Jesus have crucified their own
sinful selves. They have given up their old selfish
feelings and the evil things they wanted to do.
[25]We get our new life from the Spirit, so we
should follow the Spirit. [26]We must not be proud
or make trouble with each other or be jealous of
each other.

Help Each Other

6 Brothers and sisters, if someone in your
group does something wrong, you who are
spiritual should go to that person and gently help
make him right again. But be careful, because you
might be tempted to sin, too. [2]By helping each
other with your troubles, you truly obey the law
of Christ. [3]If anyone thinks he is important when
he really is not, he is only fooling himself. [4]Each
person should judge his own actions and not compare himself with others. Then he can be proud
for what he himself has done. [5]Each person must
be responsible for himself.

SERVICE

Free to Serve

The 1970s. "Feathered" hair, disco, the Bee Gees.

And Watergate.

The scandal of Watergate led to the first resignation by an American president since the nation was founded. It was a turbulent time, full of suspicion, intrigue, distrust, and power-hungry leaders. In the middle of it was Charles W. Colson.

Chuck Colson was a presidential aide for Richard Nixon. He was one of several White House personnel who were sentenced to prison for their involvement in the Watergate scandal. Colson served seven months.

Before he was sent to prison, Colson became a Christian. And while in prison, he saw firsthand the tremendous obstacles facing prisoners, ex-prisoners, and their families. "Rather than rehabilitating, prisons have become breeding grounds for crime," he says.

After his release from prison, Colson could have done like many people. He could have forgotten about his prison experience and gone on with his life. But he chose not to forget. He founded Prison Fellowship, a Christian outreach to inmates. Today, Colson regularly visits prisons and works for prison reform in the United States and in countries around the world.

Because of Colson's organization, nearly forty thousand volunteers work in more than six hundred prisons in the United States alone. His dedicated concern has resulted in the changed lives of thousands of inmates and families.

Chuck Colson turned his freedom into an opportunity to help those in prison. **Galatians 5:13–26** talks about the relationship between freedom and service. Read the passage to discover why God sets people free.

- How does Colson's choice to serve prisoners reflect this passage?
- How have you used your freedom in Christ as an avenue to serve others?

CONSIDER . . .

- using some of your "free time" to serve other people.
- becoming a pen pal with a prison inmate, or contacting Prison Fellowship, Box 17500, Washington, DC 20041, to see how you can serve in your area.

FOR MORE, SEE . . .

- Leviticus 19:17–18
- 1 Corinthians 10:23–24
- Philippians 2:4–7

[6]Anyone who is learning the teaching of God should share all the good things he has with his teacher.

Life Is like Planting a Field

[7]Do not be fooled: You cannot cheat God. People harvest only what they plant. [8]If they plant to satisfy their sinful selves, their sinful selves will bring them ruin. But if they plant to please the Spirit,[d] they will receive eternal life from the Spirit. [9]We must not become tired of doing good. We will receive our harvest of eternal life at the right time if we do not give up. [10]When we have the opportunity to help anyone, we should do it. But we should give special attention to those who are in the family of believers.

Paul Ends His Letter

[11]See what large letters I use to write this myself. [12]Some people are trying to force you to be circumcised[d] so the Jews will accept them. They are afraid they will be attacked if they follow only

SIDELIGHT: Paul may have had a lot to say, but he probably didn't have good handwriting (Galatians 6:11). From Galatians 4:13-15, some scholars think he might have had poor eyesight, because he thanks them for their generosity in being willing to take out their eyes and give them to him.

FRIENDS

When Friends Fail

Scott Perkins couldn't believe his eyes. There was Jason Haas, smoking a cigarette and laughing with the rest of the lunchtime crowd in the student parking lot.

"Didn't I tell you he was a phony?" Denise Rambo whispered. "I wish he'd stop coming to church altogether and hang out with his real friends."

"Hmmm," Scott thought. "I wonder what's going on here."

The next morning, he bumped into Jason between classes. "Wanna grab a burger for lunch?" Scott asked.

Jason looked down. "I don't think so."

Scott put his hand on Jason's shoulder. "Hey, you haven't been yourself lately. I wish we could talk about it."

Jason brushed him off. "I know what you want to talk about—you and Denise and everyone else. You're gonna be all nice and buy me a burger and then jump all over my case for being a big, bad sinner. Well, I don't want to hear it."

He turned to leave, but Scott grabbed his arm. "Wait a second. Number one, you're no bigger or worse a sinner than I am. Number two, I know if I suddenly had a total personality change I'd want my friends to investigate. And number three, you're buying your own burger."

Jason smiled. "Okay. You win. There are a couple of things I wouldn't mind talking about. And you're probably the only guy I know who'd care enough to listen."

Scott understood what it meant to be a real friend. Read **Galatians 6:1–10** to learn about the responsibilities of Christian friendship.

- Who most closely lived out this scripture: Scott or Denise?
- When have you acted out this scripture to help a fellow Christian who's done something wrong? When has another Christian gently corrected you? What were the results of either time?

CONSIDER . . .

- developing a friendship with an older Christian. Discuss your own areas of weakness with your new friend and ask him or her to help you avoid stumbling into sin.
- starting a prayer group with your friends. Discuss ways to draw closer and watch out for one another.

FOR MORE, SEE . . .

- Proverbs 27:6, 9–10
- Luke 22:31–32
- Hebrews 10:24–25

the cross of Christ.[n] 13Those who are circumcised do not obey the law themselves, but they
want you to be circumcised so they can brag
about what they forced you to do. 14I hope I
will never brag about things like that. The cross
of our Lord Jesus Christ is my only reason for
bragging. Through the cross of Jesus my world
was crucified, and I died to the world. 15It is
not important if a man is circumcised or uncircumcised. The important thing is being the
new people God has made. 16Peace and mercy to
those who follow this rule—and to all of God's
people.

17So do not give me any more trouble. I have
scars on my body that show[n] I belong to Christ
Jesus.

18My brothers and sisters, the grace of our Lord
Jesus Christ be with your spirit. Amen.

cross of Christ Paul uses the cross as a picture of the gospel, the story of Christ's death and rising from the dead to pay for our sins. The cross, or Christ's death, was God's way to save us.

that show Many times Paul was beaten and whipped by people who were against him because he was teaching about Christ. The scars were from these beatings.

EPHESIANS

Why Read This Book:

- Discover the blessings we have because we belong to Christ (Ephesians 1–3).
- Learn how to be united in our relationships with others (Ephesians 4–6:4).
- Gather the armor you need to follow God (Ephesians 6:10–20).

Behind the Scenes:

Has anything ever happened to you that was so great that you couldn't help but burst into song? When you read the book of Ephesians, you get the feeling the author felt that way about being a Christian.

The book is like a grand musical celebration of the Christian faith. It sings about God, Christ, human redemption, the church, God's power, and unity in Christ. Many people describe it as the climax of the New Testament.

Probably intended for several churches in Asia, including Ephesus, the book focuses on God's eternal purpose in establishing the universal church on earth. No matter what their background or nationality, all people are called to become part of Christ's body, which is both a privilege and a responsibility.

The first part of the book (Ephesians 1–3) uses prayers and praise to describe God's plan to unite all things in Christ. The second part (Ephesians 4–6) describes Christians' role in fulfilling God's plan.

As Christians, we come from various backgrounds, and attend different churches. Yet we share in the same blessings from God, and are called to live our lives according to Christ's example.

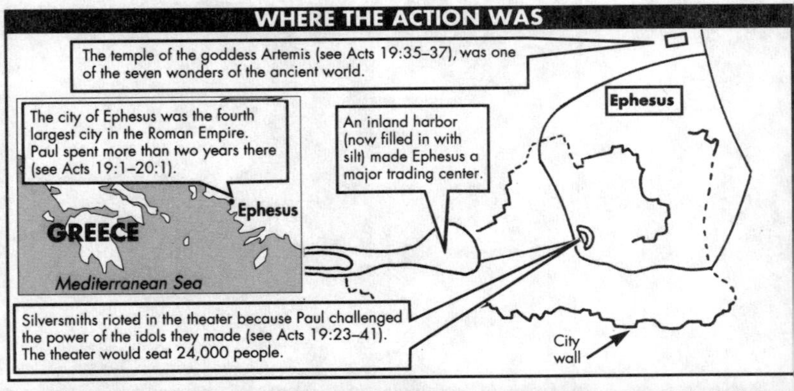

WHERE THE ACTION WAS
The temple of the goddess Artemis (see Acts 19:35–37), was one of the seven wonders of the ancient world.
The city of Ephesus was the fourth largest city in the Roman Empire. Paul spent more than two years there (see Acts 19:1–20:1).
Ephesus
GREECE
Mediterranean Sea
An inland harbor (now filled in with silt) made Ephesus a major trading center.
Ephesus
Silversmiths rioted in the theater because Paul challenged the power of the idols they made (see Acts 19:23–41). The theater would seat 24,000 people.
City wall

WHEN THE ACTION WAS

BC/AD	20AD	30AD	40AD	50AD	60AD	70AD
Jesus was born	The church began soon after Jesus went to heaven		Paul began his missionary work	Paul may have written Ephesians in prison		Fire destroyed Rome
	Jesus began his ministry	Paul became a Christian		Paul worked in Ephesus for more than two years	Romans destroyed the Temple in Jerusalem	

1 From Paul, an apostle[d] of Christ Jesus. I am
an apostle because that is what God wanted.
To God's holy people living in Ephesus, believers in Christ Jesus:
2Grace and peace to you from God our Father
and the Lord Jesus Christ.

Spiritual Blessings in Christ

3Praise be to the God and Father of our Lord
Jesus Christ. In Christ, God has given us every
spiritual blessing in the heavenly world. 4That is,
in Christ, he chose us before the world was made
so that we would be his holy people—people
without blame before him. 5Because of his love,
God had already decided to make us his own children through Jesus Christ. That was what he
wanted and what pleased him, 6and it brings
praise to God because of his wonderful grace. God
gave that grace to us freely, in Christ, the One he
loves. 7In Christ we are set free by the blood of
his death, and so we have forgiveness of sins.
How rich is God's grace, 8which he has given to
us so fully and freely. God, with full wisdom and
understanding, 9let us know his secret purpose.
This was what God wanted, and he planned to do
it through Christ. 10His goal was to carry out his
plan, when the right time came, that all things in

FORGIVENESS

Putting Up Bail

"Now I've done it," Bob Logan thought as he slammed his fist into the dashboard. The nose of his car was buried in someone's hedge, and red and blue lights were flashing in his rear-view mirror.

To make matters worse, Bob had been drinking. He hoped the police officer would be kind. More than that, he hoped his dad would be. This was the third time this year Bob had wrecked his car, and he figured his dad would explode when he found out.

Bob was arrested and allowed one phone call home. His mother cried as he told her what had happened. No one bailed Bob out; he spent the night in jail. He thought he would never be able to face his parents again.

In the morning, an officer yelled at Bob to get up and follow him. Bob left the stench of the cell and stepped into the white light of the police station. The first person Bob saw was his dad, standing with his hat in his hands, looking at the floor.

"Thanks . . ." Bob started and then stopped, unsure of how his dad would react. His dad looked up, and Bob saw the compassion in his eyes.

"Come on, Son," he said, "let's get out of here."

As they walked out of the station, Bob tried to explain. "Dad, I'm so sorry. It'll never happen again. I promise."

"Bob, you've made some big mistakes—mistakes that could've killed you," his dad responded.

Bob tried to speak, but his dad stopped him. "Son, I love you, and we're going to get through this together."

Although Bob's father forgave him, Bob still suffered some heavy consequences: He lost his license for ninety days, and it took him six months to repay the bail money. But Bob's relationship with his dad remained strong.

Being forgiven by his dad set Bob free. **Ephesians 1:1–10** describes how our Heavenly Father has set us free.

- How is Bob's experience of forgiveness like the forgiveness described in this passage? How is it different?
- According to this passage, what are the benefits of God's forgiveness to those who are in Christ?

C O N S I D E R . . .

- forgiving someone and setting that person free.
- making a card that says "Christians Aren't Perfect, Just Forgiven." Put it by your bed and think about its meaning each time you see it this week.

F O R   M O R E ,   S E E . . .

- Psalm 103
- Romans 3:21–26
- Colossians 1:13–14

heaven and on earth would be joined together in Christ as the head.

> **SIDELIGHT:** Many scholars believe this letter was originally circulated among many churches, since the earliest manuscripts do not include the words "in Ephesus" in Ephesians 1:1. In the second century A.D., one source called this letter the "letter to the Laodiceans"—another city in Asia Minor.

11In Christ we were chosen to be God's people, because from the very beginning God had decided this in keeping with his plan. And he is the One who makes everything agree with what he decides and wants. 12We are the first people who hoped in Christ, and we were chosen so that we would bring praise to God's glory. 13So it is with you. When you heard the true teaching—the Good News[d] about your salvation—you believed in Christ. And in Christ, God put his special mark of ownership on you by giving you the Holy Spirit[d] that he had promised. 14That Holy Spirit is the guarantee that we will receive what God promised for his people until God gives full freedom to those who are his—to bring praise to God's glory.

Paul's Prayer

15That is why since I heard about your faith in the Lord Jesus and your love for all God's people, 16I have not stopped giving thanks to God for you. I always remember you in my prayers, 17asking the God of our Lord Jesus Christ, the glorious Father, to give you a spirit of wisdom and revelation[d] so that you will know him better. 18I pray also that you will have greater understanding in your heart so you will know the hope to which he has called us and that you will know how rich and glorious are the blessings God has promised his holy people. 19And you will know that God's

GOD'S POWER

Batteries Included

Tony DeFazio might never have turned around except for the ministry of Richard Parks. A street kid, Tony ran away from his home in Newport, Oregon, when he was only eleven years old. He lived on handouts for a while but soon found that selling drugs earned him a better living. He was in and out of various homes and schools for seven years.

Then when he was eighteen, he met Richard on a street corner in Portland. Richard, a reformed street kid himself, was dedicated to getting kids off the streets through his work in an inner-city church. Richard found Tony a place to live and helped him get a job in a nearby gas station. He helped turn Tony around.

Tony was just one of many kids whom Richard reached with his love. When the local police heard about Richard's ministry, they asked how they could get involved. They figured their additional resources would expand the program, add energy and make it more effective.

After learning about the program, one officer remarked: "That's great. We'd be glad to help. But can we leave out the stuff about Jesus?"

Overhearing the question, Tony replied: "Hey man, you might as well take out the batteries. Jesus is what makes it work!"

Tony knew God's power was what had changed his life. This same power is available to all Christians, as we read in **Ephesians 1:15–23**.

- According to this passage, how is God's power different from earthly powers?
- How does this passage say to tap into God's power supply?

C O N S I D E R . . .

- writing a radio commercial announcing the benefits of God's power. Read the commercial to a friend or family member.
- applying God's power to your life in an area in which you have felt weak. Pray and work together with God to change that weakness.

F O R M O R E , S E E . . .

- 1 Chronicles 29:11–12
- Acts 1:7–8
- Ephesians 3:20–21

power is very great for us who believe. That power is the same as the great strength [20]God used to raise Christ from the dead and put him at his right side in the heavenly world. [21]God has put Christ over all rulers, authorities, powers, and kings, not only in this world but also in the next. [22]God put everything under his power and made him the head over everything for the church, [23]which is Christ's body. The church is filled with Christ, and Christ fills everything in every way.

We Now Have Life

2 In the past you were spiritually dead because of your sins and the things you did against God. [2]Yes, in the past you lived the way the world lives, following the ruler of the evil powers that are above the earth. That same spirit is now working in those who refuse to obey God. [3]In the past all of us lived like them, trying to please our sinful selves and doing all the things our bodies and minds wanted. We should have suffered God's anger because of the way we were. We were the same as all other people.

[4]But God's mercy is great, and he loved us very much. [5]Though we were spiritually dead because of the things we did against God, he gave us new life with Christ. You have been saved by God's grace. [6]And he raised us up with Christ and gave us a seat with him in the heavens. He did this for those in Christ Jesus [7]so that for all future time he could show the very great riches of his grace by being kind to us in Christ Jesus. [8]I mean that you have been saved by grace through believing. You did not save yourselves; it was a gift from God. [9]It was not the result of your own efforts, so you can-

PEACE

Enemy in My House

Ellie Gamble and her father were best friends. She had always run to him when she was hurt. But when Ellie was in junior high, everything changed. Her father began spending more time away from home. And when he was home, he and Ellie's mother fought all the time.

One day after school, Ellie found her mother lying across her bed, crying. The closet doors hung open, and her father's clothes were gone. Ellie's father had been having an affair and had moved out. Ellie couldn't believe it. She felt betrayed. How could her dad walk out on her like this?

Within three months, Ellie's parents were together, trying to restore their marriage. But Ellie couldn't see herself loving her father again. She avoided him. She even put a "No Men Allowed" sign on her bedroom door.

When Ellie went away to college, she was relieved to get away from the tense relationship with her dad. But during her freshman year, she heard the gospel and decided to follow Christ.

Her life began to change. She realized God wanted to rebuild her relationship with her dad. While home one weekend, Ellie cried as she told her dad she forgave him and asked him to forgive her.

From that point on, there was peace in Ellie's home—the kind of peace that made her homesick for time with her father.

God's love brought peace between Ellie and her dad. Read **Ephesians 2:4–22** to see how Christ also broke down the walls and established peace between the Jews and those who were not Jews.

- How was Ellie's broken relationship with her dad like the broken relationship between Jewish and non-Jewish people? How was it different?
- How can Christ break down walls of hatred between you and other people you know?

CONSIDER . . .

- asking God to reveal any walls in your relationships that need to be broken down.
- making peace with someone from whom you feel separated by giving that person a brick or rock and explaining that you want to break down the "wall" between you.

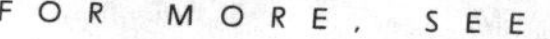

FOR MORE, SEE . . .

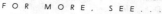

- Psalm 120:6–7
- Romans 9
- Hebrews 12:14–15

not brag about it. 10God has made us what we are. In Christ Jesus, God made us to do good works, which God planned in advance for us to live our lives doing.

One in Christ

11You were not born Jewish. You are the people the Jews call "uncircumcised."[n] Those who call you "uncircumcised" call themselves "circumcised."[d] (Their circumcision is only something they themselves do on their bodies.) 12Remember that in the past you were without Christ. You were not citizens of Israel, and you had no part in the agreements[n] with the promise that God made to his people. You had no hope, and you did not know God. 13But now in Christ Jesus, you who were far away from God are brought near through the blood of Christ's death. 14Christ himself is our peace. He made both Jewish people and those who are not Jews one people. They were separated as if there were a wall between them, but Christ broke down that wall of hate by giving his own body. 15The Jewish law had many commands and rules, but Christ ended that law. His purpose was to make the two groups of people become one new people in him and in this way make peace. 16It was also Christ's purpose to end the hatred between the two groups, to make them into one body, and to bring them back to God. Christ did all this with his death on the cross. 17Christ came and preached peace to you who were far away from God, and to those who were near to God. 18Yes, it is through Christ we all have the right to come to the Father in one Spirit.[d]

19Now you who are not Jewish are not foreigners or strangers any longer, but are citizens together with God's holy people. You belong to God's family. 20You are like a building that was built on the foundation of the apostles[d] and prophets.[d] Christ Jesus himself is the most important stone[n] in that building, 21and that whole building is joined together in Christ. He makes it grow and become a holy temple in the Lord. 22And in Christ you, too, are being built together with the Jews into a place where God lives through the Spirit.

uncircumcised People not having the mark of circumcision as the Jews had.
agreements The agreements that God gave to his people in the Old Testament.
most important stone Literally, "cornerstone." The first and most important stone in a building.

GOD'S LOVE

Unbelievable!

Imagine that the thickness of the page you are reading is the distance from Earth to the sun (93 million miles). With this scale, consider the following:

- The distance to the nearest star in our galaxy would be a 71-foot-high stack of paper.
- The diameter of our own galaxy (100,000 light years) would be a 310-mile stack.
- The edge of our known universe would be a 31 million-mile pile of paper.

And that's just the beginning! Astronomers tell us our galaxy is a family of more than 100 billion stars and that there are as many as 100 billion other galaxies in the universe. Each of these galaxies may have hundreds of millions of planets like our Earth.

Unfathomable? Incomprehensible? Beyond understanding?

Yes. But something even more vast than the universe is God's love for us. Read Paul's prayer in **Ephesians 3:14–21** to see how great God's love is.

- How accurate a comparison is God's love to the universe?
- How does knowing that God's love for you has no limits affect you?

CONSIDER . . .

- making a sign about God's love for you. Hang it where you will see it each morning, and remember that God's love for you has no limits.
- gazing at the stars on a clear night. For each star you see, thank God for a way he has shown his love for you.

FOR MORE, SEE . . .

- Psalm 36:5–10
- John 13:34–35
- Romans 8:35–39

Paul's Work in Telling the Good News

3 So I, Paul, am a prisoner of Christ Jesus for
you who are not Jews. 2Surely you have
heard that God gave me this work through his
grace to help you. 3He let me know his secret by
showing it to me. I have already written a little
about this. 4If you read what I wrote then, you
can see that I truly understand the secret about
the Christ.[d] 5People who lived in other times
were not told that secret. But now, through the
Spirit,[d] God has shown that secret to his holy
apostles[d] and prophets.[d] 6This is that secret: that
through the Good News[d] those who are not Jews
will share with the Jews in God's blessing.
They belong to the same body, and they share
together in the promise that God made in Christ
Jesus.
7By God's special gift of grace given to me
through his power, I became a servant to tell that
Good News. 8I am the least important of all God's
people, but God gave me this gift—to tell those
who are not Jews the Good News about the riches
of Christ, which are too great to understand fully.
9And God gave me the work of telling all people
about the plan for his secret, which has been hidden in him since the beginning of time. He is the
One who created everything. 10His purpose was
that through the church all the rulers and powers
in the heavenly world will now know God's wisdom, which has so many forms. 11This agrees
with the purpose God had since the beginning of
time, and he carried out his plan through Christ
Jesus our Lord. 12In Christ we can come before
God with freedom and without fear. We can do
this through faith in Christ. 13So I ask you not to
become discouraged because of the sufferings I
am having for you. My sufferings are for your
glory.

SIDELIGHT: To describe Jesus as the "most important stone" or cornerstone (Ephesians 2:20) makes him essential for the "building." When construction workers started building, they would first place one stone—the cornerstone—and then line up all the walls based on this stone.

CHURCH

Friends or Foes?

After several months of fighting among Westside Church members, the get-rid-of-the-pastor side won. Pastor Howard fought back tears as he announced his resignation on Sunday morning. He packed up his office and home, and moved away within a month.

Many church members on the keep-the-pastor side were angry and disillusioned; most of them left the Westside Church within six months. Some went to other churches. But some stayed away from the church for years.

Those who stayed at Westside Church hired a new pastor—one they were sure they would like much better than Pastor Howard. But in less than two years, the church members were fighting again. They ordered the new pastor to leave, and the cycle began again.

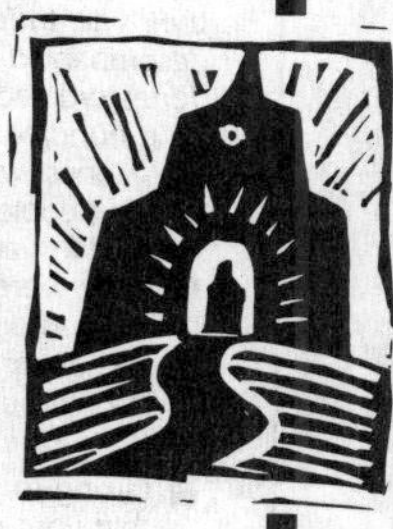

After watching the church destroy itself for the second time, one of the young people commented, "I don't think you can even call this place a church—anyway, I don't think it's what God meant for the church to be."

This teenager's perception fits the description of the church in **Ephesians 4:1–6**. Read this scripture to see what God wants the church to be like.

- If Westside Church members had applied these verses to their situation, how would the outcome have been different?
- How can you use this passage to promote unity within your church?

CONSIDER . . .

- encouraging your youth group to pray weekly for your church to be united.
- talking to your pastor about creating an annual "Unity Award" for church members who consistently promote unity in your church.

FOR MORE, SEE . . .

- Psalm 133
- Titus 3:9–11
- 1 Peter 3:8–12

The Love of Christ

14So I bow in prayer before the Father 15from
whom every family in heaven and on earth gets
its true name. 16I ask the Father in his great glory
to give you the power to be strong inwardly
through his Spirit.[d] 17I pray that Christ will live in
your hearts by faith and that your life will be
strong in love and be built on love. 18And I pray
that you and all God's holy people will have the
power to understand the greatness of Christ's
love—how wide and how long and how high and
how deep that love is. 19Christ's love is greater
than anyone can ever know, but I pray that you
will be able to know that love. Then you can be
filled with the fullness of God.
20With God's power working in us, God can do
much, much more than anything we can ask or
imagine. 21To him be glory in the church and in
Christ Jesus for all time, forever and ever. Amen.

The Unity of the Body

4 I am in prison because I belong to the Lord.
God chose you to be his people, so I urge you
now to live the life to which God called you. 2Al
ways be humble, gentle, and patient, accepting
each other in love. 3You are joined together with
peace through the Spirit,[d] so make every effort to
continue together in this way. 4There is one body
and one Spirit, and God called you to have one
hope. 5There is one Lord, one faith, and one bap
tism. 6There is one God and Father of everything.
He rules everything and is everywhere and is in
everything.

> **SIDELIGHT:** Christian unity is central to the book of Ephesians. The word "one" appears seven times in Ephesians 4:4–6 alone!

7Christ gave each one of us the special gift of
grace, showing how generous he is. 8That is why
it says in the Scriptures,[d]
"When he went up to the heights,
he led a parade of captives,
and he gave gifts to people." *Psalm 68:18*

CULTS

Hazardous to Your Health

Jim Jones was an ordained minister who thought he was the messiah. Jones demanded total allegiance from his followers, telling them he was going to create the perfect society—free from hate, crime, and lack of anything.

People believed him. They sold everything they had and gave it to Jones. Nearly a thousand people followed Jones to Guyana in South America, where he established a settlement called Jonestown.

In 1978, Leo Ryan, a United States representative from California traveled to Jonestown to investigate rumors that Jones was holding some people against their will. In fear of being caught, Jones had Ryan and three journalists who accompanied Ryan killed. Then to destroy all evidence of his lies and deceit, Jones ordered his followers to take poison in a religious ceremony. More than nine hundred people—including Jones himself—died in what is now called the "Jonestown Massacre."

The people in Jonestown didn't recognize Jim Jones's lies. **Ephesians 4:11–16** warns us to be mature so we can recognize false teachings.

- How were the people in Jim Jones's church like the babies described in this passage?
- Has anyone ever tried to lead you down the wrong path like this passage talks about? How did the truth help you stay on God's path?

C O N S I D E R . . .

- talking to your pastor or other church leader about the elements of truth that your own church emphasizes.
- asking your pastor or youth leader to lead a study on a new "religious movement" to discover whether or not it is founded on the truth.

F O R M O R E , S E E . . .

- Proverbs 4
- Romans 1:18–32
- Philippians 4:8–9

9When it says, "He went up," what does it
mean? It means that he first came down to the
earth. 10So Jesus came down, and he is the same
One who went up above all the sky. Christ did
that to fill everything with his presence. 11And
Christ gave gifts to people—he made some to be
apostles,[d] some to be prophets,[d] some to go and
tell the Good News,[d] and some to have the work
of caring for and teaching God's people. 12Christ
gave those gifts to prepare God's holy people for
the work of serving, to make the body of Christ
stronger. 13This work must continue until we
are all joined together in the same faith and
in the same knowledge of the Son of God. We
must become like a mature person, growing un-
until we become like Christ and have his perfection.

14Then we will no longer be babies. We will
not be tossed about like a ship that the waves
carry one way and then another. We will not be
influenced by every new teaching we hear from
people who are trying to fool us. They make plans
and try any kind of trick to fool people into following the wrong path. 15No! Speaking the truth with
love, we will grow up in every way into Christ,
who is the head. 16The whole body depends on
Christ, and all the parts of the body are joined and
held together. Each part does its own work to
make the whole body grow and be strong with
love.

The Way You Should Live

17In the Lord's name, I tell you this. Do not
continue living like those who do not believe.
Their thoughts are worth nothing. 18They do not
understand, and they know nothing, because they
refuse to listen. So they cannot have the life that
God gives. 19They have lost all feeling of shame,
and they use their lives for doing evil. They continually want to do all kinds of evil. 20But what
you learned in Christ was not like this. 21I know
that you heard about him, and you are in him, so
you were taught the truth that is in Jesus. 22You
were taught to leave your old self—to stop living
the evil way you lived before. That old self becomes worse, because people are fooled by the
evil things they want to do. 23But you were taught
to be made new in your hearts, 24to become a
new person. That new person is made to be like
God—made to be truly good and holy.

25So you must stop telling lies. Tell each other
the truth, because we all belong to each other in

ANGER

Handle With Care

Clarisse Olson wasn't having a good day. Her boyfriend broke up with her before her first class. She got her math test back and knew her parents would not be pleased with the score. She missed lunch. And then she mouthed off at her P.E. teacher.

She shook her head as she recalled the incident.

"Come on, Clarisse," Mr. Eaton had yelled. "You can't do push-ups with your fanny in the air. Try fifty more, and do them right this time!"

Clarisse felt the anger well up inside her as she started over again.

"One . . . two . . . three . . ." she counted.

"I'd like to see you do fifty push-ups, you fat slob," Clarisse mumbled—a little louder than she intended.

Now she was sitting in the detention room while everyone else in school was in a pep assembly for the homecoming game.

"If only I'd kept my mouth shut," Clarisse moaned.

Sometimes our anger can get us into trouble. Read the warning about anger in **Ephesians 4:25—5:2**.

- According to this passage, did Clarisse's anger lead to sin or not?
- How can you be angry, and yet not sin?

C O N S I D E R . . .

- listing three things that make you angry. Beside each one, write a brief description of how you can handle the situation without sinning.
- resolving to deal quickly with things that make you angry.

F O R M O R E , S E E . . .

- Psalm 4
- Proverbs 22:24–25
- James 1:19–20

the same body.[n] 26When you are angry, do not
sin, and be sure to stop being angry before the end
of the day. 27Do not give the devil a way to defeat
you. 28Those who are stealing must stop stealing
and start working. They should earn an honest
living for themselves. Then they will have something to share with those who are poor.

29When you talk, do not say harmful things, but
say what people need—words that will help others become stronger. Then what you say will do
good to those who listen to you. 30And do not
make the Holy Spirit[d] sad. The Spirit is God's
proof that you belong to him. God gave you the
Spirit to show that God will make you free when
the final day comes. 31Do not be bitter or angry
or mad. Never shout angrily or say things to hurt
others. Never do anything evil. 32Be kind and loving to each other, and forgive each other just as
God forgave you in Christ.

Living in the Light

5 You are God's children whom he loves, so
try to be like him. 2Live a life of love just as
Christ loved us and gave himself for us as a sweet-
smelling offering and sacrifice to God.

3But there must be no sexual sin among you,
or any kind of evil or greed. Those things are not
right for God's holy people. 4Also, there must be
no evil talk among you, and you must not speak
foolishly or tell evil jokes. These things are not
right for you. Instead, you should be giving thanks
to God. 5You can be sure of this: No one will have
a place in the kingdom of Christ and of God who
sins sexually, or does evil things, or is greedy.
Anyone who is greedy is serving a false god.

6Do not let anyone fool you by telling you
things that are not true, because these things will
bring God's anger on those who do not obey him.
7So have nothing to do with them. 8In the past
you were full of darkness, but now you are full of
light in the Lord. So live like children who belong
to the light. 9Light brings every kind of goodness,
right living, and truth. 10Try to learn what pleases
the Lord. 11Have nothing to do with the things
done in darkness, which are not worth anything.
But show that they are wrong. 12It is shameful
even to talk about what those people do in secret.
13But the light makes all things easy to see, 14and
everything that is made easy to see can become
light. This is why it is said:

"Wake up, sleeper!
Rise from death,
and Christ will shine on you."

15So be very careful how you live. Do not live

Tell . . . body. Quotation from Zechariah 8:16.

DECISION MAKING

Who's Gonna Know?

Rob was having the time of his life on tour in Germany with his community orchestra—and no parents! There were chaperones, of course, but Rob was making his own decisions and loving every minute of it.

On Saturday night, Rob's friends went out to get their first taste of German beer. Most band members were excited to take advantage of Germany's lax alcohol laws.

Rob wasn't sure. He didn't feel quite right about going. It seemed to be an okay thing to do in Germany, but it wasn't something he would do at home.

But then he thought, "Who's gonna know?"

"I'd know," Rob finally told himself, after remembering the advice in **Ephesians 5:6–20**. See how this passage can help you make tough decisions.

- What principles do you find in this passage that Rob may have used in making his decision?
- How can you use the passage's advice in a decision you face now?

CONSIDER . . .

- praying and writing about what God wants you to do with your life.
- writing a letter to a friend who's facing a tough decision. Include the passage's advice on decision making.

FOR MORE, SEE . . .

- 1 Kings 18:1–40
- Romans 12:1–2
- James 1:5–8

like those who are not wise, but live wisely. [16]Use every chance you have for doing good, because these are evil times. [17]So do not be foolish but learn what the Lord wants you to do. [18]Do not be drunk with wine, which will ruin you, but be filled with the Spirit.[d] [19]Speak to each other with psalms, hymns, and spiritual songs, singing and making music in your hearts to the Lord. [20]Always give thanks to God the Father for everything, in the name of our Lord Jesus Christ.

Wives and Husbands

[21]Yield to obey each other because you respect Christ.

[22]Wives, yield to your husbands, as you do to the Lord, [23]because the husband is the head of the wife, as Christ is the head of the church. And he is the Savior of the body, which is the church. [24]As the church yields to Christ, so you wives should yield to your husbands in everything.

[25]Husbands, love your wives as Christ loved the church and gave himself for it [26]to make it belong to God. Christ used the word to make the church clean by washing it with water. [27]He died so that he could give the church to himself like a bride in all her beauty. He died so that the church could be pure and without fault, with no evil or sin or any other wrong thing in it. [28]In the same way, husbands should love their wives as they love their own bodies. The man who loves his wife loves himself. [29]No one ever hates his own body, but feeds and takes care of it. And that is what Christ does for the church, [30]because we are parts of his body. [31]The Scripture says, "So a man will leave his father and mother and be united with his wife, and the two will become one body."[n] [32]That secret is very important—I am talking about Christ and the church. [33]But each one of you must love his wife as he loves himself, and a wife must respect her husband.

Children and Parents

6 Children, obey your parents as the Lord wants, because this is the right thing to do. [2]The command says, "Honor your father and

"So . . . body." Quotation from Genesis 2:24.

FAMILY

Wolf Packs

When people think of wolves, they sometimes visualize a lonely silhouette on a hill, howling at the moon. Some picture the predator, sneaking up on an unsuspecting flock of sheep.

Much the opposite is true of wolves. While wolves do hunt, they most often prey on the sick or old animals in a herd, leaving the healthy animals to reproduce and protect the others. And wolves are seldom lonely. They live together with other wolves in families called packs.

Within the pack, adult wolves work together to hunt and to feed the younger members of the family. After a time of training, the young wolves take their place alongside the adults to hunt and to care for the next generation. Wolves rarely fight among themselves. But they will stand together, defending their home from attack by outsiders.

Experts believe wolves stay together as families because they have a kind of love for each other. Human family members also have certain responsibilities that help maintain order. Read about these responsibilities in **Ephesians 6:1–4**.

- How is a wolf pack like the family described in this passage? How is it different?
- From this passage, what is your role in your family?

CONSIDER . . .

- writing out one thing you could do to improve your role in your family. Then do it.
- obeying your parents this week, even when they ask you to do something you don't want to.

FOR MORE, SEE . . .

- Proverbs 23:22–25
- Matthew 15:3–9
- Colossians 3:18–21

mother."[n] This is the first command that has a
promise with it— 3"Then everything will be well
with you, and you will have a long life on the
earth."[n]

4Fathers, do not make your children angry, but
raise them with the training and teaching of the
Lord.

Slaves and Masters

5Slaves, obey your masters here on earth with
fear and respect and from a sincere heart, just as
you obey Christ. 6You must do this not only while
they are watching you, to please them. With all
your heart you must do what God wants as people
who are obeying Christ. 7Do your work with enthusiasm. Work as if you were serving the Lord,
not as if you were serving only men and women.
8Remember that the Lord will give a reward to
everyone, slave or free, for doing good.

9Masters, in the same way, be good to your
slaves. Do not threaten them. Remember that the
One who is your Master and their Master is in
heaven, and he treats everyone alike.

Wear the Full Armor of God

10Finally, be strong in the Lord and in his grea
power. 11Put on the full armor of God so that yo
can fight against the devil's evil tricks. 12Our figh
is not against people on earth but against the rul
ers and authorities and the powers of this world'
darkness, against the spiritual powers of evil i
the heavenly world. 13That is why you need to pu
on God's full armor. Then on the day of evil yo
will be able to stand strong. And when you hav
finished the whole fight, you will still be standing
14So stand strong, with the belt of truth tie
around your waist and the protection of right liv
ing on your chest. 15On your feet wear the Goo
News[d] of peace to help you stand strong. 16An
also use the shield of faith with which you ca
stop all the burning arrows of the Evil One. 17Ac
cept God's salvation as your helmet, and take th
sword of the Spirit,[d] which is the word of God
18Pray in the Spirit at all times with all kinds c
prayers, asking for everything you need. To d
this you must always be ready and never give up
Always pray for all God's people.

"Honor . . . mother." Quotation from Exodus 20:12; Deuteronomy 5:16.
"Then . . . earth." Quotation from Exodus 20:12; Deuteronomy 5:16.

FOLLOWING GOD

Spiritual Armor-All

Kremmling, Colorado, was a small mountain town of fifteen hundred where nothing out of the ordinary ever happened. Then police found a graffiti-emblazoned shack where someone had set up an altar with a satanic bible and plotted to vandalize churches and sacrifice animals.

"Major things like this never happen in Kremmling," Jody Cordova said. "It's kind of scary. I wrack my brain trying to figure out the people in town who would do this."

The townspeople were frightened. Some were even hysterical, threatening to carry handguns while taking children trick-or-treating on Halloween.

People were puzzled and concerned. They couldn't believe the dark side of the spiritual world could invade their little town the way it had.

Ephesians 6:10–20 warns not to be caught off guard in spiritual battles. Read the passage to see how Christians can protect themselves.

- How might this passage help the people of Kremmling respond to their situation? Which piece of armor would help them most?
- Which pieces of your armor are weakest? Which are strongest?

C O N S I D E R . . .

- writing on a bookmark the words to represent each of the pieces of armor in the passage. Keep the bookmark in one of your school books to remind you to stay prepared.
- choosing the pieces of your armor that are weakest. Begin to strengthen those pieces this week.

F O R M O R E , S E E . . .

- 1 Samuel 17
- Matthew 8:28–34
- James 4:7–10

[19]Also pray for me that when I speak, God will give me words so that I can tell the secret of the Good News without fear. [20]I have been sent to preach this Good News, and I am doing that now, here in prison. Pray that when I preach the Good News I will speak without fear, as I should.

> **SIDELIGHT:** The "shield of faith" in Ephesians 6:16 is a comparison to the large Roman shield used by heavily armed soldiers. This shield was designed to protect against burning darts, one of the most dangerous weapons of the time. When the dart hit the shield, it sunk into wood, and the flame was extinguished.

Final Greetings

[21]I am sending to you Tychicus, our brother whom we love and a faithful servant of the Lord's work. He will tell you everything that is happening with me. Then you will know how I am and what I am doing. [22]I am sending him to you for this reason—so that you will know how we are, and he can encourage you.

[23]Peace and love with faith to you from God the Father and the Lord Jesus Christ. [24]Grace to all of you who love our Lord Jesus Christ with love that never ends.

PHILIPPIANS

Why Read This Book?

- Discover how serving other people serves Christ (Philippians 1—2).
- Learn why growing in faith is so important (Philippians 3).
- Learn Paul's secret of having joy amidst suffering (Philippians 4).

Behind the Scenes:

Paul spent his life telling the Good News of Jesus Christ and starting new churches. But what did he get for it? He was put on trial, run out of town, stoned, beaten with rods, and thrown in prison several times. In addition, other Christians misunderstood and opposed him.

In short, Paul had plenty of reason to be gloomy and depressed. But, as we learn in Philippians, Paul felt just the opposite. In fact, this short letter from Paul is probably the most upbeat, cheerful book in the Bible.

Part of the reason he was happy was that the Christians in Philippi had heard about his imprisonment and had taken up a collection for him. Their love and concern made Paul deeply grateful, and Paul thanks them in this letter.

But the most important reason for Paul's happiness is clear in the letter. "To me the only important thing about living is Christ," he writes, "and dying would be profit for me" (Philippians 1:21).

The Romans could chain Paul's body, but they couldn't chain Paul's heart. And in this letter to his friends at Philippi, the apostle shares his secret for facing difficult circumstances with a song on his lips and joy in his heart.

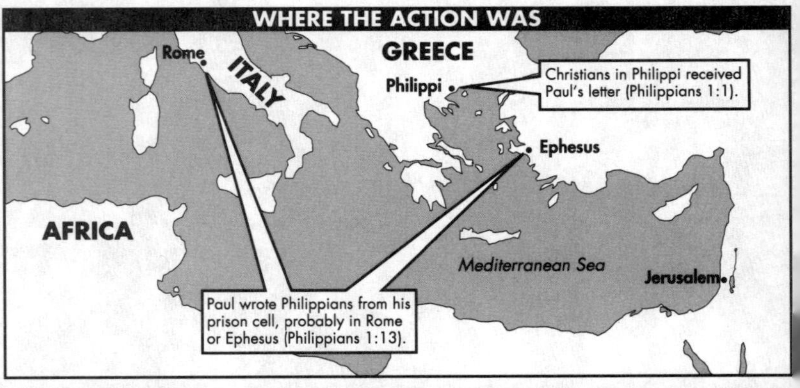
WHERE THE ACTION WAS
GREECE
Rome
ITALY
Philippi
Christians in Philippi received Paul's letter (Philippians 1:1).
Ephesus
AFRICA
Mediterranean Sea
Jerusalem
Paul wrote Philippians from his prison cell, probably in Rome or Ephesus (Philippians 1:13).

WHEN THE ACTION WAS

Above the timeline: Jesus was born (BC/AD) · The church began soon after Jesus went to heaven · Paul began his missionary work · Fire destroyed Rome

BC/AD — 25AD — 50AD — 75AD — 100AD

Below the timeline: Jesus began his ministry · Paul started the church in Philippi · Paul wrote Philippians · Romans destroyed the Temple in Jerusalem

1 From Paul and Timothy, servants of Christ
Jesus.
To all of God's holy people in Christ Jesus who
live in Philippi, including your elders[d] and deacons:[d]
2 Grace and peace to you from God our Father
and the Lord Jesus Christ.

Paul's Prayer

3 I thank my God every time I remember you,
4 always praying with joy for all of you. 5 I thank
God for the help you gave me while I preached
the Good News[d]—help you gave from the first
day you believed until now. 6 God began doing a
good work in you, and I am sure he will continue
it until it is finished when Jesus Christ comes
again.
7 And I know that I am right to think like this
about all of you, because I have you in my heart.
All of you share in God's grace with me while I
am in prison and while I am defending and proving the truth of the Good News. 8 God knows that
I want to see you very much, because I love all
of you with the love of Christ Jesus.
9 This is my prayer for you: that your love will
grow more and more; that you will have knowl-

SIDELIGHT: A woman, Lydia, was the first person baptized in Europe. She was probably a leader in the early Philippian church (see Acts 16:11-15), but she may not have stayed there long, since she made a living as a traveling merchant who sold purple-dyed cloth.

FRIENDS

First-String Help

Wyatt Jordan was a sure bet to make second-string quarterback, right behind his best friend Todd Andrews. That is, until Todd suddenly quit the team.

Steve Lowry congratulated Wyatt the morning after Todd quit. Steve was especially excited; now he would be second-string quarterback, right behind Wyatt.

"Yeah, thanks," Wyatt said with a lot less enthusiasm. He knew there was only one reason his friend would quit the team: Things must be getting worse at home. It had been a rough summer at the Andrews's family farm, with financial problems and Todd's dad being sick.

Of course, Todd's mom had insisted that her son play football. "Your brothers can bring in the harvest without you or your father," she had said. But at the first practice, Todd warned Wyatt that he might have to give up football to work on the farm.

During Wyatt's first practice as the starting quarterback, Coach Larson put the ball in Wyatt's hands.

"You're my man now," the coach said and blew his whistle.

"This is ridiculous," Wyatt thought. "The only reason I picked up a football in the first place was because of Todd. How can I do this when I know he's having a tough time right now?"

Wyatt walked off the field toward the coach, stopping first to give Steve the football. "Where are you going?" an astonished Steve asked.

"Farming," Wyatt answered.

Wyatt is the kind of friend we all want when we are having problems. Read **Philippians 1:3–11** to discover how Paul felt about friends who helped him when life was difficult.

- How do Wyatt's actions reflect the kind of friendship Paul is thankful for in this passage?
- How does the kind of friendship displayed in this passage make a difference in relationships?

C O N S I D E R . . .

- praying Philippians 1:9–11 for each of your friends.
- making a scrapbook for a friend, with mementos of what his or her friendship has meant to you. Then present the scrapbook to your friend.

F O R M O R E , S E E . . .

- Exodus 17:8–13
- Mark 14:32–42
- Philemon 10–14

edge and understanding with your love; 10that you will see the difference between good and bad and will choose the good; that you will be pure and without wrong for the coming of Christ; 11that you will do many good things with the help of Christ to bring glory and praise to God.

Paul's Troubles Help the Work

12I want you brothers and sisters[n] to know that what has happened to me has helped to spread the Good News.[d] 13All the palace guards and everyone else knows that I am in prison because I am a believer in Christ. 14Because I am in prison, most of the believers have become more bold in Christ and are not afraid to speak the word of God.

15It is true that some preach about Christ because they are jealous and ambitious, but others preach about Christ because they want to help. 16They preach because they have love, and they know that God gave me the work of defending the Good News. 17But the others preach about Christ for selfish and wrong reasons, wanting to make trouble for me in prison.

18But it doesn't matter. The important thing is that in every way, whether for right or wrong reasons, they are preaching about Christ. So I am happy, and I will continue to be happy. 19Because you are praying for me and the Spirit of Jesus Christ is helping me, I know this trouble will bring my freedom. 20I expect and hope that I will not fail Christ in anything but that I will have the courage now, as always, to show the greatness of Christ in my life here on earth, whether I live or die. 21To me the only important thing about living is Christ, and dying would be profit for me. 22If I continue living in my body, I will be able to work for the Lord. I do not know what to choose — living or dying. 23It is hard to choose between the two. I want to leave this life and be with Christ, which is much better, 24but you need me here in my body. 25Since I am sure of this, I know I will stay with you to help you grow and have joy in your faith. 26You will be very happy in Christ Jesus when I am with you again.

27Only one thing concerns me: Be sure that you live in a way that brings honor to the Good News of Christ. Then whether I come and visit you or am away from you, I will hear that you are standing strong with one purpose, that you work together as one for the faith of the Good News, 28and that you are not afraid of those who are against you. All of this is proof that your enemies will be destroyed but that you will be saved by God. 29God gave you the honor not only of believing in Christ but also of suffering for him, both of which bring glory to Christ. 30When I was with you, you saw the struggles I had, and you hear about the struggles I am having now. You yourselves are having the same kind of struggles.

2 Does your life in Christ give you strength? Does his love comfort you? Do we share together in the spirit? Do you have mercy and kindness? 2If so, make me very happy by having the same thoughts, sharing the same love, and having one mind and purpose. 3When you do things, do not let selfishness or pride be your guide. Instead, be humble and give more honor to others than to yourselves. 4Do not be interested only in your own life, but be interested in the lives of others.

Be Unselfish like Christ

5In your lives you must think and act like Christ Jesus.

6Christ himself was like God in everything.
But he did not think that being equal with God was something to be used for his own benefit.
7But he gave up his place with God and made himself nothing.
He was born to be a man
and became like a servant.
8And when he was living as a man,
he humbled himself and was fully obedient to God,
even when that caused his death — death on a cross.
9So God raised him to the highest place.
God made his name greater than every other name
10so that every knee will bow to the name of Jesus —
everyone in heaven, on earth, and under the earth.
11And everyone will confess that Jesus Christ is Lord
and bring glory to God the Father.

Be the People God Wants You to Be

12My dear friends, you have always obeyed God when I was with you. It is even more important that you obey now while I am away from you. Keep on working to complete your salvation with fear and trembling, 13because God is working in you to help you want to do and be able to do what pleases him.

14Do everything without complaining or arguing. 15Then you will be innocent and without any wrong. You will be God's children without fault. But you are living with crooked and mean people all around you, among whom you shine like stars in the dark world. 16You offer the teaching that

brothers and sisters Although the Greek text says "brothers" here and throughout this book, Paul's words were meant for the entire church, including men and women.

gives life. So when Christ comes again, I can be
happy because my work was not wasted. I ran the
race and won.
[17]Your faith makes you offer your lives as a sacrifice in serving God. If I have to offer my own
blood with your sacrifice, I will be happy and full
of joy with all of you. [18]You also should be happy
and full of joy with me.

Timothy and Epaphroditus

[19]I hope in the Lord Jesus to send Timothy to
you soon. I will be happy to learn how you are.
[20]I have no one else like Timothy, who truly cares
for you. [21]Other people are interested only in their
own lives, not in the work of Jesus Christ. [22]You
know the kind of person Timothy is. You know he
has served with me in telling the Good News,[d] as
a son serves his father. [23]I plan to send him to you
quickly when I know what will happen to me. [24]I
am sure that the Lord will help me to come to you
soon.
[25]Epaphroditus, my brother in Christ, works
and serves with me in the army of Christ. When
I needed help, you sent him to me. I think now
that I must send him back to you, [26]because he
wants very much to see all of you. He is worried
because you heard that he was sick. [27]Yes, he was
sick, and nearly died, but God had mercy on him
and me too so that I would not have more sadness. [28]I want very much to send him to you so
that when you see him you can be happy, and I
can stop worrying about you. [29]Welcome him in
the Lord with much joy. Give honor to people like
him, [30]because he almost died for the work of

DEATH

After AIDS

For Dale Pullen, a childhood filled with rejection became a life of rejection. His parents' failed marriage contributed to his own broken marriages. A need to escape problems led to drug and alcohol addictions. A desire for some kind of acceptance led to homosexuality. And homosexuality led to AIDS.

Abandoned by family and friends, Dale faced death alone. He was ready to end his life when Jeanne Cottrell, a Christian friend, invited Dale into her home. Through Jeanne's caring, Dale eventually decided to follow Christ.

What changes occurred in the heart of this beaten, lonely man! He experienced the release of forgiveness from his past. For the first time in his life, he felt genuine acceptance and unconditional love. And he had a place to belong with people who cared for him.

As his body weakened, Dale's spirit grew stronger and stronger. He was revitalized by his newfound hope in Christ. Dale directed his energy to reaching out with the love of Jesus to those who needed it most.

He visited AIDS patients at a local hospital and shared his story with many dying people who had also been rejected. He spoke at churches and support groups, and he explained how God's love reaches even those whom some find unlovable. He spent his time eagerly giving and receiving love.

"I don't know how long I'm going to live, but I want to live the rest of my days for the Lord," Dale told his friends.

After several months, Dale died. Those who were touched by Dale's life felt a tremendous loss. But at the same time, they rejoiced because they knew Dale was at peace and happy to be with Jesus.

Paul faced death peacefully under different circumstances. Read **Philippians 1:21–27** to see Paul's attitude toward living and dying.

- How were Dale's and Paul's attitudes about life affected by what they thought about death?
- According to this passage, what is the purpose of life and death?

CONSIDER . . .

- thinking of the number one reason you have to live, then putting more energy into that activity.
- discussing your feelings about death with a Christian friend. Think about how your priorities look from a heavenly perspective.

FOR MORE, SEE . . .

- Psalm 42
- Romans 14:7–8
- Galatians 2:20–21

Christ. He risked his life to give me the help you
could not give in your service to me.

> **SIDELIGHT:** If Epaphroditus's sickness had been a fever (see Philippians 2:26–27), he might have been treated by hanging a bag around his neck, a bag that included seven hairs from seven old dogs—a common treatment in New Testament times.

The Importance of Christ

3 My brothers and sisters, be full of joy in the
Lord. It is no trouble for me to write the
same things to you again, and it will help you to
be more ready. 2Watch out for those who do evil,
who are like dogs, who demand to cut[n] the body.
3We are the ones who are truly circumcised.[d] We
worship God through his Spirit,[d] and our pride is
in Christ Jesus. We do not put trust in ourselves
or anything we can do, 4although I might be able
to put trust in myself. If anyone thinks he has a
reason to trust in himself, he should know that I
have greater reason for trusting in myself. 5I was
circumcised eight days after my birth. I am from
the people of Israel and the tribe[d] of Benjamin.
I am a Hebrew, and my parents were Hebrews. I
had a strict view of the law, which is why I became a Pharisee.[d] 6I was so enthusiastic I tried to
hurt the church. No one could find fault with the
way I obeyed the law of Moses. 7Those things
were important to me, but now I think they are
worth nothing because of Christ. 8Not only those
things, but I think that all things are worth nothing compared with the greatness of knowing
Christ Jesus my Lord. Because of him, I have lost
all those things, and now I know they are worthless trash. This allows me to have Christ 9and to
belong to him. Now I am right with God, not because I followed the law, but because I believed
in Christ. God uses my faith to make me right
with him. 10I want to know Christ and the power
that raised him from the dead. I want to share in
his sufferings and become like him in his death.
11Then I have hope that I myself will be raised
from the dead.

Continuing Toward Our Goal

12I do not mean that I am already as God wants
me to be. I have not yet reached that goal, but I
continue trying to reach it and to make it mine.

cut The word in Greek is like the word "circumcise," but it means "to cut completely off."

CHURCH

Sticking Together

When a flock of geese fly south for the winter, they fly in a V-shaped formation. If they didn't, they would never reach their destination.

Researchers have found that the V-shaped formation helps geese fly at least 71 percent farther than they could fly alone, because each bird creates an updraft for the one behind it, making flying easier.

If one goose falls out of formation, the wind resistance slows down the bird. If it doesn't act quickly, it will not be able to keep up with its flock. So, it quickly gets back into formation.

Like geese, Christians need to work together in the church. Read **Philippians 2:1–11** to learn how.

- How is the geese's V-shaped formation like the passage's description of Christians working together?
- How does being with other Christians encourage you in your faith?

CONSIDER . . .

- writing your name and the names of other people in a V-shaped pattern to symbolize how you support each other. Thank God for people in the church who lead and support you.
- talking to your youth leader or a Sunday school teacher about how you can create an "updraft" to support and encourage others in your church.

FOR MORE, SEE . . .

- Psalm 133:1–3
- Mark 9:33–37
- Acts 2:44–47

Christ wants me to do that, which is the reason
he made me his. 13Brothers and sisters, I know
that I have not yet reached that goal, but there is
one thing I always do. Forgetting the past and
straining toward what is ahead, 14I keep trying to
reach the goal and get the prize for which God
called me through Christ to the life above.
15All of us who are spiritually mature should
think this way, too. And if there are things you do
not agree with, God will make them clear to you.
16But we should continue following the truth we
already have.
17Brothers and sisters, all of you should try to
follow my example and to copy those who live
the way we showed you. 18Many people live like
enemies of the cross of Christ. I have often told
you about them, and it makes me cry to tell you
about them now. 19In the end, they will be destroyed. They do whatever their bodies want,
they are proud of their shameful acts, and they
think only about earthly things. 20But our home-
land is in heaven, and we are waiting for our Savior, the Lord Jesus Christ, to come from heaven.
21By his power to rule all things, he will change
our simple bodies and make them like his own
glorious body.

POPULARITY

Impressive!

Mark Lester was assigned to work with class president Barry Clark on a biology class project. Who could have foreseen that working together a few nights a week for a month might actually lead to a friendship?

Barry and Mark had little in common. Barry was popular, owned a fancy car, and partied with the "in" crowd. Mark had a few friends from church, rode a bike, and spent his weekends with the youth group.

But one Friday night at the basketball game, Barry asked Mark to sit with him in the bleacher section informally reserved for football players, cheerleaders—anybody but Mark Lester. Not even in his wildest dreams could Mark have pictured himself sitting in the bleachers right in front of Tracy Watkins and spending more time talking to her than watching the game!

Mark was so enamored with his sudden change of fortune that he had to ask Tracy to repeat herself. The next time, she said it so loudly everyone heard her—including Barry. "If you can find a way to get us some beer, I'll go out with you after the game," she shouted above the crowd's roar.

Barry's expression said he was very impressed. Mark pretended to watch the basketball game for a second. It was the final quarter, and time was running out. But another clock was ticking in the bleachers. Mark knew the more important contest was taking place right where he sat.

"Well," he began, then hesitated.

Tracy frowned and glanced at Barry, who grinned, leaned forward, and teased, "If you won't take her out, Mark, I guess I'll have to."

Mark gripped the bleacher with both hands and, with all the enthusiasm he could muster, grinned back at Barry through gritted teeth. "Go for it, Barry," he stuttered. The clock ran out. The buzzer sounded. The game had been close, but Mark knew he had won.

Mark had chosen to be popular with God rather than people. Read **Philippians 3:8–11** to see how Paul had a similar attitude.

- How does Mark's decision reflect Paul's philosophy in this passage?
- How can "knowing Christ" be greater than what the world offers?

C O N S I D E R . . .

- giving up something that might make you popular if it stands in the way of your knowing Christ.
- asking a parent to recall the popular people in his or her high school, then finding out what has happened to them.

F O R M O R E , S E E . . .

- Joshua 24:14–27
- John 5:41–44
- Galatians 1:9–10

What the Christians Are to Do

4 My dear brothers and sisters, I love you and
want to see you. You bring me joy and make
me proud of you, so stand strong in the Lord as
I have told you.
[2]I ask Euodia and Syntyche to agree in the
Lord. [3]And I ask you, my faithful friend, to help
these women. They served with me in telling the
Good News,[d] together with Clement and others
who worked with me, whose names are written
in the book of life.[n]
[4]Be full of joy in the Lord always. I will say
again, be full of joy.
[5]Let everyone see that you are gentle and kind.
The Lord is coming soon. [6]Do not worry about
anything, but pray and ask God for everything you
need, always giving thanks. [7]And God's peace,
which is so great we cannot understand it, will
keep your hearts and minds in Christ Jesus.
[8]Brothers and sisters, think about the things

> **SIDELIGHT:** When Paul said our "homeland is in heaven" (Philippians 3:20), he literally said Christians live in a colony of heaven. The Philippian Christians would have seen this as a great privilege, since Philippi was a colony of the Roman Empire (see Acts 16:12). Being a colony meant Philippi had special privileges, including self-government, exemption from control by regional governments, and exemption from many taxes.

book of life God's book that has the names of all God's chosen people (Revelation 3:5; 21:27).

PERSISTENCE

Sticking With It

Wilma Rudolph dreamed of competing in the Olympics. But she had everything stacked against her.

She was born prematurely in a Tennessee shack, weighing only four and one-half pounds. Scarlet fever and polio struck, partially paralyzing her left leg, and forcing her to wear a steel brace.

Wilma remembers: "My father was the one who sort of babied me and was sympathetic. . . . My mother was the one who made me work, made me believe that one day it would be possible for me to walk without braces." Wilma's mother told her that, with persistence, she could follow her dreams in life.

So at age nine, Wilma did away with the braces. Four years later she developed a rhythmic stride and entered her first race. She came in last.

But she didn't give up.

"I worked very hard for the next four years," Wilma recalls. "I was self-motivated and motivated by my family. It took sheer determination to be able to run a hundred yards and remember all of the mechanics that go along with it. It takes steady nerves and being a fighter to stay out there."

In the 1960 Olympics, Wilma Rudolph set the world record in the 100-meter dash. She also won the 200-meter sprints and ran the anchor leg for the United States 400-meter relay team. She was the first American woman to win three gold medals in track and field at a single Olympiad.

Wilma Rudolph learned the lesson of **Philippians 3:12–21**. Read the passage to discover the key to persistence.

- In light of the passage, why was Wilma persistent?
- What was Paul's spiritual goal, according to this passage? How can this passage help you persist in reaching such a goal?

CONSIDER . . .

- watching part of a sports event on television. Look for evidences of persistence, then apply what you learn to a challenge you face.
- setting a specific goal to help you grow in your faith and persisting to meet that goal this week.

FOR MORE, SEE . . .

- Psalm 37:23–24
- Luke 9:57–62
- 1 Timothy 6:11–16

that are good and worthy of praise. Think about
the things that are true and honorable and right
and pure and beautiful and respected. 9Do what
you learned and received from me, what I told
you, and what you saw me do. And the God who
gives peace will be with you.

> **SIDELIGHT:** The words joy and rejoice occur in some form sixteen times in Philippians (for example, Philippians 4:4). Even in prison, Paul's thoughts were focused on joy!

Paul Thanks the Christians

10I am very happy in the Lord that you have
shown your care for me again. You continued to
care about me, but there was no way for you to
show it. 11I am not telling you this because I need
anything. I have learned to be satisfied with the
things I have and with everything that happens.
12I know how to live when I am poor, and I know
how to live when I have plenty. I have learned the
secret of being happy at any time in everything
that happens, when I have enough to eat and
when I go hungry, when I have more than I need
and when I do not have enough. 13I can do all
things through Christ, because he gives me
strength.

14But it was good that you helped me when I
needed it. 15You Philippians remember when I
first preached the Good News[a] there. When I left
Macedonia, you were the only church that gave
me help. 16Several times you sent me things I
needed when I was in Thessalonica. 17Really, it is

PEACE

Beyond Understanding

The ringing telephone pierced the night. "Hello, Mrs. Gibson. This is Officer Rogers with the highway patrol."

Norma's throat tightened, but she managed to gulp: "Yes, what is it?"

"It's your daughter, Cassandra. There's been an accident." Shocked, Norma sobbed uncontrollably and dropped the phone. Her husband, Neil, grabbed it and learned that Cassandra was still alive, but that she had extensive head injuries and was unconscious. The Flight for Life helicopter was flying her to an Oklahoma City hospital.

When Neil and Norma arrived at the hospital, Cassandra was in a coma. Her head was bruised and swollen. Her back was broken, and her body lay lifeless. Her heart had stopped once in the helicopter, but the paramedics had restarted it. Surgeons were inserting a catheter into Cassandra's skull to relieve the pressure on her brain.

During the surgery, Norma prayed in the hospital chapel. As she read her Bible, an overwhelming peace filled her. She couldn't explain what she felt, especially with her daughter so close to death. All she knew was that God seemed near and that he would take care of Cassandra.

For days, Neil and Norma rarely left Cassandra's side. Norma's prayers surprised even her, because they were filled with thanksgiving rather than questioning or pleading. Her heart was filled with God's peace.

It took a long time for Cassandra to recover, and much of what happened in the weeks after the accident is now a blur to her. But every hour is vivid to Neil and Norma. They were joyful that their daughter was alive.

In **Philippians 4:1–9**, Paul describes the secret to having a joy that is greater than life's difficulties. Read it to understand Norma's experience.

- Which actions or attitudes from this passage did Norma have that resulted in peace?
- Which ones can most help you experience God's peace?

C O N S I D E R . . .

- listing the nine steps to peace—one step from each verse in this passage. Choose one step you can take to experience God's peace.
- planning with a friend to pray together during difficult times.

F O R   M O R E ,   S E E . . .

- Psalm 25
- Luke 6:17–23
- John 14:27–29

not that I want to receive gifts from you, but I want you to have the good that comes from giving. 18And now I have everything, and more. I have all I need, because Epaphroditus brought your gift to me. It is like a sweet-smelling sacrifice offered to God, who accepts that sacrifice and is pleased with it. 19My God will use his wonderful riches in Christ Jesus to give you everything you need. 20Glory to our God and Father forever and ever! Amen.

21Greet each of God's people in Christ. Those who are with me send greetings to you. 22All of God's people greet you, particularly those from the palace of Caesar.[a]

23The grace of the Lord Jesus Christ be with you all.

COLOSSIANS

Why Read This Book?

- Learn the importance of following only Jesus Christ (Colossians 1).
- Discover how to respond to false teachers (Colossians 2).
- Find guidelines for living a Christian life (Colossians 3—4).

Behind the Scenes:

ESP. Astrology. Witchcraft. Ghosts. UFOs. Tarot cards. Ouija boards. The Loch Ness monster. Mysterious things can intrigue and attract us.

We are not the only people who can be fascinated with these kinds of things. Early Christians in Colosse were attracted to the same kinds of mysterious or supernatural things. Someone apparently came into the church and began teaching people to worship angels and cosmic powers. Jesus is fine, they argued, but these other mysterious powers controlled human destiny and gave secret knowledge (Colossians 2:16–23).

This letter to the Colossians challenges these false teachers. But instead of picking apart their arguments, the letter goes on the offensive, telling the Colossians the truth about Jesus Christ. "He ranks higher than everything that has been made," the letter states. "Christ is all that is important" (Colossians 1:15, 3:11).

The letter's advice to the Colossians is good advice for all people in all times. When we feel tempted to look for power in other, mysterious things, this book reminds us of the source of true power. And when someone suggests we need to do something else for salvation, Colossians assures us that Jesus is all we need.

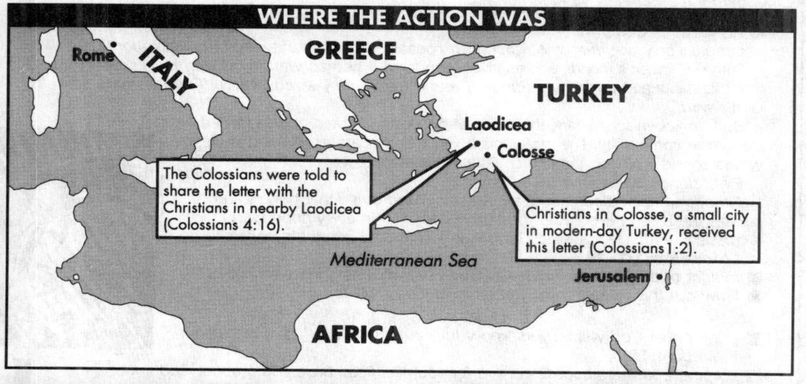

WHERE THE ACTION WAS
Rome
ITALY
GREECE
TURKEY
Laodicea
Colosse
The Colossians were told to share the letter with the Christians in nearby Laodicea (Colossians 4:16).
Christians in Colosse, a small city in modern-day Turkey, received this letter (Colossians 1:2).
Mediterranean Sea
Jerusalem
AFRICA

WHEN THE ACTION WAS
Jesus was born
The church began soon after Jesus went to heaven
Paul began his missionary work
Fire destroyed Rome
BC/AD
25AD
50AD
75AD
100AD
Jesus began his ministry
Paul became a Christian
Paul wrote this letter to the Colossians
Romans destroyed the Temple in Jerusalem

1 From Paul, an apostle[d] of Christ Jesus. I am
an apostle because that is what God wanted.
Also from Timothy, our brother.
2To the holy and faithful brothers and sisters[n]
in Christ that live in Colosse:
Grace and peace to you from God our Father.
3In our prayers for you we always thank God,
the Father of our Lord Jesus Christ, 4because we
have heard about the faith you have in Christ
Jesus and the love you have for all of God's people. 5You have this faith and love because of your
hope, and what you hope for is kept safe for you
in heaven. You learned about this hope when you
heard the message about the truth, the Good
News[d] 6that was told to you. Everywhere in the
world that Good News is bringing blessings and
is growing. This has happened with you, too,
since you heard the Good News and understood
the truth about the grace of God. 7You learned
about God's grace from Epaphras, whom we love.
He works together with us and is a faithful servant
of Christ for us. 8He also told us about the love
you have from the Holy Spirit.[d]
9Because of this, since the day we heard about
you, we have continued praying for you, asking
God that you will know fully what he wants. We
pray that you will also have great wisdom and
understanding in spiritual things 10so that you will
live the kind of life that honors and pleases the
Lord in every way. You will produce fruit in every
good work and grow in the knowledge of God.
11God will strengthen you with his own great

brothers and sisters Although the Greek text says "brothers" here and throughout this book, Paul's words were meant for the entire church, including men and women.

GOD'S WILL

A Life Pleasing God

From childhood, Robert Beck knew he wanted to be a missionary to Africa. Every day he kept his goal foremost in his mind. He read magazine articles and books and watched TV news reports and documentaries on Africa. In school he wrote stories and reports about the African people.

After graduating from high school, Robert earned a bachelor's degree, then completed seminary. After almost twenty years of education, Robert finally was ready to start on his goal. He began a church in Africa.

Robert preached regularly at the mission church. He taught children about God's love. He befriended the people when they were sick and lonely, and cheerfully devoted all his time to his vision of God's will.

But after only one year in Africa, Robert contracted malaria and died of complications.

Some of Robert's friends and relatives wondered if he had wasted his life. "How's it fair that this happened to such a promising young man?" they asked bitterly. "Can this really be God's will?"

Back at Robert's seminary, the news of his death shocked and saddened the whole community. The professors asked whether any graduating student would consider serving the church Robert had started.

Eight signed up to serve.

Although Robert died young, he lived "the kind of life that honors and pleases the Lord in every way" and produced "fruit in every good work" (Colossians 1:10). He followed God's will, just as Paul urged his readers to do in **Colossians 1:1–14**.

- In light of this passage, how was God's will accomplished with Robert?
- How can this passage help you discover God's will for your life?

CONSIDER . . .

- praying that God will let you "know fully what he wants" for your future (Colossians 1:9).
- keeping a journal about God's will for your life. Read Bible verses about God's will (see below) and write your thoughts as you apply those verses to decisions you are facing.

FOR MORE, SEE . . .

- Psalm 40:8–10
- Matthew 6:9–13
- Mark 3:31–35

power so that you will not give up when troubles
come, but you will be patient. 12And you will joyfully give thanks to the Father who has made you
able to have a share in all that he has prepared for
his people in the kingdom of light. 13God has freed
us from the power of darkness, and he brought us
into the kingdom of his dear Son. 14The Son paid
for our sins, and in him we have forgiveness.

The Importance of Christ

15No one can see God, but Jesus Christ is exactly like him. He ranks higher than everything
that has been made. 16Through his power all
things were made—things in heaven and on
earth, things seen and unseen, all powers, authorities, lords, and rulers. All things were made
through Christ and for Christ. 17He was there before anything was made, and all things continue
because of him. 18He is the head of the body,
which is the church. Everything comes from him.
He is the first one who was raised from the dead.
So in all things Jesus has first place. 19God was
pleased for all of himself to live in Christ. 20And
through Christ, God has brought all things back
to himself again—things on earth and things in
heaven. God made peace through the blood of
Christ's death on the cross.

SIDELIGHT: The city of Colosse (Colossians 1:2) was once a major mill town, known for its wool-working and cloth-dying industries. In fact, a widely used dark red wool cloth was known as colossinum. However, the city had declined by the time this letter was written, and may have been devastated by a major earthquake in A.D. 60 or 61.

21At one time you were separated from God.
You were his enemies in your minds, and the evil
things you did were against God. 22But now God
has made you his friends again. He did this
through Christ's death in the body so that he
might bring you into God's presence as people
who are holy, with no wrong, and with nothing
of which God can judge you guilty. 23This will

FORGIVENESS

The Face of Hatred

Just before Leonardo da Vinci began painting the Last Supper, he argued bitterly with a fellow painter. Da Vinci was so enraged that he decided to paint the face of his enemy as the face of Judas Iscariot. That way the hated painter's face would be preserved for ages in the face of the disciple who betrayed Jesus.

Da Vinci painted the face of Judas quickly. At first he took delight as everyone who came by recognized the face of the other painter in Judas.

Work on the other disciples' portraits continued. Da Vinci tried several times to start Jesus' face, but couldn't make any progress. Something seemed to baffle him, frustrating his best efforts.

In time, da Vinci saw his hatred of the other painter as the problem holding him back from finishing his work. Only after repainting the face of Judas was he able to paint Jesus' face and complete his masterpiece.

In his work on the Last Supper, da Vinci learned something important about forgiveness. **Colossians 1:15–29** has a similar lesson as it explains how Christ came to forgive—to end the separation between God and people.

- How was Leonardo da Vinci's separation from his fellow painter like humanity's separation from God as described in the passage?
- How do you feel when you are forgiven? How do you feel when you forgive someone else?

CONSIDER . . .

- confessing your sin to God, and, if you can, to an adult you trust. It may help you feel God's forgiveness.
- closing your eyes and thinking about the face of someone you need to forgive. Then imagine the face of Jesus next to that person's, and ask God to help you forgive that person.

FOR MORE, SEE . . .

- Psalm 79:8–9
- Luke 6:37–38
- Romans 5:1–11

happen if you continue strong and sure in your
faith. You must not be moved away from the hope
brought to you by the Good News that you heard.
That same Good News has been told to everyone
in the world, and I, Paul, help in preaching that
Good News.

Paul's Work for the Church

24I am happy in my sufferings for you. There are
things that Christ must still suffer through his
body, the church. I am accepting, in my body, my
part of these things that must be suffered. 25I became a servant of the church because God gave
me a special work to do that helps you, and that
work is to tell fully the message of God. 26This
message is the secret that was hidden from everyone since the beginning of time, but now it is
made known to God's holy people. 27God decided
to let his people know this rich and glorious secret
which he has for all people. This secret is Christ
himself, who is in you. He is our only hope for
glory. 28So we continue to preach Christ to each
person, using all wisdom to warn and to teach
everyone, in order to bring each one into God's
presence as a mature person in Christ. 29To do
this, I work and struggle, using Christ's great
strength that works so powerfully in me.

2 I want you to know how hard I work for
you, those in Laodicea, and others who have
never seen me. 2I want them to be strengthened
and joined together with love so that they may be
rich in their understanding. This leads to their
knowing fully God's secret, that is, Christ himself.
3In him all the treasures of wisdom and knowledge are safely kept.

4I say this so that no one can fool you by arguments that seem good, but are false. 5Though I am
absent from you in my body, my heart is with you,

CULTS

Fatal Attraction

DeAnne Shackly was an average high school senior. Her grades were average: Bs and Cs in most subjects. Her interest in school was average: She thought school was okay, but she would much rather play tennis or watch television. Her social life was average: an occasional date or evening out with some friends.

DeAnne couldn't wait to graduate from high school and get on with life. She didn't know what she wanted, but she knew it had to be more interesting than what she was doing.

One day after school, DeAnne went to the beach. There, some members of a religious group approached her. DeAnne had never heard of the group. But because they offered her a chance to belong, to take part in something greater than herself, she joined them.

After two years DeAnne decided the cult had manipulated her for its own ends. The group had offered "answers" to tough questions, but then told her to stop asking questions—to "just believe." It used her to raise money by selling flowers, candy, and other things, but when she asked where all the money was going, she was told it wasn't her concern.

Finally, she dropped out. She felt sick about the two years she had wasted. "Why was I attracted to that group?" she later asked herself. "I was a typical kid with a comfortable lifestyle. Why did I change my life so drastically? I wasn't that unhappy."

The Colossian Christians experienced a similar attraction to false beliefs. **Colossians 2:1–15** warns the early Christians not to be fooled by empty teachings.

- How might DeAnne's response to the cult have been different if she had listened to the warnings in this passage?
- How can you recognize false teachers today, according to the passage?

C O N S I D E R . . .

- making a list of Paul's warnings about false teachers. Refer to it when someone offers you quick, appealing answers to tough questions.
- asking your pastor or youth leader to get literature from cult groups and asking his help evaluating the groups' claims in light of scripture.

F O R M O R E , S E E . . .

- Deuteronomy 13:1–5
- Matthew 24:23–25
- 2 Peter 2:17–22

and I am happy to see your good lives and your strong faith in Christ.

> **SIDELIGHT:** Unlike most of Paul's letters, the letter to the Colossians was written to a church Paul apparently never visited (Colossians 2:1). Scholars suggest that the church may have been started by Epaphras, a native of the city who was in prison with Paul (Colossians 4:12).

Continue to Live in Christ

6As you received Christ Jesus the Lord, so continue to live in him. 7Keep your roots deep in him and have your lives built on him. Be strong in the faith, just as you were taught, and always be thankful.

8Be sure that no one leads you away with false and empty teaching that is only human, which comes from the ruling spirits of this world, and not from Christ. 9All of God lives in Christ fully (even when Christ was on earth), 10and you have a full and true life in Christ, who is ruler over all rulers and powers.

11Also in Christ you had a different kind of circumcision,[d] a circumcision not done by hands. It was through Christ's circumcision, that is, his death, that you were made free from the power of your sinful self. 12When you were baptized, you were buried with Christ, and you were raised up with him through your faith in God's power that was shown when he raised Christ from the dead. 13When you were spiritually dead because of your sins and because you were not free from the power of your sinful self, God made you alive with Christ, and he forgave all our sins. 14He canceled the debt, which listed all the rules we failed to follow. He took away that record with its rules and nailed it to the cross. 15God stripped the spiritual rulers and powers of their authority. With the cross, he won the victory and showed the world that they were powerless.

Don't Follow People's Rules

16So do not let anyone make rules for you about eating and drinking or about a religious feast, a New Moon[d] Festival, or a Sabbath[d] day. 17These things were like a shadow of what was to come. But what is true and real has come and is found in Christ. 18Do not let anyone disqualify you by making you humiliate yourself and worship angels. Such people enter into visions, which fill them with foolish pride because of their human way of thinking. 19They do not hold tightly to Christ, the head. It is from him that all the parts of the body are cared for and held together. So it grows in the way God wants it to grow.

20Since you died with Christ and were made free from the ruling spirits of the world, why do you act as if you still belong to this world by following rules like these: 21"Don't eat this," "Don't taste that," "Don't even touch that thing"? 22These rules refer to earthly things that are gone as soon as they are used. They are only man-made commands and teachings. 23They seem to be wise, but they are only part of a man-made religion. They make people pretend not to be proud and make them punish their bodies, but they do not really control the evil desires of the sinful self.

Your New Life in Christ

3 Since you were raised from the dead with Christ, aim at what is in heaven, where Christ is sitting at the right hand of God. 2Think only about the things in heaven, not the things on earth. 3Your old sinful self has died, and your new life is kept with Christ in God. 4Christ is our life, and when he comes again, you will share in his glory.

5So put all evil things out of your life: sexual sinning, doing evil, letting evil thoughts control you, wanting things that are evil, and greed. This is really serving a false god. 6These things make God angry.[n] 7In your past, evil life you also did these things.

8But now also put these things out of your life: anger, bad temper, doing or saying things to hurt others, and using evil words when you talk. 9Do not lie to each other. You have left your old sinful life and the things you did before. 10You have begun to live the new life, in which you are being made new and are becoming like the One who made you. This new life brings you the true knowledge of God. 11In the new life there is no difference between Greeks and Jews, those who are circumcised[d] and those who are not circumcised, or people who are foreigners, or Scythians.[n] There is no difference between slaves and free people. But Christ is in all believers, and Christ is all that is important.

12God has chosen you and made you his holy people. He loves you. So always do these things: Show mercy to others, be kind, humble, gentle, and patient. 13Get along with each other, and forgive each other. If someone does wrong to you, forgive that person because the Lord forgave you. 14Do all these things; but most important, love each other. Love is what holds you all together in

These . . . angry Some Greek copies add: "against the people who do not obey God."
Scythians The Scythians were known as very wild and cruel people.

perfect unity. [15]Let the peace that Christ gives
control your thinking, because you were all called
together in one body[n] to have peace. Always be
thankful. [16]Let the teaching of Christ live in you
richly. Use all wisdom to teach and instruct each
other by singing psalms, hymns, and spiritual
songs with thankfulness in your hearts to God.
[17]Everything you do or say should be done to obey
Jesus your Lord. And in all you do, give thanks to
God the Father through Jesus.

Your New Life with Other People

[18]Wives, yield to the authority of your husbands, because this is the right thing to do in the
Lord.
[19]Husbands, love your wives and be gentle
with them.
[20]Children, obey your parents in all things, because this pleases the Lord.
[21]Fathers, do not nag your children. If you are
too hard to please, they may want to stop trying.

> **SIDELIGHT:** If you feel like you have read some of Colossians somewhere else, you might be right. The book is filled with passages that closely parallel Ephesians (for example, compare Colossians 3:16-17 with Ephesians 5:19-20). In fact, about half of Ephesians' 155 verses also have similarities to verses in Colossians.

[22]Slaves, obey your masters in all things. Do not
obey just when they are watching you, to gain
their favor, but serve them honestly, because you
respect the Lord. [23]In all the work you are doing,

body The spiritual body of Christ, meaning the church or his people.

FOLLOWING GOD

Wake Up!

In high school, George shyly kept to himself. His few friends thought he was a nice guy, but nobody, including himself, thought he had much talent or potential. In fact, they seemed rarely to think anything of him. That was okay with George, since he rarely thought about anything anyway. He was content just to exist without any goals, dreams, or ideas.

About the only thing George enjoyed was driving around town in his car. It seemed a way to pass empty hours. But one day another car slammed into George's, sending his car off the road toward a tree. George was thrown from the car just before it smashed into the tree.

When George regained consciousness, he kept hearing the police say how lucky he was. George suffered minor injuries, but the car was totaled.

George's near tragedy awakened him to the reality of his empty life. Deciding he wanted to live for more than driving his car, he poured himself into many new interests, including filmmaking. A few years after his accident, George Lucas entertained millions with American Graffiti, the Star Wars trilogy, and the Indiana Jones movies.

George Lucas was lucky: He lost his car, but gained a new purpose in life. **Colossians 3:1–10** tells Christians to "wake up" to a whole, new life that is far more important than any new career.

- How does George Lucas's awakening to life illustrate Paul's challenge to live a different way in Christ? How is it different?
- In light of this passage, how is your "old life" different from your "new life in Christ"?

C O N S I D E R . . .

- writing on one side of a sheet of paper things that are different because of your "new life in Christ." On the back, write out temptations you can avoid because of this new life. Thank God for giving you strength.
- trying a new skill or interest that might help you follow God's will. Focus your attention on gifts you believe God has given you.

F O R M O R E , S E E . . .

- Habakkuk 3:2
- Luke 9:24
- Revelation 21:1–5

work the best you can. Work as if you were doing
it for the Lord, not for people. 24Remember that
you will receive your reward from the Lord,
which he promised to his people. You are serving
the Lord Christ. 25But remember that anyone who
does wrong will be punished for that wrong, and
the Lord treats everyone the same.

4 Masters, give what is good and fair to your
slaves. Remember that you have a Master in
heaven.

What the Christians Are to Do

2Continue praying, keeping alert, and always
thanking God. 3Also pray for us that God will give
us an opportunity to tell people his message. Pray
that we can preach the secret that God has made
known about Christ. This is why I am in prison.
4Pray that I can speak in a way that will make it
clear, as I should.

5Be wise in the way you act with people who
are not believers, making the most of every opportunity. 6When you talk, you should always be
kind and pleasant so you will be able to answer
everyone in the way you should.

News About the People with Paul

7Tychicus is my dear brother in Christ and a
faithful minister and servant with me in the Lord.
He will tell you all the things that are happening
to me. 8This is why I am sending him: so you may
know how we are and he may encourage you. 9I
send him with Onesimus, a faithful and dear
brother in Christ, and one of your group. They
will tell you all that has happened here.

10Aristarchus, a prisoner with me, and Mark,
the cousin of Barnabas, greet you. (I have already
told you what to do about Mark. If he comes,
welcome him.) 11Jesus, who is called Justus, also
greets you. These are the only Jewish believers
who work with me for the kingdom of God, and
they have been a comfort to me.

12Epaphras, a servant of Jesus Christ, from your
group, also greets you. He always prays for you
that you will grow to be spiritually mature and
have everything God wants for you. 13I know he
has worked hard for you and the people in Laodicea and in Hierapolis. 14Demas and our dear
friend Luke, the doctor, greet you.

15Greet the brothers in Laodicea. And greet
Nympha and the church that meets in her house.
16After this letter is read to you, be sure it is also
read to the church in Laodicea. And you read the
letter that I wrote to Laodicea. 17Tell Archippus,
"Be sure to finish the work the Lord gave you."

18I, Paul, greet you and write this with my own
hand. Remember me in prison. Grace be with
you.

1 THESSALONIANS

Why Read This Book:

- Be encouraged to stand up for your faith even when those around you make fun of you (1 Thessalonians 2—3).
- See the importance of growing strong in faith (1 Thessalonians 4—5).

Behind the Scenes:

Summer camp was sensational. You had fun. You made friends. You grew in your faith. Around the campfire the final night, you were sure your life would never be the same because of your renewed faith. Then you went home. Your enthusiasm wore off as you faced the realities of everyday life. Would your new commitment last?

The Thessalonians might have felt the same way. Paul had come to their city, and they had become Christians. Then, suddenly, Paul was run out of town, and the new Christians were left in a hostile city without their leader. Could they stick to their faith? Would their faith keep growing?

Paul wrote this letter to encourage the new Christians and to explain why he left so quickly. He says how happy he is that they are "hanging in there" through all the troubles they face. He challenges them to keep growing in their faith. And he encourages them to look beyond persecution to the day when the Lord will come again.

Just as the letter encouraged the Thessalonians, it encourages new (and longtime) Christians today. It challenges us to hold firmly to our faith and to press on toward becoming mature Christians—even when we don't feel the spiritual "highs" we might have experienced at first.

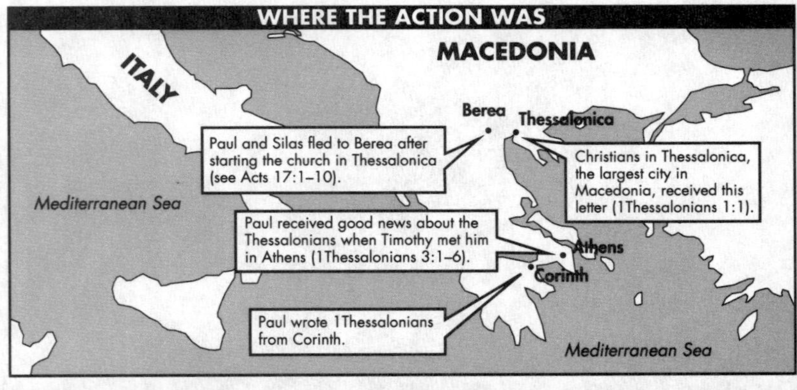

WHERE THE ACTION WAS
MACEDONIA
ITALY
Berea
Thessalonica
Athens
Corinth
Mediterranean Sea
Mediterranean Sea
Paul and Silas fled to Berea after starting the church in Thessalonica (see Acts 17:1–10).
Christians in Thessalonica, the largest city in Macedonia, received this letter (1Thessalonians 1:1).
Paul received good news about the Thessalonians when Timothy met him in Athens (1Thessalonians 3:1–6).
Paul wrote 1Thessalonians from Corinth.
WHEN THE ACTION WAS
Jesus was born
The church began soon after Jesus went to heaven
Paul began his missionary work
Fire destroyed Rome
BC/AD
25AD
50AD
75AD
100AD
Jesus began his ministry
Paul became a Christian
Paul wrote 1 Thessalonians
Romans destroyed the Temple in Jerusalem

1

1 From Paul, Silas, and Timothy.
To the church in Thessalonica, the church in God the Father and the Lord Jesus Christ:
Grace and peace to you.

The Faith of the Thessalonians

2We always thank God for all of you and mention you when we pray. 3We continually recall
before God our Father the things you have done because of your faith and the work you have done because of your love. And we thank him that you continue to be strong because of your hope in our Lord Jesus Christ.
4Brothers and sisters,[n] God loves you, and we
know he has chosen you, 5because the Good
News[d] we brought to you came not only with words, but with power, with the Holy Spirit,[d] and with sure knowledge that it is true. Also you know how we lived when we were with you in order to help you. 6And you became like us and
like the Lord. You suffered much, but still you accepted the teaching with the joy that comes

> **SIDELIGHT:** If all the New Testament books appeared in the Bible in the order they were actually written, 1 Thessalonians might come first (with the possible exception of Galatians or James). It is believed to have been written only twenty years after Jesus was crucified and rose from the dead.

Brothers and sisters Although the Greek text says "Brothers" here and throughout this book, Paul's words were meant for the entire church, including men and women.

SPIRITUAL GROWTH

Spreading Love Around

Maria Mayo sat quietly in her pew through the whole organ postlude. She couldn't get the pastor's sermon on using God-given talents out of her head. She knew she had talents such as playing the guitar, but she had never thought of how she might use them for God.

Then Maria began remembering all her church friends. One friend played the piano, another played drums, and two could sing. Maybe they should form a Christian band.

Maria approached her friends, and they agreed. After practicing for several months, the band began volunteering to perform at retreats, youth gatherings, children's camps, and church services. Maria thoroughly enjoyed the band and hoped the music was helping people grow in faith.

But she really couldn't tell.

Several years later, Maria was asked to lead music for a denominational youth gathering. After an opening service, one teenager grabbed her and asked, "Did you lead music at Circle R seven summers ago?"

Maria vaguely remembered that the old band had played there. The young person continued, "That summer was the first time I heard about Jesus. I'm starting college now and want to go into the ministry. Thanks for the seed you planted."

Even though Maria didn't know how God was using her at the time, Maria spread the Good News—just as Paul spread the Good News. In **1 Thessalonians 1:1–10** we read about how the Thessalonians heard the Good News, grew in faith, and "became an example to all the believers."

- How might Paul say Maria's faith is like the Thessalonians' faith?
- The passage describes how the Thessalonians grew through several stages in their faith. What stage is your faith in?

CONSIDER . . .

- deciding how God might use you to be an example of faith to those around you. Look in the passage for specific ideas.
- taking a potted plant to someone who needs cheering up—as a symbol of your spiritual growth.

FOR MORE, SEE . . .

- Jeremiah 17:7–8
- 1 Corinthians 12:1–11
- Hebrews 5:12–14

from the Holy Spirit. [7]So you became an example to all the believers in Macedonia and Southern Greece. [8]And the Lord's teaching spread from you not only into Macedonia and Southern Greece, but now your faith in God has become known everywhere. So we do not need to say anything about it. [9]People everywhere are telling about the way you accepted us when we were there with you. They tell how you stopped worshiping idols and began serving the living and true God. [10]And you wait for God's Son, whom God raised from the dead, to come from heaven. He is Jesus, who saves us from God's angry judgment that is sure to come.

Paul's Work in Thessalonica

2 Brothers and sisters, you know our visit to you was not a failure. [2]Before we came to you, we suffered in Philippi. People there insulted us, as you know, and many people were against us. But our God helped us to be brave and to tell you his Good News.[d] [3]Our appeal does not come from lies or wrong reasons, nor were we trying to trick you. [4]But we speak the Good News because God tested us and trusted us to do it. When we speak, we are not trying to please people, but God, who tests our hearts. [5]You know that we never tried to influence you by saying nice things about you. We were not trying to get your money; we had no selfishness to hide from you. God knows that this is true. [6]We were not looking for human praise, from you or anyone else, [7]even though as apostles[d] of Christ we could have used our authority over you.

But we were very gentle with you, like a mother caring for her little children. [8]Because we loved you, we were happy to share not only God's Good News with you, but even our own lives. You had become so dear to us! [9]Brothers and sisters, I know you remember our hard work and difficulties. We worked night and day so we

> **SIDELIGHT:** Most pastors and missionaries are not in it for the money. Paul certainly wasn't (1 Thessalonians 2:5, 9). In addition to his missionary work, Paul also worked as a tentmaker (see Acts 18:3) so he wouldn't have to take money from the churches he started.

LEADERSHIP

Gentle Leadership

She didn't look like a dynamic leader. She didn't look like a dynamic anything. In fact, you probably wouldn't notice her in a crowd—smoky gray hair, out-of-fashion glasses, thin figure, pencil behind her ear. Yet in the twenty years she taught high school English, Elsie Cannery powerfully influenced her students' lives. She gently prodded and encouraged them to use their creativity and sharpen their thinking skills.

Elsie was available to her students night and day. She told them to call her at home any time they needed to talk to someone about school or any part of their lives.

Ninety percent of her students went on to graduate from college.

As Elsie Cannery made a difference in her students' lives, the apostles made a difference in the new Christians' lives. See the similarities in **1 Thessalonians 2:1–13**.

- How are Elsie Cannery's leadership qualities like those of the apostles?
- How is your leadership style similar to the one Paul describes in the passage? How is it different?

CONSIDER . . .

- listing all the words you can to describe Christian leadership. Read the passage to give you ideas. Check the "leadership" words that also describe you. How strong is your leadership ability?
- thinking about one leader you admire a lot (a family member, friend, pastor, teacher). Talk to that person. Ask how he or she chose a profession. Ask about the qualities to strive for as a leader.

FOR MORE, SEE . . .

- Proverbs 12:14
- Ephesians 2:9–10
- James 2:14–17

would not burden any of you while we preached God's Good News to you.

10When we were with you, we lived in a holy and honest way, without fault. You know this is true, and so does God. 11You know that we treated each of you as a father treats his own children. 12We encouraged you, we urged you, and we insisted that you live good lives for God, who calls you to his glorious kingdom.

13Also, we always thank God because when you heard his message from us, you accepted it as the word of God, not the words of humans. And it really is God's message which works in you who believe. 14Brothers and sisters, your experiences have been like those of God's churches in Christ that are in Judea.[n] You suffered from the people of your own country, as they suffered from the Jews, 15who killed both the Lord Jesus and the prophets[d] and forced us to leave that country. They do not please God and are against all people. 16They try to stop us from teaching those who are not Jews so they may be saved. By doing this, they are increasing their sins to the limit. The anger of God has come to them at last.

Paul Wants to Visit Them Again

17Brothers and sisters, though we were separated from you for a short time, our thoughts were still with you. We wanted very much to see you and tried hard to do so. 18We wanted to come to you. I, Paul, tried to come more than once, but Satan stopped us. 19You are our hope, our joy, and the crown we will take pride in when our Lord Jesus Christ comes. 20Truly you are our glory and our joy.

3 When we could not wait any longer, we decided it was best to stay in Athens alone 2and send Timothy to you. Timothy, our brother, works with us for God and helps us tell people the Good News[d] about Christ. We sent him to strengthen and encourage you in your faith 3so none of you would be upset by these troubles. You yourselves know that we must face these troubles. 4Even when we were with you, we told you we all would have to suffer, and you know it has happened. 5Because of this, when I could wait no longer, I sent Timothy to you so I could learn about your faith. I was afraid the devil had tempted you, and then our hard work would have been wasted.

6But Timothy now has come back to us from you and has brought us good news about your faith and love. He told us that you always remember us in a good way and that you want to see us just as much as we want to see you. 7So, brothers and sisters, while we have much trouble and suffering, we are encouraged about you because of your faith. 8Our life is really full if you stand strong in the Lord. 9We have so much joy before our God because of you. We cannot thank him enough for all the joy we feel. 10Night and day we continue praying with all our heart that we can see you again and give you all the things you need to make your faith strong.

11Now may our God and Father himself and our Lord Jesus prepare the way for us to come to you. 12May the Lord make your love grow more and multiply for each other and for all people so that you will love others as we love you. 13May your hearts be made strong so that you will be holy and without fault before our God and Father when our Lord Jesus comes with all his holy ones.

A Life that Pleases God

4 Brothers and sisters, we taught you how to live in a way that will please God, and you are living that way. Now we ask and encourage you in the Lord Jesus to live that way even more. 2You know what we told you to do by the authority of the Lord Jesus. 3God wants you to be holy and to stay away from sexual sins. 4He wants each of you to learn to control your own body[n] in a way that is holy and honorable. 5Don't use your body for sexual sin like the people who do not know God. 6Also, do not wrong or cheat another Christian in this way. The Lord will punish people who do those things as we have already told you and warned you. 7God called us to be holy and does not want us to live in sin. 8So the person who refuses to obey this teaching is disobeying God, not simply a human teaching. And God is the One who gives us his Holy Spirit.[d]

> **SIDELIGHT:** The church in Thessalonica would have been in an excellent position to love all the "Christians in all of Macedonia" (1 Thessalonians 4:10). The city was the capital of its province, so its residents had contact with people from all over the province.

9We do not need to write you about having love for your Christian family, because God has already taught you to love each other. 10And truly you do love the Christians in all of Macedonia. Brothers and sisters, now we encourage you to love them even more.

11Do all you can to live a peaceful life. Take

Judea The Jewish land where Jesus lived and taught and where the church first began.
learn . . . body This might also mean "learn to live with your own wife."

care of your own business, and do your own work
as we have already told you. 12If you do, then
people who are not believers will respect you, and
you will not have to depend on others for what
you need.

The Lord's Coming

13Brothers and sisters, we want you to know
about those Christians who have died so you will
not be sad, as others who have no hope. 14We
believe that Jesus died and that he rose again. So,
because of him, God will raise with Jesus those
who have died. 15What we tell you now is the
Lord's own message. We who are living when the
Lord comes again will not go before those who
have already died. 16The Lord himself will come
down from heaven with a loud command, with
the voice of the archangel,[n] and with the trumpet call of God. And those who have died believing in Christ will rise first. 17After that, we who
are still alive will be gathered up with them in the
clouds to meet the Lord in the air. And we will
be with the Lord forever. 18So encourage each
other with these words.

Be Ready for the Lord's Coming

5 Now, brothers and sisters, we do not need to
write you about times and dates. 2You know

archangel The leader among God's angels or messengers.

HAPPINESS

Creating Happiness

Jorge and Juanita Hernandez were having a horrible spring as they watched their parents' unhappy marriage disintegrate. Dinners were filled with tension, evenings filled with fighting, mornings filled with angry silence.

In time, their parents decided to divorce.

On one hand, Jorge and Juanita were relieved because the constant tension would end. But they were sad because their family, as they knew it, would also end. They would have to live with one parent and visit the other.

Jorge spent the next several weeks stewing about the divorce, watching television, being alone, and skipping church and school activities. "I don't care what my parents do, and I don't care what I do," Jorge told Juanita.

Juanita thought just the opposite. "I'm hurting, but I know others are hurting worse than I am," she replied. "I want to help some of those people."

So Juanita signed up for a youth group trip to Mexico. On the trip, Juanita and other group members sang songs in prisons, presented puppet plays, read stories, and played with the village kids. Although she was sad about her parents, she dealt with that sadness by reaching out to others.

Her Mexico experience gave Juanita a new perspective on happiness. "I saw how others with a lot less than I have are happy," she said. "In some ways we need to make our own happiness."

In the midst of her sadness, Juanita created happiness for herself by reaching out to others. Read about similar feelings of happiness and joy in **1 Thessalonians 3:9–13**.

- What encouragement would Juanita find by reading this passage? What parts of this passage show the meaning of true happiness, even when things aren't going well?

CONSIDER . . .

- writing on your calendar what makes you happiest each day of the upcoming week. See if there's a pattern. Are you happiest when you are reaching out to others?
- choosing one thing that makes you happy and doing that for someone else. For example, if you're happy when a friend calls you on the phone and says, "I was just thinking about you," think of another person, and call him or her.

FOR MORE, SEE . . .

- Psalm 43:4–5
- Proverbs 8:3–36
- James 5:7–11

very well that the day the Lord comes again will
be a surprise, like a thief that comes in the night.
3While people are saying, "We have peace and we
are safe," they will be destroyed quickly. It is like
pains that come quickly to a woman having a
baby. Those people will not escape. 4But you,
brothers and sisters, are not living in darkness,
and so that day will not surprise you like a thief.
5You are all people who belong to the light and to
the day. We do not belong to the night or to darkness. 6So we should not be like other people who
are sleeping, but we should be alert and have self-
control. 7Those who sleep, sleep at night. Those
who get drunk, get drunk at night. 8But we belong to the day, so we should control ourselves.
We should wear faith and love to protect us, and
the hope of salvation should be our helmet. 9God
did not choose us to suffer his anger but to have
salvation through our Lord Jesus Christ. 10Jesus
died for us so that we can live together with him,
whether we are alive or dead when he comes.
11So encourage each other and give each other
strength, just as you are doing now.

Final Instructions and Greetings

12Now, brothers and sisters, we ask you to appreciate those who work hard among you, who
lead you in the Lord and teach you. 13Respect
them with a very special love because of the work
they do.

Live in peace with each other. 14We ask you,
brothers and sisters, to warn those who do not
work. Encourage the people who are afraid. Help
those who are weak. Be patient with everyone.
15Be sure that no one pays back wrong for wrong,
but always try to do what is good for each other
and for all people.

16Always be joyful. 17Pray continually, 18and
give thanks whatever happens. That is what God
wants for you in Christ Jesus.

19Do not hold back the work of the Holy
Spirit.[d] 20Do not treat prophecy[d] as if it were
unimportant. 21But test everything. Keep what
is good, 22and stay away from everything that is
evil.

23Now may God himself, the God of peace,
make you pure, belonging only to him. May your

DEATH

We Have Hope

Dennis Harwell was in high school when his parents had a baby girl. The birth was a major celebration, because Dennis's parents had wanted another child since he was four years old. Years of trying, years of crying, years of suffering through three miscarriages finally produced Dennis's baby sister, whom they named Sarah.

Dennis and his parents were overjoyed with the new addition to their family. They fixed up a nursery and designed a playroom. They planned a special outing each weekend. They thoroughly enjoyed their new family member.

Their joy lasted six short months. One morning they woke up to discover Sarah had died in her sleep. Dennis and his parents were numb with grief. The doctors determined the cause of death was Sudden Infant Death Syndrome (SIDS). They told the family not to blame themselves, that it is virtually impossible to prevent a SIDS death.

Although Dennis and his parents felt a bit comforted by the doctors, they were still devastated by Sarah's death. As Dennis tried to work through his grief, he read **1 Thessalonians 4:13–14**. Dennis shared the passage with his parents, and they were all comforted by its words of hope.

- How were Dennis and his family comforted by this passage?
- How does it feel to know that someday you will see Christian loved ones who have died?

CONSIDER . . .

- writing a memorial letter to someone you loved who has died. Keep the letter as a reminder of this special person.
- thinking of someone who has recently lost a loved one. Call, write, visit, or take that person out to eat. Offer a little comfort.

FOR MORE, SEE . . .

- Isaiah 25:7–8
- Romans 8:37–39
- 2 Timothy 1:9–10

whole self—spirit, soul, and body—be kept safe
and without fault when our Lord Jesus Christ
comes. [24]You can trust the One who calls you to
do that for you.
[25]Brothers and sisters, pray for us.

[26]Give each other a holy kiss when you meet.
[27]I tell you by the authority of the Lord to read this
letter to all the believers.
[28]The grace of our Lord Jesus Christ be with
you.

FOLLOWING GOD

Get Ready!

A beginning-of-the-year notice was issued to all seniors at Franklin High: "A surprise senior fitness test will be given near the end of the school year," the notice read. "You won't know the exact day or time. You will be tested on strength, flexibility, and endurance. The highest scorer will receive a $1,000 scholarship to the college of his or her choice. This is your only notice. Be prepared!"

Steven Killain read the notice and decided to prepare right away for the test. He wanted to win the scholarship money, so it meant getting in shape, staying in shape, and staying alert for the test.

He regularly jogged, stretched, and lifted weights. He ate nutritious foods. Some of his friends thought he was crazy. "Why don't you relax a while?" they asked. "You'll have plenty of time to get ready later."

But Steve wanted to be ready whenever or wherever the test was announced. He wanted to win.

When the test was announced, all seniors competed. Most were not physically fit. Most could not even finish the long-distance run, jumping jacks, or push-ups. Not only did Steve complete all test areas, he took first place in all of them. Steve won the $1,000.

In **1 Thessalonians 5:1–11** we read about being alert and ready for the Lord's coming. Like Steve, we don't want to be caught unprepared.

- What "be prepared" qualities did Steve possess that you also see recommended for believers in this passage?
- How can you grow more awake and alert in following God so that you are not caught unprepared when the Lord comes?

CONSIDER . . .

- consciously going through one day's activities as if it were the day Jesus were coming. How did you act differently? the same?
- hanging a "Be Prepared" sign in your closet to remind you to live each day to the fullest and be ready for Christ's return.

FOR MORE, SEE . . .

- Daniel 12:1–13
- Matthew 22:1–14
- 2 Peter 3:8–13

2 THESSALONIANS

Why Read This Book:

- Learn how God is with us now and in the future (2 Thessalonians 1).
- Find hope and comfort in God's love in the midst of life's tough times (2 Thessalonians 2—3).

Behind the Scenes:

You are about to graduate. You have passed all your classes, but you still have one English test left to go. You don't think the test will make any difference on your grade or transcript. How hard will you study?

The Thessalonian Christians were in a similar situation. They had been told that "the day of the Lord" (Christ's Second Coming) had already come, and some believed it. As a result, they didn't think they had anything to worry about, since they would all go to heaven soon. So they quit work, sat around lazily, meddled in other people's business, and depended on the church for charity. Worst of all, people decided they didn't really have to worry about growing spiritually.

Second Thessalonians challenged these actions, saying the day of the Lord had not come and would not come for some time. Instead of sitting lazily, waiting for the end, Christians should be working hard and seeking to grow in their faith.

Sometimes it can be tempting to be so excited about God's gift of eternal life that we stop working. Second Thessalonians reminds us that God has a purpose for us on earth, and we are called to do God's work in this world. We are called to keep growing in our faith even in the face of persecution.

WHEN THE ACTION WAS

Jesus was born — The church began soon after Jesus went to heaven — Paul began his missionary work — Fire destroyed Rome

BC/AD — 25AD — 50AD — 75AD — 100AD

Jesus began his ministry — 2 Thessalonians may have been written — Romans destroyed the Temple in Jerusalem

1 From Paul, Silas, and Timothy.
To the church in Thessalonica in God our
Father and the Lord Jesus Christ:
2Grace and peace to you from God the Father
and the Lord Jesus Christ.

Paul Talks About God's Judgment

3We must always thank God for you, brothers
and sisters.[n] This is only right, because your faith
is growing more and more, and the love that every one of you has for each other is increasing.
4So we brag about you to the other churches of
God. We tell them about the way you continue
to be strong and have faith even though you are
being treated badly and are suffering many tro
bles.
5This is proof that God is right in his judgmen
He wants you to be counted worthy of his kin
dom for which you are suffering. 6God will c
what is right. He will give trouble to those wh
trouble you. 7And he will give rest to you who a
troubled and to us also when the Lord Jesus a
pears with burning fire from heaven with his pov
erful angels. 8Then he will punish those who c
not know God and who do not obey the Goc
News[d] about our Lord Jesus Christ. 9Those peop
will be punished with a destruction that conti
ues forever. They will be kept away from the Lo

brothers and sisters Although the Greek text says "brothers" here and throughout this book, Paul's words were meant fo the entire church, including men and women.

SUFFERING

When a Dream Dies

It was unbelievable! Doug Hutchcraft would be able to play junior varsity football. And he was just a sophomore. His summer of intense training and his "killer instinct" were paying off. Maybe he would reach his lifelong dream of playing professional football.

During preseason workouts, Doug was ruthless. Once he noticed another guy's blood on his jersey after a workout, and he wouldn't let his mom wash the jersey.

Then one day during the cool-down drills after a scrimmage, Doug caught a cleat in the turf, spun around, and fell—with another guy on top of him. He heard a snap. "I tried to stand," Doug said. "It was impossible. My right knee felt like water."

Doug spent his whole sophomore year waiting for the badly torn ligament in his knee to heal. But at the beginning of the next season, Doug's coaches said he would need a doctor's release to play. So he went to see the team doctor of the New York Giants. "I can't sign a release allowing you to play," the doctor told him. "If you play football with this injury, you won't get through the season without ruining your knee for the rest of your life."

Doug's dream of playing football died. "I felt bitter," he later said. "I didn't think I deserved it. I had led a clean life, unlike most of the other players I knew. So why did God seem to be coming down so hard on me?"

The answer to Doug's question came later when he realized how football had replaced God in his life. "It hit me: I hadn't been living for the only thing that endures," he said. "Even if I'd been successful in the sport, the glory might have lasted six or eight years more, only if I got to the pros. But what was that compared to eternity?"

When the Thessalonians received this letter, they also were wondering why they had to suffer for their faith. **Second Thessalonians 1:1–12** encourages them to hang on because God will be victorious in the end.

- What perspective on their suffering might Doug and the Thessalonians have gotten from this letter?
- How might knowing you will experience peace with God in the future help you through troubles right now?

CONSIDER . . .

- praying for God's comfort and strength to help you through troubles you are facing at home, school, church, or work.
- writing all of the troubles you're now experiencing. Pray that God will strengthen you and help you grow in your faith through these troubles.

FOR MORE, SEE . . .

- Isaiah 9:2–7
- Matthew 7:7–11
- 1 Peter 3:8–22

and from his great power. 10This will happen on the day when the Lord Jesus comes to receive glory because of his holy people. And all the people who have believed will be amazed at Jesus. You will be in that group, because you believed what we told you.

> **SIDELIGHT:** In the first century, being a Christian could be hazardous to your health (2 Thessalonians 1:4). The Roman historian Tacitus describes how Emperor Nero tortured Christians in Rome by dipping them in tar and setting them on fire to illuminate his race track at night.

11That is why we always pray for you, asking our God to help you live the kind of life he called you to live. We pray that with his power God will help you do the good things you want and perform the works that come from your faith. 12We pray all this so that the name of our Lord Jesus Christ will have glory in you, and you will have glory in him. That glory comes from the grace of our God and the Lord Jesus Christ.

Evil Things Will Happen

2 Brothers and sisters, we have something to say about the coming of our Lord Jesus Christ and the time when we will meet together with him. 2Do not become easily upset in your thinking or afraid if you hear that the day of the Lord has already come. Someone may say this in a prophecy[d] or in a message or in a letter as if it came from us. 3Do not let anyone fool you in any way. That day of the Lord will not come until the turning away[n] from God happens and the Man of Evil, who is on his way to hell, appears. 4He will be against and put himself above anything called God or anything that people worship. And that Man of Evil will even go into God's Temple[d] and sit there and say that he is God.

5I told you when I was with you that all this would happen. Do you not remember? 6And now you know what is stopping that Man of Evil so he will appear at the right time. 7The secret power of evil is already working in the world, but there is one who is stopping that power. And he will continue to stop it until he is taken out of the way. 8Then that Man of Evil will appear, and the Lord Jesus will kill him with the breath that comes from his mouth and will destroy him with the glory of his coming. 9The Man of Evil will come by the power of Satan. He will have great power, and he will do many different false miracles,[d] signs, and wonders. 10He will use every kind of evil to trick those who are lost. They will die, because they refused to love the truth. (If they loved the truth, they would be saved.) 11For this reason God sends them something powerful that leads them away from the truth so they will believe a lie. 12So all those will be judged guilty who did not believe the truth, but enjoyed doing evil.

You Are Chosen for Salvation

13Brothers and sisters, whom the Lord loves, God chose you from the beginning to be saved. So we must always thank God for you. You are saved by the Spirit[d] that makes you holy and by your faith in the truth. 14God used the Good News[d] that we preached to call you to be saved so you can share in the glory of our Lord Jesus Christ. 15So, brothers and sisters, stand strong and continue to believe the teachings we gave you in our speaking and in our letter.

16-17May our Lord Jesus Christ himself and God our Father encourage you and strengthen you in every good thing you do and say. God loved us, and through his grace he gave us a good hope and encouragement that continues forever.

Pray for Us

3 And now, brothers and sisters, pray for us that the Lord's teaching will continue to spread quickly and that people will give honor to that teaching, just as happened with you. 2And pray that we will be protected from stubborn and evil people, because not all people believe.

3But the Lord is faithful and will give you strength and will protect you from the Evil One. 4The Lord makes us feel sure that you are doing and will continue to do the things we told you. 5May the Lord lead your hearts into God's love and Christ's patience.

The Duty to Work

6Brothers and sisters, by the authority of our Lord Jesus Christ we command you to stay away from any believer who refuses to work and does not follow the teaching we gave you. 7You yourselves know that you should live as we live. We were not lazy when we were with you. 8And when we ate another person's food, we always paid for it. We worked very hard night and day so we would not be an expense to any of you. 9We had the right to ask you to help us, but we worked to take care of ourselves so we would be an example for you to follow. 10When we were with you, we gave you this rule: "Anyone who refuses to work should not eat."

11We hear that some people in your group refuse to work. They do nothing but busy them-

turning away Or "the rebellion."

selves in other people's lives. [12]We command
those people and beg them in the Lord Jesus
Christ to work quietly and earn their own food.
[13]But you, brothers and sisters, never become
tired of doing good.

SIDELIGHT: Slouches, beware! If you don't work, you don't eat. That's what 2 Thessalonians 3:11–13 says to people who sat around waiting for Christ's Second Coming. The original Greek language is a pun. It could be translated, "No loaf for loafers!"

[14]If some people do not obey what we tell you
in this letter, then take note of them. Have nothing to do with them so they will feel ashamed.
[15]But do not treat them as enemies. Warn them
as fellow believers.

Final Words

[16]Now may the Lord of peace give you peace
at all times and in every way. The Lord be with
all of you.
[17]I, Paul, end this letter now in my own handwriting. All my letters have this to show they are
from me. This is the way I write.
[18]The grace of our Lord Jesus Christ be with
you all.

GOD'S LOVE

Tough Times

The Jefferson family experienced the pits of despair. Mr. Jefferson, a fantastic, energetic, loving husband and father, was killed in a car accident. He left a wife, an eighteen-year-old daughter, and a sixteen-year-old son. How would the family survive this horribly lonely and tough time?

Their church rallied around them. People volunteered to mow their yard and repair their house. Church members cooked and served meals every day right after the death and once a week throughout the following year. The church collected a special offering for their immediate expenses and found a job for Mrs. Jefferson. Church friends supported the family throughout that tough first year with phone calls, visits, cards, and gifts.

The Jeffersons wrote this thank-you to their congregation: "Through your prayers, dear friends, we have been comforted. Through your kind acts we have been soothed. We experienced God's love through you and your love. You made an unbearable experience bearable."

As the church comforted the Jeffersons, **2 Thessalonians 2:13—3:5** promises that God's love will comfort Christians who suffer.

- How is the love shown to the Jeffersons by their congregation like the love that comforted the early Christians?
- How does God's love comfort you through tough times?

CONSIDER . . .

- circling the word love each time you read your Bible over the next several days. Count the number of "loves." Notice how God's love for you is stressed throughout the Bible. Consider starting your reading with the passages listed below.
- letting God's love shine through you. Think of someone who is sad or lonely (for example, a new person at school or an elderly church member who has lost a spouse). Surprise that person with a present or a card.

FOR MORE, SEE . . .

- Psalm 89:1–2
- Matthew 11:28–30
- Romans 5:6–8

1 TIMOTHY

Why Read This Book:

- Learn how to guard against false teaching (1 Timothy 1).
- Find out what to look for in a good church leader (1 Timothy 2—5).
- See what is really important in life (1 Timothy 6).

Behind the Scenes:

When you begin using a computer, you could just turn it on and start punching keys, hoping you will hit the right ones to make something happen. But, more likely, you will begin by reading the machine's operations manual. There you will find step-by-step things to do to use the machine correctly.

The first Christians didn't have experience running a church. Many times they tried different things, hoping they were right. But they also needed an "operations manual."

First Timothy was just what they needed. It gives church leaders specific guidance on running a church: choosing leaders, dealing with false teachings, and order in worship, for example. It's called a "pastoral letter" because it focuses on the work of pastors. The two other pastoral letters in the Bible are 2 Timothy and Titus.

Just because 1 Timothy was originally written about church leaders doesn't mean pastors are the only ones who can benefit from reading it. The book helps all Christians learn the differences between true and false teachings. And it gives practical guidance on how to live as Christians.

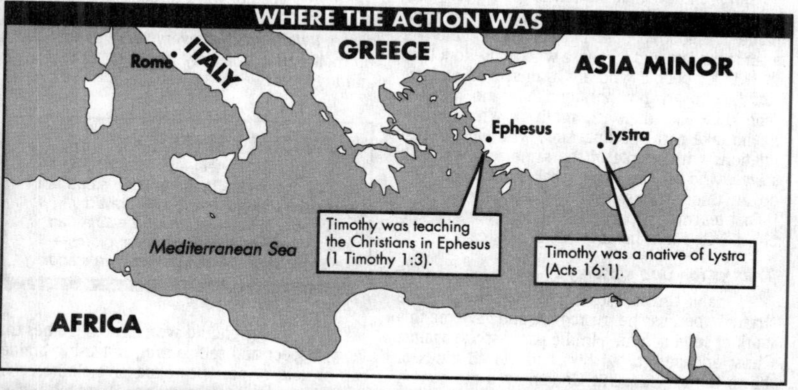
WHERE THE ACTION WAS
GREECE
Rome
ITALY
ASIA MINOR
Ephesus
Lystra
Timothy was teaching the Christians in Ephesus (1 Timothy 1:3).
Mediterranean Sea
Timothy was a native of Lystra (Acts 16:1).
AFRICA

WHEN THE ACTION WAS

Jesus was born — BC/AD
The church began soon after Jesus went to heaven
Jesus began his ministry
25AD
Paul became a Christian
Timothy traveled with Paul on numerous trips
50AD
I Timothy may have been written
Fire destroyed Rome
Romans destroyed the Temple in Jerusalem
75AD
100AD

1 From Paul, an apostle[d] of Christ Jesus, by the
command of God our Savior and Christ Jesus
our hope.
2To Timothy, a true child to me because you
believe:
Grace, mercy, and peace from God the Father
and Christ Jesus our Lord.

> **SIDELIGHT:** Genealogies were hot fads in Bible times (1 Timothy 1:4). Alexander the Great even made up his own family tree, linking him with such Greek gods as Hercules and Achilles.

Warning Against False Teaching

3I asked you to stay longer in Ephesus when I
went into Macedonia so you could command
some people there to stop teaching false things.
4Tell them not to spend their time on stories that
are not true and on long lists of names in family
histories. These things only bring arguments; they
do not help God's work, which is done in faith.
5The purpose of this command is for people to
have love, a love that comes from a pure heart
and a good conscience and a true faith. 6Some
people have missed these things and turned to
useless talk. 7They want to be teachers of the law,
but they do not understand either what they are
talking about or what they are sure about.
8But we know that the law is good if someone
uses it lawfully. 9We also know that the law is not
made for good people but for those who are
against the law and for those who refuse to follow
it. It is for people who are against God and are
sinful, who are not holy and have no religion,
who kill their fathers and mothers, who murder,
10who take part in sexual sins, who have sexual
relations with people of the same sex, who sell
slaves, who tell lies, who speak falsely, and who
do anything against the true teaching of God.
11That teaching is part of the Good News[d] of the
blessed God that he gave me to tell.

Thanks for God's Mercy

12I thank Christ Jesus our Lord, who gave me
strength, because he trusted me and gave me this
work of serving him. 13In the past I spoke against
Christ and persecuted him and did all kinds of
things to hurt him. But God showed me mercy,
because I did not know what I was doing. I did
not believe. 14But the grace of our Lord was fully
given to me, and with that grace came the faith
and love that are in Christ Jesus.
15What I say is true, and you should fully accept
it: Christ Jesus came into the world to save sinners, of whom I am the worst. 16But I was given
mercy so that in me, the worst of all sinners,
Christ Jesus could show that he has patience
without limit. His patience with me made me an
example for those who would believe in him and
have life forever. 17To the King that rules forever,
who will never die, who cannot be seen, the only
God, be honor and glory forever and ever. Amen.
18Timothy, my child, I am giving you a command that agrees with the prophecies[d] that were
given about you in the past. I tell you this so you
can follow them and fight the good fight. 19Con-
tinue to have faith and do what you know is right.
Some people have rejected this, and their faith has
been shipwrecked. 20Hymenaeus and Alexander
have done that, and I have given them to Satan
so they will learn not to speak against God.

Some Rules for Men and Women

2 First, I tell you to pray for all people, asking
God for what they need and being thankful
to him. 2Pray for rulers and for all who have authority so that we can have quiet and peaceful
lives full of worship and respect for God. 3This is
good, and it pleases God our Savior, 4who wants
all people to be saved and to know the truth.
5There is one God and one way human beings can
reach God. That way is through Christ Jesus, who
is himself human. 6He gave himself as a payment
to free all people. He is proof that came at the
right time. 7That is why I was chosen to tell the
Good News[d] and to be an apostle.[d] (I am telling
the truth; I am not lying.) I was chosen to teach
those who are not Jews to believe and to know
the truth.
8So, I want the men everywhere to pray, lifting
up their hands in a holy manner, without anger
and arguments.

> **SIDELIGHT:** Though many Christians kneel and fold their hands to pray, the early Christians often stood with their hands raised when they prayed (1 Timothy 2:8). In the art of the Christian catacombs—underground burial places—praying figures are always depicted standing.

9Also, women should wear proper clothes that
show respect and self-control, not using braided
hair or gold or pearls or expensive clothes. 10In-
stead, they should do good deeds, which is right
for women who say they worship God.
11Let a woman learn by listening quietly and
being ready to cooperate in everything. 12But I do
not allow a woman to teach or to have authority
over a man, but to listen quietly, 13because Adam
was formed first and then Eve. 14And Adam was

not tricked, but the woman was tricked and became a sinner. 15But she will be saved through
having children if they continue in faith, love, and
holiness, with self-control.

Elders in the Church

3 What I say is true: Anyone wanting to become an elder[d] desires a good work. 2An elder must not give people a reason to criticize him,
and he must have only one wife. He must be self-
controlled, wise, respected by others, ready to
welcome guests, and able to teach. 3He must not
drink too much wine or like to fight, but rather
be gentle and peaceable, not loving money. 4He
must be a good family leader, having children
who cooperate with full respect. 5(If someone
does not know how to lead the family, how can
that person take care of God's church?) 6But an
elder must not be a new believer, or he might be
too proud of himself and be judged guilty just as
the devil was. 7An elder must also have the respect of people who are not in the church so he
will not be criticized by others and caught in the
devil's trap.

Deacons in the Church

8In the same way, deacons[d] must be respected
by others, not saying things they do not mean.
They must not drink too much wine or try to get
rich by cheating others. 9With a clear conscience

FORGIVENESS

Accidents Happen

Tyler Hanson and Troy Carr crouched low when they heard a twig snap. Peering through the brush, they saw the buck.

"I'll circle to his left. You circle to his right," Troy whispered.

Tyler nodded and started crawling to the right.

As the buck wandered closer, Tyler slowly rose and pointed his rifle.

But Troy's shot pierced the silence first, and Tyler fell to the ground before he could shoot.

When Tyler awoke eight hours later at the hospital, he couldn't see. He had been shot in the eye, his doctors explained. A glass eye would replace his destroyed eye.

Tyler seethed. "How could his best friend do this to him?" he asked himself.

When Troy visited Tyler for the first time, Tyler refused to speak to him. He folded his arms and wouldn't face Troy. When Troy hung around too long, Tyler exploded. "Get out of here! Leave me alone!"

After Tyler settled down, he and Troy talked. The buck had jumped right before Troy pulled the trigger. "It was an accident. I jerked the gun to hit him," Troy explained. "But instead, I hit you. Please, don't hate me."

It took weeks for Tyler to talk to Troy—let alone forgive him. But finally Tyler realized forgiveness was the only way to heal the bitterness inside him. And when he forgave Troy, the two became close again.

"Yes, I lost my eye," Tyler told Troy two months after the accident, "but I didn't need to lose a friend, too."

Tyler and Troy understood the importance of mercy and forgiveness, which is what **1 Timothy 1:12–17** is all about. Read what the writer says about mercy.

- How is Troy like the writer in this passage? How are they different? Why were Troy and the writer of 1 Timothy thankful for the forgiveness they received?
- How might God's forgiveness help you deal with the sins you've committed?

CONSIDER . . .

- praying about the wrongs you have done and asking God for forgiveness. Write "You are forgiven" on a note, and post it on your mirror.
- inviting someone you need to forgive to an ice cream shop. Buy the person a treat, talk about the problem, and forgive the person. Ask your forgiven friend to forgive you.

FOR MORE, SEE . . .

- Genesis 50:15–21
- Matthew 6:14–15
- 2 Corinthians 2:5–10

they must follow the secret of the faith that God
made known to us. 10Test them first. Then let
them serve as deacons if you find nothing wrong
in them. 11In the same way, women[n] must be
respected by others. They must not speak evil of
others. They must be self-controlled and trustworthy in everything. 12Deacons must have only one
wife and be good leaders of their children and
their own families. 13Those who serve well as deacons are making an honorable place for themselves, and they will be very bold in their faith in
Christ Jesus.

The Secret of Our Life

14Although I hope I can come to you soon, I am
writing these things to you now. 15Then, even if
I am delayed, you will know how to live in the
family of God. That family is the church of the
living God, the support and foundation of the
truth. 16Without doubt, the secret of our life of
worship is great:

He was shown to us in a human body,
proved right in spirit,[d]
and seen by angels.
He was preached to those who are not
Jews,
believed in by the world,
and taken up in glory.

A Warning About False Teachers

4 Now the Holy Spirit[d] clearly says that in the
later times some people will stop believing
the faith. They will follow spirits that lie and
teachings of demons.[d] 2Such teachings come from
the false words of liars whose consciences are destroyed as if by a hot iron. 3They forbid people to
marry and tell them not to eat certain foods which
God created to be eaten with thanks by people
who believe and know the truth. 4Everything God
made is good, and nothing should be refused if it
is accepted with thanks, 5because it is made holy
by what God has said and by prayer.

Be a Good Servant of Christ

6By telling these things to the brothers and sis-

women This might mean the wives of the deacons, or it might mean women who serve in the same way as deacons.

PRAYER

Pray for All People

"I'm shipping out tonight to Saudi Arabia. I'll see you when I get back."

Darlene Wachs hung up the phone. Saudi Arabia? Her boyfriend Greg Richter was going to Saudi Arabia with the U.S. armed forces. She didn't even know where Saudi Arabia was!

She said a quick prayer, asking God to keep Greg safe.

Darlene swallowed the lump in her throat and searched for a world atlas. She was terrified something could happen to Greg, but she wanted at least to know where he was going.

During the worship service on Sunday, her pastor said, "Let's pray for all people," and then listed different parts of the world, including Saudi Arabia. Darlene's mind usually wandered during those prayers, since the places seemed so far away and irrelevant to her life. But this time she paid attention.

What happened in Saudi Arabia really did affect her life.

When Darlene's boyfriend suddenly went overseas, she understood the importance of praying for all people. **1 Timothy 2:1–4** expands our prayer concerns beyond ourselves and reminds us God cares for the whole world.

- How does praying for a country such as Saudi Arabia fit the message of this scripture?
- Which countries and rulers should you pray for today?

C O N S I D E R . . .

- reading the international section of your newspaper. Ask members of your church to pray for the people mentioned there.
- looking at a world atlas, and praying for people in different parts of the world. Pray for them each evening.

F O R M O R E , S E E . . .

- Psalm 46
- Ephesians 6:18–20
- James 5:13–18

ters,[n] you will be a good servant of Christ Jesus. You will be made strong by the words of the faith and the good teaching which you have been following. 7But do not follow foolish stories that disagree with God's truth, but train yourself to serve God. 8Training your body helps you in some ways, but serving God helps you in every way by bringing you blessings in this life and in the future life, too. 9What I say is true, and you should fully accept it. 10This is why we work and struggle: We hope in the living God who is the Savior of all people, especially of those who believe.

11Command and teach these things. 12Do not let anyone treat you as if you are unimportant because you are young. Instead, be an example to the believers with your words, your actions, your love, your faith, and your pure life. 13Until I come, continue to read the Scriptures[d] to the people, strengthen them, and teach them. 14Use the gift you have, which was given to you through prophecy[d] when the group of elders[d] laid their hands on[n] you. 15Continue to do those things; give your life to doing them so your progress may be seen by everyone. 16Be careful in your life and in your teaching. If you continue to live and teach rightly, you will save both yourself and those who listen to you.

> **SIDELIGHT:** When 1 Timothy 4:8 talks about training your body, the original Greek word for training is the same as gymnastics in English. And the word gymnastics comes from the word for nude, since athletes worked out in the nude. Today we just have to put up with gang showers!

Rules for Living with Others

5 Do not speak angrily to an older man, but plead with him as if he were your father. Treat younger men like brothers, 2older women like mothers, and younger women like sisters. Always treat them in a pure way.

3Take care of widows who are truly widows. 4But if a widow has children or grandchildren, let them first learn to do their duty to their own family and to repay their parents or grandparents. That pleases God. 5The true widow, who is all alone, puts her hope in God and continues to pray night and day for God's help. 6But the widow who uses her life to please herself is really dead while she is alive. 7Tell the believers to do these things so that no one can criticize them. 8Whoever does not care for his own relatives, especially his own family members, has turned against the faith and is worse than someone who does not believe in God.

9To be on the list of widows, a woman must be at least sixty years old. She must have been faithful to her husband. 10She must be known for her good works — works such as raising her children, welcoming strangers, washing the feet of God's people, helping those in trouble, and giving her life to do all kinds of good deeds.

11But do not put younger widows on that list. After they give themselves to Christ, they are pulled away from him by their physical needs, and then they want to marry again. 12They will be judged for not doing what they first promised to do. 13Besides that, they learn to waste their time, going from house to house. And they not only waste their time but also begin to gossip and busy themselves with other people's lives, saying things they should not say. 14So I want the younger widows to marry, have children, and manage their homes. Then no enemy will have any reason to criticize them. 15But some have already turned away to follow Satan.

16If any woman who is a believer has widows in her family, she should care for them herself. The church should not have to care for them. Then it will be able to take care of those who are truly widows.

17The elders[d] who lead the church well should receive double honor, especially those who work hard by speaking and teaching, 18because the Scripture[d] says: "When an ox is working in the grain, do not cover its mouth to keep it from eating,"[n] and "A worker should be given his pay."[n]

19Do not listen to someone who accuses an elder, without two or three witnesses. 20Tell those who continue sinning that they are wrong. Do this in front of the whole church so that the others will have a warning.

21Before God and Christ Jesus and the chosen angels, I command you to do these things without showing favor of any kind to anyone.

22Think carefully before you lay your hands on[n] anyone, and don't share in the sins of others. Keep yourself pure.

23Stop drinking only water, but drink a little wine to help your stomach and your frequent sicknesses.

brothers and sisters Although the Greek text says "brothers" here and throughout this book, Paul's words refer to the entire church, including men and women.
laid their hands on The laying on of hands had many purposes, including the giving of a blessing, power, or authority.
"When . . . eating," Quotation from Deuteronomy 25:4.
"A worker . . . pay." Quotation from Luke 10:7.
lay your hands on The laying on of hands had many purposes, including the giving of a blessing, power, or authority.

24The sins of some people are easy to see even
before they are judged, but the sins of others are
seen only later. 25So also good deeds are easy to
see, but even those that are not easily seen cannot
stay hidden.

6 All who are slaves under a yoke[d] should
show full respect to their masters so no one
will speak against God's name and our teaching.
2The slaves whose masters are believers should
not show their masters any less respect because
they are believers. They should serve their masters even better, because they are helping believers they love.
You must teach and preach these things.

False Teaching and True Riches

3Anyone who has a different teaching does not
agree with the true teaching of our Lord Jesus
Christ and the teaching that shows the true way
to serve God. 4This person is full of pride and understands nothing, but is sick with a love for arguing and fighting about words. This brings jealousy,
fighting, speaking against others, evil mistrust,
5and constant quarrels from those who have evil
minds and have lost the truth. They think tha
serving God is a way to get rich.
6Serving God does make us very rich, if we ar
satisfied with what we have. 7We brought noth
ing into the world, so we can take nothing out
8But, if we have food and clothes, we will be satis
fied with that. 9Those who want to become ricl
bring temptation to themselves and are caught i
a trap. They want many foolish and harmfu
things that ruin and destroy people. 10The love c
money causes all kinds of evil. Some people hav
left the faith, because they wanted to get mor
money, but they have caused themselves mucl
sorrow.

Some Things to Remember

11But you, man of God, run away from all thos
things. Instead, live in the right way, serve God
have faith, love, patience, and gentleness. 12Figh
the good fight of faith, grabbing hold of the lif
that continues forever. You were called to hav
that life when you confessed the good confessio
before many witnesses. 13In the sight of God, wh
gives life to everything, and of Christ Jesus, I giv

MONEY

More and More

Disappointed by her mom's refusal to buy the expensive dress she wanted for her junior prom, Janice Nielsen vowed her senior prom would be different.

So, at the start of her senior year, Janice landed a job as a cashier in a video store. All year she worked hard. From each paycheck, she diligently put away money for the prom dress and other prom expenses.

During March and April, Janice tried on dress after dress. She wanted to buy just the right one—the one that would make her happy.

The morning after the prom, Janice sat in her room and cried. The night had been wonderful. Her dress was beautiful. The limousine ride was fun. But now it was all over. The hundreds of dollars she had spent had not brought the happiness she expected.

She felt betrayed, especially when she compared her senior prom to her junior prom. After all, she had had just as much fun at the junior prom, even though her dress had cost much less.

Janice thought money would buy her happiness. As you read **1 Timothy 6:6–16**, consider what truly makes Christians rich.

- What advice in this passage could help Janice understand the ultimate result of the love of money?
- When do you get caught up in wanting more? How could the advice in the passage help you avoid that trap?

CONSIDER . . .

- analyzing your use of money in three categories: spending, saving and giving. Based on what you read in the passage, what do you need to do with your money?
- beginning a tithe (giving 10 percent of your income) to your church.

FOR MORE, SEE . . .

- Joshua 7:19–26
- Proverbs 15:27
- Hebrews 13:5–6

you a command. Christ Jesus made the good confession when he stood before Pontius Pilate. [14]Do
what you were commanded to do without wrong
or blame until our Lord Jesus Christ comes again.
[15]God will make that happen at the right time. He
is the blessed and only Ruler, the King of all kings
and the Lord of all lords. [16]He is the only One who
never dies. He lives in light so bright no one can
go near it. No one has ever seen God, or can see
him. May honor and power belong to God forever. Amen.

[17]Command those who are rich with things of
this world not to be proud. Tell them to hope in
God, not in their uncertain riches. God richly
gives us everything to enjoy. [18]Tell the rich people
to do good, to be rich in doing good deeds, to be
generous and ready to share. [19]By doing that, they
will be saving a treasure for themselves as a strong
foundation for the future. Then they will be able
to have the life that is true life.

[20]Timothy, guard what God has trusted to you.
Stay away from foolish, useless talk and from the
arguments of what is falsely called "knowledge."
[21]By saying they have that "knowledge," some
have missed the true faith.

Grace be with you.

SIDELIGHT: Saying that Jesus Christ is "King of all kings and the Lord of all lords" (1 Timothy 6:15) was a bold statement in the midst of the persecution the early Christians faced. Near the end of the first century, the Roman emperor Domitian demanded that his subjects address him as "Lord and God." Christians who refused were threatened, exiled, and put to death.

2 TIMOTHY

Why Read This Book:

- Be encouraged to keep following God, even when you face danger for doing it (2 Timothy 1—2).
- Find out how to make it through tough times (2 Timothy 3—4).

Behind the Scenes:

People who know they are soon to die often divide up their belongings and ask those around them to finish the projects they have started. Paul knew he was facing death (2 Timothy 4:6–8), so he wrote this letter to hand off the baton of ministry for Timothy to carry on.

Second Timothy captures what a retiring leader would say to a new leader. It gives lots of encouragement. It gives advice on how to become a leader. And it says that the road will be rocky and rough at times, but we should remain strong anyway.

While 1 Timothy gives instructions on how to run a church, 2 Timothy is a personal letter—like one you would write to a close friend. It encourages Christians facing tough times, since the Roman leader was persecuting Christians. And it can encourage us to stick to our faith today, even when people try to pull us away.

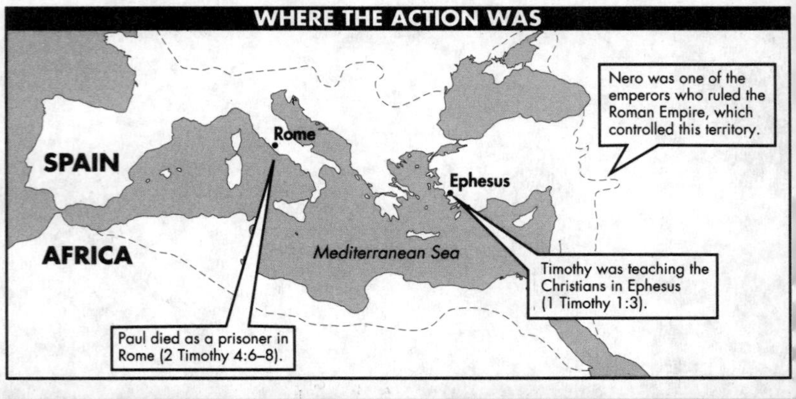
WHERE THE ACTION WAS
Nero was one of the emperors who ruled the Roman Empire, which controlled this territory.
Rome
SPAIN
Ephesus
AFRICA
Mediterranean Sea
Timothy was teaching the Christians in Ephesus (1 Timothy 1:3).
Paul died as a prisoner in Rome (2 Timothy 4:6–8).

WHEN THE ACTION WAS

BC/AD	25AD	50AD	75AD	100AD
Jesus was born	The church began soon after Jesus went to heaven	Timothy traveled with Paul on numerous trips	Fire destroyed Rome	
	Jesus began his ministry; Paul became a Christian	2 Timothy may have been written	Romans destroyed the Temple in Jerusalem	

1 From Paul, an apostle[d] of Christ Jesus by the
will of God. God sent me to tell about the
promise of life that is in Christ Jesus.
2To Timothy, a dear child to me:
Grace, mercy, and peace to you from God the
Father and Christ Jesus our Lord.

Encouragement for Timothy

3I thank God as I always mention you in my
prayers, day and night. I serve him, doing what I
know is right as my ancestors did. 4Remembering
that you cried for me, I want very much to see
you so I can be filled with joy. 5I remember your
true faith. That faith first lived in your grandmother Lois and in your mother Eunice, and I
know you now have that same faith. 6This is why
I remind you to keep using the gift God gave you
when I laid my hands on[n] you. Now let it grow,
as a small flame grows into a fire. 7God did not
give us a spirit that makes us afraid but a spirit of
power and love and self-control.
8So do not be ashamed to tell people about our
Lord Jesus, and do not be ashamed of me, in
prison for the Lord. But suffer with me for the
Good News.[d] God, who gives us the strength to
do that, 9saved us and made us his holy people.
That was not because of anything we did ourselves but because of God's purpose and grace.
That grace was given to us through Christ Jesus
before time began, 10but it is now shown to us by
the coming of our Savior Christ Jesus. He de-

laid my hands on The laying on of hands had many purposes, including the giving of a blessing, power, or authority.

SHARING FAITH

What to Say?

Megan Taylor abruptly dropped out of church. She had been going regularly for several months, so the group noticed her absence immediately. Her friend Jeanne Murray went over to Megan's house to ask what was wrong.

"I'm just not good enough to be a Christian," Megan replied. "I sometimes swear when I get mad. I think bad things sometimes. And I just don't feel like I set a good example for other people."

"But you don't need to be perfect or know all the answers," Jeanne said.

Megan just shook her head, and Jeanne struggled to find the right words to help her friend. "You're always so giving, and Christians are giving," Jeanne said.

"I'm not more giving than anybody else," Megan replied.

Jeanne didn't know how to respond. The more she thought, the more frustrated she became. She finally blurted out, "You are a Christian, Megan. But if I were really a good friend, I'd know how to help you."

Megan paused. "You're right. You're absolutely right."

"Huh?" a puzzled Jeanne asked.

"You just told me why I can still be a Christian," Megan said. "We've been friends a long time, right? But sometimes we don't feel like we're good friends. It's the same with being a Christian. At times, I may feel like a failure. But as long as I'm trying, I'm doing okay. You really helped me, Jeanne. Thanks."

As Jeanne walked home, she still wondered how she had helped Megan. So, she simply thanked God for giving her the words to say. Jeanne's willingness to witness was a lot like **2 Timothy 1:3–14**.

- How did Jeanne share her faith with Megan? How was her experience like and unlike the passage?
- What does this passage say about sharing your faith with others?

C O N S I D E R . . .

- telling your family why you are a Christian. Ask how family members see you sharing your faith.
- dropping a postcard to someone struggling with his or her faith, encouraging that person like 2 Timothy offers encouragement.

F O R M O R E , S E E . . .

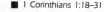

- Exodus 4:1–12
- Luke 9:1–6
- 1 Corinthians 1:18–31

stroyed death, and through the Good News he
showed us the way to have life that cannot be
destroyed. 11I was chosen to tell that Good News
and to be an apostle[d] and a teacher. 12I am suffering now because I tell the Good News, but I am
not ashamed, because I know Jesus, the One in
whom I have believed. And I am sure he is able
to protect what he has trusted me with until that
day.[n] 13Follow the pattern of true teachings that
you heard from me in faith and love, which are
in Christ Jesus. 14Protect the truth that you were
given; protect it with the help of the Holy Spirit[d]
who lives in us.

> **SIDELIGHT:** Like his mentor Paul (2 Timothy 1:8), Timothy also experienced persecution for his faith, according to Hebrews 13:23. He was imprisoned but released. Paul was apparently executed while a prisoner in Rome.

15You know that everyone in the country of
Asia has left me, even Phygelus and Hermogenes.
16May the Lord show mercy to the family of Onesiphorus, who has often helped me and was not
ashamed that I was in prison. 17When he came to
Rome, he looked eagerly for me until he found
me. 18May the Lord allow him to find mercy from
the Lord on that day. You know how many ways
he helped me in Ephesus.

A Loyal Soldier of Christ Jesus

2 You then, Timothy, my child, be strong in
the grace we have in Christ Jesus. 2You
should teach people whom you can trust the
things you and many others have heard me say.
Then they will be able to teach others. 3Share in
the troubles we have like a good soldier of Christ
Jesus. 4A soldier wants to please the enlisting officer, so no one serving in the army wastes time
with everyday matters. 5Also an athlete who takes
part in a contest must obey all the rules in order
to win. 6The farmer who works hard should be
the first person to get some of the food that was
grown. 7Think about what I am saying, because
the Lord will give you the ability to understand
everything.

8Remember Jesus Christ, who was raised from
the dead, who is from the family of David. This
is the Good News[d] I preach, 9and I am suffering
because of it to the point of being bound with
chains like a criminal. But God's teaching is not
in chains. 10So I patiently accept all these troubles
so that those whom God has chosen can have the
salvation that is in Christ Jesus. With that salvation comes glory that never ends.

11This teaching is true:

If we died with him, we will also live with
him.
12 If we accept suffering, we will also rule
with him.
If we refuse to accept him, he will refuse to
accept us.
13 If we are not faithful, he will still be
faithful,
because he cannot be false to himself.

A Worker Pleasing to God

14Continue teaching these things, warning people in God's presence not to argue about words.
It does not help anyone, and it ruins those who
listen. 15Make every effort to give yourself to God
as the kind of person he will accept. Be a worker
who is not ashamed and who uses the true teaching in the right way. 16Stay away from foolish,
useless talk, because that will lead people further
away from God. 17Their evil teaching will spread
like a sickness inside the body. Hymenaeus and
Philetus are like that. 18They have left the true
teaching, saying that the rising from the dead has
already taken place, and so they are destroying
the faith of some people. 19But God's strong foundation continues to stand. These words are written on the seal: "The Lord knows those who belong to him,"[n] and "Everyone who wants to
belong to the Lord must stop doing wrong."

20In a large house there are not only things
made of gold and silver, but also things made of
wood and clay. Some things are used for special
purposes, and others are made for ordinary jobs.
21All who make themselves clean[d] from evil will
be used for special purposes. They will be made
holy, useful to the Master, ready to do any good
work.

22But run away from the evil young people like
to do. Try hard to live right and to have faith, love,
and peace, together with those who trust in the
Lord from pure hearts. 23Stay away from foolish
and stupid arguments, because you know they
grow into quarrels. 24And a servant of the Lord
must not quarrel but must be kind to everyone,
a good teacher, and patient. 25The Lord's servant
must gently teach those who disagree. Then
maybe God will let them change their minds so
they can accept the truth. 26And they may wake
up and escape from the trap of the devil, who
catches them to do what he wants.

day The day Christ will come to judge all people and take his people to live with him.
"The Lord . . . him" Quotation from Numbers 16:5.

The Last Days

3 Remember this! In the last days there will be
many troubles, [2]because people will love
themselves, love money, brag, and be proud.
They will say evil things against others and will
not obey their parents or be thankful or be the
kind of people God wants. [3]They will not love
others, will refuse to forgive, will gossip, and will
not control themselves. They will be cruel, will
hate what is good, [4]will turn against their friends,
and will do foolish things without thinking. They
will be conceited, will love pleasure instead of
God, [5]and will act as if they serve God but will not
have his power. Stay away from those people.
[6]Some of them go into homes and get control of
silly women who are full of sin and are led by
many evil desires. [7]These women are always
learning new teachings, but they are never able to
understand the truth fully. [8]Just as Jannes and
Jambres were against Moses, these people are
against the truth. Their thinking has been ruined,
and they have failed in trying to follow the faith.
[9]But they will not be successful in what they do,

SIDELIGHT: When 2 Timothy 3:2 cautions Timothy about people who love only themselves and money, it pegs the culture of Ephesus, where Timothy ministered. Nicknamed the treasure house of the ancient world, the major seaport city of Ephesus was famous for selfish, materialistic living.

PATIENCE

Worth the Wait

For thirty years, Rosa Parks bristled at the inequalities all around her. Because she was black, she had to ride in the back of the bus. Her skin color made everything more difficult for her in the segregated South.

On her way home from work in 1955, in Montgomery, Alabama, Rosa boarded a bus and filled a vacant seat. She was exhausted. Her neck, shoulders and back ached from sewing alterations all day. A few white people boarded the bus after Rosa, and they all found seats, except for one white man.

The bus driver asked someone to give up a seat, meaning that a black person was to give up a seat for the white person. Since Rosa sat in a seat closest to the front and closest to the aisle, everyone looked at her. But Rosa would not budge. Finally two police officers arrested her.

Rosa's arrest stirred an uproar in the black community. People were furious at the unfairness of forcing a black woman to give up her seat on a bus to a white man just because of her skin color.

People gathered at Dexter Avenue Baptist Church to organize a bus boycott that made history and brought Martin Luther King, Jr., to national attention. The 381-day boycott required intense patience and endurance as the organizers set up car pools to transport workers who relied on bus transportation. The boycott succeeded when Montgomery buses were ordered desegregated in 1956. No longer would blacks be forced to give up their seats for whites.

Because of Rosa Parks's patience and the patience of the boycott leaders, the civil rights movement of the 1950s and 1960s was born. By refusing to budge and by being patient to see segregation crumble, Rosa showed the patience reflected in **2 Timothy 2:8–13**.

- How are the patience and suffering mentioned in this passage like the patience and suffering of blacks in the boycott?
- How could this passage help you to be more patient during tough times?

CONSIDER . . .

- asking God for patience to deal with a problem you are facing, and then being patient.
- talking with your family about creating a rule for silently counting to fifteen when someone tries a family member's patience.

FOR MORE, SEE . . .

- Numbers 11:4–20
- Romans 8:16–18
- 1 Peter 4:12–19

because as with Jannes and Jambres, everyone
will see that they are foolish.

Obey the Teachings

10But you have followed what I teach, the way
I live, my goal, faith, patience, and love. You
know I never give up. 11You know how I have
been hurt and have suffered, as in Antioch, Iconium, and Lystra. I have suffered, but the Lord
saved me from all those troubles. 12Everyone who
wants to live as God desires, in Christ Jesus, will
be hurt. 13But people who are evil and cheat others will go from bad to worse. They will fool others, but they will also be fooling themselves.
14But you should continue following the teachings you learned. You know they are true, because you trust those who taught you. 15Since you
were a child you have known the Holy Scriptures[d] which are able to make you wise. And that
wisdom leads to salvation through faith in Christ
Jesus. 16All Scripture is given by God and is useful
for teaching, for showing people what is wrong in
their lives, for correcting faults, and for teaching
how to live right. 17Using the Scriptures, the
person who serves God will be capable, having
all that is needed to do every good work.

4 I give you a command in the presence of
God and Christ Jesus, the One who will
judge the living and the dead, and by his coming
and his kingdom: 2Preach the Good News.[d] Be
ready at all times, and tell people what they need
to do. Tell them when they are wrong. Encourage
them with great patience and careful teaching,
3because the time will come when people will
not listen to the true teaching but will find many
more teachers who please them by saying the
things they want to hear. 4They will stop listening
to the truth and will begin to follow false stories.
5But you should control yourself at all times, accept troubles, do the work of telling the Good
News, and complete all the duties of a servant of
God.

BIBLE STUDY

Take Time to Learn

Reading the Bible is important, right? But do you do it? Many Christian teenagers don't, indicates Teenage Magazine:

- Thirteen percent of Christian teenagers say they never read their Bible.
- Only eight percent say they read the Bible every day.
- Forty-four percent say they read the Bible only when they feel like it.
- And the rest, thirty-five percent, read the Bible a few times a week, or less.

Why don't Christian teenagers read the Bible? Teenagers say the top five reasons are:

1. They get busy.
2. They would rather do something else.
3. They think the Bible is boring.
4. They don't know how to study the Bible.
5. They forget to read it.

The Bible has been called the most printed and the least read of all books. Adults and teenagers alike cannot grow as Christians without the life-changing guidance of the Bible. Teenagers might get a lot from the Bible if they read it knowing the value of scripture as described in **2 Timothy 3:14–4:5**.

- According to this passage, of what value is Bible study to the Christian's life?
- What can you do to make Bible study an important part of your everyday life?

C O N S I D E R . . .

- asking your youth minister or pastor for tips on how to make Bible study easier and more effective.
- spending one week reading through one of the Gospels (Matthew, Mark, Luke, or John) with a friend, meeting every day at lunch to discuss what you have learned in your reading.

F O R M O R E , S E E . . .

- Psalm 119:97–104
- John 5:39
- 2 Timothy 1:13–14

6My life is being given as an offering to God,
and the time has come for me to leave this life.
7I have fought the good fight, I have finished the
race, I have kept the faith. 8Now, a crown is being
held for me—a crown for being right with God.
The Lord, the judge who judges rightly, will give
the crown to me on that day[n]—not only to me
but to all those who have waited with love for
him to come again.

Personal Words

9Do your best to come to me as soon as you
can, 10because Demas, who loved this world, left
me and went to Thessalonica. Crescens went to
Galatia, and Titus went to Dalmatia. 11Luke is the
only one still with me. Get Mark and bring him
with you when you come, because he can help
me in my work here. 12I sent Tychicus to Ephesus. 13When I was in Troas, I left my coat there
with Carpus. So when you come, bring it to me,
along with my books, particularly the ones written on parchment.[n]

> **SIDELIGHT:** Have trouble misplacing things? Take heart. So did the apostle Paul. He left his coat in Troas (2 Timothy 4:13), which was more than a hundred miles from Ephesus, and close to a thousand miles from Rome—the two places he might have been when he asked the people to send the coat to him. This coat was probably a heavy cloak that would have kept Paul warmer in a damp prison cell.

14Alexander the metalworker did many harmful things against me. The Lord will punish him
for what he did. 15You also should be careful that

day The day Christ will come to judge all people and take his people to live with him.
parchment A writing paper made from the skins of sheep.

PERSISTENCE

Dream Big

He always dreamed of playing football, but many obstacles blocked his dream.

His church discouraged playing the game. His parents weren't keen on the idea, but eventually they let him try out for the sport. In seventh grade, he went out for the team—even though he was too small to fit in a uniform.

Once on the field playing defense, the odds of his making the team seemed even worse. "The coach put me up against the biggest fullback on the team," he recalls. "I didn't know what to do. I yelled and grabbed him around the legs. He carried me for a few yards, and I finally tackled him."

After that first courageous tackle, the coach let the boy play. Although he lacked size, the coach saw a "won't-give-up" persistence in the kid. And he showed an intensity the coach rarely saw.

Many years later, after high school and college football, this persistent player was drafted by the Chicago Bears. And in 1985 and 1988 Mike Singletary, the 6-foot, 230-pound linebacker, was named the NFL Defensive Player of the Year.

His seventh-grade persistence paid off for Mike Singletary. He lives the message of persistence in **2 Timothy 4:6–18**.

- How is Mike Singletary like the writer of 2 Timothy, especially in verse 16 of this passage?
- What hobby, sport, or talent have you considered giving up on? How should you decide whether to stick with it or not?

C O N S I D E R . . .

- identifying someone who has stuck with something after almost quitting. Write or call that person, encouraging him or her to hang in there.
- looking at the people around you—friends, family, teachers. Choose one person you can talk to when you feel like quitting.

F O R M O R E , S E E . . .

- 1 Samuel 17:1–54
- Acts 20:24
- 1 Corinthians 9:24–27

he does not hurt you, because he fought strongly
against our teaching.
16The first time I defended myself, no one
helped me; everyone left me. May they be forgiven. 17But the Lord stayed with me and gave me
strength so I could fully tell the Good News[d] to
all those who are not Jews. So I was saved from
the lion's mouth. 18The Lord will save me when
anyone tries to hurt me, and he will bring me
safely to his heavenly kingdom. Glory forever and
ever be the Lord's. Amen.

Final Greetings

19Greet Priscilla and Aquila and the family of
Onesiphorus. 20Erastus stayed in Corinth, and I
left Trophimus sick in Miletus. 21Try as hard as
you can to come to me before winter.

Eubulus sends greetings to you. Also Pudens, Linus, Claudia, and all the brothers and sisters in Christ greet you.

22The Lord be with your spirit. Grace be with
you.

TITUS

Why Read This Book:

- Find out what it takes to be a Christian leader (Titus 1).
- Discover how to live as a Christian (Titus 2—3).

Behind the Scenes:

Suppose you knew a group of people who lied, bickered, and were greedy? Most likely you would write them off as evil people and wouldn't hang around with them. And what if these people said they were Christians? You would probably call them hypocrites—then switch churches.

Yet that is the kind of people Titus encountered when he went to Crete, an island infamous for its tough people. Years earlier, a poet from the island had written: "Cretans are always liars, evil animals, and lazy people who do nothing but eat" (Titus 1:12).

But instead of writing off these people, Titus had gone to work with them, helping them grow in their faith. It was a tough missionary assignment. The letter to Titus encourages the leader and gives the people practical advice on how to overcome their past, sinful practices and to begin living a new life in Christ.

This short letter is full of help for effective Christian living. It summarizes the basics of the Christian faith, and encourages all people to live lives that are pleasing to God.

WHEN THE ACTION WAS

Jesus was born	BC/AD	
The church began soon after Jesus went to heaven	25AD	Jesus began his ministry
Paul began his missionary work		Paul became a Christian
Fire destroyed Rome	50AD	Titus may have been written
	75AD	Romans destroyed the Temple in Jerusalem
	100AD	

1 From Paul, a servant of God and an apostle[d] of Jesus Christ. I was sent to help the faith of God's chosen people and to help them know the truth that shows people how to serve God. 2That faith and that knowledge come from the hope for life forever, which God promised to us before time began. And God cannot lie. 3At the right time God let the world know about that life through preaching. He trusted me with that work, and I preached by the command of God our Savior.

4To Titus, my true child in the faith we share:

Grace and peace from God the Father and Christ Jesus our Savior.

Titus' Work in Crete

5I left you in Crete so you could finish doing the things that still needed to be done and so you could appoint elders[d] in every town, as I directed you. 6An elder must not be guilty of doing wrong, must have only one wife, and must have believing children. They must not be known as children who are wild and do not cooperate. 7As God's manager, an elder must not be guilty of doing wrong, being selfish, or becoming angry quickly. He must not drink too much wine, like to fight, or try to get rich by cheating others. 8An elder must be ready to welcome guests, love what is good, be wise, live right, and be holy and self-controlled. 9By holding on to the trustworthy word just as we teach it, an elder can help people by using true teaching, and he can show those who are against the true teaching that they are wrong.

> **SIDELIGHT:** When Titus 1:8 says elders must accept others into their homes, it means more than just giving them a glass of iced tea. If a stranger stopped at the door, a hospitable person was expected to feed, lodge, protect, and clothe the stranger, if necessary. The Greek word for hospitality literally meant "lover of strangers."

10There are many people who refuse to cooperate, who talk about worthless things and lead others into the wrong way—mainly those who say all who are not Jews must be circumcised.[d] 11These people must be stopped, because they are upsetting whole families by teaching things they should not teach, which they do to get rich by cheating people. 12Even one of their own prophets said, "Cretans are always liars, evil animals, and lazy people who do nothing but eat." 13The words that prophet said are true. So firmly tell those people they are wrong so they may become strong in the faith, 14not accepting Jewish false stories and the commands of people who reject the truth. 15To those who are pure, all things are pure, but to those who are full of sin and do not believe, nothing is pure. Both their minds and their consciences have been ruined. 16They say they know God, but their actions show they do not accept him. They are hateful people, they refuse to obey, and they are useless for doing anything good.

Following the True Teaching

2 But you must tell everyone what to do to follow the true teaching. 2Teach older men to be self-controlled, serious, wise, strong in faith, in love, and in patience.

3In the same way, teach older women to be holy in their behavior, not speaking against others or enslaved to too much wine, but teaching what is good. 4Then they can teach the young women to love their husbands, to love their children, 5to be wise and pure, to be good workers at home, to be kind, and to yield to their husbands. Then no one will be able to criticize the teaching God gave us.

6In the same way, encourage young men to be wise. 7In every way be an example of doing good deeds. When you teach, do it with honesty and seriousness. 8Speak the truth so that you cannot be criticized. Then those who are against you will be ashamed because there is nothing bad to say about us.

9Slaves should yield to their own masters at all times, trying to please them and not arguing with them. 10They should not steal from them but should show their masters they can be fully trusted so that in everything they do they will make the teaching of God our Savior attractive.

11That is the way we should live, because God's grace that can save everyone has come. 12It teaches us not to live against God nor to do the evil things the world wants to do. Instead, that grace teaches us to live now in a wise and right way and in a way that shows we serve God. 13We should live like that while we wait for our great hope and the coming of the glory of our great God and Savior Jesus Christ. 14He gave himself for us so he might pay the price to free us from all evil and to make us pure people who belong only to him—people who are always wanting to do good deeds.

15Say these things and encourage the people and tell them what is wrong in their lives, with all authority. Do not let anyone treat you as if you were unimportant.

The Right Way to Live

3 Remind the believers to yield to the authority of rulers and government leaders, to obey

them, to be ready to do good, [2]to speak no evil
about anyone, to live in peace, and to be gentle
and polite to all people.
[3]In the past we also were foolish. We did not
obey, we were wrong, and we were slaves to
many things our bodies wanted and enjoyed. We
spent our lives doing evil and being jealous. People hated us, and we hated each other. [4]But when
the kindness and love of God our Savior was
shown, [5]he saved us because of his mercy. It was
not because of good deeds we did to be right with
him. He saved us through the washing that made
us new people through the Holy Spirit.[d] [6]God
poured out richly upon us that Holy Spirit through
Jesus Christ our Savior. [7]Being made right with
God by his grace, we could have the hope of receiving the life that never ends.
[8]This teaching is true, and I want you to be sure
the people understand these things. Then those
who believe in God will be careful to use their
lives for doing good. These things are good and
will help everyone.
[9]But stay away from those who have foolish
arguments and talk about useless family histories
and argue and quarrel about the law. Those things
are worth nothing and will not help anyone. [10]Af-
ter a first and second warning, avoid someone
who causes arguments. [11]You can know that such
people are evil and sinful; their own sins prove
them wrong.

Some Things to Remember

[12]When I send Artemas or Tychicus to you,
make every effort to come to me at Nicopolis, because I have decided to stay there this winter.
[13]Do all you can to help Zenas the lawyer and

FOLLOWING GOD

The Fun Factor

Tom Harrington didn't think Christianity was much fun. There were so many rules and commandments. No getting drunk. No swearing. No messing around with girls. No making fun of other people. To be a Christian, he thought, meant wearing a stern face, singing slow hymns and eating tuna casseroles at potluck dinners.

His view of Christianity brightened when he saw in his youth minister's office a painting of a laughing Jesus.

Tom never imagined Jesus laughing before. He had always thought of Jesus as quiet and somber—someone who never smiled and spoke only in wise-sounding tones. Could Jesus really be fun?

This image of Jesus laughing made Tom look again at the stories of Jesus in the Gospels. He saw hints of Jesus' humor and began to see in the stories the Jesus of the painting. He started going to youth group, where he met Christians who had fun. They had joy, too, even when life wasn't great.

As Tom grew in faith, his own view of fun changed. Instead of calling friends to go get drunk, he called a Christian friend. Sometimes they just talked and laughed. Other times they watched comedies. Whatever they did, they enjoyed it, without hurting themselves.

Like Tom, the early Christians also had trouble knowing how Christians should live. **Titus 2:11—3:7** describes the joy of living a Christian life that is freeing and hopeful, not dull and rigid.

- How does the picture of a laughing Jesus match the good news of God's gift that is described in this passage?
- How could you implement these guidelines in your life and enjoy following them at the same time? What in the passage gives reason to celebrate following God?

CONSIDER . . .

- looking around your church for positive, fun, or joyful images of faith in paintings, pictures, banners, and books. Think about how these images of joy compare to the world's view of fun.
- meeting with your Christian friends and thinking of ideas for joyful ways to follow Christ.

FOR MORE, SEE . . .

- Isaiah 6:1–8
- Ephesians 4:31–32
- Philippians 4:4–9

Apollos on their journey so that they have everything they need. 14Our people must learn to use
their lives for doing good deeds to provide what
is necessary so that their lives will not be useless.
15All who are with me greet you. Greet those
who love us in the faith.
Grace be with you all.

SIDELIGHT: The reason Paul says he plans to spend the winter in Nicopolis (Titus 3:12) was that ships stopped sailing during the stormy winter months. The practice would have made it hard to get to Grandma's for Christmas!

PHILEMON

Why Read This Book:

- Learn how to treat fellow Christians (Philemon 4–7).
- Discover how to see others as friends in Christ (Philemon 8–21).

Behind the Scenes:

Onesimus, a slave, deserved to die. He had stolen from his master, then run away. Under Roman law, a runaway slave had no rights. Disobedience meant possible beatings, tortuous brandings on the face and even crucifixion.

But something had happened since Onesimus had left his master. He had become a Christian through Paul's influence. And making the matter even more complicated, his master Philemon was also a Christian. Onesimus knew he should return to his master, but he also knew he could die if he went back.

So Paul wrote this letter to persuade Philemon to forgive Onesimus and welcome him back as a Christian friend. Instead of telling Philemon to punish Onesimus, Paul asked that the wrongdoing be charged to Paul.

Though we no longer live with slavery, we, like Philemon, may be tempted to look down on people because of the color of their skin, the amount of money they have, or what they wear. And we may treat them as second-class citizens and think we are first class. Philemon challenges all of us to rethink those prejudices.

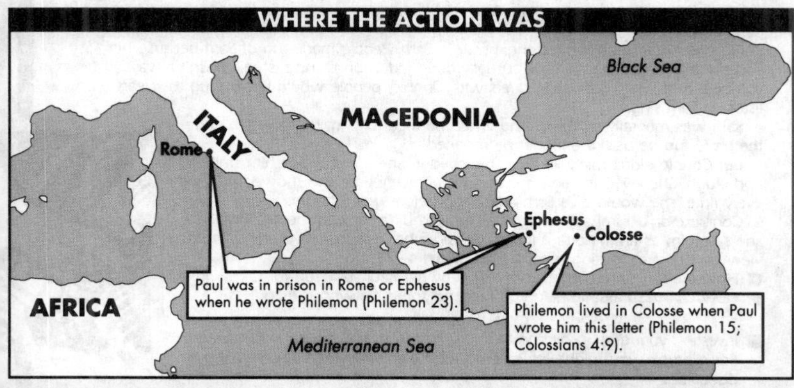

WHERE THE ACTION WAS
Black Sea
MACEDONIA
ITALY
Rome
Ephesus
Colosse
AFRICA
Mediterranean Sea
Paul was in prison in Rome or Ephesus when he wrote Philemon (Philemon 23).
Philemon lived in Colosse when Paul wrote him this letter (Philemon 15; Colossians 4:9).
WHEN THE ACTION WAS
Jesus was born
The church began soon after Jesus went to heaven
Paul began his missionary work
Fire destroyed Rome
BC/AD
25AD
50AD
75AD
100AD
Jesus began his ministry
Paul became a Christian
Paul wrote Philemon
Romans destroyed the Temple in Jerusalem

1 From Paul, a prisoner of Christ Jesus, and from Timothy, our brother.

To Philemon, our dear friend and worker with us; 2 to Apphia, our sister; to Archippus, a worker with us; and to the church that meets in your home:

3 Grace and peace to you from God our Father and the Lord Jesus Christ.

Philemon's Love and Faith

4 I always thank my God when I mention you in my prayers, 5 because I hear about the love you have for all God's holy people and the faith you have in the Lord Jesus. 6 I pray that the faith you share may make you understand every blessing we have in Christ. 7 I have great joy and comfort, my brother, because the love you have shown to God's people has refreshed them.

Accept Onesimus as a Brother

8 So, in Christ, I could be bold and order you to do what is right. 9 But because I love you, I am pleading with you instead. I, Paul, an old man now and also a prisoner for Christ Jesus, 10 am pleading with you for my child Onesimus, who became my child while I was in prison. 11 In the past he was useless to you, but now he has become useful for both you and me.

12 I am sending him back to you, and with him I am sending my own heart. 13 I wanted to keep him with me so that in your place he might help me while I am in prison for the Good News.[a] 14 But I did not want to do anything without asking you first so that any good you do for me will be because you want to do it, not because I forced you. 15 Maybe Onesimus was separated from you for a short time so you could have him back forever— 16 no longer as a slave, but better than a slave, as a loved brother. I love him very much, but you will love him even more, both as a person and as a believer in the Lord.

17 So if you consider me your partner, welcome

SIDELIGHT: Slavery was common in the Roman Empire in Paul's day. According to some estimates, there were about sixty million slaves in the Empire—up to half the total population.

FRIENDS

A Friend in Everyone

Everyone liked Connie Klein. But nobody liked Sam Bush—except Connie.

After school, Connie would visit Sam. They would go biking, go for long walks in the park, or listen to music.

No one understood what Connie saw in Sam. People made fun of Sam because his socks didn't match. His shirt was usually buttoned wrong, and his hair wasn't always combed. And when Sam sang duets with Connie, people would rather plug their ears than listen to Sam sing.

Sam was mentally disabled. And when he tried to sing, he moaned. And the more fun he had, the louder he moaned.

But Connie didn't mind. In fact, she loved it. She loved to see him smile and laugh. She loved to see his eyes light up every time she showed up. And every time, she would give Sam a big hug before going home.

Connie didn't dismiss Sam because he was different from herself. Instead she saw him as an important friend. Consider her reasons as you read Paul's view on Christian relationships in **Philemon 4–21**.

- How are Onesimus and Sam alike? Why did Paul stand up for Onesimus?
- How can this passage help you befriend someone who is friendless?

C O N S I D E R . . .

- investing your time in getting to know kids in special education programs. For example, you might volunteer to tutor elementary-age kids with learning disabilities.
- asking someone you don't like very well to join you for popcorn. Get to know the person by asking a lot of questions.

F O R M O R E , S E E . . .

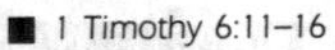

- 1 Samuel 20:1–42
- Matthew 25:34–46
- 1 Timothy 6:11–16

Onesimus as you would welcome me. 18If he has
done anything wrong to you or if he owes you
anything, charge that to me. 19I, Paul, am writing
this with my own hand. I will pay it back, and I
will say nothing about what you owe me for your
own life. 20So, my brother, I ask that you do this
for me in the Lord: Refresh my heart in Christ. 21I
write this letter, knowing that you will do what
I ask you and even more.
22One more thing—prepare a room for me in
which to stay, because I hope God will answer
your prayers and I will be able to come to you.

Final Greetings

23Epaphras, a prisoner with me for Christ Jesus,
sends greetings to you. 24And also Mark, Aristarchus, Demas, and Luke, workers together with
me, send greetings.
25The grace of our Lord Jesus Christ be with
your spirit.

HEBREWS

Why Read This Book:

- Discover how Jesus Christ fulfilled God's promises (Hebrews 1—7).
- Learn about the sacrifice Jesus made for us (Hebrews 8—10).
- Be challenged to stay strong in your faith (Hebrews 11—13).

Behind the Scenes:

Imagine a courtroom scene. The jury has heard persuasive testimony from many different people. Now the jury is about to go behind closed doors to come to a verdict about whether Christianity does hold the truth. But first the lawyers will present their closing arguments.

The book of Hebrews is like a closing argument in defense of Christianity. Using careful logic and referring often to testimony, the writer shows that Jesus Christ is the Son of God and worthy of our faith. The book compares and contrasts Jesus with all of Old Testament history and argues that Jesus is the climax of everything in the past.

So, the author concludes, "Let us look only to Jesus, the One who began our faith and who makes it perfect. . . . Think about Jesus' example. . . . So do not get tired and stop trying" (Hebrews 12:2–3).

We don't know how the original readers responded to the eloquent argument in Hebrews. But we do know that the book has become a treasured source of encouragement and hope for Christians through the centuries. Just as this letter encouraged its first readers to hold strong to their faith, it can do the same for us today.

WHEN THE ACTION WAS

Jesus was born
The church began soon after Jesus went to heaven
Paul began his missionary work
Fire destroyed Rome

BC/AD — 25AD — 50AD — 75AD — 100AD

Jesus began his ministry
Paul became a Christian
Hebrews was written
Romans destroyed the Temple in Jerusalem

God Spoke Through His Son

1 In the past God spoke to our ancestors
through the prophets[d] many times and in
many different ways. 2But now in these last days
God has spoken to us through his Son. God has
chosen his Son to own all things, and through him
he made the world. 3The Son reflects the glory of
God and shows exactly what God is like. He holds
everything together with his powerful word.
When the Son made people clean from their sins,
he sat down at the right side of God, the Great
One in heaven. 4The Son became much greater
than the angels, and God gave him a name that
is much greater than theirs.

> **SIDELIGHT:** No one really knows who wrote Hebrews. Suggestions have included Paul, Apollos, Luke, Barnabas, Clement of Rome, Silas, Philip, and Priscilla. In the third century, Origen probably had the right idea when he wrote, "Who wrote the epistle God alone knows certainly."

5This is because God never said to any of the
angels,

"You are my Son.
Today I have become your Father." *Psalm 2:7*

Nor did God say of any angel,

"I will be his Father,
and he will be my Son." *2 Samuel 7:14*

6And when God brings his firstborn Son into the
world, he says,

"Let all God's angels worship him."[n] *Psalm 97:7*

7This is what God said about the angels:

"God makes his angels become like winds.
He makes his servants become like flames
of fire." *Psalm 104:4*

8But God said this about his Son:

"God, your throne will last forever and ever.
You will rule your kingdom with fairness.
9You love right and hate evil,
so God has chosen you from among your
friends;
he has set you apart with much joy."
Psalm 45:6-7

10God also says,

"Lord, in the beginning you made the earth,
and your hands made the skies.
11They will be destroyed, but you will remain.
They will all wear out like clothes.
12You will fold them like a coat.
And, like clothes, you will change them.
But you never change,
and your life will never end." *Psalm 102:25-27*

13And God never said this to an angel:

"Sit by me at my right side
until I put your enemies under your
control."[n] *Psalm 110:1*

14All the angels are spirits who serve God and
are sent to help those who will receive salvation.

Our Salvation Is Great

2 So we must be more careful to follow what
we were taught. Then we will not stray
away from the truth. 2The teaching God spoke
through angels was shown to be true, and anyone
who did not follow it or obey it received the punishment that was earned. 3So surely we also will
be punished if we ignore this great salvation. The
Lord himself first told about this salvation, and it
was proven true to us by those who heard him.
4God also proved it by using wonders, great signs,
many kinds of miracles,[d] and by giving people
gifts through the Holy Spirit,[d] just as he wanted.

Christ Became like Humans

5God did not choose angels to be the rulers of
the new world that was coming, which is what
we have been talking about. 6It is written in the
Scriptures,[d]

"Why are people important to you?
Why do you take care of human beings?
7You made them a little lower than the angels
and crowned them with glory and honor.
8 You put all things under their control."
Psalm 8:4-6

When God put everything under their control,
there was nothing left that they did not rule. Still,
we do not yet see them ruling over everything.
9But we see Jesus, who for a short time was made
lower than the angels. And now he is wearing a
crown of glory and honor because he suffered and
died. And by God's grace, he died for everyone.

10God is the One who made all things, and all
things are for his glory. He wanted to have many
children share his glory, so he made the One who
leads people to salvation perfect through suffering.

11Jesus, who makes people holy, and those who
are made holy are from the same family. So he is
not ashamed to call them his brothers and sisters.[n] 12He says,

"Then, I will tell my fellow Israelites about
you;

"Let . . . him." These words are found in Deuteronomy 32:43 in the Septuagint, the Greek version of the Old Testament, and in a Hebrew copy among the Dead Sea Scrolls.
until . . . control Literally, "until I make your enemies a footstool for your feet."
brothers and sisters Although the Greek text says "brothers" here and throughout this book, the writer's words were meant for the entire church, including men and women.

I will praise you in the public meeting."
Psalm 22:22

13He also says,
"I will trust in God." *Isaiah 8:17*
And he also says,
"I am here, and with me are the children
God has given me." *Isaiah 8:18*

14Since these children are people with physical
bodies, Jesus himself became like them. He did
this so that, by dying, he could destroy the one
who has the power of death — the devil — 15and
free those who were like slaves all their lives because of their fear of death. 16Clearly, it is not
angels that Jesus helps, but the people who are
from Abraham.[n] 17For this reason Jesus had
to be made like his brothers in every way so he
could be their merciful and faithful high priest in
service to God. Then Jesus could bring forgiveness for their sins. 18And now he can help those
who are tempted, because he himself suffered
and was tempted.

Jesus Is Greater than Moses

3 So all of you holy brothers and sisters, who
were called by God, think about Jesus, who
was sent to us and is the high priest of our faith.
2Jesus was faithful to God as Moses was in God's
family. 3Jesus has more honor than Moses, just as
the builder of a house has more honor than the
house itself. 4Every house is built by someone, but
the builder of everything is God himself. 5Moses
was faithful in God's family as a servant, and he
told what God would say in the future. 6But
Christ is faithful as a Son over God's house. And
we are God's house if we keep on being very sure
about our great hope.

We Must Continue to Follow God

7So it is as the Holy Spirit[d] says:
"Today listen to what he says.
8Do not be stubborn as in the past
when you turned against God,
when you tested God in the desert.
9There your ancestors tried me and tested me
and saw the things I did for forty years.
10I was angry with them.
I said, 'They are not loyal to me
and have not understood my ways.'
11I was angry and made a promise,

Abraham Most respected ancestor of the Jews. Every Jew hoped to see Abraham.

SHARING FAITH

Can You Tell the Difference?

When she graduated from college, Bev Johnson became a short-term missionary at a school in Japan. Each day she led a Bible study and taught English to the Japanese.

Each day an elderly woman came to the Bible study. She sat quietly in the back of the room and rushed out when it ended. And each day Bev grew more curious about the silent woman.

One day after the Bible study, Bev walked quickly to the woman and began a conversation. The woman spoke excellent English. She told Bev she had heard of Jesus since she was a young girl. The woman owned a Bible and knew much of it by heart.

"Are you a Christian?" Bev asked.

"No, no I'm not," the woman said, "but I've seen Christians, and I'm watching to see if Jesus makes any difference in their lives."

From that incident, Bev learned how people need to see Jesus in Christians. Read how Jesus can shine through us in **Hebrews 2:9–18**.

- How does the older woman's statement to Bev relate to this passage?
- Why do you think God, in Jesus, became a person for us to know?

CONSIDER . . .

- listing all the ways Jesus showed what God is like, such as loving all people, and so on. Choose one of those ways to show how you follow Christ.
- letting at least one other person know this week how Christ has made a difference in your life.

FOR MORE, SEE . . .

- Isaiah 57:14–21
- Matthew 20:29–34
- John 11:28–43

'They will never enter my rest.' "[n]

Psalm 95:7-11

12So brothers and sisters, be careful that none of you has an evil, unbelieving heart that will turn you away from the living God. 13But encourage each other every day while it is "today."[n] Help each other so none of you will become hardened because sin has tricked you. 14We all share in Christ if we keep till the end the sure faith we had in the beginning. 15This is what the Scripture[d] says:

"Today listen to what he says.
Do not be stubborn as in the past
when you turned against God." *Psalm 95:7-8*

16Who heard God's voice and was against him? It was all those people Moses led out of Egypt. 17And with whom was God angry for forty years? He was angry with those who sinned, who died in the desert. 18And to whom was God talking when he promised that they would never enter his rest? He was talking to those who did not obey him. 19So we see they were not allowed to enter and have God's rest, because they did not believe.

> **SIDELIGHT:** If Hebrews had been submitted as a term paper, it probably would have gotten a good grade for research and documentation. The book quotes from the Old Testament more than eighty times, including Psalm 95:7-11 in Hebrews 3:7-11.

4 Now, since God has left us the promise that we may enter his rest, let us be very careful so none of you will fail to enter. 2The Good News[d] was preached to us just as it was to them. But the teaching they heard did not help them, because they heard it but did not accept it with faith. 3We who have believed are able to enter and have God's rest. As God has said,

"I was angry and made a promise,
'They will never enter my rest.' " *Psalm 95:11*

But God's work was finished from the time he made the world. 4In the Scriptures[d] he talked about the seventh day of the week: "And on the seventh day God rested from all his works."[n] 5And again in the Scripture God said, "They will never enter my rest."

6It is still true that some people will enter God's rest, but those who first heard the way to be saved did not enter, because they did not obey. 7So God planned another day, called "today." He spoke about that day through David a long time later in the same Scripture used before:

"Today listen to what he says.
Do not be stubborn." *Psalm 95:7-8*

8We know that Joshua[n] did not lead the people into that rest, because God spoke later about another day. 9This shows that the rest[n] for God's people is still coming. 10Anyone who enters God's rest will rest from his work as God did. 11Let us try as hard as we can to enter God's rest so that no one will fail by following the example of those who refused to obey.

12God's word is alive and working and is sharper than a double-edged sword. It cuts all the way into us, where the soul and the spirit are joined, to the center of our joints and bones. And it judges the thoughts and feelings in our hearts. 13Nothing in all the world can be hidden from God. Everything is clear and lies open before him, and to him we must explain the way we have lived.

Jesus Is Our High Priest

14Since we have a great high priest, Jesus the Son of God, who has gone into heaven, let us hold on to the faith we have. 15For our high priest is able to understand our weaknesses. When he lived on earth, he was tempted in every way that we are, but he did not sin. 16Let us, then, feel very sure that we can come before God's throne where there is grace. There we can receive mercy and grace to help us when we need it.

5 Every high priest is chosen from among other people. He is given the work of going before God for them to offer gifts and sacrifices for sins. 2Since he himself is weak, he is able to be gentle with those who do not understand and who are doing wrong things. 3Because he is weak, the high priest must offer sacrifices for his own sins and also for the sins of the people.

4To be a high priest is an honor, but no one chooses himself for this work. He must be called by God as Aaron[n] was. 5So also Christ did not choose himself to have the honor of being a high priest, but God chose him. God said to him,

"You are my Son.
Today I have become your Father." *Psalm 2:7*

6And in another Scripture[d] God says,

"You are a priest forever,

rest A place of rest God promised to give his people.
"today" This word is taken from verse 7. It means that it is important to do these things now.
"And . . . works." Quotation from Genesis 2:2.
Joshua After Moses died, Joshua became leader of the Jewish people and led them into the land that God promised to give them.
rest Literally, "sabbath rest," meaning a sharing in the rest that God began after he created the world.
Aaron Aaron was Moses' brother and the first Jewish high priest.

a priest like Melchizedek."[n] Psalm 110:4
7While Jesus lived on earth, he prayed to God
and asked God for help. He prayed with loud cries
and tears to the One who could save him from
death, and his prayer was heard because he
trusted God. 8Even though Jesus was the Son of
God, he learned obedience by what he suffered.
9And because his obedience was perfect, he was
able to give eternal salvation to all who obey him.
10In this way God made Jesus a high priest, a
priest like Melchizedek.

Warning Against Falling Away

11We have much to say about this, but it is hard
to explain because you are so slow to understand.
12By now you should be teachers, but you need
someone to teach you again the first lessons of
God's message. You still need the teaching that is
like milk. You are not ready for solid food. 13Any-
one who lives on milk is still a baby and knows
nothing about right teaching. 14But solid food is
for those who are grown up. They have practiced
in order to know the difference between good and
evil.

6 So let us go on to grown-up teaching. Let us
not go back over the beginning lessons we
learned about Christ. We should not again start
teaching about faith in God and about turning
away from those acts that lead to death. 2We
should not return to the teaching about bap-

Melchizedek A priest and king who lived in the time of Abraham. (Read Genesis 14:17-24.)

FOLLOWING GOD

When the Going Gets Tough . . .

Isabella Baumfree was an African-American slave born to a Dutch owner in Ulster County, New York, about 1797. She was separated from her family and sold twice before she was twelve. Slave life was never easy. Even after she was set free in 1827, she barely survived as a domestic helper in New York City.

After the Civil War began, Isabella left New York to "travel up an' down the land showin' the people their sins an' bein' a sign unto them." She even changed her name to Sojourner Truth.

Sojourner Truth became famous for her unique style of preaching. Although she couldn't read or write, she preached a message of freedom for slaves, women, and the poor. She spoke in a heavy Dutch accent, knew the Bible well, and drew stares by wrapping a turban around her head.

Because blacks—especially black women—were routinely oppressed, Sojourner Truth found the going difficult. But she kept at it, hardened by her life of slavery and struggle. Her fame spread; she even met with President Lincoln in 1864.

Fame doesn't always equal popularity, as Sojourner Truth found out. She often preached and lectured before hostile audiences. Many times she was told her mission was hopeless. "I don't care any more for your talk than I do for the bite of a flea," someone told her.

"Perhaps not," she replied, "but the Lord willing, I'll keep you scratchin'."

Sojourner Truth knew following God requires commitment and endurance. So did the writer of Hebrews. And, in **Hebrews 4:1–13**, the writer promises that endurance and commitment will not go unrewarded.

- How was Sojourner Truth's persistence in her mission like the challenge of the passage to stay obedient to God? How did she embody the theme of verses 12–13?
- What does the passage say about those who truly follow God versus those who just say they do?

CONSIDER. . .

- taking an unpopular stand on an issue because you believe it's what God wants you to do.
- listing things you would honestly die for. Decide how to follow those priorities better this week.

FOR MORE, SEE. . .

- Deuteronomy 33:26–29
- Luke 10:25–37
- Acts 7:51–60

tisms,[n] about laying on of hands,[n] about the raising of the dead and eternal judgment. 3And we
will go on to grown-up teaching if God allows.
4Some people cannot be brought back again to
a changed life. They were once in God's light, and
enjoyed heaven's gift, and shared in the Holy
Spirit.[d] 5They found out how good God's word is,
and they received the powers of his new world.
6But they fell away from Christ. It is impossible to
bring them back to a changed life again, because
they are nailing the Son of God to a cross again
and are shaming him in front of others.

7Some people are like land that gets plenty of
rain. The land produces a good crop for those who
work it, and it receives God's blessings. 8Other
people are like land that grows thorns and weeds
and is worthless. It is in danger of being cursed by
God and will be destroyed by fire.
9Dear friends, we are saying this to you, but we
really expect better things from you that will lead
to your salvation. 10God is fair; he will not forget
the work you did and the love you showed for
him by helping his people. And he will remember
that you are still helping them. 11We want each

baptisms The word here may refer to Christian baptism, or it may refer to the Jewish ceremonial washings.
laying on of hands The laying on of hands had many purposes, including the giving of a blessing, power, or authority.

GOD'S LOVE

Storm Trackers

When people on the Atlantic coast hear hurricane warnings, most board up their windows and evacuate the coastline. They know hurricanes can whip across the ocean with winds of more than 150 miles per hour and raise the ocean level by twenty feet.

But while most people are getting away from a hurricane, storm trackers aboard their WC-130 aircraft are headed straight into the storm. It takes ten to forty-five seconds to fly through the swirling clouds around the eye of the storm. Once in the storm's eye, the crew flies from one end of the eye to the other, tracking the hurricane's path and measuring its conditions.

These missions are extremely dangerous. The plane can be struck by lightning, or its jet engines sometimes stall because of the sheets of water kicked up by the storm. At times the winds are so strong that one pilot cannot steer the plane alone.

"Everything is whipping around," says storm tracker Scott Maddox, describing a typical mission. "You have one pilot with both hands on the throttle and the other one on the automatic pilot, using it to bring the plane straight and level in air that is battering it in all directions."

Why do they go on these dangerous missions? Because without their efforts, more people would lose their lives in hurricanes. While satellite pictures warn when a hurricane is approaching land, they cannot measure wind speeds, barometric pressure, temperatures, or sea swells in the middle of the storm. That information is vital for forecasting when, where, and with how much force a hurricane will hit land.

Because they risk their lives on dangerous missions, storm trackers gain information that saves people's lives. Because of his love, God sent his Son Jesus on an even more deadly mission: to come to earth to save us and pay for our sins. Read about this unbelievable love in **Hebrews 4:14—5:10**.

- How do the storm trackers illustrate the kind of self-sacrificing love that is described in this passage? What makes God's love even more amazing?
- How does knowing about God's love and Christ's sacrifice for you affect the way you live?

CONSIDER...

- looking in the newspaper this week for stories of people who take great risks to save the lives of others. Thank God for these human examples of the kind of love God has for people.
- writing "Thanks for Your Love, God" at the top of a sheet of paper. Then fill the paper with words that show how you have experienced God's love. Keep the sheet in your Bible as a reminder, and add to it when you think of something new.

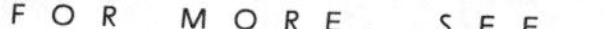

FOR MORE, SEE...

- Daniel 9:1–9
- Matthew 7:7–11
- Romans 3:21–26

of you to go on with the same hard work all your
lives so you will surely get what you hope for.
12We do not want you to become lazy. Be like
those who through faith and patience will receive
what God has promised.

> **SIDELIGHT:** Many scholars believe Hebrews may have originally been a sermon, partly because the author mentions speaking in several places (for example, Hebrews 6:9). If it was originally a sermon, it would have taken about fifty minutes to read aloud—not too long for an early Christian worship service. Their services often included "breaking bread" (communion), teaching, preaching, singing, praying, prophesying, and reading letters. Hope they had padded pews!

13God made a promise to Abraham. And as
there is no one greater than God, he used himself
when he swore to Abraham, 14saying, "I will
surely bless you and give you many descendants."[n] 15Abraham waited patiently for this to
happen, and he received what God promised.
16People always use the name of someone
greater than themselves when they swear. The
oath proves that what they say is true, and this
ends all arguing. 17God wanted to prove that his
promise was true to those who would get what he
promised. And he wanted them to understand
clearly that his purposes never change, so he
made an oath. 18These two things cannot change:
God cannot lie when he makes a promise, and he
cannot lie when he makes an oath. These things
encourage us who came to God for safety. They
give us strength to hold on to the hope we have
been given. 19We have this hope as an anchor for
the soul, sure and strong. It enters behind the curtain in the Most Holy Place in heaven, 20where
Jesus has gone ahead of us and for us. He has
become the high priest forever, a priest like Melchizedek.[n]

The Priest Melchizedek

7 Melchizedek[n] was the king of Salem and a
priest for God Most High. He met Abraham
when Abraham was coming back after defeating
the kings. When they met, Melchizedek blessed
Abraham, 2and Abraham gave him a tenth of everything he had brought back from the battle.
First, Melchizedek's name means "king of goodness," and he is king of Salem, which means "king
of peace." 3No one knows who Melchizedek's father or mother was,[n] where he came from, when
he was born, or when he died. Melchizedek is
like the Son of God; he continues being a priest
forever.
4You can see how great Melchizedek was.
Abraham, the great father, gave him a tenth of
everything that he won in battle. 5Now the law
says that those in the tribe[d] of Levi who become
priests must collect a tenth from the people—
their own people—even though the priests and
the people are from the family of Abraham. 6Mel-
chizedek was not from the tribe of Levi, but he
collected a tenth from Abraham. And he blessed
Abraham, the man who had God's promises.
7Now everyone knows that the more important
person blesses the less important person. 8Priests
receive a tenth, even though they are only men
who live and then die. But Melchizedek, who received a tenth from Abraham, continues living, as
the Scripture[d] says. 9We might even say that Levi,
who receives a tenth, also paid it when Abraham
paid Melchizedek a tenth. 10Levi was not yet
born, but he was in the body of his ancestor when
Melchizedek met Abraham.

> **SIDELIGHT:** If you think Melchizedek (Hebrews 7:1) is a hard name to say, try the Bible's longest name: Maher-Shalal-Hash-Baz, the name of Isaiah's son (Isaiah 8:1).

11The people were given the law[n] based on a
system of priests from the tribe of Levi, but they
could not be made perfect through that system.
So there was a need for another priest to come,
a priest like Melchizedek, not Aaron. 12And when
a different kind of priest comes, the law must be
changed, too. 13We are saying these things about
Christ, who belonged to a different tribe. No one
from that tribe ever served as a priest at the altar.
14It is clear that our Lord came from the tribe of
Judah, and Moses said nothing about priests belonging to that tribe.

Jesus Is like Melchizedek

15And this becomes even more clear when we
see that another priest comes who is like Melchiz
edek.[n] 16He was not made a priest by human
rules and laws but through the power of his life
which continues forever. 17It is said about him

"I . . . descendants." Quotation from Genesis 22:17.
Melchizedek A priest and king who lived in the time of Abraham. (Read Genesis 14:17-24.)
No . . . was Literally, "Melchizedek was without father, without mother, without genealogy."
The . . . law This refers to the people of Israel who were given the law of Moses.

"You are a priest forever,
a priest like Melchizedek." *Psalm 110:4*
18The old rule is now set aside, because it was
weak and useless. 19The law of Moses could not
make anything perfect. But now a better hope has
been given to us, and with this hope we can come
near to God. 20It is important that God did this
with an oath. Others became priests without an
oath, 21but Christ became a priest with God's
oath. God said:
"The Lord has made a promise
and will not change his mind.
'You are a priest forever.' " *Psalm 110:4*
22This means that Jesus is the guarantee of a better agreement[n] from God to his people.
23When one of the other priests died, he could
not continue being a priest. So there were many
priests. 24But because Jesus lives forever, he will
never stop serving as priest. 25So he is able always
to save those who come to God through him because he always lives, asking God to help them.
26Jesus is the kind of high priest we need. He
is holy, sinless, pure, not influenced by sinners,
and he is raised above the heavens. 27He is not
like the other priests who had to offer sacrifices
every day, first for their own sins, and then for the
sins of the people. Christ offered his sacrifice only
once and for all time when he offered himself.
28The law chooses high priests who are people
with weaknesses, but the word of God's oath
came later than the law. It made God's Son to be
the high priest, and that Son has been made perfect forever.

Jesus Is Our High Priest

8 Here is the point of what we are saying: We
have a high priest who sits on the right side
of God's throne in heaven. 2Our high priest serves
in the Most Holy Place, the true place of worship
that was made by God, not by humans.
3Every high priest has the work of offering gifts
and sacrifices to God. So our high priest must also
offer something to God. 4If our high priest were
now living on earth, he would not be a priest,
because there are already priests here who follow
the law by offering gifts to God. 5The work they
do as priests is only a copy and a shadow of what
is in heaven. This is why God warned Moses
when he was ready to build the Holy Tent:[d] "Be
very careful to make everything by the plan I
showed you on the mountain."[n] 6But the priestly
work that has been given to Jesus is much greater
than the work that was given to the other priests.
In the same way, the new agreement that Jesus
brought from God to his people is much greater
than the old one. And the new agreement is based
on promises of better things.
7If there had been nothing wrong with the first
agreement,[n] there would have been no need for
a second agreement. 8But God found something
wrong with his people. He says:
"Look, the time is coming, says the Lord,
when I will make a new agreement
with the people of Israel
and the people of Judah.
9It will not be like the agreement
I made with their ancestors
when I took them by the hand
to bring them out of Egypt.
But they broke that agreement,
and I turned away from them, says the
Lord.
10This is the agreement I will make
with the people of Israel at that time, says
the Lord.
I will put my teachings in their minds
and write them on their hearts.
I will be their God,
and they will be my people.
11People will no longer have to teach their
neighbors and relatives
to know the Lord,
because all people will know me,
from the least to the most important.
12I will forgive them for the wicked things they
did,
and I will not remember their sins
anymore." *Jeremiah 31:31-34*
13God called this a new agreement, so he has
made the first agreement old. And anything that
is old and worn out is ready to disappear.

The Old Agreement

9 The first agreement[n] had rules for worship
and a man-made place for worship. 2The
Holy Tent[d] was set up for this. The first area in the
Tent was called the Holy Place. In it were the
lamp and the table with the bread that was made
holy for God. 3Behind the second curtain was a
room called the Most Holy Place. 4In it was a
golden altar for burning incense[d] and the Ark[d]
covered with gold that held the old agreement.
Inside this Ark was a golden jar of manna,[d]
Aaron's rod that once grew leaves, and the stone
tablets of the old agreement. 5Above the Ark were
the creatures that showed God's glory, whose
wings reached over the lid. But we cannot tell
everything about these things now.

greement God gives a contract or agreement to his people. For the Jews, this agreement was the law of Moses. But now God has given a better agreement to his people through Christ.
Be . . . mountain." Quotation from Exodus 25:40.
rst agreement The contract God gave the Jewish people when he gave them the law of Moses.

6When everything in the Tent was made ready
in this way, the priests went into the first room
every day to worship. 7But only the high priest
could go into the second room, and he did that
only once a year. He could never enter the inner
room without taking blood with him, which he
offered to God for himself and for sins the people
did without knowing they did them. 8The Holy
Spirit[d] uses this to show that the way into the
Most Holy Place was not open while the system
of the old Holy Tent was still being used. 9This is
an example for the present time. It shows that the
gifts and sacrifices offered cannot make the conscience of the worshiper perfect. 10These gifts and
sacrifices were only about food and drink and special washings. They were rules for the body, to be
followed until the time of God's new way.

The New Agreement

11But when Christ came as the high priest of
the good things we now have, he entered the
greater and more perfect tent. It is not made by
humans and does not belong to this world.
12Christ entered the Most Holy Place only once—
and for all time. He did not take with him the
blood of goats and calves. His sacrifice was his
own blood, and by it he set us free from sin forever. 13The blood of goats and bulls and the ashes
of a cow are sprinkled on the people who are unclean,[d] and this makes their bodies clean again.
14How much more is done by the blood of Christ.
He offered himself through the eternal Spirit[n] as
a perfect sacrifice to God. His blood will make our
consciences pure from useless acts so we may
serve the living God.
15For this reason Christ brings a new agreement from God to his people. Those who are
called by God can now receive the blessings he
has promised, blessings that will last forever. They
can have those things because Christ died so that

Spirit This refers to the Holy Spirit, to Christ's own spirit, or to the spiritual and eternal nature of his sacrifice.

SIN

Unexpected Forgiveness

Dawn Hammond and Craig Meadows had been dating for about a year. Both were sixteen. When Dawn stopped coming to youth group meetings, Donna Richards, her youth leader, dropped by after school to see if she was okay.

She obviously wasn't.

Dawn confessed her relationship with Craig had gotten very physical. "I think I'm pregnant," she said.

She and Craig had had sex on a date four weeks earlier. "It just happened. We didn't plan it," she kept saying.

"Have you told your parents?" Donna asked.

"No!" she screamed. "They would absolutely die if they knew!"

"That's not the main issue," Donna said. "They need to know, and you need their help."

Donna promised to stay with Dawn until her parents came home from work. When Dawn told them the news, they were upset at first, but they assured Dawn they loved her. What she had done was wrong, but it didn't change the way they felt about her. She was their daughter.

Dawn learned a hard lesson about sex before marriage. She also learned a lot about the kind of forgiveness and acceptance written about in **Hebrews 9:11–28**.

- How was forgiveness by Dawn's parents like and unlike the forgiveness described in this passage? How did the price Dawn's parents paid in the story differ from the price Christ paid in the passage?
- How are our sins forgiven, according to the passage?

CONSIDER . . .

- talking with a trusted adult about a sin you're struggling with.
- defining the word "sin," using this passage and the ones listed in "For More, See . . ." for guidance. Find out whether your friends agree with your definition. Check it out with your youth leader too.

FOR MORE, SEE . . .

- Genesis 4:1–12
- Romans 3:21–26
- Romans 6:12–14

the people who lived under the first agreement
could be set free from sin.
16When there is a will,[n] it must be proven that
the one who wrote that will is dead. 17A will
means nothing while the person is alive; it can be
used only after the person dies. 18This is why even
the first agreement could not begin without blood
to show death. 19First, Moses told all the people
every command in the law. Next he took the
blood of calves and mixed it with water. Then he
used red wool and a branch of the hyssop plant
to sprinkle it on the book of the law and on all the
people. 20He said, "This is the blood that begins
the Agreement that God commanded you to
obey."[n] 21In the same way, Moses sprinkled the
blood on the Holy Tent[d] and over all the things
used in worship. 22The law says that almost everything must be made clean by blood, and sins cannot be forgiven without blood to show death.

Christ's Death Takes Away Sins

23So the copies of the real things in heaven had
to be made clean[d] by animal sacrifices. But the
real things in heaven need much better sacrifices.
24Christ did not go into the Most Holy Place made
by humans, which is only a copy of the real one.
He went into heaven itself and is there now before God to help us. 25The high priest enters the
Most Holy Place once every year with blood that
is not his own. But Christ did not offer himself
many times. 26Then he would have had to suffer
many times since the world was made. But Christ
came only once and for all time at just the right
time to take away all sin by sacrificing himself.
27Just as everyone must die once and be judged,
28so Christ was offered as a sacrifice one time to
take away the sins of many people. And he will
come a second time, not to offer himself for sin,
but to bring salvation to those who are waiting for
him.

10 The law is only an unclear picture of the
good things coming in the future; it is
not the real thing. The people under the law offer
the same sacrifices every year, but these sacrifices
can never make perfect those who come near to
worship God. 2If the law could make them perfect, the sacrifices would have already stopped.
The worshipers would be made clean, and they
would no longer have a sense of sin. 3But these
sacrifices remind them of their sins every year,
4because it is impossible for the blood of bulls and
goats to take away sins.
5So when Christ came into the world, he said:
"You do not want sacrifices and offerings,
but you have prepared a body for me.
6You do not ask for burnt offerings
and offerings to take away sins.
7Then I said, 'Look, I have come.
It is written about me in the book.
God, I have come to do what you want.' "

Psalm 40:6-8

8In this Scripture[d] he first said, "You do not want
sacrifices and offerings. You do not ask for burnt
offerings and offerings to take away sins." (These
are all sacrifices that the law commands.) 9Then
he said, "Look, I have come to do what you
want." God ends the first system of sacrifices
so he can set up the new system. 10And because
of this, we are made holy through the sacrifice
Christ made in his body once and for all time.
11Every day the priests stand and do their religious service, often offering the same sacrifices.
Those sacrifices can never take away sins. 12But
after Christ offered one sacrifice for sins, forever,
he sat down at the right side of God. 13And now
Christ waits there for his enemies to be put under
his power. 14With one sacrifice he made perfect
forever those who are being made holy.

> **SIDELIGHT:** *When Hebrews 10:1 talks about making "the same sacrifices every year," it refers to the annual Jewish holiday of Yom Kippur. On this day, the high priest would symbolically transfer the sins of Israel to a goat (known as a scapegoat). Then the goat would be carried away to the desert where it—along with the sins—would be lost and forgotten (see Leviticus 16:7-10, 20-22).*

15The Holy Spirit[d] also tells us about this. First
he says:
16"This is the agreement[n] I will make
with them at that time, says the Lord.
I will put my teachings in their hearts
and write them on their minds." *Jeremiah 31:33*
17Then he says:
"Their sins and the evil things they do—
I will not remember anymore." *Jeremiah 31:34*
18Now when these have been forgiven, there is no
more need for a sacrifice for sins.

Continue to Trust God

19So, brothers and sisters, we are completely
free to enter the Most Holy Place without fear

will A legal document that shows how a person's money and property are to be distributed at the time of death. This is the same word in Greek as "agreement" in verse 15.
"This . . . obey." Quotation from Exodus 24:8.
agreement God gives a contract or agreement to his people. For the Jews, this agreement was the law of Moses. But now God has given a better agreement to his people through Christ.

because of the blood of Jesus' death. 20We can
enter through a new and living way that Jesus
opened for us. It leads through the curtain—
Christ's body. 21And since we have a great priest
over God's house, 22let us come near to God with
a sincere heart and a sure faith, because we have
been made free from a guilty conscience, and our
bodies have been washed with pure water. 23Let
us hold firmly to the hope that we have confessed,
because we can trust God to do what he promised.
24Let us think about each other and help each
other to show love and do good deeds. 25You
should not stay away from the church meetings,
as some are doing, but you should meet together
and encourage each other. Do this even more as
you see the day[n] coming.
26If we decide to go on sinning after we have
learned the truth, there is no longer any sacrifice
for sins. 27There is nothing but fear in waiting for
the judgment and the terrible fire that will destroy
all those who live against God. 28Anyone who refused to obey the law of Moses was found guilty
from the proof given by two or three witnesses.
He was put to death without mercy. 29So what do
you think should be done to those who do not

day The day Christ will come to judge all people and take his people to live with him.

CHURCH

Family of Friends

Jeremy Carr had had a rough life. His parents were divorced, and he had bounced between one parent and the other. When he signed up for summer youth camp, everyone was surprised, since he had shown little interest in church before.

After they arrived at the camp, the campers were split into groups of ten, each including an adult counselor. The group would stay together for a week.

Jeremy started acting up immediately. His counselor and the other kids tried to include him, but he ignored their kind gestures. He acted rude, obnoxious and selfish.

Finally the camp director, Cheryl Bolte, met with him after supper. When she asked Jeremy what he didn't like about his group, he said, "All they do is sit around and talk about their problems. I'm bored."

Cheryl explained to Jeremy that they were trying to build relationships, and that he was choosing not to be a part. "You don't have to participate, but you must respect other people's feelings," she said.

Jeremy spent the next day listening. He watched the group care for each other. Before he knew it, he told the group about his family and how much he hated moving back and forth between parents.

The group listened. Then one of the guys spoke. "We will be family for you, if you'll let us," he offered Jeremy, and the others agreed.

Jeremy couldn't believe it at first. But through the week, the campers' concern and their openness to him convinced him.

On the last day of camp, Jeremy thanked the group. "I've never known what it meant to have a real family, until this week," he said. "I know things still won't be easy at home, but I know at least ten people who care."

Fortunately for Jeremy, he experienced the love of a group of committed Christians who wouldn't give up on him. In **Hebrews 10:19–39**, the writer talks about this kind of commitment to the family of God.

- While at camp, how well did Jeremy's group live up to this passage's message?
- According to this passage, why do we need the church?

C O N S I D E R . . .

- praying for someone at church whom you think is incredibly rude or obnoxious. Then pray for help in understanding that person.
- accepting the care and concern of others if they invite you to church youth group meetings or outings. You may find new friends there.

F O R M O R E , S E E . . .

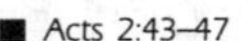

- Isaiah 65:1–2
- Matthew 16:13–20
- Acts 2:43–47

respect the Son of God, who look at the blood of
the agreement that made them holy as no different from others' blood, who insult the Spirit[d] of
God's grace? Surely they should have a much
worse punishment. 30We know that God said, "I
will punish those who do wrong; I will repay
them."[n] And he also said, "The Lord will judge
his people."[n] 31It is a terrible thing to fall into the
hands of the living God.
32Remember those days in the past when you
first learned the truth. You had a hard struggle
with many sufferings, but you continued strong.
33Sometimes you were hurt and attacked before
crowds of people, and sometimes you shared with
those who were being treated that way. 34You
helped the prisoners. You even had joy when all
that you owned was taken from you, because you
knew you had something better and more lasting.
35So do not lose the courage you had in the
past, which has a great reward. 36You must hold
on, so you can do what God wants and receive
what he has promised. 37For in a very short time,

"The One who is coming will come
and will not be delayed.
38The person who is right with me
will live by trusting in me.
But if he turns back with fear,
I will not be pleased with him." *Habakkuk 2:3-4*

39But we are not those who turn back and are
lost. We are people who have faith and are saved.

What Is Faith?

11 Faith means being sure of the things we
hope for and knowing that something is
real even if we do not see it. 2Faith is the reason
we remember great people who lived in the past.
3It is by faith we understand that the whole
world was made by God's command so what we

"I . . . them." Quotation from Deuteronomy 32:35.
"The Lord . . . people." Quotation from Deuteronomy 32:36; Psalm 135:14.

FAITH

A Voice in the Dark

A youth group was enjoying a week of climbing and cave exploration at Flat Rock, near Fredericksburg, Texas. David Yankton, an experienced wilderness guide, led the group. He'd brought along his six-year-old daughter, Kelly Jo, to hike with them.

On the second day, David led the group as it explored a nearby cave. He allowed just one flashlight. At the entrance there was plenty of light and the group moved along rapidly. As they sank deeper into the cave, however, the darkness thickened. Finally, the cave was so dark the hikers couldn't walk a step without clear directions from the person in front of them.

At one point in the darkness, Kelly Jo panicked and screamed out what the rest of the group felt: "Daddy, don't leave me!"

From the darkness came David's calming voice. "Kelly Jo, I'm right in front of you, leading the way." That was all she needed to hear. In fact, the whole group felt better after hearing David's voice.

The writer of Hebrews wanted Christians to understand how faith sometimes requires believing in things that can't be seen or heard. The writer gives examples in **Hebrews 11:1–16** of others who acted in faith even though they didn't know exactly where or how God was leading them.

- How were Kelly Jo and the group like some of the examples the writer mentions in this passage?
- When have you trusted in God even though you didn't know what was going to happen? How does that experience help you trust God now?

C O N S I D E R . . .

- trying something new in your faith, such as singing in the choir, or helping with mission or service projects.
- listing the ways you trust others, such as letting someone drive you somewhere or relying on others for food. Compare the list with the ways you trust God will take care of you.

F O R M O R E , S E E . . .

- Genesis 12:1–5
- Mark 4:35–41
- Romans 4:13–25

see was made by something that cannot be seen.

4It was by faith that Abel offered God a better sacrifice than Cain did. God said he was pleased with the gifts Abel offered and called Abel a good man because of his faith. Abel died, but through his faith he is still speaking.

5It was by faith that Enoch was taken to heaven so he would not die. He could not be found, because God had taken him away. Before he was taken, the Scripture[d] says that he was a man who truly pleased God. 6Without faith no one can please God. Anyone who comes to God must believe that he is real and that he rewards those who truly want to find him.

7It was by faith that Noah heard God's warnings about things he could not yet see. He obeyed God and built a large boat to save his family. By his faith, Noah showed that the world was wrong, and he became one of those who are made right with God through faith.

8It was by faith Abraham obeyed God's call to go to another place God promised to give him. He left his own country, not knowing where he was to go. 9It was by faith that he lived like a foreigner in the country God promised to give him. He lived in tents with Isaac and Jacob, who had received that same promise from God. 10Abraham was waiting for the city[n] that has real foundations—the city planned and built by God.

11He was too old to have children, and Sarah could not have children. It was by faith that Abraham was made able to become a father, because he trusted God to do what he had promised. 12This man was so old he was almost dead, but from him came as many descendants as there are stars in the sky. Like the sand on the seashore, they could not be counted.

13All these great people died in faith. They did not get the things that God promised his people, but they saw them coming far in the future and were glad. They said they were like visitors and strangers on earth. 14When people say such things, they show they are looking for a country that will be their own. 15If they had been thinking about the country they had left, they could have gone back. 16But they were waiting for a better country—a heavenly country. So God is not ashamed to be called their God, because he has prepared a city for them.

17It was by faith that Abraham, when God tested him, offered his son Isaac as a sacrifice. God made the promises to Abraham, but Abraham was ready to offer his own son as a sacrifice. 18God had said, "The descendants I promised you will be from Isaac."[n] 19Abraham believed that God could raise the dead, and really, it was as if Abraham got Isaac back from death.

20It was by faith that Isaac blessed the future of Jacob and Esau. 21It was by faith that Jacob, as he was dying, blessed each one of Joseph's sons. Then he worshiped as he leaned on the top of his walking stick.

22It was by faith that Joseph, while he was dying, spoke about the Israelites leaving Egypt and gave instructions about what to do with his body.

23It was by faith that Moses' parents hid him for three months after he was born. They saw that Moses was a beautiful baby, and they were not afraid to disobey the king's order.

24It was by faith that Moses, when he grew up, refused to be called the son of the king of Egypt's daughter. 25He chose to suffer with God's people instead of enjoying sin for a short time. 26He thought it was better to suffer for the Christ[d] than to have all the treasures of Egypt, because he was looking for God's reward. 27It was by faith that Moses left Egypt and was not afraid of the king's anger. Moses continued strong as if he could see the God that no one can see. 28It was by faith that Moses prepared the Passover[d] and spread the blood on the doors so the one who brings death would not kill the firstborn[d] sons of Israel.

29It was by faith that the people crossed the Red Sea as if it were dry land. But when the Egyptians tried it, they were drowned.

30It was by faith that the walls of Jericho fell after the people had marched around them for seven days.

31It was by faith that Rahab, the prostitute,[d] welcomed the spies and was not killed with those who refused to obey God.

SIDELIGHT: If you think you have had a hard life, read Hebrews 11:32-38. When verse 37 talks about being "cut in half," it may refer to the prophet Isaiah, who, according to tradition, met this fate.

32Do I need to give more examples? I do not have time to tell you about Gideon, Barak, Samson, Jephthah, David, Samuel, and the prophets.[d] 33Through their faith they defeated kingdoms. They did what was right, received God's promises, and shut the mouths of lions. 34They stopped great fires and were saved from being killed with swords. They were weak, and yet were made

city The spiritual "city" where God's people live with him. Also called "the heavenly Jerusalem." (See Hebrews 12:22.)
"The descendants . . . Isaac." Quotation from Genesis 21:12.

strong. They were powerful in battle and defeated
other armies. 35 Women received their dead relatives raised back to life. Others were tortured and
refused to accept their freedom so they could be
raised from the dead to a better life. 36 Some were
laughed at and beaten. Others were put in chains
and thrown into prison. 37 They were stoned to
death, they were cut in half, and they were killed
with swords. Some wore the skins of sheep and
goats. They were poor, abused, and treated badly.
38 The world was not good enough for them! They
wandered in deserts and mountains, living in
caves and holes in the earth.
39 All these people are known for their faith, but
none of them received what God had promised.
40 God planned to give us something better so that
they would be made perfect, but only together
with us.

Follow Jesus' Example

12 We have around us many people whose
lives tell us what faith means. So let us
run the race that is before us and never give up.
We should remove from our lives anything that
would get in the way and the sin that so easily
holds us back. 2 Let us look only to Jesus, the One
who began our faith and who makes it perfect. He
suffered death on the cross. But he accepted the
shame as if it were nothing because of the joy that

PERSISTENCE

Learning to Win

It seemed to Sylvia Snyder that Coach Riker had no trust in the girls' basketball team. "The woman's impossible to please," Sylvia complained to her parents.

Sylvia remembered the end of the previous season when Coach Riker said they had the talent to be one of the state's best teams. "The question is, do you want to be the best?" she had asked.

"Yes!" they had all shouted. So, Sylvia and her teammates dedicated themselves to that goal.

When practice began again, Coach Riker worked the girls hard. Each daily practice turned into three grueling hours of pain and sweat. The coach never let up on them. She made them run extra laps, enforced a curfew, and monitored their grades. Sylvia was so frustrated she was ready to quit.

"I don't think I can take it anymore," Sylvia told her youth minister. "Coach Riker won't let up on us. She thinks practice is the most important thing in the world."

Sylvia's youth minister heard her frustration. "I know it's tough for you," he said. "But you and the rest of the team made a commitment at the end of last season. You knew it wouldn't be easy, so hang in there at least until the end of this season."

The season did end. The girls played hard and won the district. They went on to win third place at the state tournament. At the end of their final game, they carried out Coach Riker on their shoulders.

The next Sunday, the youth minister asked Sylvia whether she was glad she didn't quit. "I just didn't realize at the time that Coach Riker knew what she was doing," Sylvia said. "All of it—the practices, drills, monitoring our homework—helped us achieve our goal."

The writer of Hebrews knew life is often difficult. Things don't always go the way we plan. **Hebrews 12:1–13** explains the importance of being persistent in our lives as Christians.

- How could Sylvia's attitude have been different if she had read this passage?
- How does this passage apply to being persistent in your own life?

C O N S I D E R . . .

- taking on the next step of the hardest task, school project, or job you are facing.
- making a goal for your spiritual life for the next week (such as reading from your Bible three times). Tell your goal to two friends so they can pray for you and encourage you to stick with your goal. Talk about what you are learning from your reading.

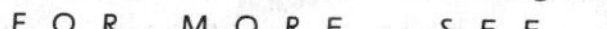

F O R M O R E , S E E . . .

- Isaiah 42:1–4
- Luke 18:1–5
- Ephesians 6:10–18

God put before him. And now he is sitting at the
right side of God's throne. 3Think about Jesus' example. He held on while wicked people were doing evil things to him. So do not get tired and stop
trying.

God Is like a Father

4You are struggling against sin, but your struggles have not yet caused you to be killed. 5You
have forgotten the encouraging words that call
you his children:

"My child, don't think the Lord's discipline is
worth nothing,
and don't stop trying when he corrects you.
6The Lord disciplines those he loves,
and he punishes everyone he accepts as his
child." *Proverbs 3:11-12*

7So hold on through your sufferings, because
they are like a father's discipline. God is treating
you as children. All children are disciplined by
their fathers. 8If you are never disciplined (and
every child must be disciplined), you are not true
children. 9We have all had fathers here on earth
who disciplined us, and we respected them. So it
is even more important that we accept discipline
from the Father of our spirits so we will have life.
10Our fathers on earth disciplined us for a short
time in the way they thought was best. But God
disciplines us to help us, so we can become holy
as he is. 11We do not enjoy being disciplined. It is
painful, but later, after we have learned from it,
we have peace, because we start living in the right
way.

Be Careful How You Live

12You have become weak, so make yourselves
strong again. 13Live in the right way so that you
will be saved and your weakness will not cause
you to be lost.

14Try to live in peace with all people, and try
to live free from sin. Anyone whose life is not holy
will never see the Lord. 15Be careful that no one
fails to receive God's grace and begins to cause
trouble among you. A person like that can ruin
many of you. 16Be careful that no one takes part
in sexual sin or is like Esau and never thinks about
God. As the oldest son, Esau would have received
everything from his father, but he sold all that for
a single meal. 17You remember that after Esau did
this, he wanted to get his father's blessing, but his
father refused. Esau could find no way to change
what he had done, even though he wanted the
blessing so much that he cried.

18You have not come to a mountain that can be
touched and that is burning with fire. You have
not come to darkness, sadness, and storms. 19You
have not come to the noise of a trumpet or to the
sound of a voice like the one the people of Israel
heard and begged not to hear another word.
20They did not want to hear the command: "If
anything, even an animal, touches the mountain,
it must be put to death with stones."[n] 21What
they saw was so terrible that Moses said, "I am
shaking with fear."[n]

22But you have come to Mount Zion,[n] to the
city of the living God, the heavenly Jerusalem.
You have come to thousands of angels gathered
together with joy. 23You have come to the meeting of God's firstborn[n] children whose names are
written in heaven. You have come to God, the
judge of all people, and to the spirits of good people who have been made perfect. 24You have
come to Jesus, the One who brought the new
agreement from God to his people, and you have
come to the sprinkled blood[n] that has a better
message than the blood of Abel.[n]

25So be careful and do not refuse to listen when
God speaks. Others refused to listen to him when
he warned them on earth, and they did not escape. So it will be worse for us if we refuse to
listen to God who warns us from heaven. 26When
he spoke before, his voice shook the earth, but
now he has promised, "Once again I will shake
not only the earth but also the heavens."[n] 27The
words "once again" clearly show us that everything that was made—things that can be
shaken—will be destroyed. Only the things that
cannot be shaken will remain.

28So let us be thankful, because we have a kingdom that cannot be shaken. We should worship
God in a way that pleases him with respect and
fear, 29because our God is like a fire that burns
things up.

13 Keep on loving each other as brothers
and sisters. 2Remember to welcome
strangers, because some who have done this have
welcomed angels without knowing it. 3Remem-
ber those who are in prison as if you were in
prison with them. Remember those who are suffering as if you were suffering with them.

4Marriage should be honored by everyone, and
husband and wife should keep their marriage

"If . . . stones." Quotation from Exodus 19:12-13.
"I . . . fear." Quotation from Deuteronomy 9:19.
Mount Zion Another name for Jerusalem, here meaning the spiritual city of God's people.
firstborn The first son born in a Jewish family was given the most important place in the family and received special blessings. All of God's children are like that.
sprinkled blood The blood of Jesus' death.
Abel The son of Adam and Eve, who was killed by his brother Cain (Genesis 4:8).
"Once . . . heavens." Quotation from Haggai 2:6, 21.

pure. God will judge as guilty those who take part
in sexual sins. 5Keep your lives free from the love
of money, and be satisfied with what you have.
God has said,

"I will never leave you;
I will never forget you." *Deuteronomy 31:6*

6So we can be sure when we say,

"I will not be afraid, because the Lord is my
helper.
People can't do anything to me." *Psalm 118:6*

7Remember your leaders who taught God's
message to you. Remember how they lived and
died, and copy their faith. 8Jesus Christ is the
same yesterday, today, and forever.

9Do not let all kinds of strange teachings lead
you into the wrong way. Your hearts should be
strengthened by God's grace, not by obeying rules
about foods, which do not help those who obey
them.

10We have a sacrifice, but the priests who serve
in the Holy Tent[d] cannot eat from it. 11The high
priest carries the blood of animals into the Most
Holy Place where he offers this blood for sins. But
the bodies of the animals are burned outside the
camp. 12So Jesus also suffered outside the city to
make his people holy with his own blood. 13So let
us go to Jesus outside the camp, holding on as he
did when we are abused.

14Here on earth we do not have a city that lasts
forever, but we are looking for the city that we
will have in the future. 15So through Jesus let us
always offer to God our sacrifice of praise, coming
from lips that speak his name. 16Do not forget to
do good to others, and share with them, because
such sacrifices please God.

17Obey your leaders and act under their authority. They are watching over you, because they are
responsible for your souls. Obey them so that they
will do this work with joy, not sadness. It will not
help you to make their work hard.

18Pray for us. We are sure that we have a clear
conscience, because we always want to do the
right thing. 19I especially beg you to pray so that
God will send me back to you soon.

20-21I pray that the God of peace will give you
every good thing you need so you can do what he

WORSHIP

Why Doesn't God Talk?

On the Thursday before Easter at the children's home, the children enjoyed a candlelight service in the chapel. The kids entered in their usual loud way. But, as soon as they saw the candles they became very quiet. Their eyes showed anticipation, as if something were about to happen.

After a moving service, Jason, Jenny, and Tina—three older children who lived at the home—came to talk to the chaplain. They wanted to know why God doesn't always seem as close as he was that evening.

"If God would talk to me, you know, out loud, it would be a lot easier to be a Christian," Jenny said.

The others agreed. "Why doesn't God just speak to us in church?" Jason asked.

Seven-year-old Kimberly, who had been listening, suddenly spoke up. "God does talk to you," she said to the other three. "Maybe you just don't always listen."

The writer of Hebrews describes how God speaks to us in worship. The writer of Hebrews knew that his readers, like the kids at the children's home, needed guidance for hearing God's message in worship. In **Hebrews 12:18–25** you will find more on hearing God in worship.

- Would the writer of Hebrews agree or disagree with Kimberly? Why or why not?
- How might you be more open to God's talking with you, according to the passage?

CONSIDER . . .

- spending a few minutes in prayer just before you go to a worship service this week, asking God to help you hear him better.
- volunteering to take a more active role one week in your church's worship service. See your pastor or minister of worship to see how you can participate.

FOR MORE, SEE . . .

- Exodus 3:1–6
- Psalm 95
- Matthew 21:12–16

wants. God raised from the dead our Lord Jesus,
the Great Shepherd of the sheep, because of the
blood of his death. His blood began the eternal
agreement that God made with his people. I pray
that God will do in us what pleases him, through
Jesus Christ, and to him be glory forever and ever.
Amen.
22My brothers and sisters, I beg you to listen
patiently to this message I have written to encour
age you, because it is not very long. 23I want you
to know that our brother Timothy has been le
out of prison. If he arrives soon, we will both
come to see you.
24Greet all your leaders and all of God's people
Those from Italy send greetings to you.
25Grace be with you all.

SERVICE

When You See It

The Seventh Street Church youth group regularly went on outings. One night when the kids were returning in a church van from a pizza party, they saw an elderly woman waving for help in a bad section of town. Her car was broken down and she was alone. The kids immediately wanted to stop and help.

The car's battery was dead, and no one had jumper cables. The woman was afraid to leave her car there, and the kids didn't want to leave her there. So they decided to push her car to the nearest service station.

Eleven kids and one youth minister began pushing the woman's old Ford LTD through two miles of the worst section of town. More than once, people offered to take the car off their hands. The group pushed for what seemed forever. When a service station came into view, everyone cheered.

The woman was so grateful that she cried. "Not even my neighbors are so kind to me," she said. She took each member of the group by the hand and gave each one a hug and a smile.

As the group boarded the van for home, the woman thanked them again. "It takes special people to see a need and meet it where it is," she said.

The writer of Hebrews reminds Christians that serving each other is important. **Hebrews 13:1–8** offers several examples of how to love and care for others.

- How does the youth group's willingness to help compare with the message of the passage?
- What specific teachings from the passage apply to your life today?

CONSIDER . . .

- calling someone who has done something for you recently and letting that person know you appreciate the caring.
- doing something for someone in need. Look for needs you can meet, such as cutting grass or running an errand.

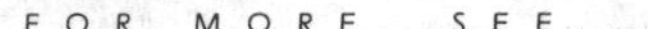

FOR MORE, SEE . . .

- Psalm 146
- Matthew 15:21–28
- Luke 7:1–10

JAMES

Why Read This Book:

- Learn how to handle temptation, testing and trouble (James 1).
- Understand the connection between what you believe and what you do (James 2—3).
- See what can happen when you let God be in charge of your life (James 4—5).

Behind the Scenes:

If someone says, "Would you mind taking out the garbage?" it's easy to forget or find some excuse for not doing it. But suppose someone says, "Take out the garbage!" It's hard to ignore the demand or find an excuse not to do it.

The book of James is like the second example. Its guidance is so clear that it is hard to ignore. "Do not become angry easily" (James 1:19). "Never think some people are more important than others" (James 2:1). "Do not tell evil lies about each other" (James 4:11). In fact, James has more than fifty direct commands in just five chapters!

While much of the New Testament focuses on what Christians believe, James focuses on how Christians behave. Some early Christians apparently thought they could do whatever they wanted because God would forgive them anyway. But James warns them that "if people say they have faith, but do nothing, their faith is worth nothing" (James 2:14).

This short book is loaded with advice on putting our faith into action. It covers many areas of life we continue to struggle with: handling money, relations between the rich and poor, bragging, judging others, being patient. The book is as practical today as when it was written almost two thousand years ago.

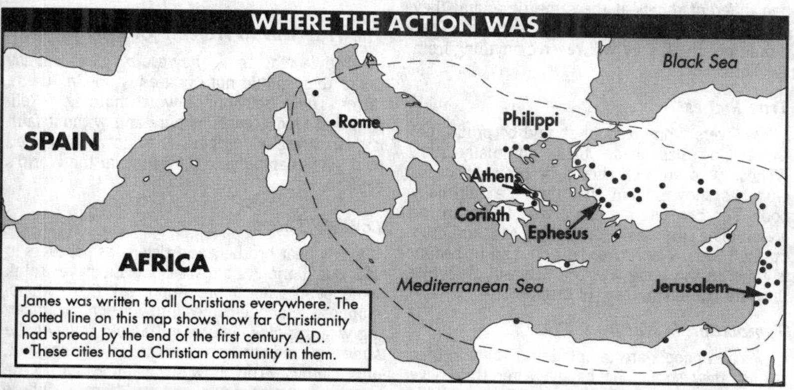

James was written to all Christians everywhere. The dotted line on this map shows how far Christianity had spread by the end of the first century A.D.
•These cities had a Christian community in them.

WHEN THE ACTION WAS

- **BC/AD** — Jesus was born
- **20AD** — Jesus began his ministry
- The church began soon after Jesus went to heaven
- **30AD** — Paul became a Christian
- **40AD**
- Paul began his missionary work
- **50AD** — James may have been written
- **60AD** — Fire destroyed Rome
- **70AD** — Romans destroyed the Temple in Jerusalem

1 From James, a servant of God and of the
Lord Jesus Christ.
To all of God's people who are scattered every-
where in the world:

Greetings.

Faith and Wisdom

2My brothers and sisters,[n] when you have
many kinds of troubles, you should be full of joy,
3because you know that these troubles test your

> **SIDELIGHT:** James was a common name in the first century, so we are not positive who wrote this letter. One theory is that the author was a brother of Jesus. This James became the leader of the Jerusalem church and later was put to death because of his faith.

faith, and this will give you patience. 4Let your
patience show itself perfectly in what you do.
Then you will be perfect and complete and will
have everything you need. 5But if any of you
needs wisdom, you should ask God for it. He is
generous and enjoys giving to all people, so he
will give you wisdom. 6But when you ask God,
you must believe and not doubt. Anyone who
doubts is like a wave in the sea, blown up and
down by the wind. 7-8Such doubters are thinking
two different things at the same time, and they
cannot decide about anything they do. They
should not think they will receive anything from
the Lord.

True Riches

9Believers who are poor should be proud, because God has made them spiritually rich.
10Those who are rich should be proud, because
God has shown them that they are spiritually
poor. The rich will die like a wild flower in the
grass. 11The sun rises with burning heat and dries
up the plants. The flower falls off, and its beauty
is gone. In the same way the rich will die while
they are still taking care of business.

Temptation Is Not from God

12When people are tempted and still continue
strong, they should be happy. After they have
proved their faith, God will reward them with life
forever. God promised this to all those who love
him. 13When people are tempted, they should not
say, "God is tempting me." Evil cannot tempt
God, and God himself does not tempt anyone.
14But people are tempted when their own evil desire leads them away and traps them. 15This desire
leads to sin, and then the sin grows and brings
death.

16My dear brothers and sisters, do not be fooled
about this. 17Every good action and every perfect
gift is from God. These good gifts come down
from the Creator of the sun, moon, and stars, who
does not change like their shifting shadows.
18God decided to give us life through the word of
truth so we might be the most important of all the
things he made.

Listening and Obeying

19My dear brothers and sisters, always be willing to listen and slow to speak. Do not become
angry easily, 20because anger will not help you
live the right kind of life God wants. 21So put out
of your life every evil thing and every kind of
wrong. Then in gentleness accept God's teaching
that is planted in your hearts, which can save you.

22Do what God's teaching says; when you only
listen and do nothing, you are fooling yourselves.
23Those who hear God's teaching and do nothing
are like people who look at themselves in a mirror. 24They see their faces and then go away and
quickly forget what they looked like. 25But the
truly happy people are those who carefully study
God's perfect law that makes people free, and
they continue to study it. They do not forget what
they heard, but they obey what God's teaching
says. Those who do this will be made happy.

The True Way to Worship God

26People who think they are religious but say
things they should not say are just fooling themselves. Their "religion" is worth nothing. 27Reli-
gion that God accepts as pure and without fault
is this: caring for orphans or widows who need
help, and keeping yourself free from the world's
evil influence.

Love All People

2 My dear brothers and sisters, as believers in
our glorious Lord Jesus Christ, never think
some people are more important than others.
2Suppose someone comes into your church meeting wearing nice clothes and a gold ring. At the
same time a poor person comes in wearing old,
dirty clothes. 3You show special attention to the
one wearing nice clothes and say, "Please, sit here
in this good seat." But you say to the poor person,
"Stand over there," or, "Sit on the floor by my
feet." 4What are you doing? You are making some
people more important than others, and with evil

brothers and sisters Although the Greek text says "brothers" here and throughout this book, James' words were meant for the entire church, including men and women.

thoughts you are deciding that one person is better.

SIDELIGHT: Wearing a gold ring (James 2:2) was a sign of great wealth in New Testament times. People who wanted to show off their wealth would cover their fingers with rings, often several on each finger. They would even rent rings when they particularly wanted to impress people. Imagine the limousine they would hire to go to the senior prom!

5Listen, my dear brothers and sisters! God
chose the poor in the world to be rich with faith
and to receive the kingdom God promised to
those who love him. 6But you show no respect to
the poor. The rich are always trying to control
your lives. They are the ones who take you to
court. 7And they are the ones who speak against
Jesus, who owns you.
8This royal law is found in the Scriptures:[d]
"Love your neighbor as you love yourself."[n] If
you obey this law, you are doing right. 9But if you
treat one person as being more important than
another, you are sinning. You are guilty of breaking God's law. 10A person who follows all of God's
law but fails to obey even one command is guilty
of breaking all the commands in that law. 11The
same God who said, "You must not be guilty of
adultery,"[d,n] also said, "You must not murder
anyone."[n] So if you do not take part in adultery
but you murder someone, you are guilty of breaking all of God's law. 12In everything you say and
do, remember that you will be judged by the law
that makes people free. 13So you must show
mercy to others, or God will not show mercy to
you when he judges you. But the person who
shows mercy can stand without fear at the judgment.

Faith and Good Works

14My brothers and sisters, if people say they
have faith, but do nothing, their faith is worth
nothing. Can faith like that save them? 15A
brother or sister in Christ might need clothes or
food. 16If you say to that person, "God be with
you! I hope you stay warm and get plenty to eat,"
but you do not give what that person needs, your

"Love . . . yourself." Quotation from Leviticus 19:18.
"You . . . adultery." Quotation from Exodus 20:14 and Deuteronomy 5:18.
"You . . . anyone." Quotation from Exodus 20:13 and Deuteronomy 5:17.

BIBLE STUDY

A Word From Your Sponsor

If you're a typical teenager, by the time you graduate from high school, you'll have watched eighteen to twenty thousand hours of television. An hour of television may carry fifteen to twenty-five advertisements. Thus, a typical eighteen year old has seen about three to four hundred thousand advertisements.

How many of those ads do you think eighteen year olds can remember?

Probably no one could recall more than a few hundred. Even lower would be the number of ads to which the typical teenager responded by purchasing the product.

We simply tune out much of what we hear.

But **James 1:17–27** says we can't afford to "tune out" when we hear God's teaching. Tune in the passage.

- What does James say about those "who hear God's teaching and do nothing"—the way most of us treat commercials?
- According to James, who is "the truly happy person?" How might your life change if you were to remember and act on more of God's teaching?

C O N S I D E R . . .

- telling a Christian friend what you read in the Bible today. Doing so can help you remember it and apply it to your own life.
- taking notes the next time you hear a sermon in church.

F O R M O R E , S E E . . .

- Joshua 1:6–9
- Psalm 119:1–16
- Luke 11:27–28

words are worth nothing. 17In the same way, faith
that is alone—that does nothing—is dead.
18Someone might say, "You have faith, but I
have deeds." Show me your faith without doing
anything, and I will show you my faith by what
I do. 19You believe there is one God. Good! But
the demons[d] believe that, too, and they tremble
with fear.
20You foolish person! Must you be shown that
faith that does nothing is worth nothing? 21Abra-
ham, our ancestor, was made right with God by
what he did when he offered his son Isaac on the
altar. 22So you see that Abraham's faith and the
things he did worked together. His faith was
made perfect by what he did. 23This shows the full
meaning of the Scripture[d] that says: "Abraham believed God, and God accepted Abraham's faith,
and that faith made him right with God."[n] And
Abraham was called God's friend.[n] 24So you see
that people are made right with God by what they
do, not by faith only.
25Another example is Rahab, a prostitute,[d] who
was made right with God by something she did.
She welcomed the spies into her home and
helped them escape by a different road.
26Just as a person's body that does not have a
spirit is dead, so faith that does nothing is dead!

Controlling the Things We Say

3 My brothers and sisters, not many of you
should become teachers, because you know
that we who teach will be judged more strictly.
2We all make many mistakes. If people never said
anything wrong, they would be perfect and able
to control their entire selves, too. 3When we put
bits into the mouths of horses to make them obey

"Abraham . . . God." Quotation from Genesis 15:6.
God's friend These words about Abraham are found in 2 Chronicles 20:7 and Isaiah 41:8.

JUDGING OTHERS

A Perfect Ten?

Peggy Reynolds and her friends moved down the food line in the music camp dining hall. Two guys serving food watched Peggy and the other girls, and grinned. When she got near them, they reached under the counter, pulled out two cardboard signs with numbers, and put them on a high ledge behind them. "Nine" and "five," Peggy thought, reading the cards. "I wonder what they mean?"

When Peggy's friend Marie got to the same place in line, the guys changed the numbers to an "eight" and a "six." By now everybody had stopped eating to watch. When the next girl in line received a "nine" and a "seven," people cheered. "They're rating us," Peggy suddenly realized. Her face turned red.

Peggy and her friends laughed uncomfortably as the two guys continued to rate girls as they passed in line. Then Terri Smith got in line. She wasn't "perfect" looking and was a bit overweight. Peggy dreaded how the guys might rate Terri. But as she passed through the line, the guys just ignored her. They didn't rate her at all. Then, when other "better looking" girls came up in the line, the guys resumed their rating game.

But the game wasn't funny to Peggy. She felt judged, and imagined how hurt Terri probably felt.

Sometimes it may seem like fun to judge other people, but being judged is rarely funny. Read in **James 2:1–17** what James wrote about treating people as though they are more important than others.

- What does James say is wrong with judging people like the guys were rating the girls at the camp?
- When have you unfairly judged someone because of clothes or grades or skill at sports? What makes us fall into doing things like that?

CONSIDER. . .

- thinking about one person you have judged. The next time you see this person, say, "Hi."
- watching this week how often you put people down. Whenever you realize you have put someone down, quickly say something that builds the person up too.

FOR MORE, SEE. . .

- 1 Samuel 16:7
- Matthew 7:1–5
- Romans 12:14–16

us, we can control their whole bodies. 4Also a ship is very big, and it is pushed by strong winds. But a very small rudder controls that big ship, making it go wherever the pilot wants. 5It is the same with the tongue. It is a small part of the body, but it brags about great things.

A big forest fire can be started with only a little flame. 6And the tongue is like a fire. It is a whole world of evil among the parts of our bodies. The tongue spreads its evil through the whole body. The tongue is set on fire by hell, and it starts a fire that influences all of life. 7People can tame every kind of wild animal, bird, reptile, and fish, and they have tamed them, 8but no one can tame the tongue. It is wild and evil and full of deadly poison. 9We use our tongues to praise our Lord and Father, but then we curse people, whom God made like himself. 10Praises and curses come from the same mouth! My brothers and sisters, this should not happen. 11Do good and bad water flow from the same spring? 12My brothers and sisters, can a fig tree make olives, or can a grapevine make figs? No! And a well full of salty water cannot give good water.

True Wisdom

13Are there those among you who are truly wise and understanding? Then they should show it by living right and doing good things with a gentleness that comes from wisdom. 14But if you are selfish and have bitter jealousy in your hearts, do not brag. Your bragging is a lie that hides the truth. 15That kind of "wisdom" does not come from God but from the world. It is not spiritual; it is from the devil. 16Where jealousy and selfishness are, there will be confusion and every kind of evil. 17But the wisdom that comes from God is first of all pure, then peaceful, gentle, and easy to please. This wisdom is always ready to help those who are troubled and to do good for others. It is always fair and honest. 18People who work for peace in a peaceful way plant a good crop of right-living.

Give Yourselves to God

4 Do you know where your fights and arguments come from? They come from the selfish desires that war within you. 2You want things, but you do not have them. So you are ready to kill and are jealous of other people, but you still cannot get what you want. So you argue and fight. You do not get what you want, because you do not ask God. 3Or when you ask, you do not receive because the reason you ask is wrong.

BRAGGING

Spain's Greatest Matador . . . Almost

Though only twenty-one years old, Jose Cubero had leaped to fame as one of Spain's most spectacular matadors. In bullfight after bullfight, he had daringly whirled and dodged his way to triumph.

It was no surprise, then, when he made especially quick work of a bull during a routine bullfight. Thrusting his sword one last time, Jose watched the bull collapse onto the dirt of the arena. Jose had performed well, and he knew it. He turned arrogantly to bask in the crowd's applause.

Enjoying the roaring cheers, Jose was unaware that the bull behind him was not dead. The bull suddenly rose and lunged, one of its horns piercing the matador from the back. Jose Cubero, a rising young star, was dead.

When we have done well, we like to get people's attention. We like to listen to the cheers. But James reminds us in **James 3:13–18** to do "good things with a gentleness that comes from wisdom." Boasting of our actions is a dangerous practice.

- What else might James have told Jose Cubero about bragging?
- What do you think makes people eager to brag? Why might Christians have less need to brag?

CONSIDER . . .

- noticing, as you watch television today, which characters brag. How do you feel about these characters?
- writing on a card this saying: "There's no limit to the amount of good you can do if you don't care who gets the credit." Place it where you will see it.

FOR MORE, SEE . . .

- Daniel 4:28–37
- Luke 14:7–11
- Philippians 2:3–11

You want things so you can use them for your
own pleasures.
4So, you are not loyal to God! You should know
that loving the world is the same as hating God.
Anyone who wants to be a friend of the world
becomes God's enemy. 5Do you think the Scripture[d] means nothing that says, "The Spirit[d] that
God made to live in us wants us for himself
alone."[n] 6But God gives us even more grace, as
the Scripture says,

"God is against the proud,
but he gives grace to the humble."

Proverbs 3:34

7So give yourselves completely to God. Stand
against the devil, and the devil will run from you.
8Come near to God, and God will come near to
you. You sinners, clean sin out of your lives. You
who are trying to follow God and the world at the
same time, make your thinking pure. 9Be sad, cry,
and weep! Change your laughter into crying and
your joy into sadness. 10Don't be too proud in the
Lord's presence, and he will make you great.

You Are Not the Judge

11Brothers and sisters, do not tell evil lies about
each other. If you speak against your fellow believers or judge them, you are judging and speaking against the law they follow. And when you are
judging the law, you are no longer a follower of
the law. You have become a judge. 12God is the
only Lawmaker and Judge. He is the only One
who can save and destroy. So it is not right for you
to judge your neighbor.

Let God Plan Your Life

13Some of you say, "Today or tomorrow we
will go to some city. We will stay there a year, do
business, and make money." 14But you do not
know what will happen tomorrow! Your life is
like a mist. You can see it for a short time, but
then it goes away. 15So you should say, "If the
Lord wants, we will live and do this or that."
16But now you are proud and you brag. All of this
bragging is wrong. 17Anyone who knows the right
thing to do, but does not do it, is sinning.

"The Spirit . . . alone." These words may be from Exodus 20:5.

GOD'S WILL

Lump on an All-Star's Arm

"Cancer came into my life as a small thing," remembers all-star baseball pitcher Dave Dravecky, talking about the small lump that had appeared on his throwing arm.

"The San Francisco Giants had clinched the division," Dave says. "We were making ready for what every baseball player works for, and most never experience: postseason play. So I had things on my mind other than a little, painless lump."

But the lump on his arm didn't go away. It grew. The next year the tumor had to be removed, along with 50 percent of Dave's deltoid muscle. "Short of a miracle," the cancer specialist said, "Dave will never pitch again."

Through therapy and exercise, Dave did come back. But in his second game the next season, he broke his arm, and his career came to an abrupt and painful halt.

"There's a bittersweet quality to my retirement from baseball," he says. "I've learned to put my life in God's hands. I had to learn to do what was within my grasp, one day at a time, and leave control of the rest to God."

James 4:13–17 reminds us that the future is in God's hands.

- What would both Dave Dravecky and James say we should expect from the future?
- What are you hoping and planning to do in the next several months? When you think about these plans, does God come into your mind?

CONSIDER . . .

- evaluating your dreams for the future in light of this passage on God's will.
- writing on an envelope, "It's in God's hands." Whenever you are worried about something in the future you cannot control, write out your worry on a slip of paper and place it in the envelope.

FOR MORE, SEE . . .

- Psalm 139
- Proverbs 16:1, 9
- Luke 12:22–31

A Warning to the Rich

5 You rich people, listen! Cry and be very sad
because of the troubles that are coming to
you. 2Your riches have rotted, and your clothes
have been eaten by moths. 3Your gold and silver
have rusted, and that rust will be a proof that you
were wrong. It will eat your bodies like fire. You
saved your treasure for the last days. 4The pay you
did not give the workers who mowed your fields
cries out against you, and the cries of the workers
have been heard by the Lord All-Powerful. 5Your
life on earth was full of rich living and pleasing
yourselves with everything you wanted. You
made yourselves fat, like an animal ready to be
killed. 6You have judged guilty and then murdered innocent people, who were not against you.

Be Patient

7Brothers and sisters, be patient until the Lord
comes again. A farmer patiently waits for his valuable crop to grow from the earth and for it to receive the autumn and spring rains. 8You, too,
must be patient. Do not give up hope, because the
Lord is coming soon. 9Brothers and sisters, do not
complain against each other or you will be judged
guilty. And the Judge is ready to come! 10Brothers
and sisters, follow the example of the prophets[d]
who spoke for the Lord. They suffered many hard
things, but they were patient. 11We say they are
happy because they did not give up. You have
heard about Job's patience, and you know the
Lord's purpose for him in the end. You know
the Lord is full of mercy and is kind.

Be Careful What You Say

12My brothers and sisters, above all, do not use
an oath when you make a promise. Don't use the
name of heaven, earth, or anything else to prove
what you say. When you mean yes, say only yes,
and when you mean no, say only no so you will
not be judged guilty.

The Power of Prayer

13Anyone who is having troubles should pray.

PATIENCE

Endless Paddling

"Come on, guys! Hurry up!" Sherri Rohrer's youth leader called from a silver canoe a hundred yards ahead. Sherri felt she would never catch up, let alone finish the ten-day trip.

They had broken camp at 9:00 A.M. It was now 3:00 P.M., and they still had miles to paddle. The wind blew against them, and the hard paddling took its toll on many out-of-shape bodies. "I can't wait to get there," Sherri complained to her canoeing partner. "Where's a motor for this thing? My arms feel dead."

As Sherri lifted her paddle out of the water, she watched the drops fall back into the dark Maine river. She thought about how she had waited all year for this trip. She and the other group members had worked hard—spaghetti dinners, car washes, bake sales. Her excitement had grown as the trip date approached. It had been hard to wait.

Now that the trip was here, she sometimes wondered whether it had been worth all the excitement. She grew tired of still waiting—for rest, for dinner, and for free time to relax.

As Sherri had trouble being patient on the canoe trip, Christians sometimes tire of waiting for things to get better. **James 5:7–11** encourages believers to keep a patient faith, because things will get better.

- How might James's advice help Sherri?
- What does James say we can look forward to if we are patient? How can knowing that Jesus is coming help you be patient today?

C O N S I D E R . . .

- listing things you are waiting for. Ask God to give you hope while you wait.
- getting a calendar and marking the date of an upcoming "big event" in your life. Sprinkle short notes on dates along the way to encourage you while you wait.

F O R M O R E , S E E . . .

- Job 2:11–13; 42:10–17
- Isaiah 40:27–31
- Matthew 7:7–11

Anyone who is happy should sing praises. [14]Anyone who is sick should call the church's elders.[d] They should pray for and pour oil on the person[n] in the name of the Lord. [15]And the prayer that is said with faith will make the sick person well; the Lord will heal that person. And if the person has sinned, the sins will be forgiven. [16]Confess your sins to each other and pray for each other so God can heal you. When a believing person prays, great things happen. [17]Elijah was a human being just like us. He prayed that it would not rain, and it did not rain on the land for three and a half years! [18]Then Elijah prayed again, and the rain came down from the sky, and the land produced crops again.

SIDELIGHT: Using oil as medicine was a common practice in Bible times (James 5:14). The good Samaritan in Jesus' parable poured oil on the victim's wounds (Luke 10:34). People who had headaches probably had the greasiest heads in town!

Saving a Soul

[19]My brothers and sisters, if one of you wanders away from the truth, and someone helps that person come back, [20]remember this: Anyone who brings a sinner back from the wrong way will save that sinner's soul from death and will cause many sins to be forgiven.

1 PETER

Why Read This Book:

- See the benefits of the salvation God offers you (1 Peter 1:3—2:10).
- Discover how Christians should live (1 Peter 2:11—4:11).
- Learn how to grow even when suffering (1 Peter 4:12—5:11).

Behind the Scenes:

You may have experienced the old prank: Someone writes "KICK ME" on a sheet of paper, then puts it on your back without your knowing it. Suddenly everyone starts laughing at you. Some kick you. You feel angry and embarrassed.

The Christians who received 1 Peter had similar feelings, though the reasons were much different and much more serious. They had become Christians in a pagan culture. And the Christian label brought ridicule, persecution, and suffering.

Some of these Christians might have felt embarrassed about their faith. They may have been tempted to get rid of the Christian "label." Maybe being a Christian wasn't worth all this pain.

This letter encourages the early Christians to stick with their faith, even in the midst of their suffering. It gives them practical advice on how to live with the pain. It reminds them that their circumstances don't have to control their joy and hope in life. God is in control, and he cares about their suffering.

Sometimes it is hard being a Christian. People may make fun of our choices. They may call us names. But this letter encourages us to stay strong in our faith, for in the end God will give victory to his faithful.

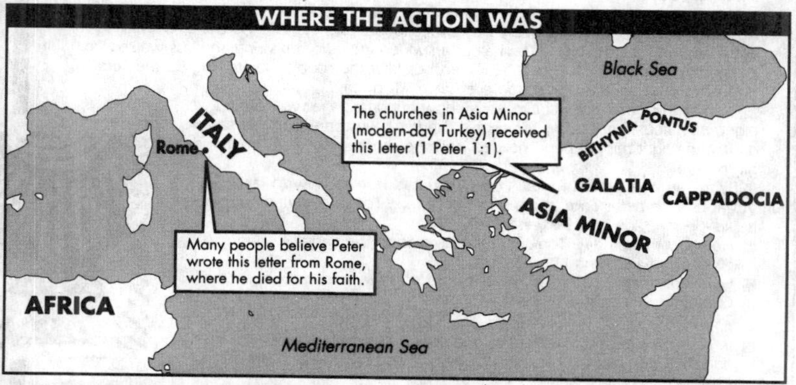
WHERE THE ACTION WAS
Black Sea
The churches in Asia Minor (modern-day Turkey) received this letter (1 Peter 1:1).
PONTUS
BITHYNIA
ITALY
Rome
GALATIA
CAPPADOCIA
ASIA MINOR
Many people believe Peter wrote this letter from Rome, where he died for his faith.
AFRICA
Mediterranean Sea

WHEN THE ACTION WAS

BC/AD — 25AD — 50AD — 75AD — 100AD

- Jesus was born
- The church began soon after Jesus went to heaven
- Fire destroyed Rome, and Roman persecution of Christians began
- Jesus began his ministry
- Paul began his missionary work
- 1 Peter may have been written
- The Roman emperor increased persecution of Christians

1 From Peter, an apostle[d] of Jesus Christ.
To God's chosen people who are away from
their homes and are scattered all around the countries of Pontus, Galatia, Cappadocia, Asia, and Bithynia. 2God planned long ago to choose you by
making you his holy people, which is the Spirit's[d]
work. God wanted you to obey him and to be
made clean by the blood of the death of Jesus
Christ.
Grace and peace be yours more and more.

We Have a Living Hope

3Praise be to the God and Father of our Lord
Jesus Christ. In God's great mercy he has caused
us to be born again into a living hope, because
Jesus Christ rose from the dead. 4Now we hope
for the blessings God has for his children. These
blessings, which cannot be destroyed or be
spoiled or lose their beauty, are kept in heaven for
you. 5God's power protects you through your
faith until salvation is shown to you at the end of

HAPPINESS

The Hope Giver

Tony Melendez amazed 100 million TV viewers in 1987 as he played the guitar with his feet and sang for Pope John Paul II. "Tony," the Pope said, after embracing the performer, "you are giving hope to all of us. My wish to you is to continue giving this hope to all the people."

Born without arms, Tony is normal in every other way. But he had struggled for years to be accepted.

Without persistence, Tony might never have graduated from high school. When he transferred from special education into a "normal" English class, all eyes watched him when he walked into the classroom. He shrugged off his backpack, pulled out a notebook with his toes and put it on the floor. Then he grabbed a pencil between his two biggest toes and began taking notes. Even the teacher had stopped the discussion of Moby Dick to watch. Everyone stared in silence.

"Somebody had to break the silence," Tony recalled. "Hope the floor is clean," he said with a grin. "If it isn't, I'll have to turn in a dirty paper." The students and teacher roared with laughter, then class continued. It was one of the many awkward times he had to show his strength.

Still, Tony was afraid to go to school dances—afraid he would be rejected by girls. But he finally faced his fears and went alone. He stood along the side watching, wondering if everyone was watching him. Then all of a sudden a girl from his English class walked up, looked him in the eye, and said "Go!" Seconds later the couple was tearing up the floor. "I've been dancing almost nonstop ever since," Tony says.

"I don't think that girl will ever know how important she was to me that night. At various times in my life people like her have come along to say or do just the right thing when I needed it. These sensitive ones are the hope givers."

By the time he played for the Pope, Tony had learned how to face obstacles with persistence and a sense of humor. Tony's enduring happiness is like the message of **1 Peter 1:3–9**.

- How did the girl give Tony hope? According to the passage, who gives every Christian "living hope"?
- How does being a Christian give you hope? How does your being a Christian give hope to others?

CONSIDER . . .

- writing down five good and five bad things that could happen to you and thinking how faith in Christ could give you happiness in any situation.
- interviewing someone who has suffered great tragedy, but whose life still is characterized by joy.

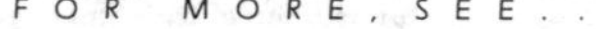

FOR MORE, SEE . . .

- Job 5:17
- John 15:11
- James 1:2–4

time. 6This makes you very happy, even though
now for a short time different kinds of troubles
may make you sad. 7These troubles come to prove
that your faith is pure. This purity of faith is worth
more than gold, which can be proved to be pure
by fire but will ruin. But the purity of your faith
will bring you praise and glory and honor when
Jesus Christ is shown to you. 8You have not seen
Christ, but still you love him. You cannot see him
now, but you believe in him. So you are filled
with a joy that cannot be explained, a joy full of
glory. 9And you are receiving the goal of your
faith — the salvation of your souls.

10The prophets[d] searched carefully and tried to
learn about this salvation. They prophesied about
the grace that was coming to you. 11The Spirit[d] of
Christ was in the prophets, telling in advance
about the sufferings of Christ and about the glory
that would follow those sufferings. The prophets
tried to learn about what the Spirit was showing
them, when those things would happen, and
what the world would be like at that time. 12It
was shown them that their service was not for
themselves but for you, when they told about the
truths you have now heard. Those who preached
the Good News[d] to you told you those things with
the help of the Holy Spirit who was sent from
heaven — things into which angels desire to look.

A Call to Holy Living

13So prepare your minds for service and have
self-control. All your hope should be for the gift of
grace that will be yours when Jesus Christ is
shown to you. 14Now that you are obedient children of God do not live as you did in the past. You
did not understand, so you did the evil things you
wanted. 15But be holy in all you do, just as God,
the One who called you, is holy. 16It is written in
the Scriptures:[d] "You must be holy, because I am
holy."[n]

17You pray to God and call him Father, and he
judges each person's work equally. So while you
are here on earth, you should live with respect for
God. 18You know that in the past you were living
in a worthless way, a way passed down from the
people who lived before you. But you were saved
from that useless life. You were bought, not with
something that ruins like gold or silver, 19but with
the precious blood of Christ, who was like a pure
and perfect lamb. 20Christ was chosen before the
world was made, but he was shown to the world
in these last times for your sake. 21Through Christ
you believe in God, who raised Christ from the
dead and gave him glory. So your faith and your
hope are in God.

22Now that you have made your souls pure by
obeying the truth, you can have true love for your
Christian brothers and sisters.[n] So love each
other deeply with all your heart. 23You have been
born again, and this new life did not come from
something that dies, but from something that cannot die. You were born again through God's living
message that continues forever. 24The Scripture
says,

"All people are like the grass,
and all their glory is like the flowers of the
field.
The grass dies and the flowers fall,
25 but the word of the Lord will live forever."
Isaiah 40:6-8

And this is the word that was preached to you.

Jesus Is the Living Stone

2 So then, rid yourselves of all evil, all lying,
hypocrisy,[d] jealousy, and evil speech. 2As
newborn babies want milk, you should want the
pure and simple teaching. By it you can grow up
and be saved, 3because you have already examined and seen how good the Lord is.

4Come to the Lord Jesus, the "stone"[n] that
lives. The people of the world did not want this
stone, but he was the stone God chose, and he
was precious. 5You also are like living stones, so
let yourselves be used to build a spiritual temple — to be holy priests who offer spiritual sacrifices to God. He will accept those sacrifices
through Jesus Christ. 6The Scripture[d] says:

"I will put a stone in the ground in
Jerusalem.
Everything will be built on this important
and precious rock.
Anyone who trusts in him
will never be disappointed." *Isaiah 28:16*

7This stone is worth much to you who believe.
But to the people who do not believe,

"the stone that the builders rejected
has become the cornerstone."[d] *Psalm 118:22*

8Also, he is

"a stone that causes people to stumble,
a rock that makes them fall." *Isaiah 8:14*

They stumble because they do not obey what God
says, which is what God planned to happen to
them.

9But you are a chosen people, royal priests, a
holy nation, a people for God's own possession.
You were chosen to tell about the wonderful acts
of God, who called you out of darkness into his
wonderful light. 10At one time you were not a
people, but now you are God's people. In the past

"You must be . . . holy." Quotation from Leviticus 11:45; 19:2; 20:7.
brothers and sisters Although the Greek text says "brothers" here and throughout this book, Peter's words were meant for the entire church, including men and women.
"stone" The most important stone in God's spiritual temple or house (his people).

you had never received mercy, but now you have
received God's mercy.

Live for God

11Dear friends, you are like foreigners and
strangers in this world. I beg you to avoid the evil
things your bodies want to do that fight against
your soul. 12People who do not believe are living
all around you and might say that you are doing
wrong. Live such good lives that they will see the
good things you do and will give glory to God on
the day when Christ comes again.

Yield to Every Human Authority

13For the Lord's sake, yield to the people who
have authority in this world: the king, who is the
highest authority, 14and the leaders who are sent
by him to punish those who do wrong and to
praise those who do right. 15It is God's desire that
by doing good you should stop foolish people from
saying stupid things about you. 16Live as free people, but do not use your freedom as an excuse to
do evil. Live as servants of God. 17Show respect
for all people: Love the brothers and sisters of
God's family, respect God, honor the king.

LOVE

Given, Not Earned

The argument was brutal. Rochelle Mattison's parents didn't want her to go to the party. They didn't know the guy throwing it, didn't know his parents, didn't know who was going to be there, and didn't know what the teenagers would be doing.

"You're eighteen years old, Rochelle," her father said. "We won't forbid you to go. But if you ignore our wishes on this, don't expect us to honor your wishes on other things . . . including the use of the car."

They thought withholding the car would stop her.

But it didn't. "I'm tired of you using the car to force me to do what you want," she shot back. "Just keep the car! I don't need it! I've got friends who'll take me to parties!"

With that, she stormed out, called her friends from a pay phone, and headed for the party. Rochelle savored her apparent victory.

But then she arrived at the party. It was wild. Heavy drinking. Too many people. No adults around. She wanted to leave. But her "friends" had left without her, and everyone else at the party had been drinking. She was left to walk seven miles home. She stood alone outside, wondering what to do.

"Hey, Beautiful! Want a lift?" a voice said from a car pulling up behind her. Rochelle felt a surge of fear, and looked for somewhere to run. But when she glanced over her shoulder at the car, she saw her dad's smiling face.

She got in. Dad spoke first. "Dina called," he explained. "She said they tried to find you before they left but it was too crowded. They wanted to get out of there before their car got blocked in."

"I didn't think you'd be willing to come and get me," Rochelle said. "Not after the things I said and did."

Dad pulled the car over and turned to look at her. "Hey," he said. "You're my daughter. I love you. Nothing you say or do can ever change that."

Rochelle learned something about true love that night. **First Peter 1:17–23** talks about the kind of love Rochelle felt from her dad.

- According to the passage, how is Rochelle's dad's love for her like God's love for us?
- How might your life change if you trusted and accepted God's love as described in 1 Peter?

CONSIDER . . .

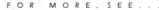

- comparing your parents' love with God's love. Share your observations with your mom or dad.
- talking with a grandparent, aunt, or uncle about times when someone had to discipline your mom or dad. How was that person's love like God's love for you?

FOR MORE, SEE . . .

- Deuteronomy 7:7–9
- Romans 4:1–8
- 1 John 4:7–10

Follow Christ's Example

18Slaves, yield to the authority of your masters
with all respect, not only those who are good and
kind, but also those who are dishonest. 19A person
might have to suffer even when it is unfair, but if
he thinks of God and stands the pain, God is
pleased. 20If you are beaten for doing wrong, there
is no reason to praise you for being patient in your
punishment. But if you suffer for doing good, and
you are patient, then God is pleased. 21This is
what you were called to do, because Christ suffered for you and gave you an example to follow.
So you should do as he did.
22"He had never sinned,
and he had never lied." *Isaiah 53:9*
23People insulted Christ, but he did not insult
them in return. Christ suffered, but he did not
threaten. He let God, the One who judges rightly,
take care of him. 24Christ carried our sins in his
body on the cross so we would stop living for sin
and start living for what is right. And you are
healed because of his wounds. 25You were like
sheep that wandered away, but now you have
come back to the Shepherd and Protector of your
souls.

SIDELIGHT: Because the early Christians were viewed suspiciously, 1 Peter 2:12 urges them to "live good lives" so people would not accuse them of wrongdoing. Among other things, early Christians were falsely accused of eating children because they followed Jesus' command to eat his body and drink his blood in the Communion (also called the Lord's Supper) (see 1 Corinthians 11:23-26).

SELF-ESTEEM

Paying the Price

More than anything, Frank Simms wanted to join the Lords. What a great feeling it would be, he thought, to wear the gang jacket, to be accepted by the guys, to be tough.

But membership in the Lords came with a price. One of the initiation rites was to beat up another guy, steal his expensive shoes, then wear those shoes the next day.

Jimmy Pantelli was chosen as Frank's target. Frank worked out a plan for the attack and left home late one afternoon with a baseball bat. He cornered Jimmy and told him to hand over his shoes.

But Jimmy refused, and a fight broke out. By the time it was over, Frank had been arrested, and Jimmy had been taken to the hospital.

Three months later, Frank still sat in jail, awaiting trial for attempted murder. Jimmy still lay in a coma. Frank wondered why it had all backfired. Why hadn't Jimmy just given him the shoes?

"I wanted to be somebody, that's all," Frank explained. "I just wanted to belong." But nothing could help him feel less guilty for wrecking Jimmy's life, nor reduce the serious consequences of his crime.

Frank was paying the price for his violent attempts to be accepted. **First Peter 2:2–10** shows how Jesus offers a different foundation for building self-esteem.

- If Frank were to read and follow this passage, what would it tell him about feeling chosen, accepted, and important?
- Whenever you feel shaky in your self-esteem, how might this passage help you improve your view?

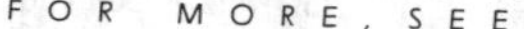

CONSIDER . . .

- listing the groups you would like to belong to, along with the need they could fill for you. What price would you pay to belong, and how would your self-esteem benefit from belonging?
- choosing one person whom you think would truly help you change for the better, and befriend that person.

FOR MORE, SEE . . .

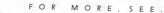

- Isaiah 8:12–14
- Hosea 2:23
- 2 Corinthians 6:3–10

Wives and Husbands

3 In the same way, you wives should yield to your husbands. Then, if some husbands do not obey God's teaching, they will be persuaded to believe without anyone's saying a word to them. They will be persuaded by the way their wives live. 2Your husbands will see the pure lives you live with your respect for God. 3It is not fancy hair, gold jewelry, or fine clothes that should make you beautiful. 4No, your beauty should come from within you—the beauty of a gentle and quiet spirit that will never be destroyed and is very precious to God. 5In this same way the holy women who lived long ago and followed God made themselves beautiful, yielding to their own husbands. 6Sarah obeyed Abraham, her husband, and called him her master. And you women are true children of Sarah if you always do what is right and are not afraid.

SIDELIGHT: When 1 Peter 3:3–4 says true beauty comes from the inside, it would not have made the jewelry merchants happy. In those times, women would decorate their hair with elaborate combs and hairpins, some of which were made of gold.

7In the same way, you husbands should live with your wives in an understanding way, since they are weaker than you. But show them respect, because God gives them the same blessing he gives you—the grace that gives true life. Do this so that nothing will stop your prayers.

Suffering for Doing Right

8Finally, all of you should be in agreement, understanding each other, loving each other as family, being kind and humble. 9Do not do wrong to repay a wrong, and do not insult to repay an insult. But repay with a blessing, because you yourselves were called to do this so that you might receive a blessing. 10The Scripture[d] says,

"A person must do these things
to enjoy life and have many happy days.
He must not say evil things,
and he must not tell lies.
11He must stop doing evil and do good.
He must look for peace and work for it.
12The Lord sees the good people
and listens to their prayers.
But the Lord is against
those who do evil." *Psalm 34:12-16*

13If you are trying hard to do good, no one can really hurt you. 14But even if you suffer for doing right, you are blessed.

"Don't be afraid of what they fear;
do not dread those things." *Isaiah 8:12-13*

15But respect Christ as the holy Lord in your hearts. Always be ready to answer everyone who asks you to explain about the hope you have, 16but answer in a gentle way and with respect. Keep a clear conscience so that those who speak evil of your good life in Christ will be made ashamed. 17It is better to suffer for doing good than for doing wrong if that is what God wants. 18Christ himself suffered for sins once. He was not guilty, but he suffered for those who are guilty to bring you to God. His body was killed, but he was made alive in the spirit. 19And in the spirit he went and preached to the spirits in prison 20who refused to obey God long ago in the time of Noah. God was waiting patiently for them while Noah was building the boat. Only a few people—eight in all—were saved by water. 21And that water is like baptism that now saves you—not the washing of dirt from the body, but the promise made to God from a good conscience. And this is because Jesus Christ was raised from the dead. 22Now Jesus has gone into heaven and is at God's right side ruling over angels, authorities, and powers.

Change Your Lives

4 Since Christ suffered while he was in his body, strengthen yourselves with the same way of thinking Christ had. The person who has suffered in the body is finished with sin. 2Strengthen yourselves so that you will live here on earth doing what God wants, not the evil things people want. 3In the past you wasted too much time doing what nonbelievers enjoy. You were guilty of sexual sins, evil desires, drunkenness, wild and drunken parties, and hateful idol worship. 4Nonbelievers think it is strange that you do not do the many wild and wasteful things they do, so they insult you. 5But they will have to explain this to God, who is ready to judge the living and the dead. 6For this reason the Good News[d] was preached to those who are now dead. Even though they were judged like all people, the Good News was preached to them so they could live in the spirit as God lives.

Use God's Gifts Wisely

7The time is near when all things will end. So think clearly and control yourselves so you will be able to pray. 8Most importantly, love each other deeply, because love will cause many sins to be forgiven. 9Open your homes to each other, without complaining. 10Each of you has received a gift to use to serve others. Be good servants of God's various gifts of grace. 11Anyone who speaks should speak words from God. Anyone who

serves should serve with the strength God gives
so that in everything God will be praised through
Jesus Christ. Power and glory belong to him forever and ever. Amen.

Suffering as a Christian

12My friends, do not be surprised at the terrible
trouble which now comes to test you. Do not
think that something strange is happening to you.
13But be happy that you are sharing in Christ's
sufferings so that you will be happy and full of joy
when Christ comes again in glory. 14When people
insult you because you follow Christ, you are
blessed, because the glorious Spirit,[d] the Spirit of
God, is with you. 15Do not suffer for murder,
theft, or any other crime, nor because you trouble
other people. 16But if you suffer because you are
a Christian, do not be ashamed. Praise God because you wear that name. 17It is time for judgment to begin with God's family. And if that judging begins with us, what will happen to those
people who do not obey the Good News[d] of God?
18"If it is very hard for a good person to be
saved,
the wicked person and the sinner will
surely be lost!"[n]
19So those who suffer as God wants should
trust their souls to the faithful Creator as they continue to do what is right.

The Flock of God

5 Now I have something to say to the elders[d]
in your group. I also am an elder. I have seen
Christ's sufferings, and I will share in the glory
that will be shown to us. I beg you to 2shepherd
God's flock, for whom you are responsible. Watch
over them because you want to, not because you
are forced. That is how God wants it. Do it because you are happy to serve, not because you
want money. 3Do not be like a ruler over people
you are responsible for, but be good examples to
them. 4Then when Christ, the Chief Shepherd,

"If . . . lost!" Quotation from Proverbs 11:31 in the Septuagint, the Greek version of the Old Testament.

SUFFERING

The Cost of Faith

"Hey, man," said Bill Miller to his friend Jose Castano. "I don't want to hear about your Jesus! Leave me alone!"

The words broke Jose's heart. Bill had been his best friend since eighth grade. But now, three years later, their friendship was in jeopardy because Jose had become a Christian and had let his friends know.

Bill had confronted Jose at a friend's party, accusing him of "thinking you're better than everyone else" because Jose had chosen not to drink anymore.

"Let me know when you get over this religion stuff," Bill had said. "Maybe then we can be friends again." At that, Bill left Jose standing alone. Jose feared he had just lost his best friend.

"No one ever told me that being a Christian could hurt this bad or cost so much," Jose muttered to himself as he went home after the party. "Maybe it's just not worth it. I thought being a Christian meant life got better, not more painful."

As we grow in faith, we change. Sometimes friends change with us. Sometimes they don't. This change may cause some pain. **First Peter 4:12–19** reminds us that being a Christian does not insulate us from pain and suffering. In fact, Peter lets us know that we can expect it as we grow in Christ. He also reminds us that some things are worth suffering for.

- What comfort or understanding might this passage give to Jose in the loss of his friendship with Bill?
- When have you paid a cost for your faith? How did you grow from that experience?

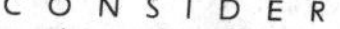

CONSIDER . . .

- praying for a friend whom you know is suffering right now.
- reading about the life of a Christian martyr. Your pastor can help you find such a story.

FOR MORE, SEE . . .

- Psalm 56:1–4
- John 15:18–21
- 1 Peter 2:19–25

comes, you will get a glorious crown that will never lose its beauty.

SIDELIGHT: If you were a star athlete in Peter's day, you might receive a palm branch (suitable for hanging) and a wreath of olive leaves, parsley, celery leaves, or ivy. These wreaths were a source of great pride, but, like a bouquet of roses, they didn't last long. Maybe that is one reason 1 Peter 5:4 urges chasing crowns that would not need watering!

5In the same way, younger people should be willing to be under older people. And all of you should be very humble with each other.

"God is against the proud,
but he gives grace to the humble."

Proverbs 3:34

6Be humble under God's powerful hand so
he will lift you up when the right time comes.
7Give all your worries to him, because he cares
about you.
8Control yourselves and be careful! The devil,
your enemy, goes around like a roaring lion looking for someone to eat. 9Refuse to give in to him,
by standing strong in your faith. You know that your Christian family all over the world is having the same kinds of suffering.
10And after you suffer for a short time, God, who gives all grace, will make everything right. He will make you strong and support you and keep you from falling. He called you to share in his glory in Christ, a glory that will continue forever. 11All power is his forever and ever. Amen.

SIDELIGHT: When 1 Peter 5:13 mentions Babylon, it probably refers to Rome, the capital of the Roman Empire. (The comparison comes from the common practice of using Babylon as a "code name" for Rome.) By the time 1 Peter was written, the historic city of Babylon was just a small, insignificant village.

Final Greetings

12I wrote this short letter with the help of Silas, who I know is a faithful brother in Christ. I

WORRYING

Weighty Worries

Dwight Evans has played baseball with the Boston Red Sox for almost two decades. He has hit more than 350 home runs, batted in 1,200 runs and had 2,000 hits. His salary matches his accomplishments. He shouldn't have much to worry about, right?

But he does. His two teenage sons suffer from neurofibromatosis, a genetic disorder that causes tumors on the skin. Both sons have had numerous surgeries and radiation treatments. Since the disease is incurable, their future remains uncertain.

"It's very easy to feel sorry for ourselves," Evans says. What keeps Evans and his wife from being overwhelmed with worries? Their faith. "I can't tell you the number of times we've just gotten down on our knees and prayed," he explains. "We have faith in God to carry us through."

Like the Evans family, the early Christians needed assurance that God would deliver them from worries. Bible texts such as **1 Peter 5:6–11** helped them put life in perspective.

- How might this passage give hope and comfort to the Evans family?
- How does the passage, especially verse 7, speak to whatever worries you right now?

CONSIDER . . .

- memorizing verse 7 to encourage you when worries get you down.
- keeping a list of troubles and prayers. Over time, review the list, remembering how God helped you endure various problems.

FOR MORE, SEE . . .

- Proverbs 3:3–5
- Matthew 11:28–30
- Revelation 2:8–11

wrote to encourage you and to tell you that this is the true grace of God. Stand strong in that grace.

13The church in Babylon, who was chosen like
you, sends you greetings. Mark, my son in Christ, also greets you.
14Give each other a kiss of Christian love when you meet.

Peace to all of you who are in Christ.

2 PETER

Why Read This Book:

- Be assured that the Christian faith is true (2 Peter 1).
- Learn how to respond to false teaching (2 Peter 2).
- Anticipate Christ's return (2 Peter 3).

Behind the Scenes:

Walking on rocks is fairly easy if you have a good pair of shoes. But what happens when even a small pebble inches its way inside your shoe? The pain and annoyance are almost unbearable. Something has to be done!

Think of 2 Peter as dealing with a pebble in the church's shoe. The early church expected false teachings outside the church, and these Christians had learned to protect themselves from those false teachings. But then, like an annoying pebble, false teachings entered the church. Some people were accepting the teachings as truth. But 2 Peter challenged them to get rid of the "pebble" before it caused more problems.

This hard-hitting letter urges believers to counteract false "knowledge" with true knowledge. It exposes the false beliefs of those who said Jesus would not come again. And it attacks those who lived sinful lives by abusing their freedom in Christ. Christ is coming again, the letter proclaims. And Christians should live moral lives as they wait for that return.

This short letter challenges us today, just as it challenged its original readers. Watch out for false teachers. Live lives that follow God's commands. And wait with anticipation for Christ to come again.

WHEN THE ACTION WAS

BC/AD	25AD	50AD	75AD	100AD
Jesus was born	The church began soon after Jesus went to heaven	Paul began his missionary work	Fire destroyed Rome	
	Jesus began his ministry		2 Peter may have been written	The Roman emperor increased persecution of Christians

1 From Simon Peter, a servant and apostle[d] of
Jesus Christ.
To you who have received a faith as valuable
as ours, because our God and Savior Jesus Christ
does what is right.
2Grace and peace be given to you more and
more, because you truly know God and Jesus our
Lord.

SIDELIGHT: *If you want to read a short version of 2 Peter, check out Jude. About nineteen of the twenty-five verses in Jude are similar to verses in 2 Peter.*

God Has Given Us Blessings

3Jesus has the power of God, by which he has
given us everything we need to live and to serve
God. We have these things because we know
him. Jesus called us by his glory and goodness.
4Through these he gave us the very great and precious promises. With these gifts you can share in
being like God, and the world will not ruin you
with its evil desires.
5Because you have these blessings, do your best
to add these things to your lives: to your faith, add
goodness; and to your goodness, add knowledge;
6and to your knowledge, add self-control; and to
your self-control, add patience; and to your patience, add service for God; 7and to your service
for God, add kindness for your brothers and sisters in Christ; and to this kindness, add love. 8If
all these things are in you and are growing, they
will help you to be useful and productive in your
knowledge of our Lord Jesus Christ. 9But anyone
who does not have these things cannot see
clearly. He is blind and has forgotten that he was
made clean from his past sins.
10My brothers and sisters,[n] try hard to be certain that you really are called and chosen by God.
If you do all these things, you will never fall.
11And you will be given a very great welcome into
the eternal kingdom of our Lord and Savior Jesus
Christ.
12You know these things, and you are very
strong in the truth, but I will always help you remember them. 13I think it is right for me to help
you remember as long as I am in this body. 14I
know I must soon leave this body, as our Lord
Jesus Christ has shown me. 15I will try my best so
that you may be able to remember these things
even after I am gone.

We Saw Christ's Glory

16When we told you about the powerful coming of our Lord Jesus Christ, we were not telling
just smart stories that someone invented. But we
saw the greatness of Jesus with our own eyes.
17Jesus heard the voice of God, the Greatest
Glory, when he received honor and glory from
God the Father. The voice said, "This is my Son,
whom I love, and I am very pleased with him."
18We heard that voice from heaven while we
were with Jesus on the holy mountain.
19This makes us more sure about the message
the prophets[d] gave. It is good for you to follow
closely what they said as you would follow a light
shining in a dark place, until the day begins and
the morning star rises in your hearts. 20Most of all,
you must understand this: No prophecy in the
Scriptures[d] ever comes from the prophet's own
interpretation. 21No prophecy ever came from
what a person wanted to say, but people led by
the Holy Spirit[d] spoke words from God.

False Teachers

2 There used to be false prophets[d] among
God's people, just as you will have some
false teachers in your group. They will secretly
teach things that are wrong—teachings that will
cause people to be lost. They will even refuse to
accept the Master, Jesus, who bought their freedom. So they will bring quick ruin on themselves.
2Many will follow their evil ways and say evil
things about the way of truth. 3Those false teachers only want your money, so they will use you
by telling you lies. Their judgment spoken against
them long ago is still coming, and their ruin is
certain.
4When angels sinned, God did not let them go
free without punishment. He sent them to hell
and put them in caves of darkness where they are
being held for judgment. 5And God punished the
world long ago when he brought a flood to the
world that was full of people who were against
him. But God saved Noah, who preached about
being right with God, and seven other people
with him. 6And God also destroyed the evil cities
of Sodom and Gomorrah[n] by burning them until
they were ashes. He made those cities an example
of what will happen to those who are against God.
7But he saved Lot from those cities. Lot, a good
man, was troubled because of the filthy lives of
evil people. 8(Lot was a good man, but because he
lived with evil people every day, his good heart
was hurt by the evil things he saw and heard.) 9So
the Lord knows how to save those who serve him
when troubles come. He will hold evil people and

brothers and sisters Although the Greek text reads "brothers" here and throughout this book, Peter's words were meant for the entire church, including men and women.
Sodom and Gomorrah Two cities God destroyed because the people were so evil.

punish them, while waiting for the Judgment
Day. 10That punishment is especially for those
who live by doing the evil things their sinful
selves want and who hate authority.
These false teachers are bold and do anything
they want. They are not afraid to speak against
the angels. 11But even the angels, who are much
stronger and more powerful than false teachers,
do not accuse them with insults before the Lord.
12But these people speak against things they do
not understand. They are like animals that act
without thinking, animals born to be caught and
killed. And, like animals, these false teachers will
be destroyed. 13They have caused many people to
suffer, so they themselves will suffer. That is their
pay for what they have done. They take pleasure
in openly doing evil, so they are like dirty spots
and stains among you. They delight in trickery
while eating meals with you. 14Every time they
look at a woman they want her, and their desire
for sin is never satisfied. They lead weak people
into the trap of sin, and they have taught their
hearts to be greedy. God will punish them!
15These false teachers left the right road and lost
their way, following the way Balaam went. Balaam was the son of Beor, who loved being paid
for doing wrong. 16But a donkey, which cannot
talk, told Balaam he was sinning. It spoke with a
man's voice and stopped the prophet's crazy
thinking.
17Those false teachers are like springs without
water and clouds blown by a storm. A place in the
blackest darkness has been kept for them. 18They
brag with words that mean nothing. By their evil
desires they lead people into the trap of sin — people who are just beginning to escape from others
who live in error. 19They promise them freedom,
but they themselves are not free. They are slaves
of things that will be destroyed. For people are
slaves of anything that controls them. 20They
were made free from the evil in the world by
knowing our Lord and Savior Jesus Christ. But if
they return to evil things and those things control
them, then it is worse for them than it was before.
21Yes, it would be better for them to have never
known the right way than to know it and to turn
away from the holy teaching that was given to
them. 22What they did is like this true saying: "A

BIBLE STUDY

God's Love Letter

Have you ever received love letters? No doubt you read them differently than you would read junk mail or a form letter inviting you to join Latin club. Indeed, author Mortimer Adler says that when we read a love letter, we:

- read every word three ways,
- read between the lines,
- weigh each sentence,
- perceive the color of each word, and,
- look for deep meaning, even in the punctuation.

When you are in love, you read a love letter over and over, carefully, and in depth.

If the Bible were a letter, what kind of letter would it be for you? Would it be "junk mail"? Would it be boring "required reading" such as a literature assignment? Or, would it be a "love letter" from God to you?

The writer of **2 Peter 1:16–21** guarantees that the life and message of Jesus Christ is not "junk mail." It's a love letter from God.

- Why might someone who loves God learn more from the Bible than someone who doesn't love God?
- How might reading more of God's "love letters" in the Bible help you face life's problems and decisions?

CONSIDER . . .

- listing reasons why people study the Bible, and then choosing which one is your top reason.
- reading the Gospel of Matthew over the next month (one chapter per day) as if it were addressed particularly to you.

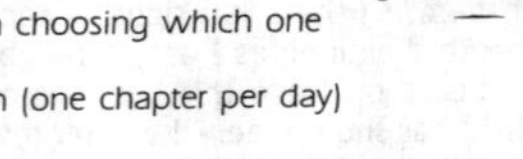

FOR MORE, SEE . . .

- Jeremiah 23:25–29
- Acts 17:11
- Hebrews 4:12–16

dog goes back to what it has thrown up,"[n] and, "After a pig is washed, it goes back and rolls in the mud."

Jesus Will Come Again

3 My friends, this is the second letter I have written you to help your honest minds remember. [2]I want you to think about the words the holy prophets[d] spoke in the past, and remember the command our Lord and Savior gave us through your apostles.[d] [3]It is most important for you to understand what will happen in the last days. People will laugh at you. They will live doing the evil things they want to do. [4]They will say, "Jesus promised to come again. Where is he? Our fathers have died, but the world continues the way it has been since it was made." [5]But they do not want to remember what happened long ago. By the word of God heaven was made, and the earth was made from water and with water. [6]Then the world was flooded and destroyed with water. [7]And that same word of God is keeping heaven and earth that we now have in order to be destroyed by fire. They are being kept for the Judgment Day and the destruction of all who are against God.

[8]But do not forget this one thing, dear friends: To the Lord one day is as a thousand years, and a thousand years is as one day. [9]The Lord is not slow in doing what he promised—the way some people understand slowness. But God is being patient with you. He does not want anyone to be lost, but he wants all people to change their hearts and lives.

[10]But the day of the Lord will come like a thief. The skies will disappear with a loud noise. Everything in them will be destroyed by fire, and the earth and everything in it will be burned up.[n]

"A dog . . . up" Quotation from Proverbs 26:11.
will be burned up Many Greek copies say, "will be found." One copy says, "will disappear."

FUTURE

Party Now?

"Why shouldn't I party?" protested sixteen-year-old Joe Williams at a youth group meeting. "The world might not even be around when I'm twenty."

Joe didn't see much hope for the future. He read newspapers and newsmagazines to keep up with world events. The more Joe read, the more he became a sarcastic pessimist.

"We're either gonna die in a nuclear war or from poisoning our environment," he would say. His cynical attitude began to affect his views on life issues. He still received good grades, but he no longer enjoyed learning

At one time in junior high, Joe had held to high values about issues such as sex, alcohol use, and the environment. In his dark gloom about the future, however, those values seemed irrelevant to him.

"I just hang out, watch some TV, and look out for a good time," he said. "I want to live it up now while I still can."

Joe said his dark view of the future might have something to do with his uncertainty about God. "I don't even know if God can get us out of this mess, or even if he cares," he said. "I'm living for now and for me. I wish there were hope somewhere, but I don't see any right now."

Joe's views of the future negatively affected how he lived every day. In contrast, **2 Peter 3:8–13** offers a hopeful message that can positively affect how we live now.

- If Joe were to read this passage, what hope or encouragement about the future might he find?
- How does knowing that the future rests in God's hands influence the way you live your life?

CONSIDER . . .

- living like God is in complete control of your day.
- setting three important goals to reach in the next five years, based on your reading of the passage.

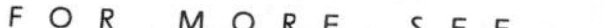

FOR MORE, SEE . . .

- Isaiah 65:17–25
- Mark 13:32–37
- Revelation 21:1–5

11In that way everything will be destroyed. So
what kind of people should you be? You should
live holy lives and serve God, 12as you wait for
and look forward to the coming of the day of God.
When that day comes, the skies will be destroyed
with fire, and everything in them will melt with
heat. 13But God made a promise to us, and we are
waiting for a new heaven and a new earth where
goodness lives.

> **SIDELIGHT:** According to 2 Peter 3:15–16, you are in good company if you sometimes have trouble understanding Romans or other books that Paul wrote. Peter did too. This passage is a rare example of a New Testament author giving another New Testament book the authority of Scripture.

14Dear friends, since you are waiting for this to
happen, do your best to be without sin and without fault. Try to be at peace with God. 15Remem-
ber that we are saved because our Lord is patient.
Our dear brother Paul told you the same thing
when he wrote to you with the wisdom that God
gave him. 16He writes about this in all his letters.
Some things in Paul's letters are hard to understand, and people who are ignorant and weak in
faith explain these things falsely. They also falsely
explain the other Scriptures,[d] but they are destroying themselves by doing this.

17Dear friends, since you already know about
this, be careful. Do not let those evil people lead
you away by the wrong they do. Be careful so you
will not fall from your strong faith. 18But grow in
the grace and knowledge of our Lord and Savior
Jesus Christ. Glory be to him now and forever!
Amen.

1 JOHN

Why Read This Book:

- Find out how to grow closer to God (1 John 1—2).
- See what it's like to be part of God's family (1 John 3—4).
- Be assured of life with God after death (1 John 5).

Behind the Scenes:

When you read the book of 1 John, you almost have the feeling that a grandfather has gathered his grandchildren around a fire to talk. You can see his love for them sparkling in his eyes, and you know from the way they look at him that they respect him a great deal.

As he talks to his "children," as he calls them, you can feel the warmth. He reassures them of God's love for them. He gently coaxes them to believe in and follow God.

But he also has another purpose. He is worried that the younger Christians are hearing mixed messages about Jesus Christ. People—known as gnostics—are saying that Jesus wasn't really human; he was only divine. Furthermore, they were arguing that they could do whatever they wanted to do with their bodies, because the physical body was separate from the spiritual nature.

The grandfather knows these ideas are wrong. Jesus was both fully human and fully divine. And what the body does certainly affects the spirit—for better or worse. So the grandfather challenges the false teaching and urges his children to stick to the truth.

Of course, 1 John isn't really a fireside chat between a grandfather and his grandchildren. It's a letter or sermon written to Christians to help them grow in their faith and to counteract the false teaching that was gaining influence among the early Christians.

Yet the true spirit of the letter comes through when we imagine the love and warmth that comes when we sit around a fireplace, listening to the advice of a wise grandfather. Not only did the words encourage and challenge the original hearers to keep following God, but they challenge and encourage us today.

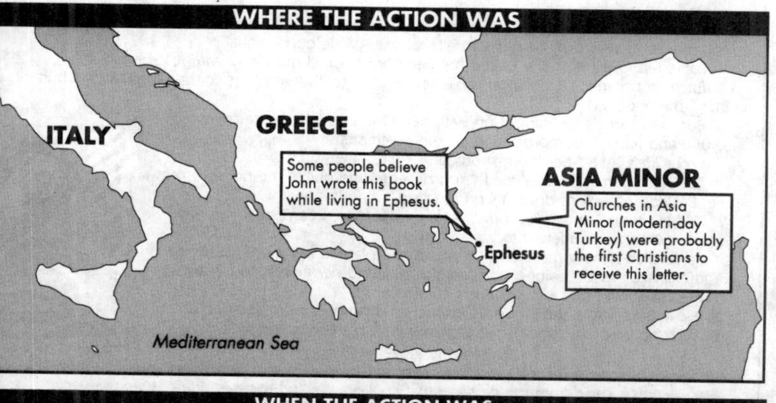
WHERE THE ACTION WAS
ITALY
GREECE
ASIA MINOR
Some people believe John wrote this book while living in Ephesus.
Churches in Asia Minor (modern-day Turkey) were probably the first Christians to receive this letter.
Ephesus
Mediterranean Sea
WHEN THE ACTION WAS
Jesus
The church began soon after Jesus went to heaven
Paul began his missionary work
Fire destroyed Rome
I John was written
25AD
50AD
75AD
100AD
Jesus began his ministry
Paul became a Christian
Romans destroyed the Temple in Jerusalem

1 We write you now about what has always
existed, which we have heard, we have seen
with our own eyes, we have looked at, and we
have touched with our hands. We write to you
about the Word[n] that gives life. 2He who gives
life was shown to us. We saw him and can give
proof about it. And now we announce to you that
he has life that continues forever. He was with
God the Father and was shown to us. 3We announce to you what we have seen and heard, because we want you also to have fellowship with
us. Our fellowship is with God the Father and
with his Son, Jesus Christ. 4We write this to you
so you can be full of joy with us.

God Forgives Our Sins

5Here is the message we have heard from
Christ and now announce to you: God is light,[n]
and in him there is no darkness at all. 6So if we
say we have fellowship with God, but we continue living in darkness, we are liars and do not
follow the truth. 7But if we live in the light, as
God is in the light, we can share fellowship with
each other. Then the blood of Jesus, God's Son,
cleanses us from every sin.

8If we say we have no sin, we are fooling ourselves, and the truth is not in us. 9But if we confess our sins, he will forgive our sins, because we
can trust God to do what is right. He will cleanse
us from all the wrongs we have done. 10If we say
we have not sinned, we make God a liar, and we
do not accept God's teaching.

Jesus Is Our Helper

2 My dear children, I write this letter to you
so you will not sin. But if anyone does sin,
we have a helper in the presence of the Father—
Jesus Christ, the One who does what is right. 2He

Word The Greek word is "logos," meaning any kind of communication. Here, it means Christ, who was the way God told people about himself.
light Here, this word is used as a symbol of God's goodness or truth.

SIN

No Excuses

Lanie Pritchard remembers the first time she lied to her mom about where she was going. "Janet, Kate, and I are going to a movie," she lied without looking straight into her mom's eyes.

Could her mom tell she was lying? Lanie couldn't tell, so she quickly left the house.

The party blared away when the three girls arrived. "See, it wasn't so hard to fool your mom," Janet teased Lanie.

Still, Lanie was tense the whole evening. When she got home, her mom asked about the movie. "It was okay," Lanie casually replied. "Well, good night."

Lanie felt relieved as she closed her bedroom door. "I got away with it," she thought.

Each lie became easier. Soon Lanie lied with ease. "What Mom doesn't know won't hurt her," she reasoned.

But then Lanie's lies caught up with her. One evening she came home drunk and found her mom sitting on the porch steps.

"Your life's a lie!" her mom shouted.

"It's not my fault," Lanie cried. "You never let me out of the house unless I lie. Besides, other kids do it. It's no big deal."

"I don't think I know you now," Mom said. "And, I can't trust you anymore. What has happened to you . . . to us?"

Lanie didn't know the answer. Instead, she blamed her mom for her lies and excused her behavior by comparing herself to her friends. Yet **1 John 1:1—2:2** shows that excuses don't eliminate sin.

- How is Lanie's situation similar to the sin described in these verses?
- Why do you think John so strongly emphasizes confessing sin?

C O N S I D E R . . .

- apologizing to someone who has been hurt by your sins.
- selecting a verse from the passage that conveys the "no excuses" idea. Write the verse on a small card and memorize it.

F O R M O R E S E E . . .

- Genesis 3:1–13
- Psalm 51:1–13
- Luke 15:11–24

is the way our sins are taken away, and not only
our sins but the sins of all people.

> **SIDELIGHT:** Perhaps the biggest heresy (wrong doctrine) that the early church faced involved the gnostic understanding of evil. Gnostics—whose name came from the word for "knowledge"—believed evil was simply an error that grew out of ignorance; the person who did wrong was not really responsible. First John responded that people are responsible for their sins and must be forgiven to be right with God (1 John 1:9; 2:2).

[3]We can be sure that we know God if we obey
his commands. [4]Anyone who says, "I know God,"
but does not obey God's commands is a liar, and
the truth is not in that person. [5]But if someone
obeys God's teaching, then in that person God's
love has truly reached its goal. This is how we can
be sure we are living in God: [6]Whoever says that
he lives in God must live as Jesus lived.

The Command to Love Others

[7]My dear friends, I am not writing a new command to you but an old command you have had
from the beginning. It is the teaching you have
already heard. [8]But also I am writing a new command to you, and you can see its truth in Jesus
and in you, because the darkness is passing away,
and the true light is already shining.

[9]Anyone who says, "I am in the light,"[n] but
hates a brother or sister,[n] is still in the darkness.
[10]Whoever loves a brother or sister lives in the
light and will not cause anyone to stumble in his
faith. [11]But whoever hates a brother or sister is in
darkness, lives in darkness, and does not know
where to go, because the darkness has made that
person blind.

[12]I write to you, dear children,
because your sins are forgiven through
Christ.
[13]I write to you, parents,
because you know the One who existed
from the beginning.
I write to you, young people,
because you have defeated the Evil One.
[14]I write to you, children,
because you know the Father.
I write to you, parents,
because you know the One who existed
from the beginning.
I write to you, young people,
because you are strong;
the teaching of God lives in you,
and you have defeated the Evil One.

[15]Do not love the world or the things in the
world. If you love the world, the love of the Father is not in you. [16]These are the ways of the
world: wanting to please our sinful selves, wanting the sinful things we see, and being too proud
of what we have. None of these come from the
Father, but all of them come from the world.
[17]The world and everything that people want in
it are passing away, but the person who does
what God wants lives forever.

Reject the Enemies of Christ

[18]My dear children, these are the last days. You
have heard that the enemy of Christ[d] is coming,
and now many enemies of Christ are already
here. This is how we know that these are the last
days. [19]These enemies of Christ were in our fellowship, but they left us. They never really belonged to us; if they had been a part of us, they
would have stayed with us. But they left, and this
shows that none of them really belonged to us.

[20]You have the gift[n] that the Holy One gave
you, so you all know the truth. [21]I do not write
to you because you do not know the truth but
because you do know the truth. And you know
that no lie comes from the truth.

[22]Who is the liar? It is the person who does not
accept Jesus as the Christ. This is the enemy of
Christ: the person who does not accept the Father
and his Son. [23]Whoever does not accept the Son
does not have the Father. But whoever confesses
the Son has the Father, too.

[24]Be sure you continue to follow the teaching
you heard from the beginning. If you continue to
follow what you heard from the beginning, you
will stay in the Son and in the Father. [25]And this
is what the Son promised to us—life forever.

[26]I am writing this letter about those people
who are trying to lead you the wrong way.
[27]Christ gave you a special gift that is still in
you, so you do not need any other teacher. His
gift teaches you about everything, and it is true,
not false. So continue to live in Christ, as his
gift taught you.

[28]Yes, my dear children, live in him so that
when Christ comes back, we can be without fear
and not be ashamed in his presence. [29]If you

light Here, this word is used as a symbol of God's goodness or truth.
brother or sister Although the Greek text says "brother" here and throughout this book, the writer's words were meant for the entire church, including men and women.
gift This might mean the Holy Spirit, or it might mean teaching or truth as in verse 24.

know that Christ is all that is right, you know that
all who do right are God's children.

We Are God's Children

3 The Father has loved us so much that we are
called children of God. And we really are his
children. The reason the people in the world do
not know us is that they have not known him.
2Dear friends, now we are children of God, and
we have not yet been shown what we will be in
the future. But we know that when Christ comes
again, we will be like him, because we will see
him as he really is. 3Christ is pure, and all who
have this hope in Christ keep themselves pure like
Christ.
4The person who sins breaks God's law. Yes,
sin is living against God's law. 5You know that
Christ came to take away sins and that there is no
sin in Christ. 6So anyone who lives in Christ does
not go on sinning. Anyone who goes on sinning
has never really understood Christ and has never
known him.
7Dear children, do not let anyone lead you the
wrong way. Christ is all that is right. So to be like
Christ a person must do what is right. 8The devil
has been sinning since the beginning, so anyone
who continues to sin belongs to the devil. The
Son of God came for this purpose: to destroy the
devil's work.
9Those who are God's children do not continue
sinning, because the new life from God remains
in them. They are not able to go on sinning, because they have become children of God. 10So we
can see who God's children are and who the
devil's children are: Those who do not do what
is right are not God's children, and those who do
not love their brothers and sisters are not God's
children.

We Must Love Each Other

11This is the teaching you have heard from the
beginning: We must love each other. 12Do not be
like Cain who belonged to the Evil One and killed
his brother. And why did he kill him? Because the
things Cain did were evil, and the things his
brother did were good.

FOLLOWING GOD

Life at the Top

Lynn Hill has always been at the top of everything. When she was a kid, she was at the top of trees, telephone poles, even street lights. Now she is on top of cliffs and mountains as one of the world's leading rock climbers. She is one of the few people who has defied gravity and scaled cliffs that are "steeper" than vertical.

Lynn has gotten to be so good because she dedicates her life to her climbing. A picture taken the day after her wedding shows how important climbing is to her. It shows her and her new husband—also a climber, of course—in full wedding attire hanging from a rope off cliffs near their home.

Lynn knows how important it is to not become lax in her climbing techniques. Once she fell seventy-five feet down a cliff because she forgot to tie a simple knot on her safety rope. A tree branch slowed her fall and saved her life, though she was injured.

"The rock is a tool for learning and understanding," she says. "When you get to the top, you've conquered something inside as well."

Lynn's dedication to climbing illustrates the kind of dedication Christians should have in following God. **First John 3:1–24** encourages Christians not to be distracted from following God.

- What parallels do you see between Lynn's dedication to rock climbing and the passage's guidance about being a Christian?
- How have other Christians encouraged you and kept you dedicated to following God?

C O N S I D E R . . .

- thinking about everything you did in the past twenty-four hours. Decide which things helped you follow God and which ones did not.
- asking a Christian friend to help you overcome a sin that keeps you from following God, with the kind of dedication Lynn has for rock climbing.

F O R M O R E , S E E . . .

- Psalm 95:1–11
- Romans 7:14–25
- Ephesians 5:1–11

13Brothers and sisters, do not be surprised when the people of the world hate you. 14We know we have left death and have come into life because we love each other. Whoever does not love is still dead. 15Everyone who hates a brother or sister is a murderer,[n] and you know that no murderers have eternal life in them. 16This is how we know what real love is: Jesus gave his life for us. So we should give our lives for our brothers and sisters. 17Suppose someone has enough to live and sees a brother or sister in need, but does not help. Then God's love is not living in that person. 18My children, we should love people not only with words and talk, but by our actions and true caring.

SIDELIGHT: When 1 John 3:13 told believers not to be surprised that the world hates them, it was speaking to an everyday reality for Christians at that time in Asia Minor. Even the Roman historian Tacitus, who lived during that time, wrote that Romans hated the Christians.

19-20This is the way we know that we belong to the way of truth. When our hearts make us feel guilty, we can still have peace before God. God is greater than our hearts, and he knows everything. 21My dear friends, if our hearts do not make us feel guilty, we can come without fear into God's presence. 22And God gives us what we ask for because we obey God's commands and do what pleases him. 23This is what God commands: that we believe in his Son, Jesus Christ, and that we love each other, just as he commanded. 24The people who obey God's commands live in God, and God lives in them. We know that God lives in us because of the Spirit[d] God gave us.

Warning Against False Teachers

4 My dear friends, many false prophets[d] have gone out into the world. So do not believe every spirit, but test the spirits to see if they are from God. 2This is how you can know God's Spirit:[d] Every spirit who confesses that Jesus Christ came to earth as a human is from God. 3And every spirit who refuses to say this about Jesus is not from God. It is the spirit of the enemy of Christ,[d] which you have heard is coming, and now he is already in the world.

4My dear children, you belong to God and have defeated them; because God's Spirit, who is in you, is greater than the devil, who is in the world. 5And they belong to the world, so what they say is from the world, and the world listens to them. 6But we belong to God, and those who know God listen to us. But those who are not from God do not listen to us. That is how we know the Spirit that is true and the spirit that is false.

Love Comes from God

7Dear friends, we should love each other, because love comes from God. Everyone who loves has become God's child and knows God. 8Whoever does not love does not know God, because God is love. 9This is how God showed his love to us: He sent his one and only Son into the world so that we could have life through him. 10This is what real love is: It is not our love for God; it is God's love for us in sending his Son to be the way to take away our sins.

11Dear friends, if God loved us that much we also should love each other. 12No one has ever seen God, but if we love each other, God lives in us, and his love is made perfect in us.

13We know that we live in God and he lives in us, because he gave us his Spirit.[d] 14We have seen and can testify that the Father sent his Son to be the Savior of the world. 15Whoever confesses that Jesus is the Son of God has God living inside, and that person lives in God. 16And so we know the love that God has for us, and we trust that love.

God is love. Those who live in love live in God, and God lives in them. 17This is how love is made perfect in us: that we can be without fear on the day God judges us, because in this world we are like him. 18Where God's love is, there is no fear, because God's perfect love drives out fear. It is punishment that makes a person fear, so love is not made perfect in the person who fears.

19We love because God first loved us. 20If people say, "I love God," but hate their brothers or sisters, they are liars. Those who do not love their brothers and sisters, whom they have seen, cannot love God, whom they have never seen. 21And God gave us this command: Those who love God must also love their brothers and sisters.

Faith in the Son of God

5 Everyone who believes that Jesus is the Christ[d] is God's child, and whoever loves the Father also loves the Father's children. 2This is how we know we love God's children: when we love God and obey his commands. 3Loving God means obeying his commands. And God's commands are not too hard for us, 4because everyone who is a child of God conquers the world. And this is the victory that conquers the world — our faith. 5So the one who wins against the world is

Everyone . . . murderer If one person hates a brother or sister, then in the heart that person has killed that brother or sister. Jesus taught about this sin to his followers (Matthew 5:21-26).

the person who believes that Jesus is the Son of
God.
6Jesus Christ is the One who came by water[n]
and blood.[n] He did not come by water only, but
by water and blood. And the Spirit[d] says that this
is true, because the Spirit is the truth. 7So there
are three witnesses that tell us about Jesus: 8the
Spirit, the water, and the blood; and these three
witnesses agree. 9We believe people when they
say something is true. But what God says is more
important, and he has told us the truth about his
own Son. 10Anyone who believes in the Son of
God has the truth that God told us. Anyone who
does not believe makes God a liar, because that
person does not believe what God told us about
his Son. 11This is what God told us: God has given
us eternal life, and this life is in his Son. 12Who-
ever has the Son has life, but whoever does not
have the Son of God does not have life.

We Have Eternal Life Now

13I write this letter to you who believe in the
Son of God so you will know you have eternal life.
14And this is the boldness we have in God's presence: that if we ask God for anything that agrees
with what he wants, he hears us. 15If we know he
hears us every time we ask him, we know we
have what we ask from him.
16If anyone sees a brother or sister sinning (sin
that does not lead to eternal death), that person
should pray, and God will give the sinner life. I
am talking about people whose sin does not lead
to eternal death. There is sin that leads to death.
I do not mean that a person should pray about

water This probably means the water of Jesus' baptism.
blood This probably means the blood of Jesus' death.

LOVE

The First Step

"But I don't even like her," Michelle Benson complained to Angie Stone after the camp Bible study. "So how am I going to love her?"

No one could remember what started the feud between Cindy and Michelle. They had known each other since childhood, and seemed always in conflict. They accused each other of telling lies; they fought over boyfriends; they over-competed in classes.

Angie suggested that Christian love goes beyond liking what others do. "It's a conscious decision to care," Angie explained.

Michelle frowned. "No matter what she does, I have to love her?"

"Loving people who love us is easy," said Angie. "Loving difficult people makes Christian love unique."

Michelle walked away, frustrated by Angie's words. During the week at camp, however, Michelle watched others build new relationships and mend damaged ones. People who had not gotten along at first seemed to make peace with each other.

At the last campfire, the camp director urged the kids to settle differences with those whom they had hurt during the year. Michelle wanted to go to Cindy, but held back, fearing rejection.

Suddenly she saw Cindy coming straight toward her with tears in her eyes. "I'm sorry," Michelle heard Cindy say. The girls hugged and cried. Healing began.

Loving others even when you don't like them is tough, but it is possible. In **1 John 4:7–12**, look for unique qualities of Christian love in action.

- How did Michelle's initial attitude toward Cindy influence her relationship with God, according to this passage?
- Why is loving others easier when you understand how God loves you?

CONSIDER . . .

- making the first move to mend a damaged relationship with a family member or friend.
- asking several friends to go out for hamburgers, including someone who is difficult for you to love. Try to get to know that person better.

FOR MORE, SEE . . .

- Deuteronomy 6:5
- Matthew 5:43–48
- 1 Peter 4:8–9

that sin. 17Doing wrong is always sin, but there is
sin that does not lead to eternal death.
18We know that those who are God's children
do not continue to sin. The Son of God keeps
them safe, and the Evil One cannot touch them.
19We know that we belong to God, but the Evil
One controls the whole world. 20We also know
that the Son of God has come and has given us
understanding so that we can know the True
One. And our lives are in the True One and in his
Son, Jesus Christ. He is the true God and the eternal life.
21So, dear children, keep yourselves away from
gods.

DISCOURAGEMENT

Hope Breakers and Makers

Did you ever experience a day when everything went wrong? Sometimes the day seems like one disappointing event after another. These disappointments can be called "hope breakers." Hope breakers can lead to outright discouragement if they persist. Which of these hope breakers seem familiar to you?

- threats of war in the world
- fights with your parents
- an accident in the family car
- breaking up with a girlfriend/boyfriend
- making a poor grade on a test
- doubting your Christian beliefs
- too much homework
- criticism from others
- feeling alone

Hope can overcome discouragement. Hope reminds you of a brighter future. Which of the events below are hope makers for you?

- feeling good about your life
- scoring high on a hard test
- giving and receiving Christian love from others
- making the team
- enjoying a beautiful day
- knowing God loves you
- getting a fantastic job
- having a great time with friends
- renewing a broken friendship

John offered reassurance and hope to Christians who had experienced too many hope breakers. Read John's hope-making ideas in **1 John 5:1–15**.

- How do the hope breakers and hope makers described above compare to the ones in this passage?
- What phrases in this passage offer you the most hope?

CONSIDER . . .

- writing out the promises and assurances in this passage. Post the list on your locker door.
- acting as a hope maker to a discouraged friend by offering encouragement, time or help.

FOR MORE, SEE . . .

- Psalm 42
- John 15:18–27
- Romans 8:35–39

2 JOHN

Why Read This Book:

- Learn ways to show Christian love (2 John 1–6).
- Examine the danger of listening to false teachers (2 John 7–11).

Behind the Scenes:

The musical-movie The Music Man tells about a swindling, traveling salesman who goes into gullible towns offering to start bands for the kids. Then when people get excited and give him money for uniforms and instruments, he slips out of town, laughing about the trick.

The early Christians faced a similar situation. Because they were always open and loving to strangers, false teachers would take advantage of their openness. These teachers would get into the church and begin spreading false teachings. (For a description of the teachings, see the introduction to 1 John).

Second John was written to warn churches not to welcome people who bring false teaching into the church. The short letter encourages them to keep loving each other. But, at the same time, it urges them to stay far away from false teachers.

As Christians, we too need to be open and loving to each other. But we also need to be on guard against people who present teachings that contradict the Bible. Second John challenges us to carefully evaluate others' statements before accepting them as true.

While 2 John warns against welcoming false teachers, 3 John gives the other side of the issue. It focuses on the importance of being hospitable toward fellow believers. Read the two letters together for a balanced picture.

WHEN THE ACTION WAS

Jesus was born — The church began soon after Jesus went to heaven — Paul began his missionary work — Fire destroyed Rome — 2 John was written

BC/AD — 25AD — 50AD — 75AD — 100AD

Jesus began his ministry — Paul became a Christian — Romans destroyed the Temple in Jerusalem

[1]From the Elder.[n]
To the chosen lady[n] and her children:
I love all of you in the truth,[n] and all those
who know the truth love you. [2]We love you because of the truth that lives in us and will be with
us forever.
[3]Grace, mercy, and peace from God the Father
and his Son, Jesus Christ, will be with us in truth
and love.
[4]I was very happy to learn that some of your
children are following the way of truth, as the
Father commanded us. [5]And now, dear lady, this
is not a new command but is the same command
we have had from the beginning. I ask you that
we all love each other. [6]And love means living the
way God commanded us to live. As you have
heard from the beginning, his command is this:
Live a life of love.
[7]Many false teachers are in the world now who
do not confess that Jesus Christ came to earth as
a human. Anyone who does not confess this is a
false teacher and an enemy of Christ.[d] [8]Be careful
yourselves that you do not lose everything you
have worked for, but that you receive your full
reward.

SIDELIGHT: If other books in the New Testament are letters (such as 1 Corinthians), then 2 John is more like a postcard. With only thirteen verses, it is the shortest book in the Bible. One reason it may have been short is so it could fit on a single sheet of papyrus, the paper of the day (2 John 12).

Elder "Elder" means an older person. It can also mean a special leader in the church (as in Titus 1:5).
lady This might mean a woman, or in this letter it might mean a church. If it is a church, then "her children" would be the people of the church.
truth The truth or "Good News" about Jesus Christ that joins all believers together.

CULTS

Christian Frauds

Amy Vanderhoof had just turned sixteen when she was approached by a friendly guy at the mall who engaged her in a conversation about God. The guy's enthusiasm about his beliefs impressed Amy. He invited her to a Bible study the next Tuesday evening. Already active in her church, Amy thought it sounded fun, so she went.

The Bible study began with upbeat songs. Then the teacher began his talk. He started calmly, but grew more energized as he taught. He held the Bible while he spoke, and he even referred to a Bible story Amy recognized. It all sounded real, acceptable, and safe.

Amy grew more involved. After attending several more Bible studies, she agreed to go with the group on a weekend retreat.

She never returned home.

Frantically, her parents tried to contact her, but the leaders kept them away. Soon her parents learned that she had "voluntarily" moved to a cult center in another state. Despite constant effort, Amy's parents never heard from her again.

Although the cult leaders used scripture, prayer, and other Christian-sounding ideas, Jesus Christ wasn't their focus. Since the beginning, false teachers have plagued the church. False teachers greatly concerned the writer of 2 John. Check out John's criteria for a false teacher in **2 John 7–11**.

- How could John's warning have helped Amy?
- What current false teachers or groups do you recognize from John's description?

C O N S I D E R . . .

- becoming aware of cults operating in your area. What do they believe? How do they recruit?
- seeking to understand more of Christ's teachings so that you will know when a false teacher "goes beyond" them (verse 9).

F O R M O R E , S E E . . .

- Daniel 6:7–23
- John 14:5–7
- 2 Timothy 4:3–5

[9]Anyone who goes beyond Christ's teaching and does not continue to follow only his teaching does not have God. But whoever continues to follow the teaching of Christ has both the Father and the Son. [10]If someone comes to you and does not bring this teaching, do not welcome or accept that person into your house. [11]If you welcome such a person, you share in the evi[l] work.

[12]I have many things to write to you, but I d[o] not want to use paper and ink. Instead, I hope t[o] come to you and talk face to face so we can be ful[l] of joy. [13]The children of your chosen sister[n] gree[t] you.

3 JOHN

Why Read This Book:

- Consider how Christians can support one another (3 John 1–8).
- See how much damage one negative leader can do (3 John 9–11).

Behind the Scenes:

Suppose a visitor walked in to your Sunday school class. Would you welcome him or her? Would you invite the visitor home for dinner? And suppose the visitor expressed different views from yours during the discussion. Would you be open to those views? Or would you cut the person off?

The two central characters in 3 John would answer those questions quite differently. Gaius (3 John 1) would probably welcome the visitor and listen closely to his or her views. Diotrephes (3 John 9) would probably shun the visitor and squelch his or her opinions.

The situation in 3 John was different from a Sunday school class, of course. Gaius was welcoming missionaries sent by "the Elder" (3 John 1), and the writer thanks him for it. Diotrephes refused to welcome these missionaries. In fact, he tried to kick out of the church anyone who did welcome them.

Like 2 John, 3 John focuses on welcoming and showing love to fellow Christians. Taken together, these two letters tell a lot about the church. On the one hand, Christians are called to love, accept, and serve one another in Christ. At the same time, Christians are to be on guard against false teachers. These two themes are as relevant to Christians today as they were back then.

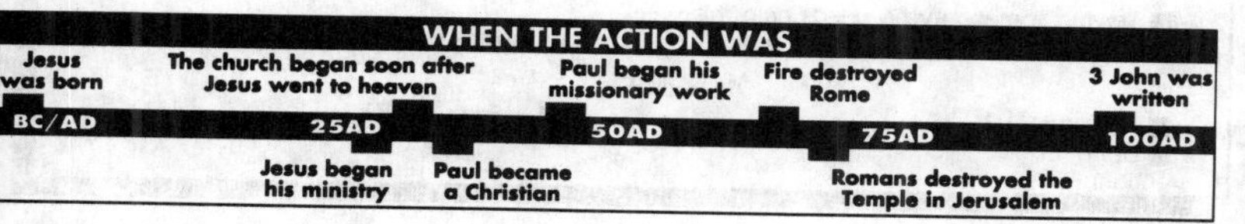

WHEN THE ACTION WAS
Jesus was born
The church began soon after Jesus went to heaven
Paul began his missionary work
Fire destroyed Rome
3 John was written
BC/AD
25AD
50AD
75AD
100AD
Jesus began his ministry
Paul became a Christian
Romans destroyed the Temple in Jerusalem

1From the Elder.[n]

To my dear friend Gaius, whom I love in the truth:[n]

2My dear friend, I know your soul is doing fine, and I pray that you are doing well in every way and that your health is good. 3I was very happy when some brothers and sisters[n] came and told me about the truth in your life and how you are following the way of truth. 4Nothing gives me greater joy than to hear that my children are following the way of truth.

5My dear friend, it is good that you help the brothers and sisters, even those you do not know. 6They told the church about your love. Please help them to continue their trip in a way worthy of God. 7They started out in service to Christ, and they have been accepting nothing from nonbelievers. 8So we should help such people; when we do, we share in their work for the truth.

> **SIDELIGHT:** Since motels in ancient times were notoriously dirty, flea-infested, and expensive, travelers often stayed in people's homes—without any advance notice (3 John 5–8). "Oh, Mom! Guess who's coming to dinner."

9I wrote something to the church, but Diotrephes, who loves to be their leader, will not listen to us. 10So if I come, I will talk about what Diotrephes is doing, about how he lies and says evil things about us. But more than that, he refuses to

Elder "Elder" means an older person. It can also mean a special leader in the church (as Titus 1:5).
truth The truth or "Good News" about Jesus Christ that joins all believers together.
brothers and sisters Although the Greek text says "brothers" here and throughout this book, the writer's words were meant for the entire church, including men and women.

SERVICE

Thanks for Coming

"Dear Mack,

"Thank you for coming so far away to teach me 'bout Jesus. I have fun. I miss you, but I'll read the Bible you gave me. I love you!— Wesley."

Mack Kemper smiled when he read the scrawled words on notebook paper. The unexpected thanks made Mack's week.

For five busy days, five hundred miles from home, twenty-two teenagers had used songs, crafts, and recreation to show Jesus' love to children in a small church. Eight-year-old Wesley Wilke was among the children who heard the exciting news about Jesus.

The summer trip had been Mack's first mission project. He didn't know what to expect, or whether the kids would like him. But Wesley had taken a special liking to Mack. Toward week's end, Wesley had asked Mack how he could make Jesus his friend. Mack had handed his own Bible to Wesley and had prayed with him. On the last day, Wesley had given Mack the short letter.

At the teenagers' final meeting before returning home, Mack read Wesley's letter. "I think I understand a little more about the song 'Jesus Loves Me, This I Know,' " Mack explained. "Now, I've seen it in action." From the back of the room the simple song began and grew as others joined in.

Mack found out how Christian service often helps the giver as much as the receiver. Read how John stressed the value of Christian service in **3 John 5–8**.

- How did Wesley benefit from Mack's serving? How did Mack benefit from the serving?
- How can John's idea of Christian service help both those receiving and those giving the service?

CONSIDER . . .

- serving someone who needs help this week.
- asking to serve on your youth group's or church's missions or outreach committee.

FOR MORE, SEE . . .

- Proverbs 11:24–25
- John 13:4–17
- 1 Peter 5:2–7

accept the other brothers and sisters; he even stops those who do want to accept them and puts them out of the church.

11My dear friend, do not follow what is bad; follow what is good. The one who does good belongs to God. But the one who does evil has never known God.

12Everyone says good things about Demetrius, and the truth agrees with what they say. We also speak well of him, and you know what we say is true.

13I have many things I want to write you, but
I do not want to use pen and ink. 14I hope to see
you soon and talk face to face. 15Peace to you. The
friends here greet you. Please greet each friend there by name.

JUDE

Why Read This Book:

- Test others' beliefs against the truth of Jesus Christ (Jude 1–4).
- Focus on the dangers of listening to false teachers (Jude 5–16).
- Be challenged to stay strong in your faith (Jude 17–24).

Behind the Scenes:

Termites can destroy a building before you even know they are there. The wood might look fine from the outside, but inside the termites have hollowed the beams. If you don't discover the damage soon enough and get rid of the insects, the building can become so weak that it can't be salvaged.

The early church had to deal with false teachers who were like termites in the church. They had sneaked into the church with lies about Jesus and salvation. Unless the church got rid of the false teachers, they could weaken or even destroy the church.

Jude urges the church to get rid of the termites!—"to fight hard for the faith that was given the holy people of God" (Jude 3). These false teachers evidently believed that their freedom encouraged them to follow the modern philosophy: "If it feels good, do it." These people will be punished by God in the end, the author says, but in the meantime their loose morals, hypocrisy, rejection of authority, and divisiveness were infecting the church.

How should the Christians deal with the false teachers? By being strong in their own faith, Jude says. By praying. By focusing on God's love. By waiting patiently for Jesus Christ. And even though Christians hate and avoid what these sinful people do, Christians should reach out to them with God's love (Jude 20–23).

As Christians, we regularly encounter people who believe and act differently from us. How do we respond to them? The book of Jude offers positive guidance.

WHEN THE ACTION WAS

Jesus was born
The church began soon after Jesus went to heaven
Paul began his missionary work
Fire destroyed Rome

BC/AD — 25AD — 50AD — 75AD — 100AD

Jesus began his ministry
Paul became a Christian
Jude may have been written
Romans destroyed the Temple in Jerusalem

[1]From Jude, a servant of Jesus Christ and a
brother of James.

To all who have been called by God. God the Father loves you, and you have been kept safe in Jesus Christ:

[2]Mercy, peace, and love be yours richly.

God Will Punish Sinners

[3]Dear friends, I wanted very much to write you
about the salvation we all share. But I felt the
need to write you about something else: I want
to encourage you to fight hard for the faith that
was given the holy people of God once and for all
time. [4]Some people have secretly entered your
group. Long ago the prophets[d] wrote about these
people who will be judged guilty. They are against
God and have changed the grace of our God into
a reason for sexual sin. They also refuse to accept
Jesus Christ, our only Master and Lord.

[5]I want to remind you of some things you already know: Remember that the Lord saved his
people by bringing them out of the land of Egypt.
But later he destroyed all those who did not believe. [6]And remember the angels who did not
keep their place of power but left their proper
home. The Lord has kept these angels in darkness, bound with everlasting chains, to be judged
on the great day. [7]Also remember the cities of

FOLLOWING GOD

Standing Alone

At a large youth convention, thirty-two teams competed for a $500 prize in a Bible quiz game called the "Holy Word Squares." Most teams had five members. But one team had only one person, a shy thirteen-year-old named Chris Bailey.

Chris was short, skinny and wore heavy glasses. He had been so excited about the Bible quiz that he had tried to find four other youth-group kids to team up with him. But they were not interested; they had other things to do besides practice for a Bible game.

Their rejection didn't stop Chris. He entered the competition alone—a one-person "team." For weeks before the contest, Chris studied the Bible and "scrimmaged" with his youth minister. He got better and better.

When Chris's youth group got to the convention, the other kids went swimming while Chris began to compete. No one took him seriously, until he won a preliminary round. Then he won the next round. Then the semifinals. By the final game, everyone was curious about this one-person team.

More than seven hundred people eagerly awaited the final round with Chris against a five-member team. First, the other team won. Then Chris won. The tournament all came down to one, tie-breaking game.

Each side answered question after question. When the round was almost over, Chris took the lead. Then he correctly answered the final question. He had won!

As Chris raised his arms in victory, his youth group swarmed around him in celebration. The crowd gave him a screaming, standing ovation.

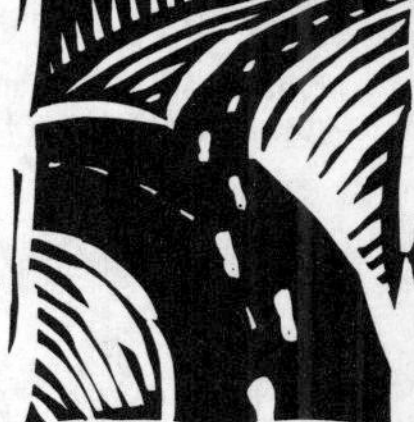

His group cheered again when he announced that he was giving the prize money to the group. Pizza was on him!

Despite the way he was treated at first, Chris stuck with what he believed. His story illustrates the kind of determination and faith **Jude 17–25** urges all Christians to have as they seek to follow God.

- How was Chris's solitary stand like the ways Jude tells believers to keep following God?
- What situations do you encounter in which this passage can encourage you to keep following God?

C O N S I D E R . . .

- rating from one to ten your willingness to act on your faith, with ten as the highest. Why did you rate yourself as you did?
- practicing sharing your faith with a Christian friend. Then share it with a non-Christian friend.

F O R   M O R E ,   S E E . . .

- Psalm 113
- 1 Thessalonians 5:12–22
- 1 Peter 2:4–10

Sodom and Gomorrah[n] and the other towns around them. In the same way they were full of sexual sin and people who desired sexual relations that God does not allow. They suffer the punishment of eternal fire, as an example for all to see.

8It is the same with these people who have entered your group. They are guided by dreams and make themselves filthy with sin. They reject God's authority and speak against the angels. 9Not even the archangel[n] Michael, when he argued with the devil about who would have the body of Moses, dared to judge the devil guilty. Instead, he said, "The Lord punish you." 10But these people speak against things they do not understand. And what they do know, by feeling, as dumb animals know things, are the very things that destroy them. 11It will be terrible for them. They have followed the way of Cain, and for money they have given themselves to doing the wrong that Balaam did. They have fought against God as Korah did, and like Korah, they surely will be destroyed. 12They are like dirty spots in your special Christian meals you share. They eat with you and have no fear, caring only for themselves. They are clouds without rain, which the wind blows around. They are autumn trees without fruit that are pulled out of the ground. So they are twice dead. 13They are like wild waves of the sea, tossing up their own shameful actions like foam. They are like stars that wander in the sky. A place in the blackest darkness has been kept for them forever.

14Enoch, the seventh descendant[d] from Adam, said about these people: "Look, the Lord is coming with many thousands of his holy angels to 15judge every person. He is coming to punish all who are against God for all the evil they have done against him. And he will punish the sinners who are against God for all the evil they have said against him."

16These people complain and blame others, doing the evil things they want to do. They brag about themselves, and they flatter others to get what they want.

A Warning and Things to Do

17Dear friends, remember what the apostles[d] of our Lord Jesus Christ said before. 18They said to you, "In the last times there will be people who laugh about God, following their own evil desires which are against God." 19These are the people who divide you, people whose thoughts are only of this world, who do not have the Spirit.[d]

20But dear friends, use your most holy faith to build yourselves up, praying in the Holy Spirit. 21Keep yourselves in God's love as you wait for the Lord Jesus Christ with his mercy to give you life forever.

22Show mercy to some people who have doubts. 23Take others out of the fire, and save them. Show mercy mixed with fear to others, hating even their clothes which are dirty from sin.

Praise God

24God is strong and can help you not to fall. He can bring you before his glory without any wrong in you and can give you great joy. 25He is the only God, the One who saves us. To him be glory, greatness, power, and authority through Jesus Christ our Lord for all time past, now, and forever. Amen.

SIDELIGHT: Don't look for the quotation by Enoch in the Old Testament (Jude 14–15). This is a direct quote from a book known as 1 Enoch, which is part of the sixty-five documents known as the Pseudepigrapha. Christians don't consider these books part of scripture, but the books were widely read and quoted in New Testament times.

Sodom and Gomorrah Two cities God destroyed because they were so evil.
archangel The leader among God's angels or messengers.

REVELATION

Why Read This Book:

- Hear warnings about problems in churches (Revelation 1—3).
- See God's power against the forces of evil (Revelation 4—11).
- Be comforted by God's promise of hope for all his people (Revelation 12—22).

Behind the Scenes:

A blood-red moon. A lamb with seven horns and seven eyes. Locusts with golden crowns. White, red, black, and pale horses. A giant, red dragon. A sea of glass mixed with fire.

These images sound like they are straight out of a science-fiction movie. But they are not; they are from the book of Revelation, the last book of the Bible. They make the book exciting and mysterious . . . and confusing.

This book can be so difficult to understand because it is "apocalyptic" literature. This literature uses mysterious visions and symbolic language to describe God's victory over the troubles of this world. Most often, this kind of literature was written during tough times, when the church was being persecuted. One reason for using the images and symbols was to use symbols that Christians would understand, but others would not.

That's certainly true of the book of Revelation. At the time, Christians were under attack by the Roman authorities. The Romans demanded that all people worship the emperor. Many Christians refused, and many were executed.

The book of Revelation was written to give hope and courage to these persecuted Christians. Scholars view the symbols, events and visions in Revelation in different ways. Some of the major perspectives include:

- The book describes the first-century situation, and all the events described in it have taken place.
- The book contains predictions for a long chain of events that will conclude with Christ's Second Coming.

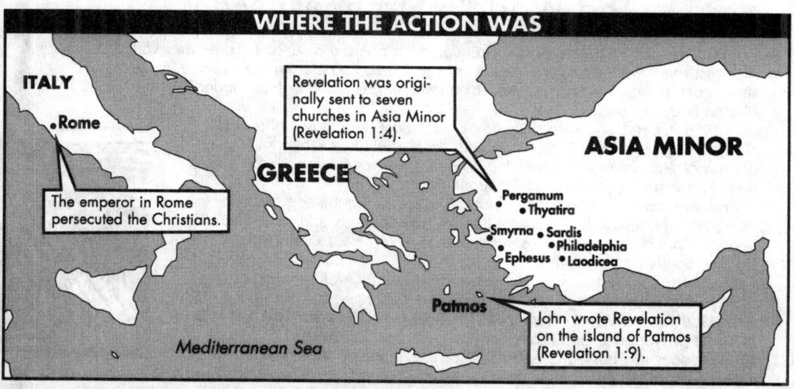

WHERE THE ACTION WAS
ITALY
Rome
Revelation was originally sent to seven churches in Asia Minor (Revelation 1:4).
ASIA MINOR
GREECE
The emperor in Rome persecuted the Christians.
Pergamum
Thyatira
Smyrna
Sardis
Philadelphia
Ephesus
Laodicea
Patmos
John wrote Revelation on the island of Patmos (Revelation 1:9).
Mediterranean Sea

WHEN THE ACTION WAS

BC/AD	25AD	50AD	75AD	100AD

Above the timeline:
- Jesus was born (BC/AD)
- The church began soon after Jesus went to heaven
- Paul began his missionary work
- Fire destroyed Rome
- The book of Revelation was written

Below the timeline:
- Jesus began his ministry
- Paul became a Christian
- Romans destroyed the Temple in Jerusalem

Behind the Scenes (cont.):

- The visions describe the final days before the end of the world, and do not relate directly to biblical times.
- The book does not predict the future; rather, it uses symbolic language to teach religious truth about God's victory over evil.

Regardless of the specific perspective, central themes are clear. God is powerful. Jesus Christ reigns forever. Those who suffer for Christ will ultimately share his victory. Revelation gives a message of hope and encouragement for all people in all times.

John Tells About This Book

1 This is the revelation[n] of Jesus Christ,
which God gave to him, to show his servants
what must soon happen. And Jesus sent his angel
to show it to his servant John, 2who has told everything he has seen. It is the word of God; it is
the message from Jesus Christ. 3Happy is the one
who reads the words of God's message, and
happy are the people who hear this message and
do what is written in it. The time is near when all
of this will happen.

Jesus' Message to the Churches

4From John.
To the seven churches in the country of Asia:

Grace and peace to you from the One who is
and was and is coming, and from the seven spirits
before his throne, 5and from Jesus Christ. Jesus is
the faithful witness, the first among those raised
from the dead. He is the ruler of the kings of the
earth.

He is the One who loves us, who made us free
from our sins with the blood of his death. 6He
made us to be a kingdom of priests who serve God
his Father. To Jesus Christ be glory and power
forever and ever! Amen.

7Look, Jesus is coming with the clouds, and everyone will see him, even those who stabbed him.
And all peoples of the earth will cry loudly because of him. Yes, this will happen! Amen.

8The Lord God says, "I am the Alpha and the

revelation A making known of truth that has been hidden.

GOD'S POWER

The World's Strongest Man

As a teenager, Paul Anderson concentrated on one big goal: to become the world's strongest man. He turned down a full college football scholarship to work on his weight-lifting goal. By age twenty-one, Anderson had packed 300 rock-hard pounds on his 5-foot, 10-inch body.

In 1956 Anderson won the Olympic gold medal in heavyweight weight-lifting. One year later in Toccoa, Georgia, he back-lifted a table holding 6,270 pounds of auto parts and a safe full of lead. This weight-lifting feat remains unbroken in the Guinness Book of World Records.

Anderson turned professional and moved from weight-lifting to power-lifting. As a professional he could squat-lift 1,200 pounds and dead-lift 820 pounds. Anderson's popularity soared, and in 1974 he was inducted into the Georgia Sports Hall of Fame.

Paul Anderson's amazing power earned him the title of the world's strongest man. His strength, however, is small compared to God's power. See what God's all-powerful nature involves as you read **Revelation 1:4–18**.

- What power does God have that no human can claim?
- How does this passage's expression of God's power affect your life?

CONSIDER . . .

- watching for evidence of God's power around you while you go through this day.
- designing a symbol or logo representing God's power described in these verses.

FOR MORE, SEE . . .

- Psalm 46
- Isaiah 40:12–31
- Luke 18: 27–39

Omega.[n] I am the One who is and was and is coming. I am the Almighty."

9I, John, am your brother. All of us share with Christ in suffering, in the kingdom, and in patience to continue. I was on the island of Patmos,[n] because I had preached the word of God

> **SIDELIGHT:** The island of Patmos, where John wrote Revelation (Revelation 1:9), was the Alcatraz of the Roman Empire. Religious and political prisoners were banished to this island prison, which is only about ten miles long.

and the message about Jesus. 10On the Lord's day I was in the Spirit,[d] and I heard a loud voice behind me that sounded like a trumpet. 11The voice said, "Write what you see in a book and send it to the seven churches: to Ephesus, Smyrna, Pergamum, Thyatira, Sardis, Philadelphia, and Laodicea."

12I turned to see who was talking to me. When I turned, I saw seven golden lampstands 13and someone among the lampstands who was "like a Son of Man."[n] He was dressed in a long robe and had a gold band around his chest. 14His head and hair were white like wool, as white as snow, and his eyes were like flames of fire. 15His feet were like bronze that glows hot in a furnace, and his voice was like the noise of flooding water. 16He held seven stars in his right hand, and a sharp double-edged sword came out of his mouth. He looked like the sun shining at its brightest time.

17When I saw him, I fell down at his feet like a dead man. He put his right hand on me and said, "Do not be afraid. I am the First and the Last. 18I am the One who lives; I was dead, but look, I am alive forever and ever! And I hold the keys to death and to the place of the dead. 19So write the things you see, what is now and what will happen later. 20Here is the secret of the seven stars that you saw in my right hand and the seven golden lampstands: The seven lampstands are the seven churches, and the seven stars are the angels of the seven churches.

To the Church in Ephesus

2 "Write this to the angel of the church in Ephesus:

"The One who holds the seven stars in his right hand and walks among the seven golden lampstands says this: 2I know what you do, how you work hard and never give up. I know you do not put up with the false teachings of evil people. You have tested those who say they are apostles[d] but really are not, and you found they are liars. 3You have patience and have suffered troubles for my name and have not given up.

4"But I have this against you: You have left the love you had in the beginning. 5So remember where you were before you fell. Change your hearts and do what you did at first. If you do not change, I will come to you and will take away your lampstand from its place. 6But there is something you do that is right: You hate what the Nicolaitans[n] do, as much as I.

7"Every person who has ears should listen to what the Spirit[d] says to the churches. To those who win the victory I will give the right to eat the fruit from the tree of life, which is in the garden of God.

To the Church in Smyrna

8"Write this to the angel of the church in Smyrna:

"The One who is the First and the Last, who died and came to life again, says this: 9I know your troubles and that you are poor, but really you are rich! I know the bad things some people say about you. They say they are Jews, but they are not true Jews. They are a synagogue[d] that belongs to Satan. 10Do not be afraid of what you are about to suffer. I tell you, the devil will put some of you in prison to test you, and you will suffer for ten days. But be faithful, even if you have to die, and I will give you the crown of life.

11"Everyone who has ears should listen to what the Spirit[d] says to the churches. Those who win the victory will not be hurt by the second death.

To the Church in Pergamum

12"Write this to the angel of the church in Pergamum:

"The One who has the sharp, double-edged sword says this: 13I know where you live. It is where Satan has his throne. But you are true to me. You did not refuse to tell about your faith in me even during the time of Antipas, my faithful witness who was killed in your city, where Satan lives.

14"But I have a few things against you: You have some there who follow the teaching of Balaam. He taught Balak how to cause the people of Israel to sin by eating food offered to idols and by taking part in sexual sins. 15You also have some who follow the teaching of the Nicolaitans.[n] 16So

Alpha and the Omega The first and last letters of the Greek alphabet. This means "the beginning and the end."
Patmos A small island in the Aegean Sea, near the coast of Asia Minor (modern Turkey).
"like . . . Man" "Son of Man" is a name Jesus called himself. See dictionary.
Nicolaitans This is the name of a religious group that followed false beliefs and ideas.

change your hearts and lives. If you do not, I will
come to you quickly and fight against them with
the sword that comes out of my mouth.
17"Everyone who has ears should listen to what
the Spirit[d] says to the churches.

"I will give some of the hidden manna[d] to everyone who wins the victory. I will also give to
each one who wins the victory a white stone with
a new name written on it. No one knows this new
name except the one who receives it.

To the Church in Thyatira

18"Write this to the angel of the church in Thyatira:

"The Son of God, who has eyes that blaze like
fire and feet like shining bronze, says this: 19I
know what you do. I know about your love, your
faith, your service, and your patience. I know that
you are doing more now than you did at first.
20"But I have this against you: You let that
woman Jezebel spread false teachings. She says
she is a prophetess,[d] but by her teaching she leads
my people to take part in sexual sins and to eat
food that is offered to idols. 21I have given her
time to change her heart and turn away from her
sin, but she does not want to change. 22So I will
throw her on a bed of suffering. And all those who
take part in adultery[d] with her will suffer greatly
if they do not turn away from the wrongs she
does. 23I will also kill her followers. Then all the
churches will know I am the One who searches
hearts and minds, and I will repay each of you for
what you have done.
24"But others of you in Thyatira have not followed her teaching and have not learned what
some call Satan's deep secrets. I say to you that
I will not put any other load on you. 25Only continue in your loyalty until I come.
26"I will give power over the nations to everyone who wins the victory and continues to be
obedient to me until the end.
27'You will rule over them with an iron rod,
as when pottery is broken into pieces.'

Psalm 2:9

28This is the same power I received from my Father. I will also give him the morning star. 29Ev-
eryone who has ears should listen to what the
Spirit[d] says to the churches.

To the Church in Sardis

3 "Write this to the angel of the church in Sardis:

"The One who has the seven spirits and the
seven stars says this: I know what you do. People
say that you are alive, but really you are dead.
2Wake up! Make yourselves stronger before what
you have left dies completely. I have found that
what you are doing is less than what my God
wants. 3So do not forget what you have received
and heard. Obey it, and change your hearts and
lives. So you must wake up, or I will come like a
thief, and you will not know when I will come to
you. 4But you have a few there in Sardis who have
kept their clothes unstained, so they will walk
with me and will wear white clothes, because
they are worthy. 5Those who win the victory will
be dressed in white clothes like them. And I will
not erase their names from the book of life, but I
will say they belong to me before my Father and
before his angels. 6Everyone who has ears should
listen to what the Spirit[d] says to the churches.

SIDELIGHT: Mathematicians, arise! Numbers have an important role in Revelation, with many having symbolic significance. For example, seven (Revelation 3:1) symbolizes completeness; four signifies the created universe (Revelation 7:1), and twelve symbolizes the church or Israel (Revelation 21:12-14).

To the Church in Philadelphia

7"Write this to the angel of the church in Philadelphia:

"This is what the One who is holy and true,
who holds the key of David, says. When he opens
a door, no one can close it. And when he closes
it, no one can open it. 8I know what you do. I
have put an open door before you, which no one
can close. I know you have a little strength, but
you have obeyed my teaching and were not afraid
to speak my name. 9Those in the synagogue[d] that
belongs to Satan say they are Jews, but they are
not true Jews; they are liars. I will make them
come before you and bow at your feet, and they
will know that I have loved you. 10You have
obeyed my teaching about not giving up your
faith. So I will keep you from the time of trouble
that will come to the whole world to test those
who live on earth.
11"I am coming soon. Continue strong in your
faith so no one will take away your crown. 12I will
make those who win the victory pillars in the temple of my God, and they will never have to leave
it. I will write on them the name of my God and
the name of the city of my God, the new Jerusalem,[n] that comes down out of heaven from my
God. I will also write on them my new name.
13Everyone who has ears should listen to what the
Spirit[d] says to the churches.

Jerusalem This name is used to mean the spiritual city God built for his people. See Revelation 21-22.

To the Church in Laodicea

14"Write this to the angel of the church in Laodicea:

"The Amen,[n] the faithful and true witness, the beginning of all God has made, says this: 15I know what you do, that you are not hot or cold. I wish that you were hot or cold! 16But because you are lukewarm — neither hot, nor cold — I am ready to spit you out of my mouth. 17You say, 'I am rich, and I have become wealthy and do not need anything.' But you do not know that you are really miserable, pitiful, poor, blind, and naked. 18I advise you to buy from me gold made pure in fire so you can be truly rich. Buy from me white clothes so you can be clothed and so you can cover your shameful nakedness. Buy from me medicine to put on your eyes so you can truly see.

19"I correct and punish those whom I love. So be eager to do right, and change your hearts and lives. 20Here I am! I stand at the door and knock. If you hear my voice and open the door, I will come in and eat with you, and you will eat with me.

21"Those who win the victory will sit with me on my throne in the same way that I won the victory and sat down with my Father on his throne. 22Everyone who has ears should listen to what the Spirit[d] says to the churches."

John Sees Heaven

4 After the vision of these things I looked, and there before me was an open door in heaven. And the same voice that spoke to me before, that sounded like a trumpet, said, "Come up here, and I will show you what must happen after this." 2Immediately I was in the Spirit,[d] and before me was a throne in heaven, and someone was sitting on it. 3The One who sat on the throne looked like precious stones, like jasper and carnelian. All around the throne was a rainbow the color of an emerald. 4Around the throne there were twenty-four other thrones with twenty-four elders sitting on them. They were dressed in white and had golden crowns on their heads. 5Lightning flashes and noises and thundering came from the throne. Before the throne seven lamps were burning, which are the seven spirits of God. 6Also before the throne there was something that looked like a sea of glass, clear like crystal.

In the center and around the throne were four living creatures with eyes all over them, in front and in back. 7The first living creature was like a lion. The second was like a calf. The third had a face like a man. The fourth was like a flying eagle. 8Each of these four living creatures had six wings and was covered all over with eyes, inside and out. Day and night they never stop saying:

"Holy, holy, holy is the Lord God Almighty.
He was, he is, and he is coming."

9These living creatures give glory, honor, and thanks to the One who sits on the throne, who lives forever and ever. 10Then the twenty-four elders bow down before the One who sits on the throne, and they worship him who lives forever and ever. They put their crowns down before the throne and say:

11"You are worthy, our Lord and God,
to receive glory and honor and power,
because you made all things.
Everything existed and was made,
because you wanted it."

5 Then I saw a scroll in the right hand of the One sitting on the throne. The scroll had writing on both sides and was kept closed with seven seals. 2And I saw a powerful angel calling in a loud voice, "Who is worthy to break the seals and open the scroll?" 3But there was no one in heaven or on earth or under the earth who could open the scroll or look inside it. 4I cried hard because there was no one who was worthy to open the scroll or look inside. 5But one of the elders said to me, "Do not cry! The Lion[n] from the tribe[d] of Judah, David's descendant,[d] has won the victory so that he is able to open the scroll and its seven seals."

6Then I saw a Lamb standing in the center of the throne and in the middle of the four living creatures and the elders. The Lamb looked as if he had been killed. He had seven horns and seven eyes, which are the seven spirits of God that were sent into all the world. 7The Lamb came and took the scroll from the right hand of the One sitting on the throne. 8When he took the scroll, the four living creatures and the twenty-four elders bowed down before the Lamb. Each one of them had a harp and golden bowls full of incense,[d] which are the prayers of God's holy people. 9And they all sang a new song to the Lamb:

SIDELIGHT: Ancient scrolls (Revelation 5:1) were created by beating papyrus (a reed found in the Nile River) into sheets (often about 8″ × 10″) and sewing them together. A scroll of Revelation—written on both sides to save money—would have been about fifteen feet long.

Amen Used here as a name for Jesus; it means to agree fully that something is true.
Lion Here refers to Christ.

"You are worthy to take the scroll
and to open its seals,
because you were killed,
and with the blood of your death you
bought people for God
from every tribe, language, people, and
nation.
10You made them to be a kingdom of priests
for our God,
and they will rule on the earth."
11Then I looked, and I heard the voices of many
angels around the throne, and the four living creatures, and the elders. There were thousands and
thousands of angels, 12saying in a loud voice:
"The Lamb who was killed is worthy
to receive power, wealth, wisdom, and
strength,
honor, glory, and praise!"
13Then I heard all creatures in heaven and on
earth and under the earth and in the sea saying:
"To the One who sits on the throne
and to the Lamb
be praise and honor and glory and power
forever and ever."
14The four living creatures said, "Amen," and
the elders bowed down and worshiped.
6 Then I watched while the Lamb opened the
first of the seven seals. I heard one of the
four living creatures say with a voice like thunder,
"Come!" 2I looked, and there before me was a
white horse. The rider on the horse held a bow,
and he was given a crown, and he rode out, determined to win the victory.
3When the Lamb opened the second seal, I
heard the second living creature say, "Come!"
4Then another horse came out, a red one. Its rider
was given power to take away peace from the
earth and to make people kill each other, and he
was given a big sword.
5When the Lamb opened the third seal, I heard
the third living creature say, "Come!" I looked,
and there before me was a black horse, and its
rider held a pair of scales in his hand. 6Then I
heard something that sounded like a voice coming from the middle of the four living creatures.
The voice said, "A quart of wheat for a day's pay,
and three quarts of barley for a day's pay, and do
not damage the olive oil and wine!"

WORSHIP

Worship's Many Faces

Christians are free to worship in varied and unique ways. There is no one right way to worship, as evidenced by the thousands of denominations and churches through the ages. Many churches today worship in ways shaped by traditions hundreds of years old. For example:

- Some Christians lift their voices in song, but use no musical instruments in their worship services.
- Many Christians sing hymns accompanied by pipe organs. They may use familiar prayers and liturgies through the service.
- Other Christians have informal worship styles that include contemporary music and spontaneous applause.
- Some Christians raise their hands above their heads when they pray and worship.
- And some Christians hold meetings without a formal program or a minister. Instead of a set order of worship, they gather in silence. They speak when they feel moved to pray, read a Bible passage or share a thought.

As these examples show, Christians worship God in many different ways. But they all have the central purpose of worship in mind that is found in **Revelation 5:11–14**.

- How do different expressions of worship capture the worship described in this vision?
- What feelings about worship does the passage bring out in you?

CONSIDER . . .

- finding ways your church has incorporated this passage in its worship services.
- planning a worship service with other young people. Ask your pastor to let you share in leading worship for the whole church.

FOR MORE, SEE . . .

- Psalm 100
- Isaiah 6:1–8
- John 4:19–24

7When the Lamb opened the fourth seal, I
heard the voice of the fourth living creature say,
"Come!" 8I looked, and there before me was a
pale horse. Its rider was named death, and Hades[n] was following close behind him. They were
given power over a fourth of the earth to kill people by war, by starvation, by disease, and by the
wild animals of the earth.

9When the Lamb opened the fifth seal, I saw
under the altar the souls of those who had been
killed because they were faithful to the word of
God and to the message they had received.
10These souls shouted in a loud voice, "Holy and
true Lord, how long until you judge the people of
the earth and punish them for killing us?" 11Then
each one of them was given a white robe and was
told to wait a short time longer. There were still
some of their fellow servants and brothers and
sisters[n] in the service of Christ who must be
killed as they were. They had to wait until all of
this was finished.

12Then I watched while the Lamb opened the
sixth seal, and there was a great earthquake. The
sun became black like rough black cloth, and
the whole moon became red like blood. 13And the
stars in the sky fell to the earth like figs falling
from a fig tree when the wind blows. 14The sky
disappeared as a scroll when it is rolled up, and
every mountain and island was moved from its
place.

15Then the kings of the earth, the rulers, the
generals, the rich people, the powerful people,
the slaves, and the free people hid themselves in
caves and in the rocks on the mountains. 16They
called to the mountains and the rocks, "Fall on us.
Hide us from the face of the One who sits on the
throne and from the anger of the Lamb! 17The
great day for their anger has come, and who can
stand against it?"

The 144,000 People of Israel

7 After the vision of these things I saw four
angels standing at the four corners of the
earth. The angels were holding the four winds of
the earth to keep them from blowing on the land
or on the sea or on any tree. 2Then I saw another
angel coming up from the east who had the seal
of the living God. And he called out in a loud
voice to the four angels to whom God had given
power to harm the earth and the sea. 3He said to
them, "Do not harm the land or the sea or the
trees until we mark with a sign the foreheads of
the people who serve our God." 4Then I heard
how many people were marked with the sign.
There were one hundred forty-four thousand
from every tribe[d] of the people of Israel.

5From the tribe of Judah twelve thousand
were marked with the sign,
from the tribe of Reuben twelve thousand,
from the tribe of Gad twelve thousand,
6from the tribe of Asher twelve thousand,
from the tribe of Naphtali twelve thousand,
from the tribe of Manasseh twelve thousand,
7from the tribe of Simeon twelve thousand,
from the tribe of Levi twelve thousand,
from the tribe of Issachar twelve thousand,
8from the tribe of Zebulun twelve thousand,
from the tribe of Joseph twelve thousand,
and from the tribe of Benjamin twelve thousand were marked with the sign.

The Great Crowd Worships God

9After the vision of these things I looked, and
there was a great number of people, so many that
no one could count them. They were from every
nation, tribe,[d] people, and language of the earth.
They were all standing before the throne and before the Lamb, wearing white robes and holding
palm branches in their hands. 10They were shouting in a loud voice, "Salvation belongs to our
God, who sits on the throne, and to the Lamb."
11All the angels were standing around the throne
and the elders and the four living creatures.
They all bowed down on their faces before the
throne and worshiped God, 12saying, "Amen!
Praise, glory, wisdom, thanks, honor, power, and
strength belong to our God forever and ever.
Amen!"

13Then one of the elders asked me, "Who are
these people dressed in white robes? Where did
they come from?"

14I answered, "You know, sir."

And the elder said to me, "These are the people
who have come out of the great distress. They
have washed their robes[n] and made them white
in the blood of the Lamb. 15Because of this, they
are before the throne of God. They worship him
day and night in his temple. And the One who sits
on the throne will be present with them. 16Those
people will never be hungry again, and they will
never be thirsty again. The sun will not hurt
them, and no heat will burn them, 17because the
Lamb at the center of the throne will be their
shepherd. He will lead them to springs of water
that give life. And God will wipe away every tear
from their eyes."

Hades The unseen world of the dead.

brothers and sisters Although the Greek text says "brothers" here and throughout this book, both men and women would have been included.

washed their robes This means they believed in Jesus so that their sins could be forgiven by Christ's blood.

The Seventh Seal

8 When the Lamb opened the seventh seal,
there was silence in heaven for about half an
hour. 2And I saw the seven angels who stand before God and to whom were given seven trumpets.
3Another angel came and stood at the altar,
holding a golden pan for incense.[d] He was given
much incense to offer with the prayers of all
God's holy people. The angel put this offering on
the golden altar before the throne. 4The smoke
from the incense went up from the angel's hand
to God with the prayers of God's people. 5Then
the angel filled the incense pan with fire from the
altar and threw it on the earth, and there were

SIDELIGHT: Since no one had invented lick-and-seal envelopes in Bible times, people would fold or roll up documents, tie string around them, and press a lump of clay over the knot (Revelation 8:1). Then the sender would stamp the hardening clay with a special ring or seal, which was intended to be broken only by the appropriate person.

SADNESS

The Worst Year of Her Life

Lexie Byers had looked forward to her junior year. She did not know it would be her life's worst.

Early in the fall her mother was diagnosed with leukemia. Her dad quit his job to help care for her mom. Money, time, and energy were scarce. And, Lexie carried a difficult class load.

"I had to take care of the house, feed everyone, and plow through my schoolwork," she recalls. "It was tough, but I got along somehow."

One day, however, her mother entered the hospital for one final, risky operation to fight the leukemia. "When the surgeons came out of the operating room, I could tell by the way they looked at me that she was gone," she says.

After the funeral, Lexie's life changed dramatically. Her father, in deep grief, wandered about the house. One day Lexie found a For Sale sign in their front yard. "It's too painful for me to live here," her father said.

Lexie watched her dad fall apart. Unable to find work and desperately lonely, her father returned to his hometown. Lexie faced the difficult choice: either live with her older sister and finish at her present school, or go with her father. Even though she missed her dad, Lexie stayed with her sister.

What sustained her through this sad time? "Christian friends and a caring church got me through the experience," she says. "I couldn't pray, because I was mad at God. All I'd do was cry. These friends just kept loving me, even when I was unlovely."

Lexie went on to college, where she's majoring in engineering. Her father, in time, overcame his grief and went on with his life. "My world fell apart in eleventh grade," Lexie reflects. "Our family suffered a lot. But with God's help, we made it through, and that's what matters."

Everyone experiences pain, disappointment, and uncontrollable events. When those sad times seem overwhelming, Christians can turn to passages such as **Revelation 7:9–17** for a message of hope.

- What hope could Lexie gain from these verses?
- How could these verses help you deal with sadness in your life?

C O N S I D E R . . .

- doing something positive to help you get out of the blues. Try visiting a friend, watching a comedy film, or exercising.
- visiting someone who is having a sad time. Take fresh flowers, cookies, or a small gift to show you care.

F O R M O R E , S E E . . .

- Psalm 40:1–3
- Ecclesiastes 3:1–8
- Hebrews 10:23–25

flashes of lightning, thunder and loud noises, and
an earthquake.

The Seven Angels and Trumpets

6Then the seven angels who had the seven
trumpets prepared to blow them.
7The first angel blew his trumpet, and hail and
fire mixed with blood were poured down on the
earth. And a third of the earth, and all the green
grass, and a third of the trees were burned up.
8Then the second angel blew his trumpet, and
something that looked like a big mountain, burning with fire, was thrown into the sea. And a
third of the sea became blood, 9a third of the
living things in the sea died, and a third of
the ships were destroyed.
10Then the third angel blew his trumpet, and a
large star, burning like a torch, fell from the sky.
It fell on a third of the rivers and on the springs
of water. 11The name of the star is Wormwood.[n]
And a third of all the water became bitter, and
many people died from drinking the water that
was bitter.
12Then the fourth angel blew his trumpet, and
a third of the sun, and a third of the moon,
and a third of the stars were struck. So a third of
them became dark, and a third of the day was
without light, and also the night.
13While I watched, I heard an eagle that was
flying high in the air cry out in a loud voice,
"Trouble! Trouble! Trouble for those who live on
the earth because of the remaining sounds of the
trumpets that the other three angels are about to
blow!"

9 Then the fifth angel blew his trumpet, and I
saw a star fall from the sky to the earth. The
star was given the key to the deep hole that leads
to the bottomless pit. 2Then it opened up the hole
that leads to the bottomless pit, and smoke came
up from the hole like smoke from a big furnace.
Then the sun and sky became dark because of the
smoke from the hole. 3Then locusts[d] came down
to the earth out of the smoke, and they were
given the power to sting like scorpions.[n] 4They
were told not to harm the grass on the earth or
any plant or tree. They could harm only the people who did not have the sign of God on their
foreheads. 5These locusts were not given the
power to kill anyone, but to cause pain to the
people for five months. And the pain they felt was
like the pain a scorpion gives when it stings someone. 6During those days people will look for a way
to die, but they will not find it. They will want to
die, but death will run away from them.
7The locusts looked like horses prepared for
battle. On their heads they wore what looked like
crowns of gold, and their faces looked like human
faces. 8Their hair was like women's hair, and their
teeth were like lions' teeth. 9Their chests looked
like iron breastplates, and the sound of their
wings was like the noise of many horses and chariots hurrying into battle. 10The locusts had tails
with stingers like scorpions, and in their tails was
their power to hurt people for five months. 11The
locusts had a king who was the angel of the bottomless pit. His name in the Hebrew language is
Abaddon and in the Greek language is Apollyon.[n]
12The first trouble is past; there are still two
other troubles that will come.
13Then the sixth angel blew his trumpet, and I
heard a voice coming from the horns on the
golden altar that is before God. 14The voice said
to the sixth angel who had the trumpet, "Free the
four angels who are tied at the great river Euphrates." 15And they let loose the four angels who had
been kept ready for this hour and day and month
and year so they could kill a third of all people on
the earth. 16I heard how many troops on horses
were in their army—two hundred million.
17The horses and their riders I saw in the vision
looked like this: They had breastplates that were
fiery red, dark blue, and yellow like sulfur. The
heads of the horses looked like heads of lions,
with fire, smoke, and sulfur coming out of their
mouths. 18A third of all the people on earth were
killed by these three terrible disasters coming out
of the horses' mouths: the fire, the smoke, and
the sulfur. 19The horses' power was in their
mouths and in their tails; their tails were like
snakes with heads, and with them they hurt
people.
20The other people who were not killed by
these terrible disasters still did not change their
hearts and turn away from what they had made
with their own hands. They did not stop worshiping demons[d] and idols made of gold, silver,
bronze, stone, and wood—things that cannot see
or hear or walk. 21These people did not change
their hearts and turn away from murder or evil
magic, from their sexual sins or stealing.

The Angel and the Small Scroll

10 Then I saw another powerful angel coming down from heaven dressed in a
cloud with a rainbow over his head. His face was
like the sun, and his legs were like pillars of fire.
2The angel was holding a small scroll open in his

Wormwood Name of a very bitter plant; used here to give the idea of bitter sorrow.
scorpions A scorpion is an insect that stings with a bad poison.
Abaddon, Apollyon Both names mean "Destroyer."

hand. He put his right foot on the sea and his left
foot on the land. 3Then he shouted loudly like the
roaring of a lion. And when he shouted, the
voices of seven thunders spoke. 4When the seven
thunders spoke, I started to write. But I heard a
voice from heaven say, "Keep hidden what the
seven thunders said, and do not write them
down."

5Then the angel I saw standing on the sea and
on the land raised his right hand to heaven, 6and
he made a promise by the power of the One who
lives forever and ever. He is the One who made
the skies and all that is in them, the earth and all
that is in it, and the sea and all that is in it. The
angel promised, "There will be no more waiting!
7In the days when the seventh angel is ready to
blow his trumpet, God's secret will be finished.
This secret is the Good News[d] God told to his
servants, the prophets."[d]

8Then I heard the same voice from heaven
again, saying to me: "Go and take the open scroll
that is in the hand of the angel that is standing on
the sea and on the land."

9So I went to the angel and told him to give me
the small scroll. And he said to me, "Take the
scroll and eat it. It will be sour in your stomach,
but in your mouth it will be sweet as honey." 10So
I took the small scroll from the angel's hand and
ate it. In my mouth it tasted sweet as honey, but
after I ate it, it was sour in my stomach. 11Then
I was told, "You must prophesy[d] again about
many peoples, nations, languages, and kings."

The Two Witnesses

11 I was given a measuring stick like a rod,
and I was told, "Go and measure the
temple[d] of God and the altar, and count the people worshiping there. 2But do not measure the
yard outside the temple. Leave it alone, because
it has been given to those who are not God's people. And they will trample on the holy city for
forty-two months. 3And I will give power to my
two witnesses to prophesy[d] for one thousand two
hundred sixty days, and they will be dressed in
rough cloth to show their sadness."

4These two witnesses are the two olive trees
and the two lampstands that stand before the
Lord of the earth. 5And if anyone tries to hurt
them, fire comes from their mouths and kills their
enemies. And if anyone tries to hurt them in
whatever way, in that same way that person will
die. 6These witnesses have the power to stop the
sky from raining during the time they are prophesying. And they have power to make the waters
become blood, and they have power to send every
kind of trouble to the earth as many times as they
want.

7When the two witnesses have finished telling
their message, the beast that comes up from the
bottomless pit will fight a war against them. He
will defeat them and kill them. 8The bodies of the
two witnesses will lie in the street of the great city
where the Lord was killed. This city is named
Sodom[n] and Egypt, which has a spiritual meaning. 9Those from every race of people, tribe,[d] language, and nation will look at the bodies of the
two witnesses for three and one-half days, and
they will refuse to bury them. 10People who live
on the earth will rejoice and be happy because
these two are dead. They will send each other
gifts, because these two prophets brought much
suffering to those who live on the earth.

11But after three and one-half days, God put the
breath of life into the two prophets again. They
stood on their feet, and everyone who saw them
became very afraid. 12Then the two prophets
heard a loud voice from heaven saying, "Come up
here!" And they went up into heaven in a cloud
as their enemies watched.

13In the same hour there was a great earthquake, and a tenth of the city was destroyed.
Seven thousand people were killed in the earthquake, and those who did not die were very afraid
and gave glory to the God of heaven.

14The second trouble is finished. Pay attention:
The third trouble is coming soon.

The Seventh Trumpet

15Then the seventh angel blew his trumpet.
And there were loud voices in heaven, saying:

"The power to rule the world
now belongs to our Lord and his Christ,[d]
and he will rule forever and ever."

16Then the twenty-four elders, who sit on their
thrones before God, bowed down on their faces
and worshiped God. 17They said:

"We give thanks to you, Lord God Almighty,
who is and who was,
because you have used your great power
and have begun to rule!
18The people of the world were angry,
but your anger has come.
The time has come to judge the dead
and to reward your servants the prophets[d]
and your holy people,
all who respect you, great and small.
The time has come to destroy those who
destroy the earth!"

19Then God's temple[d] in heaven was opened.
The Ark[d] that holds the agreement God gave to
his people could be seen in his temple. Then there
were flashes of lightning, noises, thunder, an
earthquake, and a great hailstorm.

Sodom City that God destroyed because the people were so evil.

The Woman and the Dragon

12 And then a great wonder appeared in
heaven: A woman was clothed with the
sun, and the moon was under her feet, and a
crown of twelve stars was on her head. 2She was
pregnant and cried out with pain, because she
was about to give birth. 3Then another wonder
appeared in heaven: There was a giant red dragon
with seven heads and seven crowns on each
head. He also had ten horns. 4His tail swept a
third of the stars out of the sky and threw them
down to the earth. He stood in front of the
woman who was ready to give birth so he could
eat her baby as soon as it was born. 5Then the
woman gave birth to a son who will rule all the
nations with an iron rod. And her child was taken
up to God and to his throne. 6The woman ran
away into the desert to a place God prepared for
her where she would be taken care of for one
thousand two hundred sixty days.

7Then there was a war in heaven. Michael[n]
and his angels fought against the dragon, and the
dragon and his angels fought back. 8But the
dragon was not strong enough, and he and
his angels lost their place in heaven. 9The giant
dragon was thrown down out of heaven. (He is
that old snake called the devil or Satan, who tricks
the whole world.) The dragon with his angels was
thrown down to the earth.

10Then I heard a loud voice in heaven saying:
"The salvation and the power and the
kingdom of our God
and the authority of his Christ[d] have now
come.
The accuser of our brothers and sisters,
who accused them day and night before
our God,
has been thrown down.
11And our brothers and sisters defeated him
by the blood of the Lamb's death
and by the message they preached.
They did not love their lives so much
that they were afraid of death.
12So rejoice, you heavens
and all who live there!
But it will be terrible for the earth and the
sea,
because the devil has come down to you!
He is filled with anger,
because he knows he does not have much
time."

13When the dragon saw he had been thrown
down to the earth, he hunted for the woman who
had given birth to the son. 14But the woman was
given the two wings of a great eagle so she could
fly to the place prepared for her in the desert.
There she would be taken care of for three and
one-half years, away from the snake. 15Then the
snake poured water out of its mouth like a river
toward the woman so the flood would carry her
away. 16But the earth helped the woman by opening its mouth and swallowing the river that came
from the mouth of the dragon. 17Then the dragon
was very angry at the woman, and he went off to
make war against all her other children — those
who obey God's commands and who have the
message Jesus taught.

18And the dragon stood on the seashore.

SIDELIGHT: The reign of the Roman Emperor Nero (often paralleled with the first beast in Revelation 13) was marked by terrible crimes, destruction, and persecution of Christians. When he sent someone to murder his own mother, she bared her body and cried, "Strike my womb because it bore a Nero!"

The Two Beasts

13 Then I saw a beast coming up out of the
sea. It had ten horns and seven heads,
and there was a crown on each horn. A name
against God was written on each head. 2This
beast looked like a leopard, with feet like a bear's
feet and a mouth like a lion's mouth. And the
dragon gave the beast all of his power and his
throne and great authority. 3One of the heads of
the beast looked as if it had been killed by a
wound, but this death wound was healed. Then
the whole world was amazed and followed the
beast. 4People worshiped the dragon because he
had given his power to the beast. And they also
worshiped the beast, asking, "Who is like the
beast? Who can make war against it?"

5The beast was allowed to say proud words and
words against God, and it was allowed to use its
power for forty-two months. 6It used its mouth to
speak against God, against God's name, against
the place where God lives, and against all those
who live in heaven. 7It was given power to make
war against God's holy people and to defeat them.
It was given power over every tribe,[d] people, language, and nation. 8And all who live on earth will
worship the beast — all the people since the beginning of the world whose names are not written in
the Lamb's book of life. The Lamb is the One who
was killed.

9Anyone who has ears should listen:
10If you are to be a prisoner,
then you will be a prisoner.

Michael The archangel—leader among God's angels or messengers (Jude 9).

If you are to be killed with the sword,
then you will be killed with the sword.
This means that God's holy people must have patience and faith.
11Then I saw another beast coming up out of
the earth. It had two horns like a lamb, but it
spoke like a dragon. 12This beast stands before the
first beast and uses the same power the first beast
has. By this power it makes everyone living on
earth worship the first beast, who had the death
wound that was healed. 13And the second beast
does great miracles[d] so that it even makes fire
come down from heaven to earth while people
are watching. 14It fools those who live on earth by
the miracles it has been given the power to do. It
does these miracles to serve the first beast. The
second beast orders people to make an idol to
honor the first beast, the one that was wounded
by the deadly sword but sprang to life again. 15The
second beast was given power to give life to the
idol of the first one so that the idol could speak.
And the second beast was given power to command all who will not worship the image of the
beast to be killed. 16The second beast also forced
all people, small and great, rich and poor, free and
slave, to have a mark on their right hand or on
their forehead. 17No one could buy or sell without
this mark, which is the name of the beast or the
number of its name. 18This takes wisdom. Let the
one who has understanding find the meaning of
the number, which is the number of a person. Its
number is six hundred sixty-six.

The Song of the Saved

14 Then I looked, and there before me was
the Lamb standing on Mount Zion.[n]
With him were one hundred forty-four thousand
people who had his name and his Father's name
written on their foreheads. 2And I heard a sound
from heaven like the noise of flooding water and
like the sound of loud thunder. The sound I heard
was like people playing harps. 3And they sang a
new song before the throne and before the four
living creatures and the elders. No one could
learn the new song except the one hundred forty-
four thousand who had been bought from the
earth. 4These are the ones who did not do sinful
things with women, because they kept themselves pure. They follow the Lamb every place he
goes. These one hundred forty-four thousand
were bought from among the people of the earth
as people to be offered to God and the Lamb.
5They were not guilty of telling lies; they are without fault.

The Three Angels

6Then I saw another angel flying high in the air.
He had the eternal Good News[d] to preach to
those who live on earth—to every nation, tribe,[d]
language, and people. 7He preached in a loud
voice, "Fear God and give him praise, because the
time has come for God to judge all people. So
worship God who made the heavens, and the
earth, and the sea, and the springs of water."
8Then the second angel followed the first angel
and said, "Ruined, ruined is the great city of Babylon! She made all the nations drink the wine of
the anger of her adultery."[d]
9Then a third angel followed the first two angels, saying in a loud voice: "If anyone worships
the beast and his idol and gets the beast's mark on
the forehead or on the hand, 10that one also will
drink the wine of God's anger, which is prepared
with all its strength in the cup of his anger. And
that person will be put in pain with burning sulfur
before the holy angels and the Lamb. 11And the
smoke from their burning pain will rise forever
and ever. There will be no rest, day or night, for
those who worship the beast and his idol or who
get the mark of his name." 12This means God's
holy people must be patient. They must obey
God's commands and keep their faith in Jesus.
13Then I heard a voice from heaven saying,
"Write this: Happy are the dead who die from
now on in the Lord."
The Spirit[d] says, "Yes, they will rest from their
hard work, and the reward of all they have done
stays with them."

The Earth Is Harvested

14Then I looked, and there before me was a
white cloud, and sitting on the white cloud was
One who looked like a Son of Man.[n] He had a
gold crown on his head and a sharp sickle[n] in his
hand. 15Then another angel came out of the temple and called out in a loud voice to the One who
was sitting on the cloud, "Take your sickle and
harvest from the earth, because the time to harvest has come, and the fruit of the earth is ripe."
16So the One who was sitting on the cloud swung
his sickle over the earth, and the earth was har-
vested.
17Then another angel came out of the temple in
heaven, and he also had a sharp sickle. 18And then
another angel, who has power over the fire, came
from the altar. This angel called to the angel with
the sharp sickle, saying, "Take your sharp sickle
and gather the bunches of grapes from the earth's
vine, because its grapes are ripe." 19Then the an-

Mount Zion Another name for Jerusalem; here meaning the spiritual city of God's people.
Son of Man "Son of Man" is a name Jesus called himself. See dictionary.
sickle A farming tool with a curved blade. It was used to harvest grain.

gel swung his sickle over the earth. He gathered
the earth's grapes and threw them into the great
winepress[d] of God's anger. 20They were trampled
in the winepress outside the city, and blood
flowed out of the winepress as high as horses' bri-
dles for a distance of about one hundred eighty
miles.

The Last Troubles

15 Then I saw another wonder in heaven
that was great and amazing. There were
seven angels bringing seven disasters. These are
the last disasters, because after them, God's anger
is finished.
2I saw what looked like a sea of glass mixed
with fire. All of those who had won the victory
over the beast and his idol and over the number
of his name were standing by the sea of glass.
They had harps that God had given them. 3They
sang the song of Moses, the servant of God, and
the song of the Lamb:

"You do great and wonderful things, *Psalm 111:2*
Lord God Almighty. *Amos 3:13*
Everything the Lord does is right and true,
Psalm 145:17
King of the nations.
4Everyone will respect you, Lord, *Jeremiah 10:7*
and will honor you.
Only you are holy.
All the nations will come
and worship you, *Psalm 86:9-10*
because the right things you have done
are now made known." *Deuteronomy 32:4*

5After this I saw that the temple (the Tent[d] of
the Agreement) in heaven was opened. 6And the
seven angels bringing the seven disasters came
out of the temple. They were dressed in clean,
shining linen and wore golden bands tied around
their chests. 7Then one of the four living creatures
gave to the seven angels seven golden bowls filled
with the anger of God, who lives forever and
ever. 8The temple was filled with smoke from the
glory and the power of God, and no one could
enter the temple until the seven disasters of the
seven angels were finished.

The Bowls of God's Anger

16 Then I heard a loud voice from the temple saying to the seven angels, "Go and
pour out the seven bowls of God's anger on the
earth."
2The first angel left and poured out his bowl on
the land. Then ugly and painful sores came upon
all those who had the mark of the beast and who
worshiped his idol.
3The second angel poured out his bowl on the
sea, and it became blood like that of a dead man,
and every living thing in the sea died.
4The third angel poured out his bowl on the
rivers and the springs of water, and they became
blood. 5Then I heard the angel of the waters saying:

"Holy One, you are the One who is and who
was.
You are right to decide to punish these evil
people.
6They have poured out the blood of your holy
people and your prophets.[d]
So now you have given them blood to
drink as they deserve."

7And I heard a voice coming from the altar saying:

"Yes, Lord God Almighty,
the way you punish evil people is right and
fair."

8The fourth angel poured out his bowl on the
sun, and he was given power to burn the people
with fire. 9They were burned by the great heat,
and they cursed the name of God, who had control over these disasters. But the people refused to
change their hearts and lives and give glory to
God.
10The fifth angel poured out his bowl on the
throne of the beast, and darkness covered its kingdom. People gnawed their tongues because of the
pain. 11They also cursed the God of heaven because of their pain and the sores they had, but
they refused to change their hearts and turn away
from the evil things they did.
12The sixth angel poured out his bowl on the
great river Euphrates so that the water in the river
was dried up to prepare the way for the kings
from the east to come. 13Then I saw three evil
spirits that looked like frogs coming out of the
mouth of the dragon, out of the mouth of the
beast, and out of the mouth of the false prophet.[d]
14These evil spirits are the spirits of demons,[d]
which have power to do miracles.[d] They go out
to the kings of the whole world to gather them
together for the battle on the great day of God
Almighty.
15"Listen! I will come as a thief comes! Happy
are those who stay awake and keep their clothes
on so that they will not walk around naked and
have people see their shame."
16Then the evil spirits gathered the kings to-

SIDELIGHT: Revelation 16:15 isn't a warning to wear pajamas in bed. According to Jewish laws of the time, the captain of the Temple would check up on the Temple police at night. If someone was asleep on duty, his clothes were taken off and burned, and he was sent away naked and disgraced. Anyone want an extra cup of coffee?

gether to the place that is called Armageddon in the Hebrew language.

17The seventh angel poured out his bowl into the air. Then a loud voice came out of the temple from the throne, saying, "It is finished!" 18Then there were flashes of lightning, noises, thunder, and a big earthquake—the worst earthquake that has ever happened since people have been on earth. 19The great city split into three parts, and the cities of the nations were destroyed. And God remembered the sins of Babylon the Great, so he gave that city the cup filled with the wine of his terrible anger. 20Then every island ran away, and mountains disappeared. 21Giant hailstones, each weighing about a hundred pounds, fell from the sky upon people. People cursed God for the disaster of the hail, because this disaster was so terrible.

The Woman on the Animal

17 Then one of the seven angels who had the seven bowls came and spoke to me. He said, "Come, and I will show you the punishment that will be given to the great prostitute,[d] the one sitting over many waters. 2The kings of the earth sinned sexually with her, and the people of the earth became drunk from the wine of her sexual sin."

3Then the angel carried me away by the Spirit[d] to the desert. There I saw a woman sitting on a red beast. It was covered with names against God written on it, and it had seven heads and ten horns. 4The woman was dressed in purple and red and was shining with the gold, precious jewels, and pearls she was wearing. She had a golden cup in her hand, a cup filled with evil things and the uncleanness of her sexual sin. 5On her forehead a title was written that was secret. This is what was written:

THE GREAT BABYLON
MOTHER OF PROSTITUTES
AND OF THE EVIL THINGS OF THE EARTH

6Then I saw that the woman was drunk with the blood of God's holy people and with the blood of those who were killed because of their faith in Jesus.

When I saw the woman, I was very amazed. 7Then the angel said to me, "Why are you amazed? I will tell you the secret of this woman and the beast she rides—the one with seven heads and ten horns. 8The beast you saw was once alive but is not alive now. But soon it will come up out of the bottomless pit and go away to be destroyed. There are people who live on earth whose names have not been written in the book of life since the beginning of the world. They will be amazed when they see the beast, because he was once alive, is not alive now, but will come again.

9"You need a wise mind to understand this. The seven heads on the beast are seven mountains where the woman sits. 10And they are seven kings. Five of the kings have already been destroyed, one of the kings lives now, and another has not yet come. When he comes, he must stay a short time. 11The beast that was once alive, but is not alive now, is also an eighth king. He belongs to the first seven kings, and he will go away to be destroyed.

12"The ten horns you saw are ten kings who have not yet begun to rule, but they will receive power to rule with the beast for one hour. 13All ten of these kings have the same purpose, and they will give their power and authority to the beast. 14They will make war against the Lamb, but the Lamb will defeat them, because he is Lord of lords and King of kings. He will defeat them with his called, chosen, and faithful followers."

15Then the angel said to me, "The waters that you saw, where the prostitute sits, are peoples, races, nations, and languages. 16The ten horns and the beast you saw will hate the prostitute. They will take everything she has and leave her naked. They will eat her body and burn her with fire. 17God made the ten horns want to carry out his purpose by agreeing to give the beast their power to rule, until what God has said comes about. 18The woman you saw is the great city that rules over the kings of the earth."

Babylon Is Destroyed

18 After the vision of these things, I saw another angel coming down from heaven. This angel had great power, and his glory made the earth bright. 2He shouted in a powerful voice:

"Ruined, ruined is the great city of Babylon!
She has become a home for demons[d]
and a prison for every evil spirit,
and a prison for every unclean[d] bird and unclean beast.
3She has been ruined, because all the peoples of the earth
have drunk the wine of the desire of her sexual sin.
She has been ruined also because the kings of the earth
have sinned sexually with her,
and the merchants of the earth
have grown rich from the great wealth of her luxury."

4Then I heard another voice from heaven saying:

"Come out of that city, my people,
so that you will not share in her sins,
so that you will not receive the disasters that will come to her.
5Her sins have piled up as high as the sky,

and God has not forgotten the wrongs she
has done.
6Give that city the same as she gave to others.
Pay her back twice as much as she did.
Prepare wine for her that is twice as strong
as the wine she prepared for others.
7She gave herself much glory and rich living.
Give her that much suffering and sadness.
She says to herself, 'I am a queen sitting on
my throne.
I am not a widow; I will never be sad.'
8So these disasters will come to her in one
day:
death, and crying, and great hunger,
and she will be destroyed by fire,
because the Lord God who judges her is
powerful."

9The kings of the earth who sinned sexually
with her and shared her wealth will see the
smoke from her burning. Then they will cry and
be sad because of her death. 10They will be afraid
of her suffering and stand far away and say:

"Terrible! How terrible for you, great city,
powerful city of Babylon,
because your punishment has come in one
hour!"

11And the merchants of the earth will cry and
be sad about her, because now there is no one to
buy their cargoes — 12cargoes of gold, silver, jewels, pearls, fine linen, purple cloth, silk, red cloth;
all kinds of citron wood and all kinds of things
made from ivory, expensive wood, bronze, iron,
and marble; 13cinnamon, spice, incense,[d] myrrh,[d]
frankincense,[d] wine, olive oil, fine flour, wheat,
cattle, sheep, horses, carriages, slaves, and human
lives.

14The merchants will say,

"Babylon, the good things you wanted are
gone from you.
All your rich and fancy things have
disappeared.
You will never have them again."

15The merchants who became rich from selling to
her will be afraid of her suffering and will stand
far away. They will cry and be sad 16and say:

"Terrible! How terrible for the great city!
She was dressed in fine linen, purple and
red cloth,
and she was shining with gold, precious
jewels, and pearls!
17All these riches have been destroyed in one
hour!"

Every sea captain, every passenger, the sailors,
and all those who earn their living from the sea
stood far away from Babylon. 18As they saw the
smoke from her burning, they cried out loudly,
"There was never a city like this great city!" 19And
they threw dust on their heads and cried out,
weeping and being sad. They said:

"Terrible! How terrible for the great city!
All the people who had ships on the sea
became rich because of her wealth!
But she has been destroyed in one hour!
20Be happy because of this, heaven!
Be happy, God's holy people and apostles[d]
and prophets![d]
God has punished her because of what she
did to you."

21Then a powerful angel picked up a large
stone, like one used for grinding grain, and threw
it into the sea. He said:

"In the same way, the great city of Babylon
will be thrown down,
and it will never be found again.
22The music of people playing harps and other
instruments, flutes, and trumpets,
will never be heard in you again.
No workman doing any job
will ever be found in you again.
The sound of grinding grain
will never be heard in you again.
23The light of a lamp
will never shine in you again,
and the voices of a bridegroom and bride
will never be heard in you again.
Your merchants were the world's great
people,
and all the nations were tricked by your
magic.
24You are guilty of the death of the prophets
and God's holy people
and all who have been killed on earth."

People in Heaven Praise God

19 After this vision and announcement I
heard what sounded like a great many
people in heaven saying:

"Hallelujah![n]
Salvation, glory, and power belong to our
God,
2 because his judgments are true and right.
He has punished the prostitute[d]
who made the earth evil with her sexual
sin.
He has paid her back for the death of his
servants."

3Again they said:

"Hallelujah!
She is burning, and her smoke will rise
forever and ever."

4Then the twenty-four elders and the four living creatures bowed down and worshiped God,
who sits on the throne. They said:

"Amen, Hallelujah!"

Hallelujah This means "praise God!"

5Then a voice came from the throne, saying:
"Praise our God, all you who serve him
and all you who honor him, both small and
great!"

> **SIDELIGHT:** Bowing (Revelation 19:4) was a common greeting in Bible times. However, there was more variety than we have with handshakes. Depending on whom you were greeting, you could lightly nod your head or give a complete, bend-at-the-waist, face-down bow.

6Then I heard what sounded like a great many
people, like the noise of flooding water, and like
the noise of loud thunder. The people were saying:
"Hallelujah!
Our Lord God, the Almighty, rules.
7Let us rejoice and be happy
and give God glory,
because the wedding of the Lamb has come,
and the Lamb's bride has made herself
ready.
8Fine linen, bright and clean, was given to her
to wear."
(The fine linen means the good things done by
God's holy people.)
9And the angel said to me, "Write this: Happy
are those who have been invited to the wedding
meal of the Lamb!" And the angel said, "These
are the true words of God."
10Then I bowed down at the angel's feet to
worship him, but he said to me, "Do not worship
me! I am a servant like you and your brothers and
sisters who have the message of Jesus. Worship
God, because the message about Jesus is the spirit
that gives all prophecy."[d]

The Rider on the White Horse

11Then I saw heaven opened, and there before
me was a white horse. The rider on the horse is
called Faithful and True, and he is right when he
judges and makes war. 12His eyes are like burning
fire, and on his head are many crowns. He has a
name written on him, which no one but himself
knows. 13He is dressed in a robe dipped in blood,
and his name is the Word of God. 14The armies
of heaven, dressed in fine linen, white and clean,
were following him on white horses. 15Out of the
rider's mouth comes a sharp sword that he will
use to defeat the nations, and he will rule them
with a rod of iron. He will crush out the wine in
the winepress[d] of the terrible anger of God the
Almighty. 16On his robe and on his upper leg was
written this name: KING OF KINGS AND LORD OF
LORDS.
17Then I saw an angel standing in the sun, and
he called with a loud voice to all the birds flying
in the sky: "Come and gather together for the
great feast of God 18so that you can eat the bodies
of kings, generals, mighty people, horses and their
riders, and the bodies of all people—free, slave,
small, and great."
19Then I saw the beast and the kings of the
earth. Their armies were gathered together to
make war against the rider on the horse and his
army. 20But the beast was captured and with him
the false prophet[d] who did the miracles[d] for the
beast. The false prophet had used these miracles
to trick those who had the mark of the beast and
worshiped his idol. The false prophet and the
beast were thrown alive into the lake of fire that
burns with sulfur. 21And their armies were killed
with the sword that came out of the mouth of the
rider on the horse, and all the birds ate the bodies
until they were full.

The Thousand Years

20 I saw an angel coming down from
heaven. He had the key to the bottomless pit and a large chain in his hand. 2The ange
grabbed the dragon, that old snake who is th
devil and Satan, and tied him up for a thousan
years. 3Then he threw him into the bottomles
pit, closed it, and locked it over him. The ange
did this so he could not trick the people of th
earth anymore until the thousand years wer
ended. After a thousand years he must be set fre
for a short time.
4Then I saw some thrones and people sitting o
them who had been given the power to judge
And I saw the souls of those who had been kille
because they were faithful to the message of Jesu
and the message from God. They had not wo
shiped the beast or his idol, and they had not re
ceived the mark of the beast on their foreheads o
on their hands. They came back to life and rule
with Christ for a thousand years. 5(The others tha
were dead did not live again until the thousan
years were ended.) This is the first raising of th
dead. 6Happy and holy are those who share in thi
first raising of the dead. The second death has n
power over them. They will be priests for Go
and for Christ and will rule with him for a tho
sand years.
7When the thousand years are over, Satan w
be set free from his prison. 8Then he will go o
to trick the nations in all the earth—Gog and M
gog—to gather them for battle. There are s
many people they will be like sand on the se
shore. 9And Satan's army marched across th
earth and gathered around the camp of God's pe
ple and the city God loves. But fire came dow

from heaven and burned them up. 10And Satan,
who tricked them, was thrown into the lake of
burning sulfur with the beast and the false
prophet.[d] There they will be punished day and
night forever and ever.

People of the World Are Judged

11Then I saw a great white throne and the One
who was sitting on it. Earth and sky ran away
from him and disappeared. 12And I saw the dead,
great and small, standing before the throne. Then
books were opened, and the book of life was
opened. The dead were judged by what they had
done, which was written in the books. 13The sea
gave up the dead who were in it, and Death and
Hades[n] gave up the dead who were in them.
Each person was judged by what he had done.
14And Death and Hades were thrown into the
lake of fire. The lake of fire is the second death.
15And anyone whose name was not found written
in the book of life was thrown into the lake of fire.

The New Jerusalem

21 Then I saw a new heaven and a new
earth. The first heaven and the first earth
had disappeared, and there was no sea anymore.
2And I saw the holy city, the new Jerusalem,[n]
coming down out of heaven from God. It was prepared like a bride dressed for her husband. 3And
I heard a loud voice from the throne, saying,
"Now God's presence is with people, and he will
live with them, and they will be his people. God
himself will be with them and will be their God.
4He will wipe away every tear from their eyes,
and there will be no more death, sadness, crying,
or pain, because all the old ways are gone."

SIDELIGHT: To dress the bride (Revelation 21:2) in Bible times was about as expensive as it can be today. The bride's face was made up to look glossy and shiny. Her hair was braided with gold and pearls. She was dressed in inherited family treasures. People borrowed what they couldn't buy.

5The One who was sitting on the throne said,
"Look! I am making everything new!" Then he
said, "Write this, because these words are true
and can be trusted."

Hades The place of the dead.
new Jerusalem The spiritual city where God's people live with him.

DEATH

Fear of Dying

"Thank you for flying with us," crackled the flight attendant's voice over the intercom after the jet landed. "And we encourage you to be extra careful on the most dangerous part of your journey: driving to your final destination in a car."

Many people fear flying, yet the odds of dying in a commercial airplane crash are only about 1 in 800,000. You're more likely to die by choking on food than in a plane crash.

In fact, all of the following are more dangerous than flying, based on the number of fatalities for each: car accidents, falls, fires and burns, drownings, shootings, poisonings.

Many people fear the way they will die more than they fear death itself.

The Bible, however, promises Christians that God has overcome death. **Revelation 21:1–6** offers a hopeful description of life with God beyond death.

- What does this picture of heaven say to people's many fears about dying?
- How does the passage speak to your own fears about death?

CONSIDER . . .

- selecting a story about death from the newspaper and using it to discuss your feelings about death with a friend or trusted adult.
- imagining what someone who has died might be experiencing in heaven. Thank God for his gift of eternal life that overcomes death.

FOR MORE, SEE . . .

- Psalm 23
- Luke 23:32–43
- 1 Corinthians 15:12–23

6The One on the throne said to me, "It is finished. I am the Alpha and the Omega,[n] the Beginning and the End. I will give free water from the spring of the water of life to anyone who is thirsty. 7Those who win the victory will receive this, and I will be their God, and they will be my children. 8But cowards, those who refuse to believe, who do evil things, who kill, who sin sexually, who do evil magic, who worship idols, and who tell lies—all these will have a place in the lake of burning sulfur. This is the second death."

9Then one of the seven angels who had the seven bowls full of the seven last troubles came to me, saying, "Come with me, and I will show you the bride, the wife of the Lamb." 10And the angel carried me away by the Spirit[d] to a very large and high mountain. He showed me the holy city, Jerusalem, coming down out of heaven from God. 11It was shining with the glory of God and was bright like a very expensive jewel, like a jasper, clear as crystal. 12The city had a great high wall with twelve gates with twelve angels at the gates, and on each gate was written the name of one of the twelve tribes[d] of Israel. 13There were three gates on the east, three on the north, three on the south, and three on the west. 14The walls of the city were built on twelve foundation stones, and on the stones were written the names of the twelve apostles[d] of the Lamb.

15The angel who talked with me had a measuring rod made of gold to measure the city, its gates, and its wall. 16The city was built in a square, and its length was equal to its width. The angel measured the city with the rod. The city was twelve thousand stadia[n] long, twelve thousand stadia wide, and twelve thousand stadia high. 17The angel also measured the wall. It was one hundred forty-four cubits[n] high, by human measurements, which the angel was using. 18The wall was made of jasper, and the city was made of pure gold, as pure as glass. 19The foundation stones of the city walls were decorated with every kind of jewel. The first foundation was jasper, the second was sapphire, the third was chalcedony, the fourth was emerald, 20the fifth was onyx, the sixth was carnelian, the seventh was chrysolite, the eighth was beryl, the ninth was topaz, the tenth was chrysoprase, the eleventh was jacinth, and the twelfth was amethyst. 21The twelve gates were twelve pearls, each gate having been made from a single pearl. And the street of the city was made of pure gold as clear as glass.

22I did not see a temple in the city, because the Lord God Almighty and the Lamb are the city's
temple. 23The city does not need the sun or th
moon to shine on it, because the glory of God i
its light, and the Lamb is the city's lamp. 24By it
light the people of the world will walk, and th
kings of the earth will bring their glory into i
25The city's gates will never be shut on any day
because there is no night there. 26The glory an
the honor of the nations will be brought into i
27Nothing unclean[d] and no one who does shame
ful things or tells lies will ever go into it. Onl
those whose names are written in the Lamb'
book of life will enter the city.

22 Then the angel showed me the river
the water of life. It was shining like cry
tal and was flowing from the throne of God an
of the Lamb 2down the middle of the street of th
city. The tree of life was on each side of the rive
It produces fruit twelve times a year, once eac
month. The leaves of the tree are for the healin
of all the nations. 3Nothing that God judges guil
will be in that city. The throne of God and of th
Lamb will be there, and God's servants will wo
ship him. 4They will see his face, and his nam
will be written on their foreheads. 5There wi
never be night again. They will not need the lig
of a lamp or the light of the sun, because the Lo
God will give them light. And they will rule
kings forever and ever.

6The angel said to me, "These words can b
trusted and are true." The Lord, the God of th
spirits of the prophets,[d] sent his angel to show h
servants the things that must happen soon.

7"Listen! I am coming soon! Happy is the or
who obeys the words of prophecy in this book

8I, John, am the one who heard and saw the
things. When I heard and saw them, I bowe
down to worship at the feet of the angel wh
showed these things to me. 9But the angel said
me, "Do not worship me! I am a servant like yo
your brothers the prophets, and all those wh
obey the words in this book. Worship God!"

10Then the angel told me, "Do not keep secr
the words of prophecy in this book, because th
time is near for all this to happen. 11Let whoev
is doing evil continue to do evil. Let whoever
unclean continue to be unclean. Let whoev
is doing right continue to do right. Let wh
ever is holy continue to be holy."

12"Listen! I am coming soon! I will bring m
reward with me, and I will repay each one of yo
for what you have done. 13I am the Alpha and th
Omega,[n] the First and the Last, the Beginnin
and the End.

14"Happy are those who wash their robes[n]

Alpha and the Omega The first and last letters of the Greek alphabet. This means "the beginning and the end."
stadia One stadion was a distance of about two hundred yards; about one-eighth of a Roman mile.
cubits A cubit is about half a yard, the length from the elbow to the tip of the little finger.
wash their robes This means they believed in Jesus so that their sins could be forgiven by Christ's blood.

that they will receive the right to eat the fruit from
the tree of life and may go through the gates into
the city. 15Outside the city are the evil people,
those who do evil magic, who sin sexually, who
murder, who worship idols, and who love lies and
tell lies.
16"I, Jesus, have sent my angel to tell you these
things for the churches. I am the descendant[d]
from the family of David, and I am the bright
morning star."
17The Spirit[d] and the bride say, "Come!" Let
the one who hears this say, "Come!" Let whoever
is thirsty come; whoever wishes may have the
water of life as a free gift.
18I warn everyone who hears the words of the
prophecy of this book: If anyone adds anything to
these words, God will add to that person the disasters written about in this book. 19And if anyone
takes away from the words of this book of prophecy, God will take away that one's share of the
tree of life and of the holy city, which are written
about in this book.
20Jesus, the One who says these things are true,
says, "Yes, I am coming soon."
Amen. Come, Lord Jesus!
21The grace of the Lord Jesus be with all.
Amen.

ETERNAL LIFE

A Bit of Heaven

Three hundred teenage tourists gathered in the Swiss Alps, 7,100 feet above sea level. Rising even higher on one side were craggy, snow-capped peaks. A huge glacier stretched out on the other side, seemingly unaffected by the warm July day.

The group gathered for outdoor worship, which began with a trio of alpine horns echoing hymns across the valley. The minister shared the Good News of Christ. Then voices joined together to close the service with familiar choruses of praise to God.

The day passed quickly, filled with hugs, songs, shouts of pleasure, helping hands, huge smiles, and incredible sights. As the teenagers waited to return to Grindelwald on Europe's longest chair lift, several girls talked about the experience.

"I hope heaven's like this," said one of the girls.

"Heaven's going to be even better!" said another.

God's promise of eternal life in heaven is even better! Read the promise in **Revelation 22:12–21**.

- What do you think made the girls think of heaven during their outing in Switzerland? How do you think the mountain experience compares to heaven itself?
- What difference does God's promise of eternal life make in your everyday living?

CONSIDER . . .

- remembering a time when you felt overwhelmed by nature's majesty as a reminder of God's greatness.
- asking yourself what you need to do to respond to the invitation in verse 17: "Let whoever is thirsty come; whoever wishes may have the water of life as a free gift."

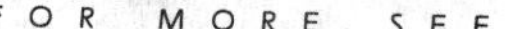

FOR MORE, SEE . . .

- Psalm 16:9–11
- Matthew 19:16–30
- John 4:5–42

Dictionary

A

Aaron (AIR-ohn) *older brother of Moses.*
- before the king of Egypt, Exodus 4:14-16; 5:1-5; 7:1-2
- death of, Numbers 20:22-29

Abba (AB-uh) *word for "father" in Aramaic.*
- Jesus called God "Abba," Mark 14:36
- we can call God "Abba," Romans 8:15; Galatians 4:6

Abednego (a-BED-nee-go) *one of the three friends of Daniel whom God protected from the fiery furnace.*
- refused the king of Babylon's food, Daniel 1:3-17
- thrown into the fiery furnace, Daniel 3

Abel (AY-bul) *the second son of Adam and Eve.*
- born to Adam and Eve, Genesis 4:2
- approved by God, Genesis 4:3-4; Hebrews 11:4
- murdered by Cain, Genesis 4:8; 1 John 3:12

Abib (ah-BEEB) *first month of the Jewish calendar, about the time of year as our March or April; also called "Nisan"; means "young ears of grain."*
- the time the Israelites left Egypt, Exodus 13:3-4
- the time for the Feast of Unleavened Bread, Exodus 23:15; 34:18

Abigail, sister of David (AB-eh-gale) 1 Chronicles 2:13-17

Abigail, wife of Nabal
- brought food to David, 1 Samuel 25:14-35
- became David's wife, 1 Samuel 25:36-42

Abijah, king of Judah (a-BY-jah) 1 Kings 15:1-8; 2 Chronicles 13:1–14:1

Abijah, son of Jeroboam
- death of, 1 Kings 14:1-18

Abijah, son of Samuel, 1 Samuel 8:1-3

ability
- given by God, 2 Corinthians 3:5-6
- through Christ, Philippians 4:13
- differing abilities, 1 Corinthians 12:7-11

Abimelech, king of Gerar (a-BIM-eh-lek)
- tried to take Sarah as his wife, Genesis 20

Abimelech, king of the Philistines
- tried to take Rebekah as his wife, Genesis 26:6-11

Abimelech, son of Gideon
- birth of, Judges 8:29-31
- murdered his brothers, Judges 9:1-6
- defeated the people of Shechem, Judges 9:22-45
- burned the Tower of Shechem, Judges 9:46-49
- death of, Judges 9:50-55

Abishai (a-BISH-eye) *nephew of King David.*
- served in David's army, 2 Samuel 23:18-19; 1 Chronicles 18:12-13
- saved David's life, 2 Samuel 21:15-17

Abner (AB-nur) *commander of Saul's army.*
- at Goliath's defeat, 1 Samuel 17:55-57
- made Ish-Bosheth king of Israel, 2 Samuel 2:8-10
- later loyal to David, 2 Samuel 3:6-21
- killed by Joab, 2 Samuel 3:22-27

Abraham (AY-bra-ham) *father of the Jewish nation.*
- called from Ur by God, Genesis 12:1-4
- lied about Sarai, Genesis 12:10-20
- separated from Lot, Genesis 13
- God's agreement with, Genesis 15; 17
- name changed, Genesis 17:3-6
- father of Isaac, Genesis 21:1-7
- offered Isaac as a sacrifice, Genesis 22:1-19
- father of the faithful, Romans 4
- God's friend, James 2:23

Absalom (AB-sah-lum) *one of David's sons.*
- turned against David, 2 Samuel 15–18:8
- killed by Joab, 2 Samuel 18:9-15

abstain (ab-STAIN) *to keep from doing something.*
- from food offered to idols, Acts 15:20
- from evil, 1 Thessalonians 5:22
- from lust, 1 Peter 2:11

abyss (uh-BISS) See "bottomless pit."

accept
- a prophet not accepted, Luke 4:24
- accepted by God, Acts 10:35; 15:7-8; Romans 14:3
- each other, Romans 14:1; 15:7
- Jesus, John 12:48

accuse
- Jesus accused by the Jews, Matthew 27:12-13; Mark 15:3; Luke 6:7
- Paul accused by the Jews, Acts 23:27-29; 26:7
- the Devil, as the accuser, Revelation 12:10

Achaia (a-KA-yuh) See "Greece."

Achan (AY-can) *an Israelite who disobeyed God during the battle of Jericho, Joshua 7*

Achish (AY-kish) *king of the Philistine city of Gath.*
- David pretends to be insane, 1 Samuel 21:10-15
- David in his army, 1 Samuel 27; 29

actions
- judged by, Proverbs 20:11; Matthew 11:19; Galatians 6:4
- of love, 1 John 3:18
- of goodness, Matthew 5:16

Adam (AD-um) *the first man.*
- created by God, Genesis 1:26–2:25
- disobeyed God, Genesis 3
- compared to Christ, 1 Corinthians 15:21-22,45-49

adder, *a poisonous snake.* See "snake."

Adonijah (ad-oh-NY-jah) *David's fourth son.*
- son of Haggith, 2 Samuel 3:4
- tried to become king, 1 Kings 1
- killed by Solomon, 1 Kings 2:12-25

Adoni-Zedek (a-DOH-ny-ZEE-dek) *an Amorite king of Jerusalem.*
- defeated by Joshua, Joshua 10:1-28

Adullam (a-DOO-lum) *a city about thirteen miles from Bethlehem.*
- David hid in a cave there, 2 Samuel 23:13

adultery (ah-DUL-ter-ee) *breaking a marriage promise by having sexual relations with someone other than your husband or wife.*
- "You must not be guilty of adultery," Exodus 20:14
- Christ teaches about, Matthew 5:27-32; Luke 16:18
- woman caught in adultery, John 8:1-11

advice
- given by Ahithophel, 2 Samuel 15:30–17:23
- given to Rehoboam, 1 Kings 12:1-15
- teachings about, Proverbs 11:14; 12:5,15; 19:20

Agabus (AG-uh-bus) *a Christian prophet.*
- warned the people, Acts 11:27-30
- warned Paul about going to Jerusalem, Acts 21:10-11

Agag (AY-gag) *king of the Amalekites.*
- captured by Saul, 1 Samuel 15

agreement *a contract, promise, or covenant.*
- with Noah, Genesis 9:1-17
- with Abraham, Genesis 15; 17:1-14
- Ark of the Agreement, Exodus 25:10-22; 1 Samuel 4–5; 2 Samuel 6:1-15
- with the Israelites, Exodus 19:3-8,24; Deuteronomy 29
- new agreement, 2 Corinthians 2:12–3:18
- difference between the old and new agreements, Hebrews 8–10

Agrippa (uh-GRIP-pah) See "Herod Agrippa."

Ahab (AY-hab) *evil king of Israel who was married to Jezebel.*
- worshiped Baal, 1 Kings 16:29-33
- had Naboth killed, 1 Kings 21
- death of, 1 Kings 22:1-40

Ahasuerus (ah-HAZ-oo-EE-rus) *Hebrew word for the Greek name Xerxes.* See "Xerxes."

Ahaz, *twelfth king of Judah,* 2 Kings 16; 2 Chronicles 28

Ahaziah, king of Judah (ay-ha-ZY-uh) 2 Chronicles 22:1-

Ahaziah, son of Ahab
- king of Israel, 1 Kings 22:40-53

Ahijah, great-grandson of Eli (a-HY-jah) 1 Samuel 14:1-23

Ahijah, the prophet
- told Jeroboam the kingdom would be divided, 1 Kings 11:29-39
- told that Jeroboam's son would die, 1 Kings 14:1-18

Ahimelech, the high priest (a-HIM-eh-lek)
- helped David, 1 Samuel 21:1-9

Ahimelech, the Hittite warrior, 1 Samuel 26:6

Ahithophel (a-HITH-oh-fel) *gave advice to King David.*
- helped Absalom rebel against David, 1 Samuel 15:31; 16:15–17:23

Ai (AY-eye) *a city completely destroyed by the Israelites,* Joshua 7–8:28

Akeldama (a-KEL-dah-mah) *field bought with the money Judas received for betraying Jesus,* Matthew 27:3-10; Acts 1:18-19

alabaster (AL-a-bass-ter) *light-colored stone with streaks or stripes through it,* Matthew 26:7; Mark 14:3; Luke 7:37

alamoth (AL-a-moth) *a musical word, which may mean "like a flute" or "high-pitched,"* Psalm 46

All-Powerful, *a name for God,* 1 Chronicles 11:9; Psalm 24:10; Isaiah 6:3-5; Malachi 3:1-17

Almighty, *a name for God.*
- "I am God Almighty," Genesis 17:1
- "I appeared to Abraham . . . by the name, God Almighty," Exodus 6:3
- "Holy, holy, holy is the Lord God Almighty," Revelation 4:8

almond
- design of the lampstands in Holy Tent, Exodus 25:31-36
- Aaron's stick produced, Numbers 17:8

aloes (AL-ohs) *oils from sweet-smelling sap of certain trees; used to make perfume and medicine and to prepare bodies for burial,* Psalm 45:8; Proverbs 7:17
- used to prepare Jesus' body for burial, John 19:39

Alpha and Omega (AL-fah and oh-MAY-guh) *the first and last letters of the Greek alphabet, like our A and Z.*
- used to describe Jesus, Revelation 1:8; 21:6; 22:13

altar (ALL-ter) *a place where sacrifices, gifts, or prayers were offered to a god.*
- built by Noah, Genesis 8:20
- built by Abraham, Genesis 22:9
- for burnt offerings, Exodus 27:1-8
- for incense, Exodus 30:1-10
- corners of, Exodus 27:2; 30:10; 1 Kings 1:50
- for the Temple, 2 Chronicles 4:1

Amalekites (AM-a-lah-kites) *fierce, fighting people who descended from Esau; they were enemies of Israel and were finally wiped out during the time of Hezekiah.*
- enemies of Israel, Exodus 17:8-16; 1 Samuel 15
- destroyed by King Hezekiah, 1 Chronicles 4:43

Amasa (AM-a-sa) *leader of Absalom's army when he rebelled against David,* 2 Samuel 17:25
- made leader of David's army, 2 Samuel 19:13
- killed by Joab, 2 Samuel 20:1-10

Amaziah (am-ah-ZY-uh) *the ninth king of Judah,* 2 Kings 14; 2 Chronicles 25

amen (AY-MEN or AH-MEN) *Hebrew word for "that is right,"* 1 Chronicles 16:36; Psalm 106:48; 1 Corinthians 14:16
- "Amen. Come, Lord Jesus!" Revelation 22:20

Ammonites (AM-on-ites) *descendants of Lot's son, Ben-Ammi,* Genesis 19:36-38
- enemies of Israel, Judges 10:6–11:33; 1 Samuel 11; 2 Samuel 10:1-14
- worshiped Molech, 1 Kings 11:5

Amon (AM-on) *the fifteenth king of Judah,* 2 Kings 21:18-26; 2 Chronicles 33:20-25
- an ancestor of Jesus, Matthew 1:10

Amorites (AM-or-ites) *a group of wicked people who worshiped false gods and lived in Canaan when the Israelites arrived.*
- defeated by Israel, Numbers 21:21-32; Joshua 10:1–11:14

Amos (AY-mos) *a prophet who warned Israel of God's punishment for disobedience.*
- a shepherd from Tekoa, Amos 1:1
- his visions, Amos 7–9:10

Anak/Anakites (A-nak/AN-uh-kites) *a group of large, fighting people who lived in Canaan when the Israelites arrived.*
- feared by the twelve spies, Numbers 13:22,28,33; Deuteronomy 1:26-28
- defeated by Joshua, Joshua 11:21-23

Ananias, husband of Sapphira (an-uh-NY-us)
- killed for lying to the Holy Spirit, Acts 5:1-6

Ananias, a Christian in Damascus
- helped Saul of Tarsus, Acts 9:10-19; 22:12-16

Ananias, the high priest
- at Paul's trial, Acts 23:1-5

Andrew, *a fisherman and brother of the apostle Peter.*
- chosen by Jesus to be an apostle, Mark 1:16-18; 3:13-19
- brought Peter to Jesus, John 1:40-42
- waited with the apostles in Jerusalem, Acts 1:13

angel (AIN-jel) *a heavenly being.*
- rescued Lot from Sodom, Genesis 19:1-22
- led Israel to Canaan, Exodus 23:20-23; 32:34
- announced Jesus' birth, Matthew 1:20-21; Luke 1:26-37; 2:8-15
- helped Jesus, Matthew 4:11; Luke 22:43
- helped the apostles, Acts 5:19-20; 12:6-10
- will bring judgment, Matthew 13:24-50; 24:31
- archangel, 1 Thessalonians 4:16; Jude 9
- less than Christ, Hebrews 1:4-14; 1 Peter 3:22
- rebellious angels, 2 Peter 2:4; Jude 6
- serving in heaven, Revelation 7–10

anger, *wrath.*
- of God toward people, John 3:36; Romans 1:18; 2:5-6; Colossians 3:5-6
- saved from God's anger by Christ, Romans 5:9; 1 Thessalonians 1:10; 5:9
- warnings against, Matthew 5:21-22; Ephesians 4:26,31; James 1:19-20

animal
- created by God, Genesis 1:20-25
- to be ruled by people, Genesis 1:26
- named by Adam, Genesis 2:19-20
- saved by Noah, Genesis 6:19-20
- clean, Leviticus 11:1-3,9; Deuteronomy 14:3-6
- unclean, Leviticus 11:4-8,10-12,26-44; Deuteronomy 14:7-8

Annas (AN-us) *a high priest of the Jews during Jesus' lifetime,* Luke 3:2; John 18:13
- questioned Peter and John, Acts 4:5-22

anoint (uh-NOINT) *to pour oil on.*
- to appoint a priest, Exodus 28:41; 40:13
- to appoint a king, 1 Samuel 10:1; 16:12-13; 2 Kings 9:6
- the Holy Tent, Numbers 7:1
- to heal sickness, Mark 6:13; James 5:14

Anti-Christ (AN-tee KRYST) See "enemy of Christ."

Antioch in Pisidia (AN-tee-ahk) *a small city in the country of Pisidia.*
- Paul preached there, Acts 13:14-15

Antioch in Syria, *third largest city in the Roman Empire.*
- Saul and Barnabus preached there, Acts 11:19-26
- followers first called "Christians" there, Acts 11:26
- Peter in Antioch, Galatians 2:11-12

- Paul preached there, Acts 13:14-15

Apollos (uh-POL-us) *an educated Jew from Alexandria.*
- taught by Aquila and Priscilla, Acts 18:24-28
- preached to the Corinthians, 1 Corinthians 1:12; 3:4-6
- friend of Paul, Titus 3:13

apostle (uh-POS-'l) *someone who is sent off. Jesus chose these twelve special followers and sent them to tell the Good News about him to the whole world.*
- twelve chosen by Jesus, Mark 3:14-19
- Matthias chosen, Acts 1:12-26
- Paul chosen, 1 Corinthians 15:3-11; 2 Corinthians 12:11-12
- duties and powers of, Luke 9:1-6; Acts 5:12-16; 8:18
- leaders of the church, Acts 15; 16:4; 1 Corinthians 12:28
- false apostles, 2 Corinthians 11:13; Revelation 2:2

appearance
- not to judge by, 1 Samuel 16:7; John 7:24
- deceiving, Matthew 23:27-28
- of Jesus, Isaiah 53:2; Philippians 2:7

Aquila (AK-wi-lah) *a Jewish Christian from Rome.*
- friend of Paul, Acts 18:2-3; Romans 16:3-5
- taught Apollos, Acts 18:24-28

Arabah (AIR-uh-bah) *the Hebrew word for the Jordan Valley.* See "Jordan Valley."

Arabah, Sea of, See "Dead Sea."

Aram (AIR-um) *a country northeast of Israel,* 1 Kings 11:25; 15:18; 2 Kings 5:1; Isaiah 7:1
- known as "Syria" in the New Testament, Matthew 4:24; Acts 15:23

Aramaic (AIR-uh-MAY-ik) *the language of the people in the nation of Aram.*
- common language of the Jews, 2 Kings 18:26; John 19:13,17,20; Acts 21:40

Ararat (AIR-uh-rat) *a group of mountains located in what is now Turkey and the Soviet Union.*
- Noah's boat landed there, Genesis 8:14

Araunah (a-RAW-nah) *a Jebusite who was also called Ornan.*
- sold his threshing floor to King David, 2 Samuel 24:15-25; 1 Chronicles 21:18-28

archangel (ark-AIN-jel) *the leader of God's angels,* 1 Thessalonians 4:16; Jude 9

Areopagus (AI R-ee-OP-uh-gus) *a council or group of important leaders in Athens.*
- Paul spoke there, Acts 17:16-34

argue
- the apostles argued, Mark 9:33-37; Luke 9:46-48
- avoid arguments, Philippians 2:14; 2 Timothy 2:23-26; Titus 3:9
- Michael argued with the devil, Jude 9

Aristarchus (air-i-STAR-kus) *a man from Thessalonica who often traveled with Paul,* Acts 27:2; Colossians 4:10; Philemon 24

ark, Noah's, *the huge boat that Noah built to save his family from the flood God sent to cover the earth.* See "boat."

Ark of the Agreement, *a special box made of acacia wood and gold. Inside were the stone tablets on which the Ten Commandments were written. Later, a pot of manna and Aaron's walking stick were also put into the Ark. It was to remind the people of Israel of God's promise to be with them.*
- building of, Exodus 25:10-22; 37:1-9
- crossing the Jordan River, Joshua 3:1-17
- captured by the Philistines, 1 Samuel 4–7:1
- touched by Uzzah, 2 Samuel 6:1-8; 1 Chronicles 13
- placed in the Temple, 2 Chronicles 5:2-10
- contents of, Hebrews 9:4-5

Ark of the Covenant, See "Ark of the Agreement."

armor
- of Saul, 1 Samuel 17:38-39; 31:9-10
- of God, Ephesians 6:10-17

arrest
- John the Baptist arrested, Matthew 14:3; Mark 6:17
- Jesus arrested, Matthew 26:50-57; Mark 14:44-50; John 18:1-14
- Peter arrested, Acts 12:1-4
- Paul arrested, Acts 28:17-20

Artaxerxes (ar-tah-ZERK-sees) *the title or name of Persian kings,* Ezra 4:7; Nehemiah 2:1
- his letter to Ezra, Ezra 7:11-26

Artemis (AR-tuh-mis) *a goddess that many Greeks worshiped,* Acts 19:23-41

Asa (AY-sah) *the third king of Judah,* 1 Kings 15:9-24; 2 Chronicles 14–16

Asaph (AY-saf) *a leader of singers when David was king,* 1 Chronicles 16:5,7; 25:1-2; 2 Chronicles 5:12
- songs of, Psalms 73–83

ascension (uh-SIN-shun) *lifted up; used to describe Jesus' return to heaven,* Acts 1:2-11; 2:32-33

ashamed
- of Jesus, Mark 8:38; Luke 9:26; 2 Timothy 1:8
- for suffering as a Christian, 1 Peter 4:16

Ashdod (ASH-dahd) *one of the five strong, walled cities of the Philistines; called Azotus in the New Testament.*
- Ark of the Agreement there, 1 Samuel 5:1-8
- later called "Azotus," Acts 8:40

Asherah (ah-SHIR-ah) *a Canaanite goddess thought to be the wife of the god Baal.*
- worshiped by Israelites, 1 Kings 14:14-15,22-23; 15:13
- worship forbidden, Exodus 34:13-14; Deuteronomy 16:21-22

Ashkelon (ASH-keh-lon) *one of the five important cities of the Philistines,* Judges 1:18; Zephaniah 2:4,7
- thirty of its men killed by Samson, Judges 14:19

Ashtoreth (ASH-toh-reth) *a goddess of the people of Assyria and Canaan. At times the Israelites forgot God and built idols to worship her.* Judges 2:13; 1 Samuel 7:3-4; 12:10
- worshiped by Solomon, 1 Kings 11:5,33

Asia (AY-zhuh) *the western part of the country now called "Turkey."*
- Paul preached there, Acts 19:10,26
- seven churches of, Revelation 1:4

assembly (a-SEM-blee) *a meeting; a group of people gathered for a purpose.*
- of the church, Hebrews 10:24-25
- conduct in, James 2:1-4

assurance (uh-SHURE-ans) *with confidence; without doubts.*
- about the gospel, 1 Thessalonians 1:5
- before God, Hebrews 10:22-23; 1 John 5:14-15
- faith as, Hebrews 11:1

Assyria (uh-SEER-ee-uh) *a powerful nation north and east of Israel.*
- enemy of Israel, 2 Kings 15:19-20; 17:3-6
- enemy of Judah, 2 Kings 18:13–19:36; Isaiah 36–37:37

Astarte (ah-STAR-tay) *another name for the goddess Ashtoreth.* See "Ashtoreth."

Athaliah (ath-uh-LY-uh) *the only woman who ruled over Judah,* 2 Kings 11; 2 Chronicles 22:10–23:21

Athens (ATH-enz) *the leading city of the country of Greece.*
- Paul preached there, Acts 17:16-34

atonement (uh-TONE-ment) *to remove or forgive sins.*
- through animal sacrifices, Exodus 30:10; Leviticus 17:11; Numbers 25:13
- through faith in the blood of Jesus' death, Romans 3:25; Hebrews 2:17; 9:22; 10:11-12

Atonement, Day of, See "Cleansing, Day of."

Augustus Caesar (aw-GUS-tus SEE-zer) *or Caesar Augustus, the first Roman emperor,* Luke 2:1

authority (uh-THAR-uh-tee) *power or right to control.*

- proper use of, Matthew 20:25-26; Luke 22:24-30; Titus 2:15
- respect for, Luke 20:20-26; Romans 13:1-7; 1 Timothy 2:2; 1 Peter 2:13-17; Hebrews 13:17
- Jesus' authority, Matthew 7:29; 9:6; Mark 11:27-33; Luke 5:24; John 5:19-29

B

Baal (BAY-el) *a god of the Canaanites; "Baal" was the common word for "master, lord." He was known as the son of Dagon, or the son of El, who was known as the father of the false gods.*
- worshiped by Israelites, Judges 2:10-11; Jeremiah 11:13
- Elijah defeated prophets of Baal, 1 Kings 18:1-40
- Baal worship destroyed by Jehu, 2 Kings 10:18-28

Baal-Zebub, See "Beelzebul."

Baasha (BAY-ah-shah) *the third king of Israel,* 1 Kings 15:27–16:7; 2 Chronicles 16:1-6; Jeremiah 41:9

Babel (BAY-bel) *a tower built to reach the sky,* Genesis 11:1-9

baby
- Moses as, Exodus 2:1-10
- Solomon determined mother of, 1 Kings 3:16-28
- Elizabeth's, Luke 1:39-44
- Jesus as, Luke 2:6-21
- as a symbol of new Christians, 1 Peter 2:2

Babylon (BAB-uh-lun) *city on the Euphrates River; capital of Babylonia.*
- captives in Babylon, Psalm 137:1; Jeremiah 29:10
- destruction predicted, Jeremiah 51:36-37
- as a symbol of evil, Revelation 14:8; 17:5

Babylonians (bab-e-LONE-e-unz) *people of the country Babylonia.* Also called "Chaldeans."
- capture warned by Jeremiah, Jeremiah 21; 25
- captured the people of Judah, 2 Kings 20:12-18; 24–25; Jeremiah 39:1-10
- Daniel in Babylon, Daniel 1–4
- released Israelite captives, Ezra 2

Balaam (BAY-lum) *a prophet from Midian.*
- asked by Balak to prophesy, Numbers 22–24; 2 Peter 2:15-16; Revelation 2:14
- death of, Numbers 31:8

balm, *oil from a plant used as medicine,* Genesis 37:25; Jeremiah 8:22; 51:8; Ezekiel 27:17

Baptist, John the (BAP-tist) *someone who baptizes. John, a relative of Jesus, was called this because he baptized many people.* Matthew 3:1-6
- condemned Pharisees and Sadducees, Matthew 3:7-10
- preached about Jesus, Matthew 3:11-12
- baptized Jesus, Matthew 3:13-17
- in prison, Matthew 11:1-6; Luke 7:18-23
- described by Jesus, Matthew 11:7-12; 17:10-13; Luke 7:24-28
- death of, Matthew 14:1-12; Mark 6:14-29
- baptism of, Matthew 21:25-26; Acts 10:37; 18:25; 19:3-4
- Jesus mistaken for, Matthew 16:13-14; Mark 8:27-28; Luke 9:18-19

baptism (BAP-tiz-em) *dipping or immersing.*
- by John, Matthew 3:6; Mark 1:4; Luke 3; Acts 19:3
- of Jesus, Matthew 3:13-17
- examples of, Acts 2:38-41; 8:36-38; 16:15,33
- with fire, Matthew 3:11; Luke 3:16
- with the Holy Spirit, Mark 1:8; Acts 1:5; 11:16

Barabbas (bah-RAB-us) *a robber who had murdered someone in Jerusalem.* He was freed instead of Jesus. Matthew 27:15-26; Mark 15:6-11

Barak (BAY-rak) *a leader of Israel's army when Deborah was judge,* Judges 4–5

Bar-Jesus, See "Elymas."

barley (BAR-lee) *a type of grain.*
- harvest of, Ruth 1:22; 2:17,23; 2 Samuel 21:9
- loaves of, John 6:9-13

barn
- storing in, Matthew 6:26
- rich man's, Luke 12:16-20

Barnabas (BAR-nah-bus) *an encourager who helped the apostles,* Acts 4:36; 11:23
- worked with Paul, Acts 11:26; 13–15
- influenced by hypocrites, Galatians 2:13

Bartholomew (bar-THOL-oh-mew) *one of the twelve apostles of Jesus,* Matthew 10:3; Mark 3:18; Luke 6:14; Acts 1:13

Bartimaeus (bar-teh-MAY-us) *a blind man who was healed by Jesus,* Mark 10:46-52

Baruch (BAH-rook) *a friend of the prophet Jeremiah,* Jeremiah 36

Bathsheba (bath-SHE-buh) *the mother of Solomon and wife of David,* 2 Samuel 11–12:25; 1 Kings 1–2; 22

beatitude (bee-A-ti-tyood) *blessed or happy; often used for Jesus' teaching in Matthew 5:3-12; Luke 6:20-22.*

Beelzebul (bee-EL-ze-bull) *false god of the Philistines; in the New Testament it often refers to the devil.*
- name for Satan, Matthew 12:24; Mark 3:22; Luke 11:15

Beersheba (beer-SHE-buh) *the town farthest south in the land of Judah,* 2 Samuel 3:10; 2 Chronicles 30:5
- Abraham made an agreement there, Genesis 21:14-34

beg
- Jesus begged by demons, Matthew 8:28-34; Mark 5:1-13; Luke 8:26-33
- Jesus begged by people, Matthew 14:36; Mark 7:24-26,32; 8:22

beggar
- Bartimaeus, Mark 10:46-52
- Lazarus, Luke 16:19-31
- at Beautiful Gate, Acts 3:1-10
- man born blind, John 9:1-12

Bel, a false god of the Babylonians, Jeremiah 50:2; 51:44

believe
- in God, Acts 16:34; Romans 4:24
- in Jesus, Matthew 18:6; John 12:44; 14:11-12; 1 John 5:10
- in the Good News, Mark 1:15; 11:24; Acts 15:7
- rewards of believing, Matthew 21:22; John 20:31; 1 Thessalonians 2:13
- a lie, 2 Thessalonians 2:11

believers (be-LEE-vers) *the followers of Jesus,* John 3:16; Acts 4:32; 5:14; Galatians 6:10

Belshazzar (bell-SHAZ-er) *a ruler of Babylon,* Daniel 5

Belteshazzar (BELL-teh-SHAZ-er) *the Babylonian name that Nebuchadnezzar gave to Daniel,* Daniel 4:8; 5:12

Benaiah (bee-NAY-uh) *the captain of David's bodyguard,* 2 Samuel 23:20-23
- commander of Solomon's army, 1 Kings 2:34-35

Ben-Hadad (ben-HAY-dad) *two or three Syrian kings who often fought against Israel,* 1 Kings 20:1-34; 2 Kings 6:24–8:15

Benjamin (BEN-jah-min) *the youngest son of Jacob and Rachel.*
- birth of, Genesis 35:16-20
- reunited with Joseph, Genesis 42–45

Bernice (bur-NY-see) *the oldest daughter of Herod Agrippa I,* Acts 25:13–26:32

Bethany (BETH-uh-nee) *a small town about two miles from Jerusalem.*
- home of Mary, Martha, and Lazarus, John 11:1; 12:1
- home of Simon, Mark 14:3

Bethel (BETH-el) *a town about twelve miles north of Jerusalem.*
- named by Jacob, Genesis 28:10-19
- Jeroboam built idols there, 1 Kings 12:26-33

Bethesda (be-THES-da) See "Bethzatha, pool of."
Bethlehem (BETH-le-hem) *a small town five miles from Jerusalem.*
- hometown of King David, 1 Samuel 16:1,13
- birthplace of Jesus, Matthew 2:1; Luke 2:15-17

Bethsaida (beth-SAY-ih-duh) *a city in Galilee and home of Peter, Andrew, and Philip,* John 1:44; 12:21
- rejected Jesus, Matthew 11:20-21; Luke 10:13

Bethzatha, pool of (beth-ZAY-tha) *a pool in Jerusalem near the Sheep Gate.*
- Jesus healed a man there, John 5:1-18

betray (be-TRAY) *to turn against.*
- families against each other, Mark 13:12-13
- Jesus betrayed, Matthew 26:20-25; Mark 14:18-46; John 13:2-30

birds
- created by God, Genesis 1:20-21
- saved by Noah, Genesis 6:19-20; 7:1-3
- unclean, Leviticus 11:13-19
- cared for by God, Matthew 6:25-27; Luke 12:24

birth
- spiritual birth, John 1:13; 3:3-8; 1 Peter 1:23

bishop, See "elder."
bitter
- water, Exodus 15:22-25; Numbers 5:18-27; Revelation 8:11
- herbs, Exodus 12:8

bitterness (BIT-er-nes) *sorrow or pain; anger or hatred.*
- warning against, Acts 8:23; Ephesians 4:31; James 3:14

blasphemy (BLAS-feh-mee) *saying things against God or not showing respect for God.*
- examples of, 1 Timothy 1:13; Revelation 13:6
- warnings against, Matthew 12:31-32; Mark 3:28-29
- Jesus accused of, Matthew 9:3; 26:65; Mark 2:6-7; John 10:36

blessing (BLES-ing) *a gift from God; asking God's favor on.*
- promised to Abraham, Genesis 12:1-3
- Isaac blessed Jacob, Genesis 27:1-41
- from God, Acts 3:25; Romans 10:12; 15:27; Hebrews 6:7
- by Jesus, Mark 10:16; Luke 24:50; John 1:16
- by each other, Luke 6:28; 1 Corinthians 4:12; 1 Peter 3:9

blind
- the blind healed, Matthew 9:27-31; 15:30; Mark 8:22-26; John 9
- Saul struck blind, Acts 9:8-9
- spiritually blind, Matthew 23:16-26; John 9:35-41; 2 Peter 1:5-9

blood, *sometimes used to mean "death."*
- water turned into, Exodus 7:14-24
- used in the Passover, Exodus 12:13-23
- not to be eaten, Leviticus 3:17; Deuteronomy 12:16; 1 Samuel 14:31-34
- of animal sacrifices, Leviticus 1; 3; 4; Hebrews 9:12-13; 10:4
- of Christ, Matthew 26:28; Romans 5:9; Hebrews 9:14; 1 John 1:7

boasting, See "bragging."
boat, *ark.*
- built by Noah, Genesis 6:11-21
- of the apostles, Matthew 4:21-22; John 21:3-11
- used by Jesus, Matthew 8:23; 13:2; 14:13-34

body
- made of dust, Genesis 2:7; 3:19
- health of, Proverbs 3:7-8; 4:20-22; 14:30
- attitudes toward, Matthew 6:25; Romans 6:13; Ephesians 5:29
- warnings against misuse, Romans 8:13; 1 Corinthians 6:18-20; 1 Thessalonians 4:5

body of Christ, *sometimes means Jesus' human body; also a way of describing Christians.*
- Christ's physical body, John 2:19-21; 19:38; Acts 2:31; 1 Corinthians 11:24; 1 Timothy 3:16; 1 Peter 3:18
- the Church as Christ's spiritual body, Romans 12:5; 1 Corinthians 12:12-31; Ephesians 1:23; 4:4; 5:23

bone
- "whose bones came from my bones," Genesis 2:23
- Ezekiel's vision of, Ezekiel 37:1-14
- none of Jesus' bones to be broken, John 19:36

book, *parchments, scroll.*
- Book of the Teachings, Deuteronomy 30:10; Joshua 1:8; 2 Chronicles 34:14-32; Ezra 8
- book of life, Philippians 4:3; Revelation 3:5; 13:8; 20:12; 21:27
- "Jesus did many other miracles. . .not written in this book." John 20:30
- "the whole world would not be big enough for all the books," John 21:25

bottomless pit, *the place where the devil and his demo[ns] live,* Luke 8:31; Revelation 9:1-11; 11:7; 17:8; 20:1-3
box of Scriptures, *small leather boxes that some Jews tied to their foreheads and left arms; also called "phylacteries" or "frontlets."*
- held the Law of Moses, Deuteronomy 6:6-8
- Jesus criticized misuse of, Matthew 23:5

bragging, *boasting.*
- warnings against, Proverbs 27:1; 2 Corinthians 10:12 18; James 4:16; Jude 16
- about the Lord, 1 Corinthians 1:31; 2 Corinthians 10:17; Galatians 6:14

bread, *the most important food in New Testament time[s] usually made of barley or wheat.*
- to feed 5,000 people, Matthew 14:13-21; Mark 6:30-44; Luke 9:10-17; John 6:1-13
- to feed 4,000 people, Matthew 15:32-39; Mark 8:1-[10]
- Jesus, the bread of life, John 6:25-59
- "A person does not live by eating only bread." Matthe[w] 4:4; Luke 4:4
- "Give us the food we need for each day." Luke 11:3
- in the Lord's Supper, Luke 22:19; Acts 20:7; 1 Corinthians 10:16; 11:17-34

bread that shows we are in God's presence, *twelve loaves of bread that were kept on the table in the Holy Tent and later in the Temple; also called "Bread of the Presence" or "showbread,"* Leviticus 24:5-9
- eaten by David, Matthew 12:3-4; Mark 2:25-26; Luk[e] 6:4

bride, Song of Solomon 4:8-12
- belongs to the bridegroom, John 3:29
- of Christ, Revelation 21:2,9

bridegroom
- sun compared to, Psalm 19:5
- Jesus compared to, Matthew 9:15; Mark 2:19-20; Lu[ke] 5:34
- Jesus' story of, Matthew 25:1-13
- at Jesus' first miracle, John 2:9

brother, *a family member; people from the same coun[try] or Christians.*
- physical brothers, Proverbs 18:24; Matthew 19:29; Mark 12:18-23
- Jesus' brothers, Matthew 13:55; Mark 3:31; John 2:[12]; 7:3; Acts 1:14; 1 Corinthians 9:5
- spiritual brothers, Romans 8:29; 12:10; 1 Timothy 6[:2]; Hebrews 2:11; 1 Peter 2:17

burn
- sacrifices, Exodus 29:10-42; Leviticus 1–4
- incense, Exodus 30:7-8; Numbers 16:40; Jeremiah 48:35; Luke 1:9
- Jericho burned by Israelites, Joshua 6:24
- idols burned by Josiah, 2 Kings 23:4-20
- jealousy like a fire, Psalm 79:5

• chaff, Matthew 3:12; Luke 3:17
• lake of burning sulfur, Revelation 21:8

burnt offerings, *a whole animal sacrificed as a gift to God.*
• rules about, Leviticus 1; 6:8-13; Numbers 28–29
• less important than obedience, 1 Samuel 15:22; Psalm 51:16-19
• less important than love, Hosea 6:6; Mark 12:32-33

bury, Matthew 8:21-22; Luke 9:59-60
• Abraham buried Sarah, Genesis 23
• Jacob not to be buried in Egypt, Genesis 47:29-30; 50:1-14
• strangers, Matthew 27:7
• in baptism, Romans 6:4

C

Caesar (SEE-zer) *a famous Roman family; used as the title of the Roman emperors.*
• Augustus, Luke 2:1
• Tiberius, Luke 3:1; 20:22; John 19:12
• Claudius, Acts 11:28; 17:7; 18:2
• Nero, Acts 25:8; 27:24; Philippians 4:22

Caesarea (SES-uh-REE-uh) *a city on the Mediterranean Sea,* Acts 10:1; 21:8; 23:32

Caesarea Philippi (SES-uh-REE-uh fih-LIP-eye) *a city at the base of Mount Hermon,* Matthew 16:13; Mark 8:27

Caiaphas (KAY-uh-fus) *the Jewish high priest from A.D. 18 to 36.*
• plotted to kill Jesus, Matthew 26:3-5; John 11:45-54
• father-in-law to Annas, John 18:13
• at Jesus' trial, Matthew 26:57-67
• questioned Peter and John, Acts 4:5-22

Cain, *the first son of Adam and Eve.*
• killed his brother Abel, Genesis 4:1-24; 1 John 3:12

Caleb (KAY-leb) *one of the twelve men Moses sent to spy out Canaan.*
• explored Canaan, Numbers 13–14
• given the city of Hebron, Joshua 14:6-15

calf
• gold idol, Exodus 32:1-20; 1 Kings 12:26-30; 2 Kings 10:28-29
• fatted, Luke 15:23,27,30

camel, Genesis 37:25; 1 Samuel 30:17; 1 Kings 10:2
• Rebekah watered Abraham's camels, Genesis 24:10-20
• "easier for a camel to go through the eye of a needle," Matthew 19:24; Mark 10:25; Luke 18:25
• "swallows a camel," Matthew 23:24

Cana (KAY-nah) *a small town near the city of Nazareth in Galilee.*
• place of Jesus' first miracle, John 2:1-11

Canaan (KAY-nun) *land God promised to the Israelites,* Leviticus 25:38; Numbers 13:2; 33:51; Psalm 105:11

Capernaum (kay-PUR-nay-um) *a city on the western shore of Lake Galilee.*
• Jesus lived there, Matthew 4:12-13
• Jesus healed there, Matthew 8:5-13; Luke 4:31-41
• rejected Jesus, Matthew 11:23-24

capital, *the top of a pillar, usually decorated with beautiful carvings.*
• in the Temple, 1 Kings 7:16-20; 2 Kings 25:17

captive
• Israelites as captives, Deuteronomy 28:41; 2 Kings 25:21; Jeremiah 30:3

cassia (CASH-ah) *a pleasant-smelling powder. Its odor is like the bark of the cinnamon plant.* Exodus 30:23-24; Psalm 45:8

census (SIN-sus) *a count of the number of people who live in an area.*
• the Israelites counted, Numbers 1:2; 26:2
• ordered by David, 1 Chronicles 21:1-2
• ordered by Augustus Caesar, Luke 2:1-3

centurion (sin-TUR-ree-un) *a Roman army officer who commanded a hundred soldiers.*
• centurion's servant healed by Jesus, Matthew 8:5-13; Luke 7:1-10
• at Jesus' death, Matthew 27:54; Mark 15:39; Luke 23:47
• Cornelius, Acts 10

Cephas (SEE-fuss) *the Aramaic word for "rock"; in Greek, "Peter." Jesus gave this name to the apostle Simon.* John 1:42

chaff (CHAF) *the husk of a head of grain. Farmers would toss the grain and chaff into the air. Since the chaff is lighter, the wind would blow it away, and the good grain would fall back to the threshing floor.*
• sinners to be destroyed like chaff, Psalms 1:4; 35:5; Matthew 3:12; Luke 3:17

Chaldeans, See "Babylonians."

change of heart and life, *repentance.*
• commanded, Matthew 3:2; Mark 1:15; Luke 13:3; Acts 3:19; 17:30
• causes of, Romans 2:4; 2 Corinthians 7:9-10
• examples of, Matthew 12:41; Luke 11:32

chariot
• Egyptians' chariots destroyed, Exodus 14:5-28
• of fire, 2 Kings 2:11; 6:17
• Ethiopian taught in a chariot, Acts 8:27-31

Chemosh (KEE-mosh) *a god of the Moabites,* Jeremiah 48:13
• worshiped by Solomon, 1 Kings 11:7

cherubim (CHAIR-uh-bim) *heavenly beings with wings and the faces of men and animals.*
• guarded the garden of Eden, Genesis 3:24
• on the Ark of the Agreement, Exodus 25:18-22; 1 Kings 6:23-28
• seen by Ezekiel, Ezekiel 10:1-20

children
• of God, John 1:12; Romans 8:14; 1 Peter 1:14; 1 John 3:1-10
• training of, Ephesians 6:4; Colossians 3:21
• obedience of, Ephesians 6:1; Colossians 3:20; 1 Timothy 3:4
• become like, Matthew 18:3-4
• "Let the little children come to me," Matthew 19:14; Mark 10:14; Luke 18:16

chosen
• Israelites chosen by God, Deuteronomy 7:7-8; 9:4-5; Isaiah 44:1
• people chosen by God, Romans 8:33; Ephesians 1:4-5; 2 Timothy 2:10; 1 Peter 1:2; 2:9
• Jesus chosen by God, Hebrews 1:2; 1 Peter 2:4

Christ (KRYST) *anointed (or chosen) one. Jesus is the Christ, chosen by God to save people from their sins.*
• active in creation, John 1:1-3; Colossians 1:15-17; Hebrews 1:2,10
• equal with God, John 5:23; 10:30; Philippians 2:6; Colossians 2:9; Hebrews 1:3
• purpose of his death, Romans 5:6; 14:9; Hebrews 9:28; 1 Peter 3:18
• gives life, John 5:21; 6:35; 10:28; 11:25; 14:6
• as Savior, Matthew 1:21; John 12:47
• as judge, Matthew 10:32-33; 25:31-46; John 5:22; Acts 17:31
• living in Christians, John 17:23; Romans 8:10; 2 Corinthians 1:21; Ephesians 3:17
• his return, Acts 1:11; 1 Thessalonians 5:1-11; Hebrews 9:28; 2 Peter 3:10
• enemy of, 1 John 2:18,22; 4:3; 2 John 7

Christians (KRIS-chuns) *Christ's followers,* Acts 11:26; 26:28; 1 Peter 4:16

church
• established by Christ, Matthew 16:18
• Christ as its head, Ephesians 1:22; 5:23; Colossians 1:18

- Christ died for, Ephesians 5:25
- activities of, Acts 12:5; 1 Corinthians 14:26-40; 1 Timothy 5:16; Hebrews 10:24-25

circumcision (SIR-kum-SIH-zhun) *the cutting off of the foreskin of the male sex organ; each Jewish boy was circumcised on the eighth day after he was born; this was done as a sign of the agreement God had made with his people, the Jews.*
- commanded by God, Genesis 17; Leviticus 12:1-3
- spiritual circumcision, Philippians 3:3; Colossians 2:11

city of refuge, See "safety, city of."

Claudius (CLAW-dee-us) *the fourth Roman emperor. He ruled from A.D. 41 to 54.* Acts 11:28; 17:7; 18:2

clean, *the state of a person, animal, or action that is pleasing to God. Under the Teachings of Moses, unclean animals could not be eaten. People who were considered clean could live and serve God normally.*
- clean and unclean animals, Deuteronomy 14:1-21; Mark 7:19; Acts 10
- clean and unclean people, Leviticus 13
- spiritually clean, Ephesians 5:26; Hebrews 9:14; 2 Peter 1:9

Cleansing, Day of, *the Day of Atonement; the most special day of the year for the Israelites when the high priest could go into the Most Holy Place. Animals were sacrificed for the sins of the people as a sign that people were cleansed of their sins for a year.*
- rules about, Leviticus 23:26-32; 25:9

cloud
- Israel led by pillar of cloud, Exodus 13:21
- cloud as small as a fist, 1 Kings 18:44
- Jesus leaves and will return in clouds, Luke 21:27; Acts 1:9; 1 Thessalonians 4:17; Revelation 1:7

Colossae (koh-LAH-see) *a city in the country of Turkey,* Colossians 1:1-2

comfort, *to help ease someone's pain, grief, or trouble.*
- bad comforters, Job 16:2
- by shepherd's rod, Psalm 23:4
- from God, Isaiah 49:13; Matthew 5:4; 2 Corinthians 1:3-4
- from the Holy Spirit, John 14:16-18

commands
- to be taught, Deuteronomy 6:1-7; Matthew 5:19
- to be obeyed, Deuteronomy 8:6; Proverbs 19:16; John 15:10
- a new command, John 13:34
- to love, Galatians 5:14; 1 Timothy 1:5; 2 John 6

communion (KUH-myu-nyun) See "Lord's Supper."

complain
- Pharisees complained, Luke 5:30
- disciples complained, John 6:61
- warnings against, Philippians 2:14

concubine (KON-kyu-bine) See "slave woman."

condemn (kun-DIM) *to judge someone guilty of doing wrong,* John 3:16-18; Romans 2:1; 8:1

coney, See "rock badger."

confess
- admitting sin, Psalm 32:5; Proverbs 28:13; James 5:16; 1 John 1:9
- admitting Christ is Lord, Romans 10:9-10; Philippians 2:11; 1 Timothy 6:12; 1 John 4:2-3

confidence (KON-fuh-dens) *a feeling of assurance; trust.*
- from the Lord, 2 Thessalonians 3:4; 2 Timothy 1:7
- in Christ, Philippians 4:13
- before God, 1 John 3:21

conscience (KON-shunts) *a person's belief about what is right and wrong.*
- Paul's good conscience, Acts 23:1
- commanded to have a good conscience, 1 Timothy 3:9; Hebrews 9:14
- a troubled conscience, Hebrews 10:22; 1 John 3:20
- a corrupt conscience, 1 Timothy 4:2; Titus 1:15

contentment, *satisfaction.*
- Paul learned, Philippians 4:11
- with possessions, Luke 3:14; 1 Timothy 6:6; Hebrews 13:5

conversion (kon-VER-zhun) *a person's turning toward God and becoming a Christian.*
- examples of, Acts 9:1-22; 11:19-21; 1 Thessalonians 1

coral (KOR-al) *a type of limestone that forms in the ocea* Job 28:18; Ezekiel 27:16

Corinth (KOR-inth) *a large seaport in the country of Greece.*
- Paul preached there, Acts 18:1-11
- Paul's letters to the church there, 1 and 2 Corinthians

Cornelius (kor-NEEL-yus) *a Roman army officer in charg of a hundred soldiers,* Acts 10

cornerstone, *the most important stone at the corner of the base of a building; Jesus is called the cornerstone of the new law.*
- Christ as the cornerstone, Ephesians 2:20; 1 Peter 2:4

council (KOWN-s'l) *or meeting; the highest Jewish cour in the days of Jesus.*
- Jesus before the council, Matthew 26:57-68; Mark 14:53-65
- apostles before the council, Acts 4:1-22; 22:30–23:10
- Stephen before the council, Acts 6:18–7

courage
- need for, Joshua 1:6-9; Psalm 27:14; 1 Corinthians 16:13; Philippians 1:20
- examples of, Acts 4:13; 5:17-32; 20:22-24

court, courtyard, *part of a building that has walls, but n roof. The Temple had four courts:*
- the Court of the Non-Jews (Gentiles), a large open are just inside the walls of Herod's Temple, Mark 11:1 17; John 10:23; Acts 3:11
- the Court of Women, the next area, where both men and women were allowed, Mark 12:41-44
- the Court of Israel, the inner area of the Temple, whe only Jewish men were allowed
- the Court of the Priests, the innermost court in the Temple, where only priests were allowed, Matthew 23:35

covenant (KUV-eh-nant) See "agreement."

covet (KUV-et) *to want strongly something that belongs someone else.*
- forbidden by God, Exodus 20:17; Romans 13:9; Hebrews 13:5

creation
- of the world, Genesis 1–2; Job 38–41; Psalm 8; Isaiah 40:21-26; John 1:1-3; Hebrews 11:3

creator, *one who makes something out of nothing.*
- God as our Maker, Deuteronomy 32:6
- "Remember your Creator," Ecclesiastes 12:1

Crete (KREET) *an island in the Mediterranean Sea.*
- Paul visited there, Acts 27:7; Titus 1:5

cross, *two rough beams of wood nailed together; criminals were killed on crosses.*
- Jesus died on a cross, Matthew 27:31-50; Mark 15:2 37; Luke 23:26-46; John 19:16-30
- importance of, 1 Corinthians 1:18; 2:2; Galatians 6:1 Ephesians 2:16; Colossians 2:13-14
- as a symbol of death to oneself, Matthew 10:38; Luke 9:23; Romans 6:6; Galatians 5:24

crown, *a special band worn around the head.*
- a king's crown, Psalm 21:2-3; Song of Solomon 3:11; Revelation 12:3
- of thorns, Matthew 27:29; Mark 15:17; John 19:2
- of victory, 1 Corinthians 9:25; 2 Timothy 4:8; 1 Peter 5:4

crucifixion (kroo-suh-FIK-shun) *to be killed on a cross. See "cross."*

ubit (KU-bit) *a measurement in Bible times; about eighteen inches,* Revelation 21:17

ud, *an animal's food that is chewed slightly, swallowed, brought up, then chewed more completely a second time,* Leviticus 11; Deuteronomy 14

up
- of the king of Egypt, Genesis 40:11
- of Joseph, Genesis 44:1-17
- of Lord's Supper, Matthew 26:27-29; Mark 14:22-25; Luke 22:17-20; 1 Corinthians 11:25-29
- of anger, Isaiah 51:17-23
- of water, Matthew 10:42; Mark 9:41

upbearer, *the officer who tasted and served the king his wine.*
- to the king of Egypt, Genesis 40
- Nehemiah, cupbearer to Artaxerxes, Nehemiah 1:11

urse
- from God, Deuteronomy 11:26-29; John 7:49; Galatians 3:10-13
- forbidden to people, Matthew 15:4; Romans 12:14; James 3:9-10
- response to, Luke 6:28; 1 Corinthians 4:12

urtain
- of the Holy Tent, Exodus 26:1-2; 36:9
- of the Temple, Matthew 27:51; Mark 15:38; Luke 23:45

ush, *a country in Africa,* Genesis 2:13; Psalm 68:31; Isaiah 18; 20

ush, grandson of Noah, Genesis 10

yprus (SY-prus) *an island in the Mediterranean Sea,* Acts 11:19-20; 13:4; 15:39

yrene (sy-REE-nee) *a city in North Africa,* Acts 2:10; 6:9
- Simon of, Matthew 27:32; Mark 15:21; Luke 23:26

yrus (SY-rus) *a king of Persia,* Daniel 1:21
- sent captives home, Ezra 1; 6
- chosen by God, Isaiah 44:28–45:13

D

agon (DAY-gon) *a false god of the Philistines,* Judges 16:23; 1 Samuel 5:2-7; 1 Chronicles 10:10

amascus (duh-MAS-kus) *a city forty miles east of Lake Galilee.*
- a chief city of Syria, 1 Kings 15:18; 2 Chronicles 24:23
- condemned by Amos, Amos 1:3,5
- Paul converted there, Acts 9:1-22

an, a city
- Israel's most northern city, Judges 20:1; 2 Samuel 16:11

an, son of Jacob, Genesis 30:6; 49:16-17; Joshua 19:40-48

aniel (DAN-yel) *a Hebrew captive taken to Babylon as a young man.*
- taken to Babylon, Daniel 1:1-6
- became king's servant, Daniel 1:7-21
- explained Nebuchadnezzar's dreams, Daniel 2; 4
- read the writing on the wall, Daniel 5
- thrown into lions' den, Daniel 6
- his visions, Daniel 7; 8; 10
- a prophet, Matthew 24:15

arius Hystaspes (dah-RYE-us his-TAHS-peez) *a ruler of Persia who allowed the Jews to finish rebuilding the Temple,* Ezra 5–6

arius the Mede, *the king of Persia who made Daniel an important ruler under him,* Daniel 5:31–6:28; Haggai 1:1; Zechariah 1:1

arkness, *having no light; a symbol of evil.*
- before creation, Genesis 1:2
- as a plague, Exodus 10:21-23
- at Jesus' death, Matthew 27:45; Mark 15:33; Luke 23:44-45
- spiritual, John 1:5; Romans 13:12; Colossians 1:13
- as punishment, Matthew 8:12; 2 Peter 2:17; Jude 6; 13

avid (DAY-vid) *Israel's greatest king.*
- son of Jesse, 1 Samuel 16:13-23
- played harp for Saul, 1 Samuel 16:14-23
- killed Goliath, 1 Samuel 17
- friend of Jonathan, 1 Samuel 18:1-4; 19:1-7; 20
- chased by Saul, 1 Samuel 18–19; 23:7-29
- protected Saul, 1 Samuel 24; 26
- became king, 2 Samuel 2:1-7; 5:1-14
- married Bathsheba, 2 Samuel 11–12:25
- reign of, 2 Samuel 5–1 Kings 1
- not allowed to build the Temple, 2 Samuel 7:1-17
- death of, 1 Kings 2:1-11
- Jesus as son of David, Matthew 22:42-45; Luke 1:27; 20:41-44

deacon (DEE-kun) *a person chosen to serve the church in special ways,* Philippians 1:1; 1 Timothy 3:8-13

Dead Sea, *large lake at the south end of the Jordan River. Several small streams flow into it, but it has no outlet. It is so salty that nothing lives in it. It is also called the "Sea of Arabah," the "Salt Sea," and the "Eastern Sea."* Genesis 14:3; Numbers 34:3,12; Joshua 3:16

deaf, *unable or unwilling to hear.*
- healed, Matthew 11:5; Luke 7:22
- and dumb spirit, Mark 9:25

death
- a result of sin, Genesis 2:16-17; Romans 5:12; 6:23; 1 Corinthians 15:21
- Christ's victory over, 1 Corinthians 15:24-26,54-57; 2 Timothy 1:10; Hebrews 2:14; Revelation 1:18
- spiritual death, Ephesians 2:1; Colossians 2:13

Deborah (DEB-oh-rah) *the only woman judge over Israel,* Judges 4–5

Decapolis (dee-KAP-oh-lis) *ten towns in an area southeast of Lake Galilee,* Matthew 4:25; Mark 5:20; 7:31

Delilah (dee-LYE-luh) *an evil Philistine woman whom Samson loved,* Judges 16:4-20

Demas (DEE-mus) *a Christian who helped the apostle Paul when Paul was in prison.*
- worked with Paul, Colossians 4:14; Philemon 24
- left Paul, 2 Timothy 4:10

Demetrius (deh-MEE-tree-us) *a silver worker in Ephesus,* Acts 19:23-27,38

demon, *an evil spirit from the devil. Sometimes demons lived in people, but Jesus could force them out.*
- people possessed by, Matthew 8:28-32; 9:32-33; Mark 7:24-30; 9:17-29
- Jesus accused of demon possession, Mark 3:22; John 7:20; 8:48; 10:20-21
- demons recognized Jesus, Mark 1:23-26; 3:11-12; 5:7-8; Acts 19:15; James 2:19

deny (di-NY) *refusing to believe the truth.*
- denying Christ, Matthew 10:32-33; 2 Timothy 2:12; 1 John 2:22-23
- Peter denied Christ, Matthew 26:34-35,69-75

descendants (de-SIN-dants) *family members who are born to a person or his children; grandchildren, great-grandchildren, great-great-grandchildren and so on,* Genesis 13:14-16; 15:12-16

devil (DEV-'l) *Satan; a spirit and the enemy of God and humans.*
- Jesus tempted by, Matthew 4:1-11; Luke 4:1-13
- children of, John 8:41-44; Acts 13:10; 1 John 3:7-10
- people to oppose, Ephesians 4:27; 6:11; James 4:7

Didymus (DID-ee-mus) *another name for Thomas, one of Jesus' apostles,* John 11:16; 20:24; 21:2

disciple (dih-SYE-p'l) See "follower."

disease
- a result of sin, Exodus 15:26; Deuteronomy 7:15; 28:60-61
- healed by Jesus, Matthew 4:23-24; 15:30-31; 21:14; Luke 7:21
- healed by apostles, Acts 5:12-16; 9:32-35; 14:8-10; 19:11-12; 28:8-9

disobedience
• brought sin, Romans 5:19
• to be punished, 2 Corinthians 10:6; Hebrews 4:11
divide
• heavens and earth, Genesis 1:6-8
• Red Sea, Exodus 14:16,21
• family against itself, Matthew 12:25; Mark 3:25; Luke 11:17
divorce
• teachings about, Deuteronomy 22:13-19,28-29; 24:1-4; Matthew 5:31-32; 19:1-12; 1 Corinthians 7:10-16
dog
• drinking water like a dog, Judges 7:5-6
• returns to its vomit, Proverbs 26:11; 2 Peter 2:22
• licked Ahab's blood, 1 Kings 22:38
• licked Lazarus's sores, Luke 16:20-21
door
• Jesus as the door, John 10:1
• "Knock, and the door will open," Luke 11:9-10
• "I stand at the door and knock." Revelation 3:20
donkey
• Balaam's, Numbers 22:21-30
• jawbone of, Judges 15:15-17
• ridden by Jesus, Matthew 21:1-7
Dorcas (DOR-kus) *Tabitha; a Christian woman known for helping the poor.*
• raised from the dead, Acts 9:36-43
dove, *a small bird similar to a pigeon; often a symbol for love, peace, and the Holy Spirit.*
• sent out by Noah, Genesis 8:8-12
• form taken by the Spirit of God, Matthew 3:16; Mark 1:10
• sellers of, John 2:14-16
dreams
• Joseph's, Genesis 37:1-11
• the king of Egypt's, Genesis 41:1-36
• Nebuchadnezzar's, Daniel 2; 4
• angel appeared to Joseph, Matthew 1:20-21; 2:13,19
• "your old men will dream dreams," Acts 2:17
drunkenness
• Noah became drunk, Genesis 9:20-23
• warnings against, Romans 13:13; 1 Corinthians 6:10; Ephesians 5:18; 1 Peter 4:3

E

eagle
• "to rise up as an eagle," Isaiah 40:31
earth
• creation of, Genesis 1:9-10; Jeremiah 51:15
• belongs to God, Exodus 19:5; Psalm 24:1
earthquake
• experienced by Elijah, 1 Kings 19:11-12
• at the death of Jesus, Matthew 27:51-54
• at Jesus' resurrection, Matthew 28:2
• experienced by Paul and Silas, Acts 16:25-26
Ebal (EE-buhl) *a mountain in Samaria next to Mount Gerizim.*
• place to announce curses, Deuteronomy 11:29; 27:12-13; Joshua 8:30-35
Eden, garden of (EE-den) *the home God created for Adam and Eve,* Genesis 2:8–3:24; Ezekiel 36:35; Joel 2:3
Edom (EE-dum) *Esau; the land where Esau's descendants lived.*
• the land of Esau, Genesis 36:8-9
• refused to let Israelites pass through, Numbers 20:14-21; Judges 11:17-18
• broke away from Judah, 2 Kings 8:20-22
• to be punished, Jeremiah 49:7-22; Ezekiel 25:12-14; Obadiah
education
• of Moses, Acts 7:22
• of children, Deuteronomy 6:1-7
• brings wisdom, Proverbs 8:33; 22:6
Eglon (EGG-lon) *a king of Moab,* Judges 3:12-25
Egypt (EE-jipt) *a country in the northeast part of Africa.*
• Joseph there, Genesis 39–50
• Israelites there, Genesis 46:5-34; Exodus 1; Acts 7:9-38
• Israelites left, Exodus 12:31-51
• Jesus there, Matthew 2:13-15
Ehud (EE-hud) *the second judge of Israel,* Judges 3:12-30
elder (EL-der) *older men who led God's people; appointed leaders in the church.*
• leaders of the Jews, Numbers 11:16-25; Deuteronomy 19:11-12; Matthew 21:23; Acts 4:5-7
• leaders of the church, Acts 11:30; 14:23; 15:2; 16:4
• duties and qualities, Acts 20:28; 1 Timothy 3:1-7; Titus 1:6-9; 1 Peter 5:1-3
Eleazar (el-ee-A-zar) *son of Aaron.*
• birth of, Exodus 6:23-25
• Moses became angry with, Leviticus 10:16-20
• a high priest, Numbers 3:32
• divided the promised land, Numbers 34:17
election, *process of selecting.* See "chosen."
Eli (EE-lye) *a priest and the next-to-last judge of Israel.*
• trained Samuel, 1 Samuel 1:9-28; 2:11; 3
• didn't discipline his sons, 1 Samuel 2:12-36
• death of, 1 Samuel 4:1-18
Elihu (ee-LYE-hew) *the fourth of Job's friends to try to explain Job's troubles,* Job 32–37
Elijah (ee-LIE-juh) *a prophet who spoke for God.*
• fed by ravens, 1 Kings 17:1-6
• brought boy to life, 1 Kings 17:7-24
• against prophets of Baal, 1 Kings 18:1-40
• condemned Ahab, 1 Kings 21:17-29
• taken to heaven, 2 Kings 2:1-12
• appeared with Jesus, Matthew 17:1-13; Mark 9:2-13; Luke 9:28-36
Elisha (ee-LYE-shuh) *the prophet who took Elijah's place as God's messenger.*
• received Elijah's spirit, 2 Kings 2:9-14
• helped a Shunammite woman, 2 Kings 4:1-36
• miracles of, 2 Kings 2:19-22; 4:38-44; 6:1-7
• healed Naaman, 2 Kings 5
• death of, 2 Kings 13:14-20
Elizabeth (ee-LIZ-uh-beth) *the wife of Zechariah, a priest.*
• mother of John the Baptist, Luke 1:5-25,57-66
• visited by Mary, Luke 1:39-45
Elkanah (el-KAY-nuh) *the father of Samuel,* 1 Samuel 1–2:11
Elymas (EL-ih-mus) *Bar-Jesus; a magician in the city of Paphos in Cyprus,* Acts 13:4-12
Emmaus (ee-MAY-us) *a town seven miles from Jerusalem*
• Jesus appeared to disciples near there, Luke 24:13-39
encourage
• encouragement from God, Romans 15:4-5
• Christians to encourage each other, 1 Thessalonians 5:14; 2 Timothy 4:2; Hebrews 3:13; 10:24-25
• examples of encouragement, Acts 11:23; 13:15; 15:31-32
endurance, See "patience."
enemy
• attitude toward, Exodus 23:4-5; Matthew 5:43-48; Luke 6:27-36; Romans 12:20
• God's enemies, Romans 5:10; Philippians 3:18-19; James 4:4
enemy of Christ, *the anti-Christ,* 1 John 2:18,22; 4:3; 2 John 7
Enoch (E-nuk) *a man who walked with God,* Genesis 5:21-24; Hebrews 11:5
enrollment, See "census."
envy, See "jealousy."
Epaphras (EP-ah-fruhs) *a Christian who started the church at Colossae,* Colossians 1:7-8; 4:12-13; Philemon 23
Epaphroditus (ee-PAF-ro-DYE-tus) *a Christian in the church at Philippi,* Philippians 2:25-30; 4:18

ephah (EE-fah) *a common measurement for dry materials, about twenty quarts,* Exodus 16:36

Ephesus (EF-eh-sus) *the capital city in the Roman state of Asia.*
- Paul's work there, Acts 18:18-20; 1 Corinthians 16:8-9
- church there, Ephesians 1:1; Revelation 2:1-7

ephod (EF-ahd) See "vest, holy."

Ephraim (EE-frah-im) *Joseph's younger son,* Genesis 41:50-52; 48:8-20
- descendants of, Numbers 26:35; Joshua 16:5-10

equality (ee-KWAHL-eh-tee) *being identical in value.*
- in death, Ecclesiastes 3:19-20
- of Jewish and non-Jewish people, Romans 10:12
- in Christ, Galatians 3:26-28

Esau (EE-saw) See "Edom."

Esther (ES-ter) *a Jewish girl who became the wife of Ahasuerus, King of Persia,* Esther 1–10
- became queen, Esther 1–2:18
- learned of the plan to kill the Jews, Esther 3–4
- saved the Jews, Esther 5–8

eternal, See "forever."

eternal life, *the new kind of life promised to those who follow Jesus.*
- conditions for, Mark 10:17-31; John 3:14-15; 12:25; 17:3; Galatians 6:7-8
- source of, John 6:27-29; 10:28; Titus 1:2; 1 John 5:11-12

Ethiopia, *earlier called "Cush."* See "Cush."

eunuch (YOU-nuk) *a man who cannot have sexual relations. In Bible times, eunuchs were often high officers in royal palaces or armies.* 2 Kings 9:32; Esther 2:3; Isaiah 56:3-5; Acts 8:26-40

Euphrates (you-FRAY-teez) *a long, important river in Bible lands.*
- in the garden of Eden, Genesis 2:10-14
- a boundary, Genesis 15:18; 1 Kings 4:21; 2 Kings 24:7

Eutychus (YOU-ti-cus) *a young man in the city of Troas who was brought back to life,* Acts 20:7-12

evangelist (ee-VAN-juh-list) *someone who tells the Good News.*
- Philip, the evangelist, Acts 21:8
- as a gift from Christ, Ephesians 4:11

Eve (EEV) *the first woman.*
- created by God, Genesis 2:18-25
- tricked by Satan, Genesis 3; 2 Corinthians 11:3; 1 Timothy 2:13-14

everlasting, *living forever; eternal.*
- God, Genesis 21:33; Nehemiah 9:5; Isaiah 40:28
- Christ, Isaiah 9:6
- kingdom, Daniel 4:3; 2 Peter 1:11
- fire, Matthew 18:8,25,41
- gospel, Revelation 14:6

evil
- warnings against, Amos 5:15; Romans 12:9; 1 Thessalonians 5:22
- to be punished, Proverbs 24:20; Isaiah 13:11

evil spirit, See "demon."

eye
- "eye for eye," Exodus 21:23-24; Matthew 5:38
- wood in, Matthew 7:3-5; Luke 6:41-42

eyewitness, *one who sees an occurrence and reports on it.*
- of Jesus' life, Luke 1:2; 2 Peter 1:16; 1 John 1:1

Ezekiel (ee-ZEEK-yel) *a prophet during the time the Jews were captured by the Babylonians,* Ezekiel 1:3
- his vision of dry bones, Ezekiel 37:1-14

Ezra (EZ-ra) *the leader of a group of Israelites who were allowed to return to Jerusalem from Babylon,* Ezra 7–10; Nehemiah 8

F

faith (FAYTH) *belief and trust.*
- definition of, Hebrews 11:1
- sources of, Romans 1:20; 10:17
- examples of, Matthew 8:5-10; 15:21-28; Hebrews 11
- power of, Matthew 17:20-21; Ephesians 6:16
- made right with God by, Romans 4:3; 5:1; Philippians 3:9
- salvation by, Mark 16:15-16; John 5:24; 20:31; Romans 10:9; Galatians 2:16
- blessings by, Galatians 3:1-14; Ephesians 3:12; 1 Peter 1:5
- continue in, 2 Corinthians 13:5; Colossians 1:23; 1 Timothy 1:19; 2 Timothy 2:22
- lack of, Matthew 8:26; 14:31; 16:8

faithful (FAYTH-ful) honest, loyal, *true.*
- God is faithful, Deuteronomy 32:3-4; Isaiah 49:7; 2 Timothy 2:13; Hebrews 3:6; Revelation 19:11
- God's people must be faithful, Matthew 25:21; Revelation 2:10; 14:12; 17:14

fall, *sometimes used to describe the first sin.*
- Adam and Eve sinned, Genesis 3

false
- gods, Exodus 20:3; Deuteronomy 4:28; 1 Chronicles 16:26
- prophets, Deuteronomy 13:1-11; 18:22; Jeremiah 14:13-16; Matthew 7:15
- Christs, Matthew 24:24; Mark 13:22
- apostles, 2 Corinthians 11:13
- brothers, Galatians 2:4
- teachers, 2 Peter 2:1

family
- of believers, Galatians 6:10; Hebrews 2:11; 1 Peter 4:17

famine (FAM-un) *a time of hunger when there is very little food.*
- in Egypt, Genesis 41:30-31,53-57
- in Moab, Ruth 1:1
- in Israel, 1 Kings 17:1
- in Jerusalem during Claudius's rule, Acts 11:27-28

fasting (FAST-ing) *giving up food for a while.*
- to show sorrow, 1 Samuel 1:11-12; 2 Samuel 12:15-22
- of Jesus, Matthew 4:1-2
- how to fast, Matthew 6:16-18
- combined with prayer, Ezra 8:23; Luke 5:33; Acts 13:1-3

father
- to be honored, Exodus 20:12; Ephesians 6:2
- commands to, Colossians 3:21
- God as Father, Matthew 6:9; 23:9; 2 Corinthians 6:18; Galatians 4:6; Hebrews 12:4-11

fear, *a feeling of being afraid, or one of deep respect.*
- of God, Matthew 10:26-31; Luke 23:40
- overcoming, 2 Timothy 1:7; Hebrews 13:6; 1 John 4:18
- "your salvation. . .with fear and trembling," Philippians 2:12

feast (FEEST) *a special meal and celebration for a certain purpose.*
- Feast of Dedication, an eight-day celebration for the Jews that showed they were thankful that the Temple had been cleansed again, John 10:22
- Feast of Harvest, see "Feast of Weeks."
- Feast of Purim (PURE-rim) reminded the Israelites of how they were saved from death during the time of Queen Esther, Esther 9:18-32
- Feast of Shelters, "Feast of Booths" or "Feast of Tents"; reminded the Israelites of how God had taken care of them when they left Egypt and lived in tents in the wilderness, Exodus 23:16; Deuteronomy 16:13-17
- Feast of Unleavened Bread, or "Passover"; reminded the Israelites how God brought them out of Egyptian slavery, Exodus 12:1-30; Numbers 28:16-25; Deuteronomy 16:1-8
- Feast of Weeks, or "Pentecost," the "Feast of Harvest," or the "Day of Firstfruits"; a feast of thanksgiving for the summer harvest, Exodus 34:22; Leviticus 23:15-22; Numbers 28:26-31

Felix (FEE-lix) *the Roman governor of Judea from A.D. 52 to 54.*
- put Paul on trial, Acts 23:23-24; 24

fellowship (FEL-o-ship) *sharing friendship and love with others.*
- with Christ, Matthew 18:20; 1 Corinthians 1:9; 1 John 1:3
- with the Holy Spirit, 2 Corinthians 13:14; Philippians 2:1
- with believers, Acts 2:42; 1 John 1:7

Festus (FES-tus) *governor of Judea after Felix.*
- put Paul on trial, Acts 25–26

fighting
- against evil, 2 Corinthians 10:3-6; Ephesians 6:12
- "fight the good fight," 1 Timothy 1:18
- "I have fought the good fight." 2 Timothy 4:7

fire, *used by God as a sign of his presence and power.*
- the burning bush, Exodus 3:1-6
- pillar of, Exodus 13:21-22
- chariot of, 2 Kings 2:11
- wrong kind of, Numbers 26:61
- fiery furnace, Daniel 3:25
- baptism of, Matthew 3:11
- of punishment, Matthew 5:22; 13:41-42; Mark 9:43; 2 Thessalonians 1:8; Hebrews 10:27
- everything destroyed by fire, 2 Peter 3:10
- evidence of the Holy Spirit, Acts 2:3

firstborn (FIRST-born) *the oldest child in a family; the firstborn son in a Jewish family received a double share of his father's wealth and became the leader of the family when his father died.*
- Esau sold his rights, Genesis 25:27-34
- Israelites as God's firstborn, Exodus 4:22; Jeremiah 31:9
- death of, Exodus 11:1-8
- given to God, Exodus 13:1-16

firstfruits (FIRST-fruits) *the first and best crops and animals the Israelites raised and gave to God at harvest time,* Exodus 34:26; Numbers 28:26; Deuteronomy 18:3-4

fish
- clean and unclean, Deuteronomy 14:9-10
- used in miracles, Matthew 14:17; Luke 5:1-7; John 21:1-13

flax (FLAKS) *a plant used to make clothing and ropes,* Exodus 9:31; Isaiah 19:9
- used by Rahab, Joshua 2:6

flood, Genesis 6:9–8; Matthew 24:37-39; 2 Peter 3:5-6

follower (FAHL-o-wer) *a person who is learning from someone else; a "disciple."*
- of John, Matthew 9:14; 11:2; Mark 2:18
- of Christ, Matthew 11:1; 28:18-20; John 19:38; Acts 6:1-7; 11:26

fool, *someone who is not wise,* Proverbs 10:8-23; 17:7-28; 26:1-12
- examples of, Matthew 7:24-27; 25:1-13
- rejects God, Psalms 14:1; 53:1; Romans 1:20-23

footwashing, *done as an act of hospitality in Bible times because people wore sandals.*
- examples of, 1 Samuel 25:41; Luke 7:44; John 13:1-17

forever
- God's love continues forever, 1 Chronicles 16:34; Psalm 136
- praise God forever, Psalm 44:8; Romans 9:5
- be with God forever, 1 Thessalonians 4:17; 1 John 2:17
- Jesus lives forever, Hebrews 7:24
- "word of the Lord will live forever," 1 Peter 1:25

forgiveness
- of others, Matthew 6:14-15; 18:21-35; Mark 11:25; Luke 17:3-4
- by God, Luke 24:47-48; Acts 10:43; Ephesians 1:7; 1 John 1:9
- not given, Matthew 12:31-32; Mark 3:28-29; Luke 12:10; John 20:19-23
- "Father, forgive them," Luke 23:34

fornication (for-ni-KAY-shun) *having sexual relations with someone to whom you are not married.* See "adultery."

fountain, Proverbs 10:11; 13:14; 14:27; 16:22

frankincense (FRANK-in-senz) *a very expensive, sweet smelling perfume,* Exodus 30:34; Revelation 18:13
- given to Jesus, Matthew 2:11

freedom, *having liberty; not being a slave.*
- given to Jesus, Matthew 2:11
- in Christ, 2 Corinthians 3:17; Galatians 5:1; Hebrews 2:15
- from sin, Romans 6; 8:2; Hebrews 9:15
- to be used wisely, 1 Corinthians 8:9; Galatians 5:13; 1 Peter 2:16
- "truth will make you free," John 8:32

friend
- characteristics of, Proverbs 17:17; 18:24
- of Jesus, John 15:13-15
- Abraham, as a friend of God, James 2:23

frontlet, See "box of Scriptures."

fruit, *often used to mean "result."*
- spiritual, Matthew 7:15-20; John 15:1-17; Colossians 1:10
- of the Spirit, Galatians 5:22

fulfill (full-FILL) *to give the full meaning or to cause something to come true.*
- prophecy fulfilled, Matthew 2:14-15,17-18; Luke 4:16-21; 24:44-46; John 19:24

furnace
- Shadrach, Meshach, and Abednego thrown into, Daniel 3
- hell compared to, Matthew 13:42

G

Gabriel (GAY-bree-el) *an angel of God.*
- seen in a vision, Daniel 8:16; 9:21-27
- announced Jesus' birth, Luke 1:8-20,26-38

Gad, *a prophet*
- David's seer, 1 Samuel 22:5; 2 Samuel 24:11-19

Gad, son of Jacob
- birth of, Genesis 30:9-11
- land of, Deuteronomy 33:20-21; Joshua 22:1-4
- tribe of, Numbers 26:15

Gadarenes (gad-uh-REENZ) *people who lived in Gadara, southeast of Lake Galilee,* Matthew 8:28-34

Galatia (guh-LAY-shuh) *a district of Asia,* Acts 16:6; 18:23; Galatians 1:2; 1 Corinthians 16:1

Galilee (GAL-i-lee) *the country between the Jordan River and the Mediterranean Sea,* 2 Kings 15:29; Matthew 4:23; 21:11; John 7:1

Galilee, Lake (GAL-i-lee) *or "Sea of Galilee," "Sea of Kinnereth," "Lake of Gennesaret," "Sea of Tiberias"; a lake thirteen miles long and eight miles wide.*
- Jesus preached there, Matthew 4:12-22; 8:23-27; John 6:1-2,16-21

Gallio (GAL-ee-oh) *a Roman governor in the country of Achaia.*
- refused to punish Paul, Acts 18:12-17

Gamaliel (guh-MAY-lee-el) *a Pharisee and Jewish teacher of the Law of Moses.*
- prevented deaths of Peter and John, Acts 5:17-40
- Paul's teacher, Acts 22:1-3

gate
- Samson removed, Judges 16:3
- narrow, Matthew 7:13-14
- of heaven, Revelation 21:21

Gath, *one of the Philistines' five strong cities,* Joshua 13:3; 1 Samuel 21:10-12
- captured Ark taken there, 1 Samuel 5:1-10
- home of Goliath, 1 Samuel 17:4

Gaza (GAY-zuh) *one of the Philistines' five strong cities,*

Joshua 13:3; Judges 1:18; 1 Samuel 6:17; Amos 1:6; Acts 8:26
• Samson in prison there, Judges 16
gazelle (gah-ZEL) *an animal of the antelope family; known for its beauty and speed,* Deuteronomy 12:15; 1 Chronicles 12:8
Gedaliah (ged-uh-LYE-uh) *made governor of Judah by Nebuchadnezzar after capturing Jerusalem,* 2 Kings 25:22-26; Jeremiah 39:14–41:18
Gehazi (geh-HAY-zye) *a servant of the prophet Elisha.*
• and the Shunammite woman, 2 Kings 4:8-37
• and Naaman, 2 Kings 5:1-27
Gehenna, See "Hinnom."
genealogy (jee-nee-AHL-o-jee) *a list of the descendants in a family.*
• of Jesus, Matthew 1:1-17; Luke 3:23-38
generosity (jen-uh-RAHS-et-ee) *unselfishness.*
• shown to Ruth, Ruth 2:14-16
• to the needy, Nehemiah 8:10
• rewarded, Proverbs 11:25; Matthew 7:11
Gennesaret, Lake of, See "Galilee, Lake."
Gentiles (JEN-tiles) *anyone not Jewish.*
• received the Good News, Acts 10:44-45; 11:18; Romans 11:11-15; Ephesians 3:6-8
• conflict with the Jews, Acts 15:5-11; Galatians 2:11-14
Gerasenes (GER-un-seenz) *or "Gadarenes."* See "Gadarenes."
Gerizim (GER-i-zim) *a mountain next to Mount Ebal about thirty miles north of Jerusalem.*
• blessings announced from there, Deuteronomy 11:29; 27:12; Joshua 8:33
Gethsemane (geth-SEM-uh-nee) *a garden of olive trees just outside Jerusalem.*
• Jesus arrested there, Matthew 26:36-56; Mark 14:32-50
Gibeah (GIB-ee-uh) *a city about three miles north of Jerusalem,* Judges 19:12–20:43; 1 Samuel 10:26
Gibeon (GIB-ee-uhn) *a town about six miles northwest of Jerusalem.*
• Joshua defeated Amorites there, Joshua 9–10
Gideon (GID-ee-uhn) *the judge who led Israel to defeat the Midianites,* Judges 6:1–8:35
• angel appeared to, Judges 6:11-24
• destroyed Baal idol, Judges 6:25-32
• defeated Midianites, Judges 6:33–8:21
• the sign of the fleece, Judges 6:36-40
• built an idol, Judges 8:22-27
• death of, Judges 8:28-32
• hero of faith, Hebrews 11:32-34
gifts, *talents or abilities.*
• spiritual, Romans 12:6-8; 1 Corinthians 7:7; 12; 14:1-25; Ephesians 4:7
Gihon (GYE-hohn) *a spring outside the walls of Jerusalem,* 1 Kings 1:38-39; 2 Chronicles 32:30; 33:14
Gilead (GIL-ee-ad) *the area that Israel owned east of the Jordan River,* Numbers 32; Deuteronomy 3:10-16
Gilgal (GIL-gal) *the first place the Israelites camped after entering the promised land,* Joshua 4:19–5:12
gittith (GIT-tith) *probably a musical word and a musical instrument,* Psalms 8; 81; 84
giving
• examples of generous giving, Mark 12:43; Acts 10:2; 11:29-30; 2 Corinthians 8:3-5
• proper attitude toward, Matthew 6:3-4; Romans 12:8; 1 Corinthians 13:3; 2 Corinthians 9:7
gleaning (GLEEN-ing) *to gather grain left in the field after harvest,* Ruth 2
glory, *visible sign of God's greatness.*
• appeared in a cloud, Exodus 16:10; 24:16-17
• seen by Moses, Exodus 33:18-23
• "The heavens tell the glory of God," Psalm 19:1
• seen by Ezekiel, Ezekiel 1:26-28; 3:23; 8:4
• at Jesus' birth, Luke 2:8-14
• of Jesus, Luke 9:28-32
• seen by Stephen, Acts 7:55
• in the temple in heaven, Revelation 15:8
gluttony (GLUH-tun-ee) *eating too much.*
• warnings against, Deuteronomy 21:20; Proverbs 23:20-21
• Jesus accused of, Matthew 11:19; Luke 7:34
goat
• for a sin offering, Leviticus 9:3
• divided from sheep, Matthew 25:32-33
• blood of, Hebrews 9:12-13; 10:4
God, *the One who made the world and everything in it.* See also "glory."
• the creator, Genesis 1; Acts 17:24; Romans 1:25
• nearness of, Acts 17:27-28; James 4:8
• goodness of, Matthew 19:17; Acts 14:17; Romans 2:4; 1 John 4:7-11
• eternal nature of, Psalm 102:24-28; 1 Timothy 1:17; 6:16
• names of, Exodus 3:13-14; 1 Timothy 6:15; Hebrews 12:9; James 1:17; 5:4
• power of, Job 9:4-19; Isaiah 40:12-31; Matthew 19:26
• mercy of, Exodus 20:6; Numbers 14:18; Ephesians 2:4
• justice of, Psalm 67:4; Acts 17:31; Romans 2:2
golden calf, *an idol made to worship false gods.*
• made by Aaron, Exodus 32:1-24
• made by Jeroboam, 1 Kings 12:26-33
golden rule, *a name often used for Jesus' command: "Do to others what you want them to do to you,"* Matthew 7:12; Luke 6:31
Golgotha (GOL-guh-thuh) *Calvary; the hill where Jesus was crucified,* Matthew 27:33; Mark 15:22; John 19:17
Goliath (go-LYE-eth) *the giant from Gath whom David killed,* 1 Samuel 17
Gomorrah (goh-MOR-ruh) *an evil city near Sodom.*
• destroyed by God, Genesis 18:17–19:29; Matthew 10:11-15; 2 Peter 2:6
Good News, *also called the "gospel." Jesus died on the cross, was buried, and came back to life so people can be saved.* Mark 1:1; Acts 5:42; 13:26-39
• power of, Romans 1:16-17; Colossians 1:5-6; 1 Corinthians 15:2
• preached by the apostles, Luke 9:6; Acts 8:25; Philippians 1:5,12-14
Goshen (GO-shen) *an area in the Nile delta of Egypt.*
• home for Joseph's family, Genesis 45:9-10; 47:1-6,27
gospel (GOS-p'l) *"good news." The first four books of the New Testament are called the gospels because they tell the good news of what Jesus has done for us. See "Good News."*
gossip
• to be avoided, Romans 1:28-32; 2 Corinthians 12:20; 1 Timothy 5:13
government (GUV-er-ment) *group of people in charge of managing and making laws for people in a country, state, or city.*
• to be obeyed, Matthew 22:15-21; Romans 13:1-7; Titus 3:1; 1 Peter 2:13-17
governor
• Joseph, governor of Egypt, Genesis 42:6
• Nehemiah, governor of Judah, Nehemiah 5:14
• Pilate, governor of Judea, Matthew 27:2
• Felix, governor of Judea, Acts 23:26
grace, *God's kindness and love shown to us, even though we do not deserve them.*
• source of, Ephesians 3:7; Hebrews 4:14-16
• saved by, Acts 15:11; Romans 3:24; Ephesians 2:5-8; 2 Timothy 1:9
• misuse of, Romans 6; Galatians 5:4; Jude 4
grandchildren
• a blessing, Ruth 4:15; Proverbs 17:6
• inherit grandparents' wealth, Proverbs 13:22
grave, See "tomb."
Great Sea, See "Mediterranean Sea."

Greece, *once the most powerful nation in southeast Europe. Northern Greece was called "Macedonia." Southern Greece was called "Achaia."*
- Paul preached there, Acts 16:11-12; 20:1-6

greed, *selfish desire for more than one's share of something.*
- never satisfied, Proverbs 27:20
- beware of, Luke 12:15
- love of money, 1 Timothy 6:10

Greek
- the language of Greece, John 19:20; Acts 21:37; Revelation 9:11
- the people from Greece, Acts 14:1; 16:1; Colossians 3:11

grief
- of David for Absalom, 2 Samuel 18:33
- of the disciples, Matthew 17:23; John 16:6

guidance (GYD-ns) *direction.*
- by God, Exodus 13:21
- of the humble, Psalm 25:9
- of the Holy Spirit, John 16:15

guilt, *fact of having done wrong; regret, shame.*
- for improper worship, 1 Corinthians 11:27
- for breaking the Law, James 2:10
- cleansed of, Job 33:9; Isaiah 6:7; Hebrews 10:22

H

Habakkuk (ha-BAK-uk) *a prophet who wrote about the same time as Jeremiah,* Habakkuk 1–3

Hades (HAY-deez) *the world of the dead,* Revelation 6:8; 20:13-14

Hagar (HAY-gar) *Sarah's slave girl.*
- gave birth to Ishmael, Genesis 16
- sent away by Sarah, Genesis 21:8-21

Haggai (HAG-ay-eye) *a prophet in Jerusalem when the Israelites came back from Babylon,* Ezra 5:1; 6:14; Haggai 1–2

half-tribe, *one of the two parts of the tribe of Manasseh. One half-tribe settled east of the Jordan and the other settled west of the Jordan.* Joshua 1:12-15; 13:8-9; 22

Ham, *the son of Noah,* Genesis 6:10; 9:18-19; 10:6

Haman (HAY-man) *the chief officer under Ahasuerus, King of Persia.*
- planned to kill the Jews, Esther 3–6
- hanged, Esther 7

hands, laying on, *a ceremony where a person places his hands upon another.*
- for healing, Mark 5:23; 6:5; Luke 4:40
- to receive the Holy Spirit, Acts 8:17-19; 19:6
- for blessing, Mark 10:16; Acts 13:3

Hannah (HAN-uh) *the mother of Samuel,* 1 Samuel 1–2:21

happiness
- of the people of God, Psalms 144:15; 146:5; Proverbs 16:20; Matthew 5:3-12
- comes from wisdom, Proverbs 3:13

Haran (HAY-ran)
- Abraham's brother, Genesis 11:26-31
- home of Abraham, Genesis 11:31–12:5

harlot, See "prostitute."

harp, *the favorite musical instrument of the Jews.*
- first played, Genesis 4:21
- played by David, 1 Samuel 16:23; 18:10-11
- to praise God, Psalms 33:2; 71:22; 150:3

harvest
- of the poor, Ruth 2
- as a symbol, Matthew 9:37-38; 13:24-30,39; Revelation 14:14-16

hate
- seven things God hates, Proverbs 6:16-19
- a time to, Ecclesiastes 3:8
- of the world toward Jesus, John 15:18
- equal to murder, 1 John 3:15
- commands against, Galatians 5:19-21; 1 John 4:19-21

head
- a part of the body, Genesis 3:15; Psalm 23:5; Matthew 8:20; 1 Corinthians 12:21; Revelation 14:14
- a leader, Ephesians 1:22; 5:23; Colossians 1:18

heal
- a time to, Ecclesiastes 3:3
- by faith, Matthew 9:21-22; James 5:15
- "Doctor, heal yourself." Luke 4:23

heart, *the mind or feelings; not the physical heart that pumps blood,* Deuteronomy 6:5; Matthew 22:37

heaven
- *the home of God,* Matthew 5:34; Mark 16:19; John 3:13; Revelation 4
- angel spoke from, Genesis 21:17; 22:11
- opened, Matthew 3:16; Acts 7:56; 10:11
- fire from, 2 Kings 1:10-14; 1 Chronicles 21:26
- third heaven, 2 Corinthians 12:2
- the new heaven, Revelation 21:1-4
- kingdom of, Matthew 3:2; 5:3,19-20

Hebrews (HEE-brooz) *another name for the Jewish people,* Exodus 7:16; 2 Corinthians 11:22; Philippians 3:5

Hebron (HEE-bron) *a city about twenty miles southwest of Jerusalem,* Genesis 13:18; Numbers 13:22; 2 Samuel 2:1-11

heir (AIR) *the person who inherits what belongs to a relative. Because through Christ we can be adopted children of God, Christians are heirs to God's riches.*
- Abraham's heir, Genesis 15:3-4
- heir of God, Romans 8:17; Galatians 4:7

hell
- home of the devil and his angels, 2 Peter 2:4
- future home of sinners, Matthew 10:28; 23:33; Revelation 21:8
- descriptions of, Matthew 13:42; Mark 9:47-48; James 3:6; Revelation 14:11

helmet
- worn in battle, 1 Samuel 17:5; Ezekiel 23:24
- a symbol of salvation, Isaiah 59:17; Ephesians 6:17; 1 Thessalonians 5:8

help
- the stone of help, 1 Samuel 7:12
- the Holy Spirit as helper, Romans 8:26; Philippians 1:19
- from God, Psalms 46:1; 121:1-2; Isaiah 41:10
- commanded, 1 Thessalonians 5:14; Hebrews 6:10

Herod I (HEH-rud) *"Herod the Great"; king of Palestine from 40 to 4 B.C.,* Matthew 2:1; Luke 1:5

Herod Agrippa I (uh-GRIP-a) *King of Palestine from A.D. 41 to 44,* Acts 12:1

Herod Agrippa II, *King of Palestine from A.D. 52 to 70,* Acts 25:13–26:32

Herod Antipas (AN-ti-pus) *King of Palestine from 4 B.C. to about A.D. 39,* Matthew 14:1; Mark 6:14; Luke 23:7

Herodias (heh-ROW-dee-us) *the granddaughter of Herod I.*
- asked for John's head, Matthew 14:3-12; Mark 6:17-28; Luke 3:19

Hezekiah (hez-eh-KY-uh) *one of the good kings of Judah.*
- destroyed idols, 2 Kings 18:1-8; 2 Chronicles 29–31
- attacked by Assyria, 2 Kings 18:9–19:37; 2 Chronicles 32:1-23; Isaiah 36–37
- life extended by God, 2 Kings 20:1-11; Isaiah 38
- death of, 2 Kings 20:12-21; 2 Chronicles 32:24-33

higgaion (hig-GI-on) *probably a time to think quietly during a song,* Psalm 9:16

high place, *a place to worship gods,* 1 Kings 14:23; 2 Chronicles 31:1; 33:3

high priest, *the most important religious leader of the Jewish people.*
- rules for, Leviticus 21:10-15
- of the Jews, Exodus 29:30; Numbers 35:25; Matthew 26:3; Acts 23:2

• Jesus as, Hebrews 2:17; 3:1; 4:14–5:10; 8:1-6
Hilkiah (hil-KY-ah) *high priest when Josiah was King,* 2 Kings 22–23; 2 Chronicles 34
Hinnom, Valley of (HIN-num) *an area where trash was burned just outside of Jerusalem; also called "Gehenna,"* Joshua 15:8; 18:16; Nehemiah 11:30
Hiram (HY-rum) *King of Tyre when David and Solomon were kings over Israel.*
• supplied trees for Solomon's Temple, 2 Samuel 5:11; 1 Kings 5:1-18; 9:11-27; 10:22
Hittites (HIT-tites) *people who lived in what is now Turkey,* Genesis 23:1-16; Exodus 3:8; Joshua 1:4; 1 Samuel 11:3
holy (HO-lee) *pure, belonging to and willing to serve God.*
• holiness of God, Leviticus 11:45; Isaiah 6:3; Hebrews 12:10; Revelation 4:8
• holy kiss, Romans 16:16
• people to be holy, Ephesians 1:4; Colossians 1:22-23; 3:2; 1 Peter 1:15-16
Holy of Holies, See "Most Holy Place."
Holy Place, *a room in the Holy Tent and the Temple,* Exodus 26:31-35; 28:29; Leviticus 6:30; 1 Kings 8:10-11
Holy Spirit (HO-lee SPIH-rit) *one of the three persons of God. The Holy Spirit helped the apostles do miracles and led men to write God's word; he lives in Christians today.*
• in creation, Genesis 1:2
• living in Christians, John 14:15-17; 1 Corinthians 6:19; Galatians 4:6
• as a helper, John 14:25-26; 16:7-15; Romans 8:1-27; Galatians 5:22-25
• filled with, Luke 1:15; Acts 2:4; 7:55; 11:23-24
• sin against, Matthew 12:31; Acts 5:3; 1 Thessalonians 5:19; Hebrews 10:29
Holy Tent, See "Meeting Tent."
honest
• heart, Luke 8:15
• people, 2 Kings 12:15
• answer, Proverbs 24:26
• commanded, Mark 10:19; Philippians 4:8
honor
• for the old, Leviticus 19:32
• from God, 1 Samuel 2:30
• comes from humility, Proverbs 15:33
• to the deserving, Romans 13:7
• shown to parents, Exodus 20:12; Matthew 15:4
• shown to God, Proverbs 3:9; John 5:23; Revelation 4:9
• not shown to a prophet in his own town, Matthew 13:57
hope, *looking forward to something you really expect to happen.*
• reason for, Romans 5:3-5; 15:4; 2 Thessalonians 2:16; 1 Peter 1:13
• nature of, Romans 8:24-25
• results of, Colossians 1:5; Hebrews 6:18
Hophni (HOF-nee) *an evil son of Eli the priest,* 1 Samuel 2:12-34; 3:11–4:18
Horeb, Mount, See "Sinai."
horses, Exodus 14:9; 1 Kings 10:26-29; Psalm 33:16-17; James 3:3
Hosanna (ho-ZAN-ah) *a shout of joy in praising God,* Matthew 21:9,15; Mark 11:9; John 12:13
Hosea (ho-SEE-uh) *a prophet who lived about seven hundred years before Christ.*
• his unfaithful wife, Hosea 1
• his warnings to Israel, Hosea 2; 4–14
hospitality
• of Abraham, Genesis 18:1-16
• teachings about, Romans 12:13; 1 Timothy 3:2; 5:9-10; 1 Peter 4:9
hosts, *armies; God is called the "Lord of hosts."* See "Lord of hosts."
Huldah (HUL-duh) *a woman prophet,* 2 Kings 22:14-20; 2 Chronicles 34:22-28
humble (HUM-bul) *not bragging or calling attention to yourself.*
• Moses as example of, Numbers 12:3
• humility commanded, Luke 14:7-11; 22:24-27; Ephesians 4:2; Philippians 2:3
• Jesus' humility, Philippians 2:5-8
hunger
• feeding the hungry, Matthew 25:34-35; Romans 12:20
• spiritual, John 6:35; 1 Peter 2:2
husband
• responsibilities of, 1 Corinthians 7:3-5; Ephesians 5:25-33; Colossians 3:19; 1 Peter 3:7
hymn (HIM) *a song that teaches us about God or praises him,* Matthew 26:30; Ephesians 5:19; Colossians 3:16
• Jesus and apostles sang, Matthew 26:30; Mark 14:26
• teachings about, Ephesians 5:19; Colossians 3:16
hypocrisy (hi-POK-ri-see) *acting as if one is good when that is not true,* Matthew 23:28; 1 Peter 2:1
hypocrite (HIP-oh-krit) *a person who acts as if he is good but isn't.*
• warnings about, Matthew 6:2,5,16; 7:3-5; Luke 13:15-17
• Pharisees as hypocrites, Matthew 15:1-9; 23:13-32
hyssop (HIS-op) *a small bushy plant; marjoram,* Exodus 12:22; Leviticus 14:4,6; John 19:29

I

Iconium (eye-KOH-nee-um) *a city in Galatia where Paul preached,* Acts 14:1-7,19-23
idol (EYE-d'l) *a statue of a false god.* See also "Baal," "Chemosh," "Molech."
• worship of, 2 Kings 17:12-17; Acts 17:16-23; 19:24; Romans 1:25
• warnings against worship of, Leviticus 19:4; Deuteronomy 6:14-15; 1 Corinthians 5:10-11; 6:9-10
• Baal, 1 Kings 18:17-40
• Chemosh, Numbers 21:29
• Molech, Jeremiah 32:35
ignorance (IG-nur-rance) *a lack of knowledge.*
• not an excuse, Leviticus 5:17
image, *likeness.*
• God's, Genesis 1:26-27
• Caesar's, Luke 20:24
• the Lord's, 2 Corinthians 3:18
• Jesus in God's image, Hebrews 1:3
immorality (IM-mor-RAL-i-tee) *evil; sinfulness.* See also "sin."
• warnings against, 1 Corinthians 5:9-11; 6:9-10; Galatians 5:19-21; Ephesians 5:5
immortality (IM-mor-TAL-i-tee) *life after death,* Job 14:1-14; Daniel 12:1-2; 1 Corinthians 15:12-58; 2 Timothy 1:10. See also "eternal life."
impossible
• people cannot do, Matthew 19:26
• for God to lie, Hebrews 6:18
• without faith to please God, Hebrews 11:6
incense (IN-sents) *a spice burned to make a sweet smell.*
• altar of, Exodus 30:1-10,34-38; Revelation 8:3-5
• used in worship, Psalm 141:2
• as a gift, Matthew 2:11
inheritance (in-HEH-ri-tence) *something valuable that is handed down within a family.*
• of land, Numbers 36:8; Deuteronomy 3:28; Psalm 25:13
iniquity, See "sin."
inn, *a place for travelers to spend the night,* Luke 2:7; 10:34
innocence (IN-uh-sens) *not guilty of sin.*
• of Adam and Eve, Genesis 2:25
• declared by Job, Job 34:5

- declared by Pilate, Matthew 27:24

inspiration (IN-spi-RAY-shun) *"God-breathed." It is used to mean that the Bible writers wrote what God wanted them to write.* 2 Timothy 3:16; 2 Peter 1:20-21

Isaac (EYE-zak) *the son of Abraham and Sarah.*
- birth of, Genesis 21:1-4
- offered as a sacrifice, Genesis 22:1-19
- married Rebekah, Genesis 24
- tricked by Jacob, Genesis 27
- hero of faith, Hebrews 11:20

Isaiah (eye-ZAY-uh) *prophet who lived about seven hundred years before Christ.*
- became a prophet, Isaiah 6:1-8
- prophesied to Hezekiah, 2 Kings 19–20
- prophecies fulfilled, Matthew 3:3; 4:14; 13:14-15

Ish-Bosheth (ish-BOW-sheth) *son of Saul,* 2 Samuel 2:8–4

Ishmael (ISH-may-el) *son of Abraham and Hagar.*
- birth of, Genesis 16:2-16
- sent away from Abraham's camp, Genesis 21:8-21

Israel, kingdom of (IZ-rah-el) *the northern kingdom which had ten tribes.*
- beginning of, 1 Kings 11:27–12
- fall of, 2 Kings 17:1-18
- rulers of, 1 Kings 15:25–16; 22:51-53; 2 Kings 13; 14:23–17:6

Israel, son of Isaac, *Hebrew for "he who wrestles with God." Jacob's name was changed to Israel when he struggled with an angel at Bethel.* Genesis 32:22-28; 35:9-10. See also "Jacob."
- name given to Jacob's descendants, Genesis 49:28; Exodus 4:22; Psalm 22:23; Romans 9:3-5

Issachar (IS-uh-car) *a son of Jacob and Leah,* Genesis 30:18
- his descendants, Numbers 1:28-29; 26:23

ivory (EYE-voh-ree) *a creamy white bone that comes from elephant tusks,* 1 Kings 10:18; 22:39; Psalm 45:8

J

Jabbok River (JAB-ok) *a stream about fifty miles long that runs into the Jordan River,* Numbers 21:24; Joshua 12:2; Judges 11:13

Jabesh Gilead (JAY-besh GIL-ee-ad) *a small town on the east side of the Jordan River,* Judges 21:6-14; 2 Samuel 2:4-7

Jabin, king of Hazor (JAY-bin) *led a group of kings against the Israelites,* Joshua 11:1-11

Jabin, king of Canaan, *defeated by Israel when Deborah was judge,* Judges 4

Jacob (JAY-cub) *one of the sons of Isaac.*
- cheated Esau, Genesis 25:29-34
- tricked Isaac, Genesis 27:1-29
- his dream of a ladder to heaven, Genesis 28:10-22
- tricked by his sons, Genesis 37:10-22
- moved to Egypt, Genesis 45:25–47:12
- hero of faith, Hebrews 11:20-21

Jacob's Portion (JAY-cubs POR-shun) *a name for God, meaning he cares for Jacob's people,* Jeremiah 10:16; 51:19

jailer, *a keeper of a jail.*
- of Paul and Silas, Acts 16:23

Jairus (jay-EYE-rus) *a ruler of the synagogue.*
- Jesus brought his daughter back to life, Matthew 9:18-26; Mark 5:21-43; Luke 8:40-56

James, brother of Jesus, Matthew 13:55; Acts 12:17; 21:18
- later an apostle, Galatians 1:19

James, son of Alphaeus, *an apostle,* Matthew 10:3; Mark 3:18; Luke 6:15; Acts 1:13

James, son of Zebedee, *an apostle of Jesus and a brother of the apostle John,* Matthew 10:2; Mark 10:35; Acts 12:2

Japheth (JAY-fith) *one of Noah's three sons,* Genesis 5:32; 7:13; 9:18-27; 10:1-5

Jashar, Book of, *a book mentioned in the Bible, but not part of it,* Joshua 10:12-13; 2 Samuel 1:17-27

Jason (JAY-son) *a Christian in Thessalonica,* Acts 17:5-9

jealousy
- to describe God, Exodus 20:5; 34:14; Deuteronomy 5:9
- examples of, Genesis 37:11; 1 Samuel 18:19; Matthew 27:18; Acts 5:17
- warnings against, Romans 13:13; 1 Corinthians 13:4; 1 Timothy 6:4; 1 Peter 2:1

Jebusites (JEB-you-sites) *people who lived around Jerusalem before the time of David,* Joshua 15:63; Judges 19:10-11; 2 Samuel 4:6-8

Jehoahaz, son of Jehu (jeh-HO-uh-haz) *King of Israel who lived about eight hundred years before Christ,* 2 Kings 13:1-9

Jehoahaz, son of Josiah, *King of Judah for only three months,* 2 Kings 23:31-34; 2 Chronicles 36:1-4

Jehoash (jeh-HO-ash) *a king of Israel,* 2 Kings 13:10–14:16

Jehoiachin (jeh-HO-uh-kin) *the next-to-last king of Judah.*
- surrendered to Babylon, 2 Kings 24:8-17
- in Babylon, 2 Kings 25:27-30

Jehoiada (jeh-HO-yah-duh) *the chief priest in Jerusalem during Joash's rule,* 2 Kings 11– 12; 2 Chronicles 22:11–24

Jehoiakim (jeh-HO-uh-kim) *king of Judah about 600 B.C.,* 2 Kings 23:34–24:6
- tried to kill Jeremiah, Jeremiah 26:1-23
- burned Jeremiah's scroll, Jeremiah 36:1-23

Jehoram (jeh-HOR-am) *or "Joram"; the fifth king of Judah,* 2 Kings 8:16-29; 2 Chronicles 21:4-20

Jehoshaphat (jeh-HOSH-uh-fat) *one of the good kings of Judah.*
- faithful to God, 2 Chronicles 17:1-9
- appointed judges, 2 Chronicles 19:4-11
- defeated Moab and Ammon, 2 Chronicles 20

Jehovah (jeh-HOVE-uh) *a name for God; also translated "LORD,"* Exodus 3:15; 6:3; Deuteronomy 28:58; Psalm 83:18

Jehu (JEE-hew) *an army captain who became king of Israel.*
- appointed as king, 2 Kings 9:1-13
- killed Joram and Ahaziah, 2 Kings 9:14-29
- stopped Baal worship, 2 Kings 10:18-35

Jephthah (JEF-thuh) *one of the judges of Israel.*
- fought the Ammonites, Judges 11:1-29,32-33
- his vow, Judges 11:30-31,34-39
- fought the people of Ephraim, Judges 12:2-7

Jeremiah (jer-eh-MY-ah) *a prophet who warned the people of Judah,* Jeremiah 1–52
- became a prophet, Jeremiah 1:1-10
- songs of, 2 Chronicles 35:25
- his prophecies fulfilled, 2 Chronicles 36:21-22; Matthew 2:17; 27:9
- wrote a scroll, Jeremiah 36

Jericho (JEHR-ih-ko) *probably the oldest city in the world,* Mark 10:46; Luke 10:30; 19:1
- fall of, Joshua 2–6
- rebuilt, 1 Kings 16:34

Jeroboam, son of Jehoash (jeh-ro-BO-am) *a king of Israel,* 2 Kings 14:23-29; Amos 7:7-17

Jeroboam, son of Nebat, *first ruler of the northern kingdom of Israel.*
- given ten tribes by God, 1 Kings 11:26-40
- built idols, 1 Kings 12:26-33
- warned by God, 1 Kings 13:1-34
- death of his son, 1 Kings 14:1-20

Jerusalem (jeh-ROO-suh-lem) *"Zion" or "City of David"; the greatest city of Palestine.*
- the City of David, 2 Samuel 5:6-7
- captured by Babylonians, 2 Chronicles 36:15-23

- Jews returned to, Ezra 1–2
- the new Jerusalem, Galatians 4:26; Hebrews 12:22; Revelation 3:12; 21–22

Jesse (JEH-see) *father of King David,* 1 Samuel 16–17; 1 Chronicles 2:13-15; Luke 3:32; Romans 15:12

Jesus (JEE-zus) *"Savior"; the son of God.* See also "Christ," "Son of David," "Son of Man."
- birth and childhood of, Matthew 1–2; Luke 1–2
- temptation of, Matthew 4:1-11; Mark 1:12-13; Luke 4:1-13
- miracles of, Matthew 8–9; Mark 6:30-56; Luke 17:11; 22:50-51; John 2:1; 11
- appeared with Moses and Elijah, Matthew 17:1-13; Mark 9:2-13; Luke 9:28-36
- forced men from the Temple, Matthew 21:12-13; John 2:13-17
- the Last Supper, Matthew 26:17-30; Luke 22:1-20; John 13
- trial and death of, Matthew 26:57–27:66; Mark 15; Luke 22:66–23:56; John 18–19
- appearances after resurrection, Matthew 28; Mark 16; Luke 24; John 20–21; 1 Corinthians 15:5-8
- Son of God, Matthew 3:16-17; 26:63-64; John 1:14

Jethro (JETH-row) *father of Moses' wife,* Exodus 2:16-21
- advised Moses, Exodus 18

Jews (JOOZ) *first, the tribe of Judah; later, any of the twelve tribes,* Ezra 4:12; Esther 3–10; Acts 2:5
- against Jesus, John 5:16-18; 7:1,32-36; 10:25-42
- Jesus, king of, Matthew 2:2; 27:11-14,29; John 19:17-22
- and non-Jewish people, 1 Corinthians 12:13; Galatians 3:28; Colossians 3:11

Jezebel (JEZ-eh-bell) *the evil wife of King Ahab.*
- married Ahab, 1 Kings 16:31
- killed the Lord's prophets, 1 Kings 18:4-14
- killed Naboth, 1 Kings 21:1-23
- death of, 2 Kings 9:30-37

Jezreel (JEZ-reel) *the name of a town and a valley near the Jordan River,* Judges 6:33; 1 Kings 21:1; 2 Kings 8:29

Joab (JO-ab) *the commander of King David's army,* 2 Samuel 2:12-3; 10–11; 14; 18– 20; 24; 1 Kings 1–2

Joanna (jo-ANN-uh) *a woman Jesus healed,* Luke 8:2-3; 23:55–24:11

Joash, Gideon's father (JO-ash)
- protected Gideon, Judges 6:28-32

Joash, son of Ahaziah, *became king of Judah when he was seven,* 2 Kings 11–12; 2 Chronicles 22:10–24

Job (JOBE) *a wealthy man who honored God.*
- ruined by Satan, Job 1–2:10
- wealth restored, Job 42:7
- example of patience, James 5:11

Joel (JO-el) *a prophet who wrote the book of Joel,* Joel 1–3; Acts 2:16

Johanan (jo-HAY-nan) *a Jewish army captain,* Jeremiah 40:8–43

John, the apostle, *one of the sons of Zebedee.*
- called by Jesus, Mark 1:19-20
- at Jesus' transfiguration, Mark 9:2
- with Jesus in Gethsemane, Mark 14:33-42
- in the early church, Acts 3–4
- writer of Revelation, Revelation 1:1-4,9

John the Baptist, *Jesus' relative and the son of Elizabeth and Zechariah the priest.*
- birth of, Luke 1:5-25,57-80
- preached at the Jordan River, Matthew 3:1-12
- baptized Jesus, Matthew 3:13-17
- killed by Herod, Matthew 14:1-12

John Mark, See "Mark."

Jonah (JO-nah) *a prophet whom God told to preach to the city of Nineveh.*
- ran from God, Jonah 1:1-3
- swallowed by a fish, Jonah 1:4–2:10
- went to Nineveh, Jonah 3
- complained to God, Jonah 4
- the sign of, Matthew 12:38-41; 16:4; Luke 11:29-32

Jonathan (JAH-nah-thun) *the oldest son of King Saul.*
- David's friend, 1 Samuel 18:1-4
- saved David's life, 1 Samuel 19:1-7; 20
- death of, 1 Samuel 31:2

Joppa (JOP-uh) *a city on the coast of Palestine,* Jonah 1:3
- Peter preached there, Acts 9:36-42; 10:9-36

Joram (JO-ram) *son of Ahab; also a king of Israel,* 2 Kings 3:1-3; 8:29; 9:14-29

Jordan (JOR-d'n) *the only large river in Palestine.*
- Israelites crossed, Joshua 3
- Jesus baptized in, Matthew 3:13-17; Mark 1:9-11

Jordan Valley, *the valley along the Jordan River,* Deuteronomy 1:1; 3:17; Joshua 11:2

Joseph of Arimathea (JOZ-uf) *took the body of Jesus down from the cross and buried it in a tomb Joseph had dug for himself,* Matthew 27:57-60; Mark 15:42-46; Luke 23:50-54

Joseph of Nazareth, *husband of Mary, Jesus' mother.*
- angel appeared to, Matthew 1:18-24
- went to register in Bethlehem, Luke 2:4-7
- took Jesus to the Temple, Luke 2:21-52

Joseph, son of Jacob, *one of the twelve sons of Israel.*
- sold into slavery, Genesis 37
- put into prison, Genesis 39
- interpreted dreams, Genesis 40–41
- reunited with family, Genesis 42–50

Joshua (JAH-shoo-ah) *leader of the Israelites into the promised land.*
- spied out Canaan, Numbers 13
- chosen to replace Moses, Numbers 27:12-23; Deuteronomy 34:9-10
- conquered Canaan, Joshua 1; 3–12
- death of, Joshua 23–24

Josiah (jo-SY-uh) *king of Judah about 640 to 609 B.C.*
- became king, 2 Kings 22:1-2
- found the lost laws of God, 2 Kings 22:3-20
- gave the law to the people, 2 Kings 23:1-30

Jotham, youngest son of Gideon (JO-tham) Judges 9:1-21,57

Jotham, son of Uzziah, *a king of Judah,* 2 Kings 15:32-38; 2 Chronicles 27

joy, Psalm 43:4; John 15:11; 17:13; 1 Thessalonians 1:6
- a fruit of the Holy Spirit, Galatians 5:22
- God as the source, Psalms 43:4; 45:7; Romans 15:13
- joy from the Holy Spirit, Luke 10:21; Romans 14:17; Galatians 5:22; 1 Thessalonians 1:6

Jubilee (JOO-bih-lee) *a Jewish celebration that took place once every fifty years. Israelites were to let the soil rest, to free their slaves, and to return land and houses to their first owners or their descendants.* Leviticus 25; 27:17-24; Numbers 36:4

Judah, son of Jacob (JOO-duh) Genesis 29:35
- saved Joseph, Genesis 37:26-27
- deceived by Tamar, Genesis 38
- reunited with Joseph, Genesis 43–44
- tribe of, Numbers 1:26-27; 26:20-22; Joshua 15
- Jesus, a descendant of, Matthew 1:2-3; Luke 3:33-34; Revelation 5:5

Judah, kingdom of, *the southern kingdom when Israel split in two.*
- beginning of, 1 Kings 11:27–12:20
- rulers of, 1 Kings 14:21–15:24; 22:41-50; 2 Kings 8:16-29; 11–12; 14–16; 18–24
- fall of, 2 Kings 24:18–25:22

Judas Iscariot (JOO-dus is-CARE-ee-ut) *apostle who handed Jesus over to be killed.*
- chosen by Jesus, Matthew 10:4; Mark 3:19
- apostles' treasurer, John 12:4-6; 13:27-29
- betrayed Jesus, Matthew 26:14-16,47-50; Luke 22:1-6; John 6:70-71; 13:2,21-30

• death of, Matthew 27:3-5
Judas, brother of Jesus, Matthew 13:55; Mark 6:3
Judas, son of James
• an apostle, Luke 6:16; Acts 1:13
Jude (JOOD) *brother of James,* Jude 1
Judea (joo-DEE-uh) *the land of the Jews,* Matthew 2:1; 3:1; Luke 1:5; 3:1; Acts 1:8
judges (JUHG-es) *leaders of Israel prior to the kings,* Judges 2:16-19; 3:7–4; 10–12; 1 Samuel 8:1-5
judging
• warnings against, Matthew 7:1-5; 1 Corinthians 4:5; James 4:11-12
• good kinds of judging, 1 Corinthians 5:12; 6:2; 10:15
• God's judging of people, Matthew 11:22; Acts 17:31; 2 Peter 2:9; 3:7
Judgment Day (JUJ-ment) *the day Christ will judge all people,* Matthew 11:20-24; 12:33-37; 2 Peter 2:9-10; 3:7-13
Julius (JOOL-yus) *a Roman soldier in charge of Paul while Paul was taken to Rome,* Acts 27:1-3
justify (JUS-teh-fy) *to make someone right with God,* Romans 3:24; 5:1; Galatians 2:16; Titus 3:7

K

Kadesh/Kadesh Barnea (KAY-desh BAR-nee-uh) *a town in the Desert of Zin,* Numbers 20:1-21; Joshua 10:41
Kenites (KEE-nites) *a tribe of early metal workers,* Genesis 15:19; Judges 1:16; 4:11; 1 Samuel 27:10
Kerethites (KAIR-uh-thites) *King David's bodyguards,* 2 Samuel 8:18; 1 Kings 1:38
Keturah (keh-TOO-ruh) *Abraham's second wife,* Genesis 25:1-4; 1 Chronicles 1:32-33
key, *something that solves or explains.*
• to God's kingdom, Matthew 16:19
• to death, Revelation 1:18
Kidron Valley (KEH-dron) *a valley between Jerusalem and the Mount of Olives,* 2 Samuel 15:23; John 18:1
• idols burned there, 1 Kings 15:13; 2 Kings 23:4
kill
• Cain killed, Genesis 4:10-11
• laws against, Exodus 20:13
• of baby boys, Exodus 1:16; Matthew 2:16
• Jesus killed, Matthew 27:31-50; Mark 15:20-37; Luke 23:25-46; John 19:16-30
kindness
• of God, Exodus 34:6-7; Jeremiah 9:24; Romans 2:4; Ephesians 2:4-7
• commanded, 2 Corinthians 6:6; Ephesians 4:32; Colossians 3:12; 2 Peter 1:5-7
king
• King of kings, 1 Timothy 6:15; Revelation 17:14
kingdom (KING-d'm) *the kingdom of heaven is God ruling in the lives of his people.*
• the nature of, Matthew 5:19-20; 19:14; Luke 17:20-21; Romans 14:17
• parables of, Matthew 13:24-52; 18:23-35; 20:1-16; 25:1-30; Mark 4:30-33; Luke 13:18-21
• belongs to, Matthew 5:3,10; 19:14
Kiriath Jearim (KEER-yath JEE-ah-rim) *a town in the hills about twelve miles west of Jerusalem,* 1 Samuel 6:20–7:20; 1 Chronicles 13:5-6; 2 Chronicles 1:4
Kish, *father of Saul,* 1 Samuel 9:1-2
Kishon (KY-shon) *the name of a valley and a stream,* Judges 4:13; 5:21; 1 Kings 18:40
kiss, *a greeting of friendship, love, or respect.*
• of Judas, Matthew 26:48-49; Mark 14:44-45; Luke 22:47-48
• holy kiss, Romans 16:16; 1 Corinthians 16:20; 1 Peter 5:14
Kittim (KEH-tim) *the island of Cyprus,* Genesis 10:4; Numbers 24:24; 1 Chronicles 1:7; Isaiah 23:1,12
kneel
• Solomon kneeled before God, 1 Kings 8:54
• Daniel kneeled before God, Daniel 6:10
• everyone to kneel before Jesus, Philippians 2:10
knock
• "knock, and the door will open," Matthew 7:7
• at the door, Luke 13:25
• Peter knocked, Acts 12:13,16
• Jesus knocks, Revelation 3:20
knowledge
• tree of, Genesis 2:9,17
• value of, Proverbs 1:7; 8:10; 18:15; 24:5; 2 Peter 1:5-6
• lack of, Hosea 4:6; Romans 1:28
• limitations of, 1 Corinthians 8:1-2; 13:2,8-10
Kohath (KO-hath) *a son of Levi,* Exodus 6:16-20; Numbers 3:17-19
Kohathites (KO-hath-ites) *descendants of Kohath.*
• worked in the Holy Tent and Temple, Numbers 3:27-31; 4:1-20; 1 Chronicles 9:17-32
Korah (KO-ruh) *the musician,* Psalms 42; 44–49; 84
Korah, son of Izhar, *rebelled against Moses,* Numbers 16:1-40

L

Laban (LAY-ban) *father of Leah and Rachel.*
• Jacob worked for, Genesis 29:13-30
• divided his flocks with Jacob, Genesis 30:29-43
• chased Jacob, Genesis 31:19-55
Lachish (LAY-kish) *a city about thirty miles southwest of Jerusalem.*
• Joshua defeated, Joshua 10
lake
• of Galilee, Luke 5:1-2; 8:22-23,33
• of fire, Revelation 19:20
• of sulfur, Revelation 20:10; 21:8
lamb (LAM) *an animal that the Jews often offered as a gift to God.*
• as sacrifice, Genesis 4:4; Exodus 12:3-10; Leviticus 3:6-11; 4:32-35; 5:6; 14:24-25
• Jesus, the lamb of God, John 1:29,36; 1 Corinthians 5:7; 1 Peter 1:19; Revelation 5–7
Lamech, a descendant of Cain (LAY-mek) Genesis 4:18-24
Lamech, son of Methuselah, *the father of Noah,* Genesis 5:28-31
lamp, *a small bowl that held a wick and burned olive oil, thus giving light,* Matthew 25:1-13; Luke 8:16-18
• "Your word is like a lamp for my feet," Psalm 119:105
lampstand, *a holder for a lamp.*
• in the Holy Tent, Exodus 25:31-40; Numbers 8:1-4
• in the Temple, 1 Kings 7:49
• symbol of the church, Revelation 1:12-13,20
language
• world spoke only one, Genesis 11:1,6
• confused at Babel, Genesis 11:7,9
• Aramaic, 2 Kings 18:26; Ezra 4:7; John 19:20
• Latin, John 19:20
• Greek, John 19:20; Acts 21:37
Laodicea (lay-ah-deh-SEE-uh) *a town in what is now Turkey,* Colossians 4:13-16; Revelation 3:14-22
Last Supper, *the meal Jesus ate with his followers the night before his death,* Matthew 26:17-30; Mark 14:12-26; Luke 22:7-20; 1 Corinthians 11:23-26
Latin (LAT-in) *the language spoken by the Romans during New Testament times,* John 19:20
laughter
• Sarah laughed, Genesis 18:12
• mouths filled with, Psalm 126:2
• sorrow better than, Ecclesiastes 7:3
• changed into crying, James 4:9
law
• as rules, Romans 4:15; 6:14-15; Galatians 5:18

• as God's rules or teachings, Psalm 119; Romans 7:22; 8:7; James 1:25; 1 John 3:4
Law of Moses, See "Teachings of Moses."
laying on of hands, See "hands, laying on."
Lazarus of Bethany (LAZ-uh-rus) *a brother to Mary and Martha and a friend of Jesus,* John 11:1-45; 12:1-11
Lazarus, the beggar, Luke 16:19-31
laziness
• brings poverty, Proverbs 10:4
• not to be fed, 2 Thessalonians 3:10
leadership
• blind, Matthew 15:14
• of own family, 1 Timothy 3:5
• elders worthy of honor, 1 Timothy 5:17
Leah (LEE-uh) *a wife of Jacob,* Genesis 29:15-35; 30:9-21; 49:31
leather, Leviticus 13:47-59; Matthew 3:4
leaven, See "yeast."
Lebanon (LEH-beh-nun) *a country north of Israel.*
• cedars of, 1 Kings 5:1-11; Ezra 3:7
• prophecy of Lebanon's fall, Isaiah 10:34
Legion (LEE-jun) *a man who had many evil spirits in him,* Mark 5:9; Luke 8:30
lend
• money, Exodus 22:25
• borrower, a servant to lender, Proverbs 22:7
• sinners to sinners, Luke 6:34
• to enemies, Luke 6:35
leprosy (LEH-prah-see) *bad skin disease. A person with leprosy was called a leper and had to live outside the city.* Leviticus 13:45-46
• disease of Naaman, 2 Kings 5:1-27
• healed by Jesus, Matthew 8:2-3; Luke 7:11-19
Leviathan (lee-VI-ah-than) *a sea monster; possibly a crocodile,* Job 3:8; 41:1; Psalm 74:14; Isaiah 27:1
Levites (LEE-vites) *descendants of Levi, one of Jacob's sons.*
• served as priests, Numbers 1:47-53; 8:5-26; Deuteronomy 10:8-9; 18:1-8
• towns assigned to, Joshua 21
liar
• better to be poor, Proverbs 19:22
• Satan as a, John 8:44
• Cretans as, Titus 1:12
• to be punished, Revelation 21:8
lid on the Ark of the Agreement, *the mercy seat; the gold lid on the Ark of the Agreement,* Exodus 25:17-22; Hebrews 9:5
life
• breath of, Genesis 2:7
• book of, Philippians 4:3; Revelation 3:5; 21:27
• in the blood, Leviticus 17:14
• length of, Psalm 90:10
• true life, John 12:25
• "I am the. . .life." John 14:6
• eternal, John 5:24-29; 6:35-51
light
• creation of, Genesis 1:3-4
• of the world, Matthew 5:14
• God is, 1 Timothy 6:16; 1 John 1:5
• Jesus is, John 1:4-9; 3:19-20; 8:12; 12:46
• God's word is light, Psalm 119:105
• symbol of God's presence, 2 Corinthians 4:6; Ephesians 5:8-9; 1 Peter 2:9
linen (LEH-nin) *a type of cloth made from the flax plant.*
• used for priests' clothes, Exodus 28:39-42; Leviticus 6:10
• used for royal clothes, Esther 8:15
• Jesus' body wrapped in, Matthew 27:59
lion
• killed by Samson, Judges 14:5-18
• killed by David, 1 Samuel 17:34-37
• devil like a lion, 1 Peter 5:8
lips
• touched by hot coal, Isaiah 6:5-7
loaves
• used to feed five thousand, Matthew 14:17-19
• used to feed four thousand, Matthew 15:34-38
locust (LO-cust) *an insect that looks like a grasshopper. They travel in large groups and can destroy crops.*
• as a plague, Exodus 10:3-19; Deuteronomy 28:38-42; Joel 1:1-4; Nahum 3:15-17
• food for John the Baptist, Matthew 3:4; Mark 1:6
Lord, *master or one who is in control; ruler of all the world and universe.*
• God as Lord, Exodus 3:15; 7:16; Psalms 31:5; 106:48
• Jesus as Lord, Acts 2:36; 1 Corinthians 8:6; Philippians 2:11; 1 Peter 3:15
• Holy Spirit as Lord, 2 Corinthians 3:18
Lord of hosts, *one of the names used for God; also called "Lord All-Powerful" and "Lord Sabaoth,"* 1 Chronicles 11:9; Psalm 24:10; Isaiah 6:3-5; Malachi 3:1-17
Lord's day
• the first day of the week, Acts 20:7; Revelation 1:10
• as the Judgment Day, 1 Corinthians 5:5; 2 Corinthians 1:14; 1 Thessalonians 5:2; 2 Peter 3:10
Lord's Prayer, *the name often given to the model prayer Jesus taught his followers,* Matthew 6:9-13; Luke 11:1-4
Lord's Supper, *the meal Jesus' followers eat to remember how he died for them; also called "communion."*
• beginning of, Matthew 26:26-29; Mark 14:22-25; Luke 22:14-20
• examples of, Acts 20:7; 1 Corinthians 10:16; 11:17-34
Lot, *Abraham's nephew,* Genesis 11:27-30
• divided land with Abram, Genesis 13
• captured, Genesis 14:1-16
• escaped destruction of Sodom, Genesis 19:1-29
• death of wife, Genesis 19:15-26
lots, *sticks, stones, or pieces of bone thrown like dice to decide something. Often God controlled the result of the lots to let people know what he wanted them to do.*
• Canaan divided by, Numbers 26:55-56
• Jonah found guilty by, Jonah 1:7
• Jesus' clothes divided by, Luke 23:34
• Matthias chosen by, Acts 1:26
love, *a strong feeling of affection, loyalty and concern for someone.*
• love of God commanded, Deuteronomy 6:5; 11:1; Matthew 22:36-38
• of God for people, Psalm 36; John 3:16; Romans 5:8; 8:39; Ephesians 1:4; 1 John 4:10-11
• of people for God, 1 Corinthians 8:3; 1 John 5:3
• of Christ for people, John 13:1; 15:9; Romans 8:35; Galatians 2:20; 1 John 3:16
• of people for Christ, Matthew 10:37; 1 Corinthians 16:22; 1 Peter 1:8
• of people for each other, Leviticus 19:18; Luke 6:27-35; John 13:34-35; 1 Corinthians 13; 1 John 4:7
Luke, *a non-Jewish doctor who often traveled with the apostle Paul,* Colossians 4:14; 2 Timothy 4:11
lust, *wanting something evil.*
• to be avoided, Proverbs 6:25; Matthew 5:28; Colossians 3:5; 1 Thessalonians 4:5
• typical of the ungodly, Romans 1:26; 1 Peter 4:3
Lydia (LID-ee-uh) *a woman from the city of Thyatira who sold purple cloth,* Acts 16:13-15,40
lying
• warnings against, Ephesians 4:25; Colossians 3:9; Revelation 21:8
• devil as a liar, John 8:44
• to the Holy Spirit, Acts 5:1-6

lyre (LIRE) *a musical instrument with strings, similar to a harp,* 1 Chronicles 15:16; Psalms 33:2; 81:2

Lystra (LIS-tra) *a city of Lycaonia.*
- Paul preached there, Acts 14:6-20; 16:1; 2 Timothy 3:11

M

Macedonia (mas-eh-DOH-nee-uh) *the northern part of Greece.*
- Paul preached there, Acts 16:6-10; 20:1-6; 1 Corinthians 16:5-9; Philippians 4:15

Machpelah (mack-PEE-luh) *the land Abraham bought from Ephron, the Hittite.*
- Sarah buried there, Genesis 23:7-19
- Abraham buried there, Genesis 25:7-10
- Jacob buried there, Genesis 49:29-33; 50:12-13

magic (MAJ-ik) *trying to use the power of evil spirits to make unnatural things happen.*
- magicians of Egypt, Genesis 41:8; Exodus 7:11-12
- condemned, Leviticus 19:26; 20:27; Deuteronomy 18:10-12
- Simon the magician, Acts 8:9-24
- Elymas the magician, Acts 13:6-11
- Ephesian magicians burn their books, Acts 19:17-19

mahalath (mah-HAY-lath) *probably a musical word; may be the name of a tune or may mean to dance and shout,* Psalms 53; 88

Malachi (MAL-uh-ky) *a prophet who lived about the time of Nehemiah. He wrote the last book of the Old Testament.* Malachi 1:1

man, *humankind; a male.*
- created by God, Genesis 1:26-27; 2:7-23
- born of woman, Job 14:1
- important to God, Psalm 8:4-8
- woman created for, 1 Corinthians 11:9

Manasseh, son of Hezekiah (mah-NASS-uh) *a king of Judah for fifty-five years,* 2 Kings 21:1-17; 2 Chronicles 33:1-20

Manasseh, son of Joseph, *older brother of Ephraim. His descendants were the tribe of Manasseh.* Genesis 41:51; 46:20; 48:1-20
- descendants of, Numbers 1:34; 26:29-34; Joshua 13:8-13; 17
- eastern half-tribe, Joshua 1:12-17; 22
- western half-tribe, Joshua 21:5,25; 22:7

manger (MAIN-jur) *a box where animals are fed,* Luke 2:6-17

manna (MAN-ah) *the white, sweet-tasting food God gave the people of Israel in the wilderness. It appeared on the ground during the night so they could gather it in the morning.*
- God sent to Israel, Exodus 16:11-36; Joshua 5:10-12
- kept in the Ark, Exodus 16:31-34; Hebrews 9:1-4

Manoah (mah-NO-uh) *the father of Samson,* Judges 13

Marduk (MAR-dook) *a god of the Babylonians. The Babylonians believed that people were evil because Marduk had created them from the blood of an evil god.* Jeremiah 50:2

Mark, *John Mark; a cousin to Barnabas; traveled with Paul and Barnabas and wrote the Gospel of Mark,* Acts 12:12,25; 13:5; Colossians 4:10; 2 Timothy 4:11
- left Paul, Acts 13:13
- traveled with Barnabas, Acts 15:36-41

marketplace, *usually a large open area inside a city where people came to buy and sell goods,* Matthew 20:3; Mark 7:4; 12:38; Luke 7:32; Acts 16:19

marriage
- teachings about, Mark 10:6-9; 1 Corinthians 7:1-16; Hebrews 13:4; 1 Timothy 5:14
- authority in, Ephesians 5:21; Colossians 3:18

Mars Hill, See "Areopagus."

Martha (MAR-thuh) *the sister of Mary and Lazarus who lived in Bethany.*
- criticized Mary, Luke 10:38-42
- at death of Lazarus, John 11:17-44

martyr (MAR-ter) *"witness"; one who knows about something. Later, martyr came to mean a person who was killed for being a witness.*
- Stephen, first Christian martyr, Acts 7:54-60
- James killed, Acts 12:2
- heroes of faith killed, Hebrews 11:32-37

Mary Magdalene (MAG-duh-lun) *a follower of Jesus from the town of Magdala; the first person to see Jesus after he came back to life.*
- at Jesus' death, Matthew 27:55-56,61
- saw Jesus after his resurrection, Matthew 28:1-10; Mark 16:1-11; John 20:10-18

Mary, mother of Jesus
- engaged to marry Joseph, Matthew 1:18-25; Luke 2:4-5
- angel appeared to, Luke 1:26-45
- birth of Jesus, Luke 2:6-21
- with Jesus in Jerusalem, Luke 2:41-52
- at wedding in Cana, John 2:1-10
- at Jesus' death, John 19:25-27
- with the apostles, Acts 1:14

Mary of Bethany, *sister of Martha and Lazarus, and a friend of Jesus.*
- sat at Jesus' feet, Luke 10:38-42
- at death of Lazarus, John 11:1-45
- poured oil on Jesus' feet, John 12:1-8

maskil (MAS-kil) *probably a description of the kind of song that some of the Psalms were,* Psalms 32, 42, 44, 45

master, *lord; ruler.*
- "No one can serve two masters." Matthew 6:24
- not to be called, Matthew 23:10
- to be obeyed, Ephesians 6:5
- how to treat slaves, Ephesians 6:9
- in heaven, Ephesians 6:9; Colossians 4:1
- Jesus as, Luke 5:5; 8:24; 17:13

Matthew (MATH-you) *also called Levi; a tax collector; wrote the Gospel of Matthew,* Matthew 9:9-10; 10:3; Acts 1:13

Matthias (muh-THY-us) *chosen to be an apostle after Judas Iscariot killed himself,* Acts 1:15-26

meat
- given by God in the wilderness, Exodus 16:1-15; Numbers 11:4-34; Psalm 78:27
- eating meat sacrificed to idols, Acts 15:20; 1 Corinthians 8; 10:25-32

Medes (MEEDS) *the people who lived in Media, which is called "Iran" today,* 2 Kings 17:6; Ezra 6:2; Esther 1:3-19; Daniel 5:28; 6:8-15

mediator (MEE-dee-a-ter) *a go-between.*
- Jesus as, 1 Timothy 2:5

medicine
- happy heart as, Proverbs 17:22

Mediterranean Sea (med-ih-teh-RANE-ih-an) *a large sea west of Canaan; also called the "Great Sea" or the "Western Sea,"* Numbers 34:6-7; Joshua 1:4

medium (MEED-ee-um) *a person who tries to help living people talk to the spirits of the dead.*
- condemned, Leviticus 19:31; Deuteronomy 18:11-13; Isaiah 8:19-20
- of Endor, 1 Samuel 28
- Josiah destroyed mediums, 2 Kings 23:24

Meeting Tent, *"Tabernacle" or "Holy Tent"; a special tent where the Israelites worshiped God. It was used from the time they left Egypt until Solomon built the Temple in Jerusalem.*
- description of, Exodus 25–27
- set up, Exodus 39:32–40:36

Megiddo (meh-GID-oh) *important town in northern Israel where many battles were fought. The book of Revelation tells about a great battle between good and evil at "Armageddon," which means "the hill of*

Megiddo." Joshua 12:8-21; 2 Kings 23:29-30; Revelation 16:16

Melchizedek (mel-KIZ-ih-dek) *priest and king who worshiped God in the time of Abraham,* Genesis 14:17-24
- Christ compared to, Hebrews 5:4-10; 7

Mene, mene, tekel, parsin (MEE-nee, TEE-kul, PAR-sun) *the words written on the wall by a mysterious hand at Belshazzar's feast,* Daniel 5

Mephibosheth (me-FIB-o-sheth) *crippled son of Jonathan,* 2 Samuel 4:4
- David's agreement with, 2 Samuel 9
- tricked by Ziba, 2 Samuel 16:1-4; 19:24-30

Merab (MEE-rab) *daughter of King Saul,* 1 Samuel 14:49; 18:17-19

Merarites (mee-RAY-rites) *descendants of Merari, a son of Levi; they were responsible for caring for the frame of the Holy Tent,* Numbers 3:17,33-37; 4:29-33

mercy (MUR-see) *kindness and forgiveness.*
- God's mercy to people, Exodus 34:6; Deuteronomy 4:31; Luke 1:50; Ephesians 2:4
- people's mercy to each other, Matthew 5:7; James 2:13

mercy seat, See "lid on the Ark of the Agreement."

Mesha (MEE-shuh) *an evil king of Moab,* 2 Kings 3:4-27

Meshach (MEE-shack) *friend of Daniel who was put in the fiery furnace,* Daniel 1–3

messenger, 1 Samuel 23:27; 1 Kings 19:2
- John the Baptist as, Matthew 11:10; Mark 1:2; Luke 7:27
- of Satan, 2 Corinthians 12:7

Messiah (muh-SYE-uh) *"anointed one"; the Greek word for Messiah is "Christ." Christians believe that Jesus is the Messiah or the Christ.* John 1:40-41; 4:25-26

Methuselah (meh-THOO-zeh-lah) *lived 969 years, longer than anyone else in the Bible; the son of Enoch and the grandfather of Noah,* Genesis 5:21-27

Micah (MY-cuh) *a prophet who told the people of Israel and Judah about their sins,* Micah 1–7

Micaiah (mi-KAY-uh) *a prophet of God,* 1 Kings 22:8-28; 2 Chronicles 18

Michael (MY-kul) *the archangel of God,* Jude 9; Revelation 12:7

Michal (MY-kul) *a daughter of Saul and wife of David,* 1 Samuel 18:20-29; 19:11-17; 2 Samuel 3:13-16
- criticized David, 2 Samuel 6:16-23

Michmash (MIK-mash) *a hilly area about seven miles northeast of Jerusalem,* 1 Samuel 13:23–14:23; Isaiah 10:28

Midian (MID-ee-un) *a son of Abraham; his descendants were called "Midianites,"* Genesis 25:1-6
- Joseph sold to, Genesis 37:18-36
- Jethro, a descendant of, Exodus 2:15-21
- enemy of Israel, Judges 6–7

midnight
- when the firstborn of Egypt died, Exodus 12:29
- Paul and Silas freed from jail, Acts 16:25-26
- Paul preached until, Acts 20:7

miktam (MIK-tam) *a kind of song that may describe some of the Psalms. It may mean that it is a sad song or a song about danger.* Psalms 16; 56–60

mildew (MIL-doo) *a growth that appears on things that have been damp for a long time,* Leviticus 13:47-59; 14:33-54

milk, 1 Peter 2:2

millstones, *huge stones used for grinding grain into flour or meal,* Deuteronomy 24:6; Matthew 18:6; Luke 17:1-2
- used to kill Abimelech, Judges 9:53; 2 Samuel 11:21

minister (MIN-i-ster) *servant; one who lives serving God and others,* Romans 15:15-16; Colossians 4:7

miracle (MEER-ih-k'l) *"wonderful thing"; a great event which can be done only by God's help. Miracles are special signs to show God's power.*
- purpose of, Exodus 10:1-2; Mark 2:8-12; John 2:11; Acts 3:1-10
- over nature, Exodus 14:21-22; Joshua 10:12-13; Matthew 8:23-27; 14:22-32; 21:18-22
- of healing, Matthew 8:14-17; 9:27-31; Mark 7:31-37; Acts 14:3
- of bringing people back to life, Mark 5:21-43; John 11:1-44; Acts 9:36-43

Miriam (MEER-ee-um) *the sister of Moses and Aaron.*
- watched over Moses, Exodus 2:1-8
- song of, Exodus 15:19-21
- punished, Numbers 12:1-15
- death of, Numbers 20:1

mistress (MISS-tres) *a female head of the household,* Proverbs 30:21-23
- Hagar as, Genesis 16:4-9

Mizpah (MIZ-pah) *the place where Jacob and Laban made a pile of stones to remind them of their agreement not to be angry with each other,* Genesis 31:44-49

Mizpah, *the city, a few miles north of Jerusalem,* Judges 11:29-34; 1 Samuel 7:5-16; 2 Kings 25:23

Moab (MO-ab) *the country on the east side of the Dead Sea.*
- fought with Israel, Numbers 22:1–25:9; Judges 3:12-30
- home of Ruth, Ruth 1:2,4
- rebelled against Israel, 2 Kings 3:4-27

mob
- against Paul, Acts 17:5; 21:30-36

Molech (MO-lek) *a god of the Canaanite people. Those who worshiped Molech often sacrificed their own children to him by burning them on altars.* Leviticus 18:21; 20:1-5; 2 Kings 23:10; Jeremiah 32:35

money, *Many kinds of money were used in Bible days–gold, silver, and copper.*
- proper attitudes toward, Luke 16:13; Hebrews 13:5; 1 Timothy 3:3; 6:10

moneychangers, *people who traded money from other countries for Jewish money.*
- of the Temple, Matthew 21:12-13; Mark 11:15-17; Luke 19:45-46; John 2:13-16

Mordecai (MOR-deh-kye) *a man who helped Esther to save the Jews from death.*
- discovered a plot, Esther 2:19-23
- asked Esther to help, Esther 4
- honored by the king, Esther 6

Moriah (moh-RYE-uh) *the land where Abraham went to sacrifice Isaac,* Genesis 22:2
- site of the Temple, 2 Chronicles 3:1

mortar (MORE-tar) *a stone bowl where grain is ground into flour by pounding; also, the sticky material that holds bricks together,* Genesis 11:3; Exodus 1:14

Moses (MO-zez) *the man who led God's people out of the land of Egypt; the author of the first five books of the Old Testament.*
- birth of, Exodus 2:1-10
- in Midian, Exodus 2:11–4:17
- led Israel out of Egypt, Exodus 4:18–12:51; 13:17-31
- received the law, Exodus 20–31
- struck the rock, Numbers 20:1-13
- death of, Deuteronomy 31:14–34:12

Most Holy Place, *the inner and most special room in the Holy Tent and the Temple.*
- rules about, Leviticus 16:2-20
- in the Temple, 1 Kings 6:16-35
- entered by Christ, Hebrews 9:3-25

mother-in-law
- law about, Deuteronomy 27:23
- of Ruth, Ruth 1:3-4
- Peter's, Matthew 8:14-15; Luke 4:38-39
- family against, Matthew 10:35; Luke 12:53

mothers
- treatment of, Exodus 20:12; 21:15,17; Leviticus 19:3;

Proverbs 1:8; 13:1; 23:22, 25; Matthew 15:4; 1 Timothy 5:2,4

Mount of Olives, *a hill covered with olive trees near Jerusalem; site of the garden of Gethsemane,* Matthew 21:1; 24:3; John 8:1
- David cried there, 2 Samuel 15:30
- Jesus prayed there, Luke 22:39-53
- Jesus ascended from there, Acts 1:6-12

Mount Sinai (SYE-nye) *a mountain in the Sinai Peninsula.*
- Lord spoke with Moses there, Exodus 24:16; Acts 7:30,38
- law given on, Exodus 31:18

Mount Zion (ZI-on) *one of the hills on which Jerusalem was built; later, it became another name for the whole city of Jerusalem; also a name for heaven.*
- hill of Jerusalem, 2 Kings 19:31; Psalm 48:2,11; Isaiah 24:23
- as heaven, Hebrews 12:22; Revelation 14:1

mourning (MORN-ing) *showing sadness, especially when someone has died.*
- examples of, Genesis 50:3; Deuteronomy 34:8; 1 Samuel 31:11-13

murder
- laws against, Exodus 20:13; Deuteronomy 5:17; Matthew 5:21
- committed by Barabbas, Mark 15:7
- devil as a murderer, John 8:44
- full of, Romans 1:29

music
- to the Lord, Judges 5:3; Ephesians 5:19
- in the Temple, 1 Chronicles 25:6-7

myrrh (MUR) *sweet-smelling liquid taken from certain trees and shrubs; used as a perfume and a painkiller,* Genesis 37:25; 43:11; Proverbs 7:17
- given to Jesus, Matthew 2:11; Mark 15:23
- used in Jesus' burial, John 19:39-40

mystery (MIH-ster-ee) *a secret.*
- revealed by God, Daniel 2:28
- of the message of Christ, Romans 16:25-26; Colossians 2:2; 4:3
- of Gentiles also being saved, Ephesians 3:1-6; Colossians 1:25-27
- of life after death, 1 Corinthians 15:51

N

Naaman (NAY-uh-mun) *a commander of the Aramean army; healed by Elisha of a skin disease,* 2 Kings 5; Luke 4:27

Nabal (NAY-bal) *husband of Abigail.*
- refused to help David, 1 Samuel 25:2-13
- saved by Abigail, 1 Samuel 25:14-35
- death of, 1 Samuel 25:36-38

Naboth (NAY-both) *killed by Jezebel so she could steal his vineyard,* 1 Kings 21

Nadab (NAY-dab) *son of Aaron.*
- saw God, Exodus 24:1-11
- death of, Leviticus 10:1; Numbers 3:4; 26:61

Nahum (NAY-hum) *a prophet of God; wrote the book of Nahum,* Nahum 1–3

naked
- Adam and Eve, Genesis 2:25
- realization of nakedness, Genesis 3:7-10
- born, Job 1:21

Naomi (nay-OH-me) *mother-in-law of Ruth,* Ruth 1:1-5
- returned to Bethlehem, Ruth 1:6-22
- encouraged Ruth, Ruth 2:19–3:4
- became a grandmother, Ruth 4:13-17

Naphtali (NAF-tuh-lye) *the sixth son of Jacob; his descendants were the tribe of Naphtali,* Genesis 30:7-8; Numbers 26:48-50; Joshua 19:32-39

nard, *an expensive perfume which was imported from India,* Song of Solomon 4:13; Mark 14:3; John 12:3

Nathan (NAY-thun) *a prophet during the time of David and Solomon,* 1 Kings 1
- told David not to build the Temple, 2 Samuel 7:1-17
- told David the parable of the lamb, 2 Samuel 12:1-25

Nathanael (nuh-THAN-yul) *one of Jesus' twelve apostles; probably called "Bartholomew."* John 1:43-51

nation
- formed and spread, Genesis 10:32
- against nation, Mark 13:8
- Good News preached to every one, Revelation 14:6

Nazarene (NAZ-uh-reen) *a person from the town of Nazareth. Jesus was called a Nazarene, so his followers sometimes were also called Nazarenes.* Matthew 2:21-23; Acts 24:5

Nazareth (NAZ-uh-reth) *the city in Galilee where Jesus grew up,* Matthew 2:21-23; Luke 4:16-30; John 1:45-46

Nazirite (NAZ-e-rite) *a special promise made to God, which had rules about eating certain foods and cutting the hair.*
- rules for, Numbers 6:1-21
- made by Samson, Judges 13:2-7; 16:17

Nebo, god of the Babylonians (NEE-boh) Isaiah 46:1

Nebo, the mountain
- Moses died there, Deuteronomy 34:1-5

Nebuchadnezzar (neb-you-kud-NEZ-zur) *a Babylonian king.*
- conquered Jerusalem, 2 Kings 24–25; 2 Chronicles 36
- his dreams, Daniel 2; 4
- and fiery furnace, Daniel 3

Nebuzaradan (NEB-you-ZAR-ah-dan) *the commander of Nebuchadnezzar's army.*
- captured Jerusalem, 2 Kings 25:8-12; Jeremiah 39:8-14; 40:1-6

Neco (NECK-o) *king of Egypt from 609 to 594 B.C.*
- killed King Josiah, 2 Kings 23:29-37; 2 Chronicles 35:20-27
- captured Jehoahaz, 2 Chronicles 36:1-4
- defeated by Nebuchadnezzar, Jeremiah 46:2

Nehemiah (NEE-uh-MY-uh) *led the first group of Israelites back to Jerusalem from Babylon.*
- sent to Jerusalem, Nehemiah 2
- rebuilt walls of Jerusalem, Nehemiah 3–4; 6
- as governor, Nehemiah 8:9; 10:1

neighbor
- teachings about, Exodus 20:16-17; Leviticus 19:13-18; Proverbs 3:27-29; Matthew 19:19; Luke 10:25-37

Nephilim (NEF-eh-lim) *people who were famous for being large and strong. The ten spies who were afraid to enter Canaan had seen the Nephilim who lived there.* Genesis 6:4; Numbers 13:30-33

Ner (NUR) *father of Kish,* 1 Chronicles 8:33; 9:36,39

net
- fishing with, Matthew 4:18; Luke 5:5,6; John 21:6-11
- kingdom of heaven like, Matthew 13:47

new
- a new song, Psalms 40:3; 98:1
- a new name, Isaiah 62:2; Revelation 2:17
- new mercies every morning, Lamentations 3:22-23
- a new heart, Ezekiel 18:31; 36:26
- a new life, Romans 6:4; Ephesians 4:23-24; Colossians 3:10; 1 Peter 1:3
- a new agreement, Jeremiah 31:31; 1 Corinthians 11:25; Hebrews 8:8; 9:15; 12:24
- a new heaven and earth, 2 Peter 3:13; Revelation 21:1

New Moon, *a Jewish feast held on the first day of the month. It was celebrated with animal sacrifices and the blowing of trumpets. It was to dedicate the month to the Lord.* Numbers 10:10; 2 Chronicles 2:4; 8:13; Psalm 81:3; Isaiah 1:11-17

Nicodemus (nick-uh-DEE-mus) *an important Jewish ruler*

and teacher. *Jesus taught him about spiritual life.* John 3:1-21; 7:45-53; 19:38-42

night, *can refer to ordinary darkness or be a symbol of distress, judgment, or evil.*
- created by God, Genesis 1:5; Psalm 19:1-2
- time of distress, Psalms 30:5; 42:8; 77:6
- time of judgment, John 9:4
- symbol of evil, 1 Thessalonians 5:5
- no night in heaven, Revelation 21:25

Nile River, *a river in Africa more than twenty-five hundred miles long.*
- baby Moses placed there, Exodus 2:1-10
- turned to blood, Exodus 7:14-25
- produced plague of frogs, Exodus 8:1-15

Nineveh (NIN-eh-vuh) *one of the oldest and most important cities in the world. For many years it was the capital of Assyria.* Genesis 10:8-11
- Jonah preached there, Jonah 1:1-2; 3–4; Matthew 12:41
- Nahum prophesied against, Nahum 1–3

Noah (NO-uh) *saved his family and the animals from the flood.*
- built the boat, Genesis 6:8-22
- saved from the flood, Genesis 7–8
- agreement with God, Genesis 9:1-17

Nob, *a town where priests lived during the days of King Saul,* 1 Samuel 21:1

noise
- joyful, Psalm 66:1
- of many people, Isaiah 17:12
- skies will disappear with, 2 Peter 3:10

noon
- sun to go down at, Amos 8:9
- bright light at, Acts 22:6

O

oath, *a promise or vow.*
- rules about, Matthew 5:33-37; 23:16-22; James 5:12
- God's oath, Hebrews 6:16-18
- examples of, 1 Samuel 14:24-28; 1 Kings 1:29-30; Psalm 132:1-12

Obadiah (oh-buh-DYE-uh) *a prophet of God who warned the Edomites they would be punished,* Obadiah 1-21

obedience
- to God, Leviticus 25:18; Deuteronomy 27:10; Acts 5:29
- to parents, Ephesians 6:1; Colossians 3:20
- to government, Romans 13:1-7; Titus 3:1-2; Matthew 22:17-21
- punishment for disobedience, Ephesians 5:6; 2 Thessalonians 1:8; 1 Timothy 1:9

offering (AW-fer-ing) *a gift or sacrifice.* See "sacrifice."
- brought by Cain, Genesis 4:3-5
- of non-Jewish people, Romans 15:16
- of Christ, Hebrews 10:5-18

Og (AHG) *the king of Bashan who was defeated by the Israelites,* Numbers 21:33-35; Deuteronomy 3:1-11

oil, *in Bible times usually means olive oil; used for cooking, medicine, burning in lamps, and anointing.* See "anoint."
- for lamps, Exodus 25:5-6; Matthew 25:1-10
- as medicine, Luke 10:34
- in offerings, Leviticus 2; 14:12-31
- in cooking, 1 Kings 17:10-16

ointment, See "perfume."

olive (OL-iv*) a small fruit; its oil was used in anointing ceremonies and as medicine.* See "oil."
- leaf, Genesis 8:11
- trees, Deuteronomy 6:11; 1 Samuel 8:14; Habakkuk 3:17; John 18:1

Omega, See "Alpha and Omega."

Omri (AHM-rih) *an evil king of Israel,* 1 Kings 16:15-28

Onesimus (oh-NES-ih-mus) *the slave of a Christian named Philemon,* Colossians 4:9; Philemon

Onesiphorus (OH-nih-SIF-uh-russ) *a Christian friend of Paul who lived in Ephesus,* 2 Timothy 1:16-18; 4:19

onyx (AHN-ix) *a precious stone with layers of black and white running through it,* Genesis 2:12; Job 28:16
- used in the holy vest, Exodus 25:7; 28:9-14; 39:6-7,13

Orpah (OR-pah) *the sister-in-law of Ruth,* Ruth 1:3-14

Ophir (OH-fur) *a land known for its gold and beautiful trees. Its location is uncertain.* Psalm 45:9; Isaiah 13:12
- Solomon traded with Ophir, 1 Kings 9:28; 10:11; 1 Chronicles 29:4

oven, *fire was built in the bottom of a clay barrel to bake bread,* Exodus 8:3; Leviticus 2:4; Hosea 7:4

oxen
- not to be coveted, Exodus 20:17
- as offering, Numbers 7:12-83
- not to be denied food, Deuteronomy 25:4; 1 Corinthians 9:9
- Elisha plowed with, 1 Kings 19:19-21
- pulled the cart containing the Ark, 1 Chronicles 13:9

P

pain
- of a woman in childbirth, Genesis 3:16; Isaiah 13:8; Romans 8:22; Galatians 4:19,27
- not found in the new Jerusalem, Revelation 21:4

palace
- of David, 2 Samuel 5:11-12
- of Solomon, 1 Kings 7:1-12

palm tree, *a tall tree with long, fan-shaped branches growing out of the top; gives dates for food and wood for building,* Exodus 15:27; Nehemiah 8:15
- Jericho, city of, Deuteronomy 34:3; Judges 1:16; 3:13
- branches spread before Jesus, John 12:12-13

papyrus (puh-PY-rus) *a tall reed that grows in swampy places; used to make paper,* Job 8:11; 9:26

parable (PARE-uh-b'l) *a story that teaches a lesson by comparing two things.*
- of the kingdom of God, Matthew 13; 20:1-16
- of the lost sheep, coin, and son, Luke 15:1-31
- of the Judgment Day, Matthew 25

Paradise (PARE-uh-dice) *"garden"; a place where God's people go when they die,* Luke 23:43; 2 Corinthians 12:3-4

Paran (PAY-ran) *a desert area between Egypt and Canaan,* Genesis 21:20; Numbers 10:12; 12:16; 13:1-26

parchment (PARCH-ment) *a writing material made from the skin of sheep or goats,* 2 Timothy 4:13

parents
- responsibilities of, Ephesians 6:4; Colossians 3:21

Passover Feast (PASS-o-ver FEEST) *an important holy day for the Jews in the spring of each year. They ate a special meal on this day to remind them that God had freed them from being slaves in Egypt.*
- first Passover, Exodus 12:1-30
- commanded, Numbers 9:1-14
- celebrated by Jesus, Matthew 26:2,17-19

patience (PAY-shentz) *to handle pain or difficult times calmly and without complaining.*
- of God, Romans 2:4; 2 Peter 3:9
- teachings about, 1 Corinthians 13:4,7; Hebrews 6:12
- comes from the Holy Spirit, Galatians 5:22
- commanded, Romans 12:12; Ephesians 4:2; 1 Thessalonians 5:14; James 5:7-8

Patmos (PAT-mus) *a small, rocky island in the Aegean Sea between Greece and Turkey,* Revelation 1:9

Paul, *the Roman name for "Saul." Saul was a Jew, born in the city of Tarsus. He became an apostle and a great servant of God.*
- conversion of, Acts 9:1-22

- name changed from "Saul," Acts 13:9
- healings by, Acts 14:8-10; 19:11-12; 20:7-12; 28:1-11
- imprisoned, Acts 23:35–28:31
- death of, 2 Timothy 4:6-8

peace
- from God, Psalm 29:11; John 14:27; Romans 5:1
- commanded, Romans 12:18; 14:17-19; Colossians 3:15
- Prince of Peace, Isaiah 9:6
- from the Holy Spirit, Galatians 5:22

pearl (PURL), Matthew 7:6; 1 Timothy 2:9; Revelation 21:21
- parable of, Matthew 13:45-46

Pekah (PEE-kuh) *an evil king of Israel,* 2 Kings 15:25–16:9; Isaiah 7:1-10

Pekahiah (peck-uh-HI-uh) *an evil king of Israel,* 2 Kings 15:22-26

Pelethites (PELL-eh-thites) *King David's bodyguards,* 2 Samuel 15:18; 20:6-7,23

Peninnah (pe-NIN-uh) *a wife of Elkanah,* 1 Samuel 1:2-6

Pentecost (PEN-tee-cost) *a Jewish feast day celebrating the summer harvest. The apostles began telling the Good News on Pentecost after Jesus died.* Acts 2:1-41; 20:16; 1 Corinthians 16:8

perfect
- describing Jesus, Hebrews 2:10; 5:9; 7:28
- describing God, Psalm 18:30; Matthew 5:48
- God's perfect law, James 1:25
- will of God, Romans 12:2
- love, 1 John 4:18
- people made perfect, 2 Corinthians 13:11; Hebrews 10:1-14; 11:40; 12:23

perfume
- used in idol worship, Isaiah 57:9
- poured on Jesus' feet, Mark 14:3-9; Luke 7:36-39; John 12:3

Pergamum (PER-guh-mum) *a town in the Roman province of Asia in what is now Turkey,* Revelation 2:12-17

persecution (PUR-seh-CUE-shun) *trying to hurt people. Christians in the New Testament times were often persecuted by being put in jail or killed.*
- blessings with, Matthew 5:11-12; 1 Peter 3:8-17
- examples of, Acts 8:1-4; 1 Peter 3:13-15
- response to, Matthew 5:44; Romans 12:14; 1 Corinthians 4:12; 2 Corinthians 12:2
- of Christians, Matthew 13:21; 2 Timothy 3:12

Persia (PUR-zhuh) *a powerful country during the last years of the Old Testament; now called "Iran."*
- defeated Babylon, 2 Chronicles 36:20-23
- let captives return to Jerusalem, Ezra 1:1-11

Peter, *a fisherman; he and his brother, Andrew, were the first two apostles Jesus chose. First called " Simon" or "Peter," Jesus changed his name to "Cephas," which means "rock."*
- called to follow Jesus, Matthew 4:18-20
- walked on water, Matthew 14:22-33
- at the Last Supper, John 13:1-11
- defended Jesus, John 18:10-11
- denied Jesus, Mark 14:66-72; Luke 22:54-62
- preached the Good News, Acts 2:14-40
- an elder in the church, 1 Peter 5:1

pharaoh (FAY-row) *the title given to the kings of Egypt.*
- made Joseph ruler of Egypt, Genesis 40–47
- made Israelites slaves, Exodus 1–14

Pharisees (FARE-ih-seez) *"the separate people"; they followed the Jewish religious laws and customs very strictly. Jesus often spoke against them for their religious teachings and traditions.*
- practices of, Matthew 9:14; 15:1-9; Mark 7:1-13; Luke 7:30
- against Jesus, Matthew 12:14; 22:15; John 8:1-6
- criticized by Jesus, Matthew 5:20; Matthew 23

Philadelphia (fill-uh-DEL-fee-uh) *a city in the country now called "Turkey,"* Revelation 3:7-13

Philemon (fih-LEE-mun) *a Christian in the city of Colossae,* Philemon 1-25

Philip, the apostle (FIL-ip) *friend of Peter and Andrew.*
- called by Jesus, John 1:43
- brought Nathanael to Jesus, John 1:44-50
- brought Greeks to Jesus, John 12:21-22

Philip, the evangelist, *a Greek-speaking Jew chosen to serve in the church in Jerusalem.*
- preached in Samaria, Acts 8:5-13
- preached to the Ethiopian, Acts 8:26-39
- his daughters prophesied, Acts 21:8-9

Philip, the tetrarch, *son of Herod I and Cleopatra.*
- ruler of Iturea and Trachonitis, Luke 3:1

Philippi (fih-LIP-eye) *a city in northeastern Greece,* Philippians 1:1; 4:15
- Paul in jail there, Acts 16:11-40

Philistines (FIL-ih-steens) *people who were Israel's enemy for many years; worshiped false gods.*
- Samson defeated, Judges 15–16
- captured the Ark of the Agreement, 1 Samuel 4–6
- David defeated, 1 Samuel 17–18; 2 Samuel 5:17-25; 21:15-22

Phinehas, son of Eleazar (FIN-ee-us) *a priest and grandson of Aaron,* Numbers 25:1-13

Phinehas, son of Eli, *an evil priest,* 1 Samuel 1:3; 2:34; 4:4-11

Phoebe (FEE-beh) *a woman in the church in Cenchrea,* Romans 16:1

Phoenicia (foh-NEE-shuh) *an early name for the land on the east coast of the Mediterranean Sea; called "Lebanon" today,* Mark 7:26; Acts 11:19; 15:3

phylactery (fil-LAK-tur-ee) See "box of Scriptures."

pigs
- considered unclean, Leviticus 11:7
- snout of, Proverbs 11:22
- "don't throw your pearls before pigs." Matthew 7:6
- demons sent into, Matthew 8:30-33; Mark 5:11-13; Luke 8:32-33
- fed by prodigal son, Luke 15:15-16

Pilate, Pontius (PIE-lut, PON-shus) *the Roman governor of Judea from A.D. 26 to 36,* Luke 3:1; 13:1
- handed Jesus over to be killed, Matthew 27; Mark 15; Luke 23; John 18:28–19:38

pillar (PILL-ur) *a large stone that is set upright; also a tall column of stone that supports the roof of a building.*
- of Jacob, Genesis 28:18-22
- to worship false gods, 2 Kings 17:9-12
- in the Temple, 1 Kings 7:6,15-22
- of cloud and fire, Exodus 13:21-22; 14:19-24; 33:8-10

Pisgah, Mount (PIS-guh) *one of the high spots on Mount Nebo where Moses stood to see into the promised land,* Numbers 23:14; Deuteronomy 3:27; 34:1

plague (PLAYG) *a disaster. God sent ten plagues on the land of Egypt so the Egyptians would set the Israelites free.*
- on the Egyptians, Exodus 7–11
- on the Israelites, Exodus 32:35; Numbers 11:31-33; 16:41-50; 25:1-9

plumb line (PLUM LINE) *a string with a rock or other weight on one end. People used it to see if a wall was straight.*
- symbol for God's judging, 2 Kings 21:10-13; Amos 7:7-8

pomegranate (PAHM-gran-it) *a reddish fruit about the size of an apple,* Numbers 13:23; Joel 1:12
- design on priests' clothing, Exodus 28:33-34
- design of Temple decorations, 1 Kings 7:18-20

poor
- God's care for, Psalm 140:12; Proverbs 22:22-23; Matthew 11:5; James 2:5

• treatment of, Leviticus 19:9-10; Matthew 25:34-36; Luke 14:12-14
possessions
• promised land given to Israelites, Genesis 17:8; Numbers 32:22; Joshua 1:11
• proper attitudes toward, Ecclesiastes 5:10– 6:6; Luke 12:13-21; Acts 2:45; 1 John 3:17
• danger of, Matthew 19:22
• sold by Christians, Acts 2:45
Potiphar (POT-ih-fur) *an officer for the king of Egypt. He put Joseph in charge of his household.* Genesis 39
pottage (POT-edge) *a thick vegetable soup or stew,* Genesis 25:29-34; 2 Kings 4:38-41
potter (POT-ur) *a person who makes pots and dishes out of clay.*
• as a symbol of God, Jeremiah 18:1-6
power
• of Jesus, Matthew 24:30; 28:18; Luke 6:19
• of the Spirit, Luke 4:14; Acts 1:8; Romans 15:19
• of Satan, Acts 26:18
• of the apostles, Luke 9:1; Acts 4:33
praetorium (pray-TORE-ee-um) *the governor's palace in New Testament times,* Matthew 27:27; Acts 23:35
praise (PRAYZ) *to say good things about someone or something. God's people can praise him by singing, praying, and by living the way he tells us to live.* 1 Chronicles 16:4-7; Psalms 103; 104; 145–150
prayer
• teachings about, Matthew 5:44-45; 21:18-22; Philippians 4:6; James 5:15-16
• Jesus' model prayer, Matthew 6:5-15
preach, *to give a talk on a religious subject; to tell the Good News.*
• Jonah preached to Nineveh, Jonah 3:2-4
• John preached, Matthew 3:1; Mark 1:4; Luke 3:3
• Jesus preached, Matthew 4:17; Mark 2:2; Luke 4:43-44
• Good News preached, Acts 8:25,40; Galatians 2:7; 1 Thessalonians 2:9
• preaching commanded, 2 Timothy 4:2
Preparation Day (prep-a-RAY-shun DAY) *the day before the Sabbath day. On that day the Jews prepared for the Sabbath.* Luke 23:54; John 19:14,31
pride
• warnings against, Romans 12:3; 1 Corinthians 13:4; Philippians 2:3; James 4:6
priest (PREEST) *in the Old Testament, a servant of God who worked in the Holy Tent or Temple. See also "high priest."*
• clothes for, Exodus 28
• appointing of, Exodus 29:1-37
• rules for, Leviticus 21–22:16
Priscilla (prih-SIL-uh) *a friend of Paul,* Acts 18:1-4,18-19; Romans 16:3-4
• taught Apollos, Acts 18:24-26
prison
• Joseph in prison, Genesis 39:20–41:40
• Peter in prison, Acts 5:17-20
• Paul in prison, Acts 16:23-34
prodigal (PRAH-dih-gul) *careless and wasteful.*
• the prodigal son, Luke 15:11-32
promise
• from God, Joshua 1:3; 1 Kings 8:20; Galatians 3:14; Ephesians 3:6
• first commandment with, Ephesians 6:2
• Lord is not slow in keeping, 2 Peter 2:9
prophecy (PRAH-feh-see) *a message; God speaking through chosen people called "prophets,"* Ezekiel 14:9; 1 Thessalonians 5:20; 2 Peter 1:20-21
prophesy (PRAH-fes-sy) *to speak a prophecy,* Acts 2:17-18. See "prophecy."
• a spiritual gift, 1 Corinthians 14:1-5
prophet (PRAH-fet) *a messenger; one who is able, with God's help, to tell God's message correctly. Sometimes prophets told what would happen in the future.* Matthew 11:13-14
• how to judge, Deuteronomy 13:1-5; 18:21-22
• examples of, Ezra 5:1; Jeremiah 1:1-9; Matthew 3:3
• false prophets, Deuteronomy 13:1-5
prophetess (PRAH-feh-tess) *a female prophet,* Exodus 15:20; Judges 4:4; 2 Kings 22:14; Luke 2:36. See "prophet."
prostitute (PRAH-sti-toot) *a person who sells his or her body for sex.*
• warnings against, 1 Corinthians 6:15
• examples of, Genesis 38:15-16; Jeremiah 3:1-3; Hosea 3:2-3; Matthew 21:32
proverbs (PRAH-verbs) *wise sayings. The book of Proverbs contains many wise sayings that tell how to live a good and happy life.* 1 Kings 4:32; Proverbs
psalm (SAHM) *a song. The book of Psalms is like a songbook.* Ephesians 5:19; Colossians 3:16
publican (PUB-leh-kun) See "tax collector."
Publius (POOB-lih-us) *an important man of the island of Malta,* Acts 28:7-8
Pul, See "Tiglath-Pileser."
punishment
• of Cain, Genesis 4:13
• everlasting, Matthew 25:46; 2 Thessalonians 1:8-9
• for rejecting Jesus, Hebrews 10:29
• by government, Romans 13:4; 1 Peter 2:14
pure
• gold, Exodus 25:11-39; 37; 1 Kings 6:20-21
• heart, Psalm 51:10; Matthew 5:8
• describing Jesus, Hebrews 7:26
• describing people, Job 4:17; 15:14; Philippians 1:10; Titus 1:15
• water, Hebrews 10:22
Purim, See "Feast of Purim."
purple, *a color that, in Bible times, was worn by kings, queens, and other rich people. Purple cloth was expensive because the purple dye came from special shellfish.* Exodus 25:1-4; Judges 8:26; Mark 15:17; Acts 16:14

Q

quail (KWALE) *a brownish-white bird.*
• given by God to Israel, Exodus 16:11-13; Numbers 11:31-34; Psalm 105:40
quarrel
• Israelites quarreled with Moses, Exodus 17:1-7
Queen Goddess, *Ishtar; a goddess of the Babylonians,* Jeremiah 7:18; 44:15-29
Queen of Heaven, See "Queen Goddess."
queen of Sheba, See "Sheba, queen of."
question
• Solomon questioned by queen of Sheba, 1 Kings 10:1-3
• Jesus questioned, Mark 8:11; Luke 23:9; John 8:6
• asked by Jesus, Matthew 21:24
• apostles questioned by Jews, Acts 4:7; 5:27
quiet
• words, Ecclesiastes 9:17
• riot quieted, Acts 19:35-36
• life, 1 Thessalonians 4:11; 1 Timothy 2:2
Quirinius (kwy-RIN-ee-us) *the Roman governor of Syria when Jesus was born,* Luke 2:1-3
quiver (KWIH-vur) *a bag to hold arrows,* Psalm 127:5; Isaiah 49:2

R

Rabbah (RAB-uh) *the capital city of the Ammonites,* 2 Samuel 11:1; 12:26-29; Ezekiel 25:5
rabbi/rabboni (RAB-eye/rah-BONE-eye) *teacher. Jesus' followers often called him "rabbi" as a sign of respect.* John 1:38; 20:16

Rachel (RAY-chel) *a wife of Jacob and the mother of Benjamin and Joseph.*
- married Jacob, Genesis 29:1-30
- gave birth to Joseph, Genesis 30:22-24
- stole Laban's idols, Genesis 31:19-35
- death of, Genesis 35:16-20

Rahab, the dragon (RAY-hab) *In a well-known story, Rahab was defeated. Egypt was sometimes called Rahab to show that it would be defeated.* Job 9:13; Isaiah 30:7

Rahab, the prostitute, *a woman in Jericho. She hid the Israelite spies and helped them escape.*
- hid the spies, Joshua 2:1-21
- rescued from Jericho, Joshua 6:16-25
- an example of faith, Hebrews 11:31; James 2:25

rainbow
- a sign of God's agreement with people, Genesis 9:8-17

raisin, 1 Samuel 25:18; 30:12; 1 Chronicles 12:40

ram, *a male sheep.*
- offered instead of Isaac, Genesis 22:13
- used for burnt offerings, Exodus 29; Leviticus 8:18-29; Numbers 28:11–29:37
- with two horns, Daniel 8:3-22

Ramah (RAY-muh) *a town about five miles north of Jerusalem,* Jeremiah 31:15; Matthew 2:18

Rameses (RAM-eh-seez) *one of the cities built by the Israelites when they were slaves in Egypt,* Exodus 1:11; 12:37; Numbers 33:3

Ramoth Gilead (RAY-moth GIL-ee-ad) *one of the cities of safety on the east side of the Jordan River,* Joshua 20:8; 1 Kings 4:13; 2 Kings 8:28–9:14

ransom, *a payment that frees a captive.*
- Jesus as a ransom for sins, Matthew 20:28; 1 Timothy 2:6; Hebrews 9:15

Rapha (RAY-fa) *a leader of a group of people in Canaan who may have been giants. The descendants of Rapha are called "Rephaites."* 2 Samuel 21:15-22; Joshua 13:12

raven, *a large black bird similar to a crow which eats dead things.*
- sent out by Noah, Genesis 8:7
- fed Elijah, 1 Kings 17:4-6

read
- the Book of the Teachings, Joshua 8:34-35; Nehemiah 8:2-9
- reading the teachings commanded, Deuteronomy 17:18-19; 31:9-13
- brings happiness, Revelation 1:3

Rebekah (ree-BEK-uh) *the wife of Isaac and the mother of Jacob and Esau.*
- married Isaac, Genesis 24
- gave birth to Jacob and Esau, Genesis 25:19-26
- helped deceive Isaac, Genesis 27
- buried at Machpelah, Genesis 49:31

redeem (ree-DEEM) *to buy something back or to buy a slave's freedom.*
- property, Leviticus 25:23-34; Ruth 4:3-6
- slave, Leviticus 25:47-49
- redeemed by God, 1 Corinthians 6:20; Galatians 4:5; Titus 2:14

Red Sea, *Sea of Reeds; a large body of water between Africa and Arabia.*
- Israelites crossed, Exodus 13:17–14:31

refuge, *a place of safety or protection.*
- God as our refuge, Deuteronomy 33:27; 2 Samuel 22:3; Psalms 18:2; 31:2; 71:3; 91:2
- city of, Numbers 35:6-34; Joshua 20

Rehoboam (ree-ho-BO-um) *son of Solomon who took his place as king.*
- became king, 1 Kings 11:41-43
- Israel rebelled against, 1 Kings 12:1-24
- strengthened Judah, 2 Chronicles 11:5-17
- disobeyed God, 2 Chronicles 12

rejoice
- commanded to, Matthew 5:11-12; Romans 12:15; Philippians 4:4; 1 Peter 4:13
- examples of, 1 Samuel 6:13; Nehemiah 12:43

remission (rih-MISH-un) See "forgiveness."

remnant (REM-nant) *a small part that is left; a name used for the Jews who were left alive after their captivity in Babylon.*
- of Israelites who returned to Jerusalem, Ezra 9:15; Nehemiah 1:2; Isaiah 10:20-22

repent (ree-PENT) *being sorry for doing something wrong and not continuing to do that wrong. See "change of heart and life."*

Rephaites, See "Rapha."

respect
- to parents, Leviticus 19:3; 1 Timothy 3:4
- between husbands and wives, Ephesians 5:33; 1 Peter 3:7
- to all people, 1 Peter 2:17; 3:16

rest
- on the seventh day, Genesis 2:2; Exodus 31:15; Hebrews 4:4
- given by the Lord, Psalm 95:11; Jeremiah 6:16; Matthew 11:28
- heaven as a place of rest, Revelation 14:13

resurrection (REZ-uh-REK-shun) *a dead person's coming back to life.*
- of Jesus, Matthew 28:1-10; Mark 16; Luke 24; John 20–21; Acts 2:24-32; Romans 1:4
- of God's people, John 6:39; Acts 24:15; 1 Corinthians 15; Philippians 3:10-11; Hebrews 11:35

Reuben (ROO-ben) *oldest of Jacob's twelve sons.*
- birth of, Genesis 29:32
- tried to save Joseph, Genesis 37:18-29
- descendants of, Exodus 6:14; Numbers 1:20; Joshua 13:15-23

revelation (rev-uh-LAY-shun) *showing plainly something that has been hidden,* 2 Corinthians 12:1; Revelation 1:1-3

revenge
- warnings against, Leviticus 19:18; Romans 12:19; 1 Thessalonians 5:15; 1 Peter 3:9

reward
- in heaven, Matthew 5:12
- for obedience, Psalm 19:11
- for what a person does, Matthew 6:1-18; 10:42; 16:27; Colossians 3:24
- children as a reward, Psalm 127:3

Rhoda (ROAD-uh) *a servant girl in the home of John Mark's mother,* Acts 12:6-17

righteousness (RY-chuss-ness) *being right with God and doing what is right.*
- explained, Romans 3:19-26; 2 Corinthians 5:21; 6:4-7; Philippians 3:8-9
- Abraham as an example of, Romans 4:3
- right living, 2 Corinthians 6:7; Ephesians 5:9; 1 Timothy 6:11; 1 Peter 2:24

robber
- Temple as a hideout for, Jeremiah 7:11; Matthew 21:13
- attacked man on road to Jericho, Luke 10:30
- killed with Jesus, Matthew 27:38-44; John 18:40

roof
- spies hid there, Joshua 2:6
- David saw Bathsheba from there, 2 Samuel 11:2
- built room for Elisha there, 2 Kings 4:8-10
- man lowered through, Mark 2:3-4
- Peter prayed there, Acts 10:9

Rock, *often used as a name for God. As a large rock is strong and provides a hiding place, so God is strong and protects us from our enemies.* Genesis 49:24; 2 Samuel 22:32-49; Psalm 19:14

rock badger (ROK BAD-jur) *a coney; a small, tailless animal like a rabbit that hides among the mountain gorges and rocky areas of Arabia,* Psalm 104:18; Proverbs 30:26
Rome, *the capital city of the Roman Empire at the time of Christ,* Acts 2:10; 18:2; Romans 1:7
- Paul sent there, Acts 23:11; 28:14-15

Ruth (ROOTH) *a widow from Moab.*
- moved to Judah, Ruth 1
- worked in Boaz's field, Ruth 2
- married Boaz, Ruth 3–4
- birth of Obed, Ruth 4:13-22

S

Sabbath (SAB-uth) *means "rest"; the seventh day of the Jewish week; the Jews' day to worship God. They were not allowed to work on this day.*
- commands about, Exodus 20:8-11; 31:12-17
- Jesus is Lord of, Matthew 12:1-13; Mark 2:23-28; Luke 6:1-11

sackcloth (SAK-cloth) *a type of clothing made from rough cloth; worn by people to show their sadness,* Genesis 37:33-35; Esther 4:1; Matthew 11:21
sacrifice (SAK-rih-fice) *to give something valuable to God.*
- burnt sacrifices, Leviticus 6:8-13
- drink sacrifices, Leviticus 23:13; Numbers 15:5; 28:7
- penalty sacrifices, Leviticus 7:1-10
- fellowship sacrifices, Leviticus 3; 7:11-27
- sin sacrifices, Leviticus 4
- limits of, Hebrews 9; 10
- living sacrifice, Romans 12:1

Sadducees (SAD-you-seez) *a Jewish religious group that didn't believe in angels or resurrection; they believed only the first five books of the Old Testament were true.*
- challenged Jesus, Matthew 22:23-33
- arrested Peter and John, Acts 4:1-3
- arrested the apostles, Acts 5:17-42
- Paul spoke to the council, Acts 23:1-9

safety, city of, *city of refuge. In Bible times, someone who had accidentally killed another person could go to a city of safety for protection. As long as he was there, the dead person's relative could not punish him.*
- rules about, Numbers 35:6-34; Joshua 20

saffron (SAF-ron) *a purple flower; parts of it are used as a spice,* Song of Solomon 4:14
saint, *holy person; another word for "Christian,"* Acts 9:41; Romans 1:7; 1 Corinthians 14:33
Salem (SAY-lem) *means "peace"; an old name for Jerusalem.*
- home of Melchizedek, Genesis 14:18; Hebrews 7:1-2

Salome, daughter of Herodias (sah-LO-mee)
- had John the Baptist killed, Matthew 14:3-12; Mark 6:17-29

Salome, wife of Zebedee, t*he mother of the apostles James and John,* Mark 15:40; 16:1
salt
- used to preserve foods, Job 6:6; Mark 9:50
- Lot's wife turned into salt, Genesis 19:15-26
- "You are the salt of the earth," Matthew 5:13

Salt Sea, See "Dead Sea."
salvation (sal-VAY-shun) *being rescued from danger; being saved from sin and its punishment.*
- as God's gift, John 3:16; Ephesians 2:8; Titus 2:11
- through Christ, Acts 4:12; 1 Thessalonians 5:9; 1 Timothy 1:15; Hebrews 5:7-9
- as a helmet, Ephesians 6:17; 1 Thessalonians 5:8
- urgency of, 2 Corinthians 6:2; Hebrews 2:3
- rejoice in, Psalms 9:14; 13:5; 51:12; Isaiah 25:9

Samaritan (sah-MEHR-ih-ton) *a person from the area of Samaria in Palestine. These people were only partly Jewish, so the Jews hated them.* John 4:9
- Jesus taught a Samaritan woman, John 4:1-42
- story of the good Samaritan, Luke 10:25-37

Samson (SAM-son) *one of Israel's judges; he was famous for his great strength.*
- birth of, Judges 13
- married a Philistine, Judges 14–15
- tricked by Delilah, Judges 16:4-22
- death of, Judges 16:23-31
- hero of faith, Hebrews 11:32

Samuel (SAM-u-el) *the last judge in Israel.*
- birth of, 1 Samuel 1:1-20
- worked in the Temple, 1 Samuel 1:21–2:26
- became a prophet, 1 Samuel 3
- appointed Saul as king, 1 Samuel 10
- appointed David as king, 1 Samuel 16:1-13
- death of, 1 Samuel 25:1

Sanballat (san-BAL-lat) *governor of Samaria who tried to stop Nehemiah from rebuilding the walls of Jerusalem,* Nehemiah 4–6
sanctify (SANK-teh-fy) *to make holy or ready for service to God,* John 17:17-19; 1 Corinthians 6:11; 1 Peter 1:2
sanctuary (SANK-choo-air-ee) See "Holy Place."
sand
- Abraham's descendants as numerous as, Genesis 22:17; 32:12
- Job's days as numerous as, Job 29:18
- house built on, Matthew 7:26-27

Sanhedrin (san-HEE-drin) See "council."
Sapphira (sah-FY-ruh) *wife of Ananias.*
- lied to the Holy Spirit, Acts 5:1-11

Sarah (SAIR-uh) *wife of Abraham,* Genesis 11:29-30
- gave Hagar to Abraham, Genesis 16:1-6
- name changed from "Sarai," Genesis 17:15-16
- gave birth to Isaac, Genesis 21:1-7
- death of, Genesis 23

Satan (SAY-ton) *means "enemy"; the devil; the enemy of God and man.*
- encouraged David to sin, 1 Chronicles 21:1
- tested Job, Job 1:6-12; 2:1-7
- tempted Jesus, Luke 4:1-13
- a fallen angel, Luke 10:18-19
- to be thrown into lake of fire, Revelation 20:10

Saul, king of Israel
- appointed king, 1 Samuel 9–10
- disobeyed God, 1 Samuel 15
- tried to kill David, 1 Samuel 19; 23:7-29
- death of, 1 Samuel 31

Saul of Tarsus, Acts 13:9. See "Paul."
savior
- God as Savior, Psalm 25:5; Isaiah 45:21; Luke 1:47; 1 Timothy 1:1
- Christ as Savior, Luke 2:11; John 4:42; Ephesians 5:23; Titus 2:13

scarlet (SCAR-let) *a bright red color,* Exodus 26:1; Joshua 2:18; Isaiah 1:18; Matthew 27:28
scepter (SEP-tur) *a wand or a rod that the king holds; a sign of his power,* Esther 4:11; Psalm 60:7
scourge (SKURJ) *to beat someone with a whip or stick,* 1 Kings 12:11
- Jesus scourged, Matthew 27:26; Mark 15:15
- Paul scourged, Acts 21:32; 2 Corinthians 11:24

scribe, *to write, to count, and to put in order. In New Testament times scribes were men who wrote copies of the Scriptures.*
- Ezra as scribe, Nehemiah 8:1
- against Jesus, Matthew 15:1-9
- condemned by Jesus, Matthew 23:13-36

Scriptures (SCRIP-churs) *special writings of God's word for people. When the word Scriptures is used in the New Testament, it usually means the Old Testament. Later, it came to mean the whole Bible.*

• fulfilled, Matthew 26:52-54; John 19:24,28,36
• given by God, 2 Timothy 3:16
scroll, *a long roll of paper used for writing,* Deuteronomy 17:18; Jeremiah 36; Revelation 5:1-5
Scythians (SITH-ee-unz) *a group of wandering people who lived near the Black Sea,* Colossians 3:11
Sea of Galilee, See "Galilee, Lake."
Sea of Reeds, See "Red Sea."
seal, *a tool with a design or picture carved on it. Kings pressed this seal into wax and used it like a signature. Sometimes these seals were worn as rings.*
• examples of, 1 Kings 21:8; Esther 8:8
seed
• created by God, Genesis 1:11,12,29
• parables of, Matthew 13:1-43
seer, *another name for prophet.* See "prophet."
Selah (SEE-lah) *probably a musical direction; used in the Psalms. It may mean to pause. The word was not intended to be spoken when reading the psalm.* Psalms 3:2,4,8; 89:4,37,45,48
Sennacherib (sen-AK-ur-ib) *king of Assyria from 705 to 681 B.C.*
• attacked Jerusalem, 2 Kings 18:13–19; 2 Chronicles 32:1-23; Isaiah 36–37
Sermon on the Mount, *a sermon Jesus preached as he was sitting on the side of a mountain near Lake Galilee,* Matthew 5–7
serpent, See "snake."
servant
• of the Lord, Deuteronomy 34:5; Joshua 2:8; 1 Kings 11:32; Luke 1:38
• Jesus as a, Philippians 2:7
• parable of, Matthew 25:14-30
• Jesus' followers to be, Matthew 20:25-27
Seth, *the third son of Adam and Eve,* Genesis 4:25-26; 5:6-8; Luke 3:38
Shadrach (SHAYD-rak) *a friend of Daniel.*
• taken into captivity, Daniel 1
• became a leader, Daniel 2:49
• saved from the furnace, Daniel 3
Shallum, king of Israel (SHAL-um) *ruled for only one month in 752 B.C.,* 2 Kings 15:10-15
Shalmaneser (shal-mah-NEE-zer) *a king of Assyria,* 2 Kings 17:1-6; 18:9
Shaphan (SHAY-fan) *an assistant to King Josiah,* 2 Kings 22:3-14; 2 Chronicles 34:8-21
sharing
• commanded, Luke 3:11; Romans 12:13; 1 Timothy 6:18
• examples of, Acts 2:42-47; 4:32; 2 Corinthians 8:1-4
Sharon (SHAIR-un) *the plain in Palestine along the coast of the Mediterranean Sea,* 1 Chronicles 5:16; 27:29; Song of Solomon 2:1; Isaiah 33:9
sheaf (SHEEF) *a bundle of grain stalks that have been cut and tied together,* Genesis 37:7; Leviticus 23:10; Job 24:10
Sheba, queen of (SHE-buh) *a queen who came to visit Solomon and see his wealth,* 1 Kings 10:1-13
Shebna (SHEB-nuh) *the manager of the palace for King Hezekiah,* 2 Kings 18:17–19:4; Isaiah 36:1–37:4
sheep
• God's people compared to, Ezekiel 34; John 10:1-18; 1 Peter 2:25
• parable of, Luke 15:1-7
Shem, *Noah's oldest son,* Genesis 6:10; 7:13; 10:21-31
sheminith (SHEM-ih-nith) *a musical term in the Psalms that means an octave (eight notes); may mean to use an instrument with eight strings,* Psalms 6; 12
shepherd
• David as, 1 Samuel 17:15,34-36
• Lord as, Psalm 23
• Jesus, the good shepherd, John 10:1-18
• elders as, 1 Peter 5:1-4
Sheshbazzar (shesh-BAZ-ur) *governor of the Jews in 538 B.C.,* Ezra 1:7-11; 5:13-16
shiggaion (shi-GY-on) *probably a musical term; used in the Psalms; may mean that the psalm is a sad song,* Psalm 7
shigionoth (shi-GY-o-noth) *probably a musical term,* Habakkuk 3:1
Shiloh (SHY-lo) *a town north of Jerusalem.*
• location of the Holy Tent, Joshua 18:1,8; Judges 18:31; Jeremiah 7:12
Shimei (SHIM-ee-i) *a relative of King Saul.*
• cursed David, 2 Samuel 16:5-14
• asked forgiveness, 2 Samuel 19:16-23
• death of, 1 Kings 2:36-46
ship, 1 Kings 9:26-28; 22:48; Acts 27
Shishak (SHY-shak) *king of Egypt during the time of Solomon and Rehoboam.*
• attacked Jerusalem, 1 Kings 14:25-28; 2 Chronicles 12:1-9
showbread, See "bread that shows we are in God's presence."
Shunammite (SHOO-nah-mite) *a person from Shunem, a town in northern Israel.*
• Shunammite woman took care of Elisha, 2 Kings 4:8-17
• her son raised from the dead, 2 Kings 4:18-37
• given back her land, 2 Kings 8:1-6
sickle (SICK-ul) *a tool for cutting grain,* Revelation 14:14-19
Sidon (SY-don) *a Phoenician city on the coast of the Mediterranean Sea,* Genesis 10:19; Matthew 11:21-22; Mark 7:31; Acts 27:3-4
siege mound (SEEJ) *dirt piled against a city wall to make it easier for attackers to climb up and attack the city,* 2 Samuel 20:15; Isaiah 37:33; Jeremiah 6:6
signet ring (SIG-net RING) *a ring worn by a king or other important person. It had his seal on it.* Genesis 41:42; Esther 3:10; 8:2-10; Daniel 6:17. See "seal."
Sihon (SY-hon) *a king of the Amorites when the Israelites came out of Egypt.*
• refused to let Israelites pass, Numbers 21:21-31; Deuteronomy 2:24-37
Silas (SY-lus) *also "Silvanus"; a teacher in the church in Jerusalem who often traveled with Paul.*
• sent to the Gentiles, Acts 15:22-23; 17:16
• joined Paul in Corinth, Acts 18:5
• helped with Peter's letter, 1 Peter 5:12
Siloam, pool of (sy-LO-um) *a pool of water in Jerusalem,* John 9:1-12
Silvanus (sil-VAY-nus) See "Silas."
Simeon of Jerusalem (SIM-ee-un) *a godly man who saw baby Jesus in the Temple,* Luke 2:25-35
Simeon, son of Israel, *one of the twelve sons of Israel,* Genesis 29:33; 42:23-36
• descendants of, Numbers 1:22-23; 26:12-14
Simon, brother of Jesus (SY-mun) Matthew 13:55
Simon of Cyrene (sy-REE-ni) *carried the cross of Jesus,* Matthew 27:32; Mark 15:21; Luke 23:26
Simon Peter, See "Peter."
Simon, the magician, *tried to buy the power of the Holy Spirit,* Acts 8:9-24
Simon, the Zealot, *an apostle of Jesus,* Matthew 10:4; Mark 3:18; Luke 6:15; Acts 1:13
sin, *a word, thought, or act against the law of God.*
• offering for, Leviticus 4; 6:24-30; Hebrews 7:27; 10:4-12
• committed by everyone, Romans 3:23; 1 John 1:8-10
• Christ died for, Romans 4:25; 1 Corinthians 15:3; 1 Peter 2:24; 1 John 2:2; 3:5
• results of, Isaiah 59:2; Romans 6:23; Ephesians 2:1; Hebrews 12:1

Sinai (SY-ny) *a mountain in the desert between Egypt and Canaan.*
- Moses received the Ten Commandments there, Exodus 19–20

singing, *a way of praising God and teaching each other,* Judges 5:3; Psalm 30:4; Ephesians 5:19; Colossians 3:16

Sisera (SIS-er-uh) *captain of a Canaanite army,* Judges 4

slave
- rules about, Exodus 21:1-11,16,26-32; Ephesians 6:5-9; 1 Timothy 6:1-2

slave woman, *concubine; she bore children for her master but was not considered equal to a wife.*
- Hagar as, Genesis 16:1-3
- of Solomon, 1 Kings 11:2-3

sleep
- God never sleeps, Psalm 121:4
- danger of, Proverbs 6:10-11
- Eutychus fell asleep, Acts 20:9
- to awake from, Romans 13:11
- a gift from the Lord, Psalm 127:2

sling, *a weapon for throwing rocks,* Judges 20:16; 1 Samuel 17:39-50; 2 Kings 3:24-25

slothful (SLAWTH-ful) *lazy and undependable,* Proverbs 6:6-11; 13:4; Matthew 25:26; Hebrews 6:12

sluggard, See "slothful."

snake
- sticks became snakes, Exodus 7:8-13
- bronze snake made by Moses, Numbers 21:4-9; John 3:14
- Paul bitten by, Acts 28:1-6

Sodom (SOD-um) *a town known for its evil people.*
- destroyed, Genesis 18:17–19:29
- symbol of evil, Matthew 10:11-15; 11:20-24; Revelation 11:8

soldier
- arrested Jesus, John 18:12-13
- made fun of Jesus, Matthew 27:27-31; Luke 23:11
- at Jesus' death, Matthew 27:32-37; Luke 23:26-38,47; John 19:1-3,16-24,28-35
- lied about Jesus' resurrection, Matthew 28:11-15
- Cornelius, Acts 10:1
- guarded Peter, Acts 12:6
- Christian compared to, 2 Timothy 2:3-4

Solomon (SOL-o-mon) *a son of David; famous for his wisdom.*
- became king, 1 Kings 1:28-53
- wisdom of, 1 Kings 3:1-15; 4:29-34
- made a wise decision, 1 Kings 3:16-28
- built the Temple, 1 Kings 6; 7:13-51
- visited by the queen of Sheba, 1 Kings 10:1-13; Matthew 12:42
- married many women, 1 Kings 11:1-8
- death of, 1 Kings 11:40-41

Solomon's Porch (SOL-o-mon's PORCH) *a covered courtyard on the east side of the Temple,* 1 Kings 7:6; John 10:23; Acts 3:11; 5:12

Son of David, *a name the Jews used for the Christ because the Savior was to come from the family of King David,* Matthew 1:1; 9:27; 15:22; 21:9

Son of Man, *a name Jesus called himself. It showed that he was God's Son, but he was also a human being.* Matthew 24:30; Mark 13:26; Luke 21:27; 22:69-70

sorcery (SOR-sir-ee) *trying to put magical spells on people or harming them by magic,* Acts 8:9-25; 19:18-19
- warnings against, Leviticus 19:26; Deuteronomy 18:14-15; 2 Kings 17:17

soul (SOLE) *what makes a person alive. Sometimes the Bible writers used words like "heart" and "soul" to mean a person's whole being or the person himself.*
- "destroy the soul and the body," Matthew 10:28
- losing, Matthew 16:26
- "all your heart and all your soul," Matthew 22:37
- joined with the spirit, Hebrews 4:12

sower, *someone who plants seeds to grow into crops,* Matthew 13:1-43; 2 Corinthians 9:6

Spirit (SPIH-rit) See "Holy Spirit."

spirit, *the part of humans that was made to be like God because God is spirit. The New Testament also talks about evil spirits.* Isaiah 26:9; 1 Thessalonians 5:23; James 2:26
- evil spirit, Matthew 12:43; Mark 1:23; 5:2; Luke 4:33

spiritual gifts, *special talents or abilities that God gives his people,* Romans 12:6-8; 1 Corinthians 12:1-11; 14; Ephesians 4:7-13

spring, *a natural fountain,* Genesis 7:11; Exodus 15:27

staff, *a shepherd's walking stick,* Exodus 4:1-5; 7:8-12; Numbers 20:6-11; Psalm 23:4

steal, See also "robber."
- commands against, Exodus 20:15; Matthew 19:18; Romans 13:9; Ephesians 4:28

Stephen (STEE-ven) *one of the seven men chosen to serve the church in Jerusalem; the first martyr for Christ.*
- chosen to serve the church, Acts 6:5-6
- killed by the Jews, Acts 6:8–7:60

stoning, *a way of killing someone by throwing rocks at him.*
- commanded, Deuteronomy 17:2-7
- Naboth stoned, 1 Kings 21:13
- Stephen stoned, Acts 7:54-60
- Paul stoned, Acts 14:19

strength
- love God with all your strength, Deuteronomy 6:5; Mark 12:30
- God as the source, Psalms 18:1; 73:26; Philippians 4:13; 1 Peter 4:11

stronghold, *a fortress, a well protected place,* 1 Samuel 22:4; 2 Samuel 5:17

suffering
- proper attitude toward, 2 Corinthians 1:3-7; James 5:10
- value of, Romans 8:17-18; 1 Peter 3:8-17
- of Jesus, Isaiah 53:3-10; Luke 24:26,46; Philippians 3:10; Hebrews 2:18

swaddling clothes, *pieces of cloth that were wrapped around a newborn baby in Jesus' time,* Luke 2:7-12

sword
- of fire, Genesis 3:24
- a weapon, Joshua 5:13; 1 Samuel 17:45; Matthew 26:51-52
- the word of God, Ephesians 6:17; Hebrews 4:12

Sychar (SY-kar) *a small town in Samaria near Jacob's well,* John 4:5-6

synagogue (SIN-uh-gog) *"a meeting." By the first century, the Jews met in synagogues to read and study the Scriptures. The building was also used as the Jewish court and as a school.*
- Jesus taught in, Matthew 4:23; Mark 1:21; Luke 4:16-17
- Paul spoke there, Acts 17:1,10

Syria (SEER-ee-uh) *an area north of Galilee and east of the Mediterranean Sea; called "Aram" in Old Testament times.* See "Aram."
- enemy of Israel, 1 Kings 11:25; 20:1-34; 2 Kings 13:22-25
- learned about Jesus, Matthew 4:24

T

tabernacle (TAB-er-NAK-'l) See "Meeting Tent."

tablets of the agreement, *two flat stones on which God wrote the Ten Commandments.*
- given to Moses, Exodus 19–20; 24:12-18
- broken by Moses, Exodus 32:15-19
- the second tablets, Exodus 34:1-4

- in the Most Holy Place, Hebrews 9:4

Tabitha (TAB-eh-thuh) See "Dorcas."

Tabor, Mount (TAY-bur) *in the Valley of Jezreel about twelve miles from Lake Galilee,* Judges 4:6-16; Psalm 89:12

tambourine (tam-bah-REEN) *a musical instrument that is beaten to keep rhythm,* Exodus 15:20; 1 Samuel 18:6; Psalm 81:2

Tarshish (TAR-shish) *a city somewhere on the western side of the Mediterranean Sea,* Jonah 1:3; 4:2

Tarsus (TAR-sus) *the most important city in Cilicia, which is now the country of Turkey,* Acts 9:30; 11:25-26
- home of Paul, Acts 9:11; 21:39; 22:3

tax collector, *a Jew hired by the Romans to collect taxes,* Matthew 9:10-11
- Matthew, Matthew 10:3; Luke 5:27
- Zacchaeus, Luke 19:1-10

teacher
- Jesus called a, Matthew 8:19; Mark 10:17; John 1:38; 3:2
- in the church, Romans 12:7; Ephesians 4:11; 1 Timothy 4:13
- false, 1 Timothy 4:1-5; 2 Peter 2:1
- to be judged more strictly, James 3:1

teaching
- commanded, Deuteronomy 6:1-7; Matthew 28:20; 2 Timothy 2:2,14-15; Titus 2

Teachings of Moses, *or the "Law of Moses,"* Deuteronomy 31:24-26; Joshua 23:6; Nehemiah 8
- purpose of, Romans 3:20; 5:20; Galatians 3:21-25
- limitations of, Romans 8:3; Galatians 2:19; Hebrews 10:1

temple (TEM-p'l) *a building where people worship. God told the Jewish people to worship him at the Temple in Jerusalem.*
- Solomon's Temple, 1 Kings 6–8; 2 Chronicles 2–7
- the Temple rebuilt, Ezra 3
- the body as a temple, John 2:19-22; 1 Corinthians 3:16-17; 6:19-20; 2 Corinthians 6:16

temptation (temp-TAY-shun) *the devil's attempt to get us to do something wrong.*
- Jesus tempted, Matthew 4:1-11; Luke 4:1-13; Hebrews 4:15-16
- a way of escape from, 1 Corinthians 10:13
- source of, James 1:13-15

Ten Commandments, *the rules God gave Moses on Mount Sinai,* Exodus 20:1-20; 31:18; 34:1-28; Deuteronomy 5:1-22

tent
- Abram's tents, Genesis 13:18
- peg, Judges 4:21-22
- makers of, Acts 18:3

Tent, See "Meeting Tent."

Thaddaeus (THAD-ee-us) *one of the twelve apostles,* Matthew 10:3; Mark 3:18

thankfulness, Psalm 107:1; 1 Thessalonians 5:8; Hebrews 12:28

Theophilus (thee-AHF-ih-lus) *the person to whom the books of Luke and Acts were written,* Luke 1:1-4; Acts 1:1

Thessalonica (THES-ah-lah-NY-kah) *the capital of the country of Macedonia, which is now northern Greece,* 1 Thessalonians 1:1; 2 Thessalonians 1:1
- Paul preached there, Acts 17:1-9

Thomas (TOM-us) *Didymus; one of the twelve apostles,* Matthew 10:2-3
- questioned Jesus, John 14:5-7
- saw Jesus after resurrection, John 20:24-29; 21:2

thorn, *sharp points on a branch or stem of a plant.*
- as a curse on Adam, Genesis 3:17-18
- crown of, Matthew 27:29; Mark 15:17; John 19:2-5

threshing floor, *a place where farmers separated grain from chaff. This was done by beating the stalks on the hard ground, throwing them in the air, and letting the wind blow the chaff away.*
- angel visited Gideon there, Judges 6:11
- David bought, 2 Samuel 24:16-25

throne
- king's throne, 1 Kings 10:18-19
- God's throne, Matthew 5:34; Hebrews 4:16; Revelatio 3:21; 4

Thummim (THUM-im) *the Urim and Thummim may hav been gems. They were attached to the holy vest of the high priest and were used to learn God's will.* Exodus 28:29-30; Leviticus 8:8; Deuteronomy 33:8

Thyatira (THY-ah-TY-rah) *an important city in Asia famous for its purple cloth,* Acts 16:13-14; Revelation 1:11; 2:18-29

Tiberius Caesar (tie-BEER-ee-us SEE-zur) *Roman emperc during the last half of Jesus' life,* Luke 3:1

Tiglath-Pileser (TIG-lath-peh-LEE-zur) *king of Assyria wh helped Ahaz;* also called "Pul."
- attacked Israel, 2 Kings 15:19-20
- rescued Ahaz, 2 Kings 16:7-10

Tigris (TY-gris) *a great river in the eastern part of the Bib lands,* Genesis 2:14; Daniel 10:4

Timothy (TIM-oh-thee) *close friend and helper of the apostle Paul.*
- helped Paul, Acts 16:1-3; 17:13-16; 1 Corinthians 4:1 2 Corinthians 1:19
- instructed by Paul, 1 and 2 Timothy

tithe (TIETH) *"tenth." The Jews were told to give one-tenth of what they earned to God.* Leviticus 27:30-32; Deuteronomy 12:1-6; Luke 11:42; 18:12

Titus (TIE-tus) *trusted friend and helper of the apostle Paul.*
- helped Corinthians, 2 Corinthians 7:6-7,13-15; 8:6,16,23
- appointed elders, Titus 1:4-5
- Paul's instructions to, Titus 1–3

Tobiah (toe-BY-uh) *tried to keep Nehemiah from rebuilding the walls of Jerusalem,* Nehemiah 2:10-20; 6:10-19; 13:4-9

tomb
- of Lazarus, John 11:38-44
- of Jesus, Matthew 27:57–28:15; Mark 15:42–16:30; Luke 23:50–24:12; John 19:38–20:9

tongue
- lying tongue hated by God, Proverbs 6:16-17
- cannot be tamed, James 3:2-12

tower of Babel, See "Babel."

transfiguration (tranz-fig-you-RAY-shun) *"to change." Jesus was transfigured in front of Peter, James, and John when his face and clothes began to shine brightly.* Matthew 17:1-9; Mark 9:2-9; Luke 9:28-3

tree
- of knowledge of good and evil, Genesis 2:9; 3:3
- of life, Genesis 2:9; Revelation 2:7; 22:2,14
- people compared to, Psalms 1:3; 92:12; Jeremiah 17:8 Matthew 3:10; 12:33
- cross described as a tree, Galatians 3:13

trespass, See "sin."

tribe, *all descendants of a certain person. The twelve tribes of Israel were descendants of the twelve son of Jacob, who was later named "Israel."* Numbers 1–2
- Canaan divided among, Joshua 13:7-33; 15–19

triumphal entry (tri-UMF-ul) *the time Jesus entered Jerusalem just before his death,* Matthew 21:1-11; Mark 11:1-19; Luke 19:28-44; John 12:12-15

Troas (TRO-az) *one of the most important cities in northwest Asia,* Acts 16:8-10; 20:5-12; 2 Corinthia 2:12

Trophimus *(TROF-eh-mus) non-Jewish Christian who*

traveled with Paul, Acts 20:3-4; 21:27-29; 2 Timothy 4:20

trumpet (TRUM-pet) *in Bible times it was made from animal horns; used to call an army together or announce something important,* Numbers 10:2-10; Joshua 6:4-20; 1 Corinthians 15:52

trust
- a duty, Luke 16:11; 1 Corinthians 4:2; Titus 2:10
- in God, Psalm 20:7; Proverbs 3:5; 16:20; Romans 4:5; 10:11; 1 Peter 2:6
- in lesser things, Psalms 49:13-14; 118:9; Proverbs 11:28; Isaiah 2:22

truth
- speaking honestly, Psalm 15:2; Proverbs 16:13
- God's message, John 17:17; Romans 1:25; Ephesians 1:13; 1 John 1:6

tunic (TOO-nik) *a kind of coat,* Exodus 28:39-40; John 19:23

Tychicus (TIK-ih-kus) *Christian from Asia who did important jobs for Paul,* Acts 20:4; Ephesians 6:21-22; Colossians 4:7-9

Tyre (TIRE) *large, important city in Phoenicia, which is now part of the country of Lebanon,* Mark 7:24-31; Acts 12:20
- Hiram, king of, 2 Samuel 5:11; 1 Kings 9:10-14; 2 Chronicles 2
- a wicked city, Matthew 11:21-22; Luke 10:13-14

U

uncircumcised, See "circumcision."

unclean, *the state of a person, animal or action that was not pleasing to God. In the Old Testament God said certain animals were unclean and were not to be eaten. If a person disobeyed the rules about being clean, he was called unclean and could not serve God until he was made clean again.* See "clean."
- unclean animals, Leviticus 11; Acts 10:9-15
- unclean people, Leviticus 12–15
- God declared everyone to be clean, Acts 10

unleavened bread (un-LEV-'nd BREAD) *bread made without yeast.*
- used in the Passover Feast, Exodus 12:20; Deuteronomy 16:1-4

Unleavened Bread, Day of, *the first day of the Feast of Unleavened Bread or Passover,* Matthew 26:17; Luke 22:7

upper room, *upstairs room in a house.*
- Jesus and his followers met there, Mark 14:14-15; Luke 22:9-12

Ur, *a great city thousands of years ago; today in the country of Iraq.*
- home of Abram, Genesis 11:28-31

Uriah (you-RY-uh) *a soldier in King David's army.*
- killed by David, 2 Samuel 11

Urim (YOUR-im) See "Thummim."

Uzzah (UZ-uh) *touched the Ark of the Agreement and died,* 2 Samuel 6:1-8; 1 Chronicles 13:1-14

Uzziah (uh-ZY-uh) *a king of Judah,* 2 Kings 15:13-15; 2 Chronicles 26; Isaiah 6:1

V

Vashti (VASH-ty) *the wife of Ahasuerus, king of Persia,* Esther 1:1-20

veil (VALE) *a head covering usually worn by women; also, a curtain in the Temple.*
- worn by women, Genesis 24:65; Song of Solomon 4:1; Isaiah 3:19
- the Temple veil, Matthew 27:51; Mark 15:38; Luke 23:45

vest, holy, *"ephod"; a special type of clothing for the priests in the Old Testament. The holy vest for the high priest had gold and gems on it.*
- description of, Exodus 25:7; 28:6-14; 39:2-7
- one made by Micah, Judges 17:1-5; 18:14-20
- worn by David, 2 Samuel 6:14

vine
- fruit of the, Matthew 26:29; Mark 14:25; Luke 22:18
- Jesus as the, John 15:1-11

vineyard
- Naboth's, 1 Kings 21
- parables of, Matthew 20:1-16; 21:28-46; Mark 12:1-12; Luke 20:9-19

virgin (VUR-jin) *person who has not had sexual relations,* Deuteronomy 22:13-29; Isaiah 7:14; Matthew 1:23; Luke 1:34

vision (VIZ-zhun) *like a dream. God often spoke to his people in visions.*
- of Abram, Genesis 15:1
- of Daniel, Daniel 2:19
- of Peter and Cornelius, Acts 10:1-16
- of Paul, Acts 16:9

vow, *a special and serious promise often made to God.*
- rules about, Numbers 30; Deuteronomy 23:21-23
- the Nazirite, Numbers 6:1-21
- of Jephthah, Judges 11:29-40
- of Paul, Acts 18:18

W

war
- rumors of, Matthew 24:6-7; Mark 13:7-8; Luke 21:9-10
- spiritual, 2 Corinthians 10:3-4
- will end, Micah 4:1-3

watchman
- examples of, 2 Samuel 18:24-27; Psalm 130:6
- prophets as watchmen, Ezekiel 3:17; Micah 7:4

water
- in creation, Genesis 1:1-2,6-10
- bitter, Exodus 15:22-27
- from a rock, Exodus 17:1-7
- for David, 2 Samuel 23:15-17
- drink of, Matthew 10:42; Mark 9:41
- Jesus walked on, Matthew 14:22-36
- turned to wine, John 2:1-11
- living water, John 4:1-15

"Way, the," *one of the earliest names given to Christians. Jesus said he was "the way" to reach God.* Acts 9:1-2; 19:9,23; 22:4; 24:14,22

wedding, Matthew 22:1-14; Luke 14:8; John 2:1-11

Western Sea, See "Mediterranean Sea."

widow
- examples of, Ruth 4:10; 1 Kings 17:8-24; Luke 21:2-4
- care for, Deuteronomy 24:17-22; 1 Timothy 5:3-16; James 1:27

wife
- man united with, Genesis 2:24
- the good wife, Proverbs 31:10-31
- teachings about, 1 Corinthians 7:1-16
- responsibility of, Ephesians 5:21-24,33; Colossians 3:18; 1 Peter 3:1

wine
- danger of, Proverbs 20:1; Ephesians 5:18
- at wedding in Cana, John 2:1-11
- for the stomach, 1 Timothy 5:23

winepress, *a pit where grapes were mashed to get the juice out. The winepress is sometimes used to describe how enemy armies will defeat people as if they were grapes crushed in a winepress.*
- examples of, Judges 6:11; Matthew 21:33
- as a symbol of punishment, Lamentations 1:15; Revelation 14:19-20; 19:15

wisdom (WIZ-d'm) *understanding what is really important in life. This wisdom comes from God.* Proverbs 1:1-2,7; 2; 4
- Solomon asked for, 1 Kings 4:29-34

• source of, James 1:5
• a parable about, Matthew 25:1-13

wise men, "magi"; *men who studied the stars,* Genesis 41:8; Exodus 7:11; Matthew 2:1-12

witchcraft, *using the power of the devil to do magic.*
• warnings against, Deuteronomy 18:10-12; Galatians 5:19-21
• examples of, 2 Kings 9:22; 2 Chronicles 33:6

witness, Acts 1:8,22; 2:32; 22:14-15

woman
• created by God, Genesis 2:22-23
• how to treat a, 1 Timothy 5:2,14

word, *in the Bible often means God's message to us in the Scriptures. Jesus is called the "Word" because he shows us what God is like.*
• like a lamp, Psalm 119:105
• like a sword, Hebrews 4:12
• living in God's people, John 15:7; Colossians 3:16; 1 John 2:14
• lasts forever, Matthew 24:35; 1 Peter 1:25
• people's words, Proverbs 12:25; 25:11; Matthew 12:36-37
• as a message, 1 Peter 1:24-25; 1 John 2:14
• Jesus as the "Word," John 1:1-5,14; 1 John 1:1-2

world, *the planet Earth; also the people on this earth who follow Satan.*
• as the Earth, 2 Samuel 22:16; Psalm 18:15
• as a symbol of wickedness, Romans 12:2; Ephesians 2:2

worship, *to praise and serve God.*
• commanded, Exodus 34:14; Luke 4:8; John 4:20-24

X-Y

Xerxes (ZERK-sees) *a king of Persia; also called "Ahasuerus,"* Esther 1–10

yeast (YEEST) *an ingredient used to make breads and cakes rise; used in the New Testament to stand for a person's influence over others.* See also "unleavened bread."
• as a symbol for influence, Mark 8:15; Luke 13:21

yoke, *a wooden frame that fits on the necks of animals to hold them together while working.*
• examples of, Deuteronomy 21:3; 1 Kings 19:19-21

youth
• "Remember your Creator," Ecclesiastes 12:1
• teachings about, 1 Timothy 4:12

Z

Zacchaeus (za-KEE-us) *Jewish tax collector in the city of Jericho,* Luke 19:1-8

Zadok (ZAY-dok) *priest who helped King David,* 2 Samue 15:24-36; 17:15-21; 1 Kings 1:18-45

Zarephath (ZAIR-eh-fath) *a Canaanite town where the prophet Elijah helped a widow,* 1 Kings 17:8-24; Luke 4:25-26

Zealots (ZEL-ots) *a group of Jewish men also called "Enthusiasts." They hated the Romans for controlling their home country, and they planned t force the Romans out.*
• Simon, the Zealot, Matthew 10:4; Mark 3:18; Luke 6:15; Acts 1:13

Zebedee (ZEB-uh-dee) *a fisherman on Lake Galilee,* Matthew 4:21-22; 20:20; Mark 1:19-20; Luke 5:10 John 21:2

Zechariah, father of John the Baptist, (ZEK-uh-RY-uh) *Jewish priest,* Luke 1:5-25,57-80

Zechariah, king of Israel, *ruled for only six months; killed by Shallum,* 2 Kings 14:29; 15:8-11

Zechariah, son of Berekiah, *a prophet who wrote the next-to-the-last book in the Old Testament,* Ezra 5: Zechariah 1–14

Zechariah, son of Jehoiada, *a priest who taught the people to serve God,* 2 Chronicles 24:20-25

Zedekiah, son of Josiah, (zed-ee-KY-uh) *the last king of Judah,* 2 Kings 24:16–25:7

Zedekiah, son of Kenaanah, *a false prophet during the time of King Ahab,* 1 Kings 22:1-24

Zedekiah, son of Maaseiah, *a false prophet in Babylon during the time of Jeremiah,* Jeremiah 29:21-23

Zephaniah (zef-uh-NY-uh) *a prophet who lived when Josiah was king of Judah; wrote the short book of Zephaniah,* Zephaniah 1:1

Zerubbabel (zeh-RUB-uh-bull) *governor of Jerusalem aft the Jews had been in captivity in Babylon for sever years.*
• returned from exile, Ezra 2:2
• built the altar of God, Ezra 3:1-6
• rebuilt the Temple, Ezra 3:7-10; 5:2

Ziba (ZY-buh) *a servant of Saul,* 2 Samuel 9:1-11; 16:1-4; 19:24-30

Zimri (ZIM-rye) *a king of Israel,* 1 Kings 16:11-20

Zion (ZY-on) *a hill inside the city of Jerusalem.* See "Mount Zion."

Ziph (ZIF) *a city about twenty-five miles south of Jerusalem,* 1 Samuel 23:14-28; 26:1-25

Zipporah (zih-PO-ruh) *the wife of Moses,* Exodus 2:15-2 4:24-26; 18:1-3

zither (ZITH-ur) *a type of musical instrument that had about forty strings on it,* Ezekiel 3:5,7,10,15